Dos Passos

Dos Passos
A LIFE

Virginia Spencer Carr

DOUBLEDAY & COMPANY, INC.

GARDEN CITY, NEW YORK

1984

Library of Congress Cataloging in Publication Data

Carr, Virginia Spencer.
Dos Passos: A Life.
Includes index.
1. Dos Passos, John, 1896–1970—Biography.
2. Novelists, American—20th century—Biography.
I. Title.
PS3507.743Z548   1984   813'.52[B]
ISBN 0-385-12964-5

Library of Congress Catalog Card Number: 79-7230

In memory of my parents,
Wilma Bell Spencer and Louis Perry Spencer,
and of my brothers,
John Raymond Spencer and Melville Louis Spencer,
and for my daughters,
Karen, Catherine, and Kimberly.

Contents

BOOK III

"MR. JACK"
SQUIRE OF SPENCE'S POINT, 1949–70

A NOTE FROM THE AUTHOR

For seven years I was immersed in the life and writings of John Dos Passos. Even my one-year residence in Poland—as a Fulbright lecturer at the University of Wrocław in 1980–81, when I was physically separated from interview sources and most of my materials—became an integral part of this book. I taught American literature to a hearty and close-knit group of Polish students during the period that immediately followed the birth of Solidarity—a period of stress, turmoil, and hardship for a courageous people living under the red cloak of their "friends" to the East. I carried to Poland the rough draft of a half-completed manuscript and enough source materials to write additional chapters covering ten years of Dos Passos' life; these being irreplaceable, however, I shipped them home early when an American official in a nearby consulate warned me that if a state of war was declared, I would have less than twenty-four hours' notice to leave the country, and would be allowed to take only one suitcase. Experiencing socialism as a way of life—and Communism as a struggling country's political knife—helped me plumb the depths of the young Dos Passos' ambivalences with a subjectivity I could not have gained otherwise.

Among the many people who contributed generously to the making of *Dos Passos: A Life,* the most important was my friend and research associate, Maxine Brown, who traveled with me every mile and byway—including Poland—from the book's genesis in the summer of 1976. She worked unstintingly through each phase of the research and writing, combing research centers across the United States, reading and taking notes, collating materials, organizing, transcribing, editing, and proofreading draft after draft as the book evolved. For these and other tasks that made my work easier through this project, and for her encouragement and companionship, I am grateful.

My rendering of Dos Passos' life would not be possible without the reminiscences, insights, letters, and other materials shared by those who knew him personally and gave liberally of their time, energies, and often bed and board. I appreciate, especially, the help of Elizabeth Dos Passos, who gave me access to materials, granted permission for me to quote from her husband's writings—both published and unpublished—offered leads to elusive sources, granted countless interviews, and extended every possible courtesy and encouragement during the evolvement of this biography; upon my request she also read the manuscript and offered suggestions where she felt I had erred in fact or nuance. I thank Christopher Holdridge, Dos Passos' stepson; Lucy Dos Passos Coggin, his daughter;

and Rodney Coggin, his son-in-law. All were generous in sharing the facets of Dos Passos as they knew him.

I am indebted to many others who contributed their recollections both through personal interviews and letters: Daniel Aaron, Phil Alexander, Louis Auchincloss, Oliver Austin, Louis Azrael, Sara Azrael, Ellen Barry, Grace Bell, Joan Bergstrom, James Bready, George Bricka, Mary James Brown, William Slater Brown, Betty Bruce, T. Otto Bruce, William F. Buckley, Jr., Brodnax Cameron, Julia Sprigg Cameron, Hazel Carden, Herb Carden, William T. Carden, Manoel da Silveira Cardozo, John Chamberlain, Harold Clurman, Elizabeth W. Cope, Crystal Ross Dabney, Virginia Dehn, Frances Foley Dickinson, Honoria Murphy Donnelly, John Dorsey, Cyril F. dos Passos, John David Dos Passos, John David Dos Passos II, Maria Amália dos Passos, Otis Douglas II, Katharine Merrill Smith Durand, Yvette Eastman, Helen Sawyer Farnsworth, Jerry Farnsworth, James T. Farrell, Carl Feiss, Ellen Feiss, William O. Field, Clifford Forster, Andrew H. Gantt, W. Horsley Gantt, Antonio Gattorno, Isabel Gattorno, Adelaide Lawson Gaylor, Eben Given, Howard B. Gotlieb, Paul Green, Esmee Griffith, Mildred Griffith, W. Fairfax Griffith, Mary Hackett, William H. Harding, Joseph Hawthorne, Lois Sprigg Hazell, Mary Welsh Hemingway, Larry Holdridge, Jean Kaeselau, Evelyn Lawson, John Leggett, John Lehmann, Madelene L'Engle, Isaac Don Levine, Ruth Levine, Marion Lowndes, Susan Lowndes, Mary McCarthy, Richard A. Macksey, Jerre Mangione, Beulah Marvin, Walter Rumsey Marvin, Frances Massey, R. Bruce Massey, Charles Mayo, Madelaine Hemingway Miller, Robert Nathan, Howard A. Nicholson, Charles Norman, Diana Norman, Joel O'Brien, Gwinn F. Owens, Olga Owens, Dudley Poore, Constance Poster, Lucy Virginia Ralston, Lucy Virginia Gordon Ralston, Jere Real, Curt Richter, Francis M. Rogers, Dorothy Hillyer de Santillana, Jean Shay, Cecil Woodrow Shuler, Katharine Dos Passos Shuler, Mary Dos Passos Singleton, Scottie Fitzgerald Smith, Robert Solley, Benjamin Sonnenberg, James Cresap Sprigg, Jr., Frances Steloff, Lorene Thompson, Lovell Thompson, Calvin Tomkins, Alice Vorperian, Heaton Vorse, Adelaide Walker, Harvey Weldon, Martha Weldon, Hazel Hawthorne Werner, Morris R. Werner, Isabel Foley Whelan, C. Dickerman Williams, Virginia Williams, Elena Mumm Wilson, Elizabeth Burroughs Woodhouse, Gurden Worcester, John Worthington, Tiny Worthington, Marguerite Young, and Steve Zebrock.

A number of friends and acquaintances of Dos Passos contributed materials and reminiscences through letters when a personal interview was not feasible, and for their help, too, I am grateful: Roger Baldwin, Simone de Beauvoir, Marian H. Blakeman, Florence Schmidt de Bottari, William Cates, John Cheever, Joan Colebrook, Malcolm Cowley, Mura Dehn, Margaret Devereaux, Benjamin W. Early, Sidney Fairbanks, Oriana Fallaci, P. W. Filby, Celia E. Francis, Peter M. Grosz, John Hughes Hall, Daphne Hellman, Lillian Hellman, Leicester Hemingway, C. Wright Houghland, Sr., John Knox Jessup, Alfred Kazin, Robert Kotlowitz, Elinor Langer, James Laughlin, Joshua Logan, J. Russell Lynes, Eugene Lyons, Archibald MacLeish, Selden Rodman, Mark Schorer, Robert Sherrod, Herman Shumlin, Paul Shyre, Joseph Slater, Carlton Sprague Smith, Philip Hillyer Smith, Alice Hunt Sokoloff, Elaine Steinbeck, Donald Ogden Stewart, Harold Sugg, Ralph de Toledano, James Sibley Watson, Jr., Faith Weston, Toni Willison, and Rosalind Wilson.

I appreciate, too, the assistance of other Dos Passos scholars through their published works, letters, or interviews: Georges-Albert Astre, George J. Becker, Maurice-Edgar Coindreau, Kenneth W. Holditch, Hartwig Isernhagen, Martin Kallich, Melvin Landsberg, Townsend Ludington, John Magee, Michael Palmer, Donald Pizer, Jack Potter, Virginia Reinhart, Robert Rosen, David Sanders, Charles Swick, Linda Wagner, James Westerhoven, and William White.

The staffs of countless libraries were generous also. I am indebted to Joel Holmes, Callie McGinnis, and the reference staff of the Columbus College Library in Columbus, Georgia, especially to David Anderson, Erma Banks, Merne Posey, Sharon Self, Fred Smith, Sandra Stratford, and Elwood White, who helped me daily for many months.

The major repository of unpublished Dos Passos materials is the Manuscript Division of the Alderman Library at the University of Virginia, Charlottesville; and I thank Joan St. Clair Crane, Curator of the American Literature Collections; Anne Freudenberg, Assistant Curator; and Gregory Johnson, Michael Plunkett, and Helen Troy, Public Service Assistants who generously helped me during my several visits to the Manuscripts Division and, later, in delving through materials and answering many questions through letters.

I also appreciate the help extended me by Nancy Johnson and Hortense Zera at the American Academy and Institute of Arts and Letters in New York City; Darlene Holdsworth, Special Collections Assistant, Amherst College Library, Massachusetts; Howard B. Gotlieb, Director, Special Collections, Mugar Memorial Library, Boston University, Massachusetts; Virginia Storey and the reference staff of the W. C. Bradley Memorial Library, Columbus, Georgia; Elizabeth L. White, Local History Librarian, Brooklyn Public Library, New York City; John Ingram, Manuscripts Cataloguer, The John Hay Library, Brown University Library, Providence, Rhode Island; Marie Byrne, Manuscripts Division, The Bancroft Library, University of California, Berkeley; Diane Elizabeth Nassir, Manuscript Curator, Department of Special Collections, University of California, Santa Barbara; Jane Colokathis, Library Research Specialist, The Joseph Regenstein Library, The University of Chicago, Illinois; Pauline Anderson, Director, and Mrs. Ben Sylvester, Jr., Archivist, The Choate Rosemary Archives, Andrew Mellon Library, The Choate School, Wallingford, Connecticut; Dorothy E. Mosakowski, Special Collections Assistant, Robert Hutchings Goddard Library, Clark University, Worcester, Massachusetts; Bruce Brown, Librarian, Case Library, Colgate University, Hamilton, New York; Kenneth A. Lohf, Librarian for Rare Books and Manuscripts, Columbia University Libraries of the City of New York; Ellen B. Wells, Associate Librarian, and Jane E. Woolston, Assistant, Department of Rare Books, Cornell University Library, Ithaca, New York; Ruby Fielding, Librarian, Dalton Junior College Library, Georgia; Betty Shaw, Librarian, Dalton Public Library, Georgia; Walter W. Wright, Chief of Special Collections, Dartmouth College Library, Hanover, New Hampshire; Stuart Dick, Special Collections Librarian, Morris Library, University of Delaware, Newark; John Sharpe, Curator of Rare Books, Albert Nelius, Reference Librarian, and Sharon E. Knapp, Cataloguer, Manuscript Division, William R. Perkins Library, Duke University, Durham, North Carolina; Laura V. Monti, Chairwoman, Rare Books and Manuscripts, The University Libraries, The University of Florida, Gainesville; George M. Barringer, Special Collections Librarian, The University

Library, Georgetown University, Washington, D.C.; Robert M. Willingham, Jr., Assistant Librarian, University of Georgia Libraries, Athens; Sarah D. Jones, Librarian, Julia Rogers Library, Goucher College, Towson, Maryland; Kathleen S. Miller and Jennifer Zukowski, University Archives, Harvard University Library, Cambridge, Massachusetts; Rodney C. Dennis, Curator of Manuscripts, The Houghton Library, Harvard University, Cambridge, Massachusetts; Jo August, Curator, The Ernest Hemingway Collection, John F. Kennedy Library, Boston, Massachusetts; M. C. Beecheno, Manuscripts Department, The Milton S. Eisenhower Library, and Jane Katz, Assistant, Special Collections, Evergreen House Foundation, The Johns Hopkins University, Baltimore, Maryland; Nancy McCall, Assistant Archivist, The Johns Hopkins Medical Institutions, Baltimore, Maryland; Paul Myers, Curator, Theatre Collection, Library and Museum of the Performing Arts, The New York Public Library at Lincoln Center, New York City; Mary Ceibert, Assistant Rare Book Room Librarian, and Maynard Brichford, University Archivist, University Library, University of Illinois at Urbana-Champaign; Kenneth W. Duckett, Curator, Special Collections, Morris Library, Southern Illinois University at Carbondale; Sandra Taylor, Curator of Manuscripts, The Lilly Library, Indiana University, Bloomington; Frank Paluka, Head, Special Collections, The University Libraries, The University of Iowa, Iowa City; John C. Broderick, Chief, Manuscript Division, The Library of Congress, Washington, D.C.; Eric S. Flower, Head, Special Collections, Raymond H. Fogler Library, University of Maine at Orono; Ruby Y. Weinbrecht, Librarian, Mary Washington College, Fredericksburg, Virginia; Charlotte B. Brown, Archivist, McKeldin Library, University of Maryland, College Park; Robert DeRusha, Assistant Archivist, University of Massachusetts, Amherst; Harriet C. Jameson, Head, Department of Rare Books and Special Collections, University Library, The University of Michigan, Ann Arbor; Robert Buckeye, Special Collections, Abernethy Library, Middlebury College, Vermont; Ruby J. Shields, Research Assistant, Minnesota Historical Society, St. Paul; Margaret Howell, Rare Book and Manuscripts Librarian, University of Missouri Library, Columbia; Tim Gorelangton, Assistant, Special Collections, The University Library, The University of Nevada, Reno; Donald E. Spencer, The National Archives and Records Service, Washington, D.C.; Theodore Grieder, Curator, Elmer Holmes Bobst Library and Fales Library, New York University, New York City; K. C. Gay, Curator, The Poetry Collection of the Lockwood Memorial Library, State University of New York at Buffalo; Evert Volkersz, Head, Department of Special Collections, and Frank Melville, Jr., Memorial Library, State University of New York at Stony Brook; Jean R. McNiece, Lola Szladits, Robert F. Wiseman, and John D. Stinson in the Rare Books and Manuscripts Divisions of The New York Public Library, New York City; Diana Haskell, Curator of Modern Manuscripts, the Newberry Library, Chicago, Illinois; Harry McKown, Reference Archivist, Southern Historical Collection, Wilson Library, The University of North Carolina at Chapel Hill; Mary H. Proper, Reference Librarian, The Nyack Library, New York; Phillip Zorich, Librarian, Special Collections, University of Oregon, Eugene; Jack D. Haley, Assistant Curator, Western History Collections, The University of Oklahoma, Norman; Jackie Kingsolver, Assistant, Special Collections, Joint University Libraries, Peabody College, Scarritt College, and Vanderbilt University, Nashville, Tennessee; Evelyn Hart, Head, Peabody Institute Library, Baltimore, Maryland; Barbara E. Deibler, Rare Books Librarian, State Library of Pennsylvania, Harrisburg;

Charles W. Mann, Chief, Rare Books and Special Collections, The University Libraries, The Pennsylvania State University, University Park; Lyman W. Riley, Assistant Director for Special Collections, The Charles Patterson Van Pelt Library, University of Pennsylvania, Philadelphia; William A. Felker, Head, General Information Department, The Free Library of Philadelphia, Pennsylvania; Christine A. Ruggere, Curator, Historical Collections, Library of the College of Physicians of Philadelphia, Pennsylvania; Alexander P. Clark, Curator of Manuscripts, and Agnes B. Sherman, Manuscripts Assistant, Seeley G. Mudd Manuscript Library, Princeton University, New Jersey; William J. Stewart, Acting Director, Franklin D. Roosevelt Library, National Archives and Records Service, Hyde Park, New York; Mary M. Huth, Assistant Librarian, Department of Rare Books, Manuscripts and Archives, The University of Rochester Library, New York; Clark L. Beck, Jr., Assistant Curator, Special Collections Department, Archibald Stevens Alexander Library, Rutgers, The State University of New Jersey, New Brunswick; Carolyn A. Davis, Manuscripts Librarian, The George Arents Research Library, Syracuse University, New York; Daniel C. Williamson, Rare Book Bibliographer, Samuel Paley Library, Temple University, Philadelphia, Pennsylvania; Ellen S. Dunlap, Research Librarian, Humanities Research Center, The University of Texas, Austin; Ann S. Gwyn, Head, Special Collections Division, Howard-Tilton Memorial Library, Tulane University, New Orleans, Louisiana; Clark Thayer, Modern Letters Bibliographer, McFarlin Library, The University of Tulsa, Oklahoma; Frances Goudy, Special Collections Librarian, Vassar College Library, Poughkeepsie, New York; Daniel A. Yanchisin, Special Collections Librarian, James Branch Cabell Library, Virginia Commonwealth University, Richmond; Louis H. Manarin, State Archivist, Virginia State Library, Richmond; Patricia Herron, Reference Librarian, Petersburg Public Library, Virginia; Dione Miles, Reference Archivist, and Mary Karshner, Research Assistant, Archives of Labor and Urban Affairs, Walter P. Reuther Library, Wayne State University, Detroit, Michigan; Robert G. Mittelstadt, Library Specialist, Archives and Manuscripts Division, Suzzallo Library, University of Washington, Seattle; Eleanor Nicholes, Special Collections Librarian, Wilma R. Slaight, Archivist, and Stephanie Welch, Archives Assistant, Margaret Clapp Library, Wellesley College, Massachusetts; Elisabeth A. Swiam, Special Collections Librarian and University Archivist, Olin Library, Wesleyan University, Middletown, Connecticut; David Crosson, Research Historian, Archives of Contemporary History, Division of Rare Books and Special Collections, The University of Wyoming, Laramie; Donald Gallup, Curator, Collection of American Literature, Peter Dzwonkoski, Assistant to the Curator, and Stephen C. Jones, Public Services Assistant, The Beinecke Rare Book and Manuscript Library, and Judith A. Schiff, Chief Research Archivist, Manuscripts and Archives, Sterling Memorial Library, Yale University, New Haven, Connecticut.

I thank, also, Mary A. Dye and Helen Straw Hinkle of the Genealogical Society of Allegany County, Maryland; Mary C. Lipham, Archivist, and Patsy R. Acree, Assistant Archivist, of the Hall of Records, Annapolis, Maryland; Stanley T. Kusper, Jr., County Clerk, Bureau of Vital Statistics, Chicago, Illinois; the Admissions Office and Registrar, University of Missouri—Columbia; James P. McGrath, Clerk of the Adoption Court of New York City; Margaret C. Lunt, Registrar of the Probate Court, Hancock County, Ellsworth, Maine; Fern Kelley, City Clerk, Ellsworth, Maine; Robert L. Neal, Director,

Allegany County Library System, Maryland; L. John Gernand, Registrar and Archivist, The Phillips Collection, Washington, D.C.; Mary McIsaac, Archivist, The School of the Art Institute of Chicago, Illinois; Frederic P. Claussen, Registrar, Barnstable County Probate Court, Massachusetts; Vera Dickey and Marjorie P. Pyburn, The Sidwell Friends School, Washington, D.C.; Raymond W. Walker, Clerk of the Circuit Court, Cumberland, Maryland; Margaret E. Law, Registrar, Harvard University, Cambridge, Massachusetts; Miriam Stewart, The Drawing Department, Fogg Art Museum of Harvard University, Cambridge, Massachusetts; Nancy Holyoke, Mary Norris, and Helen Stark, reference staff, *The New Yorker;* Hannah Bruce, Diana Franklin, and Lillian Owens, *Time* and *Life* Archives, New York City; Fred R. Brandt and Richard Woodward, The Virginia Museum of Fine Arts, Richmond; Alex Wilkinson, Provincetown Art Association, Massachusetts.

Many others assisted in the making of *Dos Passos: A Life* in a variety of ways. I thank Ghreta and John Vincent Adams, Jane Allport, Charles Anderson, Katherine Archer, Lawrence P. Ashmead, Stanley D. Bachrack, Nona Balakian, Leslie Bates, Betty Berne, Lewis Berne, Frank Blackford, Michael Blankfort, Jay Bochner, George S. Bolster, Edgar M. Branch, Carol Brandt, Arthur Cantor, Eltse B. Carter, Monique Chefdor, Elliott Coleman, Mrs. Reginald Gorton Combe, Mary Comer, Phil Comer, George Cress, Richard Cruce, Laura Curran, John Dalmas, Chris Dickey, Madeline Dickinson, George Dudley, Cathy Eckdall, Bethel Edrington, David Eisendroth, Jean Elliot, Sherrard Elliot, Gene Fedorka, Rodney Fielding, John Fleischauer, Lenemaja Friedman, Rowland E. Fullilove, Dorothy Gallagher, Jan Gannon, Spencer Garrard, Mary Garst, Atalissa S. Gilfoyle, Dwight E. Gray, Miriam Gurko, Gusti's Restaurant, Washington, D.C., Harington Harlow, Curtis Harnock, Director, and the Executive Board, Yaddo Artists Colony, John T. Harrison, James Boswell Howard III, Nancy Hubbard, Karin Isernhagen, Edward C. Janes, Werner Janssen, Andy Jenkins, Oliver Jensen, David J. Johnson, Joanna Kirkpatrick, Alfred A. Knopf, Leah Koontz, Clason Kyle, Sylvia Lazerow, Jean Lowrey, Rodney Luery, Beatrice McMillan, Jordan Massee, John S. Mayfield, Francisco J. Mendonça, Bruce Mitchell, Agnes Mongan, Edwin Morgan, Linda Mulgrew, Scott Murrie, Carolyn Nash, the New York *Times Book Review,* Martin S. Ochs, Arnold R. Oliver, Thomas Parker, Cleo Mitchell Paturis, Edwin Peacock, Phil Phelps, Robert Phillips, Nicholas Potter, Ted Purdy, Ann Kubie Rabinowitz, Bonnie Robbins, Peter Romanofsky, Robert Saliba, L. D. Soderlind, Donald E. Spencer, Margit Spencer, Joseph Steinmetz, Dan Streetman, Mary Ellen Stumpf, Patricia Sumner, Anthea Tatton-Brown, Kenneth Thompson, Lois Thompson, Joseph J. Thorndike, Jr., Lynn Tudor, Eva Ulrich, Giorgio Voghi, Ruth Wall, Deborah Wallner, Maggie H. Whaley, R. A. Whitaker, Martha Willett, Florence Wislocki, and John Ziegler.

I extend special thanks to the linguists who translated French, Spanish, German, or Italian letters, articles, and other documents: Philip Battle, Pedro Campa, Caryl Lloyd, Mario Mion, and Zaiga Mion; to the secretarial staff of the Languages and Literature Department of Columbus College, Georgia, especially to Georgia Allison, Pamela Chappell, Melanie Haynes, and Audrey Wolfe, who typed several drafts of the manuscript; to Jeanette Cable, who prepared much of the final draft; to Maxine Brown and Sharon Sudderth, who read galley proof; to Julia Payne, who typed, proofread, and performed sundry other chores; to Francis J. Brooke and Sue Dezendolet, who allowed me to carry a reduced teaching load during a crucial period of writing and provided a typist when I needed one most; to John E. Anderson and Thomas Y. Whitley, who granted a three-month leave from teaching; to Roy Tanner and the Columbus College Foundation, who gave me an interest-free loan to free me from teaching for six months while on an unpaid leave; to Paul VanderGheynst, who supported my project in countless ways as Dean of the College of Arts and Letters at Columbus College, Georgia; to Cyril F. dos Passos, Lois Sprigg Hazell, Robert Nathan, and Dudley Poore, who read much of the early manuscript; and to Manoel da Silveira Cardozo and Elizabeth Dos Passos, who read the final draft.

I am especially grateful to Carolyn Blakemore and Ken McCormick, my editors at Doubleday, and to their assistants, Robert Frese and Joan Ward; to my copy editor, Scott Sack, and to my literary agent, Roberta Pryor.

And, finally, to Kenneth G. Gale, my son-in-law, and to my three daughters, to whom this biography is dedicated—Karen, Catherine, and Kimberly—who encouraged and supported me and, at times, took short shrift, yet did not complain, my heartfelt thanks—and my apologies, dear ones.

*"Dos Passos has invented only one thing,
an art of storytelling.
But that is enough. . . .
I regard Dos Passos as the greatest writer
of our time."*

Jean-Paul Sartre
Paris, 1938

Book I

JACK MADISON

1896–1912

PROLOGUE

In 1912 John Randolph Dos Passos wrote Ida Little Pifer
("my dear cousin fourteen hundred times removed"):
    I want you—if you can secure the time—
    to consult the birth register of Chicago
    to see if anyone by the name of Dos Passos
    was dropped there in the month of January
        —in 1895, 1896, or 1897—
    and let me drive it home by asking you
    to send the information at once. . . .
    When you are asking a favor
    you might as well go the whole figure:
    Do me the favor and do it quickly.

John Randolph—his friends called him John R.—was sixty-eight,
and the birth of his bastard son January 14, 1896,
should have been no mystery (least of all to him).
Even his recently deceased wife knew about "Master Jack" Madison,
but John R. likedbeingmysterious.
He was already married to Jack's mother
when he directed Ida to make inquiry.
The well-born Lucy Addison Sprigg Madison
had loved him feverishly for three decades,
was convinced that somedaytheywouldwed.
Jack called his father "Dedi,"
told inquisitive classmates
that Dedi was his guardian;
he was fourteen when John R. confided:
"Our marriage is no longer a secret—
the name Madison must be forever stopped."
A cocky little man, John R. intimidated his wife and son,
ruled the roost at home—or wherever he dispatched them—
and was a rooster of the courts as well.

He mademoneyandspentit
and never stopped working
and never let his mind sit in neutral.

John R. was christened John Rodrigues in 1844
(insisted later the "R" stood for Randolph),
the fourth of nine children:
Manoel, Joseph, David, John, Eugene, Benjamin;
and the girls, Joaquina, Francesca, and Harriet.
His father, Manoel Joaquim dos Passos, was eighteen
when he left his native village, Ponta do Sol,
on the island of Madeira and journeyed to America
(rumors had it he had killed a man in a brawl, fled the country).
Six brothers and sisters remained at home
and missed their hot-headed brother
who believed he had to go to America to be his own man.
Manoel landed in Baltimore, mended boots and shoes
for a stern master until the City of Brotherly Love beckoned.
In a shop of his own at last he cobbled fine leathers,
but nine children drained his purse and he stayed poor.
His well-born wife, Lucinda Ann ("Lucy") Cattell,
and her sister, Jamina, were from Haddonfield, New Jersey;
Methodists with a Quaker bent, Lucy's parents shuddered
that she could do little to assuage
her husband's dish-throwing tantrums
set off when a meal displeased him,
regretted that she had married a Roman Catholic.
Manoel's children cowered and left home early.

An incurable romantic, young John R.
thought of taking to the sea as a cabin boy
and vowed to skipper his own yacht some day;
was routed from the Union Army by dysentery
and said he had been a drummer but never mentioned combat
until years later when he reported
having fought valiantly against the Rebels.
"Be a priest," advised Papa upon his return,
but John R. held out for the courts and marketplace,
met a Philadelphia barrister, William S. Price,
who took him into his law office and loved him like the son he never had.
At night John R. sat at the feet of George Sherwood,
who lectured on the wiles of lawyerhood
at the University of Pennsylvania,
but most of what John R. knew he taught himself.

At six A.M. on his twenty-first birthday
he got himself admitted to the bar,
argued in the District Court and the Court of Common Pleas
for the City and County of Philadelphia.
It was the year General Lee surrendered at Appomattox
and Lincoln was assassinated.

By 1867 John R. had wearied of Philadelphia,
thought opportunities more golden in New York
and went to get some.
He practiced first in the old office of Aaron Burr,
defended a Frenchman who had killed his wife in a jealous rage,
maneuvered the charge from murder to manslaughter,
and people who counted took note.
Soon John R. was successfully defending other opportunists.
When Edward S. Stokes was convicted of first-degree murder
(having gunned down Jim Fisk, a rival suitor,
in the lobby of the Grand Central Hotel),
all Manhattan was aghast.
Everyone knew the prominent Stokes family,
and most knew, too, Jim Fisk's itch for trouble;
A Vermont peddler, Fisk had worked his way
through Southern cotton and bogus Erie Railroad stock
into a scheme with Jay Gould to buy up the nation's gold
on Black Friday when Wall Street tumbled.
Gould cleared eleven million on the deal,
but Fisk was not so lucky.
John R. was hired by Mrs. Stokes for the defense team,
and when her son's guilty verdict was overturned,
most of the credit went to the young lawyer
who had dazzled his opponents.

He also dazzled the daughter of DeWitt Clinton Hays,
president of The Bank of Manhattan
(known later as Chase Manhattan),
and treasurer of The New York Stock Exchange.
Mary Dyckman Hays was bright, comely, and good-hearted,
attributes in combination with her father's sterling qualities
which did not go unheeded by John R.,
who courted her with such fervor
that she and her father quickly agreed to the marriage,
rejoiced when she bore him a son, Louis Hays
(their first child had died in infancy, a daughter, unnamed),
and they were happy—for a time.

John R.'s wants were simple,
and he knew how to get them:
With a new firm name, Dos Passos Brothers
(his partner, his brother Benjamin),
and an office overlooking The New York Stock Exchange,
John R. had politicians and capitalists alike
scrambling for his favor,
entertaining him at Delmonico's,
and clamoring for his services.
He trotted each morning in Central Park
with The Liver Brigade, riders who tipped their hats
before squaring off an hour later in the marketplace.
When thrown from his horse, John R. made headlines.
He made them again for his new ritual: pedestrianism.
"Rich Men Who Walk" featured his brisk daily saunter
from his fashionable brownstone at Eighteen East Fifty-Sixth
(a wedding gift from his generous father-in-law)
to Wall Street and back, regardless of the weather,
but nothing in print matched John R.'s flamboyance.
Heads swiveled as he strutted past
in a cutaway jacket tailored in London,
worn like a uniform for almost every affair—both night and day—
(including his presentation to the Court of Edward VII),
his bushy waxed mustaches glistening ear to ear
beneath a black silk hat.
He eschewed an overcoat, did not own one, he boasted;
his one concession to the elements an opera cloak
thrown rakishly over his shoulders
before he set out for the theatre or concert hall.
Never without his cherry walking stick,
John R. twirled it with a flourish
and cut an international figure at home and abroad.

He also made headlines for setting up
the American Sugar Refining Company,
for establishing the Sugar Trust,
for earning the largest fee on record
($500,000.00, so the papers reported);
for lending a million dollars at six per cent
to support Cuba's revolution;
for approving of American imperialism
("keep the Philippines—a nation should retain its colonies");
for being an authority on everything.

He dispatched letters
to editors, governors, Congressmen, the President,
ever alert to allies in a position
to convert opinion to legislation;
stumped for William McKinley,
rued his assassination,
saw the nation sliding downhill,
accused Teddy Roosevelt of selling out the American people,
insisted that the trend of the Party
which had once saved the Union now foreboded ill,
believed salvation lay with the British,
urged all English-speaking peoples of the world to unite
("let there be one citizenship, one currency,
one standard of weights and measures,
unlimited commercial intercourse,
an international Supreme Court");
proposed that farmers be allowed to borrow money
at half the normal rate
from new financial institutions comprised of stockholders
mechanics, artisans, laborers,
a new breed of capitalists: THE COMMON MAN.
He also feared the country's drift toward socialism,
struck out against it repeatedly,
warned of its dangers.
He conceived a new electoral procedure for the United States Senate,
crusaded for civil law reform, for criminal law reform,
wrote definitive law texts, pitied the poor,
established the office of Public Defender,
opposed suffrage ("women do not want it," he argued),
stiffened when attackers ridiculed his views
or dubbed them archaic;
but no one ever said he lacked conviction—
and he always spoke his mind.
He would not have known how to straddle a fence,
but vaulted back and forth as his theories—
and the world—changed.

A sermonizer always,
John R. penned hundreds of missives to Lucy,
and later, to their son,
admonishing them as a dutiful pastor whose errant sheep
need guidance in selecting the proper pasture in which to graze:
    Seek—and if you cultivate the mind and soul—ye shall find;
    Believe not that religion is founded upon miracles

or faith or logic—they are mere trappings;
Read Peter's denial of Christ—some falsehoods are justified;
Know that churches have their place
(just as I have mine);
This Sabbath morning I preach
from the Grand Union Hotel in Saratoga Springs.
John R. orated:
   on friendship
   on the hereafter,
   on the proper use of time,
   on the importance of habit,
   on the habit of reading the Bible,
   on the relationship of duty to beauty,
   on the rewards of daily self-examination,
   on the eight-hour work day (he was against it),
   on the necessity of sunshine to illuminate virtue,
   on the misfortunes of young men who have no Socrates,
and the fount never went dry.
His sermons to Lucy were without salutation
(or signature, the discretion of a married man),
but his scrawl was readily identified—
liberally punctuated by dashes—
his rush of rhetoric declaiming THE TRUTH—THE TRUTH—THE TRUTH—
Know that I am with you (IN SPIRIT)—
wherever you are—
Be patient—
And somedaywewillwed—
(he promised her)
when I am free—

1

Jack may have been illegitimate, but he came from good stock.

Lois Sprigg Hazell to Virginia Spencer Carr
5 May 1977

The Cresaps and Spriggs from whom Jack Madison descended on his mother's side were colorful, illustrious ancestors. His mother—Lucy Addison Sprigg Madison—was the fourth generation of her family born in Cumberland, Maryland, the seat of Allegany County and most important town in the state's rugged northwest panhandle.

The town was perched on the edge of the Potomac River where it rose as a narrow stream in the Allegheny Mountains and wriggled its way on a southeasterly course to the lower end of Chesapeake Bay. Strangers who journeyed through the region from north to south were startled to find themselves in Maryland for a time. Natives were proud of their heritage and the freedoms historically associated with their state. Those who lived in its westernmost counties looked to Cumberland for their resources, leadership, and culture.

As a child, Lucy Addison Sprigg was enthralled by the tales her father and his twin, Sarah Elizabeth, told of their pioneering forebears, the Cresaps and Spriggs. The Cresaps were the first whites to settle among the Indians of Allegany County. Thomas Cresap, who emigrated in 1710 from the village of Skipton in Yorkshire, England, preferred the frontier to towns already settled along the coast. Pushing westward, he came to a small valley nestled among the mountains; a good-sized stream snaked through this valley, which seemed an ideal homesite. Cresap went home for his wife Hannah Johnson and their five children, then returned to the region and called it "Skipton" in honor of the town of his birth. With the aid of his sons, he built a home and stockade, and soon other pioneering families arrived to homestead with him. The mountainous terrain tended to isolate them from the rest of the state, but the settlers soon discovered a gigantic natural pass that they dubbed "the Narrows," its vertical rock walls stretching from sky to meadow down as though cleaved by a giant machete. Word spread East that wagon trains could easily migrate West through the narrow gap, but many families who had intended to push on became so enamored of the region that they chose to remain rather than risk the unknown hazards beyond. By the time Lucy Addison Sprigg was born (January 9, 1856) in the shadow of the Narrows, Cumberland was a thriving transportation center, with both the Baltimore & Ohio Railroad and the recently completed Chesapeake and Ohio Canal providing vital links between East and West. Boats and barges of freight and settlers steamed up the canal daily, their destination Allegany County.

It was Thomas Cresap's youngest child, Michael, from whom Lucy was descended. Michael Cresap died young, having commanded the first troops mustered in Maryland when General Washington's army laid siege to Boston in 1775. Sarah, his youngest daughter, married into the prominent Sprigg family of Cumberland. Osborn and Sarah Sprigg had five children; the eldest, Michael Cresap Sprigg, continued the line of Lucy Sprigg's forebears, having chosen as his bride one Mary Lamar, a proper Cumberland woman of hardy stock whose father had distinguished himself as a colonel in the Revolutionary War. Outspoken in matters of community concern, Michael was sent twice to the Maryland legislature, then elected to the United States Congress. Of his ten children, only four survived infancy: William Osborn, Louisa Ann, and the first of two sets of twins: James Cresap and Sarah Elizabeth.

It was James Cresap Sprigg who fathered Lucy. A renegade of sorts, young James chose not to remain in Cumberland after the birth of his first two children, Floyd Addison and Lucy Addison. When talk of secession erupted in 1857, he moved his family to Petersburg, Virginia. Sprigg was not an inflamed sectionalist, but his sympathies lay with the South. He was a builder of roads and bridges, and Virginia had far more need of him than Maryland, he reasoned. His wife's people lived in Washington, D.C.—a Union bastion—but she agreed that they should remain in Virginia. Their five other children were born in Petersburg. During the war when a new baby was imminent, the older children were farmed out to various Sprigg or Addison households thought to be safe from enemy lines. During one such lying-in—for the birth of William Mercer in 1863— Lucy, seven, was sent to North Brighton, New York, to the home of an Addison relative. A spunky child, Lucy fought her own "civil war" with her Yankee cousins and playmates. She wrote her mother: "When anybody says to me that General Grant is the best, I say not better than General Lee and Jeff Davis."

The James Cresap Sprigg family continued to make their home in Petersburg after the war, although the children and Mrs. Sprigg frequently visited the Addison clan in Washington. The Addisons claimed the brilliant eighteenth-century British essayist and poet Joseph Addison as a direct ancestor, but were even prouder of their own rank in Washington society. Sprigg's children were so strung out in ages that Lucy, his oldest daughter, was already married and about to become a mother herself when his youngest child was born. Lucy had been courted at sixteen by Ryland Randolph Madison, a fourth-generation nephew of President James Madison and a descendant of the esteemed Randolphs of Virginia—in short, a proper suitor.

Young Madison's propensity for hard liquor was established early. At twenty-one he seemed unwilling to settle down to the responsibilities of a family; consequently, his son James grew up with little awareness of his father. It is likely that Lucy Sprigg Madison never left home (at least not to live with her husband), and if Madison himself returned to his father-in-law's roof to be with his wife and infant son, it was only briefly. James was reared with his mother's two baby sisters, a confusing relationship for the children. James's "Aunt Mamie" (Mary Lamar) was only three when he was born, and his "Aunt Lilly" was younger than he. Lucy Sprigg Madison assisted her mother in the care of her son, but she herself was a child of sorts.

The family home in Petersburg was largely a matriarchal structure. James Cresap Sprigg moved alone to Washington after the war to take a job as surveyor in the General Land Office of the U.S. Department of the Interior and left his oldest son, Addison, to be the mainstay of the family; Addison, however, died at twenty-one in 1873—the same year his sister Lilly and nephew James were born—a death that nearly devastated his mother. Meanwhile, Lucy was no happier at home than her father had been. When he told her there was an opening in his office for a copyist she wasted no time in applying. By now, James was four. To take a job outside the home was almost unheard of among nineteenth-century women reared in what was considered a genteel Southern tradition, but Lucy Madison insisted, leaving young James in her mother's care and moving alone to the District of Columbia.

The first decade of her life in Washington was marked by a series of almost annual moves. Lucy lived first in the upstairs of a narrow row house at 211 A Street, S.E. After residing there a few months she took a room in the "Court District" to be closer to her work, first at 311 D Street, N.W., then at 340 C Street, N.W., just a block away. By this time she had been a copier of government documents and records at the General Land Office for some three years. In 1880 her father—having become something of a real estate entrepreneur on the side—purchased a home at 2020 G Street, N.W., and moved his family up from Petersburg. Lucy, too, came home to live, but kept her job, thriving on the freedom she experienced outside the confines of her family. The only way for proper Southern women to contribute to the sagging economics of a household was to take in paying guests (they were never referred to as boarders). Mrs. Sprigg's guests during this period were three government clerks recommended by her husband (two widows and a twenty-nine-year-old spinster) and a grocery checker who was given a room in exchange for doing odd chores about the house.

Several years after the family moved to Washington, Sprigg bought still another house for them, this one at 1710 F Street, N.W., not far from the G Street residence. Eventually his wife and the younger children moved into the F Street home and Sprigg maintained his living quarters in the other house. Mrs. Sprigg was apparently aware that her husband had a continuing liaison with one "Mrs. Camp" and there was an implicit understanding that he was free to come and go without question. In the 1880s, divorce was seldom an acceptable alternative to marriage even if adultery was the issue. The injured party usually made the best of the situation and tried to protect the rest of the family from the inevitable gossip. Gossip was inevitable concerning Lucy as well. For Lucy to have left a child at home to be reared by its grandmother when the mother herself did not *have* to work was not quite the same as taking to the streets, but she was criticized soundly. Her return home redeemed her somewhat, but she moved out again in 1885, this time to 530 Twenty-first Street, N.W.

What prompted Lucy's latest exodus may have been a new gentleman friend, whom she met through her father. John R. Dos Passos was James Sprigg's business associate and a prominent New York lawyer whose practice took him frequently to the nation's capital, where he hobnobbed with congressmen, dined at the Metropolitan Club, rode horseback in Rock Creek Park, and enjoyed other pastimes unrelated to his profession, such as the acquisition of land and houses, through which his friendship with Sprigg developed.

Sprigg's work with the General Land Office often took him to Virginia, especially to the Tidewater and Northern Neck regions, where he was exposed to a number of good land buys, large estates for the most part. Plantation sales were common in the 1880s as formerly indentured servants and field hands died off and homeowners could not afford to replace them. Many farms had not been worked since the war, and surviving families had sold off their land bit by bit or abandoned their property in hopes that it might be better coped with later. Though Sprigg had little money to invest in large land tracts, he had a knack for hearing about good buys before anyone else did and hated to see property slip away if he could enhance his own position in the process. With Sprigg's help, John R. became the absentee owner of more than a dozen houses and parcels of land in the District of Columbia and of several land tracts in the Northern Neck of Virginia.

John R. may well have begun seeing Lucy Sprigg Madison—and courting her—as early as 1883 when his business dealings first evolved with Sprigg. Never one to ignore a pretty face, he was charmed by his friend's daughter. Sprigg apprised John R. that she was living apart from her husband, had a young son (by this time James was ten), and worked for a living. In 1885, John R. asked permission of Lucy to invite young James to his home in New York City to meet his own son, Louis. James was ecstatic. He had never been that far north before and was thrilled at the prospect of visiting all the wondrous places his mother's friend had promised to show him. A few days after his twelfth birthday, the boy accompanied John R. to his fashionable brownstone at 18 East Fifty-sixth Street. Although Louis was three years younger than James, they got along well during their week together, according to James's letter to his mother on February 13, 1885: "Louis is a very nice boy. We went to the Eden Musée this afternoon and it was a very nice place. I am just having a splendid time. . . . Mr. Dos Passos' house is beautiful. Mrs. Dos Passos is a very nice lady, but a little lame."

In 1887 Lucy quit her job, took James from her mother's home, and moved with him to a modest two-story row house on a tree-lined, cobblestone street in Georgetown. James, now fourteen, was glad to be living in a home of their own at last. Lucy did not own the house at 2816 Olive Street, but for all practical purposes it was theirs. In nearby Rock Creek Park James rode horseback in the company of his mother's friend, who came often from New York to visit. Lucy enjoyed her role as a genteel lady of leisure. For the first time since her marriage she had a live-in servant with whom she could leave James. She made a number of visits to her relatives in Virginia, Maryland, and New York, where she also saw John R. By now, Lucy had begun listing herself as "widow" in the city directories, but in fact, she was not. She and Ryland Madison remained married for thirty-one years, a status changed only by his death in Cumberland, Maryland, on his wife's birthday in 1903. Family members may have promoted her pose as widow.

Several family members chose to believe there was no impropriety between Lucy and her friend. The fact that she moved into a house owned by him (at 2022 F Street, N.W.) after leaving her Olive Street address is not in itself incriminating. John R. may have thought of it only as helping the daughter of an old friend to whom he owed a debt; or he may have thought of Lucy as an apt tenant for one of his recently acquired houses, which he would rather have occupied than empty, and offered it to her for little or no rent. Yet when she gave up her government job at the General Land Office, she gave up her income. There is no evidence that Lucy had private funds from any source other than John R. She had no inheritance, nor was her father's income—or inclination, for that matter—sufficient to support her and James in a home of their own. Lucy was undoubtedly encouraged to believe that someday Dos Passos would have his freedom and marry her. It is probable, too, that Dos Passos played the misunderstood husband whose life at home left much to be desired. With a flamboyant personality, flair for the grand gesture, and inordinate powers of persuasion, he could have talked the blindfold off the goddess of justice herself with only half a tongue. It is unlikely that Lucy was aware of how emotionally involved she had become in the relationship until it was too late to extricate herself, even if she had wanted to.

Unaware that James Madison had been a guest in the Dos Passos home in New York as early as 1885, several members of the Sprigg clan believed a horseback-riding accident four years later to be the event that first brought John R. and Lucy together. The New York *Times* reported the incident in two long paragraphs, with the headline: JOHN R. DOS PASSOS ILL—SUFFERING FROM THE EFFECTS OF AN ACCIDENT IN WASHINGTON. The story persisting among family members was that he was not taken to a hotel, as reported to the newspaper after the accident, but to the F Street address, the house owned by him, but occupied by Lucy. Since the house was situated three blocks from the lower end of Rock Creek Park, John R. was probably riding in the vicinity with James, or with Lucy herself, and insisted on being taken there, instead of to a hotel or hospital. It was Lucy who nursed his head wound and helped him through the siege of "brain fever" that followed until he was well enough to return to New York City.

The name "Lucy Sprigg Madison" appeared almost annually in city directories of the District of Columbia from 1876 to 1890, then disappeared from official records for the next four years before surfacing once more as the "resident" of 1023 Vermont Avenue, N.W. This time she was back home with her mother and younger siblings. She sometimes went to Texas to visit her sister, Lilly, for months at a time, but more often she stayed on West End Avenue in New York City with her sister, Mary Lamar (now married to an architect, James Riely Gordon). The Gordons were devoted to Lucy, sympathized with her plight, and enjoyed the intrigue of having a prominent attorney call upon her in their home.

No matter where Lucy traveled, her lover's letters followed her, long missives in which John R. poured out his feelings of love and devotion and expressed himself on a variety of public and private topics (including his health and bodily functions). Lucy spent several summers during the early 1890s in Spring Lake, New Jersey, usually at the Monmouth Hotel. Here John R. joined her several times a month, yet typically wrote her two or three times a week even though he often arrived before his letters did. On August 21, 1892, he wrote: "I wonder in my heart if you feel as isolated without me today as I do without you, my sweet Lucia? If you do I pity you. I am listless, sad—without the pride of occupation." His letters always began or ended with an observation of his feverish desire for their next meeting, or of his impatience in the interim.

Lucy Madison returned to Washington, D.C., in the late winter of 1896 after an absence of several months and moved into the first home purchased in her own name, an elegantly furnished, three-story structure at 1201 Nineteenth Street, N.W. Accompanying her were a nanny and a newborn infant. Preceding their arrival was the whispered announcement that Lucy had adopted a baby boy in Chicago and was going to rear him as though he were her own. He resembled John R., however, and to those who also knew Louis Dos Passos, the baby was a ringer for his half-brother. Lucy named her infant Jack Madison and told her relatives that she had taken him from a North Shore Chicago hotel, where he had been born on January 14, 1896, to a wretched unwed woman without visible means of support. The infant's father had abandoned them, she added. Whatever the family's private thoughts may have been, no one accused Lucy to her face of having given birth to the child herself. According to official records, the birth went unnoticed and unreported in Cook County, Illinois. When Dos Passos asked Ida Little Pifer, his cousin who lived for a time in Chicago, to search the birth records for any "Dos Passos" child born in 1895, 1896, or 1897, she turned up nothing. Years later, John R. Dos Passos, Jr., conducted his own search, but found no record of his birth.

Amidst lamentations by various members of the Sprigg and Addison clan regarding the new disgrace to which the family had fallen heir, Lucy confided to her brother, William—and perhaps to one or more of her other siblings—the truth about her son's birth, yet so far as the outward story went, Jack Madison was adopted. His young cousins heard rumors over the years that there was something secretive about his parentage, but they did not dream of asking "Aunt Lucy" herself about it until her niece and namesake, Lucy Virginia Gordon—Mary Lamar's daughter—raised the question. A curious and forthright person, young Lucy Virginia, fifteen, was certain that her loving relationship with her aunt merited a candid answer. "Aunt Lucy, is there any truth that my Cousin Jack is *not* your adopted child at all, but truly your *real* son?" The anguished lady, distressed by the question, replied, "Absolutely not! I would swear on a stack of Bibles that I am telling you the truth—Jack is not my own child." So far as Lucy Virginia was concerned, the matter was closed. Regardless of what anyone else thought, Lucy Virginia and her aunt now had a secret to which no one else was privy. She alone had dared to ask and had learned "the truth," she concluded. Those who believed Jack Madison to be a love child were aware also that John R. was already a married man, although they may not have known that Lucy, too, still had a spouse. John R. himself had no legal basis for divorce, since adultery was the only grounds in the state of New York; moreover, his wife had no intention of initiating a divorce. To those who knew of his dual life, he reported that his wife was mentally ill so that his philandering might be more acceptable.

2

Nothing is so beneficial to a man as to be happily married—no state so wretched as when these relations are inharmonious.

John R. Dos Passos to Ida Little Pifer
16 March 1900

Before Jack Madison was a year old, his mother left Washington and took him to Europe. The relocation was John R.'s idea. It was less expensive—as well as less complicated—for him to maintain a mistress and child with an ocean's distance between them and his legitimate family and professional affairs in New York City and Washington. John R. promised Lucy they would be married as soon as he was free; in the meantime, he insisted they could have a more open relationship on the Continent than in the United States, where they could pose as man and wife. Young Jack grew up calling his mother's companion "Dedi." If asked, he was instructed to tell people simply that Dedi was his guardian.

Since John R.'s business involving trust and corporation law took him frequently to Europe, he usually arranged his schedule so that he could stay on the Continent or in England for at least three weeks at a time. Whenever possible, he summoned Lucy from wherever she happened to be to join him. Though she sometimes took their young son with her, she usually traveled alone, leaving him with two maiden friends who shared a home in London. Jack Madison grew up calling his mother's friends, Kate Gee and Sophia Louisa Meakin, "Aunt Kate" and "Auntie Loo." So far as he was concerned, they were his only aunts until he met his mother's family in New York and Washington, D.C. Until he attended boarding school in London, young Jack lived almost exclusively in the company of older women. It was years before there was an opportunity for a meaningful father/son association, and by then Jack was too accustomed to Dedi as his guardian for there to be any warm camaraderie in their relationship.

During 1898 and 1899 Jack and his mother spent their summers in Wiesbaden, Germany. The rest of the time they made the bustling French-speaking city of Brussels their home. Here the child became fluent in French before he knew a word of English. Lucy, too, learned French, though never as well as her young son did. John R. had a good ear for language and taught himself enough grammar to write letters to her in French. While his skills were limited, this fact never dampened his enthusiasm for the habit. Besides writing in French, another ploy of the wary lawyer was not signing letters to his mistress or beginning them with any salutation. He spoke of his illegitimate son as "Monsieur Singe" or "Mr. Monkey," a nickname used until Jack entered preparatory school. Dos Passos spoke of Lucy in letters to her and Jack as "The Princess," a name her son sometimes used, too, though he usually called her "Mother."

In 1899, while Lucy was living in Brussels with her son and having to content herself with seeing John R. three or four times a year, her health became a problem. She was plagued first by pains in her back and abdominal tract. She felt listless and spent most of her time in bed or indoors. Doctors could not agree on her condition, but she was often bedridden with chills, fever, and headaches. Some thought she had suffered a stroke and had a severe kidney disorder; later, Bright's disease and aphasia were diagnosed. Each time Jack returned from play, accompanied by a nanny, he feared that something dreadful might have happened to his mother in his absence. Her nurse kept the shades drawn, and Jack and other visitors were admitted to the bedchamber for brief audiences held in a whisper.

Not only was Lucy physically ill during much of her life abroad from 1899 to 1901, but she also was depressed and vexed that her lover seemed content for her to live indefinitely in Europe. She had wearied of her nomadic existence, of living from cable to cable, of seldom knowing in advance when he expected her to rush to his side. It seemed that he was never with her when she needed him most. Unable to attend her mother's funeral in 1900, she experienced both sorrow and relief—she would not have to bear the inevitable stares and encounters with the various Sprigg and Addison relatives who disapproved of her life and were relieved that she had put an ocean between them. For almost four years Lucy and her son left their trail across Europe—Brussels, Wiesbaden, Paris, London—living out of steamer trunks, waiting in railroad depots, visiting flower stalls and postcard shops, and posting hundreds of letters and picture postcards to America, asking: "Here is where we are staying this week . . . write me next at Aunt Kate's and Auntie Loo's. . . . We got your cable . . . why was there no letter waiting? . . . When do you sail? . . . Why can't Jack have his operation [hernia repair] in America? . . . You should see how much M. Singe has grown. . . . My headaches are becoming worse. . . . Who dare interfere with your mail? . . . My eyes and heart were so full of tears I could not even look at you as we parted." Lucy also longed to return to America so that Jack might begin to know his country firsthand. More and more she found herself caught up in talk with her son about the United States and what they would see and do when she was well and could travel. Most of all, they would be able to spend more time with Dedi, she told him, convinced that prayers and words—once spoken—would make it so.

Meanwhile, it had not taken Mary Hays Dos Passos long to surmise that the child from Washington, D.C., who had visited them in 1885 had a mother in whom her husband was more than casually interested. John R. had been something of a dandy among the ladies before his marriage, but Mary was jealous and hurt by his outrageous flirtations observed and reported to her after they were married. When Mary confided to her father what she knew of her husband's infidelities, she wondered if she should seek a divorce. "Absolutely not! Your husband will get over it. You must be firm and let him know you do not approve," replied Hays. The family did not believe in divorce, he reminded her; some things must be endured. Mary had had little cause to rejoice of late. Her mother had died in 1890 and her sister, Catherine, in 1892. With her father's death in 1895, she felt she had lost her last prop. She had only Eugene, her brother (seventeen years her junior), and Louis, her son, for emotional support. She could not blame her dismay upon her husband's illegitimate child, since Jack Madison had not even been born when her father died, but John R.'s dalliance over the years had irrevocably estranged her. Louis, devoted to his mother, blamed his father for her unhappiness. When Mary begged her son not to return to Princeton for his sophomore year, he did as she requested. A few months later, he fell in love with Constance Beardsley and married her, but there was never a question of his moving out; Louis simply moved his bride into the house with him and his mother.

Mary kept up a brave face to outsiders. Except for John R.'s confidential secretary, probably no one outside the family knew the precise nature of Mary's relationship with her husband. When John R. was at home, he slept in his library, which he shared with his pet black snake, Socrates, which he allowed out of its glass cage at night to sleep on a cushioned chair. Mary recovered from her distress and continued to plan meals, supervise the servants, and maintain an elegant home. She also welcomed into their home John R.'s sister Fannie, whom she nursed for many months through a fatal illness. John R. and Mary continued to take their meals together, but had apparently stopped talking to one another by this time. When Cyril dos Passos, John R.'s nephew—who became a law partner upon the death of Benjamin, his father—was invited to dinner as a young man, he was surprised to discover that his aunt and uncle did not exchange a word; each acted as though the other were not present. He was forced to engage them separately in conversation on entirely different subjects. "It was not a pleasant meal," observed Cyril later.

Lucy had been led to believe that John R. intended to divorce his wife, but in actuality, he had no grounds; even if he had, such action would have been detrimental to his career. He was also a Roman Catholic; he had been born one and had never left the church despite his not attending mass or supporting it in other obvious ways. He never would have had the church's sanction to dissolve the marriage. Mary, who had the grounds for a divorce, had chosen to stay married. It was during Mary's bereavement over her father's death and her subsequent unhappiness that John R. began to pass her condition off as "a mental illness" and to tell Lucy that he could not "in good conscience" desert his infirm wife by divorcing her.

Over the years John R. regretted not having a better relationship with Louis. He had disagreed with Mary over his rearing, but had not had his way, having been too consumed by his affair with Lucy and his career to assert himself in the matter. John R. faulted Louis for being "a mama's boy" and hated his having dropped out of Princeton. Yet he realized, too, that his estrangement from Mary and its effect upon their son was largely his own doing. It distressed him that he had no influence on Louis' behavior, and that it was Mary to whom his son turned for advice.

John R. stayed home no more than necessary. His passion for acquiring property had taken on the obsessiveness of a professional gambler, especially in regard to his holdings in Virginia. Through James Cresap Sprigg, Lucy's father, he had learned about a spread of waterfront property in the Northern Neck of Virginia that reportedly could be had for "practically nothing." First he bought an estate known as Sandy Point, the plantation home of Colonel George Eskridge, whose ward—Mary Ball—was the mother of George Washington. Washington, James Monroe, Robert E. Lee and his father, "Lighthorse Harry" Lee, a renowned Revolutionary War commander—all were born in the vicinity, and the entire area was rich in local color. Before long, John R. found himself the baron of seven ancient plantations and some seven thousand acres of valuable farm and timber lands that spread over twelve miles of waterfront on the Potomac River at the point that it spilled into a five-mile-wide estuary. He had no idea what he would eventually do with the property, but he liked owning it.

According to those who knew him best, John R. made money so that he could spend it. In the spring of 1901 when he became dissatisfied with his Washington assets and considered liquidating them, he wrote Ida Little Pifer, his cousin who sometimes assisted him in business dealings, that he felt "hard up" because $500,000 had slipped through his fingers of late, with another $250,000 likely to go within the week. "If that keeps on, I'll get me to a nunnery and go into an active law practice, such as defending criminals," he complained. An impulsive investor, John R. kept little liquid cash, but always knew how to get it. For a time he owned the Pilgrim Gold Mine in California, an investment to satisfy a personal craving when he decided that he was a "Gold Democrat." But he lost money on the mine and unloaded it as soon as possible. He also gambled huge amounts in land speculation in Mexico City, became a major stockholder in Mexican railroads, and invested in countless other enterprises, such as the Arkansas *Gazette,* which he bought outright to help win a lawsuit. He owned two boats—first a sleek Gloucester schooner, then a one-hundred-foot steam yacht, the *Gaivota* (Portuguese for "sea gull"), so that he might have easy access to his Virginia property, which could be reached in less than a day from Washington via the Potomac, whereas by land the journey took some forty-eight hours.

While John R. continued his egocentric pursuits at will, convinced that he was in control of his destiny as well as the destinies of many of those around him, Lucy chafed and fumed and threatened to come home from Europe and throw off her three-year yoke of exile without her lover's approval. In June 1901 he was astonished to discover Lucy at his elbow as he sat in the Reading Room of the Library of Congress. She had written Mary Lamar Gordon that she was sailing to New York with Jack, now five, and asked that she meet the ship. Once in New York, Lucy telephoned John R. at his office and learned from his confidential secretary, Joseph Schmidt, that he was working in Washington in the Library of Congress. Schmidt took care of John R.'s personal affairs and was accustomed to handling mail and messages from Lucy, whose relationship with his employer he understood implicitly. Once informed of John R.'s whereabouts, Lucy left Jack with her sister in New York, caught the Limited to Washington, took a hotel room, and sought out her lover in the Library of Congress, where she found him sitting with Ida Little Pifer, whom she had never met. Their meeting was recorded in John R.'s note to Ida on June 14, 1901: "I was very glad to have had the opportunity to present my dearest friend to you yesterday afternoon. It was a surprise all around, for she came into the building unexpectedly. She is coming to see you, and you are sure to fall in love with her. She is gentle, vivacious, full of womanly qualities—withal a lady which embraces everything. We have known each other many many years." He asked Ida to reserve a room for Lucy at The Cairo, a residence hotel where Ida lived.

After a few days at The Cairo, Lucy went to New York to fetch Jack and returned once more to Washington, this time to the house at 1201 Nineteenth Street, N.W. Despite her surface bravado, the act of coming home had terrified Lucy. Among her Addison/ Sprigg clan living in Washington (her mother—an Addison—had been born and reared in Washington), only her brother Will welcomed her. One of Lucy's cousins was now a United States congressman and another, the rector of Trinity Episcopal Church, but according to Lucy's niece, Lois Sprigg Hazell, none of the Addisons came to call. Will Sprigg, a doctor, and his wife—the former Lucy Derby Page—visited them in their Locomobile, the first steam-powered automobile Jack had ever seen. It was one of three in all the city, and heads swiveled as they drove by. With the Spriggs were their two children, William Mercer, Jr., and Lois, who was Jack's age.

Lois was amused by her young cousin, whom she considered a man of the world because her parents reported he had traveled to "far countries" and had just returned from a place spoken of in a mysterious voice as "abroad." She was impressed, too, that unlike most other children their age, Jack—at five—could read. She was also intrigued by his strange accent. "Talk French to me, Jack," she urged. She laughed at his "tewwibles" and "vewys," since his *r*'s in English came out sounding like *w*'s. He also had a habit of hesitating between phrases, as though he had to think about the pronunciation, yet thought faster than he could get the words out. He seemed the shyest boy Lois had ever met, and she took to him immediately. Jack gave her his lead soldiers, many of them headless with broken arms and legs, but treasures to a little girl who formerly had played only with dolls and tea sets.

As soon as possible Jack was enrolled in first grade at the Sidwell Friends School for boys and girls at 1812 I Street, N.W. Founded in 1811 by the Society of Friends for the children of its members, the school took pride in its rigorous program designed to enhance the mental, moral, and physical well-being of its students. It had long since become nonsectarian, but still operated according to Quaker principles. Jack liked his teachers and curried favor, but hated school. He had never played with other children before, and the experience did not sit well with him now. The school boasted one of the finest gymnasiums for children in the city, but when he learned that he was expected to perform upon its bars, flying rings, tumbling pads, and other apparatus, he was thrown into a panic. In team play Jack was jeered because of his poor coordination and inability to do anything with a ball except bounce it. He had never played catch in his life and dreaded having to compete on the playground under the scrutiny of classmates, who snubbed or teased him for his awkwardness and strange way of talking. When his teachers observed him squinting while reading or looking at the blackboard, they recommended his seeing an eye doctor, who put him into thick-lensed glasses, which brought on new self-consciousness.

Lucy was almost as lonely in Washington as she had been in Europe and resented John R.'s not coming down from New York every weekend to see her and to bear some of the responsibility in the day-to-day rearing of their son. Though her physical health had improved considerably since her first serious attack two years earlier, her condition was delicate, and she was in need of emotional nurturing from the man to whom she had devoted her life for eighteen years. Lucy understood only vaguely the demands of her lover's profession and his multifarious ventures on the side and concluded that she would see as much of him in Europe, where they could take extended holidays together, as she had that winter in America. She also could not envision spending a hot, muggy summer in Washington. In the spring, Lucy announced that she was returning to Brussels at the close of Jack's school term. Jack saw their prospective journey as the end of his misery as a student until Dedi told him that he would be expected to continue his education in an English boarding school that fall. John R. was convinced that a British education was superior to anything offered in America. Lucy resisted her lover's directive that their son be enrolled in boarding school in September because she thought he was too young, but John R. insisted that sitting at the feet of Oxford- and Cambridge-trained masters and learning how to live and play with other boys his age was precisely what the boy needed.

Meanwhile, John R. had been working that year on a long, visionary manuscript in which he proposed unification of all the English-speaking peoples of the world. King Edward VII, who succeeded his mother to the throne in 1901, was the key to the salvation of the British Empire, insisted John R., who thought that he, too—through his new book, *The Anglo-Saxon Century and the Unification of the English Speaking People*—had a role to play in England's future. John R. favored imperialism and proposed that the United States look for peaceful means to annex other English-speaking nations, who in turn would benefit by unification with a larger political body. A first move was for Canada and the United States to unify into a single American Republic. He reasoned that if he could engineer international mergers in big business, why not between countries? The manuscript was ready by midsummer for simultaneous publication the following January in both London and New York.

John R. had persuaded Lucy to delay her departure for Europe until he finished his book and could go with her. On July 23, 1902, he was aboard the SS *Vanderland* en route to Southampton, the typescript of his book in tow to show to his British publisher, and Lucy and Jack in a connecting stateroom. The voyage itself marked their first crossing of the Atlantic together. This trip to England, John R. was presented at court. "My mother and I have come to see him in his court uniform before he goes to be presented to King Edward," wrote Jack in *The Best Times* years later as though it were a diary entry. "He's wearing short pants just like I am, and a frilled shirt and black stockings and strutting up and down in front of the tall rainstreaked windows reciting Othello's address to the

Venetian senate. I am eyeing him with mixed feelings." Although Jack was careful to refer to John R. as his guardian and to address him as Dedi, he had at least a vague understanding at the time that the man who played such an important role in his and his mother's lives was his father.

Before returning to America, John R. embarked on a goodwill sweep through England, Scotland, and Wales to talk with influential people about his unification proposal, but nothing came of it. Jack remained in London with his mother's friends Kate Gee and Louisa Meakin while she traveled with John R. In Edinburgh, John R. was desolate when he received word that Fannie, his favorite sister, had died. "Poor Fannie—the link without which I seem to be able to have no chain of pleasure—gone forever," he lamented in a letter to Ida Little Pifer on August 4, 1902. By the time he and Lucy had returned to London, she had convinced him to allow her to delay their son's formal education abroad until he was seven, a reprieve of four months. In early September John R. accompanied Lucy and Jack to Folkestone, an English resort town seven miles from Dover, where he put them on a ship bound for Brussels to resume their lives as citizens of the world.

3

When you write me, I drop everything on earth. I can hear only one voice—yours. I see only one spot on earth—that upon which you stand.

Lucy Addison Sprigg Madison to John R. Dos Passos
July 1903

Abroad again for most of the next four years, Lucy lived largely for the letters and cables from her lover announcing when and where they should meet next. Although she saw less of John R. than in Washington—which was precious little, she reminded him—she was far happier in Europe than in America. At least she was assured of having him to herself for several days at a time once they were together. More and more John R.'s counsel was sought abroad as capitalists throughout Europe learned that the name "Dos Passos" was a persuasive element in reconciling financial conflicts. He planned three or four trips abroad a year and whenever possible scheduled his legal chores to coincide with the desirable seasons in the various countries to which he was summoned. In the summer and winter he avoided London and met Lucy in southern Italy or on the French Mediterranean; in the fall, they joined in Paris. Wiesbaden, Vienna, Berne, Bologna, Brussels, London, Paris—all became their trysting places. They met as often as possible in Bologna, where John R. had established an apartment for them, but most of the time Lucy and Jack resided in Brussels or London.

Jack, too, was more at ease abroad than in Washington. He was happy, also, because his education in a London boarding school had been delayed, this time because of illness. He would have been sent to school at seven had the doctors not decided that he needed an operation to correct a hernia. The operation itself was a simple procedure, but complications following the surgery put the boy to bed for nearly a month. Lucy blamed his illness on the operation. She was certain it had been botched and would have to be repeated.

What the doctors did not realize was that Jack was suffering from rheumatic fever, a condition not diagnosed until years later at Johns Hopkins Hospital in Baltimore. Lucy was upset, too, because she was ill with a flare-up of her kidney ailment. London, where they were at midsummer in 1903, was plagued by unseasonable heat and humidity, which in combination had always given Lucy what she referred to as "sinking spells." The nanny retained to care for Jack also nursed Lucy. In a long, disjointed note to John R. from the Grand Hotel in Folkestone, England, Lucy complained that the doctor had "ordered Jack out of hot London immediately, his three weeks in bed over," yet he was still too ill to cross the Channel. "Were it not for Jack's condition, I would take the first steamer to America," she threatened. "We would have gone straight to Bologna, but Jack was ordered to stay here. I sent you two cables, but not a sign has there been of their reception and I am wild for fear you are ill." A second letter from Lucy announced that Jack needed further surgery. She would not have it done in Europe, she vowed. John R. cabled in reply that he was sailing immediately for England and they must stay put until he arrived.

John R. soothed his mistress and son as best he could, but insisted that Jack needed recuperation in a mild, healthful climate more than he needed an operation. Madeira, the land of his forebears, was just the place, he urged. It was time for Jack to get acquainted with his Portuguese roots. John R. had business elsewhere in Europe, but planned to join them as soon as possible in Funchal, the capital. "Eyes and heart were so full of tears I could not even look at you as we parted," wrote Lucy in a distraught missive from the ship en route to Lisbon, from which they took a crowded, foul-smelling steamer to the island. Later, Jack recalled a gentleman who fed him incredibly sweet strawberries as he stretched out on a chaise lounge on deck. "Jack was ill for three days, but on Friday seemed quite himself. Up to that time he had eaten nothing but some ice and a little potatoes," said Lucy, who promised John R. not to press her petition to have their son operated on in America. "I have taught Jack to know and love you, and that no matter how strange our life may be, someday you will make it plain that you are the only one we can trust. . . . I have lived an inner life few can realize, although often I have rebelled, crying out to myself he does not love me or how can he live away from me when he knows the suffering it entails. I am his wife before God, but he lives away from me. I must go with our child." Lucy claimed in her letter that she could have had title and wealth and not been a "wanderer on the face of the earth" had she not chosen to be faithful to John R. throughout the long years she had awaited his freedom so they might marry. Never once had she been faithless, she vowed.

Within the week John R. had joined them at Reid's Hotel in Madeira, where they stayed for over a fortnight while Jack recovered his health and appetite basking in the sun and frolicking in a small pool of ocean water hollowed from a natural rock at the base of the cliff on which their hotel perched. In an essay written a dozen years later for an English professor at Harvard, Jack recalled trying to swim, which he had attempted unsuccessfully in formal lessons the summer before in Boulogne-sur-Mer in northern France. "How hard I tried to strike out boldly as I saw other people do who bathed in the real ocean beside the pool! No use, hardly did my feet leave the bottom before there was a frightened agonized splutter and a great gulp of burning salt water. Then after tearful coughing, I would be urged to try again with the same miserable results." He remembered, too, "a nice oldish gentleman with two large white moustaches—the American consul I think—who used to bring my mother a gigantic bunch of pink and apricot tinted roses every morning." Jack made no reference to his father—or "guardian"—in the essay, but the gentleman bearing roses was undoubtedly John R., who was photographed during his stay holding a bouquet of roses beside a plaque bearing the name REID's HOTEL. An acquaintance who mailed a postcard to Lucy from Madeira a few days after their departure and signed it "your loving friend, Henrietta," sent "kisses to Jack and many remembrances to our D.P." By this time, John R. had escorted his mistress and son back to the mainland and put them on an Italian liner bound for Bologna, where they were to spend the fall and early winter, while he himself was on his way back to America.

In January 1904 Jack accompanied his mother to England to be enrolled on his eighth birthday in boarding school at Peterborough Lodge in the London suburb of Hampstead. Lucy was free at last to return alone to New York City. For six weeks she stayed in the home of her sister, Mary Lamar, and saw John R. almost daily. She would have liked to move into her house in Washington for the winter so that they could enjoy a modicum of privacy, but it had been rented out on a long-term lease and the tenants chose not to vacate. In the spring she was back in London in the home of her friends Kate Gee and Sophia Louisa Meakin, with whom Jack, too, often stayed. The women probably knew the precise relationship between Jack and John R., but supported the guardian/ward pose without comment. Lucy took to her sickbed that spring while staying in her friends' home in Kew Gardens and was referred to as "the Baby," a name Jack began to use, too, in addressing his mother. In turn, he became known as "Little Man" and was treated as though he were his mother's suitor and escort. Jack took pride in his role as companion and champion of her virtue and health. When company came, he sat in the parlor and joined in their adult conversations over tea and cakes. Many of his mother's friends and acquaintances abroad were American widows—or perhaps mistresses like herself—who traveled freely with independent incomes. Their paths crossed often in the various European resort hotels and tearooms they frequented. Jack's mother's friends made a great fuss over him and usually tucked a separate note or card in for him in their letters to her. One such correspondent sent Jack a card from the French Riviera depicting a beach setting with two children in the foreground astride a donkey. The one-line message read: "This must be Baby and her Little Man at play."

Lucy, too, wrote hundreds of postcards to her son over the years as a means of both entertaining him and keeping in touch without taking time for a letter. He delighted in the pictures and she relished finding unusual cards, which she began sending addressed to "Master Jack Madison" when he was barely two years old. Jack saved all of his picture postcards. One of his favorite pastimes was spreading his collection over the bed or rug and studying each card again and again. He was ten and staying in Kew Gardens with his surrogate aunts when Lucy mailed him a scene of three infants dressed in frilly bonnets sitting upright in a single, oversized perambulator sucking milk from huge rubber nipples attached to three hoses stretching to the udders of a cow grazing contentedly a few feet away. "How do you like this type of nourishment?" his mother had scrawled beneath the picture.

During his first year at Peterborough Lodge, Jack was the school's only American-

born student, but few of his British chums took him for one. He seemed more European
—both in appearance and manner—than American. In the fall of 1904 when another
American boy was enrolled, they were introduced by one of the masters, who expected
them "to fall upon each other's necks," Jack recalled years later. Instead, the newcomer
eyed him suspiciously and demanded to know who he was for, for President. "When I
said Judge Parker he promptly punched me in the nose. It was forty years before I could
properly appreciate Theodore Roosevelt." Jack recalled John R.'s having spoken enthusiastically of Alton B. Parker, Roosevelt's opponent, and until the encounter with his bullying
compatriot, he had given little thought to the need to think for himself and to be
accountable for his decisions, which had been left largely to other people. For the most
part, Jack was an obedient child who performed as his elders requested. Approval by them
meant more to him than what his peers thought. With adults Jack was attentive, cheerful,
and outgoing, but with children his own age he was withdrawn, quiet, and often stammered. He preferred to sit on the sidelines and watch rather than to be a participant in an
event, except in the classroom, where he gained approval from his masters for his quick
mind and achievements.

At the end of his summer term in 1906, when he withdrew officially to return to
America, Jack stood first in his class in Latin, second in French, and third in algebra. The
headmaster urged Lucy to allow her son to continue his education at Peterborough Lodge
in the fall, but she was determined to resume her life in the United States. She wanted
Jack to take up studies in the land of his birth; yet more to the point, she felt that her
emotional and physical well-being depended upon John R.'s being more accessible to her,
and her to him. Already over fifty, Lucy felt that she could ill afford to let happiness—and
life itself—continue to pass her by.

4

My dear, one has to fight for himself in this world . . .

Lucy Addison Sprigg Madison to Jack Madison

Jack was ten in the summer of 1906 when he packed his valise and steamer trunk and said good-bye to his masters at Peterborough Lodge. He did not intend to be back because he was going to a prep school in America, he told them. His father had also talked with him about his vast land holdings in Virginia and promised to let him take the wheel of the *Gaivota* and sail it down the Potomac. Enamored of the sea—just as John R. himself had been as a youth—Jack fancied himself a sailor and dreamed of becoming a midshipman at the United States Naval Academy at Annapolis so that he might command his own ship someday. But first he must get through preparatory school, his father reminded him. By the time John R. decided where to send him and had made the necessary arrangements, however, Jack had missed the opening of the fall term. They had settled upon a new school, Choate, in Wallingford, Connecticut, where a foresighted founder set up shop in four cottages in an out-of-the way crossroads in 1896, the year of Jack's birth. John R. had studied at length the curriculum and approved its sound program in classical languages, history, mathematics, and English, all essentials for one's being groomed for any respectable profession, he maintained. Jack may have imagined himself a naval commander, but John R. was convinced that with a little prodding he could be maneuvered into a law career.

Lucy intended to move back into her home in Washington and did not like the idea of her "Little Man" being as far away from her as New England, but John R. insisted he could easily watch out for him at Choate, since Wallingford, a few miles north of New Haven, was less than two hours by train from New York City. They would have "manly discourses," he promised Lucy. As a self-made man, John R. saw himself a fit mentor to shape his young son's destiny. Every man needed a Socrates, he reasoned.

"We are glad to welcome to the school this term a new Lower School scholar, Jack Madison," the headmaster, Mark Pitman, was quoted in the *Choate Brief* in its February 1907 issue. Pitman was uncertain where to place their new young scholar, now eleven, when he arrived to begin the second semester at Choate. Jack's formal education had been sporadic, but good, and his studies abroad with private tutors and two and a half years in a British boarding school gave him a decisive academic edge over other boys his age. It was decided that if he did well during his first term, he could go into the third form in the fall. The headmaster's welcome was more reflective of the cordiality of the masters than of the feelings of the students, who were skeptical that the scrawny child who blinked shyly at them through thick-lensed glasses could be any kind of asset to their school.

From the beginning, Jack was an oddity at Choate. He was the youngest and smallest boy in the student body. At first he was housed in the home of the headmaster and his wife rather than in one of the cottage/dormitories. Jack did nothing well that winter for which he might gain peer approval. So far as the other boys were concerned, acceptable performance in the classroom did not count. Hazing began with his new nickname, "Four-eyes," which the boys used when the masters were not at hand. Jack's myopia had become more pronounced. He held his books close to his face, squinted, and peered. The boys imitated him and teased him and called him "Frenchy" because of his accent, a strange conglomerate of British-schoolboy English, French, and "Southern." His masters called him "Maddie."

Timid about personal encounters, Jack hated the competitive sports most Choate boys thrived on and went to great lengths to avoid a confrontation in which he was expected to assert himself or display prowess. He was once goaded into a fist fight, but it proved a brief and unwilling exchange. He remembered later having cried about it in the privacy of his room. He also recalled the exclamations of encouragement by a classmate who had witnessed the scuffle, a rare gesture among those who observed his harassment. No match for the others in team play, Jack retreated to his room to study or read when the athletes took to the field or cavorted without supervision. Only when he could be assured of solitude did he emerge to tramp over the ten hilly, wooded acres owned by the school.

During the four and one half years Jack was at Choate, Wallingford was only a village. An agricultural community of some five thousand people, the town boasted, also, a few mills and a silver factory. There was little to distinguish Wallingford from other New England towns. During the winter, snow blanketed the hills for weeks. After classes and on weekends the boys hurried to their sleds and hitched rides behind the tradesmen's sleighs and were towed for miles around the countryside, their cheeks red from the cold before they dropped off to trudge back to the cottages and dress for dinner.

When John R. sent ice skates to Jack his first winter at Choate, he discovered in his son a trait he hoped he would soon outgrow. After a week passed and there had been no acknowledgment, John R. made no attempt to conceal his aggravation. "Have you received the skates?" he demanded, repeating the question three times. "If you have them, don't take the time to reply for I know that with your studies and your necessary recreation you have all that you can attend to. I can wait until some rainy day when you have nothing else to do—and then you can return the punches in order that I may strike back violently." John R.'s "punches" were calculated to provoke action. Jack's problem was that he was not only forgetful and preoccupied, but he also was not happy with his gift. He had no desire to expose to the other boys his awkwardness on ice skates.

Despite his reclusiveness and tendency to back off from a fight, Jack was not a sissy. He sometimes enjoyed a scuffle or an impromptu wrestling match if it was an exchange in good humor and occurred outdoors. His one fight had been in his dormitory/cottage, and he did not want a repeat of that. Occasionally he was cajoled into sledding or tobogganing with the others. His one close friend was Franklin ("Skinny") Nordhoff, who entered Choate during Jack's second year there. Nordhoff, slightly older, but behind Jack in school, liked the woods and fields almost as much as he did. In the spring they canoed on Lake Quinnipiac—or Community Lake, as it was called then—a smooth, half-mile wide body of water fed by the Quinnipiac River, which flowed near the campus. After Jack became a student in the upper school, John R. bought him a canoe. When he and Nordhoff were granted overnight camping privileges, they stowed their gear in the canoe and paddled upriver for several miles before making camp and roasting bullfrogs over an open fire, a meal they thought much tastier than the rations provided by the school's kitchen. Years later Dos Passos returned to Choate to reminisce with masters and the new crop of students about some of his experiences there.

> A chill of half delicious fright still goes down my back when I remember a hound baying around our camp one night. We had been reading *The Hound of the Baskervilles*. He was circling, coming closer and closer. We were in a cold sweat but we went to sleep in spite of the hound and daylight came with the early mosquitoes and no harm was done. Even then the Quinnipiac seemed to others a pretty sordid little stream smelling of whale oil soap from the silver factories up around Meriden, but for us it was the Amazon.

He and Nordhoff sometimes trapped and killed squirrels, muskrats, and other small rodents for their hides, which they brought home to tan. Choate students routinely attended classes on Saturdays and had a structured Sabbath; therefore, when Jack and Nordhoff tramped back to their cottage at dusk on a Sunday night, laden with spoils after spending two days upriver, jealousy crackled among their classmates for days afterward and rekindled Jack's estrangement from his peers.

Once he learned to swim, he was happiest at Silver Pond, in which he plunged as soon as the ice began to break up, a habit he attributed to his father's influence. Over the years Jack had watched John R. bathe among the ice floes in the Potomac, into which he leaped in all seasons and swam great distances. In planning holiday excursions, John R. did not care where they went so long as they could be near the water. It did not matter whether it was a Maine cove, the French Mediterranean, the Rhine, a lake in the English countryside, or the Potomac, John R. swam daily and soon had his young son swimming at his side. Jack's love for hiking and the outdoors stemmed largely from his father, too. John R. had a long stride for a short man, and he made the most of it. As a youngster, Jack tried to imitate his father's walk. When he grew older and taller than John R., he still was challenged to keep pace. Eventually Jack developed a smooth, effortless stride, and with his long steps was able to outdistance all but the hardiest of walking companions. On the farm in Virginia with John R. and his mother a few days before his first winter at Choate, Jack arose early each morning so that he might hike with his father over the frosty countryside before breakfast. At first Jack had been skeptical of swimming among the ice floes, but John R. would not tolerate a laggard. Jack tired easily in the cold water and was forced to retreat to the dock before his father did, but he was proud of his efforts, nonetheless, and appreciated his lean hardness as his muscles developed. He also liked to poke around by himself, curious about almost everything. Fascinated by the sea birds that ran with mincing steps and flipped up small crustaceans from the beach at low tide, Jack entertained himself outside for hours. His father introduced him to *Robinson Crusoe,* which he read with a passion, and he longed to put his wits to the task of solitary survival and dreamed of how he might do it.

Something else Jack got from his father was his middle name, which he used for the first time at Choate. He was presented as Jack *Rodrigo* Madison. Lucy clung to the conviction that her son would claim his full birthright someday, but in the meantime it would do no harm, she reasoned, to nudge him a step closer to identification with his father by having him use a name that was a derivative of John R.'s legal name, "Rodrigues." John R. concurred with her wishes. To Lucy, a Southerner, the perpetuation of heritage through use of family names was important. The names "Lucy," "Cresap," "Sprigg," and "Addison" had been used many times by four generations of her forebears in America, but she wanted Jack to wear the badge of his father's ancestry. At the beginning of his senior year at Choate, an *e* was introduced to the spelling, thus converting the name to "Roderigo"; hereafter Jack's official records bore that name—even after he dropped "Madison" and signed himself "John R. Dos Passos, Jr."

Dedicated to the pursuit of happiness for John R. and their son, Lucy tended to forget that she had another son, James (and that her lover had a firstborn son, Louis, to whom he was responsible). She was certain that Jack would distinguish himself in law or some other noble profession, but about the future of James she was not so sure. By this time James was in his middle thirties, yet she still suffered spurts of doubt and guilt over what she considered her neglect of him. During one such moment she wrote Jack at Choate: "Just think . . . two lovely sons! God will have blessed me, indeed, for I feel James will be all right. Ah James. I have not done just right by James. His is a lovely nature, and I have neglected him for Dedi, and he has never complained. I thank God for His Mercy, for James has suffered much. . . . Thank Him with me, my darling, as I thank Him from my heart for all my sweet boys—I have three—rich indeed am I—and now, my sweetheart, may His blessings always be around you." Lucy liked thinking of John R. as one of her "sweet boys," but Jack never quite knew how to respond to such letters. At this point in his life his mother was the dearest person in the world to him, yet he had difficulty identifying James, whom he seldom saw, as his own flesh and blood. At about the same time that Lucy wrote to Jack of his half brother, whom he had seen perhaps only a dozen times by then, John R. also had a few things to say to Jack about James:

> The Princess is very well—but a little nervous about being alone and wanting to have James here. I'll try to arrange to have him come if I can get some suitable place for him, but I still

distrust his ability to command himself. He is as weak as any mortal ever made and at bottom lacks real manhood. His love for his mother must be superficial else it would cause him to be noble and strong to make her happy. I'll try him again, however. Men make themselves by finding out early their weaknesses and controlling them.

James's chief problem—like that of his father and some of his other Madison antecedents —was that he was given to drink. Lucy blamed herself, as well as her now deceased husband, for James's misfortunes; she also believed he could be rehabilitated if he avoided the corruption of his friends and life in the city. James had lost one job after another because he could not handle his liquor. Lucy urged John R. to put him "in charge of something" at the farm, where she had begun staying while Jack was in school and John R. was in New York City. Lucy's optimism for James was not shared by John R., though he had once had high hopes for James and had encouraged him to go to law school. In 1895, John R. paid James's expenses upon his acceptance into the summer session of law school at the University of Virginia. James attended the lectures and completed the term, but for some reason never went back. He was twenty-two at the time and full of resolutions and good intentions, but each fell by the wayside. His half brother had not been born then, and other than John R., James had no rival for his mother's affection. Once she took up life abroad, he saw little of her, or of his Cresap grandparents who had helped rear him. After James dropped out of law school he read Blackstone and studied on his own for a time, but his interest flagged when he was no longer in a structured program. For a year or so he worked in a law office in Washington, D.C., but apparently never passed the bar examination or pursued a career in law.

John R. had no patience with men who drank more than they could handle and prided himself on his own freedom from excesses of any kind. He rarely drank hard liquor—partook of rye whiskey when he did—and never kept liquor in his law office. He enjoyed wine with dinner, but even a little went to his head and he sipped sparingly. After dinner he retreated to his library to read or write letters, and he always had a manuscript in progress. Although some of John R.'s correspondents may have believed him intoxicated when he lifted his pen and sallied forth in rhapsodic meanderings, such headiness was rarely due to alcohol. Rather, it was his innate grandiloquence at flood tide, when he violated every tenet he routinely preached to Lucy and his son regarding restraint and moderation.

Boldly gregarious, John R. liked having people around him and was happiest at center stage with an attentive audience regardless of its size. His idea of a special treat for Jack at Choate was arranging for him to miss his Saturday afternoon classes so that he might join him in the city for dinner at Delmonico's. John R. had outfitted his son on his twelfth birthday with a tuxedo, and each Delmonico dinner was a full-dress occasion. Jack was instructed to take the train down from New Haven, check into the Murray Hill Hotel, change his clothes, and meet him at the restaurant at 7 P.M. New experiences were a source of consternation for Jack if the occasion was not a result of his own initiative, and his first command performance at Delmonico's was no exception. He dressed nervously and set out on foot for the restaurant at Fifth Avenue and Forty-fourth Street. John R. strode down from Fifty-sixth to join him and arrived a few minutes after the hour. In a social situation, John R. preferred to be the one *awaited*. The grand entry appealed to his sense of pageantry. If it was business, on the other hand, he liked being there first; not just being prompt, but being *early* abetted his controlling edge. For Jack and his father, such dinners at Delmonico's were never quiet *tête-à-têtes*. Although John R. was insistent in hearing details of life at Choate and they exchanged bits of news about "The Princess" and the Virginia farm, there was little opportunity for intimate conversation. The dinners were marked by much scraping of chairs. Jack fidgeted between courses, smiled amiably, popped up and down as various friends, clients, and other business acquaintances paused to talk or lingered at their table over coffee and dessert, fought to stay awake, and stammered tentative replies to countless questions. Jack recalled later his embarrassment while sitting in state at Delmonico's huddled in "acute misery" as John R. "joshed with the waiters or indulged in boastful talk with some friend who would sit down for a moment at his table." He had a dim recollection, too, of wresting the floor from John R. when someone asked a question about beavers. "Beavers were something I knew about. Though I was fearfully shy, before I knew what I was doing, I had launched into a disquisition on beavers, their lodges and dams, their habits and virtues. John R.'s friends stared at me in astonishment, but he listened carefully and kept drawing me out—like a witness in court—until I'd told all I knew." It is not unlikely that many of John R.'s acquaintances had figured out the relationship between Jack and his guardian, but it would have been indecorous to have commented upon it—at least to John R.—even in private.

John R. wrote often to his young ward at Choate. If there was no special news, he wrote of the weather but heightened interest through evocative imagery by relating the weather in some way to its probable effect upon Jack. In one letter John R. spoke of that day's "full grown blizzard with whiskers and all the accompaniments of frigid manhood. After snowing all day it is now turning cold and the weather man predicts 10 to 12 above zero for tomorrow morning. Certainly he will not neglect you and he may give you enough ice for a full summer's supply—and it even may continue so that when you come to Washington you will find a little for skating." Almost every letter concluded with "God bless you and protect you" and was signed "Affectionately, Dedi."

For every letter that Lucy wrote Jack, John R. wrote at least a dozen. When Jack's mother was ill, John R. wrote for both of them. They expected to hear from Jack at least three or four times a week, and unless John R. was with Lucy—so that her immediate thoughts were taken up by him—she was upset if she did not receive a letter from Jack daily. "I have missed your letters, darling, dreadfully. For two days I have not received one, but find that you are on a trip up or down that charming river," she chided Jack before shifting to thoughts of a trip she wanted them to take together. "Oh! How happy I will be! I am simply longing for the days to pass, and you—you count them all. . . . I am so tired, darling, of waiting, but will try to be patient a little longer."

During the summer of 1909, after Jack's second full year at Choate, John R. took him and Lucy by steamer to Squirrel Island, Maine, where he tarried with them a few days before pressing business demanded his return to the city. While Lucy and Jack were dallying on their own in Portland, Maine, Lucy decided she wanted to go abroad for the rest of the summer and suggested in a letter to John R. that he find a reason to travel to

France and to take her and Jack. Although John R. had insisted many times that Jack do and say nothing that might annoy or upset his mother, he invariably perturbed Lucy himself, and was, in turn, distressed. "Each letter from you contains expressions calculated to make me unhappy, restless," he replied. "I don't know of what material I am made to withstand these assaults from all sides and at all times. . . . I cannot go to Europe at present for reasons altogether of a business nature. . . . Certainly the appeal from M. Singe to go so that he can be at Rheims on a certain date to witness aerial performances does not affect me. Such an utterance, although suggestingly made, shows some disorganization of ideas—it should be sternly checked." John R. also accused his mistress of having no regard for money. She could go to Europe if she must, he concluded. "Far be it for me to interfere with your dearest wish." Then he made a counterproposal: "a real old-fashioned yachting trip up and down the coast and Sound."

Ultimately, as usual, it was John R.'s wishes that prevailed. He suggested that Lucy and Jack remain in Maine for two or three more weeks while he finished his business and had the *Gaivota* brought up to Philadelphia, where the three of them met it and took aboard, also, William S. Price—in whose office John R. had apprenticed while studying for the bar—and Price's cigar-smoking daughter, Mary Brown. They cruised up and down the Delaware River before depositing their guests in Philadelphia, then headed down the western coast of New Jersey (in Delaware Bay), stopped off at Cape May briefly, and rounded the southern tip of the state. A week later they were steaming up the inland waterway to the lower coast of Long Island, then into the Sound. The *Gaivota* had three staterooms belowdecks, quarters for a crew of four, which included a cook and steward, a sitting room, library, galley, dining room, and several baths. Aboard, Lucy played the role of "The Princess" with a flourish, as did John R. as the colorful "Commodore," who dressed in a cap and yachting outfit and manned the wheel when it suited him—assisted by Jack—and the rest of the time held court for his guests by reciting Shakespeare, presiding at charades, and selecting records for his windup Victor talking machine.

John R. was proud of Jack for his accomplishments at Choate for the year just ended. Jack stood second in his class in his fourth form (tenth grade) and on Class Day was awarded the prize for "Excellence in English" and honorable mention for "Excellence in Classics." By now he had also distinguished himself in the writing of expository themes, an achievement also reflected in his letters home. Jack wrote John R. and his mother of the books he was reading, the subjects of his essays, his canoe trips, hikes, and ramblings around the town and countryside, having long since abandoned the confines of Choate's acreage. He was the envy of his school chums when allowed to keep as a pet the raccoon John R. had captured on the Virginia farm and shipped to him. When the animal escaped and was at large for two days until Jack recovered him near Silver Pond, John R. urged him to dub his furry friend "Ulysses," make a classical scholar of him, and write a story. "The meanderings of a coon—you can show his good sense and gratitude in returning to captivity," he suggested. John R. prided himself on his own flair for storytelling, especially in his letters to Jack, who found them more interesting than his mother's, despite his father's preachy tone. John R. also made up tales that he passed off as dreams, as did a number of his literary models. His language abounded with metaphor and simile, though it often lacked originality. "I am at my library desk again, calm and placid as a mill pond," he mentioned in one letter, and in another likened himself to a May morning, "calm and serene in the midst of an affray."

John R. felt left out if Jack did not engage him in literary discussions of his reading assignments for English and history. When Jack announced his intention to "take a peep into the <u>Odyssey</u>," his father recommended that he read the *Iliad* immediately, too, and commit the best of the passages to memory. Convinced of the benefits of memorization, John R. advised his son to begin memorizing the *Aeneid* as well: "Commit Virgil to memory little by little—especially as an exercise for the mind. The mind is like the body and one by skillful training can become a mental prize fighter—with all the muscles of the mind, so to speak, in magnificent order and with all of the powers of retention and endurance that a trained physical athlete befits." John R. apologized for "drifting into a sermon," but reminded Jack that his cousin in Madeira, to whom he had been introduced in Lisbon when he was eight, "could recite the whole <u>Aeneid</u>. . . . He was a great man in his Latin and Greek." Self-educated in the classics, John R. was proud of his own ability to read and write Latin. Jack received a number of letters from John R. in which long passages from Virgil were quoted from memory, a feat intended not so much to show off as to set an example that it could be done easily. Enamored of the Greeks, John R. told his son that of all the people he knew, the Greeks interested him most. "They were so elegant and refined. I especially delight in Thucydides—the greatest historian possibly the world ever read. . . . Byron said, 'See Naples and then die.' I say, read Thucydides and then live—live to remember him and dote upon him." John R. announced that he wanted to take Jack to Greece someday so that they might ruminate and throw themselves back through the centuries to see how inferior people of the twentieth century were so far as art and the theater were concerned. "We sometimes think our civilization is far ahead of ancient times, but I opine not. In sculpture we are incomparably behind, and I guess in one way or another their wants and tastes were satisfied even better than ours can be."

John R. had also taught himself French, having found it useful in his travels abroad both in his private life and legal and business affairs. Once Jack became at ease in his life at Choate, John R. insisted that they write one another in French. "I'll keep your French alive by writing to you in that language—and it will certainly be a sufficient exercise for you to read and correct my bad French." His many errors notwithstanding, John R.'s letters to Jack in French were marked by an overt tenderness. While his comments may have made Jack somewhat uncomfortable at times, since his manner was often patronizing and mawkish, his love for his son and his faith in his living up to his high expectations brooked no misunderstanding.

Lucy, too, expected Jack to display exemplary behavior at all times. "Be careful, my darling, and do nothing I would disapprove of. Prove yourself worthy, my precious boy, of the confidence I have always placed in you," she urged. Jack would rather be drawn and quartered than upset his mother, yet he did—inadvertently—again and again. When he confessed to a minor oversight or misadventure, Lucy treated it as a grave iniquity that he must eternally repent and never repeat. Seldom was an infraction dealt with lightly, then dismissed. Jack was almost as bad as his mother in complaining about the infrequency of letters if she, too, did not write three or four times a week. If she did not feel up to writing, he expected a servant or nurse to write in her stead and report fully on her condition. When he did not receive a letter or token of remembrance on his fourteenth birthday—January 14, 1910—he could not resist chiding her for having forgotten it. He also reproached her for not using the fountain pen he had given her for Christmas. "I am so glad you got me this fountain pen—and was truly sorry you had to remind me of it," she replied. In her defense she added that she had not forgotten his birthday; she had asked a servant to remind her, and the servant had forgotten.

With Jack away at Choate, Lucy was alone in her house in Washington most of the time. Occasionally a distant cousin, Lil Cragin, came in to stay with her at night, and Lizzie, a maid, was there off and on, but Lizzie was given to drink and unreliable. "Oh Jack, it is necessary for me to have someone with me. . . . It is not intended for man or woman to be alone all the time, nearly all the time," she lamented in a letter dated January 18, 1910, and signed "Lovingly, your baby-mother, Lucy S. Dos Passos." Jack was doubtless startled by the signature, though by this time he was almost certainly aware of his birthright and that it was only a matter of time before his father and mother were married. Despite John R.'s legal tie to Mary Hays Dos Passos, Lucy had been convinced for years that she was his wife "before God," and that someday God would grant them peace and happiness. Yet she also felt guilty in praying that they soon be free to wed because only Mary's death would make it possible. Lucy's distress was so great during the winter and spring of 1909–10 that she may not have even realized that she had signed the name "Dos Passos" to her son's letter.

In letter after letter she expressed her longing for him to come home to keep her company. She did not mean that she expected him to abort his schooling at Choate, however; she simply wanted him at hand so that they could walk and talk and have tea together as in their happy days of old. Sometimes she wrote to Jack with the fervor of a youthful lover, her notes fraught with seductive imagery. "My darling Jack, oh what a pleasure it is for me to write to you and to love you to my heart's content. My arms are weary to hold you close to my heart for it does seem so long since I saw you. . . . Thank you very much for the lovely pressed flowers. It was so sweet and thoughtful, my darling —you know how I will cherish them," she said in an undated letter posted from Washington while he was at Choate. In another letter she apologized for the burden she placed upon him, adding: "You know, darling, what a baby you have to deal with. But I am not a troublesome baby, only a lonely one."

In the spring of 1910 Lucy suffered a mild stroke, which was undiagnosed for a time, but the malady affected her eyes and she could not see to read or write. Lil Cragin was with Lucy at the time and informed John R., who assured her by return mail that he was leaving in a few hours "to see the best woman any patient, man, or doctor ever dealt with." Since Lucy must not try to read, he said that he was sending only a single word that embraced "every hope, prayer, wish, entreaty, that a million hearts filled with the purest affection could utter or feel" for her recovery. John R. kept Jack fully apprised of his mother's condition. A week after she was stricken, he wrote Jack that he had had a letter from her that morning, and though her handwriting was almost illegible, she was somewhat better. "I am sorry not to give you very cheerful news, but we must accept it as it is and hope for the best." Lucy's great fear was that she herself might not survive John R.'s wife, and thus that they might never marry and escape their bondage. However, surely God would not be that unkind, she reasoned.

Lucy's stroke made it impossible for her to travel to Choate that spring to see Jack perform onstage in the Dramatics Club's presentation of Arthur Pinero's *Dandy Dick,* in which he played Sheba, one of the two female leads. He had been cast the year before as Lucy in Sheridan's *The Rivals.* Still the smallest boy in his class—as well as the youngest —Jack played the ingenue well. His delicate face, thin, well-shaped nose with a slight tilt at the end, and dark eyes—his strongest feature—in combination with "a sweet smile," as his cousin described him, afforded a "pretty look" even without his wig and makeup. Despite the teasing by the boys in his dormitory/cottage, Jack found it amusing to play such roles and was disappointed when he did not get a major part in the play presented by his sixth form class, William Gillette's comedy, *The Private Secretary.* On January 9, 1911, he complained in his diary that he had hoped to be cast as Miss Ashford, since he did not get the lead, but had ended up with the Eva Webster role. "I feel very badly about not getting a better one," he said. "It's the smallest part in the play—except that of John and Knox." In the circus presented by his sixth form class, Jack was cast as "Princess Eva, the Charioteeress." Later, his Greek teacher, Clara St. John (whose husband, George, was named headmaster in 1908 to succeed Mark Pitman), bragged about his "captivating performances" and "instinctive dramatic sense," but admitted that he was "less convinc-ing" in *The Private Secretary* because his voice had deepened and he had "shot up to six feet." Mrs. St. John spoke, too, of what she described as Jack's "special quality." His charm and intelligence, his "ability to mix harmoniously with his fellows and delightfully with older people, his integrity and his spirit of cooperation, and his ambition, mature beyond his years, are all unforgettable." It would be an injustice, she continued, if she did not mention his "great lovability . . . latent power. He was in no way a 'sissy.' " She also commended his sensitive perceptions, "quick sympathies and social adjustments beyond his years."

5

All seem to take well to my marriage who speak—and those who do not speak I do not care for.

John R. Dos Passos to Ida Little Pifer
28 October 1910

On October 28, 1910, the Baltimore *News* reported: "NOTED LAWYER KEPT WEDDING A SECRET. J. R. Dos Passos and Mrs. L. S. Madison Married Last June." It also reported that his first wife, Miss Mary Hays, had died "about two years ago," and that the new Mrs. Dos Passos had spent twenty years traveling abroad, "with occasional visits to this country" before her return to America "nearly a year ago" when she took possession of her home in Washington, which had been leased to another family for seven years. She and Mr. Dos Passos had reportedly met "on one of his annual European trips." Mrs. Dos Passos was "the wife of the late J. R. Madison, and had one son, James Madison, a New York lawyer." In addition to his description as "one of the most prominent lawyers in the country" with extensive real estate interests in Washington, John R. was described as a graduate of the University of Pennsylvania and an accomplished linguist.

The announcement had a semblance of truth, but little of it was accurate. John R. had married Lucy on June 21, 1910, in Wilmington, Delaware, and he was a prominent lawyer of a Philadelphia family. They were making their home at 1201 Nineteenth Street, N.W., in Washington, where he owned considerable real estate, mainly small lots and houses. He had written several books on law and was a member of the Metropolitan Club in Washington. All of these facts were included in the marriage notice. But Mary Hays had died on March 20, 1910—just three months and a day before her husband took his mistress to the altar—and Mary's family must have shaken their heads in disbelief and frustration in reading that the first Mrs. Dos Passos had "died about two years ago." The omission of James Madison's half brother Jack from the wedding account was a glaring error, too, to those who knew of Lucy's unbridled love for her second-born son. Moreover, she was not the widow of "J. R. Madison," but Ryland R., and her son, James, had never been a New York lawyer. Nor did Lucy spend twenty years abroad, as reported. She may have joined John R. in Europe for a clandestine meeting or two as early as 1890—some six years before the birth of their son—but she did not take up residence in Europe until 1896, when Jack was an infant. Lucy was back in Washington during part of 1901 and 1902, and again during most of Jack's school years at Choate. She and John R. did not *meet* in Europe (she had never been abroad before they were lovers), nor did the few night classes he attended at the University of Pennsylvania qualify him as a graduate of that institution.

The events immediately preceding the death of Mary Hays Dos Passos and the activities leading up to John R.'s second marriage were recorded in a number of letters of the period. On March 5, 1910, John R. wrote Jack that he had important things to discuss with him before leaving for Europe March 17. On March 8, Lucy wrote Jack that John R. had assured her that "he has told you everything so you will know what to do. I shall be glad for him to arrange all my things satisfactorily for it is a long time since I have felt my affairs were in order, and you will be near me." Before Jack left for his spring holidays from Choate to be with his mother in Washington, John R. sent him the keys to his safe deposit vault in New York City, accompanied by a directive: "In case anything should happen, you and your mother should go at once to the safe deposit company and take all of her holdings and yours in a satchel and put them in a safe deposit vault in Washington."

The veiled language and mysterious goings-on had been prompted by the sudden, critical illness of Mary Dos Passos, a pulmonary infection from which there was little likelihood she would recover. John R. was reluctant to go abroad under the circumstances, but rationalized that his pressing business in England and Germany demanded his departure as soon as possible. In the event of Mary's death in his absence, he did not want the contents of a safe deposit box intended for his eyes alone to prove embarrassing. John R. was at sea on March 20 when he received a cable announcing that his wife's condition had worsened; a second cable several hours later announced her death. "My God—I received a sudden shock, and you know the thoughts I had," he wrote Lucy the next day from the mid-Atlantic. "I sent a cable to you immediately and I am sure that you were as sad as I. She went finally, thank God, to her final rest. She had her faults—but I see now only the virtues. She led an irreproachable life. She was a weak woman, very weak, but with many qualities. What should I say now? You must recover your health immediately because our future must begin soon. The world can say no more and we will be free to show them what kind of woman and man we are." Two days later he apologized for not having written the day before: "I was in an emotional state fearing and thinking all day long that I did not give proper treatment to that poor woman. This morning I am a bit more calm. Her funeral took place yesterday and the poor woman is now in the ground. . . . She will soon be forgotten. We have another life we are beginning. We will try to be healthy and strong—and we will show the world now that we are not ordinary. . . . We can do things that we want without fearing critics." At the end of the voyage, John R. closed a fourteen-page letter to Lucy—written a few pages a day throughout his crossing—with the comment: "My deepest love to M. Singe. We must soon change his name."

When the ship docked in Plymouth, John R. also posted a letter to his son Louis, to whom he observed: "The heart-rending tragedy is over—she is buried, and there is left to you her splendid memory. Never was a boy blessed with a more devoted mother." He added that since he was not a hypocrite, it was his opinion that "her love caused her to overlook your true interests. She was so afraid lest your health be affected by going away from home or study that she never would sympathize with my views. . . . You have been living a neutral life—no one knew whether there was anything in you. It would be quite unworthy of the memory of such a mother not to show the world that at a proper time, being reared under such influences produces legitimate results." John R.'s letter to Louis implied that he resented his wife's insistence that their son abort his college education. Louis had gone into real estate with a large, reputable firm, Dwight Helmsley, a few years before his mother's death, and it never occurred to him that there was anything "neutral" about his life, or that people may have wondered if "there was anything" in him. Moreover, he had never anticipated any need to demonstrate "legitimate results" of such rearing.

Upon arrival in London, John R. wrote Jack that "a great deal had passed" since they were last together, and that he could not go into particulars then but promised that they would soon be united in such a way that would make the three of them "very happy." John R. did not return from Europe until May 8. By this time, having suffered an attack of gout and rheumatism, he announced his intention to go directly to the farm to rest after a brief visit with Lucy in Washington. "Dedi looked much better when he left. . . . Pray for him, my darling, and that we may at last be happy," she urged Jack, now back at Choate finishing up his fifth form (junior year).

For a time the letters Jack received from his mother and father were largely progress reports of the other's health. Despite her need for an operation, she was improving on her own, said John R., who presently was more worried about her inability to manage money than her general condition. "I have told her she must draw no more checks. Hasten the hours, Je Joko, so that you can take charge of 1201 [the house in Washington] and all bills and visitors can be referred to M. Singe." Jack came home in early June, disappointed that his mother had been unable to attend his Class Day ceremonies on May 30. Although he was not awarded any of the top prizes for academic excellence this year, he received honorable mentions in English, classics, mathematics, and Bible study; he was also cited for his leadership as editor in chief of the Choate *News.* Jack worked as literary editor of his newspaper, too.

Upon the death of Mary Dos Passos, John R. spent little time at his home in New York, but worked long hours at his law office so that he might be free for another yachting cruise with Lucy. This time they left Jack at home. On June 19 they departed from the yacht basin in Washington, steamed down the Potomac and across the Delaware Canal, then up the Delaware River to Wilmington, where Lucy's cousin, Judge Wilmer J. Latimer, awaited them in his chambers. With him was George L. Wolfe, a doctor of divinity, who performed the wedding ceremony, witnessed only by Lucy's cousin, the judge. In view of the recent death of John R.'s first wife, the couple decided to keep the wedding a secret from all but a handful of intimates: Jack, John R.'s confidential secretary, Joseph Schmidt; Lucy's brother and sister, Will Sprigg and Mary Lamar Gordon; John R.'s cousin, Ida Little Pifer; and Lucy's servant, Lizzie. The truth would get out eventually, but there was no need to rush it, John R. reasoned. Having been accustomed to subterfuge all these years, he saw no reason to break the pattern just yet.

In September Jack reentered Choate, again under the name "Madison," and told no one that his parents had married until a letter from his father dated October 12, 1910, revealed that their secret had been exposed. "Hereafter your letters must be addressed to Lucy Sprigg Dos Passos and the name of Madison forever stopped. We will attend to yours later. I think you had better quietly give out the fact to Mr. St. John—if you wish—I leave it with you—but I think *yes.*" Jack confided to his headmaster, but to no one else. John R. had been able to keep the news of his marriage out of the New York papers, but the Baltimore *News* got hold of the story through an unacknowledged Washington source, which may have accounted for its errors, since the principals involved were elusive.

Among the countless directives, requests, and suggestions Jack received from his father during his Choate years was his insistence that he keep a diary. "The Diary. The Diary. The Diary. Keep a Diary and get rich," urged John R. Resistant at first, Jack complied. His first entry read:

> Jan. 9 [1911]: I have finally determined to keep a diary which I will try to make as interesting as possible to myself. I wish to make it a greater success than any of my former attempts and will try to write it up each evening before I go to bed. So hail, thou patron divinity of diaries —which ever of the Muses thou art—look propitiously upon my attempts to keep a diary & instill me with a desire for literary fame. May this diary be as interesting as that of Pepys, as historical as that of Everett, as useful as Franklin's, so once again "Hail, Muse of Diaries, all hail."

Jack's desire for literary fame, rather than keeping a diary to "get rich," became his prime motivation in his evolving commitment to the pursuit of letters. His entries were sporadic, but he managed to jot down impressions, observations, notable experiences, and, on rare occasions, his feelings. John R. also wanted him to keep a diary as a means of accounting for the way he spent his money. After a six-week lapse, he recorded: "Alas! . . . Am again in a state of bankruptcy. It is only when I am in that condition that I write in my diary at all." A month later he threw up his hands so far as his diary was concerned: "If I do it, I'll do it, but if I don't, I won't and that is all." He was depressed because his father did not send encouraging news of his mother. "I hate to think of it, but I am afraid that she will never get well," Jack appended to a journal entry that winter. Having resolved that he alone would decide when and if he kept a diary, he became more at ease with it and more intimate in what he said. Perhaps his most telling entry in the spring of 1911 was his lament that he was without friends:

> Everyone is very nice to me but—that is all, I have no friends—there is no one who cares a rap about me. No one ever seems to speak to me unless it is necessary; no one ever comes into my room to talk to me. If I go into anyone else's room, I feel that I am not wanted. How happy I could be if I could only have one true friend who did not treat me like a damned little

fool. Is it because I am younger than most of the fellows I am with that they neither respect me, like me, dislike me, hate me? I should rather be hated by every one in the school than looked upon as a nonentity. . . . Perhaps I am a "hated little stuck up fool"—I certainly try not to be—but it does hurt me to feel that if I should die tonight it would not make any lasting impression on any one. . . . But I do not care what misery I go through now if I can only in the future be great—Be the greatest man that ever lived—Be such a man that they will all treasure the remembrance of me and say with pride: "I went to school with John R. Dos Passos" (if I ever do assume that name). But I suppose it is morbid foolishness to write all this —and does no good to anyone. . . . But if I can make myself great—oh if I can—

Upon the marriage of his father to his mother, Jack's name was legally Dos Passos. No formal adoption was required, since he was already his father's—his guardian's—son. The problem lay in his not feeling free to use it. He entered preparatory school as Jack Madison and he left with that name. Although he told the headmaster of his parents' marriage, he probably did not confide that John R. was his real father. Jack's consternation stemmed from the limbo in which he hung at year's end, being neither Madison nor Dos Passos. In his diary on June 17, 1911, he noted that the date marked his final hours at Choate and that he was bidding his school farewell without regret. "Mr. St. John said goodbye rather coldly, but I must expect that, as I have lost favor with him greatly lately. I did not get a diploma, either, which surprised me a good deal, for I really think that I deserved one." Jack offered nothing ostensible for his failure to be handed a diploma. His records later demonstrated that he graduated *cum laude* in the upper third of his class. On Class Day he was awarded the top literary prize, "Excellence in English," and commended for his superior performance in class and for his editorship of the *Choate News*. In his second year as literary editor he had persuaded the English master who supervised student publications to allow him to produce a special literary supplement, since there had been no official literary magazine for several years. Jack recruited short fiction and published a significant batch of student writers under the masthead *New Fiction Supplement*. Buried within was his first published story, "The City of Burnished Copper," which, like the various news stories and feature articles he had written during his three years on the *Choate News* staff, appeared anonymously. All the others had bylines, but he did not. It was as though he chose to bear no name than to represent himself as someone he was not. Not being awarded a diploma may have had a simple explanation: St. John may have been instructed not to use the name "Madison" on it, since he would soon be authorized to use "Dos Passos"; or Jack may have committed some infraction of Choate's rules and thus have had the diploma temporarily withheld. But nothing was entered in Jack's permanent record to indicate that he did not receive a diploma. Whether he did or not, however, was not as important as Jack's puzzlement as to why he was singled out and branded different from his classmates who did receive diplomas. Again and again he was reminded of his second-class status: his birthright as a bastard son. He found that he had been denied by his father for obvious reasons, but accepted what he could not change. Yet when his parents eventually were able to marry, he had expected his life to take on a new dimension: he would be *somebody* at last. It seemed to him that at every turn he was stymied in achieving status. He may well have seen the marriage announcement by this time, too.

Why was only James Madison mentioned, and who was Jack Madison/Dos Passos? he may have pondered.

When the *Choate Brief* caught up with Jack that summer at Bay Head, New Jersey, where he had gone with his mother to visit Will Sprigg's family, who had a summer home on the beach, a flood of memories returned. He was reminded anew of the badgering he had fallen heir to over the years by seeing himself in his yearbook identified as "Little Maddie, the class co-ed" who had been a "hit in girls' parts for the past three years." He was dubbed "Best Student" and "Class Grind," and "How thrilling!" was given as his "favorite expression." Jack's fourteen classmates were bound for Yale, Harvard, Amherst, Cornell, Leheigh, Williams, and MIT in the fall, but not he. Although he was one of two at Choate who already had gained admission to Harvard at year's end, he was barely fifteen. John R. thought it would be to his advantage to delay his entrance a year, however, so that a little seasoning could set in. Having his temperament described as "meek" in the yearbook confirmed Jack's view of how others saw him, and he did not want to be tagged with such a submissive label indefinitely. Disposition, age, and circumstance—as well as an overbearing father—all had contributed to his behavior among his peers, and he longed to be free of the strictures of academe and the censuring eyes that had fallen upon him during his four and half years at Choate.

When John R. suggested a six-month "Grand Tour" with a tutor/companion, Jack eagerly accepted, relishing the prospects of going abroad for the first time without his father and mother along to pamper him and direct his steps. Having already traveled extensively throughout Europe, which held little sense of mystery for him, Jack longed for the exotic sounds, sights, and culture of northern Africa and the Middle East. He wanted to view ancient Islamic civilizations, Egypt and the Nile Valley, to ponder firsthand the architectural feats of pyramids, mosques, and temples, Byzantine art, and to pore at length over the ruins and splendors of Greece, Italy, and the isles of the Mediterranean Sea.

For once the keeping of a daily journal became important to Jack. Having virtually abandoned his diary during the summer after leaving Choate, he took it up again on November 15, 1911, the day he and one "Mr. Jones"—whom he called "Uncle Virgil"— embarked from Manhattan's East River docks aboard the SS *Baltic* for Liverpool. Only John R. was there to see them off. Confined to her bed, Lucy remained in Washington her blood pressure having soared to dangerous heights that fall. "Write often to cheer 'The Princess' and make her laugh," John R. called to his son before the ship slipped its berth. Jack complied as best he could. "I should like the Baby to keep all the postals I send her in one pile and in chronological order," he suggested, wanting to have them for himself upon his return. Jack's cards and notes to his mother may have seemed fatuous or doltish to others, but she treasured each one. An outsider might have thought them written to a child. "Best love to the dear little Baby," began one postal card. "Does the dear Baby remember when it took me to Cannes with it and how we went over the factory for making glacé fruits together? I sent Aunt Kate a box of them for Christmas from there. I would have sent Baby one had she been able to eat any of it." No matter where he was headed next, he expected a cache of mail awaiting him. From Rome he wrote Lucy: "I do not know why I expected to get so many letters from the dear Baby, but I did. And when I went to the bank this morning I found only one! I hope to get a lot more soon, however, hoping that poor Jack has not been entirely forgotten." If his mother was not up to writing, he counted on hearing from Lucy's nurse, and if he should hear from neither of them, he threatened to withhold information and details regarding his journey.

To his father, Jack wrote long letters swollen with picturesque observations and impressions of all that he saw. He described his fellow tourists and natives encountered, wrote of his current, voracious readings of ancient history and literature, and spoke of his awe inspired by the "countless wonders wrought by human hands" that exceeded his "boldest imaginings." John R. informed him that he had already dusted off his Homer "to get the jump" on him in Grecian history and legend. When Jack reported reading about Alcibiades—an Athenian general and protégé of Socrates—John R. urged him to share his impressions. Jack's reply was a five-hundred-word discourse revealing his ingestion of Alcibiades both as a person and a man of history. In summarizing, he said that the general had been "one of the most dangerous men possible. If he had been totally bad, he could have done no harm, but it was his great good qualities, which if united with a moral courage and a disinterested patriotism would have made him a great man, that gave him his immense power to do evil." Jack's letter demonstrated that he, too, had a historian's sense of the past. He saw history as a developing process and understood that what happened was colored—chameleon-fashion—by the chronicler's vision of it. Although barely sixteen, Jack already was demonstrating an ability to discern and record life both visually and critically. The literary techniques for which he was known later had begun to evolve.

By the first of January 1912 Jack and his tutor had completed one fourth of their projected tour, having gone from Liverpool to London, then to Paris, Avignon, Marseilles, and the Mediterranean coast. They tarried only briefly in Cannes, Nice, Monte Carlo, and other areas Jack described as "resort towns," but lingered in Pisa and Rome. Jack yearned to see every conceivable marvel of ancient and modern man that lay between central Italy and its western shores, and then to tour the islands. From Naples they traveled to Brindisi, a seaport on the southeastern coast of Italy, to board a steamer for Egypt. Mid-January found them in Alexandria and Cairo, the capital, where Jack proposed they join a camel caravan to view the pyramids of Giza. They traveled next by train to Asyūt to begin a six-hundred-mile trip upriver into the interior of the desert. Jack tried to do it all: they pored over art treasures from morning to night, combed the temples of Luxor and Karnak, maneuvered among the almsmen stationed before the giant Sphinx, paid their respects to the dead at the necropolises of Thebes, and tramped unknowingly over the tomb of the boy king Tutankhamen, discovered ten years later in the Valley of the Tombs of the Kings, the very area they had traversed. Although most tourists ended their journey up the Nile at Aswan, the last major city before the river spilled into Lake Nasser, Jack insisted they continue to Ballana, a small settlement situated a few kilometers from the Egyptian/ Sudan border. On their way back to Cairo, they inspected the pyramid of King Zoser (the most ancient stone building in the world, the Step Pyramid dates from nearly three thousand years before the birth of Christ), then visited still another burial ground, the necropolises of Memphis.

The second week of February Jack and his companion/tutor were aboard the SS *Saidiyeh* en route to Constantinople (Istanbul). They stayed four days in the fabled city among its Ottoman and Byzantine relics, the painted and gilded porcelain, jewels, and gold and silver-threaded robes found in the palaces of its mighty sultans, trekking from mosques and palaces to the Grand Oriental Bazaar, their heads reeling as they tumbled each night into their beds at the Pera Palace Hotel after an exotic meal and an evening walk up one of the city's seven hills to view the setting sun drop behind the towering minarets and bridges into the sea.

Upon arrival in Athens Jack wrote his father that the trip thus far had cost them more than they anticipated because of his unscheduled visit to Constantinople. Although he had spent only seventy dollars on that leg of their journey, it meant that they would have to miss Florence and Venice, he lamented. "Still I'm awfully glad we went," he added. Jack had hoped to have at least three weeks in the Ionian Islands and Greece, then to explore more of central and northern Italy. As it was, they had only enough cash for a whirlwind tour of Greece and a straight-line crossing of Italy to Paris, then on to London and the steamer. John R. immediately cabled money to Athens and urged them to travel as they saw fit. The postal cards and letters Jack mailed "the dear Baby" and his father during the next six weeks bore such postmarks as Delphi, Corfu, Trieste, Venice, Florence, Rome, Milan—all records of their journey to examine later—and his diary bulged with almost daily entries. In Italy they skittered up and down the calf of the Italian boot like a cobbler's cross-stitch and saw the country and its artifacts from almost every vantage. After a week in Rome they set off by train for Milan, and by April 15 were back in Paris. Since they started their tour in London, where they stayed a week, they stopped only briefly this time. Jack wanted to look in again on his mother's friends Kate Gee and Sophia Louisa Meakin, who still seemed more like his real family to him than most of his blood relatives he had met in America.

In none of his letters home did Jack mention being "helplessly smitten" with the younger daughter of a family of New Zealanders whom they kept running into on their travels, but in his published memoirs, later, he confessed his infatuation. He spoke also of his mortification in catching the girl "on the forward deck of the steamer, one moonlight night on the Aegean, flirting in French with a young Turk named Talaat Bey." His infatuation and disillusionment became the substance of a short story published the end of his freshman year at Harvard, his seasoning behind him.

By mid-May Jack was back in Washington with his mother, whose condition was much as he had left it. Upon the death of Mary Dos Passos, John R.'s New York housekeeper, Mary Harris—who had also served as Mary's nurse—came to Washington to keep house for Lucy, who was incapable of performing more than rudimentary chores for herself. Having Jack at home for part of the summer freed John R., who was little disposed to attend to the countless details necessary to run the household for an ailing wife. His time was taken up then in trying to finish a text on law reform; in June John R. was busily campaigning for Woodrow Wilson (then governor of New Jersey), who sought to wrest the Democratic nomination for the presidency from the prime contender, James Beauchamp Clark.

Home at last after seven months of almost constant movement abroad, Jack found Washington even more stultifying than he remembered it. Whenever possible he temporarily eluded his chores through reading (Jack wrote in his diary that spring of having discovered H. G. Wells's "tales of the marvelous" and of devouring Poe's horror stories, in which he identified with the victim), or through desperate walks, as though driven by demons along Washington's scorching streets, the city already unseasonably hot. Although Jack loved his mother, petted her, and did all he could to make her comfortable, he longed to be in New York or even at the political convention in Baltimore, where he envisioned his father helping shape important world decisions. Even the haven of the farm, where John R. had taken him and Lucy in early June, and the cooling breezes coming off the Potomac brought little relief. Impatient to be gone, Jack announced to his father that he wished to go to Cambridge early in order to secure his rooms and prepare for the fall semester at Harvard, and if time permitted to take some side trips on his own.

John R. accompanied his son to Boston to help him get situated. On July 13 he wrote Lucy that he had engaged that day in "pleasant talks" with the dean and bursar and had arranged for Wanamaker's to send someone to Cambridge "to arrange everything for the young gentleman who is to occupy the rooms." They dined that evening on John R.'s favorite dish, codfish tongues and broiled honeycomb tripe. The day had been long and celebratory both for Jack and his father. Even on his Grand Tour Jack had registered in hotels and received his mail as *"Master James Madison,"* but as of July 13, 1912, the name was relegated to past history. He had signed the register at Young's Hotel in Boston as *"John Roderigo Dos Passos, Jr."*

"We have made history today. The boy has begun his career," John R. announced with pride.

The first flood of adverse criticism against Three Soldiers I was prepared for. Manhattan Transfer was called "an explosion in a sewer," a phrase which entertained me no end. Even in those early days I read press criticism as little as possible because I had very little respect for the ladies and gentlemen who wrote the pieces. The real campaign against my work started with The Big Money. Mike Gold, a fanatic with a delicate nose for heresy, had been hailing me as a proletarian writer and fellow traveller. Suddenly he smelt a social-fascist rat. Adventures of a Young Man upset the applecart. The Commies decided I was a goddamn reactionary and let loose. The amount of influence the Communists have had on the liberal ingangs that have made a hash of non-partisan literary criticism in this country would make an interesting study.

In spite of the strong tide of prejudice I've managed to publish what I please and make a moderately good living doing it, largely because of the continued sale of foreign translations.

Publico ergo damnatus. As Truman used to say: if you can't stand the heat keep out of the kitchen.

John Dos Passos to Jon Bracker
23 May 1970

Book II

"DOS"

JOHN R. DOS PASSOS, JR.

1912–47

PROLOGUE

those spring nights the streetcar wheels screech grinding in a
rattle of loose trucks round the curved tracks of Harvard Square dust
hangs in the powdery arclight glare allnight till dawn can't sleep

haven't got the nerve to break out of the bellglass

four years under the ethercone breathe deep gently now that's
the way be a good boy one two three four five six get A's in some
courses but don't be a grind be interested in literature but remain
a gentleman don't be seen with Jews or Socialists

and all the pleasant contacts will be useful in Later Life say hello
pleasantly to everybody crossing the yard

sit looking out into the twilight of the pleasantest four years of
your life

grow cold with culture like a cup of tea forgotten between an
incenseburner and a volume of Oscar Wilde cold and not strong like
a claret lemonade drunk at a Pop Concert in Symphony Hall

four years I didn't know you could do what you Michelangelo
wanted say

Marx

    to all

the professors with a small Swift break all the Greenoughs in the
shooting gallery

but tossed with eyes smarting all the spring night reading *The
Tragical History of Doctor Faustus* and went mad listening to the
streetcar wheels screech grinding in a rattle of loose trucks round
Harvard Square and the trains crying across the saltmarshes and the
rumbling siren of a steamboat leaving dock and the blue peter flying
and millworkers marching with a red brass band through the streets
of Lawrence Massachusetts

it was like the Magdeburg spheres the pressure outside sustained
the vacuum within

and I hadn't the nerve

to jump up and walk outofdoors and tell
them all to go take a flying
Rimbaud
at the moon

"Camera Eye 25"
The 42nd Parallel

6

The Harvard Years, 1912–16

Let us hope that . . . he will enter college fresh, ambitious, and determined to make the name he bears illustrious—not in riches, but in learning.

John R. Dos Passos, Sr., to his wife, Lucy
13 July 1912

When the brick and wrought-iron fence went up around the Harvard Yard in 1904, Henry James observed that the venerated buildings within seemed a cloister amid American commercialism. Harvard men were expected to pursue the art of tasteful living unmindful of the adversities of the outside world, to depart as gentlemen of letters and assume leadership roles in the pulpits, courts, and counting houses of America, or move into other intellectual arenas according to the dictates of time, purse, or conscience.

John Dos Passos, Jr. ("Dos," as he became known at Harvard), was one of 662 freshmen who found themselves in the throes of change when they began classes in September 1912. They were learning what was expected of them as Harvard men, but were caught up, also, in their school's competitive pursuit of international fame. For forty years President Charles W. Eliot had led the school from narrow New England provincialism to world prominence as a distinguished university. Unwilling to let Harvard rest on its laurels as the oldest academic institution in America, Eliot saw to it that it was the richest, largest, and greatest of its time. Nor did he brook any slack in its strides. By the end of his regime, Eliot had gathered a faculty of some five hundred superior minds unequaled in any other collective body in America, doubled the undergraduate enrollment (to more than two thousand students), and boasted that Harvard had almost as many graduate students as the combined classes of baccalaureate candidates. In all, more than four thousand students ranged over the Harvard Yard during the 1912–13 academic year.

Eliot's liberalism knew few bounds. He was convinced that the university's liberally educated graduates could successfully take their places in the outside world if they had chosen their courses wisely and had been consistent and serious in their efforts. Under Eliot's open elective system, students had no prescribed curricula for baccalaureate degrees in liberal arts. They attended classes four years, took four credits a year, and avoided getting excessive D's. In the philosophy department they selected from among such distinguished professors as William James, Hugo Münsterberg, and Josiah Royce. In English they signed waiting lists for George Pierce Baker, Le Baron Russell Briggs, Chester Noyes Greenough, George Lyman Kittredge, William Allan Neilson, Bliss Perry, or Barrett Wendell—all of whom enjoyed national reputations and attracted hundreds of students annually who were more willing to await a vacancy than choose a professor who had no special attraction. Bliss Perry, for example, had six hundred sign up for English literature in 1913. He allowed three hundred in the course and told the rest to wait a year. Dos Passos was one who stayed.

Harvard's growth and greatness under Eliot were deemed insufficient by his successor, Abbot Lawrence Lowell, installed in 1909 after many years service to the university as a faculty member. Long a foe to Eliot's open elective system, Lowell inaugurated a plan of "concentration and distributions." Students took at least six courses in one department and distributed a half dozen others elsewhere among three general groups of their choice. Additional courses could be elected from any department. Each student was assigned a single faculty member who advised him carefully on an individual basis throughout his undergraduate years. Those who showed special promise were encouraged to go into the university's newly conceived honors program. Lowell was convinced that his faculty expected too little of students and urged them to find new ways to stimulate harder work, to develop a sounder basis for grade differentials, and to award A's to only the most competitive achievers.

Most Harvard graduates considered themselves well educated and expected their sons to follow them to Cambridge, live in the same dormitories (the private dormitories on Mount Auburn Street's "Gold Coast" maintained waiting lists so that sons might occupy the identical rooms their fathers had), and pursue like careers. Time may have dimmed memories of their own academic achievements or caused vast distortions regarding them, but Harvard fathers expected better-than-average grades of their sons regardless of their own performances. John R. was by no means a Harvard man and his son had no Harvard heritage, but he took pride in his being at Harvard and expected great things of him. Dos Passos' grades at the end of his freshman year may have disappointed his father, but his one C and four B's were decidedly above average for his class. Robert Nathan, a classmate, expressed the prevailing attitude of a Harvard undergraduate of that era: "A C meant you weren't a brain, that you were just an ordinary sort (I got almost nothing but C's). It was never stylish to make a D in a course. A B meant that there was some hope for you in the world outside. An A—and a cum laude or magna cum laude—was rather dazzling to the ordinary student, but only what proud parents expected." As Dos Passos' freshman year was drawing to a close, John R. wrote him that he hoped he would receive good grades and become "one of the distinguished few," and not only to study for his examinations, but to "know the fields" he had completed. "It is necessary to lay the foundation for the future, for perhaps after having finished college you will not have the chance to engage in systematic study. I am sure that your college life will prove useful." Although Dos Passos may have appreciated the spirit of his father's letter, he lacked his confidence regarding the eventual usefulness of college life. John R. took his son's significant achievement for granted, but the young man himself had no idea that he would graduate *cum laude.*

Another Harvard legacy to which young Dos Passos was not heir as a freshman concerned his choice of rooms. He had no idea when he traveled to Cambridge with his father during the summer of 1912 and selected Matthews Hall that he was moving into quarters traditionally assigned only to seniors and graduate students. Freshmen were not supposed to live in the Harvard Yard. The ornate qualities of Matthews Hall, a majestic Gothic structure, nonetheless appealed to the sixteen-year-old youth who had spent most of his impressionable early life amid Europe's splendors. When Matthews was built in 1872 on the northeast corner of the Yard—along with Weld Hall across from it (elegantly Elizabethan with its towering twin skylights), it was called the finest college dormitory in America. The hall had been renovated and central heat added by the time Dos Passos moved into room #22, a three-room suite that rented unfurnished for $240 for the academic year. Most rooms ranged from $60 to $200, although some students paid $350 for the most commodious quarters. It was not extraordinary that John R. engaged a decorator from Wanamaker's to furnish his son's suite. His sitting room with a fireplace and three large windows afforded a view of busy Harvard Square, as did his bedroom; a third room, tiny by comparison, accommodated his chiffonier and wardrobe and served as a dressing room.

Having selected the wrong dormitory, Dos Passos was slow to make friends. Moreover, nearsighted and bookish-looking in his thick-lensed glasses, he had scarcely a physical attribute that might commend him on sight to his classmates. A spurt of growth during the summer before his final year at Choate had added three inches to his lean frame, but he had gained no weight. John R. wrote Lucy in the fall of their son's freshman year that he looked as "straight as a bean pole and as stiff." He no longer resembled Pisa's Leaning Tower, but "might well be picked as the best pole for a shad," added John R. Ungainly as well as tall, Dos Passos abandoned his single effort to make a team when he failed to impress the freshman crew coach during practice in the spring. Unsuccessful in his half-hearted attempt to become an athlete, he had no desire to be a manager of a soccer or lacrosse team, positions for which several of his classmates competed. If he did not "make something" he would become a "runt," warned one paternalistic senior who lived in his hall. Being a runt meant not making the Institute—the initial screening organization from which "higher clubs" drew their members—and thus being destined for a humdrum social life while at Harvard. If one did not achieve the first rung of Harvard clubdom, he was automatically excluded from fraternity life as well as membership in most other organizations. Coping with such social politics was beyond Dos Passos. Later, when he congratulated a friend still in prep school for the ribbons he had recently won in a track meet, he also cautioned him: "Don't get too husky, please—husky people invariably have a brain the size of a pea and are awful bores. At least I find them so at college here." He admitted that he had once placed fourth in a hundred-yard dash at Choate and from time to time had considered doing something to develop his body, but balked because of his dislike for organized athletics. He said, too, that he hated golf and ice skating ("I always freeze to death; furthermore, I skate very badly"), yet lamented that there was no place to ski nearby, an activity he had engaged in two or three times on Choate's gently rolling hills. The thought of skiing appealed to him more than "landing with a thud on the frozen surface of the Charles." During football season Dos Passos attended several pep rallies, beer nights, and smokers at the invitation of another relatively unpopular student who condescended to take him along, "but no one much bothered with me," he admitted, "except socialists and Jews." The then prevailing attitude at Harvard regarding Jews insured their being "treated politely, yet as personae non gratae," said Robert Nathan, himself a Jew.

John R. continued to write long letters to his son two or three times a week—usually in French—and his mother scrawled a few lines when she was able, but Dos Passos reacted to such missives much as he had during his days at Choate. To his father's sermons he turned a deaf ear and skimmed his letters for news of his mother. He derived comfort in keeping alive his friendship with Clara St. John, the wife of Choate's headmaster, to whom he wrote three or four times during the year to report that things were "going well" for him at Harvard. Actually, they were. He lived a solitary existence for the most part, his letters and diary entries of the period attesting to his general lack of involvement in campus activities or other internal affairs of the university, excepting classes, which he attended regularly. The din that arose sporadically outside the Harvard gates provoked only mild discussion or controversy within the sanctum. Students sat smoking and talking on the steps of lecture halls or loitered in little groups in the Yard before their dormitory entrances discussing next week's game with Princeton or Yale, but most of the headlines that blazoned across the Boston *Transcript* or *Globe* and the New York *Times* in 1912 elicited scant comment from Harvard men. Dos Passos moved in and out of the gates more freely than many students because of his compulsion to take to the hills beyond Cambridge and to tramp about greater Boston. An innate curiosity to observe his environment was strong, but he managed to stay relatively detached and uninvolved emotionally. Although he may have taken note of the labor agitation and violence that rocked nearby Lawrence and Salem and read that Theodore Roosevelt, the Progressive party's candidate to oppose Wilson, had been shot in an assassination attempt, he made no mention of such incidents in letters home.

Parades, riots, strikes, protests, woman's suffrage, a presidential election—all did relatively little to pipe Dos Passos and his classmates outside the gates of Harvard Yard, but avant-garde art did. Headlines that marked the controversial Armory Show's opening of Postimpressionists in New York City—the International Exhibition of Modern Art— set off a flurry of excitement in Boston's Copley Hall in the spring of 1913 after its run at the Art Institute of Chicago. Many paintings from the original exhibition had been dropped because of the size of the gallery (for the most part, works by Americans). What remained were the most startling pieces of modern European art, some 240 in all. Harvard professors and students—as well as proper Bostonians—hastened to join gawking viewers queued three-deep before Marcel Duchamp's Cubist painting *Nude Descending a Staircase,* and a bust, *Mlle. Pogany,* by Constantin Brancuşi, the most controversial works in the exhibition. Even those who admired the Duchamp painting for its successful depiction of continuous action through a series of overlapping figure outlines were puzzled or disturbed by the Brancuşi sculpture with its egg-shaped head, sinuous arms curving upward to the face, and great bulbous eyes. Despite the traditionalists' disdain, defending critics hailed the Brancuşi bust for its triumph of impressionism over realism and line for line's sake.

Dos Passos, untutored in art, accompanied a new friend and fellow student, Edward Nagel, to the exhibit. Nagel was the stepson of Gaston Lachaise, already a prominent sculptor, and Nagel was an art major. Dos Passos recalled years later that the Armory Show at Copley Hall had been a jolt to him, but he did not remember specific paintings. "In spite of all the kidding about the Nude Descending a Staircase, I didn't recognize it when I saw it again at the Museum of Modern Art," he added, explaining that the most he derived from cubism at the time was a "tingling feeling that a lot of odd things I didn't know about were happening in the world." It was the beginning of his looking at a picture directly as an "excitement for the eye," an experience that had been preceded a few weeks earlier by a visit to the Museum of Fine Arts in Boston to view the paintings of James Whistler. Curious because he had heard Whistler's work spoken of in the same breath with the piano pieces of Debussy (to which he had just been introduced), Dos Passos saw the paintings and thought them comparable to the music. Harvard students in 1912 were full of "callow snobadmiration for the nineties," and it seemed to him that Whistler's pastels and Debussy's pieces were in the "fashionable mood of gentle and European snobmelancholy." The titles of Whistler's paintings affected him more than the works themselves, Dos Passos added. "Still, I must have been visually stirred because I soon got hold of a box of pastels and began to make dovecolored smudges of my own. The trouble was that it immediately became obvious that almost any combination of pastel blurs was as agreeable to look at as any other, and my enthusiasm for that sort of thing began to flag." Nonetheless, his attempt was the beginning of Dos Passos' lifetime avocation as a painter.

He was seventeen when he ranged among the avant-garde paintings and sculpture of the Armory Show when it came to Boston. At the time he was more interested in literature than art, having decided to concentrate on courses within the general field of English, and was fortunate to have assigned as his faculty advisor Chandler Post, who became his Greek teacher. Post held simultaneous appointments in the classics, Romance languages, and fine arts departments and took a special liking to students who esteemed the language and culture of ancient civilizations and were put off by the materialism, crassness, and vulgarity commonplace in contemporary American society. It seemed to Dos Passos that he and his mentor saw eye to eye. For his first year of study he chose courses in advanced Greek, Latin, and French, introductory German, a survey of European civilization, and freshman composition.

Despite his having matriculated to Harvard with a vague notion of studying law, Dos Passos inwardly rebelled against following his father's profession. He respected John R.'s intelligence, his success as a corporate lawyer, and his willingness to press his convictions even though his stand was often an unpopular one. To young Dos Passos, there was much in his father's character and personality to admire, but he resented him, too. Having perceived his mother as a victim of a chain of events that led her to subjugate her entire being to a man to whom she was not married for over a quarter of a century, he was far more sympathetic of her suffering—which he had observed at close range—than of any problem involving his errant father. He envied his father's fame and deplored his own sense of being a nonentity, but if he was ever going to *be* somebody, he reasoned, it would have to be in a direction quite different from his father's. If he could not turn his bent for literature and history, his attraction to languages and the poetic word, into a life work, he did not know what he would be when he got out on his own. He knew that he did not give a fig for riches—which his father had dangled as a goal—but he did want to be a success. Moreover, the interior life found in books appealed to Dos Passos far more than anything connected with jurisprudence.

A yellowed copy of Van Gogh's *Letters* and a French translation of *Crime and Punishment* (he had just discovered Dostoevski) were tucked under his arm the day he roamed the gallery in Copley Hall. He said later that his books excited him more than did the visual art of the exhibition. Dos Passos' reading habits were never restricted to class assignments. Rather, he delighted in discovering books on his own and eagerly took up the writings of Flaubert, Laforgue, Mallarmé, Rimbaud, and Verlaine; Voltaire's *Candide,* Stendahl's *Le Rouge et le Noir,* Anatole France's *Île des Penguins,* Rabelais' *Gargantua* and *Pantagruel;* and read countless other French editions. Such eclecticism also included H. G. Wells, Oscar Wilde, George Meredith, and Laurence Sterne; most of the popular Victorian poets; the leading Imagists of both England and the United States; Hafiz, FitzGerald (especially the *Rubáiyát of Omar Khayyám),* Baudelaire; Apuleius, Catullus, Juvenal, Martial, and Petronius (all of whom he read in Latin); and a host of Russian novelists in French and English translations. Sir James Frazer's *The Golden Bough* also made an impact upon Dos Passos during this period. He took no courses in American literature, but read a number of selected native poets, novelists, philosophers, and social critics. He especially admired the writings of Jefferson, Thoreau, Whitman, Twain, Crane, James (both Henry and William), Veblen, and Bertrand Russell.

What Dos Passos most longed for at Harvard was recognition of the literary ability that had earned him plaudits at Choate, and he set out to get it. Of the six official undergraduate publications to which Harvard men aspired, he eliminated all but two. Since writing journalistically was furthest from his mind, the daily newspaper, the *Harvard Crimson* (known as *The Crime),* was out. His sense of humor qualified him for the *Lampoon,* but he wanted to do more than entertain; moreover, he was not enough concerned with the foibles of society to attack them with "trenchant pencil and sarcastic pen," the avowed motive of the *Lampoon.* The *Harvard Illustrated Magazine* seemed too mundane, smug, and superficial for him (the epitome of its concerns was seen in the lead editorial of the "Yale Game Issue" his sophomore year: "One would hardly think it necessary to add emphasis to the warnings which have come from Washington in order to impress upon Harvard men the necessity of strict silence concerning the war. . . . Harvard has enough troubles, football and otherwise, of her own to care for without borrowing any of those three thousand miles away"). Dos Passos ruled out *The Signet,* a publication devoted to the arts, which operated more like a social club for "nice boys who wrote sonnets" than a publication staff. The only serious contenders for Dos Passos' creative ventures were the *Harvard Advocate,* published every two weeks, and the *Harvard Monthly,* both dedicated to literature as art.

The University's oldest publication was the *Harvard Advocate,* founded in 1866. Known for its inveterate conservatism, the magazine proclaimed its writings "brief, readable, and frankly popular in conception of things literary." The *Harvard Monthly* began in 1885 as an avant-garde rival. It claimed to be a "forum for the intelligent discussion of all questions relating to the policy and conditions of the university" and vowed to keep its offerings on a high, idealistic, literary plane. Both magazines declared that their readers were provided a balanced fare of verse, fiction, essays, reviews, and literary polemics. Their staffs were sociable and friendly despite their rivalry and at times considered merging. Their offices were on the top floor of Memorial Union, and when one group threw a beer night or "punch," the other was automatically invited. Board members were gay and witty in their commingling, and at parties it was impossible to distinguish a *Harvard Advocate* editor from a *Harvard Monthly* one. Many students contributed to both magazines and were known loosely as "Harvard aesthetes," a label they eschewed.

The roots of the aesthetic movement at Harvard lay in its one-time cult hero Oscar Wilde, who concluded his lecture tour of America in 1882 with a challenge to the "vulgar herd." He accused Americans of being sterile in their artistic sensibilities, of seeing no marvel in art, no meaning in beauty, and no message in the past. Quick to rally, Bostonians picked up their aesthetic banners and waved them with a vengeance for three decades. Art, music, literature—all were pursued in the name of "art for art's sake" in repudiation of Wilde's claim that the country reeked with ugliness, industrialism, and Philistinism at the expense of goodness and beauty. By the turn of the century, most of the mauve afterglow—as Dos Passos described it—and effete sophistication with which countless Harvard men had adorned themselves in the 1880s and 1890s had died out. Even then, however, there were attempts to rekindle the ardors of the past through the writings of Wilde, the art nouveau illustrations of Aubrey Beardsley and other contributors to *The Yellow Book,* a lively but short-lived quarterly of the 1890s, and morose reflections upon Francis Thompson's "The Hound of Heaven." Young men sat cross-legged in purple pajamas, sipped exotic liqueurs in rooms heavily hung with brocades and silks, and burned incense before curious bronze figures under dim lights. Finding such posturing inane, Dos Passos later satirized it in a tale published in the *Harvard Monthly* entitled "An Aesthete's Nightmare." He relished Gilbert and Sullivan's satire of Wilde in the operetta *Patience* and was bored by most of the decadent verse associated with imitators of the Pre-Raphaelites, but found *The Yellow Book* humorous. The editorial staffs of both the *Harvard Advocate* and the *Harvard Monthly* tried to shake off the surviving vestiges of effete romanticism by declaring they would publish nothing that smacked of preciosity.

Dos Passos preferred the *Harvard Monthly* to the *Advocate* and got up the nerve near the end of his freshman year to submit a short story entitled "The Almeh." The piece contained no well-made plot or conventional development of character, but it was an effective slice of life, low-keyed and rich in sensory detail. In tone and revelation it resembled James Joyce's "Araby." "The Almeh," which evolved from his recent journey to North Africa and the Middle East, concerned two prep school boys on tour in Cairo. Jack Hazen, a crass, athletic American, had little patience with Dick Mansford, his young British friend with a newly discovered inclination to paint. Mansford, enamored of the picturesque, romantic aspects of the ancient city, was smitten when he accidentally glimpsed the face of a voluptuous, dark-eyed Egyptian maiden, and combed the city in search of her. His dreams were shattered upon discovering that she was not the woman of class he had fantasized, but a cheap bazaar dancer. Even more distressing was learning that she was to be the bride of his donkey boy. That evening the youth captured her beauty in oils during an all-night "orgy" of painting, yet his disenchantment was reinforced when he saw the girl again, this time in his donkey boy's fly-infested hut. The story's theme of disillusionment was telescoped in the final scene when Mansford observed her squatting in the doorway of the hut as she cooked the midday meal and heard her shouting shrewishly to her naked nephews at play outside.

"The Almeh" was accepted by the *Harvard Monthly* for publication in its final issue of the 1912–13 academic year. By then it was July and Dos Passos was back in Virginia with his mother and had no inkling that the piece was to be published. John Walcott, a Choate friend who was now at Harvard, wrote: "Allow me to offer my congratulations to the distinguished new writer of the *Harvard Monthly!* . . . It is really fine, and now with your volumes of manuscripts written during the summer you will be an editor by Christmas," he predicted. Dos Passos was proud of his accomplishment because freshmen were rarely published by the *Harvard Monthly*, but he bemoaned his luck that the story did not appear till after most students had left for the summer holidays.

He stayed with his mother in Virginia scarcely a month this time, the old wanderlust upon him once more. From Washington in mid-July, he traveled by train to Lake Ontario, where he took a river steamer up the Rideau Canal to Ottawa, then to Montreal and Quebec by cruise ship. For a time he traveled alone, took pleasure in practicing his French on the natives (in the spring of 1913 he passed the required oral examination in French for a baccalaureate degree in liberal arts, unusual for a freshman), liked the feel and steady hum of the motors underfoot and the continuously moving scenery, and scrutinized his fellow passengers with rising interest. Snatches of conversations and impressions of what he was experiencing were set down in his journal each day to become grist for his creative mill upon his return to Harvard. By early September Dos Passos was impatient to get back to Cambridge, having concluded that life there was not such a netherworld after all. Over the summer he had put on weight and now blended into his Harvard environment with new self-assurance. He had improved his lot considerably by being published in the *Harvard Monthly*. Students who read the magazine were alert to the names and faces of its contributors and, as a result, often made sociable overtures. The fledgling author benefited, also, by moving in the fall from the Harvard Yard to 32 Ware Hall, a private dormitory on Harvard Street (at the edge of the campus) where residents were a homogeneous mixture of underclassmen. Every day he saw others with whom he had classes. They dropped in upon one another for tea, often dined together, and attended the ballet or theater. Weekend activities usually included a concert at Symphony Hall.

Most Harvard men took their weekday meals on campus at Memorial Hall; the food suited unimaginative palates and the students who were more concerned with the expeditious use of the time than with what they ate. On Saturday evenings, however, Dos Passos made dining out an occasion. Gourmet concoctions having been his usual fare while abroad, he missed the Continental cuisine on which his taste buds had developed and sought out new restaurants. Such new friends as Kenneth Murdock, S. Foster Damon, and

Frederick van den Arend found it sporting to accompany Dos Passos about the city in pursuit of the perfect dinner on forays that soon took on the nature of a game, their progressive supper itinerary changing weekly. After eating in a multitude of French, Italian, and Greek restaurants (and an occasional American one), they concluded where the best individual courses could be found and progressed through the evening accordingly. One establishment was chosen for its steamed oysters, raw kibbe, or roasted Italian peppers, another for its lobster bisque or clams *au beurre blanc* and dry white wine, a third for its beef bordelaise and asparagus, *poulet au riesling,* shrimp scorpio, or baked bluefish with rosemary—with such side dishes as Armenian stuffed artichokes, eggplant cooked in sesame oil, and Sicilian broccoli—and a final restaurant for its strawberries in liqueur, baked papaya, or pineapple flan. Dos Passos and his friends were as choosy about their wines, table service, orchestral accompaniment, and atmosphere as they were with the succulent dishes. Although the perfect meal with its appropriate accouterments often eluded them, their adventuresome evenings were long and ebullient. Sometimes a symphony concert, ballet, play, or variety show at the old Colonial Theatre was sandwiched in between courses. Among their favorite restaurants were such venerated establishments as the Athenia, Parthenon, Thorndike, Venice, the Hotel Touraine, Wirth's, and the Boar's Head (at Richie's Grill).

Their mode of locomotion was by foot, Dos Passos' long strides setting the pace. Even in the winter they walked. It was a rare night that snow or rain drove them to public transportation. Dos Passos was especially fond of tramping alone in the rain. In a letter to a friend after "a tremendously long ramble through Boston," he wrote of the "wonderful atmosphere of gaiety and a sort of paganism" in the city on a rainy night when the "reflections of the orange and yellow lights are so gay on the wet streets." He was drawn to the cheaper parts of town and to the marketplace. "It is wonderful what beautiful faces you sometimes see at such times—ugly gargoyle-grotesques, too—still it is all very alive and exciting when not done up in stays like the life of us cotton-wool plutocrats," he added.

Dos Passos' letters abounded with colorful language. He referred to his wanderings at night as his "main amusement of late," during which he had seen enough "to keep a painter busy a century." In the spring he wrote of hiking out on a hillside with several classmates and picnicking on cold roasted chicken, cheeses, bread, and jellies: "I've never known anything so delightful. . . . a wonderful red-orange sunset, fading gradually through rosy-purple and violet to a sort of dim lavender with a yellow sheen. We climbed into a big oak tree—as if we were Bonnie Prince Charlie being pursued by the King's men—and watched it, then walked back to Cambridge through the gloaming." In another letter he spoke of his walking cure to be applied "when you have reached the last stage of boredom and are surrounded on all sides by blue devils." He suggested setting out alone without heed to direction and "chanting your favorite poet (or your own works, according to taste) to the May breezes as you walk." If the cure is a success, the patient will be hoarse, tired, temporarily lost, but contented once more when he finds his way home at last.

Another solace was either rowing alone on the Charles River or running late at night along Cambridge's quiet streets for three or four miles. More than once he surprised himself by taking off his glasses and stepping into a boxing ring in the school's gymnasium. To a prep school acquaintance he volunteered: "Imagine . . . I box nowadays! I have a friend who knows nothing about boxing—and I know nothing about it—so we have a charming time hammering at each other and at the air. If we ever do happen to hit each other, we apologize profusely. We nearly weep for fear of hurting one another. It is screamingly amusing." Dos Passos had come a long way from the painfully self-conscious encounters suffered with his peers at Choate. His wry sense of humor and ability to laugh at himself had evolved quite naturally of late along with other marks of maturity that sustained his occasional ventures as an athlete.

Seldom did Dos Passos allow himself to become bored. If alone, he was either asleep or doing something he enjoyed. Writing creatively was also a means of entertaining himself. He savored words and phrases, was intrigued by the sensuousness of language, the sense of motion, line, and color that words conveyed, and considered much of what was appearing in Harvard's various student publications drivel. He was convinced that the stories he had begun to spin were as good as the usual offerings, and possibly better. He was also put off by the current crop of periodicals that served as typical reading fare of Harvard men—and by American literature in general—and was restless in his anticipation for what was new and experimental in modern art and music to set in, also, in the writing of his American contemporaries.

Clubs did not interest Dos Passos unless they were tied to his literary goals. He had not made the Institute. "My blood did not run thin enough for the very best clubs," he offered. As a sophomore he was invited into the Classical Club and Cercle Français, organizations he embraced because they promoted the study and culture of Latin, Greek, and French and provided a measure of sociability in the process. Confident by this time that he was well grounded in these languages, Dos Passos abandoned his formal study to read them on his own. In their place, he signed up for basic Spanish, taught by Chandler Post. Before long he was reading novels and plays by modern Spanish writers and yearned to put his newly acquired skills to work in Spain, as well as in the classroom and his armchair at home.

Caught up as he was in the cultures of other countries, Dos Passos wrote stories about them, too. Just before Christmas of 1913 he submitted a second tale, "The Honor of the Klepht," to the editors of the *Harvard Monthly* and was overjoyed when it, too, was accepted. Its appearance in the February 1914 issue prompted several board members of the magazine to seek him out, and even strangers approached him to compliment him on it. This story was like its predecessor, "The Almeh," in its theme of love and disillusionment and in its reflection of Dos Passos' preoccupation with the romantic past and exotic, distant lands. "The Honor of the Klepht" took its title from a band of Byzantine Greeks who swept down from the hills of Mount Parnassus to warn a tiny village of an impending Turkish raid and massacre. Yet before the young klepht leader could rescue Louka, the maiden he loved, she was abducted and the other villagers killed. Not knowing if the girl, too, had been killed, the bereaved chieftain led his band in a heroic attack upon the marauders only to discover his beloved in the leader's tent—no longer in her goat-girl rags but in silks—now a sultana herself with a slave girl to fan her. "Louka is dead!" he shouted as he threw himself upon the Turkish ranks in a passionate attack, then leaped off a cliff into the sea. Though an apprentice piece, the tale had merit in comparison to the rest of the offerings in the *Harvard Monthly* that year.

"The Honor of the Klepht" was Dos Passos' only publication as a sophomore. In the spring of 1914 he came down with scarlet fever and for eight weeks was quarantined in Harvard's Stillman Infirmary while health officials tried to keep the outbreak from reaching epidemic proportions. Impatient to be released and feeling abandoned by those who had been stricken but recovered quickly, he worried about his grades, found it difficult to concentrate, and felt sorry for himself in general. In May he was spied pacing inside the Stillman fence near the bank of the Charles River, watching the racing shells, hearing the coxswain's cries, and hoping that someone he knew might stroll by to relieve his boredom. A friend who chanced upon him wrote the headmaster of his plight, and soon there were commiserating letters from Clara and George St. John. St. John feared that his young friend's earlier encounters with rheumatic fever—first in Brussels, then at Choate—might have weakened his overall constitution and urged him to take better care of himself.

Dos Passos resented having more difficulty shaking off relatively common diseases than most of his Harvard friends and acquaintances had. It was an enigma to him that a person who loved the outdoors and fresh air as much as he did had to take to his sickbed more often than those who smoked heavily and drank hard liquor. He did neither at Harvard, and even fine wines he sipped sparingly. Dos Passos' robust countenance and addiction to outdoor exercise were deceptive, for they implied a better state of health than was actually his. Friends were impressed by what seemed his boundless energy, his habit of almost constant motion even during conversation indoors. He never just sat, relaxed, and conversed at a leisurely pace; rather, he stood, paced, fidgeted, and thrashed about the room as though impatient to terminate the exchange and move along, which was seldom the case. His shy, hesitant mannerisms in speaking were misleading, too. Although he seemed nervous, he was not. A characteristic gesture was to duck his head, then peer up at his listener and venture an idea that might be punctuated by an "ah . . . ah . . . ah" before launching into a stream of rhetoric, yet he was neither dogmatic nor arrogant in forcing his opinions upon others. If there were disagreements he often suggested with a wry smile that his adversary take another look at their essential differences.

For the most part, Dos Passos liked his studies during his sophomore year and attended classes regularly. In addition to his Spanish course, he took English 41 (survey of English literature), Comparative Literature 12, and American government. Bliss Perry, his English professor, viewed writing as a highly personal craft to be improved upon only by practice. As an editor of *The Atlantic Monthly* for eight years before coming to Harvard, Perry had seen considerable writing—both good and bad—come across his desk. While he believed that mechanical correctness could be taught in the classroom, writing as an art rested primarily upon self-discipline, he insisted. Anyone whose ambition was to write should be encouraged to create in whatever form appealed to him, be it verse, prose, drama, or fiction. Competent guidance aided his progress, as did training in Latin and Greek composition, he added. The most successful students had a broad base in the classics. Although taking courses in composition would never make writers of them, working on their own and exposing their work to intelligent, critical readers might. Perry's supportive philosophy coincided with Dos Passos' own, and under his professor's tutelage he wrote a great deal during his sophomore year. He also resolved to take a composition course each semester he was in school. Much of Dos Passos' work went into a journal that he showed to no one.

Dos Passos' extended illness during the spring of 1914 cost him one half credit of his comparative literature class. The rest of his work he was able to complete satisfactorily before returning to Washington in June. He finished the year with three B's and two C's, a feat under the circumstances. He would like to have lingered in Cambridge to recuperate from the pressures of finishing up his course work without having sufficiently recovered his strength, but his parents were impatient for his arrival so that they could set out to the farm together. Lucy's doctor thought a change of scenery might have a salubrious effect upon her. John R. had kept their son apprised of her rapidly deteriorating condition, but his remarks were phrased in vague terms. Although he informed Jack—John R. never called his son "Dos"—that Lucy needed surgery, he never explained why. When it was canceled, John R. reported only that she was too weak to undergo it safely. The doctor, too, was obscure in his own diagnosis and treatment. For weeks he had her on a milk diet. Lucy's mental condition at times seemed worse than her physical problems. After a second stroke, her memory had become—in John R.'s words—"very bad." She now bordered on senility, he reported to his son. Any improvement they had hoped for upon moving her to Virginia failed to materialize. The sultry weather of the Northern Neck in June and July sapped Lucy's scant energies, and the breezes off the river provided only temporary relief from soaring temperatures, which rose even higher in August. Dos Passos, too, suffered from the heat and humidity, yet felt guilty if he whiled away the hours fishing, swimming, or lounging on a half-submerged log at the river's edge instead of sitting in the sickroom and reading to his mother, or otherwise communing with her. Never one to engage in trivial conversation for long, he tried, nonetheless, to entertain her by recounting humorous anecdotes of the people encountered in their sparsely populated community, but there was little that he could tell of life in Cambridge to which she might relate. He enjoyed, as always, digging in the vegetable and flower beds and brought great armloads of sweet peas, roses, zinnias, and marigolds into his mother's bedroom, but when boredom set in he chafed and lamented to himself that his meager creative efforts were weak and without inspiration. He missed the intellectual excitement of being among others who shared his artistic temperament.

Dos Passos' half brother James was on the scene daily, having been made manager of the property known as Cherry Grove. Although John R. spoke disparagingly of his stepson from time to time because of his drinking, James was able to assist in the running of the farm with more authority than was generally attributed to him. James supervised Otis, the hired hand, saw to the harvesting of the cash crop, tomatoes (which involved many laborers), and wrote explicit progress reports to John R. and Dos Passos. James wrote Dos Passos in the spring of 1914 that "Miss Blondine had dropped a fine heifer calf," said he had finished digging the fish pond Dos Passos had designed, planted the lawn with grass seed, and ordered from the Drears catalogue the various flower and vegetable seeds requested. Dos Passos relied on James to follow through on his various landscaping schemes dreamed up while at Harvard. They closed their letters to each other "Affectionately." John R. treated his stepson with civility (and generosity when it came to his education), but did not embrace him with the warmth reserved for his own sons. James wrote of his stepfather to Dos Passos: "We do not write each other often, but it does not mean the heart is cold—at least on my part."

In August 1914, the heat and boredom now unbearable, Dos Passos bolted the farm once more and set out with his friend John Walcott on an ocean voyage to the Outer Banks of Newfoundland. Impressions of this venture were not preserved because Dos Passos lost his diary in the wilds of Placentia Bay. The journal contained all of his literary jottings of the previous year, a loss of many potential manuscripts, Dos Passos lamented. In a letter to a prep school friend he wrote of swimming in icy, pale green water that stung his limbs and made him feel as though he were bathing in green champagne. After bathing, he and Walcott cavorted on the deserted, white beach "like Green fauns." To Dos Passos, it was a "red-letter swimming day."

Once back at Harvard for the fall, he commenced a new diary, this one labeled "Volume II." On the first page he announced rather cavalierly the fate of its predecessor, then began afresh to comment upon everything he was doing relative to the arts, to which he became increasingly devoted as the year progressed. He catalogued the performances he saw, the books and plays he read, and his impressions and criticisms of every cultural event of which he had firsthand knowledge. Although Dos Passos' entries were often sophomoric, they revealed a serious attempt to define his tastes and develop a critical vocabulary. On September 26, 1914, for example, he wrote that of the two plays he had just seen in Boston's Colonial Theatre, George M. Cohan's *The Miracle Man* and Philip Bartholomae's *Miss Daisy*, the latter was "an unusually excellent little musical comedy, very spritely and not at all vulgar. No chorus! Hurrah!" Two nights later he saw a play called *Drugged*, "a crude melodrama with one good scene and a sensational title" and "excellently acted" by John Mason. He described *Wanted 22,000*, viewed October 3, as "a most snappy and—in jerks—excellently written play. Cast including Glendinning excellent. Each part written with consummate skill, as was to be expected of Clayton Hamilton and A. E. Thomas, but the sudden transitions between farce and tragedy were horrifying. The idea is ever so clever and well worked out—with the exception of the heroine, who was an interesting actress—but the other women in the cast were abominable." He spoke of Henry Bernstein's *The Secret* as a good David Belasco production, but said that "some of the company was poor . . . a rather needless, but interesting play. Is it all 'technique'? Not really satisfying, but absorbing; over-emotional at times and lost by translation." Upon returning from Symphony Hall one night, he wrote of reading Rudolf Besier's *Lady Patricia,* "a most amusing and entertaining play, almost a farce in its deliciously extravagant lines; most excellently written, with rather good technique and awfully funny situations." He then remarked on a concert and opera. "Beethoven's Eroica Symphony very beautiful, especially the funeral march and scherzo. Strauss's Don Juan most interesting contrasted with aria from Serse by Handel, which followed it. This was sung magnificently by Amato."

By the end of October he was on a reading spree of Henry James. *The Europeans* was "a delightful, entertaining little story," the satire "exquisite," and the characterization "wonderfully careful and delicate," he wrote in his diary. The "strokes" of James's portraits were "so fine, so miniature" that they reminded him of the "delicacy of Fra Angelico, or better, of some of the more refined Dutch portrait painters." He thought *Daisy Miller* "an interesting character study . . . almost too subtle . . . minute, almost microscopic, but hardly very vivid." The dialogue reminded him of Oscar Wilde. After reading *The Portrait of a Lady* Dos Passos was convinced that James's women were "marvelous." Other works commented on that fall were George Sand's *Elle et Lui,* Thackeray's *Vanity Fair,* and Turgenev's *Fathers and Sons.* The Turgenev novel disappointed him. He had expected something more radical, incendiary, yet found the characterization excellent. "Construction is rather lacking," he added. "There is a sort of pointlessness to the book which is quite unexpected. It seems lacking in universality . . . in significance for our generation." More and more Dos Passos found himself at odds with what he read. On the one hand, he clung to the notion of "art for art's sake," the byword of the aesthete; on the other, he wanted to be entertained. He expected relevance to his own generation and situation, universality as well as particularization. "I am not easy to please," he concluded. Dos Passos experienced another ambivalence, too. While he expected realism in plot, characterization, and setting, and applauded James for his finely drawn, truthful depiction of life and his "delicate subtlety," he himself was becoming more effete and pretentious—even precious—in his own behavior. The trappings of the Harvard aesthete were upon him, a fact reflected in his literary diary as well as in his daily living.

When Dos Passos returned to Harvard in the fall of 1914, he selected rooms this time at 33 Ridgely Hall on Mount Auburn Street. Ridgely was a private dormitory some distance from the Harvard Yard and occupied chiefly by young men whose allowances enabled them to squander more money than the moderate allotments to which most Harvard undergraduates were privy. Students who did not live on Mount Auburn Street— especially those whose fathers had not lived on the "Gold Coast" in the 1890s when the street first became popular—spoke of those who *did* live there (in tones tinged by envy) as "the gilded collegians." Also living on "the Gold Coast" were a few of the more flamboyant professors, such as George Lyman Kittredge, from whom Dos Passos took Shakespeare and "English and Scottish Ballads and Early Metrical Romances." Forceful, aristocratic, fierce-looking, "Kitty"—as he was popularly known—might have been taken for a Viking warrior in another age. He was easily spotted on his characteristic charge across Harvard Square in the midst of rush-hour traffic, his folded umbrella or cane raised like a baton and brandished at the cars teeming around him. With flashing blue eyes, white hair, and full white beard, he was sometimes stopped on the street at Christmastime by children with their Christmas lists. Taxi drivers were known to call out, "Step on it, Santa Claus, or they'll run over your beard!" Students loved the tale concerning a maid who viewed Kittredge for the first time when admitting him for tea and was so startled by his appearance that she clapped a hand to her breast and inhaled a breathy "My God!"

"Not God, madam—Kittredge!" he thundered as he strode into the foyer. Compared to the ostentatious antics of Kittredge, those of Dos Passos and his confreres at Harvard were relatively mild. The men took to gathering in the late afternoon for tea and hot chocolate, or on rare occasions, port and rum toddies. Their social habits were not unlike those of Fanshaw, a character Dos Passos created for a novel of his Harvard period, *Streets of Night* (1923). Fanshaw was a Harvard man who lived on Mount Auburn Street and possessed a number of characteristics similar to Dos Passos himself. Fanshaw took his byword from *The Book of Tea* (a volume then in vogue among students): "A man without tea was a man without poise, refinement." Dos Passos and his friends devoted their mornings to the rigorous routine of going to classes, reading, and studying; their afternoons—and sometimes their entire day—were spent in passionate pursuit of their individual creative endeavors, be it verse, prose, or painting. At 5 P.M., however, they arose and groomed themselves, donned gray gloves, pocketed their calling cards, and began a punctilious ritual of visitations. From door to door they progressed according to whim and fancy, either alone or in pairs. Sometimes there was no "host" to receive them because everyone was out calling on someone else. If they missed each other, they walked up Brattle Street for tea at the Cock House or converged for chocolate pudding at the Merle or the Green Lantern.

Dos Passos' friends during the 1914–15 school year included several board members of the *Harvard Monthly*. One was Robert Nathan, the first member of his class to be invited to join the magazine's editorial staff. A coveted position, it was gained after publishing at least six pieces in the *Harvard Monthly* and exhibiting a keen interest in literary affairs in general. Nathan lived only a few doors from Dos Passos' Auburn Street quarters (26); thus they saw each other fairly often. Nathan did not participate in the full-dress visitations and teas in which the others engaged, however. His recollection was of having occasionally gone through a keg of beer with such Auburn Street cronies as Frank Dazey and "a fellow named Peterson," but of not being fully accepted by many of his classmates because he was a Jew. Nathan was next in line to become president of the *Harvard Monthly*, but said that as a Jew, he was excluded from the office. As R. Stewart Mitchell—who did become chief editor—explained it to him: "If you were to be elected president of the <u>Harvard Monthly</u>, then the Signets would have to take you in . . . and the Signets don't really want to take in a Jew." Years later when asked about anti-Semitism at Harvard (Nathan left a semester short of graduation because married students were not allowed to remain in school and he had already committed himself to matrimony), he replied:

> Yes, there was always some prejudice everywhere. A few very wealthy Jews (and therefore well connected in banking circles) were "accepted"—their Jewishness overlooked—but they were few. On the other hand, it was never blatant, either at Exeter—my prep school—or Harvard; the Jews made their own friends, both Jewish and otherwise. There was a Jewish "frat" at Harvard—but none of my friends (or perhaps only one or two) had anything to do with it; it consisted mainly of boys who happened to be rooming in the same house in the Yard. The Institute never even considered me. I was a little hurt by the <u>Harvard Monthly</u>, but I can't remember getting very upset about it. It just seemed a natural part of nature. . . . I never felt the least anti-Semitism in Dos.

After leaving college, Nathan, too, wrote a "Harvard novel," *Peter Kindred* (1919), which aptly reflected the anti-Semitism of the period.

Closer friends to Dos Passos than Nathan who were on the *Harvard Monthly* staff during his junior year were E. Estlin ("E.E.") Cummings, Gilbert Seldes, and Harold Weston, all seniors. Cummings had lived with his family on nearby Irving Street until he was a senior, when he moved into Thayer Hall in the Harvard Yard. He and Dos Passos found themselves in several classes together, and Cummings began inviting him home for dinner. Dos Passos found the old-fashioned Cambridge household of the Cummings family much to his liking. It seemed "a link with the Jameses and all the generations of old New Englanders back to Emerson and Thoreau," he observed later. Edward Cummings (for whom his son was named) was the most prominent Unitarian minister in Boston at the time, having succeeded Edward Everett Hale to the pulpit at South Congregational Church. Dr. Cummings was a Harvard graduate and a former assistant professor of sociology there, but gave up teaching for the pulpit. He hoped his son would follow a more traditional approach and distinguish himself as a professor of classics at Harvard. Though young Cummings displayed exceptional facility with languages at the Cambridge Latin School and won distinction at Harvard for his translations of the Greek lyrical poets, he was more interested in a career as a poet than as a teacher.

Dos Passos, too, was writing poetry in 1914–15, but was reluctant to submit it to the scrutinizing eyes of the editorial board of the *Harvard Monthly.* He may also have thought it foolish to compete for space with Cummings, Seldes, Nathan, and two other senior board members he already knew well—S. Foster Damon and Scofield Thayer—all of whom were proven poets, when he could contribute prose, about which he felt more confident.

His next submission to the *Harvard Monthly* was a review of *Insurgent Mexico,* by John Reed, a recent Harvard graduate (class of 1910). A protégé of Charles Townsend Copeland, John Reed was already something of a legend at Harvard. He had been arrested and jailed briefly in Paterson, New Jersey, upon visiting the scene of a historic silk workers' strike and refusing to leave when ordered to do so by a truculent policeman. News of the event filtered up to Harvard because impounded with Reed were two labor leaders, William D. ("Big Bill") Haywood, founder and leader of the Wobblies (the I.W.W.—Industrial Workers of the World); and Carlo Tresca, a fiery young Italian newspaperman and anarchist; and some fifty textile workers. A few weeks later, Reed, with the aid of Mabel Dodge and other habitués of her salon on lower Fifth Avenue, staged a reenactment of the Paterson strike in Madison Square Garden for which they imported a thousand men, women, and children who actually had participated in the strike. Some twenty thousand people attended the one-night pageant depicting the impoverished conditions of the workers and their families, the brutality of the police, and the rallying speeches by labor leaders, but the money raised was insufficient to cover expenses, let alone aid the poverty-stricken workers.

Dos Passos had followed with interest the heady career of Reed, though he himself sublimated any such inclinations while at Harvard. He felt certain loyalties as the genteel son of a capitalist whose professional success depended upon the growth of industrialism. Although Dos Passos was passively resistant to the socialist agitation about him, he kept abreast of what was going on. While John R. was writing tracts for publication and traveling over the countryside in opposition to the eight-hour work day, his son was steeping in a growing socialist brew on the Harvard campus. Unlike most other American colleges, which had begun to clamp down on faculty and students vocal in their unrest, Harvard placed no restrictions on the activities of political groups. In 1914 the newly formed Harvard Socialist Club had some sixty official members. When John Spargo, a British spokesman for revisionist Marxism, came to Harvard to speak, over three hundred cheering students were in his audience. Almost unawares, the college community found itself concerned with labor problems at home, the war raging in Europe and its effect upon the United States, and Mexico's latest insurrection (Francisco ["Pancho"] Villa was leading his growing band of guerillas against the Nationalists). Reed, who had been in Mexico on assignment by *Metropolitan Magazine* and *The World* to determine firsthand what was going on in the guerilla camp of Villa, accompanied Villa on horseback into the thick of battle and sent back reports to the American people. When the saddle-weary journalist—after three months in the field—returned to the United States, his experiences were incorporated into the single volume, *Insurgent Mexico,* published in October 1914 and reviewed by Dos Passos in the November issue of the *Harvard Monthly,* his third piece accepted for publication. Dos Passos paid little attention to the politics, economics, and ethics involved in Mexico's war, but measured, instead, Reed's aesthetics and applauded his objective reporting and method of arresting the moment as a war correspondent under fire, his descriptive skills enabling him to evoke romantically both facts and impressions of the life and scenery of Mexico. Dos Passos had an opportunity to meet Reed in person a few months later during one of Reed's periodic trips to Harvard to visit Copeland, known for his intellectual soirées on Saturday nights.

"Copey"—as most of his students called him—handpicked everyone in his classes and met them on an individual basis. Disdainful of large classes in traditional lecture halls, he chose to receive his young charges in the sanctity of his living quarters, 15 Hollis Hall, in the Harvard Yard. Students came to him by appointment and read their themes aloud. Though they complimented themselves on being among the chosen few, they quaked at the prospects of the seemingly absurd indignities and barbed witticisms to which they sometimes fell heir. In the wintertime Copeland sipped tea, threw another log on the fire, leaned back in his chair, and listened beneath closed lids to the creative oblations of his students. It was not unusual for him to go to sleep during a reading. A good essay awakened him, a feat for which he commended its writer. If the theme was outrageously poor, he feigned sleep and punctuated the reading with explosive snores. Copeland was a funny little man with a bulbous head, which he topped with a large, black derby in cold weather or a stiff-brimmed straw hat when it was hot. He moved across the Yard with a gait between a march and a trudge, his stiff-jointed motion suggestive of a child's windup toy. Heavy mustaches, a penchant for checks and plaids, and the oversized derby planted squarely on his forehead gave Copeland the look of a racetrack tout.

Almost everyone who had a class with Copey felt affection for him and trotted in and out of his rooms as though he were a classmate whose help they depended on regularly. He gave generously of his time in private conferences and preferred to counsel students on the craft of writing (or to talk about anything else that concerned them) than to engage in his own work, such as enhancing his chance of promotion through scholarly publications. Copeland, a graduate of Harvard, had returned in 1893 after dropping out of law school to lecture on English literature. President Eliot was critical of his unconventional teaching habits and other idiosyncrasies and refused to promote him, but Eliot's successor, Lowell, awarded him professorial status. Both Copeland and Kittredge were members of the same graduating class (1882), but the Shakespearean scholar had fared better with faculty promotions than Copeland had and already was a full professor by the time Dos Passos arrived at Harvard.

Copeland's fame rested in part on his dramatic readings. On Saturday nights "Copey's Circle"—as the young men were known—congregated in his rooms in droves. Unobtrusive students and campus leaders, athletes, scholars, radicals, conservatives, editors, men of the Institute and men of *runtdom*—the socially accepted and the nobodies— all sat close-legged on the floor of his apartment, sandwiched in along the walls or in front of the fireplace at his feet while he sat in an armchair under a dim lamp, smoked, and read from the works of his favorite poets and writers. They also talked and listened. It did not matter to the professor whether his guests were in his classes or merely aspired to be. They gazed at each other and around the walls jammed floor to ceiling with books and photographs inscribed by the men and women who were personally significant to him, and ventured their ideas, surprising even themselves that they verbalized and thought more penetratingly than they imagined possible. For all his preachments and posturings, Copeland had a knack for bringing out the best in them. A single light bulb, sometimes a candle on the mantelpiece, and a smouldering fire were the only illumination in the room, but to his disciples, the brilliance of the atmosphere seemed dazzling. Sometimes a famous writer, actor, or other luminary (such as John Reed) dropped in to talk with them informally, but the prevailing light was Copeland's.

Although his students read their themes aloud to him and were subject to instant criticism during his daytime sessions with them, he usually kept the papers and wrote cryptic evaluative comments upon them later. On an early essay by Dos Passos, Copeland scribbled only the phrase "decidedly attractive." Of a later piece, entitled "Madeira," the professor observed: "A vividly delightful bit of natural-sounding recollection. It is only after you have *done* that the listener asks himself: 'Odds jittickins! Can the child have been but six?' The dash of hot fragrant oil adds extraordinarily to the vividness of that part of the description." In the margin, Copeland added: "The best thing you've done in English 12—a catalogue of odors compiled by D.P. would be worth having!" Dos Passos' sensitivity to smells was his strongest sensory perception, compensation, perhaps, for his myopia. Throughout his life people observed him sniffing. Whether indoors or out, Dos Passos caught the waft of fragrances or other odors unnoticed by most people and catalogued them mentally for recall later. His ability to capture, then to re-create through language, the odors, sounds, colors, lines, textures, rhythms, and moods—all were refined constantly under the critical eye and ear of Copeland.

A month after his review of *Insurgent Mexico* was published, Dos Passos' third short story appeared in the *Harvard Monthly* (December 1914): "The Poet of Cordale." Unlike his earlier fiction, this tale was set in an imaginary small town in rural Pennsylvania; the time, the present. Corby Harwick, the protagonist, peddled hardware products over the countryside in a horse-drawn buggy; at heart, he was a poet. He was especially enamored of the sensuous, exotic lines of the *Rubáiyát* and whiled away the time in rapturous recitations. When the Reverend Beals invited him to recite a poem for a Fourth of July "speaking" in the town hall, Harwick was ecstatic. His wife's insistence that the poem was inappropriate for the poetic tastes of Cordale led him to choose "Barbara Frietchie," but he was determined to deliver a few lines of Khayyám for an encore. Cheered wildly after his first recitation, Harwick launched in on his revered Persian poet. As the expressions on his listeners' faces evolved from attentiveness to restlessness, then to shocked surprise, his pastor and members of The Temperance Union left their seats and the crowded hall rocked with confusion. Unable to comprehend what he had done wrong, the bewildered poet groped his way to his buggy and drove off. Suddenly he spied the little brown volume at his side and hurled it into the shrubs, then tightened his puzzled horse's reins and sobbed. "The Poet of Cordale" was superior to Dos Passos' earlier stories. The dialect of the tale was effective and its overall style more fluid and natural than its predecessors.

Dos Passos submitted next to the *Harvard Monthly* two book reviews, both more pedestrian than his critique of John Reed's *Insurgent Mexico.* In the February (1915) issue he complimented Dutch novelist Louis Couperus (whose *Small Souls* had been recently translated into English) for his "vivid depiction of struggling small souls" whose trivial lives afforded little opportunity for greatness. Dos Passos spoke of satire as the novelist's chief instrument and liked its use in *Small Souls* because it was "cold and unemotional without a trace of didacticism." A third review by Dos Passos was of a travel book, *Brittany with Bergère,* written by another recent Harvard graduate, William Whitelock. Whitelock told of his three-week tour of Brittany with Bergère, his horse, who was presented as the heroine of the journey. Dos Passos commended the book for its informal, personal style and for its brevity. He thought it a marked improvement over the "ponderous, heavily-gilt volume" produced by travel writers a generation earlier.

The March issue (1915) of the *Harvard Monthly* contained both the travel-book review and a sketch entitled "Malbrouck," whose protagonist was a young Parisian woman who sat up one night with her wakeful troubled son. The child insisted that she sing to him "Malbrouck," a dirge for a slain warrior whose body lay unclaimed on a distant battlefield. "Mother doesn't want to sing that, dearie, one hears so much about war," she replied as she gazed at their sparsely furnished garret, yet sang it finally, her voice trembling and catching. At the end she broke down in tears, unable to cope with fears that her own husband, too, might be lying that moment undiscovered in the cold mud flats of Flanders, his fight "for the glory of France" over.

"Malbrouck" was Dos Passos' first implicit comment in print upon the war in Europe. The preceding November—the same month his review of *Insurgent Mexico* appeared—German forces were pushing toward the waiting French lines, having already invaded Belgium and occupied Brussels, Dos Passos' childhood home. By March, enemy bombs were falling on London. John Reed came to Harvard not only to see Copeland, but also to make an impassioned plea before a disturbed audience of students and faculty that field artillery, bayonet warfare, bombs, and life in the trenches were no means by which disputes should be settled. The war was still Europe's war, Reed urged. Harvard men, in turn, were divided in what they saw as America's role in the war. A machine gun company had been newly authorized for students and many were at that moment marching in reserve officers' uniforms in their university regiment. The *Harvard Crimson* took a vigorous stand against summer training camps for students, declared them an unwarranted menace, and urged membership in Harvard's chapter of the Collegiate Anti-Militarism League, formed to protest growing support to arm the country.

Alumnus Theodore Roosevelt was one of the country's strongest proponents of armament. In an editorial in the *Harvard Advocate* in 1915, Roosevelt wrote:

> Harvard ought to take the lead in every real movement for making our country stand as it should stand. Unfortunately, prominent Harvard men sometimes take the lead the wrong way. This applies pre-eminently to all Harvard men who have had anything to do with the absurd and mischievous professional-pacificist or peace-at-any-price movements which have so thoroughly discredited this country during the past five years. . . . Much harm has been done to America by crooked politicians and by crooked business men; but they have never done as much harm as these professional pacificists have sought to do and partially succeeded in doing. They have weakened the moral fibre of our people. They have preached base and ignoble doctrines to this nation.

Such attacks had little effect on Harvard men of Dos Passos' ilk, who continued to intellectualize why the United States should stay out of war. Most vowed not to serve militarily if troops were sent to Europe and to go to war only if it was a dire case of self-defense and then only in a noncombatant role.

Dos Passos was saddened by the fall of Brussels and feared for the safety of his surrogate aunts living in London, but managed to remain relatively aloof from politics and lived for the most part among his fellow aesthetes on a plane dominated by literature. From time to time, eyewitness reports of atrocities on the battlefield probably shattered their calm detachment, their sensitive retinas taking in the bitterness, conflict, and tragedy surrounding them, yet most of their writings appearing in the *Harvard Monthly* in 1914 and 1915 belied the suggestion.

The most important pronouncement to Dos Passos personally during the spring of 1915 was a note from Wright McCormick, secretary of the *Harvard Monthly* editorial board, informing him of his election to the board and inviting him to tea to meet the other initiates. Two other new board members were R. Stewart Mitchell, a modernist, and Robert S. Hillyer, a traditionalist, selected for their contributions as poets. At the time, Dos Passos knew them only through their poetry, but before the year was up lifelong friendships had developed. The *Harvard Monthly* became their literary proving ground—just as it was for Dos Passos—and hurled all three of them into a trajectory of American letters to which they dedicated themselves the rest of their lives.

Dos Passos' first fiction as a board member appeared in the May 1915 issue. Variously interpreted, "An Aesthete's Nightmare" provoked a negative letter to the editor of the *Harvard Crimson*. It was the first published criticism of his work. The tale (with a Harvard setting) concerned a devotee of art—known only as the Aesthete—who went from room to room showing his friends his most recent acquisition of art, a small marble copy of the *Venus de Milo*. Once home, he placed the replica on the table before him so that its torso was illuminated with just the right amber light from his lamp, settled himself amid the pillows on his divan (actually, a cot draped with an Eastern rug), and contemplated it. To the Aesthete, the "little Venus" had sat leadenly and unimaginatively upon the shelf of an insensitive, secondhand Boston merchant until being transmogrified by its new setting. During his reverie the aroma of incense rose from his lotus-shaped burner before a Buddha on the mantelpiece and permeated the room. After inhaling the fragrant bouquet of a precious golden liqueur and letting the drops linger on his tongue, the Aesthete, clad in Turkish slippers and a pale crepe dressing gown, fell asleep, his bosom swollen with pride in the luxurious atmosphere of his own creative art. Suddenly a weird change came over him as he slept. He imagined himself a Vandal in the act of sacking ancient Rome, invading Aphrodite's temple, and destroying her statue and himself in the process. The Aesthete awoke to discover his own Venus statue in fragments on the floor, his amber lamp and liqueur bottle shattered, too. The tale ended with his seizing a hammer and destroying every *objet d'art* in his room, hurling his Buddha through the window, and tearing down the curtains in a fit of "Homeric laughter." Put off by Dos Passos' portrait of the Aesthete, the letter writer to the *Crimson* declared that the extreme aesthete was rare at Harvard and the protagonist in the story atypical. Then he chided: "Mr. Dos Passos would never have to resort to such obvious objects of art as the Venus de Milo, a Buddha, and Parrish's 'Pirate Ship' if he had ever seen the animal in the wild state in his native lair—in Oxford, for instance." Such aesthetic snobbery no doubt irked Dos Passos, who considered himself no stranger to European art galleries. Some fifty years later, a reader saw the tale as a rebellion "against a marble, unattainable ideal of womanhood," one which "set living vandalism above dead culture." He also thought the tale indicated Dos Passos' amusement at Harvard "devotees of exotic taste." Yet Dos Passos saw himself as a devotee of exotic taste, and though his satire is obvious, there is an underlying tragic note in his tale. Lacking genuine aesthetic sensibility, Dos Passos' fictional aesthete could not cope when his contrived aesthetics failed him. To Dos Passos, true aestheticism was revitalizing and set art free from vapid posturing. The destroyer in his tale was not a true aesthete. His nightmare and the ensuing shattering of his various idols was his self-illumination and the means by which he arrived at his essential being, insisted Dos Passos.

He, too, was wrestling with an identity crisis of sorts. Choate's "Maddie" had become Harvard's "Dos," and life within the ivy-clad walls of the Harvard Yard seemed at once shallow, stifling, and devoid of meaning. He had achieved his immediate goal, a berth on the *Harvard Monthly,* and with it, prestige and a meaningful creative outlet, yet at the same time he felt himself carried along only in the slipstream of events. The labor agitation at home, aggression in Europe, America's imminent involvement—all quickened his expanding social consciousness and gave him cause to ponder the direction of his life. Though a pacifist in theory, Dos Passos approved of military service from the point of view of sociability. "It would make young men rub shoulders more, get to know people outside of their class—to be *actually,* instead of only theoretically democratic," he told a friend. Such positive thoughts, however, were negated in the next breath:

> The devil of it is that military affairs lead the other way. Just think of the insufferable snobbery of army officers, of the swagger everything in uniform puts on when it runs up against a poor civilian—and the messy picture of a military democracy, poet and peasant, doctor and butcher, arm in arm, sweating together, marching together, hero-izing together, to the tune of a patriotic song. . . . Plus when you have an army you immediately want to use it, and a military population in a government like ours would be absolutely at the mercy of

any corrupt politician who got into the White House, or of any millionaire who could buy enough newspapers.

The attack by a German submarine on May 7, 1915, upon the sleek luxury liner the *Lusitania*—in which hundreds of American and British citizens lost their lives—provoked new outbursts from otherwise uninvolved Harvard students. Many urged immediate military retaliation by the United States; others signed up for the War Department's summer training camp. Dos Passos was proud of his father's indignant response in a signed, three-column lead article in *The World* on May 11 after the German government tried to justify the sinking: "No one, as I understand, seriously contends that the wholesale slaughter of the innocent passengers on the *Lusitania* can be justified, mitigated, or even explained under any fixed or known rule of international law. But new principles are sought to be created to cover the case, and specious reasons are given to support them. No rule, however, can be added to that vacillating body of law called the law of nations which could justify or excuse inhuman and uncivilized conduct by a belligerent." Dos Passos appreciated the spirit of humanitarianism that flourished in John R.'s rhetoric, yet mere verbalization was not enough. He felt he should be doing something other than staying in school, but was stymied for a workable option. Part of the problem, Dos Passos reflected later, was that it was his fate to be born at the end of an era, to enter college after "Victorian scholarship had fulfilled its cycle." The afterglow of the "great Transcendentalists had not quite faded from the Cambridge sky," and William James was dead. "There had been a young poet named Tom Eliot, an explosive journalist named Jack Reed. They had moved out into the great world of hellroaring and confusion. I felt I'd come too late."

While the nation was shoring up its military defenses and recoiling from the sinking of the *Lusitania,* Dos Passos suffered a personal crisis. On May 12, 1915, Mary Harris wrote to apprise him of his mother's grave condition:

> The dear Baby is very good and patient and does not suffer any pain at all. Everything goes very quietly and smoothly. Miss Fretincel takes night duty and goes to bed at 6:30 a.m., when I come on for day duty. She sleeps until eleven or twelve o'clock and comes back on duty after luncheon so that I can go out and get a couple of minutes in the fresh air. We do not leave the Baby alone for one minute. As this had to come it is a great blessing that it happened before we left Washington. The doctor comes every day and brought the specialist with him again yesterday. . . . I have her room a bower of roses, a vase on the mantlepiece, one on the chiffonier, and two on the dressing case.

His father's words were more ominous: "I have just talked to Mrs. Harris. Your mother is gradually sinking and we must prepare for the worst. In fact, I have been so prepared, yet I had always a ray of hope. I shall leave for Washington probably at one o'clock instead of four and I'll telegraph you as soon as I arrive as to conditions."

On May 15 Dos Passos received the inevitable message that his mother was dying and that he should come home at once. Although he had grown up in the shadow of her chronic illnesses, he was unprepared for her death. In the past he had been able to put aside his father's interminable missives (sometimes without reading them), skimming only for news of "Baby," unwilling to allow the tedious sermonizing to invade at will his bell-jar environment. The death message broke through Dos Passos' quasi-etherized condition and left him in a state of quiet shock. Years later he was able to write of it in an autobiographical "Camera Eye" section of his novel *1919:*

> the bellglass cracked in a screech of slate pencils (have you ever never been able to sleep for a week in April?) and He met me in the gray trainshed my eyes were stinging with vermillion bronze and chromegreen inks that oozed from the spinning April hills His mustaches were white the tired droop of an old man's cheeks She's gone Jack grief isn't a uniform and the [he could not bring himself to write the word "body" and left a space instead] in the parlor the waxen odor of lilies in the parlor (He and I must bury the uniform of grief) then the riversmell the shimmering Potomac reaches the little choppysilver waves at Indian Head there were mockingbirds in the graveyard and the roadsides steamed with spring April enough to shock the world [in the fictional account Dos Passos changed the month from May to April, another apparent evasion of reality].

Dos Passos balked at returning to Harvard, but the gesture fell on deaf ears. He knew even as he protested that he was no closer to giving more than voice to his destiny than he had been when his mother was alive. Until he graduated, he would have to content himself only with decisions regarding his day-to-day activities within the circumscribed arena of Cambridge and its adjacent byways. As a child when he had objected to a course of action—with his mother as his antagonist—he yielded readily because he did not want to upset her, a characteristic exemplified in his novel *Manhattan Transfer* (1925). Dos Passos put much of himself into the character of Jimmy Herf, who was sixteen when his chronically ill mother died of a stroke. Like his creator, Herf was unusually dependent upon his mother for emotional and physical succor and nourishment, as was "Muddy," Lucy's fictional counterpart, dependent upon her son: "We mustn't have any secrets from each other dear. Remember you're the only comfort your mother has in the world." When Muddy told the boy to put his rubbers on before he went outside, he replied: "But it's not raining at all." She countered: "Do as Mother wants you dear . . . and please don't be long. I put you on your honor to come right back. Mother's not a bit well tonight and she gets so nervous when you're out in the street. There are such terrible dangers." Similarly, Dos Passos gently rebelled against his mother, then quietly acquiesced. Such conversations between Herf and his mother pervaded *Manhattan Transfer,* the dialogue having been drawn virtually unchanged from Dos Passos' bank of vivid memories.

Where his father was concerned, he remained a closet rebel. Dos Passos handled John R.'s private preachments well. If the confrontation was direct, he usually admitted the error in his judgment or behavior—stammering and ducking his head with eyes slightly averted under his father's steady gaze—then backed off from the issue. When public issues were involved and his father's profile prominent, Dos Passos was sometimes embarrassed. He was proud of John R.'s outraged response to the sinking of the *Lusitania,* but disconcerted by his stand against suffrage for women. It was one thing for Harvard officials to deny Emmeline Pankhurst, a British suffragette leader, a hall in which to lecture; but for his father to claim that women would be so corrupted if given the franchise that he would sooner give up his own vote than grant it to them was quite another. He resented such high-mindedness and bigotry, yet was guarded in how he voiced his objections. Even when he differed with John R., Dos Passos could not help admiring his individualism in the face of opposition or when he took unpopular stands. It was an innate trait to which he himself fell heir and exercised increasingly as he gained maturity.

Dos Passos returned to Cambridge a few days after his mother's funeral determined to house his grief and resentment within as best he could and get on with the task of finishing his junior year. He made up his assignments and stayed in town to help get out the July issue of the *Harvard Monthly*. His grades at year's end were commendable given his adversities: C's in botany, comparative literature, Browning, philosophy; B's in Chaucer, composition, fine arts; and an A in advanced Greek.

In the spring before his mother's death Dos Passos finished another short story, "An Interrupted Romance," for publication in the June issue of the *Harvard Monthly*. The tale depicted an American youth in Paris, Francis Thomas, who was more interested in the girl he observed and admired from his park bench along the Champs-Élysées than in his studies at the Sorbonne. When he saw her talking warmly with an old gentleman, another habitué of a nearby bench, he was frantic to meet her and imagined all manner of improbable entries. A dropped handkerchief provided the opportunity Thomas awaited, but upon "screwing up his courage" and approaching her the next day, he was interrupted by the unexpected appearance of his stout aunt and her two giggly daughters from Chicago who bore down upon him and swept him away to help them locate the Arc de Triomphe. It was the last he saw of the girl and her companion despite a daily surveillance of their bench. "Interrupted Romance" revealed the influence of Henry James upon Dos Passos. The subtle tone, theme of resignation and unrequited love, and light satire of the youth's Baedecker-bearing kin "loose in Paris"—all were unmistakably Jamesian.

The writings of Joseph Conrad affected Dos Passos during this period, too. In an essay/review of *Lord Jim* in the July issue of the *Harvard Monthly*, Dos Passos commended Conrad for his remarkable narrative method, characterization, and deep sense of humanity. The novel abounded with color and other evocative images, he said. Conrad's shorter tales, "Chance," "Youth," and "Heart of Darkness" were praised, also, for their "wealth of sensuous, impressionistic details."

Having stayed in Cambridge until midsummer to help edit the *Harvard Monthly*, Dos Passos would have preferred to linger and poke around Boston at his leisure, but his father urged him to come home as soon as possible. The farm in Virginia held too many somber memories, however, and Dos Passos was in no hurry to return. An ambivalent pull compelled him to return to Washington before setting off on another distant vacation trek, but the stillness, emptiness, and staleness of the house without his mother's presence were almost more than he could bear. The heavy drapes in her large, airy bedroom were drawn against the sun, and without the bright sunlight streaming in through the big bay windows and the fragrance of rose and lavender that he associated with her bedchamber, his sense of *home* was gone. Lucy's will left everything to John R. (the house, its contents, her jewelry) except a cash bequest of $1,000 for James Madison. The single mention of Dos Passos in the will (identified as "my son John Roderigo Madison") was in relationship to

John R., who was named as her son's guardian and trustee during his minority. The will, signed in September 1910—a few months after Lucy's marriage—named John R. as executor. Lucy's estate was small (the house was assessed at $6,903, the furniture at $1,000 and the jewelry at $600). John R. assured Dos Passos that the Washington property was his whenever he wanted it, but he chose to let everything remain in his father's name. The jewelry went into a safe-deposit box and the furniture stayed in the house.

Feeling untethered, rootless, Dos Passos found himself thinking more and more about the "gentleman's ambulance corps" then forming at Harvard for service in France. When he mentioned to his father that "joining up" might be an alternative to returning to his studies in the fall, John R. soundly vetoed it. He did not want his son dead; it was as simple as that, he told him. He must stay in college and complete his education, perhaps even go to law school, John R. suggested. No, there would be no career in law, Dos Passos countered, but conceded that architecture was a possibility. Buildings had fascinated him both aesthetically and structurally since his childhood. His early exposure to European and Middle Eastern design and construction had stimulated his appreciation, and the several courses he took with Chandler Post advanced it appreciably. Post's lectures on art history, Hispanic architecture and culture, and the works of leading contemporary Spanish painters and sculptors stirred latent cravings in Dos Passos to sketch and paint what he saw. He had been so stimulated, in fact, that he recommended Post's course to his friend Cummings, who had begun to paint himself. Cummings had graduated *magna cum laude* in June and decided to stay on at Harvard an additional year for a master's degree in English, but at Dos Passos' insistence agreed to take Post's course (Fine Arts 9). Cummings claimed later to have learned more about painting from Chandler Post than from any other source in his career. Both men attributed Post as the chief impetus for their lifelong enamorment of Spain and its people.

Dos Passos' plan after leaving Washington was to travel West and take in the World's Fair. The Panama-Pacific International Exposition had recently opened in San Francisco, ostensibly a celebration of the newly completed Panama Canal. The exposition also boasted a number of architectural feats of its own and he was curious to see them. Vacation plans were usually *his* decision exclusively, but Dos Passos sought his father's advice for matters of practical concern. Before leaving Cambridge he wrote John R. that he was moving to a dormitory in the Harvard Yard (29 Thayer Hall) and wanted to store some things and move the rest into his new quarters before heading West. "What do you advise?" Dos Passos asked his father. John R. replied to his son's questions in his accustomed fashion: he sent money and a set of numbered directives as though he were dictating a memorandum to a client. The letter concluded: "Keep this as your Baedecker's guide and read it every hour until it is fully impressed upon your mind. Or have it stamped on copper and hang it around your neck." John R.'s chiding was both comic and functional. Dos Passos *was* forgetful. Though he may have resented being treated as a perennial child, he also relied upon his "punchings." Similarly, an important facet of John R.'s sense of fulfillment as a father—and, earlier, as a husband—rested upon his opportunity to advise: he was a counselor-at-law and a counselor-at-home. It was a way of life, an emotional ingredient essential not only to his professional life, but also to his manhood and survival itself. John R. and John R. Jr. were stitched from the same fabric and permanently bonded. Each provided the other with one of the most significant relationships of his life. Dos Passos may have had more satisfying interdependencies, but none was more influencing.

When he returned to Harvard in September 1915, Dos Passos had made a new friend: Walter Rumsey Marvin, a fifteen-year-old prep school student at St. Paul's in Concord, New Hampshire, whom he had met aboard the Shasta Limited en route to the exposition in San Francisco. Dos Passos was standing on the observation platform—his favorite vantage when traveling by train—when one of Marvin's gregarious cousins, a youth slightly younger than Dos Passos, struck up a conversation and invited him to join his cousin, his brother, and him at their seats. Shy about initiating conversation with a stranger, Dos Passos was pleased to be taken in tow once someone else made the first move. Soon the boys were exchanging travel backgrounds, likes, dislikes, pedigrees, and discovering affinities: Marvin had spent several years in a private school in Switzerland, spoke French fluently, admired the beauties and antiquities of Italy (he had lived in Capri for five months, for which Dos Passos envied him), appreciated the classics, had a keen sense of history, and dabbled in poetry. Like Dos Passos, he was an Easterner (Montclair, New Jersey) who had been surrounded by an abundance of material advantages. The son of a capitalist, he intended to run his paternal grandfather's chocolate factory in Pittsburgh. Marvin was bright with a sophistication that belied his years, yet was free of affectation.

Dos Passos found him an ideal companion with whom he was loath to part when they reached San Francisco. Several days later they chanced upon one another at the exposition and viewed the exhibits together. Even more surprising was their fortuitous meeting atop the sandstone cliffs of Ocean Beach in San Diego while Dos Passos was visiting his Sprigg relatives. He and Marvin stretched out in the sun and talked for hours, agreeing when they parted to see one another again in the East. The difference in their ages never came up that summer, said Marvin, who was impressed that "a Harvard man" had found him interesting.

On the train home, Dos Passos wrote his new friend a long letter. Rarely had he met anyone with so many things in common, he admitted, not did he intend "to let such a person slip through" his fingers. As though to justify the missive, he listed their mutual interests: "food, first and foremost . . . next to literature. Reading is useful; then there is always travel. I think we both have the disease. Italy's another thing to chat about—all lovers of Italy have something in common." Such mutuality made for "splendid subjects" for letters, he reminded Marvin, then tossed out a few titles of books he had read of late, such as Byron's *Childe Harold's Pilgrimage,* which he found "a task to finish." He planned "to wash the taste away with a draught of Stevenson" and recommended *Travels with a Donkey in the Cévennes* and *An Inland Voyage.*

Dos Passos had no idea when he urged Rumsey Marvin to write that he was launching a correspondence destined to continue a lifetime. Years later Marvin concluded that he seldom had an important original idea after his first meeting with Dos Passos: "We didn't *share* views (especially regarding politics). All my ideas came from him. He was my idea of a renaissance gentleman, and he was my number one friend all my life. I was tremendously influenced by his use of language and was continually tossing off *his* phrases as though I had thought them up myself. I sometimes felt guilty about that." For Dos Passos, the friendship could not have evolved at a better time. More than any other single factor, it helped him get over his mother's death. Writing to Marvin about anything that struck his fancy was also a means of exploring his own feelings. He had been a private person all his life. There was about him a genteel reserve, a barrier of sorts erected between his inner life and the gregariousness that had begun to manifest itself at Harvard. His friends there did not pry into his personal life. Any inquisitiveness on their part was kept in check by his reserve. Dos Passos could have counted on one hand those outside his family who knew about his illegitimacy (it was years before Marvin had any inkling). From his point of view, there was nothing to tell or not to tell. The past had passed. Dos Passos wrote bits and pieces of himself and his family again and again in his fiction, but at Harvard he was too close to it. His letters to Marvin in the fall of 1915 exuded enthusiasm. He loved having someone to talk to with whom he could share anything he chose. It was one thing to verbalize his ideas to classsmates or fellow board members of the *Harvard Monthly* and to record in his literary diary his reactions to things he read and saw, but it was quite another to shape his ideas on paper to a respondent, to someone who would write back, match confidence for confidence, and seek advice in return. Dos Passos also delighted in playing with the language. Evocative images spilled over the bright yellow sheets on which he wrote while sprawled at his window seat, a position he relished compared to sitting straight-legged at his desk. Apologizing often to Marvin for his poor calligraphy, Dos Passos admitted that his scrawls resembled "the wanderings of an intoxicated hen." He said that he hated "formal letters like sin—anything else is a joy and relief, particularly if one says all sorts of mad things most people wouldn't dream of putting in letters. . . . I dote on long fat ones. They are so charming to read during a lecture hour! Be sure to keep me supplied." If Dos Passos wrote letters during classes, his professors probably were unaware of it. Lecture halls were large for the most part. His courses as a senior included philosophy and religion of Greek poets and the Hellenistic period; anthropology; history of the physical and biological sciences; and two English courses: Shakespeare (from Kittredge) and English 5 (a composition course with the dean of the faculty, Le Baron Russell Briggs).

As Boylston Professor of Rhetoric and Oratory, Briggs held the most esteemed chair of the English department, a chair once occupied by John Quincy Adams (and awarded several years later to Copeland). English 5 was the most advanced composition course at Harvard, and students and faculty alike wondered how Briggs had time for it. As President Lowell's chief assistant, he was involved daily in administrative decisions and in meetings with various professors and committees. He was also president of Radcliffe, Harvard's sister college. Yet through it all, the dean never noticeably slighted his students. Unlike most Harvard professors, who went to class twice a week and arranged for a "grader" or someone else to meet students for a third contact hour during the week, Briggs met them thrice weekly and insisted that they write something at every meeting— even if it was only a twenty or thirty-minute exercise. Like Bliss Perry, he believed that students improved only through practice and graded all of his papers himself. He held open house each Wednesday night in the Brattle Street home he shared with his wife and family (his son, Le Baron, Jr., was a classmate of Dos Passos). Although the dean's informal get-togethers were never the popular successes that Copeland's were, they were respectfully attended.

Dos Passos wrote affectionately of Dean Briggs after leaving Harvard. He said that he regretted not having taken better advantage of the dean's accessibility and openheartedness, which he blamed on his own "idiot sophistication . . . as a horrid little prig." To Dos Passos, the dean was hopelessly old-fashioned in his teaching methods, "but no one could help being moved by his lovely candor, his tenderhearted irony, and the salty small town way he had of putting things." He said that he admired, too, his professor's "old-fashioned schoolmaster's concern for the neatness of the language, a Yankee zest for the shipshape phrase, an old-fashioned gentleman's concern for purity of morals . . . his sharp nose for sham and pretense." While the dean was sometimes referred to as "Mother Briggs" in testimonies later, he was described by countless students as "the best-loved professor" encountered anywhere.

If Dos Passos felt handicapped by Dean Briggs's provincialism, he overcompensated for it by rebounding at times to the other extreme by using precious language. When he wrote Rumsey Marvin during the winter of 1916 that the bitter cold evoked memories of sun, sand, and bare feet—the residue of their summer encounter in San Diego—he added: "At this moment I'd like nothing better than to be lying somewhere in the sun in a bathing suit—it is such a wonderful feeling, the sun licking you all over with its warm velvet tongue—Whee!" Dos Passos knew he was waxing poetic and blamed such sensuous evocations on "an overdose of modern poetry" induced by his latest reading jag. Though he had not abandoned the classicists or Elizabethans, he assured Marvin, he had enlarged his sphere. His letters were soon peppered with what became his favorite oath: "By the gods of Flaubert, Homer, modern realism, and new poetry!"

Dos Passos not only was reading the new poetry, but was writing it as well. It is "a sinning path," he admitted; "once you've started, you're doomed. It is write, write, write, to the accompaniment of much soulful socking of pencil ends." It was chiefly the French poets who launched him, most notably Verlaine and Rimbaud. He was also enamored of Richard Aldington, whose newly published *Images* he sent to Marvin. Dos Passos' literary orgy—as he termed it—included Emile Verhaeren, a Belgian poet whose *Belgium's Agony* had just been translated into English and was attracting considerable notice; Ezra Pound's anthology of modern poets, *Des Imagistes* (1914); Frank Stewart Flint's collected verses, *Cadences* (1915); and the exquisite poems of a young Bryn Mawr graduate, Hilda Doolittle ("H.D."), Aldington's wife.

The two friends continued to write long, thoughtful missives to each other throughout the year regarding the verse of poets they admired, and to react critically to their own creative efforts, sometimes replying within the hour. In one letter, they exchanged views regarding what was a "fit subject for poetry." Dos Passos contended that "prize fights are every bit as good a subject . . . as fine ladies and illicit love affairs." What was the *Iliad* anyway, he reasoned, but "a succession of rather sweaty and infinitely bombastic prize fights, . . . though an excessive and artificial use of <u>sweat</u> and <u>swear</u> to make poems seem manly and modern is abominable and heinous and to be brought before the tribunals of taste and good sense. . . . Yet every subject under the sun which has anything to do with human beings—man, woman, or child—is susceptible of poetic treatment." Marvin sent his own apprentice work to Dos Passos for judgment as well as poems of his classmates. Of a friend's poem, Dos Passos replied: "It's damnably good—particularly the first line in the descriptive bits. The diction is a bit flabby in places, unoriginal, unalive, but on the whole it's one of the decentest poems I've seen in a school paper."

Dos Passos paid considerable attention to Marvin's poetic diction and encouraged him at every turn:

> You must write more. I like your smash in "And went away" but somehow it might smash a little more successfully. The line about "huddled clouds" before "snow" in one of your winter things is the best you have done. It has real gumption. Try some more stuff on that order. The game is to get musical-picture words and pack them with the desired emotion. Of course the best results come when they appear of themselves, and when your poems come as easily as sausage from a sausage machine—even then—it takes a shocking lot of work.

He also told Marvin that it did not "hurt a bit to imitate form in poetry so long as you have your own ideas. You'll find, too, that squashing an idea into a given form so transforms it that it ends up being yours anyway."

Marvin thrived on his friend's criticism. In one letter he wrote: "I received your letter about an hour ago. Thank you ever so much for criticizing my poem. It's funny, but I had some vague uneasy feelings about a number of the points you criticize. . . . Once I have written a thing, it is with difficulty that I can revise it. I like to have you look over my things, for then you can put your finger just where the trouble is while I have only happy notions."

Dos Passos benefited, too, by passing judgment upon his friend's verses because it gave him practice as an editor of the *Harvard Monthly*. Submissions were passed among the editors, who scribbled evaluative comments on the margins or back of a piece that was subsequently accepted or rejected by general agreement. If the editor himself had written it, it usually went in unless there was strenuous opposition. Disgruntled contributors sometimes accused the editors of discrimination or unfair promotion of self-interest. Many whose Muse had descended upon them in the robes of *vers libre* were likewise disappointed when they learned that the newly organized Harvard Poetry Society did not see fit to issue invitations to them. Under the aegis of Dean Briggs a group of ten or twelve men (including Estlin Cummings and S. Foster Damon, who, like Cummings, stayed on for a master's degree in English and was probably the most knowledgeable in the arts of all the "Harvard aesthetes") got together to read their poetry. They gathered around a large table in the dimly lit sanctum of the *Harvard Monthly* office every two or three weeks—a flexible date that depended chiefly upon word getting around that they had created a new batch of poems of sufficient number to warrant their meeting—and read and criticized each poem.

When the Poetry Society first banded together in late September 1915, Dean Briggs surmised that members would be less restrained if personalities were not involved and announced that he would read each piece anonymously. Everyone smiled politely after each poem and offered faint—or fulsome—praise or sat in stony silence. At the next session they decided to read their own poems. Now the atmosphere crackled under the parries and thrusts of diverse personalities. Most of the poets in the group had no criteria to apply other than their personal responses as to whether or not the work was "alive." No sound methods of aesthetic analysis were in vogue. One spoke only of impressions. The poets of the Harvard Poetry Society were reacting to staid traditionalism and genteel prejudices inherent in the English faculty as a whole as well as to the literary radicalism of the Imagists.

With the exception of Robert Hillyer, who bore the unofficial title of "outraged standard-bearer" of the traditionalists, most of the poets acknowledged a debt to Harriet Monroe, who chastised Americans for their neglect of poetry and foresaw a new poetic era, which she marked by establishing in 1912 (and editing until her death in 1936) the Chicago-based *Poetry: A Magazine of Verse*. The magazine pervaded the intellectual milieu of Boston. The same year that *Poetry* was launched, an anthology entitled *The Lyric Year* appeared with one hundred verses by one hundred different poets. The volume slid into obscurity before the decade was out, but a number of poems in it were recognized and valued for their new cadences and themes. Among them was a poem entitled "Renascence" by a Vassar undergraduate, Edna St. Vincent Millay. Millay was also one of the first poets to appear in *Poetry*, along with such others who already had gained fame as Ezra Pound, Marianne Moore, Amy Lowell, and William Carlos Williams, all of whom were being read and admired by most members of the Poetry Society. Briggs had serious reservations regarding the direction modern poetry was taking, but was ineffectual in influencing the modernists regarding meter, line, and diction. Robert Hillyer and Joseph Auslander were the only staunch conservatives in the group. Leading the experimentalists were Dos Passos, Cummings, whose often explosive lyrics protested the "dreary conventions of modern society," S. Foster Damon, and R. Stewart Mitchell. Other charter members of the Poetry Society—sometimes known as Harvard's "inner circle of aesthetes"— were Dudley Poore, Cuthbert Wright, William A. Norris, and John Brooks Wheelwright.

The majority of its meetings were closed to outsiders because members were more interested in providing a lively arena for discussion of their own poems than in listening to those who had already achieved significant recognition. They were also reluctant to allow into their group petty rhymsters or proven serious poets. From time to time, however, the group declared certain meetings open to candidates for membership. When the poets invited Amy Lowell to come read and talk about *vers libre,* the meeting was open so that Lowell could be assured a good-sized audience. As leader of the movement of Imagism (the appearance of her third book of verse, *Men, Women, and Ghosts,* was imminent) and the sister of the president of Harvard, Lowell was well known to Cambridge students, whom she sometimes invited to her literary salon in nearby Brookline. She was also a formidable lady known for her salty language, eccentric behavior, and troupe of dogs who accompanied her everywhere. For forty-five minutes she read to the attentive group—from whom she was partially obscured by a thick cloud of black Manila cigar smoke—then sat back and awaited questions. First to shoot to his feet was one of the youngest poets, John Brooks Wheelwright, whose New England pedigree matched that of the celebrated guest. Wheelwright posed what he considered a serious question: "What do you do, Miss Lowell, when you want to write a poem and haven't anything to say?"

The august lady peered stonily at the youth until he foided silently into his seat, then gazed around the room, the cloud of smoke having cleared momentarily, and awaited the next query. Three or four questions followed, which she deigned to answer in good grace. Finally Cummings rose and asked her opinion of Gertrude Stein.

"Do you like her work?" she countered.

"Why, . . . yes," he replied after a pause.

"*I* don't," Miss Lowell retorted, whereupon she snubbed out her cigar, gathered her skirts about her, and swept out under full sail into the night. The startled group sat woodenly for a moment, then fell upon the beer and pretzels in mock astonishment that the *grande dame* had not seen fit to linger.

A number of other luminaries were brought on campus that year by the Harvard poets. Robert Frost attracted hordes of townspeople as well as students of the Cambridge community. His *A Boy's Will* (1913) and *North of Boston* (1914) gained him fame in England for his new poetry and assured him a triumphant return to the United States in 1915. The lecture by William Butler Yeats on poetic drama drew a standing-room-only crowd. Conrad Aiken, a recent graduate of Harvard, came to read from his book of poetry *The Jig of Forslin* (1916), for which he was just beginning to achieve literary distinction. Vachel Lindsay, whose reputation was already well established by *General William Booth Enters into Heaven and Other Poems* (1913), was admired by a number of the poets in his audience, but he put off others because of his exaggerated theatrical intonation and gestures. Still another guest was John Gould Fletcher, whose early volumes of poetry, *Irradiations—Sand and Spray* (1915) and *Goblins and Pagodas* (1916), aligned him firmly with Amy Lowell and her Imagist confreres.

Malcolm Cowley, a freshman at Harvard in 1916, recalled being a guest at one or two meetings at which there were no outside poets and hearing Damon, Hillyer, and Dos Passos read from their works. "Damon's poems were chaste in form, but rather less chaste in sentiment. The reading was almost apologetic, with a notable lack of drama. When he came to an especially outrageous line, his flat New England Seaboard voice became flatter and more noncommittal." About the other two, Cowley remembered only that Hillyer looked like "a wicked cherub" as he read, and that Dos Passos' voice "sounded soft and low" as he "peered at his manuscript from behind thick lenses."

Being a poet at Harvard was no easy calling, nor was the Harvard Poetry Society a haven for tender skins. Dos Passos was a charter member of the group because he had at least ventured into publication in the *Harvard Monthly* as a poet. Under the influence of his fellow poets and the entire movement toward freedom of expression in every genre of the creative arts, Dos Passos found himself writing almost as much poetry as fiction his senior year. He sent Rumsey Marvin the November 1915 *Harvard Monthly*, which contained his first published poem, "Prairies." In an accompanying note, he described it as "ragged, modern, and—I fear—very bad."

> 'Tis green and gold the world is;
> Green with the green of wheat fields
> And of waving, feathery grasses;
> Gold with the golden sunlight

> *And with the hoards of cornflowers spilt*
> *Over the rolling and endless prairie.*
>
> *A green that verges to greyness*
> *Where shadows of faint mists roam,*
> *A gold of velvet and softness*
> *When fleeces of wind-combed clouds*
> *Veil the golden sun and deepened*
> *The darkling shades of the prairie.*
>
> *And sparkling gold the air is*
> *Pale, laughing and luminous gold.*
> *The winds on the face of the prairie*
> *Sweep the great spaces unhindered,*
> *Swaying the plumes of the tall grass*
> *On the rolling and endless prairie.*

Dos Passos told Marvin that the important thing a poem should do is capture an idea or emotion in a picture or figure of speech without restraints of meter or other traditional trappings, yet look and sound like a poem. Marvin thought it a marvelous poem. The lines were richly alliterative and rhythmical, yet had no structured meter. The rhythm was sprung in the manner of Gerard Manley Hopkins, whose poems were not published until 1918 (posthumously), thus unknown to the wave of young poets writing while Dos Passos was at Harvard. The Imagists referred to such seemingly unstructured lines as "unrhymed cadences," a phrase coined by F. S. Flint. The *g* sounds in Dos Passos' poem *(green, gold, grasses)* used repetitively conveyed movement and helped unify his idea; the liquid *l*'s *(gold, world, fields, sunlight, spilt, rolling, endless, velvet, fleeces, clouds, veil, darkling, sparkling, pale, laughing, luminous, plumes, tall)* contributed to the mellifluous and euphonious flow of the poem and provided internal rhyme. Its regular line lengths (characterized by four—or three, depending upon how it was read—stressed syllables irregularly spaced, thus sprung), its three stanzas of six lines each, its archaic *'Tis*, and its inversion *('Tis green and gold the world is/ . . . And sparkling gold the air is)*—all gave the poem a traditional look as a frame for its modernity.

A second poem, "Saturnalia," appeared in the January *Harvard Monthly*, his paean to *vers libre*:

> *In earth's womb the old gods stir,*
> *Fierce chthonian deities of old time*
> *With cymbals and rattle of castanets,*
> *And shriek of slug-horns, the North Wind*
> *Bows the oak and the moaning fir,*
> *On russet hills and by roadsides stiff with rime.*
>
> *In nature, dead, the life gods stir*
> *From Rhadamanthus and the Isles,*
> *Where Saturn rules the Age of Gold,*

> *Come old, old ghosts of bygone gods;*
> *While dim mists earth's outlines blur,*
> *And drip all night from lichen-greened roof-tiles.*
>
> *In men's hearts the mad gods rise*
> *And fill the streets with revelling,*
> *With torchlight that glances on frozen pools,*
> *With tapers starring the thick-fogged night,*
> *A-dance, like strayed fireflies,*
> *'Mid dim mad throngs who Saturn's orisons sing.*
>
> *In driven clouds the old gods come,*
> *When fogs the face of Apollo have veiled;*
> *A fear of things, unhallowed, strange,*
> *And a fierce free joy flares in the land.*
> *Men mutter rhymes in language dead,*
> *By night, with rumbling drum,*
> *In quaking groves where the daedal spirits are hailed.*
>
> *To earth's brood of souls of old,*
> *With covered heads and aspen wands,*
> *Mist-shrouded priests do ancient rites;*
> *The black ram's fleece is stained with blood,*
> *That steams, dull red on the frozen ground;*
> *And pale votaries shiver with the cold,*
> *That numbs the earth, and etches patterned mirrors on the ponds.*

Drawing on his knowledge of the classics and mythology, Dos Passos chose as his unifying metaphor the ancient Roman Festival of Saturn, which he depicted revived by the old *life gods* of the underworld in orgiastic celebration, freeing Apollo, the god of poetry, his face too long *veiled.* Dos Passos did not eliminate rhyme in his poem, but gave it freedom. Whereas the first four lines of each stanza are unrhymed, the fifth catches the rhyme of the first line, and the sixth, the rhyme of the second line (the fourth and fifth stanzas add a seventh rhymed line, but the basic pattern is retained. As with "Prairies," the rhythm is not metered, but cadenced; each line contains four or five stresses, except for the final line, which has five or six stresses and is offset from the rest of the stanza. The poem is an effective combination of the classical and modern both in content and method. Though it was as free as many of the poems then being published that Dos Passos admired, he, too, was marching to the drum of the moderns.

During the winter of 1915–16, R. Stewart Mitchell—known by his friends as "The Great Auk" because of his long face—hit upon the idea of putting together a volume of verses written that year by selected members of the Harvard Poetry Society. From time to time the *Harvard Advocate* issued collections of its best poetry and prose, and the *Harvard Monthly* published a book of poems in 1910; therefore Mitchell saw no reason why Harvard's new poets could not collect their own poems regardless of whether they had appeared previously in any publication. The plan seemed feasible, since Mitchell's aunt was a friend of Laurence J. Gomme, who owned a bookshop and a small publishing house in New York City. Gomme had brought out handsome limited editions of the poems of Edna St. Vincent Millay, Alfred Joyce Kilmer, Hilaire Belloc, and John Jay Chapman, but never before had published a limited edition of the work of a group of poets. Mitchell's aunt spoke to Gomme on behalf of the young poets, who in turn agreed to submit the manuscript to his poetry reader, Clement Wood, for a recommendation.

With Mitchell acting as editor, some seventy poems were collected under the title *Eight Harvard Poets* (1917). Contributors were Dos Passos, Cummings, Damon, Hillyer, Poore, Wright, Norris, and, of course, Mitchell—all members of the Harvard Poetry Society. Each submitted what *he* himself considered his best. Dos Passos offered the fewest, seven; Cummings, whose work was picked to lead off the volume, eight; and the others, eight to eleven. Clement Wood told Gomme that he had reservations regarding certain offerings, but recommended their publication as a collected volume. He said that he liked Cummings' work least. He objected to Cummings' "lapses of bad grammar, . . . dreadful inversion, and silly archaisms." It was Woods's opinion that "more maturity would rub these artificial excrescences from his work and let him say in a thoroughly understandable manner what he is getting at. Take him all in all, he is only fair." Damon's work, too, left much to be desired, said the poetry reader, who found Damon "inclined to be too much only a fair distiller of overused poetic material." Wood liked most of the poems of the other six contributors. Two of Dos Passos' poems, "Salvation Army" and "Incarnation," he described as "good"; "Memory" and "Night Piece" were awarded "honorable mention."

Gomme agreed to publish the volume with the stipulation that the poets would receive no royalties for the first five hundred copies. They had to commit themselves to buying thirty copies each at one third the retail price ($1.00); if additional printings were in order and subsequent copies sold, the eight poets were to divide a 10 percent royalty (a little over a penny per book for each contributor). A number of problems beset *Eight Harvard Poets* before its publication, most of which Gomme blamed on the war. Rising cost of materials and the improbability of sufficient sales to make the venture worthwhile prompted him to seek a release from the contract. Many months had passed since the agreement was signed; by this time each poet had left Harvard and gone his separate way. Gomme wrote Mitchell in late 1916 that he himself had decided to go into war work and would close his publishing house and The Little Book Shop Around the Corner, out of which he operated. Since he had no other books pending, Gomme said that he would be ruined financially if he proceeded with the project, but the Harvard poets were not put off. Ultimately, it was Dos Passos' father who rescued the project. Convinced that his son was determined to pursue a literary career regardless of the consequences, he agreed to put up $750 to underwrite the printing costs so that Gomme would not risk any of his own money in the venture.

A number of poems in the collection were in the traditional sonnet form and posed no problem in the editing, such as the sonnets of Robert Hillyer, who was awarded before his graduation the Garrison Prize for Poetry and became the only undergraduate in the history of the school to have a collection of poems *(Sonnets and Other Lyrics)* published by the university (1917). Cummings' four sonnets, on the other hand, were decidedly *new*. Every word, including the pronoun *i*, was in lowercase. Dos Passos, having assumed some of the editing chores, anticipated a problem with the printer as well as harsh criticism from readers (especially those in the Harvard community, who were more resistant to what was new in art than were readers in New York City or in the greater Boston area) and asked Cummings what he intended to do about the *i*'s in his poems. "The poems must stand as they are," replied the poet. "It was the beginning of my style," Cummings reflected later. He was dismayed, however, when the volume finally appeared. Though Gomme had agreed to publish the poems precisely as Cummings instructed, an enterprising typesetter took it upon himself to capitalize every pronoun and lead word according to the rules.

Of the seven poems by Dos Passos published in *Eight Harvard Poets*, four had appeared earlier in the *Harvard Monthly:* "Saturnalia," "Salvation Army," "Memory," and "Incarnation." Three other poems written during his senior year appeared in the *Harvard Monthly*, but were never republished elsewhere: "Prairies," "From Simonides," and "Philosophy." Though he continued to be self-effacing regarding his practice and achievement as a poet, Dos Passos was doing well in his own poetry most of the things that he admired in the work of the new poets. By and large, his use of rhyme was subtle and without scheme. He used none of the traditional metrical patterns, but relied on unrhymed cadence. In "Salvation Army," for example, a drum *pounds out the hymn* on a busy street at Christmastime. The poem's cadenced lines are irregular in length, yet bound by rhymed couplets; analogous to the form is *a woman's thin, raucous voice* that carries *salvation's tune* in ironic juxtaposition with other women who *shout their wares* in the *dinning market stalls*. The mood is fittingly somber, unrelieved by *gaudy angels, tinsel cherubim*. The tune that emanates from the tiny band is *monotonously importune*. As the song *fades away/Among the silent, dark array/Of city houses where no soul stirs,/The crowd thins, the players are alone*.

"Memory," his longest poem—some sixty-eight lines—is laden with rhyme without scheme. Its jagged lines reflect the narrator's memory of a journey by steamer, which snaked in and out amid the reeds and water weeds *between rounded hills*. He recalled a young girl's *eyes in sunshine* and the way he stood watching the *sunlight lose itself* in her hair and talking with her of *meaningless things*. The *hoarse whistle shrieked for a landing* and she left him. As he watched her disappear, *a slim blue figure amid the wharf's crowd*, he registered his sense of loss: *I never even knew your name./. . . With a grinding swing/And see-saw of sound/The steamer slunk down the canal*. For the final stanza, Dos Passos dipped into his memory for an image from "The City of Burnished Copper," his first published fiction *(The Choate School News Fiction Supplement)*, which recounted the fabled discovery of a lost city by a "lunatic" dying of brain fever (it was an image he used again some ten years later in "The Moon Is a Gong," a poetic drama written for the New Playwrights Theatre. The poem concluded:

> That night from a dingy hotel room
> I saw the moon like a golden gong,
> Redly loom

> *Across the lake; like a golden gong*
> *In a temple, which a priest ere long*
> *Will strike into throbbing song*
> *To wake some silent twinkling city to prayer.*
> *The lake waves were flakes of red gold*
> *Burnished to copper,*
> *Gold, red as the tangled gleam*
> *Of sunlight in your hair.*

"Incarnation," too, is a memory poem rich in color imagery. Like "Salvation Army," its rhymed couplets and occasional alternating lines of rhyme tend to lock in the *turbulent darkness* and sense of moral aloneness in which the poet/narrator is caught. After the first two stanzas, the rhyme yields. The verse is totally free in the final stanza, thus reinforcing the freedom felt by the speaker when his vision of the woman's face flames once more through his soul. The stanza concludes:

> *Incessantly the long rain falls;*
> *Slanting on black walls.*
> *But through the dark interminable streets*
> *Along pavements where the rain beats*
> *Its sharp tattoo, and gas-lamps shine*
> *Greenish gold in the solitude,*
> *The vision flames through my mood*
> *Of that Italian woman's face,*
> *Through the dripping windowpane.*

Dos Passos was clearly a modernist, but his *vers libre* did not look as strikingly different as the new poems of Cummings, who was more single-minded as a poet. Cummings took English versification (English 12) that year from Briggs, whereas Dos Passos was in Briggs's prose composition class, in which traditional forms of poetry were studied. Though the writing of poetry sharpened Dos Passos' use of language, and gave him free play in experimentation—essential to him as a writer of prose—he was more interested in self-expression as a fictionist. As a senior he contributed to each issue of the *Harvard Monthly* one or more pieces, which included six short stories, four editorials, two book reviews, a personal reminiscence, and a long essay.

"Romantic Education" was the lead fiction in the October issue of the magazine. Ricker, its protagonist, is a stammering, unimaginative engineer whose challenge is to learn how to live. "Ah, you do not live, you Americans," he is told by a faded but once beautiful Spanish opera singer with whom he takes up. She recommends Spain or Italy to him, where "it is hot, where people really live," instead of Paris or London, cities cloyed by tourists, she warned. Easily embarrassed, he is like a "school girl from a convent." Under her influence he is filled with a rush of longing for beauty and life, but he dares not break his mold. In the final scene the reader sees him sitting in the Café Vibert in Paris, where "Americans who desire to be naughty are taken by their couriers." At his side is a heavily scented, jaded woman whose "overpowdered, coarse face" is distorted in "a nasty leering smile" as he sips champagne and speaks "painfully unfluent French" to her. For a moment he is reminded of the Spanish opera singer whose suggestions he had sidestepped. His current brush with the "real world" is neither what she intended for him, nor what he envisioned, but merely "a romantic education."

Still another Dos Passos tale of disillusionment in the October *Harvard Monthly* was "First Love." In this story a prep school boy is awakened from his reverie of first love while reading a Latin assignment in study hall. The love passages between Aeneas and Dido set him off upon his own dialogue of love with an imaginary Juliet. Not only does the master catch him in the act of pouring out his fantasies on paper and destroys them, but also blames the boy for the caricature of himself discovered on the back of the paper, though, in truth, the drawing had been slipped to him by a classmate who had rudely intruded into his private world moments earlier. In a final ironic statement, the boy's penalty is "five black marks for drawing in study period."

Dos Passos' next tale, "Orientale," appeared in the November *Harvard Monthly*. It, too, depicts a naive, conservative young man (Tommy) who is concerned with appearances and lives a dull, unimaginative life. An effective foil to Tommy is his resourceful older cousin, Agnes Leviker, who relieves her widow's grief by reading Hafiz and Fitz-Gerald. Fantasizing herself into the realm of the *Rubáiyát of Omar Khayyám,* Mrs. Leviker commences an extravagant redecoration of her home in an Eastern motif. The story has a tables-turned ending when the woman learns that her Persian decorator, a posturing aesthete, has fled the country and left her with a staggering bill for carpets, wall hangings, Persian miniatures, jewelry, and the like that she thought he had *given* her. Instead of paying the bill, she was inspired to open "a select oriental store" in her basement, whereupon she wrote Tommy: "You must patronize it, and make all your friends come and spend money. I'm tired of being one of the idle rich. You'll be shocked."

More and more, characters who rebelled in some fashion against society's dictates fascinated Dos Passos and became a primary means of getting his own ambiguous feelings objectified so that he might deal with them. Harvard men were becoming increasingly rebellious against their conservative milieu. Everything new in art, literature, music, and dance was a protest against the traditional. Dos Passos' innate shyness and genial manner made him ill-equipped for direct statement by which he might register his disapproval of things; instead, he developed characters and fictional situations whereby he could humorously and ironically ridicule, censure, or otherwise attempt to correct what he took to be the follies and vices of the individual and society. Cummings was going through a similar rebellion. Skinny and plagued by acne, he was painfully bashful, a private person who kept much of what he felt to himself. Like Dos Passos, he avoided crowds and was highly selective in the few friends he chose. Breaking away from his parents' surveillance by moving into the Harvard Yard and otherwise rejecting his father's dominance were acts paralleled by his protests and break with conventionality in the arts. He learned the newest dances and pursued women with a passion that led to the bed whenever possible. Cummings made no secret of his brothel engagements and alcoholic excesses. His rebellion was a more direct statement than that which Dos Passos allowed himself.

Even Dos Passos' attempt to speak directly in the lead editorial published in the *Harvard Monthly* in the same issue with "Orientale" was couched in an extended metaphor. Under the title "The Evangelist and the Volcano," it had the tone of a latter-day parable. He depicted crass, insensitive tourists—Canadians and Americans—being conveyed in a horse-drawn carriage over uneven roads amid "gorgeous solemn mountains" to which they were oblivious, "chattering empty-headedly" instead about the war. One attributed the war to the "evil designs" of George V and the Kaiser, another to "all them Kings and Queens . . . getting land for their princeling." "It ought to be stopped," pronounced a third. Dos Passos likened the American attitude to "an Evangelist preaching a sermon to a volcano—from a safe distance." The editorial was his first signed comment on what he called his country's "supercilious disapproval" of the war. "Above all we must realize that we are not isolated onlookers, that our destinies as well as those of the warring nations are being fought out on French and Turkish battlefields . . . and come to understand that such a huge catastrophe is above and apart from all praise and blame." To Dos Passos, the war might just as well be happening on the moon for all the effect it was having upon the thought of the American people.

His fictional tale "The Shepherd," published in the January *Harvard Monthly,* was similarly allegorical, but its concern was not the Great War; rather, it was the age-old innocence-versus-experience theme: a youth's thirst for adventure and worldly knowledge juxtaposed with his unwillingness to relinquish maternal sustenance. Told in muted tones and rhythms that at times took on an Old Testament cadence, the circular tale revolved around the fifteen-year-old youth who climbed a mountain, then "abandoned himself to a slow round of thought." He knew that he was at a pinnacle moment, that "time did not exist [and] his whole life seemed concentrated in this one moment of passive reflection." Suddenly he thought of his mother and his eyes welled with tears: "He ached with love and tenderness towards her. She was the center of his world. In spirit he prostrated himself before the fragrant shrine of her sweetness and gentleness." The memory stirred him while he vacillated between the adventure that lay before him and the drab fate he had left behind, his former life bare except for books. Then a mist rose from the valley and settled over the mountain, and a "mysterious lonely terror" swept over him. Losing the way during his attempt to return to his mother and the little village in which he had been reared, the boy was forced to seek shelter overnight with a shepherd who offered him food and fed his soul with fearsome tales of pain and passion. Once more the boy's thoughts "flared with longing" as his body stood poised on "the threshold of all experience, of all adventure." Then he saw his mother, her head down, walking slowly toward him. Again he felt young and helpless:

> The glittering vision of his desire shattered like a bubble. . . . The gold and scarlet were tinsel and tawdry. . . . As he kissed her slightly wrinkled cheeks, and saw the tears on them, he felt infinitely tender, felt that he must protect his mother against all the world. The dazzling vision of freedom faded away. He felt all the dim pleasure of renunciation. But in his mind lingered the memory of the glint of the firelight in the black eyes of the shepherd on the mountain.

Dos Passos' parabolic fiction was a poignant depiction of the complexities of his own dilemma.

Memories of his mother pursued Dos Passos relentlessly that winter and spring. As the first anniversary of her death approached, Dos Passos wrote an elegiac lament and submitted it for anonymous publication in the April issue of the *Harvard Monthly*. Explicitly personal, *"Les Lauriers Sont Coupés"* combined his sense of loss with sensuous reminiscences of his childhood in Brussels, a city that now stirred uneasily in the hands of the Kaiser's soldiers. The reader was reminded of the war and the present condition in Belgium only by the singular statement "So much has intervened—both for me and for Brussels—since then." The evocative piece concluded with the few lines his mother crooned him as she sat beside his bed "in her silk evening gown that was so soft to stroke":

> *"Voici l'herbe qu'on fauche et les lauriers qu'on coupe.*
> *Nous n'irons plus aux bois, les lauriers sont coupés."*

> [Behold the grass they mow and the laurel trees they cut.
> We'll go to the woods no more, the laurel trees are cut.]

Dos Passos said that with those words he sank "off to sleep amid dim solemn gardens and the pale sadness of autumn woods." *"Les Lauriers Sont Coupés"* was one of the best pieces of prose to appear in the *Harvard Monthly* during Dos Passos' entire editorship of the magazine. It ranked significantly with his later prose.

"A Pot of Tulips" (December 1915) and "The Cardinal's Grapes" (February 1916) were other fictional offerings by Dos Passos as a senior. Both tales comment upon the aesthete whose artistic sensitivity has been artificially cultivated. The protagonist of "A Pot of Tulips" is Stanhope Whitcombe, a professional poet who has "been able to strike so exactly the note required by the magazine-reading public that half the periodicals in the country filled their empty spaces with his verse" (of "a very inflamed, purple order. Shame and flame always rhymed together"). Whitcombe is shy almost to the point of paralysis, his turbid dreams well concealed by "an exterior of calm placidity," his vapid posturing reinforced by oriental rugs and hangings, Japanese bronzes, and ornate furniture with which he surrounds himself. He lacks only a love affair, he decided ("his life had not tallied with his poems"). The object of his avowed affection is a self-possessed, rational young woman who runs a flower shop. The florist rejects his recitations of passion, but agrees to a closely monitored affair until she discovers he lied regarding his reasons for purchasing the various plants from her (the pot in which the azaleas were brought clashed with his brick-red curtains, but perhaps the pot of tulips would be suitable, he reasoned). At the story's close, the girl has left him and the pot of tulips lies broken on the asphalt outside his window. The ending is reminiscent of the silly youth in "An Aesthete's Nightmare" who belatedly came to his senses and threw his false gods out the window, as did the "poet of Cordale," who discarded his copy of the *Rubáiyát* when it failed him.

The fat Cardinal of "The Cardinal's Grapes" is first cousin to Dos Passos' American aesthetes. Though the Cardinal lives in Italy and the nervous, bumbling youth who picks and bruises the Cardinal's grapes is the son of his steward, Fra Giacomo, the story is as much a commentary on the affectation and cultism practiced by the self-prostituting aesthetes of Harvard as it is on the vanity, hypocrisy, and excesses of life common the world over. To the true artist, contends Dos Passos, aestheticism is revitalizing; to the imposter, it is stagnating. His Eminence becomes a central metaphor for what Dos Passos deems wrong with the aesthetic movement. The prelate is a connoisseur of grapes, not art, a fact that in itself would not be cause for indictment, but this fat servant of God behaves as he imagines the Pope himself acts:

> Comfortably the Cardinal settled himself in his wide-armed chair. He leaned back into the cushions, and shook the red-plush slippers from his feet, stretching each toe separately under the silk stockings. The flowered dressing-gown nestled cosily about his portly form. On a gilt tabouret at his right hand was a *Sèvres* bowl full of immense white grapes in splendid bunches —each grape perfect and veined on one side with purple. Languidly he picked up a bunch and held it before him, where the light from the bracket of candles on the wall behind him might strike it. Then, with the other hand, where his episcopal rings glistened, he pulled off the grapes one by one. They made a little click as they left the stem. Since the doctors had cut off his wine, the Cardinal had become a connoisseur of grapes; so it was with especial pleasure that he rubbed each one between his thumb and forefinger and put it delicately into his mouth.

The Cardinal reminisces briefly about his own days spent in the vineyards and the time he found a basket of white grapes like those he ate now. He could still feel "their sticky juice on his fingers in the hot sunlight of the vineyard." He is jerked back to the present when he realizes that someone has allowed his grapes to fall upon the ground. The culprit, Tommaso, is sent for and threatened with flogging if he ever again sends the Cardinal an imperfect grape. The lad trembles, and tears roll down his cheeks as he kneels on the stone floor of the churchman's library. He does not tell the Cardinal that he had been kissing a girl when he allowed the grapes to become bruised. The tale's final scene depicts the boy kneeling once more, this time during a feast at high mass, with the girl at his side. When His Eminence enters the church, Tommaso whispers boastfully: "There is the Cardinal. You know, I talked to him in his own library." Dos Passos' message is implicit. Tommaso had the makings of a rebel, but he cowered when put to the test and revealed himself cut from the same cloth as the Cardinal. After misrepresenting his encounter with the churchman—for which he is embraced and admired by his sweetheart—Tommaso performs another empty pretense of piety as he prays before the Virgin Mary and perhaps fools even himself. Dos Passos implies that Tommaso himself is well on the way to becoming a Cardinal one day. "The Cardinal's Grapes" and "The Shepherd" reveal the author's ability to make the faraway and foreign close and familiar, and the past, immediate. Both tales function as effective, modern-day allegories. The revelation of character and situation through irony and understatement makes the "The Cardinal's Grapes" Dos Passos' best piece of fiction of his Harvard years. It was his last as well.

The spring of his senior year was a busy time for him for many reasons. He also pondered the war and what his role should be in it. The editing of *Eight Harvard Poets* and the problems besetting the volume before it went to press were taxing; and he was preparing several pieces for publication in the *Harvard Monthly* before graduation in June. For the May 1916 issue of the magazine he reviewed two recent books of poetry: *The Catholic Anthology* and *Georgian Poetry, 1913–1915*. Neither was so bad as "certain annual collections of current verse of the embalming, Egyptian fashion," he insisted, nor was either so significant as Pound's anthology, *Des Imagistes,* the first of the Imagist anthologies. Though most of the verse in *The Catholic Anthology* "straggled over dull pages," he commended the volume for its "sense of satire." Certain poems by T. S. Eliot, Edgar Lee Masters, Harold Munro, and Ezra Pound were worthy of mention, but affectation seemed the rule rather than the exception, he concluded. He preferred *Georgian Poetry, 1913–1915* for the "aliveness and closeness to the soil" found in many of the poems, yet was disappointed in the English volume because of its paucity of war poetry. It was inconceivable to Dos Passos that the poets took no note of the fact that the war "had split the centuries apart." They clung instead to the "purple moorland" and ignored the city. It was as though the nineteenth century had superimposed itself upon the twentieth despite the war.

The June issue of the *Harvard Monthly* carried three contributions by Dos Passos, each different in form and content, but related nevertheless. The first was an editorial, "A Conference on Foreign Relations," calling attention to a conference at Western Reserve University concerning international relations and foreseeing important results if its members could stir public opinion sufficiently to convince the government to abandon its *laissez-faire* dogmas of the past. The civilized world must never again slip into the "path of competitive armament" that inevitably leads to war, urged Dos Passos. America must "throw its weight against the powers of darkness" through "constructive pacifism" and an awakening from its "provincial slumbers" of isolation.

Dos Passos' two other pieces were "Philosophy," a short poem in free verse, and "A Humble Protest," a richly textured essay of some twenty-five hundred words, his longest nonfiction piece yet published. Fittingly juxtaposed, they might have been entitled "Before" and "After." "Philosophy" was the poet's plea for what once was, yet could be again: a simple life in which a person has both the time and inclination to ponder old verities, attempt to fathom his universe and himself, expand his imagination, and create. Dos Passos' persona is an older man who beholds the beauty in nature and at last is able to move *the ivory chessmen of his thoughts.* As his beard *sinks on his breast,* a youth comes singing down the road and *kicks up with bare brown feet/The red-tinged dust.* The poem is an apt prologue to "A Humble Protest" against a way of life in which modern youth is "shod." America's young men have grown up "to the tune of Science," all "lustily singing, comfortable in companionship, the paeon of the new shibboleth." The password resounds in "rhymes of pleasant optimism," a beat drummed out relentlessly by a beguiling "steel-girded goddess" leading a twentieth-century torch parade of human thought. She is accompanied by her handmaidens, Industrialism and Mechanical Civilization, who serve her every whim. The essay posed several questions: "How do thought and art fare under the rule of Science? . . . Has life become more intense, art greater, thought more profound in our age than in the reign of Elizabeth? . . . What happened to 'Know thyself' of the Greeks?" It seemed to Dos Passos that modern man had lost his sense of proportion. He had pored "over the cells of his epidermis" so long that he had forgotten "his body as a unit"; he had become so obsessed with the tabulation of fact and the elements on the "other end of the telescope and microscope" that he had lost the ability to focus on what was at hand. "How long will the squirrel contentedly turn his wheel and imagine he is progressing," Dos Passos queried, and is man not "crouching on a runaway engine" yet insensately "shoveling in fuel" at the same time with no thought as to where he was being taken? And had not the energies of the scientific spirit gone berserk in building "a silly claptrap of unnecessary luxuries, a clutter of inessentials?" It was time to examine the balance sheet of industrialism, he insisted. Man's materialistic lusts had outstripped his ability to harness them or to put them to constructive use. The same civilization had produced Wagner and Von Tirpitz, the *Eroica* Symphony and the ruins of Rheims. The nation that had thrived on "great living art" had slipped back almost overnight into barbarism. Man's desire to fathom and to create were in danger of being smothered. What does modern man intend to do about it, he asked. Dos Passos offered no pat answers, no panacea; his questions were merely "a humble protest." In combination, the message of the three pieces served the author both as peroration and valediction at the close of his Harvard career.

Before graduation he wrote a final piece for the July issue of the magazine, a review of *The War in Eastern Europe,* a new book by John Reed and Boardman Robinson. It was not as brilliantly written as *Insurgent Mexico,* but had "great vividness of style, a delightful sense of humor, and almost a novelist's sympathy for all sorts and conditions of men," observed Dos Passos, who complimented American correspondents as a whole for their vigorous style and humanistic, impartial treatment, which he saw as "journalistic English at its best." Although the United States had not joined in the fighting, he continued, "its pens had not been idle." He did not intend to allow his pen to be idle either. A few days before graduating *cum laude* from Harvard on June 26, 1916, with an A.B. degree in English, he wrote Rumsey Marvin a prophetic letter: "Rejoicing in my large and examless freedom [he had been excused from final examination], I have been making vows. Firstly I am going to start educating myself. It's wonderful how much college interferes with one's education. Secondly I am going to write huge amounts each day. Thirdly I am going to wander far and wide over the face of the globe. Small order!" He did not know precisely where he was going, but he meant to record each step of the way. On Class Day (June 20, 1916), he wrote again to Marvin:

> I've marched and counter-marched in processions and heard endless orations. Now it is dark and the Yard is hung with Japanese lanterns, is lilting with the music of three bands and two fountains, and I have a pink in my buttonhole—you know their wistful far away odor—all conduces to a mood of pleasant aloofness. I've been wandering among the crowd and listening to their footsteps and feeling a strange half-melancholy. What little family I have I would not let come—so I feel like Virgil and Dante in a pleasant Purgatorio—interested but aloof. . . . Wish you were here—it is very fascinating—glow of lanterns and ripple of voices above a low grind of footsteps—through it all runs like a gilt thread, the brazen sound of the band, then the occasional militia uniform. . . . Let's hope the "cannon's opening roar" won't follow.

Dos Passos felt a curious detachment on the eve of his graduation. Harvard had not been unkind to him, yet he had bemoaned his plight and railed against the system many times there. In response to a letter from one "Mr. Oliver" a few years after his graduation, Dos Passos said that his four years at Harvard were "a disastrous waste of time and that most of the attitudes and exploiting class manners" were more of a hindrance than a help in understanding the world he lived in. "I must admit that the taste for good writing was in the air there. . . . All the things I learned specifically in the courses on writing I have had to reject (outside of the plain essentials of prose composition—the unity coherence and emphasis stuff anybody picks up in any high school or freshman English course), but reading Chaucer, a little Greek, the Elizabethans, etc. have been fundamental in my development as a writer."

He was more explicit in his letter to Rumsey Marvin regarding Harvard and his attitude regarding university life in general:

I am cynical about American colleges. They do pump so much twaddle into one at American schools—so much watery heroics. I'm awfully glad you've decided to get educated, but if you think college'll do that for you, you've got another guess coming. Don't go to Williams I beg —it is the home and original abiding place of the YMCA man. Shall it be Harvard or Yale? It really doesn't matter if you don't take either of them seriously. If it weren't for the existence of President Lowell and other annoyances I would urge my beloved Harvard more strenuously— and I wouldn't mind Yale a bit if it weren't for Tap Day. . . . The Harvard kind of snobbery does not irritate me so much as the Yale kind—I mean the sort of thing those sacred "frats" breed—but the intellectual life in any of them is slim enough. . . . If one doesn't take them too seriously, one can chug very happily through four years and emerge without having one's intellect utterly mossed over. The only thing I don't think you ought to do is let your studies interfere with your education—I mean your reading. I found that school and college inter- fered most damnably—and all real education you get yourself anyway. . . . It doesn't matter much what you take—you do your own educating outside—but Military Tactics, be sensible! Even if everyone else in that godforsaken country has lost his head completely! Just imagine: Fortifications 1, Rape 4b, Poison Gas II, History of Bayonets 6. I cannot imagine anything more stale, flat, and unprofitable! Why go to college at all if not to study the humanities. The thing is to read good literature and cultivate things you're interested in and let the rest go hang!

7

Summer 1916

It's a wonderful blowy day and the hollyhocks are nodding and bowing like tall ladies at a country dance—the poppies are all a-flutter and the lavender comes in puffs of glorious fragrance through the window. Soon I shall bathe in the river and read Pierre Nozière of the beloved Anatole in a bathtowel dressing gown—En effet je suis étourdi [Indeed, I am quite stupid].

Dos Passos to Dudley Poore
5 July 1916

Dos Passos had been apprehensive about returning to his boyhood home at Spence's Point in Virginia, his formal schooling now behind him and his future yet uncharted. The preceding summer, grief over his mother's death still fresh, he had lingered on the farm only a few days, then bolted for California to visit relatives and take in the Panama-Pacific International Exposition in San Francisco. The youthful sorcerer who had eased his sorrow was Rumsey Marvin, with whom he launched a voluminous correspondence of extravagant prose similar to the letters he now wrote to Dudley Poore. His letters to each were laced with French phrases, newly coined expressions, and purposefully bastardized spellings of popular American idioms. With the sensuousness of a Pre-Raphaelite aesthete, he was open to every sensate experience that came his way. He also played the minstrel poet while strolling the banks of the Potomac, whistling, and talking to the birds. Though he eventually settled down to a routine of writing, his linguistic ability was called forth primarily to give form to his pleasures. Notes to Marvin were fraught with imagistic overlay. When Dos Passos invited him to visit the farm, he tempted him by adding: "You'd love the bathing here. At night the water is often phosphorescent and wildly exciting to swim in. Your arms and legs are as if they had flaming draperies, and you trail jewelled bubbles behind you. . . . There is a sort of jellyfish which lights up like a milky star when you hit it—I don't know anything more gorgeous." Almost every sensation was dressed in precious rhetoric, yet in the process he rid himself of much extravagant prose at a young age and went on to more measured expression. He also shared with Marvin prosaic details of his day. "I'm about to settle down to a month's hard work amid the rural serenity," he wrote in early summer. "I have a program each day—think of that! How long I'll keep to it, heaven knows! You'll be amused to hear it:

6 A.M.	Get up, run for 15 minutes on beach.
	Bathe.
8—	Breakfast.
to 10	Work in garden.
10–12	Write.
12—	Bathe.
1:30	Lunch.

Then siesta and writing and reading until 5:00 P.M.
Then horseback ride followed by bath.
Some program!"

To Arthur McComb, a friend still at Harvard, he spoke of his "new joy," sailing: "I have an impromptu sailboat made out of a canoe—in which I skim the bay more or less ungracefully. Today a boom came undone and I came to grief, receiving the mast in the nose and being cast, like Jonah, upon the waters. The affair ended by the whole equipage being trundled ashore and swamped in the surf. You should have seen me dragging mast, canoe, paddles, etc. out of the breakers. Apart from that I read, write, garden, ride, and mostly, pine for jocund companionship. No plans yet."

Years later when Dos Passos wrote about the summer of 1916 he recalled his impatience to be on the road: "The breathless July days, the dusty roads, the cornfields curling in the drought seemed hideous that hot Virginia summer. I wanted to see the war, to paddle up undiscovered rivers, to climb unmapped mountains." He said he had "greedily gulped" the ten-volume edition of Romain Rolland's *Jean-Christophe* with a great deal of "youth against the world" enthusiasm, yet had no sooner finished the book when he began an essay to "demolish the *Jean-Christophe* cult." Rolland's epic novel, some seven thousand pages long and published over a nine-year period (1904–12), had won for him a Nobel Prize for literature in 1915. It was said, however, that the award was more for his courageous stand for pacifism (which the prize committee supported) than for the works. Dos Passos credited Rolland for having stimulated his own pacifist belief, but faulted *Jean-Christophe* as a novel because it did not tally with the sum of its parts. Rolland's title character, an idealistic hero who died alone in Paris—unrecognized as the world's greatest composer of modern music—was not enough of a man of action for Dos Passos' heady tastes, which were inclined toward the writings of Bertrand Russell, who had recently gone to jail as a conscientious objector. Rolland was not a doer. Caught in Switzerland at the start of the war, he preached pacifism and launched a vigorous attack against war of any kind, a stand for which he was criticized by French countrymen and German nationalists alike.

"I kept mounting my fiery steed and riding off in all directions," conceded Dos

Passos in writing of his summer's activities after graduating from Harvard. He had been dogged off and on throughout his senior year by the status of American letters. Other than Whitman, Dickinson, Crane, and Twain—whose works he had read extensively—most other American writers lacked substance, he insisted. Harvard offered no course in American literature, nor did any other university except Princeton. Dos Passos observed to Rumsey Marvin that "one of the prime reasons American literature isn't is that we as a nation have not that feeling of the infinite beauty and infinite poetry underlying things—love, war, sunsets, tin pans, lawnmowers, etc." Unless Marvin were ready for a three-hour discourse on the subject, he would not go into detail, he added. Rather than venting his literary peeves only in letters and no longer having the *Harvard Monthly* for his formal arguments, Dos Passos decided to seek a national readership. Since the only magazine he read regularly was *The New Republic,* it was to editor Herbert Croly to whom he addressed a long treatise entitled "Against American Literature."

A reader could not survive for long on the "rice-pudding fare" cooked up by contemporary American authors, he contended. Such hybrid works were much poorer than their parent stock. He likened the current crop of books by American writers to the cities they lived in: "They're all the same. Any other nation's literature would take a lifetime to exhaust." The heart of the problem lay in its rootlessness.

> In other countries literature is the result of long evolution, based on primitive folklore, on the first joy and terror of man in the presence of the trees and scented meadowlands and dimpled whirling rivers, interwoven with the moulding fabric of old dead civilizations, and with threads of fiery new gold from incoming races. . . . This artistic stimulus, fervid with primitive savageries, redolent with old cults of earth and harvest, smoked and mellowed by time, is the main inheritance of the civilizations, the woof upon which individual artists may work the warp of their own thoughts. America lacks it almost completely. . . . We find ourselves floundering without rudder or compass, in the sea of modern life, vaguely lit by the phosphorescent gleam of our traditional optimism. . . . The only substitute for dependence on the past is dependence on the future. Here our only poet found his true greatness. Walt Whitman abandoned the vague genteelness that had characterized American writing . . . and, founding his faith on himself, on the glowing life within him, shouted genially, fervidly his challenge to the future.

Those who managed to cut through Dos Passos' lush verbiage to the last page of his essay found two concluding observations to help justify the ordeal: one, that the weaknesses inherent in American literature help account for the sudden vogue of Russian literature, and two, that the snares of industrialism had cut off any retreat to the past (when literature flowered) and allowed now only the course of following Whitman's lead and pressing on. Surely something more than steel and oil and grain could be wrung from the melting pot of America, he insisted. Dos Passos' rhetoric may have resembled Oscar Wilde's more than that of his hero, Walt Whitman, but there was nothing lacking in his spirit. Dos Passos put his essay in the mail in September and prepared to abandon his idyllic life in Virginia in favor of New York City and new commitments.

Before leaving the farm, he applied for service with Herbert Hoover's Commission for Relief in Belgium. Some three hundred thousand Belgians were about to be deported to Germany, and Great Britain and the United States stepped up their efforts to provide additional relief of food, medicine, and clothing. Since America was technically neutral, volunteer teams went into Belgium to insure that supplies were distributed fairly. Young men were being recruited for six-month enlistments in Hoover's relief team, and Dos Passos was eager to be one of them. His ultimate goal of becoming a professional writer, however, was always in the forefront.

Meanwhile John R. prayed that his son might somehow be induced to change his mind and take up law. In 1916 John R. was seventy-two years old and crippled with gout. He needed to slow his pace and envisioned DOS PASSOS BROTHERS & SONS emblazoned on the doors of his office. For years he had relied upon his brother Benjamin's son, Cyril, for much of his legwork, but his nephew, a brilliant attorney, was overworked and would have welcomed the assistance of young Dos Passos. John R. yearned for his son to commit his mind and energies to America's judicial system instead of running full tilt into battle on behalf of vague, idealistic causes.

John R. frequently wrote long, rambling letters to his housekeeper that differed little from those he once wrote his wife. "Jack is here with his friends. Every now and then I have a pang of regret that he is in this big den of so-called pleasure. I am afraid lest his lovely nature may be affected and he become as others," began one letter.

> But he is launched into life now—must take his chance. He has been reared as no other boy in the world has been. My judgment, tact, nature, and experience have always been lavished upon him. He has never known a want—he has never expressed a desire that has not been gratified. And from the day of his birth till now I cannot pick a flaw in his character or conduct. All has been—so far as his wants are concerned—moderation and conservatism. Not trained qualities, but qualities which were born within him. Will this lovely character, like a flower, wilt? I must not worry, but I must hope. I will get him to Spain or Belgium as soon as possible. Horrible thought!—for the latter is almost like putting him in confinement. Yet he wants to go—he must go on—he is in the hands of destiny. If he be not wiped out he will prove a bright and particular star in the firmament of literature. God bless him!

Dos Passos' application for service with the Commission for Relief in Belgium was denied. "For the present my age is too tender," he explained to Arthur McComb. When he became twenty-one, he would be eligible, he continued. Unwilling to wait until January, however, Dos Passos contacted Eliot Norton, his father's friend, a New York attorney who was signing up volunteers for his brother Richard's volunteer ambulance corps then forming for service in France. Comprised of Harvard graduates, the Norton-Harjes Ambulance Corps was to function under the auspices of the American Red Cross. Aghast when he learned that his son had already applied for such a mission, John R. had no intention of consenting to the venture and engineered a compromise. Since Dos Passos had always been enamored of buildings and had an aptitude for sketching, he would be suited for a career in architecture, concluded John R. If his son was determined to go abroad that year, he could go to Spain to study under the Spanish masters, become fluent in the language, and, best of all, be safe there, John R. reasoned. The very idea of his thinking that he could drive ambulances in the thick of battle when he had acute myopic vision and had never even been behind the wheel of any motorized vehicle was appalling to John R. The matter was closed. He would stake his son's every need in Spain, or he could stay home—it was as simple as that, the wily man insisted.

Young Dos Passos had other thoughts. He had not arrived at this twenty-first year without learning a few tricks of his mentor's, for John R. had been a tactician all his life. It was time for the pupil to put his own artful maneuvering to use. To Arthur McComb he confided:

> I am sailing on the Espagne to Bordeaux, thence to Madrid . . . where I have letters to three poets and other amusing people. I shall . . . study architecture and the Bible like mad—also Cervantes, Calderón, Homer, and Virgil's Georgics. Then in the spring I shall go to Paris and make every endeavor to get to the front by hook or by crook—let's hope it'll be the Rhine. . . . I have spent the morning being looked at suspiciously by an official who looked like a jailbird, and swearing allegiance to the United States, and that I should support the Constitution (of all baroque absurdities!); also in filling out numberless blanks and signing photos of myself for the benefit of Mr. Wilson.

"Stay home where you belong," replied McComb, who was more radical in his antiwar convictions than Dos Passos. "I might suggest, Mr. Pacifist," Dos Passos shot back, "War is a human phenomenon you can't argue out of existence. You people are like Christian Scientists with yellow fever. All your praying and ought not's won't change the present fact."

Dos Passos enjoyed the heady talk of art, poetry, anarchism, socialism, war, and free love that he found rampant among his literary cohorts and artist friends now in Greenwich Village. Before learning of his rejection by the Commission for Relief in Belgium, he sought out Cummings, who had left home over his parents' objections to support himself as an artist in the city. Arthur Winslow ("Tex") Wilson, a former editor of the *Harvard Monthly* who had abandoned poetry for painting and was already well ensconced in Village life, invited Cummings to share a flat. Soon Cummings, too, had joined the ranks of several hundred unknown artists who prowled the Village from their lofts and cold-water walk-ups. Dos Passos envied his friends there who did not have to go anywhere else to prove themselves. Wilson was already signing his paintings (when he signed them at all) "Winslow Wilson" and Dos Passos surmised that he would be recognized eventually for his stunning portraits and seascapes. He was convinced that Cummings, too, was assured a reputation as a painter and saw Dudley Poore as the best poet of the lot from Harvard who aspired to a career in letters.

Dos Passos believed that he, too, could thrive creatively if he was in physical proximity to people who valued the expression of ideas more than the dull accounting of personal experiences. Although he knew well the need to retreat to his room (or wherever the writing area might be), he also had to emerge often to be with people. Had he had his friends near him during his summer in Virginia, he might have taken pleasure in staying on there indefinitely. When elsewhere, he thought longingly of returning to the farm; yet once there and without a companion against whom he might bounce ideas, he was impatient to be gone. He realized, too, that having completed four years of accountability to his Harvard professors, he was ready to be his own person for a change, but so long as his father was alive, he would have to play the game of compromise as best he could.

Before leaving for Spain, Dos Passos wrote Rumsey Marvin: "I really am interested in architecture—and I think the grinding study necessary will be good for my lazy and undisciplined soul." The boost he needed was a letter from Herbert Croly with a check enclosed: "I am sorry to have delayed so long in giving you a decision about your manuscript entitled 'Against American Literature.' I am glad to say, however, that it is accepted and is likely to be published next week." Dos Passos could hardly wait to inform Marvin: "I've finally broken into print. Next week or the week after an essay of mine is coming out in The New Republic—they are paying thirty bones for it. My value has risen 100% in my own estimation. I already (since this morning) look upon myself as an established light of literature. It is with great difficulty I keep from stopping people on the street and telling them what a charming magazine The New Republic is."

His departure for Europe aboard the *Espagne* could not have been more splendidly heralded had he been escorted to his ship by a fleet of clanging fire engines. Instead, he walked quietly out of his father's house, a large portmanteau in one hand and a copy of *The New Republic* of October 14, 1916, grasped firmly in the other. Dos Passos thought it fitting that he had turned his public face from American literature on the same date he was departing the country as well. He had had enough of the American scene for a while. "I did not care to wait to bid adieu with hands and handkerchief so we kissed and parted an hour before he started," John R. wrote Mary Harris that night.

> From my office window I could see her go down the bay—a noble ship! The air is full of rumors of submarines . . . [but] I would as soon tried to restrain an angry lion from seizing its prey as to have protested against Jack's going. It is his destiny! . . . He is out of the nest. . . . A nobler boy—a more completely educated character—a finer scholar—never went forth. . . . He is his own guide now—and I am alone! Well! What of it? This is living—the branch has broken from the tree and goes to plant itself in a foreign soil.

John R. sent his housekeeper—and now his confidante—the article in *The New Republic* and predicted that his son would make "many more dollars and much fame." Again he mused upon their leave-taking. "His conduct was beautiful. He walked out of the door with me as if he were going for a stroll. We had no regrets to express to each other, and no sighs were made. It was simply a kiss and an au revoir." It was John R.'s last embrace of his son. Three months later, he was dead.

8

Winter in Castile, 1916

My life is a mad scramble after a bus I never catch, and juggling oranges the while!

Dos Passos to Rumsey Marvin
Madrid, 12 December 1916

The tune "I Didn't Raise My Boy to Be a Soldier" resounded again and again over the radio in the United States during the fall of 1916 as domestic forces for and against war squared off against one another in the shadow of the November elections. "Preparedness!" was the cry of the country, and being a soldier was part of it, although "being prepared" did not necessarily mean going to war, insisted proponents of the policies of President Woodrow Wilson. Military camps sprang up first in the Northeast as a result of what was now being viewed as an international crisis, and college deans began instituting courses in military science. At Harvard alone some eight hundred men enrolled in the initial program. Third-year students signed up for duty in the new military camp for officers at Plattsburgh, New York, where Yale and Princeton sent their budding officers, attended summer encampment, and returned to their classes in the fall as seniors. Recruitment officers were on hand in June to sign up a fresh batch before they could be lured by worldly affairs into other arenas. There was snob appeal among Ivy League men to claim their places among the *crème de la crème* of military preparedness, but Dos Passos' friends at Harvard steered clear of any involvement that was not pacifist in sentiment and commitment. Dos Passos was disappointed when he heard that Edmund Wilson, whom he had met at Princeton, was an officer-trainee at Plattsburgh during the summer of 1916, but rejoiced that he had had the good sense to get out after three months. In the fall Wilson launched his professional literary career as a reporter for the New York *Evening Sun.*

Dos Passos' father himself could have written the lyrics to "I Didn't Raise My Boy to

Be a Soldier." As he saw it, it was a simple equation. To be a soldier was to be dead. John R. was convinced that it was a matter of time before the United States was drawn into the war. Only a miracle could keep America from sending troops to foreign shores. The President insisted that strict neutrality be maintained no matter what happened on the European front, and industrialists hammered their plea to the people that maintaining diplomatic relations with Germany was vital to the nation's economy. Neutral countries were convinced that the war could not be won by either side but would end in a negotiated peace.

John R. believed that his son would be safe in Spain. The towering Pyrenees and the Castilian spirit of "live and let live" insured that the Iberian people would remain neutral, he reasoned. Alfonso XIII had been fiercely insistent on remaining neutral as a means of playing peacemaker for the entire Western world. Wilson had similar ideas, but conditions soon evolved to make him change his country's stance to armed neutrality, a pendulum that began to swing in October 1916 when the European front shifted to the shoals of the United States itself. Just five days before the *Espagne* left port with Dos Passos aboard, a single German U-boat raider that had ridden anchor in Newport only hours earlier sent torpedoes into a fleet of merchant ships off Nantucket, then headed for the safety of the open sea. Six freighters bearing British, Dutch, and Danish flags sank while American sailors worked frantically to pluck some two hundred survivors from lifeboats and wreckage. Until now Kaiser Wilhelm had honored his pledge not to attack any neutral vessel, but a crisis was on the horizon.

Wilson tried to live up to his campaign promise to keep America out of war, but his position became untenable when marauding submarines partook of the hospitality of American ports, then intercepted foreign merchant ships bearing essential imports and exports. Passenger liners of neutral countries were assured that they might continue their runs without interference, but the *Espagne* was headed for Bordeaux, where floating mines had been spotted in the harbor. Had the imperial family of Franz Josef of Austria not been a major stockholder of the French line under which the *Espagne* sailed, John R. would not have allowed his son aboard. Even so, eighty passengers canceled their reservations after the U-boat incident off Nantucket.

On both ends of the crossing, the *Espagne* ran without lights, its portholes muffled. Passengers slept in their clothes, and some in life preservers, yet the voyage itself was uneventful. Upon arrival in Bordeaux, Dos Passos confessed to Rumsey Marvin that he had traversed the ocean "in a coma:" "I just lay around and looked at the sea and felt the damp caressing breath of it and sort of melted into it." The letters he intended to write, the reading he had hoped to do, the poems he might have completed—all suffered the same torpor. His very being seemed in limbo; he had turned his back on his former life and a new one was still beyond reach.

Dos Passos had boarded his ship on Estlin Cummings' twenty-second birthday, and he regretted not being on hand to help him celebrate. Cummings was in New England at the time for the marriage of their classmate, James Sibley Watson. The weddings of Dos Passos' friends depressed him, so he did not mind missing that. "A friend married is a friend lost," he wrote Rumsey Marvin upon hearing of Watson's plans to marry Hildegarde Lassell. Whether or not he approved of the bride had nothing to do with his disappointment. He thought Watson's wife was charming, ethereal, artistically talented, and brilliant—all fetching traits—but because friends were such "damnably rare commodities," he told Marvin, he preferred them without the infringement of a wife. He was not bothered when Scofield Thayer got married. In the spring of 1916 Thayer took Elaine Orr to Cambridge to introduce her to his friends. He wanted them to be comfortable with his fiancée, before the wedding. It proved a strategic move on Thayer's part because his friends became enamored of her. She in turn did everything possible after the marriage to make Thayer's friends a part of their daily lives and otherwise support the old relationships.

Years later, Dos Passos remembered Elaine Orr as "the Blessed Damozel, the fair, the lovable, the lily maid of Astolot. . . . She seemed the poet's dream." Cummings himself fell in love with Thayer's bride and eventually married her. In reminiscing about those years, Dos Passos recalled that "those of us who weren't in love with Cummings were in love with Elaine." Cummings' biographer, Richard S. Kennedy *(Dreams in the Mirror,* 1980), commented upon the "sexual coloration" of the *Harvard Monthly* staff and the friends who gathered about them later in New York:

> Only one of them, Stewart Mitchell, was an overt homosexual. Nevertheless, an innocent homoeroticism marked their devotion to each other: their intense loyalty when a friend was in need, their eager promotion of a friend's artistic career, and their genuine enjoyment of each other's company. Their heterosexual drives were strong but they seemed still to be outgrowing a sexual immaturity brought about, to a great extent, by the repressions of the American home and church and by the ethos of the boys' school and men's college, where the friendship of young fellows together, is the basis of life and any attention to women is a secondary matter, even a diversion. Elaine [Orr] provided a sisterly presence for these young men.

In the late summer of 1916, when Rumsey Marvin wrote that he was in love, Dos Passos replied that he sometimes fell "in love with a face or a glint of light on hair or an intonation of the voice," but that the "conventional fluffiness of respectable mating" did not attract him. "It rather spoils things," he added. "If one is feeling well and properly in tune with earth and sky, he is already in love with every man, woman, and child in sight." Three months short of his twenty-first birthday when he sailed for Spain, Dos Passos was still the stammering, bashful dreamer who probably lacked firsthand carnal knowledge of a woman. A number of his friends and classmates anticipated visiting a house of prostitution for their sexual christening upon reaching their majority, but they would have been surprised had he harbored such thoughts. Dos Passos had no concrete sense of what coming of age might mean for him other than his vague ambitions for a literary career, yet his antennas were out as always and waiting only to be fine-tuned to whatever external stimuli lay within his wavelength. He recognized, too, that it took more than good intentions and willpower to set his coiled mainspring into motion.

Again and again throughout his winter in Spain, Dos Passos reproached himself for his inability to accomplish what he had laid out in his mind. He acknowledged his frustration to Rumsey Marvin:

> Oh dear, I have so much to tell you that it brings on a sort of paralysis. Things to be said jostle and tread on each other's heels. . . . I've been trying unsuccessfully to write all the morning

and have got into a most irritated state. It always makes me furious how slowly I turn out things. . . . You talk about pressed for time, I never have a moment. It is strange: with nothing to do but things I want to extremely badly, I have an awful time getting anything actually completed. I find myself frittering frightfully. I guess I shall have to turn over some new leaves or bust from sheer desperation.

Dos Passos was taking Spanish literature and language at the Centro de Estudios Históricos in Madrid, where many fellow students practiced their English on him. He improved his Spanish similarly and for a time helped a sociologist on a translation of one of John Dewey's books in exchange for Spanish lessons. In letters to his father and friends back home, Dos Passos admitted that his knowledge of Spanish was almost nil, but that it was amusing to try to make himself understood. By mid-November he was "jabbering at every chance a confused tongue" of his own invention that people even understood. "If not rattled too fast, I can understand spoken Spanish fairly well," he boasted to his father. Going to the theater in Madrid as often as possible helped considerably, too, he said.

"This is the most musical city I've ever been in. Everything jingles and rings," Dos Passos wrote John R., who delighted in his son's descriptions of Madrid. Their letters arrived in spurts because of the irregular departures of steamships from both sides of the Atlantic. "What letters! 'Letters from Madrid' by Monsieur Singe, deluxe edition, price five dollars!" exclaimed John R. upon receipt of several in November. He referred to them as "books": "Another book—'Reflections of a Young Man in Madrid'—by the same author has just arrived. Another, 'An Architect's Impressions of the Buildings of Madrid.' That will be enough for the first three months—otherwise you'll produce more books than Voltaire."

Almost everything Dos Passos saw went into letters and his literary diary. He also began to write poems once more. From the window of his pension just off the Puerta del Sol, the largest and noisiest square in the city, he looked down upon young girls selling tuberoses and wreaths to cover tombs of relatives and lovers on All Souls' Day, on shawl-muffled women with their market baskets stuffed with green vegetables, on black-robed priests crossing to buy red sausages or tripe at a shop on the corner, on a youth who ground coffee at his cart beside a wizened man blowing coals until mocha-colored smoke curled lazily into the sky, on a milkman with his pony *slung with silvery metal jars,* on an old woman without teeth whose roasted chestnuts were displayed invitingly *like marriageable daughters,* and on four blind musicians who scraped *with violin and flute the interment of a song.* Such scenes abounded in Dos Passos' literary jottings during his stay in Madrid.

Immersed as he was in the sights and sounds of Madrid, he gulped down Cervantes, Calderón, and Lope de Vega in great quaffs, then shifted to the contemporary man of letters Unamuno, or to Juan Ramón Jiménez, a poet with whom he had tea one afternoon (later, Jiménez won a Nobel Prize in literature). Dos Passos pored over the picaresque novel Lazarillo de Tormes and the fiction of Pío Baroja, a Basque novelist who reminded him of Gorki. He recognized in the stirring novels of Blasco-Ibáñez—who took his text from the world at large—that here was a kindred spirit of Whitman. When he discovered Antonio Machado, the "poet of Castile," he began to translate him. He also admired the

"Catalan poet," Joan Maragall i Gorina, and struggled to capture his nuances and rhythms in English. The contemporary playwright Jacinto Benavente y Martínez also held his attention. Perhaps his favorite poet was Jorge Manrique, best known for a single epic poem upon the death of his father. For days after discovering Manrique's poetry, Dos Passos carried the slim volume in his pocket. There was no apparent order to his reading. He jumped back and forth across the centuries at will.

As Dos Passos talked with new friends, read, attended the theater, and sought out Spain's art treasures, he was struck repeatedly by how remarkably layered was its culture. He wrote Marvin that a "wonderful thing about Spain" was its anachronisms:

> I've never been anywhere where you so felt the strata of civilization—Celt-Iberians, Phoenicians, Greeks, Romans, Moors and French have each passed through Spain and left something there, alive. Roman Italy is a sepulchre. Roman Spain is living actuality in the way a peasant wears his manta, in the queer wooden plows they use, in the way they sacrifice to the dead—not consciously, of course—but with a thin veil of Catholicism. The pottery you see in the markets is absolutely Greek in shape. The music and the dances are strangely Semitic and Phoenician Moorish—even the little cakes in the pastry shops are Moorish, oriental—the sort of things odalisques with henna-stained fingers eat in The Arabian Nights. It's the most wonderful jumble: the peaceful Roman world; the sadness of the Semitic nations, their mysticism; the grace—a little provincialized, a little barbarized—of a Greek colony; the sensuous dream of Moorish Spain; and little yellow French trains and American automobiles and German locomotives—all in a tangle together!

Dos Passos was discomfited when his father asked about his plans to enroll in architecture at the University of Madrid. He was already taking a drawing course and sketching courtyards, squares, marketplaces, and cathedrals and marveled at the seemingly infinite variety of architectural styles. He was more interested in drawing people than buildings, however. When Rumsey Marvin urged him to "talk architecture" in his next letter, Dos Passos replied that he would try to be more learned about Spanish cathedrals someday, but meanwhile, his architecture consisted only of drawing plaster casts for two hours each day. "And a jolly mess I've made of it so far!" he added. Dos Passos was bored when his drawing instructor set him to copying a Florentine bust. He thought it ridiculous to spend his time copying Italian Renaissance art when he had all of Spain from which to draw.

An activity he enjoyed especially was setting out early to tramp the countryside with a companion or climbing high into the long brown range of the Sierra de Guadarrama, which sliced through the two plains comprising "Old and New Castile." From the summit he glimpsed Segovia across the ruddy yellow plain to the north, and to the south he gazed upon a flaxen-colored plain that faded into the mists at the foot of snow-crested mountains behind Toledo. The view was incredible, and he liked to linger long enough to watch the sun drop behind the mountains before making his way back into the city in the gloaming, his favorite time outdoors. "I've never seen such sunsets," recalled Dos Passos in his own twilight years, having watched suns drop from the sky almost all over the world. In his memoirs, he wrote: "They stir up your soul the way a cook stirs a pot of broth but with what a golden spoon."

Dos Passos had no trouble finding *simpático* companions eager to match his stride wherever he chose to go. Carlos Posada, a law student, could hardly wait to lay aside his briefs to accompany his new friend into the Sierra de Guadarrama for a weekend of hiking and mountain climbing. Another was José ("Pepe") Giner, "a black-bearded little man" who led Dos Passos to art treasures that had never found their way into the museums and galleries of Madrid. Still a third companion was José ("Pepe") Robles, a lean, handsome youth with whom he struck up a conversation one night on a third-class coach returning to Madrid from Toledo. Like Dos Passos, Robles was a student at the Centro de Estudios Históricos. Soon they, too, were hiking companions.

Winter had already set in when two Harvard classmates, Roland Jackson and Lowell Downes, showed up. By now, he had moved to the university's Residencia de Estudiantes. Jackson and Downes had come to tramp the provinces of Spain while they sorted out what to do about the war. Jackson was certain that military conscription would go into effect soon and planned to enlist in the artillery instead of being drafted. His father, a Denver judge, wanted him to go to law school, but the youth was more inclined to follow the example of Helen Hunt Jackson (his father's sister), whose social consciousness was demonstrated through her pen in such novels as *A Century of Dishonor* and *Ramona*. Roland Jackson did not want to write law briefs or books, but music. His dream was to help unite the world through new and startling music. Meanwhile, he would fight if necessary, he conceded.

Dos Passos was pleased to see his Harvard chums. Although he had liked them since their meeting during freshman orientation, he did not get to know them well until they combed Madrid together. Each morning he maintained a ritual of classes and writing, having thrown off his lethargy through new companions, then met Jackson and Downes after the siesta for an evening of dinner, music, or the theater. The Spanish people loved the theater and revered their playwrights even more than their poets. Dos Passos resolved in Spain that he, too, would someday try his hand at writing plays.

Perhaps his most heady experience to date occurred in the company of Jackson and Downes one evening when they called for him at his lodging and they strolled together to the Café Oro del Rhín on the Plaza de Santa Ana not far from the theater they were to attend after dinner. They feasted on roast pigeon and downed stein after stein of dark beer while debating countless topics over treacly German music. Dos Passos read them a poem by Jorge Manrique that he had been carrying about with him and knew much by heart. Manrique was a Castilian nobleman who shut himself up in his great dust-colored mansion after the death of his father and did not emerge until he had re-created "the rhythms of death sweeping like a wind over the world." Dos Passos recited to his friends: *"Nuestras vidas son los ríos/que van a dar en la mar/que es el morir* [Our lives are rivers on their way to the sea which is death]." The poem thrilled him as he created in his mind's eye the entire tableau of the old man's death and of his son who had written furiously night and day behind locked doors until the epic was complete.

The trio debated that night what they were doing in Spain, and Dos Passos asked: "Why anywhere else than here?" It was reminiscent of the jailed Thoreau's answer to Emerson's "Why are you here?"

"Waldo, why are you not here?" Thoreau replied. Dos Passos recalled, too, his vow to Rumsey Marvin not to return from Spain until he had "come to grips with old lady adventure—sort of a search for the Holy Grail." It seemed to Dos Passos this very night in Madrid that he was about to catch a glimpse of the grail he sought. As the trio walked across the plaza from the café to the theater, flushed now by the alcohol as well as by the stirring rhythms of Manrique's poem, they spoke of death and of how the Spanish people knew how to die and to honor their dead, and of how they also knew how to live. If only his own people could be jarred out of their paralyzed existences, there might be hope for America yet, Dos Passos reasoned. Manrique had the right idea. There was dignity in death, but death gained after a life well lived, not in the senseless killings on the raging battlefields of Europe. Would that his own countrymen could learn to live like the noble and free-spirited souls encountered all around him, he voiced to his friends.

When they stepped into the darkened theater to watch a famous Andalusian gypsy, Pastora Imperio, perform her "Dance of Death," it seemed to Dos Passos as though her snapping fingers were re-creating the rhythms of Manrique's poem. Pastora Imperio was "the last of the great flamencos." She whirred fast, "like dry locusts in a hedge on a summer day," her graceful, full-bosomed body coiling and uncoiling with sudden rushes and pauses that caught one's blood and froze it "suddenly still like the rustling of a branch in silent woods at night." Never had Dos Passos witnessed such a stunning combination of sound and movement, he said. "Manrique's poem and Pastora's dancing were the two greatest experiences of my life," he proclaimed in retrospect many years later. Thoughts and feelings that had previously danced only on air were about to take malleable form, he realized that night. It was the beginning of his idyll of Spain, *Rosinante to the Road Again* (1922).

The book Dos Passos conceived depicted Telemachus, the quester, and his sensuous, carefree companion, Lyaeus, who rambled the byways of Spain in search of "a gesture," which he saw embodied in Pastora's dance and the Andalusian life from which it sprang. To Dos Passos, *lo flamenco* was "the tough swaggering gesture, the quavering song well sung, the couplet neatly capped, the back turned to the charging bull, the mantilla draped with exquisite provocativeness. . . . It was neither work nor getting ready to work. . . . it was making the road so significant that one needs no destination." He realized the night Pastora danced that the Spanish picaro knew how to live, that his dusty road was paved with adventure because he himself had eyes, ears, a nose, and stout heart with which to ingest it.

When the music at the German beer hall suddenly seemed too cloying for their inflamed spirits, Dos Passos challenged his companion to set out on the road with him that very evening. Roland Jackson declared that it was much too late for him to venture into the Spanish countryside and returned to his pension, but Dos Passos and Downes strode out into the cold and brilliantly clear, moon-drenched night. Toledo lay before them, and Dos Passos suggested that they walk all the way. Seldom were they alone on the road. At sunup they overtook jingling carts piled high with produce, exchanged greetings with donkey boys, and inspected the panniers brimming with bright green lettuces, purple cabbages, and glistening red bell-shaped peppers. Strangers they were never to see again proffered them the hospitality of the road. It was not today, they kept telling themselves. It was three hundred years ago and the Andalusian countryside of Don Quixote and Sancho Panza. Dos Passos took his text from Cervantes. He, too, tilted at windmills, read tales of knight-errantry, rode his own Rosinante in a confusing and often futile attempt to redress all manner of grievances. It seemed to him that he was both Don Quixote, mystic dreamer, and Sancho Panza, fat-bellied sensualist—there was no middle ground.

A few miles short of Toledo—at the train depot of Torrejón de Ardoz—the two footsore companions from America paused to rest and to debate whether their destination should be Toledo or if they should simply press on without chart or compass, their direction the whim of the moment. Almost at once—their decision still hanging—Dos Passos remembered a dinner engagement at the American Embassy back in Madrid that very evening. He knew no one at the embassy, but the invitation was the result of one of his father's letters of introduction. The anticipation of spending that night in formal attire with someone he did not know and had no real desire to know was worse than being strung up by his thumbs, he reasoned, yet he had committed himself and he must go. Life was deterministic, he lamented. Nonetheless, the events of the last eighteen hours had left upon him an "imperishable glow."

At dinner with his fellow Americans at the embassy that night, Dos Passos collided once more with events that had been making news in his country since his departure. His father had kept him abreast of political news, but they were at odds concerning presidential candidates. The battle was between labor and capital, contended John R. Labor endorsed Woodrow Wilson for a second term. To John R., labor and socialism were synonymous. Charles Evans Hughes, the Republican candidate, opposed the eight-hour workday signed into law by Wilson in 1916, as did John R., who stumped on Hughes's behalf at every opportunity. "It is not that I am against government setting the hours and wages," John R. insisted in a fiery campaign speech in New York City. "Labor must understand that it is not the whole country, or the whole world. . . . Socialism should be dealt with here and elsewhere without gloves. . . . Not a single man in our country seems to know or appreciate where we are drifting." He was furious when he saw huge advertisements placed by Wilson's Business Men's League in leading newspapers throughout the country just before the election:

YOU ARE WORKING—NOT FIGHTING!
ALIVE AND HAPPY—NOT CANNON FODDER!
WILSON AND PEACE WITH HONOR?
or
HUGHES WITH ROOSEVELT AND WAR?

Theodore Roosevelt's support of Hughes had become a liability. *The New Republic,* the New York *Times,* the New York *Evening Post, The Nation, Pearson's Magazine,* the Scripps newspapers, and a number of other leaders of independent thought shifted suddenly from Hughes to Wilson. Even so, the American people went to bed the night of November 8 convinced that Hughes had won, but awoke to the President's reelection, Wilson having garnered a majority of both popular and electoral votes.

Dos Passos was elated by Wilson's victory. "I was mad for Wilson, the Peacemaker." John R. insisted that with Wilson elected, the world was going to the devil, "as you know —being his advocate!" In another, he jabbed: "Your friend, the President, evades the rules of international law. He does what he likes. As in the case of Mexico, everything he does aggravates the war instead of working against it." Dos Passos eventually saw his father's side of the matter. Each move the President took after his reelection brought the nation closer to the brink of war.

On January 14, 1917, Dos Passos celebrated his twenty-first birthday with friends in Madrid after a two-week hiking trip through southern and eastern Spain. "The great day has come. My Jack is his own master," John R. wrote him that morning. "He is free. He is free from enslavement to his father. He's free to climb a tree and to do anything—even to pay his own bills. I salute you!" John R.'s letters to his son in Spain abounded with such questions as "How are you? Where are you today? . . . How did you spend Christmas? . . . How did you celebrate your birthday? . . . Did you get my cable? . . . What do you want me to do with the bulky manuscript that arrived today with no instructions? . . . Did you hear about the bombardment of Funchal? You know I still have relatives and friends there. . . . What are you reading? . . . Wouldn't it be lovely to be at the farm together? . . . How is your Spanish coming? . . . When will you start your architecture course? . . . When are you coming home?" It vexed him that it took seven or eight weeks from the time he plied his son with questions until he had answers.

His feelings were ambivalent regarding his son's return to the United States. He yearned to see him, but was afraid for him to risk another crossing. The ocean had become more perilous upon the Kaiser's announcement of a blockade covering most of the shipping lanes from the North Atlantic to the Mediterranean Sea. By now Germany was attacking without warning any neutral vessel that strayed from the narrow safety zones. According to a bulletin in late 1916, one American passenger ship a week was to be allowed to pass unmolested from New York to Falmouth. John R. was afraid that once his son was twenty-one, he would do something foolish and deadly, such as join the ambulance service in France and get himself killed.

He was also disturbed by painful attacks of gout in his feet that winter. One morning he could barely pull his shoes over his swollen feet and found it impossible to walk to the office, a habit he was reluctant to abandon even at age seventy-three. His son Louis prevailed upon him to be driven during the height of his misery, but John R. crouched in his seat and removed his hat so that he would not be seen along the way or be recognized alighting from the vehicle. He vowed later that he would rather stay home than venture into an automobile again. People who knew him concluded that there was not a vainer man his age in the entire city. He still kept a mirror, comb, and mustache wax at the office with which he groomed himself periodically, and he had frequent engagements with his manicurist and barber. "A gay dog," his friends called him behind his back. According to George Bricka, the husband of a niece, he was such a womanizer that Louis was reluctant to introduce him to his new fiancée, Grace Quinn. "She was twenty-two and beautiful. Louis worried that his father might try to woo her for himself," said Bricka. Some thought that John R. flirted outrageously with Louis' first wife," he added. "John R. never let being married himself interfere with his appreciation of an attractive woman," observed the daughter of his confidential secretary.

John R. wrote his son Jack on January 9 of his doctor's assurance that his heart, stomach, and blood pressure were satisfactory, but that he was still suffering the discomforts of his latest gout attack. "I shall try to stir his ambition before our next session," he joked. Dos Passos heard nothing of his father's health until January 27, when a cable announced that he was dangerously ill. Only hours later the death message itself arrived. Stunned and bereaved, Dos Passos pondered his next move. His father's words resounded in his ears: "The great day has come. My Jack is his own master. He is free. He is free from enslavement to his father. He's free to climb a tree and to do anything. . . . I salute you!"

9

Death of a Father—Alone in New York, Winter and Spring 1917

It gives you a queer catching of the breath to find yourself suddenly alone in the world—you see, my father died yesterday in New York. . . . It is silly to make a fuss about anything as obvious and humdrum as death—except perhaps to be glad when people you love die suddenly, without the long sordidness of disease.

> John Dos Passos to Rumsey Marvin
> Residencia de Estudiantes, Madrid
> 30 January 1917

There was no question of the funeral's being delayed until Dos Passos could get home. Had he been able to book passage immediately, it still would have taken two weeks to reach the States. He dreaded the scene awaiting him: "the tinsel grief, the red eyes and black crepe . . . the silliness of people making themselves miserable because they think they ought to." It was life that had been important to his father, not death. Like Pastora, the flamenco dancer, John R. had known how to live. For as long as his son had known him, his heart seemed filled with the gusto of life. No matter how much one might have disagreed with him, there was little quarrel with the fact that most of his actions were motivated by good intentions.

After the shock of the death message subsided, Dos Passos turned first to Rumsey Marvin to share his feelings:

In time of crisis there are just two things to do: sit on the stairs and weep, or send cablegrams. I have been doing the latter and feel—I suppose—comforted. . . . Only one feels as if all one's protection against the knocks and pains of life had been pulled away, for one hasn't much except the love of others to retire into. It's like a man who has been walking hours and hours through a blizzard trying to reach a tiny light that promises warmth and food and rest from the straining exertion—and suddenly the light has gone out.

On February 10 he wrote Arthur McComb that he was trying to get home to America, but dreaded the "black-gloved relations and the discreet shuffle of initiative parchment—wills and all abominations" that would greet him. Once matters were settled at home, he intended to return to Spain for a few months to round out his ideas of it, he added.

Because of the German blockade prohibiting ships from leaving any port except Falmouth (traffic had also been halted in American harbors in an attempt to preserve the country's neutrality), Dos Passos was unable to leave Bordeaux until some three weeks after his father's funeral. The SS *Touraine* was the first ship to leave from a southern European port since the imposing of the blockade. On February 20, 1917, Dos Passos began a letter to Rumsey Marvin:

> The mouth of the Gironde is full of shipping—steamers, sailing vessels, waiting, I suppose, to get up their courage to go out. The *Touraine* is an old, slow, and rather uncomfortable steamer and I imagine will roll like a log. Strange to say, she is full—first class, second class, and steerage. Last night we lay with all lights out—and tonight passengers are not to be allowed to go to bed and must sit with clothes and life-preservers on, all ready to take to the boats.

The next day he added: "I did go to bed—and slept undisturbed by mines or submarines —and today I believe we are out of danger. You can't imagine how amusing it was to see all the passengers roaming about with life-belts on in the dark." Still at sea, Dos Passos added a few more lines on March 2:

> Fire Island Light is now astern of us, and after a trip of thirteen days we are pretty nearly done in. . . . Everything must be in wild excitement about war. The latest rumor is that a secret treaty has been made between Mexico and Germany deeding Mexico "the three southern provinces of the United States"—whatever that means. But it's too absurd even for German diplomacy; so it probably springs from the fecund brain of a New York reporter. . . . Oh Rummy, I dread the arrival in New York. I wish people wouldn't make such a fuss about the most ordinary things like death and birth and marriage. There is enough incidental pain connected with them anyway without encumbering them with conventions and childish trivialities.

Dos Passos arrived at his paternal home on March 4 and confronted one of the first of the conventional trappings associated with his father's death and burial. John R. was one of two thousand New Yorkers who died of pneumonia and other respiratory infections in a single week. Area deaths had been high throughout January, but numbers rose at an alarming rate after a blizzard from the northwest blanketed the city for days and kept people shut up within germ-ridden quarters. Some took ill from prolonged exposure to the cold. Knowing his father, Dos Passos assumed that he had not allowed himself to stay indoors despite his gout-swollen feet. According to Cyril dos Passos, he had been at the office when stricken and died at home the next day. The same page in the New York *Times* that had carried the health department's report of record deaths also carried John R.'s obituary. A 10:30 A.M. mass was said on January 30 at St. Patrick's Cathedral, followed by a private interment. "Kindly omit flowers," the notice concluded. The obituary also presented considerable biographical data, since John R. had stature as an international figure. He had thrown his "remarkable talents into service for his country and fellow man as a soldier in the Pennsylvania state militia" at the onset of the War Between the States and had been wounded in the battle of Antietam. Recognized both in Europe and the United States as one of the most prominent lawyers of his time, John R. was a friend of statesmen, presidents, and kings—of the renowned and the unrenowned—a good and generous man who would be missed by all who knew him. As expected, the obituary also listed the principal survivors of the deceased: "Both were at his bedside when he died: his son, Louis Dos Passos, who resided at 18 East 56th Street, and his nephew and partner in the firm of Dos Passos Brothers, Cyril F. dos Passos." Of John R. Dos Passos, Jr., there was no mention.

A number of readers of the New York *Times* that day were doubtless puzzled by the omission of John R.'s second-born son and namesake from the obituary. Not for several years had Dos Passos been denied his paternity. John R. had been outrageously proud of his younger son, whom he saw destined to be "a bright and particular star in the firmament of literature." The two or three friends who knew of Dos Passos' illegitimacy knew also that his parents had finally married. They thought it strange that he should suddenly be eliminated now as a legitimate survivor. Being three thousand miles from his father's bedside at death was hardly cause for him to be denied now. Whatever the circumstances or sources of the death notice, the fact that Dos Passos was John R.'s son remained unaltered. His "queer catching of the breath" when he first found himself "suddenly alone in the world"—as he expressed it to Rumsey Marvin before leaving Spain—probably repeated itself more than once in the days following his return home. His half brother Louis drove him to Woodlawn Cemetery some twenty miles north of midtown New York to show him the grave site. The cemetery was known as "the resting place of the famous." John R. lay not far from headstones marking the graves of such men as Jay Gould, Admiral Farragut, General Archibald Gracie, Herman Melville, and Joseph Pulitzer. His first wife, Mary Hays Dos Passos, was buried next to him, and on the other side of Mary lay their first child, the unnamed daughter who had died at birth. The rest of the DeWitt Clinton Hays clan, one of the oldest and best-known families of New York City, were ranged about them.

There was something incongruous about John R.'s having been buried at Woodlawn Cemetery among his first wife's family, just as there was something amiss in the obituary that failed to acknowledge the existence of a child by his second wife. It was as though his life with Lucy Sprigg Madison and their love child—legitimatized by their marriage—had never existed. At the reading of the will his executors—his son Louis, his nephew Cyril, and his private secretary, Joseph Schmidt—reportedly discovered that John R. had left instructions for his body to be conveyed to Virginia aboard the *Gaivota* and interred beside his second wife, Lucy, in the old Yeocomico churchyard adjacent to their waterfront property. He also requested that his burial not be accompanied by long faces, dirges, or other signs of mourning; rather, he wanted his friends, neighbors, and family to come from far and wide as though the event was an after-Christmas barbecue or fox hunt. His funeral should be an occasion of feasting, music, and dancing—a final fling as the "Commodore" and generous friend of the people he had grown to love on the Northern Neck.

John R.'s New York relatives claimed no prior knowledge of such wishes. So far as they were concerned, the funeral mass at St. Patrick's and his interment in the Hays family plot were in accord with his position, as well as with his love of ritual. They gave him what they thought he wanted. John R.'s father had been a Roman Catholic (his mother, a Quaker); though Louis Dos Passos had been reared a Methodist, his mother's faith, he was reportedly in the process of becoming a Roman Catholic so that he could marry Grace Quinn, a devout Catholic whose help he sought in planning the funeral.

A sidelight on John R.'s religious fervor was heard in the eulogy by Henry Wollman delivered on May 3, 1917, before an impressive gathering of the New York County Lawyers Association: "Mr. Dos Passos was not actively affiliated with any church; yet every Sunday he was on his yacht, he called his crew around him and delivered a sermon to them." Wollman, a lawyer, knew the deceased personally and also had researched rather thoroughly the published records pertaining to his exemplary life, which had been dedicated to his family and his profession, but he either missed or chose to ignore a New York *Times* article published upon the reading of the will. In a brief news story of the appraisal of the John R. Dos Passos estate on March 7, *both* sons were acknowledged. Yet Wollman's eulogy declared: "Mr. Dos Passos for many years before his death was a widower. He and his son Louis, who was his only child, were just like two brothers, but the father always maintained that he was the younger brother." Surely some of his colleagues were aware of *both* sons, and no doubt one or two could have disputed the length of his widowerhood. John R. was a widower for only ninety days when he was between wives, and he was one again for almost two years before his own death. The same inaccuracies were repeated when Wollman's entire address was published in the July 1917 issue of *Case and Comment*.

The New York *Times* article of March 7 declared that the principal portion of the estate—valued at "about one million dollars"—divided equally between his sons, Louis Hays Dos Passos, of 18 East Fifty-sixth Street, and John R. Dos Passos, Jr., of 214 Riverside Drive. "The son Louis gets all his father's pictures and art objects and the other son receives his jewelry." Dos Passos was also left his father's clothes and his "miscellaneous library." Louis' actual portion included the rugs and furniture in his father's home and all the jewelry except two pieces specified for his half brother: John R.'s gold watch and his black scarf pin. Cash bequests included two thousand dollars for his niece, Annie Kelley (the daughter of John R.'s sister Fannie); two thousand dollars for his brother Joseph; two thousand five hundred dollars for Mary Harris "as a partial token for her unceasing and faithful services in my family." To Cyril dos Passos he left "the good will, name, and business of Dos Passos Brothers" and his law library. On March 9 the will was filed by the clerk of the court in Westmoreland County, Virginia. It had been signed, dated, and witnessed in New York City on August 5, 1916, scarcely five months before John R.'s death.

Though the facts of Dos Passos' welcome home by other members of his father's family were unknown by outsiders, there was probably considerable strain experienced by both half brothers. Instead of remaining under his paternal roof upon his return from Spain (where he had suggested that Rumsey Marvin write him next and where he habitually stayed when his father was alive), Dos Passos moved almost immediately to the home of his mother's sister, Mary Lamar Gordon (thus the Riverside Drive address in the *Times* article of March 7). Mrs. Gordon was the wife of James Riely Gordon, architect known through the East for his courthouse designs. Their only child was Lucy Virginia, who was three when her cousin was born. There were several other cousins, aunts, and uncles scattered about the country, but none whom he knew better (except Lois Sprigg, who lived in Washington). The Gordons were never fond of John R. because of his failure to marry Lucy until she was over fifty and had lost her health; moreover, they never admitted (unless to themselves alone) that the child Lucy reared as Jack Madison was, indeed, *her* child. As they saw it, "poor foolish Lucy" had devoted her life to rearing an abandoned offspring of one of John R.'s hapless mistresses. Mary Lamar Gordon did not talk about the nature of the long-standing relationship between her sister and John R. She avoided the word "lover," although one niece speculated that she was probably supportive of her sister's illicit romance because "Aunt Mary Lamar loved intrigue. As long as I can remember there was a lot of gossip about Aunt Lucy's involvement with 'Uncle John'; also, we were all told that 'Cousin Jack' was Aunt Lucy's *adopted* child, though none of us actually believed it," added Lois Sprigg Hazell many years later. When young Jack Madison was growing up—first in Europe, then in Washington, and later at Choate and Harvard—the more distant relatives had no idea he even existed. It was obvious from John R.'s obituary and eulogy that many others as well were unaware that he had a second son. Although Cyril dos Passos knew who "Master Jack" was before his parents married, he was close-mouthed about it, just as members of Lucy's family were. According to Cyril dos Passos, John R.'s private secretary was aware of the situation, too. But as Joseph Schmidt's daughter, Florence Schmidt de Bottari, said:

> A good private secretary doesn't talk about his employer's life, family, or business outside the office. What I know I've gleaned since 1917. Until World War I, I didn't know there was a J.R., Jr. The summer of 1917 (I was then a lower senior in college) I spent several weeks at Cintra (J. R. Sr.'s farm in Virginia) with my father, and with Louis Hays Dos Passos and Grace Quinn, who later became Louis' wife. My mother had remained in New York with my brother who was facing "the draft." They joined us later. On our way home, we—the Schmidts—stopped in Washington to visit the Robertsons. Mr. Robertson, known as <u>Scott</u>, had been the captain of J. R. Sr.'s boat. Mrs. Robertson talked much. Apparently her husband had passed on to her whatever he knew. Later, my mother gave up some information, learned not from father, but from Aunt Fannie Mitchell, J. R. Sr.'s sister.

Schmidt's daughter also remembered meeting James Madison in Virginia during the summer of 1917. Madison "drove his horse and buggy to Cintra [the farm] one day to pay us—the Schmidts—a visit." She was told that Madison lived at Cherry Grove, John R.'s estate that formerly had been the family home of Mary Ball, George Washington's mother. "I was unaware then that there was any family connection with James Madison," said Schmidt's daughter, who was surprised to learn that Madison was "the <u>other</u> half-brother."

Similarly, Louis Dos Passos did not tell his own children about the existence of his half brother Jack, or even about his father's second marriage. They first heard about it when they were almost grown, from their garrulous Irish nurse, Rose Mulligan. By this time, Mary Dyckman Dos Passos (born in 1920) and her brother John David (born in

1926) were living with their parents on Park Avenue, where Louis moved with his wife Grace several years after the settling of his father's estate (the old family home on East Fifty-sixth Street was torn down a few years later to make way for a multistory office building).

For young Dos Passos to have returned to his paternal home upon his father's death and discovered that he was once more an *unacknowledged* son—no matter what the circumstances—must have been a painful opening of an old wound that he had long since dismissed as having healed; it was a difficult time for his half brother Louis as well. The disposition of his father's estate as revealed by his will was probably an unexpected blow to Louis. Whereas the house at 18 East Fifty-sixth Street was what Dos Passos thought of as his *paternal* home, he also had a *maternal* home, a home he inherited upon his mother's death. On November 20, 1915, some six months after her death, John R. deeded over every other material possession associated with his second wife—except for the farm in Virginia—to *their* son. The document read:

> In consideration of one dollar and in fulfillment of a trust reposed in me by his mother I hereby sell, assign, transfer, and set over to John R. Dos Passos, Jr., all of the jewelry and precious stones contained in my box in the safe deposit vault in the above mentioned building [the American Security and Trust Company, Washington, D.C.] and all of the silverware, china, glass, and furniture of all description contained in the house belonging to John R. Dos Passos, Jr., at 1201 Nineteenth Street, N.W., Washington, D.C.

Now, upon John R.'s own death, his New York City home was to be shared—"share and share alike"—by *both* sons. Louis was offended and no doubt wondered what business his half brother had owning one house and half of another one when he had probably no intention of living in either one of them. Louis had been the dutiful son to his father, as well as to his mother, all these years. It may have rankled him, too, that it was the illegitimate, second son who had his father's good name. As the obedient, caring son, Louis had devoted himself to his mother, knowing full well his father's philandering habits. It was Louis who stayed at his mother's bedside when she lay dying, not his father, who was already on the high seas when she died. When John R. finally was free to marry Lucy, Louis continued to live in the family home. Here, too, his father lived during the week. John R.'s weekends were spent with his wife on the farm during the summers, and in the home he maintained for her in Washington during the winter months. While Dos Passos was traipsing over the countryside of Spain, his head spinning in the clouds with poetry and other self-indulgences, the gainfully employed son Louis was tending to business at home. Louis was secretary-treasurer of the American Krupp-System Diesel Engine Company in New York and had an interest in its sister corporation, the American Krupp Gun Company. Shortly after his father's death Louis became the chief representative of the German-based company. The disposition of his father's estate was difficult for Louis to accept, and relations continued to be taut between the half brothers for many years.

Dos Passos loathed details involving money; moreover, having relied all his life upon his father for letters of credit, letters of introduction (which created insufferable obligations in themselves, he lamented), instructions for the handling of most of his financial affairs, he had absolutely no business acumen. All he knew was that he wanted to separate himself now from such dealings as quickly as possible. On March 10, 1917—one week after his return home—he wrote to Rumsey Marvin:

> Apollonius of Tyana used to pray on entering a city that the wise might remain poor. There is something to be said for the idea. In fact I agree with him so much that it is with a certain joy and much amusement that I am watching the rapid evaporation of The Estate. It's rather grisly, isn't it, how soon a living man becomes nothing more than a collection of stocks and bonds and debts and real estate? Eventually I shall scrape up enough of the debris to keep the wolf from the door. . . . The annoying thing is that I can't do anything until the estate is settled and I am wasting a lot of time when I might be writing. At present I am living up here at my aunt's—but before long I shall find a room somewhere where I can stack my books and retire into monastic seclusion.

Mary Lamar Gordon volunteered to assist in handling his inheritance, since he was determined to return to Europe as soon as practicable. Mrs. Gordon was well intentioned, and he was grateful for the offer, but she had little business sense or practical experience in investing money or dealing with property. At least she was on the scene, which was more than he intended.

Meanwhile, Dos Passos wasted no time in taking the necessary steps to join the Norton-Harjes Ambulance Corps. He had been back in New York only four days when he submitted his application to Eliot Norton, whose brother Richard was director of the Red Cross Ambulance Service. How soon he could be inducted and trained as an ambulance driver was to depend upon funding for the all-volunteer program. On March 22, the Newport (Rhode Island) *News* confirmed that a gift of a quarter of a million dollars had been given by Robert W. Goelet of New York City so that two additional sections of the Norton-Harjes Ambulance Corps might be formed and sent to the European front. More than one hundred motor ambulances were already in operation. Goelet's gift stipulated that the full number—eighty men in all—be recruited, trained, and sent abroad together; moreover, they were to proceed directly to the front upon arrival in France. "We will sail in about a month," announced Norton, who already had a waiting list of applicants.

Years later, Dos Passos observed to Charles Norman, whose biography of Estlin Cummings *(e. e. cummings: The Magic Maker,* 1964) was in progress, that he "wanted to get into the ambulance service to see what the war was like." As an enthusiastic pacifist, he had "a horror of serving in the army." He also reasoned that with his myopic vision, ambulance duty was the only way he could approach the front. Dos Passos was certain that if he was not notified soon that his application for the Norton-Harjes Ambulance Corps was accepted, he would be drafted.

On April 6, 1917, headlines from the New York *Times* depicted the country poised on the brink of war. After a sixteen-hour debate, the House of Representatives voted 373 to 50 for war and requested three billion dollars and one million men to help carry it off. Upon the President's declaration of war on Germany, Dos Passos wrote Rumsey Marvin that he was trying to do three things at once: "enlist in the mosquito fleet, be an ambulance attendant, and get a job as an interpreter or something of the sort with the first expeditionary force. . . . Don't think that I've gone militarist or believe in conscription

—far from it. I merely want to see a little of the war personally—and, then too, I rather believe that the deeper we Americans go into it, the harder we put our shoulders to the muskets and our breasts to the bayonets, the sooner the butchery will stop." He was skeptical of getting into anything because of his eyes, he admitted, but was attempting to rid himself of various encumbrances, such as money, so that he would be ready if given the opportunity. Everything connected with the settling of his father's estate was distasteful. "I hate money more than ever. I feel like taking a cockle and script, giving my goods to the poor and my body to be burned, and making a pilgrimage to Jerusalem." One had to take some such step to "achieve freedom from utter asininity," he added. "A constant stripping process is needed before one can live naked and clean—in the full blast of experience." As he expressed it in his memoirs: "The executors of my father's estate tried to interest me in various propositions. But what use was an income to a man who expected to get killed within the year? Even if I did survive, the Revolution would sweep away stocks and bonds, landed interests, property rights. I signed a contract of sale on my mother's house in Washington . . . to raise some needed cash and let it go at that. 'Naked I came into the world' was to be my motto."

Most people who knew John R. assumed that there was considerable money in his estate. Though he made a great deal of money, he was a lavish spender; moreover, the upkeep of two women, his yacht, and three separate households with a son in each (including his stepson, James Madison), a situation that prevailed for much of his lifetime, had cost him dearly. On January 17, 1918, the New York *Times* reported that upon the estate's being probated and fully appraised, the adjusted gross figure was $195,738, and the net, $80,192. Stocks and bonds were reportedly worth $72,873, and claims outstanding against Dos Passos Brothers law firm totaled $22,000. The estate was still unsettled on July 19, 1919, when the New York *Times* announced that a reappraisal for transfer tax purposes was necessary because the appraiser of the case "declined to list among the debts of the estate a note of the American Krupp Gun Company for $102,927, which the decedent guaranteed; and also refused to allow a claim of $25,000 for legal expenses. The estate also objected to the appraisal values of certain stocks." Despite evidence to the contrary, rumors persisted for years that Dos Passos had rejected a million-dollar inheritance as an "aesthetic stumbling block."

Dos Passos wrote Rumsey Marvin in April 1917 that he was trying to get some work done while awaiting his acceptance in the Norton-Harjes Ambulance Corps. "I've been leading a terrifically uninteresting and unprofitable existence since I got back from Spain. Puttering about money matters and arranging my apartment—weird place. The furniture has not yet arrived so we sit on the floor on cushions and stretch out on Turkish rugs. . . . My Irishman—Wright McCormick—is taking one of the rooms of my floor, which has been officially named and christened the Labyrinth." Dos Passos had wasted little time moving from his aunt's home on Riverside Drive into a flat of his own at 15 East Thirty-third Street. He and Wright McCormick (who had been secretary of the *Harvard Monthly* when they met) shared the third floor of strangely connected rooms where their friends came to argue socialist doctrine and talk of revolution over wine and Turkish coffee. McCormick was a reporter for the New York *Times*. "Don't believe the New York Times," Dos Passos advised Marvin that spring. "You see, I live with a man who's on it and knows its inner workings. Believe rather the Call or the New Republic or the Ladies' Home Journal. I vow before Jehovah that half the ills of the country are caused by the fact that all educated and intelligent Americans believe the New York Times as if it were Direct Revelation—or Tablets found on a Mountain by a reputable Brigham Young." He said, too, that by the time he got back from the war Marvin would disown him. "I'll be so red, radical, and revolutionary. Did I tell you about sitting next to Emma Goldman's table in the cafe at the Brevort some time ago? It was wonderful—the people I was with knew lots of her myrmidons, and we were the outer circle of her glory. . . . She has a charmingly munchy fashion of eating sandwiches and patting her myrmidons on the head and kissing them in a motherly fashion."

Dos Passos wrote in his memoirs of his pacifist attitudes during this period and of his conviction that America's entrance into the war was only a means of prolonging a "futile massacre." He said that he and his housemate spent their spare time going to radical meetings:

> We protested night and day. We were carried away by a brilliant speech of Max Eastman's at a mass meeting in Stanford White's Madison Square Garden; we approved the shrill denunciations of Emma Goldman. We read each issue of *The Masses* damp from the press. My admiration for Woodrow Wilson had turned to virulent hatred. Conscription seemed a personal betrayal. The new freedom had become the new servitude. We signed petitions. We protested the declaration of war. . . . Bob La Follette, Gene Debs, Max Eastman were our heroes. . . . In Russia revolution had put an end to war. It was the red dawn of an era of peace, freedom and justice. The Russians were socialists. It was socialists who had taken action to stop the butchery. Suddenly I believed I was a socialist. Even then I think I marveled a little at the suddenness with which passionate convictions develop in the youthful mind. It was a contagion. In the spring of 1917 some people caught socialism the way others caught the flu.

These were heady times, and Dos Passos readily embraced the attitudes and vocabulary of radicalism. Whereas his incendiary remarks were voiced only in letters or to friends who talked revolution but did little about it, such left-wing liberals as Emma Goldman, Alexander Berkman, Max Eastman, Randolph Bourne, Floyd Dell, Michael Gold, Lincoln Steffens, Elizabeth Gurley Flynn, and countless others were speaking out in public, getting arrested, and declaring themselves conscientious objectors to the war and conscription. They were also declaiming their opinions in *The Masses* until the government banned it from the mails and indicted its editors for conspiring to obstruct the draft.

In a new introduction to a reissue of *One Man's Initiation: 1917,* his first novel, written some fifty years after the book's original publication date, Dos Passos spoke of his attitude when America first entered the war:

> Like a good many young Americans today I had convinced myself that war was the greatest evil. Though not old enough to vote in 1916 I had been all for Woodrow Wilson: "He kept us out of war." His declaration of war against the Central Powers almost immediately after being sworn in for a second term in the spring of 1917 was a bitter disappointment. In my disillusionment I began listening seriously to the Socialists. Their song was that all that was needed to abolish war was to abolish capitalism. By that time it was clear to every man of independent mind that the war was a senseless bloody massacre which served no purpose but to destroy the delicate fabric of civilization. Why shouldn't the working people, who had everything to lose

and nothing to gain from war and aggression, knit that fabric up again? We were young hotheads. We took to shouting all the warcries of the Socialist dogma.

His jeremiads became increasingly bitter the longer he stayed in New York. To Arthur McComb he observed that spring that his only hope was "in revolution—in wholesale assassination of all statesmen, capitalists, warmongers, jingoists, inventors, scientists; in the destruction of all the machinery of the industrial world, equally barren in destruction and construction. . . . I'm going to France with the Norton-Harjes Ambulance as soon as I can take a course in running a machine. . . . They say it takes eleven days to die of poison gas. And what of our beloved Russian Republic?" McComb replied that only in Russia "does the sacred flame burn brightly. There they have the courage to really revolutionize and only there (and in Germany) can one talk of peace."

Dos Passos' tone in his letters usually took on the hue of the person to whom he wrote. When writing to Dudley Poore, he was the "Renaissance gentleman" painting dainty word pictures of life as he envisioned it in the Norton-Harjes "gentleman's ambulance corps." Dos Passos urged Poore to join up with him so that they might venture together to Europe "to sniff the ocean, see Bordeaux, partake of its wines and chocolates and smell its smells . . . feel the delightful jog-jog, jog-jog, jog, jog, jog of a French railway . . . have a glimpse of Paris in June . . . then become brawny and muscular and mahogany-colored." Then they would seat themselves upon "piles of skulls" and discuss Changchow to our hearts' content while shells splash us with bits of gentlemen 'doing their bit.' . . . And best of all, the numbing influence of reality would purge our minds of the horror that steams like a deadly vapor from all the world."

Dos Passos made light of having to take a course in automotive operation and maintenance, but it vexed him to think that his whole involvement in the war was to be linked with a machine. Along with other perturbations, he had become increasingly antimechanistic during his few months at home. He also worried that his poor vision might trip him up in the end and keep him from qualifying for ambulance duty, no matter how capable he might be in the operation of a motor vehicle under normal conditions. Dos Passos had inherited his father's aversion to any substitution for pedestrianism except when traveling over great distances and had absolutely no curiosity regarding what went on under the hood of an automobile. With ambivalence he reported to an automotive training school in New York City in mid-May.

Though he spent considerable time in activities that fanned his radical embers or helped insure that he would be among the first Americans to proceed to the front (when he did leave, his ship was only two days behind the convoy bearing the first American combat troops to France), he continued to work daily at his avowed profession. Soon after his return from Spain, he wrote Rumsey Marvin that he did not know how long he would be able "to stand New York," but wanted to finish up what he was presently writing before doing anything else. The manuscript begun in Spain—which he referred to as his "novel thing"—was "The Dance of Death," a long work seeded by the flamenco dancer, Pastora. Another was an essay, "Young Spain," which Waldo Frank accepted for publication in the July issue of *The Seven Arts,* a short-lived magazine noted for its opposition to the "money cult of twentieth-century American life and aestheticism without revolution." "I just received $50 for an article on Spain for The Seven Arts—I feel quite a money-maker," Dos Passos boasted in early June. It was his second sale.

Dos Passos took pride in being a writer, but knew that it would be years before he could support himself by writing alone and was repelled by the idea of living off his father's estate. He did not want to sail to Europe with the Norton-Harjes Ambulance Corps as a charity case, however, or let his father's friend, Eliot Norton, know how little money was actually available from his inheritance (perhaps a face-saving move to protect his father's image); therefore, he decided to sell his maternal home in Washington. Relieving himself of the responsibility of the house was important, too, in keeping his resolution to live "naked and clean." Dos Passos had no difficulty finding a buyer. Mary Lamar Gordon, his aunt, volunteered that her friend, James Brown Scott, wanted to buy it. Scott was secretary of the Carnegie Endowment for International Peace. Upon his aunt's advice, Dos Passos met Scott in Washington and agreed to his proposal, to sell the house for six thousand dollars (in three installments over the next three years at 6 percent interest, payable semiannually). He named his aunt his "attorney in fact," which legally empowered her to act as his agent in subsequent financial transactions (until such power was revoked). He also turned over to her for safekeeping the jewelry he had been left by his mother and father. Once his father's estate was settled, Mrs. Gordon was to care for his portion of it and invest it or do with it as she saw fit on his behalf. In effect she had *carte blanche* to handle every facet of his affairs. "I have just sold part of my poor disputed inheritance. Uncles shake their heads and see the beginning of the process of 'running through'—and they all tremble for fear they'll have to support the black sheep when the process is concluded," Dos Passos wrote to Dudley Poore on May 8. In addition to buying Dos Passos' house, James Brown Scott offered to assist him by using his influence to help get him into the ambulance corps. Dos Passos never knew the extent of Scott's aid, but when he sailed for France in June, he carried a letter of introduction addressed to the "Diplomatic and Consular Officers of the United States of America in Great Britain and France" and signed by Robert Land, Secretary of State.

Dos Passos' candidacy for the "gentleman's ambulance corps" was also endorsed by his headmaster at Choate, George St. John, who wrote admiringly of his "sterling character, high ideals, and genuine ability." Norton, too, spoke on Dos Passos' behalf. Had Dos Passos remained in the United States for another month he might well have been arrested and prosecuted under the Espionage Act of June 15, 1917, which prohibited any evidence of disloyalty to the government. Speaking out against conscription, discouraging recruitment, or uttering or writing any disloyal or abusive language relative to the President's proclamation of war was a criminal offense.

Before leaving port aboard the SS *Chicago* on June 20, 1917, Dos Passos fired off two sternly worded missives that might have landed him in jail had they fallen into the wrong hands. To Arthur McComb he urged: "Read my letters carefully. I may try to transmit censorable news. Nagel—the name—will stand for chances of revolution and the psychological fringes thereof. I've heard that things are very near the breaking point in France." He also commented upon the twenty thousand petitions reportedly signed and in the registration booths of the Socialist party urging the repeal of the Selective Service Act of

1917. His postscript was a caricature of Elihu Root and Theodore Roosevelt hanging from the arc lights of Fifth Avenue while two stick figures labeled "Harvard Intelligencia" danced the "Carmagnole." He called his sketch "A Revolutionist's Vision of Fifth Avenue." To Rumsey Marvin he confessed: "I don't believe in the 'spiritual good' of war and I expect to have one hell of a time until I get accustomed to taking ambulance loads of pulverized people about."

10

One Man's Initiation, 1917

Where're we going, boys?
Oh, we're bound for the Hamburg show
To see the elephant and the wild kangaroo—
And we'll all stick together
In fair and foul weather—
For we're going to see the damn show through!

The men aboard the SS *Chicago* sang such rally-round-the-flag lyrics again and again. To Dos Passos, the entire crossing from New York to the mouth of the Gironde in southern France was one long song. The gentlemen-volunteers of the Norton-Harjes Ambulance Corps boarded their transport at the foot of West Fifteenth Street while a spirited band played Hawaiian music and throngs of *bon voyage* well-wishers danced in and out among the packing cases. Even the winches sang as the last of the supplies and two long guns destined for use by United States Army troops in France were hoisted aboard. Dos Passos wrote Arthur McComb that the ship was "laden with fear, patriotism, and young men in uniform."

He had been aboard since midmorning in anticipation of a noon-hour departure, but by 5 P.M. the ship was still in port. The festive air surrounding his boarding had long since dissipated. By the time the final whistle blew, the crowd on the wharf consisted chiefly of weary longshoremen and a few teary-eyed stragglers. After the band retired—hours before the *Chicago* slipped from its pier—most of the noise and merriment came from within the vessel. The bar was already littered with empty champagne bottles when the passengers streamed once more on deck, glasses or beer mugs in hand, to shout good-byes to the faithful few who had lingered on the dock, their faces indistinguishable to the men squinting into the setting sun as the figures on the dock faded from view.

Women, too, were aboard the *Chicago:* volunteer nurses, society women with thinning, blue-tinted hair eager to do "their bit alongside the men," debutantes seeking one last fling chaperoned by brightly rouged maiden aunts or an apprehensive French teacher. Although some appeared jittery at the prospects of a crossing through submarine-infested waters, most looked forward to the ten-day journey in the company of eager, young college men bound for war. A few fastened coy looks upon would-be suitors, who lost little time before introducing them to the ship's lifeboats, favorite trysting grounds for groping couples who had eyed each other shyly only hours earlier.

Dos Passos did not join in the conviviality at the bar or wave to the crowd when the engines themselves announced that the ship was under way. Uncomfortable with good-byes, he had solicited no one to see him off. He could handle a "so long" in writing, but physical partings that stood on ceremony had always been awkward for him. Actually, there was no one in New York City at the time other than Wright McCormick for whom he had any particular feelings. Estlin Cummings had already sailed for France with an earlier group of volunteer drivers, as had Robert Hillyer and Dudley Poore. Dos Passos hoped that they might all turn up in the same section, but Poore was destined for the American Field Service.

Dos Passos stayed in his stateroom—shared with two other Norton-Harjes volunteers he had never laid eyes on until they stowed their gear—to finish his letters to Marvin and several other friends, then asked the tugboat captain who had guided them from the harbor to mail them. For a while he tarried on deck to watch the receding silhouette of Manhattan in the darkening sky before heading to the bar and smoking room. "The trip was one long party," he wrote later. Someone was always at the piano to guide them through sentimental medleys from the ubiquitous *YMCA Songbook,* a sheaf of mimeographed lyrics handed to each passenger in the lounge area. In boisterous, drunken voices, both with and without piano accompaniment, the men and their female companions sang until not only their voices, but also the bar itself was dry. Dos Passos himself had little ear for music and even less ability to stay on key, but readily joined the others in their nightly songfests.

After a week at sea, he wrote McComb that he had found five socialists aboard. "Imagine!—and there may be more—Glory Hallelujah!" He mentioned by name only John Howard Lawson, a 1914 Williams College graduate who had signed on with the predominantly Harvard men of the Norton-Harjes. His bright brown eyes peering out over a hawklike nose, Lawson looked much like Cyrano de Bergerac, and his dark, unruly hair behaved as though it had never encountered a brush. It seemed to Dos Passos that Lawson had a drastic idea about every subject that surfaced, and away from the group for ten minutes, Lawson returned with a tale of some abracadabra adventure that had befallen him in his absence. Dos Passos observed that shipboard life had improved considerably upon his meeting with Lawson, already a produced playwright. Lawson agreed with Dos Passos that the American theater had been chronically ill for too long, and that one of the things they should do upon their return to New York was to carry their revolutionary zeal to the American stage.

Dos Passos also encountered two zealots whose "mumbo-jumbo"—as he called it—disturbed him: Theodore Roosevelt, Jr., and his brother Archie, sons of the former President. He thought of them as "Princes of the Blood" in their military garb of the American Expeditionary Forces en route to Europe on a special mission and overheard one of them saying: "When this is over, the United States'll be the greatest military nation in the world." Such rhetoric under the guise of patriotism sickened him. As he saw it, the best his nation *should* hope for was a negotiated peace by sane men, not militarists or "merchants of death" the likes of the Roosevelt clan.

In a long letter to McComb while still at sea, Dos Passos urged him to try to get out at least "one red hot issue" of the *Harvard Monthly* before its ultimate suppression. "If I had something to blow off steam in, I'd love to lambaste conscription and the daily press and the intellectual classes and Harvard's attitude." He promised that if he were not destitute come fall, he would donate one hundred dollars to help get out such an issue.

Most of his voyage had been spent lying on deck, his head cradled by a life preserver, his mind in a "grey, cloudy nirvana," he told McComb. One of the things he said he had managed to do, however, was separate himself from his "web of memories." Shortly before docking at Bordeaux, he emerged from his torpor and wrote a poem that began: *I have no more memories.*

> *Before,*
> *My memories with various strands*
> *Had spun me many misty-colored towns,*
> *Full of gleams of halfheard music,*
> *Full of sudden throbbing scents*
> *And rustle of unseen passers-by—*
> *Vague streets rainbow glowing*
> *For me to wander in . . .*
>
> *Today,*
> *As if a gritty stinking sponge*
> *Had smeared the slate of my pale memories,*
> *I stand aghast in a grey world,*
> *Waiting . . .*
> *I have no more memories.*
> *Sea and the grey brooding sky—*
> *Two halves of a flameless opal—*
> *Glow soft and sullenly*
> *In a vast sphere about me*
> *As I, very drowsy, lie*
> *On deck; by the rise and fall*
> *Of the sound of spumed water*
> *Lulled into dreaminess,*
> *Into a passionless mood*
> *Of utter lassitude,*
> *A dull Nirvana where stir*
> *Negations without stress. . . .*

The *Chicago* reached its port on July 1 a few hours after a harrowing submarine scare at dawn; a sailor had mistaken a barnacled log for a periscope and alarmed the entire ship. As the vessel entered the estuary, Dos Passos observed the spars of a submerged steamer. Boatloads of survivors were still scrambling ashore when he shouldered his duffel bag and strode with his fellow drivers down the cobbled streets to the railroad station to board a train to Paris. *"Vive l'Amérique!"* shouted welcoming villagers who clapped and cheered from doorways and windows as wildly as though he and his companions were arrayed in battle gear and headed for the front. Although most of the men were in civilian clothing, the French mistook neither their mission nor their nationality. Wilson's declaration of war had made them comrades-in-arms, and the natives loved them one and all.

Among the new arrivals in Bordeaux that morning, Dos Passos probably spoke the most fluent French. He found it amusing to help his compatriots order food and drink at the curbside café outside the railway station. The men envied his ability to walk up to strangers and engage them in conversation. French girls had gathered on street corners and doorways to toss pink roses and white daisies into the men's outstretched arms as they made their way to the station, and he was plied by his buddies with such questions as: "How long before our train? . . . What'd she say? . . . Hey, man, how did you learn to parley-voo so well? . . . How do I ask for cognac?" Laments and warnings about "precautions" rippled through the section as prostitutes beckoned in hopes that *les Américains* might be free to tarry briefly on their own. Dos Passos loved being back in France. As he saw it, the imminence of destruction and threat of catastrophe had brought out the people's finest qualities. He observed before boarding the train that there was little evidence of the war having touched Bordeaux except for the absence of young men in civilian garb. Of the French countryside he never tired. It reminded him of long-forgotten picture books of fairy tales his mother had read him. Even from afar he readily pictured the red-tiled roofs clustered around the town's church steeple, which caught the sun and dazzled the eye. Fields nodded with cornflowers, daisies, and ripening grain. Scarlet poppies stretched in every direction. The long overland trip to Paris took many hours as the slow-moving train paused at village after village along the way, its ancient cars filling up with more passengers than the tiny compartments could seat. The names of the towns —Poitiers, Tours, Orleans—evoked for Dos Passos thoughts of ancient wars. Surely there was a poem in all this, he mused, opening his diary and jotting down lines from which he might work later. "Poitiers—July 2," his entry began:

> *Wide grey-green fields,*
> *Dappled with swaying vermillion,*
> *Everywhere glowing with stains of poppies,*
> *Poppies spring from old sad fields*
> *Of a battle long fought out . . .*
> *How many years, oh God,*
> *Before the blood of battles springs up*
> *Into the arrogant glowing youth*
> *Of poppies?*

Wartime Paris was new to Dos Passos. The City of Lights was dark and quiet when the ambulance men detrained at the little station on the Quai d'Orsay. He felt as though he was walking into the pages of a mystery novel when he stepped through black felt blackout curtains to enter the hotel assigned to the Norton-Harjes men. Early the next morning they reported to headquarters at 7 rue François Premier for swearing-in ceremonies led by A. Herman Harjes, the French banker who had donated thousands of dollars and many ambulances to provide French war relief. The millionaire banker had agreed to pool his efforts with Richard Norton, who launched the American Ambulance Corps in 1914 with two cars and four drivers. By the time Dos Passos enlisted with the Norton-Harjes, the service had grown to thirteen sections comprised of six hundred American volunteer drivers and three hundred ambulances.

The Norton-Harjes organization was closely aligned with the American Field Service, established in 1915 by A. Piatt Andrew, a political economics professor at Harvard whose efforts at recruitment there paid off more handsomely than Richard Norton's did. Though their benefits in the field were comparable, the men of the American Field Service prided themselves in their posh headquarters at 21 rue Raymouard atop Passy, a hill in suburban Paris. An enormous château, it served also as post office and clubhouse. The American Field Service had many transport sections, which the Norton-Harjes did not have, and over eight hundred ambulance drivers. Ambulance driving was considered more hazardous duty than *camion* driving and filled up first. The volunteers of both units worked without pay, though the French government insisted on giving each American driver five cents a day, the equivalent wage of the French military troops. The Norton-Harjes trained its men for two and a half to three weeks before sending them into active duty, whereas American Field Service men trained for a week. Many thought the *esprit de corps* better in the Norton-Harjes. The men in it were "better disciplined and a more snappily dressed outfit" than their competitors, for whom wearing a uniform was sometimes optional. When fatalities were tallied after the two services were disbanded (all American ambulance services in Europe were federalized by the government in 1918), the American Field Service reported twenty-one Harvard students killed and a total of one hundred fifty-one in all. The Norton-Harjes outfit claimed no fatalities. Among the American Field Service drivers who survived and became known later for their distinguished careers in writing were Louis Bromfield, Malcolm Cowley, Harry Crosby, Julian Green, Dashiell Hammett, Sidney Howard, and William Seabrook. Ernest Hemingway was neither in the Norton-Harjes nor the American Field Service, but arrived in Europe after these groups disbanded and served with the American Red Cross in Italy. The most notable Norton-Harjes men in the field of letters were Dos Passos, E. E. Cummings, Robert Hillyer, John Howard Lawson, and William Slater Brown.

The need for ambulance and *camion* drivers was dire when Dos Passos arrived in France, and he wanted to get on with his training and into the field as soon as possible. His first step after registering at the Norton-Harjes headquarters on July 3, 1917, was to report to a fashionable shop on the rue de la Paix to be fitted for a uniform. Each volunteer paid for the materials and tailoring of his outfit—just as he had done for his transportation overseas—and provided whatever sustenance necessary during his interim in Paris. Dos Passos was reminded by Norton-Harjes officials of his gentleman volunteer status and cautioned to avoid any form of public mischief, then given credentials that entitled him to roam the city at will while his uniform was being readied. The French *gendarmes* had orders to arrest on sight any young man out of uniform unless he had an official pass granting him immunity.

As a Norton-Harjes man, Dos Passos' contract was also with the American Red Cross, in which he agreed to serve for a minimum of six months. Free in Paris at last, he was delighted to come upon three cronies from Harvard: Robert Hillyer, Frederick van den Arend, and Dudley Poore. Poore left shortly after their encounter for his training camp with the American Ambulance Field Service, but Hillyer and Van den Arend were still awaiting uniforms and assignments and had already been in Paris a week. Together they set off to wander the city and began referring to themselves as "Athos, Porthos, and D'Artagnan"—the Three Musketeers—and succeeded in putting out of mind for the time being the grim realities of war.

Since prostitution was legal in France, Paris teemed with painted whores who no longer held court under lampposts, but frequented the nightclubs and cafés where French soldiers and sailors on leave congregated almost around the clock. Other than the roisterous trappings of harlotry and the uniformed French and Americans, there were few visual manifestations of war to the casual observer. Dos Passos noted sandbags nestled against the stained glass windows of churches and chapels, and the casements of government buildings had been shielded against street skirmishes, but Paris gave little appearance of being a fortified city. An occasional cripple still dressed in a dusty uniform freshened Dos Passos' thoughts of his own mortality. He could not shake easily from his mind the chubby boyish face of a soldier whose triangular black patch rested "where the nose should have been." He looked long into the man's eyes a few inches above "a mechanical contrivance with shiny little black metal rods" that replaced his jaw and was reminded of an injured animal "full of meek dismay," he wrote later.

The essential Paris he had always loved remained unchanged. The courtyard of the Louvre, flower beds of the Tuileries, the Luxembourg Palace with its exquisite gardens, children at play on the Champs-Élysées, Punch and Judy shows he had delighted in as a child, cuisine that catered to discriminating palates no matter how ill-stocked chefs found their larder—all provoked intensely pleasurable sensations. The "musketeers" followed the quais along the Seine to Notre Dame, peered curiously at everything they saw, poked leisurely in bookstalls, and at dusk climbed to the top of Montmartre, which Dos Passos deemed the single most exciting place in the world. The view of Paris darkening in the sunset alone was worth the arduous ascent. He wrote Rumsey Marvin that he especially liked the people there because only the jolliest succeeded in the climb. He reported having watched "an incredibly beautiful performance of Les Ballets Russes," spent two evenings at the Folies-Bergère, and had "several long thrilling nights" at the opera. "If you want to find out how I feel about Paris, go hear Louise," he urged. Alone in his hotel room at the end of a long day, he devoured the poems of Rimbaud.

From his Harvard friends Dos Passos learned that he had just missed Cummings, who departed Paris under a cloud of notoriety because of an unsanctioned holiday spree. Cummings and a new friend, William Slater Brown, had eluded their official duties for a month. The entire affair was absurd from the onset, said Brown, who had accompanied

Cummings to Paris on the train from Boulogne, the SS *Touraine*'s port of entry. In seats some distance from the rest of their group, they had detrained at their proper destination a few blocks from Norton-Harjes headquarters unaware that everyone else had left the train at the wrong stop and were miles from their assigned hotel. Cummings and Brown went directly to headquarters for assignment, but found the offices closed for the day. Early the next morning when they again attempted to check in, they learned that the rest of the group had failed to report. "Stay where you are until your records and the other men catch up with you. Meanwhile, get your uniforms fitted and await an official summons to rejoin your unit," they were told.

"It wasn't our fault no one came looking for us," recalled Brown. "It took days to get our uniforms made, and we didn't like them when we got them, though the girls we picked up liked them and wanted us to go out on the town dressed that way. They were of worsted wool and khaki, and those big Sam Browne belts we were supposed to wear made us look like aviators." A. Herman Harjes himself summoned Cummings and Brown back to headquarters and rebuked them for not reporting immediately upon getting their uniforms. "The least you might have done was report to the garage and learn how to service an ambulance," he said sternly. "But we would never have considered that even for a moment," observed Brown. "When we finally were assigned a unit, Estlin was to have gone into a deluxe Harvard section—#10, I think it was—and I was to go into an ordinary unit since I was from Columbia University, not Harvard. But Estlin insisted on joining my unit—#21—and they let him. Harvard elitism or snob-elegance was definitely not his thing."

Dos Passos had hoped to be in Cummings' unit, but had he been with him and Brown, he probably would have been as outspoken in his dissidence. Cummings and Brown did little to conceal their contempt for military discipline and authority and flagrantly violated the rules prohibiting fraternization with the French soldiers *(les poilus)*, from whom they sought a more accurate pulse of the war than anything gleaned from their countrymen. "It didn't take long for our superiors to brand us trouble-makers. By late September 1917, both Estlin and I were jailed on suspicion of espionage," said Brown. "I didn't know Dos then, but I learned later that he found it hard to keep out of trouble, too. We were in jail for three months—I imagine he would have been right there with us."

Dos Passos was in Paris a fortnight before being wrenched from his jolly meanderings among friends and sent to a training camp north of Paris where he knew no one. Sandricourt was an erstwhile hunting preserve named for its former owner, a French marquis. There the men were supposed to practice driving on narrow, pocked roads and to learn the rudiments of servicing their vehicles (Model-T Fords and French Fiats). Instead, there was not a single ambulance either to drive or tinker with for almost two weeks. The men were bored and frustrated. Most of their time was to be spent in close-order drills. Dos Passos complained of being taken advantage of and said that if he had wanted to behave as a soldier, he would have become one. When mail caught up with him at Sandricourt, he learned that he had just missed being a soldier technically as well. Wright McCormick wrote him that his name had been drawn in the first lottery, a marathon conscription process that took sixteen hours to complete. McCormick telephoned the draft board that Dos Passos was already serving his country in Europe as an ambulance driver. "They took it quite badly" and accused him of having "run away," reported McCormick. Draft officials intended to communicate immediately with his commanding officer and retrieve him if possible.

Dos Passos and his compatriots of the Norton-Harjes heard the tom-tom of guns from the north and were impatient to experience the war firsthand. His outfit had finally acquired two ambulances, but had scant time to become acquainted with them before being ordered to Paris for assignment to a field unit. Dos Passos wrote Rumsey Marvin that he was relieving his boredom at Sandricourt by taking up profanity. "One swears and filthifies largely and joyfully and waits with faint hope for the moment of release." Until his assignment there, Dos Passos' expletives had seldom gone beyond a "gosh, oh gee" or a "goddamn." He announced, too, that his "pacifism-at-any-price" had become more fierce. As he saw it, life's grotesqueries were "a jumble of swooningly pleasant yet strangely sinister and despairing times." It was as though he were an "Alice in Wonderland with the world at stake instead of the March Hare's watch."

Back in Paris, Dos Passos was reunited with Robert Hillyer, Frederick van den Arend, and John Howard Lawson, who completed their training in a neighboring camp at the same time and were assigned to the same unit as Dos Passos, Section Sanitaire 60, now quartered *en repos* at Châlons-sur-Marne. Having no duties yet, they spent their leisure swimming in abbreviated, striped French tights that would have shocked bathers at Atlantic City, sailing fleets of paper boats in mock naval fights, and listening to the "charmingly noisy French chefs" who prepared the evening meals in their mess quarters. In his new environment, Dos Passos wrote frequently to friends in the States and began to record once more his observations in long, reflective passages in his diary. He said he sneered at tragedy one moment, then giggled impishly at it the next, amazed at his frivolity. Despite the ornate imagery abounding in his various entries, he was also using more concrete, objective detail in pinning down his environment, which he described, then reflected upon. He wrote one day of sitting in a tangled grape arbor of a beer garden beside an ancient inn, the temporary barracks for his section at Châlons-sur-Marne. After describing the inn and garden, he allowed his thoughts to slip back in time to the wedding parties that might have sat in "that very spot, flushed with champagne" and felt the world "soft and warm with the phallic glow." Then his mood darkened, and he shifted to the "evils of capitalism" and wrote wrathfully of "swag-bellied old fogies in frock-coats," ministers in "their damn smug pulpits," bankers, brokers, meatpackers, businessmen—all making a "God-damned mess" of organized society. It seemed to Dos Passos at age twenty-one that "all young men were terribly decent. . . . If only *we* governed the world! Down with the middle-aged!" he cried.

In early August his unit was ordered to the tiny village above Bar-le-Duc—known as Erize-la-Petite—which he described as "the damndest godforsakenest hole" one could encounter. Already an evacuated town, it straggled along two sides of the main road to Verdun. The road itself was known as the Voi Sacrée (Sacred Way). The few houses that had withstood German bombardment stood ludicrously above the rubble. For two weeks Dos Passos' section was encamped in the region near Erize-la-Petite, where day by day hundreds of *camions* filled with troops—many driven by American volunteers—converged upon their staging area, joined by countless ambulance units of the Norton-Harjes and American Field Service. Caissons of ammunition drawn by sweating mules moved daily along the white, chalky road toward the front. In early August the rains came, lightly at first and then in a deluge. While *en repos* at Châlons-sur-Marne he had recorded "the pleasant look and sound" of rain falling in "lucid pensive drops" from the "smallish horsechestnut trees with a faint kiss on the puddly gravel," but from his new location in the staging area he wrote of the somber countryside that "lowered under heavy rain and drizzling rain and mist and cat-and-dog rain—but always rain." Drivers and vehicles became mired in "muddy manure," and restless men and machines "trampled to soup" the entire rank scene, now "unbelievably gloomy" and a symbol of all the "intense brooding boredom of war."

The horror stories of battle he had heard on the train coming up from Bordeaux had gone the rounds of each ambulance section before the men of the Norton-Harjes ever approached the front. "We are too near the front for any damned heroics, thank God," Dos Passos wrote in his diary after returning from a walk in the rain along the Verdun road, where everything was "dank and damp and mouldy-smelling like a tomb." Although he still had seen nothing of combat, he spoke of building a "snail shell of hysterical laughter against the hideousness of war." His caustic rhetoric became increasingly marked with battlefield images. He wrote of the victims of cant and hypocrisy who lay "choking on a poison" worse than German gas, and of old verities now "putrid and false." All the chatter about the heroics of war, the platitudes alleging allegiance to one's country "right or wrong"—all were the makings of a "rollicking, grotesque dance of death," he said. Dos Passos had a passion to set it all down in words, then to "banish despair with delirious laughter and thus reveal the stupidity and utter asininity of war." If only he might catch horror on the wing and freeze it for posterity so that distant people might read and be forewarned before they committed *others* to such slaughter, he lamented. On August 15, 1917, the eve of his going to the front, Robert Hillyer and he had decided to collaborate on an antiwar novel. Their creative efforts might be paltry at best, they conceded, but at least they could amuse themselves through them to relieve their boredom. Since each ambulance driver alternated twenty-four hours on duty and twenty-four off, they decided to work separately on alternate chapters on their free days and get together at night to read each other what they had written. With enthusiasm they spoke now of their "G.N.," their "Great Novel."

Heavy rains delayed the anticipated major Allied offensive, but the weather cleared the second week of August and once more the French *camions* rolled through the battered village of Erize-la-Petite toward Verdun. One of the men in his unit counted three hundred *camions* loaded with men streaming by during the few hours from dusk until he retired to his tent for the night. All night long troops passed the Norton-Harjes encampment in *camions* and on foot. It seemed to Dos Passos that all of France was sweeping past him while he sat on the sidelines.

Later, in a novel of his own, *One Man's Initiation: 1917,* which spun off from his collaboration with Hillyer after the project was abandoned, Dos Passos captured the mood of that night in a conversation between Martin Howe (a quasi-autobiographical character) and a young French soldier en route to the front:

"I tell you, fellers, there's goin' to be an attack. This concentration of sanitary sections means something. . . . Probably I'll come back in your little omnibus."

"I hope you won't."

"I'd be very glad to. A lucky wound! But I'll probably be killed. This is the first time I've gone up to the front that I didn't expect to be killed. So it'll probably happen."

Martin Howe could not help looking at him suddenly. The aspirant sat at ease on the stone margin of the well, leaning against the wrought iron support for the bucket, one knee clasped in his strong, heavily veined hands. Dead he would be different. Martin's mind could hardly grasp the connection between this man full of latent energies, full of thoughts and desires, this man whose shoulder he would have liked to have put his arm round from friendliness, with whom he would have liked to go for long walks, with whom he would have liked to sit long into the night drinking and talking—and those huddled, pulpy masses of blue uniform half-buried in the mud of ditches.

"Have you ever seen a herd of cattle being driven to abattoir on a fine May morning?" asked the aspirant. . . . "The herd can be driven by a boy of six . . . or a prime minister!"

As troop movements continued toward the Verdun front, so too did the routine of the ambulance men quicken. Drivers pored over maps, memorized the areas identified only as "P1," "P2," "P3," and noted the locations of each dressing station and field hospital. Each morning the vehicles were deployed—like elephants in a Barnum and Bailey spectacular, said Dos Passos—in convoy from one staging area to another in practice runs while dodging potholes and learning the rudiments of transporting casualties. The men were expected to keep a strict accounting of how many *couches* and *assises* (litter casualties and those who had been injured, but could be transported sitting up) they handled on each run, and where they had been picked up and delivered for treatment.

Dos Passos' section of twenty ambulances was comprised chiefly of French Fiats, but several of the men were assigned Model-T Fords. Dos Passos and his partner, James Parshall, appreciated having a Model-T because it was lighter than a Fiat and easier to handle in dodging shell holes. The Fiats were new and hard to crank, but they were appreciated by most drivers for their superior brakes, sturdier transmissions, and wheels of solid iron. It was only when they sank to their hubcaps in the chalky mud during blinding rains that their drivers cursed and kicked them. Dos Passos learned to tease his little Ford motor to life as readily as his partner did, but Parshall was a better driver. Their ambulance bucked and pitched and behaved as if it had a mind of its own. Hills had to be taken in low gear, and sometimes their recalcitrant vehicle refused to make the ascent. There was little straightaway in their driving. The roads over which they maneuvered bore such tags as "Deadman's Turn," "Dip of Death," "Dead Man's Gulley" "Le Mort Homme," "Hell's Half Acre," and "R4 in No Man's Land." At night they ran without lights through pitch black forests. Since the ambulances had no windshields, either the driver's partner or an orderly—if available, orderlies made the run to help with the wounded—rode on the front fender or walked (with a white handkerchief tucked into his epaulet) to help navigate amidst the shell craters and animal carcasses. Since Dos Passos had difficulty seeing potholes and other obstructions, his partner insisted on driving if there was shelling in the area. Dos Passos took the wheel on more quiet roads leading to the dressing stations or base hospitals. Just before going into action, Edward E. Harding, one of the men in Dos Passos' unit, made up their battle cry, "The Helmet Song of Section 60":

> *Put on your old gray bonnet*
> *With the strap a hangin' on it,*
> *And we'll go thru shrapnel and thru shell—*
> *Then on roads of desolation,*
> *We will cure your constipation*
> *With a wild night ride in Hell!*

With a cold and almost constant drizzle alternating with heavy downpours throughout much of August, Dos Passos and his friends found it impossible to keep their vehicles tuned, greased, and oiled, and tinkered with their engines almost daily, since their lives, as well as those of the men they transported, depended as much upon their mechanical ingenuity as upon their driving skills. Among the eight French soldiers assigned to each section, one was usually a mechanic who handled serious breakdowns, but finding spare parts was a perpetual problem. French soldiers served as cooks and menial laborers, but provided no military protection for the American *ambulancier*'s transitory outposts. Sometimes the drivers were assigned to a French infantry division and quartered next to it, but often they were on their own. Each night the American drivers stood two-hour shifts of sentry duty to help secure their vehicles from sabotage or theft.

The men of Section 60 got along well together. They gave each other haircuts, played checkers—they had no money to gamble, therefore did little cardplaying—and sat around smoking, drinking, singing, and swapping yarns. Lacking musical instruments, some played tunes on their combs. Many slept in their ambulances on hammocks strung in the stretcher compartments to avoid the sleek, well-fed trench rats that invaded their tents. It was impossible to keep even the insides of their vehicles clean, since the men tramped through foot-deep mud to and from mess quarters, latrine, and bed. Dos Passos wrote in his diary of lying on a cot on one of the stretchers in the car and listening to the rain and the "rather pleasant sound of slightly drunken voices quarreling" in the distance while he tried to concentrate on Rimbaud's poems. It was Saturday night, he said, and nearly everyone was "soused on the strong red army wine—nicknamed pinard (bull piss) —which they dole us in seemingly limitless quantities." The big guns sounding in the distance resembled "deep measured snoring." He admitted that if it were not for the "most charming and graceful spirit of comradeship" enlivening the "dry dustiness of it all," the situation would be intolerable.

Even the practical jokes were accepted in good spirits. Dos Passos awoke one morning to the "meow-meow" of a scrawny, flea-bitten cat whose sharp-clawed paws were kneading his chest. Upon discovering that it was his friend, Edward Harding, who had slipped the mournful creature into his ambulance during the night, he retaliated by absconding with the prankster's ambulance from a neighboring village, where he found it parked while Harding was enjoying the hospitality of the natives during his off-duty evening. Harding and his partner were forced to walk a dozen kilometers back to their encampment in a downpour.

Dos Passos got along well with James Parshall, his lanky Texan partner, once they fell into a driving routine and the sharing of their tiny living quarters. Since Parshall did the hazardous driving, Dos Passos made it up to him by scrounging wine and victuals from the French. If he supplied the eggs, he was able to wangle omelettes from the cooks assigned to his section. A fellow ambulancier observed that Dos Passos could easily have been taken by the natives as one of their own had he not been in uniform. No one else in his unit managed to convert his meager allotment into vintage wine, eggs, and fresh vegetables as advantageously as did Dos Passos.

On August 15, 1917, Dos Passos noted in his diary that he was going the next day "to a devilish hot section" of the front. Section 60 of the Norton-Harjes had been ordered to replace Section 21 of the American Field Service. Rumor had it that the men they were relieving had suffered such trauma and fatigue that the entire unit had "gone yellow and revolted." Dos Passos wrote McComb several days before proceeding to the combat area that none of the French soldiers he had talked with "spoke gibberish about the glories of war. . . . Of Nagel in France—remember what I told you—there are increasing indications. I've come to firmly believe that the only thing that can save America is Nagelism there." He said that whenever he got drunk with French soldiers, he heard countless stories of "petitions and complaints" protesting *gendarmes* who had been used to hunt down deserters and who then strung them up on meat hooks in an abattoir. The French soldiers also told him horror stories of the mutinies that swept their ranks during the spring.

Dos Passos had no free time during his first week on the front to write letters, diary jottings, or work on his collaborative venture with Hillyer, whom he barely saw. The men slept in their clothes the eve of their advance. At dawn they proceeded in convoy to the town of Brocourt under a barrage of heavy German artillery. For a few moments they had driven along feeling relatively secure; then the bombardment commenced and the men dove frantically into dugouts and shell craters while fragments of men and horses sprayed their vehicles. Dos Passos carried his first casualties that day. The men snaked their ambulances in and out from the hospital at Brocourt to several first aid stations in forward positions. As quickly as they could pull up to an aid post, *brancardiers* raced out with stretchers of hastily bandaged men. The drivers lifted them aboard and fastened each man into wall cots that let down in stacks on each side. Three *couches* and six *assises* was the official maximum load, but the ambulance men sometimes piled eleven or twelve aboard at one time. It was not unusual to see one or two of the less critically injured soldiers hanging from the running boards or sitting on fenders. They also squeezed in beside the driver while his partner crouched in the rear trying to comfort and hold down the wounded as the ambulance pitched and jolted over the shell-scooped roads. Before long, a spirit of competition evolved among the drivers and sections as each tried to outperform the others in cases handled in a day's and week's tally.

Dos Passos lamented that he had let his "beastly diary" go for over a week and feared that many of the things he wanted to express would lose their impressiveness. "But, gosh, I want to be able to express later all of this, all the tragedy and hideous excitement," he wrote in a rush of boyish exuberance. "I must experience more of it—and more—the grey crooked fingers of the dead, the dark look of dirty mangled bodies, their groans and joltings in the ambulance, the vast tomtom of the guns, the ripping tear shells make when they explode, the song of shells outgoing, like vast woodcocks—their contented whir as they near their mark—the twang of fragments like a harp broken in the air, the rattle of stones and mud on your helmet."

Dos Passos' friend Harding expressed himself similarly in his diary of the Avocourt/ Verdun offensives. He wrote of a chance he took going into French trenches for casualties after the soldiers had advanced up Dead Man's Hill: "Dead men all around, but didn't mind it any more. . . . Oh God, it's great. Shells all around, trees coming down, horses dropping all around, and had to look hard at a pile of flesh that had been a man just as we turned past the battery. Going along with artillery shooting in front and behind and over you for the day is terrible, but after that you rather eat it." Dos Passos told, too, of the degree to which one could get used to almost anything: "In some ways the high point for me at the Avocourt offensive was the day I caught myself quietly opening a can of sardines for my lunch in the rear of a dressing-station while some poor devil of a *poilu* was having his leg sawed off on the operating table up front. God knows I was still morbidly sensitive to other people's pain, but I had learned to live in the world and stand it."

The men of Dos Passos' section worked up to seventy hours without relief. If they slept at all, it was to lie down on a stretcher in an underground dressing station. These deep dugouts, known as *abris,* were close to the front line trenches. The trenches themselves were only some two hundred yards from the German trenches. The injured lay in the *abris* until they could be taken by ambulance to the hospital in Brocourt, a heavily shelled town within range of the German 220-mm guns. After a week in the field, Dos Passos fumed to Marvin:

> I've been so vastly bitter that I can produce nothing but gall and wormwood. The war is utter damn nonsense—a vast cancer fed by lies and self-seeking malignity on the part of those who don't do the fighting. . . . None of the poor devils whose mangled dirty bodies I take to the hospital in my ambulance really give a damn about any of the aims of this ridiculous affair. They fight because they are too cowardly and too unimaginative not to see which way they ought to turn their guns. . . . Jane Addams' account that the soldiers were fed rum and ether before attacks is true. No human being can stand the performance without constant stimulants. It's queer how much happier I am here in the midst of it than in America, where the air was stinking with lies and hypocritical patriotic gibber. . . . We've carried tons of wounded Germans and have found them very pleasant and grateful and given just as much fare as the French. The prisoners and their captors laugh and chat and kid each other along at a great rate. In fact, there is less bitterness about the war at the front than there is over an ordinary Harvard-Yale baseball game. It's so damned remarkable how universally decent people are if you'll only leave them to themselves.

A friend in the States had sent Dos Passos a recent copy of *The New Republic,* but he complained that its "meaningless, smug phraseology" was nauseating. America was an utter anathema, he insisted, to be coped with similarly to the way the giant cannons "roared and farted and spit their venom." Again and again, his recourse was profanity, a battery of rhetoric, and a sense of humor. His complaints in letters and in his diary were directed against the establishment rather than the ghastly environment in which he had voluntarily placed himself. Although a number of his fellow drivers were "scared green, too terrorstruck to think," he said that his own reaction was "a curious hankering after danger." When one shell came, he wanted another to follow "nearer, nearer. I constantly feel the need of the drunken excitement of a good bombardment. I want to throw the dice at every turn with the roisterer, Death. And through it all I feel more alive than ever before." Dudley Poore said of his "remarkable indifference to danger" that he had an unlimited endurance and an "admirable coolness under fire" that amazed him. "According to *ambulanciers* who knew him in France and later in Italy, where he drove even worse vehicles, Dos was completely fearless," reported another Harvard colleague, J. Sibley Watson, who did not see action himself but had friends who observed Dos Passos on many occasions during the fighting.

The ambulance men were instructed to keep their mouths open when under fire so that eardrums would not be shattered by the barking salvos that sounded like the cracking of giant whips. The men soon recognized the various "insane noises" and could identify the short, snappy punch of the powerful French 75s—which caused a concussion strong enough to stall Dos Passos' Model-T—and the screeching boom of the impressive German artillery. The drivers also learned to time and anticipate the frequency of the bombardments so they could slip from their *abri* and race to another location between attacks. They knew, for example, that they had fifteen minutes in which to make a run if the "Boche 75s were raising hell," said Edward Harding. Although the *abris* were two tiers deep and fortified by heavy crossed logs and sandbags, they pitched and rocked like a ship at anchor when the shelling got heavy. A more fearsome noise than the battery of big guns was the constant "swishing and whistling of gas-shells, like endless pails of dirty water being thrown on gravel" as they landed upon the roofs of ambulances and on the ground around the *abris*. In 1917 gas warfare was being waged only by the Germans. During a gas attack the air turned a misty, ghoulish-looking green. If an ambulance driver encountered an area under gas, there was no hope for anyone to survive without a mark unless he could locate a nearby *abri* for immediate refuge. Although casualties being transported often had masks affixed to their faces, it was almost impossible for the driver to wear one. Keeping a mask positioned so gas would not seep in required his pressing it against his face with one hand while steering with the other. Even the best drivers needed both hands on the wheel. The Germans had developed both "mustard gas" and "vomiting gas," which they lobbed in upon Allied lines regularly. Since the gas had no odor and could not be discerned at night by its greenish color, it was one of the most effective and frightening weapons of the war.

Gas seeped into the dugouts deep underground. Dos Passos' comment to Rumsey Marvin of having spent five hours under poison gas in the *abri* during his first night on duty revealed little of the actual events of the evening. The gas attack had begun a few minutes after midnight while he was on a run with Parshall. Caught in the attack, they searched frantically for the entrance of the *abri* to which they had been dispatched. They were fortunate to have no casualties in their ambulance at the time. It took them fifteen minutes to grope their way in, according to Edward Harding, who helped drag them to the lower tier of the dugout and strapped gas masks on them. Dos Passos was ordered out again that night, this time with Harding. "Man, did it take nerve," said Harding later. "Couldn't see at all thru masks and dead horses and shell holes all around us and gas even came thru our masks. As Dos and I poked our heads out the door, a Hun shell lifted a tree two feet in diameter from in front of the entrance and laid it over the dugout. Still wearing masks at 8:00 A.M. as gas is hell. I have used six masks in eight straight hours." Dos Passos himself did not write of this incident in his diary, but re-created it later in *One Man's Initiation: 1917.*

The Norton-Harjes men of Section 60 spent most of their first week of the Verdun offensive in the dressing stations and field hospitals near the front lines. The *abris* in which they dozed and rested were dank, smelly, and cold. Even in mid-August the men saw their breaths in the light cast by the acetylene lamp hanging at one end of the dugout. Sometimes they went to bed to stay warm if the cots were not already occupied by casualties. Bunks were straw-filled and infested with lice, fleas, and other crawling vermin. Dos Passos complained of "beating back cooties" and of his relief to be washing off the grime and fleas after two nights in a dugout. If there were no beds available in the *abris*, they spread chicken wire or branches on the floor, covered it with their ponchos, then pulled one or two blankets over themselves. When not under attack they slept for two or three hours, but awoke numb with cold. The men called their dugouts rat holes, but considered themselves fortunate to be there instead of in the trenches, where rodents twelve inches long ranged in abundance. Before settling down at night in their *abris*, the *ambulanciers* went gaming for the rats with pitchforks or baseball bats. Despite the cold, infestation, and wretched odors of the mud that oozed in through chinks in the walls, the men managed to maintain an air of warm congeniality. When off duty, they sat around a table near the lamp drinking *pinard*, talking, arguing, writing letters, poring over journals, and playing checkers or cards. Often they entertained themselves by emptying their pockets and displaying their various trophies of the day. Among the collectibles were empty shells, German helmets, maps, signal lights, revolvers, and even unfinished letters found in trenches when they went in to pick up casualties, trenches occupied alternately by the Germans and the French. Other than the men of the Norton-Harjes and the American Field Service, there were no American combat troops in Dos Passos' immediate sector. By the time the men had been in the field two weeks, they looked out from sunken eyes and cheeks, and most suffered dysentery from the gas. Their weight had fallen off fifteen to twenty-five pounds no matter how successful they may have been in foraging for food.

On their days off, Dos Passos and his partner sometimes lay on the hood or roof of their vehicle to sunbathe, but sunny days were infrequent. A special treat was finding a hot shower behind the lines. The French troops went without bathing, observed Dos Passos, except for their monthly forced baths in the river Meuse, a ritual performed with their trousers on. It was not unusual for a man to slip in the cold, fast-moving currents and drown before help could reach him. Perhaps what the men of the Norton-Harjes enjoyed most—in a curiously detached fashion—was watching the Lafayette Escadrille duel with the Imperial German Military Air Service. They sat on boxes outside their dugouts or crawled upon their vehicles to observe with utter fascination the deadly aerogymnastics. Day and night the pilots engaged in combat, but to the observers below their exchanges appeared as innocuous as porpoises at play until a machine plummeted earthward in a puff of white smoke. At night the planes resembled shooting stars, their port and starboard lights flickering from each wing while searchlights swept the heavens as they dipped and rose and banked for the kill. Punctuating such dogfights were star shells exploding like gigantic fireworks, sending streaks of brilliant whites, reds, and yellows across the sky. The men below sometimes gambled on how long an air duel would last. At night it was impossible to determine whether the victor was a pilot of the Lafayette Escadrille or of the Imperial German Military Air Service.

Dos Passos wrote Rumsey Marvin a few days after the worst of the Verdun offensive was over that nothing had affected him so much as the *camion* loads of men "grinding through the white dust clouds on the road to the front . . . drunk and desperate, shouting, screaming jokes, spilling wine over each other—or else asleep with ghoulish, dust-powdered faces." He said that he brought some of them back later in his ambulance, or else "saw them piled on little two-wheeled carts, tangles of bodies with grey crooked fingers and dirty protruding feet, to be trundled to the cemeteries, where they are always busy making their orderly little grey wood crosses."

After the ambulance men of the Norton-Harjes and the American Field Service had been in France long enough to witness the war firsthand, many tried to defect and join combat outfits. To join the Army, however, they were told they must return home first—at their own expense—enlist as privates, then train in the States before being allowed to return to Europe in a combat status. The men found, too, that once they had been sworn in as volunteers, the American Red Cross was reluctant to discharge them short of their six-month commitment. Some two months after Dos Passos' arrival in France, the men of Section 60 received a letter from Richard Norton announcing that he and his brother Eliot had resigned their commands. Both the Norton-Harjes and the American Field Service were being taken over by the United States government. Two days after Norton's letter of August 27, 1917, was read to the men, he appeared in person in Dos Passos' encampment, accompanied by an American Red Cross official, an army major, and a prominent newspaperman from Emporia, Kansas, William Allen White, to convey his personal regrets that their service was being terminated. "It is America's mistake," White told them. The first reaction by the men was utter consternation. They did not want to abandon their mission while their services were needed. They knew, too, that some six hundred French had been killed in one day alone during the Verdun offensive, and the drivers themselves had conveyed ten times that number of casualties during the same period. As they saw it, the newly conscripted American soldiers would be grossly inadequate for the job. On August 28, the Norton-Harjes Ambulance Corps was placed under the direction of Colonel J. R. Kean, the organization to be known now as the Medical Corps of the American Expeditionary Forces. American Field Service drivers were transferred directly to the United States Army Ambulance Service. On August 30, every man in Dos Passos' section officially resigned as Norton-Harjes men, but agreed to continue working as a part of Colonel Kean's Medical Corps until mid-October, when they were to be processed out. Norton urged the drivers to continue their good work by enlisting in the United States Army. A new ruling permitted them to enlist in Paris so that their service would be continued with little restructuring of original units. The "catch"—as most of the men saw it—was that upon enlistment they would be army privates. Having to assume the lowest noncommissioned rank after enjoying the relative freedom and quasi-officer status as "gentlemen volunteers" kept many from joining up. The men were also required to commit themselves for the duration of the war. About half the drivers in each of the volunteer services elected to return to the United States, and most of the others became army privates in France. Dos Passos was one of the few who did neither, but elected to find some other nonmilitary organization that would allow him to remain "on the fringes of the great butchery" in Europe.

On September 12 Richard Norton arrived at Remicourt, a village in the Argonne, for his farewell address to the Norton-Harjes men. "As gentlemen volunteers you enlisted in this service, and as gentlemen volunteers I bid you farewell," he said. "What a wonderful phrase, 'gentlemen volunteers,' " observed Dos Passos in a tongue-in-cheek note to McComb upon Norton's departure. The phrase delighted Dos Passos, punctuated as it was by a shell exploding thirty feet away. He reported that the drivers clapped on their "tin helmets and crouched like scared puppies under a shower of pebbles and dust," and that the "fat-jowled gentlemen in the uniform of the United States Army" who accompanied Norton "lost their restraint and their expression of tense interest (often seen in people about to be seasick) and bolted for the <u>abris</u>." The drivers had the immense satisfaction of watching Norton, "his monocle gleaming in his eye," ignore his cowering associates and walk calmly up the ranks shaking hands with every man in turn.

Dos Passos told McComb that he intended to remain a "gentleman volunteer." In pursuit of that ambition his possibilities were to work in some "rear-line ambulance service," help with a prisoner exchange service being set up, or join an organization rumored being formed in Italy that would carry casualties across the Alps and lakes of northern Italy. He intended to take whatever materialized first, but looked forward to being *en repos* in Paris for a few days. His official affiliation was now with the American Red Cross, which had sworn him in on July 3, 1917. It also provided him his discharge, dated October 20, which read: "This is to certify that J. R. Dos Passos served under me in the <u>Section Sanitaire Américaine No. 60</u> for three months." It affirmed that his service was entirely satisfactory and that he left only because the service had been taken over by the United States Army. The document was essential to his being allowed to enlist in the Red Cross for ambulance service in Italy. Dos Passos signed up almost immediately for the newly formed American Red Cross Section I, which was to proceed in convoy to the Italian front as soon as sufficient ambulances could be acquired.

Meanwhile, he met up in Paris with Dudley Poore, John Howard Lawson, and Frederick van den Arend, who had also signed on for service in Italy. Poore was still undergoing treatment for shrapnel wounds suffered on the front and had to catch up with them in Italy. Dos Passos had hoped to see Cummings and Brown in Paris, but they had already been jailed on suspicion of espionage and were languishing in a French concentration camp while awaiting a commission's examination to determine their fate. The hearing could result in one of three actions: they could be declared innocent and set free; they could be declared "undesirables" and deported; or they could be indicted, tried by a French military court, and if found guilty, executed or imprisoned for the rest of the war. Dos Passos tried futilely to communicate with Cummings and wrote his father that he would do anything he could to help. Yet Dos Passos himself had difficulty staying out of trouble. In the fall before his discharge from the Norton-Harjes, he and seven fellow dissidents were jailed briefly for their protest concerning inadequate food rations. Upon learning about Cummings' and Brown's plight, his excoriations of the establishment intensified. Cummings was imprisoned three months before being pardoned and sent home; Brown was detained considerably longer (Cummings—with Brown as unofficial collaborator—immediately wrote a novel about their incarceration, *The Enormous Room*).

In Paris Dos Passos acquired a new friend, Thomas Cope, during the fall of 1917 before his departure for Italy. Cope was a handsome, angular youth from Philadelphia who shared Dos Passos' pacifist convictions and his fascination for architecture. His father, an architect, was acclaimed for his Gothic designs of academic buildings on the campuses of Princeton, Bryn Mawr, and Washington University in St. Louis. Young Cope had worked for his father for a time because he enjoyed sketching, but he preferred sculpting. A fourth-generation Philadelphian, Cope told Dos Passos that he was certain their grandmothers had known each other, since Dos Passos' paternal grandmother, Lucinda Cattell, had been a staunch Philadelphia Quaker, as was Cope's family on his mother's side. Cope's mother, an ardent and militant pacifist, was firm in her stance that he volunteer his services to any outfit that would not expose him to battlefield activities. His compromise, he told Dos Passos, was to join a Friends' reconstruction detachment. The two men argued about whether the "morally decent thing to do" was simply to go to jail as conscientious objectors.

Dos Passos did not like having to leave Cope behind when his ambulance convoy headed for Italy. He regretted, too, that he would no longer have Robert Hillyer for a companion. A family emergency had called Hillyer home just before the federalization of the Norton-Harjes, but before leaving he gave Dos Passos *carte blanche* to proceed with their collaboration alone. While in Paris, Dos Passos spent his mornings working on the novel and kept his afternoons and evenings free to "eat the lotus," as he referred to his idle hours in a letter to Rumsey Marvin. "The wistfulness of russet fall in the Luxembourg gardens, cold twilights walking up Montmartre to get escargots in a certain little restaurant in the tip top of Paris, the refined gluttony of *pâtisseries,* concerts with lots of César Franck—oh, many are the seeds of my autumnal lotuses," he wrote of his "atrociously delightful month" in Paris. He also mentioned wandering constantly through "dimly seen crowds, peeping in on orgies of drink and women, and vague incomplete adventures." Marvin, still in prep school, was fascinated by his friend's mysterious and sensuous references to women. Dos Passos was equally obscure in his published memoirs years later when he described his "period of waiting in Paris" marked by "long walks in search of architecture and petites femmes . . . rigajig, coucher avec (alas the remorseful prophylaxis that followed)." Marvin attributed Dos Passos' vagueness and ambivalent phrasing regarding his amorous adventures to his "being such a gentleman." He also thought Dos Passos was "a tease and a born story teller." Though Dos Passos was closemouthed about his own experiences with women, he did not hesitate to give counsel when requested. When Marvin asked him how to handle "the Temptations of St. Anthony," he replied:

> I'm afraid they've been filling you up with the Y.M.C.A. idea of the period of storm and stress in a young man's life. . . . The storms of desire to reproduce the species are such a jolly

natural sort of thing that instead of torturing oneself about them, I think one should accept them—at their cash value. Not that I mean you should run to the first scarlet woman on Main Street . . . but you should realize that life is a sweaty, semeny business, and that one shouldn't be shocked by its commonplace mechanism any more than by the digestive juices. . . . I honestly think all the purity gag, mixed up with facts of scientific misinformation about venereal diseases that American youth has its mind polluted with is simply disgusting.

In mid-November, Dos Passos set out from Paris in a slow-moving convoy of French Fiats and Model-T Fords in much worse shape than those pressed into service for the men of the Norton-Harjes. He did not complain because the journey was pleasant enough as they wended their way from Paris to Fontainebleau, then south into the Loire Valley and on to Lyons and the valley of the Rhone. By the time they reached Marseilles, several of their vehicles were out of commission. According to Dos Passos, their section leader had left the staff car in Avignon because he had run it up a tree. One ambulance burned in the square, and Dos Passos himself had an accident in Marseilles. While attempting to back his French Fiat into a line of ambulances, he slammed into a fender of the vehicle parked next to him with such a crash that he was reproved by the section chief. Dos Passos regretted the accident mainly because he was afraid that if his vision were discovered to be as myopic as it was, he might be summarily dismissed and sent home. A second accident occurred three months later in northern Italy. After delivering an ambulanceload of "light *assises*" and stopping off at a small *trattoria* for dinner and a prolonged evening of imbibing "astringent red wine" with villagers, he ran his Fiat into the back of a wagon. Other than a feeling of annoyed shame and a much-bent mudguard and steering gear— which sent their vehicle into the garage for repairs—Dos Passos was none the worse for that incident either.

Before leaving Marseilles, Dos Passos observed a startling performance at a cheap, wharfside café when the waitresses and barmaids entertained the patrons by lifting their skirts and seizing gratuities in "their private parts," as he expressed it in his memoirs. He noted that the women could exercise their talents only if the coins were placed at the corner of the table. "Oh god oh Montreal—what a spectacle." In his diary he spoke of the "unshockingness of the performance" and added: "Bah, one has seen it every day of one's life." Never before had he seen so many prostitutes exhibiting their wares, an observation later recorded in a "Camera Eye" section in his novel *1919*. His reminiscence began and ended with the phrase "Eleven thousand registered harlots said the Red Cross Publicity Man infest the streets of Marseilles."

In Milan at last in early December, Dos Passos amused himself during a "very bad musical show" by writing in his journal:

I am too far away to hope to understand and I am sleepy and it's dull and I wish I had the sense to amuse myself with literature. The people I'm with want to go whoring. I wish I did. It is such a simple naive way of amusing oneself. Why people think it is worth the trouble I can't imagine. Of course love, attraction, the most temporary sort of affair is different. But a barrel with a bunghole in it seems to be their only idea of a woman. I suppose it's only by going out and getting them that one makes adventures, but good God—why not wait? Things do turn up in time.

In Milan, Dos Passos was assigned an Italian Fiat that broke down before the convoy could get under way. His new ambulance partner was Sidney Fairbanks, who lost no time finding himself "a steady whore" and thought it "perfectly charming" that their ambulance section was ordered on to Bassano without him and Dos Passos. For almost a month the Italian mechanics in the Red Cross Motor Garage experimented with ways to keep the tiny engine running, and every day Dos Passos added another jingle to his diary, its variations a spinoff of four basic lines:

> *Fiat 4, Fiat 4*
> *O mécanicien of Milano*
> *When will she roll, my Fiat 4?*
> *Piano, signore, va piano.*

Dos Passos had little confidence in the mechanics at the auto park, whom he spoke of as "bastardly dastards." He also disliked the Italian foot soldier and put no stock, either, in the Italian officers encountered. "God, they are a nasty crew. Even the rather decent ones have the same disease. Their overbearing nastiness to anyone they don't lick the boots of is disgusting." If they discovered silverware poorly washed, they simply hurled them at the steward, and if peasant women refused their favors, they "practically raped them on the spot," he said.

In Dolo—between Padua and Venice—at year's end, Dos Passos and his partner caught up with their unit, which was languishing in a villa without ever having advanced into the field. In a letter to Arthur McComb he complained bitterly of two American Red Cross majors who came in drunk to wish the drivers a happy new year: "God! The things they said. We are here for propaganda it seems, more than for ambulance work. We will be used in the most conspicuous way possible—we must show Italy that America is behind them. That is to say, America has entered—with England and France—into the publicity contest as to who shall save Italy." It was true that morale had been low that winter, due in part to the Italian Army's having suffered thousands of casualties at Caporetto when the Austrians stormed across the border and sent them into rapid retreat. Though the United States Army was still nowhere in evidence, a number of French troops were there, and the Italian government hoped that the presence of the American Red Cross would be taken as a harbinger of the American Expeditionary Forces expected to mass as a strike force in several weeks.

It seemed to Dos Passos that the term "front" in Italy was preposterous. In France the "poor devils" at least knew where the battle lines were and queued to await their turn to be shot down, but in Italy the troops spent their time "playing hide and seek in the mountains." In January the American drivers moved on to Bassano, which underwent frequent artillery attacks and bombings on clear, moonlit nights, yet Dos Passos still felt remote from any combat zone. One day he hiked high into the Dolomites in the direction of the so-called front to see what was going on. He learned later that he had climbed in full view of Austrian sharpshooters who might have picked him off at will. At an outpost in the valley of the river Brenta—also claimed to be the front—he reported seeing the men entertain themselves by lobbing hand grenades into the river and shooting off machine guns whenever they took a notion. As he saw it, the Italians and Austrians were playing "tattoos to each other on them."

Dos Passos found that the men they were bringing down from the mountains suffered from dysentery and frostbite, not bullet or shrapnel wounds. The days offered little relief from boredom for him until Dudley Poore arrived on February 8, 1918, along with an amusing cohort, Fred Bird, who had participated in some of Dos Passos' escapades while in the same Norton-Harjes section in France. That night Dos Passos recorded in his diary that he had been caught in an artillery attack while he, Poore, and their partners were in town on a pretense of buying condensed milk for the section. Their real purpose was to stock up on food and alcohol for a reunion celebration upon their return to camp. "There was nothing like a little shelling of Bassano to liven things up," he observed. From their camp later, they heard the batteries making "a great racket" and saw bombers passing over in four waves attacking the city, yet the next day when he went into the town to witness "smoking ruins and entrails smeared about the paving stones," Dos Passos found only a few collapsed roofs, a room or two rearranged, and perhaps a garden "given a new conformation."

Dos Passos' cynicism darkened the longer he stayed in Italy. "Bitter hate is the only protection one has against the cozening influences of a world rampant with colossal asininity," he carped. Excoriations against the American government, the Italian Army, and his superior officers of the American Red Cross intensified during his six months there. His heaviest barrage was reserved for American capitalists, politicians, and clergymen. "Something in preachifying makes me profoundly miserable," he wrote Rumsey Marvin. He equated the "nasal moaning of hymns" to the "pasty-faced, Y.M.C.A. do-gooders" and feared being cornered and asked to join in the singing of "Onward, Christian Soldiers," which had been taken as a battle cry by the general population. "It is God who has summoned us to this war," preached the Reverend Randolph H. McKinn from a Washington, D.C., pulpit in 1917, as did thousands of other clergymen every Sunday throughout the country. "It is in the profoundest and truest sense a Holy War," he continued. "Yes, it is Christ, the King of Righteousness, who calls us to grapple in deadly strife with this unholy and blasphemous power." To countries in Europe, religious crusades were standard trade, but the United States had never fought a "Holy War" before. Dos Passos ranted against the duping of his countrymen in such a fashion. He was able to work off some of his resentment and anger in the manuscript that eventually became *One Man's Initiation: 1917.* In it he assigned to his protagonist, Martin Howe, the same sense of helplessness and futility which had plagued him in France, and even more so, in Italy:

> It was the fifth time that day that Martin's car had passed the cross-roads where the calvary was. Someone had propped up the fallen crucifix so that it tilted dark despairing arms against the sunset sky where the sun gleamed like a huge copper kettle lost in its own steam. The rain made bright yellowish stripes across the sky and dripped from the cracked feet of the old wooden Christ, whose gaunt, scarred figure hung out from the tilted cross, swaying a little under the beating of the rain. Martin was wiping the mud from his hands after changing a wheel. He stared curiously at the fallen jowl and the cavernous eyes that had meant for some country sculptor ages ago the utterest agony of pain. Suddenly he noticed that where the crown of thorns had been about the forehead of the Christ someone had wound barbed wire.

He smiled, asking the swaying figure in his mind, "What do You think of it, old boy? How do You like Your followers? Not so romantic as thorns, is it, that barbed wire?" . . . The road was filled suddenly with the tramp and splash of troops marching, their wet helmets and their rifles gleaming in the coppery sunset. Even through the clean rain came the smell of filth and sweat and misery of troops marching. The faces under the helmets were strained and colourless and cadaverous from the weight of the equipment on their necks and their backs and their thighs. The faces drooped under the helmets, tilted to one side or the other, distorted and wooden like the face of the figure that dangled from the cross. . . . One of the stragglers who floundered along through the churned mud . . . suddenly began kicking feebly at the prop of the cross with his foot, and then dragged himself off after the column. The cross fell forward with a dull splintering splash into the mud of the road.

Dos Passos' antagonism was fueled, too, by friends at home. When Marvin expressed surprise that the *ambulancier*'s "seditious utterings about governments and war in general" had escaped the censor, and acknowledged that he was selling war bonds and had signed up for a three-year course in military tactics when he entered Yale in the fall, Dos Passos replied: "Military Tactics! Be sensible—even if everyone else in that godforsaken country has lost his head completely. . . . What the devil do you want such a bloody lot of training for anyway? I swear, you people in America are daft on the subject. Training does nothing but eradicate original ideas and stultify the mind to the state of a drill-sergeant." Dos Passos glowered when he read a clipping sent him from the New York *Times Magazine,* dated December 30, 1917. PASSIVISM DIAGNOSED AS DISEASE OF THE MIND, declared its five-column headline. Dr. Mary Keyt Isham's article was subtitled: "Suffering a Genuine Pleasure to Peace-at-Any-Price Pacifists Who Cannot Help Standing By and Watching Spectacle of Prussian Cruelty." Isham's theory was that pacifists were perverts who thrived on German terrorism. The Kaiser and the "Peace-at-Any-Price Pacifists" were of the same fabric, she insisted.

Another newspaper clipping Dos Passos received that winter was an advertisement for the movie *Beast of Berlin: The Kaiser,* playing at the Broadway Theatre on Forty-first Street. "See for yourself. See the picture that will make even a pacifist fight," the advertisement boasted. Although such movies were intended to convert pacifists, the convictions of most were too strong to be shaken in such fashion. Most of the draftees went to war because they felt it their patriotic duty to comply; others went because it was against the law *not* to go. Wright McCormick wrote Dos Passos upon being drafted that he had debated his course of action for days before giving in and felt now that he had forfeited his "right to everything, especially to all expression of opinion." His self-respect had fled.

In 1917–18, there was no middle ground for American citizens concerning the war. They were either loyal or disloyal. If against the war, they were dubbed pro-German. Perhaps what annoyed Dos Passos most about his fellow ambulance drivers who supported the war was their banner of nationalism waved at every turn. Such patriotic cant repulsed him. When dinner conversation "degenerated" to topics of war or the YMCA, "the organizational breeding ground of patriotism," he bolted to seek his own kind.

Dos Passos was frustrated, too, because his efforts to find out what had happened to Cummings and Brown had fallen on deaf ears. "I sympathize with him so thoroughly," Dos Passos wrote Cummings' mother, "and my letters being anything but prudent, I expected I'd be in the same boat. But the censor evidently didn't notice me so I'm still 'at large,' as the blood-and-thunder militarists would say of us," he concluded. Apprehension on his own behalf was quickened when he got news of the "Heine affair." One of his fellow drivers of German parentage, Heine Krieger, had been forced to resign because the Italian censors had intercepted a letter "speaking slightingly of the Italians." The Red Cross had sought his arrest and court-martial. He also was accused of divulging military information, criticizing the Allies, and using "low language" with a "low moral tone" in his letters home. Dos Passos had no personal knowledge of the young soldier, but he was certain that the entire affair was attributable to his parentage. "God! How filthy. . . . And how much of just this sort of sheer meanness and small-mindedness is going on everywhere. It makes you long for a desert island or an ivory tower—somewhere you'd never see anything so small as a man again."

A few days later he heard of a court-martial in the States in which a youth was sentenced to death for refusing to report for military duty when drafted. "Won't it be strange if it comes to that in my case?" he reflected. "Might happen pretty soon too—it'll just be luck if it doesn't as I see it. God! They'll probably even do their best to take the dignity out of death for a conscientious objector." He noted in his diary on March 1, 1918, that there was talk of who was going to be expelled from Italy for the contents of certain letters taken "exception to by the Italian government. Awful curious situation—the Sword of Damocles." He was sure that John Howard Lawson, Frederick van den Arend, and he were the prime candidates. The letter that led to his serious difficulties with American Red Cross officials and resulted in his expulsion from Italy was no worse than a dozen others he had written that winter, but the one in question was mailed from Bassano to José ("Pepe") Giner, his Spanish friend in Madrid, and written in French.

> From a distance, the war must seem a bit theoretical, but here, or anywhere on the front, I assure you, it is quite different. Here there is boredom, slavery to military stupidity, the most interesting misery, the need for warmth and bread, the need to be clean. There is nothing beautiful about modern war. . . . It is nothing but an enormous, tragic digression in people's lives. It is rather up to those of you who live in countries outside of the struggle to continue working for the progress of this poor tormented civilization of ours. . . . It is up to you who quietly, tumultuously make revolutions, who try, perhaps in vain, to evolve towards a purpose for our lives, it is up to you to safeguard all the beautiful things of humanity, while the rest of us struggle brutally, with a suicidal passion. . . . It is only in your Spain and in Russia, it seems to me, that the conquest is not yet complete—that is why I love Spain so much. And my poor country . . . it seems to me that with the war, and with the passage of the military service law, that freedom there is extinguished for a long time to come, and the day of triumph of the plutocracy has arrived. In this connection, one of my best friends is now in Madrid—Arthur McComb—who, being an unshakable anti-militarist, has had to leave the United States and will stay in Spain, I think, for a long time. He is an intelligent fellow and very likable, and I have taken the liberty of telling him to go to see you.

The letter, undated, was probably written in April. McComb had finished up his work at Harvard in February, and instead of allowing himself to be drafted, chose voluntary exile in Spain. He was not alone in such an action, but most draft dodgers chose Mexico or Canada to wait out the war.

Dos Passos' censors prepared a translation of the offending missive, then passed it along to one Major Bates of the American Red Cross, with whom Dos Passos had had a run-in in Paris. Bates, having already pegged Dos Passos a troublemaker and pacifist, immediately forwarded the letter to Major Guy Lowell, the American Red Cross official who had propagandized the *ambulanciers* on New Year's Eve. Appended to the letter was Bates's recommendation that he be dishonorably discharged. "In spite of my repeated warnings, a general notice on the subject, the example of Heine who was discharged from their section, this man has still endangered the cordial relations existing between us and the Italians. I have no sympathy for him. It is about time we had another object lesson. . . . We have no reason for action in the cases of the men with him except that knowing their pacifist ideas we need not give them further employment in the American Red Cross."

Dos Passos, Poore, Lawson, and Van den Arend—all "suspects"—were on holiday at the time. They had left March 15 on a two-week walking tour of southern Italy: Bologna, Rome, Naples, Pompeii, Sorrento, Positano, Paestum, Salerno, and Florence. Just before leaving, Dos Passos had heard rumors that "the hounds" had taken up "the scent." He proceeded less cautiously than did the others. Feeling the net tightening, he relished the cat-and-mouse game with the censors. He had been reading *Crime and Punishment* that spring and identified with Raskolnikov, not out of any sense of guilt that he had perpetrated a crime, but rather that he found reading the novel extinguished his reality and made him live, in a sense, only in the novel. Dos Passos was also alert to the various rumors regarding what would happen to an ambulance man convicted of being pro-German. From one source he heard that anyone discharged dishonorably from the American Red Cross would not be allowed to leave the war zone by way of Paris—where he might linger and get lost—but would be shipped nonstop to the United States by way of Geneva.

Still unaware of the turn of events surrounding his letter to Giner and Bates's recommendation for his discharge, Dos Passos seemed deliberately sporting in the course over which he led the censors. A letter of May 7 to McComb had two lines obliterated by the censor, who inserted a warning slip suggesting that he urge his correspondent to write more legibly, put no more than twenty lines on the page, and limit letters to four pages. His letter to his friend in Spain had begun: "Again I throw a leaf to the winds of the postal service and of the censorship. A card of April 23 has just reached me, and I stop in the midst of a paragraph of Chapter II, Part II of a certain novel-thing to write you again."

Dos Passos saw as his chief task now the completion of his novel, which was two-thirds finished. He was handicapped in that his large, airy quarters in a once elegant villa in Bassano were unheated, and he was physically miserable throughout the winter and early spring. The two gasoline stoves acquired for his barrackslike room provided only enough heat to boil water for tea, in which he floated figs and added Campari. His fingers stayed blue and stiff when not kept to the flame, he groused. There was no way to take the chill from the room. Between ambulance runs the men sat wrapped in blankets. In his diary, he wrote: "And people say that cold is stimulating—Bosh!" Dos Passos now suffered from week-long headaches—something new for him—and was plagued repeatedly by colds and bronchial attacks.

Boredom was another adversary. On April 7, 1918, his cursory remark in his diary was "Ecco! Here am I, bored at Borgo [a village near Bassano]—have finished my books, got disgusted with my novel." The next day, he entered: "At Gherla—bored, mon ami, bored to tears. Oh God, I want to go to sea or to Greece or to Spain or to anywhere away from the Italian rear. I've been trying to draw—I can't draw—I want to novelize—I can't novelize." Dos Passos' diary and sketchbooks contained a number of drawings of bridges, villas, churches, fat-robed priests, and mountainous countryside. He did more sketching in Italy than he had done in France. In the spring when the sun was high enough to take the bite out of the air, Dos Passos hiked with Dudley Poore to a nearby village or a grassy knoll beside the Brenta to draw and while away the hours. "I've gone quite dippy about early Italian fresco painting," he informed Rumsey Marvin. "God, I've never seen such gorgeous, unimaginably interesting decoration as those people—even the rather poor ones —could do." He told of having first glimpsed Giotto's frescoes of the life of Christ in the Arena Chapel near Padua and thought them the finest painting he had seen. Fifty years later he observed in his memoirs that he still pictured the Gospels "in the simple sweet stately terms of Giotto's figures." Again and again Dos Passos gave evidence of his need to live vicariously through other people's art and literature—though their subject matters were different—at the same time he was trying to write something decent of his own. His novel found its life in what he himself had lived and was experiencing at the moment, yet his creative life was heavily dependent upon the writings of others. If caught somewhere without a book, he was beside himself with frustration.

On April 9 he ranted:

Stuck in the damn mud hole of Borgo. Again the noise of wailing goeth up to heaven. . . . Was ever a creature more dependent on literature for life and stimulus. I can't live passively— God—I must either be on the move externally, or internally via literature. I'm like a dope fiend about it. . . . The lack of reading matter has induced me to peep inside the covers of magazines—always a bad thing to do—for it leaves you with a miserable mental nausea. Even for purposes of satire and collection of phrases, such utter mediocrity, such asinine revamping of conventional phrases, it is absolutely sickening. I shall climb up the Campanile to write.

Dos Passos was in the bell tower only briefly when an Italian soldier poked his head through the trap door and ordered him down because he had no *permesso*. "Damn their asinine rules," he muttered, and with every rung of his descent hurled a new curse at the military. "Everywhere in Europe—in America—little bumptious sergeants are chasing poor devils off the steeples that afford them the only spots in a crowded world where they can look at their poor stock of dreams—the way a soldier pulls out and looks over lovingly the few grimy cards and passes and state papers he carries in his pocket book. . . . It's humiliating to be alive."

Lawson and Van den Arend were Dos Passos' chief sounding boards in Italy. When he read them "Book One" of his novel, now entitled "The Walls of Jericho," they complained that the narrative was "too jerky" and that the "unfortunate reader wallowed desperately in a slough of constant misunderstandings." As he saw it, the happenings themselves were unimportant; it was the impression of events that counted. At the end of a catalogue of things he wanted to be sure to include in his novel, he wrote: "Damn—what on earth is the use of making lists of things—it's like making lists of things you want to do or be in life. You just chug along without regarding them all anyway, so you might just as well not tabulate them." More useful to him were the jottings of the thoughts and actions of the characters who romped through his diary at will.

Dos Passos had hoped to finish his novel before his American Red Cross enlistment was up the end of May, but when he set out for Rome on June 1 with Jack Lawson, Dudley Poore, and Frederick van den Arend to investigate the possibilities of an assignment elsewhere, the book was still considerably short of completion. He had heard of a volunteer ambulance service being formed in Palestine and Greece—also sponsored by the American Red Cross—and thought of joining it as a means of extending his stay abroad. "We are in Rome pending all sorts of things under the ridiculous accusations of being pro-German, but I think we are managing to prove our innocence to Red Cross officials. The whole affair is wonderfully absurd and diverting. It shows the canker is growing," he wrote McComb on June 9. To the authorities he admitted only to being injudicious in his letters to McComb and José Giner. He did not worry so much about being jailed as being sent home by way of Geneva, thus having no opportunity to plead his case to American Red Cross officials in Paris who outranked their counterparts in Rome. Charges against Lawson, Van den Arend, and Poore were dropped, but the Italian censors insisted on making a case against Dos Passos as a lesson to other volunteers and urged his immediate expulsion from Italy. None of the four was allowed to reenlist, but Lawson surprised the others with his announcement that the American Red Cross had hired him to stay in Rome to write publicity.

On June 20 Dos Passos left alone by train for Paris with instructions to report immediately to his superiors there. When Van den Arend and Poore caught up with him in Paris, they found him working as a stretcher-bearer in response to pleas that all off-duty men help evacuate the hundreds of wounded American and French soldiers at Château-Thierry, where Allied forces had launched a costly counterattack against German troops waging their last major offensive of the war. Paris itself was under assault by "Big Bertha," a new long-range German cannon. Dos Passos' job was the transporting and dumping of bucketloads of amputated limbs from the operating room of a base hospital on the outskirts of the city. "The world never seemed quite so divided into black and white again. It is impossible to cling to dogmatic opinions in the face of these pathetic remnants of shattered humanity," he observed after the grisly experience was well behind him.

Dos Passos was also traipsing daily between the headquarters of the American Red Cross and the American Expeditionary Forces while authorities of both outfits debated his fate. For a month he argued his case amidst warnings that if he attempted to travel either to Spain or Switzerland he would be arrested. A complicating factor of the entire affair was his failure to report as ordered to his draft board for a physical examination back in the fall of 1917 just after his departure for Europe with the Norton-Harjes. The fact that Wright McCormick had notified the draft board of his service to his country as a volunteer ambulance driver in France had never been appropriately recorded. When Dos Passos was placed on a delinquent list and ordered to Albany, New York, to report to the adjutant general not later than January 3, 1918, he was as unaware of the new order as he was of the first one. His aunt—having power of attorney—could have appeared in his stead, but she had no direct knowledge of the situation until March, when she, too, received notification of her nephew's dire straits. Again Dos Passos was ordered to report to his draft board, but he insisted later that he had never received that notice either. Mary Lamar Gordon sought the help of James Brown Scott, who was influential in high circles as president of the Carnegie Endowment for International Peace. He was also a major in the Judge Advocate General's Department. Scott advised her to petition the local draft board to allow her nephew to report for a physical examination by an American army doctor near the Italian front rather than being required to return home to be examined. It was not until Dos Passos faced charges in Rome and was threatened with expulsion from the country that he learned of his precarious status with his draft board at home.

In Paris, he was told that his choices were either to return voluntarily to the United States as ordered by the draft board, or be deported. Deportation would leave a permanent blight upon his record and keep him from ever being allowed back in France, he was warned. For a time he thought he might be allowed to enlist in the American Field Service, but the examining doctor was horrified when he learned that he could not read even the top letter of the eye chart, yet had served two tours of duty as an ambulance driver. Van den Arend and Poore had been persuaded by Tom Cope, still in Paris with a Quaker reconstruction outfit, to join him for a six-month hitch, a service Dos Passos would gladly have performed, but he was ineligible for that duty also. Robert Hillyer was back in Paris, this time in the uniform of the United States Army. "Bobby's a lieutenant and joy-rides with a colonel round about Tours," Dos Passos reported to Lawson. "Oh, the irony of it all," he wailed. Scott appealed to the American Embassy in Paris, to the postmaster general (Albert Sidney Burleson), and to his congressman (Senator Claude Swanson) with the ploy that the young *ambulancier*'s pacifistic statements "in certain letters" had been tactless, foolish, and ill-timed, but hardly criminal, and urged that the authorities allow him to "continue risking his life for his fellow-countrymen on the field of battle." Despite Scott's efforts, Dos Passos was ordered to return immediately to the United States. He made one final appeal to Scott in hopes that the decision could be reversed if he promised "never again to express unorthodox opinions while in the service of the United States." Dos Passos' declaration that he would throttle all "unorthodox opinions" was as foolish and outrageous as had been his statements that got him into difficulty in the first place, but he was ready to promise anything to be able to return to the war zone while a war was still in progress. His fear was that it might end before he could get back. He also was not ready to go home because he had not lived out his novel. He could not finish it as he chose while the horrors and thrills of the war itself were still going on and he himself was excluded. Before leaving Paris he wrote McComb that the "wretched thing has wormed itself into all sorts of ideas" and had made him "discharge a shocking lot of ammunition prematurely." He described his book as "a history of a young person named Martin Howe, nicknamed Fibbie for his habit of telling yarns in his youth. There are chapters at prep school, at Harvard, in New York, and finally the orgy of lies culminating in the war in a sort of whirlwind." It had enough eating, drinking, and fornicating in it to keep it from appearing in English, he said, and feared that it would die a smouldering "stink-box" in his own pocket instead of a "gas bomb thrown at the head of the American public," but insisted that he had to write it as he saw fit.

On August 10, the SS *Espagne*, the same ship on which he had traveled to Europe in 1916 when he set out for Spain to bide his time until he could see the war firsthand, now conveyed him west. Envious of McComb's being "safe in Spain" at the moment while his own fate was uncertain, he vowed not to stay in the United States but to find some way to "climb in through the back window" of McComb's "ivory tower." He also addressed a letter to Lawson in Rome the day he sailed. Though gentlemen volunteers were "no longer in style," he lamented, he intended to throw himself "at the feet of Washington" and arise "whiter and more patriotic than the lily." As the ship entered the open sea at the mouth of the Gironde beyond Bordeaux, Dos Passos opened a new yellow notebook and jotted down the refrain of a ballad going the rounds aboard ship about Sinbad the sailor, who was *in bad in Tokyo and Rome . . . and twice as bad at home.*

The cash with which he had purchased his first-class ticket home had been cabled him by Scott. It was an installment payment for the purchase of his home by Scott. Dressed again as a civilian, Dos Passos appreciated the fact that no one took him for a pacifist ambulance driver sent home in disfavor. He carried on with his fellow passengers as though he had donned the mask of writer incognito to freshen his stock of grievances while partaking of the amenities of the first-class deck. He tucked his beret into his suitcase, dressed for dinner, chatted amiably with a two-star general who read French, and even listened to a "Y.M.C.A. man" discourse on the eventual triumph of democracy. Perhaps his most uncharacteristic activity aboard ship was to pass the collection plate at the Sunday Protestant church service. Not once did he snicker at the "hymn-droning" or the pathetically played "Largo," he boasted later. Although it was tempting to succumb to his usual lethargy once he felt a ship's engines beneath him and reveled now in the untainted ocean breezes after the stench of war, this time Dos Passos felt obsessed by the need to finish his novel. The first three parts, virtually complete, had been left with Dudley Poore in Paris for safekeeping, and he was ready to begin work on the final section. There was much to be compressed into the closing chapters of the book because he had not yet put his hero into the volunteer ambulance service, the part of his story line that concerned him more than anything else. With his fictional hero heading toward the front and Dos Passos himself pointed resolutely in the opposite direction—his fate uncertain—Part IV was on the verge of having a life of its own.

Throughout the ten-day crossing, he scribbled furiously each morning and sometimes well into the afternoon. The more he worked on the new section, severed as it was from all that led up to it, the greater coherence it had as an entity in itself. Just as Dos Passos himself had broken with his home and family and set off for Europe as a gentleman volunteer without entanglements of the past, so too was he able to begin anew on his novel and write the comparable life of its protagonist, Martin ("Fibbie") Howe. He had no idea just *how* it would all turn out; he knew only that he must get it on paper quickly. Upon his return home he would have to concentrate on clearing himself of his delinquency charge and convince the United States Army that there was not a pacifist bone in his body. The trick would be to get the Army to overlook his myopic vision and accept him. The name "Fibbie Howe" drummed a tattoo as he debarked the *Espagne* and headed for a telephone in lower Manhattan to call Mary Lamar Gordon. At this point in his life he thought of her as his "fairy godmother aunt" who worked miracles when it suited her. When he learned that she was ensconced in the Sprigg family's summer cottage on the ocean at Bay Head, New Jersey, and not available to help intercede for him, his spirits fell. He would have to face the censorious eyes of his draft board officials alone.

11

Return to France, 1918–20

The days succeed one another sordid, without a jot of variety. O the inexpressible sordidness of army life—the filth and greasiness of it.

diary, 12 December 1918

James Brown Scott, whom Dos Passos identified as his "other guardian angel," had offered to mediate on his behalf in a letter to the formidable chairman of the local draft board, George Gordon Battle, whose reputation for indifference to the pleas of young men trying to explain away their brash behavior as draft evaders was well known in his district. "If only Aunt Mamie, my silver-tongued orator, were at my side," Dos Passos lamented as he approached Battle's office the afternoon of his arrival in New York buoyed only by letters from Scott and American Red Cross officials in Paris that vouched for his innocence regarding any intentional wrongdoing in failing to report for his physical examination as ordered. Appropriately contrite, Dos Passos managed to get the draft board chairman to set aside his delinquency charge and promised to report the next morning to the medical examiner as an eager candidate for the United States Army.

So fervent were his pleas to those administering his physical that the eye examiner gave him time to memorize the eye chart. He was amused that someone who could not even read the *E* on the top line wanted *in* the Army, in contrast to the able-bodied men who pulled every ruse they knew to avoid induction or to wriggle *out* of the Army before their hitch was up. Dos Passos was optimistic when he boarded the train for Bay Head a few hours later to apologize in person to his aunt for being such a nuisance and to spend a few days on the beach while awaiting disposition of his case.

As a little boy, Dos Passos had often gone to Bay Head with his mother. After her death he continued to show up unannounced on the doorstep of one of the several cottages owned by his various Sprigg relatives who had been vacationing there for decades. The smiling little summer resort into which he had thrown himself again provided a disquieting contrast to the grotesqueries he had experienced over the past year. The town with its square houses lined up like wooden soldiers at the edge of the ocean, its noisy boardwalks, and its parade of gawking summer people who wore their innocence like a badge seemed innocuous enough on the surface, but Dos Passos was sure that just beneath the veneer were strange and bizarre incidents awaiting birth. Perhaps he would put it into a novel someday, he mused. It seemed to him that he had only to listen to the conversation of his various kinfolk in residence that summer and the characters and plot fairly leaped upon the page. To jostle his memory later when he had time to pursue it, he made a few notes in his diary intended as "the bones of a new novel," which he identified now as "The Family Connection."

For now, however, he had his present novel to bring to a close and retreated to the hull of an old boat in the shade of the boardwalk to write. He watched the bathers— though unobserved himself—feasted upon a box of chocolates, listened to the slap of waves on the shore, and gave his mind license to romp the present and the past. He had written a poem his last day at sea, a ballad entitled "Figaro Sings in the Steerage," an ironic *envoi* to his crossing, since he himself sang from the first-class deck. In the broken hull of the tiny vessel under the boardwalk, he felt moved to start a new poem. "Cannot we let the old gods die?" he asked. "O who will take a drum and pound out the new tune? . . . And where are the songs that should slay the old lies?" Dos Passos did not make a poem of the new lines then, but the questions he raised were with him when he ended his interlude at Bay Head and caught a train to the city to pursue his induction into the Army.

The patina of the "City of Destruction," as he dubbed New York once more, had none of the appeal that Europe's people and antiquities had held for him of late, and he vowed to escape its loathsome abrasiveness as quickly as possible. He did not dare risk spending time in Greenwich Village with his old cohorts because he needed to avoid contact with those whose visibility as pacifists might undermine his efforts to don military khaki. He hoped to be able to sidestep the usual basic training for enlisted men and be sent immediately to an ambulance section in France. His year as a driver at the French and Italian fronts, fluency in French, and ability to communicate in Italian should make him sufficiently valuable to the Army so that his talents and experience would not be wasted, he reasoned. With fresh resolve, Dos Passos hastened to Washington to call upon Scott for help in expediting what he considered an "appropriate chain of events."

On August 28, 1918, Scott arrived late for their appointment and Dos Passos did not wait for him, having decided that it had been "morally impossible" for Scott to keep the engagement. Scott, in turn, took Dos Passos' defection as further evidence of his "positive genius for doing the wrong thing." When they met the next day, however, Dos Passos played the prostrate supplicant. He pleaded shame, stupidity, and boorishness for his unwitting actions and urged Scott to give him another chance to prove his desire to serve his country as a soldier. Scott and Dos Passos had a long session together on August 30, and Scott promised to help him further in any way possible. As Dos Passos saw it, his entire destiny lay in Scott's hands, but his contrite demeanor with Scott took on a different hue in his thoughts recorded in his diary. There was no doubt about it, opined Dos Passos:

Scott was "a governor through and through," whose oligarchic attitude was unassailable. "The idea of individual liberty does not exist" for him. Dos Passos concluded that no matter how sympathetic a man like Scott might be toward "the little man," if he were called upon to adjudicate a case between the individual and the national government, the solitary figure would go down on his knees. He was convinced that it was Scott's intimate friendship with his aunt that had enabled his own tiny ember of freedom to smoulder, and if he did not play Scott's game, he would be prohibited from leaving the country under any circumstances.

Mrs. Gordon was as anxious as her nephew that he be taken into the Army. On September 23, she received a night letter from James Brown Scott:

Congratulations upon nephew's entrance into service. He should make present conveyance of all property real personal and mixed he now owns or which he becomes entitled to under probate of father's will. This should be for consideration of one dollar love and affection as lawyer in New York may advise. In any event conveyance would be absolute not by way of trust as he must rely upon your good faith. This is suggestion accordance your request but he must take advice of New York lawyer as to form. Will be in New York Sunday evening September 29 and all day Sunday and hope to see you then.

Meanwhile, Dos Passos was unaware of his assignment to active duty in the Army or of the collaboration between his aunt and her chief advisor as to the disposition of his material possessions. He had asked Rumsey Marvin to meet him in Stamford, Connecticut, for a walking trip. Marvin had taken a job for the summer in the shipyards at Mystic, Connecticut, with Reginald Marsh, their families having been friends for many years. Marsh was sketching some of the scenes of shipyards and laborers that brought him fame later. Marvin was struck by the fact that he had two remarkable and talented friends, but fretted that if he himself did nothing creative with his mind and hands, he was destined for a dreary career in his grandfather's chocolate factory. It delighted him to watch Dos Passos pull a sketchbook from his knapsack and pause to draw from time to time. Their first day on the trail they hiked to Danbury, where they stopped at dusk at "Mrs. Smith's Boarding House." According to Marvin, "Dos's appearance put off the landlady, who feared that she might be arrested for harboring a couple of spies. His accent made him seem like a foreigner, and with his swarthy complexion and dressed in rumpled clothing and his black beret, he gave her a bit of a fright." They tramped some thirty-six miles in all: from Danbury to New Milford, then north along the Housatonic River until it bent almost to the New York State line, then traveled south again. Dos Passos impressed Marvin with the idea that he was "taking one last fling as an unfettered spirit in the face of an uncertain future."

Several days after his walking trip, Dos Passos went to Cambridge to visit old haunts there. In his diary on September 17, 1918, he noted that of the few places he had been intimate with—Cambridge, the farm in Virginia, London, Brussels—Cambridge was both the best loved and the most hated. For four days he stayed with Edward Massey, his Harvard friend who had studied playwriting with George Pierce Baker. Massey encouraged him during his visit to try his hand at playwriting, too. A play Dos Passos eventually wrote, "The Moon Is a Gong," had its genesis that fall in Cambridge, although the setting itself was Greenwich Village. He also worked on Fibbie Howe's story in an attempt to bring it to a close before his own status significantly changed. Dos Passos realized that once in the Army, he would of necessity part company with his fictional counterpart whose story involved ambulance driving, not soldiering. Upon his return to his aunt's Riverside Drive apartment, he learned that he was due to report to Camp Crane in Allentown, Pennsylvania, on September 26. The United States Army had accepted him at last.

Nothing that Dos Passos envisioned about life in the Army was as offensive to him as its actuality. As a newly inducted member of the Army Medical Corps, he found himself attached to a "Casuals Company." Not only was Camp Crane no ordinary military installation; it had once been a county fair grounds. The barracks were formerly livestock exhibition halls with such names as "Long Horned Cattle Exhibit" and "Poultry and Pigeons." As Dos Passos saw it, the entire camp was comprised of undesirables. "Characters whom other outfits found indigestible tended to sift down into the Medical Corps. . . . All were misfits and oddballs of various kinds," he explained. "The sergeants found us too awkward to drill so they set us to washing windows. When the windows were washed, we swept out the barracks. When the barracks were swept we swept the autumn leaves off the desolate spaces of the old fairground." Two days after his arrival at Camp Crane, Dos Passos discovered he should not have been sent there in the first place. He had been classified for "special service" because of his restricted vision. Without a waiver allowing him to remain there, he was to be processed out of the Army and returned to civilian life. Although he had been tentatively promised an assignment in an ambulance section, red tape had tied up both the waiver of his physical disabilities—which should have come from the Office of the Adjutant General—and his new orders. Meanwhile, he complained that he was "neither fish, fowl, or good red herring," but a poor unbusied soul in Hades, "unable to cross the Styx or even to wear a uniform."

For six weeks Dos Passos languished at "Syphilis Valley"—as its inmates called Camp Crane—and ticked off one by one his days of "captivity." Diary entries and letters were headed by such phrases as "first day of captivity," "seventh day of captivity," and his counting went on and on. "Organization is death—organization is death—organization is death," he muttered with each rub of the windowpane. He wailed later that he had dragged his extension ladder all over camp and scrubbed some one million windows in the process. He knew that if he railed against the establishment as injudiciously as he had in Italy he might find himself permanently incarcerated at Camp Crane or out of the service entirely, but his "blood boiled" when he was ordered to sweep out the quarters of the noncoms. What made matters worse was the influenza epidemic that caused twenty army camps to throw up a strict quarantine. Soldiers dropped like ripe cherries at Camp Crane and other bases across the country before they could even get overseas. There was something ignominious about being in the Army and dying before they reached the trenches or heard the cannons of war, thought Dos Passos. Half as many soldiers died in army camps from influenza during the fall and winter of 1918–19 as those mortally wounded in combat in France during the entire war.

Both Mary Lamar Gordon and James Brown Scott had breathed a great sigh of relief when Dos Passos was inducted into the Army, and they did not relish the thought of his being at large again. Once more Scott set out to use his influence to see that Dos Passos was allowed to stay in military service. After Mrs. Gordon wired her nephew that the waiver was being sent at last, he wrote Scott: "I feel like a burglar explaining how it pained him to take the family silver; but I assure you my uneasiness in troubling you is thoroughly genuine, as is my gratitude." Scott urged Mrs. Gordon to see that Dos Passos "convey at once—if he had not already done so—all of his property in accordance with the manner outlined. One never knew if the misfortunes of war should be his lot," Scott added. Her job was to convince her nephew to avail himself of the $10,000 war risk insurance policy before being shipped overseas, Scott insisted in a letter on October 4. Enclosed were the appropriate documents with her name as beneficiary already inserted. She should forward them for Dos Passos' signature, which must be done within four months of his induction, he explained. In November Scott urged Mrs. Gordon to exercise her power of attorney and sign the forms herself for her "charming but somewhat preoccupied nephew." When she hesitated, he insisted that she act immediately "before the opportunity is forever lost," since her "engaging but somewhat irresponsible nephew" had failed to take the initiative himself. Whatever questions Mrs. Gordon may have put to Dos Passos directly regarding the disposition of his affairs, he either ignored or told her to proceed as she saw fit. Other than meeting his immediate needs of body and spirit—a little food and tobacco, some books, and an opportunity to write—he had no pressing concerns.

Dos Passos saw the raw materials all about him from which he expected to carve his next novel, referred to now as "The Sack of Corinth" (published later as *Three Soldiers),* but his technique as a writer did not permit him to create a manuscript while he was playing out the script daily. To help insure the necessary distance as well as to preserve the essence of what he did, heard, felt, and observed, Dos Passos crammed everything he could into his diary each night. Conversations with fellow soldiers—characterized and even identified by name—were entered almost verbatim. The propaganda he was fed at every turn would be successful in making most men eager to rush to the front lines, kill Germans, rape their women, wave the American flag, and return home victorious and beribboned, he predicted. He also wrote glowingly to McComb and others of the "simple and sublime amiability of the average American soldier," whose pliable nature made him "fit clay" for almost any molding, but the important question concerned the identity of the potter. In his diary he observed that he had more hopes for the United States since getting into the Army than ever before. As a writer of fiction, he knew that he, too, was a molder, but at Camp Crane he saw no need to *create* characters when they were at hand for the asking. The three soldiers who found their way into "The Sack of Corinth" as the principal characters were lifted bodily from Dos Passos' boot camp environment and subsequent happenings in France after shipping out as an acting quartermaster sergeant. His own thin disguise as John Andrews involved only a slight tampering of facts.

Dos Passos was sure that if he had not had books and his own writing as outlets, he could not have survived the endless waiting, the day-in-day-out boredom of jobs completed and repeated, the barbed wire fences and quarantine of Camp Crane, the rumors abounding "from that great council chamber, the can," that the war would be over before he got to go anywhere, and if it should be, that he might be forced to rot in the same camp for the term of his enlistment. The married men wailed that they would be forced to go overseas "to clean up the shit," and the single men did not care what they did so long as they did it on foreign soil. Dos Passos wrote McComb that he was "nearly crazy with the waiting and the fear" that he would not make it to the front before the armistice. He said, too, that he was glad to be in the Army so that he might see things "from the bottom up" for a change. Having divested himself of class and his "moneyed background," he appreciated the opportunity to crouch in the pits with the common man.

McComb's reply from the American Embassy in Madrid, where he now worked, revealed that his and Dos Passos' differences were more than regional. Whereas he had been more outspoken in his radicalism than Dos Passos and they agreed on such topics as anarchy, class, and individual freedom, McComb took issue with Dos Passos' new perspective: "I do not quite agree with you that one sees best from below. It is hard to attain a serenity of spirit without a certain background, and money enough to dissolve the petty ennui is almost an essential part of that background. Stoics can do without, of course, but how hateful, fanatical, and violent the 'simple common man' can be is shown by a Bolshevik. My class, your class, the silent bourgeoisie was never guilty of these things." Dos Passos thought McComb's words quite a turnabout for one who recently had written such fervent lines as his proclamation that "only in Russia does the sacred flame burn brightly. There they have the courage to really revolutionize, and only there (and in Germany) can one talk peace." Dos Passos surmised that McComb's job at the American Embassy had cooled his revolutionary passion. His friend was even more explicit after reading the part of the manuscript that became *One Man's Initiation: 1917:* "I am going to quarrel entirely with your general philosophy and more particularly with your apparent conclusion. You can say that you were only giving an objective picture, but I think I detect the revolutionary tinge and for me it is no solution at all. If anything I am more of a 'moderate' than when I last saw you. I am entirely undeceived about the Bolshevik revolution which has turned out to be the most hateful of tyrannies—the arbitrary rule of undisciplined and facile theorists of the lower classes." As a "piece of work," however, the manuscript was "nothing less than admirable," added McComb, urging Dos Passos to get it to a British publisher as soon as possible, rather than to an American publisher, whose "moral sensibilities would be offended. . . . You will have to pick a publisher with care."

For a time Dos Passos thought he would concentrate on getting Part IV published (the ambulance service days of Fibbie Howe). The earlier sections, left with Dudley Poore, might end up being scrapped, he informed Tom Cope from Camp Crane. He wanted Cope to read the manuscript in Poore's possession to see if it might make a book in itself. When he told Cope that he was glad to have had the experience of knowing the Army firsthand, despite its drawbacks, as a means of helping round out his education, his friend scoffed:

> You say your education is not complete? Does one need to read the <u>Cosmopolitan</u>? . . . know ragtime? . . . draw comic supplements . . . lend money on security . . . play a hand organ . . . dance a clog dance a la vaudeville . . . play football, baseball, and prize fight . . . tell the difference between a one-step and a corrugated waltz? Does education

comprise all 57 varieties? . . . Must one know why Burrows Screens are rustless or rats don't die in the house, or Gordon's particular codfish are invertebrate? Bah! My education is good enough!

Dos Passos also asked Edward Massey to read and criticize Part IV, which he proposed Massey retain for the time being—since he had received orders assigning him to a newly created ambulance section (#541) which was to proceed at once to Camp Merritt, New Jersey, for embarkation to France. He had hoped to have a weekend pass to travel to Boston before leaving Camp Crane, but no one was granted leave because of the quarantine. The danger of his manuscript's falling into the censors' hands made heading overseas risky. He could end up sitting out the war in a stockade. More to the point, he did not want to risk losing it. Finally, Dos Passos decided to put the manuscript in the mail to Massey, who read it and thought it too radical for him to send out of the country until after the war. He did not want to get into trouble with his theater board or the censors.

Dos Passos also sent Massey the scenario that had been brewing since his visit to Bay Head when he first came home from France. The play was incomplete, but Massey encouraged him to develop it. "I've no doubt you've got something quite good there, but it is very chaotic just now." Massey found it difficult to determine when Dos Passos was "deadly serious" and when he was "kidding," but surmised that the funeral scenes were "straight satire" and others verged on burlesque. He had seen nothing like it anywhere, he told Dos Passos, but cautioned him not to let "that sort of burlesque fantasy" become an entire evening's play. Dos Passos had more important things to work on than experimental theater, however, and put the play aside once more. Later, it was Massey himself who produced the play that eventually came out of it ("The Moon Is a Gong") and encouraged Dos Passos to pursue a career in the theater.

Leaving Camp Merritt on November 11, 1918, Dos Passos was headed for the open sea aboard the SS *Cedric* when rumors spread that the war had already ended. The *Cedric* was in convoy with a dozen other troop transports, cargo carriers, warships, and destroyers, its destination England. Dos Passos' acting-quartermaster-sergeant status put him in charge of the mess hall, and for a week he lived in the bowels of the ship supervising the preparation and service of nine meals a day (the troops ate in three shifts). On other crossings, Dos Passos had suffered from a queasiness of stomach, but upon surviving this "sordid hell in the black hole" he saw no reason ever to be seasick again. In his diary he noted that it was remarkable how much more the human organism was capable of standing than he had ever guessed. The dangers encountered behind the wheel of his ambulance in France and the grisly realities of war experienced while transporting dismembered parts from a base operating room had not caused him the personal distress inherent in his kitchen police duties.

To compound the horror of the crossing, an influenza epidemic broke out aboard ship, and dozens of men were buried at sea. The virus swept his own company upon arrival in Camp Winnal Downs, their temporary quarters on a rainswept moor not far from Winchester in southern England. As acting quartermaster sergeant, Dos Passos had to make out the hospitalization orders. On November 27, he recorded his own reprieve from the disease: "After four days of miscellaneous and most grievous disease I feel well enough to start to scribble notes again. I think I've had symptoms of all known diseases: pneumonia, T. B., diptheria, diarrhea, dispepsia, sore throat, whooping cough, scarlet fever and beri-beri, whatever that is. Americans crab so—I wonder if all people do when you get them in unusual positions. Hell—I can't write with everybody singing, crabbing, mainly crabbing." He was convinced that his own death had been warded off by a bottle of rum. Had he given in to his aches and pains and sent himself to the hospital for treatment—just as dozens of others had done in his company—he was sure he would not have come back. Each day carpenters worked at outfitting his men with neat white crosses. Dizzy with fever but braced by rum, Dos Passos managed to board the steamboat at Southampton on November 28 for the channel crossing and arrived in Le Havre, hung over, skinny, and weak, yet fit for duty, he insisted. The ultimate destination of his outfit was an American Army base camp in Ferrières-en-Gâtinais, some fifty-eight kilometers south of Paris.

Dos Passos' acting-quartermaster-sergeant status was arrived at because he could type, though only with two fingers. Once in France he became the chief interpreter for his outfit. Since there was little need for an ambulance section in France after the armistice, the men spent much of their time in close-order drill. Dos Passos was no more adept at it now than he had been while training for the Norton-Harjes, but his new assignment as drillmaster proved catastrophic when he was asked to march his troops for a visiting colonel. He might have been given permanent quartermaster-sergeant status had he not commanded them into a stone wall. The inspecting officer was not impressed by his attempt to reassemble the men after they laughed uproariously and broke ranks. On the spot he was admonished and stripped of his rank. By this time almost every man he had gone overseas with was at least a private first class, but he remained a private for the rest of his military career.

Dos Passos was happier in France with his present outfit than he had been since his early days with the Norton-Harjes. The men considered themselves fortunate to be a part of "O'Reilly's Traveling Circus," a name they took from their Irish sergeant, William J. O'Reilly, a natural leader whose sense of humor held him in good stead. Although Dos Passos complained of having to live with his "neck in a collar," of being hungry and having to panhandle food and drink for three weeks because his army pay had been mysteriously held up, and of being endlessly bored, he accepted his discomfort and restrictions as material for his novel. Into his diary during this period went such comments as "the unforgettable scene with the whore in the back room of the Cheval Blanc—a page out of Artzibasheff—must go in the Sack of Corinth word for word . . . also the girl with the red cheeks and the Café de Madeleine where the boys cluster like flies on a wet day . . . and the whores and the man who is going to marry the French girl."

Had Dos Passos been granted an occasional pass to get into Paris to see his friends there, he would not have objected to his present assignment, but he wanted to retrieve his "Seven Times Round the Walls of Jericho" manuscript from Dudley Poore, read it to Jack Lawson—who had given up his public relations job in Rome and was in Paris writing a play—then revise the work and try to get it published. Robert Hillyer was still in Paris, too, and Dos Passos was eager for him to react critically to the manuscript, since it was the work they had begun originally in collaboration.

Dos Passos hoped that if he did nothing to mar his army record, he could be discharged in Paris. It was rumored that a select group of enlisted men serving with the American Expeditionary Forces in Europe would be allowed to pursue advanced degrees at the Sorbonne and in such other universities as Caen, Dijon, and Lyons. Several universities in England were also participating. The assignment was to depend upon the student's anticipated course of studies. Dos Passos vowed to take up anything that might prove "pleasing to official ears," be it icthyology, hermetic languages, or anthropology, so long as he could do it at the Sorbonne and get to stay in Paris. Those chosen for the program would remain in the Army, but serve on "detached duty" status. Tuition and books would be provided, and they would receive their regular army pay and a food and housing allowance of three additional dollars a day. Dos Passos wrote the Army Overseas Educational Commission in Paris of his qualifications and aspirations to study anthropology, but thought he had a better chance of being selected if he petitioned in person, too. The only way he could wangle a trip into Paris for such a purpose was to transfer to another section, which would require his traveling to Headquarters Company in Paris for the processing of his orders. His new section, S.S.U. 523, was assigned to the Thirty-fifth Division of the French infantry—also quartered in Saussheim Alsace, but his primary mission was accomplished in the interim. Of the ninety-four men selected to participate in the study-abroad program of the Army Overseas Educational Commission in seven French universities, Dos Passos was the only *ambulancier* from his section—and one of ten in all —assigned to the Sorbonne.

Until March 6, 1919, when his orders to the Sorbonne came through, Dos Passos had made one or two trips a week into Paris on every imaginable ruse. Marcus S. Goldman, a private first class who handled the paperwork for the various assignments, remembered Dos Passos years later as "a very suspicious man" who kept checking on his application. Goldman, who was successful in getting his own application approved, was Dos Passos' classmate at the Sorbonne that spring. On March 17 Dos Passos wrote Marvin:

> I am free—at least provisionally. Libertad—libertad!—as Walt would have cried, tearing another button off his undershirt. I loll in the grove of Academe . . . at the Sorbonne—a large monumental place that has up to the writing given me no other impression but that of massy dullness—but I live in a pleasant room on the Montagne Ste.-Geneviève, near the Pantheon, where I typewrite from morning till night with intervals for food—delicious sizzly Paris food—and concerts, preparing the manuscript of "Seven Times Round the Walls of Jericho" for a journey to London and a promenade in publishers' wastebaskets. Furthermore, another novel and a play are clamouring for a hearing. . . . There is, alas, so remarkably little time in twenty-four hours. Why don't days have forty-eight?

An important aspect of Dos Passos' literary life that spring was having receptive friends at hand who enjoyed listening to him read his manuscript aloud. A new addition to his group was Griffin Barry, a young journalist who had spent a year in Russia with John Reed and was now a stringer for the United Press in Paris. Dos Passos liked Barry, whom he described as "a small rosyfaced man who knew everything and everybody . . .

the insider incarnate. There was hardly anybody he hadn't been to bed with." Lawson's room at 45 Quai de la Tournelle on the Left Bank was usually the site of their gatherings over wine and Camembert cheese. The room hummed with Barry's radical friends and the "lingo of Mabel Dodge's salon in New York," said Dos Passos. Another intimate of their group was Kate Drain, a volunteer nurse's aide Dos Passos had met in Paris between stints with the Norton-Harjes and his ambulance service in Italy. All of the men were fond of Kate Drain, who became pregnant by Lawson, married him, and accompanied him to the States to bear their child.

A new addition to their coterie that spring was Trilby Ewer, foreign editor to the London *Daily Herald.* Ewer listened to a reading of some of Dos Passos' "Seven Times Round the Walls of Jericho" and suggested that his friend George Allen, editor and publisher of Allen & Unwin, in London, might be interested in taking a gamble on it. "But not the whole thing," he added. Fibbie Howe's story as an ambulance driver had the best possibility of being published, proposed Ewer. Dos Passos wrote Dudley Poore, who had been selected to study at Emmanuel College in Cambridge, that the early manuscript was "positively horrid" and would need considerable revision if it were not to be abandoned altogether. He intended to enlarge Part IV, "put in steam heat and enameled bath tubs and call it 'France—1917' or something of the sort and try to publish it that way. Really, it's rather fun suddenly having two children instead of one," he added. It took his reading all four parts aloud and heeding his friends' criticism to realize that the manuscript had no business as a single novel. The character Fibbie Howe was insufficient to link the entire story line.

Dos Passos intended to take the ten-day leave due him upon completion of the spring term at the Sorbonne to go to London to follow up on Ewer's suggestion that Allen & Unwin look at his manuscript. Meanwhile, he applied for a discharge at Gièvres, a mustering-out station for those who waived their rights to be sent home at the expense of the American government. Poore, too, asked to be released from the Army in Europe. Until his "France—1917" manuscript was out of the way, Dos Passos was unable to concentrate on "Sack of Corinth," his tale of three soldiers that he had mulled over since his incarceration behind the barbed wire of Camp Crane as a raw recruit. He also looked forward to getting on with his burlesque/fantasy, "The Moon Is a Gong," which Edward Massey had urged him not to allow to fall by the wayside. He told Rumsey Marvin that he had in mind a fourth project, too, a collection of essays culled from his writings in Spain and New York after his father's death. A New Year's resolution to take up painting or drawing once more prompted him to attend a still-life drawing class on Montparnasse, where a franc allowed him to contemplate "a lady's nude contortions" several nights a week. Caught up in a variety of activities, he found himself suddenly back in bed with a new outbreak of rheumatic fever, which forced him to remain indoors for two weeks.

Paris in the spring was a time to be outdoors, he fumed. By mid-May he had his strength back and wrote to Poore: "I am staying in, trying to work, to scribble, to scrawl over pages—but I can't manage it! The day is too gorgeously hot and green and white and vigorous. The carts rattle so along the quais and the little boats shriek on the river with such demoniac glee and the people who are unloading the barges shout so jollily and the warm wind tugs so at my paper. How do people manage to live through the spring? I have never felt it more insanely." As often as possible Dos Passos tramped into the countryside—sometimes with Robert Hillyer or Tom Cope—on overnight excursions along the Seine to such charming villages as St.-Germain, Maisons-Laffitte, Herblay, and Conflans-Ste.-Honorine, all a few miles northwest of Paris. He also rode the train to the historic towns of Rouen and Chartres, where he lolled for hours admiring their cathedrals, his fascination for architecture as alive as ever. His sketchbook went almost everywhere he did, as did his diary and a few sheets of paper and envelopes for his letter-writing. Landscapes, village scenes, red-faced priests, and old women in black shawls sketched in attitudes of prayer came home with him to 45 Quai de la Tournelle, the room he acquired when Jack Lawson and Kate Drain returned to the States. He attended classes faithfully and was a sufficiently successful student to be invited to begin a Ph.D. program at the Sorbonne, but he knew that he was largely marking time until he could shed his uniform permanently and behave precisely as he saw fit.

For a time, Dos Passos was enamored of Germaine Lucas-Championnière, to whom Tom Cope introduced him at a concert. An accomplished pianist, she frequently played for Dos Passos when he came for tea at the invitation of her mother, who welcomed him to their home at 52 rue de Clichy as though he were a member of the family. They shared an enthusiasm for Debussy's *Pelléas and Mélisande,* which Dos Passos told Dudley Poore he had seen a third time and found it "as delightful as ever, even more so." Dos Passos' fictional account of their relationship and of his life in Paris in 1919 in a novel *(Chosen Country)* written some thirty years later suggests that for a time he contemplated asking the French woman to marry him but felt that he was not ready at that stage of his life to take on the responsibilities of a wife.

In late June Dos Passos was informed that everyone from his old unit—to which he was formally attached while on temporary duty as a student at the Sorbonne—had been sent home already or mustered out at Gièvres except him. He had anticipated being given leave on June 30, but learned that if his discharge was not at hand by that date, he would be ordered directly to the United States while still in service. Once again Dos Passos petitioned James Brown Scott for help. Scott, in Paris at the time to help set up arrangements for the signing of the peace treaty at Versailles, listened to Dos Passos' newest tale of woe and agreed to intervene. Trying to gain release from the Army before being shipped home was one challenge, but getting a passport approved on short notice to allow him to remain in Europe was quite another. After an interview with Dos Passos in Paris, Scott directed a letter to the Honorable Robert Woods Bliss at the American Embassy: "I have had a long talk with John R. Dos Passos, Jr., about his intentions for the future in case a passport be issued to him, and I find them 'honorable.' He wants to take his Doctor's degree at the Sorbonne; he wants to prepare himself for a literary career; and he hopes in the near future to become a foreign correspondent for the press." When Mary Lamar Gordon heard of Scott's "latest goodness to that nephew of mine," she apologized for what she considered Dos Passos' imposition and indiscretion:

> I am so sorry that he went to you to obtain his discharge. I am simply disgusted with him. Please do not allow him to worry you anymore. I suppose he feels that you are the only friend

he has on earth who <u>can</u> help him. What has he decided to do to make an honest living? I <u>sincerely</u> hope that Europe will prove so alluring to him that he will remain over there. He spoke of teaching English at some university. Encourage it. He <u>must go to work.</u>

Mary Lamar Gordon minced no words about not wanting her nephew back in New York City. It was not simply a matter of his becoming gainfully employed. She preferred that an ocean remain between them so that she did not have to be reminded constantly of his shortcomings. She thought it scandalous that he intended to make his living by writing.

With the aid of Scott, Dos Passos was allowed to remain in France beyond the June 30 deadline, since his discharge had been inexplicably held up. Meanwhile, he was assigned to a labor battalion at the American discharge camp at Gièvres, where he complained in still another letter to Scott that his daily chore was to move piles of scrap iron —the same scrap iron—back and forth across the tracks at the depot of the camp. He also apologized for his "constant begging of favors":

> You are the first person, though, I ever asked a favor of, and you will be the last. . . . If it had been possible for me to get myself into a mood of resignation I should never have troubled you in the first place. But I seem to have been organized without an atom of submission in me. It really needs constant restraint to keep from fleeing pell mell across the fields and hedges, away from all this hideousness, away from all this stupid despair.

Dos Passos was convinced that one "Mr. Thaw" had "nipped the application in the bud" while it was still in the Office of the Adjutant General's headquarters in Paris. He told Scott that he had actually seen his discharge application with an approval stamp upon it when he had last been in the office, yet it had never been received by the discharge processing office in Tours. So convinced was Dos Passos that he was destined to die of hard labor in his present state of "non-being"—as he called it—that he felt he must do something more than write letters to effect a change. In still another letter to Scott on July 4, 1919, he wrote: "I wonder if you have ever known the bitterness of being utterly helpless, of being utterly unable to affect your destiny in any way. Life under these conditions is utterly worthless."

A week later he took matters into his own hands and went AWOL to locate his papers himself. To evade the military police constantly on alert for soldiers without leave papers, he slipped away from camp early one morning, boarded one train, then another and still another, as he made his way to army headquarters in Tours, where he pled his case to a sympathetic sergeant. A search through file after file finally yielded Dos Passos' entire service jacket, which contained the missing papers. Until his total military file turned up, it was as though John R. Dos Passos, Jr., ASN 2,532,118, Private, United States Ambulance Service Section Unit 523 of the United States Army, had never existed.

On July 11, 1919, Private Dos Passos reappeared for roll call at the discharge camp in Gièvres without anyone's having been aware that he had been absent from the camp for twenty-two hours. He strode through the door of the company commander's quarters, handed over the appropriate document on which was written the phrase "honorable discharge . . . by reason of convenience of the Government," with a character assessment of "excellent," and walked out a free man. Three days later—on Bastille Day—Dos Passos arrived in Paris in a gray suit borrowed from Tom Cope. It had been one hundred thirty years to the day that the Bastille had erupted, signaling the onset of the French Revolution. Dos Passos knew something of how its prisoners must have felt as they emerged from their dungeons and cellblocks. Never again would he wittingly put himself into such a collar, he vowed. "It is such a good old sparkling jolly world when you are not the underdog," he wrote Rumsey Marvin. "At last I am a man once more and not a soldier. Now that it's over I must admit that it was frightful and that it had me in a state of despair such as I've never suffered before. . . . It is a good thing for everyone to be the underdog once in a while, I suppose, but it's frightfully demoralizing. It takes all the guts out of you."

More than anything else now, Dos Passos wanted to get to England to peddle his novel. Trilby Ewer had given him a letter of introduction to George Allen in hopes that Allen & Unwin would seriously consider publishing it, but Dos Passos did not let himself get optimistic about the prospects. He was afraid, also, that his delay in being discharged had eliminated him from consideration of a free-lance spot with the *Daily Herald,* a position for which Ewer had recommended him. In June while Dos Passos was languishing at the discharge camp in Gièvres, Ewer wrote him that the *Daily Herald* could use him as a stringer in Madrid if he could get there immediately. A basis for his appeal to James Brown Scott for help in getting discharged in France was that he would lose his opportunity to be hired as a free-lance journalist by the *Daily Herald,* which he called "the only occupation at which I can make my living without unduly stunting my real work."

In London within a week of his discharge, Dos Passos left his "France—1917" manuscript with the editors of Allen & Unwin, who promised a reading, but offered him little encouragement regarding publication. As an American "doughboy," he had recorded his experiences and impressions of the war—just as countless other young men had —and the editors saw no reason to believe that Dos Passos' manuscript might offer any more than a dozen others on the subject. Money and materials were still in short supply with the war recently over, they reminded him; their firm, too, was in an economic straitjacket. Even if the editors liked the novel and thought it had potential for a life of its own among British readers, they still might insist on his putting up an advance against publishing costs, they warned him. It might be as much as fifty pounds. But if Allen & Unwin liked it, he would come up with the appropriate sum, he promised.

The London *Daily Herald* was more definite. The editor there told Dos Passos that he still had a job as a stringer in Spain if he wanted it, and furnished him with the necessary identification and instructions for transmitting stories. Dos Passos rejoiced that he was a *bona fide* journalist at last, untried, but committed, at any rate. He was impatient now to cross the Pyrenees and bask in his favorite of all lands—Spain—where he intended to travel with Dudley Poore.

Before leaving London, Dos Passos had one more mission to perform: a visit with his mother's friends Kate Gee and Sophia Louisa Meakin. The women had fared poorly during the war, yet managed to send him boxes of chocolates, cakes, and teas to brace his spirits and energies while driving ambulances in France and Italy. Several packages had caught up with him during his reassignment in France. They had been too poor to return to their old home in Kew Gardens, but with money Dos Passos sent them from the initial installment payment for the purchase of his house in Washington, which he had sold to James Brown Scott—another reason that made him feel freer to seek Scott's help—the ladies had been able to return to the home they had vacated before the war. They loved Dos Passos like the son they never had, and probably no soldier or ambulance driver was prayed for more fervently than he. Wright McCormick complained to Dos Passos that spring that he had received a letter obviously intended for "the aunties" and wondered if they had received the gutsy, high-spirited one intended for him. Dos Passos' visit marked the first glimpse they had had of each other in five years. The women fed him tea cakes and ices and pampered him no end, as though he were still "Master Jack Madison," then sent him off for Paris the first of August.

With the exception of Kate Gee and Sophia Louisa Meakin, Dos Passos discovered after his few days in London that he was not much fonder of the Anglo-Saxon world there than he was of New York City. The intellectual atmosphere of England was "as soggy and depressing as the food," he complained. His chief criticism of fellow Americans was that they were "too half-hearted, no matter what the issue." If something seemed awry, they voiced their disapproval with such flaccidity and gentility that one could only guess how they stood on the issues. As he saw it, they failed to *stand* at all, but *sat* upon cushioned seats in the bleachers at the fifty-yard line—never one to miss a show—and looked on "in well-modulated dismay." Dos Passos said that at least he "howled," even if he could do nothing to reverse a bad procedure.

In several letters during the summer and fall of 1919, he spoke of fate's having taken the upper hand over free will of late. Whether he put much stock in such beliefs or not, he gave considerable lip service to the "nasty old women with needle and thread" who were "forever putting the wrong patches side by side in the crazy quilt of destiny." In another letter he complained of "those three old ladies" who sat knitting "somewhere behind the curtain of conjecture" and playing "sorry tricks" on him. He spoke, too, of the turning "wheel of Karma" spinning out his destiny. Yet it was his nature to take matters into his own hands, such as when he had gone AWOL to Tours to search out his service jacket. He reasoned that even though fate conspired against him, it was his duty to raise a rumpus. He had described his basic constitution aptly when he informed Scott that he had been structured without an "atom of submission" regardless of how the dice rolled. By this time, the American who stood best as a symbol or model for Dos Passos' attempt to control his own destiny regardless of the odds was Walt Whitman. He considered the old bard of Long Island his spiritual father. If only Whitman had scattered his seed sufficiently for a handful of like souls to spring up in his stead and emit their own "bardic yap," lamented Dos Passos to Rumsey Marvin, whom he lectured now in hopes that Marvin would not make some of the mistakes that Dos Passos' father had made. Both Marvin and his father possessed admirable "gumption," he said, but his father's had been applied chiefly to capitalistic endeavors, and he did not want Marvin's gumption misplaced:

> If you want to take up manufacturing, for god's sake take up the scientific end of it. You want to be a brain that creates; not a parasite living off other people's brains, off other people's work. . . . My father who had the best brain I've ever known was a tragic example. He was

poor and energetic and lively, and in his day the only thing for a poor boy to do was to make a fortune. But he got so entangled in that famous "business" that when he wanted to start being a person instead of a business man he couldn't disentangle himself, and all through his life he could only really live—use his brain (not his wits)—creatively in odd moments. He never had time. It was the tragedy of his generation.

With little more than the clothes on their backs, Dos Passos set out with Dudley Poore on a walking trip through northern Spain. For six weeks they meandered in the heart of the Basque Provinces, hiking, crossing the Picos de Europa and descending on the seats of their pants, talking with villagers, sitting around campfires with generous-hearted shepherds in the dark Asturian valleys, resting alongside powdery roads beneath a brilliant sun while they sketched the rugged terrain and awesome beauty at every glance. Their bathtub was the sea, and their meals, the hospitality of the house or whatever their rapidly diminishing pesos could acquire for them. Dos Passos was more at ease with himself now than at any time since the death of his father. In Santander, they met up with Arthur McComb, whom Dos Passos had not seen since 1917 when he left for France with the Norton-Harjes. McComb joined them again in Oviedo for another walking junket before the trio took the train together to Madrid.

Madrid brought back countless memories. One night he sat alone at the same white marble table in the German beer hall, Café Oro del Rhín, where he had sat with his friends from Harvard, Roland Jackson and Lowell Downes, during the winter of 1916–17. America had not yet entered the war, and Jackson—an avowed idealist—wondered what might happen if a soldier sat down with his so-called enemy over a drink and talked out their hatred and desires. "Perhaps one might even laugh the hatred out of the other's eyes," Jackson had ventured, his conclusion comparable to that of Thomas Hardy's persona in "The Man He Killed." Upon his return to the States Jackson became an artilleryman. Almost the day he arrived on the French front, he was killed. Dos Passos had been deeply troubled by his friend's death. Although he had watched hundreds of men die and had scooped up carnage he hoped never to see again, he had never lost a friend before. As with most things that happened to him personally over the years, such happenings and feelings eventually went into his fiction or his poetry, but it was usually long after the incident itself or the contributing experience had faded. Then he re-created it impressionistically on his own canvas, be it sketch pad, diary, or letters. Once his letters were dispatched, they were out of reach for concrete reference in the future, yet the mere act of writing things down in any form etched them upon his mind. His ability to catalogue and store smells worked similarly. One of the things that had lured him back to Spain was the pungency of the land and its people. There was nothing cloying about the Iberian Peninsula. It seemed to Dos Passos that Spain was an ideal place in which to write his "Sack of Corinth" novel. When he mentioned the manuscript now in letters to Rumsey Marvin and other friends, his mute identification was a drawing of three stick figures roughly shaded as soldiers. The night he sat alone in the Café Oro del Rhín, the need to get on with his own antiwar tale heavy upon him, Dos Passos took out his notepad and addressed a few lines to his dead friend:

It would be fun, you said,
sitting two years ago at this same table,
at this same white marble café table,
if people only knew what fun it would be
to laugh the hatred out of soldiers' eyes . . .

—If I drink beer with my enemy,
you said, and put your lips to the long glass,
and give him what he wants, if he wants it so hard
that he would kill me for it,
I rather think he'd give it back to me—
You laughed, and stretched your long legs out
  across the floor.

I wonder in what mood you died,
out there in that great muddy butcher-shop,
on that meaningless dicing-table of death.
Did you laugh aloud at the futility,
and drink death down in a long draught,
as you drank your beer two years ago
at this same white marble café table?
Or had the darkness drowned you?

If there had been doubt before, Dos Passos knew now that he was not cut out to be a correspondent for a labor newspaper. Although he sent dispatches intermittently to the London *Daily Herald* that were published, neither he nor his editors felt he had made any significant contribution as a labor journalist of the Iberian Peninsula. It was not that he lacked interest in such matters as syndicalism, socialism, and trade unions, he admitted, but that he was distracted by his physical surroundings and preferred to traipse the countryside without having to account to anyone for what he saw and did. When he wanted most to play the journalist was the fall of 1919. Having heard that a royalist plot to overthrow the Portuguese republic was imminent, Dos Passos set off in a great hurry for Lisbon. At the border he was arrested on suspicion of subversion. His inability to speak Portuguese did not square with his surname and swarthy look. No one accepted the validity of his presence in Portugal as a reporter until he was conveyed under guard—he also had to pay the expenses of his armed escort—to the American consulate in Lisbon. Finally he was identified and given license to roam the city. On October 8, he wrote Stewart Mitchell that he was sitting upon the soil of his ancestors,

> drinking coffee in solitary grandeur at a small white table on the Avenida da Libertade. I have been in Lisbon a week, journalizing. The Portuguese, I find, are a good people, somewhat dirty, somewhat thievish, somewhat humble, lacking that superb haughtiness which seems to be the heritage of the Arabs to Spain, but a people full of goodness. Their main vice is their language, of which I disapprove entirely. It jibes in no way with my ideas of what a language should be. . . . How can you stay in a country where they call your name Dsh Pass-sh.

Think of it! My honorable ancestors called themselves Dsh Pass-sh. Do you wonder that I don't believe in God?

The revolution he had gone to Portugal to witness did not materialize, and he did not like what he saw of the Republican government. "I found the politicians grandiloquent and evasive. Their air of ineffectual benevolence rubbed me the wrong way." The temperament of the Spaniards suited him far better, he said. "I found it a relief to get back to the haughty idiosyncracy of the Spanish. From beggar to grandee the Spaniards carried their burdens with style."

To Rumsey Marvin on November 17 from Granada, he wrote that he had wasted a month in Portugal in "a very foolish business," and on his return "had the bad taste to go to bed with a damn fool rheumatic fever." He and Poore had planned a walking trip to Cádiz, but were forced to hole up in Granada. "As soon as I dare I shall trek for Madrid, as this absurd illness caught me in a dreadful English pension . . . and in the midst of jolly preposterous Spain to be caught in an atmosphere of moral malignancy and Scotch parsimony is too awful for words. My friend and I have our meals with three old hags who sit and hate the Huns and make moral judgments on the Spaniards. I swear it takes many a Byron, many a Marlowe, and many a Shelley to expiate the sins of the Anglo-Saxon race." Dos Passos had never been so ill. For a time Poore nursed him around the clock, then sent for a nurse from Gibraltar. Neither the local doctor—who thought Dos Passos had Maltese fever—nor a German specialist from Madrid was able to prescribe anything that had an appreciable effect upon his fever and swollen joints, but after a month the disease ran its course and he ventured out, feeling more scarecrow than human, into the crisp autumn air. What had bothered him most throughout his ordeal was not working on his "Sack of Corinth" manuscript. His illness also made it impossible to write articles for the London *Daily Herald* he had counted on to pay his room and board at the pension, buy medicine, and help finance the publication of his "France—1917" manuscript. He needed seventy-five pounds as his share of the expense. Allen & Unwin tried to find an American publisher to take it on as a joint venture, but could find no one in the United States willing to gamble on it.

Dos Passos said later that he could not recall precisely where the money had come from to pay his publisher. He probably petitioned his aunt for it. Although the money he solicited from her from time to time was, in effect, his own, he did not like asking for it. Most of the time he and his friends simply *gave* money to each other rather than thinking of it as a loan. They did not take advantage of each other's generosity, and never asked for money if there was not a genuine need. When Dos Passos wrote Rumsey Marvin in the spring of 1920 that "the economic monster licks his chops and sniffs outside my door," he was not seeking a handout; he was aggravated because he needed more time to finish his novel and did not want to interrupt his work to write an article or do something else pedestrian as a means of support.

Dos Passos was unimpressed by the few copies of *The New Republic* he had seen while in Spain during the winter of 1919–20 and thus was heartened when Stewart Mitchell wrote that he and several classmates planned to start a new magazine in which they might "unburden" their souls. The next he heard of the venture was from Robert

Hillyer, then back in New York, who reported that Mitchell had been named managing editor of the resurrected *Dial,* which had foundered after being brought from Chicago to New York in 1916 and was now edited by Scofield Thayer and James Sibley Watson, Jr., who had bought the defunct magazine from owner Martyn Johnson. The first issue of the new *Dial* (January 1920) was bad, said Hillyer. "They published a perfect sheaf of awful unnamables by Estlin and some line drawings by him of trollops with their limbs spread wide apart. . . . Then they had the Boom! Boom! Boom! of several foreign greatnesses, such as Gilbert Canaan and other writers of a costly nature. Shades of The Seven Arts!"

Dos Passos saw the initial issue a few days later and let fly his own judgment to Mitchell: "To get away with a literary magazine at this moment in America, The Seven Arts will have to be gone one better. . . . You are certainly a vivider person and have greater intelligence than any of the seven artists. For God's sake, impose yourself—forget your nice manners, take off your coat, and be willing to make an ass of yourself. . . . We who have worshipped freedom and writing as God—shall we be annihilated by destiny filling up the precious printed pages with spacefillers?" The magazine was so flat it could well have been *The Atlantic Monthly* back in 1889, unless "The Atlantic had life in those days," he added and also disagreed with Hillyer regarding Cummings' contributions. He especially liked Cummings' "Buffalo Bill's defunct." The magazine could at least give its readers "juicier meat for their 35¢." In closing he urged Mitchell to shape *The Dial* for people of his own bent who wanted to express themselves freely yet remain Americans.

Dos Passos had begun to think of returning to the United States. In early February he wrote Jack Lawson from Madrid that he had almost finished his military novel, which he was inclined to hate "with a hate passing all hates hitherto hated," and was bored:

> Spain remains joyously preposterous, but I—I have not been. . . . I have been living a cabbage-like existence . . . unable to escape a regular three meals a day getup and go to bed existence. I have taken to going to a thing called an Ateneo where there is a library, where I write slowly and solemnly and heavily amid an atmosphere of literati. . . . My money is exhausting itself rapidly—I suffer from the limitations of space and time. . . . I must have excitement. I must do something preposterous. Therefore America!

Yet he was determined not to leave Spain until he finished "The Sack of Corinth," which he thought of now as *Three Soldiers.* In mid-March he wrote Rumsey Marvin that he was "sitting in this wretched library-place trying to write chapter four of the last lap of Three Soldiers, feeling about as fluent as an empty tea pot." To counteract his lethargy, Dos Passos went to Barcelona, where he found a room with a view of the harbor. Here he met up with Lawson's wife, Kate Drain, and his sister, Adelaide. Lawson himself was in Paris recuperating from typhoid fever. Dos Passos and his companions disported together for ten days. Each morning he worked in his bright, airy room, then joined the women for lunch and a swim. They baked on the broad, white beaches, tramped into the hills and along the harbor, and took a three-day excursion to Majorca. In Palma, he put the women on a ship bound for Alicante and returned alone to Barcelona. The middle of April, his manuscript virtually complete, he hastened to Carcassonne, a walled town on the Aude River in southern France. Having survived the war intact, it was one of the few fortified medieval towns extant in Europe. Here, he was joined by Lawson, who journeyed with

Louis Hays Dos Passos with his parents, John R. and Mary Hays Dos Passos, about 1887. (Mary Dos Passos Singleton)

Left, James Madison, son of Lucy Addison Sprigg Madison and Ryland R. Madison, about 1891. (Lois Sprigg Hazell) Right, Lucy Addison Sprigg Madison, about 1889, several years after her affair began with John R. Dos Passos. (Elizabeth Dos Passos)

Louis Hays Dos Passos and his father, John R. Dos Passos, about 1900. (Mary Dos Passos Singleton)

Mary Hays Dos Passos, about 1900, during the peri
that her husband maintained she was mentally
(Photo by L. Alman & Co., Courtesy of Mary L
Passos Singleton)

 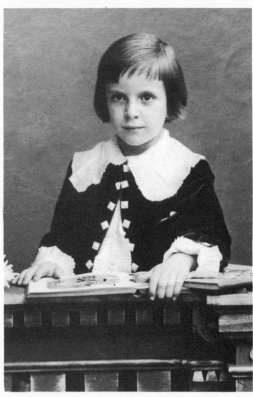

Left, *Jack Madison, about 1899, probably in Brussels. (Elizabeth Dos Passos)* Right, *Jack Madison in Washington, D.C., about 1902, when he was enrolled at the Sidwell Friends School. (Elizabeth Dos Passos)*

Jack Madison in London, about age ten, when he was enrolled at the Peterborough Lodge School. (Photo by Alfred Ellis & Walery, Courtesy Lois Sprigg Hazell)

Left, *John R. Dos Passos, probably about 1911, shortly after his marriage to Lucy Madison. (Mary Dos Passos Singleton)* Right, *Lucy Madison Dos Passos, about 1911. (Lois Sprigg Hazell)*

John R. Dos Passos, Jr., Harvard University, Class of 1916, from the Harvard Year Book. *(By permission of the Houghton Library, Harvard University)*

The Gaivota, *the yacht of John R. Dos Passos, Sr. (Elizabeth Dos Passos)*

The White House, also known as Cintra, at Sandy Point, Virginia, on the Northern Neck, where Dos Passos Jr. spent much of his boyhood, and where his mother died. (Mary Dos Passos Singleton)

Dos Passos, second from left. Photo taken in Milan, Italy, December 12, 1917, upon the attachment of three American Red Cross Ambulance Sections to the Italian Army. (Elizabeth Dos Passos)

A detachment of the Norton-Harjes Ambulance Corps in the field awaiting orders, France, 1917. (William H. Harding)

Robert Hillyer in uniform of Norton-Harjes Ambulance Corps, Paris 1917. (By permission of George Arents Library, Syracuse University)

Thomas Cope, a Quaker pacifist whom Dos Passos met in Paris after World War I. (Elizabeth W. Cope)

him along the verdant, coastal land beside the Gulf of Lions to Marseilles. Having completed *Three Soldiers* at last, Dos Passos thought it a fitting locale in which to celebrate. "O there is nowhere more epic than Marseille, nowhere bawdier, more farcical, jollier, wilder, more seething with humors. . . . Everyone eating, hating, loving, struggling, starving, fornicating—a bath in raw humanity," he wrote Marvin on April 30. In May he was back in Paris, where he announced to Mitchell that "a silly little thing" of his was being published in London after a squabble about "bad language." He had compromised by eliminating some "disrespectful references to Jesus," and in return was "allowed to keep several whores and one prophylaxis." He said he was also "preparing to peddle the second great American novel—called <u>Three Soldiers</u>—or something of the sort. Wonderfully untimely, isn't it?" July found him in London arguing with his publisher in person. "The printers refuse to print <u>One Man's Initiation</u>—they say it's indecent! So more expurgations and changes must be made. The poor thing will be gelded for fair by the time it comes out," he wrote Tom Cope. In the event of a lawsuit, the printers—rather than the author, publisher, or editor—were held responsible. The passage in question had to do with a soldier's kicking the prop out from under a cross from which a wooden Christ figure dangled. When the cross fell, Dos Passos had his protagonist, Fibbie Howe, address the fallen Christ as "Old Boy." The word "you" could be used in place of "Old Boy" providing the *y* was not capitalized, "unless you really feel it's your duty," he added. The word ended up being capitalized, just as he had feared. Dos Passos insisted that he was willing to have almost anything omitted, but refused to be paraphrased. He said later that he regretted having given in to any bowdlerization of his novel.

In addition to *Three Soldiers,* Dos Passos submitted to Allen & Unwin the manuscript of the revised "Seven Times Round the Walls of Jericho," which the publisher's reader liked for its "vitality without vulgarity," although he suggested that they wait to see what happened to the ambulance tale in the way of sales and reader response before making a second commitment. *Three Soldiers* also favorably impressed the reader as a "fine piece of realism and a powerful anti-militarist document." He was sure its appeal would be limited, however, since readers wanted to forget the tragedy and move on to more positive aspects of living. Disappointed, Dos Passos retrieved his manuscripts and resolved to find a publisher in the States.

"I don't know why I'm going back, except that there was no particular point in my staying in Europe," he wrote Tom Cope from aboard the SS *Espagne* on August 7. The date was almost two years to the day that he had set sail on the same ship and headed west. It was also the ship he had traveled on to Bordeaux as an *ambulancier*. Again he traveled first-class. So long as he had money in the bank, Dos Passos had no intention of traveling again in the bowels of a ship. Having been locked in with the masses once, he intended to take them on his own terms from now on. Though he sympathized with the masses and identified with the underdog, it was the individual who counted, whatever his station in life. *Three Soldiers* was his document of the dehumanization of the individual. Personal liberty was one's most precious possession, and if he lacked that, the dehumanizing process was irreversible, declared Dos Passos. Having been unsuccessful in placing the novel with a British publisher, he rationalized now that it would be more fit for an American audience. If his countrymen gagged on it, so much the better. Now that the

Great War was over, he wanted the men who remained at home to set policy to know that to the foot soldier, war was ridiculous, demeaning, hateful, and deadly. If his book gave his countrymen pause before committing other young men to someone else's insanities on foreign soil, he would have made the best contribution possible as an American citizen. Dos Passos had lived almost a quarter century already, and if he had his father's good luck he would come close to tripling that mark, he reasoned. So long as there was life—no matter how the fates measured it—he intended not to let his pen run dry.

12

The New York Literary Scene
and Retreat to the Near East,
1920–22

I suspect it will take a damn short time to get fed up with God's country.

Dos Passos to Tom Cope
at sea, late August 1920

The last leg of Dos Passos' journey home was aboard a dilapidated steamer caught in Havana, since the *Espagne* was destined for ports in Latin America before its run to New York. The balmy journey northward was "given over to the study and culture of the gin fizz," Dos Passos wrote Jack Lawson, who was still recuperating in Paris. Prohibition had become the law of the land during his absence. He was amused by the "marvelous amount of snooping" about the dock by "little men with satchels and hungry eyes" who cast cryptic phrases to the debarking passengers after a host of "square-jawed men with clubs" scrambled up the gangplank to intimidate the innocent and ferret out the ingenious containers bearing the outlawed spirits. New York struck him "like a badly drawn cartoon," he said. "Everybody looks and dresses like the Arrow-collarman." Whereas he had once said that he wanted to get to Europe during the fighting before "everything went belly-up," his observation upon returning to the "City of Destruction" was that everything was already "belly-up" back home. "Labor's belly up completely—the only hope is in the I.W.W. (which no one mentions even in a whisper) and in the Non-Partisan League which has just captured the Democratic primaries in North Dakota and I think in Montana, too." He was certain that Warren G. Harding would defeat Woodrow Wilson in the November elections, though he intended to vote for Eugene Debs. Deb's fifth presidential campaign was being conducted from the federal penitentiary in Atlanta, where he was serving a ten-year sentence for antiwar speeches in violation of the Espionage Act. In a letter to Lawson on October 11, 1920, Dos Passos said he kept meeting "extraordinary people in all walks of life, mild little people who say with a worm-will-turn expression

'I'm going to vote for Debs,' like little boys say damn just because they're scared of the sound of it." His missive concluded with six exclamations of "Belly up."

Mary Lamar Gordon was not pleased when her nephew turned up on her doorstep once more, having hoped he would travel to the Middle East or anywhere that insured an ocean or a continent between them. James Brown Scott, who continued to serve as Mrs. Gordon's legal and financial advisor in matters where Dos Passos was concerned, reasoned that with her nephew's propensity for trouble, she would do well to induce him to take out a ten-thousand-dollar, twenty-year war risk insurance endowment policy and to make her his beneficiary. The payments could come from Dos Passos' inheritance, which she was administering. If he died before the policy matured, she would be fitly compensated. Dividends could go directly to her, Scott suggested. In letter after letter, beginning in January 1920, while Dos Passos was still in Europe, Scott implored Mrs. Gordon to send her "incorrigible nephew" the appropriate papers, which Scott himself had prepared. If he failed to take action in the matter, she must sign the papers herself as "attorney in fact," Scott insisted.

Dos Passos had not agreed to the new policy upon his return to New York in September, and Mrs. Gordon was reluctant to affix her own name to the document. Meanwhile, Scott himself paid six monthly premiums—for which he billed Mrs. Gordon when Dos Passos finally signed for the new insurance—so that the original war risk policy would not lapse. Since Dos Passos was planning to be in Washington to spend Christmas day with his cousin, Lois Sprigg, and her family, Mrs. Gordon suggested he pay a visit to his benefactor. Three days later, Scott informed her that Dos Passos had agreed to the new endowment policy. Scott warned her, however, that her nephew had the looks of one who intended to deprive her of the benefits accruing from the policy. Scott had suggested that dividends go directly to Mrs. Gordon, but Dos Passos explained that since his only livelihood was his writing, he might well use such benefits himself. Scott assured Mrs. Gordon that her nephew was fond of her. "Considering his fine intellect, you really cannot call him spiteful," he added.

Although Scott's correspondence with Mary Lamar Gordon remained formal, they had begun to see each other socially. She apologized often for the trouble that her irresponsible nephew had caused him, but Scott seemed not to mind, since it gave him an excuse for frequent correspondence and for seeing her when she came to Washington or he was in New York. On November 6, 1920, Scott's secretary wrote Mrs. Gordon: "Dr. Scott was so sorry to have missed you when you were in Washington the other day. He . . . will be in Washington Wednesday and Thursday of the coming week and hopes to see you if you have returned. He has asked me to write you not to communicate regarding the football tickets, etc., until then."

Dos Passos stayed at his aunt's home at 214 Riverside Drive—which he still considered his permanent address for mail purposes—while he looked for a place of his own to stay during the fall and winter. "I've been amused, though glutted with relatives, ever since I've been here," he wrote Jack Lawson on September 12. He said he had been a "goddam loafer" on the ship coming home. "Instead of writing the play I wrote absurdities for the Dionysus novel which may be called 'Quest of the Core.' However I feel murderously energetic, slit'em up and slash'em and blow'em up with T.N.T. so—if I ever can find a place to lay my weary hind quarters—have hopes." The Gordons took a dim view of Dos Passos' literary efforts, though they usually refrained from explicit comment. What little bit Mrs. Gordon had read of his in print foreboded ill for all concerned, as she saw it. Dos Passos found the straitlaced atmosphere surrounding the Gordons stultifying and spent as little time there as possible.

In early November after finding a room of his own at 213 East Fifteenth Street (facing Stuyvesant Square), Dos Passos wrote Hillyer that New York was "silly and rather stupendous—I mean skies—buildings—garbage cans." His room was two blocks from the offices of *The Dial*, which had a "charming house with paradise bushes in the back yard on 13th Street, a lovely dark stenog named Sophia. . . . They speak only French during office hours and are genteel, though I admit, delightful," he wrote Lawson. Dos Passos stopped in from time to time to drink tea with its editors—Thayer, Watson, and Mitchell—and renewed his acquaintance with Edward Nagel, whose stepfather, Gaston Lachaise, also enjoyed the hospitality of *The Dial*, since his studio was in the neighborhood. Also important to their crowd were Cummings and William Slater Brown, who returned to the Village in October 1920 from seclusion in New Hampshire, where Cummings finished *The Enormous Room*, his account of their incarceration at La Ferté-Macé. Dos Passos read the tale and thought it splendidly told, though a horror to have lived.

By this time, Cummings was in love with Elaine Orr, whose wedding to Thayer Dos Passos had attended in 1916. Upon their return to New York the following year, Thayer had established separate residences for them, having reportedly declared: "Love should be free and a mere social institution should not interfere with sexual adventure." The daughter Elaine Orr bore in December 1919 was not Thayer's but Cummings'. Although Thayer seemed quite aware of Cummings' relationship with his wife, he appeared not to mind, and he raised the child as his own. Cummings' paternity was kept secret from his daughter until she was an adult. At every opportunity Thayer promoted Cummings' career as an artist and poet and considered his wife's lover one of his best friends. Dos Passos fell in handily with the crowd who gathered at Elaine Orr's spacious, first-floor apartment at 3 Washington Square North for afternoon tea and conversation or an extended cocktail hour before dinner. "Jesus, the alcohol," he exclaimed in a letter to Lawson on November 2. "Prohibition will send the entire population of New York into D.T.'s if it continues. You go into a restaurant and innocently order clam bouillon and before you know it you are guzzling vitriolic cocktails out of a soup tureen. You order coffee and find yourself drinking red ink. You order tea and find it's gin. . . . The smallest wayside inns to which one wanders in New Jersey become before you've sat down, fountains and cataracts and Niagaras of Canadian whiskey."

On November 1, Dos Passos received his author's copies of *One Man's Initiation: 1917* and celebrated with Village friends his new status as published novelist. Outside of their immediate crowd, no one in New York was aware of his book. Reviewers in London ignored it, too. Dos Passos' surrogate aunt, Kate Gee, wrote on November 16:

> I feel so proud of my little Jack that I am like a peacock with three tails. I remember the little inky fingers painfully learning to write and the little brain puzzling over lessons, and now the result: a real live author, and a clever one at that. Your book arrived and I read it at once. It is

graphically told and keeps one's attention going, but oh, it is appallingly sad and realistic. It makes me shiver when I think of the sights you saw and the dreadful things you had to do and so young. . . . I can only feel thankful you came out alive. . . . Publishers are a fraud. . . . They do not push your book at all. For a short time it was in the window, but only in a corner. Now it is not there at all. I do not think they advertise it.

He was not surprised later to learn that only sixty-three copies were sold during the first six-month royalty period. Even worse, he feared that his *Three Soldiers* manuscript might not even have the opportunity to suffer a similar fate.

Three Soldiers made the rounds to some fourteen publishing houses before Eugene F. Saxton, editor and publisher of George H. Doran, decided to gamble on it. Dos Passos was rankled when Saxton insisted that some of the strong language be toned down, but compromised, just as he had with Allen & Unwin:

If you people give me my Jesuses, sonsofbitches, etc., I'll give you some alleviation in other quarters. If you like, some of the Jesuses can be spelt Jez'—but I don't want them cut out. I think it's very important to put down the American lingo as it is, and I think that people will get accustomed to it very easily. No particularly messy hell was raised over Cummings' Enormous Room. . . . As for Justice Ford, I think he's got to be fought and I consider cutting out a word giving aid and comfort to the enemy. Freedom of the press does not mean compromise. It means publishing what Tom Dick and Harry damn please and letting people lump it if they don't like it.

He closed his letter with "wrathfully yours" and added a postscript: "I want my *sonsofbitches* especially."

By this time, Dos Passos had an agent, Brandt and Kirkpatrick, to whom Jack Lawson had shown all but the last section of "Seven Times Round the Walls of Jericho" in the summer of 1919 upon Lawson's marriage to Kate Drain. The firms of both Alfred A. Knopf and Boni & Liveright had expressed interest then in publishing the manuscript, but nothing came of it. Now Carl Brandt concentrated on getting *Three Soldiers* published. Not only did he persuade George H. Doran to accept *Three Soldiers*—scheduled originally for publication in June 1921, but delayed until September—but also *Rosinante to the Road Again,* a collection of Dos Passos' essays on Spain that had begun to appear in *The Dial, The Liberator,* and *The Freeman. The Dial* had published his "Antonio Machado: Poet of Castile" in June 1920, but turned down two essays that *The Freeman* accepted: one, an approving piece on a Basque novelist and anarchist, Pío Baroja, entitled "A Novelist of Disintegration," and the other, on Blasco Ibáñez, whom he saw as "An Inverted Midas." Dos Passos gathered that these pieces were not compatible with *The Dial's* newly avowed nonpolitical stand and testily commented to Lawson: "The Dial and I have little communication so there is no danger of their good manners being corrupted." He was pleased upon his return from Europe by his success in placing articles with other important periodicals, too. Max Eastman, who edited *The Liberator,* published a political piece on Portugal in April 1920, and another on striking farmers in Spain, in October. Albert Nock and Van Wyck Brooks published thirteen of the *Rosinante to the Road Again* essays in *The Freeman* before the collection itself was published in the spring of 1922. "America and the Pursuit of Happiness" appeared in still another magazine, which

Dos Passos considered one of the best on the racks. "I've finally made The Nation," he boasted to Lawson after his essay repudiating what he saw as "the abuse of government's authority and every instance of bullying intolerance" was published in the December 29, 1920, issue of *The Nation*.

Three Soldiers was in galley proofs in the spring of 1921 when Dos Passos and Cummings decided to bolt New York "on a dead run, la vie littéraire getting all at once too much for me"—as he put it to Rumsey Marvin in a letter apologizing for not seeing him before shipping out aboard a Portuguese steamer bound for Lisbon. Almost on the spur of the moment the two of them had persuaded the captain of the SS *Mormugão*, berthed in New Bedford, Massachusetts, to take them on as passengers. The ancient freighter's engines broke down their first night out, and the vessel rolled and bucked in the giant troughs of rough seas until almost dawn. Though not optimistic that he would still be afloat by sun-up, Dos Passos managed to control his seasickness by tossing down shots of brandy every half hour. Finally he and Cummings were able to crawl hand over hand to their cabin and brace themselves in their bunks until sleep overtook them. When they awoke, they were steaming on course into the sun and had won for themselves the respect of the officers and crew. "And now I am on the sea in the warm sopping air of the Middle Atlantic and extraordinarily content, and thanking my stars that I am no longer struggling to keep my head above water in the noisome angular whirlpool of New York," Dos Passos told Marvin.

He had no intention of being in New York when *Three Soldiers* appeared. He and Cummings had agreed that a six- or eight-week walking trip through the crisp spring air of Portugal and Spain would enable them to dispel the taint each felt he had suffered in the city. Dos Passos also felt the pull of Teheran, Baghdad, Damascus, and Beirut, his appetite for such remarkable and mysterious places whetted long ago by his passion for ancient history and the travels of his youth. Cummings intended to lay over in Paris, since Elaine Orr and their daughter, Nancy, would be there. Scofield Thayer's behavior had become increasingly neurotic, and he had persuaded Sigmund Freud to take him on as a patient. Orr had established residency in Paris, where she intended to file for a divorce, since Thayer was no longer interested in even the semblance of a marriage.

The SS *Mormugão* was three weeks in crossing the Atlantic, its first port the coaling station of Horta, the chief seaport on Fayal (an island in the central Azores). The ship wended from island to island, first in the Azores, then to Madeira and its capital, Funchal, where Dos Passos had dinner at Reid's Hotel, which he remembered fondly from his visit at age seven when he was recuperating from his hernia operation. By the time they reached Lisbon, they were "so at home with the ship's company that it was a wrench to leave the smelly unsteady old Mormugão," he reported. When he took Cummings to see the fifteenth-century paintings of Nuno Gonçalves, Cummings told him he preferred Rembrandt. Similarly, Cummings was not impressed by the Manueline architectural style popularized by King Manuel I. It was rank, said Cummings. In Oporto, a harbor town in the heart of the wine district in northern Portugal, Dos Passos spent more time searching for a dentist to treat Cummings' ulcerated tooth than in sampling the wines, to which both had looked forward. On April 21, Cummings wrote his mother that he had drawn twenty-five pounds on his letter of credit from a bank in Seville upon learning that Dos

Passos had been paying for him "in Dosian fashion." Cummings added that he did not wish his friend to "go broke" on his account.

From Seville they traveled by train to the Basque town of St.-Jean-de-Luz, on the French side of the Pyrenees, where they met Jack Lawson, who accompanied them to Oloron-Ste.-Marie, then helped ship their luggage on to Paris so that they were free to traverse a pass in the Pyrenees still blanketed by deep snow. Not much of a hiker himself, Lawson proceeded alone by train to Toulouse. From the tiny village of Accous, they set out on foot in search of Col d'Iseye, a mountain pass known to fair-weather climbers only. Even in good weather it was a dangerous climb. An ancient shepherd warned them to keep on the rocks, but when they recognized what seemed a short cut they left the rocks and struck out through the drifts, into which they sank at times to their hips. Suddenly they found themselves on the top of a ridge, their choice either to backtrack or risk a hazardous descent. In a letter to his mother upon reaching Paris, Cummings spoke of their predicament:

> Dos went first, waist-deep; I lowered the baggage (his musette and an extraordinary bundle of mine) . . . then I followed "in his steps," which was easier as I wore low shoes. . . . We went rushing and tumbling downward . . . on and on and on. No bottom. We hit a river, and Dos discovered its direction—so we followed. Always snow. . . . Finally we came to patches of furze—finally again to trees. . . . My G. how it rained! After resting under a huge spruce and chocolating, we started down again, down a perpendicular meadow . . . my pants-seat disappearing rather rapidly.

At last they heard cowbells and encountered peasants, who offered them a ride in an oxcart for the twelve kilometers remaining before they reached Biel—not their original destination, but a fit haven until they could push on again to Paris, this leg of their journey by train.

In Paris, Dos Passos stayed again in Lawson's flat at 37 Quai d'Anjou while working on two final pieces for his *Rosinante to the Road Again* manuscript, which he sent to John Farrar at George H. Doran with a note that he hoped they were not "too g.d. rotten." One of them, "Two Visiting Professors," he carried with him to Rome, where it was accepted by *Broom,* an international "little magazine" dedicated to the arts that Harold Loeb and Alfred Kreymborg then published abroad (in 1923 it was moved to the Village under the editorship of Matthew Josephson and Malcolm Cowley). The *Broom* piece appeared as "A Funeral in Madrid" in the April 1922 issue a week after its publication in *Rosinante to the Road Again.* Dos Passos urged Farrar not to put his Spanish words and other foreign phrases in italics, since the entire book dealt with Spain. The use of italics would distort the emphasis, he explained. He also asked that his contractions be spelled without apostrophes and dashes used instead of quotation marks to denote conversations. He did not feel strongly enough about such matters to insist "if the honor of the house of Doran" were at stake, he added. Farrar declined Dos Passos' request and published the book with conventional punctuation.

Before leaving New York, Dos Passos had carefully gathered up a number of what he hoped were his best poems for consideration by George H. Doran. Most had been written during his ambulance-driving days and in Spain and Paris both during and after his architectural studies in Madrid. Several, however, were the fruit of his new writings upon settling in the Village in the fall of 1920. *The Dial* accepted two for publication in its June and October 1921 issues before Dos Passos returned to Europe. *Vanity Fair* selected five, and others appeared in *Bookman, The Measure,* and *Current Opinion.* He took his poetry seriously and craved recognition as a poet as well as a novelist and writer of nonfiction. "Anything happened about the verse?" he probed John Farrar before leaving Paris for Venice, where he puttered in hopes that Dudley Poore and Stewart Mitchell would arrive for a final fling in western Europe before he boarded the Orient Express for Constantinople. Venice that summer was "a sort of highfaluting Coney Island," he reported. There was music from morning till night, "spaghetti tenors yodeling in barges on the Grand Canal, fine swimming and exhibition of legs of ladies of pleasure at the Lido, little boats chugging in every direction toodling and jingling, general bawdy brouhaha." He had with him his "Seven Times Round the Walls of Jericho" manuscript, which he intended to revise for a third and final time. If *Three Soldiers* sold as poorly as *One Man's Initiation: 1917,* Dos Passos predicted he would not have the heart to bother with still another revision or to try to find a new publisher for what he persisted in calling "the G.N." ("the Great Novel"). Literature was a "dirty occupation," he observed to Robert Hillyer. "Wish to God my father had apprenticed me to a cobbler."

He was going to Turkey to meet Paxton Hibben, a former artillery captain, diplomat, foreign correspondent, and writer, who now was secretary for the Russian Committee of the Near East Relief (N.E.R), organized by the Red Cross in 1920. They had met in New York the preceding winter, then saw one another again in Paris in June. Hibben was on his way to investigate conditions in the Soviet republics wrapped around the eastern shore of the Black Sea. The lands were wracked by drought, famine, disease, and political repression. Hibben told Dos Passos that if he wished to meet him in Constantinople in July, he would try to get his superiors to accept him for work with the Near East Relief as a means of traveling into the Soviet Union. Dos Passos had yearned to return to Asia Minor since his brief visit to Constantinople at age sixteen.

After a grueling two-day journey across the Balkan Peninsula, Dos Passos stepped off the Orient Express into a hotbed of intrigue, assassination, and homeless White Russian refugees. A pool of blood from an assassinated Levantine diplomat was still fresh on an overstuffed chair in the lobby of the Pera Palace Hotel when he checked in. Turkey had sided with Germany and Austria-Hungary during the war in an effort to regain some of its lost territory, but found itself being carved into even smaller pieces. The Greeks controlled the Aegean port of İzmir, and Constantinople was supervised by the Allies. Dos Passos noted that the British, French, and Italians seemed to vie for ineffectual administration because of their "military stupidity." Had it not been for Admiral Mark L. Bristol, who commanded the American naval detachment in the eastern Mediterranean, he would not have relinquished his prejudice "against brass hats" so readily, he said. Bristol also served as the American high commissioner to Turkey and directed American relief operations. The Greeks and Turks had been involved for some time in a senseless "grubby little war" in which they pillaged, raped, maimed, and murdered each other in seesaw skirmishes in villages and towns near the Aegean and the Sea of Marmara. In an effort to rally the American public to do something to help stop it, Bristol invited a number of foreign correspondents aboard one of his destroyers for a cruise to interview refugees in some of the port cities. Dos Passos was among them, having wrangled press credentials from *Metropolitan Magazine* and the New York *Tribune.* Before leaving New York, he had secured commitments for articles with each. A long piece entitled "Out of Turkish Coffee Cups" appeared on October 2, 1921, in the New York *Tribune* with Dos Passos' byline, but he confided to Rumsey Marvin after three months in the Near East: "I'm no more a journalist than I am a guinea pig and the sooner I go home and get to work writing and stop playing Richard Harding Davis the better."

Paxton Hibben was unable to get approval for Dos Passos to accompany the group to Batum, chief port of the Transcaucasian Soviet Federated Socialist Republic, but Hibben managed to smuggle him aboard the Italian steamer *Aventino,* on which the relief committee also was traveling. At each port along the Black Sea Dos Passos was not allowed to go ashore. The Turks and Greeks alike feared that any foreigner was a spy, especially one who had no credentials. Dos Passos, who had prided himself on being a "fairly able picker of locks in passport barriers," fumed and cursed when he was detained aboard ship for two days upon arrival in Batum on August 7, 1921, while a Soviet official drew up a travel document allowing him to proceed by train to Tiflis, the capital. Hibben had managed to convince a Russian officer that Dos Passos was "favorable to their cause."

Dos Passos crowded aboard the Tiflis express—comprised of an engine, three sleeping cars, and a caboose—with several hundred other passengers, most of whom had stormed the train before it stopped. "Soldiers in white tunics, peasant women with bundles, men with long moustaches and astrakhan caps, speculators with peddlers' packs and honest proletarians with loaves of bread"—all shoved and wriggled aboard. Clots of people perched in the coal car and clung to the roofs, doors, and windows. Dos Passos' documents entitled him to a sleeping berth, but he chose to bed down on an overhead baggage rack after discovering that the insect powder he had sprinkled over his berth stimulated the lice, rather than immobilized them. Upon reaching Tiflis, he learned that twenty people were dying daily of cholera, and from typhus, twice that number. Countless others succumbed of whom records were not kept. From the Near East Relief quarters, where he was permitted to pitch a folding cot, he spent three weeks roaming the city and observing the relief agency at work. Many of his observations were published later in an article in *The Liberator,* "The Caucasus Under the Soviets" (November 1922), but he was not as explicit then in his criticism as later, when he minced no words in an expanded piece entitled "The Relievers" in *Orient Express,* a book of essays dealing with his travels of 1921–22 in the Near East. The black market traffic among members of the N.E.R. was outrageous, he reported: "The real energy of the relievers goes into the relief of Things. To a casual eye Tiflis is bare of Things, nothing in the shopwindows, houses empty as the tents of arabs, but towards the N.E.R. there is a constant streaming of diamonds, emeralds, rubies, silver-encrusted daggers, rugs, . . . watches, filigree work, silver mesh bags, furs, amber." Hibben was similarly explicit in his *American Report on the Russian Famine: Findings of the Russian Commission of the Near East Relief.*

From Tiflis, Dos Passos traveled in the boxcar of a freight train with a Persian doctor en route home to Teheran from medical school in Germany. Hibben had arranged documents for both Dos Passos and the doctor to proceed through the Georgian Soviet Social-

ist Republic to Yerevan (in the Armenian S.S.R.), then on to the Nakhichevan Autono-
mous Soviet Socialist Republic (in the Azerbaijan S.S.R.), bordering Persia (Iran). They
had the car to themselves except for an Armenian interloper attended by two youths. Dos
Passos got along well with Hassan Tabataba, his Persian companion. He had converted a
gold Turkish pound into a suitcase of paper rubles, which gave them bargaining power
with the authorities and merchants encountered along the way, and Tabataba's facility
with the various dialects and languages contributed to their safe passage. Squads of Cheka
police looked in on them from time to time, but did not question the locked wooden chest
Dos Passos had been prevailed upon to deliver for an Armenian family upon reaching
Tabrīz, an interim destination in northwestern Persia. Their boxcar was also the propaganda car, which was invaded daily by Soviet officials whose job was to pick up bundles of
Pravda and *Izvestia* for distribution to the outermost regions of the U.S.S.R.

Much of their journey was detailed by Dos Passos in such articles as "In a New
Republic" *(The Freeman,* October 5, 1921), "One Hundred Views of Ararat" *(Asia,* April
1922), and "Opinions of the Sayyid" *(Asia,* June 1922). Most of his diary jottings he
saved, however, for development in his book of travel essays, *Orient Express,* published in
1927. Dos Passos related how they slept on folding cots provided by Hibben, heated their
tea on a tiny alcohol stove, dined off black rye bread pocked with gravel, tins of sardines,
smoked caviar, six watermelons, Kakhetian wine, and washed in irrigation ditches whenever they had a chance. The stench of sour clothing, filth, garbage, and death permeated
the open boxcar each time the train stopped. In his memoirs of the trip, he wrote:

> War had ground the country down to cinders. The soldiers on the armored trains we passed
> had a hungry feverish air. . . . Where starving people weren't dying of typhus they were
> dying of cholera. The flatcars and boxcars that made up our train were packed with refugees
> escaping from what? Where bound? Nobody seemed to know. In one station corpses were
> stacked like cordwood behind the stove. When a woman died in the car behind us her body
> was left on a red and yellow striped mat beside the tracks.

As soon as Dos Passos and Tabataba crossed the border they got seats in a conventional
passenger compartment while proceeding through northwestern Persia to the trade center
of Tabrīz, but from there across the rugged, mountainous terrain to Teheran, the capital,
there was no rail service. Leaving Dos Passos in the hotel in Tabrīz, the Persian doctor
took several of his gold pounds to the bazaar and returned with an ancient phaeton drawn
by four "ill-favored white horses" and held together by rope and a few bolts. It would be a
thirteen-day trip if there were no major problems, he announced.

After three days on the trail, Dos Passos wrote McComb that he felt like the
"unfortunate Phaethon" himself as their contraption leaped "from crag to crag like a
flea," floundered through marshes, and tore over trackless hillsides with remarkable success. The searing sun stung him like a lash, and his nose was "an enormous and tender
beet." Their tumultuous progress was relieved occasionally by an unexpected "delicious
valley full of violent green trees and watercresses and little moist breezes and a sound of
birds singing." When they paused to rest or to spend the night in a caravansary, the driver
and his grimy assistant—who joggled behind the carriage in a sling when he was not
crouched in the tiny luggage compartment behind the seat—broadcast to the curious

onlookers the marvelous skills of their Persian passenger. In moments the courtyard was wriggling with suppliants seeking healing. Sometimes Dos Passos himself assisted in the doctoring. He reported later having held a patient down by sitting on his head while an ulcer was being carved from his back. After several hours of public service each evening, the medico was paid with whatever barter was available: usually a chicken or two, or eggs, rice, dates, and melons. Sometimes the village khan offered the visiting American and his Persian companion the hospitality of his hut or villa. Here they drank tea and "discussed the fate of Islam" and other subjects until the evening meal was produced on a large brass tray. Chicken, rice, cheese, yogurt, honey, butter, and fruit were served without utensils on what Dos Passos described as an oval of "delicious flat slightly corrugated bread."

At one point their phaeton was intercepted by a fierce-looking horseman and a band of road guards who bargained for their safe passage through a notorious stretch of badlands. Dos Passos respected the leader's wreath of cartridge belts entwining his upper torso and his tale of an unfortunate traveler who had been drawn and quartered when he opted to decline protection. By the time they reached Teheran, the doctor had done battle with malaria and recuperated, and Dos Passos was just coming down with it, his discomfort augmented by the knowledge that only one gold pound stood between him and insolvency. Dos Passos daily braved chills and fever to totter from the Hôtel de France to the cable office in hopes that an editor had seen fit to dispatch payment for one of the various articles recently submitted. When nothing appeared for two weeks, he was forced to spend his few remaining silver krans on a cable to Mary Lamar Gordon requesting two hundred dollars.

Dos Passos described Teheran as an "amazing and dilapidated oasis of French provincialism . . . overhung by purplish mountains with patches of snow on them." From his hotel window he watched "withered and yellowed dignitaries" jiggle by "like dry peas in a pod" in carriages that had been old before their passengers were born. He was also struck by the "grand people on horses with flowing manes and long silky tails such as one sees in Japanese prints" and by the peasants who combed the narrow, winding streets wearing domed felt hats, brilliant robes, and henna-tinted beards. The beginning of the Moslem New Year was celebrated while Dos Passos was in Teheran, but when he witnessed a processional commemorating the death of Husein, grandson of Mohammed the Prophet, he felt oddly discomfited to be "staring at their strange penance as if it were a wild animal act at the circus."

It was already early fall when Dos Passos persuaded a young Armenian who communicated in "missionary American" to drive him in a Model T Ford to the Iraqi border, where he was assured he could proceed by train to Baghdad. Other than its aura and shades of the *Arabian Nights* and the city's architecture, Dos Passos found little in Baghdad that appealed to him. The food was terrible, his tiny room in the seedy Hotel Maude was furnished only with the cot he had brought with him, and the British appeared to be in competition with the rats for control of the city. The British, who had defeated the Turks in 1917 and administered the region until King Faisal I was installed in 1921, were bored and ready to go home. Dos Passos observed that the British troops amused themselves by drinking beer each night in the Hotel Maude, the junior officers' mess, hurling beer bottles at the rats and singing bawdy songs. He had had his own run-in with a rat, which bit him on the lip when he tried to bat him off his chest while abed. Compounding his difficulty was another malaria attack. "The great goggle-eyed banshee of malaria takes to me with more enthusiasm than I enjoy," he told Jack Lawson in a letter in late November. In three weeks' time he was cured and impatient to be on his way after a British army doctor treated him with large doses of quinine.

Dos Passos had become increasingly weary of travel. He wrote almost everyone he knew during the latter stages of his Near East sojourn that he was returning to America to settle in and either produce bona fide works of literature or abandon the trade altogether and "take up chess or knitting." From Teheran he wrote Robert Hillyer: "As to my possibilities in wordmongering, I have never been deeper in the dumps. Things I write become every day more putrid." He had dragged out his decrepit "Seven Times Round the Walls of Jericho" "for the nth time," he said, and saw no reason for optimism. In Baghdad, Dos Passos was in better spirits. On October 23, he wrote Lawson: "I have purged myself of my morgue. . . . I think now I'll be able to get to work with some sort of steadfastness. . . . I am very keen to get back into everybody's midst." Dos Passos was frustrated because he had not hit upon a suitable way to leave Baghdad. He spurned the obvious, a hop in a British army plane to Marseilles. A steamship ticket from Basra, the closest port on the Persian Gulf, to Marseilles by way of the Suez Canal might be entertaining, but such a journey cost far more than he had available, he admitted. To Tom Cope he wrote: "I've decided that this wandering about the world's hotels is a low form of existence. . . . If one's got to travel, one should have the courage of one's convictions, take a staff and a begging bowl and a jar of hashish like a proper dervish and a fig for the city-bred world." The trouble with his kind of self-styled journalism, he continued, was that it required his "fussing with bigbugs. . . . One comes into contact with nobody but personages, chambermaids and drummers."

Dos Passos considered himself fortunate, however, when he met Gertrude Bell, a remarkably talented and resourceful woman who was also chief of British Intelligence for the entire Iraqi region. When he told her that he wished to go overland from Baghdad to Damascus—some five hundred miles across the Syrian Desert—she did not scoff or declare the journey impossible, as did other Westerners to whom he broached the subject; instead, she put him in touch with Jassem-er-Rawwaf, a caravan master who had much to gain from such a crossing if he managed to smuggle into Syria a cache of opium, Persian rugs, bales of tobacco, and several hundred camels in defiance of heavy French tariffs, and thus double his profits. Taking an American along could complicate things, allowed Jassem. Extra "safety money" would be demanded of him by rival Bedouins once word leaked that there was a "mad American" about to set out. On November 13, 1921, Dos Passos wrote Tom Cope:

> I'm sitting on pins and needles in the world's worst hotel. For three weeks I've been trying to get out of Baghdad. Every day the caravan has been about to leave in two days. First it was that there was a squabble between one of the sheikhs to whom safety money had been paid and his son, who demanded a share and said he'd plunder said caravan if he didn't get it. Then for another week, when that was arranged we waited through the sheer mercy of Allah. I couldn't discover any other reason. Now the bridge is repaired over the Euphrates, and I rot in the Hotel Maude and revile my typewriter. All this because I've been seized with an insane

desire to go overland to Damascus, a thing that is regarded in these parts with as much horror as a journey up Everest.

A week later, he was still fuming in Baghdad. In exchange for the twenty gold Turkish pounds Dos Passos had paid the caravan master for his safe delivery in Damascus, he had been promised his own tent and a camel for the journey, but had to agree to dress as an Arab and let his beard grow out. He was also to furnish his own food. Dos Passos spent the rest of his meager funds on two saddlebags of canned goods and a traveling outfit: a loose-fitting aba of brown with a broad white stripe worn over his khaki shirt and pants, a black and white *ishmak* draped about his head, and an agal to secure his headdress. Had it not been for his steel-rimmed spectacles, he might have passed for a proper, turbaned Bedouin until he opened his mouth to venture the few phrases of Arabic he had learned; then all was lost. "Arabic is the most difficult language I ever came up against. The sounds are enormously diverse and difficult and the grammar is unbelievable," he wrote Rumsey Marvin.

What Dos Passos wanted most was to be able to explain in Arabic "the mysteries of cookery" to his camel driver. The camels had been sent on early from Baghdad to Ramadi, the caravan's staging area on the southern bank of the Euphrates, and Dos Passos and Jassem followed in an ailing Model T Ford. By the time they set out across the desert, it was early December. The weather was relatively mild at first, but before long bone-chilling winds and rains beset them. At dusk Dos Passos warmed his stiff feet and hands before a fire of dry camel dung in the lee afforded by stacked bales of cargo. He also drank "endless tiny cups of the most delicious coffee . . . coalblack and almost as bitter as quinine." Each evening he shivered in his "gaudy ten-sided crimson-lined tent" through which the wind and rain leaked no matter how taut the guys were pulled. Although the "chilblains" that had plagued him in northern Italy during the war returned, he insisted that he was "as jolly as a lark" and wrote light-spirited diary entries extolling the virtues of such a trip. "There never was a pleasanter method of traveling. It's great sport," he told Marvin. To Stewart Mitchell he wrote: "This caravan across the desert is the finest thing I ever did in my life."

For a time they seemed merely to drift westward with the sands. Once the news fanned out across the desert that an American was a part of the caravan, rival tribes of the Bedouin already contracted to provide Dos Passos' safe conduct through the desert rode in on their ponies with rifles blazing. Each man tried to look as fearsome as possible before pitching his tent and sitting down in a genial, civilized manner to negotiate the American's continued safe passage. To Dos Passos, his Bedouin foes were as charming as his allies. On December 8, he wrote Marvin: "Last night it was discovered to the horror of a delightful man with a curly beard who brings me coffee and dates at intervals while I sit in splendor in my tent that I was chatting amiably about the weather with one of Ibn Khubain's merry men, who are out to cut our throats—or at least our pursestrings—and feeding him cigarettes." Dos Passos was reprimanded for consorting with the enemy. "I was sorry to have him driven off," added Dos Passos. "He was one of the nicest people I've struck." The caravan master was forced to pay an extra five pounds (Turkish) to ransom Dos Passos' huge suitcase—which he referred to as his "hippo"—although Dos Passos told him that he would gladly give it up to the raiders. It had been trouble enough already. Jassem-er-Rawwaf insisted on Dos Passos' retaining possession of it as a point of honor, however.

Other marauding bands stalked their caravan, too. Some days Dos Passos and his camel driver jog-trotted for eleven-hour stretches at top speed around red sandstone cliffs, across pancake-flat mesas, stony gulches, and up and down grassy uplands in a breakneck attempt to elude them. Before the journey was half over, Dos Passos had used up his own rations, having been instructed to bring enough only for two weeks, but they were on the desert for over a month. While still a week from Damascus the entire band went on half rations—a handful of fried dates and rice—and the camels fed off their own stores and a little water. Dos Passos dreamed of roast goose. He sometimes lost track of the days, but knew that both Christmas and New Year's Day had come and gone while he was on the desert. When they approached the Syrian border, there was the new hazard: the need to maneuver through the dry mountains and sand dunes without being spotted by the French camel corps or customs officers on patrol.

Their last night out, there was "deep talk" around the caravan leader's fire as strange faces appeared and disappeared. In Jassem's tent was heard the "clink of coins being counted from palm to palm." Dos Passos was not surprised upon emerging from his tent the next morning to discover that practically the entire caravan had disappeared. He assured his leader that he had no head for figures in the event that anyone asked him about the size of the caravan or the nature of its cargo. French officials who interrogated Dos Passos later were more interested in how he had entered the country without a passport than in anything else, and dismissed him without further questions when the document was produced by an officer of the American consulate. Dos Passos was examined, too, by officers of British Intelligence, who invited him to lunch and treated him as "a nine days' wonder." The American consul borrowed a tuxedo for him and took him to a party given by the French high commissioner.

To his surprise, Dos Passos discovered that during the five months he had gone without mail he had become something of a celebrity. He wrote Rumsey Marvin on January 10 from Beirut, a short train ride from Damascus:

> Tumbled into Damascus the other day in the company of the Sayyid Mahomet on a grey stallion on a castrational saddle without stirrups. . . . After thirty-nine days of desert, ten of them cold as Christmas (it was) and very hungry for our food ran low and at the end we had nothing but rice and castawi—fried dates, delicious, one of the great elemental patriarchal foods. The Arabs, the people I came over with, the Agail from the Nejel—Central Arabia, were the finest people I've ever known. I felt like kissing their feet I was so fussy and gawky beside them. I've never known people so intense, so well balanced, so gentle. I actually found myself crying after I said goodbye to them. But now I've shaved off my beard and replaced the agal and ishmak by a hat and sent my aba to the wash and live at the best hotel in Beirut in the fattest most uninspired ease, and write letters in response to the little journalistic turds Three Soldiers seems to have induced; envelopes full of them were awaiting for me here— fragrant and foul.

Jack Lawson wrote Dos Passos that *Three Soldiers* had made him "as famous as Wrigley's" and that one could escape the "grandiose rumpus" neither in subways nor churches. Tom Cope told him that there had been so many reviews and articles that he was now being compared to Shakespeare. Dos Passos replied that his publishers with their genius for publicity "deserved the gold-enameled urinal. They could probably make George Eliot go like hotcakes, or the Lamentations of Jeremiah." Cope offered him a bed at 6 Patchin Place in Greenwich Village if Dos Passos wanted to use his room as a hideaway upon his return. A letter from Frederick van den Arend informed him that the book was raising "one hell of a hullabaloo" and predicted that he would have on his trail the Grand Wizard of the Ku Klux Klan, the American Legion, General Pershing, and hordes of indignant mothers of heroes. Van den Arend envied his having "tweeked self-righteous America by the nose," but added that if Dos Passos succeeded, too, "in making America see how dreadfully she bulldozed herself with phrases, how pitifully she is ridden with the same vices for which she reviled the Germans, how brutally she squashes individuality," he would have done more to increase the humaneness and decency in all of them than had the "glorious company of whining Liberals." Van den Arend said that he understood at last why Dos Passos had been "so bent upon volunteering" himself into the Army. Rumsey Marvin chided him for having "overdone the black side of things. Surely every man in the Army went on at least one gay drunk."

According to Cummings, Dos Passos "shot through Paris on his way to America via England," but took time for "several really remarkable parties." Cummings told his mother that Dos Passos "paid left and right" for things, then was forced to borrow eight hundred francs to get home on because he had received no royalties from *Three Soldiers*. They were fortunate to have their "family backers," he added.

The book and its initial reviews set off a rage of controversy among readers, who discharged a volley of letters to the editors of various newspapers and magazines and provoked additional reviews. A banner headline across the front page of the New York *Times Book Review* declared that *Three Soldiers* had insulted the Army. The reviewer, Coningsby Dawson, admitted that his military service had been with the Canadian forces, but insisted that "this is the kind of book that anyone would have been arrested for writing while the war was yet in progress." *Three Soldiers* was "a nationwide insult." Two weeks later, still another front page of the New York *Times Book Review* was devoted to Dos Passos and his novel. The second *Times* reviewer, Harold Norman Denny, explained that he had served in the American Army, thus was qualified to criticize the book according to the way the war actually was. Nowhere during his two years in the Army did he encounter such despicable and craven soldiers as Dos Passos presented as typical. Denny found it incredible that Dos Passos himself was "not a slacker," yet could not resist concluding his review with the comment: "Perhaps it is malicious to point out, but the paper cover surrounding *Three Soldiers* is of an intense, passionate yellow." The editor of *Foreign Service* was tempted to allow *Three Soldiers* "to die the ignominious death it deserves," but the "urge to nail a lie" was "too strong." Dos Passos was guilty of slandering the officers and men of the American Expeditionary Forces "for commercial gain" and he should be "locked up" and "made to pay for it," he insisted. James Sibley Watson, writing for readers of *The Dial* under the name "W. C. Blum," applauded the book for its harmonious expression of a "well-chewed rage," and Francis Hackett contended in *The New Republic* that "apart from its brilliant expressiveness and its beauty, *Three Soldiers* should be welcomed for its candor. It shows what sins have been committed in this country's name." Henry Seidel Canby informed readers of the New York *Evening Post Literary Review* that *Three Soldiers* was the first book about the war by an American written with "sufficient passion and vividness of detail to count as literature. . . . This is by no means a perfect book, but it is a very engrossing one, a first-hand study, finely imagined and powerfully created."

Sherwood Anderson, who had just won the *Dial* prize, wrote Dos Passos a personal letter extolling its virtues, to which he replied: "Since it seems to be a time for the passing of gold-embossed chamber pots, let me blurt out that there's nobody in the country such a note means so much from as you." A. Hamilton Gibbs read the manuscript before it was published and wrote Carl Brandt, Dos Passos' agent: "It's magnificent . . . a combination of Barbusse and Sassoon and Frankau, an extraordinary mixture of poetry and terrible prose pictures one after the other without a thought of sequence or so-called rules. . . . To put my bluebottles in the same envelope with it makes me feel like a sidewalk artist telling Rubens how to draw."

Dos Passos probably did not see the inscription a young war veteran wrote in the flyleaf of *Three Soldiers* and sent to a friend in New Orleans: "This is the truest damn book ever written."

13

"Scuttling About the World . . .
Like a Cockroach Running Away from a Light,"
1922–26

Tried to make a speech at a beastly dinner in New York and made a hideous mess of it. . . . I'm all for the mute inglorious Milton stuff and resent highly the attempts of Doran's publicity staff to turn me into a prize cow. That's what drove me away from New York.

Dos Passos to Rumsey Marvin
March 1922

Upon debarking the SS *Aquitania* in New York in late February 1922, Dos Passos dutifully visited his aunt, Mary Lamar Gordon, then retreated to Cambridge to work on *Streets of Night,* a book-length manuscript that languished despite his good intentions. He told Edmund Wilson in the spring that it was a novel about "the devitalized gentility of modern Boston . . . a tragedy of impotence." Its characters and story line contributed to his inertia. As with *Three Soldiers,* his principal cast was a trio: Fanshaw, who bore a striking resemblance to John Andrews, the quasi-autobiographical protagonist of his war novel; David Wendell, Fanshaw's best friend, who chose suicide to break the bonds of conventionality; and Nancibel Taylor, a violinist from whose point of view the story unfolds. Dos Passos wrote Arthur McComb that "poor Miss Nancibel Taylor waits and waits . . . and her two young gentlemen have been crossing the Cambridge Bridge for some two or three weeks." Later, he referred to his heroine as "that tiresome bitch" and complained that never had he "undertaken a piece of work more anti-sympatico and less successful."

Dos Passos hid away "in a fine little room up three flights on a back street nobody knows" (at 19 Farwell Place) in Cambridge, where he saw Robert Hillyer—now back at Harvard as an instructor of English—Stewart Mitchell, and Dudley Poore. Of their intimate Harvard group, only Cummings and McComb—both still in Europe—were missing. "It was delightful even if one did feel like a <u>haut,</u> and even if everybody talked about the same things they used to talk about seven years ago," said Dos Passos. They roamed the streets of Cambridge by night much as they had before and dined at such familiar haunts as the Parthenon, the Posillipo, the Old Oyster House, and Gee Fong's, a Cantonese restaurant where "every dish was as perfect as a poem translated by Waley." Dos Passos observed that prohibition had not set well with Bostonians. "The 'wine' and 'gin' people feed one here are simply vomitose—infinitely worse than New York."

Rumsey Marvin had urged Dos Passos to stop in New Haven on his way back to New York, hoping to prevail upon him to talk to his literary society at Yale. "I can't do it, and don't want to learn," Dos Passos replied. If he spoke anywhere, he explained, people would hear of it and he would not be able to refuse as stoutly as he had in the past. His books spoke for themselves and the less he had to say about them, the better, he told his editor. Promotion was the publisher's job, he added. "Do let me creep in and out of New Haven unheralded and unsung," he pleaded with Marvin. Two weeks later Dos Passos apologized for having "scooted through New Haven" but explained that he had no money. "At the moment I languish stony broke at 45 Barrow Street, third floor—on the eve of great riches."

Dos Passos' first royalties for *Three Soldiers*—received in April—came to eight thousand dollars. "Never had so much in my life, though I owe about $2,500 of it. At any rate it will solve the question of the next trip to foreign parts when the question arises," he informed McComb. "I shan't write any more damn fool little articles until I am broke again." Meantime, *Rosinante to the Road Again* was published March 18, 1922, and met with a fair amount of critical acclaim, although sales were slight (some 2,360 copies in all). Reviewers noted that the book was valuable more for its revelation of the man who wrote *Three Soldiers* than for its picture of Spain. The consensus was, as the anonymous reviewer for *The Nation* put it, that Dos Passos was "an amateur at social diagnosis," but his literature was professional. Stewart Mitchell did not allow his friendship with Dos Passos to interfere with an honest assessment. *Rosinante to the Road Again* was a "work of unusually good journalism" despite its vagaries. "Dos Passos is at his best on the high-road: he paints better than he explains. For all his diving and spinning [Dos Passos is] a pilot who loves life—and words, perhaps, most of all." Most of the critics thought the book an asset to his reputation and placed him among the most gifted of the younger American writers.

Readers who had been bothered by the verbal excesses in his Spanish book or were put off by the poetic passages in *Three Soldiers* were further estranged by his sensuous lines in *A Pushcart at the Curb,* the book of poetry published by Doran in October. Louis Untermeyer appreciated Dos Passos more as a poetic writer of prose than as a poet, but spoke admiringly of the poems for their "moving brilliance" and the poet's "amazing versatility" and "swift sensitivity." Mark Van Doren thought that an occasional image had "blood on it" and noted a few satiric lines, but faulted Dos Passos for his "imagist stare— cold, sullen, eyeless contemplation of life in terms of aesthetic experience." Van Doren said that he had expected considerable freshness from Dos Passos, but found him "stale enough to startle." Dos Passos' editor did not push for a large first edition. Of the 1,313 copies produced, 544 were remaindered. *A Pushcart at the Curb* was his only book-length manuscript of poems. Upon the publication of *Streets of Night* in November 1923, and his play, "The Moon Is a Gong," which he rewrote several times in 1922–23, Dos Passos turned his back on what he began to perceive as aesthetic dalliance. The precise form his creative energies would take next was unknown to him, but he knew that he had reached a juncture. The paralysis motif in which the struggling aesthete succumbed to the demands of a hostile, oppressive society was at odds with Dos Passos' own fierce determination to direct his destiny. While he anguished over the completion of *Streets of Night,* his next novel, *Manhattan Transfer,* was already gestating. Jimmy Herf, his new protagonist, was tougher than his predecessors, Martin "Fibbie" Howe, John Andrews, and Fanshaw, though still a quasi–Dos Passos persona. Herf's chief domain was not a military camp, combat front, Paris, or Cambridge, but metropolitan New York, a spiritual wasteland whose inhabitants were troubled, anxious people as bleak as their surroundings.

When Dos Passos returned to New York from Cambridge in the spring of 1922, he was accompanied by Dudley Poore, who had been working on an M.A. degree in English at Harvard until jolted by the word "shame" scrawled on a postcard by Dos Passos upon his emergence from the Syrian Desert. "The gesture did not sit well with me and led me to abandon my plan for the M.A., which I needed if I were ever to seek a teaching job," reflected Poore years later. "Dos was generous in attributing to his friends the possession of talents equal to his own, which none of us had. Not that I blame Dos. Myself, I do blame for being so easily deflected from a path I ought to have been firm enough to persist in following. I sometimes wonder what he thought I should do instead." Dos Passos and Poore shared a room at 45 Barrow Street until Elaine Orr Thayer invited them to occupy rooms in the rear of her home at 3 Washington Square North, known as Washington Mews. Poore, whom Dos Passos described as knowing a "most dreadful lot about Romanesque sculpture and has pictures of inconceivable things," decided to try his hand in the city as an art critic and free-lance writer. Poore also sketched and dabbled with watercolors, but did not take himself seriously as an artist or writer. "Dudley and I are in Greenwich Village (but not of it) and live in rapt contemplation of a photodrawing by Antonio Pollaiuolo," Dos Passos wrote McComb after viewing an exhibition of Florentine artists of the fourteenth and fifteenth centuries at the Fogg Art Museum in Cambridge that spring. He said that he was impatient to return to Italy, having "registered a vow to learn all about, and see all the paintings of the scientists—Pollaiuolo, Castagno, Masaccio, Buffalmacco, Della Francesca and pupils—before many more years spin round the barberpole. . . . I must go before I spend all my Three Soldiers money, as I'll never have a chance again for ages. I want to see every piece of plaster a scientist ever put brush to, if I can."

Bored by his efforts to complete *Streets of Night,* which he described now as "stale, flat and unprofitable" and a "garbage pail of wilted aspirations," he turned again to painting. "I've never liked this fantastic city so much," he said, despite its grimy, hectic veneer. "I paint and scribble and dine in Italian restaurants and talk to bums on park benches and the days fly by like flocks of ducks—whirr and they're gone," he observed to McComb, who urged him to finish his book and hie himself back to Europe. McComb saw a feature on Dos Passos as a watercolorist in the Sunday New York *World Magazine,* and chided: "You are now a capitalist, you know. . . . I realize quite vividly that you're a celebrity." He advised Dos Passos to be careful not to allow himself to become public property. New York would be superb if it were not for the persistent "aviary squawkings of the literary gentry," replied Dos Passos.

Adelaide Lawson thought he had considerable talent as a painter and encouraged him to spend more time at it. Before long, they were taking classes together at the Art Students League, where he met Hamilton Easter Field, a wealthy Quaker who lived in Brooklyn Heights and took in needy artists. Field invited him to paint at his little colony in Ogunquit, Maine, known later as the Thurnscoe School of Modern Art. "It was at Ogunquit that I first met Dos," recalled Elizabeth Burroughs Woodhouse, a sculptor (who was married to artist Reginald Marsh for a time).

> I didn't think of him as a writer then, though I knew he had published. He was painting just like everybody else, working then in oils mainly. Hamilton Field had taken over a number of fishermen's shacks on the south end of the harbor, and we descended on him in a swarm. There were some twenty or thirty of us at times. Some of us lived on an island just out from Ogunquit. Adelaide Lawson was there, too, dressed in her outlandish garbs. I remember her painting beside Dos and saying, "Dos, I want a baby." Dos acted as though he never heard her and just went on painting.

According to Lawson, a number of their mutual friends speculated that she and Dos Passos might marry someday. "It occurred to me once or twice, too, and we were fond of each other, but never lovers. He was a wonderful escort and had many women friends. Ours was an easy relationship all our lives, and we never fell out. Even after I married Wood Gaylor Dos was always dropping by and leaving his sketches and watercolors with me. Most of them he never reclaimed." Lawson saw Dos Passos as "shy and modest about his talent as a painter," yet those who knew he painted thought him a good artist. She was pleased when he finally consented to join her and sculptor Reuben Nakian in a public exhibition of their work at the Whitney Studio Club (at 147 West Fourth Street), where it opened January 3, 1923, and ran for three weeks. When he was given engraved invitations to an opening reception to mail to friends, he was reluctant to take any for fear that he might appear to be taking his painting too seriously, she said. "Come and bring a lot of drunks," Dos Passos scribbled on the invitation to F. Scott Fitzgerald (to whom Edmund Wilson introduced him that winter). On Wilson's invitation he jotted: "Follow the green line to the cocktail shaker. Any person caught looking at a picture will be fined for infringement of rules."

Robert Nathan did not see Dos Passos' art at the Whitney Studio Club, but did remember visiting his studio apartment in Washington Mews with Robert Hillyer one night that winter and seeing the paintings ranged around the room on the floor. "There were a great many, and none were hung. I don't recall any single painting, just a general daubishness, which I took to be modern. What I remember better is our sitting on cushions on the floor because there was no furniture except an elaborate buhl chest—a family treasure, no doubt—and a cot. There was considerable imbibing, and suddenly Hillyer stripped and cavorted naked in the moonlight—by himself, like a fawn under a full moon." Nathan had written a "Harvard novel," *Peter Kindred,* which received considerable critical acclaim, a recently published second novel, *Autumn,* and a book of poetry, *Youth Grows Old.* By this time, Nathan, Hillyer, and Dos Passos had garnered considerably more literary notice than their other Harvard classmates, including Cummings. Nathan, too, was living in the Village, but his path seldom crossed Dos Passos' unless they happened upon each other at the Brevoort or the Lafayette Hotel tearoom.

A motivating factor in Dos Passos' renewed interest in painting was his eye trouble. During the preceding summer he had been seldom free from stabbing headaches, and his eyes felt like "hard opaque pebbles." James Sibley Watson's wife, Hildegarde, heard of his ailment and recommended his reading Dr. William D. Bates's recently published and controversial book, *Perfect Sight Without Glasses*. Willing to try anything at this point, Dos Passos took a studio apartment in Washington, D.C. (2174 Wyoming Avenue N.W.) so that he could be close to the doctor's treatment center and began rigorous eye exercises designed both to relieve his headaches and to correct his myopic vision. Bates ordered him to stop work, rest, take off his glasses, and exercise his eyes by reading fine print several times a day. Painting and sketching without his glasses—as well as with them—required frequent shifts in his field of vision; therefore eye therapy and painting were to be encouraged, said Bates. While practicing his new regimen back in Manhattan, Dos Passos began carrying a minuscule Old Testament that he would whip out periodically from a hip pocket and pull to his nose to recapture his place; squinting at the verses, he would then read aloud to friends to demonstrate his progress. Such antics were amusing, but those who saw him were alarmed as he strode down congested streets without his glasses, hearing the traffic more than seeing it, cars and pedestrians a colorful blur as they—or he —streaked by.

His eye problems could not have come at a worse time, Dos Passos wrote Arthur McComb from Hickory Nut Gap, North Carolina, in October 1922. Frederick van den Arend's family had invited him to their vacation retreat in the mountains to work on his *Streets of Night* manuscript without further distraction. "It was all damned annoying just as I was battling hardest with that tiresome bitch, Miss Nan Taylor," he reported to McComb. At month's end he wrote Hillyer: "I've been in Washington having my eyes polished and down in North Carolina cooling my fevered brow. I had rather a scare as the aforesaid peepers were in a horrid state, but now they are moderately luminous, my novel's finished, and I'm Queen of the May."

He intended to return to Europe in the spring, but resolved to stay in New York through the winter in an effort to finish the play he had labored over intermittently since its conception while awaiting orders at Camp Crane to go overseas. In his diary he had written: "Here is an idea for the play thing that has thrust itself so obtrusively into my consciousness—the scene in the garden in Greenwich Village with skyscrapers in the background and garbage cans in the foreground—enter the Garbage Man." A few months later he spoke of it as a "fantasy with music" in which a boy climbed a skyscraper and struck the moon with a sunflower stalk while his lover strolled in the garden. In the fall of 1920 he described it as a "historical pastoral comical realistical fantastic lyrical tragical farcical morality." It was an "utterly futile play," he admitted, but one that dogged him and insisted on being written. He thought of it first as "The Moon Is a Gong." Then it became "The Garbage Man: A Parade of Singing." During the winter of 1922–23 when he worked at it again, both his play and new novel, *Manhattan Transfer*, were close kin to one another in content and expressionistic method. The entire theater scene was part and parcel of the "belly up" condition of all Manhattan, he complained. The only thing that had impressed him on the New York stage of late was Eugene O'Neill's *The Emperor Jones*, which "just missed" being good despite Charles Sidney Gilpin's playing the Brutus Jones role "to perfection." The only hopeful sign he had seen in American theater was its "undressedness and the raw jokes that get by," he wrote Jack Lawson. He and Lawson saw eye to eye when it came to theater criticism, and it was Dos Passos to whom Lawson turned for a preface to his own expressionistic play, *Roger Bloomer*, before its production in the fall of 1923. Their cities would be filled with robots, not men, unless the theater was allowed to serve as a "direct organ of group consciousness," predicted Dos Passos in his preface. O'Neill had issued his own warning against the "grinding machine of industrial life" in *The Hairy Ape*, which Dos Passos saw produced in the spring of 1922 and applauded for its "poignance and superb material," though it was "not entirely solidified," he added. Some of the techniques Dos Passos had begun to experiment with in *Manhattan Transfer* were not unlike what he and Lawson were doing in their plays. For Dos Passos, both play and novel used the mosaic of New York City as its backdrop. Like the play, his new novel was developing amid a cacophony of sounds and rhythms.

Dos Passo found it easier to write about the city when he was not in it. New York distracted and jangled him. He was aboard the SS *Roussillon* on March 8, 1923, when he wrote a friend that he felt he had been wasting his time "stewing in New York" all winter. "Like the young monk in Siberia my existence was growing drier and drier until at last I managed to elope with this excellent empty ex-German boat which is carrying me —I don't know exactly where—probably towards Italy, first." He debarked in Hamburg, traveled south through Germany by train, then stopped off in Strasbourg to visit a woman he had met in New York in September at a memorial service for Wright McCormick, whose death in a mountain-climbing accident in Mexico on August 27, 1922, had stunned them both. "There was an instant affinity with Dos when we met at the services for Mickey, our relationship bonded, in a sense, by the friend who had meant a great deal to us both. Mickey and I were very close, but not sweethearts," recounted Crystal Ross years later. "Since I was leaving for France in mid-September, Dos and I didn't have much time together then, but we wrote often and during the three years that followed we discovered that our values were the same, our backgrounds similar, and almost everything we saw and did was in terms of each other." Ross, a Texan, had gone that fall to Strasbourg to study comparative literature at the university.

Not only was Crystal Ross entreating Dos Passos to meet her in Paris or Strasbourg during the winter or spring of 1923, but two other women were also urging him to put in his appearance on foreign soil. Mildred Sweeney, a widow he had seen off and on when their paths crossed in Europe, begged him to stop off in Geneva, Switzerland, but his reply was evasive. Sweeney was a friend of Arthur McComb and Dudley Poore, too, but she seemed to have pursued Dos Passos' attentions more than the others. His French friend, Germaine Lucas-Championnière, and her mother beseeched him to join them for Easter—and for as long as he would stay—in their summer cottage in Plessis, a village twenty kilometers from Nantes, near the Bay of Biscay on the Loire River. After a few days in Paris, where he journeyed from Strasbourg, Dos Passos appeared on the doorstep of the Lucas-Championnières the day before Easter unannounced save for his own soft tap, having walked from the train station in Nantes. He thrived on meeting up with friends on his travels and appreciated the hospitality of bed, board, and good company for a night or two, but seldom allowed himself to be pinned down in advance to a specific arrival date. He preferred to keep his engagements loose and to be the one to set them.

Unwilling to burden himself with more than he could hang from his own lean shoulders, he arrived in Plessis with only his musette. He intended to live out of it for a month while he roved southern France and caught up with Poore and McComb in Italy. It was a lively weekend with the Lucas-Championnières. They rowed on the Acheneau River, fell over each other in sack races with Germaine's friends, imbibed the sweet, rich muscatel for which their region was known, and exchanged modest, humorous tales of their happenings since they had last sat at table. At sunset he walked out alone to sketch the sky against the trees and village rooftops. His cot that night was in a tiny room above the stables. He had never slept better, he boasted the next morning before shouldering his musette and heading for the Loire to take a boat downriver, then on to Florence and Rome to pore over the paintings and sculpture of the Florentines whose work he had recently viewed in the Fogg Art Museum. Not since the Armory Show a decade earlier had his artistic impulses been so inflamed.

By early June he was back in Paris, where Donald Ogden Stewart introduced him to Gerald and Sara Murphy, fellow Americans who impressed Stewart more than anyone else he had met abroad that year. To Stewart, Murphy was "intelligent, perceptive, gracious, and one of the most attractive men" he had ever known. His wife was the "perfect complement to these virtues." Murphy had gone to Yale (as had Stewart), studied architecture, and rejected a lucrative career in Mark Cross, his father's leather goods company, to live abroad as he saw fit. Stewart described the Murphys as having the "gift of making life enchantingly pleasurable for those who were fortunate enough to be their friends." Dos Passos was not impressed by Gerald Murphy at their first meeting. He thought him "cold and brisk and preoccupied . . . a dandified dresser . . . a poseur." Upon their second encounter, his opinion changed. Murphy had invited Dos Passos to join him and Fernand Léger for lunch, and afterward they strolled the quais together. Murphy had been studying art with Léger, with whom he now exchanged a lively conversation as they walked, each delighting in pointing out to the other such things as a tugboat's red funnel, the flukes of an anchor, winches and coils of rope on a deck, the profile of a woman glimpsed through red geraniums in a window box on a passing barge—all viewed for their shapes and colors. Never had Dos Passos' eye taken in so much along the Seine, which had seemed only banal before. Dos Passos said later that he liked Léger's "butcher's approach to painting, violent, skillful, accurate" and thought his two companions "set each other off." Juxtaposed with Léger's "visual fury" was Murphy's rational and discriminating perceptions marked by "mathematical elegance." Murphy's "cool originality" belied any sense that he may have been merely a "wealthy amateur." Léger proclaimed Murphy the "only American painter in Paris" when he exhibited a "boldly composed" and "technically assured" oil painting (entitled *Razor)* that caused considerable stir at the Salon des Indépendants in the spring of 1923. As Léger saw it, Murphy demonstrated the single "really American response to the new postwar French painting." Most of Murphy's formal training in art had been with Nathalia Gontcharova, an exiled Russian artist.

Gontcharova was also designing the sets for Igor Stravinsky's ballet *Les Noces* at its world premiere in Paris in mid-June. When she let it be known a week before the opening that she did not have sufficient personnel to get the sets ready, Dos Passos and Murphy insisted on helping. Each morning they reported to a loft near the Place des Combats to heat glue pots, mix paints, and spread them over vast, odd-shaped canvases. Twice they worked until dawn amidst great confusion, and Dos Passos marveled that everything fell into place at the last moment. George Balanchine, then a young Russian choreographer, came from Moscow for the stunning premiere that electrified the Parisian world of art, music, and dance. "We were all mad for Diaghilev's Ballet Russe," said Dos Passos, who hoped that the ballet would do for his own time what tragedy had done for the Greeks. Stravinsky's *Le Sacre du Printemps* was the height of what could be accomplished on the stage," he declared, and the great Sokolova had "carried dancing as far as it could go." For months Stravinsky's rhythms "underlay everything we heard, his prancing figures moved behind everything we saw."

Despite his growing fondness for the Murphys, Dos Passos did not take to their large-scale entertaining, which he assumed was their habit, rather than an exception, and refused to attend their champagne dinner party aboard a chartered barge on the Seine to celebrate the opening. "I was shy and I hated small talk and I didn't like having to answer questions about my writing. I cultivated the pose of sidewalk proletarian to whom riches were vanity," he said. The party became legendary, and he was sorry that he missed it. Almost everyone connected with the modern movement in Paris was there: Pablo Picasso, Darius Milhaud, Jean Cocteau, Igor Stravinsky, Sergei Diaghilev, Gontcharova, Mikhail Larionov, Marcelle Meyer, Ernest Ansermet (who conducted *Les Noces*), and poets Tristan Tzara and Blaise Cendrars. Scofield Thayer was one of the few Americans invited.

Cummings, also in Paris at the time, had attended a rehearsal of the ballet with Dos Passos, but sat in the back row and slipped away without allowing himself to be introduced to the Murphys. His attitude concerning money and lavish entertaining was not unlike Dos Passos'. Elaine Orr was in the city, too, with their daughter, Nancy. A favorite activity of Dos Passos that spring was tramping about Paris with Cummings and Nancy (now three) and accompanying them to the Tuileries garden and to the Cirque Médrano to see the Fratinelli clowns and acrobats. Cummings' propensity for getting into trouble became legendary in Paris that year. What was referred to as his "famous episode of *le pisseur*" was in high contrast to the extravagant dinner party of the Murphys, but the tale became almost as well known. Dos Passos himself was one of the principals of the scenario. He had been back in Paris only briefly when he met Cummings and their old classmate, Gilbert Seldes, for dinner at the Café de la Paix. Seldes was in Paris on business for *The Dial*, having replaced Stewart Mitchell as its managing editor. After a long, bibulous evening at table, the trio headed on foot down a dark alley toward a cabaret recently discovered by Cummings near the Place St.-Michel. They were discoursing noisily as they walked when Cummings paused to urinate against a building. Suddenly out of the mist two gendarmes appeared and seized him. *"Un pisseur!"* they shouted and marched him to the nearest police station with Dos Passos and Seldes at their heels protesting loudly that the gentleman being arrested was "America's greatest poet." They threw in, too, that he had served on the front to save *la belle France* from the *boche,* their declamations interspersed with *"vive la France"* and *vive l'Amèrique!"* Such railings served only to increase the tempo of their march to the station. When Dos Passos tried to follow them into the *poste de police,* he was pushed out the door. Then he tried to force his way in and ended up in the street. Not since his prep school skirmish with a bullying classmate had Dos Passos been so physically aggressive. The action surprised himself as well as everyone else to whom the incident was repeated later. "Never had three men become sober so quickly," said Seldes, when it occurred to them that Cummings might be ejected from France permanently if the old record of his incarceration in La Ferté-Macé was dredged up. After several fitful hours he was released but ordered to appear for a hearing the next day. With the aid of writer Paul Morand, who was also an influential official at the Quai d'Orsay, the charges were dropped, and Cummings returned to Seldes' flat to celebrate and found posters proclaiming *"Reprieve Pisseur Americain!"*

The Murphys, who had left Paris for Cap d'Antibes soon after their party for the Diaghilev troupe, urged Dos Passos to join them there. They had been introduced to the French Riviera in 1922 by Cole Porter, whose musical career Murphy helped launch while both were at Yale. The accommodating manager of the Hôtel du Cap at Cap d'Antibes had agreed to stay open for the remainder of the summer with a skeleton staff—instead of closing at the end of the spring tourist season—so the Murphys could enjoy the beach and have a place in which to entertain and put up their guests until their own villa was ready for occupancy. Dos Passos arrived the first of August to find several of his friends already ensconced. Donald and Clara Stewart were there, Archibald and Ada MacLeish, Philip and Ellen Barry, Marc Connelly and his mother, and Cole Porter and his wife, who lived in Venice. Here he met for the first time Pablo Picasso and his family, who came over daily from nearby Juan-les-Pins. Whereas the French and British knew the Riviera only as a winter resort, Americans such as Murphy and Porter thought the summer temperature there perfect. Dos Passos called the swimming off the rocks "delicious" and likened it to the remarkable bathing off Reid's Hotel in Madeira. "The cult of the sun had barely begun," he said, and Antibes was "just the quiet untrampled provincial seaport they had dreamed of discovering." He had already left when Gertrude Stein swept in with Alice B. Toklas in pursuit of Picasso. She wanted to swap a portrait he had painted for her for one she had recently seen hanging at the Rosenberg Gallery.

After a week at Cap d'Antibes, Dos Passos proceeded down the Mediterranean coast to Nerja, Spain, some one hundred kilometers east of the country's southernmost tip, near Málaga. "I've been spending a week in one of the sideshows they forgot to close when the Eden Amusement Company boarded up its doors for an indefinite closure," he wrote Eugene Saxton, his editor, on August 19, 1923. "Places have no right to be so outrageously delightful as Nerja." He said that he would be in New York in time to read the page proofs of the final chapter of *Streets of Night,* which he had rewritten abroad. On August 30 he sailed for home from Bordeaux.

Streets of Night appeared November 9, 1923. Dos Passos avoided the city for over a month, choosing instead to remain in seclusion in a remote kosher boarding house at 119

Boardwalk on the beach at Rockaway Park, Queens. His few days at Cap d'Antibes and in Nerja, Spain, had made him unwilling to return to the relatively close quarters afforded by Greenwich Village life and prompted him to seek a beach environment away from anyone he knew so that he might write without interruption. His headaches had returned and his eyes had never fully recovered from their discomfort of the preceding summer. Bates, with whom he resumed treatment, insisted that he again go without glasses and adhere stringently to his eye exercises. In late November he wrote Rumsey Marvin that he was sorry to have been "so mum," but had written no one all fall. "Have been living a most hermit existence out at Rockaway Park practicing a new theory about my eyes. Haven't worn glasses since October 24 and I think my sight has improved a little. It's terribly tedious but worth spending years on if it works. Anyhow, my headaches have stopped."

Dos Passos returned to the city a day or two before Christmas, which he spent with Scott and Zelda Fitzgerald. He had met them in the fall of 1922 soon after *The Beautiful and the Damned* and *Tales of the Jazz Age* had endeared the Fitzgeralds to countless thousands across the country. Fitzgerald had admired *Three Soldiers* and recommended it to Max Perkins, his editor at Scribner's, as "the book of the autumn," but said later that he "lost faith" in Dos Passos' work after reading *Streets of Night*. Although Fitzgerald liked Dos Passos as a person, he thought Cummings and Hemingway revealed more genius and viewed Dos Passos only as "a strong, valuable talent." Edmund Wilson's introduction of Dos Passos to his Princeton classmate had led to Fitzgerald's initial luncheon invitation in a luxury suite at the Plaza, where they were joined by Sherwood Anderson, whom Dos Passos also met for the first time. Despite what appeared to be a "golden innocence" about the Fitzgeralds, he was put off by their plying him with questions in poor taste. "Their gambit was to put you in the wrong. You were backward in your ideas. You were inhibited about sex. These things might perfectly well have been true but my attitude was that they were nobody's goddamn business," he complained later. After lunch, Fitzgerald invited him to accompany them in a touring car they had hired for the day for a house-hunting mission in Great Neck, Long Island. They also called upon Ring Lardner, whose mansion was not unlike several others they saw that day. Dos Passos had looked forward to meeting Lardner, whose use of the American idiom in his fiction he admired, but the man himself—"a tall sallow mournful man with a higharched nose" who stood beside the fireplace looking out from "dark hollow eyes, hollow cheeks, and helplessly drunk"—was a disappointment. When they left, Fitzgerald observed that "everybody had to have his private drunkard," and that Lardner was his. On their way back to Manhattan they passed a carnival, and Zelda and Dos Passos clamored that they stop and "be allowed to take some rides." Fitzgerald glowered in the car and swigged a bottle of gin in their absence. Dos Passos described his strange ride with Zelda on the Ferris wheel:

> Carnivals, amusement parks, the flash of colored lights on faces in the dark, the view over misty suburbs twinkling with lights, these were things I liked to try to paint. I tried to explain my infantile excitement to Zelda. She wouldn't listen. Zelda and I kept saying things to each other but our minds never met. . . . The gulf that opened between Zelda and me, sitting up on that rickety Ferris wheel, was something I couldn't explain. It was only looking back at it years later that it occurred to me that, even the first day we knew each other, I had come up

against that basic fissure in her mental processes that was to have such tragic consequences. Though she was lovely I had come upon something that frightened and repelled me, even physically.

Dos Passos met the Fitzgeralds at the beginning of what became known as their "Great Neck period," soon to be immortalized in *The Great Gatsby*. It seemed to him that they were celebrities in the "Sunday supplement sense of the word." They relished and cultivated it at every turn. The idea of his ever becoming their kind of celebrity set his teeth on edge, he said. Nonetheless, he was amused a few days after their initial encounter to see himself caricatured on an "overture curtain" for the 1922 *Greenwich Village Follies*. He and Fitzgerald were depicted in a truck racing across Seventh Avenue with Edmund Wilson, John Peale Bishop, and Gilbert Seldes—all headed for Washington Square, where Zelda, the focal point of the curtain, disported at the edge of the fountain in a dazzling white bathing suit.

Often uncomfortable in the company of the Fitzgeralds during the winter of 1923–24 and put off by their extravagant drinking habits and overall ostentation, Dos Passos retreated after Christmas to a small apartment in Hamilton Easter Field's old house at 110 Columbia Heights in Brooklyn, where his spectacular view was the Brooklyn Bridge and waterfront. Here he began work in earnest on his novel of the city, *Manhattan Transfer,* and resided intermittently over the next four years. He found that he worked much better in the relative seclusion of Brooklyn Heights than in his other favorite haunt, Greenwich Village. Hart Crane moved into Field's house a few months later, and he and Dos Passos became friends.

"Jesus I am broke—haven't had a five-dollar bill in two months," Dos Passos complained to Rumsey Marvin in February 1924. "I'm going south to Savannah and New Orleans if I can scrape up some cash." Meanwhile, he was deep in his new novel. "Everything else is the bunk," he said. Several weeks later he turned up in New Orleans, where he rented a spacious room at 510 Esplanade in the French Quarter for two dollars and fifty cents a week. "New Orleans suits me to a T. I don't know anybody so I live cheap and work continuously and spend the rest of the time doing voodoo on the eyes," he said. "It's a fine town . . . full of noise and jingle and horse racing and crap shooting and whoring and bawdry. Why don't you come down?" he suggested to Marvin, who had recently taken a job on a newspaper in Goldsboro, North Carolina. When he complained that he was tired of eating alone and had no one to drink with, either, Marvin urged him to look up a friend, William McComb, now a reporter for the New Orleans *Item*. Soon Dos Passos and McComb were meeting each evening for dinner and exploring the town together. Dos Passos' several letters to Marvin from New Orleans were filled with his impressions of the city and its people. Each had taken to describing at length the town or area in which he found himself that the other did not know. Dos Passos' letters to Marvin after his graduation from Yale in 1922 until the end of the decade were filled with such requests as "tell me more about Pittsburgh" or "write me of Wilmington" or of Salisbury or Goldsboro—all places in the South of which Dos Passos lacked firsthand knowledge.

"I sort of hoped you'd turn up here," he wrote Rumsey Marvin after he had been in New Orleans a month:

There's a regular Frankie and Johnny café called the Original Tripoli full of vice niggermusic and rotten booze. There are streets and streets of scaling crumbling houses with broad wrought iron verandahs painted in Caribbean blues and greens. There's a square with a fine cathedral and wharves and ships galore and the air is full of the smell of molasses from the sugar refineries. There are levees along the Mississippi to walk on, bayous leading into Lake Pontchartrain, winter-scorched palms and palmettos everywhere. The streets are full of inconceivable old geezers in decrepit frockcoats, of tall negresses with green and magenta bandanas on their heads, of whores and racingmen and South Americans and Central Americans of all colors and shapes.

Dos Passos urged Marvin to join him on a walking trip to Florida, but set out alone the end of March. For a week he walked through much of northern and central Florida, then hopped a freight in Venice, a tiny settlement on the Gulf a few miles south of Sarasota, and crossed to the western shore of Lake Okeechobee, over which he was ferried in a motor launch. In Sebring, he boarded Henry Flagler's luxury passenger train for Palm Beach, where he alighted at the foot of the Royal Poinciana Hotel. Six stories high and a mile in circumference, the building was the largest wooden-structured hotel in the world in 1893, when it was built. When Dos Passos arrived, Palm Beach—known originally as Lake Worth—had been a winter home for wealthy Northern socialites for three decades. Much of the state had been settled by hordes of "commoners" attracted by the land boom, he observed wryly in a letter to Germaine Lucas-Championnière on April 3. "One arrives on foot, works a year, buys an orange grove from his wages, then in five years travels in a limousine, in ten years is the founder of a city, is a millionaire or a senator—it's the American Eden. . . . The fruit is forbidden to no one except those who cannot buy it."

Dos Passos did not linger in Palm Beach, but crossed to the mainland and produced enough cash to buy a train ticket to Key West, the end of the line. Later, he reminisced:

I'll never forget the dreamlike crossing of the Keys on the Old Flagler viaduct. In those days Key West really was an island. It was a coaling station. There was shipping in the harbor. The air smelt of the Gulf Stream. It was like no other place in Florida. . . . The English speaking population was made up of railroad men, old Florida settlers, a few descendants of New Englanders from such allwhite settlements as Spanish Wells in the Bahamas. There was not a trace of a cracker drawl in their speech. One remembered that Key West had been northern territory all through the Civil War. There were a couple of drowsy hotels where train passengers on their way to Cuba or the Caribbean occasionally stopped over. Palms and pepper trees. The shady streets of unpainted frame houses had a faintly New England look. Automobiles were rare because there was no highway to the mainland, only the viaduct that carried the singletrack railroad.

Nowhere else in America, except perhaps among the sand dunes of Cape Cod—to which Dos Passos had retreated for a few days just before his graduation from Harvard—had he felt so completely untouched by civilization as he did in Key West that spring. He had made good progress on his novel in New Orleans despite having to rest his eyes and exercise them periodically, and in Key West, where he stayed for almost a fortnight, he continued to work well. Each day he bathed in the clear, bright sea, which changed from green to purplish-blue as he swam over coral beds to deep water. He relaxed in the sun, hiked the beaches, watched fishermen unload their catches, and dined at night on Rioja wine and fresh seafood in small, darkly lit Spanish and Cuban restaurants. Life in Key West was "delicious," he observed.

Before leaving New Orleans, Dos Passos wrote Marvin that he might be going to Russia in April or May at the request of the Kamerny Theatre in Moscow. He was to help arrange productions for an American tour, and all of his expenses were to be paid. If that did not materialize, he was "looking lustfully towards Mexico." Marvin countered with a suggestion that he stop in Goldsboro on his way north, or, better yet, meet him for a walking trip along the sand dunes of Cape Hatteras. The letter did not reach him, however, until he was back in New York and on the verge of leaving for Europe. Moscow was out and so was Mexico, Dos Passos told Marvin without elaborating. Instead, he was off to Paris, he said.

In June he was in Paris, where he fell into a warm camaraderie with Ernest Hemingway and his wife, Hadley, who had returned from Toronto soon after the first of the year with their three-month-old son, John Hadley Nicanor. Gertrude Stein, the infant's godmother, called him "Bumby" and the name stuck. Bumby was named for his mother and for Nicanor Vilata, a renowned matador whom Hemingway and Hadley had met in Pamplona the preceding summer. The best matadors and bravest bulls came to Pamplona from all over Spain for the week-long fiesta of San Fermín, marked by daily bullfights, drinking, singing and dancing in the streets each night, religious processions, special masses, and fireworks—all to celebrate the encounter between man and beast in the bullring.

Hemingway, an organizer, was happiest when planning an excursion that included friends. It was also a means of keeping himself at center. Dos Passos needed no urging to return to Spain. He had not been to Pamplona during his various sojourns in the past and looked forward to it now especially because Crystal Ross had agreed to go, too. Others in their group that year included Donald Ogden Stewart, William and Sally Bird (Bird ran the Continental branch of the Consolidated Press and had published Hemingway's first collection of sketches, *in our time*), Robert McAlmon, Erik ("Chink") Dorman-Smith, a British army captain Hemingway had met during the war and now one of his and Hadley's best friends, and George O'Neil, the nineteen-year-old son of a friend of Hadley's family in St. Louis. Hemingway and O'Neil were sparring partners in Paris and had skied some together.

Upon arrival in Pamplona, Dos Passos and Ross discovered that Hemingway had booked a double room for them, having assumed that the couple was sleeping together. Resentful of Hemingway's presumption, Ross insisted on taking the single room reserved for Stewart, who in turn moved in with Dos Passos. "I couldn't have stood the American part of the crowd if there hadn't been a young woman along," Dos Passos wrote later. "I was discovering the truth of Ben Franklin's old saying: 'A man and woman are like a pair of scissors. Neither one is any good without the other.' Between us we built ourselves a sort of private box from which we looked out at all these goings on, in them but not of them." Hemingway made no mention of Ross's being in their group that summer in Pamplona in his several accounts of it over the years, although he mentioned everyone else who accompanied them, an omission he probably intended as retaliation for her having disputed the sleeping arrangements he had made.

Hemingway chided Dos Passos for not joining him and the other men in their crowd in proving their mettle by racing down the street in front of the bulls being driven to the ring each morning, but the event was not Dos Passos' idea of a good time. He did find himself face to face with a Pamplona bull quite by accident, however. The beast had jumped a fence in the stadium and charged down the passage along which Dos Passos happened to be walking at the moment. The others had only a fleeting glimpse of the horns and Dos Passos disappearing over the wall into the lower tier of seats. When they teased him of it later, he said that he was simply finding an elevated spot from which to make some sketches. Stewart took pride in his own injury, sustained when he ventured into the ring during "pre-fight warm-ups" and was tossed into the air twice by a bull. Hemingway congratulated him upon his bravery, and Stewart ignored as best he could the discomfort of two cracked ribs. He said he felt as though he had just scored a winning touchdown.

At the close of the festival, Crystal Ross set out for Paris with Stewart by bus. She needed to return to Strasbourg, and Stewart was not fit enough to accompany the others on a fishing expedition into some of the most rugged countryside of the Spanish Pyrenees. Ross volunteered to transport back to Paris several parcels and the dirty laundry of Dos Passos, Smith, and O'Neil, who planned a two-week walking trip of some four hundred sixty kilometers from Burguete to Andorra la Vella, the capital of an independent republic nestled high in the Pyrenees. En route to Pamplona, Ross had hiked with Dos Passos through the Roncesvalles Pass from St.-Jean-Pied-de-Port (the town in which they de-trained on the French side of the Pyrenees), but she was no match for his strides and did not want to attempt another long hike at his side. Although she considered herself a good walker, she had finished their earlier trek on the back of a donkey.

Hemingway's wife outdid the men with her trout-fishing in a pool below a waterfall of the Irati River high in the Basque country of Navarre, but had no interest in accompa-nying the hikers through the Pyrenees. Hemingway set out with them, but returned to their fishing camp before nightfall. He was never the hiker Dos Passos was. At the last minute McAlmon decided to hike with them, but dropped out after six days. He had tried to walk in canvas slippers, then in tennis shoes, which he termed a foolish mistake and attributed to his aborting the journey in Biescas, twenty-five kilometers short of the French border. "Silence and solitude were a delight after the gabblegabble round the tables under the portales at Pamplona," Dos Passos wrote later. He was happiest on the high trails where scenery unrolled "on either side like the painted panorama they used to unroll during the Rhine music in *Siegfried.*" Villagers encountered along the way offered them goat's cheese, black bread, tortillas, and honey, having assumed they were headed for the border with contraband. The only wayfarers Dos Passos and his band encountered were *contrabandistas,* who searched their musettes and sometimes lingered in a spirit of friendliness to break bread with them. Toward the end of their trek, their feet sore and bruised, legs aching, and bodies protesting the gruelling pace (one day they hiked sixty-five kilometers), they began to swig from a flask of brandy. They also had a skin full of native liquor known as *agua de gigante,* which proved so potent that a few sips enabled them to extend their hiking day by another five or ten kilometers. The weather was fair during most of their trip, but a thunderstorm struck their last night out and they tumbled down the mountainside in the dark, their way illuminated by great zigzags of lightning. It was midnight when they pounded on the door of the only inn they could find open in Andorra la Vella and were led to "an evil-smelling room" with three beds. "The minute we stretched out in dry clothes the bedbugs came like shock troops, wave after wave," reported Dos Passos later. Chink Dorman-Smith leaped from his bed, dressed himself, and spent the night in a chair, but Dos Passos and young O'Neil managed to sleep soundly. Smith's attitude was that it did not "behove an officer in His Majesty's army to suffer indignities at the hands of the natives. I esteemed him for it," said Dos Passos.

He was in Cap d'Antibes a few days later "working in a red plush room at the Murphys' place" when he wrote Jack Lawson that his trip to Russia was off. "Numerous insane things have been happening. . . . I found myself—I know not how—at a lot of bullfights in Pamplona and a ferocious fiesta with a lot of fake bohemians. Then I was walking up the spine of the Pyrenees thirteen days from Roncesvalles to Andorra in the company of a very comic English captain and a morose young man named George." He said that he was being entertained then "with great elegance and a great deal of gin fizz. The Riviera in summer is a strange and rather exciting place. The people are very bastard and peculiar and the landscape is obstructed by villas full of artificial countesses under the influence of opium or spirits or spaniels. Has to be seen to be believed." The countess he alluded to was the wife of Count Étienne de Beaumont, both of whom were at Cap d'Antibes that summer. Calvin Tomkins' saga of the Murphys, *Living Well Is the Best Revenge,* described the Beaumonts as "Proustian characters who were great connoisseurs and patrons of the avant-garde." According to Murphy, the count and his wife "threw fantastic 'Soirées de Paris' in Montmartre. You'd go to each one and find everybody else there, too." De Beaumont was easily recognizable that summer as the outrageous fictive count in Raymond Radiguet's recently published *Le Bal du Comte d'Orgel.* Given neither to gossiping nor name-dropping, Dos Passos spoke of no one by name but his hosts in his letter to Lawson. He made no mention of Rudolph Valentino—then in the prime of his career—who had been a guest of the Murphys for a week and was probably still there, nor did he mention to Lawson or to anyone else to whom he wrote that summer such comings and goings into the Murphy household as actor Monty Woolley, who had been a class ahead of Murphy at Yale; Donald Ogden Stewart, who had already retrieved his wife in Paris after their Pamplona venture and was in Antibes before Dos Passos arrived; Gilbert Seldes, who brought his bride there for their honeymoon; Archibald and Ada MacLeish; Picasso and his family; Philip and Ellen Barry; or Cole Porter—all of whom were members of the Murphy ménage while Dos Passos, too, was in residence. Perhaps the most talked about that summer were Scott and Zelda Fitzgerald, whose extravagant antics on the Riviera were well known by this time. The Fitzgeralds rented a villa high above the sea in nearby St.-Raphaël, but came daily to swim and sunbathe with the Murphys and their other guests at the little seaweed-strewn beach known as La Garoupe, which Murphy (dressed in his striped sailor's jersey and white work cap) raked each morning before dispensing sherry and hors d'oeuvres and escorting the entire crowd back to the terrace of their home for lunch. When Dos Passos arrived, the Murphys were still at the Hôtel du Cap, but in August they moved to the Villa America, their own unpretentious, two-story villa located just below the Antibes lighthouse. From the villa's upstairs windows and its rooftop sundeck was a sweeping view of sea and mountains. Its balconies and porches, shaded patio, rock garden, lush foliage, and intimate descending terraces afforded just the kind of entertaining Sara Murphy enjoyed. "But it was not parties that made our life then such a gay time," she stressed. Rather, it was the "great affection between everybody. You loved your friends and wanted to see them every day. . . . It was like a great fair."

To Sara Murphy, everyone was young. Zelda turned twenty-four that summer, and Fitzgerald was twenty-eight. Her affair with Édouard Jozan, a French naval aviator, had gone on for two months under everyone's eyes including her husband's. When Fitzgerald finally recognized Zelda's dalliance for what it was and insisted that she stop seeing Jozan, she complied, yet might have died a few nights later upon overdosing on sleeping pills had Fitzgerald not enlisted the Murphys' aid. Gossip of the Fitzgeralds was rampant when Dos Passos arrived at Villa America, but he made no reference to them in letters to anyone during this period. It was only in his memoirs years later that he spoke candidly of his impressions of the Fitzgeralds:

> By this time Scott and Zelda were very much in the Antibes picture. Scott, with his capacity for hero worship, began to worship Gerald and Sara. The golden couple that he and Zelda dreamed of becoming actually existed. The Murphys were rich. They were goodlooking. They dressed brilliantly. They were canny about the arts. They had a knack for entertaining. They had lovely children. They had reached the highest rung on mankind's ladder. *Fortunatus* incarnate. Scott sometimes found odd ways of expressing his devotion, such as the night when the Murphys invited a lot of rather stuffy French people, including a brace of duchesses, to dinner in the garden. Scott and Zelda got drunk on cocktails and instead of coming to the table crawled among the vegetables on all fours tossing an occasional tomato at the guests. A duchess who got a blob of ripe fruit down the back of her décolleté was emphatically not amused. It was many months before they were invited again to Villa America. In fact they were formally forbidden to cross its threshold.

Dos Passos was given the Murphys' small guesthouse, the Bastide, where he wrote each morning uninterrupted by the other guests who stayed in the villa or the Ferme des Orangers (a former donkey stable at the edge of an orange grove across the road from the Villa America). The Murphys had set the donkey stable up as a fully equipped cottage for those who preferred to do for themselves and to emerge only when they wanted the sociability of the others or one of Sara Murphy's special dishes. Dos Passos rose early and got considerable writing done before noon, when he joined the others for a swim to the mouth of the cove and back. Then they sipped cold sherry in the sun before trooping up the hillside for lunch. He thought it a "marvelous life," but four or five days with the Murphy crowd was usually his limit. "It was like trying to live in heaven," he once wrote. "I had to get back down to earth. It was different when we were up to something special." Sometimes they drove over to Juan-les-Pins to a new casino or to a provincial local movie theater. Fernand Léger, who came down to the Villa America that summer, was fond of the old movie house, which presented only one film a week, featured a chain-smoking piano player, and "smelled of feet." Léger was devoted to the Murphys and visited them often on the Riviera. According to Dos Passos, the Murphys soon discovered the need for "evasive action before the onrush of French high society. They enjoyed the painters more than the pernickety men of letters. Léger, with his marvelous knack of making everything he saw, everything he heard, everything he tasted a special composition of his own, was their favorite as he was mine." Dos Passos thought Picasso less genial than most Spaniards. Picasso seemed "sardonic, earthily cynical . . . impenetrable even in moments of relaxation and laughter." Yet even Sara Murphy and Picasso became friends, he observed.

Dos Passos left Antibes the end of August for Strasbourg. Before leaving Pamplona to go their separate ways, he and Crystal Ross had talked about marriage. As he saw it, a formal engagement was unnecessary. He was twenty-eight and ready to get married immediately if she was. Most of his friends were married by this time, but until he got to know Ross (whom he called "Crys") he had not known anyone he wanted to marry. When he heard that summer of Rumsey Marvin's being "merry in love" and "comfortably fed in Wilmington," Dos Passos replied that there was something "so silly about running around the world like a dancing mouse." The comment may have revealed more of his situation than he intended. He did not allude to Crystal Ross in his letter to Marvin, preferring to wait until something as serious as marriage was a *fait accompli* before speaking of it. Dos Passos pressed her to marry him then or to set a wedding date in the near future, but she put him off, pleading an obligation to her father for financing her studies and also her own desire to finish her doctorate before assuming a wife's role. Her parents simply would not understand if she married now, she told him, and they would never forgive her if she married someone to whom they had not been properly introduced. They would also need time to get accustomed to the idea.

Dos Passos stayed in Strasbourg a week, then left for Paris after getting Ross to agree to meet him in Bruges, Belgium—a town he had remembered fondly from his youth—in September. He wanted her to go with him to London for her holidays between terms. Again he implored her to marry him, right then in Bruges, or in London if she preferred. He would even return with her to Texas if she insisted. Whatever her decision, however, he said he needed to return to New York as quickly as possible. His editor, Eugene Saxton, had written to urge him to deliver his novel, *Manhattan Transfer*—which he had tried to work on throughout his European junket—by the spring of 1925 at the latest so that a fall publication date could be assured. Saxton had moved to Harper & Brothers upon George H. Doran's merger with Doubleday and asked Dos Passos to move with him. It was a small advance by Harper & Brothers for the new novel that had enabled him to travel now.

In Paris after telling Crystal Ross good-bye and preparing to entrain for Le Havre to board his ship the end of September, Dos Passos telescoped for Rumsey Marvin something of his activities over the last three months:

> Almost went to Russia, took a colossal thirteen-day walk instead along the top of the Pyrenees ending in a thunderstorm and a flood and a blind sliding down a gorge into Andorra at midnight. Then had some of the most marvellous swimming ever had at Antibes on the Mediterranean, ate a great deal of choucroute in the rain under the dripping eaves of Strasbourg and drank riesling, muscat in romantische Schlösser popeyed with Weltschmerz und weibliche Liebe until the cows came home.

Marvin relished his letters from Dos Passos, but usually found himself more tantalized than informed of his actual doings and yearned for more details of his romance. Although

Dos Passos made no mention of marriage, Marvin hoped that his friend had found someone with whom he might build a lasting tie. Dos Passos had never before been this explicit to Marvin regarding a romantic involvement. Ross spoke later of their leave-taking of 1924, which she said was difficult for both of them. "I loved Dos very much, but I simply wasn't ready to commit my life to him or to anyone else just then, though we considered ourselves engaged and I had a ring. I went back to Strasbourg to finish my studies and he went to New York, but we agreed to meet again in a few months."

Upon his return to the States, Dos Passos stayed first at 11 Bank Street, then took his old room back in Brooklyn at 110 Columbia Heights. Still in the house during the winter of 1924–25 was Hart Crane, with whom he often dropped into a nearby Italian speakeasy for dinner. Sometimes William Slater Brown or Morris Werner, a newspaperman and biographer (Werner's *P. T. Barnum* was published that year), joined them, as did Cummings, now back in New York after a brief marriage to Elaine Orr Thayer. She had already left Cummings for Frank MacDermot, an Irishman she had met on her return to Europe two months after marrying Cummings. Dos Passos, Cummings, and Crane took to spending bibulous weekends with Brown, Edward Nagel, Gaston Lachaise, Matthew Josephson, and a host of others—though not all at the same time—in an old farmhouse in the Catskills outside Woodstock. They painted, wrote, or sculpted during the day, then caroused half the night, their motley ensemble resembling at times a revolving artists' colony. Dos Passos found it difficult to work on his novel under such convivial circum-stances, although he was more structured in his writing habits than many who joined them on such weekends. Also there from time to time were Malcolm Cowley, Kenneth Burke, James Light, Mary Blair, and Sue Jenkins—all of whom had been classmates at Peabody High in Pittsburgh and thought of such gatherings as informal class reunions. Blair married Edmund Wilson in 1923, and Jenkins (formerly married to Light) married Brown and moved to a farmhouse in a remote orchard outside Sherman, Connecticut. By late 1925 the original group, including Dos Passos, had dispersed.

No matter where Dos Passos was, he did not hang around long if there was a crowd at hand and he had work to do. He was fond of Hart Crane and admired his poetic gift, but preferred his company early in the evening before he became "helpless in drink," which was often, during the time they lived under the same roof in Brooklyn Heights. It seemed to Dos Passos that Crane had everything within him to be a "first-rate poet and first-rate man," yet somehow had been "put together wrong." Dos Passos saw Crane's frequent cruising of the Brooklyn waterfront for homosexual encounters with sailors as an "adolescent addiction" he was unwilling to give up. "You couldn't get mad at him any more than you could at a refractory colt," said Dos Passos after the poet's suicidal plunge into the Caribbean a few years later when he was barely thirty-three.

Although Dos Passos considered himself engaged, Crystal Ross's playful, ambiguous letters did little to reassure him. She addressed him usually as "Darling" and insisted that she loved him, but kept him off balance by such comments as "Dos for God's sake don't count on me—I'm trying hard not to count on you," or "Don't be alarmed by this tenderness of mine—it won't last and for God's sake don't let's analyze." When the ring he had given her had broken, she wrote: "O Dos the ring can't be fixed. I'm so sorry—maybe he can do another exactly the same. . . . I sort of hate you (tho I don't blame you in view of my tremulo-appreciation) for not knowing that I'd accept it the way you gave it. I think that's about all I hate you for—and I love you for lots—O I do—at this moment, that is."

Dos Passos wrote Ross in April that *Manhattan Transfer* lacked only the finishing touches and that his play, "The Moon Is a Gong," was to be produced by the Harvard Dramatic Club May 12, 1925, but that the "big news" was his invitation to spend the summer at Cap d'Antibes as the guests of Gerald and Sara Murphy. They wanted him to meet them in Marseilles June 1 for a cruise aboard their small sloop they had not yet put to the wind. *The Picaflor,* a superannuated racing sloop, was being readied for its maiden voyage with Murphy at the helm. Since Ross expected to finish her studies at the University of Strasbourg in May, Dos Passos proposed that they meet in Italy, or if that was not feasible, for her to hurry to Boston for the opening of his play. "Pretty damned sure that I'm hopelessly in love with you, or at least hankering for the sight of, and to be seen by you," she replied, but warned that her family expected her to proceed directly to Texas. She also piqued his curiosity by adding that "a Texas boy, a pal," had invited her on "just the sailing tour that your Murphy proposes, and in June. If I had dreamed of you in the same waters I couldn't have resisted." Ross asked Dos Passos' indulgence regarding her family. "I've seen so many family formations and I live one across such geography that it's getting under the quick. . . . If you pull my right ear I say Mama, if you pull my left I say DaDa and when you pinch my nose I yell Bub-ba! If I care enough about you I will make you and Dad love each other. That will be a spectacle." Dos Passos had no intention of cultivating a relationship with Ross's family. He had spent enough time getting out from under his own family and establishing his independence. If he finally did manage to get his fiancée to the altar, he was determined to maintain as much distance as possible between them and the rest of the Ross clan.

Despite her good intentions, Ross did not make it home in time to see "The Moon Is a Gong." On May 12, 1925, the little auditorium in Brattle Hall on the Harvard University campus fairly rocked with the play's blaring syncopations of jazz and broken dialogue, the cacophony of shouting voices, horns, and grinding machines resounding against a backdrop Dos Passos had designed for the scene at Union Square, which caught the pulse of the city at night—all in an extravagant, expressionistic staging that combined burlesque and vaudeville with romantic lyricism and tragedy. A TALL FEATHER FOR THE CAP OF HARVARD PLAYERS, announced the headline in the Boston *Evening Transcript*'s theater section the day after its premiere. The reviewer—who signed himself "H.T.P."—commended Edward Massey for having chosen the play. Not within his memory had the critic viewed a production by the Harvard Dramatic Club that moved with such "fluency, certainty, gusto" or won "so large and eager an audience." He likened the play to John Howard Lawson's *Roger Bloomer* and *Processional: A Jazz Symphony of American Life,* but thought Dos Passos outshone Lawson in his "poetic impulse, poetic vision, and poetic sense of spaced, rhythmed speech." The play ran again on May 15 in a Boston theater. Its genteel audience was less appreciative than Harvard viewers had been of such avant-garde efforts, but it was considered a success in Boston as well.

Meanwhile, Rumsey Marvin had been trying to line up another walking trip with Dos Passos, his earlier attempts over the preceding two years having failed, and hoped that they could meet in Wilmington, North Carolina, to comb the Outer Banks together. Dos Passos replied that even if he could scrape up the cash for such a venture, it would mean backing out of his commitment to cruise with the Murphys:

> I'm crazy to take a walking trip round Hatteras with you, Rummy, but it would cost pretty near a hundred dollars to get down and back and I absolutely haven't the money and I can't get any deeper in debt. Christ I'm getting fed up with this piddling literary existence. It's a year now since I've had any money at all that wasn't immediately swallowed up by debts. . . . I'm sore as a crab about it. Hell it's rotten to lose control of one's destiny. . . . But if I went I'd have to give up my three months on the Mediterranean and I can't do that.

He did not mention the uncertainty of his plans with Crystal Ross, who wrote that she was sailing for the States the end of May. Just as he feared, Ross's family was at the dock to welcome her, as was he. He had hobbled from his sickbed to greet her, his joints having become swollen once more from the illness that had stalked him on and off all spring. His condition had worsened in June, and he had been forced to beg off from his cruise with the Murphys until late summer. From Midtown Hospital at 231 East Fifty-seventh Street, he wrote Robert Hillyer in June:

> I've been in the clutches of a rheumatic fever or arthritis which has ruined me in every way, reduced me to an immovable painful vegetable. Still I'm much better now and I am promised that the cutting out of certain ingrown tonsils where the tenement-house conditions among the streptococci were just disgraceful will put me on my feet again. It's all hellishly annoying as if it weren't for this disease I'd be sailing towards Stromboli at this minute. . . . I sit here this accursed Sunday afternoon in a fuzzy hospital bathrobe looking out through a rusty flyscreen at the backyards and clotheslines and paradise bushes and I feel about as alive as an opened tomato can.

Dos Passos was vexed, too, because he had been unable to persuade Crystal Ross to take their so-called engagement seriously enough to marry him without further delay. Her parents did not encourage the relationship—perhaps were not even aware of it except as a casual friendship—and did not like it when she insisted on staying in New York for a few days rather than accompanying them to Dallas. Instead, she took a room at the Lafayette Hotel, shopped, and met Dos Passos for lunch or dinner. They went to the theater several times, but he was barely ambulatory and it was not a good time for him to press his case as her suitor. She had written him of a teaching job her father had lined up at the University of Texas, and, once in New York, she told him that she had to return to Texas soon to fulfill her obligations at home. She also admitted that she may not be geared up to the kind of life that seemed essential to his career. Dos Passos, too, may have sensed that each of them had needs the other would be unable to fill. Ross's letters to him abounded with scratched-out words and phrases, dashes, ellipses, irregularly positioned question marks, parentheses, single and double underlinings and squiggles, all interpolated in a rush of loosely constructed prose, sometimes half in French, half in English, in a style that mirrored what seemed her unstructured approach to life in general. Almost as soon as Ross left New York, he found himself back in Midtown Hospital and wondered if he had lost his fiancée in the process.

The muggy weather exacerbated Dos Passos' condition, and he welcomed pleas by the Murphys to sun himself on the French Riviera as soon as he felt like traveling. Hemingway, too, had been after him to return to Paris: "Jesus I wish you were over here so we could get drunk like I am now and have been so often lately." Hemingway also thanked Dos Passos for his influence on Horace Liveright's decision to publish an American edition of *In Our Time,* but urged him to intervene now and convince Liveright "not to be a damn fool" by making him delete some of the original manuscript. Hemingway was upset because his editor insisted that "Up in Michigan" was not fit for publication because "the girl got yenced." Although he offered another Nick Adams story in its place, "The Battler," he insisted that the other proposed cuts were unnecessary. Dos Passos was asked to write a blurb for the jacket of the new edition, which he was happy to do. He was still bristling from his own battle royal with Harper & Brothers, of which he spoke now in a letter to Robert Hillyer after putting to sea in late July. He had just finished reading the galley proof of *Manhattan Transfer:*

> For some reason letter writing has been impossible since I've been sick. I'm stiff and very mediocre in health but my morale has improved. I'm in steerage on the <u>Paris</u> being transported eastward. . . . It took a great deal of aspirin to get me through smut talks with Harper and his brother. Did you know that Kerist was not blasphemous, but that <u>Christ!</u> was? And when a chaste vaudeville lady spoke of "three a day," Harper and his brother thought three men? . . . Still my next novel, after the battle with the gelding shears was found to be not quite castrated—perhaps half a testicle remained on the left side. So it was in a state of collapse and by pure reflex that I landed sprawling on the <u>Paris</u> yesterday morning. Literature, Mr. Hillyer, is a lousy trade. Locomotion even under the most adverse conditions always cheers me up. . . . New York last week was like being rolled naked in metal filings.

Dos Passos was aboard ship when he wrote John Howard Lawson that his publisher took the word "fanny" for "penis" and wanted it changed. Such naiveté seemed incredible to Dos Passos, despite his own apparent innocence and ingenuousness, which sometimes astounded his friends. He had commiserated with Lawson that summer because the Theatre Guild had balked at producing *Nirvana,* Lawson's new play. "The Guild, as I have long suspected, are the illegitimate offspring of female dogs," Dos Passos told him. Both Lawson and he agreed that the time was ripe for a new theater with a social message. They had no idea how they would go about building such a revolutionary theater group, but felt that its place was assured. Their own plays were proof enough that such a theater was in the making, they agreed.

By the time Dos Passos arrived in Paris, the crowd that had accompanied Hemingway to Pamplona earlier in the summer for the bull fights and fiesta of San Fermín had dispersed, and Hemingway's fictionalized version of their week there and the events leading up to it was already well under way. Although Paris had often served Dos Passos as a place through which to pass for several days while en route elsewhere, he was always pleased to drop in for a few hours of leisure at such familiar haunts as the Closerie de Lilas, where he could generally find someone he knew to drink a vermouth cassis with him. Hemingway was not in Paris when Dos Passos arrived, having found an inexpensive hotel just across the French border in which he secluded himself to work on his novel instead of returning to Paris. He said later that he had tried to stay out of Paris that summer because Bill Smith, an old boyhood friend, was there. Smith had a drinking problem and was given to spells of depression. He had been in Pamplona earlier with Hemingway and had been no trouble, but Hemingway said he could not write if Smith were nearby because Smith's depression tended to rub off on him. Smith, now thirty, lived in Provincetown with his older sister, Katharine ("Katy"). He wrote Hemingway that spring that he was getting ready to head for Paris to look for an editing or newspaper job. It had been three years since they last saw each other, having become estranged upon Hemingway's verbal assault on one of Smith's brothers who formerly had been a good friend. Smith wrote Katy after returning to Paris from Pamplona that she ought to "flash over" and visit. "You would love Paris and you can live here a good deal more cheaply."

Pauline Pfeiffer, with whom Katy had gone to school in St. Louis, wrote Katy that summer from Paris with a similar message. Pauline was chic, articulate about women's fashions, and a recently hired writer for *Vogue*'s Paris office. "I have just bid Bill godspeed to the bulls," she wrote Katy on June 24, 1925. "Really, my dear, you have two super brothers. I would marry either of them. I have a little money of my own, have a calm, even temper. Don't you think you could arrange something for me? However, the object of this letter is not to marry myself off . . . but to plead with you with all my charm, which you know is now considerable, to come on over here this autumn." Regardless of such pleas, Katy stayed in Provincetown that summer, and before long Pauline had taken up with Hemingway, not one of the Smith brothers. Hadley Hemingway, also a close friend of Katy, did not know Pauline until after her husband met her. Katy had been a bridesmaid in Hadley's wedding, and Hadley, too, was urging Katy to come visit her and Hemingway that summer in Paris. Had she gone to Europe then, she probably would have met Dos Passos either through Hadley or Pauline in 1925, instead of three years later, and the course of both of their lives might have been altered considerably.

As it was, marrying Crystal Ross was still the most important thing in Dos Passos' personal life that he had been bent on doing that seemed beyond his control. In the spring of 1926 when Ross wrote that she had decided to marry Lewis M. Dabney, the Texan she had been seeing upon her return from Europe, Dos Passos probably wondered if he were the same "Texas pal" who had invited her on the Mediterranean cruise the preceding summer. Disheartened by her decision, he regretted that she had not seen fit to talk it over with him. Not to have married him was one thing—he could accept that—but for her to have chosen someone else while he still considered them to be engaged to each other was another. When Rumsey Marvin wrote that he was about to become engaged, Dos Passos replied:

> I never understood exactly why people get engaged. The only time I ever did the most disastrous things happened. But I feel that there's a great deal to be said for immediate matrimony always. If I once got started I'd probably have to become a Mormon to cover my confusion. What I mean is that if he and she are crazy about each other it is sheer tempting God to stay apart, come what may. And if people aren't crazy about each other, being engaged won't help them. But my private life is such a disorganized menagerie of ill-fed desires that

I'm no authority on Hymen. St. Paul had the last word anyway, when he said it was better to marry than burn.

His friends were not aware of it, but Dos Passos had been "burning" for a long time.

One of the places to which he retreated when in need of a change of pace, fresh air, and sunlight was the remote village of Provincetown. "There's nobody here I know, and I've lived absolutely alone with my work, a volume of Casanova, an oil cook stove named Jiminy, and a big trash burner named gog and magog," he wrote Marvin in the spring of 1926. It may have been his dismay in receiving Crystal Ross's "Dear Dos" letter breaking their engagement that prompted his seeking the seclusion of the Cape this time. "I've taken enormous walks and lived on rice and codfish tongues and I feel like a new man," he informed Marvin. "God damn it, I suppose by the time I'm eighty-five and it's too late, I will have learned how to live. As I sit on top of a sand dune in the sunny March wind and look back at my alleged life I realize it's the things you pass up that torment you, not the things you do." Marvin wondered if Dos Passos had turned to Casanova for instruction. It seemed incredible to him that his mentor and best friend, who had traveled the globe and had done more during his first thirty years than the average person did in a lifetime, could still be seeking "how to live." If anyone already knew about life, surely it was Dos Passos, his voracious appetite continually seeking heightened sensations through new places and experiences, reasoned Marvin.

Back in Cap d'Antibes at last a few weeks later, Dos Passos found another solace of sorts in his first Mediterranean cruise with Gerald Murphy and his skipper, Vladimir Orloff. Yet it might well have been the last for the lot of them. Each had sailed in the past —especially Orloff, who grew up on his grandfather's yachts on the Black Sea—but none had handled such a sleek craft as *The Picaflor* even on calm seas, let alone in a gale. When the trio unfurled the balloon jib under a gentle breeze on a moonlit night and headed for Genoa, no one anticipated the problems ahead. They had been at sea only a short time when the wind freshened, then blew in from all directions at once, and the rain fell in sheets. When the sloop's halyard snagged in the pulleys, they could not get their jib down and almost capsized. Orloff would not consent to cutting the sail loose, and the battered vessel was half swamped when they overshot the channel in a run to the port of Savona. Soon they were foundering dangerously close to the rocks in the breakwater. A lull allowed them to take in the sails and lash down the boom. They bucked at anchor for several hours until a tugboat pulled them into the harbor. Tied up to a wharf at last, they were exclaiming their good fortune in having lost nothing more than their anchors when a grinding crunch threw them upon the deck. Scrambling to their feet, they watched their rescuing tugboat carry off their bowsprit. The captain had reversed his engines by mistake. The next morning, Dos Passos accompanied Murphy into Genoa in search of new anchors while Orloff poled *The Picaflor* around the harbor to a ship's carpenter to have a new bowsprit fitted. By this time Murphy had decided to commission Orloff to design him a two-masted vessel that would be sturdy and broad enough to accommodate with reasonable safety his entire family and several guests. Orloff, whose profession was naval architecture before his flight from Russia upon the overthrow of the Czar and murder of his father, had given up a job as set designer for Diaghilev's Ballet Russe to sail as Murphy's private skipper. Murphy named his ketch after his nine-year-old daughter, Honoria, upon its launching in a Bordeaux shipyard the following winter. Again, Dos Passos was invited on the maiden voyage. From the Villa America after their near disaster at sea, Dos Passos wrote John Howard Lawson that he was "as happy as a blue bird and twice as musical, having only the faintest traces of rheumatism and free from the slightest literary itch. Nearly got thrown up on the mole at Savona in a wild storm. At the last moment when we were all ready to throw ourselves in the surf crying Mort aux vaches ["Death to the cows"] or Viva il fascio according to the taste, we were thrown a rope by a tug and hauled rather ignominiously into the harbor." Savona was "a dead town" in contrast to "how swell it seemed in 1917 when it was communist," he ventured. The change had been effected in 1922 when Benito Mussolini swept into Rome with his fascist army and declared himself dictator. Savona was now a "fantastically sinister place," said Dos Passos. In the only café they found open, they had drinks with the leading fascist gunmen, "an extraordinary set of thugs . . . obscene roistering, overfed bruisers tossing down glasses of crème de menthe. The head of the black shirt squadron let us shake the hand that had that morning shaken hands with Mussolini at Parma."

Dos Passos told Lawson that he was trying to get sent to Morocco. Through Eugene Saxton he had arranged for letters of introduction to officials in northern Morocco so that he might cover the Riffian revolt for *Harper's Magazine*. The French had gone in to help their neighbors when Abd-el-Krim attempted to drive the Spaniards from the Rif country so he could rule it himself. Abd-el-Krim led the Berber tribesmen in bloody skirmishes against both the French and the Spaniards, but the revolt was put down. "It seems Abd-el-Krim didn't shoot his prime minister out of a cannon after all," Dos Passos wrote Lawson before leaving Cap d'Antibes. Back in Paris in the fall, he learned that Hemingway, too, had considered going to Morocco, but declined, pleading the need to finish his novel. By the time Dos Passos arrived in Paris, Hemingway was already well into another manuscript, a parody of Sherwood Anderson's recently published *Dark Laughter*. "Have been working like hell," Hemingway wrote Bill Smith on December 3. "Written funny book, 28,000 words. Scott, Louis Bromfield, Dos, etc., declare it is O.K. Really think it is funny as hell. Firing it to Liveright this Saturday when it comes back from re-typers. Is called The Torrents of Spring." Hemingway had read the manuscript to a number of people, including Dos Passos and the Murphys, as a means of entertaining them. "I certainly laughed when he read it out loud but I tried to argue him out of getting it printed, at least right now," said Dos Passos. "I said it wasn't quite good enough to stand on its own feet as a parody, and that *In Our Time* had been so damn good he ought to wait until he had something really smashing to follow it with." Dos Passos also pointed out that Anderson had been kind to Hemingway—Anderson had written a laudatory blurb for the jacket of *In Our Time* (as had Gilbert Seldes, Waldo Frank, and Dos Passos)—and that publishing the book now in view of such kindness would be meanspirited and hurtful. Fitzgerald described the manuscript to Max Perkins as "a vicious parody" of Anderson. "I love it, but believe it wouldn't be popular," said Fitzgerald, who was convinced that Perkins ought to be Hemingway's editor. As Dos Passos put it later: "Scott had one of his literary crushes on Hem, the sportsman-stylist, the pugilist storyteller. . . . Scott was right. Scribner's was the publisher for Hem," but the problem was getting out of his contract with Liveright, who had an option on the next book. Since Liveright was Anderson's friend and publisher, Fitzgerald and Hemingway were convinced that *The Torrents of Spring* would be rejected, leaving both his parody and *The Sun Also Rises* to whomever he wished.

Hemingway bragged to Bill Smith in his letter of December 3, 1925, that *In Our Time* was "going well in the States. Had report from Chicago it was selling very well. Have gotten over fifty good reviews from clipping bureau." Actually, Liveright had published only thirteen hundred copies of the book, and only a little over one thousand copies were sold. Hemingway coveted Fitzgerald's ability to sell his stories with ease for big money. "Trash doesn't come as easily as it used to," confessed Fitzgerald to Max Perkins that winter. "Do you know I now get $2,500 a story from the Post?" Hemingway recounted to Smith that winter what he called "the peculiar situation" in the magazine world:

> Liberty, Post, Cosmopolitan all have one million circulation. Terrific competition to get exclusivity on authors. Scott's been raised to 3,000 bones a story by the Post after offers of 2,750 and 2,850 by Liberty and Cosmo. . . . Hearst's man came over to see me, said he had a cable from N.Y. to get in touch with me and took "Fifty Grand" story back with him. Said he was sure Ray Long [*Cosmopolitan* editor] would like it as much as he does. All horseshit of course, but a chance. Sooner or later will grab off a chunk of dough. . . . Don't say anything about what Post pays Scott as it would get him in wrong.

Dos Passos left for Morocco in early December after promising he would meet Hemingway and Hadley in Schruns, Austria, upon his return. The Murphys, who were devoted to Hemingway, said they would come, too. The preceding winter Hemingway had discovered the Austrian Vorarlberg and a small family hotel (the Taube) there, where they lived for the equivalent of twenty-eight dollars and fifty cents a week and came out ahead by subletting their flat in Paris. Just as Hemingway had delighted in getting up a crowd for his Pamplona adventures, so, too, did he look forward to having his friends come up to ski. Pauline Pfeiffer was the first to arrive that winter, having been invited to spend Christmas with them. Pauline was not a skier, but Hemingway insisted on teaching her. Hadley extended her hospitality and friendship to Pauline without reserve. She was accustomed to women being enamored of her husband, but had no idea that he had already fallen in love with Pauline by then.

Dos Passos, meanwhile, was in the port city of Oran, Algeria, on December 10, 1925, when he scribbled a postcard to Cummings: "Found a baby elephant engraved on the rocks near where the camel trail goes into Figig. If it hadn't been part of a fifty-ton boulder I'd bring him home to you." Cummings sketched elephants and had filled several sketchpads with them over the years. He especially liked depicting them in various attitudes of sexual play. Despite his joking with Cummings, Dos Passos experienced considerable melancholy as he wandered over Morocco and Algeria. He had expected to find Riffian tribesmen, led by Abd-el-Krim, in a fresh revolt, but arrived during a lull in the fighting. A few weeks later the Rif leader was captured and banished to Réunion Island, in the Indian Ocean; thus Dos Passos had seen little to report that he thought might interest his magazine readers back home. Actually, he did not feel well that winter. He spoke in his memoirs of having "messed around in Morocco" in an attempt to "ward off a fresh attack of rheumatic fever. Some doctor told me it would do me good to toast myself on the sand dunes. . . . Christmas I spent absolutely alone roaming round the mud villages of Béni-Ounif and watching caravans come in from the Tuareg country. The pink and purple mountains kept beckoning me." Other than writing about the scenery, there was little going on about which to comment, he complained to Eugene Saxton in a letter on Christmas day. Two or three days later he jotted a note to Arthur McComb, with whom he had had little correspondence of late:

> Full of melancholy reflections on the falling of hair, the loss of friends, the disappearance of ocean greyhounds. . . . It is time I hitched up my pants and mended my ways. . . . I might embrace Islam, but that would necessitate a painful operation. . . . It's much the same with communism or your own romantic antiquarianism—the nearing of the end of the year always brings on these idées noires. It is a ridiculous and repulsive spectacle that one offers, I fear, continuously scuttling about the world from place to place like a cockroach running away from a light. I am assailed by wise adages and knowing saws. The trouble is they are all quite true—rolling stones gather neither moss nor information. Here I am suddenly trying to pick up Arabic. It's undignified. It's obscene.

His emergence in Tangier in late January was comparable to his coming out of the Assyrian Desert in 1922 and finding a bag full of letters and numerous reviews of *Three Soldiers*. This time, considerable mail and the early reviews of *Manhattan Transfer* (published by Harper & Brothers November 12, 1925) awaited him. It was his fourth novel, and it stood out among the critics' reviews during a year described later as "the most notable twelve-month period in American publishing history." Readers were exposed to a variety of touted books in 1925, including Fitzgerald's *The Great Gatsby*, Lewis' *Arrowsmith*, Dreiser's *An American Tragedy*, Glasgow's *Barren Ground*, Cather's *The Professor's House*, Anderson's *Dark Laughter*, Hemingway's *In Our Time*, Jeffers' *Roan Stallion, Tamar and Other Poems*, Loos's *Gentlemen Prefer Blondes*, Bromfield's *Possession*, Wylie's *The Venetian Glass Nephew*, Eliot's *Poems, 1909–1925*, H.D.'s *Collected Poems*, Atherton's *The Crystal Cup*, Grey's *The Thundering Herd*, Mann's *Death in Venice*, Lowell's *John Keats*, Werner's *Brigham Young*, Stein's *The Making of Americans*, Parrish's *The Perennial Bachelor*, Heyward's *Porgy*, Huxley's *Those Barren Leaves*, Wodehouse's *Carry On, Jeeves!*, Woolf's *Mrs. Dalloway*, Erskine's *The Private Life of Helen of Troy*, Morley's *Thunder on the Left*, and George Moore's *Hail and Farewell*.

For some critics, *Manhattan Transfer* stood out among its rivals as "an explosion in a cesspool," as Paul Elmer More termed it. Several reviewers dismissed the book as merely another "experimental piece." To describe Dos Passos' innovative technique, they used such words as "impressionistic," "expressionistic," "super-naturalistic," "neo-realistic," "architectonic," "panoramic," "kaleidoscopic," "fragmented," and "cinemascopic." Others speculated on the authors and books from which *Manhattan Transfer* may have derived. Moses Harper insisted in *The New Republic* that it was "too much influenced by the French naturalists." Lloyd Morris informed readers of the New York *Times Book Review* that the book was a "courageous but not impressive attempt to achieve an expressionistic picture of New York" and compared it to *Ulysses*. Sinclair Lewis' essay in *The Saturday Review of Literature*, "Manhattan at Last!" was the most significant and laudatory assessment. "The first novel to catch Manhattan," avowed Lewis, and "a novel of the very first importance. . . . The dawn of a whole new school of writing." Lewis noted Dos Passos' use of the cinema with its abrupt cuts, flashbacks, and close-ups. He applauded the technique, but thought the author's "passion for the beauty and stir of life" was even more impressive. His concluding statement shocked many readers: "Just to rub it in, I consider *Manhattan Transfer* more important in every way than anything by Gertrude Stein or Marcel Proust, or even the great white boar, Mr. Joyce's *Ulysses.*" Since Lewis was considered by most of his contemporaries as the most important writer in America in 1925 (and was the first American to win the Nobel Prize for literature), his praise of Dos Passos was significant. The sales department of Harper & Brothers lost no time seeking permission to publish an expanded version of Lewis' essay in a promotion pamphlet of twenty-two pages.

The four thousand copies of the first edition of *Manhattan Transfer* had two different bindings and were released simultaneously. Each sold equally well. Fitzgerald described *Manhattan Transfer* as "astonishingly good," but Hemingway did not express himself publicly regarding the novel until he wrote a blurb for a European edition. By this time, he, too, was better known:

> In Europe, *Manhattan Transfer,* translated into many languages, has become a spiritual Baedeker to New York. He alone of American writers has been able to show to Europeans the America they really find when they come here. Even in translation his vitality, his observation, his honesty and his passion persist. He has the honesty that is the lone virtue of our dull writers; he has a broader culture than many of our self-styled Humanists and he combines with these the vigor and invention of a true creative writer. Every book he has written has been an improvement on the last and this one is no exception.

Manhattan Transfer continued to receive considerable critical acclaim both in 1926 and 1927. After its British edition was published by Constable, D. H. Lawrence called it "the best modern book about New York" he had ever read. He liked its "endless series of glimpses of people in the vast scuffle of Manhattan Island, as they turn up again and again, in a confusion that has no obvious rhythm, but wherein at last we recognize the systole-diastole of success and failure, the end being all failure, from the point of view of life; and then another flight towards another nowhere." He saw the book as "a very complete film . . . of the vast loose gang of strivers and winners and losers which seems to be the very pep of New York."

Dos Passos was in Fez, Morocco, in February when he dropped a postcard to Hemingway complaining that he was "living the life of a 55-year-old virgin lady from Brookline, Massachusetts" and regretting that he was not already in Schruns. His new novel had been "getting the rasberry" from everyone but Sinclair Lewis, he said, but was in its third printing. When Hemingway returned from New York in early March—he had left Hadley and Bumby in Schruns while he traveled to the States to confer with Max Perkins regarding Scribner's publication of *The Sun Also Rises* (Liveright had lost its option by refusing to publish *The Torrents of Spring)*—he wrote Dos Passos that *Manhattan Trans-*

fer had gone into still another printing. Perhaps his new novel would allow him to pay off his debts, replied Dos Passos. "I don't expect much more except that it might serve as the foundation of a credit system. Credit, my dear sir, is the foundation of modern finance."

He was in Tangier when John Howard Lawson cabled that he should come home to help launch a new theater venture. "I snapped at the opportunity," recounted Dos Passos, eager to be a part of the new group. Everything remained in the talking stage for over a year, but he and Lawson agreed from the onset regarding what they hoped to achieve. They believed that American theater had become so decadent that it would be impossible to revitalize it unless startling new writing and staging devices were utilized in the manner already employed in their own recently produced plays. A "new playwrights" theater would have to appeal to the rising class of workers and intellectuals much as the new Russian theater under V. E. Meyerhold and Yevgeni Vakhtangov had done. Lawson issued invitations to three others to participate in his theater venture also: Em Jo Basshe, who had been associated for a number of years with the Provincetown Theatre and now was writing plays; Francis Edward Faragoh, a Hungarian-born short-story writer who had recently turned to the theater; and Michael Gold, a ghetto-born Jew from New York whose sympathies had evolved from socialism to staunch Communism. Gold had been editor of *The Masses,* founded *The Liberator,* and was now involved in starting a new magazine, *The New Masses.* His primary interest in 1926, however, was the theater. Two years older than Dos Passos, Gold had been associated with radical causes almost as long as he could remember. Lawson envisioned himself, Basshe, Faragoh, Gold, and Dos Passos as directors and chief playwrights of what was soon to be known as the New Playwrights Theatre. Dos Passos was not only receptive, but eager to have another arena in which to joust the platitudes, pieties, and stereotypes of middle-class, capitalistic America. As he saw it, he had only just begun his protests with "The Moon Is a Gong." When Lawson cabled that "The Moon Is a Gong" was already in rehearsal with a New York cast and would be presented to Greenwich Village audiences at the old Cherry Lane Playhouse (at 40 Commerce Street) on March 12, 1926, Dos Passos assured him that he would be there, too, although not in time for the opening. Lawson had talked Edward Massey into coming down from Boston to direct the play, and the same backdrop that Dos Passos had designed for the Harvard Dramatic Club's presentation was to be used for the New York production. "The Moon Is a Gong" had the backing of Juliet Barrett Rublee, rather than being a New Playwrights Theatre production. The principals behind the scenes, however, were Lawson and his revolutionary cohorts: Basshe, Faragoh, and Gold.

Dos Passos hitchhiked a ride aboard a mail plane from Tangier to the French coast, having talked the pilot into allowing him to perch at his feet upon his cargo. "God what a cold ride," he exclaimed in recalling his first flight. Only a canvas flap sheltered him from the elements as the begoggled pilot navigated his bucking single-engine craft through sleet and rain clouds and touched down at his various ports of call in Spain, distributing mail. Dos Passos marveled that he had not thrown up upon the mail bags despite his churning stomach. He could have flown all the way to Paris, then set out immediately for the States, but he asked to be let out on the tiny airstrip of Sète beside the Mediterranean Sea. Stiff with cold, he unfolded his limbs and headed overland for Cap d'Antibes to thaw out in the sun with Gerald and Sara Murphy. For a time Dos Passos had abandoned all

thoughts of proceeding to Schruns for a week to join Hemingway and Hadley as originally planned. From the Villa America on March 6 he wrote Hemingway that he needed
to catch his "fool play" in New York before someone retitled it "Dark Laughter," thus
would have to skip the skiing holidays in the Vorarlberg. Hemingway replied that he
must come immediately and bring the Murphys. He wanted to take them to the
Madlener-Haus, a ski lodge high above the town that could be reached only by an
arduous, cross-country trek. The snow was fresh and powdery and the entire area was a
skier's delight, he said. Dos Passos had not been on skis since his schoolboy excursions at
Choate, but was game to try it again, he said, and set out with the Murphys for Schruns.
With luck and the kindness of critics—about which he was never optimistic—he might
still catch his play in New York, and in any case, a week's delay would not be catastrophic,
he reasoned.

Sara Murphy stayed on the "bunny" slopes with Hadley and Bumby or remained
indoors while the men went out daily in the company of a ski instructor, Walther Lent,
whose wife usually helped Dos Passos while Lent himself skied with Hemingway and
Murphy. "I knew from the first I'd never be any good," allowed Dos Passos. "Too damned
clumsy. . . . I just couldn't get the knack of turning corners. The best I could do was
fall down. When the slopes got too steep I used to sit down on my skis and turn them into
a sort of toboggan. Was I razzed when it was discovered arriving in Schruns that I'd worn
a hole in the seat of my pants." After a few hours on the purple-shadowed slopes,
everyone went indoors to a roaring fire and hot food. "We ate vast quantities of trout,
drank the wines and beers and slept like dormice under the great featherbeds." Herr and
Frau Lent, the Hemingways, Dos Passos, the Murphys, and a handful of other guests
stayed at the intimate, privately owned Hotel Taube, where a generous spirited Nels
family treated them as though they were kin. "We were all brothers and sisters when we
parted company," Dos Passos wrote in his memoirs. "It was a real shock to hear a few
months later that Ernest was walking out on Hadley. When you get fond of a couple you
like them to stay hitched." Their few days together in Schruns was what Dos Passos called
his "last unalloyed good time" with Hemingway and Hadley. When he learned later that
Hemingway planned to marry Pauline Pfeiffer, he wrote that he would like to knock his
and Hadley's heads together and suggested Hemingway become a Mormon.

Some thirty years after the events themselves, Hemingway described his winter in
Schruns as "a nightmare winter disguised as the greatest fun of all. That was the year that
the rich showed up . . . led by the pilot fish." He blamed Gerald Murphy—who was
impressed by what he took to be Hemingway's genius upon hearing him read parts of *The
Sun Also Rises* while it was still in manuscript—for having supported his decision to leave
Hadley. Murphy feared that Hemingway's feelings of guilt might adversely affect his
writing and gave Hemingway both money and encouragement when he learned that
Hemingway had no intention of reconciling with Hadley and was bent, instead, upon
marrying Pauline. Hemingway may have said little or nothing to Dos Passos, the
Murphys, or to Pauline herself directly in assigning blame, but he exercised scant reserve
in his writings later by attacking them for what he thought of as their duplicity in the
matter. In his memoirs, *A Moveable Feast,* Hemingway spoke of "the rich" who never did
anything for their own ends, but rather "collected people as some collect pictures and

others breed horses. . . . I had hated these rich because they had backed me and encouraged me when I was doing wrong." Had they not been led to him by "the pilot fish," who had the "irreplaceable early training of the bastard and a latent and long denied love of money," he might never have left his first wife, he implied.

14

War on the Home Front: The New Playwrights, Sacco and Vanzetti, and *The New Masses,* 1925–27

In the States everything is up shit creek and going belly-up fast.

Dos Passos to Hemingway
9 June 1927

Dos Passos arrived in New York City in late March 1926 on the tag end of the two-week run of his play, "The Moon Is a Gong," a production that baffled and offended its New York audiences. Critics predicted an early demise for the production, which seemed a bizarre combination of proletarian message and jazz revue clad in the motley garb of allegory. Gilbert Gabriel described it as a "hoarse, furious harlequinade" that spattered its "sarcasms, drolleries, tendernesses and rebellious helter-skelter, heavy handedly, with the lustiness of young gamins round an election night bonfire and the irresponsibility of poetry in knee pants." Brooks Atkinson and Alexander Woollcott tried to be equally clever in their remarks, but were less kind. The reviewer who signed himself "B.D." found only two of the dozen episodes worth keeping alive and commended a third scene because it "rang like the golden gong of truth in the speech of the old man who tends a sidewalk telescope through which the curious can look at the moon for a dime." He did not advise Dos Passos to abandon the theater altogether, but suggested that he write "another fantasy with less youthful, cocksure bitterness in it and more dramatic unity. . . . The object of a play is to be played, and no dramatist can preach to empty pews."

The criticism leveled at Dos Passos' play in New York proved that audiences there were no more ready for such radical departures from traditional forms than Bostonians were. The expressionistic plays of Eugene O'Neill and Elmer Rice had been useful fore-runners so far as technique was concerned, yet lacked the social message that the New Playwrights Theatre directors considered essential. They wished to synthesize the goals of playwright, producer, and actor. For their offerings to be successful, they had to be intellectually salutary as well as entertaining. Though their goal was social reformation, they were determined not to allow revolutionary fervor to prostitute their concept of good theater. They intended to shatter the icons and vapid posturing of complacent Americans who lacked understanding of the inner workings of a democratic society, but to avoid, at the same time, any compromise to their sense of artistic craftsmanship. The challenge was to conceive new, externalized methods by which to present inner truths.

Despite efforts during the spring and fall of 1926 to launch their new venture, the directors of the New Playwrights Theatre made little headway until late in the year when the group acquired the active patronage of Otto Kahn, who declared: "No business I have ever conducted has brought me dividends comparable to the satisfaction I have in working for the advancement of art." Kahn's reputation for shrewd benevolence to the arts— especially when the cause was somewhat revolutionary—had earned him such nicknames as "the Maecenas of Manhattan," "a modern Medici," "Kubla," "The Emperor," and, as Michael Gold called him, "my favorite millionaire." During the second season of the New Playwrights Theatre, a number of artists were invited to hang their paintings in the theater when they took over the old Cherry Lane for productions. For a time the work of Dos Passos, Louis Lozowick, William Zorach, Thomas Benton, Hugo Gellert, Adelaide Lawson, Wood Gaylor, Bernard Hartman, and a number of other painters could be found there as well as in an experimental studio at 95 Bank Street with which they were associated.

Along with his involvement with the New Playwrights Theatre—slight until March 1927, when its first two plays were presented—Dos Passos became an active contributor and member of the executive board of *The New Masses,* a new magazine. He was still in Morocco when Arthur McComb chided him in a letter of December 8, 1925: "What are you, my dear friend, at the age of thirty doing on that dismal roster of names of agitators —oh, no, seriously I mourn. . . . Why not go to Tibet and turn prayer wheels?" Mc-Comb's reference was to a New York *Times* article about the still incipient magazine. Early in the year Dos Passos had been invited to serve on the national executive committee of the newly organized Proletarian Artists and Writers League, which most people associated with Moscow rather than anything homegrown. One of the charges of the executive board was to agitate for a magazine to replace *The Masses,* silent since its governmental banning during World War I. Its successor, *The Liberator,* was popular among readers of *The Masses* until it was turned over to the Workers' party in 1922 and became a Communist organ. Dos Passos assured painter Maurice Becker, a member of the Proletarian Artists and Writers League, that he would do anything he could to help: "I'm absolutely with you. . . . The Masses was the only magazine I ever had any use for." Other writers who agreed to serve on the executive board included Michael Gold, John Howard Lawson, Mary Heaton Vorse, Genevieve Taggard, Robert Wolf, Joseph Freeman, Louis Lozowick, Simon Felshin, and Hugo Gellert. From the first issue of *The New Masses* (May 1926) until 1934, Dos Passos' name was listed as a member of the executive board. During this time he wrote for it regularly, despite its having little resources with which to pay contributors. The magazine was supported largely by the Garland Fund, a trust established by Charles Garland, who at twenty-five decided to bestow his paternal inheritance upon the cause of radicalism. Dos Passos received token payment for his book reviews, but almost everything else he wrote for *The New Masses* was a matter of charity. His dedication to left-wing reformist causes and his heady ascent to radicalism in 1926–27 were seeded by his association with the New Playwrights Theatre, *The New Masses*, and the Sacco-Vanzetti Defense Committee—all of which he was involved in at the same time.

Dos Passos' first essay for the new magazine was an important contribution to its second issue: "The *New Masses* I'd Like." He said that Michael Gold's attack upon him as a "bourgeois intellectual" had prompted him to set down his ideas regarding America's need to develop its own brand of thinking and not to be beholden to Russia or anyone else for its "phrases, badges, opinions, and banners." As he saw it, there was far more to be gained by rigorously examining the home terrain "than by sitting on the side lines of the labor movement with a red rosette in your buttonhole and cheering for the home team." He wanted a magazine "full of introspection and doubt that would be like a piece of litmus paper to test things by." Ever since the discovery of the country by Columbus, various imported systems had been its curse, he insisted. "Why not develop our own brand?" Their focus should be the masses, the people who work themselves, rather than those who work others.

Gold's essay—"Let It Be Really New!"—was juxtaposed on the same page with the Dos Passos piece. Gold agreed with "friend John" that writers in *The New Masses* "ought to set sail for a new discovery of America," but denied the charge of having loaded "the pilot's compass-box" with Moscow and revolution. There was no need for "spiritual commands" from Moscow. The need to revolt was inherent in what lay rotten in the American system, he continued. The question lay in how to go about it: "Shall we revolt blindly . . . or with full, bold hard consciousness?" Gold accused Dos Passos and Lawson of shutting their eyes to the main drifts of American life and of trying to live in "isolated sensation," rejecting generalizations, hugging "chaos to their bosoms," and condemning the heroes of their fiction to "chaos and failure." Already an avowed Communist, Gold goaded Dos Passos still further in his review of *Manhattan Transfer*. The author had been "fiercely honest" in his "barbaric poem of New York," but had not gone far enough. Dos Passos' idealism was middle-class, which he might rectify if he would commence a stringent self-education in history, psychology, and economics. Only a no-nonsense plunge into the labor movement would suffice, urged Gold. Dos Passos was already on the periphery of the labor movement, but had no intention of plunging in and emerging with a hammer and sickle between his teeth.

In a second essay published in the same issue with "The *New Masses* I'd Like"—"300 Red Agitators Reach Passaic" (a title taken from a newspaper headline)—Dos Passos was apologetic for having viewed the Passaic, New Jersey, strike scene from a safe distance. His perspective was from a motorcade of intellectuals who arrived in "their shiny sedans and taxis" and emerged into the brisk spring air clad in warm overcoats to congregate illegally for an hour or so until a member of their group was arrested. Then they dispersed quietly, leaving the strikers behind. The experience enabled Dos Passos to write poignantly and ironically of it, however, as he contrasted the observers with the observed: "the squat square women with yellow gray faces, groups of men and boys standing still, saying nothing, looking nowhere, square hands hanging at their sides, people square and still, chunks of yellow gray stone at the edge of a quarry, idle, waiting, on strike."

Dos Passos' next important piece for *The New Masses* was the result of face-to-face interviews with Nicola Sacco and Bartolomeo Vanzetti, the poor and nearly illiterate Italian-born shoemaker and fishmonger whose case had become a *cause célèbre* among radicals and intellectuals around the world. They had been convicted of the brutal robbery-murders of a payroll guard and driver in South Braintree, Massachusetts, on April 15, 1920, and had been behind bars since their arrest, soon after the murders were discovered. After visiting Sacco in the Dedham jail and Vanzetti in the Charlestown prison, Dos Passos was convinced of their innocence and wrote movingly of their plight in a *New Masses* essay entitled "The Pit and the Pendulum." In the fall, his interviews were published in the *Official Bulletin of the Sacco-Vanzetti Defense Committee of Boston, Massachusetts.* Then Gardner Jackson, chairman of the defense committee, invited him to become a member. In his new role, Dos Passos made several fact-finding and interview trips to Boston and the vicinity to develop the official document of the case, a 127-page pamphlet, *Facing the Chair: Story of the Americanization of Two Foreignborn Workmen.*

Acting upon Dos Passos' complaint during the summer of 1926 that he had been "as low as a moulting canary" and in need of exercise and excitement, Rumsey Marvin—now city editor of the Mamaroneck *Daily Times*—prevailed upon him to bolt the city for a few days and accompany him on a walking expedition around Cape Hatteras that they had talked about for several years, but had never gotten around to doing. It was late June and Dos Passos, having already written up his interviews with Sacco and Vanzetti, felt the need to retreat from civilization for a time. Marvin also invited two of his Yale classmates, C. Dickerman Williams, now assistant United States district attorney, and Hugh A. Leamy, an associate editor of *Collier's.* The men started their trek in Morehead City and proceeded north along North Carolina's Outer Banks. For three days they tramped under a scorching sun. To cool off, they stripped and swam nude, then walked without their clothes until they had dried off. Except for an occasional fisherman, they saw no one along the beaches. The Coast Guard was on the lookout for them each night and welcomed them to sleep in their lifesaving stations. They also ferried them from one bank to the next, but refused payment either for the lodging or the ferry service. In Ocracoke, the hikers paused one afternoon for a few hours to see if Leamy recuperated sufficiently from the effects of too much sun and corn liquor to continue the walk. Leamy was overweight, and the combination proved immobilizing. He was not even in shape to accept an invitation that evening from several Ocracoke maidens who invited them to square dance with them. Dos Passos, Marvin, and Williams decided to walk at night to escape the sun's blistering rays and set out for Hatteras after the dance, but could not rouse Leamy from the wheelbarrow into which he had crawled to sleep off his discomfort. The trio took turns pushing him until it was time to take to the beach again, then abandoned him—along with his wheelbarrow—on the outskirts of Ocracoke. Leamy said later that he had dropped out to research an article for his magazine. Walking Ocracoke under a full moon, they came upon wild ponies that whinnied, snorted, and tossed their heads at the intruders before galloping off. Dos Passos thought it an eerie, otherworldly scene as he watched the ponies prance over the dunes and play amid the sea grasses, the silhouettes of hulls and masts of shipwrecks casting grotesque shadows upon the fine white sands. The sojourners counted some forty vessels in one area alone. It seemed to them that the dying hulks had sought each other out for a mass burial.

Their walking trip ended five days after they set forth in Manteo, North Carolina, one hundred miles from Morehead City. They had planned to continue the walk to Kitty Hawk, but decided instead to catch the steamer preparing to leave then for Elizabeth City, Virginia, where they caught a train to Richmond. A reporter for the Richmond *News Leader* sought an interview, impressed by their journey and pleased to have an opportunity to talk with a writer of Dos Passos' stature. Dos Passos' chief contribution to the interview was his comment that the maidens in the little village of Buxton, North Carolina, were the most beautiful women he had seen in America, a remark probably provoked by one of the coastguardsmen encountered along the way who had complained that his pretty daughter had little hope of finding a husband in such a remote duty station.

In the fall of 1926 after another five months of energetic involvement with the Sacco-Vanzetti Defense Committee, work on his defense pamphlet, and a number of journalistic pieces and book reviews for *The New Masses,* Dos Passos complained again of his "damned literary existence" and set out on another walking trip, this time alone, "to clear my mind," he added. His walk took him across the Blue Ridge Mountains from Staunton, Virginia, to Covington, Kentucky. He was troubled because he could not put down his vague longings for Crystal Ross and decided to resolve his problem by going to Texas to see her. She was still single, though admittedly engaged to Dabney Lewis, her Texan. Dos Passos was not optimistic that he could convince her to marry him instead of Lewis, but he wanted to clear the air by talking over the situation and to be assured that he had her friendship, if nothing more.

Before setting out for Texas, he was asked by *The New Masses* to review *The Sun Also Rises.* Dos Passos disliked reviewing books by friends, but found himself yielding to such requests more and more. He knew that what he had to say about Hemingway's novel would rankle him, just as a review of Robert Hillyer's "Alchemy" for *The Freeman* back in the fall of 1920 had grossly upset Hillyer. He had sent a copy of the review to Hillyer, along with an apologetic note: "You are probably going to hate me. . . . But I thought I would knock it more understandingly, and more sweetly perhaps than would a harsh outsider." When Hillyer railed in protest, Dos Passos replied: "You know perfectly well that I am fond of you and you have no right to get sore however clumsily I belabour you. I am awfully sorry that silly criticism hurt you. . . . But remember that one has to take one's friends bag and baggage—and if they are lumbering oafs like myself, put up with many a dainty corn stepped on without malice." As with Hillyer, Dos Passos sent Hemingway a copy of the review before it was published. He added a personal note as well:

> I've written a damn priggish mealy mouthed review that makes me sick. The book makes me
> sick anyway, besides making me very anxious to see you, and homesick for good drinks and
> wisecracks and Pamplona and bullfights and all that sort of thing, god damn it and them. I
> never felt so rotten about anything. . . . Hem, please forgive all this rubbish. The trouble
> with me is that I'm an expatriate—from Paris. Like hell, ain't we all lil' expatriates from the
> Garden of Eden? I feel thoroughly sore about everything. Everything I write seems to be crap
> and everything everybody I like writes seems to be crap. They're going to kill Sacco and
> Vanzetti—and I saw Harry Wills's last fight—and everything is inexpressibly shitty. . . .

The Sun Also Rises is just about as bad as Streets of Night, only it's more entertaining and better written. . . . We can't any of us write and ought to take up charcoal burning. Batiking. Honestly it's pretty god damn discouraging for the American Renaissance. The thing is that writing isn't an occupation—it's a thing like raising fancy pigeons or stamp collecting. People who give up all their time to a hobby go sour or crazy or both. I'm going down to Mexico—to forget. . . . I think I'm getting stomach ulcers like Valentino. They probably affect the brain.

Dos Passos had been in Mexico five weeks when he wrote Hemingway a follow-up letter regarding *The Sun Also Rises:*

The funny thing about The Sun Also is that in sections it isn't shitty. It's only in conjunto that it begins to smell. Of course it's perfectly conceivable that it's really a swell book and that we're all of us balmy. Anyway, as I says to myself writing for The New Masses, we've all got to write a mile of turds before we die. . . . But honestly Hem (one more cut at the cold mutton), I think that all the tendency to write about friends is rotten—like putting in pieces of Don [Stewart] and various people's maiden names in The Torrents of Spring. Writers are per se damn lousy bourgeois parasitic upperclass shits and not to be written about unless they are your enemies. Trying to be nice to your friends in a book brings it all down to the level of the Hotel Algonquin and the Youth's Companion.

He told Hemingway that he had been "preoccupied with personal alarms and confusion in New York and left there like shot out of a gun." He thought it ridiculous that he had just had his thirty-first birthday and "had some jack for the first time in years," yet was "up shit creek from every point of view except financial." Had he gone any place but Mexico, Dos Passos allowed, he might have "caved in from sheer depression." Mexico was the place to be, he insisted: "The sun's hot and air's cold and there're all sorts of fantastic foods and drinks, and the people—particularly the women of Indian blood—are like stone idols." He said he hoped that "muddling along" with *The New Masses* might help him come up with something interesting. "The writing in it is pretty rotten, but some of the drawings are good. I admit though that the whole thing stinks. Still at the moment it's just about my speed." He was angry with himself, he admitted, because the new play on which he was working was "the utterest bilderdibble you ever imagined. I've got plenty of plans for writing but can't get down to them because I haven't any confidence in what I write about."

Never one to indulge a friend or acquaintance when he sniveled, Hemingway replied:

What the hell do you write a play for if it doesn't go or if you've got enough jack (or did you get the jack to write the play)? Lay off and don't try and do a damn thing and let the juice come back. You've done too bloody much writing and you are stale as hell on it. For christ sake you've published six books that I know about and I don't know how many behind my back. You ought to go to grass and not when you ought not to be writing a damn thing be working on a bloody play.

Hemingway also admitted that Dos Passos had been correct in criticizing his tendency to "stick people's names in": "I only did it at the time to kid sticking people's names in. That was why I tried to make out the writer an imbecile in the notes to the reader in Torrents.

. . . Anyway it's bad. Been working lately like in the old days and put the result away in the trunk. Publication is the fucking damn evil. I shouldn't ever have published the stories in In Our Time, nor written Torrents except for us guys to read at the time and put it away." He added that he should not have published *The Sun Also Rises,* either, but that at least he was getting "big money" for it because it was outselling everything by Bromfield and Fitzgerald.

Dos Passos was still in Mexico when Lawson wrote that the New Playwrights Theatre was being launched officially with the opening of *Loud Speaker,* another expressionistic play by Lawson, on March 2, 1927. "I'm as dumb as an ostrich that's had its feathers plucked and should be delighted to engage in any conceivable enterprise," replied Dos Passos to his friend, relieved to be roused at last from his "great state of mental and moral decay." Again Lawson summoned him—just as he had a year earlier—and again Dos Passos "rushed up from the deep" to do what he could. The next time Dos Passos wrote Hemingway, he was singing a tune quite different from his earlier blues:

> I'm in deeper and deeper in the drahma every moment. I'm now one of five directors of a little Otto Kahn–undernourished playhouse on W. 52nd Street (near an excellent old fashioned German saloon and beer swiggery). I do a lot of (against union rules) carrying about and painting of scenery and switching on and off of lights which is very entertaining—but I don't feel it's my life work. Anyway it keeps me from writing or worrying and I'm merry as a cricket. . . . Honestly Hem—I think that publication is the honestest and easiest method of getting rid of bum writing. Unpublished stuff just festers and you get to be like a horse that's pistol shy or whatever they call it when they are wonderful horses but never can start a race. I'm all for living by writing and making the best living possible out of what one writes, but the thing is that one has got to have people to throw up red flags . . . when one has produced a talented and daintily scented turd. . . . In Our Time was a goddamn good thing to publish. So was The Sun Also. It's better to publish than burn as St. Paul said.

From St. Thomas in the Virgin Islands several months later, Dos Passos wrote Hemingway that everything was "up shit creek and going belly-up fast." His new complaint was that "they are trying to send a kid up for three years for saying (in the Daily Worker) that America was a whorehouse full of two dollar whores, which though inaccurate, is hardly criminal." He also grumbled that the magazines were turning down everything he wrote and that he was "getting sour and bald. I ought to get married—and a big laugh that is." Dos Passos had gone to the West Indies on the spur of the moment. He could ill afford the time away from his involvement in the theater, but hoped that the steamer crossing would give his jangled nerves a chance to repair and that the sun would prove beneficial to his aching rheumatic joints. His condition was helped, too, by his recent discovery of "green swizzles," planters' punch, and "Barbadian enfuriators"—all made with rum—which the natives treated as staples. "My God Sir, the drinking down here is amazing!" he exclaimed to Hemingway.

Dos Passos' most immediate concern was his involvement with the Sacco-Vanzetti Defense Committee, which he made no mention of in his letter to Hemingway. After a series of appeals for a new trial, the final appeal having been rejected by the Massachusetts Supreme Court despite new evidence and certain irregularities of due process, Governor Alvan T. Fuller of Massachusetts yielded to defense committee pressure and appointed an ad hoc advisory committee to review the trial and conviction. If his committee agreed that the trial had been fair and just and the defendants' guilt established beyond reasonable doubt, he intended to consider the matter closed and allow the executions to take place as ordered. It was during the deliberations of the committee behind closed doors that Dos Passos sought respite in the Virgin Islands. On August 1, 1927, the governor's committee released its report: Sacco and Vanzetti had been fairly tried and found guilty according to the evidence presented. It saw no reason to recommend a new trial. By this time the attitude of the citizen-at-large in Massachusetts was that the condemned men should die because they were anarchist immigrants as well as convicted murderers. Their deaths were expedient as a lesson to refute radicalism the world over. The Communists had decided, too, that there was far more to be gained by their executions than by pardons or other executive clemency, which the official defense committee worked valiantly to achieve. The Citizens National Committee for Sacco and Vanzetti, organized by Isaac Don Levine, appealed for help nationwide. Everyone who could was urged to travel to Boston and take a place in the picket lines that began forming two weeks before the scheduled executions. Incensed by the committee's report, Dos Passos addressed an eight-hundred-word "Open Letter" to A. Lawrence Lowell, president of Harvard University. He wrote as a Harvard graduate who had expected that Lowell's appointment to the committee would have insured its having "at least a modicum of fair play and of historical perspective in the conduct of the investigation." Instead, his signature on the report made him a collaborator in a "judicial murder. . . . The part into which you have forced Harvard University will make many a man ashamed of being one of its graduates." The report was not the result of an open, unbiased investigation, insisted Dos Passos, but an apology for the conduct of the trial itself. His letter concluded:

> This is a matter of life and death, not only for Sacco and Vanzetti but for the civilization that Harvard University is supposed to represent. The Sacco-Vanzetti case has become part of the world struggle between the capitalist class and the working class, between those who have power and those who are struggling to get it. In a man in high office ignorance of the new sprouting forces that are remaking society, whether he is with them or against them, is little short of criminal. . . . Are you going to prove by a bloody reprisal that the radical contention that a man holding unpopular ideas cannot get a free trial in our courts is true? . . . It is upon men of your class and position that will rest the inevitable decision as to whether the coming struggle for the reorganization of society shall be bloodless and fertile or inconceivably bloody and destructive. . . . As a Harvard man I want to protest most solemnly against your smirching the university of which you are an officer with the foul crime against humanity and civilization to which you have made yourself accessory.

As August 23 approached, the ranks of picketers swelled as they gathered on the Boston Common, donned black armbands, picked up placards, and marched across Beacon Street and once or twice around the Massachusetts State House in full view of the governor's council chambers, then were arrested. They were supposed to be warned that their behavior was illegal, given seven minutes to disperse, then taken to the nearby Joy Street Station for booking. Most protestors carried such signs as GOVERNOR FULLER! WHY DID YOU CALL ALL OUR WITNESSES LIARS? and IF THEY ARE NOT INNOCENT WHY ARE YOU AFRAID OF A NEW TRIAL? One woman walked from Provincetown to Boston wearing a sandwich board declaring AMERICANS CANNOT LOOK THE WORLD IN THE FACE IF SACCO AND VANZETTI ARE MURDERED. Other placards bore a quotation attributed to Judge Webster Thayer, I WILL GET THOSE BASTARDS GOOD AND PROPER!—and beside it the statement: IT IS THE RIGHT OF EVERY CITIZEN TO BE TRIED BY JUDGES AS FREE, IMPARTIAL AND INDEPENDENT AS THE LOT OF HUMANITY WILL ADMIT. Thayer's contempt for foreigners, especially Italians—whom he referred to as "Wops" and "Dago sons of bitches"—was well publicized. Robert Benchley filed a writ of protest with the court when he heard of Thayer's outrageous remarks, and Heywood Broun wrote stirringly on behalf of the condemned men in his column in the New York *World.* When Vanzetti's sister, Luigia, arrived in New York aboard the *Aquitania* several days before the scheduled executions, she was met at the dock by Broun's wife (Ruth Hale), Dorothy Parker, and Carlo Tresca, an avowed anarchist and editor of *Il Martello,* an Italian newspaper.

Dos Passos was in Boston ten days before the executions to work with Isaac Don Levine and his Citizens National Committee for Sacco and Vanzetti, who were summoning everyone of prominence they knew to come to Boston in person to lend weight to their appeal. Most of the picketers were immigrants of myriad nationalities from the garment district. Some had traveled from as far away as Chicago. A number of protestors were Communists, such as Michael Gold, Fred Beal, and John Howard Lawson (Lawson was not a card-carrying member yet, but well on his way). Many did not consider themselves radicals, but simply patriotic Americans who viewed the trial as a gross frame-up by the Department of Justice. Those who could not come in person sent letters of appeal to the governor in chorus with Vanzetti's much-publicized plea for "justice, not mercy." Meanwhile, Vanzetti's twenty-three day hunger strike, which began the day of the release of the report by the governor's committee, helped fan sentiments throughout the world. Simultaneous demonstrations went on in Paris, Geneva, Warsaw, Berlin, Belfast, San Juan, Buenos Aires, and other population centers. Some four hundred thousand signatures accompanied petitions and letters assailing Governor Fuller or pleading for him to "prevent the legal lynching." Many of the picketers—such as Katherine Anne Porter—were arrested and booked repeatedly. With each arrest Porter found Edward James (a nephew of Henry James) awaiting her at the Joy Street Station to bail her out. Dos Passos was arrested and charged with "sauntering and loitering . . . in connection with the Sacco-Vanzetti picketing in front of the State House" and was bailed out by Eugen Boissevain, the husband of Edna St. Vincent Millay, another fervent demonstrator. Other marchers included Dorothy Parker, Mary Heaton Vorse, Susan Glaspell, Frank Shay, Zona Gale, Lola Ridge, Babette Deutsch, Helen O'Lochlain Crowe, Grace Lumpkin, James Rorty, William Gropper, Upton Sinclair, Paxton Hibben, Powers Hapgood, and dozens of others of prominence, most of whom were arrested at least once and bailed out at twenty-five dollars a head. In court on August 27 to face charges, Dos Passos appealed his ten-dollar fine on the grounds that he had been there as a reporter for the *Daily Worker.*

On the day of the executions—August 23, 1927—the Boston Common was declared off-limits to orators, a sanction never before imposed and contrary to its long tradition of freedom of assembly and speech. Demonstrations erupted through midtown Boston, but most were orderly. More uniformed policemen were on duty that day with their riot sticks and loaded handguns than ever before in the city's history. That night the largest crowd ever to gather before an execution chamber faced mounted policemen who cordoned off the area in front of Charlestown prison in anticipation of its being stormed. The day before the executions a general strike had been called by labor unions throughout the country. Although the Boston turnout was slight by comparison to demonstrations in New York, some one hundred thousand workers walked off their jobs at noon and gathered at Union Square. On August 29, fifty thousand workers assembled a second time at Union Square in defiance of not being granted a parade permit to accompany the ashes of Sacco and Vanzetti down the streets of New York to the hall in which Carlo Tresca and others awaited to deliver stirring eulogies. Writer James T. Farrell was among the New York mourners who, like Dos Passos, attributed much of the shaping of his developing radicalism to U.S. Attorney General A. Mitchell Palmer's anti-Red raids, the delirium of arrests and deportations of alleged radicals at the beginning of the decade, and the Sacco and Vanzetti executions.

In an effort to summon everyone he knew to come to Boston for a last-ditch effort to picket before the executions, Dos Passos had been unable to locate Edmund Wilson, who he was sure would come. Suddenly, in the midst of the general confusion, he received a wire from Wilson inviting him to Provincetown to a party. "You can't imagine how queerly your wire jangled my nerves," Dos Passos replied. "Jesus X Columbus, man, didn't you realize that we were all virtually mad up in Boston? You try battering your head against a stone wall sometime."

Dos Passos' eulogy to Sacco and Vanzetti appeared in the October 1927 issue of *The New Masses:*

They Are Dead Now—

This isn't a poem
This is two men in grey prison clothes.
One man sits looking at the sick flesh of his hands—
hands that haven't worked for seven years.
Do you know how long a year is?
Do you know how many hours there are in a day
when a day is twenty-three hours on a cot in a cell,
in a cell in a row of cells in a tier of rows of cells
all empty with the choked emptiness of dreams?
Do you know the dreams of men in jail?

• • •

They are dead now
The black automatons have won.
They are burned up utterly
their flesh has passed into the air of Massachusetts
their dreams have passed into the wind.
"They are dead now," the Governor's Secretary nudges
the Governor,

> *"They are dead now," the Superior Court Judge nudges*
> *the Supreme Court Judge,*
> *"They are dead now," the College President nudges*
> *the College President*
> *A dry chuckling comes up from all the dead:*
> *The white collar dead; the silkhatted dead;*
> *the frockcoated dead*
> *They hop in and out of automobiles*
> *breathe deep in relief*
> *as they walk up and down the Boston streets.*

• • •

> *they are free of dreams now*
> *free of greasy prison denim*
> *their voices blow back in a thousand lingoes*
> *singing one song*
> *to burst the eardrums of Massachusetts*
> *Make a poem of that if you dare!*

Dos Passos was ripe now for other protests. Zona Gale, also a member of the Sacco-Vanzetti Defense Committee, had supported the awarding of a scholarship to David Gordon, the eighteen-year-old youth sentenced to an indeterminate term in the New York City reformatory for his reportedly obscene poem published in the *Daily Worker* in the spring of 1926. It was Gordon, of whom Dos Passos spoke in his letter to Hemingway, who had written that America was "a whorehouse full of two dollar whores." The poem had begun:

> *America is a land of censored opportunity.*
> *Lick spit; eat dirt.*
> *There's your opportunity. . . .*

Dos Passos admitted that it was not a good poem, but disagreed that Gordon deserved three years of incarceration with hardened criminals and prison guards. Gordon had been awarded a scholarship to the University of Wisconsin by the Zona Gale Foundation, but instead was serving his term at the reformatory. Dos Passos termed it a "grim substitute for the college education he had earned by his obvious and precocious talent as a writer," and on Gordon's behalf sent a mimeographed letter to such friends as Robert Hillyer, Stewart Mitchell, Rumsey Marvin, Burton Rascoe, Hemingway, and Fitzgerald during the fall and winter of 1927–28 along with a scribbled note asking that each of them write "very mildly worded" letters on business stationery to the parole board requesting clemency: "The important thing now is not to complain about fair play or freedom of speech, but to get him out. The length of sentence is up to the Parole Board. A plea on the grounds of the boy's youth will carry more . . . than abstract complaints about the obvious infringement of human rights involved in this case." He also sent copies of the poem and of the transcript of the judge's remarks at sentencing so his friends might better "understand the atmosphere of meanness and spite that surrounded the trial." As Dos Passos saw it, most of America's best writers would be in jail if "such were the penalty for obscenity and disgust with America. . . . The boy's real crime was that he was writing for a communist publication and that he was a Russian Jew." In his letter to Hillyer about the affair, Dos Passos added: "Just sending you these little enclosures to keep you up with the progress of liberty and the pursuit of happiness." He said he had run out of copies of the transcript, but asked Hillyer to take his word for it that the two Irish Catholic justices were "as stinking as they possibly could be under the circumstances, and neither the poor kid nor his rotten lawyer who gave away the case as lawyers usually do (not C. D. Williams, who took the case up later and is a good guy) had a chance to defend themselves."

Another cause Dos Passos embraced during the winter of 1927–28 involved two other less well-publicized Italian immigrants in Brooklyn. Carlogero Cresco and Donato Carillo were charged with the murders of two Italian fascists in the Bronx on Memorial Day of 1927. In a December 12, 1927, article in the Brooklyn *Daily Eagle,* Dos Passos was identified—complete with picture—as a "picturesque Brooklyn parlor radical and novelist of 110 Columbia Heights" who had just been delivered from the "toils of the law for his placard-carrying in front of Governor Fuller's office on Beacon Hill." He was quoted as saying that he was now preparing an active campaign in support of the men: "Mussolini's effort to extend his influence to Italians in this country is damnable. I will do everything I can to help these men. The whole thing is a frame-up." The reporter acknowledged that he had interviewed Dos Passos in a cellar at 91 Charles Street in Greenwich Village, "where he is engaged in trying out new plays."

Dos Passos' work with the committee aiding Cresco and Carillo was far less involved than his efforts on behalf of Sacco and Vanzetti. He was not convinced of their innocence, he admitted, but thought the real issue was whether or not the industrial capitalist system had become so prostituted in its money-fisted grubbing that the "god damn human race" counted for nothing anymore. In his next book, in a "Camera Eye" depicting the era, he wrote:

America our nation has been beaten by strangers who have turned
our language inside out who have taken the clean words our fathers
spoke and made them slimy and foul
their hired men sit on the judge's bench they sit back with their feet
on the tables under the dome of the State they are ignorant of our
beliefs they have the dollars the guns the armed forces the powerplants
. . . we are two nations . . . we stand defeated America.

It was in such a mood that Dos Passos admitted to Robert Hillyer in the spring of 1928 that the past year had been one of great confusion and hard work. "The theatre and trying to write and private worries have almost driven me distracted. . . . I'm off for Russia (I hope) early in May. At the moment I'm in a little jerkwater boat of seasick passengers being conveyed (I hardly know why) to Key West." To hear Hemingway tell it, the amberjacks and groupers were practically leaping into the boat. "You must come down and see for yourself," he insisted. "Besides the salt air and surf will do wonders for your weary bones." Dos Passos had been in New York almost without relief for a year, and when Hemingway had suggested that he board a steamer and head for the Florida Keys and a fishing expedition, he needed no second invitation. Once again, Hemingway was rounding up "the gang." Actually, it was Dos Passos himself who was responsible for Hemingway's sojourn to Key West in the first place. He had recommended the Keys after his own hiking trip down the peninsula in the spring of 1924. "It's a vacation paradise, like no other place in Florida. You ought to try it," Dos Passos had written him. When Hemingway left Europe with Pauline for the birth of their son, Patrick, they decided to heed their friend's advice and check out Key West for themselves. If the fishing was half as good as the rumors, Hemingway wanted to stay until time for Pauline's lying-in, which was to be at her parents' home in Piggott, Arkansas. The Hemingways arrived in Key West the first of April 1928 and rented an apartment at the Trevor and Morris House on Simonton Street in the heart of Key West. Two weeks later, Dos Passos arrived, the first of their friends to rally to Hemingway's call, and checked into the only decent lodging that catered to transients, the Overseas Hotel.

As was his habit, he worked four or five hours every morning, then joined Hemingway and Pauline for lunch. Afterward, they usually went their separate ways. Dos Passos chose to walk his meal off or swim, whereas Hemingway guided a rented skiff out to the reefs for an afternoon of fishing. Dos Passos did not care much for fishing, but sometimes accompanied Hemingway for the experience and camaraderie. He loved such brushes with nature: the wild look of the coast from the sea and the way the shoreline changed as they rounded each bend, the gentle vibration of the motor, the sense of movement and the freedom it conveyed, the incredibly beautiful sky—especially at sunset—the fast-moving blue-gray clouds that brought sudden showers, and the beauty beneath the waters. Dos Passos appreciated the unhurried life that characterized the entire island. It was not that the natives were lazy; they simply did not rush. They measured time by the sun and tides, ate when they were hungry, did not push themselves to weariness, retired early, and rose with the sun. He was especially intrigued by the cigar factories and from time to time wandered in to chat with the Cuban and Spanish workers, whom he confounded regarding his ancestry. The swarthy complexion he had fallen heir to from his Portuguese ancestors tanned easily, and he might have passed for a native had the peculiar pronunciation of his *r*'s not made him suspect. His idiomatic Spanish was better than his French at this time. That the cigar workers he met were well read surprised him, but he was even more intrigued when he learned the circumstances. The workers pooled their money to hire readers while they stood at long tables without relief for hours hand-rolling each cigar. They listened to Spanish novels of the nineteenth century, Spanish translations of Dostoevski and Tolstoi, Socialist newspapers, and papers and other tracts from Cuba. "They were people who had their own ideas about things," reported Dos Passos, who was impressed that they did not parrot the preachings of others.

His memoirs, published almost forty years later, included many rich details and sensory impressions of Key West as he found it in the 1920s, but his personal reminiscences were not intended to be read for any strict accounting of time or events regarding his several stays there. Like Thoreau, who condensed two years at Walden Pond into four seasons for the sake of his dramatic narrative, so too did Dos Passos telescope two spring visits to Key West into one. In *The Best Times,* Dos Passos told of meeting Katharine Foster Smith—whom Hemingway and Pauline called "Katy"—in the spring of 1928, but he did not get to know her well until a year later, when they met again in Key West, where they had both been invited by Hemingway. By the time Katy arrived the end of April of 1928, Dos Passos was already on the verge of leaving for New York. Nor did he meet Katy's brother, Bill Smith, in 1928 or any of Hemingway's other cronies from his Paris days then, as his memoirs imply. Artists Waldo Peirce and Henry Strater arrived a few days after he left. All stayed at the Overseas Hotel, just as Dos Passos had, and converged nightly at Hemingway's apartment on Simonton Street after a round of drinking at Sloppy Joe's Bar and sundry other hangouts. As in Paris, Pamplona, or Schruns, Hemingway was happiest with attentive, adoring friends about him. He had always told a good tale and thrived on competition and an audience. Katy and her brother Bill, Peirce, and Strater stayed for almost a month. They worked each morning (Katy and Bill were writing, Peirce and Strater, painting), then joined Hemingway for an afternoon of fishing or carousing about the town. Liquor and gutsy conversation usually flowed late into the night. Neither Katy nor Pauline drank very much, but they were good sports and company for the men. By the end of May, however, Hemingway became nervous about Pauline's impending delivery and insisted they leave for Piggott even sooner than she thought necessary. Upon their departure, the band dispersed and Katy and her brother returned to Provincetown.

The lower Cape had been transformed during their absence by the summer people, who descended like locusts and threatened to ravage it of its life juices even before summer was officially on the calendar. The year-rounders avoided the tourists, but there was little escaping auto horns and raucous carryings-on as they combed the beaches and overflowed Commercial Street and "Back" Street (Bradford Street) both day and night. Happy to be home once more, Katy retreated to her study to type up the light fiction she had worked on in Key West. She probably mentioned to her two housemates, Edith Shay and Stella Roof, her brief encounter with the shy, slightly balding writer she had met in Key West, but she may have been surprised that he traipsed through her thoughts with a boldness that he, too, had not anticipated. Although she had found Peirce and Strater livelier companions than Dos Passos during the three or four days their visits to Key West had overlapped, there was something fetching about this Chicago-born author who dogged her consciousness during idle moments. Moreover, Katy had been with too many fishermen of late not to recognize that a little "chum" tossed overboard could do no harm and might even attract the catch of the day. "Pleased to have met you," she scribbled on a postal card and mailed to Dos Passos on June 22, 1928. She signed it "Home Girl," nothing more. If he could not guess who had sent it, that was his problem, she reasoned. The note might not provoke an amberjack's strike or tease a sailfish into the boat, but she was interested in only a muttonfish's nibble for the time being. Already she had dubbed Dos Passos "Monsieur Muttonfish," a name natives assigned to snapper that had been "moon-struck." Dos Passos relished the fish and chose it at every opportunity over the seafood considered more choice by others in their group.

Although he and Katy made no plans to meet again, she did not think they had seen the last of each other now that they had finally been introduced to one another. She had known about Dos Passos for several years, first from Hadley Hemingway, who had been a friend and classmate in college, and then from Pauline, with whom she had gone to school in St. Louis, and she may even have read a book or two of his. They both wondered why they had not run into each other sooner in view of their mutual friends. When they parted in Key West, Dos Passos had given her Cummings' address at 4 Patchin Place in Greenwich Village, where he assured her a card could always reach him. But he did not expect to be in New York long, he added. He intended only to meet with his agent and editor to see what money might be available to stake him on another trip abroad. Katy surmised that by the time she wrote, he might already be scrambling across the steppes and plains of Russia.

15

Visit to Russia, 1928

One sees better if one sits on the fence.

Adolph Dehn of John Dos Passos
spring 1928

Adolph Dehn's caricature of Dos Passos perched on iron spikes of a picket fence separating East from West was an apt one on the eve of the writer's departure for the Soviet Union in the spring of 1928. It might well have been Dos Passos' calling card for a time. The slim, lithe body in the sketch faced its capitalistic homeland, but the head swiveled to the rear, where the Russian sickle and hammer illuminated and dispelled the gloom hanging over factory rooftops and smokestacks. From such a vantage, Dos Passos in caricature looked upon, yet remained aloof from, both scenes. He could no more fasten upon the eyes of the bowed American workers on whose back the fat American industrialist rode—whip in hand, satisfaction on his face—than he could probe behind the brow of Kremlin bureaucrat or peasant from such a distance.

Clickety-clickety-clickety-clack
played the nimble fingers over the keys
stay detached, be objective
report only what you see
(be guarded about what you feel)
leave judgments to others.

He had gone to Key West only because he had been unable to wangle free passage to Leningrad as the custodian of a shipment of live, American-bred muskrats bound for the Soviet Union. To stay in New York against his will did terrible things to his psyche. "I'm a dead letter, an unexpanded Japanese flower, an unopened can of beans, a cocoon—

anything that's tied down, pinned, cribbed, confined, and uncomfortable," he complained. The interlude in Key West made him even more determined to get to Russia. Having missed out on the muskrat shipment, he would have ridden herd on a cage of skunks or anything else bound for the Far East via a northern port. Upon his return from Florida he had stayed in Cummings' flat only long enough for his agent (Carol Brandt, rather than Carl Brandt, her husband, was now handling his affairs at Brandt and Kirkpatrick) to get an advance from Macaulay Company for the publication of his new play, *Airways, Inc.,* in the fall. Brandt could not have placed *Airways, Inc.* with Macaulay had Harper & Brothers not declined to publish the play on the grounds that it had not yet been produced. It was slated for production by the New Playwrights Theatre as the second bill of their 1928–29 season, but its content was so explosive—a diatribe against American capitalism, the American Legion, and other "sacred cows"—that Eugene Saxton had been unable to persuade his conservative house of Harper & Brothers to publish the play under any circumstances (it was not a book on which the publisher expected to make any money; of the first and only edition, relatively few copies of the fifteen hundred copies were sold other than to libraries and the loyal band of friends who were always on the lookout for a new title). Dos Passos' advance for *Airways, Inc.* was sufficient for third-class passage aboard the Scandinavian liner the SS *United States.* Yet he could not have survived the summer and fall in the Soviet Union had it not also been for an advance on a still incipient novel to be entitled *The 42nd Parallel.* The new contract with Harper & Brothers was drawn up practically on the eve of his departure for Europe.

By the end of May 1928, Dos Passos was steaming across the Atlantic bound for Copenhagen, then a zigzag course to London, Paris, and Berlin to look up old friends before arrival in Leningrad in July. En route he had had ample time to consider his attitudes and present position. Although he may have appeared to sit with ease on the spikes of the cast iron fence separating East from West, as depicted by his friend, Adolph Dehn, they pricked both rump and conscience. Nor was he alone on the fence. Other straddlers plumped up their padding at will and gave every indication that they could sit indefinitely. His father—a role model he rebelled against and embraced with great ambivalence—had not been a fence sitter, but a vaulter who tested the wind and sprang back and forth amid loud hurrahs. Dos Passos, Jr., operated in quite a different style. He knew he was on the cusp of something momentous and had to decide where he stood in relation to his personal ideology. Was it to have intellectual meaning only, he questioned, or was its validity dependent upon translation into purposeful action? The executions of Sacco and Vanzetti left him heartsick and embittered. Nine months had passed, and he was still angry that his countrymen had permitted such a gruesome miscarriage of justice. The spinelessness of the general populace increasingly disgusted him. He had had a bellyful of the woolly-headed citizenry who allowed a few hopelessly inept elected officials and capitalistic entrepreneurs to run over them willy-nilly with hardly a bleat of protest. It seemed to him that *The New Masses* with its handful of radical editors and writers, coupled with the raucous blasts from the stage of the New Playwrights Theatre, were mere whispers amongst the thundering hoofs of a herd too shortsighted to lift their faces above the dust—Cassandras in the winds.

It was tempting for Dos Passos simply to remain neutral, but there were lessons to be learned from the Russian experience he was seeking now. He was not fool enough to think that America would find its salvation in the Soviet Union. The kernel for repair and growth lay within his own nation, he reasoned. His usual stance on foreign soil was to play affable observer and reporter. He allowed his impressions to scamper higgledy-piggledy over the canvas of his mind without feeling the need to interpret, argue, or account to anyone for his personal reactions. Yet he knew this trip would be different. This time he longed to be both observer and participant, to involve himself as directly as possible in the mainstream of life in the Soviet Union. He wanted to relate their political ideology to every facet of their existence, to discover the logic in sequential events, to pin down cause and effect regardless of the order of succession, to see what progress had been made since the Bolshevik massacre of thousands of sailors who mutinied at Kronstadt in 1921 in the midst of great drought and famine. Lenin's new economic policy had brought relief, but the power struggle between Stalin and Trotsky upon the death of their leader in 1924 caused further distress to the people and the world at large. Stalin emerged as virtual dictator in a socialist state of workers and peasants—a people's republic—to whom he promised industrial and agricultural independence from the capitalistic West. Dos Passos wondered now what effect Stalin's almost feverish process of industrialization and collectivization of agriculture was having upon the people themselves. He was sure that when he found the answers he sought, he would get down off his fence.

Already he knew how he would go about it. From Leningrad he planned to journey the countryside for the rest of the summer, to traverse the hinterlands by every conceivable mode of transportation, to range the valleys beside the Volga, cross the wide steppes, and climb the treacherous crests of the Caucasus—all the while talking to the peasants, looking into their eyes, feeling their pulses. He arrived with a vague idea of learning enough Russian so that he might communicate with peasant and worker alike, but felt that most of his answers would be nonverbal. He meant to read their faces and the way they carried themselves. In the fall he intended to end up in Moscow and live among the throngs of city folk, to visit the factories, schools, museums, and theaters. Perhaps it would be in the theater itself that he would discover most truly what was going on in the hearts and minds of the Russian people. Then he would be able to go home and square his own ambivalent feelings regarding the "new masses" of America, he reasoned.

Before leaving Leningrad, he had the good fortune to meet W. Horsley Gantt, a young physician from Virginia who had been in the Soviet Union for six years as an apprentice scientist of Ivan Pavlov. Gantt, two years older than Dos Passos, went to Russia to head up the medical team of Herbert Hoover's American Relief Administration. The organization brought in great quantities of food and drugs to aid the stricken country, which had been ravaged by drought and famine since 1920, but the American relief team was sent home after three months, its work ostensibly finished. Gantt got permission to stay on, having encountered by accident the famous Nobel Prize winner, whom he thought already dead. He had read an erroneous account of Pavlov's death and was startled to find him alive and just beginning his experiments on the conditioned reflex. Gantt had considered a career in psychiatry, but found too much confusion in Freud's answers to suit him. Through Pavlov's objective analysis of the neurological reflexes in dogs, Gantt perceived an approach to psychiatry that satisfied his pragmatic, science-based training. Soon he was one of Pavlov's most trusted assistants at his Institute for Experimental Medicine.

"I have seen Pavlov's dogs!" exclaimed Dos Passos to Cummings in a letter soon after meeting Gantt. He had little interest in his friend's laboratory experiments, however; he was more engrossed by Gantt's accounts of life in Russia. Gantt also led him about Leningrad and introduced him to his Russian friends. Most were guarded about their reminiscences of "Old Russia." Dos Passos was especially interested in talking with those who had been through the Bolshevik revolution, who had witnessed the siege and fall of Petrograd (essentially a European city) and the transfer of the capital to Asiatic Moscow; and with those who had been privy firsthand to the power struggle between the Bolsheviks and Mensheviks, to the inner workings behind Lenin's slogan of "land, bread, and peace," and to the ascendancy of Stalin upon the ouster of Trotsky from the party. In 1928 —shortly before Dos Passos' arrival in the Soviet Union—Stalin had launched the first of his scheduled Five-Year Plans, an economic policy designed to revitalize Soviet economy. In theory the plan seemed workable. It projected a production schedule for both agriculture and industry that would enable the country to overtake both western Europe and the United States in economic growth. In effect, it imposed extraordinary hardship upon peasants and factory workers alike. In their race to produce food and manufactured products for the Soviet state, they were driven almost to starvation themselves. It was one thing to suffer drought and famine through natural phenomena, but quite another to have it imposed upon them by their government.

Dos Passos posed a number of elusive questions in his diary that summer, such as "were the Georgians inveterate small proprietors or was it just the two or three innkeepers" with whom he had carried on "painfully inadequate conversations." He wondered if the waiter with a dirty apron who had just brought him his supper was happier under Communism than he would have been under the Czar. "Was he a better waiter, a better citizen, did he have more opportunity to study languages—he told me he was trying to learn French—to play chess, to make love to his wife, and raise clean healthy bright-eyed children? . . . Was all the poverty and hunger part of the clearing of the ground for magnificent new constructions, or was it the result of old-fashioned ignorant centralized oppression?" While he recognized that "one man's fact is another man's fiction," he resolved to stick to facts as best he could.

Before leaving Leningrad, Dos Passos made plans to meet Gantt in southern Russia in the foothills of the Caucasus Mountains for a two-hundred-mile trek through the wilds of a vast, untraveled land. Meantime, however, there was much that he craved to see in other Soviet republics. He journeyed by train to Moscow, where he tarried only long enough to obtain permission from the Minister of Education to join an expedition of Russians who already were on the trail en route to the remote republic of Daghestan in the southwestern region. To catch up with the group, he journeyed five days by steamer down the Volga in its zigzag course to the Caspian Sea, the most wretched body of water he said he had ever seen. The Caspian—the world's largest inland sea—lies ninety-two feet below sea level. While in Astrakhan, a port on the Volga (about as far from the sea as New Orleans is to the Gulf), Dos Passos fell into conversation with a Polish sailor who had been in England for six months and was happy to find someone with whom he could practice his English. The word he remembered best from his sojourn in an English port was "bloody," which Dos Passos readily picked up to describe his new environment. The two men drank a bottle of vodka together before the Pole traipsed off cursing the "bloody Caspian Sea" with a trail of "bloodies" following him. "Perhaps this very bloody night he would kill himself" after having one more "bloody drink." In his diary later, Dos Passos wrote: "Imagine the fate of a fine new steamship launched in the Caspian. It wasn't a sea, it was a bloody trough full of bloody slime. It smelt like a bloody purgative. It was a bloody prison. The north end was so shallow there was nowhere to dock. What was the use of keeping a ship in good shape if you never went into port? The steamers rotted and rusted and so did their crews. The bloody Caspian was one of nature's mistakes."

By the time Dos Passos reached Baku, a large port on the southeastern end of the sea, he feared that his sensitive olfactory powers had become permanently impaired. The reeking sea rivaled the stench of any water closet he had known. He could hardly wait to board a train for Grozny, three hundred miles to the northwest, where he hoped to catch up with the elusive delegation he had been chasing. Its members had been sent by the Minister of Education to comb the remote regions of southwestern Russia for the selection of new school sites. All were Russians from Moscow except one woman, whom Dos Passos described to Dudley Poore as a "300-pound 6-foot American lady journalist from the great open spaces of Mt. Rainier. God help us." Despite his being the interloper in the tiny band, he resented the position he found himself in as "reluctant squire" to his fellow American, Anna Louise Strong, a radical free-lance journalist:

> On a trip of this kind, the last thing you want is a compatriot. . . . One suspected she was the only child of a welltodo family and had been spoiled rotten as a girl. She wore a welldesigned green traveling suit with a split skirt for riding. She wasn't a very interesting woman but she made up for it by enthusiasm. It was a little like the enthusiasm of certain missionaries I had met in various dismal corners of the world, only in Anna Louise it was directed toward the Communist idea. I couldn't help admire her courage because it proved a fairly tough trip. Poor soul, her efforts to provide herself with a few creature comforts only managed to irritate the rest of us. . . . It never occurred to the Russians to put themselves out for her.

If Dos Passos had been aware that Strong was a close friend of Trotsky and an enthusiastic Bolshevik/Communist in Stalin's camp now, he might have regarded her more highly in terms of what she could convey to him about socialist life behind the scenes in the Soviet Union. She was sending back enlightening and well-regarded vignettes of life in Russia to *The Liberator,* as was Dos Passos, but both apparently remained closemouthed at the time about their observations and journalistic endeavors. He was so put off by her appearance and manner that he could not take her seriously and missed the opportunity of talking with a compatriot about the rationale behind her commitment to Communism.

He felt like Marco Polo as their band pressed more deeply into the wilds of Daghestan, whose centuries of civilization seemed to have fallen away almost overnight. Villages appeared as "cubist constructions set on cliffs above roaring gorges." They met young shepherds and grizzled old men who had never heard of Moscow or America. Although they were warned to look out for bandits who would as soon slit six throats as offer them a skin of wine, they never felt their lives to be endangered no matter whom they encountered or how threatening the terrain. The youngest Russian in their band, Nikolai Semyonovich, nearly lost his horse in quicksand when it slipped its hobble and wandered off as they bathed in an icy mountain lake. By this time it was early September, and already there was snow on the mountains south of them. Most of the time they traveled on shaggy ponies, which they mounted at dawn each day for a look at another "inspection site." One of Dos Passos' problems was the language. While he made daily use of his primer, *Russian Made Easy,* and Strong spoke fluent Russian and readily translated for him when she could, not even the native Russian speakers in their group were successful in communicating with many of the remote tribes of southwestern Russia. Each morning they started out with a fresh interpreter to help with the ever-changing dialects as they pushed deeper and deeper into the Caucasus. By the end of the day, the interpreter himself was as baffled as the outsiders and sought someone else to interpret for him. Dos Passos realized then as never before that it was not so much a question of *learning* a difficult language, but that the *language* itself was difficult.

By the time he said good-bye to the delegation, he was "sorry to leave them," he said later. "They proved excellent traveling companions, energetic and fanatically curious about peoples, languages, architecture, history, everything we ran into." He was especially taken by young Semyonovich, who seemed the student out of every Russian novel he had read. "We had long conversations in bad French and worse German, sprinkled with an occasional Russian or English expression. The poor fellow had done well at the University, attained something equivalent to a Ph.D., but his career was about to be ruined because he had the wrong class origins." Upon Dos Passos' return to Moscow three weeks after he left the group, he learned that Semyonovich had killed himself. Whether his fears were real or imaginary, Dos Passos never learned, but to the young Russian it was only a matter of time before "The Committee" charged with determining the class origins of all students would catch him. He had told Dos Passos that when it happened, he was sure it would be "the end."

Dos Passos left the group in Tiflis, then traveled by bus back into the Caucasus to join Horsley Gantt at Vladikavkaz, where they set out on foot on a more arduous journey than either had envisioned. They climbed glaciers, ascended high, snow-covered passes, traversed great rivers spanned by ancient, swinging bridges, and trudged through deep, hot valleys. For a time they were accompanied by George and Seraphima Kiryaov, a brother/sister pair who were friends of Gantt. Seraphima, eighteen, had typed for Gantt and was enamored of the handsome, lean American, with whom she felt privileged to associate in any capacity. She and her brother lost heart in the expedition, however, their second day on the trail when they learned that Gantt and Dos Passos did not intend to use pack pony or cart to carry supplies for their trek. At the first opportunity, Seraphima and her brother located a driver with a crude cart who agreed to transport the young couple and all of their knapsacks and bedrolls and meet Dos Passos and Gantt at a rendezvous point somewhere up the steep ascent ahead. By the time they met up, however, the Russians had devoured the cache of pastries and chocolates reserved for the difficult last leg of their expedition. From Kazbek, a remote town in the Georgian Soviet Socialist Republic, they planned to hike to Zaramag, then push on to Tiflis, still farther south.

Seraphima and her brother jounced along in the pony cart for several days in the company of "an Albanian bandit who claimed he knew the way to Zaramag," and the two Americans brought up the rear. Finally their guide admitted to being lost and turned off in another direction to proceed alone, and the Russian couple decided to backtrack to a highway to flag down a bus headed for Tiflis. By this time, Gantt was hiking in his bare feet, having decided after two days on the trail that his shoes did not fit properly. Dos Passos was amazed when he learned that Gantt returned home with no bruises from the ordeal.

Other than hunger and a little weight loss, neither suffered appreciably from their journey. It was the hospitality of the people that especially struck Dos Passos, who discovered that a poor peasant would readily give his last egg or water down his own tea in order that his visitor's might be more strongly brewed. Almost everyone responded kindly to them, although no one they encountered spoke English. Many took Gantt for a Russian, but the dialects defied his fluency with the cultured language of Leningrad or Moscow. Dos Passos was touched by a peasant woman's apology for offering them no hot water for tea. She explained that she could afford a fire only once a day. It had to be lit only at nightfall for the workers who came in from the fields. She would be happy for them to wait in her rude hut until that hour, she offered.

In addition to meeting the people encountered along the way, Dos Passos was grateful for the opportunity to travel with Gantt for two weeks because of the conversations the trip afforded. Years later when called upon to give testimony regarding Gantt's loyalty to the United States in connection with security proceedings involving his employment by the Soviet government (Pavlov's experiments were subsidized by the state), Dos Passos vigorously defended his friend:

> Soon after I met Dr. Gantt we took a walking trip together. Our conversations gave me every opportunity to learn his attitude toward Soviet Communism. His attitude at that time was very much more critical than mine. Dr. Gantt's attitude, a rather common one among scientists, was that political theories and political movements were out of his field; but he viewed the Soviet life around him highly objectively and appraised it with a robust common sense. . . . This critical attitude had been sharpened by daily experience with the passionate hostility which his teacher Pavlov felt towards the Soviet government. Efforts have been made since by Soviet propagandists to make it appear that Pavlov was a supporter of their system, but as letters of his still extant can prove, he was very much opposed to it. . . . Though he was not allowed to move his laboratory out of Russia, his work was subsidized by the government and he was allowed to say and write things which from anyone else would have meant prison or death. Of course Pavlov's statements were not allowed to go further than the walls of his laboratory.

Gantt conveyed to Dos Passos during their trek through the Caucasus Mountains much of Pavlov's private feelings as well as his own. At the time, Gantt was completing a book-length manuscript on the effects of war, famine, revolution, and national influence on the incidence of disease in the Soviet Union, to be published by the British Medical Association Press as *A Medical Review of Soviet Russia,* and his findings began appearing as a series of articles in the *British Medical Journal.* One of the motives of his overland journey now was to gather new data for a medical discipline he was pioneering, known later as geomedicine. The health of the Russian people in general and their economic condition had improved since Gantt's arrival in 1922, but life was by no means easy even in the cities. Food was scarce, sometimes nonexistent, and Gantt himself had gone without food for several days at a time. There was no heat in the poorly insulated buildings, even for Pavlov and his assistants in the laboratory, Gantt told Dos Passos. They worked in overcoats and wrapped their throats with scarves throughout the long, gray winters. As a result of such deprivation and bitter cold, he had contracted pneumonia and tuberculosis. Convinced that he would have to find a cure of his own, he turned to vigorous outdoor exercise. Even in subzero weather Gantt walked an hour and a half each day. After months of such a regimen, he worked himself back to rigorous health. His hiking bare-footed was nothing new, he said.

Whereas Gantt allowed himself to be drawn into private discussions on the pros and cons of Marxism—conclusions he had drawn from firsthand observations during his lengthy stay in Russia—he preferred to engage Dos Passos in such topics as free will versus determinism. Gantt took the pragmatic approach, which by its very nature required a belief in free will, he insisted. Dos Passos tended to embrace determinism at this stage in his life, but maintained that such thinking did not rule out free will for the individual. In Leningrad before they separated, and during their rugged travel together over unmarked cross-country trails, they debated a number of philosophical subjects, but Gantt had little heart for politics, neither American nor Russian. He was in medical school during the war and managed to avoid both the draft and any kind of volunteer service. Totally absorbed in scientific phenomena and the ways in which physiology could be applied to the study of physical events, he had not even bothered to register to vote. Although Dos Passos admired his single-minded devotion to his work, he knew that he could never view his sociological surroundings with such detachment.

In the gay-spirited Georgian town of Kutais, Dos Passos and Gantt had a final evening together in the comfort of the Hotel de France, marred only by a reeking toilet near their room. Gantt left the next morning for Bantum—on the Black Sea—and after a second day in Kutais, Dos Passos headed for the port city of Baku on the Caspian to catch a train to Moscow. Traveling by train in Russia was unlike any other travel he had experienced. The cars were larger than generally found in western Europe or America. There were upright seats and three tiers of bunks. Men, women, and children sprawled over every surface, their baskets and sacks bulging with babies, fruits, potatoes, potted plants, and sundry cartons of clothes and other possessions that spilled out from time to time. Dos Passos observed that train travelers in Russia seemed to eat continually from the parcels they had brought with them. Also, each time the train stopped they leaped off to haggle for more food from the local vendors. He wrote Dudley Poore that seeing Russia by train was a wild adventure in itself. "Everybody talks about everything under the sun, and I endeavor frantically to understand what people are saying. The Russian language is no joke. Under the strain of trying to learn it I've forced all the Spanish and most everything else out of my head and have managed to learn enough to make myself almost completely misunderstood wherever I go."

More important to Dos Passos than wrestling with the language was trying to collect his own thoughts. For almost three months he had traversed the wilds of southwestern

Russia by foot or pack pony, and no one had asked to see his papers. He had traveled freely and no one had threatened him or made him feel unwelcome. The generosity of the people continued to amaze him. Regardless of how little they had, they shared it, whether it was a tent or crude hut, a goatskin to wrap up in, a freshly killed lamb, or a tough, rank-smelling haunch of mutton and a taste of goat's cheese. They may never have heard of collectivization and the division of food and property in the name of Communist brotherhood or the greeting "comrade" with its implied ideology, but they shared their wealth—whatever it was—without hesitation. Dos Passos wrote Cummings from the wilds that the people were "so hospitable here and so nice that it's heartbreaking."

He and Gantt had talked at length about the fence he had been straddling and his compulsion to do something about it. "How can I stand for something if I don't put my full weight to it?" he asked Gantt, who suggested he try a more moderate approach and not be so obsessive in his commitments. "Whether I am for something or against it, I must do the same thing," he replied. The problem lay in his making the proper or right choice. His trouble in Russia was trying to decide whether he was for or against the Soviet Communist system, and even more important, what his own destiny was in relationship to it. From July through September he had traveled the valleys, steppes, and mountainous regions of untamed Russia and felt that he had slipped back in time to what seemed the eleventh century in a land as remote as a crater on the moon, yet he was no closer to a decision than he had been when he stepped off the train in Leningrad upon his arrival in the country.

Although he was convinced that the heart of a nation lay in its people, he hoped that the answer to his personal dilemma awaited him in Moscow. By the time he reached the Soviet capital, it was early October and the weather was already yielding to snow. Had it not been for the generosity of several robust explorers from the American Museum of Modern History en route home from a tiger-hunting expedition on the frozen flatlands of northern Siberia, he would not have been the happy wearer of their gift of some "magnificent fleece-lined underwear."

The Russian intelligentsia welcomed Dos Passos to Moscow. They saw him as the American Gorki, the most potentially influential revolutionary writer of the West, and were eager for him to commit his pen to Communist doctrine. He had not accepted their invitation to the tenth-anniversary celebration of the overthrow of the Czar the previous year because of his involvement with the New Playwrights Theatre, nor did he have money at the time to finance such a trip. Contrary to what the intelligentsia may have surmised, Dos Passos was not in the vanguard of his radical countrymen who had made the trek in recent years. A list of his fellow writers preceding him to the Russian capital since the Bolshevik revolution read like the mastheads and editorial boards of the leading leftist literature: Floyd Dell, Max Eastman, Joseph Freeman, Michael Gold, Lincoln Steffens, Mary Heaton Vorse, Robert Minor, Ruth Stout, Albert Rhys Williams, Claude McKay, V. F. Calverton, Scott Nearing, Theodore Dreiser, John Reed, Eugene Lyons, Anna Louise Strong, Walter Duranty—the cataloguing could go on and on. Even Sinclair Lewis and Dorothy Thompson visited Moscow before Dos Passos did. Some had gone at the invitation of the Russian government to testify to the outside world the improved economic conditions brought on by sweeping reforms since the Kronstadt revolt. By the time Dos Passos arrived, a small American colony of writers and newspapermen had rooted itself in Moscow. It centered around Walter Duranty, a New York *Times* reporter who made his apartment available to every visiting journalist. Eugene Lyons was in Moscow for six years as a United Press correspondent and writer for the Soviet news agency, Tass. Anna Louise Strong was well accepted in Moscow. She knew Trotsky and hoped he would approve of her writing his biography, an approval he gave, instead, to Max Eastman. In 1930 she began editing the first English-language newspaper in Moscow.

Dos Passos was more interested in Russians connected with the theater than with any of his journalistic countrymen, though he did see several, such as Duranty and Strong, from time to time. He especially liked talking with movie directors, whom he thought were the most interesting and lively people he had met in the city. "Eisenstein says that Meyerhold has ruined the theatre by carrying each of his productions so far in a logical direction that it is impossible to go further out," he wrote Cummings. Eisenstein was an "extremely genteel and very interesting bird," he observed. It was Eisenstein who urged him to watch Kabuki theater, which was making its first appearance in Moscow. They discussed the importance of montage. Dos Passos told him he was using it more and more in his own writing, and Eisenstein confided that he had learned much from "that old scoundrel of a capitalist, D. W. Griffith, and his *Birth of a Nation.*" Dos Passos allowed that he had, too. He also met V. I. Pudovkin, who shared Eisenstein's prestige as an avant-garde motion picture director. Pudovkin, too, was enthusiastic about the Japanese Kabuki troupe whose two-week run in Moscow provided one of the most exciting entertainments the Russian people had ever seen. "Every Russian I met seemed to have spent weeks reading up on the Japanese theatre," Dos Passos wrote upon his return home. "The shows were besieged. People invented dangerous strategems to get themselves seats. . . . They noted every move of the actors, greedily sopped up every note of the music, every stylized gesture of the dancing. The way the revolving stage was used appealed to them particularly. By the time the Kabuki players left they had drunk style to the dregs."

It seemed to Dos Passos that the enthusiasm of an average citizen of Moscow for good entertainment and well-executed artistic presentations exceeded the response of habitués of the art, music, and theater world he had encountered elsewhere. Such was the case whether viewed in the paintings of Chagall, Pimenov, or Kandinsky; in an exhibition of French impressionism that had just opened that fall in a Moscow museum; in a Moscow theater in which a Russian company was presenting O'Neill's *Desire Under the Elms;* or in the electrifying performance of the Moscow Symphony. Again and again he compared and contrasted the theaters of Moscow and New York, and each time his own theater came off a poor second. He went to the theater almost every evening and took careful notes. When he returned home he rendered his impressions in an article for *The New Republic* entitled "The New Theater in Russia." He said that most American critics who attended Russian theater were frightened because they feared they would be "caught and chopped up into mincemeat by the Gaypayoo." Also, theater habits were different in Moscow: "The show begins just about when the critic would ordinarily be eating dinner; if he didn't eat, he's hungry and if he did, it was probably in a hurry and he's getting a touch of indigestion. None of the audience is much dressed up. He is probably distracted by the raw, crude look of the building or wonders how often these dirty Russians bathe." He probably worries, too, for fear that he is hearing Communist propaganda and will be converted without realizing it. He cannot follow the translator's English and most likely has no knowledge of Russian. "The play begins without much formality; . . . bright nervous spotlights point out the action dogmatically. . . . The play lasts a long time, the intermissions are too long, the seats are hard." When the critic returns tired and yawning to his hotel, he is "afraid he may have picked up lice and writes to the folks at home that the Russian theater is much over-rated and that it's all Bolshevik propaganda anyway." By contrast, New Yorkers want "ritzy art," Dos Passos continued. "The stage in America as a purely business proposition tends to become a mere subsidiary of Hollywood. Any theater that's to continue alive has got to appeal to other than money motives and to other feelings than the dominant dollar religion." It would take more than a couple of Meyerholds and Vakhtangovs to counteract the decadent state of American theater, he insisted. Russian theater succeeded, too, because it had a permanent tradition behind it and a corporate existence. "Individual directors and policies come and go, the staff of actors changes a little from year to year, as does the repertory of plays, but the institution is an organism with a memory." Acting and directing are considered reputable professions requiring long conventional training. "Another thing that insures the vitality of the Russian theater," he continued, was the opportunity for experimentation afforded by subsidiary studios. "These studios are the germs of new theaters and at the same time the try-out grounds for new methods and ideas. It costs so little to run them that they are not dependent on the public, and there are so many of them that every conceivable line of ideas has a chance to get practical application."

Dos Passos' words were written against the backdrop of his own painful experience in fighting for the survival of the New Playwrights Theatre. He hoped to get home in time to help with the production of Upton Sinclair's *Singing Jailbirds,* then to mount his own play, *Airways, Inc.,* which he intended to direct and for which he had already designed the sets. He realized now as never before, however, that until the American theater could divorce itself from the box office and concentrate on art and theme—as did the Russians—there was little cause for hope. After the production of his own "little opus," he intended to bow out from any involvement with the American theater other than what he might do with his pen or typewriter.

Dos Passos marveled at the number of Russian theaters that had sprung up almost everywhere. There were "factory" theaters, an "army" theater, a "sanitary propaganda" theater, a theater to "re-educate prostitutes," a theater "of the revolution," small art theaters, opera theaters, studio and experimental theaters sponsored by "parent" theaters —in short, there was a theater for any organization or group who wanted to get together for a common purpose to act and to share their performances with appreciative viewers. Many were sponsored by the Central Trade Union Councils; all were subsidized in some manner, and not necessarily by the Soviet government itself—as had been the case under the Czar.

The more exposure Dos Passos had to Russian theater, the less secure he felt in his ability to make judgments about Soviet life in arenas in which he was merely an observer. As he put it:

If you are an engineer or a mechanic or a schoolteacher you can do something, but if you're a writer you're merely in the unenviable position of standing round and watching other people do the work. . . . That's why the best thing to do if you're in Moscow is to go to the theatre. Here's as much as you can digest at a sitting put into digestible form. Not knowing the language is hardly a barrier at all. You can look at the stage all the better for not following all the lines. You can look at the audience. You are part of the audience. . . . In Moscow people go to the theatre to feel part of the victorious march through history of the world proletariat.

For two and a half months—until early December 1928—Dos Passos crisscrossed Moscow and its suburbs many dozens of times talking with writers, actors, directors, Kremlin bureaucrats and party leaders, medicos, peasants, shopkeepers, soldiers, and factory workers. He visited theaters of every description by day and saw their productions at night. He inspected hospital operating rooms, production lines in factories, classrooms of children of all ages, playgrounds, sports arenas, newspaper offices, assembly halls—the questions and answers resounding in his ears until set aside by sleep.

Despite his difficulty with the language, Dos Passos was struck repeatedly by the Russian mind. Hundreds of educated members of the old governing classes had died during the Bolshevik upheaval, but their surviving countrymen "still comprised one of the world's major reservoirs of brains," he said. Moreover, contrary to the propaganda he had been fed regarding the terror-ridden faces of the Russian people, he found that the people appeared to be free of tensions, their faces smiling, contented. Most of the men and women he talked with in Moscow were optimistic that their lot was improving, and that the die had been cast for the betterment of all who would avail themselves of Communist brotherhood and social revolution. The Cheka—the terrorist organization of Bolsheviks established after the revolution of 1917—had long since ceased to exist, he reported, though it had been succeeded by a less feared secret police, the G.P.U. During his stay in Moscow he was the houseguest of a ranking official of the G.P.U. He said that Valia Gerasimova and her husband, Aleksandr Fadeev, a writer and enthusiastic Party Member, introduced him to many of their friends who were willing to talk about a variety of topics without apparent fear of having what was discussed reported. Both Gerasimova and Fadeev were staunch Stalinists, and Fadeev was the ranking proponent of Stalinism in Russia's literary world. Some forty years later when Dos Passos was writing his memoirs of the period, he consulted his notes for evidence of Russian terror he might have observed but had forgotten about, yet could find none. He said it was rare that he fastened his eye upon a grim countenance, let alone a terror-stricken one. The only thing he could remember involving terror was an evening spent with a Russian woman and her English husband, who had come to Russia to work for Communism, but now was "desperate to get out." He knew his wife would never be allowed to leave because she had "the wrong class origins." There was "no cruelty like Russian cruelty, not even Chinese," the Englishman told him. Dos Passos said he tried to argue with the man, to point out that the old terror was fading. "I told him about how freely I'd been able to travel, how easily people talked. My theory then was that the Russian revolution was entering a liberal phase."

In early December Dos Passos decided that he must no longer put off his return to the United States. He was ambivalent regarding what he had seen and heard. He would like to have sorted out his facts and impressions, but was much too close to them, he realized. Moreover, Lawson had written that his own play, *Airways, Inc.,* was already in rehearsal, and he wanted to get back to the New Playwrights Theatre to see if anything he had learned might be applicable in his own country's mode of theater, regardless of its inherent limitations. The night was cold and murky when he closed his "hippo" bag and headed for the train station. He was escorted to the depot by a theater director and her company of actors, youths who worked in factories and acted at night. He had seen them rehearsing a play for the Sanitary Propaganda Theatre, a play about cleaning one's teeth and avoiding syphilis, a play about "the world that will stand up so bright and shining when the dark murky scaffolding of today's struggle is torn away."

"They want to say goodbye," the theater director told him as he shook their hard "untrembly hands." There was something else they wanted, too, she said. "They like you very much, but they want to ask you one question. They want you to show your face. They want to know where you stand politically. Are you with us?"

Dos Passos felt his head constrict and throb. There had been too many questions of late, "too many hands shaken, too many foreign languages badly understood." He felt the eyes of his young entourage fasten hard upon him. He took another drag from his cigarette, pushed his hat back, and rocked forward slightly on the balls of his feet. His words were barely audible above the hissing of the steam engine and clanging noises as the train bucked and snorted beside the platform. "Oh . . . Oh . . . But let me see. . . . Maybe I can explain," he stammered. "But in so short a time . . . Oh, there's not time now even to begin." Already the train was moving as he ran for the steps and pulled himself aboard. Leaning out, he smiled at the group wryly and threw a wave in their direction as the gray mist swallowed them up.

He was pressed again for answers in a letter from his Soviet host, Valia Gerasimova, soon after his return home. She wrote him that he seemed "not quite real. . . . Your staying with us reminded me a little of a chapter from a sentimental novel. . . . What man are you, and what were you thinking? Your being 'tongueless' made it so difficult to understand you." Gerasimova was not referring so much to his lack of expertise in speaking Russian as to his unwillingness to be cornered. The tone of the letter was affectionate. She was obviously fond of Dos Passos. But he probably winced when she told him quite offhandedly that he was "very simple" and addressed him as "my good child Dos."

The question "Are you with us?" came back repeatedly to haunt Dos Passos. In dealing with his exodus from Moscow for his memoirs, he raised it once more: "How could I answer that question? I liked and admired the Russian people. I had enjoyed their enormous and varied country, but when next morning I crossed the Polish border— Poland was not Communist then—it was like being let out of jail." If such was his feeling, however, there was no evidence of it at the time. To the contrary, if one is to take at face value his comment to Hemingway in a letter of December 4 from Warsaw, where he detrained and spent the night. "Jesus, all you have to do to realize how swell things are in Russia is to take a look at Warsaw—the differences in people's faces, the way they walk talk eat cross the street. Warsaw's a horrible dump anyway." His only complaint to Hemingway regarding the Soviet Union was that foreign writers could "get jack out of the publisher," but could not "take it out of the country and had to drink it up in vodka and salt herring." He also acknowledged that during his two months in Moscow he had seen the sun for only a day and a half. "No wonder they all want to go to America," he observed. "There may be something in all this talk about God's country after all."

Perhaps nowhere else was Dos Passos' tendency to oversimplify more apparent than in his letters to Hemingway. As for himself, he was on his way home to take his "annual beating" in the American theater, he said. Hemingway replied that it was only a matter of time before the endeavor would have him on his *ass*. Why not lick his wounds in Key West, he ventured. The snipe hunting was especially good just then: "Shot twelve yesterday, twenty the day before yesterday and fifteen two days before that." Then, as though an afterthought, he added: "My old man shot himself on the other hand (not in the other hand—in the head), as you may have read in the paper." His offhanded report of his father's suicide reminded him in turn of something else: his "bloody book"—*A Farewell to Arms*—was finished at last and being typed.

Dos Passos saw in the New Year in New York. Key West and a reunion with Hemingway and his cronies would have to wait, he wrote him. There were a number of loose ends to tie up in the city, but he intended to head South as soon as he could.

16

The Demise of a Theatre and a New Life, 1929

It was not for me. I'd always been a morning worker and everything in the theater happens after midnight.

Dos Passos
The Best Times

When Dos Passos returned home from Moscow bursting with new ideas from his observations of theater in Russia, he found his own New Playwrights Theatre already undergoing a major overhaul. Em Jo Basshe had declared himself executive director and was making radical changes in policy in an effort to rescue the New Playwrights from the problems that had besieged it previously. A thorough housecleaning was in order, he declared: new blood, new actors, new technical directors, new management. No longer would a play run five weeks, then bow to the next one on the schedule—with four plays running each season—in the manner previously attempted. This time they would work on one until it was as nearly perfect as possible, then run it as long as they could meet expenses and pay their people decent salaries. The playwright/directors would henceforth serve only as advisors, Basshe demanded.

On December 28, 1928, Jack Lawson apprised Dos Passos of the situation, which was secondhand, since he had abandoned New York for Hollywood and was now a scriptwriter for movie mogul Samuel Goldwyn. Lawson had written Francis Faragoh a few days before Dos Passos' homecoming expressing both interest and alarm about the "N. P. Toodle in general and Airways, Inc., in particular":

It appears that Em Jo, Inc. is acting like a combination of an efficient executive and a person in the last stages of dementia praecox—or maybe those are the same things anyway! I'm amazed at what he has done, but I feel a little bit like a person going over Niagra Falls in a barrel as to what he will do next. Please give me your impressions and opinions. Personally,

> I'm inclined to think the only immediate important problem is to make a fine production of
> Airways, Inc., and after that, if Jo feels so strongly about it he should be handed the theatre on
> an enormous silver platter and call it a day.

The original board of directors was still intact on paper, yet Faragoh, too, was Hollywood-bound before the play opened, and Mike Gold had withdrawn to his old neighborhood on the East Side to work on his autobiographical novel, *Jews Without Money*. Dos Passos intended to follow suit with his own novel, *The 42nd Parallel*, to which he had devoted himself far too sporadically while in the Soviet Union, he admitted. Working with Basshe had never been easy, but Dos Passos might only have bristled at what he saw as Basshe's high-handedness had it not been for his firing of Edward Massey, who had directed both productions of "The Moon Is a Gong" and was now directing *Airways, Inc.* As Dos Passos saw it, Massey should have had *carte blanche,* and he was infuriated by Basshe's seemingly irrational act. "Don't ever write any plays," he groused to Robert Hillyer. "Believe me there's nuttin in it, kid—except worry and the loss of hair and hours and wishes causing dyspepsia after midnight." He had learned to cope with the critics by turning his back, although he defended others whom he felt had been misjudged (such as Lawson when his *Processional* had been drubbed). The machinations behind stage were more of a problem to Dos Passos. He liked designing, constructing, and painting sets, but very little of the business of play making was compatible with his habits or desires. To have written the play and designed its set and playbill was one thing, yet as chief constructionist he could not even get started in his work until after everyone else had gone home. Being a "morning person" was incompatible with most of the life of the theater in which he was engaged.

Airways, Inc. opened February 20, 1929, at the Grove Street Theater, where it struggled to survive its impoverished budget and thrashings by the critics. Brooks Atkinson had already panned most of the earlier productions of the New Playwrights. "As the only radical dramatic organization in town, they have full access to immediate and sensational themes, raw humanity, mass emotion, social idealism," but they had botched it again, he said. Their efforts had produced "sophomoric writing, flatulent thinking and noisy boredom." Similarly, he found *Airways, Inc.* a "noisy, incoherent, undisciplined play . . . burdened by murky poetry and symbolism." There were moments of interest but the play needed radical surgery. It was "not without its rewards for those who have any interest whatsoever in the pranks that the New Playwrights are usually up to," conceded Atkinson. "As it spatters across its Greenwich Village stage, *Airways, Inc.,* seems of more consequence for various individual scenes than for its achievements as an entity, as a well-rounded play. . . . The production is what such a play usually demands and gets from the employment of the suspended action of Mr. O'Neill's 'Interludism'—in this case to portray simultaneous happenings rather than to express the thoughts of characters—to the use of expressionism, constructivism and other such anti-box-set devices."

Richard Watts, Jr., reviewing for the *Herald Tribune,* judged the play "uneven, garrulous, uncoordinated and badly edited . . . a half-arresting, half-irritating work that was more moving in its intent than in its achievements." St. John Ervine told his *World* readers that Dos Passos' play had too many echoes of Elmer Rice and the "later O'Neill" —all badly done. The *Daily Worker,* itself the recipient of three benefit performances immediately after opening night, praised *Airways, Inc.,* yet regretted that its impact was weakened by too many themes. "It is hardly revolutionary," lamented A. B. Magil in the *Daily Worker,* but commended Dos Passos for having veered sharply to the left in recent years and for now being "close to Communism." Most critics attacked the play for its lack of unity, the failure of its two narratives to converge successfully, and for having as many themes "as flies in a sugar bowl," as Mike Gold described it. To Gold, *Airways, Inc.* was Dos Passos' most important work. Stephen Rathbun told readers of the New York *Sun* that it was the best play he had seen of the dramas "sponsored by this group of radicals." Edmund Wilson agreed. In an essay for *The New Republic* after the play's demise—it ran only four weeks—Wilson called *Airways, Inc.* "a remarkable play, perhaps the best that the New Playwrights have done," but thought Dos Passos "less expert as a dramatist than as a novelist." He was "more intelligent and a better artist than his associates and was able to enter into more points of view," said Wilson. Yet he faulted Dos Passos for his bias regarding capitalism because it extended "not merely to all its official representatives, but even to all those human beings whose only fault is to have been born where it prevails and to have been so lacking in perspicacity and zeal as not to have allied themselves with its opponents." Surely the life of middle-class America is not so bad as Dos Passos paints it, he chided.

Had the playwright not played the capitalist as well and put some eight hundred dollars of his own money into the production to keep it running, it would have folded after the second week. Even before it closed, he mailed a formal letter of resignation to each member of the board of directors. He believed it only a matter of time before the theater itself closed. "Perhaps it's worthwhile to sketch out my reasons," he offered. "The men who made it up have not been sure of their aims or honest about them. Half the time we have been trying to found an institution and the rest of the time trying to put over ourselves or each other, and occasionally trying to knife each other in the back." It seemed to Dos Passos that if anyone wanted "to put over new, unpopular, radical, revolutionary, or even 'good plays' in America," such plays were feasible only if presented in a theater with a repertory system. "Such a theater can be founded only when the people who try to finally realize that cooperation is not an empty phrase, but a sane and businesslike method of attaining a certain fifty percent of common aims." In reply, Lawson insisted that only Basshe and Gold had been "guilty of any lack of cooperation." He said that he doubted if the "revolutionary theatre will ever be a reality except as a one-man job, or a lot of separate one-man jobs." Lawson was upset, too, when he learned that Dos Passos had invested his own money to keep *Airways, Inc.* running and tucked a three-hundred-dollar check into the letter. He thought each director should share equally in the costs, since the show had played to empty seats much of the time. *"Airways, Inc.,* is a decidedly worthwhile play, but don't expect your taxi to find the Grove Street Theater," warned the reviewer in the *Sun,* who added that it could be discovered if one would drive a block below Christopher Street on Seventh Avenue and "look westward." The show had been closed a month when the New York *Times* reported that Basshe had resigned because of lack of support. He had neither the fortitude nor the funds to carry the endeavor on alone, said Basshe. Otto Kahn was unwilling to invest further in the project.

Once the dust had settled, Dos Passos ventured a backward glance at the New Playwrights Theatre and framed its failure neatly within the context of its accomplishments. There was no reason for the playwright/directors or anyone else associated with the theater to be ashamed of their work or to feel they had wasted their time, he insisted, then outlined the strengths and values of each play. He described his own production as "very successful: the best acting we ever had. . . . The audience accepted the elimination of the proscenium arch and curtain without batting an eyelash." The theater failed ultimately, he concluded, because the playwrights were "too preoccupied with their own works to make good producers, and because the problems involved were not seen clearly enough in the beginning." There had been too many theories, both political and artistic, and their personalities had been far too disparate for any sustained unity of effort. Still another explanation was offered by Edmund Wilson in a letter to John Peale Bishop: "Dos has broken with the social-revolutionary New Playwrights group, which I think is an excellent thing; they apparently kept trying to high-hat him by giving him to understand that Airways, Inc., was insufficiently social-revolutionary, while he on his part had certainly made a supreme effort to be as social-revolutionary as possible."

One thing certain in Dos Passos' mind, regardless of what others thought, was that he needed to repair to a remote haven. Lawson urged him to come to Hollywood and join the "M.G.M. circus"; however, Dos Passos had no intention of becoming embroiled in an organization again. He did not want to take a participant role in anything that could be handled more advantageously with his pen alone. The question he had been asked at the train station in Moscow as he prepared to leave Russia—"Are you with us?"—resounded again and again, no matter what the issue was. He knew already that he was aligned with the minority and always would be. If he was going to continue as the social revolutionary, he had to be one on his own terms. Although he lent his name and gave his pen to a number of different causes, there was never a time that he did not reckon himself an independent radical.

It was not Lawson's invitation to Hollywood, but Hemingway's to Key West that Dos Passos acted upon after submitting his resignation from the New Playwrights Theatre. "For God's sake come down," Hemingway had urged. Great schools of tarpon were running, and Hemingway had counted some one hundred in a single night. He had no money to offer, he ventured, but there was "lots of liquor off a wrecked booze boat" to share. Waldo Peirce was coming with "some jack" because his mother had just died. "My old man shot himself but it was no help financially," added Hemingway. As usual when he was happy with a turn of events concerning himself personally, he wanted others to participate in his good fortune. So long as he was catching fish and recognized as "top dog," there was nothing irascible about him. He was pleased with himself now because Max Perkins had come down in person to collect his *A Farewell to Arms* manuscript and stayed on for an eight-day fishing marathon. Perkins was enthusiastic over the manuscript —except for the profanities—and when he returned to New York reported a sixteen-thousand-dollar sale to Scribner's for magazine serialization. "The dirty words" would have to go, however, Perkins insisted.

Dos Passos arrived in mid-March 1929 to join the group already on the scene. Perkins referred to the loose fraternity of friends who gathered around Hemingway in Key West as "the Mob." Waldo Peirce and Henry Strater were there to take advantage of the incredibly clear skies, vivid colors, and lush, tropical landscape and were painting brilliant canvases. Strater also painted a portrait of Hemingway, and Peirce painted Bumby on the lap of his black nanny, Olive. Among the paintings Peirce gave away to his fishing buddies that spring were a portrait of Pauline Hemingway (holding a cigarette), a still life of a platter of dead birds, the Bumby/Olive painting, and a self-portrait. Dos Passos, too, sketched and painted in Key West, it being his habit to tuck in brushes, watercolors, and sketch pads wherever he went, but he considered himself a novice beside Peirce and Strater. He was not an avid fisherman either. Instead, he preferred to sit back and observe the hubbub around him. Each afternoon and often late into the night the men fished. It was Hemingway's habit to meet the steamer from Havana or ferryboat from Boca Chica as each crony arrived, quickly deposit his paraphernalia at the Overseas Hotel, then rush him back to sea for a fishing expedition with whoever was at hand. Usually they went out with Bra Saunders, a professional guide, or Charles Thompson, a local business-man who was never too busy running his cigar-box factory, fish house, ship's chandlery, hardware store, icehouse, or tackle shop to be prevailed upon to take Hemingway's mob trolling for tarpon.

Hemingway's sister, Madelaine, better known as "Sunny," had been in Key West since November, having come down to type his *A Farewell to Arms* manuscript and assist Pauline with baby Patrick. Hemingway had hoped that his sister would take a special interest in Dos Passos. "When he invited Dos Passos down, he built him up to me at every opportunity," recalled Madelaine. "I began to look forward to Dos's arrival and had a fine mental picture of him. But when he arrived, I was shocked to see a bald man with nervous, jumpy movements. Ernie had neglected to give me a physical picture of his friend, who was nine years older than I. Of course, I didn't play up to Dos, and Ernie was put out by my lack of interest and apparent rudeness."

If Dos Passos noticed, he did not complain. He was more interested in Pauline's houseguest from Provincetown, Katy Smith, whom he had met a year earlier during his last trip to Key West. Although he had been attracted to Katy then—and remembered especially her large, yellow "cat eyes"—there was no correspondence between them except for her casual jotting on a postcard just before he left for Russia. This time, feelings that had lain quite dormant since his broken engagement to Crystal Ross stirred. He was envious, also, of the ebullient rapport between Katy and Peirce, who had seen each other several times in Provincetown over the years. Peirce was a likable Bohemian sort. Tall, barrel-chested, he had played football at Harvard and was known for his prodigious strength and adventuresome spirit. Whether he had actually wrestled a huge tarpon ashore Dos Passos never knew, but a number of legendary feats surrounded Peirce, who looked like a young Triton—or Poseidon himself—as water streamed from the ringlets of his bushy head and beard when he hauled himself aboard Thompson's boat after cavorting in the deep.

Dos Passos saw no way to compete with Peirce when it came to machismo, but in Key West he affected a blustering stance in an effort to meld with Hemingway's band of toughies. He smoked, drank heavily on occasion, swore (his "gee whizzes" gave way to more salty expletives when in Hemingway's company), philosophized, and socialized in as manly a fashion as the others. Yet his appearance—the thick-lensed glasses (which he usually removed for a picture), his tendency to peer and squint, his receding hairline, which met the bald spot spreading forward from the crown, and his shy, stammering manner and impediment in pronouncing r's and v's—all seemed to belie Dos Passos' he-man posture in the presence of Hemingway, Peirce, and Strater.

Alone with Katy, Dos Passos was more himself. She enjoyed the revelry of the pack, but both sought each other's company and preferred being off by themselves to poke around the town, swim, picnic, or simply to sit on the porch of the old white-frame house on South Street and engage in quiet conversation while waiting for the others to return from the sea. Though no great beauty, Katy drew people easily, her charm never something "turned on" for a suitor. She would not have known how to be coquettish or seductive, but her eyes provoked a stir from all upon whose glance they fell. She appeared shy, but her spontaneous warmth never kept a stranger at bay if she wanted to develop the acquaintance. Katy habitually gave each new friend a unique nickname that even the most straitlaced recipient found amusing. She did not forget the "Monsieur Muttonfish" she had assigned Dos Passos when they first met, but shortened it now to "M. Fish."

Dos Passos wrote Edmund Wilson from Key West that spring of his "somewhat shattering" experience with the New Playwrights Theatre and that he was repairing himself by swimming, fishing, feasting on wild heron and turtle steak, and swilling Spanish wine and Cuban rum. All had done wonders for the inner man, he confided. There was no mention of his recuperation being helped along by the companionship of a woman. Yet before he and Katy separated in late April after almost a month together, they had apparently become more than casual in their affection for each other and agreed to meet in Provincetown in June.

Upon leaving Key West, Dos Passos accepted an invitation to stay in an old Penn-sylvania Dutch farmhouse in Erwinna (Bucks County), Pennsylvania, as the guest of Josephine Herbst and John Herrmann. He wanted to hole up somewhere besides New York City or the Village to try to finish his novel before taking a holiday on the Cape with Katy. As he explained later in an interview for *Writers at Work: The Paris Review Interviews,* he had had in mind from the beginning the characters and whole sweep of historical events and plotting that eventually became the *U.S.A.* trilogy: "It started to be one book, but then there was so much that I wanted to get in that it got to be three books very soon. . . . I started *42nd Parallel* with the idea of publishing a series of reportages of the times . . . in which characters appeared and reappeared. . . . It's hard to say how I came to add the portraits. I was trying different facets of my subject and trying to get something a little more accurate than fiction, at the same time to work these pieces into the fictional picture."

From Erwinna, Dos Passos was summoned to New York for the wedding of Cum-mings to Anne Barton on May 1, 1929. Most of Cummings' friends saw Anne as a party girl, a beautiful flapper who had worked for a time as an artist's model, married at seventeen, and was now an affluent divorcée at twenty-nine. Cummings had been morose since his divorce from Elaine Orr Thayer in 1924, and he hoped that marriage to Anne would be therapeutic. The early morning ceremony in All Souls Church at Fourth Avenue and Twentieth Street was followed by a wedding breakfast at the Hotel Brevoort. Edmund Wilson, who attended the breakfast, sketched his version of the event. Dos Passos was Cummings' best man:

> Dos with his withered bachelor's button—drinking at Hoboken—they had been stewed for days—married in what they called "The Church of the Holy Zebra"—Dos had put them through it—Cummings had taken several baths, one after the other: he had felt his arms and legs getting numb, as if they weren't there—Anne went to sleep and slept for days and couldn't wake up—awful moment just before ceremony (Cummings' mother and sister were there) when, after everything had been most nonchalant and amiable, they all suddenly began snapping at one another. The sad German band—we had them come to the table and play the wedding march—Cummings looked unusually washed and well and carried things off with an excellent easy distinguished manner.

While in New York for the wedding, Dos Passos asked *The New Republic* to send him to Gastonia, North Carolina, to cover the textile mill strike. Violence had broken out between the strikers in the National Textile Workers' Union, a Communist organization, and the United Textile Workers' Union, a branch of the American Federation of Labor. Morale was low after the strikers were evicted from their company-owned homes and the food supply dwindled. Their demands for a forty-hour week and a twenty-dollar-a-week minimum wage went unheeded. The management declared that the mill was operating well without them and that they had no rights or privileges as discharged employees. On April 29, 1929, sleeping strikers of the Communist group were awakened and beaten by masked men, their company building wrecked, and a sign left in their wake: WE HAVE QUIT YOUR DAMN UNION. Herbert Croly, editor in chief of *The New Republic,* turned down Dos Passos' request to go on assignment to Gastonia on the basis that he was too far to the left. Though he toyed with the idea of going anyway, he did not have the money to do it on his own and returned to the Herbst/Herrmann farmhouse in Pennsylvania to try to bring together the disparate parts of his novel.

On June 7, 1929, the strike at the Loray Cotton Mills was in its tenth week and strikers were desperate when they headed for their mill to rout the scabs and claim their old jobs. Police intervened and herded them back to their makeshift tent city, but a fight broke out between two strikers and the strikers' guard opened fire upon the police. Killed was Orville Aderholt, chief of police. A union organizer and three other policemen were wounded. Arrested were fifty-nine strikers and Fred Beal, strike organizer, who had gone to Gastonia to drum up membership in the National Textile Workers' Union, the Communist group. Dos Passos learned that Beal had eluded arrest for a time, but was captured just as he crossed the South Carolina border. Not since the execution of Sacco and Vanzetti had Dos Passos been so personally agitated by domestic events. Beal was a friend of Dos Passos by this time and also a close associate of Mary Heaton Vorse, who had been involved in labor problems for two decades. She, too, had been turned down by Herbert Croly in a request to cover the labor crisis in Gastonia and had retreated to write about other things. Vorse was at home in Provincetown when Dos Passos was informed privately of the turn of events in Gastonia and hastened to convey the news to her in person. On

June 11, Vorse noted in her diary that Dos Passos had come to Provincetown to tell her of Beal's arrest. "Here I am enjoying myself amusing myself buying things for my house and not even knowing about it," she lamented. "What a state I am in in the labor movement, jumping in for a moment having a good time then away to a grand place to write again." Dos Passos commiserated with her, since he, too, felt guilty about not being there himself as an eyewitness to record events as he saw them. Yet he also knew that he was not cut out for straight reporting, a lesson learned ten years earlier when he had tried to write news dispatches of Portugal's internal problems for the London *Daily Herald.* Having a journalist's credentials was advantageous in gaining access to newsworthy events, but he was never as successful at reporting them objectively as he was in shaping his impressions later as "reportages" worked into his fiction or rendered as sociotravel pieces. In his memoirs later, Dos Passos explained that he was not a success as a correspondent for a labor paper despite his interest in syndicalism, socialism, and trade union matters because he was "continually distracted by scenery and painting and architecture and the infinitely tragical, comical, pathetic and laughable varieties of people."

Although his ostensible motive in chasing down the Cape in early June was to talk with Mary Heaton Vorse about Beal's arrest and a plan of action to consider in aiding the arrested mill workers, he might not have gone in person had Katy Smith not been in Provincetown then, too. Katy lived only a few doors from Vorse at 571 Commercial Street. She and her brother Bill had purchased the Arequipa—as the house had formerly been known—from Vorse only a year earlier when Vorse was practically destitute. "Kate and Bill Smooley came in and offered me $2,500 for the Arequipa," she wrote in her diary on April 7, 1928. "I sat at the Smooleys' and while we drank to the new venture and while we adopted one another, suddenly I felt rather like a predatory old buzzard in a doves' nest. They are so lovely and idealistic. I liked them so much. No new friends have so warmed my heart."

The name "Smooley" derived from the surnames of Katy and Bill Smith and their two housemates, Edith Foley and Stella Roof, who had lived together in Provincetown since the summer of 1924. Katy and Edith had arrived first, not unlike countless other unknown writers who thought they were settling in only for the summer, but chose to stay the winter as well, then the next summer and winter, and the next and the next, their addiction to the town and its people now irrefutable. Stella Roof, who had been Edith's classmate at Vassar, joined them their first year in Provincetown, and Bill Smith lived there off and on when he was not traipsing off to Europe or back to St. Louis or Charlevoix, Michigan, where he had spent most of his summers since his birth. The Smiths and Foleys had been friends since their childhood, when both families routinely summered in the cool lake district of upper Michigan. Katy and her brother were from St. Louis and had graduated from the University of Missouri, where she majored in English and journalism and Bill, agriculture. Katy worked first in Chicago editing a trade magazine for a bank, then wrote copy for an advertising agency, where Edith Shay also worked, but both yearned to write fiction and decided to strike out on their own in the East. Smith readily gave up his interest in agriculture after trying to farm his father's property in Pike County, Arkansas, and decided that he wanted to be a free-lance writer, too. Stella Roof was an English and history teacher in Pueblo, Colorado, when Edith and Katy invited her to live with them in "Smooley Hall," which had six different locations in Provincetown, before they settled into the Arequipa.

Hutchins Hapgood, a veteran newspaperman and novelist who settled on the tip of the Cape soon after Vorse (Vorse and her husband, Albert, came to Provincetown in 1907, the first nonindigenous writers), was fond of the Smooleys and described their ménage in its infancy:

> The group at Smooley Hall were at that time of the essence of joyous freedom in life and booze, but never did they forget that their first job was to think and do. The girls were very interesting in that they remained women, and not merely feminists or revolutionists or writers. They had that instinctive and always subtly creative art of enhancing life through their mere existence. They were four delightful companions and they formed a unique atmosphere; all definitely under the balanced swag of desire for self-expression.

The Smooleys submitted all of their early writings under pseudonyms because they thought the magazines they wrote for were trashy. Katy knew that "Madame Charles"— the aunt who reared her and Bill upon their mother's death when she was eight and Bill, not quite four—would not approve of her fiction; nor would her father, a Greek scholar, mathematician, and university professor, even have understood the stories she readily cranked out and published under such titles as "The House of Secrets," "Masks and Marriages," "One False Step-In," "The Rescue," "Through a Glass Eye," "Plain Ann," "Bachelor Husband," "Big Boy," "The Golden Gypsy," all under pseudonyms of "Mrs. John Morse" and "Katharine Carr." Her tales were always in the first person, and her protagonist was an ingenious, determined, and plain-looking young woman whose shrewd but essentially good character enabled her to outwit her adversaries and catch her man or whatever it was she set out to get.

For five years the essential flavor and character of the Smooley household remained unchanged as they crisscrossed the town, their moves precipitated by various owners returning to the Cape to reclaim their homes, which had been let for little or no rent in favor of having someone responsible to keep the place up. Countless writers and artists had begun to come home in 1924 after extended absences abroad, and for the first time found themselves in the midst of Prohibition. Although bootlegging, rum-running, and gangsterism ran rampant on the heels of the Eighteenth Amendment in curious counterpoint to the boop-boop-a-doop of big band jazz, speakeasies, and booze emporiums in New York, Chicago, and other metropolises, Provincetown remained free of crime and hysteria, but never lacked liquor or a place to drink it. Residents of the lower Cape took Prohibition in stride as surely as they did the lashings of capricious winter storms, homes that slid off shifting dunes into the sea, and gawking summer people. It, too, would pass. The Smooleys fit into the life and landscape of the town as casually as did their name, which came to mean in Provincetown lingo "close friends."

Friends of the Smooleys knew that the door of the Arequipa was never latched unless Bill Smith was getting ready to run off his home brew, known as "The Boy" or "The Fruit of the Worm." Edith Foley used to quip: "Tis only a boy, but it has the strength of a man." All of the imbibers on the lower Cape were forced from time to time to do business with "Old Man Fall River," a Portuguese bootlegger. "I want a pint of whiskey"—spoken in Portuguese—was the only way they could buy it, but according to Eben Given, a friend of the Smooleys to whom Dos Passos was introduced in 1926 when he was last in Provincetown: "Even then it cost seventy-five cents and rotted our sockets." The Smooleys had an ancient wood-burning stove in their kitchen, which made them the envy of the neighborhood because their brew was prepared without the stench of oil fumes. Most Provincetowners had to brew their liquor on oil stoves. Dos Passos was in Provincetown that summer when it was time for Smith to harvest "The Boy." Because the ingredients were expensive, the Smooleys often took in several outside partners. When the brew was ripe, Smith pulled the shade to signal his partners—usually Charles Kaeselau, a painter and formidable boozer, and Hutchins Hapgood—to assist in the harvest. They could not resist drinking the first liquid drawn off, known as fusel oil and not meant for consumption. Before the night was over, the partners and drop-ins had drunk the entire crop and there was none left to age. As Dos Passos put it, making home brew was Bill Smith's way of "working quietly for civilization."

Eben Given reported that his part of the Cape was much given to parties. "Ring a bell or whisper 'party' and a hundred people sprang up like dragon's teeth out of the ground." Given lived five doors down Front Street (Commercial Street) from Smooley Hall with his parents and widowed sister, Thelma Verdi, a concert violinist, and was an art student at the Académie Julienne in Paris when he met Waldo Peirce, a fellow student. For a time, both Given and Peirce had courted Katy. "Eben Given used to like Katy; in fact, a lot of people were keen on Katy," said Helen Sawyer Farnsworth, a painter whom Katy called "Henkaberry." "Before Eben started going with Phyllis Duganne, I remember our teasing him and Katy. They'd go down into the kitchen of Smooley Hall—it was the basement level that opened onto the deck overlooking the harbor—and we could hear what sounded like scuffling going on. Katy never encouraged anyone to speak of marriage back then. Katy loved the single, carefree life of Smooley Hall, but when Dos Passos visited we wondered what was in the making."

Katy gave a party on June 11, 1929, to introduce Dos Passos to her friends. He stayed a week, and by the time he left they knew they not only were in love, but intended to get married. They agreed, however, not to talk about it with anyone else until it was a *fait accompli.* The sodden, immoderate behavior surrounding the wedding of Cummings and Anne Barton was still fresh enough in his mind to reinforce his vow not to make a spectacle of his own marriage. He wanted only a private ceremony in a legal chamber or home, to which Katy readily agreed, but they had no intention of getting married until he finished his book and she tied up a few loose ends, such as helping her brother Bill sell their aunt's summer home in Michigan, which had been vacant since her death the preceding year. It was their small inheritance from Madame Charles that had enabled her and Bill to purchase the Arequipa.

Perhaps the only friend to whom Dos Passos wrote that summer of his decision to marry was Frederick van den Arend, who replied from Paris on July 23, 1929: "Well Passos, you have my blessing but you'll need a damnsite more than that. However, the God that protects drunks sometimes extends his ministrations to matrimonies. I will have Masses said for you through a megaphone from minarets and trust Honorable Deity will lend an Ear." Dos Passos' observation to Hemingway was simply: "Incidentally, Katy's a hell of a swell girl—why have I been kept in ignorance of her all this time?"

Their plan when he and Katy parted in mid-June was for him to join Dudley Poore at Otisco Lake, New York (some twenty miles south of Syracuse), where Poore assured him he could work undisturbed for at least a month at his mother's remote summer cottage on the edge of the lake. Otisco was James Fenimore Cooper territory and the setting for numerous adventures of the youthful Hawkeye and Deerslayer. "It was a wonderfully productive time for Dos," said Poore. "He rose at 7 o'clock, jumped into a tub of cold spring water making loud cheerful vocal noises the while, ate breakfast, then polished off his correspondence. At 9 o'clock he was at work on his novel steadily and fast, never pausing to alter a phrase or clause. His work habits were amazing. By noon he had finished for the day." On the Fourth of July they took the day off and made the complete circuit of Otisco Lake, a twenty-five mile tramp. "At Dos's insistence we set off rockets on the lake shore that evening; not to do so would have been to fail in our duty toward the day," added Poore. He remembered that Dos Passos especially liked the hour of fading daylight. "We ate supper early in order not to miss the sunset."

Although the evergreens surrounding the edge of Otisco Lake were not his loblolly pines of the Northern Neck of Virginia, Dos Passos was reminded of his own family homestead where he had spent many of his summer holidays with his father and mother. He hardly thought of it as his property now, although he owned half of it. James Madison, his mother's firstborn, still lived there. Despite Madison's apparently sincere welcome when he stopped in from time to time during his treks up and down the coast, he still felt keenly his role of uninvited guest. Most of Dos Passos' friends had family hearths somewhere—just as the farm in Virginia had served his father well for over twenty years as a haven from the jangle of city life—but he was as rootless in 1929 as he had been a decade earlier upon his return from the war. If there were funds available to which he was entitled from his father's estate, he either did not know about it or chose not to pursue it. Everything was still resting in the custody of his aunt, Mary Lamar Gordon, and her son-in-law, Byron Ralston. Outsiders such as Lawson, Marvin, Hemingway, the Murphys all came to his financial rescue from time to time, but the only thing Dos Passos apparently collected from his kin during this period was his mail. The Ralstons' Riverside Drive apartment in New York City provided the only address with any degree of permanency for him for many years. Mrs. Gordon and the Ralstons extended their hospitality when he dropped in occasionally, but the wool of the black sheep was still upon him there, and he seldom tarried. His life from infancy on had been geared to movement, the pattern having been cut for him at birth in a Chicago hotel. He no doubt reasoned that it would be good to put down roots with Katy, to tend his own piece of land instead of being the itinerant farmer in someone else's garden or window box, to have a home base for the first time in his adult life. Katy would be a stabilizer, a rudder to keep him from chasing about at half tilt.

Meanwhile, what had commenced that summer as a "Memorial Expedition" for Katy, her brother Bill, and Edith Foley evolved into more than a revisitation of old haunts. On June 28, 1929, Katy was preparing to set out with her brother and Edith on the "Smith-Foley Michigan Memorial Expedition of 1929." She allowed that she was "still eaten up by little formless fears and spotted phobias with pale green mane and tail," but insisted she would write often because "Love must have its say." When she closed, she added: "Do write to me, darling, and tell me you miss your girl." After "girl," she trailed off with other signatures: "goil," "gerl," "gurl," "gal," "gurrl," and, finally, "Katy." On July 4, her message was "Sorry not to be with you this glorious Fourth," signed "Patriot." Two days later she wrote that they had crossed the Ohio line that day "at 4:40 exactly, four days eight minutes and one thousand miles from Smooley Hall, Provincetown. All rose to feet when crossing border." On July 8 her card, signed "Squareshooter," said: "Closing in on farm—only sixty-five miles away. Country very wild and fresh. Makes New England look like a game of clock-golf." The next day she wrote: "Lift up your heads ye gates and be ye lifted up ye Everlasting Doors: I have heard from Muttonfish. Muttonfish Darling, Old Home Week now in full swing." They had found the house in decay, "stripped and gutted by local boys and neighbors, not even the wall-paper left. Write to me as quick as you can please. I love you as the crow flies. I wish we were 1 (one)." This note was signed "Katy Marco Polo."

The family farmhouse was in such shambles that they had to live elsewhere while they labored to refurbish it enough to put it on the market. Katy wrote Dos Passos that the work would keep them in Michigan for at least a month and urged him to join them. "We pray nightly for some sucker to come along, but if any are swimming nearby they aren't apparent," Bill Smith wrote Helen Farnsworth. "There is no grog, no dancing, and no one to call on," he complained. There was no trace of their old life or friends, only a few elderly matrons whose names they had forgotten. "We drive to Boyne for a soda of an evening and creep off to bed. The yawning chorus can be heard from 7:00 P.M. on." They swam in Pine Lake (later renamed Lake Charlevoix) to cool off after a day of hammering, painting, raking, and shoveling, and rented a Boston dory to sail the lake as a special treat, but the heat was outrageous and they yearned for the salty breezes of the Cape.

Meanwhile, Dos Passos had left Otisco Lake and gone to Chicago to use the extensive newspaper morgue in the public library. To finish his manuscript, he needed actual headlines, news stories, features, slogans, advertisements, dispatches, popular songs, all a pastiche to juxtapose with his fictional narrative, which he called "Newsreels." These, he interpolated—along with the "Camera Eyes" and minibiographies—techniques he was using for the first time to help provide the clamor and fabric of everyday life. For years he had saved clippings that struck him as amusing or startling. Many he had used in *Manhattan Transfer,* though much less directly than in the new book, to help illustrate what his characters were seeing, reading, and thinking. Before leaving New York, Dos Passos asked Poore to help him find the words to a number of old popular songs. Poore was pleased to discover "There's a Broken Heart for Every Light on Broadway" in a "Newsreel" chapter of *The 42nd Parallel* because it was one that he had sent Dos Passos that summer.

Before Katy's expedition West, they had talked about meeting in Chicago and perhaps returning East together. Instead, she urged him to take the boat or train to Petoskey, Michigan: "I could meet you and then we could see each other, and while tramping the woods and fields and swimming the waters of this northern country have a cozy constructive talk. We can dope it out easily enough eye to eye." Katy was more nervous about their impending marriage than he. "I am afraid hourly and at the same time have tremendous spurts of confidence. I could feel no worse if I were expecting a brace of twins. . . . You are the only guy I could ever talk to at all and I aint able to do that." Dos Passos did not want to waste time between Katy's agreement to marry him and the event itself. Delay had destroyed his one previous engagement and he did not want to risk losing Katy.

The trio was ready to head home when he arrived in Petoskey, and on August 2, 1929, they traveled north across the Canadian border in search of liquor and a different route home. In Quebec they paused to explore the town, then dropped into the northeastern pocket of New England and across Maine to the town of Ellsworth (not far from Bangor, in Hancock County), where they decided to pause long enough for Dos Passos and Katy to take out a license and get married. Katy wanted Stella Roof to be a part of their wedding party, too. She did not think it fitting to incorporate Dos Passos into Smooley Hall without all of the Smooleys together to endorse and witness the event. Katy had no intention of breaking up her household by marrying Dos Passos. They would simply make him a Smooley, too. The Arequipa would be a home for the five of them for as long as they wished, she vowed. After sending a telegram to Stella Roof to hasten to Ellsworth, the quartet drove to Cranberry Island for the weekend. Dos Passos had spent some ten days there back in 1926 when he was finishing his Sacco and Vanzetti defense.

On Monday, August 19, 1929, they drove back to Ellsworth to meet Stella, then gathered in the study of a Unitarian minister to recite their vows after picking up the license (for one dollar) from the county courthouse. Edith and Stella served as Katy's maids of honor, and Bill Smith was Dos Passos' groomsman. Smith's chief function as best man was locating a raincoat with which to drape Dos Passos' backside after his pants had split open moments before the ceremony. In a letter to Hemingway a few days later, Dos Passos allowed that there had been some "shaky moments" until a guest of the minister had "fished some real Bourbon whiskey" from one of his lobster pots and the revelry began. "I feel so swell I don't like to mention it," he said. "We have a swell little red house for a month outside Wiscasset, money in the bank, and a small amount of magnificent Bourbon whiskey. . . . This trilogy stuff is the cats nuts to a writer because you can always think that if Vol. I is shit, Vol. II will be swell. Jesus I hope it's not the beginning of the end. If a wordfellow can live down a trilogy he can live down anything. I suppose that's what Galsworthy thought as he strained at stool over the Forsytes day after day." In customary fashion, Dos Passos combined his naive "gee-whiz" diction with a touch of the bawdy and scatological. To no one else did he write so graphically.

On October 3, Dos Passos and Katy were back in New York City, where he met with Eugene Saxton and handed over his completed manuscript of *The 42nd Parallel*. A reporter from the New York *Herald Tribune* had cornered them that day, having heard of their marriage, but got little information except confirmation of the event. The author and his bride were "married in Maine several weeks ago . . . and would sail in a few weeks for Europe," acknowledged his article the next day. "Miss Kate Smith" was identified as "about thirty years old," born in St. Louis, and engaged formerly in advertising. The couple had met in Tampa, Florida, the brief announcement concluded. Actually, in applying for their marriage license, Dos Passos had given his age as thirty-three, and Katy said that she was thirty-four. The truth of the matter was, however, that Katy's birthday was October 24, 1891. When she married, she was two months short of thirty-eight. Dos Passos himself may not have known Katy's true age. *Time*'s "Milestones" reported as much as Dos Passos chose to make public: "MARRIED: John Dos Passos, 33, author *(Three Soldiers, Manhattan Transfer),* and a Miss Kate Smith; at Ellsworth, Me. Because to him the married state is not an awesome thing, he did not publicize his wedding, could not remember exactly when it happened."

Katy's brother Bill presented his version of the affair on October 4, the same day the story broke in New York, in a letter to Hemingway:

> Well, Kate and Dos did it—I was there, ring bearer to the groom, and Knobby [Stella Roof] and Edie [Foley] were also of the party. We had the Rev. E. E. Gorileus and a very fine divine he proved to be. The little group had pulled itself together over a bottle of swell real bourbon but even so the contracting parties needed a firm hand. It gave an odd touch to start off with them being called John and Katharine. I kept looking around to see who he meant. The Rella's [the Reverend Mr. Gorileus'] voice just slowly weakened and sank during the program, but Dos's cruised all over the register, now here now there in a manner wonderful to hear. But it was soon done and a good job. The writer is prone to endorse Passos in a variety of ways. . . . I am greatly relieved that my sister has at last gotten a good Christian husband. The pair was left at Wiscasset Maine for their moon and then came down here for Dos to finish his brochure. He done so and is now in N.Y. City to try to find someone willing to publish it. There is reason to suppose Harper's will act. They plan to return here [to Provincetown] pretty soon and perhaps stayage into the Christmas season—it all depends. I do not know on what.

One of the things Dos Passos and Katy did that fall after their return to Smooley Hall was to look for a small place of their own in the fertile hills of nearby South Truro. They wanted a cottage with a small piece of land they could farm during the summer, but intended to live in Provincetown during the winter in the house that Katy and Bill owned together. Edith Shay and Stella Roof agreed to stay on in Smooley Hall for the time being, but Bill came and went as he saw fit, much as he always had. As soon as he could finish reading the galleys and page proofs of *The 42nd Parallel,* Dos Passos intended to take Katy to Europe for an extended honeymoon. Contrary to the impression he had recently given Hemingway, however, he had relatively little cash for such a junket. He did receive payment from Harper & Brothers upon turning in his book manuscript, and Jack Lawson sent him money, too. "That two hundred and some more is not a loan but part of what I owe you to even up the expenditures on the theatre. Beyond that I can loan any amount you care for—will send on five hundred or a thousand any time you want it." Lawson suggested that Dos Passos join him in Hollywood. "I can have almost anything I ask for in this Hell-hole next winter. I think it's ridiculous not to take it while the taking's good." Dos Passos had no intention of going to Hollywood, but he did envy Hemingway's success. *A Farewell to Arms* had been out only a little over a month, yet already had sold over thirty thousand copies and moved ahead of Remarque's *All Quiet on the Western Front* to head the bestseller lists. Hemingway was in Paris on October 24, 1929, when Dos Passos wrote:

Hem—do you realize that you're the King of the fiction racket? Two different publishers took me aside into soundproof rooms and after hemming and hawing asked me if I knew Mr. Hemingway. I allowed as I did. Then they screwed up their eyes, put their fingers in their noses, made moronic high signs, farted slighted to the right, crossed themselves and said: "We hear that Hemingway is discontented with Scribner's." I allowed as I didn't know anything about it and the interview was at an end. Coward McCann said "But what can we offer a man like that? We can't offer him money." Looks like you'll be able to have any number more dependents if this keeps up. I have a theory that the whole fiction market will go belly up in a couple of years—so now is the time to cash in.

To the laurels already bestowed upon *A Farewell to Arms,* Dos Passos added his own, applauding its "firstrate craftsmanship" and calling it the "best written book that has seen the light in America for many a long day" in a review that winter in *The New Masses.* The book's matchless narrative prose was "as good as anything that's been written since there was any English language." Perhaps most important of all, he concluded: "It's a magnificent novel because the writer felt every minute the satisfaction of working ably with his material and his tools and continually pushing the work to the limit of effort." He also threw a jab at what he called the "Fordized world." It was getting to be almost unthinkable for a person to take pleasure in his work, that he "should enjoy doing a piece of work for the sake of doing it as well as he damn well can." Craftsmanship was "a damn fine thing," but it was being threatened by America's passion for mechanization and subdivision of labor, he insisted. Dos Passos was thinking, also, of his own labors when he reviewed *A Farewell to Arms.* In his play, *Airways, Inc.,* he had aligned himself with the craftsman who wanted fair payment and recognition for an honest day's labor. The play was a barrage against the mechanized American world of capitalism, but the attack had fallen largely on deaf ears and empty seats in the theater of the New Playwrights. One of the satiric thrusts of *Airways, Inc.* had been that the working class itself had neither recognized its own best interests as workers, nor acted intelligently upon them. In turn, its people were evolving into self-prostituting capitalists themselves. Dos Passos hoped that his own shockingly crafted novel, *The 42nd Parallel,* would reach the people in a way that the play had not. Perhaps then the workers would get up and do something about it.

17

A Middle-Class Liberal
in the Depressed Thirties, 1930–33

I speak as a writer, and therefore as a middle-class liberal, whether I like it or not. . . . Even neutrality, with the major organs for information in the hands of the government and the industrialists, is going to be difficult, and to many even the coolest neutrality is going to look like Red radicalism.

Dos Passos in *The New Republic*
"Back to Red Hysteria," 2 July 1930

The very day Dos Passos proposed to Hemingway his "belly up" theory of the fiction market and the need to "cash in" on it, another market was undergoing dramatic change. Stocks tumbled in wild disorder as thousands of frenzied investors elbowed their way into brokerage offices across the country, mindful that the nation's speculative boom had ended. Bankers' stratagem to reassure stockholders that the economy was still sound by buying huge blocks of stock did little to stanch the flow. Wall Street's "Black Thursday" —October 24, 1929 (which was also Katy's birthday)—was superseded by an even grimmer Tuesday when sixteen million shares were dumped in a single day, a record unequaled for three decades. Bellboys and playboy industrialists alike watched their rags-to-riches empires crumble as Wall Street's collapse reverberated around the world.

The personal worlds of Dos Passos and Hemingway, however, remained relatively untouched by the calamity. "The Great Depression . . . didn't affect me very much personally," said Dos Passos. "I used to tell people I had been just as broke before the stockmarket crash as after it. It was what I saw of other people's lives that brought home the failure of New Era capitalism." Hemingway had already had his say regarding the dangers of lolling in the lotus garden of capitalism. Upon hearing of Dos Passos' marriage, he warned against succumbing to the trap Donald Ogden Stewart had sprung. Stewart had been ruined by running with the Payne Whitney family and getting a twenty-five thousand-dollar contract, said Hemingway, and John Peale Bishop had been done in by his wife's income. "Keep money away from Katy," he advised. "Eternal youth has sunk the Fitzgeralds—get old, Passos, age up Kate. Old Hem ruined by his father shooting himself—keep guns away from Katharine's old man." Dos Passos was sure that keeping money away from Katy would never be their problem. Getting it was more the rub. Nor did he anticipate any problems with Katy's erudite father regarding firearms.

When Dos Passos squired his bride of four months aboard the SS *Roussillon* on December 5, 1929, the second volume of his trilogy, *1919,* was well under way. He wired Hemingway that proofreading and home buying had delayed them, but that they would be in Paris in a fortnight and hoped to find him there. "Having big four-letter word fight —pray for me," the message concluded. *Harper's* objected to a number of words and phrases in *The 42nd Parallel* manuscript, such as "crissake," "Jeez," "Holy Jesus," "Jesus God," "God damn it to hell," "clap," "sonsofbitches," "friggin'," "shit," "I'm drunk as a pissant," "a goddam whore," "he got a hardon," "feeling her tongue in his mouth," and "they loved each other up on the sofa and she let him do everything he wanted," but Dos Passos insisted that the language of his characters authentically mirrored their lives and must be retained. Hemingway, on the other hand, had given in to Charles Scribner's demands that "balls" and "cocksucker" be eliminated from the *A Farewell to Arms* manuscript. Dos Passos had already fought over four-letter-word usage in *Three Soldiers* when Eugene Saxton was his editor at George H. Doran, but Saxton had more leeway at Harper & Brothers than at Doran, where Frank Doubleday kept a tight rein on his editors.

The 42nd Parallel had ended with its main character, Charlie Anderson, aboard ship headed for France. The year was 1918, and Anderson was off to the war as a volunteer ambulance driver, as was Richard Savage, the character about whom events swirled in *1919* with greater prominence than in *The 42nd Parallel.* Although more than a decade separated Dos Passos from his own heady experiences as a novitiate to war, the sights and sounds and smells of the past engulfed him once more en route to Europe himself. Dos Passos sat in his own shadow as he picked up his major characters and planted them firmly, one by one, into the pages of *1919.*

His arrival with Katy in Paris in December 1929 was eclipsed by news of the suicide of Harry Crosby, whose eighteenth-century townhouse at 19 rue de Lille in the Faubourg St.-Germain had served as a watering hole for American and European literati alike since the mid-twenties. Crosby's Black Sun Press had published not only his own poems and those of his wife, Caresse (the former Polly Peabody), but also the work of such writers and poets as Lawrence, Joyce, Pound, Boyle, Crane, and MacLeish. Crosby had died in the New York studio of his friend Stanley Mortimer, whose name was well known in Boston and New York City social registers (he had asked to borrow the key to Mortimer's room at the Hôtel Des Artistes for a few hours, but when Mortimer returned to his quarters several hours later, he discovered Crosby's body beside Josephine Rotch Bigelow, his twenty-two-year-old lover, also dead). The New York *Times* carried the story emblazoned across its front page December 9. The deaths appeared to be a suicide pact, but the motive was unknown, said the *Times* reporter. Friends were shocked, though aware that Crosby's long-standing courtship of death had been rehearsed many times. He also had made it clear that he did not intend to die alone. Hart Crane, Estlin Cummings, Walker Evans,

Malcolm Cowley, Matthew Josephson, and William Carlos Williams—all had just attended a farewell party for Crosby and his wife, who were getting ready to embark for Paris. Dos Passos and Crosby had known each other as Harvard classmates and had shared the horrors of Verdun as ambulance drivers during the war. Their paths crossed later in Paris several times, but Crosby's profligate life—punctuated by opium and alcohol abuse —repelled associates who could not cope with the emotional drain through which he put them, yet were attracted by his genius, essential goodness, and sense of fair play. "He was a hell of a good boy," said Hemingway.

Another prodigal who had become increasingly difficult to deal with by the literati of New York and Paris was F. Scott Fitzgerald, whose moods shifted suddenly when he imbibed. It was not so much the quantity—though he sometimes drank a great deal—as it was that he no longer could hold what little he did drink. Fitzgerald was gay and charming one moment, nasty and vicious the next. Upon their arrival in Paris, Dos Passos introduced Katy to Fitzgerald and Zelda. Fitzgerald was fond of Dos Passos and offended him less than many of his other friends, but they saw relatively little of each other that winter. Zelda, determined to be a dancer with the Ballet Russe, was busy practicing. Seven hours a day she worked under the direction of Madame Lubov Egorova—once a leading ballerina with the Ballet Russe—and now head of the ballet school for the Diaghilev troupe. "For anyone who was fond of the Fitzgeralds, it was heartbreaking to be with them," wrote Dos Passos of this period. Zelda had become nervous, underweight, paranoid with both friends and strangers, and fiercely jealous and resentful of her husband's reckless self-indulgences.

Hemingway was not the best company that winter in Paris, either, Dos Passos discovered. His irascibility then was not directed at Dos Passos, but swung pendulum fashion. On one hand, he was in high spirits because *A Farewell to Arms* now headed the bestseller lists. So far as sales went, it was as though Wall Street had never collapsed. Hemingway's sense of his own worth had never been stronger, yet he was still smarting from Fitzgerald's having recently told him that Robert McAlmon had maligned his masculinity. McAlmon reportedly accused both Hemingway and Pauline of homosexuality; moreover, Hemingway routinely "knocked Hadley about," said McAlmon. Zelda fanned the rumors by telling people that her husband had "an unnatural attachment" to Hemingway. Although this was more likely symptomatic of her own emotional instability than based on any realistic evidence, she was convinced that Fitzgerald and Hemingway were having an affair. Zelda's accusation helped compensate for her own sense of loss. During the winter of 1929–30, she complained to several friends of her husband's progressive inadequacy as a sexual partner. Fitzgerald, in turn, worried that Morley Callaghan had misinterpreted an arm extended in friendship as a sexual pass. To compound the situation, Hemingway was furious at Callaghan because a New York *Herald Tribune* article claimed that when Hemingway pushed Callaghan into a fight, Callaghan retaliated by knocking him out in one round. Fitzgerald, too, became unwittingly involved in the fracas. Although the tale was eventually retracted and Callaghan and Fitzgerald declared innocent of any wrongdoing, the friendships of all concerned were strained irreparably. Misunderstandings, exaggerations, accusations, and apologies flew back and forth across the Seine and the Atlantic during the winter of 1929–30 while Dos Passos and other onlookers withdrew as best they could. By this time, the patience of Gerald and Sara Murphy regarding Fitzgerald was wearing thin, too. Fitzgerald had fashioned his two main characters, Dick and Nicole Diver, in his manuscript still in progress *(Tender is the Night)* in part from the Murphys. What he could not glean through observation as their houseguest and during other social encounters with the Murphys, he approached head-on with a number of outlandish questions. Sara, hurt by Fitzgerald's impertinence, indignantly called him down on it, and their friendship cooled. Later, Sara insisted that she and her husband had remained sympathetic to the Fitzgeralds' plight despite their reprehensible antics.

The Murphys had troubles enough of their own during the winter of 1929–30. Patrick, their younger son, had recently been diagnosed as being tubercular. He was nine and his condition grave. Doctors encouraged his parents to take him to a sanitarium perched on the edge of a mountain in the tiny village of Montana-Vermala, high in the Swiss Alps. Determined to carry on their lives there in as normal a fashion as possible, they urged their friends to come to their mountain retreat for Christmas. They especially wanted Dos Passos to bring Katy so they might meet her. Invited, too, were Hemingway, Pauline, and Pauline's sister, Virginia Pfeiffer. Dorothy Parker was already there, and Donald Ogden Stewart was invited to come as soon as possible with his wife, Bea. The Murphys thrived on having people with them who liked each other and may have been unaware that Hemingway, Parker, and Stewart were estranged. Hemingway had made Parker the butt of a scatological poem at a party in Paris given by the MacLeishes. Parker was not present, but Stewart was and leaped to Parker's defense. If Sara knew of the breach, she did not let on to anyone who might have repeated it. She may have been aware only that Parker had written an adoring *New Yorker* profile of Hemingway in which she declared him "far and away the first American artist." It was Parker, also, who coined the phrase "grace under pressure" to characterize the Hemingway hero. At any rate, Hemingway did not behave in an unseemly fashion at the Murphys' despite his dismay at finding Parker already ensconced there. He simply vowed to leave immediately after Christmas. He did not like being beholden to someone for whom he had little personal regard. Parker's drinking bouts had become more frenzied and talked about of late, and her morose nature and acerbic humor were part and parcel of her frequent contemplation of suicide. Despite her personal problems in 1929–30, however, she was writing well and had no difficulty getting published (Parker was a regular contributor to *The New Yorker*, had just won an O. Henry Award—for her story "Big Blonde"—and her books of poetry were faring well in the marketplace). Dos Passos thought Parker handled herself well at the Murphys'. "She made her usual funny cracks with her eyes full of tears. . . . We laughed our heads off over cheese fondue. . . . We were all set on keeping the Murphys cheered up. For a while it worked."

Stewart, who delayed his visit to the Murphys' until after Hemingway left, described the situation as "infinitely more grim" than they had imagined:

> Dotty Parker, who had been visiting them for a month, tried her best to cover the horror with tenderness and laughter. . . . And here, trapped on this desolate snow-covered silent mountain, with Death seeming to be waiting mockingly in the cold clear air outside, were the two

people who had been our models for the Happy Life. They themselves gave no sign of any change. . . . Sara had outdone herself with amazing variations of Swiss cookery. . . . After dinner Gerald played new records he had discovered in Germany, including one by an unknown Marlene Dietrich from a film called *Der Blaue Engel.* Sara and he told us of the macabre life-in-death with which they were surrounded, and to which they were attempting to bring some of their own brave gaiety. When one of the patients was given his death warrant by his physician, it was now the custom for him to appear at the club with a small replica of his coffin; those who were also about to die saluted him with champagne. Sara had found some musicians and had actually persuaded them to open a night club, which had become extremely successful. At the end of the evening Gerald went to the piano and Sara, in her lovely alto, sang with him. At the end of the evening Bea and I found ourselves in our bedroom crying our eyes out. . . . Next day we fled, taking Dotty with us.

Parker's version was that she had become "utterly bored" at the Murphys' and begged the Stewarts to take her with them when they left.

Dos Passos and Katy had stayed on with the Murphys for several days after Hemingway's departure, but left before Stewart arrived. From Montana-Vermala, they traveled northward by train to Berne and Zurich, then east into Austria. He wanted to take Katy to the little Hotel Taube in Schruns, where he had spent a memorable "old-fashioned Christmas card" holiday with the Murphys and Hemingway when Hadley had been his wife. Hadley had even written to Katy from Schruns while Dos Passos himself had been there to implore her to join them for the holidays. Katy was struck now by the irony that she at last was in Schruns but Hadley was not, and that Pauline—her *other* best friend from their school days in St. Louis—was the second Mrs. Hemingway. Only the Murphys, the cornerstone of the quintet at Schruns in 1926, had not changed outwardly, although their internal family structure had cracked. The prognosis for Patrick's recovery was not good, but their continued flair for high living was a gauntlet to shake in the face of fate. When Dos Passos said good-bye to Patrick on the mountain, he did not know if he would see him again. The child bore his infirmity bravely and in good spirits, yet may have intuited that his days were numbered. Dos Passos had known Patrick since he was two and was probably fonder of him than of any other child he knew until he, too, was a father.

When Dos Passos returned with Katy to Paris in mid-January, he was already looking foward to a new project, the translation of *Le Panama ou les Aventures de Mes Sept Oncles* by Blaise Cendrars, a Swiss-born French poet whose work he had admired for several years. Dos Passos' essay on Cendrars for *The Saturday Review of Literature* in 1926 identified him as the "Homer of the Transsiberian." When they finally met in person in Paris through the Murphys, Dos Passos was taken by the man as well as his work. Like Dos Passos, Cendrars had been a wanderer during his formative years. Cendrars told him that he had traveled the globe in his youth on his own. As a young man he traipsed to Leningrad for a three-year apprenticeship in a Swiss colony of watchmakers, but abandoned his craft for poetry. Before age twenty-five, Cendrars had traveled, also, to Peking, Warsaw, Brussels, Paris, and, finally, to New York, where American critics concurred with their European peers that his new work, *La Prose du Transsibérien et de la Petite Jehanne de France* (1913), heralded promise that even greater things were in the making. Dos

Passos's essay on Cendrars and fragments of his poetry that he had translated into English were published in his travel volume, *Orient Express,* but he knew now that he wanted to work in depth on the poetry of Cendrars, whose technique was similar to his own in *The 42nd Parallel.*

Before traveling to Switzerland for Christmas with the Murphys, Dos Passos and Katy spent a few days in Paris with Cendrars, where his friends included Léger, Delaunay, Chagall, Epstein, Cocteau, Grosz, and Braque. He drove them about in his custom-made sports car, an Alpha Romeo designed by Braque. It had been fitted with a unique gear shift, which he operated with a hook attached to the stub of his right arm, having lost two thirds of his arm in a skirmish in the service of the French Foreign Legion. Upon their return to the city, Dos Passos and Katy were invited by Cendrars to Montpazier for a week in the country. "If you come to my village near Les Eyzies, you will stay at the Hôtel de Londres and eat like a God there," Cendrars promised. Dos Passos could not remember having eaten so well or as inexpensively in the period of a week. Each day the woman in charge of the dining room surprised them with some new Perigordine dish:

> There were truffles, *pot-au-feu* with garlic to make you sop up your plate—with a little wine, country style; *buisson d'écrevisses, champignons à la crème,* boletus mushrooms *à la bordelaise,* fried fish of the Dordogne and of the Garonne, *brochettes* of little birds, woodcock *à l'armagnac,* game feathered and furred, poachers' venison of which the main supplier was the curé of a neighboring village, roasts, *terrine de foie gras,* wild lettuce, peasant cheeses, figs in honey and crushed nuts, *pruneaux d'Agen, crêpes flambées,* as much strong red wine as you wanted, a bottle of Monbazillac for two, coffee, liqueurs. . . . I didn't even know there might still be wild swans in France, even in migration. What an astonishing country is the black Périgord!

Cendrars insisted on driving them daily through the scenic mountainous region of the Massif Central. They were amazed at his dexterity in handling the car on hairpin curves at high speed while gesturing toward some distant ridge or pointing out an interesting configuration of rocks or trees and shifting gears with his metal hook. It was also frightening. Such heady days were matched by Cendrars' creative discourses over dinner. Not since Dos Passos' discovery of Walt Whitman had he encountered such a kindred spirit. Before they had met that winter, Cendrars had already turned from writing poetry to prose. He also was involved in filmmaking and had collaborated as the scenarist with Léger and Milhaud for the ballet *La Création du Monde.* Cendrars' technique in each medium employed verbal montage and simultaneous narrative. It seemed to Dos Passos that the Frenchman's "obsessions and manias" were his own. Cendrars was delighted when Dos Passos promised to translate *Le Panama ou les Aventures de Mes Sept Oncles,* and to illustrate it with his own watercolors. It would mean significant interruption to his *1919* manuscript, but the priority was justified, said Dos Passos.

He and Katy stayed abroad longer than they had originally planned. In Paris, a telegram prompted their going to London for a few days. Constable, who was bringing out a British edition of *The 42nd Parallel* after the American release by Harper & Brothers, was convinced that the "Newsreel" and "Camera Eye" chapters would confound their readers, who, in turn, would criticize the book and not buy it. Since Dos Passos had been only mildly resistant to proposed cuts in the British edition of *Manhattan Transfer,* the logical solution was simply to omit the questionable pages, suggested Constable, impatient to settle the matter. Whereas he had been willing to go along with such things as deleting "bedpan" if the publisher thought the British public would truly be offended, he did not want to find *pot de chambre* in its place. To the new request to publish *The 42nd Parallel* without the "Newsreel" and "Camera Eye" chapters, Dos Passos replied by cable: ABSOLUTELY NOT. Then he headed for London with Katy to argue his convictions in person. He also insisted on reading and correcting the proof himself, even though the book was to be set from the American plates.

Meanwhile, Hemingway and Pauline had extracted from Dos Passos and Katy before leaving Europe a promise to come directly to the Florida Keys instead of going to New York or the Cape so that they might accompany Hemingway and a few other cronies on a fishing expedition to the Dry Tortugas. Yet by the time they arrived, Hemingway's mob—Bill Smith, Waldo Peirce, Henry Strater, and Max Perkins—had already come and gone. Dos Passos and Katy had moseyed by way of the Canary Islands to Havana from Cádiz aboard a tramp steamer, the *Antonio López.* The few passengers with whom they traveled on the small Spanish vessel shared an atmosphere of intimate congeniality in first-class accommodations, and the trip provided just the ambiance he needed to translate and illustrate Cendrars' *Le Panama ou les Aventures de Mes Sept Oncles.* Each morning Dos Passos pored over the original volume with a dictionary and French grammar at hand, then shifted to his paints and brushes after lunch. Besides the poem itself, he took his text from his immediate surroundings: ropes, funnels, decks, and deckhands; bare-backed sailors in dories pulling at oars, tiny fishing boats, schooners, freighters, and luxury liners hobbled to their wharves, awaiting a change of tide, villages clinging like aphids against tropic hillsides with a single peak rising in the distance. He appreciated the change of focus that painting afforded his myopic eyes. The close scrutiny, the extended arm, the steady, distant gaze, the instant decisions as he worked quickly with subtle washes and bold splashes and streaks of reds, oranges, blues, blacks, grays—all brought immense satisfaction. In Havana, where they lingered a week, Dos Passos continued painting, and by the time they reached Key West he had made countless sketches and painted some two dozen watercolors for inclusion in the Cendrars volume.

Along with a batch of personal mail, the first reviews of the Harper & Brothers edition of *The 42nd Parallel*—published February 19, 1930—caught up with Dos Passos in Key West. Having already developed a hard shell to the vagaries of critics, he was not so much worried as interested in how they would assess the book's innovative techniques. In general, *The 42nd Parallel* fared considerably better than its three chief competitors by American authors that appeared in the same week: Thornton Wilder's *The Woman of Andros,* Michael Gold's *Jews Without Money,* and Edward Dahlberg's *Bottom Dogs.* Most of the reviewers had also read *Manhattan Transfer* and now noted features in *The 42nd Parallel* that his previous fiction lacked. Although many found his technique baffling or irritating, the new book showed remarkable growth, they added. "It is not a book for those who want to know how the story comes out," advised Mary Ross in the New York *Herald Tribune Books.* The novel was too open-ended, she insisted. *"The 42nd*

Parallel is more richly textured than *Manhattan Transfer.* . . . Like all of Mr. Dos Passos' writings, the poet's acuteness of sensuous perception—sights, sounds, smells, tastes —fairly leap from the print to engulf you."

Several critics commented upon the novel's "synthesis of time, class geography and social theory," yet wondered if it was worth the effort to wrestle it into an organic whole. George Curry in the Brooklyn *Daily Eagle* said he was unconvinced that "putting on a story in the manner of a movie continuity is either high art or easier reading." The author's "smashing disregard of conventional forms" may be effective to an extent, but one tended to "wonder if a part of Mark Sullivan's *Our Times* had been picked up by mistake in the bindery of the Mssrs. Harper and thus made its way into the book." John Chamberlain in the New York *Times Book Review* referred to the interpolations of "Newsreel, "Camera Eye," and "Biography" sections as "trick stuff" to draw the readers into the book. He believed that the novel had been left "at loose ends for aesthetic purposes." The book's structure was a mirror image of the lives within. Chamberlain regretted that Dos Passos had not made his point of view more explicit and criticized the novel for its lack of a philosophical approach. He was certain that *The 42nd Parallel* was a first "panel" in a series of novels and faulted the publisher for not making that clear in publicity releases. Chamberlain contended, too, that Dos Passos was indebted to James Joyce's *Ulysses* and to John Howard Lawson's *Processional.* Henry Hazlitt, reviewing for *The Nation,* declared that the book's only unity lay in its bindings. The book's haphazard style and dreary themes were relieved only by the brilliant effects of the "Newsreels." *The New Masses* reviewer, Upton Sinclair (whom Dos Passos had applauded for his *Singing Jailbirds* production staged by the New Playwrights during the season of its demise), saw little of merit in the technical devices, yet thought the novel the most interesting he had read in years.

Edmund Wilson's review for *The New Republic* probably pleased Dos Passos more than any of the others. Wilson termed the book "by far the most remarkable, the most encouraging American novel" he had read since the end of the war. It did not approach Hemingway's skill or intensity, he contended, but its literary originality and intellectual interest were significant. Most remarkable about the novel was Dos Passos' ability to get into the minds and lives of his middle-class characters. The characterization was far superior to his achievement in *Manhattan Transfer,* continued Wilson. Although the characters still were viewed only from the outside, Dos Passos had allowed the reader to get close to the characters through the use of the colloquial American idiom. Wilson, too, was aware that the work was the first of a series of volumes. When complete, the entire body could well turn out to be the most important work yet produced by any American of Dos Passos' generation, he concluded. V. S. Pritchett saw Dos Passos as the "American stereotype." Writing for the *Spectator,* he declared that the author was "obsessed with the idea that he has got to shout the whole history of the United States since 1900 through a megaphone. He has no emotions, only moods: moods of revulsion, satire, lyricism, sensuality. . . . If he abandons mechanical stunts and devices, and leaves American history and biography to look after themselves, he has the makings of a first-class picaresque novelist—American literature's greatest present need. At the moment he is like a man who is trying to run in a dozen directions at once."

It is unlikely that Dos Passos was aware of Fitzgerald's observation to Max Perkins in a letter from Paris on May 1, 1930. In response to the pressure Perkins was putting on him to complete *Tender Is the Night,* on which he puttered for over a year and a half, Fitzgerald wrote: "I know what I'm doing—honest, Max. . . . I think time seems to go by quicker there in America but time put in is time eventually taken out—whatever this thing of mine is, it's certainly not a mediocrity like The Woman of Andros and The 42nd Parallel." Dos Passos could take anything in print the critics said, but Fitzgerald's remark would have disturbed him. The reviewers had called him and his books many things over the years, but *mediocre* was not one of them.

The 42nd Parallel was unavailable to most French readers until a translation was published in 1931, but the American and British editions were well received in France. Blaise Cendrars was exuberant. Writing Dos Passos from Hyères, France, on July 18, 1930, Cendrars described the book as "absolutely delightful." He especially liked the "Newsreels" for the sense they gave him of "being there." He saw the "Camera Eye" as a "kind of chemical reaction, mysterious, experimenting." What he admired most was his friend's "extraordinarily alive vocabulary." Cendrars urged Dos Passos to tell his French editor at Gallimard, which had published *Manhattan Transfer,* to authorize a translation immediately. "If Gallimard is not interested in publishing it, I will find someone who is," Cendrars volunteered. "I will scrutinize the translation and correct it as though it were a book of my own. You can sleep on both your ears and it'll be well done," he concluded. The French edition eventually appeared under the imprint of Au Sans Pareil after considerable interloping by Cendrars. Within a year there were also editions of *The 42nd Parallel* in German, Spanish, Swedish, Danish/Norwegian, and Czech.

Although their terminology was different, the essence of what Cendrars admired in Dos Passos' books is what Dos Passos liked about the poetry of Cendrars. In his "Foreword" to Cendrars' poem, now translated as *Panama, or The Adventures of My Seven Uncles,* Dos Passos saw Paris as his "spiritual father" and placed the poet squarely in the modernist camp:

> The poetry of Blaise Cendrars was part of the creative tidal wave that spread over the world from the Paris of before the last European war. Under various tags—futurism, cubism, voricism, modernism—most of the best work in the arts in our time has been the direct product of this explosion, that had an influence in its sphere comparable with that of the October revolution in social organization and politics and the Einstein formula in physics. Cendrars and Apollinaire, poets, were on the first cubist barricades with the group that included Picasso, Modigliana, Marinetti, Chagall; that profoundly influenced Maiakovsky, Meyerhold, Eisenstein; whose ideas carom through Joyce, Gertrude Stein, T.S. Eliot (first published in Wyndham Lewis's "Blast"). The music of Stravinsky and Prokofiev and Diaghilev's Ballet hail from this same Paris already in the disintegration of victory, as do the windows of Saks Fifth Avenue, skyscraper furniture, the Lenin Memorial in Moscow, the paintings of Diego Rivera in Mexico City and the newritz styles of advertising in American magazines.

Dos Passos' introduction to Cendrars' poetry acclaimed the new, but also took American critics to task for creating a climate in which poetry was merely "parlor entertainment for high school English classes. The stuffed shirts have come out of their libraries everywhere and rule literary taste." Dos Passos claimed that a person coming to poetry now for the first time would have difficulty finding any semblance of the "virility, intense experimentation and meaning in everyday life" that had marked it only a few years earlier. It was for the sake of the new reader of poetry and the "confusion of Humanists, stuffed shirts in editorial chairs, anthology compilers and prize poets, sonnet writers and readers of book-chats" that he had attempted to turn Cendrars' "alive informal personal everyday poems" into English, despite his convictions that poetry could not be satisfactorily lifted from the language in which it was written. "I only hope it will at least induce people to read the originals," he added.

Dos Passos and Katy lingered in the Florida Keys until early May before returning to Provincetown. His introduction for the Cendrars manuscript and the translation were virtually complete except for what he considered a touch-up here and there, but he had accomplished little on his *1919* manuscript, and was eager to direct his attention to it full-time. Katy remained ashore with Pauline when Dos Passos joined Hemingway on a ten-day fishing expedition to the Dry Tortugas. Not being an avid fisherman, however, the excursion was about a week too long for him. Moreover, the humidity had risen sharply while they were in Key West, and he found it difficult to work. His joints, too, began to ache. Even the natives wilted that spring when not fanned by ocean breezes. Katy did not like the humidity, either, and both were impatient to return to the Cape. They also had tired of living out of suitcases for almost five months. Katy loved Pauline, and the two couples got along well together that spring, but Hemingway was easier to take in short doses.

Money again was tight for Dos Passos and Katy when they returned to the Cape in the spring of 1930. Not that it had ever been loose, but when there was money, they did not deny themselves what they needed or reasonably wanted. In a financial bind, Dos Passos turned out an article or two with relative ease. He usually set down his ideas spontaneously and sent them off to the magazines he and his friends habitually read *(The New Masses, The New Republic, The Nation)*. Sometimes they sold, and sometimes they did not. He also had become adept at getting a few dollars from his publisher or a subsidiary house through his agents, Carol Brandt or Bernice Baumgarten. Although Katy could whip up a froth of light fiction for one of the women's magazines if she set her mind to it, she did almost no writing for publication during the first year and a half of her marriage.

With Bill Smith in agreement, since he was half owner of the house in Provincetown, Katy and Dos Passos decided to put it up for rent and move to their recently purchased house in South Truro. A good rental fee could stake them for the winter and pay off their mounting bill at Gaffer's, the neighborhood grocery store. The Depression had moved in like a heavy fog and settled indiscriminately over the Cape during their absence and almost everyone they knew had trouble making ends meet. A paying tenant was found to take occupancy August 1, but Dos Passos and Katy had to paint the house first and also tear out two walls in the Truro house to finish refurbishing it before they could move in. Although Dos Passos could plant and make almost anything grow, he was relatively inexperienced with a hammer and saw. With Smith and a hired man to help, however, he calculated, measured, sawed, nailed, screwed, and painted with exactness and energy. By late July both houses were ready.

Dos Passos insisted on maintaining his usual morning writing routine that summer, but work on *1919* went slowly. A number of letters to Eugene Saxton during this period contained such remarks as "the new novel is progressing about as rapidly as a snail crawling up a greased pole, though I sit dutifully at a little square table all day long—so please don't sick your bloodhounds on me just yet Mister Sheriff—at the end of the week if you think it's essential." A few months later he wrote: "About 1919 I don't know what to say—I keep piling up written typewritten pencilwritten every kind of written sheets and have a great deal of cutting to do." In a letter to John Herrmann and Josephine Herbst in July 1930, Dos Passos admitted being "broke," yet had not lost hope: "You said it—the wordfellow racket is on the rocks. Actually it's not such a bad thing as many will abandon a profession for which God knows they were never suited, leaving more room for the rest of us. Meanwhile there'll be some lean and hungry kine around. The worst thing is that the cute little European cheques I used to get from time to time have entirely stopped coming through and as for Harper's, they can't even sell books by their rich lady authors. So why should they sell mine?"

Important to Dos Passos that summer was his developing friendship with Edmund Wilson, who had married Margaret Canby in the spring and brought her to the lower Cape for the summer, along with his daughter, Rosalind (now almost seven), his stepson, Jimmy Canby, and Rosalind's nanny. The Wilson ménage moved into the old Eugene O'Neill house, the converted Coast Guard station at Peaked Hill Bar, once owned by Mabel Dodge Luhan. Wilson had rented it two years earlier and felt lucky to have acquired it for another summer. He and Margaret trekked the beach to Truro to observe the cocktail hour with Dos Passos and Katy at their "little farm sunk in a lonely and rather somber little hollow where the occasional booming of bitterns is the only sound to be heard." The countryside was "gray and dry and abandoned . . . the crooked branches and gray stems of the dead birches and the picket fence around [the house] made it look somehow like something in a queer picture by a modern primitive who gave awkward, ugly, or simple things an ominous or simply an intense value." A journal entry by Wilson described the interior and spoke of a recent evening with Dos Passos and Katy:

> Their big bare fresh brown-and-gray-painted living room, which they had made by knocking a partition out—windows on two sides, screen door on one side, kitchen opening at one end. . . . Supper of cold roast beef, Smithfield ham, potato, lettuce, canned asparagus-tip salad, Dos's special stuffed eggplant, toast made on bottom of frying pan, which gave it special richness and flavor, coffee, admirable cocktails mixed by Bill [Smith] in glass cocktail shaker. . . . The Boy Columbus [the names Dos Passos' home brew had been given, to distinguish it from Bill Smith's "The Boy"] on the stove, the lamps with big bulging chimneys which had been found in the house. . . . Neighbor who had come in, pulled out all the bureau drawers, and tried to read the manuscript on Dos's typewriter.

Margaret once told Wilson she would rather live like the Niles Spencers, whose upstairs piazza of their Provincetown home overlooked the ever-changing scenes of the beach and harbor, "than live in Truro like the Dos Passoses." Wilson spoke of Dos Passos when he jotted down bits of conversation at a party given by Niles and Betty Spencer that summer. When the assembled guests began to catalogue what they termed the nasty and good points of Lucy and Bill L'Engle, a couple included in most of their social gatherings, but absent that night, Spencer said that he "took Lucy and Bill L'Engle just like any other people and was untroubled by all the considerations agitating the rest." Mary Heaton Vorse accused the group of being snobbish, but admitted that she "couldn't stand Brownie" [the name by which most of the Provincetown-Truro crowd knew Lucy L'Engle. Katy called her "The Duchess of All the Truros"] for the things she did "at regular intervals." An example Vorse offered, continued Wilson, was that Lucy L'Engle had been her guest at a dinner party when she insisted on everyone's traipsing off to a movie "that only she wanted to see." Dos Passos apparently offered a few negative remarks on the situation, whereupon Susan Glaspell, known as the peacemaker of the crowd, remonstrated that the L'Engles were their neighbors and should not be "discriminated against because they were rich." If Wilson's story was true, it was probably obvious to the group that Dos Passos was not prejudiced against the L'Engles because they were rich. Money per se did not put him off; rather, it was how people behaved with it; in some cases, how they came by their money might also be called into question. According to Wilson, Dos Passos was annoyed because Lucy L'Engle had recently invaded his house without being invited. He had been asleep in his bedroom when Lucy L'Engle walked in unannounced. "Why, I don't think this house is so unattractive as everybody says it is," she told him when he came downstairs to investigate the intrusion.

With the possible exception of their wives, Wilson and Dos Passos probably knew each other better at this period in their lives than they knew anyone else so far as their attitudes regarding contemporary affairs and politics were concerned. Just as Rumsey Marvin had been Dos Passos' sounding board during the Harvard years, Wilson functioned similarly now. Whereas Marvin had served largely as a receiver, rather than a transmitter, in their epistolary exchanges of ideas, Wilson and Dos Passos fired ideas back and forth at close range. Each appreciated the other's mind and respected his differences. Sometimes their debates became fairly heated and were set down later on paper. Wilson wrote Allen Tate in the spring of 1930 that Dos Passos had transformed himself into a "middle-class liberal" and that the two of them had been debating the meaning of the term. The fruits of their discussion would soon be in *The New Republic,* he added. "Dos has finally come to the conclusion that since the Communist Party with its pedantic Marxism is impossible, the thing to do is to persuade some radical millionaire to hire an Ed Bernays or Ivy Lee to use the American publicity methods to convert the Americans to Communism. It is interesting to contemplate the kind of Communism this would produce." Wilson told Tate that he (Wilson) was "moving further and further to the left," and that he had moments "of trying to become converted to American Communism in the same way that Eliot makes an effort to become converted to Anglo-Catholicism. It is not that Communism in itself isn't all right, but that all that sort of thing in America seems even more unrelated to real life than Catholicism does in England."

Dos Passos' argument appeared in two forms in *The New Republic,* first in an article entitled "Back to Red Hysteria!" (July 2, 1930), then as a "Letter to the Editor": "Wanted: An Ivy Lee for Liberals" (August 13, 1930). The impetus of the first piece—other than Dos Passos' discussions with Wilson—derived from the arrest and jailing of Robert Minor (Mary Heaton Vorse's husband), and William Z. Foster for distributing leaflets and speaking out at recent unemployment demonstrations. Similar arrests were widespread. Dos Passos focused upon three court cases then being fought by the International Labor Defense with the assistance of the American Civil Liberties Union: the Newark case, the Chester case, and the Atlanta case. If convicted for "inciting to insurrection," the defendants faced a possible death penalty or from five to twenty years in prison (for circulating insurrectionary papers). The situation in Atlanta was particularly provoking to Dos Passos: "Anyone who knows the bitter sentiment in Georgia against the labor organizations, and particularly against the assumption of racial equality in labor organizations, will realize how easy it will be to get a conviction, in spite of the youth of the defendants and the extremely thin evidence upon which they are held." In the eyes of the people, the archenemy was Communism. "One important question in connection with this fight," said Dos Passos, "is the attitude of the middle-class liberals," whom he defined as everyone not "forced by his position in the economic structure of society to be pro-worker or anti-worker." Then he made his plea:

> They are the only class to which neutrality is possible in any phase of the struggle. I don't know if they can have much effect on the outcome, but their attitude certainly can affect the conditions under which the fighting is carried on. If they are genuinely neutral, they can at least demand that the war be fought under the most humane conditions possible. What is our attitude (I speak as a writer, and therefore as a middle-class liberal, whether I like it or not) about it going to be? Even neutrality, with the major organs for information in the hands of the government and the industrialists, is going to be difficult, and to many even the coolest neutrality is going to look like Red radicalism.

Dos Passos' call provoked others to action. By September 1930, an Emergency Committee for Southern Political Prisoners had been set up in New York City under the direction of Theodore Dreiser. Dos Passos agreed to be treasurer. The committee itself, formed by the John Reed Club in cooperation with the International Labor Defense, also included Sherwood Anderson, William Rose Benét, Witter Bynner, Malcolm Cowley, Waldo Frank, Josephine Herbst, Sheila Hibben, Alfred Kreymborg, Suzanne La Follette, Scott Nearing, Albert Jay Nock, Burton Rascoe, Lola Ridge, Boardman Robinson, Upton Sinclair, Louis Untermeyer, Carl Van Doren, and Edmund Wilson. Most of the committee had worked on behalf of Sacco and Vanzetti. With these names on the letterhead, Dos Passos issued a "Dear Friend" call for moral commitment and financial help:

> You have undoubtedly read in The New Freeman, The Nation, The New Republic and other journals, of the Atlanta "insurrection" cases, where six workers face the death penalty for holding protest meetings on unemployment. All over the South the authorities are arresting white and colored workers who dare organize unions together, or advocate political and social equality. This new persecution must arouse the indignation of every champion of workers' rights and race equality. The International Labor Defense, the organization defending the Atlanta and other Southern cases, is making an heroic struggle to carry on its work. But the appalling burden of hundreds of cases, resulting from the new "red hunting" hysteria, has strained its resources to the breaking point.

Dos Passos had now begun to frame for himself the answer he chose not to formulate for the director of the Sanitary Propaganda Theatre in Moscow who had queried him at the train station. His role as middle-class liberal had no connection with the Soviet Union, nor was he an activist within the American Communist Party. As he saw it, his pitch must be for the survival of humanity. In a "Discussion" entitled "Intellectuals in America," published in *The New Masses* (August 1930), he wrote the lead article in which he spoke of the "wave of redbaiting and legal lynching" against which "nobody so much as bats an eyelash." He thought the stock market crash had taught the middle-class that "participation in capital through stockholdings was . . . the sort of participation a man playing roulette has in the funds of the gambling house whether he's winning or losing. . . . It's the job of people of all the professions in the radical fringe of the middle-class to try to influence this middle-class. . . . We can't affect the class war much, but we might possibly make it more humane."

Edmund Wilson responded with his own "battlecry"—as Dos Passos termed it in applauding him later—in "An Appeal to Progressives," published in *The New Republic* on January 14, 1931. Wilson urged a Communism on native grounds: "If the American radicals and progressives who repudiate the Marxist dogma and the strategy of the Communist party still hope to accomplish anything valuable, they must take Communism away from the Communists, and take it without ambiguities, asserting that their ultimate goal is the ownership by the government of the means of production." Wilson proposed to bring Communism into line with the American democratic tradition. Dos Passos spoke similarly of the "Americanization of Marx." Dos Passos thought Wilson's piece "splendid and very neatly oiled to slip past mental obstacles." The position of the "shibboleth experts" seemed particularly important, he continued. "Are they/we really in the position of people who are marching at the head of a parade entirely unconscious of the fact that the parade turned down another street?" To Dos Passos, the most *The New Republic* could do was "stir things up and try to smoke out a few honest men who do know something about industrial life as she is lived." He favored the end result, but admitted that his difficulty was in making up his mind whether to "swallow political methods" or choose another course. "Most of the time I think the IWW theory was right—build a new society in the shell of the old—but practically all they did was go to jail. . . . The first problem is to find a new phraseology that we'll be at home with to organize mentally what is really happening now."

Since the Emergency Committee for Southern Political Prisoners had been organized by the John Reed Club of New York, Dos Passos thought it fitting to submit the lead portrait from the *1919* manuscript, "Jack Reed," to *The New Masses* for publication in its October 1930 issue. The piece was an apt follow-up to his September 3, 1930, "Letter to the Editor" of *The New Republic*: "For Southern Political Prisoners." Many people had been tried and sentenced to "barbarously long jail terms," such as the striking cantaloupe pickers in El Centro and the North Carolina textile mill workers, wrote Dos Passos, and now the "monied reaction that is fast obliterating all trace of free institutions in America" was trying to "execute six young people in Georgia under old insurrection laws passed during the civil war." He then gave the pertinent details of each case. Six months earlier two white men had been arrested in Atlanta for holding a meeting under the auspices of the Communist party at which blacks and whites were invited to discuss the unemployment situation. The men were released, rearrested, and held under a war measure passed in 1861 against agitation for a slave insurrection. Two months later, four others including two blacks were arrested in Atlanta and held on the same charges. "In neither case was there any disorder on the part of the communists, nor did the police give them a chance to make seditios utterances even if they had intended," continued Dos Passos. The state solicitor's office in Atlanta demanded the death penalty "in every case of communist agitation, to prove that the Georgia laws against social dissenters and working class organizers 'have teeth in them.' " One of the jailed women was an official in the International Labor Defense organization, which was fighting such cases. Dos Passos' letter on behalf of The Emergency Committee for Southern Political Prisoners was a plea "for any amount however small" from those who felt horror at the thought of death penalties and long jail terms for "crimes of opinion."

Dos Passos' letter evoked new contributions, but it also prompted a negative letter to the editor, which *The New Republic* published the following week. His critic warned against rushing in where others have wisely decided not to tread. "Liberals are a dangerous element in our midst. They protest loudly, create a false impression in the minds of the masses."

Exasperated by what he considered such idiot responses, Dos Passos looked forward to the relief offered by Hemingway, who had been in the northern Absaroka wilderness of Wyoming near the eastern edge of Yellowstone Park since midsummer and wanted him there, too. Pauline had been with Hemingway for a time. They were sharpening their hunting prowess in preparation for a trip to Kenya and Tanganyika the following spring, but she had returned to Piggott and Hemingway did not like to be without a cohort to impress with his woodsmanship and rifle skill. He saw Dos Passos with his wide-eyed, boyish wonder as the ideal novice for such an adventure. Pauline's "Uncle Gus" Pfeiffer would finance Dos Passos' trip, said Hemingway. Gustavus Adolphus Pfeiffer was the wealthy brother of Pauline's father, whose money derived from Hudnut perfumes. Pfeiffer had been his niece's generous benefactor a number of times already, and he gave Hemingway the new yellow Ford roadster they drove West in this year. The proposal now was for Dos Passos to hunt with Hemingway on a ten-day expedition in the mountains of Wyoming, then for them to drive East together. Dos Passos would be dropped off in New York, and Hemingway would proceed to Key West to await Pauline and Patrick's arrival by train.

Hemingway's letters to Dos Passos had always been loaded with how many birds he had shot that day and what kind, how many tarpon and sailfish he had hooked and boated, and how they had fought, how much they weighed. Now he wrote exuberantly of killing bull elks, wild rams, and bears (both brown and black) and lamented that he had not been able to get a shot at the grizzly bear he had spotted. Although Dos Passos was not a hunter—had neither the vision for it nor the sportsman's heart—he was game, nonetheless, to mosey out West and see what it was all about. He also needed to get away from the radical entanglements to which he had lent his pen during recent months and to gain some distance from his *1919* manuscript. Katy thought the trip a splendid idea. Consequently, on October 21, 1930, Dos Passos detrained alone in Billings, Montana, where he was met by Hemingway and driven some sixty miles to Lawrence Nordquist's ranch—the L-Bar-T—from which they set out the next morning on horseback with pack mules and a bounteous supply of food, liquor, guns, and ammunition. For ten days he and Hemingway combed the rugged mountain timber with Nordquist in search of big game. Dos Passos carried Hemingway's Mannlicher rifle and had a license to shoot elk, but never managed to fire on an animal in range. When he spotted a large elk close enough to lob a rock at, he fumbled with the set trigger long enough for the elk to lope off. His first letter to Katy told of being "out in these damn hills" all morning "perpetually nervous for fear of injuring the damn popgun. Have already managed to put the telescopic sight on the blink but Hem was extremely decent about it." Dos Passos much preferred sighting bears with his naked eyes, watching beavers at work, and reveling in the scenery to handling a gun. He wrote Katy that they were "in this hunting camp way up on the creek (Timber Creek) around Indian Peak up about 8000 feet. It's snowing a little—wonderful two-day ride over here from the Lord's wild country to knock your eye out. . . . Magnificent country to walk around in." The first day out they saw tracks of bear, antelope, elk, and moose, but spotted only squirrels, blue jays, crows, and chickadees. The next day Hemingway was startled by a bull elk "charging right at him but his gun jammed." In search of their saddle horses, which had strayed, Nordquist came across fresh tracks of a grizzly, reported Dos Passos. "So we may have a bear—if he stops to eat the dead horse that's laid out for bear bait a little way down the creek." His last note to Katy, dated October 30, described the "fine sparkling mountains all snowy and sitting up all around and it's cold as the dickens. . . . Hem's packing up and we'll pull out in the Ford in a day or two."

The anticipated trip East, on which they were accompanied by Floyd Allington, a winsome ranch hand who rode in the rumble seat, was interrupted the second day on the road. On November 1, they were still a number of miles west of Billings, Montana—having set out from Mammoth Hot Springs, Wyoming—and were traveling on a narrow, gravel road at dusk when the roadster careened into a gully and turned over. Upon hearing of the accident, their friends concluded that it was probably Dos Passos behind the wheel, not Hemingway, whose vision, although not good, was not as bad as Dos Passos'. Yet Hemingway was the driver. His story was that he had been blinded by headlights of an approaching car and thought the car had veered into his path. To avoid a collision, Hemingway ran off the road and the car flipped upside down. Bruised and shaken, Dos Passos and Allington escaped injury, but Hemingway was trapped beneath the wheel until the others managed to extricate him and flag a motorist, who carried him into a Billings hospital. There they discovered that Hemingway's right arm had suffered a compound fracture above the elbow. Dos Passos rationalized that the bourbon they had consumed to ward off the cold had relaxed them, thus contributed to their safety, and that Hemingway would have been hurt worse had he not also been nipping. Not even Dos Passos' glasses had been broken. Once in Billings, Dos Passos took charge of local arrangements. He wired Pauline of the accident, recovered the car and drove it to a neighboring town for repairs, met Pauline's plane, and took her to the hospital to await Hemingway's surgery. He also stayed with her until assured that the operation was a success. Dos Passos resumed his trip East by train. A letter from Katy that had crossed his in the mails caught up with him in New York. Only the day before the accident she had asked about Hemingway and suggested that Dos Passos bring him to the Cape to visit:

"How is Wonderful Wemmege? . . . We fret to see him something terrible but I suppose the fellow won't come."

Other than the severe prewinter freeze and storm that had wrecked the Cape, caused their water pipes to burst, and the house in Provincetown to stand ankle-deep in water, Katy insisted that there was little new to report. One of Edith Foley's sisters had eloped and Waldo Peirce had fathered twins and intended to marry their mother, but there was not much else to speak of except Frank Shay's new state of sobriety, which she assumed was brought on by his budding courtship of Edith Foley. Until Katy married Dos Passos, none of "the Smooley crowd"—as they were known to others—had shown any inclination toward matrimony. Even Stella Roof, whose good looks headed her into several tangled affairs, seemed determined to stay single. Their friends referred to the Smooley household as "Bachelor Hall." The men who wanted their bachelor state felt safe there, and those who were between wives counted on the Smooleys to introduce them to the eligible newcomers who were bound to show up there eventually. When Edwin Dickinson came to the Cape to study art with Charles Hawthorne, he visited Smooley Hall frequently and escorted Katy to parties until he met Edith Foley's sister, Frances, whom he married. According to Helen ("Henka") Farnsworth, "More matches were made at Smooley Hall and at Hawthorne's Cape Cod School of Art than anywhere else on the lower Cape." Henka Farnsworth had her own share of romantic intrigue. In the same letter in which Katy commented on Frank Shay's sobriety, she spoke also of Henka, whose fling with Katy's brother Bill was no secret. "Jerry Farnsworth has gone to St. Louis but Henka remains in New York, writing the sappiest letters to Mr. Weeley [Bill Smith] that ever soaked the mails. She feels however that Jerry has already suffered too much to be allowed to know this so she told him she would not write to Weeley or even let him know where she was."

Sexual involvements and other short-term attachments seldom received serious disapproval or censure. Libertines in thought as well as actions, most of the men and women in their crowd behaved according to highly individualized personal codes. Having stripped themselves of a number of conventional standards, many felt that any behavior—be it nude sunbathing and swimming in broad daylight off Corn Hill beach at the mouth of the Pamet in Truro, or an affair with the spouse of someone they all saw regularly—so long as they did not flaunt their nudity or their affairs and did not cause discomfort or consternation to others, was acceptable. As Frank Shay's daughter, Jean, put it years later: "If you didn't sleep with your neighbors—and you were single—who was there to sleep with?" Most thought it made more sense to marry than simply to cohabit if it looked as though it was going to be a permanent arrangement. Henka Farnsworth said that writer Phyllis Duganne might have gone on indefinitely in a loose living arrangement with Eben Given had it not been for a friend who admonished: "They're talking about cohabitation around here, and there's a thing on the books in Massachusetts against it. We can't have it —so you just set the date!" Given had been "wanting to marry Phyllis anyway," said Henka, and "Billie Miller, who was a little teeny feminine creature, yanked them to New York City and got them married. We all had a good laugh over that."

Before Phyllis Duganne came to the lower Cape in 1926 and bought a house in Truro, Given had been courting Katy. "I loved her. Never before had I seen such yellow eyes—and how they flashed!" For a time Frank Shay had pursued Duganne, who had a ten-year-old daughter. Shay had recently ended his marriage with Fern Forrester, an artist and magazine illustrator, and made no secret that he needed help in rearing his daughter Jean, then five. "Phyllis loved Shay's little girl and wanted to adopt her," said Given, "but she did not want Shay." The two men sometimes fought over Phyllis Duganne until it was obvious that Given had won out. Given was convinced it was his own marriage to Duganne that prompted Shay's courtship of Edith Foley. He also thought it was Katy's marriage to Dos Passos that had made Edith receptive to marrying Shay. Life had changed significantly at Smooley Hall with Dos Passos in the picture. Although Edith had been fully supportive of Katy's fast-blooming romance with Dos Passos and seemed delighted that they had married, the marriage broke up a relationship of many years, pointed out Given.

Since homosexuality was a way of life for a small minority on the Lower Cape, there were those who speculated that Katy and Edith's relationship may have been a lesbian one. Edmund Wilson was fond of Katy, but did not care for her group of female friends. He considered them something of a "lesbian enclave who had stolen Dos Passos," rather than Katy's having been stolen from them, said Mary McCarthy, Wilson's wife for a time. Wilson was jealous of the friendship Margaret Canby, his second wife, had with Katy. After Margaret's death in 1932—she broke her neck in a fall—Wilson devoted a chapter in his journal, *The Thirties* (1980), to her. One passage read: "Margaret thought that if she were a man, she'd like pale camellialike women. . . . Glimpse of her chasing Katy Dos Passos a moment in the front room of Susan Glaspell's house in Provincetown—somehow this glimpse made me feel badly: masculine impulses helplessly, awkwardly, ludicrously in little feminine body—impulse automatic, she didn't know what she was doing or why." Jean Shay, whom Edith had helped rear after marrying Jean's father, was certain that Katy would never have desired a lesbian relationship with Edith. "Katy was too pleased with the way things were: married to an international figure, able to travel freely, and able to do pretty much as she wanted."

Edith Foley was happy to be courted by Shay. "I never saw a woman more cherished and loved than Edie," said Jean Shay. "My father idolized her. To him she was the cutest, sweetest, most flamboyant, cleverest woman around—all unrealistic, of course—but it was good for my father, and for Edie, too. I think I could safely say that his great need and love for her over the years was the most important reason for her existence." Hutchins Hapgood observed that Shay was a "big and periodic drunk and fighter, brawny, healthy, and amusing" until his marriage to Edith. Then he "ceased to be a drunk but retained his other fine qualities." They were married in a quiet private ceremony in Provincetown on December 6, 1930. Shay was forty-two and his wife, thirty-six. In attendance were her sister, Frances, and Frances' husband, Edwin Dickinson, Katy, Dos Passos, and Bill Smith. After the ceremony, Katy, Frances, and other friends of the Smooleys gave a large supper party.

Though the character of Smooley Hall had changed somewhat when Katy brought Dos Passos into the household as a permanent member, no one had been forced to move out. Edith Shay and Stella Roof had lived elsewhere when the house was rented briefly during the late summer of 1930, but Smith was in residence most of the time. After the wedding, Edith and Shay lived in his old house on Back Street. At its elbow stood Shay's huge red barn, which had been converted a few years earlier into the Barnstormer Theatre. Nestled in the dunes nearby was the cottage of Frances and Edwin Dickinson. Stella Roof was invited to move in with Susan Glaspell and Norman Matson, with whom Glaspell took up after the death of her husband, George Cram ("Jig") Cook (whether Glaspell and Matson were actually married or not was a moot question for their crowd; literary records indicated that the marriage was "dissolved"). After Katy and Edith married, Stella was dubbed "the Crone," "the Old One," or simply "the Old." She and Smith had once joked about marrying each other as a means of preserving what little they could of the old Smooley life. Probably neither considered it seriously. Stella was still taking too much medicine for her own good, was drinking more and more, and becoming less and less the pretty, intelligent, and winsomely witty woman who had charmed many a man— both married and single—during her six years on the Cape. Again and again Stella turned to the bottle. Drinking bouts were followed by drying-out spells and resolutions to remain sober. Then the cycle began again. People used to say that if their home-brew tankards were empty, they could always count on finding a cache of bootleg beer at Stella's.

Bill Smith still owned the Arequipa—the Provincetown house—jointly with Katy, but was there infrequently during the winter of 1930–31. Katy wrote Henka Farnsworth that her brother was in New York working and "making contracts and connections. They is a lot of rainbows hanging over Manhattan—theatrical and movie rainbows with pots of gold at the end—but you know how they fade out. And though producers keep coming up to Dos with their vile suggestions, I say not to touch any stage money." Behind this remark was Dos Passos' letter from Dawn Powell in New York: "Clurman and Crawford and Strasberg say your play *[Fortune Heights]* is a very fine thing. . . . They say they're going to repertoire in Boston next year but I doubt if they've gotten enough moratorium money together to buy your play." The Group Theatre, conceived by Harold Clurman, Cheryl Crawford, and Lee Strasberg, was still incipient in March 1930, but the trio was voraciously reading scripts and casting about for a fitting vehicle for their opening production. When the Theatre Guild released Paul Green's *The House of Connelly*, it was selected as the Group Theatre's opening bill. Any hope by Dos Passos for the Group Theatre to select *Fortune Heights* was nullified when Claire and Paul Sifton's *1931* was presented as the second bill. The Siftons' play eked out only twelve performances, and the directors concluded that it failed because the few theatergoers who still could afford tickets did not want to be reminded on stage of the "Brother, Can You Spare a Dime" milieu. The theme alone eliminated *Fortune Heights* from further consideration.

Dawn Powell's ear was privy to almost every literary and theatrical grapevine. The poor man's Dorothy Parker, Dawn Powell held forth at a corner table of the atmospheric French café of the Hotel Lafayette while Parker was entertaining other wits at the Algonquin. By this time the tiny lady (who wrote her tales in the Children's Department of the New York Public Library because she liked the way the chairs fit her) had published dozens of humorous short stories and three satiric novels drawn from the Village characters about her—she herself was such a character—and from the gutsy tales swapped with those who came to drink with her. A friend of the directors and of many of the actors of the Group Theatre, Powell also had begun to write her own plays. The rainbow footing in a pot of gold alluded to by Katy was out there somewhere, and the opportunist ought to be able to take advantage of it, reasoned Powell, who wrote Dos Passos that the banks were closed but money was still available. "M.G.M. or somebody paid thousands to Phil Story the State Fair Man, Harper's Magazine paid Selma Robinson $250 for an eight-page pastiche, and the New Yorker offered me seventy dollars for four pages of suitably pointless dribble which I could wipe off my nose in five minutes. Carol Hill Brandt even told me she'd gotten a six thousand dollar advance on somebody's novel—and worse luck —she wouldn't lie. I hear Macmillan's and Knopf are the only publishers blooming in the depresh."

So far as Dos Passos was concerned, however, the "wordfellow racket" was hard work straight down the line. It had been a long time since he last thought of Mary Lamar Gordon as his fairy godmother, and he did not expect any hocus-pocus except what he could conjure up for himself. The thing that disgruntled him most was that his books had been allowed to go out of print. Constable refused to reissue *Manhattan Transfer* in a "cheap edition" to sell at three shillings, six pence when there were still a few copies of the original available at seven shillings, six pence. According to Patience Ross, Dos Passos' agent with Heath & Company, in London, Constable's attitude was that Dos Passos' books were not saleable to the "three shillings/six pence public." *Manhattan Transfer* was out of print in England in 1931, but according to Constable's plan, it would be 1934 before a new edition would be out. "It does seem a pity," Ross wrote to Carol Brandt. "I am never at all happy when back books of an important author are completely unobtainable." Dos Passos also pushed for a cheap edition of *The 42nd Parallel,* but Constable's reply was that they would wait until all three novels of the projected trilogy were complete before reissuing any one of them. He became increasingly disillusioned by the short shrift he felt his books were receiving at the hands of publishers. He had learned to walk away from critics and to leave the negotiations of contracts and paperwork to his agents, but his heart had hardened where publishers were concerned. Royalties dribbled in during the winter and spring of 1930–31. Upon publication of the limited signed edition of his translation of Cendrars' *Panama, or The Adventures of My Seven Uncles,* Dos Passos and Katy decided they could afford to buy a new Ford roadster. Their plan was to take the Fall River Steamship Line to Jacksonville, Florida, pick up their car, and drive to Mexico City by way of New Orleans and San Antonio, Texas. Already in Mexico were Susan Glaspell and Norman Matson, who urged Dos Passos and Katy to join them. Edmund Wilson and Margaret Canby said they would like to go, too. Wilson and his wife had visited the Dos Passoses in Provincetown for a few days in January, arriving in time to witness the old O'Neill house sliding into the sea. They had considered buying it, and when they saw it lying in the surf, they "wore an expression of people who have just missed being run over at a railroad crossing," reported Katy to Henka Farnsworth a few days later. O'Neill's son retrieved his father's desk from the house, but scavengers had stripped and picked the ancient carcass bare by the end of its second day in the sea. Not even a latch was left to the elements. The town itself was quiet enough to hear a pin drop. Almost everyone was away for the winter, Katy lamented, "and soon we too will be gone. . . . We are good and poor now and how we are going to get to Mexico I don't just see." She was sure the local grocer would get out an injunction against them when he heard they were leaving without settling their debt. "Eben is going to pay a four hundred dollar grocery bill there this month," she continued, "though only on one condition. He is going into Gaffer's with the check in his hand and let Gaffer smell the check," then jerk it back and say, "This is yours if you promise not to close in on Phyllis or the Smooleys."

Hemingway, back South after a seven-week hospital recuperation in Montana, wanted Dos Passos and Katy to come to Key West in the spring, but they were more interested in a Mexican adventure. They loved being on the highway together, but tarried only briefly in Mexico. Dos Passos was still some fifty pages short of finishing *1919,* and though he had written a good bit on the steamer coming down to Jacksonville it was difficult to produce anything but bits and pieces on the road. Katy usually drove, but he liked being behind the wheel. When they checked into their hotel in Mexico City, she left the car in a congested NO PARKING area while she ran in to inquire about a room. A policeman insisted that Dos Passos move the car, but before he could complete his sweep around the block, he entered an intersection where six roads converged and failed to notice a policeman on a slightly raised wooden platform directing traffic. He crashed into the stand and knocked the officer to the pavement. His dignity may have suffered, but the man was uninjured. Dos Passos' apology in fluent Spanish impressed the officer sufficiently so that he not only refrained from issuing a ticket, but smiled and saluted Dos Passos when he drove away.

Rid of his *1919* manuscript at last in September 1931, he asked his British agent to finagle an advance from Constable upon receipt of the manuscript rather than having to wait until publication, as was customary. He needed money to tide him over until year's end. Finally Constable agreed to advance two thirds the amount that *Manhattan Transfer* had earned as of June 30, 1931. Dos Passos' share was thirty-five pounds, twelve shillings, and six pence. He learned that summer that Hemingway had just received twenty-four thousand dollars as his share in a sale of the movie rights of *A Farewell to Arms,* but if he was jealous of his friend's good fortune, he did not comment upon it. Pauline's "Uncle Gus" Pfeiffer had also recently bought them an ancient stone house facing the harbor on Whitehead Street in Key West. "Big money" may have put Dos Passos off, but he would have liked to have a small cash flow to swim in as he saw fit. Katy had no money to speak of, but what little she could squirrel away she preferred to invest in real estate. Although she did not push Dos Passos at this time to look into his inherited share of what had been his father's land holdings in Virginia, it no doubt occurred to her—and to him as well—that someone else was reaping the rewards of that land while they were struggling to make ends meet during the throes of the Depression. Dos Passos had taken her to meet Mary Lamar Gordon—whom he seemed genuinely fond of—and also his cousin and her husband, Lucy Virginia and Byron Ralston, but it was largely a courtesy call. He knew that the Ralstons chose to maintain as much separation from their "black sheep" relative as possible. They saw him as the interloper, someone who had no claim to their family tree at all. Not only was his birth a source of embarrassment to his mother's Sprigg clan, since Mary Lamar Gordon and his mother were sisters, but his illegitimacy was denied and his very existence ignored. Now that he had become a controversial public figure, they shied away from him even more. So far as they were concerned, there was no reason for any of their friends to know of the embarrassing family connection, although the Ralstons seldom read such rabble-rousing periodicals as *The New Masses, The New Republic,* or *The Nation.* Moreover, having read a few pages of *Three Soldiers, Manhattan Transfer,* and *The 42nd Parallel,* Lucy Virginia Ralston vowed never to read any more of her cousin's "dirty books." It may have been a bit of the imp in Dos Passos that prompted him from time to time to drop off inscribed copies of his books at her Riverside Drive home.

Dos Passos' editor allowed far more leeway in publishing what the Ralstons considered obscenities than Max Perkins and Charles Scribner granted Hemingway; therefore, it came as a shock when Eugene Saxton informed him that an entire biographical portrait had to be deleted if *1919* was to be published as agreed upon. The book was already in press when the former president of Harper & Brothers, Thomas B. Wells, now a stockholder and advisor, used his influence to stop production if Dos Passos did not consent to excise his "House of Morgan" sketch from the book. To Dos Passos, the very idea was horrific. The suggestion alone reflected his quarrel with the entire monopolistic syndrome. Not only was the ironic sketch of John Pierpont Morgan one of the best in the book; it also conveyed as did no other portrait the essential theme of the novel. To be made to drop it or alter it violated the very core of his artistic and philosophical being. Saxton regretted his firm's decision, for he knew it would mean losing one of its best authors. Dos Passos told him not to worry about it. Whether it was a "lousy book" or not, he said he had a hunch there was something "fairly timely about the volume and that it ought to come out as soon as possible." He did not blame Saxton personally for the decision and did not want to lose his friendship, but business was business and so was integrity. "I'll be down in New York . . . and maybe we can have a drink together and talk about other things. Hell it's only a book after all," he concluded. The problem was not censorship per se. Morgan had arranged for a large loan to Harper & Brothers a number of years earlier, but did not call for the demand notes when due. Had the banking firm done so, it could have caused the beleaguered house to be handed over to Doubleday, explained the firm's former president. Morgan allowed the notes to be rewritten twice. "I am all for freedom of speech and uncontrolled publishing policy. Never in a single instance did Morgan try to control or influence us. He was far too wise for that," Wells told Saxton after the controversy subsided. "We have played the game decently and have nothing to be ashamed of—and we have kept a good friend."

Upon Harcourt, Brace's assumption of Dos Passos' contract for *1919* in December 1931, he stayed with his new house for the next six books. When Hemingway heard about the problem months later, he scolded: "Why the hell didn't you give me a chance to do something about Scribner's when Harper's haywired on you? Max will let you say anything about anybody. Anybody else in the outfit is so dumb they don't know what you are saying anyway. . . . What the hell has got into Harper's?" Hemingway had a short memory when it came to Scribner's heavy-handedness. Although he usually did say almost "anything about anybody," he still had to be careful *how* he said it.

Dos Passos already had enough on his mind during the fall of 1931, the status of his *1919* manuscript notwithstanding. In August, at the request of Theodore Dreiser, head of the National Committee for the Defense of Political Prisoners, he agreed to serve as chairman of the National Committee to Aid Striking Miners Fighting Starvation. Some forty thousand striking coal miners in Pennsylvania, Ohio, West Virginia, and Kentucky were starving, and especially dire was the situation in the eastern Kentucky counties of Harlan and Bell.

In his new post, Dos Passos' first act was to issue "An Appeal for Aid," published as an open letter in *The New Republic*. Nearly one hundred thousand people had been evicted from their company-owned houses and needed tents in which to sleep; infants and children needed milk. All suffered from pellagra or other malnutrition-related diseases. Relief kitchens provided relatively little aid. If a family was lucky, it huddled around a fire in a tar-paper shack and ate pinto beans, potatoes, bulldog (flour and water) gravy, and an occasional piece of fatback or cornbread if meal was available. Typhoid and dysentery were rampant. The American Red Cross refused to help on the grounds that the situation had not been brought about by "a catastrophe or an act of God." The official line was that striking miners had brought their sufferings upon themselves. If they wanted assistance, they must go back to work; In Harlan, even if they worked they must not be union members, they were told.

After his initial plea for help as chairman of the National Committee to Aid Striking Miners Fighting Starvation, Dos Passos spent five days in Wilkes-Barre and Pittsburgh investigating alleged abuses of coal miners and interviewing mine officials. On Labor Day weekend he was in the heart of the Coal Belt. Here he devoted long hours to interviewing the miners and their families in their tent camps, tar-paper shacks, and field kitchens. The note he mailed Katy on September 7 revealed that he felt sorry for himself as well as for the miners. His return ticket to New York called for his sleeping in an upper berth, which he said he hated because he could not see out. The missive was signed "Misanthrape," a fitting variation from the "ape" epithet Katy sometimes applied to him. Dos Passos often drew tiny apes in sundry postures performing whatever tasks he himself was involved in at the time. Sometimes his "ape" signatures merely mirrored his mood of the moment.

Upon Dos Passos' return from Pennsylvania, Dreiser summoned a group of concerned citizens and asked for a team of volunteers to conduct its own investigation in eastern Kentucky. Dos Passos and Charles R. Walker, his neighbor from the lower Cape, declared immediately that they would accompany Dreiser, who announced he would lead the group. Others who joined them included Walker's wife, Adelaide, Lester Cohn, Samuel Ornitz, George Maurer, Bruce Crawford, and a stenographer, Celia Kuhn. Dreiser's unofficial companion was Marie Pergain, whom Dos Passos described as "a mysterious young woman in brown who is introduced sometimes as his secretary." Their mission was to inspect the quality of living conditions and interview miners, their families, union leaders, coal mine officials, public servants, and law enforcement officers. In addition to learning the truth behind the violence, deprivation, and terror that had swept the area for a half year, they also sought to test their constitutional right to freedom of speech and freedom of assemblage, rights that had been increasingly denied in the coal mining villages dotting the hills of eastern Kentucky. The trouble stemmed from twenty-two hundred men having lost their jobs in Harlan County for attending a single United Mine Workers union meeting. The miners had met to air their protests against a drastic cut in wages and an almost equal increase in deductible services provided by company officials. Their pay statements indicated they were receiving twenty-five to thirty-five dollars a month, yet their *hard* cash (for a family of five or six) was usually less than five dollars. Script to be spent at the company store replaced cash. Miners paid for their own explosives and carbide and had a burial fund deducted monthly even though they built their own caskets and buried their dead without assistance. As violence mounted, relief kitchens were dynamited and steel-vested strikebreakers were imported by motorcade; henchmen bearing sawed-off shotguns and machine guns pointed their arms menacingly at bystanders. Bloodshed and untold brutality erupted, and miners and company guards lay dead in the wake. Whereas a number of miners were indicted and jailed for murder, the company guards and invading strikebreakers involved in the fracas ranged at will, still in possession of their firearms. It was into this environment that the Dreiser committee came on November 5, 1931.

The group detrained from the Spirit of Saint Louis at Pineville, the Bell County seat, where they were met by miners and their wives, the mayor of the town, and one Judge D. C. Jones, who reported that the governor was sending in the militia to keep order. Dos Passos told Katy that the so-called militia turned out to be "two young shavetails going as observers." He described Jones as "the famous Judge Baby Jones," who stood six feet eight inches tall and was one of the most hard-boiled-looking men he had seen. "He told us about what a fine jail they had and said everything was peaceful and smiling in Harlan County." The committee reviewed its strategy, then moved from Pineville to Harlan to commence a series of hearings in the Llewellyn Hotel, followed by a large, open meeting in the Baptist church of nearby Straight Creek (also in Harlan County). The old, white-frame church was accessible only by crossing in single file a swinging, one-way cable bridge. By no means a clandestine meeting, the assemblage was comprised of miners, their wives, and children; newspaper correspondents representing the Associated Press and United Press; a special investigator appointed by the governor of Kentucky; a major in the state militia; national guardsmen assigned to protect the committee; and union officials, most of whom came out of their own ranks. The National Miners' Union—known as the "Red Union"—came in to help only when the United Mine Workers of America could not effect an acceptable reconciliation between miners and mine operators. Each faction was equally grim in its determination not to buckle under the demands of the other.

The next day the group held a second "free-speech test meeting," this one in Wallin's Creek, Kentucky. At each session miners got up to testify as though they were witnessing at a prayer meeting. As Dos Passos reported later in a poignant piece entitled "Harlan County Sunset," an old miner had been speaking, "striding up and down the platform and banging his fist on the table like a backwoods preacher. . . . 'I love my chillun a thousand times better today than I love Herbert Hoover. . . . Dear companions ther's things happened in this state and county you couldn't believe could happen in civilized Ameriky. . . . We're on that lonesome road between starvation and heathenism.'" Then he sang a strike song and sat down. Another witness—"Aunt Molly" Jackson—testified in a "moaning blues" ballad:

> *Please don't go under those mountains*
> *with the slate ahangin' over your head,*
> *Please don't go under those mountains*

> with the slate ahangin' over your head,
> An' work for juss coal light and carbide
> an' your children acryin' for bread;
> I pray you take my council
>   please take a friend's advice;
> Don't load no more, don't put out no more
>   till you get a livin' price.

Dos Passos told of walking with a young miner from the meeting at Straight Creek and asking how he liked the speech of a bright young man from the *Daily Worker* who had spoken stirringly about the international working class, their struggles in Germany and China, and the miners' life in the Soviet Union. The young man allowed that he liked it: "Why if it warn't for the N.M.U. we'd be on our knees before the coal company beggin' for a glass of water right now." When the miner asked, "Are you in this business too," Dos Passos replied that he was a writer, and that "writers were people who stayed on the sidelines as long as they could. They were sympathizers."

The young man looked disappointed. "I thought maybe you was a lodgemember, in for a revolution too . . . because I'm in it . . . up to the neck." By this time, it was dark and Dos Passos could barely discern the face of the youth. Dos Passos wondered what he was thinking. He also realized that he had defined once more what his own position was. In recent months he had called himself "progressive radical" and "middle-class liberal." He could be a treasurer of one committee or a chairman of another; he could be a fund-raiser through a few strokes of a pen or an ad hoc committee investigator for five days in the remote hills of Kentucky. He could sympathize and empathize; he could hate and castigate. But what it all boiled down to—the great leveler—was that he stood by the sidelines, not as a spectator, a writer only, but as a coach. The world provided the occasions and he—and others like him—the protest. Dos Passos' senses absorbed and refracted. He had opinions and attitudes, but he was a man in motion; a stance would have slowed him down. He would travel with his fellows, but never sign his name on the dotted line.

The Dreiser committee stayed five days in Kentucky, then returned to write and publish their findings. The major official document of the group appeared March 31, 1932, as the *Harlan Miners Speak*, a slim volume published by Harcourt, Brace, the house to which Dos Passos had moved with his *1919* manuscript. Dos Passos did the major editing, and along with other members of the National Committee for Defense of Political Prisoners, contributed individual essays. He also published two articles in *The New Republic:* "Harlan: Working Under the Gun" (December 2, 1931) and "In Defense of Kentucky" (December 16, 1931). For the first issue of a new magazine, *The Student Review*, he contributed "Free Speech Speakin'" (January–February 1932); "Harlan County Sunset" appeared in a collection of pieces published under the title *In All Countries* (1934). Another important airing of the stench in eastern Kentucky was by another member of the Dreiser committee, Charles R. Walker, Dos Passos' friend, whose " 'Red' Blood in Kentucky: Why 100% Americans Turn Communist," appeared in *The Forum* (January 1932).

The New York *Herald Tribune* provided immediate and widespread coverage of the committee's efforts and findings in two articles—featuring photographs of Dos Passos and Dreiser—entitled "Kentucky Indicts Dreiser and 9 as Syndicalists" and "Dreiser Group Opens Attack on Extradition" (November 17, 1931). The Bell County Circuit Court of Kentucky heard testimony that "the snake doctors from New York"—the Dreiser group —had suggested "disorders and resistance to the governments of the United States and of Kentucky" in direct violation of the state's criminal syndicalism law. Each member of the committee, two newsmen, the stenographer, and Dreiser's companion, Marie Pergain—all found themselves indicted for criminal syndicalism and promulgating "a reign of terror" in the coal fields. Under Kentucky law each offender could be fined ten thousand dollars and sentenced to prison for up to twenty-one years. Earl Browder, head of the Communist Central Committee, tried to convince Dos Passos to return to Kentucky to stand trial. The resultant publicity would serve their cause well, Browder insisted. Dos Passos was put off by Browder's "sneering tone" regarding his being a liberal and told him: "If they want me badly enough, they'll find me waiting quietly at home." What Dos Passos considered the "cheap shot in the whole affair" was Dreiser's being indicted for adultery along with the criminal syndicalism charge. So, too, was his alleged paramour. The New York *Herald Tribune* reported:

> Judge Jones's first crude attempt to drag a red herring across the trail of the committee's findings of official murder, dynamiting, kidnaping and tyranny in Harlan County was a charge of adultery brought against Theodore Dreiser based upon the statement of toothpick snoopers and amateur detectives. This charge proved to be a boomerang. It only centered more attention on Judge Jones's illegal conduct on the bench and the whole machinery of gunman terror and thug rule in these coal-company owned mining towns.

Dreiser reportedly confounded everyone by declaring that he was old and impotent; therefore, "nothing immoral could have happened."

In February 1932 a delegation of the Independent Miners' Relief Committee, led by Waldo Frank, went into Harlan County with several truckloads of food and clothing. Accompanying Frank were Mary Heaton Vorse, Edmund Wilson, Malcolm Cowley, Elsie Reed Mitchell (a retired medical doctor), and Quincy Howe. On hand to greet them was Allen Taub, an International Labor Defense lawyer. A number of other liberals and leftists were involved behind the scenes, including Charles and Adelaide Walker—who risked being arrested if they reentered Harlan County after being charged with criminal syndicalism—and Sherwood Anderson, whose publicity regarding the whole affair exceeded any physical embroilment. In the spring a delegation of pastors, several groups of students, and a committee of attorneys sponsored by the American Civil Liberties Union —which had offered to defend any member of the Dreiser committee if he chose to stand trial—also went to Harlan County. The combined efforts of these groups helped put into motion an investigation by a subcommittee of the United States Senate. The plight of the miners was temporarily relieved, but they returned to the mines with almost no concessions by their employers. Objective reporters contended that the National Miners' Union acted irresponsibly in regard to the faithful few who were miners themselves in the

Harlan region. By the winter of 1932–33, there was not a union member in the mines and the "Red Union" looked elsewhere to further its aims.

Dos Passos himself remained active as chairman of the National Committee to Aid Striking Miners Fighting Starvation until early spring of 1932. Both in January and February he sent out letters calling for additional help: "Shoeless children are school-less children. Many lack even underwear. Thru the gray of any morning one can see a group of mourners behind a shack—a gash in the mountainside, a little pine coffin lowered into the earth, and the earth close around the remains of a child that did not have a chance to live. Can you give something to help bring food to the mouths of these freezing, starving children?" Countersigning the plea were the names of Dos Passos' fellow committee members: Sherwood Anderson, Roger Baldwin, Floyd Dell, Babette Deutsch, Clifton Fadiman, Waldo Frank, Michael Gold, Charles Yale Harrison, Sidney Hook, Corliss Lamont, Melvin P. Levy, Robert Morss Lovett, Lewis Mumford, Samuel Ornitz, Anna Rochester, Upton Sinclair, Lincoln Steffens, Genevieve Taggard, Mary Heaton Vorse, Charles R. Walker, and some thirty more. The document read like a "Leftist Who's Who" in answer to the "Park Avenue Four Hundred."

Edmund Wilson had been staying in Susan Glaspell's home during the fall and early winter of 1931. He had left his wife temporarily in California to return East to put his daughter, Rosalind, in school. When their spouses were elsewhere, Wilson and Katy often kept each other company. Dos Passos, by the very nature of his out-of-town missions and investigative reporting, was away frequently. They worried about each other inordinately when apart. He had not had a serious flare-up of his rheumatics in almost a decade, but he had been careful of his health and tried to be in more temperate climates than the Cape and New York afforded during the coldest weeks of winter. Katy was much given to colds and tonsillitis, accompanied by a rasping cough. She had smoked for many years, as did Dos Passos and everyone else in the Smooley household. Most of their friends thought of Katy as the frail one in the crowd and wondered how she kept up with her husband's seemingly effortless strides. Upon observing them in Mexico the preceding winter, Carlton Beals noted that Dos Passos appeared to have "a sublime indifference to Katy. His head was full of so many things that he was forever marching off. It must have taxed Katy to keep up. Just when Dos seemed striding off to grab a star, he would unexpectedly show Katy bluff tenderness and concern." Beals concluded that they "understood each other uncommonly well."

When Katy felt poorly, she usually mentioned it casually to Dos Passos with a twist of humor. In a letter addressed to "Bat-Ears darling" on September 20, 1931, she said she was leaving Wiscasset for Boston to see Dr. Robert Minor "in his white coat and two blond nurses in white dresses and chromium porcelain trimmings and attendant and switchboard girl chorus in white with rubber soles all singing 'Who's the case Get her card He charges more than she can afford'—but I think better go because tooth says so." Katy's letters to Dos Passos were almost always playful. She bantered her devotion with such exclamations as "Oh my adored Ape! Am sending a thousand kisses ahead in track-pants." When apart they wrote each other three or four times a week and shot telegrams back and forth to announce comings and goings or to update an address at which they could be reached. Katy's letter from Wiscasset closed with "I'll write where to wire in

Boston," yet she was only going to be there to see her dentist, whom she said she was also wiring. "I am wiring right and left and feel so important—almost like an Organization. Almost wired Shanghai. Adieu thou M. Fish, with love," signed "The Home Office, Kitty Kate-Face, Secretary to the President." Her letters were cleverer than his, filled with anecdotes about their friends, vignettes, bits of innocent gossip. She exaggerated, but there was never any doubt regarding what she meant to be taken as truth.

While Dos Passos was in Harlan County, Katy wrote:

> All the troops back here are pretty frantic for a message. Here comes a wire from you this minute! Oh Gee I would like to come to New York but better not as would only get drunk and throw money away—and am getting drunk here and saving money hand over fist as am fed by charity all over town. . . . Dr. Antichrist [Edmund Wilson] gives me a hot breakfast every morning, also lunch, and evenings I have Hapgood stew, Shay beans, Miller steak, Spencer duck, Parmenter roast, Clymer cutlets, and Kaselau cold meats. . . . Dr. Antichrist is a big white dove and spiritual advisor and yesterday spent the whole afternoon digging at Truro. We planted two large trees and two bushes and all the currants and gooseberries, but Oh Ape I forgot entirely where you said they were to go and you may tear them all up by the roots and me too when you get home. Don't strike me please. Oh Mr. Dos Passos I love you so much—remember you perfectly.

Three days later, she wrote:

> I am on the hermit side now after a brief whirl and won't see anyone but Dr. AntiChrist who feeds and cares for me—his little bride Margaret has disappeared in California and if you don't return before long Dr. AntiChrist and I will get married as both lonely hearts and congenial. . . . Hutch Hapgood has discovered a prophecy in an old Egyptian pyramid which says that the depression won't be over till 1936 with years and catastrophies piling up all the time—after that the millennium. Gee I hope we can last through. I should hate to be taken just before beer begins running in the streets and they lead milkwhite heifers down Fifth Avenue with garlands around their necks and roses scattering down from aeroplanes. A wind is coming up howling from the south, white water outside and the sky gray and squally. Gulls blowing and mewing, tide over the bulkhead. I'm in wild rough-weather spirits and wish you were here—we would go walking—don't think from that that I'm in any condition to go walking. I'm full of little snuffy sneezes like ballroom bananas and trimmed with shivers and bone aches. Oh dear I shall never cease to regret the loss of my health. Think I will go and get a little rum. A big shot with hot water and lemon over at AntiChrist's would be the wisest thing I could do. But oh dear I do not like the taste of rum.

She also spoke of having just read some of his *1919* manuscript:

> Oh M. Fish what a splendid slab of writing you done in Benny [the character Ben Compton]. Pure sirloin all through. . . . Tears ran off my nose where they beat them up at Everett. . . . And I never felt in anything I ever read about labor before that fierce beaten-down energy and struggle—as if you'd raked off all the slag and ashes of newspaper bunk and dead communist vocabulary and showed the live hot coals spreading underneath like a fire in a ship's hold. I think it's a scaly dragon of a section. . . . Dr. AntiChrist was talking about 1919 and said to me in a fierce squeak: Well it may well be a masterpiece. . . . How did he know?

Katy's own writing as a fictionist had gone by the boards during their early marriage. In the old days of Smooley Hall, Edith Foley, Stella Roof, and her brother Bill had shared with her the responsibilities of running the house, but with Smith only in residence occasionally and Dos Passos and Katy the primary occupants now, the brunt of its operation fell upon her. It took considerable time to see to the affairs of two households. Even when they were ensconced in one, there was always something to be done to the house or grounds of the other, and Katy often tore back and forth between them. Living in the dunes during the summer months was the main reason they had purchased a car. She also helped Dos Passos with details pertaining to his professional life. When his agent wired that publication of *1919* was being held up in London because of discrepancies between the British and American editions, Dos Passos was out of town; it was Katy who recovered the missing pages. He often wrote or wired her to locate certain documents, books, and other resource materials from among his things—or to borrow them from friends or libraries—and to forward them to his next destination. Although she did not type his manuscripts, she kept track of negotiations involving subsidiary rights, paid bills, dealt with creditors (no small matter), and shopped for food and other essentials in their daily lives.

Taking care of their pets was no small task either. Their black standard poodle, whom Katy called Liza-poodle, insisted on going everywhere they did. As soon as Dos Passos or Katy picked up the keys, Liza-poodle raced to the car to hitch a ride. Provincetowners were accustomed to seeing her perched on the narrow running board of the roadster as it traversed the lower Cape. When Katy and Dos Passos stopped at a restaurant, Liza-poodle waited outside near the car until Katy cracked the door and signaled that the coast was clear. Then the dog darted in and hid under the skirts of the tablecloth until meal's end. Other diners were unaware of her presence, even when she accepted handouts from beneath the table. Katy also bred Siamese cats. Although she usually sold the kittens, she never thought of her menagerie as a business venture. All the animals had names and were considered part of the family. Edmund Wilson, who was sometimes chided as the owner of a scrubby, ill-kempt dog, admired Katy's big, tawny Siamese. He told in his diary of observing the cat weaving in and out among the porcelain pitchers and other dishes like a snake without "so much as a rattle from the shelf." Visitors seldom came twice to the Dos Passos home if they were put off by animals. When writer Edward Dahlberg called upon them during the winter of 1931–32, it was not just the cat or Liza-poodle or her pups—Poof and Toto Blacknose—that rankled him; rather, he was offended by Dos Passos' having shown more interest in his animals than in his guest. Dahlberg had written a first novel, *Bottom Dogs* (published the same day as *The 42nd Parallel*) that was either ignored by the critics or dismissed as unimportant. Only Edmund Wilson had given the novel a boost with a few kind words in *The New Republic*. Later, seeking to help Dahlberg further, Wilson suggested that he work on his new novel in Provincetown, where Dos Passos would introduce him to the literary life on the Cape. Wilson's imp of the perverse may well have enjoyed contemplating such a meeting, since he knew Dahlberg relished talk of books and ideas and liked picking the minds of intellects and scholars. Dahlberg was offensively pedantic and considered most of his contemporaries "mediocre scribblers."

According to Eben Given, present at Dahlberg's first meeting with Dos Passos:

> The man came to the house intent on engaging Dos in earnest conversation regarding the aesthetics of literature. Dos welcomed him graciously, showed him to a chair, then addressed Liza-poodle. "Here Liza," he said, and Liza dropped to his side to be stroked and made over. Suddenly an interior door swung open with Katy's Siamese dangling from the doorknob. The cat dropped to the floor with a thud, snubbed Dahlberg, and leaped over the poodle into Dos's lap. Dos launched in on the cat's aversion to closed doors, whereupon Dahlberg leaped to his feet and beat a hasty exit. Moments later, there was a demanding knock, and Dahlberg was back at the door glowering in the dark, his eyes flashing red, nostrils distended. "I came for a serious discussion of *belles lettres* with a prominent writer, yet all I've witnessed is a three-ring circus!" he sputtered, then disappeared into the night.

Dahlberg's version of their meeting in his published memoirs differed from Given's, but his impression of Dos Passos was similar:

> My first meeting with Dos Passos was at a party. Looking for a heretic and an icon-breaker I was surprised to be in the presence of a pleasant unoriginal man, quite myopic, and with a levantine bald-looking face. I made a grave mistake: I tried to talk to him about *belles lettres*. The writing and painting roisterers seated at the table looked at me with hostility. Earnest conversation had died long ago, and what clearer proof is there than the fiction of these ephebes. Seldom is a tedious man an entertaining author. . . . I realized nobody was supposed to do anything at these bibulous soirées except vomit, fall on the floor or insult somebody. Incensed, I later wrote Dos Passos a waspish letter which became the *scandale* of the Provincetown Bohemians. One day he came to my studio and informed me he was far more interested in what a grocer had to say than in the conceptions of a novelist. . . . After that I saw Dos Passos several times, and I liked him. He did not lack probity; he spoke out of the shallows because he was mediocre, and he could do nothing else unless he were a hypocrite. I think he feared putting on airs.

Years after the initial Provincetown meeting, Dahlberg damned all "advocates of bestial provincial scribblers like Dos Passos, Faulkner, Hemingway, and those who have received the laurels while other books that are truthful are starved to death in limbo. Dos Passos used to tell me that he preferred to talk to the grocer rather than converse with an author. But Dos Passos is a lowly clerk himself of literature, and his own conversation was never any addition to one's mind."

In February 1932, Dos Passos accompanied John Peale Bishop on a fishing expedition to Nova Scotia, which he parlayed into an essay for inclusion in his next book, *In All Countries,* and later, into a long, atypical piece entitled "Atlantic Fisheries," published anonymously in *Fortune.* For a week he cruised from Boston to Halifax and back over the various western and northern banks aboard a trawler that took aboard hundreds of thousands of pounds of fish. The squat little boat pitched and bucked in the heavy surf, forcing a seasick Dos Passos to his bunk for a time, but when it snowed during their journey, and the wet rigging iced up, he gamely stayed on deck to watch the crew boat its catch. The raw pungent air chilled his rheumatic joints, and he vowed to head South as soon as he returned to Provincetown to meet Katy and take her with him. Hemingway urged him to come to Key West. His friend, Charles Thompson, had a cook who ate parched buzzard bones to cure rheumatism, wrote Hemingway. "There are plenty of buzzards in Key West," he added. "Like to try some?" If a serious health problem was in the making, Dos Passos' trip South warded it off. Trolling for sailfish for three days with Hemingway, Bra Saunders, and Katy in the balmy breezes of the Gulf Stream was far more to his liking than the bitter cold of the great northern banks. He said later that this particular interlude with Hemingway was better than any of his previous fishing cruises had been. One of the things he had done at sea this trip was to read the entire manuscript of Hemingway's recently completed *Death in the Afternoon*. The book was "hellishly good" and the "language magnificently used," he wrote Hemingway upon his departure. "I kept having the feeling I was reading a classic . . . like Rabelais or Harvey's <u>Circulation of the Blood</u>. . . . That's a hell of a good way to feel about a book not even published yet." It was the best thing Hemingway had done, he ventured, but suggested that his criticism of Waldo Frank be tempered. "God knows he ought to be deflated—at least <u>Virgin Spain</u>— but why not put it on the book basis instead of the entire lecturer?" He also admitted being put off by Hemingway's having "strapped on the longwhite whiskers" to "give the boys the lowdown about writing. . . . Don't you think that's all secrets of the profession —like plaster of Paris in a glove—and oughtn't to be spilt to the vulgar?" Two months later Hemingway reported that he had worked over the manuscript seven times and cut out everything to which Dos Passos objected. "Seemed like the best to me—God damn you if it really was," he added.

Upon leaving Key West, Dos Passos and Katy returned by steamship to Havana, then on to the port city of Progreso on the Yucatán Peninsula for a week-long excursion to the site of the pre-Columbian Mayan ruins. Katy turned the trip into an extensive travel piece for *Woman's Home Companion*. Although she combined their trip the preceding winter with the present one, a reader of her "Just over the Border" article could follow closely their trampings over the entire Mexican countryside. They were in Mexico when Harcourt, Brace brought out *1919* on March 14, 1932. His being out of the country when a new novel was published was more than a ploy to avoid the critics. It was also a case of moving on to something else and having no intention of sitting around palavering about what he had already done. He was in France when *One Man's Initiation* and *Manhattan Transfer* appeared, in Persia at the publication of *Three Soldiers*, and in Spain for *The 42nd Parallel*. In each case, he was already drawing upon his new adventures for an article or book of essays or stockpiling them in the form of a diary until metamorphosed into fiction.

They had intended originally to leave Mexico and return directly to Provincetown in April, but on reaching Tucson, they detrained from the "much too expensive Pullman" and bought a dilapidated Chrysler roadster in which to drive to California to see Jack Lawson, who had not abandoned the idea of attracting Dos Passos to Hollywood to write for M-G-M. Dos Passos had no intention of becoming a scriptwriter, but looked forward to seeing Lawson and other monied people who were faring splendidly in the West while the nation's economy spiraled downward. Traveling across country by automobile enabled him to take the pulse of the people from different economic classes. He already was at work on the sequel to *1919, The Big Money* (it was considerably later before he committed himself to the phrase as a title). This time he wanted his fictional landscape to stretch across the entire continent as he juxtaposed the exploiters with the exploited. He poked into corners, peered into their faces, pored over newspapers, observed, questioned, and gathered his facts and anecdotes as best he could in an attempt to winnow truth from the chaff of propaganda. By mid-May he was impatient to get home to Provincetown to begin pulling together some of the disparate strands of his note taking and narrative. In a breezy letter to Hemingway, Dos Passos wrote: "A lot of the characters are climbing out of windows already and I'm barely under weigh on last tome. You're damn right, the Angel of Death is the novelist's only friend. Flu and machine guns will do the rest. Whole trouble with the opus is too many drawing room bitches—never again—it's like fairies getting into a bar—ruin it in no time."

Dos Passos was far more interested in what his friends had to say about *1919* than what the critics liked or rejected, but was not naive enough to think reviews did not matter. Good ones enhanced sales, a fact not to be sneezed at during depressed times. Yet he disclaimed ever learning anything from the critics that he found useful. What Hemingway thought of the book was important to him: "The book is bloody splendid . . . four times the book The 42nd Parallel was—and that was damned good. You write so damn well it spooks me that something might happen to you," said Hemingway after finishing the book that spring. Just as Dos Passos had offered advice concerning *The Torrents of Spring, The Sun Also Rises,* and *Death in the Afternoon,* so too did Hemingway advise Dos Passos: "Watch one thing—in the third volume don't let yourself slip and get any perfect characters in—no Stephen Daedeluses—remember, it was Bloom and Mrs. Bloom saved Joyce. . . . If you get a noble Communist remember the bastard probably masturbates and is jealous as a cat—at least he has piles—weak eyes won't save him. Keep them people, people, people, and don't let them get to be symbols—remember the race is older than the economic system." Hemingway also reminded him to get weather into his "goddamned book." While in Key West, Dos Passos had borrowed two hundred dollars from Hemingway, knowing that he could repay it from a royalty check expected any day from Brandt and Brandt. Actually, he had written his own check to Hemingway to cover the loan before leaving for Mexico, yet when Hemingway cashed it, it bounced. Hemingway apprised Dos Passos of the returned check, but said he had torn it up and wanted to think of the debt as an investment. "Having a 200-seed stake in the goddamned fine way" Dos Passos was writing was payment enough, he volunteered. Although Hemingway may have enjoyed the gesture of having written off the money in the name of friendship and admiration for a fellow writer, he did not fail to deposit the debt in his memory bank as a demand note to be called at will. Despite his apparent generosity, there was usually a *quid pro quo* lurking in the background. Hemingway's comment to Dos Passos in 1932—his desire to have a "stake" in him as a writer—revealed his then incipient code of compensation. Several years later, Hemingway struck out angrily at Dos Passos over an incident having nothing to do with finances, yet couched his grievance as a much abused creditor who had decided at last to call for a long-overdue note.

A letter awaiting Dos Passos' return evoked a voice from the past. " 'A nice book' thought I of The 42nd Parallel but thought no more," wrote Tad Edwards from New

York on Lotos Club stationery on the publication day of *1919*. Edwards told him that upon reading a review of the book, he had gasped: "It must be the same Dos Passos—he of the fluent French that produced tough chicken dinners from peasant women. Maybe you will remember the sixteen-year-old innocent in S.S.O. #60. But here's something you don't know: I have a perfectly glorious pencil sketch of you lying quite plastered under a tree in Bois de Recicourt—empty bottle beside you." Edwards vowed to send the drawing to *The Graphic* or *The Mirror* unless Dos Passos promised to meet him for lunch and autograph his copy of *1919*.

Another letter awaiting Dos Passos upon his return to Provincetown in the spring of 1932 was from Blaise Cendrars, who claimed to have read *1919* in a single evening:

> What a reading! Thank you, thank you. It is every bit as delightful as the 42nd, although more monotonous since it lacks the pleasant surprise of form already given in the first volume. The Newsreels create less atmosphere because they are no longer like labels in time to distance the reader but parasitic noises, like echoes, which reverberate on and whose selection seems for that reason more arbitrary. As a story I very much like Daughter, in particular her departure by plane. I wonder how you managed to pull off this sort of stenography which is both audient and in relief and reshapes all of life for those who are voluntarily deaf and blind—all the while avoiding becoming a writing technique; in that way 1919 is really superior to 42nd and I do admire you with all my strength. For me a real feast is the ineluctable pessimism which saps the activity of all your characters and renders them ferocious—all, without a single exception—a physical (as opposed to metaphysical) pessimism which you recorded as the only evidence of life in all its human forms. That's why, despite all the party lines and despite perhaps your own personal view, this book, for me, will never be an indictment and that is the misunderstanding which awaits. I wonder how this book will be received in America.

Matthew Josephson apologized to Dos Passos for the "hatchet job" by Henry S. Canby in cutting four hundred words from his review in *The Saturday Review of Literature*. Canby had excised the core itself of his essay, lamented Josephson, because "it was angry and likened you in your attitude to George Grosz, who paints bourgeois people with pig snouts and transparent trousers and underwear." The book was unquestionably the "strongest American novel" he had read in many years, continued Josephson. "More than any of us, you have seen ahead of the times. I was delighted when Harcourt told me it was selling better than anything else around the place."

Upton Sinclair's assessment was a terse "1919 is bully" and urged Dos Passos to add to his J. P. Morgan sketch that when Morgan "wanted a woman, he tapped her on the shoulder, like King Edward VII, and no one ever refused him. He liked to undress himself, and to have them terrified, so that he could tear their clothes (ask Lincoln Steffens!). One society lady had a little cottage at Newport, who built a million dollar pier in front of it for his royal convenience. And when other children would jeer at her children, because they lived in a little cottage, the answer would be: 'But you haven't got any pier!' " Sinclair suggested that Dos Passos might also like to pass his comments along to *Harper's*.

Word had already traveled the literary grapevine regarding Dos Passos' break with Harper & Brothers. Actually, had the biographical sketch of J. P. Morgan, juxtaposed with an admiring portrait of Randolph Bourne—a hero among leftist intellectuals—not been published in *The New Masses* in November, it might have slipped through Harper & Brothers and not caught the publisher's wary eye until too late for excision before publication. All but one of the minibiographies had been published before the book itself appeared: six in *The New Masses* (which also published the portraits of John Reed, Joe Hill, Wesley Everest, and "The Body of an American") and two in *The New Republic,* "Meester Veelson" (Woodrow Wilson) and "A Hoosier Quixote" (Paxton Hibben). Only the Teddy Roosevelt portrait, "The Happy Warrior," had not been published before the book itself appeared. *The New Masses* also carried two "Camera Eyes" (41 and 42). Four other "Camera Eyes" (24, 29, 34, and 39) were published in *The Hound and Horn,* and *Pagany* published the four "Eveline Hutchins" narrative sections—all before Harcourt, Brace brought out *1919.* Dos Passos derived more income from these prepublication pieces than from any other periodical sales of a comparable period to date.

The novel appeared with considerable fanfare, and critics reviewed it positively, for the most part. Yet overall sales were poor, and the book failed to go into a second printing. Malcolm Cowley called *1919* "a landmark of American fiction" in his review for *The New Republic.* His only reservation concerned the "Camera Eyes," which prompted Hemingway to advise: "Don't let a twirp like Cowley shake your confidence in those damned swell Camera Eyes. Remember how nosepicking all those twirps were when we were all out seeing the bloody world—remember how lousy worried you were about 1919 and it turned out so damned bloody fine. Also none of it makes a godamned bit of difference." Henry Hazlitt apprised readers of *The Nation* that *1919* was superior to *The 42nd Parallel,* "which was itself the outstanding American novel of 1930." Dos Passos' books had more to offer than Hemingway's, though they were akin in tone, said Hazlitt; moreover, compared to Upton Sinclair's "wax dummies," Dos Passos' characters were "alive and convincing." Hazlitt also cited Dos Passos' "range of sympathy" as a strong point and thought the author without peer in his "awareness of American life." John Chamberlain, the New York *Times*'s first daily book reviewer, compared Dos Passos to Wilder, Hemingway, and Fitzgerald and praised him as the most adventurous, the most widely experienced, and the "man with the broadest sympathies" of all the novelists. "The language of *1919* is really a literary language" despite its "clichés, vulgarisms, curses, illiterate ellipses and shorthands of speech," continued Chamberlain. "Dos Passos has quintessentialized and distilled, compressed and foreshortened, until he is able to give the overtones of common chatter without resorting to a dreary literalism."

Lawrence Leighton insisted in his review of *1919* in *The Hound and Horn* that "in Dos Passos' ant-like accumulation of detail and forlorn liberalness there is a suggestion that he has come to be like the loathed object he looks upon." Leighton saw no "quality of imagination of divination other than the humdrum workings of the ordinary bourgeois mind" in his latest novel or in *Manhattan Transfer* or *The 42nd Parallel.*

Leftist reviewers and critics in the Soviet Union expressed hope that the book would fan radicals to give more than lip service to the Communist cause. Most of Dos Passos' fellow-traveling countrymen were not that explicit. Granville Hicks, reviewing the novel for *Bookman,* applauded Dos Passos' "revolutionary vision," which he saw as a "framework for understanding" (Hicks himself became a card-carrying Communist in 1934). Michael Gold presented a Marxist analysis of Dos Passos for *The English Journal.* He saw the first two panels of Dos Passos' panoramic novel as a beginning of the new man. "He is winning a struggle against himself" and his aristocratic heritage, said Gold; "these novels are the first fruits of victory of the militant collectivist." In the 1932 summer issue of *The Modern Quarterly,* editor V. F. Calverton presented answers to the "Whither the American Writer" questionnaire submitted to such authors and critics as Dos Passos, Anderson, Bates, Canby, Chamberlain, Cowley, Dell, Hazlitt, Hicks, and Fadiman. Dos Passos' responses were given the lead position in the piece: "Sure," he believed that American capitalism was doomed to inevitable failure and collapse; the question was when. "We've got the failure. . . . What I don't see is the collapse." He saw American capitalism changing "pretty radically . . . into a centralized plutocracy like that of ancient Rome. Ten years seems a pretty short time for that to ripen and drop off the tree. . . . Of course if enough guys shake the tree . . ." When asked about the relationship between a writer's work and the radical political party, he replied: "Some people are natural party men and others are natural scavengers and campfollowers. Matter of temperament. I personally belong to the scavenger and campfollower section." A writer's feelings regarding the party's philosophy is "his own goddam business." He did not see how a novelist or historian could be a party member under present conditions. "The Communist party ought to produce some good pamphleteers or poets . . . [but] where are they?" There was no way that becoming a communist or a socialist "could deepen an artist's work. . . . I personally think the socialists and all other radicals have their usefulness, but I should think that becoming a socialist right now would have just about the same effect on anybody as drinking a bottle of near-beer."

Dos Passos' final comment prompted Fredericka Pisek Field to criticize him publicly in her magazine, *The Golden Book,* to which he replied: "In quoting my very feeble crack at the American Socialist Party, out of my reply to Calverton's questionnaire, you twisted its meaning completely around. I don't see how you can have failed to notice that what I intended was that the Socialist Party was near beer in distinction to the Communist Party (good 7¹/2%). However much we may cavil at the Communists they mean it when they say they are fighting for socialism, i.e., the cooperative commonwealth."

The Soviet Union intelligentsia had no intention of sitting quietly by while Dos Passos charted his course among the scavengers and camp followers. They were looking for a standard-bearer and did everything they could to promote Dos Passos to the vanguard position. *Literary Digest* publicized in its July 9 (1932) issue a news item picked up from a French magazine, *Comoedia,* reporting on the preferences of Soviet writers for books produced abroad. The five leading Soviet writers of the period were named, but no work was cited so frequently as *The 42nd Parallel.* Scattered votes went to Joyce, Proust, Dickens, and Erwin Kisch (a German reporter). *"Literaturnaya Gazeta* accords almost supreme preference to John Dos Passos," concluded the piece in *Literary Digest. Living Age* published in its "Letters and the Arts" feature (October 1932) a long, adulatory statement by the editors of the journal *Literature of the World Revolution* addressed to "Dear Comrade." The letter revealed a substantial knowledge of what Dos Passos had written to date and called on the dedication of his pen to "actively expose and fight the tactics of capitalism. We count you as our friend, that is, a friend of our task. And we hope that you will come forward at once in the press as Romain Rolland did against the new tactics of imperalism, which is planning a new world war in the east and an attack on the Soviet Union."

Dos Passos also began receiving letters from people he had met in Moscow in 1928 who had been following his career since *Manhattan Transfer* and told him that the characters Jimmy Herf and Elaine (in *Manhattan Transfer)* were as familiar to the man on the street in Moscow as those in any Pushkin novel. Dos Passos had become the Soviet's star in the West, and they wanted him to know it. His friend Aleksandr Fadeev wrote that *1919* was being serialized in the magazine *Zvezda (The Star)*. "It persuades me once more that your literary work is making a new epoch in the history of the world literature. . . . We are sympathetically watching your heroic fight for the working class —we know it to be the source of your creative growth. We remember you as you were living here with us and attentively observing the life of the Soviet Union. We expect very much from your future work."

Another "Dear Comrade" letter from Moscow came from fellow American Walt Carmon, formerly managing editor of *The New Masses* and now an official in the International Union of Revolutionary Writers (I.U.R.W.), which had begun directing the activities of the John Reed Club: "Everyone here that reads, and they all do, have been reading and admiring everything you have written. I've heard talk of hardly any American's work but yours in fact. . . . You, Dreiser, Anderson, Frank and Mike [Gold]. But while they know a good deal of what the others have written they seem to know every word of yours. Your 1919 particularly is admired tremendously."

Dos Passos did not save all of his "Dear Comrade" letters, but one that did survive came from James McCann, a convict with a literary bent who served four years in San Quentin and was still in residence when he wrote: "1919 is the most realistic piece of writing that has ever crossed my bows":

> I have the first and only copy that has come into this stir so far, that in itself is an honor. . . . Damn few people will realize the depth and intensity of your book. It's too vast for their puny brains. But you may rest assured this dingbat convict read every word, was admirably entertained in some places, amazed at your temerity in others, and burnt up in still other spots when you skated along giving fact after fact, slambanging about with gusto and making the sparks fly. . . . With each chapter in 1919 you swung your work along at a higher and higher pitch until you smashed the peak with a loud crescendo, which, I might add, almost made me break outta this joint. Joe Williams, I know hundreds of them, have eaten with them, worked alongside them on tankers, cargo ships and got drunk with them in France, Germany, England, Holland. . . . John Reed is excellently done. . . . Not for nothing did they select you as one of the bigshots of the J. R. Clubs. And not for nothing are the same clubs springing up all over the land. . . . This last work makes you stand alone, the greatest of America's proletarian writers, fit to head the John Reed club, fit to claim the title, and able to write still other books like this one. On behalf of those workers and criminals incarcerated I want to thank you for a piece of literature that has never been approached in this land. Carry on, comrade.

Upon McCann's request, Dos Passos sent him a copy of *1919.* Then McCann told him that he had read all his books except the two he had never laid eyes on: *A Pushcart at the*

Curb and *The Garbage Man*. "Some mutt clouted my copy of The 42nd Parallel but I still have The Orient Express left. I can't find the damn thing anywhere and none of the guys who read my books have it so I guess I'll just have to mourn my loss, unless I can talk you outta nother one." In a second letter from McCann a few months later, Dos Passos was asked: "Are you going to make a trilogy of 42nd and 1919? It appears to me that another one, giving all the dope up to the depression would be very appropriate. . . . Sinclair has gone haywire, Lewis is not interested, Dreiser lives in the past, and Jack London is dead. It's up to you, me lad."

On June 10, Dos Passos traveled to Washington, D.C., on assignment for *The New Republic* to see how some twenty-two hundred veterans of the war were faring around their makeshift breakfast tables on the edge of a flimsy encampment of tents and tar-paper and packing-crate shelters beside the muddy Anacostia River in the southeastern district of the city. A "bonus army" of veterans calling itself the B.E.F. (Bonus Expeditionary Forces) straggled in droves that summer from the four points of the compass in dilapidated cars, buses, and trains. Some were loosely organized into companies and battalions bearing the names of the cities from which they had come. Others carried placards on which two words—THE REDS—were scrawled. The Cleveland Bonus Veterans commandeered a locomotive after railroad bosses refused them transportation to Washington in freight cars. All sought the public's attention and congressional action to alleviate their plight by giving them their "survival bonuses" early. Since veterans were already receiving pensions or other compensation such as tax exemption and priority over nonveteran civilians in their scramble for jobs, the American Legion and other veteran organizations were fearful of a backlash that might jeopardize their own tenuous gains. Gladwin Bland, on whom Dos Passos had modeled Fenian McCreary, his "Mac" character in *The 42nd Parallel,* showed up in Washington the end of June and wrote Dos Passos of the situation as he encountered it:

> The sight of the veterans camped about the city was suggestive of an immense hobo jungle. The makeshift shelters erected on lots in most cases covered with debris, took me back to the days in Frisco after the quake—The jungling up at that time, to use an insurance term, was caused by an act of God, but in the case of Washington the blame could not very well be hung on "pink whiskers." I attempted to enlighten a few of my fellow veterans as to the cause for their plight but they kind of backed away declaring: "Oh the hell with the Red propaganda." Most all the camps had signs posted which disclaimed any connection or sympathy with The Reds, poor misguided devils. . . . The only support or sympathy the Bonus Army received from Locals or camps of Veteran organizations was from those in which the radical element dominated.

Dos Passos' treatment of the veterans' predicament for *The New Republic* was muted, his words noninflammatory, but his call for action was unmistakable. It would take more than a few veteran bonuses to cast off the slough of despair and revitalize the country, he said. The piece concluded with a conversation overheard in a Washington streetcar between two mail carriers and the conductor:

> "Well, they say they'll stay here till they get the bonus if they have to stay here till 1945. . . . I guess they ought to get it all right, but how'll that help all the others out of work? . . .

Terrible to think of men, women and children starving and having to beg charity relief with all the stuff there is going to waste in this country." . . . Then began the stock conversation of this year 1932 about farmers not shipping apples, cabbage, potatoes, because they couldn't get any price, about loads of fresh fish dumped overboard, trainloads of milk poured out and babies crying for it. One of the mail carriers was from Texas and had just come back from a trip home. He'd seen them plowing under last year's unharvested cotton. "We got the food, we got the clothing, we got the man power, we got the brains," he said. "There must be some remedy."

What Dos Passos did not anticipate was Hoover's remedy. Fed up with the entire affair and convinced that he would have a hard time being reelected if the unemployed veterans, their numbers mounting steadily, were allowed to continue their roost in his own presidential yard, Hoover called for federal troops to replace the city's weary police force. General Douglas MacArthur's minutemen burned lean-tos, trampled tents, pulled down the speaker's platform that rose like a crow's nest over "shack city" on Anacostia Flats, and moved in with tanks to evict squatters from temporary federal buildings under orders at the time to be demolished. MacArthur's men routed the veterans with billy clubs, bayonets, and tear gas, and drove them limping and bloody from the city. MacArthur's chief aide was Dwight David Eisenhower, a young West Point major. Later, political analysts had no difficulty agreeing that Hoover's order was the most indefensible political blunder of his career.

Dos Passos, still on assignment for *The New Republic,* traveled directly to Chicago from Washington, D.C., to cover the Republican and Democratic conventions and with deft strokes ridiculed the antics and manipulative gestures of each party as it moved into high gear to seat its helmsman before losing the attention and good will of its delegates. The Republican rally he likened to a Barnum and Bailey spectacular poorly choreographed for a hearty troop of trained sea lions, neckless puppets, and marionettes. "The show goes on smoothly," reported Dos Passos, seating his reader alongside him in the gallery of the Chicago stadium "behind a battery of Rosslite superspots." There were two hitches in the performance, he said:

The wires of the marionettes had gotten crossed for an instant when the fat marionette of ex-Senator France appears on one side of the rostrum waving its little arms and attempting (as it turns out later) to nominate for President that sturdy rotogravure fisherman and columnist, Calvin Coolidge. We didn't get a chance to see what the spotlights would have done if they'd had to extemporize, because the offending marionette was immediately dragged off by the stagehands and the show continued according to the script.

The only other hitch occurred during the spontaneous celebration that took place when Mr. Scott [Howard Scott], lifting himself hand over hand up an astonishingly long ladder of "becauses," reached the exalted name of Herbert Hoover. The delegates marched round all right, and the tin trumpets tooted and the little flags waved, and the toy balloons that had been coyly hiding in big nets in the ceiling all through the convention were released and floated down to give the delegates something to do with their hands. The ushers threw paper streamers from the galleries and the bands played, and the organ pealed forth *I'se Been Workin' on the Railroad,* but the grand climax, when His Master's Voice poured out of the loudspeakers and a moving picture of the rotund features of the Great Engineer flicked vaguely on two huge screens, was a flop, owing to bad lighting and stage management; or perhaps for other reasons. The Presence failed to materialize.

With a week's interval between conventions, Dos Passos traveled to Detroit for a firsthand look at "the city of leisure," as he referred to it in his next dispatch to *The New Republic*. Detroit, the hardest-hit city in the United States, had one out of every seven citizens on relief. The city was on the verge of bankruptcy, and only bread and flour were available for welfare recipients. Some five thousand were being evicted from their homes each month. Several weeks before Dos Passos' visit, hunger marchers bearing Red banners were dispelled by police after bloody hand-to-hand fighting left four dead and fifty wounded. Federal relief was nonexistent. Dos Passos had already selected Henry Ford as a target in the third book in his trilogy and wanted to talk with the River Rouge Plant officials and workers and fact-find and observe for himself. He also wanted to see the new V-8 Ford evolve from nuts and bolts to engine, chassis, and body and crawl like "a new glistening insect" off the line under its own power. Later he described his superficial tour through the Rouge Plant at the elbow of a company official: "A whistle blew and the men knocked off for lunch. 'A halfhour for lunch' says the collegiate young man. 'He's lying, they only get fifteen minutes,' whispers the man next to me. The men have slumped down in their tracks and are eating their food with bent heads, no laughing or talking. The visitors are piled into a bus and safely deposited outside the main-office gates." In a "Tin Lizzie" portrait of Henry Ford, the lead minibiography of the novel in progress, Dos Passos transmuted what he had heard and witnessed at the plant into a rush of rhetoric to serve his own purposes:

> At Ford's production was improving all the time; less waste, more spotters,
> strawbosses, stool-pigeons (fifteen minutes for lunch, three minutes to
> go to the toilet, the Taylorized speedup everywhere, reachunder,
> adjust-washer, screwdown bolt, reachadjustscrewdownreachunderadjust, until
> every ounce of life was sucked off into production and at night the
> workmen went home gray shaking husks). . . .
>
> New Era prosperity and the American plan
> (there were strings to it, always there were strings to it)
> had killed Tin Lizzie.
> Ford's was just one of many automobile plants.
> When the stockmarket bubble burst,
> Mr. Ford the crackerbarrel philosopher said jubilantly,
> "I told you so.
> Serves you right for gambling and getting in debt.
> The country is sound."
> But when the country on cracked shoes, in frayed trousers, belts
> tightened over hollow bellies,
> idle hands cracked and chapped with the cold of that coldest March
> day of 1932,
> started marching from Detroit to Dearborn, asking for work and
> the American Plan, all they could think of at Ford's was machineguns.
> The country was sound, but they mowed the marchers down.
> They shot four of them dead.

Upon his return to Chicago June 25, 1932, Dos Passos wrote Katy that whereas Detroit gave him the impression that "main street was reddening up—was full of good beer and cool notherly wind," Chicago had dried up and contained nothing "but bad dago wine and needle beer." He said he had been to "a lot of rooms in the Congress Hotel (convention headquarters) and never saw a drink, except in Heywood Broun's and he just pretended the bottle standing on the table was empty although . . . it was half full. Conventions aren't what they used to be."

In his convention coverage for *The New Republic* ("Out of the Red with Roosevelt"), Dos Passos likened the Democratic convention to a "weeklong vaudeville show" in which nothing really happened. There was "courteous applause, but no feeling":

> Starting on Monday with "The Star-spangled Banner" and an inaugural address of Thomas Jefferson's read by a stout gentleman with a white gardenia in his buttonhole; through the Senator from Kentucky's keynote speech, during which he so dextrously caught his glasses every time they fell from his nose when he jerked his head to one side and up to emphasize a point; through Wednesday's all star variety show that offered Clarence Darrow, Will Rogers, Amos 'n' Andy, and Father Coughlin "the radio priest" (who, by the way, advised the convention to put Jesus Christ in the White House), all on one bill; through the joyful reading of the platform with its promise of beer now and a quietus by and by on prohibition snoopers and bootleggers; through the all-night cabaret on Thursday, with its smoke and sweaty shirts and fatigue and watered down Coca Cola and putty sandwiches and the cockeyed idiocy of the demonstrations . . . through all the convention week and the flicker of flashlight bulbs and the roar of voices there had been built up a myth, as incongruous to this age as the myth of the keeneyed pilot at the helm of the ship of state that the Republicans tried to revitalize three weeks before:—the myth of the young American working his way by honesty and brawn, from Log Cabin to President.

At the convention's close, Dos Passos walked his reader out of the stadium, across the train yards and the river, out to Michigan Avenue with its "shiny store fronts, doormen, smartly dressed girls, taxis, buses taking shoppers, clerks, business men home to the South Side and North Side," then down under Michigan Avenue to a "leisure class" that lies

> along the ledges about the roadway, huddled in grimed newspapers, grey sagfaced men in wornout clothes, discards, men who have nothing left but their stiff hungry grimy bodies, men who have lost the power to want. Try to tell one of them that the *gre-eat* Franklin D. Roosevelt, Governor of the *gre-eat* state of New York, has been nominated by the *gre-eat* Democratic party as its candidate for President, and you'll get what the galleries at the convention gave Mr. McAdoo when they discovered that he had the votes of Texas and California in his pocket and was about to shovel them into the Roosevelt band wagon, a prolonged and enthusiastic Boooooo. Hoover or Roosevelt, it'll be the same cops.

The week before the general election, all four of the major political parties staged rallies at Madison Square Garden. Dos Passos was on hand to cover them for the inaugural issue of *Common Sense,* a journal whose avowed purpose was the promotion of a new economic system for the country that was not based on competitive capitalism. Halfway measures or a patching up of capitalism was not the answer, proclaimed the magazine's editors, Alfred Bingham, Selden Rodman, and C. C. Nocolet. Bingham, a Yale graduate whose father was Hiram Bingham, a conservative United States senator from Connecticut, had recently returned from two years of travel through Europe, Asia, and the Soviet Union convinced that capitalism was doomed in the United States and envisioned for his country a "just distribution of work and wealth." Although he foresaw a high standard of living for everyone, he did not think that Marxism was the best way to achieve it and insisted that his magazine would remain independent of any political party. *Common Sense* would place before the American public radical principles that might well be acceptable if they did not appear to have been wrung from a Soviet dyebath, Bingham told Dos Passos when he solicited his essays and asked permission to carry his name on its masthead as one of twelve contributors. Dos Passos readily agreed, having become increasingly put off by the militaristic jargon of *The New Masses,* whose hard-line Communist editors seemed bent upon a violent revolution to install a Communist system modeled on the Soviet Union's. Dos Passos saw the new magazine as an apt vehicle for his own ideas since they, too, were independent of any existing party platform.

His treatment of the four political rallies held the week preceding the general election of 1932 revealed his lack of fervor for any of the presidential candidates. The Socialist rally he described as "a pink tea" at which everything was "very agreeable." The word "agreeable," which appeared again and again in his coverage of the Socialist meeting, jarred the reader with its wry blandness, the word itself and the tone of his essay catching perfectly the attitude he had expressed in Calverton's questionnaire: "I should think that becoming a socialist right now would have just about the same effect on anybody as drinking a bottle of near-beer." In his catalogue of what he saw as the highlights of the rally, Dos Passos spoke of the Socialist party's proclamation that it was the "only hope for the Negro people," of the demonstration by Columbia University, Hunter College, and New York University spokesmen who paraded the hall bearing placards announcing that they would be voting Socialist next week, of the announcement that the Socialist government of Vienna had made remarkable progress, and of the address by presidential candidate Norman Thomas to his "well-behaved audience." Thomas was "always on the edge of dropping into 'Dearly beloved brethren,' " said Dos Passos. Thomas lifted his hand high in the air "holding a large red flag in the attitude of the resurrection angel." Everyone seemed interested in hearing his speech, but the Long Island Railroad and the Staten Island ferry were "mightier than salvation by socialism," and his audience melted into the night.

By the time the Communist party wound up its campaign, its standard-bearer, William Z. Foster—by now an old hand in presidential elections, having also run in 1924 and 1928—had collapsed from a mild heart attack and was in bed when his fellow Communists rallied at Madison Square Garden November 6. Foster had "broken down under the strain of bucking a hostile continent," said Dos Passos. Foster's running mate, James W. Ford, a Negro and former Alabama steelworker whose grandfather had been lynched by Ku Klux Klansmen, was in the great hall, but the presidential nominee insisted on reading his speech himself from his sickbed (an assistant had to finish delivering it for him). Earl Browder's "well thought-out, carefully enunciated statement of the party's aim" in the election did not relieve the pall. "Is it that we're ten thousand miles from Moscow?" suggested Dos Passos. The audience listened to the announcement that

German Communists had cast two million votes and won eleven seats in the Reichstag in its recent election and felt "for a moment the tremendous intoxication with history that is the great achievement of a Communist solidarity," but Hooverville's "forgotten man" seemed remote from the Communist party's considerations.

According to Malcolm Cowley, most of the intellectuals supported Norman Thomas and the Socialist ticket, as did *The New Republic* ("in a mild fashion"), yet Cowley joined Dos Passos, Wilson, and some fifty other writers, poets, critics, and artists in signing an "open letter" published September 13 in several metropolitan newspapers. As they saw it, the two major parties were "hopelessly corrupt" and the Socialists were stalled in a mud puddle of "do-nothing" rhetoric. Only the Communist party offered hope for a capitalistic country rotten to the core, their statement continued. Only through the growth of Communist cells could the nation be restored; diseased organisms must be excised and imperialistic arms being flung to distant shores in a frantic grasp at straws must be amputated. A month later an expanded statement was published in a pamphlet entitled *Culture and Crisis: An Open Letter to the Writers, Artists, Teachers, Physicians, Engineers, Scientists and Other Professional Workers of America.* Such an alignment of white collar, or desk workers—as Dos Passos preferred to call them—with the blue collar masses was without precedent in America. It was the largest public renouncement of bourgeois allegiance on record in 1932. Those who signed the letter referred to themselves as the League of Professional Groups for Foster and Ford. Their statement concluded with the peroration:

> We strike hands with our true comrades. We claim our own and we reject the disorder, the lunacy spawned by grabbers, advertisers, traders, speculators, salesmen, the much-adulated, immensely stupid and irresponsible "business men." We claim the right to live and function. It is our business to think and we shall not permit business men to teach us our business. It is also, in the end, our business to act. . . . As responsible intellectual workers we have aligned ourselves with the frankly revolutionary Communist party, the party of the workers. In this letter we speak to you of our own class . . . telling you as best we can why we have made this decision and why we think you too should support the Communist party or the political campaign now under way.

Some twenty-five years after Franklin Delano Roosevelt's landslide victory in the 1932 general election, Dos Passos reflected upon his rationale of voting the Communist ticket that year:

> As the literal-minded young men of the F.B.I. have occasionally reminded me, I let my name be used in a list of literary people who said they were going to vote for Foster and Ford in that election. I actually did vote for them. I remember thinking how surprised some of my casual friends in Provincetown would have been if they had known it. It certainly wasn't that I wanted the communists to conduct the revolution in American government which I felt was needed. It was because I knew they had no chance of winning. It was the old theory of the protest vote. It's a perfectly good way of using the American political machinery. . . . If I'd known enough about the peculiar processes by which American exceptionalism weaves its own peculiar politics, I might have guessed that the revolution I was wanting, some of it, at least, was going to be carried through under the leadership of a sweet talking crippled man whose origins lay in Groton and Harvard and in the Hudson River aristocracy, instead of in Engels and Marx. Still in 1932, to a casual onlooker like myself, Franklin D. Roosevelt seemed

the unlikeliest man in the world to assume such a function. . . . It was somewhere during the years of the New Deal that I rejoined the United States. I had seceded privately the night Sacco and Vanzetti were executed. It was not that I had joined the communists. The more I saw of the Party the more I felt that the kind of world they wanted had nothing in common with the kind of world I wanted. I wasn't joining anybody. I had seceded into my private conscience like Thoreau in Concord jail. That protest vote in 1932 was already a step back into the American way of doing things. It indicated a certain skepticism about the Marxist millennium. So far as I can remember I hadn't quite recovered from the plague on both your houses attitude toward the two conflicting systems.

Although relatively few blacks went to the polls in 1932, efforts on behalf of the nine Scottsboro boys in Alabama did more to promote respect of the Southern black population for the Communist party than any other *cause célèbre* with which the Party was associated in the 1930s. The Scottsboro boys had been arrested in 1931 and convicted of raping Victoria Price and Ruby Bates, two white women, in a railroad boxcar. No medical evidence supported the charges, and Bates later admitted she lied in testifying against the youths. The two youngest boys were held in prison eighteen months without a conviction. Roy Wright's case ended in a mistrial, and Eugene Williams, fourteen, was given a death sentence that was later reversed by the Alabama Supreme Court because he was a juvenile. Meanwhile, the state made no effort to try them again, and they languished in prison. As treasurer of the National Committee for Defense of Political Prisoners, Dos Passos sent letters and published urgent pleas for help in raising fifteen hundred dollars so that Wright and Williams could be brought to trial again and adequately defended. Both *The New Republic* and *The Nation* carried Dos Passos' letters to the editor on behalf of the Scottsboro youths, and dollars poured in from coast to coast. Many donors wrote Dos Passos personally, such as Paul Green, who sent twenty-five dollars from Hollywood and told him that it was all he could spare at the moment, but wished "it was many times that." His letter caught the pulse of people outraged by the Sacco-Vanzetti convictions and executions who did not want to see what they considered a second major miscarriage of justice:

> Day and night it comes to me that the Scottsboro human shame can be endured no more and that a march of the righteous is demanded. . . . Think of it—Roy Wright, 14, and Eugene Williams, 14, still behind bars—after eighteen months! And no hope in sight! As I write these words they might be out playing cat with other boys in the alley, or tag, or helping in the fields, or fishing down at the old swimming hole—breathing the fresh air—happy—just boys. But all this while, the sovereign state of Alabama, the "pride" and prejudice of an erring system keeps them shackled in the shade of death. My God what are we—men or brutes! Is this the doing of the South of our fathers, the land that gave us Lee, Washington, Jefferson, and a vision of justice for all, yea even kindness to children?

Between April 1931 and October 1937, six separate trials were held in the state courts of Alabama, and three appeals were filed in the United States Supreme Court. Finally, four of the Scottsboro youths were convicted and given life sentences and five were released. By this time, many liberal organizations had joined the effort to help bring about fair trials, and Samuel Leibowitz, a prominent New York criminal lawyer, had been hired by the Communist-oriented International Labor Defense (ILD) as chief defender.

Although the plight of the Scottsboro boys in Alabama was not his immediate concern, the country's new helmsman in 1933, Franklin D. Roosevelt, shared Paul Green's conviction that the South, which "gave us Lee, Washington, and Jefferson," was in deep trouble, and so was the North. It was his job to help the American people figure out a solution and steer a new, true course. A week after his inauguration on March 4, 1933, Roosevelt delivered his first fireside chat. He apologized for the temporary closing of the banks and spoke as a wise, benevolent friend without platitudes or false promises, his performance a masterpiece of theatrics. Charles Michelson, who assisted as ghostwriter of the first fireside address, said of the President's radio audience that night: "They were ready to believe FDR could see in the dark." As Dos Passos listened to the President from his living room in Provincetown while a northeast gale drove slanting rain across the windowpanes, he had no illusions that the man could move mountains, but he was intrigued, nonetheless, by his talent for manipulation. In "The Radio Voice," an essay written after a later fireside chat, Dos Passos caught aptly Roosevelt's techniques in establishing credibility and an intimacy with the American people:

> After supper people sit around in the parlor listening drowsily to disconnected voices, stale scraps of last year's jazz, unfinished litanies advertising unnamed products that dribble sense-lessly from the radio. A brisk deferential organizing voice from N.B.C. breaks in. People wake up. People edge their chairs up to the radio. . . . There is a man leaning across his desk, speaking clearly and cordially to you and me, painstakingly explaining how he's sitting at his desk there in Washington, leaning towards you and me across his desk, speaking clearly and cordially so that you and me shall completely understand that he sits at his desk there in Washington with his fingers on all the switchboards of the federal government, operating the intricate machinery of the departments, drafting codes and regulations and bills for the benefit of you and me worried about things, sitting close to the radio in small houses on rainy nights, for the benefit of us wageearners, us homeowners, us farmers, us mechanics, us miners, us mortgagees, us processors, us mortgageholders, us bankdepositors, us consumers, retail mer-chants, bankers, brokers, stockholders, bondholders, creditors, debtors, jobless and jobholders. . . . *Not a sparrow falleth but.* . . . He is leaning cordially toward you and me across his desk there in Washington telling in carefully chosen words how the machinations of chiselers are to be foiled for you and me, and how the myriad-cylindered motor of recovery is being primed with billions for youandme and youandme understand, we belong to billions, billions belong to us, we are going to have good jobs, good pay, protected bankdeposits, a new dealing out of billions youandme. We edge our chairs closer to the radio, we are flattered and pleased, we feel we are right there in the White House. When the cordial explaining voice stops we want to say "Thankyou Frank," we want to ask about the grandchildren and the dog that had to be sent away for biting a foreign diplomat. . . . You have been listening to the President of the United States in the Blue Room.

In May after another fireside chat, Dos Passos remarked to Edmund Wilson that Roosevelt was a fascinating performer. "He's no cripple; he's a sleek wire artist. See how delicately (just 24 hours after he'd sponsored it) he handed the red hot sales tax to Congress. The upshot of it is that you and me and The Forgotten Man are going to get fucked plenty, but its almost a pleasure to be liquidated by such a bonny gentleman. And if he had false teeth and his eyes were a little farther apart he'd be the spitting image of George Washington."

Dos Passos was at Johns Hopkins in Baltimore in April 1933 when he heard Roosevelt's second address to the American people. As he explained it in a letter to Hemingway: "Brought Katy up here to have her tonsils out at cut rates and before I knew it was surrounded by medics and hog-tied in a little white bed under accusation of rheumatic fever." Katy was recuperating at the home of Horsley Gantt on April 19 when she wrote Wilson:

> Oh AntiChrist it's so awful. Oh it was better under the ether cone—oh why did they lift the ether cone off my face. They took M. Fish to the hospital yesterday helpless and unable to walk. He has the articular rheumatism in his joints so painful, can't move, oh it's horrible. A whole battery of physicians working on him there never less than two at a time, a great concourse of medicine men bewildered by science surround M. Fish. . . . Science has a great future. They don't know a thing about this and room seven dollars a day and the doctors cutting prices, but we're trapped here with the quacks making tests every minute. . . . Please write to M. Fish with consolations of philosophy as he is blue. He would like to hear from you, tried to write you a post card yesterday but fell back. . . . You can see how bad it is when I tell you Dos is asking for Proust.

The missive was signed "I am (while I last) . . . Hecuba Dos Passos." It was Wilson who had urged Dos Passos to take Proust in great gulps, believing his works to be a better tonic for his ailment than anything the doctors might prescribe. Proust did not set well with him at first, complained Dos Passos. He told Wilson that the phrases were "long and iridescent and the sentences hang out of the poultice in long slightly writhing threads" (Wilson had insisted that Dos Passos treat Proust as a compress for his swollen joints). To Katy, who had returned to Provincetown as soon as she felt well enough to travel, Dos Passos wrote: "I'm banked with Proust on every side and steaming through with considerable enthusiasm now."

Among Dos Passos' visitors to his bedside at Johns Hopkins Hospital was Scott Fitzgerald, who had been in Baltimore for several months so that he would be close to Zelda, now hospitalized at the Phipps Clinic in Baltimore after suffering a second serious mental breakdown. She had been treated for schizophrenia for eighteen months at the Prangins Sanitarium in Switzerland and was out only briefly before falling ill again. By this time, Zelda had finished her novel, *Save Me the Waltz,* brought out by Max Perkins under a Scribner's imprint in October 1932. When Fitzgerald learned that his wife's book had sold only fourteen hundred copies during its first three months, he wrote Perkins: "I do not think the sale of Zelda's book was bad when I have just learned that Dos Passos' *1919* sold only 9,000 copies. At any rate I don't see how my book *[Tender Is the Night]* is ever going to pay the debt I owe you because he [Dos Passos] is certainly more in the public eye at present than I am." Perkins replied that Fitzgerald should not compare himself to Dos Passos:

> His sales have steadily dropped. I suppose he might have sold 20,000 or more in this case if it had not been for the depression. But the truth is I do not think his way of writing and his theory make books that people care to read unless they are interested objectively in society, or

in literature purely for its own sake. . . . I know I have never taken one of them up without feeling that I was in for three or four hours of agony only relieved by admiration of his ability. They are fascinating, but they do make you suffer like the deuce, and people cannot want to do that.

On May 10, 1933, after Fitzgerald had visited Dos Passos at Johns Hopkins, Dos Passos wrote Hemingway that Zelda was apparently getting better, but that it was all "hellishly precarious—Scott's in pretty good shape—aging up damn well—a hell of a lot less flighty than he used to be." Fitzgerald, in turn, had learned to try to avoid saying anything that might prove inflammatory where Hemingway was concerned. Fitzgerald warned Perkins now that when he saw Hemingway again, he should not praise Zelda's book or even talk to him about it. "You haven't been in the publishing business over twenty years without noticing the streaks of smallness in very large personalities. Ernest told me once he would 'never publish a book in the same season with me,' meaning it would lead to ill-feeling. . . . The finer the thing he has written, the more he'll expect your entire allegiance to it as this is one of the few pleasures, rich & full & new, he'll get out of it." Similarly, Fitzgerald did not want Hemingway to know that he planned to "go on a water wagon" for at least three months during the spring of 1933 so that he might finish *Tender Is the Night* without further unnecessary delay. "Don't tell Ernest because he has long convinced himself that I'm an incurable alcoholic," Fitzgerald admonished Perkins. "I am his alcoholic just like Ring [Lardner] is mine and do not want to disillusion him, tho even Post stories must be done in a state of sobriety." Fitzgerald was still drinking when he visited Dos Passos at the hospital, however. Dos Passos wrote Katy that he had just seen Fitzgerald, who had arrived "a little under the weather" with some beer. "He and a young man he brought with him drank the beer . . . introduced me to a lot of interns and an old lady and went on his way."

Word spread rapidly among Dos Passos' friends that he was hospitalized with an illness more serious than anything he had yet known, and many well-wishers sent cards, letters, and flowers. From Provincetown, Susan Glaspell wrote: "Pretty sad was this house when we heard you were in the hospital. As I make a survey of the world, I can think of many billion people I would rather have rheumatism than you. . . . It's like a horrid joke, in bad taste, and cruel, that you went on a good errand, to have your dear wife's tonsils out, and then stayed on. Such jokes do not appeal to me at all." Gerald Murphy wrote that he was arranging for his bank to send Dos Passos a check for three hundred dollars, but warned that it might arrive "in the form of wheat or Kleenex (scrip)" and that he did not want Dos Passos to be startled if it were not immediately negotiable. The gift was merely "a chip of a little legacy" his mother had left him, said Murphy, who wanted Dos Passos "to use it for something [he] . . . shouldn't." Murphy's letter was written right after Roosevelt had closed the banks.

Hemingway, too, sent Dos Passos money even before he knew that Dos Passos was ill. In an earlier exchange of letters immediately after the closing of the banks, Dos Passos had informed Hemingway that he had not been personally affected by the President's initial "New Deal action," to which Hemingway replied: "You certainly fooled the banks by not having any dough in them. . . . I enclose 100 in case you can use it. If you need more let me know. I don't mean need, I mean if you cannot get it conveniently from our natural enemies. Deducting this I have 487.50 in bank. Can let you take another 200 or even 287.50 to simplify bookkeeping." Hemingway had sent Dos Passos the money because he wanted him and Katy to join him in Cuba in April to fish a couple of weeks, then to go together to Spain. Hemingway planned to make a documentary on Spain as a sequel to *Death in the Afternoon* and already had talked with film director Lewis Milestone about it. "It will all be perfectly simple," said Hemingway:

> We will hire a car and work this movie out writing down what we work out, places and shots in a couple of five-cent notebooks. We will . . . go around and find out what we want to do exactly. Then we will have dope and will get some money (no milestoning or big shots) and make the picture the following summer. You would do better on your damned perpetual education of Henry J. Passos to go to Spain this summer than anywhere I believe. Really, and I won't bother you or anything. We can have a damned good time doing the movie thing, i.e. getting it all set in our heads and much enjoyment withall. Then with it all clear I will sell some bastard on idea of making it even if I have to be polite.

Hemingway also insisted that Dos Passos not worry about how to finance the trip. Scribner's owed him $750 for a story, and he was due an additional $1,500 on book royalties. There was money enough for both of them, Hemingway assured him. Once he heard about Dos Passos' illness, however, he immediately proposed selling $1,000 of the common stock Gus Pfeiffer, his wife's uncle, had given them for their African safari—now planned tentatively for 1934—and giving the money to Dos Passos to pay his hospital bills and then to go on to Spain when he was well enough to travel. "Jesus Hem it's mighty handsome of you to start raising that grand," wrote Dos Passos, but conceded that he still had some money:

> If I get it off you I won't get it off our natural enemies, because it's only when I'm broke that I start to chisel on them properly. I've got a grand promised off Harcourt for the Spanish trip and am trying to make my agents pre-sell some articles, also have nicked a lot of small sums off friends so that I'm able to pay my hospital bill and even the eventual medics. Gantt is surrounding me with free medics and they are making the hospital cut rates also, so that way I'm really saving money being in here. Temperature cleared up yesterday for first time and feel pretty good, no pain for three or four days. This is a hellishly disagreeable disease, but is not chronic arthritis, in which I am damn lucky (according to the big boss medic here it always eventually leaves your carcass enormously dilapidated). Only way known to avoid recurrence is to dodge under the tropics now and then.

After consulting *Black's Medical Dictionary* for the symptoms and side effects of rheumatic fever, Hemingway sent Dos Passos one thousand dollars despite his protestations. "That's a hell of a disease," he wrote. "Would have come up to Baltimore if hadn't heard you were better. Did you run any of that 106° fever?" Then he spoke of the money:

> Listen this G is off the record. Uncle Gus gave me some stock to use to make the African trip —I cashed this out of that—there's plenty to go to Africa still and even come back from Africa. I can't make a trip to Coney Island let alone Africa with you, you ignorant Portuguese, having some lousy disease that swells the hands and saps the brain. So cash this before I change it into pennies and pelt you publicly as a hypochondriac. This won't keep you from

giving the publishers hell—nor anything else—just make it simpler to turn around. You can pay a few creditors and re-establish your borrow-ability. Hope to Christ I haven't been intrusive—but I was spooked about you. Didn't mean to be Stewart [Donald Ogden Stewart] minkcoating a pal.

Dos Passos replied: "Say Hem I didn't want to cut into your African trip like that—Jesus that means fifty less jigs on the safari. But it's frankly an enormous convenience. . . . I'm getting over this so damn slowly that I don't think I'll be able to do the necessary running around to get the material [for an article on the Scottsboro boys] before I sail." Arnold Gingrich had given him two hundred dollars to do a piece for *Esquire,* which Dos Passos said he would have to return.

Gingrich had been editing a trade journal in Chicago, *Apparel Arts,* when he hit upon the idea of publishing a magazine exclusively for men and wanted notable writers, sportsmen, and adventurers as contributors. Gingrich approached Hemingway first with the idea, having met him in December 1932 when he asked Hemingway to autograph his copy of *Death in the Afternoon.* He told Hemingway that he wanted to do for American men what *Vogue* had done for American women, but that it would not be "a sissy journal." Gingrich offered Hemingway $250 to write a nonfiction piece on hunting or fishing for the magazine's first issue. Then he asked Dos Passos—whom he had not yet met—to write an article on the Scottsboro case. When the doctors ordered Dos Passos to have bed rest and "no running around" for at least a month after his release from the hospital, Dos Passos returned Gingrich's check. Gingrich sent it back, along with a second check for $75 and a request that Dos Passos illustrate whatever he cared to send. It could be anything he had already written, said Gingrich, who wanted a star-studded cast for his first issue, planned tentatively for fall 1933 as a quarterly. The editor considered Hemingway and Dos Passos his plum contributors.

The inaugural issue of *Esquire* carried Dos Passos' opening episode of the "Charley Anderson" narrative from *The Big Money* manuscript and a full-color reproduction of a painting entitled *Port of New York.* Also published was Hemingway's "Cuban Letter" about fishing for marlin in Cuban waters, as well as pieces by such notables as Ring Lardner, James T. Farrell, Gene Tunney, Bobby Jones, Erskine Caldwell, Morley Callaghan, Joseph Auslander, William McFee, Douglas Fairbanks, Jr., Gilbert Seldes, and Dashiell Hammett. In an editor's note entitled "Backstage with Esquire," Gingrich explained:

> John Dos Passos is in Spain with his good friend Ernest Hemingway, having gone there after a summer spent at Antibes. Before returning to America, he will do the illustrations for Mr. Hemingway's "Spanish Letter," scheduled for the next issue. While everyone has heard of Dos Passos as a writer, many may be surprised to see the evidence, on page 11, that he is also an artist. As far as we know, this is the first time that one of his drawings has been reproduced in color in a periodical, although his water colors have appeared in two books. He is an author who ought to be read by everyone and could get along without being read by his admirers— we mean, that he has a tremendous following among the long haired literary audience and deserves to have it among all readers of books. No one, with the possible exception of James Joyce (and you could get us into an argument on this point very easily) has had such a pronounced influence on the contemporary novel. . . . Until someone can show us conclu-

sively that we're wrong, we lay our money in the Great American Novel Sweepstakes on the ultimate great book of which *The 42nd Parallel* and *1919* form the beginning and middle.

On May 25, 1933, Dos Passos and Katy sailed aboard the SS *Conte di Savoia*—which he described as a "wop superdeluxe liner"—for Genoa, and were to go from there to Cap d'Antibes to spend a month or more with the Murphys. A week before leaving, Dos Passos wrote Hemingway: "Gerald and Sara went and bought our tickets which was damn sweet of them. . . . This sickness has turned out to be a gigantic panhandling enterprise. The wily Portuguese shakes down his friends. Damn lucky to be equipped with same." Although his manner was breezily self-deprecatory when he spoke of his various borrowings, Dos Passos took such matters to heart and kept track of his debts. When he and Katy sailed for Europe, they had on deposit at Chemical Bank & Trust, their bank in Provincetown, $1,350. It was more money than they had had immediate access to in many years.

Gerald Murphy, Ernest Hemingway, and Dos Passos during a skiing trip at Schruns, Austria, March 1926. (By permission of the John F. Kennedy Library, # EH7281N)

Bill and Katharine Smith with their aunt, Mrs. Joseph W. Charles, about 1900. (Katharine Merrill Smith Durand)

Merrill, Bill, Katharine, and Y. K. Smith, about 1900. (Katharine Merrill Smith Durand)

Left, *Bill Smith, seated, and Ernest Hemingway. (Marion Hammett Smith)* Right, *Y. K. Smith. (Marion Hammett Smith)*

Katharine and Bill Smith, with Hadley and Ernest Hemingway, just before their wedding, September 1921 (two men in rear not identified). (By permission of the John F. Kennedy Library, # EH5529P)

"The Smooleys" of Smooley Hall: Katharine Smith,
Edith Foley, seated; Stella Roof and Bill Smith, about
1927. (Jean Shay)

Hemingway with his catch of the day, Key West, abou
1929. (Marion Hammett Smith)

Left, *Katharine Dos Passos and Robert Ball in Provincetown. (Marion Hammett Smith)* Right, *Bill Smith outside the Arequipa, Provincetown. (Katharine Merrill Smith Durand)*

Left, *Helen Sawyer Farnsworth on the beach at Truro, Massachusetts. (Helen Sawyer Farnsworth)* Right, *Robert Nathan at his home, the Parsonage, Truro, about 1934. (Robert Nathan)*

Thelma Given, Lucy L'Engle, and Lucy's daughter, Madeleine, on the beach in Wellfleet. (Madeleine L'Engle)

Frank Shay, Bill L'Engle, Bill Smith, Eben Given (kneeling), and Charles Kaeselau. (Madeleine L'Engle)

Dos Passos and Katy at home with guests Ada and Archibald MacLeish, Provincetown, about 1936. (Jean Shay)

Dos Passos and Hemingway in Spain during the Spanish Civil War, spring 1937. (Mary Hemingway)

Dos Passos and Katy frequently illustrated their letters to one another using pet names and personae. (By permission of the University of Virginia Library, Manuscript Division)

18

The French Riviera and Spain: A Summer Interlude, 1933

Damn disappointed I couldn't see more of you gents, also get around Spain more. Summer was pretty much of a fiasco. Was sick as hell in Gibraltar, but picked up on the boat and now weak but damn well.

Dos Passos to Hemingway
October 1933

Gerald and Sara Murphy left for Europe in early June with their three children, Patrick having made what doctors considered a remarkable recovery from his tubercular condition, and urged Dos Passos and Katy to join them at the Villa America, their home in Cap d'Antibes, as soon as he felt well enough to travel. "A damn handsome velvet offer," Dos Passos wrote Hemingway, adding that the Murphys had insisted they come and had even sent them their tickets to insure an early arrival.

The Murphys were ideal hosts. They made no demands upon their guests, fed them sumptuously, saw to every detail for their personal comfort and convenience, and left them largely to their own devices to spend each day as they saw fit. Until Dos Passos recovered his strength, he spent considerable time on a chaise lounge on the Murphys' outdoor terrace, where they generally took their meals. Soon he was able to walk down to the beach and bathe his still-swollen joints in the warm salt sea. Katy swam with him or sat on the beach reading or playing with the Murphy children, who were their almost constant companions. Dos Passos recuperated swiftly in the nurturing environment of the French Riviera in midsummer, and before long he was strolling with Katy and the others down the beach to the newly renovated Grand Hôtel du Cap for lunch and an afternoon's swim at the new Eden-Roc pool.

Before leaving New York, Dos Passos accepted one thousand dollars from Harcourt, Brace to do a slim volume on the Spanish republic, now in its third year after the ouster of

Alfonso XIII, who had been born a King and ruled the country for four decades. In view of the poor sales of his other books—except for *Manhattan Transfer*—and still smarting from the failure of *1919* to top the ten-thousand mark, Dos Passos saw no reason for optimism about a book on Spain. He wrote Hemingway that he was sure it would be "burned by Hitler, pissed on in the Kremlin, used for toilet paper by the anarchist syndicalists, deplored by The Nation, branded by the New York Times, derided by the Daily Worker, and left unread by the Great American Public," Nevertheless, he planned to research and write the manuscript, have it typed and delivered to his editor by early fall, and move along with *The Big Money* (his sequel to *1919*, still untitled) without another major interruption unless his health failed him once more.

Confident that he had licked his disease through the steady diet of rest, sun, and healthful fresh fruits and vegetables with which Sara Murphy had plied him, Dos Passos looked forward now to driving with Katy through the Spanish countryside and living as close to the people as he could in an effort to get to know them better. Although the political structure of the country had changed considerably since his last visit to Spain, the people of the villages and towns had not. As he saw it, the heart of Spain was still in its villages, and he wanted to observe firsthand the effects of a Republican constitution upon the lives of the peasants and workers who lived far from Madrid. The country had had over two years to settle down to its new form of government since its bloodless coup in 1931. The new Republican regime had closed down church schools, driven the Jesuits either underground or from the country, and otherwise tried to discourage Roman Catholicism, which the Socialists—now the ascendant party—associated with the fallen monarchy. A number of churches were burned, religious orders suppressed, and civil divorce made easy for the first time in Spanish history. The government had put down a monarchist uprising scarcely a year after the republic was established, and rebel leaders had either been executed or imprisoned, and grandees had fled the country.

Upon arrival in Spain in late July, Dos Passos was guardedly optimistic about the future of the Second Republic. Its Premier was Manuel Azaña y Díaz, whom Dos Passos had seen during his student days in Madrid. Then, it had been Dos Passos' habit to work in the library of the Ateneo because it was warmer than his room in the pension. He also liked working there because he could smoke and even send a waiter out for sandwiches. Azaña was secretary-general of the Ateneo back in 1916–17 when Dos Passos was an architectural student in Madrid. The Ateneo, known as the "Madrid Atheneum," served as a "watering hole" for Republicans. The leaders of the new republic came from the ranks of a rising middle class of professionals who had been nurtured by the Ateneo, where men were encouraged to think freely. In Madrid now, Dos Passos sought first an interview with Azaña, who seemed to be the man of the hour in 1933 rather than the President, Alcalá Zamora y Torres, who was expected to retire soon or be voted out of office. Azaña explained to Dos Passos that Spain had emerged from the war prosperous on the whole, with a "magnificent gold reserve," and that his government was trying now to spread that prosperity among all the classes. Spaniards were being educated, given better health care, and provided opportunities to "rise in the world. We don't want any more of our good people emigrating to America." Dos Passos listened to the Premier, then called his attention to conditions elsewhere. "Would the Pyrenees form as good a bulwark against the murderous hatreds that were sweeping Europe as they had against the sensible liberalism of the nineteenth century?" he asked, then mentioned Stalin, Hitler, and the fascist movements in France. Azaña replied that he was confident Spain had escaped the "uncivilizing influence of the war" and surmised that there might be an advantage in being a backward country. Dos Passos concluded that the prime minister was "profoundly unhappy" regardless of his protestations to the contrary.

Writing about Spain also gave Dos Passos an opportunity to see such old friends as José ("Pepe") Giner, now curator of the Palacio National. He and Katy were enthralled by Giner's private tour through the royal palace and his colorful tale of Don Alfonso's final hours in residence as king. The palace had been spared destruction in 1930 when Ramón Franco, Spain's ace aviator—and the brother of Francisco Franco—had a change of heart during a bombing raid and led his squadron away from its target. He could not bring himself to unload his bombs upon the centuries-old Bourbon palace, but dropped leaflets, instead. When Don Alfonso perceived how narrowly he escaped death, he realized that the crown with its attendant problems no longer suited him. As Dos Passos put it, Alfonso "sneaked out of the palace under cover of darkness as stealthily as a defaulting bank cashier" and the people "awoke the next morning to find themselves a republic." Giner led Dos Passos and Katy to the very wardrobe in the royal bedchambers in which he, personally, had discovered the abandoned crown of Spain stuffed into a bag of green baize.

Dos Passos also took Katy to the Escorial, the historic royal residence of Philip II, some fifty kilometers from Madrid. For hours they poked through the intriguing rooms, still furnished as Philip had left them. From there they drove to Ávila, where it seemed to them that St. Teresa might still be walking the crooked streets. Later, they strolled Segovia by moonlight, much as Dos Passos himself had done years earlier. Then he showed Katy another favorite region, Galicia, the northwesternmost region of Spain. When they arrived in the colorful town of Pontevedra, their annual festival was under way. That night they viewed an astonishing fireworks display in a crowded plaza. Dos Passos was amazed that no one was injured or set afire by the cascading sparks. From Pontevedra, they drove to Santander on the Bay of Biscay, where they heard José Giner's cousin, Fernando de los Ríos—an influential representative of Granada in the constituent Cortes—deliver an address at a huge Socialist rally in an arena generally reserved for bullfights. The Socialists in Spain in 1933 were as "innocent as a flock of sheep in the wolf country," Dos Passos noted in his journal later. Miners, mechanics, and farmers had come in mule carts, buses, on bicycles, and on foot from all over northern Spain to attend the rally. Their wives and children were there, too, with picnic baskets and bottles of wine. School children sang the "Internationale" and proclaimed the Second Republic to be "the Republic of Honest Men." Dos Passos feared that the pigeons that were supposed to "fly up into the empyrean to symbolize the reign of peace and goodwill that was to come," but dropped to the ground because they had probably been cooped up in the heat too long, were a portent that the Second Republic was destined for trouble.

Dos Passos and Katy were traveling about Spain that summer in a second-hand Fiat they had bought upon leaving Antibes. They had nested in it for some twenty-five hundred kilometers without any problems except coping with its tiny interior until a mishap occurred while journeying southwestward from Santander. They had just come upon one of the few level stretches of the entire way after driving among cliffs and gorges that Dos Passos thought rivaled the splendor of the Colorado Rockies. As they entered the valley of the Ebro and Dos Passos was complimenting their *cochecito* for its virtuous performace, the vehicle shot off the road and skittered across a meadow. Had the steering pin jostled loose a kilometer or two earlier, they might have disappeared off a precipice. As it was, they were neither hurt nor shaken, merely shocked by the audacity of their little car. Two husky Asturians happened upon the scene moments later, picked up the ailing *cochecito,* and hoisted it aboard their flatbed truck. Their deliverers hauled them and their vehicle to the next village and found a garage that would repair the car, but demurred when Dos Passos tried to force a few pesetas upon them. "You would do the same thing for us," they assured him. "But your truck wouldn't fit into my *cochecito,"* he countered, and after considerable joking got them to accept a few coins because of "the disparity of sizes."

Dos Passos and Katy were back in Madrid and ensconced at the Hotel Alfonso when he wired Hemingway in early August to inquire of his travel plans. After an exchange of several cables, Hemingway assured them that he was leaving Havana for Santander on August 7. Regardless of how enthusiastic he may have sounded at first about joining Dos Passos and Katy in Spain, romping over the countryside, and planning a film scenario together, it was soon apparent that he was more interested in other matters, such as bullfighting. He had hoped to spend six or eight weeks at the bullrings until he learned that his favorite matador, Sidney Franklin, would be unable to go into the ring because of impending surgery. At that point, Hemingway decided that the season's new crop of matadors was unimpressive and not worthy of his time.

Pauline was with Hemingway, and Katy and Dos Passos drove back to Santander from Madrid to meet them, but the couples saw little of each other after their initial meeting. Dos Passos spoke later of having a couple of long "winey lunches" with Hemingway and Claude Bowers, the United States ambassador to Spain, whom he had met in New York through Paxton and Sheila Hibben. According to Dos Passos, it was the last time he and Hemingway were able to "talk about things Spanish" without losing their tempers. When they parted that summer, Hemingway was getting ready to go on a wild boar hunt with Luis Quintanilla, a painter and revolutionist who was not happy with the tide of events of the Second Republic. For the time being, Quintanilla was content to register his rebellion in a series of satiric etchings and paintings that Dos Passos likened to the drawings of George Grosz. At this point, it was obvious to Dos Passos that Hemingway had no intention of making the Spanish film they had previously talked about. He was more intent on traveling to Africa on his first big-game safari.

Dos Passos did not object. He had been in Madrid only briefly in late August when his joints and hands began to swell. Before long, excruciating pain set in and he was forced to admit that his "hellish rheumatics" had returned in full measure. He took to his bed, but protested any suggestion that he be hospitalized. If he could manage to make it aboard ship, he preferred to seek treatment from his doctors back in the States. Katy made the necessary arrangements for their departure while he lay abed and fumed at not having accomplished as much as he had hoped. He had intended to visit each province to see for himself how the peasants and workers fared at their jobs and in their leisure in the cafés and on the squares. Labor in Spain had been organized into unions in many areas, but until now he had seen little of the effects of pooling their energies. Dos Passos realized that regardless of the Premier's confidence that the people would prosper increasingly under the Second Republic, Spain, too, was in an economic depression not unlike the rest of the world. The export market had dried up almost completely, and many of the Spanish people wore looks of quiet desperation. Dos Passos had not planned to make a large book of his impressions of the Second Republic, but he wondered now, in view of the fact that his illness had limited his travel, if he would have enough to make even a respectable slim volume.

Meanwhile, Katy booked passage for their return to the United States on September 7, but first they needed to sell their car. *"Cochecito de venta"* read their advertisement in more than one Madrid newspaper. Dos Passos interviewed several prospective buyers from his sickbed, yet all were put off by the price until a young lieutenant presented himself "looking resplendent in red and blue dress uniform" and assured them that the car and price were a perfect match. Katy gave him the keys so that he might test-drive it after sealing the bargain over a glass of sherry. In his absence, she and Dos Passos rejoiced that they had found a buyer at last, but twenty-four hours later they summoned the police because he had not returned. Finally the car turned up, and the young officer's brother appeared on their threshold to plead for mercy on behalf of his errant kin. The lieutenant was merely "a little mad," but had already been hospitalized for his uncontrollable penchant for trying out other people's cars and abandoning them. After more sherry and, this time, amid vows of "eternal brotherhood," Dos Passos, still on his sickbed, agreed not to prosecute. He wanted only to get his car back or to make a bona fide sale. The police, however, were not impressed. Although Katy's advertisement had produced another buyer, the car was ordered impounded as evidence until the thief himself was arrested and brought to trial. Dos Passos was allowed neither to reclaim the little Fiat nor sell it. As their taxi rounded the corner of the Puerta del Sol, they cast mournful eyes at their *cochecito* swathed in a gossamer cocoon of chicken wire in the courtyard of the government building where it was being detained. *"Pobrecito cochecito,"* they lamented in chorus as they spied it for the last time. They were on their way to the depot then to catch a night train for Gibraltar, where their ship awaited them.

Dos Passos was chagrined that he had had to borrow money again, this time from Hemingway's sister-in-law, Virginia Pfeiffer. Just before boarding the SS *Exchorda* in Gibraltar, Dos Passos addressed a card to Hemingway with the message: "Tell Jinny I'll send you the 300 pesetas (we needed 'em) as soon as I get home. Damn handsome of you boys to come across. Sorry I had to shake you down again." Borrowing money during the depressed thirties had become a way of life for untold thousands forced to cope with hand-to-mouth existences, but Dos Passos did not consider himself in the same category. Yet he was working as hard as he could to make ends meet, and he resented having to approach friends for loans or to be the recipient of what smacked of charity. "I wish to God my father had apprenticed me to a cobbler," he exclaimed on more than one occasion.

19

Life Under the Blue Eagle, 1933–36

The U.S. is funny as hell under the Blue Eagle—but the chances are it won't be so funny after a while when the boys really start to clamp so tight nobody but Louis Bromfield'll be allowed to publish books. Things are certainly going to get worse.

Dos Passos to Hemingway
October 1933

Dos Passos' rheumatic condition persisted over much of the winter of 1933–34. "Getting better every day. I think the disease is finally licked," he wrote Hemingway in the fall. Upon arrival in Boston, Katy took Dos Passos to Massachusetts General Hospital, where doctors ran a battery of tests and declared his vital organs undamaged. It was only a matter of time and bed rest before his complete recovery, he was assured. Once in Provincetown, he hobbled about the house and wrote a few letters, but spent most of his time in bed. Before cold weather set in, he managed to have a few days in the sun on the terrace. As usual, Dos Passos chafed when kept down for long. He wanted to finish his essays for the book on Spain, then get back to his novel. After conferring with his new editor at Harcourt, Brace, Charles A. Pearce, he decided not to limit the nonfiction book to Spain, but to include some of his earlier pieces on the Soviet Union, Mexico, and the United States as well. He would devote a section to each country and have a brief opening section to establish his persona, "A Peesatyel," a narrator/traveler who would bind the disparate essays into a single fabric.

Except for a trip to Washington, D. C., after the first of the year, Dos Passos had no intention of leaving the Cape until he accomplished at his writing table what he set out to do. By spring, if the work went well, he expected to be back in Key West. Other than finishing the Spanish pieces, the only new thing he wanted to include in his book of essays was his impression of life in the nation's capital under the "Blue Eagle," another innovation of the New Deal. Dos Passos gathered up a number of his old essays published elsewhere, gave them new titles, edited them slightly, shortened some, and organized them according to his plan. In January 1934, he submitted everything to Pearce except the pieces he planned to write on Washington. He wrote Hemingway that he wanted to witness the antics of Congress in session, which would be "roaring and tearing for inflation. These damn codes absolutely hogtie labor—leaving the boys running the monopolies in full control of the situation." He thought Roosevelt was the "cleverest politician turned out in many moons" and likened him to Spain's Azaña. "Men like Roosevelt and Azaña can keep up their slick wire walking as long as a majority of people manage to eat, but after that they have to give up the stage to more muscular and preposterous forms of hooey."

Bernice Baumgarten, Dos Passos' agent at Brandt & Brandt, and his British agent, Patience Ross, at A. M. Heath & Company, worked diligently to place to advantage everything possible. Baumgarten wrote Ross at the beginning of the summer: "I hope you don't feel that I value Dos Passos' work too highly. I honestly believe that he is among the most important of the modern authors, and that in the end his work will prove a very valuable property." Both agents worked hard to get him top dollar.

Dos Passos was in Key West, just as he had planned, when his author's copies of his book of essays, entitled *In All Countries,* arrived. The jacket design was "pretty foul," but he liked the overall look of the book and urged Baumgarten to find out how Harcourt, Brace intended to promote it:

> I don't want them to pull off another sales flop like 1919 (I know all the alibis). . . . After all I've got to eat even if I'm not Faith Baldwin. I don't think my books could have a very large circulation at present, but I'm damn sure that properly handled they could have two or three times the circulation they have got. My impression is that Harcourt, Brace have gotten it into their heads that my stuff won't sell and that they'll just carry it along for window dressing. . . . I'm afraid it's up to you to give them a little poking. This time they'll have no alibi of a lousy book market because from what I hear people are buying books like flies everywhere.

Baumgarten went in to discuss the problem in person with Pearce, who was taken aback by Dos Passos' accusatory attitude and reviewed and presented to her the facts. Harcourt, Brace had spent $3,838 on advertising, which did not include direct mail, publicity, broadsides, posters, and the like. Their advertising campaign for *1919* extended from its publication date, February 1932, until June with follow-up advertisements in various important magazines over the summer. The company's policy in promoting a book that sold for $2.50—as did *1919*—allowed for $2,500 for every 10,000 copies sold. Pearce did not feel that the company's outlay in promoting Dos Passos' book was modest by any standards. They had published a first edition of 10,250 and found no justification for a second printing, since books were still on hand. Pearce also informed Baumgarten that Dos Passos had approved of the jacket design, given certain changes. "I followed all his suggestions and showed the final sketch to everyone around here before accepting it," insisted Pearce, who thought the result effectively represented the book and also served as an apt poster design for competing with hundreds of other jackets in bookstores. "There's an enormous difference between explaining things and answering unexpected criticism. It's doubly depressing in that the more deeply I go into each detail of the whole process of publishing Dos Passos' books, the less I find for any real criticism of our activities. . . . I hate to have it on my mind that an author in whom we are all so genuinely interested should be holding to the notion that we haven't done the best for him."

What had helped set Dos Passos' tirade off in the first place was the blurb on the jacket, which said that he sometimes lectured. "I never lecture—have only made speeches a few times in my life and consider lectures an extremely bum way of passing the time," he insisted. If people read on the jacket that he lectured, they would think he was lying when he answered their requests by saying that it was not his line of work. "I don't suppose it matters a hell of a lot, but it gives a very false picture of the life and habits of yr. humble servant," he added. Pearce told Baumgarten that Dos Passos had also approved the blurb. When questioned about it, Dos Passos admitted that he was "unable to read the damn things." He merely held them in his hand and stared at them when his opinion was asked.

Baumgarten was adroit in handling Dos Passos as well as his publisher. To reassure her client, she sent him the publisher's advertisement schedule for advertisements yet to run and copies of what had already appeared. A half dozen had been run since publication date (April 19, 1934). The Sunday New York *Times* and the *Herald Tribune* were to carry large two-column ads on May 1; *The Nation*, a half-page on May 16 (a full-page ad had already run); *The New Masses*, a quarter-page on May 21; *The Atlantic Monthly*, *Harper's Magazine*, and *The American Mercury*, half-page ads in June issues; the Sunday supplements of the New York papers for three successive weeks; *The New Republic*, a second ad (a half-page had already run); and an ad in *The Saturday Review of Literature* would be out soon. As Baumgarten saw it, any writer should be pleased by such a schedule. Pearce assured Baumgarten that Harcourt, Brace thought the book excellent and "would not miss the chance to do as well as possible with it," but that salesmen had already met with "serious reluctance on the part of the booksellers" in stocking the book in great numbers.

Harcourt, Brace was publishing a second book by Dos Passos during the spring of 1934. Scarcely a month after *In All Countries* appeared, *Three Plays* was brought out, which included the first hard-cover publication of *Fortune Heights*, a slightly revised version of "The Moon Is a Gong" entitled *The Garbage Man*, and *Airways, Inc. Fortune Heights* had already been produced successfully at the Kamerny Theatre in Moscow, according to a wire from Alexander Taïrov, its Russian director, after opening night. Baumgarten told Dos Passos that Taïrov was one of the best-known directors in the world. "It is supposed to be a great honor to have him produce the play—if that means anything to you." *Fortune Heights* was also being produced by the Trades Unions Theatre in Moscow and the Alexandrinsky Theatre in Leningrad. It was premiered soon afterward in the United States by an amateur group in Chicago known as the Workers Theatre. A secretary at Brandt & Brandt who misread Dos Passos' handwriting caused Baumgarten to convey the news to Pearce that the play had been "greatly praised." When she learned that the play had been "panned unmercifully" by the Chicago critics rather than praised, she hastened to correct the error so that a misstatement did not appear in publicity blurbs.

Pearce assured Baumgarten that he had used the information, but had carefully avoided saying whether the production had been "razzed or praised."

Dos Passos' agents worked diligently to get *In All Countries* and *Three Plays* published abroad as soon as possible. "We managed to get Constable to raise their offer on In All Countries to £50 advance instead of £35" (they had sought £100), Patience Ross informed Baumgarten, the book having been sold in early February before Dos Passos completed the "Washington, D.C.," section of the manuscript. From time to time Dos Passos sought advice from Hemingway as to whether he should be satisfied with an offer. "Say do you think £250 (free from tax) is a fair outright price" for *Manhattan Transfer, The 42nd Parallel, 1919,* and the next novel as an "outright sale of royalties to last five years from publication of next novel?" he asked. It would be a way of avoiding a "gigantic English tax," he suggested, but suspected that he was "getting gypped." The offer had come from Constable, and it was tempting. Hemingway cautioned him against tying up his novel rights irrevocably but thought a five-year option was all right. Dos Passos' decision was to accept the offer, with the exception of a one- or two-volume edition of all three books comprising the trilogy to be negotiated and sold whenever he saw fit. The idea of a separate publication combining the volumes originated with Dos Passos and proved a good move. The still untitled third volume, *The Big Money,* was published in August 1936. On January 27, 1938, *U.S.A.* was brought out by Harcourt, Brace in a single volume using the original plates.

Baumgarten also prodded A. M. Heath & Company in London for a complete report on sales of Dos Passos' books on the Continent. "Mr. Dos Passos counts quite heavily on his income from foreign publication and he is very much dissatisfied," she wrote C. H. Brooks, who handled foreign sales at Heath. As of September 1934, translations of his novels into foreign languages included: *Three Soldiers,* German and Polish; *Streets of Night,* Czech; *Manhattan Transfer,* Czech, French, German, Hungarian, Italian, Polish, Spanish, Swedish; *The 42nd Parallel,* the same languages as *Manhattan Transfer* except for Polish, which was dropped (a pirated edition by the State Publishing House in Moscow also appeared); *1919,* Danish-Norwegian, German, Swedish, and a pirated Russian edition. Of the nonfiction books, only *Rosinante to the Road Again* was translated (Spanish). By year's end, *In All Countries* had been sold for Czech, French, and Portuguese editions (the latter to be published and distributed only in Brazil).

Dos Passos knew all too well how difficult it was to get payment on various foreign translations when a legitimate sale was involved. He wrote Brooks that he had tried repeatedly to commission people to get money out of Russia for him. "There's a vague rumor of an account in my name in a Moscow bank. . . . I guess the foreign market's pretty well shot to hell except for piracies." The "Joe Williams" opening segment of *1919* was already being printed in various forms in Latin America without royalties being paid on it, he said. "Half the boys won't pay because I'm a near-Communist, and therefore a comrade, and the other half won't because I'm a red." He stated categorically to his British agent, however, that he was not a Communist, but had sympathy and admiration for much that they did.

He was rankled at year's end (1934) that *1919* had been translated in only three languages plus the pirated Russian edition. Contrary to reports, he explained, the Russian edition was legitimate. "I send my stuff to Valentine Stenich in Leningrad, who's an excellent translator." A. M. Heath himself explained to Baumgarten the situation as he saw it concerning foreign sales of *1919* and *In All Countries:*

> Mr. Dos Passos does not quite realize the very considerable change that has taken place in European markets. There is a growing tendency to steer clear of left wing material and, at the same time, his work has grown more in that direction. . . . Nobody can count on any certain income from foreign publication. The publishing position everywhere and, of course, particularly in Germany, is simply chaotic and there is very little certainty about getting the money even when one makes a sale!

Heath said that he had sent *In All Countries* to a publisher in Vienna, since it "seemed wise to have this done by a firm outside Germany." The book had already been turned down by Fischer Verlag, which had published *The 42nd Parallel.* "I gather In All Countries is politically too dangerous for him to take up," wrote Brooks, who urged Baumgarten to convey to Dos Passos Heath's enthusiasm for his work, yet at the same time to explain to him the difficulties inherent in the situation. Another problem was that Dos Passos' style in his later books was even more difficult to translate than that of the earlier books.

Dos Passos had nineteen pieces published in nine different journals and magazines in 1934, more than he had ever published previously in periodicals in a single year. *The New Masses, The New Republic, New Theatre, The Saturday Review of the Brooklyn Daily Eagle, Common Sense, Esquire, Student Outlet, The American Mercury,* and *The American Spectator*—all carried one or more pieces in 1934. Theodore Dreiser had pursued Dos Passos relentlessly for articles for *The American Spectator,* edited by George Jean Nathan and Ernest Boyd. The four-page "sheet of intellectual comment" sold for ten cents, carried no advertising, and paid its contributors a penny a word (articles were limited to two thousand words; thus no one could receive more than twenty dollars per piece). Dreiser was an unpaid contributing editor to whom Dos Passos finally sent two articles for publication, which he wrote primarily for inclusion in *In All Countries:* "Notes on the Back of a Passport" and "The Persian Merchant and the Red Army Officer."

Only one of the pieces published in 1934 was written for his novel in progress, the lead minibiography: "Man with a Watch in His Hand." It was a sketch of master machinist/efficiency expert Frederick Winslow Taylor, who "died with a watch in his hand." It was published in the second issue of Arnold Gingrich's new magazine, *Esquire.* Gingrich also paid Dos Passos seventy-five dollars in January for another full-color reproduction of a painting, this one to illustrate Hemingway's "Festival in Madrid." In addition, he had two letters to the editor of *The New Republic* published and a "Foreword" to *Veterans on the March* (Workers Library Publications), a collection of short stories by war veterans edited by Jack Douglas. Still another publication in 1934 was a critical commentary for the leaflet of an exhibition of eighteen etchings of Luis Quintanilla for the opening of his show at the Pierre Matisse Gallery in New York on November 20, 1934.

Bernice Baumgarten urged Dos Passos to stop giving things away, as had been his wont in the past (he sometimes allowed reprint rights to an article or an excerpt from a book with little or no fee). In 1934, more permissions than ever before were sought for publication from works already published. When B. A. Bergman wrote Brandt & Brandt of his plan to publish in the New York *American* and other Hearst newspapers a series of pieces from the "best war books" to warn against the horrors of war and asked for one thousand words from *Three Soldiers*, Baumgarten replied: "Just before Mr. Dos Passos left for Florida I told him of the excerpt you wished to run, and he agreed with me that it would hardly be fair to grant permission without some fee." She asked for five dollars and a copy of the book when Harry Hartwick petitioned for one hundred words from *Manhattan Transfer* and two hundred words from *Orient Express* for a college textbook, *The Foreground of American Fiction*, as examples of "literary quality." Dos Passos asked Baumgarten to "try to get a few cents out of Mr. Van D." when Carl Van Doren sought permission to include something from *Orient Express* in his *Modern American Prose* anthology. She set the fee at twenty-five dollars.

Dos Passos also began to get inquiries regarding his willingness to sell his manuscripts to collectors. When one Harold S. Zimmerman of Orrville, Ohio, wrote in 1934 that he was interested in obtaining something of Dos Passos', Baumgarten told him that the only manuscripts possibly available then were *In All Countries* and the play *Fortune Heights*, but that she had no idea if Dos Passos wanted to sell them. "What price would you be prepared to pay?" she asked. Zimmerman chose not to buy either manuscript.

Although Baumgarten attended to most of Dos Passos' literary affairs, he always maintained a direct relationship with his editors so far as original work was concerned. Payment for book reviews and various articles—which he agreed to do with increasing frequency unless he was in the middle of reading proofs or was trying to pull together the final pages of a book manuscript—was made to him directly from the editor himself. When payment was slow in coming, he did not hesitate to issue a reminder. To Malcolm Cowley in the spring of 1934, he wrote: "Say—if you people have any cheques round there, send them down here [to Key West] please, and for God's sake make them as large as you can as I ruined myself running round Washington in 20-cent taxicabs in pursuit of Knowledge." He also sent along a book review of William Rollins' "whopping fine novel" *The Shadow Before* (published April 4, 1934, as "The Business of a Novelist"). Dos Passos apologized for "the accursed delay" of a list of books Cowley had solicited for a feature entitled "Good Books That Almost Nobody Has Read" and recommended five recently published books that deserved to be "kept out of the ash barrel": *Laugh and Lie Down* (1913), a first novel by Robert Cantwell and "one of the best in the last ten years"; *Daughter of Earth* (1929), an "uneven but impressive I suppose autobiographical narrative" by Agnes Smedley; *Forgotten Frontiers: Dreiser and the Land of the Free* (1932), a "profound factual and atmospheric study of the origins of Dreiser's work and the Chicago and Indiana background of our writing during the first fifteen years of the century," by Dorothy Dudley; *The American Jitters—A Year of the Slump* (1932), "Edmund Wilson's compendium of a year's reporting that has, besides a great deal of valuable information, some magnificent writing in it, the description of Hollywood architecture and the lyrical account of the Coronado Beach Hotel"; and *The Disinherited* (1933), "a springy lively narrative" by Jack Conroy of the "coming of age of a coal miner's son—as absolutely out of the soil and roads and garages and backhouses of these United States as Jack London's good early stuff." Dos Passos prefaced his list with an apology of sorts for the critics themselves:

> The fact that most professional critics are overworked and confused by the flood of books and ballyhoo about books that roars over their head every week makes it impossible for them to get any perspective on their work. The result is there is no actual critical weeding out of books that may have permanent value for one reason or another. Everything published goes down the same chute out of the overbright glare of publicity into oblivion. . . . It is important to establish a public memory for good or for usefully informative writing.

Other writers whose lists of "Good Books That Almost Nobody Has Read" were published included Edmund Wilson, Conrad Aiken, Newton Arvin, Clifton Fadiman, Harry Hansen, Clara Stillman, John Chamberlain, Isidor Schneider, Horace Gregory, Suzanne La Follette, Thornton Wilder, T. S. Matthews, and F. Scott Fitzgerald. Dos Passos' contribution was the lead list in the April 18, 1934, issue of *The New Republic*.

Dorothy Dudley, whose *Forgotten Frontiers* he had recommended, and her sister, Caroline, had been good friends of Dos Passos since the early 1920s (he and Caroline had been enamored of each other for a time) in Chicago. He had written Dorothy Dudley a year or so earlier that he had just finished reading *Forgotten Frontiers* and could not imagine why it had been received "so ignorantly by the critics, except that the critics are always glad to crap on anything that comes to them unintroduced and unbacked by some literary vested interest." He assured her that it was "an extraordinarily competent piece of work." The only thing comparable to it as a "densely packed history of American manners" was *The Education of Henry Adams,* and only D. H. Lawrence's *Studies in Classic American Literature* could match its "salty comment." Most New York critics had "never been west of the Hudson in their lives and don't know anything about the country and care less," he added, and said that he had already written a letter to the editor of *The New Republic* to protest the poor reception of *Forgotten Frontiers.* The book had certain weaknesses, but "since when have you got to agree with everything in a book to admire it as a sound and carefully wrought piece of historical work?"

In his review of William Rollins' book, *The Shadow Before,* Dos Passos had raised the question of what the legitimate business of a novelist should be. As he saw it, the novelist's duty was to create characters, then to set them "in the snarl of the human currents of his time" so that there would be an accurate permanent record of a particular phase of history. "Everything in a novel that doesn't work toward these aims is superfluous or, at best, innocent day-dreaming." What he liked about Rollins' novel was that it was not a book about a textile strike, but that it was the "living invention of certain people undergoing a textile strike. The strike, the town, the social struggle, are real and profoundly moving because the people are real, not the other way around, as is usual in novels describing topical events." Dos Passos' credo as a writer in 1934, and later as well, remained virtually unchanged from his "Statements of Belief" published in *Bookman* in 1928, when he had written:

> The only excuse for a novelist, aside from the entertainment and vicarious living his books give the people who read them, is as a sort of second-class historian of the age he lives in. The "reality" he missed by writing about imaginary people, he gains by being able to build a

reality more nearly out of his own factual experience than a plain historian or biographer can. I suppose the best kind of narrative would combine the two like Froissart or Commines, or Darwin in *The Voyage of the Beagle*. I think that any novelist worth his salt is a sort of truffle dog digging up raw material which a scientist, an anthropologist or an historian can later use to permanent advantage.

When Dos Passos reviewed William Rollins' *The Shadow Before*, he was probably still smarting from comments John Howard Lawson had made to him regarding the weaknesses inherent in his play *Fortune Heights*. The concept of the play was superb, said Lawson, but its canvas was not broad enough for a true representation of mass events, nor were the characters sufficiently rounded to enable the theatergoer or reader to see the predicament through their eyes. He also faulted Dos Passos for not having worked out ideologically the social ideas in the play. "Christ Almighty, it seems to me obvious that if you undertake certain revolutionary problems—evictions, the hunger march, things that are part and parcel of the whole life around us—you've got to have some revolutionary ground on which to stand."

Lawson was eager to talk with Dos Passos regarding their respective views of the proletariat and Communism. Lawson insisted that he was not "strictly a Marxian Stalinist," but felt the necessity to have a much closer contact with Communism and to be more actively involved in its activities. He was critical of Dos Passos' having signed an "Open Letter" to the Communist party in the March 6, 1934, issue of *The New Masses*. The letter, signed also by two dozen other writers and intellectuals such as Edmund Wilson, John Chamberlain, Robert Morss Lovett, Clifton Fadiman, and Lionel Trilling, protested the strong-arm, disruptive tactics of Communist agitators who broke up a large Socialist party rally in Madison Square Garden on February 16. In a long, chastising letter that spring, Lawson wrote Dos Passos:

> I don't blame the Communists for feeling bitter about your signing that Madison Square Garden letter. In the first place you hadn't (at least I don't think you had) investigated the case fully. You expressed a hasty emotional objection. The letter seemed to me clearly designed as a dirty attack on the Communists; what the hell difference did it make whether their conduct was nice or not at the Garden—whether they did or did not start a riot? . . . I'm convinced that the whole thing was on the shoulders of the Socialists—but anyway, the whole thing comes down to a clear question of individualistic (and careless) expression of opinion, or giving disciplined support to a movement because the movement is right, regardless of mistakes along the way. . . . The Communists are beginning to accuse you of consorting with their enemies. . . . You've always (far more than myself) followed a revolutionary idea. It seems to me that now you (and all of us) are faced with a clear-cut revolutionary choice. I maintain that there is only one revolutionary line and one revolutionary party (be as sentimental as you like about the Wobblies, but they do not represent the working class). What's needed now is not sentimental adherence, but the will to fight a disciplined difficult fight.

One evidence of Dos Passos' change was his writing for *Common Sense*, insisted Lawson. Too many people were going astray by serving "fascism and war and Jew-baiting and Negro-baiting" in the name of aesthetic integrity: "the Dreisers and Sherwood Andersons and Bunny Wilsons and Archibald MacLeishes and Hemingways and Menckens and Nathans and Heywood Brouns and Calvertons and Eugene O'Neills and Roger Baldwins and Sidney Howards." A few would discover their mistake and "start to scream like stuck pigs when it's too late," warned Lawson. He did not want Dos Passos to be one of them.

In mid-July 1934, Dos Passos was in New York City and Katy was in Provincetown when he had to make an immediate decision on an offer to fly to the West Coast for a five- to eight-week stint writing for Paramount Studios, Inc. He was invited to write a screenplay for Marlene Dietrich, who was to be directed by Josef von Sternberg, one of Hollywood's leading filmmakers. "Oh possum I'm not sure that it's not a grave tactical error but my feet are in the flypaper now and anyway it'll be a good trip and educational," he wrote Katy the night he signed a "jumbled document" and agreed to leave immediately. It was the first important decision he had made alone since their marriage that involved an extended separation, and he was abjectly apologetic about it. Even worse, there had not been time even to say good bye.

A twenty-two-hour flight aboard an ancient Ford trimotor plane that might have been found in a museum rather than in the air did little to dispel the gloom that had set in almost immediately upon Dos Passos' affixing his signature to the film contract promising "big money." The tiny craft pitched its way across country on wings that flapped "like a buzzard's," unperturbed by the air pockets and powerful updrafts as passengers hunkered over their air sickness cartons and prayed for the journey to end. Dos Passos was no exception. He staggered off the plane into the welcoming embrace of Sternberg, who exuded an air of Austrian nobility and appeared to Dos Passos to be the "last paragon of old Viennese culture." He insisted later that Sternberg had been born Joseph Stern in Brooklyn, New York, and that he had never been to Vienna; yet they spent considerable time talking about the Ring, wine festivals, and the Imperial Spanish Riding School of Vienna as though he were a native. On August 1, the *Herald Tribune* carried a misleading news brief: "John Dos Passos, playwright and novelist, has arrived in Hollywood to develop his original story, 'Caprice Espagnol,' as Marlene Dietrich's new starring vehicle. It will be directed by Joseph von Sternberg." Actually, *Spanish Caprice* was the title of a piece by Rimsky-Korsakov on which the music in the film was based. As Dos Passos explained it to Hemingway, he had been hired to "adapt an old smut story . . . a silly novel by Pierre Louÿs, now happily dead, entitled <u>La Femme et le Pantin</u>" (The Woman and the Puppet). Dos Passos was quick to label Hollywood "the world's great bullshit center."

He wrote Estlin Cummings that he and Sternberg had engaged in an interminable "round the mulberry bush conversation" in which neither talked of "what the other party had not intended to make clear." It had "so exacerbated" his rheumatic condition that he was forced to take to his bed after only a glimpse at "the Scarlet Empress," Marlene Dietrich. Dietrich sent him flowers, and Paramount Studios told him not to worry. There was no need to report to an office or work within the confines of a studio, he was told. He could just as easily work in bed. From his room at the Hollywood Plaza Hotel (overlooking Hollywood and Vine), he scribbled to Katy that he had "spilt the milk" and now had to "lap it up." He felt as though he were a small boy who had just been sent to boarding school. His new doctors had offered him a new treatment, he told Katy. He was now being injected with great quantities of cow's milk. Daily the attending physician stopped by his hotel room to administer the shots to his "Celestial buttocks."

Since almost everyone else in Hollywood had a phony name, Dos Passos decided that he should have one, too, and began signing his letters to Katy "WuFang." He told her that his ancestors did not want him writing scenarios. "By god I think they may be right. This miserable Oriental has been behaving rather badly—he lies abed all day and groans and curses when people speak to him." He had been in Hollywood almost two weeks when he addressed Katy as "dearest little andsofaraway and doesn't look like she'd ever get started Possum." Please come join him quickly, he insisted. After a week or ten days in the hotel, Dos Passos was delighted when Francis Faragoh, who had left the New Playwrights Theatre and moved to Hollywood soon after Lawson did, invited him to finish his recuperation in the home he and his wife had bought on North Orange Grove Avenue. The phony Russian food served by "phony Russian waiters" he had been eating at the hotel bored him, and he was quick to accept Faragoh's hospitality. At night, Faragoh and several of his cronies played poker at his bedside and plied him with recent goings-on both behind and in front of the cameras. Dos Passos spoke later of his amusement when he heard that Faragoh's poker-playing friends tithed a share of their winnings to the Communist party. "Communism for the high-salaried screenwriters had become a secret solemn rite," he said.

Meanwhile, Katy had promised to join him in Hollywood after spending a few days with her father in Columbia, Missouri. Instead, she stayed in the Midwest for over two weeks. She and Y. K. Smith, her brother, had set out by train from New York on August 4, 1934, having been notified of their father's hospitalization following the extraction of four infected teeth. Twelve hours after their arrival in Missouri, William Benjamin Smith, Sr., was dead from blood poisoning. Katy and her brother accompanied their father's body to Louisiana, Missouri, for interment beside their mother, then spent another ten days attending to affairs of the estate. Smith's will, signed three days before his death, left his 110-acre farm in Arkansas, bonds, and stocks—valued at four thousand dollars—to be divided equally among his three surviving children, but Katy and Y. K. decided that their younger brother, Bill, needed the bequest more than they did and deeded over their portions to him. Katy may have reasoned that her husband was on the verge of "big money" as a result of his Hollywood venture and that they would not need any of her modest inheritance. Katy's father also left an insurance policy worth twenty-three hundred dollars, which he designated was to provide for the education of his only grandchild, Katharine Merrill Smith, the daughter of Katy's deceased brother, Merrill.

The brief stint Dos Passos had envisioned among the movie moguls stretched to a weary ten weeks even before his fever left him. Katy had joined him in late August looking "awfully pale and blue, but beginning to pick up a little," he reported to Edmund Wilson. On September 18, Katy wrote the Murphys that Dos Passos was "picking up almost as fast as cold molasses." As he saw it, the entire affair had been a fiasco and there would be no encore. He told Cummings that his physical problems had been compounded by his poor progress on the script. With each successive script there was an "increasing disparity" between what he suggested and what came back "from those handsome and efficient typists." Finally it sank in that he was simply a ghostwriter. "The whole thing was being adapted by a young man named Nertz," he complained. To Edmund Wilson he wrote that once having learned his actual relationship to the script, he felt like "Queen

Marie endorsing a vanishing cream," and in his memoirs he concluded that he was lucky that *The Devil Is a Woman,* the title under which *La Femme et le Pantin* was released, had been made from a bed of pain. If he had known what was actually being screened, he would have made a terrible row, he said.

Hollywood was "wonderful" and "funny to see," and its people were almost unbelievable, he allowed to Cummings. He was especially struck by their inordinate capacity for self destruction "by cap pistol, codeine, old dueling swords, drownings, castage out of windows and off bridges. The most spectacular method is for two automobiles crowded with man, woman, and children, each doing seventy with radios tuned in to Martin Luther Thompson, to engage in a head-on collision on the public highway." It was the only way unemployment was being handled, he added. "The Hollywood people dwell in a world that I frankly don't know enough higher mathematics to conceive. . . . Like the New York literati, everybody is on the make and everything is part of something else, but the people have that frank innocent viciousness of little children left down in study hall on a rainy afternoon."

Dos Passos told Wilson that spending a few weeks "in the big money makes us feel strangely broke and parsimonious. Also we are faced with paying our debts. I don't think the big money is what it's cracked up to be." Several weeks earlier he had tucked fifty dollars into a letter to Wilson, whose health he was worried about. "Gosh I wish you'd go down to Boston and see that corps of physicians Katy had lined up for you. Please hold this fifty for a year or so. We'll probably need it more later because this is my last emergence into the big money." He also sent three hundred dollars to Hemingway to begin paying back what he owed him. The word "loan" or "debt" was seldom a part of the active vocabulary of Dos Passos and his friends. It was simply a matter of giving money as they saw fit to those who had less to spend, confident that a reversal of fortunes would reverse the cash flow, too.

Before leaving Hollywood in October, Dos Passos complained to C. A. Pearce, his editor at Harcourt, Brace, that "if you people sold more books you wouldn't have me out in the red-light district like this." Regardless of Pearce's insistence that the company was doing everything possible to promote Dos Passos' books and to keep them in print, the author himself could not resist putting on his neglected-writer hair shirt from time to time with asides that were more than tongue in cheek. He told Pearce that his illness had kept him from working at full strength and that he was far behind where he had hoped to be in putting together the final manuscript of his sequel to *1919,* but he expected to be able to submit the title, at least, before long. "Big money," the phrase that had jeered him ever since affixing his signature on the contract to write a Hollywood script, appeared in almost every letter he wrote during this period. Had it not been for his unhappy fling with Hollywood, his new novel would not have been entitled *The Big Money,* nor would Margo Dowling, his Hollywood starlet, and her promoter, Sam Margolies, have been an important part of his fictive canvas.

Dos Passos and Katy were impatient to put considerable distance between them and life behind the tarnished silver screen as soon as he could hobble up the gangplank in Long Beach and board a United Fruit Lines steamer for Havana. He was sure that if he could bake his aching limbs in the sun astride a deck chair during the voyage east, he would be ambulatory by the time they reached Caribbean waters. The journey was hard on both of them, however. Dos Passos wrote Fitzgerald that Katy had become a trained nurse, and that he had been unable even to go on deck. In Havana they lounged on the roof of the Hotel Ambos Mundos, where they paid thirty-five dollars a week for two rooms that faced the sea and Morro Castle. Their meals were also included. Hemingway, too, was in Havana when they arrived. "Hem's in wonderful shape, got a lot of dope about the marlin this summer, and discovered thirty-six unlisted varieties of fish, but had poor luck in size—they wouldn't come larger than 300 lbs.," he jested to the Murphys in a letter on October 30. He said he had just left his sickbed to take a brief look at the city. There were no tourists in evidence, and he speculated that they had been discouraged by a recent spate of terrorist bombings in butcher shops, department stores, Chinese laundries, yachts, and sailboats. Fulgencio Batista y Zaldívar was "grabbing everything for the army," and students were "breaking up furniture in clubrooms of the left wing and throwing ink on the Rivera-style frescoes," he wrote Wilson. To Robert Cantwell, then an editor at *Time,* he explained that Cuba was interesting "as a sort of social laboratory. It's like these machines they are going to put in men's rooms so that the gents can find out if they have clap or diabetes—you put in a specimen and a little bell rings and zingo you register the disease. . . . This miserable island would be a wonderful place for a man to make a careful study of capitalist contradictions and revolutionary failures." Just as he had used Hollywood as a locale for his novel in progress, so too did he use Havana.

On November 8, 1934, Katy left Dos Passos in Havana and boarded a steamer for New York in a state of near hysteria. She could not find her purse when she got to her stateroom and was convinced that it had been stolen until she received a cable from Dos Passos a few hours later announcing that it had been recovered in the taxi that delivered her to the ship. "Please Katy, let's have no more Ki-ying, you poor little thing, but orderly procedure from one task to another. Do write all the time as now I'll really be quite alarmed as to how that animal will behave off the leash. I wish I hadn't let it go. . . . Please start South soon. You'll find both pocketbook and me quietly awaiting you in Cayo Hueso. . . . Please please possum, no scampering, no mislaying of objects, no running back and forth. . . . Calma—Calma." A day or two later he wrote: "It seems an age since that poor little beast scuttled across the gangplank. Possum please do have a very good time in New York, and no more scampering scuttling or other addlepated and chicken-headed cavortings, please."

Meanwhile, Katy apologized for her behavior at departure in her own inimitable fashion:

> Oh my dearest M. Fish how terrible that the last thing you saw of me should of been a chicken head—what an augury. I almost sprang off the boat and ran after you to show you I had become calm almost at once. Oh dear me. I did quiet right down and was crying peacefully in the stateroom when your wire came. . . . Ape if you would like to cast me off I won't say a word. Oh I nearly cast myself off, but the whole thing is I think Ape, it was probably just the last of my nervous breakdown—as you know I've been having a small one and no wonder, but it could of been worse and the money really lost though I suppose morally it <u>was</u> lost, but still very good luck for such bad luck—that's the kind of luck we've been having. Ape please don't reproach me.

Katy cabled Edith Shay and her brother, Bill, of her expected arrival, and they met the ship and took her to temporary quarters at 314 East Fifty-third Street, near the river on the East Side. Edith, her husband, Frank, and Bill were living in an old, wooden frame house with Edmund Wilson, who had leased it and was renting out rooms to help pay the rent. The Shays lived downstairs with Shay's daughter, Jean, now twelve. The upstairs was occupied by a couple known only as "the Pingreys." Wilson had been living there off and on for two years. Shortly after moving in, he had described the house as "no palace," but said he liked living there. He paid sixty dollars a month and had "a faithful blackamoor" to attend him in his "hermit existence." Katy gathered that things had changed considerably for the Shays and for Wilson during the past year, but she was unprepared for the impoverished state in which she found them.

Upon arrival she wrote Dos Passos that she had shared the gin she had brought from Cuba and enjoyed "light conversation" over dinner prepared by Edith before spending "a lonesome night" in bed without "a Chinaman anywhere in the house." The setting that evening did not appear idyllic to Katy, but it was shocking by daylight. "The house is in the most fearful state you can imagine," she continued.

> The poor Shays have been unable to keep it up in any way, and sunk with it into a state of indescribable squalor. There are fleas, bedbugs (everywhere), and very terrible great rats in the Pingreys' apartment, where I am (the Pingreys have gone). . . . All day long there's a stream of bill collectors and baliffs coming, and drunks lie in the area-way, and the plumber came while I was here almost beside himself with a great hammer and pinchers in his hand and he said he was going to tear out and destroy all the plumbing because AntiX [Wilson] has never paid any of his bills for years, and his miserable creditors are nearly crazy. . . . The bank is foreclosing on the property. It's a wonderful picture of the decline of capitalism, in a way, but it's very distressing. . . . New York seemed horrible to me—so cold, dirty and grotesque after we landed, though fine from the boat. But perhaps my view is warped by the terrible conditions at 314 E. 53rd, which are solid Hogarth all down the street. Poor creatures, Pirate Wench [Frank Shay's book] was just refused today by R. K. O. They nearly took it. The disappointment was so keen that they are now all downstairs drinking up what they can find. . . . AntiX is coming back Thanksgiving.

In each letter to Dos Passos, Katy updated her reports on the Shays and their wretched environment. On November 14, she wrote of being awakened "by a fearful din and uproar . . . drunken angry voices saying 'We'll knock the door down' . . . a fearful crash and voices 'All together now, we'll break her in!' " Shay and her brother had managed to sleep through the commotion, but she awakened them, and Smith opened an upstairs window to "brain them with a chair." It was then, said Katy, that they noticed "a large pale mass lying on the area-way . . . the naked rump of a lady with her skirts over her head, who—in some way I don't understand—was identified by Frank as Mrs. Pingrey." She explained that Edith Shay had simply "given up, like the very poor do in the city, because it's no use. You can't fight the broken glass and garbage and bill collectors and plaster falling off the wall and no money for anything. If AntiX comes to inhabit the Pingreys' quarters it will just be a terrible warren of down and outers, says Edie. The Bailiffs and Catchpoles are after poor AntiX very desperately. He owes $250 back rent and they have tried to seize the furniture, and every day there is a stream of people here clamoring for payment."

When Gerald and Sara Murphy came one afternoon to pick up Katy, they gave her one hundred dollars to "pay off some of Bunny's catchpoles. . . . I'd give anything to embezzle it for myself," she told Dos Passos. The Shays would have to have money or be evicted, said Katy. It occurred to her while staying with the Shays that both she and Edith ought to get back to their writing. Although she gave no details to Dos Passos of her new scheme, she said she had thought up "an enterprise to help Edie make some money. If it goes through it will bring in a regular tidy sum." Katy's plan was to create an adult comic strip in the mode of the current crop of newspaper comics, to be published serially in a magazine such as *Woman's Home Companion.* The plot she conceived involved a bride from St. Louis (Katy's birthplace) in conflict with the groom's family from Baltimore society, and a female rival from high society. Two of the characters were named Spencer and Hackett, actual names of two of Katy's friends on the Cape; she also planned for her characters a honeymoon in Jamaica, where Dos Passos had promised to take her as soon as she felt well enough to rejoin him in Florida, and there were other characters and gimmicks intended to hook readers for a number of installments. By the time Katy left the Shays, she had worked out, with Edith's help, the first chapter of *Bride's Progress,* "The Wedding Day." The women were amused by the irony of the discrepancy between the high-fashion environment of their characters and the squalor in which the scenes were being written. In the same letter in which Katy first mentioned her new undertaking to Dos Passos, she told with relish of Shay's having met "a rat on the stairs that was too big to pass." Shay retreated to let it go by. "It was larger than Sambo . . . and went by in a very insolent way, like a Nazi officer," she added.

Katy's original intent upon arrival in New York was to visit briefly with the Shays, see the Murphys a time or two, then go to Provincetown. She did not feel well and spent most of her first week in bed. "You don't say what you're in bed with," Dos Passos scolded when she did not acknowledge the nature of her malady. "Is it a cold or another stinking headache? Or gut? Please say." Any time Katy had a cold, it usually settled in her chest, turned into a racking cough, and was hard to root out. She also suffered from migraine headaches. Earlier, when he wrote in February from Washington, D. C., to close the house in Provincetown as quickly as possible and join him there so that they could proceed directly to Key West together, he suggested that she stop off first at the Lahey Clinic in Boston for tests. "So enjoyed letter but fear the megrim. . . . Do take care of self—please don't love megrim," he cautioned. A day or two later he wrote, "Possum you will come won't you? . . . and not crawl into a hospital and have to be fetched?"

According to Horsley Gantt, Katy was pregnant at least twice—and probably three times—during the first five or six years of her marriage and miscarried each time. She had tests both at the Lahey Clinic and at Johns Hopkins to try to determine the cause. "I am reasonably sure that Dr. Long at Johns Hopkins performed a gynecological operation upon Katy in the spring of 1934, but it was not something that she and Dos talked about back then," said Gantt. On November 18, 1934, when Dos Passos was in Key West after Katy left him in Havana and took a steamer to New York in a state of agitation, she wrote that she was leaving the Shays' "hovel" in a day or two and going to "see the quacks," but gave no details of her current indisposition. By this time, Dos Passos was thoroughly annoyed by what he termed Katy's "extremely inconsiderate" behavior in not keeping him apprised of her condition.

> I can't understand your not answering my telegrams. . . . If I telegraph it means that I'm worried about you and want a reply. Not answering puts me to a lot of trouble—and worry— If I don't hear tonight I'm going to wire somebody to look you up and see what the trouble is. You must keep me informed and don't take it for granted that I've gotten a letter when it's obvious that it's on account of not receiving a letter that I've telegraphed. I don't like worrying and it just makes me sore at you and I don't like that either, so for Chris' sake don't do it again.

Dos Passos signed himself "Miserable Irascible Ape." He wired both Bill Smith and the Murphys, who replied that Katy had already left for the Cape. "Please don't play any more tricks like that," he admonished. "Ordinarily I wouldn't care so much but I lead a thoroughly isolated existence all day—am a little on the gloomy side anyway and tend to expect the worse." Katy hated being scolded. "Oh Irascible, what an awful letter," she replied. "Ape I never got any telegram from you at all." She explained that she had gone to Boston with Edith Shay "in the team" (the Ford roadster) to see the doctor and have a few tests run, but still did not specify what was wrong. She did not admit to him that she had been hospitalized in the process until her fourth day at the New England Baptist Hospital in Boston. "Oh my dear M. Fish I might as well come clean," Katy's letter began. "I fought like a tiger but they insisted they could not make the damn tests with me at large. . . . I've nothing serious and will rush out of here like a wild thing." She implied that her problem was allergy-related, but did not elaborate. Her chief complaint was that she would be "incarcerated over Thanksgiving. I only hope I don't cry all day."

Dos Passos implored Katy in letter after letter to hurry South to him. The Key West nights were long and cold, he said, and "it would be nice to have company in bed." He also plied her with requests: "Will you buy me a black typewriter ribbon . . . large manila envelopes . . . a package of Park & Davis or Abbott's vitamin A, B and D capsules . . . and you won't forget the Veblen Life and Instinct of Workmanship . . . or William Henry Chamberlin's Russia's Iron Age . . . and Carey's Decline of American Capitalism. . . . I suppose AntiX has left—and left before he got my letter asking him to send down the various books on Henry Ford he had—if he had them."

One of the first things Dos Passos had written once he felt like working in Key West was a tribute to Luis Quintanilla and his work for an exhibition brochure for Quintanilla's one-man show at the Pierre Matisse Gallery, which opened November 20, 1934. The artist himself could not be there. He was in jail in Madrid for his involvement in the October Revolution. Rumor had it that he was going to be sentenced to sixteen years in prison, given a life sentence, or be executed. A few days before the show's opening, Dos Passos wrote a number of letters on behalf of Quintanilla, whom he identified as "a hell of a nice guy" and a "damn good etcher." To Estlin Cummings he explained that Quintanilla was "(a) broke; (b) in jail; (c) and all his friends in Spain are broke, in jail, or in Paris. . . . If you can corral any buyers or stir up any admiration (if you happen to agree with me about the dry prints), it would be enormously appreciated and useful around the Cárcel Modelo" (the prison where Quintanilla was being held). Dos Passos wrote similarly to Malcolm Cowley, and added: "If you like the stuff, please try to get the boys to go to bat for it, articles and stuff like that. I'm hoping that if he's hailed as Spain's best etcher—which he is, in the great line of Goya, etc.,—it may be possible to circulate a petition of some kind that might induce the Spanish government to go a little easy on him." He also suggested that a petition on Quintanilla's behalf "might be an opening wedge for a general protest on the way they crushed the rebellion. It's not so very pretty to use Moorish troops, bombing planes and heavy artillery on your own people and towns— then of course they blamed all the damage on the revolutionaries. . . . Everybody ought to do everything they can to get him out."

Cowley responded to Dos Passos' letter with what seemed to him to be appropriate action. Since the Quintanilla exhibition was to run only until December 4, he decided to put something in the November 28 issue of *The New Republic* to help get more people to view the etchings, people who, in turn, might be willing to sign such a petition as Dos Passos proposed. Pressed for time, Cowley took the liberty of deleting several phrases from Dos Passos' letter that he considered extraneous and revised it slightly to make it resemble more closely the "Letter to the Editor" format of *The New Republic,* then wrote Dos Passos of what he had done. Dos Passos shot back instructions that Cowley must not print anything that could be construed as a plea for funds or to imply that the Spanish government might be influenced in Quintanilla's favor if the exhibition was an artistic success. He also cautioned Cowley not to mention "that son of a bitch Lerroux" (Premier Alejandro Lerroux). The magazine was already in press with Dos Passos' "Letter to the Editor" even before Dos Passos had a chance to put his second letter to Cowley in the mail. "Publishing my confidential letter was a great mistake," he admonished Cowley as soon as he saw his letter in print. "It has just about ruined the effectiveness of what we were trying to do. Having known you for years and thought of you as an honest and trustworthy guy, I couldn't imagine that you could do anything so stupid. . . . That lousy letter of mine being published makes it very difficult for us to raise the kind of protest we were trying to raise in this country." Dos Passos apologized to Cowley almost immediately for lashing out as angrily at him as he had and acknowledged that it was largely his fault for not being more explicit regarding what he had in mind.

It was Hemingway who had financed the exhibition, paid to have the etchings matted, framed, and sent to New York. He had also paid for the exhibition catalogue, written the introduction, and was the one who had asked Dos Passos to write about Quintanilla's etchings and his worth as a satirist. Part of Dos Passos' anger at Cowley was also in reaction to the reproof he anticipated from Hemingway, who was a close friend of Quintanilla. Dos Passos wrote Cowley:

> Hemingway and I both feel we stepped too heavily on the revolution business in our spiels for the catalogue. The etchings are selling pretty well in spite of the lukewarm press. These bastardly critics probably thought Hemingway and I were trying to clean up personally in some way. . . . Forgive me for taking out my accumulated bitterness against the liberal weeklies on you personally—I'm getting pretty crabbed in my old age. Also, in spite of some twenty years spent in the continuous cultivation of letters, it's increasingly more difficult for me to make myself understood either by writing or word of mouth.

Dos Passos and Hemingway, aided by Pierre Matisse himself, circulated a petition that many writers, artists, and other leftists signed in an effort to get Quintanilla released from prison. He was sentenced to sixteen years, but was released in less than a year and attributed his freedom to the trio who had made his first New York exhibition a reality.

Dos Passos and Hemingway teamed up again during the winter of 1934–35 on behalf of another foreign-born painter whose career they wished to launch in the United States, Antonio Gattorno, a thirty-one-year-old Cuban. Hemingway met Gattorno first and lured him as often as possible from his brushes and easel to fish with him in Cuban waters aboard *The Pilar.* Dos Passos was introduced to Gattorno by Hemingway in the fall of 1934 when he and Katy arrived in Havana from California and liked him, as well as his work, immediately. Gattorno's leadership in the avant-garde movement of art in Cuba was undisputed in 1934. At sixteen, Gattorno won a Cuban government scholarship to study painting in Italy and Paris (the youngest person ever to receive such an award), but when he returned to Cuba five years later, he was censured harshly for his nontraditional techniques, which differed radically from the classical nineteenth-century approach then in favor at Havana's Academy of Art. When Dos Passos saw Gattorno's work, he knew that they had much in common in their view of life as well as in their art. Hemingway asked Dos Passos to write a critique of Gattorno's art for a book of his paintings he was getting up, and Dos Passos readily agreed. Hemingway was also arranging and financing an exhibition of Gattorno's work at the Georgette Passedoit Gallery at 22 East Sixtieth Street to run January 6–25, 1935. Dos Passos was in New York for the opening and wrote:

> If you have been looking at Gattorno's paintings you see them as soon as you leave the suburbs of Havana. He seems to have painted them all. You see the men and boys with pale earth colored faces riding their chunky ponies or working in the fields under their broad straw hats or plowing the heavy land with oxen, or scattered, with their machetes in their hands, among the tall white stalks of the royal palms and the ragged intense green of banana patches and shining canefields. You see the bare footed fraily built women standing in the doors of their palm-thatched huts that have bare earth floors and walls of white-washed boards or interwoven palm fibre, and the rickety children and the chickens and the goats and the black pigs dotted over the rolling dry hills under the circling buzzards and the high piled Gulfstream clouds. And always a look of poverty, a certain malarial refinement and sadness and isolation of a transplanted race. They are the *guajiros,* the poor whites of Cuba, and Gattorno has put them on paper and canvas so well that once you have seen his paintings you continue to see the *guajiros* through his eyes.

Dos Passos and Katy were in New York for two weeks in January. She had joined him in Key West on Christmas day, and they returned to the city together a few days later so that he could work in the New York Public Library. He had lacked the necessary resource materials in Key West and said that he was looking forward to getting back to the "big city after all this salubrious rubbish." Once in New York, he jotted notes to a number of people to suggest that they take a look at Gattorno's paintings at the Passedoit Gallery. "As he's entirely unknown here I'm afraid nobody will go to see his stuff," Dos Passos wrote Waldo Frank. "Antonio Gattorno is about the only Cuban painter, and I think a youngster of great originality and talent. . . . Do you know any spectator sportsmen and art lovers and buyers (if such there be) who you could start in that direction?" Although Dos Passos himself had little money to spare, he bought an oil painting of Gattorno's and two ink drawings. He also escorted Gerald Murphy to the exhibition, and Murphy, too, bought a drawing. "I never forgot Dos Passos' help when I was a young unknown in New York," said Gattorno.

Dos Passos told Edmund Wilson that winter that he had given considerable thought during his convalescent state over the past several months regarding what he "would be willing to be shot for." The Kremlin was not on his list, he said. The steps marking the decline of his enthusiasm for the U.S.S.R. were concrete and "fairly obvious," he wrote Wilson: the Kronstadt rebellion in 1921; the massacres by Béla Kun in the Crimea; the persecution of the Socialist revolutionaries; the New Economic Policy of the Soviet Union (the N.E.P.); Trotsky's expulsion in 1927; the abolition of factory committees; and the liquidating of the Kulaks and the Workers' and Peasants' Inspection in 1929—all of which left the "Kremlin absolutely supreme. . . . I've overstated the case against the Kremlin—but I'm at last convinced that means can't be disassociated from ends, and that massacre only creates more massacre and oppression more oppression and means become ends." He told Wilson that given the American aim of freedom and a minimum of oppression, he preferred "the despotism of Henry Ford, the United Fruit, and Standard Oil than that of Earl Browder and Amster and Mike Gold. . . . Whether the Stalinist performances are intellectually justifiable or not, they are alienating the working class movement of the world. What's the use of losing your 'chains' if you get a firing squad instead?"

Wilson, who had applied for a Guggenheim grant to enable him to work at the Marx-Engels Institute in Moscow for a few months, was attempting to clarify his own views at the same time that he challenged Dos Passos' rationale for his acceptance and rejection of the various isms of the day. The two men exchanged a half dozen letters on the subject until Wilson departed for the Soviet Union. Their debate helped Dos Passos bring into focus some of the issues at stake in *The Big Money*. Once he knew what he himself thought, the characters he was having difficulty with would behave more decisively, too, he reasoned. Dos Passos was explicit in his rejection of the politics of the Soviet Union in his letter to Edmund Wilson of December 23, 1934:

Everything I saw, or heard, from Horsley Gantt and others confirms our worst suspicions. This business about Kirov looks very bad to me [Sergei Kirov, a Communist party leader in Leningrad, was murdered; in revenge, the Stalinists executed over one hundred political prisoners without a trial]. In fact it has completely destroyed my benefit-of-the-doubt attitude towards the Stalinists. It seems to be another convolution of the self-destructive tendency that began with the Trotsky-Stalin row. From now on events in Russia have no more interest—except as a terrible example—for world socialism. . . . The thing has gone into its Napoleonic stage and the progressive tendencies in the Soviet government have definitely gone under before the self-protective tendencies. . . . I think we should be very careful not to damage any latent spores of democracy that there still may be in the local American soil. It would be funny if I ended up an Anglo-Saxon chauvinist. Did you ever read my father's Anglo-Saxon Century? We are now getting to the age when papa's shoes yawn wide.

Wilson conceded that Americans who supported socialism should not try to import Russia's methods, but thought the ideas of socialism could be implemented better in the United States than in the Soviet Union. "I can't imagine an American Stalin . . . but you ought to give the Communists, with all their shortcomings, credit for playing a valuable role as agitators. . . . Their influence has been felt through the whole length of American politics. . . . You speak disapprovingly of intellectuals, theories, etc., but aren't you giving evidence, in your present disillusion about the Communists and Russia, of having cherished a typical intellectual illusion?" As Wilson saw it, Dos Passos was being "driven into Marxophobia by the present literary popularity of Marxism." In reply, Dos Passos insisted that it was not the possibility of Stalinism in America that bothered him. "It is the fact that the Stalinist C. P. seems doomed to fail and to bring down with it all the humanitarian tendencies I personally believe in." He said he had never doubted the value of the abolitionists before the Civil War, but saw no reason to give them and their methods a blanket endorsement. The recent massacre after Kirov's murder was "a sign of Stalinism's weakness and not of its strength."

Dos Passos would have never guessed from Wilson's letters that anything was amiss in his personal life other than an occasional reference to poor health—a siege of boils and the like—and he had no idea that Wilson had a serious problem with his creditors and was behaving irrationally. Instead, Wilson made such casual remarks as "The Shays, Bill Smith, and myself are getting along very pleasantly in this house. I don't much like living in New York though any more and have been getting away as much as I could." This letter was dated January 11, 1935, only a few days after Edith Shay reported that she and her husband were awakened at 2 A.M. by

> a pealing doorbell and the shouts of Frank's name from the street. . . . Then came a great splintering crash and Wilson surged in carrying the frame of the front door on his back. A powerful man, Wilson, but I do think people who find themselves locked out of their homes ought to wait a bit before breaking down doors. . . . Wilson scarcely knew what he was doing. After his striking entrance, he just scuttled past us upstairs on all fours and gaining his room threw a lot of furniture over the floor, and today is so pale and wan as to hardly be recognizable as a living man. . . . On coming down to lunch, he asked if we had heard him come in.

Whereas Wilson remarked offhandedly on January 31 to Dos Passos: "I've been leading a pretty quiet life—everything is going on painlessly here," Edith Shay reported scarcely a week later: "Oh dear, Hattie was just down saying that Mr. Wilson was getting up for lunch, so I guess I'll have to go out and bring in some food; he rarely rises until late in the afternoon. He is more restless and crazy than ever, drinking himself into frenzies nearly every night and tearing up newspapers with his teeth, and then so pitiful and sick and despondent in the brief period of sobriety that occurs between the time when he gets up and when he darts out again. I do think some good woman ought to take him in hand." On May 9—the day before Wilson sailed for the Soviet Union—he wrote Dos Passos: "We have all moved out of the 53rd Street house and left it to the sheriffs and the cats." He mentioned, too, having recently seen the motion picture Dos Passos had worked on in Hollywood, *The Devil Is a Woman*. "It is much better than anything else of Sternberg's I have seen and doesn't suffer so much from his awful taste. If you are responsible for this and for the detail, some of which is excellent, you got much further in Hollywood than most people do. It is really quite a good picture." Wilson's comments surprised Dos Passos after hearing about the movie first from Pauline Hemingway and another friend, Esther Andrews, who had seen it in Miami and thought it "unbelievably frightful" and described Marlene Dietrich as "gawky and homely."

Dos Passos and Katy were back in Key West in the spring of 1935 after spending several weeks in Jamaica, and on April 7, set off with Hemingway and Henry Strater for Bimini in the Bahamas to troll for giant tuna. Their first attempt to make the 230-mile crossing was aborted 20 miles at sea when Hemingway accidentally shot himself. He had fired at a shark that one of his crew was trying to boat after the Old Master—as Dos Passos and Katy facetiously referred to him at this time—had hooked it and brought it alongside the boat. Having already fired one shot into the fish from his rifle, he reached for his pistol to finish it off. The gaff snapped under the shark's weight as it made a final convulsive leap, causing the shaft to bounce up and strike Hemingway's hand just as he was poised to fire. The weapon discharged, and the soft-nosed bullet ricocheted from the brass railing, striking both legs and embedding itself into his left calf. Meanwhile, Dos Passos was on the bridge taking movies of the shark being boated when the mishap occurred. He did not hear the shot but saw blood pouring from Hemingway's legs as he descended to the deck. "Jeez Hem, that's a hell of a note. We'd better turn back," he said. Strater had been fighting his own shark during the fracas and was not pleased by Hemingway's shout to cut his shark loose. Katy chalked up the accident to Hemingway's imprudent exhibitionism. She had been exposed to it since he was a child, but had become increasingly disenchanted by it of late. "Katy was so mad she would hardly speak to him," said Dos Passos of his latest antic.

Six days later they set out again, this time with Hemingway playing the invalid. Once in Bimini, Dos Passos and Katy preferred to spend their time ashore instead of fishing. They sunbathed, swam, combed the pearl white beaches picking up shells, and hiked great distances along the shore. Then, for no apparent reason, his rheumatics flared up and she was bothered by intestinal and stomach pains. Dos Passos decided that they should fly back to the mainland so that he could take to his bed in Key West and she could head North for treatment back in Boston, where she had been hospitalized before, or at Johns Hopkins Hospital. Horsley Gantt arranged for her to see an internist and have tests run at Johns Hopkins. Although the precise nature of her disorder was never spoken of in letters during this period, Katy underwent surgery in Baltimore. Gantt wired Dos Passos that she had had "the little operation" and was fine. He said later: "I think it was a D. & C., but I've forgotten the details." Pauline Hemingway dashed off a cryptic message to her husband to report that "Katy has had the operation—no details yet—and Dos Passos a little seedy, doesn't swim, goes home early at night, was in bed two days." In mid-May after Katy had returned to Key West, Dos Passos informed Hemingway that it was "very lucky" she had gone to Johns Hopkins when she did because "the situation demanded very skillful handling. . . . The medico refused to charge—wants an autographed book. We feel very good about the whole thing."

Katy did not return immediately to Key West after her surgery, but traveled first to

New York to spend several days with the Murphys, whose son Baoth had died in mid-March almost without warning, having contracted spinal meningitis while put to bed with measles. Baoth, fifteen, was in prep school when stricken. His parents were unaware that he was seriously ill until they were called to his bedside, where they discovered him dying. Archibald MacLeish, a close friend of the Murphys and of Dos Passos, wrote of Baoth's final hours: "Poor kid—tortured with knives, wracked with agony. Sara kept him alive for four hours sitting beside him saying 'Breathe Baoth! Breathe Baoth!' He didn't hear her but the will came through and he went on. Sara could not believe he was dead." Dos Passos and Katy were aboard *The Pilar* with Hemingway and Pauline when word of Baoth's death arrived. Writing to Gerald and Sara the next day was difficult, but Dos Passos managed a few lines:

> You've been so brave through all this horrible time that it seems hard to write that you must go on and be brave. We admire and love you and wish so there was something we could do. . . . Perhaps later we will be able to cheer you up a little. Just now we feel it's too frightfully hard for anyone to bear. Perhaps it can be a slight too slight consolation to feel that you have friends who feel what you feel—even if dimly and far away—and that you play a large part in their thoughts and feelings. And we want you to go on living bravely and looking around at the world in spite of everything. I wish I could have said goodbye to Baoth. Trying to think of some kind of cheerful word to end a letter with I can't find any.

Katy wrote Dos Passos from the Murphys' apartment in New York City that she had gone to Easthampton for the weekend, since it was Baoth's birthday and she wanted to be with Gerald and Sara to give them something else to think about. Murphy's salvation was an internal crisis with his father's company, Mark Cross, which had gone downhill since the senior Murphy's death in 1931. "Gerald was nearly crushed by what has happened, but this forces him away from his sorrow," wrote Katy, who was more worried about Sara than Gerald. Sara laughed and joked and was as quick and talkative as before, but she brooded desperately, added Katy. Patrick Murphy's life was in danger again, too, because his tuberculosis returned. He was moved to the Trudeau Institute at Saranac Lake, New York, for treatment with Dr. Lorison Brown, a renowned specialist. Patrick's illness was almost more than Sara could bear, said Katy.

Dos Passos tried not to scold Katy about her tendency to overdraw their joint bank account, and he sometimes accused her of overdrawing their funds when she had not. Before leaving Johns Hopkins for New York, he wrote her that money had become a serious problem once more, and that she simply must not overdraw regardless of the circumstances. Katy insisted that she had not written a single check since they were together in Key West. She was recuperating in Horsley Gantt's home for several days when she wrote her brother, Y.K., to please lend her $170. "How mortifying, but sudden operation and hospital took last cent. How humiliating. Thanks darling—can repay next week. How embarrassing." Katy did not tip her hand regarding how she expected to repay her brother within a week's time, nor did she indicate why she needed the money. Whatever the reason, however, she made no reference to her call for help to her brother in any of her letters to Dos Passos during this period. She did mention that besides seeing the

Murphys, she wanted to sell "the strip," the serial she and Edith Shay had been working on in spurts for the past several months.

Whereas Dos Passos did not seem to mind living out of suitcases and being away from Provincetown for months at a time, Katy became homesick for the Cape if she was away for more than a week or two. Living on the lower Cape was essential to her well-being. She also wanted to talk over with Edith Shay, now back in Provincetown, a travel book on Cape Cod that she envisioned as another collaboration. Since the two of them knew the Cape as well as anyone else did, she reasoned, why not write about it and turn a fancy penny. Katy was also worried about the financial straits of the Shays, which she considered more desperate than her own. Sara Murphy usually presented Katy with cash for Christmas, but the Shays had no such benefactor. Dos Passos had sent Katy fifty dollars before she left Baltimore with the suggestion that she "go easy on the spendage" in New York. He said he had received two hundred dollars from Arnold Gingrich for an *Esquire* piece on Gattorno, and from it had repaid Esther Andrews the money he had borrowed a few weeks earlier, but still owed Pauline Hemingway one hundred dollars. He implied that since Hemingway was in Bimini at the time, he had been forced to ask Pauline for money.

According to records kept by Brandt & Brandt, Dos Passos had earned $720.51 in 1934. In 1935 he reportedly made only $634. Neither sum was taxable. Several payments did not have to go through his literary agent, since they were for magazine articles and book reviews contracted independently, but so far as book royalties went, these were his totals. Dos Passos was stymied in 1935 by his inability to promote his work serially. Near the end of April he sent his entire "Charlie Anderson" section of *The Big Money* to Bernice Baumgarten with the suggestion that it could be broken into segments and sold prior to publication. She had sold bits and pieces of *1919*, but was less successful with *The Big Money*, and Dos Passos could not understand why. In May he sent another batch of Charlie Anderson material—the latter part of Anderson's career—which he hoped could be published as a single story entitled "The Knowhow." Perhaps the "Margo Dowling" section could be sold to a woman's magazine, he proposed to Baumgarten. "I sure hope you can sell it because it's pretty silly that after so many years in the racket I haven't yet nailed down a decent serial market. Need jack pretty acutely, so do your best," he urged. At this point he was optimistic that it was worth "a fair-sized piece of change." His tone changed after *Redbook, Harper's Magazine, Scribner's Magazine, The New Yorker, Pictorial Review, The American Magazine, Cosmopolitan, The Atlantic Monthly, Story, The Forum, Esquire*—all turned down the Charlie Anderson section. "I hope the Margo Dowling section will be typed and ready for rejection by the first of September," he wrote Baumgarten. In response to a piece entitled "American Beauty"—which Baumgarten identified as "a new story"—*The New Yorker* replied skeptically: "Seems like some remnant of his postwar writing, and very definitely out of date." Sections from the novel known as "The Crossing" and "Bill of Fare" were also turned down by *The New Yorker* with the comment: "The Dos Passos doesn't seem at all in his usual powerful and effective manner. Are these old things that have recently come to light, or what? Whatever they are, we are of course interested in them, and I wish you would try us again with his things." *Cosmopolitan* replied to his "Home" piece: "Most of our readers felt that this was just too depressing, and despite our interest in this author's work, Mr. Burton felt obliged to mark it for rejection." Dos Passos carried "The Knowhow" piece personally to Paul Hoffman at *The Atlantic Monthly*, who reported: "Despite my own earnest efforts to bring about a favorable decision, I was defeated. . . . The others felt it somewhat below Dos's par—an opinion to which I personally do not subscribe." Dos Passos fired off frequent letters to Baumgarten suggesting various leads for his work. A typical note began: "It seems a slightly cockeyed idea, but the aim of this whole business is training editors—and the more of my stuff they read (maybe), the more likely they are to be less horrified another time. . . . I'm sorry to send you on so many wild goose chases but we may cash in on them later."

Although Dos Passos worked assiduously most of the last half of 1935 in Provincetown, his health now improved, he was still considerably short of completion of *The Big Money* in the fall, when he had hoped to be through with it. From Saranac Lake, New York, where he visited young Patrick Murphy in midsummer, Dos Passos wrote Hemingway that there was nothing like economic pressure to keep him "at the top of the dial. . . . Hoped to send you gents some jack soon but so far can't seem to sell anything. You and Pauline were certainly lifesavers last winter. . . . Too goddam busy finishing this lousy superannuated hypertrophied hellinvented novel to get diseased for a while or worry about the tottering debtstructure." He had been granted a temporary respite from money problems when Brandt & Brandt deposited $483.19 to his account June 3, his portion of Constable's advance (£150) for publishing rights to the British edition of *The Big Money*, and a few additional dollars trickled in when Harcourt, Brace remaindered the nine hundred copies on hand of *1919*, which they hoped to sell in an "Original Editions" promotion at half price ($1.25).

By August, all of his new earnings were depleted, and he wrote Katy—then in New York City trying to sell her "strip" while he remained cloistered in Provincetown—a nononsense report on their financial status: "I've been working pretty steadily and advancing slowly in my usual two steps forward and three steps backward. Nothing that looks like money has come in through the mail and I'm beginning to think I have a jinx. Bernice Baumgarten seems to have thrown up the sponge and is sending the material back. . . . I'm afraid we're in for a no-money period. . . . How we've managed to get suddenly so broke I can't imagine. . . . I'm afraid we'll have to rationalize our expenditures a little." Meanwhile, he added, the next time he was in New York he would try to pry some of his mother's jewelry out of his aunt Mary Lamar Gordon's strongbox. Dos Passos' "Aunt Mamie" still had his mother's jewelry, which he thought seriously of retrieving, then hocking or selling a piece, but he did not petition for the jewelry until almost a decade later. Dos Passos told Katy in his next letter that he was awaiting Rumsey Marvin's response to his question "Do you have any money?" He also enclosed a check for twenty dollars, which drew their bank account down to zero, he admitted, then asked what she thought of his borrowing a few dollars from their Provincetown neighbor, Niles Spencer. "I don't seem to have any borrowing capacity at the moment—wish I was in New York to help keep off the sharks," he lamented.

Gerald Murphy may not have been aware of just how dire Dos Passos' financial predicament was, but he undoubtedly had an inkling when he offered Katy a job with his firm, Mark Cross. Katy was exuberant when she wrote Dos Passos that it was "an advertiser's dream job," and that she had already started, but she did not elaborate on her duties. He learned later that she had been commissioned to design a series of plaques for Mark Cross bearing some of her clever turns of phrase. Marion Smith Lowndes, a close friend of both the Murphys and Dos Passos, recalled one of Katy's plaques, which read: BIRDS THAT FLY TOO HIGH SOMETIMES MISS THEIR NESTS. In September, Sara Murphy sent Dos Passos and Katy several hundred dollars (the exact amount was never disclosed) upon the settling of her mother's estate, which had been tied up for over fifteen years. As Sara explained it: "I have quite a lot of cash to spare and want you to have some of it. . . . The greatest compliment one friend could grant another is to accept." She wrote similarly to Hemingway that fall, also. "We have plenty and Gerald has a good job," she insisted. "I know you can make the money, but why wait? . . . There is plenty more if you need it." She also implored Hemingway not to be cross with her for sending the money without asking if he would accept it. "Friends are the dearest things we have," she told him. Hemingway apparently accepted the money, since he, too, was short of cash. In a letter to Dos Passos that winter, Hemingway complained that some of his friends behaved as though he owned stock in *Esquire* and was "a yachtsman millonario y aficionada a la literatura y los toros," and that he had only three hundred dollars to tide him and his family over until the first of the year. Dos Passos may have felt that he was being nudged by Hemingway to settle his accounts, but was in no financial position to do so.

Dos Passos joined Katy in New York City in October so that he could begin treatment with Dr. John Currence, a specialist who claimed he could eliminate painful attacks of arthritic rheumatism if his patient adhered rigorously to his prescribed regimen of injections, hot baths, "sweats," cold showers, diet, and exercise for three months. Dos Passos agreed to give the "new sawbones" a try, since it suited him anyway to be in the city for a few weeks to use the New York Public Library to complete his "Newsreels" and biographies for *The Big Money*. He also had to interpolate the "Margo Dowling," "Mary French," and "Richard Savage" sections into the Charlie Anderson material, his major story line. By the end of 1935, Dos Passos' health was better than it had been in several years. Currence's "boiling treatments" had paid off, and Dos Passos demonstrated once again his ability to withstand the rigors of a winter in the North. Perhaps he had put his rheumatics behind him for good, he reasoned. C. A. Pearce's recent remarks to Bernice Baumgarten cheered him, too. Pearce said that if *The Big Money* was on his desk by February, they had a good chance to "make a killing." Dos Passos was "so superior to the rest of the radical novelists that there is really no room for comparison. . . . If The Big Money doesn't completely alter Dos Passos' rather downhearted outlook about sales of his books, I shall be miserably mistaken. . . . If there is any element of wish-thinking in his choice of a title for his next novel, I am inclined to think that his wishes will be fulfilled." Baumgarten told Dos Passos that a small fee would soon be in the mail because of the British Broadcasting Company's recent production of *The Garbage Man*, presented twice, and that two more foreign sales were being negotiated for his book of essays, *In All Countries*, in addition to the French and Czech editions scheduled to be out soon. At year's end he thought his life was on the upswing once more and hoped that he had seen the last of his three-digit income. Yet despite the promise of money to come, he would have welcomed any three-digit figure as a bank balance during the winter and spring of 1935–36.

He would have been happier, too, if he and Katy had been able to spend more time together that winter. It seemed that their paths crossed only intermittently, for which he largely blamed himself. He had spent much of the winter and early spring at the Hotel Lafayette in New York City working and going regularly for treatments with Dr. Currence (sometimes Dos Passos interrupted a letter to say he had to "go up to be boiled again"), and Katy was back on the Cape.

Before leaving New York in January, Katy persuaded an editor at Dodge Publishing Company that she and Edith Shay could have a good-sized travel guide to Cape Cod ready in time for the onslaught of tourists in May, and for two months she and Edith chased up and down the Cape during one of New England's severest winter storms of the decade. Undaunted by rain, sleet, or snow, the two women combed the hook of the Cape for photographs and sundry other materials for their guidebook. Dos Passos worried inordinately about Katy's health and feared she would not exercise good judgment, traipsing about the raw countryside, after reading her account of driving from New York City to Provincetown with their two standard poodles, Liza-poodle and Patapouf, Patapouf's six puppies, Mrs. Cat, and four Siamese kittens:

> Oh Ape, a terrific trip down and the pups were terrible. They were all right when we started and quiet in their box, but when we got further along the sea air got to them and they began to howl and push out of the box and started to grow, and when we got across the canal you couldn't control them and one of them was barking. They got larger and stronger every minute—began to crawl over the car got up on the seat and in the gears and fell out on the road when we opened the door and we were afraid we'd have seven grown dogs by the time we got here. They arrived feeling great but I was nearly dead, the driving was so difficult—roads good in spots but lots of them just glazed ice and the towns were a muck of wrecks and slush and every car but ours clunking with chains.

Dos Passos grumbled in reply that he wished she were "out of that awful guidebook" and allowed that it was all his fault "for not stepping on it in the beginning." He was sure it would turn out "darn well" despite his qualms, but urged: "Oh please, don't be a literary lady who arrives in New York—oh please—not literary lady meets literary gent at Lafayette."

Katy replied that she and Edith were reverting to their old status as "Blondheim girls," the name by which they had been known when they first established Smooley Hall in a house on Front Street (Commercial Street) owned by artist Adolph Blondheim. "People we haven't seen for years turn up and invite us to tea and never mention our husbands at all," she teased. In addition to working on her guidebook, Katy was still trying to sell her adult "strip" that she had been writing intermittently for over a year. Having published a travel piece, "Just over the Border," in the *Woman's Home Companion* recently, she decided to submit her strip, now entitled "Bride's Progress," to Willa Roberts, a senior editor at the *Woman's Home Companion*. Katy was in New York when she reported to Dos Passos:

Ape, it's not absolutely sewed up yet, but think Woman's Home is going to take the strip. They are crazy about it. "It's a risk," Roberts said, "but we want to take it—it's so new and fresh." M. Fish, I knew they had taken the mullet when Miss Roberts swept me into the Park Lane for lunch—all at once it came over me—I was an author being lunched by an editor, and as we finished ordering the capon gelantine (very nasty indeed), Mrs. Roberts said, "I may as well admit that we are frankly struck by your idea, and are willing to try it for six months —after that, perhaps we might see." Ape, I had all I could do to keep from running up the striped umbrellas but controlled myself. . . . She also said that the Mexican article was the most successful they'd ever had—and has been their model for all their travel articles. . . . Oh I hope I can keep away from hubris.

In the spring, Katy received her first check for "Bride's Progress," which began serially in the May issue of *Woman's Home Companion.* Although Edith Shay had assisted with the initial chapter, the primary writing was Katy's and only her name was carried on the strip as its author; however, Katy shared her proceeds with Edith, on whose account she had thought up the strip in the first place.

Meanwhile, Dos Passos complained about his own wretched progress on *The Big Money* throughout his three-month stay in New York during the winter and early spring of 1935–36. Never had a book gone so slowly, he rued, nor had his literary situation been so deplorable. In one note he told Katy: "I am thinking of getting false whiskers and slipping away and just not referring to the matter again. . . . The book is growing worse than the puppies but it's not finishing," to which she replied: "M. Fish, do not feel too despondent on account of the book. Give it its head and it will make a fine finish, oh thou poor Ape." She knew the difficulties of bringing a long work to a close, although her own experience was far more limited than his. Had she not had the help of Edith Shay, whose forte was her attention to details, organizing, and editing, she would not have finished *Down the Cape: The Complete Guide to Cape Cod* as agreed upon for publication in May 1936. The book appeared under Katy's maiden name, Katharine Smith, and Edith Shay was listed as coauthor. Katy had used the name "Dos Passos" for her "Bride's Progress" strip in *Woman's Home Companion,* but may have chosen her maiden name to avoid confusion, since Dos Passos' novel was due out a few weeks later.

Tentative publication dates of *The Big Money* had been rolled back several times in 1936. On January 21, Dos Passos wrote Katy that he was about to finish the William Randolph Hearst portrait, which he had already sold to Selden Rodman for the March issue of *Common Sense. Esquire,* which had turned down the "Charlie Anderson" section, accepted the "Art and Isadora" minibiography of Isadora Duncan for its March issue and ran other excerpts from the novel each month until its publication August 1, 1936. Baumgarten was relentless in her efforts to sell Dos Passos' manuscript serially and as individual pieces. She placed "The Crossing" (earlier turned down by *The New Yorker* and *The Atlantic Monthly)* in the February issue of *Partisan Review,* the piece now retitled "Grade Crossing." Other magazines carrying prepublication excerpts included *Partisan Review and Anvil, The American Mercury,* and *The New Republic* ("The Wrights at Kitty Hawk" was in the July 8 issue of *The New Republic* and "Vag," the final episode in the novel, in the July 22 issue). Malcolm Cowley rejected an excerpt Dos Passos had sent him on January 15 with the request that if it could be used, to "please try to hitch up the price a little. Just past my fortieth birthday and feel I ought to be making more money. After all, all I ask is your top." Dos Passos' postscript to Hemingway on February 7 may have been prompted by Cowley's rejection: "Christ it's hard to get money for anything or to get any bastard to publish anything."

He was frustrated, too, because Edmund Wilson had recently approached him at a party and dunned him, he told Katy: "Dr. AntiX fixed me with a pale gold eye and said he wanted the one hundred fifty dollars back due to a change of plans." The cash dribbling in from his few magazine sales had not enabled him to put anything aside, and he had counted on repaying Wilson with royalties from *The Big Money*, still some five months away. His editor's prediction that the book would be a success provided scant comfort in such moments. "I don't know quite where to find it—maybe I can get it from Jack Lawson," Dos Passos ventured to Katy in reference to his debt to Wilson. Katy usually replied to her husband's financial lamentations with a droll remark such as "What a blow from Indian Giver AntiChrist—where will we get the money, or any money in fact, as we are now just a couple of paupers not on relief. . . . Why does that Old Navajo AntiX have to have his money back so soon? Is he fleeing somebody?"

Again, Dos Passos sought out John Howard Lawson, who never turned a deaf ear to his friend's emergent requests for money despite their relationship having become somewhat strained because of their divergent views regarding American Communism and the proletariat. Lawson helped Dos Passos settle his debt to Wilson and gave him cash to pay bills and tide him and Katy over for a while. She was in the city when Dos Passos mailed her a check for "twenty-five iron men" and attributed their windfall to Lawson. "Thought you might need it up there. Leaves me eighteen and some cash which will carry me through the week," he added. He told of going to the zoo in New York one afternoon for diversion instead of to a museum, which he preferred, because he did not have enough money for admission. Their financial distress was relieved somewhat that spring after a London attorney notified him that Sophia Louisa Meakin had died on February 15, 1936, and made him sole heir to her modest estate. Considerable stock was listed in the will that was no longer available because it had been sold to meet expenses following the death of her companion, Kate Gee, a few years earlier, but a dozen shares of DeBeers Consolidated Mines and one or two other stocks were still intact. Dos Passos requested that the stock be sold, and some $350 arrived when he needed it most.

Dos Passos and Katy avoided asking Gerald Murphy for money, preferring instead to rotate their distress signals among other friends of long duration who had also known lean times. They may have surmised that Murphy would not have treated a request for money as a loan or accepted repayment. Murphy was alert to their needs, nevertheless, and sometimes made a contribution to Dos Passos' wardrobe when he noticed that it seemed threadbare. "Beau Murphy presented me a wonderful brown suit that I haven't tried on yet," Dos Passos wrote Katy from New York during the winter of 1935–36. On February 2, 1934, he wrote her: "Wish you were here to go to Washington on the 5:53 train in company of a magnificent overcoat with which I've been outfitted by Puss and Mrs. Puss" (their pet names for the Murphys). Sara Murphy usually gave money to Katy on her birthday or for Christmas and sometimes bought her an outfit for some special occasion.

When Dos Passos and Katy set out by automobile for southern Florida in May to join Hemingway on another fishing expedition, they insisted that Sara Murphy go with them. She was still mourning the death of Baoth and had rarely left Patrick's bedside throughout his long tubercular illness. Whereas Gerald Murphy had recently spent a month in Europe on business for Mark Cross and had his company to divert him daily, Sara had no such relief and was close to a total collapse. By the time they arrived in Miami, Hemingway had already taken *The Pilar* across the Gulf Stream to Havana, where they were to meet him. On the trip down, Dos Passos pored over his galley proofs of *The Big Money,* which he finished reading at the Miami Colonial Hotel and put in the mail to Bernice Baumgarten on May 2 before boarding a plane to Cuba. He still had another set of galleys with him to read and correct for Constable, his British publisher, who had agreed to publish *The Big Money* one month after the American edition appeared. Before mailing the corrected proofs to Baumgarten, Dos Passos asked her to get for him another one thousand dollars from Harcourt, Brace and to deposit it to his account at the Chemical Bank & Trust Company in New York City so that he could afford to write checks during his vacation.

Hemingway complained later that he had barely seen Dos Passos in Havana because he had been buried under the British proofs practically the entire visit. He had invited Dos Passos to fish with him, and he was irritated to find him unwilling to engage in the old camaraderie they had once known when he had summoned Dos Passos and other "cronies to cavort in the deep." He also resented having the responsibility of entertaining Katy and Sara without Pauline's being there to help him. Even worse, the fishing was not good. Sara was on edge and impatient to return North to be with Patrick, still at Saranac Lake, and Dos Passos said that he needed to get back to Miami to put the British proofs into the mail; therefore, they had stayed only a week. Dos Passos wrote Baumgarten that "the proofs were a long job. The whole thing is too damn long. I'm thinking of changing my name to Wolfe and calling the whole thing <u>Of Time and the Sewer</u>."

Dos Passos felt guilty at never having raised his eyes from his lap during their week with Hemingway aboard *The Pilar,* where they stayed while in Havana. "Gosh Hem, it was a tough proposition for you, me bringing all the women folk to Havana, but the trip really did Sara a great deal of good." He also sent Hemingway a case of champagne. Hemingway had asked Dos Passos to leave the extra set of proofs he had with him so that he, too, could read them, and a few days after Dos Passos returned to New York, he wrote: "You must have had hell with that to proofread—it's as long as the Bible but I can see why you couldn't cut it more. The shorter those years seemed, the longer it takes to write them." Hemingway also apologized for having behaved badly during their few days together in Havana: "Will make a good trip soon with lots of exercise and no proof and no bellyaching by old Hem. . . . Would like to have a chance to not mistreat my friends sometime."

The Big Money appeared August 6, 1936, to private hurrahs by most of Dos Passos' literary friends and to considerable public acclaim by the critics. The novel was boosted into the limelight by something Harcourt, Brace's generous advertising budget could not buy, its author's photograph on the August 10 cover of *Time.* Open-collared and drawing on the stub of a cigar, a rugged-looking Dos Passos faced his readers—glasses off, no trace of myopia in his compelling, steady gaze—and under the portrait, his full name, JOHN

RODERIGO DOS PASSOS, with the arresting phrase: "Writes to be damned, not to be saved." Dos Passos was only the twelfth literary figure in a decade to appear on *Time*'s cover, and the first in two years (a notable distinction, since the magazine published fifty-two issues each year).

The choice was attributed to Dos Passos' friend Robert Cantwell, then a novelist and editor for *Time,* who suggested the feature. Cantwell drove a staff photographer, R. H. Hoffmann, and T. S. Matthews to Provincetown in July for a round of interviews and picture taking that made the Dos Passos name and face a household item to several hundred thousand readers across the country. The other literary figures who had preceded Dos Passos on the cover of *Time* during the last decade were Sinclair Lewis (1927); Eugene O'Neill (1928 and 1931); Willa Cather (1931); Philip Barry and Robinson Jeffers (1932); Noel Coward and Gertrude Stein (1933); and James Joyce, Thomas Mann, Upton Sinclair, and Maxwell Anderson (1934). Dos Passos was the only literary figure to make the cover of *Time* in 1936, a year that saw Haile Selassie as *Time*'s "Man of the Year." Adolf Hitler, Shirley Temple, Clark Gable, Eugene Talmadge, Marlene Dietrich, Emperor Hirohito, Joe DiMaggio, Chiang Kai-shek, and Salvador Dali also made *Time*'s cover in 1936. Ernest Hemingway and Virginia Woolf were the only literary figures in 1937.

Although being on the cover of *Time* sold books, Dos Passos did well on his own, aided by dozens of advertisements in major newspapers and magazines throughout the country placed almost daily by the advertising strategists of Harcourt, Brace, who did everything possible within its allotted budget to promote *The Big Money.* A week before its publication, advance sales topped seven thousand, and by the end of August the novel was in its fourth printing and on several lists of bestsellers. "What's all this nonsense about another printing? Are you sure you aren't binding up some lost sheets of <u>Anthony Adverse</u> behind that jacket?" Dos Passos teased his editor. "If this keeps up we'll be garnering in the mortgages with the October apples. . . . It'll be a long time before it makes any difference to me yet, but my creditors must be rubbing their hands."

Dozens of reviews of *The Big Money* came across Dos Passos' desk during the summer and fall of 1936, but he paid little attention to them. He believed that he was his own most severe critic, but appreciated reactions from friends. John Howard Lawson wrote that the novel was "terrifically exciting and far more completely realized than the two earlier books." Scott Fitzgerald said that after reading the novel he caught himself referring to "a Cuban boy I once knew . . . and a girl I knew who knew a Cuban boy once," characters in the "Margo Dowling" section of *The Big Money.* The characters and many of the incidents took on a life within his own experience, he explained. Upton Sinclair wrote of having read the book in two days and thought it "the best picture of present-day America" yet encountered. He liked its structure, too, and thought it less confusing to follow than the others. "Such control helps simple minds like mine," he confessed. "I read it with great interest and admiration." Edmund Wilson called *The Big Money* "a noble performance" and said he liked the "Charlie Anderson" narrative best, but thought that all of the fictional sections were "original and remarkable." Especially successful was Dos Passos' depiction throughout the trilogy—not just in *The Big Money* —of "people in those moments when they are at loose ends or drifting or up against a blank wall," as when Moorehouse had "washed up in Pittsburgh and simply lies on the bed for several days, not knowing what he is going to do next—moments when the social currents, taking advantage of the set of the character, will sweep the individual in." Wilson saw such moments and the purposeful careers of the men and women in the biographical sections as the book's "positive and negative poles." He thought Dos Passos might have preserved more of the "glamor and exhilaration of the good times which Americans thought they were having during the Boom." Although the ending of *The Big Money* suffered in comparison to the "brilliance" of the ending of *1919,* all in all, Dos Passos had allowed for "more of life and cheated less" on the actualities of human experience than any other radical writer, Wilson concluded.

Dos Passos replied that he was "darn glad" Wilson liked the book. He, too, was disappointed in the end, he admitted. "I guess I ought to have put more work in on it but I'd more or less worked myself out trying to carry the framework too long." Perhaps when the three books were published under one cover, the deficiencies would be less glaring, he suggested.

Horace Gregory launched the major big city reviews on August 9, 1936, with the full front page of the New York *Herald Tribune Books.* Gregory treated *The Big Money* within the context of the total trilogy and deemed it "one of the most impressive contributions made to the literature of our time" and its author, "one of the most important of our contemporary poets." *The Big Money* established Dos Passos' position as "the most incisive and direct of American satirists. . . . Only the most unresponsive reader would fail to appreciate the humor which is the force behind the keen stroke of Mr. Dos Passos' irony," said Gregory, who suggested that the trilogy be read in three successive sittings as "one might witness three successive performances of a single motion picture." The entire work was "an experiment in *montage* as applied to modern prose." *The Big Money* was the best of the trio, but Gregory was not completely sold on the "Camera Eye," which seemed "arty rather than artful." He also suggested that readers not confuse Dos Passos' objectives in the novel with those of "strictly Marxian critics."

J. Donald Adams' review of August 16 appeared on page two of the New York *Times Book Review.* Adams saw Dos Passos as the country's "ablest naturalistic craftsman" and thought him without peer in writing convincingly of all levels of American society. He only regretted that Dos Passos did not see fit to include in his novel a character whose life was "lived with integrity, with purpose, and by standards which are not for a day. There are many such people in America, and one of them should have been in the picture."

Malcolm Cowley reviewed *The Big Money* for *The New Republic* and faulted it for failing to include an important aspect of contemporary life, the "will to struggle ahead, the comradeship in struggle, the consciousness of new men and new forces continually rising." America might appear to be a beaten nation, but the fight was not over, he insisted. Cowley liked Dos Passos' successful merger of the art novel's emphasis on the individual and the collective novel's emphasis on society—enhanced by the technique of the "Camera Eye," he said, which supplied the "inwardness" lacking in the general narrative.

T. S. Matthews (in an anonymous review in *Time)* referred to Dos Passos as a "private historian" who believed that "a writer's modest job is to be an architect of history." His power of writing was more likely to be "exercised vertically through a century than horizontally over a year's sales." Matthews saw Dos Passos as unique among American writers. "To find the equivalent of his nationalism one must look ahead to Tolstoy's *War and Peace,* to Balzac's *Comédie Humaine,* to James Joyce's *Ulysses.*"

Herschel Brickell informed readers of the *Review of Reviews* that there was almost nothing redeeming about *The Big Money.* He doubted the reportage of the period, thought Dos Passos' portrait of America was a "figment of his imagination," termed his plot and characterization "vapid," called the book as a whole "tedious and unimportant." The Brooklyn *Daily Eagle*'s reviewer, Alvah C. Bessie, admitted that Dos Passos wrote in such an "enthralling fashion" that a reader could not put the book down until "utterly fatigued," yet his "many gifts—of sardonic comment, of painstaking and pertinent research—of brilliant narrative technique, of the elaboration of fictional incident" were insufficient to provide the reader with a book designed to "outlast its time as something more than contemporary documentation." Bessie saw as a fundamental failure the author's inability to create characters from the "inside"; moreover, there was no "cumulative increment of power observable" despite each separate novel in the trilogy having moments of "high effectiveness and emotional evocation."

A few days before publication of *The Big Money,* Dos Passos and Katy retreated to their cottage in the dunes of South Truro to hide out for the remainder of the summer. They had turned the Provincetown house over to Edmund Wilson, who rented it for six weeks for $200. When Dos Passos wrote Bernice Baumgarten for an additional $250 from his royalties, which he specified were to pay bills with, he added that the only thing he saw consistent in his life was his increasing capacity to spend money. This time the money went not for travel, but for home improvements. He and Katy remodeled the kitchen of the Provincetown house, bought a stove, curtains, linens, and other furnishings for the Truro house, refurbished "the barn"—a small structure on the Truro property—and converted it into a guest cottage. They also bought a boat. "Dos and I have gone aquatic and sail and boat all the time," Katy wrote Wilson just before he moved into their Provincetown home the first of August. She likened their holidays to a "delirious roller-coaster kind of summer . . . all very up and down, fast, yelling and out of control." Dos Passos and Katy were relieved to be out of Provincetown for a while. She wrote Sara Murphy that they had been subjected to many strange visitors that summer, "most of them crazy." Three came in one day, she continued: "One came to tell Dos that he was a babe in the wood, another to complain that his brother was persecuting him by camping in his front yard with a tent, and the third, a pale young man from Harvard preparing for a diplomatic career in communism ('when it comes')—all very fanatical and hard to get rid of." She never did see the relevancy of such visits, but Dos Passos was polite to his callers and treated their missions with seriousness.

Dos Passos began a voracious reading of American history during the summer of 1936, having put *The Big Money* behind him and not actively involved yet in the writing of a new, long manuscript. Upon reading Wilson's recent book, *Travels in Two Democracies*—which grew out of Wilson's trip to the Soviet Union—Dos Passos told him that he liked the book and felt that it paid off in the long run "to put down what happens just as it does happen. I'm not at all sure that it isn't all anybody can do that's of any permanent use in a literary way." When he wrote Theodore Dreiser in August to suggest that he visit them in South Truro, he ventured that it would be "good to chew the rag a little about the state of the nation. I'm trying to do a lot of reading this summer to find out what the damn country was like in the old days." In September he wrote Fitzgerald that he reproached himself now for sitting on his "tail at home while etcetera etcetera is on the march to Rome. . . . We're living in one of the damnedest tragic moments in history." Having just read Fitzgerald's recently serialized autobiographical piece, "The Crack-up," in *Esquire*, Dos Passos could not resist adding: "Christ man, how do you find time in the middle of the general conflagration to worry about all that stuff? . . . If you want to go to pieces I think it's absolutely O.K., but I thought you ought to write a first-rate novel about it (and you probably will) instead of spilling it in little pieces for Arnold Gingrich."

When Hemingway wrote Dos Passos from the Nordquist L-Bar-T ranch in Wyoming in October 1936 to invite him to hunt with him again, he begged off: "Can't get out there this year—wish to hell I could—no money—the B.M. is selling very moderately but it'll have to sell a hell of a lot more to do me any good." Hemingway may have thought Dos Passos' excuse a lame one, knowing full well that the book was selling well, although he had no idea what the actual sales figures were. Dos Passos' explanation did not surprise Hemingway when he read: "We've gone and increased our standard of living and something's got to be done about it. Seems like the more money you make, the farther off you are from balancing up the books. Maybe the combined volume will sell." From Hemingway's point of view, "balancing the books" should also include Dos Passos' repayment of the rest of the money he had borrowed from him of late. Dos Passos allowed to Hemingway, too, that even if he had the money to spare for a trip to Wyoming, he had to stick to "an asinine pamphlet" *(Terror in Cuba)*, published by the Workers Defense League in November 1936, for which he had been asked to write a preface.

The crux of Dos Passos' malcontent went much deeper than being short of cash or having an "asinine pamphlet" on which to work. What worried him most, he told Hemingway, was "making a living at this lousy trade. . . . One book a year makes a million dollars and everything else drags out an existence on the shelves, is remaindered, and forgotten. If people keep on using books at all by the end of this century, they sure will have a time weeding out the few sound bits of meat among the garbage." Dos Passos was still nursing his indignation upon learning that *In All Countries* was being remaindered. It had been out scarcely two years, and its single edition consisted of fifteen hundred copies. Moreover, a week before publication of *The Big Money*, he was notified that *Three Plays*, also published in 1934, was being remaindered. Of its fifteen hundred copies, some three hundred were still on hand, he was told, and only eight copies had been sold during the first six months of 1936. Harcourt, Brace gave him the opportunity to buy the books on hand at eighteen cents a copy (one half the publisher's cost), but he declined. Instead, he gave ten copies to an amateur theater group in Brooklyn that had asked permission to present *Fortune Heights.* He said he did not care what Harcourt, Brace did with the balance of the copies if they "did not try to sell them for a decent price."

After brooding about the fate of *In All Countries*, Dos Passos wrote a long letter to

C. A. Pearce to spell out the problem and a solution, which he hoped would be considered:

> Suppose you have an author, Nathaniel Twinklebottom say, whose work seems to have some permanent value. Instead of looking for El Dorado on a speculative basis with each book of his you publish and then having the officeboy sweep it out from under the desk six months later, I think your aim ought to be to build up a slow basic sale from all his works. To do that you have to begin from the ground up by convincing the booksellers that it's to their advantage to be a little less hysterical about their business, and alongside of the big wows of the moment, to keep the past works of a certain number of writers in stock instead of only their overpublicized novelties. Then, if somebody comes in to ask for the next novel of Nathaniel Twinklebottom before it's printed, instead of trying to sell him <u>Eyeless in Gaza</u>, the clerk could sell him some of Nat's past works, an early volume of poems or essays. Coming back to my own work and the fact that I have to make a living out of it, I feel very strongly that that is how it ought to be handled. . . . Somebody's got to start bringing the bookselling and publishing business back to sanity, and it seems to me that Harcourt, Brace is the firm to do it. . . . Pass these suggestions on to Messrs. Harcourt and Brace, will you? I'd like to know what they think of them.

One of the most enthusiastic personal letters Dos Passos had received that summer in support of *The Big Money* came from Alfred Harcourt, who read an advance copy of the novel and predicted its "enormous success." The firm planned to use it to launch the fall season, he said. In return, Dos Passos asked that he not simply be considered a "flash in the pan" and his book allowed to die in a year or two. Donald Brace read Dos Passos' letter to Pearce and wrote his own letter of assurance. The firm would continue to backlist him as an author, just as they did other important authors in this house. Dos Passos' ideas were already things they were doing, said Brace. Their problem was that their backlist had to be a limited one. Brace reminded Dos Passos that they had already evidenced good faith by buying from Harper & Brothers (for one thousand dollars) the plates, existing stock, and all publishing rights to everything Harper's had published: *The 42nd Parallel, Manhattan Transfer, Orient Express,* and *Panama, or The Adventures of My Seven Uncles.* Moreover, the publishing house was committed to publishing *The 42nd Parallel, 1919,* and *The Big Money* as a single-volume trilogy as soon as they could appropriately do so and not interfere with the sales of *The Big Money.* Dos Passos had not expected his letter to Pearce to result in a reversal of the order to remainder *In All Countries,* but he felt his convictions strongly and was relieved to have spoken his mind. Since he could not bring back to the bookshelves what had already been let go, at least he could get up a new collection of essays to succeed the remaindered book, he reasoned, and saw it as a project for 1937.

Just as Harper & Brothers had balked at publishing *1919* unless Dos Passos consented to their removing the J. P. Morgan portrait, so too did Constable raise serious objections to the Samuel Insull minibiography in *The Big Money.* Either the sketch or the book itself would have to go, he was told. Insull was "of English origin" and the firm did not want to run "grave risks of prosecution for defamation or libel," Bernice Baumgarten wrote Dos Passos. The offensive Insull portrait, "Power Superpower," had been overlooked earlier because it began with a focus upon Thomas Edison. The entire affair was ridiculous, countered Dos Passos, who pointed out that no change had been called for in the American edition. Finally he agreed to write a new version of the portrait. For ten days he worked over the old portrait and revised more fully than he intended. "I rather wish I'd put it in the American edition in this form. It's shorter, too, which is always a help. I think Constable will swallow it now," he wrote Baumgarten when he mailed her the new material. "I think it was using so many names that kayoed him," Dos Passos reasoned. Taking out most of the other proper names in the piece enabled Dos Passos to sharpen his focus upon Insull, about whom they had feared offending in the first place, and the entire sketch was stronger. Constable accepted the new manuscript and brought the book out on schedule, October 22, 1936.

A few days later, Dos Passos was leafing through his author's copy of the British edition when it struck him that there was something odd about the book. The controversial Insull portrait was there as he had rewritten it, and the entire edition looked good. Suddenly he realized that the final "Mary French" section was missing, and so was "Vag," the chapter with which the book ended. Thirty pages were missing. He was astounded. AUTHOR HYSTERICAL, PRESUME BINDER'S ERROR, read the British agent's cable to the publisher. All faulty copies must be recalled and distribution stopped immediately, insisted Dos Passos. Ultimately the blame was placed upon the printer, who substituted the revised Insull section and neglected to reinsert the two sections that followed it. Except for a few copies that remained untraceable, said Dos Passos' British agent, the entire edition had been rebound and the muddle cleared up, but it was Christmas before everyone breathed easily about the matter.

At year's end, negotiations were already under way for translations of *The Big Money* into French, Italian, Hungarian, and German (the German edition was to be published in Vienna, since trouble was brewing in Germany). Dos Passos had the satisfaction of learning, too, that despite *In All Countries'* having been taken out of circulation in America, the book had now been spoken for by publishers in Italy and France. In late December C. A. Pearce advised him that *The Big Money*'s sales now totaled twenty thousand copies. Counting the one thousand dollars he had drawn in May upon mailing in the galley proofs, Dos Passos received some thirty-five hundred dollars for his new book and still had a little money in the bank from which to draw to start the new year.

Although his current novel was selling better than any of his previous volumes—fiction or nonfiction—Dos Passos wrote Hemingway in January 1937 that he was "sore, broke, and sick of everything. . . . Damn sorry about not being able to pay you back any dough, but this lousy novel hasn't made any and have had to catch up on more pressing debts." He blamed Katy for some of his debts. She had a penchant for houses. One of her favorite activities during the thirties was observing foreclosure auctions from the steps of the Barnstable County courthouse. It was Katy, not Dos Passos, who had bought the cottage in South Truro, and once it was refurbished she began to look about for another good buy. She had her own bank account maintained under her maiden name, and what little money she generated on her own usually was squirreled away against the eventuality that another house she wanted came on the market. In the spring of 1936 she bought another house in an estate sale, this one financed largely from her royalties for her Cape Cod guidebook. She paid three thousand dollars for the L. D. Baker house on Bound

Brook Road in Wellfleet, a small cottage just off the beach. As poor as they were, Dos Passos considered Katy's latest purchase sheer folly. According to John Hughes Hall, who bought the house from Katy less than a year later for thirty-two hundred dollars. "She made nothing on the house—the difference between her price and mine was because of the trees she planted and for interest on the loan. Katy and Dos never lived in the house; it was just a dream of Katy's." Dos Passos did not object so much to Katy's buying houses as he did the money required for their upkeep. He was rankled when Katy's creditors took him by surprise when she was out of town. "Oh Katy please let's not run up any more bills or buy any more houses," he admonished when she was at a health spa in Virginia in November 1936 and he was in Provincetown. "I hadn't planned to be so disappointed when I got your wire saying you weren't coming till Friday, but to be here alone with all these dreadful houses and the bills pouring in is certainly not much fun," he began one letter.

> I've always lived successfully from hand to mouth without the slightest worry, but I can't combine that with unpaid bills and financial operations. Forgive these gloomy reflections. They are induced by a summons from Days to pay a coal bill I've never heard of. . . . Possum, we just can't continue leaving unpaid bills around like this. Honestly it's a mania with you not to pay bills. Let's clean it up. I feel as depressed and lethargic as an old Provincetowner. But Katy, if you should come Friday I'd feel much better, and the two hundred bucks will pay all the most pressing bills so don't worry. But it's just horrid here without you.

Dos Passos had recently borrowed two hundred dollars from Rumsey Marvin to tide them over until some book money came in, and he resented having to spend any portion of it unnecessarily. Katy had gone for health treatments for her migraine headaches, nasal polyps, and an almost chronic sinus infection, but when she stayed for three weeks and was trying to finish a travel article and drop it off on her way through New York City, he reasoned that she could come home to write. It seemed that more and more they only met each other in passing. Dos Passos, too, was feeling infirm that fall and was impatient to return to New York for another "boiling" at the hands of Currence, the specialist who had eased his rheumatics considerably during the past year. He was also due in New York to attend a meeting of the newly formed American Committee to Aid Spanish Democracy, with which he had been working since early fall. For the next eight months, most of Dos Passos' emotional and physical energies were directed toward the dilemma in Spain.

20

Disillusionment in Spain, 1937

If the Communists don't like a man in Spain, right away they shoot him.

Carlo Tresca to John Dos Passos
3 March 1937

The American Committee to Aid Spanish Democracy was one of several groups that sprang up in the United States during the late summer of 1936 upon General Francisco Franco's declaration of war against the Spanish republic on July 17. One of the chief goals of the committee was to establish a professional news bureau "sincerely unconnected with politics or labor phraseology" so that the true facts of the escalating civil war might be presented to the American public, who, in turn, could initiate steps as private citizens to try to influence Congress to reverse its nonintervention policy. Dos Passos was asked by Norman Thomas, successor to Eugene Debs as standard-bearer for the Socialist party, and Roger Baldwin, founder and director of the American Civil Liberties Union, to help organize such a bureau. Dos Passos insisted that he had neither the time nor experience necessary for such a venture, but in his stead proposed Suzanne La Follette, whom he thought "admirably suited to manage professionals and present material in Washington." Katy told Mary Heaton Vorse that winter that "Dos is up to his ears in work . . . doing publicity for Spanish democracy and it's a bitter business, with the humanitarians all tearing each other to pieces and the Communists prowling on the edges to pick off any stray heretics that may not be quite kosher with regard to Moscow."

Dos Passos and his American Committee to Aid Spanish Democracy thought it ridiculous for the United States not to allow the Spanish republic—the legally constituted government—to purchase American-made munitions, since it was already buying all it could get from the Soviet Union. Dos Passos was convinced that unless the American government intervened, the country was, in effect, handing Spain over to fascism as well as to Communism, regardless of the outcome of the war. Hemingway had mentioned to Dos Passos in the fall of 1936 that he was going to Spain as soon as he could wangle an assignment as a syndicated journalist to finance the venture. "I hope you get to go," replied Dos Passos with a tinge of envy, since he, too, had been agitating about what he should do regarding Spain. He was reluctant to interrupt his intensive reading program in American history just then because he needed it as background for his next book. Moreover, he had no money to spend on travel. It was hard enough to make ends meet as it was. "Everything I hear from Spain sounds pretty goddamn horrible—but things are always different if you see them," he told Hemingway. By now a generation removed from the men in the trenches, Dos Passos had no desire to experience a war firsthand, as he once had. Yet he was convinced that the American people were entitled to know the true story of the fight for Spanish democracy, which—if current news accounts had any validity—seemed to be draining daily into the soil that had nurtured it.

Spain's civil war had become a moral and political football in an international game as the sundry powers of the world sent in plays—and players—from the sidelines and blew the whistle upon others who marched upon the field as though it were their own game. The Spaniards themselves initiated the call for help from outside forces after Franco returned from quasi-exile in the Canary Islands and tried to figure out how to pull his disparate troops together and set up a Spanish Nationalist government in Madrid. As the rebel leader—a tactician rather than a field general—Franco was relatively powerless until he could get his army airlifted across the Strait of Gibraltar. A fleet of Communist ships was patrolling the western end of the Mediterranean Sea and would not have taken kindly to a blatant crossing. Franco petitioned Italy for transport aircraft, knowing full well that Mussolini considered the Mediterranean his personal territory and would appreciate the opportunity to gain Spain as an ally and thus secure for Italy control of the western end of the sea. Mussolini had already ignored Italy's League of Nations pact by overrunning Ethiopia (then Abyssinia) in 1935–36 and had no intention of allowing his country's combat-hardened troops to soften through inactivity. Mussolini not only provided planes to airlift Franco's army onto the mainland, but also sent aircraft engines, bombs, ammunition, cannon, automatic weapons, small arms, and assorted motor vehicles—along with some sixty thousand troops—before the war had been under way six months. Franco sought similar aid from Germany, which had withdrawn from the League of Nations in 1933 and had no qualms about aiding the Spanish rebels. Hitler wanted to test his budding Luftwaffe, halt the spread of Communism, and gain Italy and Spain as allies in the process. He also reasoned that a Spanish Nationalist government would make iron ore available to Germany—necessary for its own arms race—whereas a left-wing government would not, nor could it be trusted. Soon after the fighting began, Hitler sent engineers, technicians, transport planes, fighter planes, tank companies, batteries of aircraft guns, reconnaissance aircraft, and munitions—all of which poured into Spain through Portugal, with the cooperation of Antonio de Oliveira Salazar, who openly supported the rebel Nationalists. Many thousands of German troops—though their numbers never matched the Italian forces—were in Spain by the end of the year, and more than half the country was already in the hands of the insurgents.

The Soviet Union had much at stake in Spain, too, and quickly aligned itself with the Loyalists. Stalin rationalized that the spread of Communism under the umbrella of world revolution—a workers' revolt—could not be a priority until the threat of German and Italian fascism was eliminated. The Soviet Union had joined the League of Nations in 1934, signed a pact allying it with France in 1935, and called for a common-front alliance with antifascist forces throughout the world. Though the Soviets had trouble enough of their own at home with the purges proceeding at an alarming rate, they believed it to be in their interest to provide humanitarian aid while insisting that they were not intervening in Spain's internal affairs. In response to the Republican government's request, the Soviet Union sent in military experts and technicians as "advisors," then began shipping arms, munitions, and other accouterments of war despite the League of Nations' injunction that all member countries keep out of Spain. Since France was an ally, the Soviets were allowed to establish in Paris a central recruiting office for several International Brigades under the direction of Karol Swierczerski, a Soviet-trained Polish general (known in Spain as "General Walter"). In exchange for Soviet aid, the Spanish government turned over its remaining gold reserve as security. France would have sold arms openly to the Spanish republic, too, had Great Britain not stoutly insisted on neutrality, its own and also the neutrality of France and the United States. The Spanish Loyalists appealed first to France for help. Upon Franco's declaration of war, Spain's new Premier, José Giral, cabled Léon Blum for help in putting down "a dangerous military coup." Blum, the newly elected Premier of France and head of the French Popular Front government, promised to send arms and airplanes immediately, but was forced to rescind his agreement after various political machinations tied his hands. Finally Blum was able to ship materials into Spain by way of Mexico. British sentiments mounted regarding the Spanish Civil War. Where the working people sympathized with the Spanish Loyalists, whom they saw as their comrades, the middle and upper classes favored the Nationalists. Winston Churchill, Anthony Eden, and Stanley Baldwin insisted on rigid neutrality for England and its allies, which the London *Times* and *Daily Telegraph* supported. Clement Attlee's Labour party was supported by the *News Chronicle, Daily Herald,* Manchester *Guardian, Daily Express,* and *Daily Mirror,* which sided with the Loyalists. According to Claude Bowers (American Ambassador to Spain), Great Britain's ambassador, Sir Henry Chilton, was more interested in serving the insurgents and crippling the Republican government than in supporting it, although that was not his official position. Also siding with Franco's Nationalists were the London *Observer, Morning Post, Daily Mail,* and *Daily Sketch.*

A few weeks after the war commenced, Great Britain spearheaded a Non-Intervention International Board established for the policing of Spain's land and sea borders to prevent foreign military aid from further escalating the war. Warships flying nonintervention flags (a white flag with two black balls in the center) patrolled Spanish waters, and official observers were charged with supervising the unloading of all cargo from ships and land vehicles. The irony apparent to all participants was that the very countries that had been conveying arms to the insurgents as well as to the duly recognized regime without abatement since the beginning of the war were now vouching for their own nonintervention. Meanwhile, President Roosevelt insisted that the United States stand by its Neutrality Act of 1935—passed by Congress during the heat of the Abyssinian crisis—which made it illegal for American citizens to sell or transport arms to belligerent forces once the

President of the country in question had proclaimed a state of war. The Neutrality Act was not applicable to civil strife, but the United States government acted as though it was. Cordell Hull, Secretary of State, agreed with Great Britain that America should steer a course of strict impartiality. The rest of Roosevelt's Cabinet—Henry Morgenthau, Jr. (Secretary of the Treasury), Henry Wallace (Secretary of Agriculture), and Harold Ickes (Secretary of the Interior)—were partial to the Loyalists, as were Eleanor Roosevelt and Sumner Welles, assistant secretary of state. The President, too, was sympathetic toward the Republican cause, but sided with Hull. Consequently, Congress passed on January 11, 1937, a revised Neutrality Act that banned passport travel to Spain, made it illegal for the United States to ship war materials or cargo of any kind into Spain during its state of war, and reconfirmed a standing law that prohibited Americans from enlisting in a foreign army. The only way Americans were able to volunteer for service in Spain was through an "underground railway" established by the Communist party of the United States; consequently, the two battalions recruited in the United States (the Abraham Lincoln Battalion and the George Washington Battalion) had a high proportion of young American Communists in them. The Abraham Lincoln Battalion—numbering 550—was comprised chiefly of students (including many blacks) who had never served in the American Army. They were the youngest soldiers in all the International Brigades. When Dos Passos finally effected a plan to get to Spain himself, he complained to Edmund Wilson that "some halfwit in connection with one of the [Spanish] committees" had caused him "endless trouble" with the State Department because of a story that he and Hemingway were going to Spain as combatants. Bernice Baumgarten wrote Dos Passos upon reading the account that she was surprised to learn he meant to "join the Spanish war." She had supposed he was going only to "look things over" and to "generate a few articles" that could be useful for his next book. The erroneous account also prompted the editor of *Crítica*—a magazine published in Santiago de Chile—to cable Dos Passos for a contract to produce three articles while "fighting in Spain." He had no intention of going "as a combatant," replied Dos Passos and suggested that he might "send out little printed notices" to friends to remind them "not to believe what they read in the papers." He also wrote the chairman of the Medical Committee of the American Committee to Aid Spanish Democracy that he had been caused "grave inconvenience" because someone associated with one of the Spanish committees had used his name without authorization. His whole usefulness as a reporter in Spain had been threatened, he insisted. Dos Passos informed Wilson that he was "absolutely, completely, and irrevocably through with all committees, protests, non-paying magazines, relievers, and uplifters" whether he happened to agree with them or not. "Their ends are not my ends," he continued. "Their methods are asinine when they aren't actually damaging to the causes they pretend to serve, and to hell with 'em."

Dos Passos may have been upset, also, because he was now being labeled a Trotskyite, which, he told May Cameron of the New York *World Telegram*, was no more apt than the Communist tag hung on him, though in truth he had never been a member of any political party, he added. The new label he attributed to having been named to the American Committee for the Defense of Trotsky, which he came by as inadvertently as did Mary McCarthy, whom Dos Passos met at about this time. As McCarthy told it, a dimple-faced, shaggy-headed, earnest novelist friend (James T. Farrell) approached her at a publisher's party for Art Young and asked if she thought Trotsky was entitled to a hearing (Trotsky had been in Coyoacán, Mexico, since his arrival from Norway on January 9, 1937, and had asked for an impartial hearing to consider the conspiracy charges he faced regarding the alleged assassination plot against Stalin and other ranking Soviet officials). McCarthy replied in all honesty that she knew nothing of the facts but thought any accused person had the right to a hearing. Undaunted, Farrell pressed for her opinion of whether Trotsky should have the right to asylum. Although she eventually answered affirmatively to both questions, McCarthy was surprised and indignant when she received a letter several days later identifying her as a member of the American Committee for the Defense of Leon Trotsky. She intended to protest such a misappropriation of her name and to remove herself from the committee, but before she could do so became a victim of a persistent telephone campaign by her Communist acquaintances urging her—and warning her—to disassociate herself from the group.

In addition to such telephone harassment, McCarthy and her fellow liberal members of the Trotsky defense committee were addressed in an open letter published in *The New Masses* declaring that they were being used and urging them to recant and remove themselves from the committee immediately. Among the fifty signatures of writers, editors, and artists on the letter were such names as Newton Arvin, Heywood Broun, Theodore Dreiser, Louis Fischer, Lillian Hellman, Corliss Lamont, Max Lerner, Robert Lynd, Raymond Robins, and Lillian Wald. "Name after name fell off the Committee's letterhead. Prominent liberals and literary figures issued statements deploring their mistake," reported McCarthy. Many protested that "their names had been used without permission. When I saw what was happening, I rebounded to the defense of the Committee without a single hesitation—it was nobody's business, I felt, how I happened to be on it, and if anybody had asked me, I should have lied without a scruple."

Wilson wrote Dos Passos on February 12, 1937, that despite his intention to steer clear of the Stalin-Trotsky controversy, he was now in the middle of it. Having been named to the committee inadvertently, just as McCarthy had been, he complained that he was being bedeviled and besieged by Trotskyists and Stalinists alike as each faction hammered away at him politically and tried to pull him into its camp. It was in the fall of 1937 in connection with the new *Partisan Review*, a Trotskyite-leaning literary magazine, that Wilson met McCarthy and before long was courting her with ardor.

At about the same time, Farrell wrote Hemingway of his involvement with the defense committee and said that Dos Passos, too, was a member. It was a ticklish affair because the Communist party was conducting a vindictive campaign against everyone on it, declared Farrell: "Members are telephoned day and night, rumors are spread concerning false withdrawals from the Committee, there is a literal daily shrieking out of the mouth of the *Daily Worker*, and it goes on." Farrell predicted a riot at the mass meeting on February 9 when a telephoned speech by Trotsky would be heard from Mexico. Dos Passos had no intention of participating in the Trotsky hearing scheduled to commence April 10 in Coyoacán, Mexico, although he did tell a reporter for the *World Telegram* that he was going to Mexico, then to Spain. On February 20, 1937, when the interview was published, Dos Passos had reportedly already left. In reality, he was still in New York and did not sail for Spain until March 3 (by way of England, not Mexico). Actually, Dos Passos would have liked to go to Mexico to interview Trotsky. Trotskyist devotees from the United States were trekking to Mexico in a steady stream, he reported to Wilson March 9 while steaming from Southampton toward the French coast. The "show" down there promised to rival the "great days of Whitfield the preacher," he allowed. Among his and Wilson's mutual friends from the lower Cape already in Mexico—"attracted consciously or unconsciously by the new volcano" (Trotsky)—were Bill Smith, Coulton Waugh, Gwenyth Clymer (Waugh's sister), Herbert Solow, and Charles and Adelaide Walker. Had he not believed that "the show down there will last longer than the European show," he would not be on his way to Spain that moment, he admitted, but the opportunity to "get up some material" for *Fortune* was not to be passed up.

Dos Passos had several reasons for going to Europe at this particular time, the least of which was *Fortune*'s assignment by editor Archibald MacLeish to help finance the venture. MacLeish was also chairman of the board of directors of Contemporary Historians, chiefly a fund-raising structure for the project conceived during the winter of 1936–37: the making of a documentary movie. Dos Passos wanted to depict the heroic struggle to survive of the people of the Spanish republic, as well as their attempts to irrigate and reclaim the soil in the midst of civil war. Since the Spanish news service to apprise the American people of the true facts of the plight of the Spanish people had failed to develop, the Contemporary Historians hoped that a documentary might convince President Roosevelt to reverse his stand on nonintervention. More to the point, they wanted Congress to repeal its Neutrality Act signed into law in January 1937.

Meanwhile, Dos Passos had already lined up Joris Ivens, a promising young Dutch filmmaker, and John Ferno, Ivens' chief cameraman, to produce the documentary in accordance with the aims of the Contemporary Historians. Dos Passos had met Ivens the preceding spring upon his arrival from the Netherlands for the New York City premiere of *New Earth,* his documentary of Holland's recovery program to reclaim submerged lands from the Zuider Zee. "Ivens has just come to America not entirely in search of fortune," Dos Passos observed to Dreiser when urging him to use the complimentary ticket he had asked Ivens to send Dreiser. After viewing Ivens' film, Dos Passos was convinced that Ivens was philosophically aligned with the goals of the Contemporary Historians. Hemingway, too, had been invited to join the project (and the Contemporary Historians Board) several weeks after its conception, since he had just signed a contract with the North American Newspaper Alliance (NANA) and was going to Spain on assignment. NANA had promised him five hundred dollars for each cabled dispatch and a thousand dollars for each story that went out by mail (with no limit on the number he could send).

Dos Passos and Hemingway had become edgy with one another in New York while discussing their new project, a fact attributed by Katy to Hemingway's involvement with Martha Gellhorn, a tall, handsome woman in her late twenties who dressed and carried herself as though she were a *Vogue* model. Gellhorn had presented herself to Hemingway (accompanied by her mother) in Key West only a few weeks earlier as a novice writer in need of counsel. She had worked briefly on *The New Republic* as an editorial assistant after graduating from Bryn Mawr College and married the Marquis Bertrand de Juvenel, a French intellectual and political economist with whom she lived near St. Tropez on the French Mediterranean until her divorce two years later. She was already the author of two books, *What Mad Pursuit,* a novel, and *The Trouble I've Seen,* a collection of short stories based on her travels in the United States while a field investigator for the Federal Emergency Relief Administration in depressed areas (which won for her the friendship of Eleanor Roosevelt). Hemingway, flattered by her attention, read Gellhorn's manuscripts, took her fishing, and began addressing her as "Daughter" (he was thirty-eight and she sometimes called him "Papa"). Gellhorn was from St. Louis—as were each of Hemingway's wives—which called for more cordiality on Pauline's part than she might have extended under other circumstances. But Pauline was also wary of her husband's new friend and guessed that Gellhorn would not hesitate to transform an infatuation into an affair if given the opportunity. Pauline, too, had played that game and knew the ground rules and probable mode of development.

Matthew Josephson was in Key West that winter and attended a farewell party for Hemingway shortly before his departure for Europe. "It was by now visible to most of us in the Key West circle that the marriage of Ernest and Pauline had reached a delicate stage," observed Josephson. "She was trying to be patient and also fighting to hold him." Pauline did not accompany Hemingway to the airport when he left for New York; had she been there, she would have seen Gellhorn board the same flight, recalled Josephson. Gellhorn also accompanied Hemingway to the dinner meeting of the Contemporary Historians, at which he introduced her to Dos Passos and Katy. It was obvious from Gellhorn's comments that she intended to join Hemingway in Madrid as soon as she could arrange credentials for her new assignment as a correspondent for *Collier's.* Katy took an immediate dislike to Gellhorn and wondered how much Pauline knew about the interloper. Hemingway had a tendency to marry the women with whom he fell in love, and Katy resented his vulnerability and what she considered his weak character where women were concerned. She also did not like what she saw happening to Hemingway, the man, who seemed small-minded and meanspirited despite his generous streak, which often ran rampant. Hemingway was now being feted for having donated money and several ambulances to the Loyalists' cause and was the titular head of the Ambulance Corps Committee of the American Friends of Spanish Democracy. Had Katy known that Hemingway had written a thinly veiled portrait of his concept of Dos Passos in the characterization of Richard Gordon, a pseudo-proletarian novelist, in his recent published novel, *To Have and Have Not,* she would have been even more upset with him. In December Arnold Gingrich read the manuscript and warned Hemingway that Dos Passos had been libeled in the Richard Gordon portrait. As Carlos Baker, a Hemingway biographer, put it: "Knowing Dos did not like Gingrich, [Hemingway] . . . would merely tell Dos that Gingrich objected to a given passage, and Dos would be certain to approve it." During the winter and spring of 1937 Dos Passos and Hemingway were on the brink of an irreconcilable breach, but neither of them was aware of it.

At the suggestion of Archibald MacLeish, Lillian Hellman was also named to the board of Contemporary Historians, Inc., and invited to collaborate with Dos Passos and Hemingway as scenarists for the documentary, for which thirteen thousand dollars had to be raised if the venture was to become a reality. MacLeish, too, was credited as one of the scenarists, but his work primarily involved fund-raising and editing once the film had been shot (his job at *Fortune* also necessitated his staying in New York). Once the campaign for funds commenced, donations poured in. Margaret De Silver (probably the largest single donor), Gerald Murphy, Herman Shumlin, and several who desired anonymity concerning their charity to the Loyalists' cause gave more than five hundred dollars each, and many organizations contributed. In less than a month, a group known as the North American Committee for Spain had raised some four thousand dollars for the film.

Funds for the new Ivens documentary also came from proceeds of two other documentary films premiered as a double bill at the Cameo Theatre in New York City on January 28, 1937. Hemingway had worked on one, and Dos Passos on the other in collaboration with W. O. ("Bill") Field, a free-lance photographer, in editing footage shot by Joris Ivens' cameraman in Spain in December. According to Field, the problem was "to edit in such a way to make the Spanish problem understandable by the American public, which was then getting the two versions of the war weighted rather heavily on the Franco side." Dos Passos blamed William Randolph Hearst—he had written a scathing indictment against Hearst in his "Poor Little Rich Boy" sketch in *The Big Money*—for much of the news coverage favored the insurgents. It was largely because of Hearst's biased coverage that the American Committee to Aid Spanish Democracy had tried to establish an independent, professional news bureau. "Since that attempt had failed," said Field, "we wanted to edit a factual, non-emotional point of view supporting what was then the legitimate government of Spain."

Meanwhile, Hemingway had been working independently of Dos Passos and Field with a young Spanish novelist, Prudencia de Pereda, who already had a reel of film complete with commentary almost ready for showing under the title *Spain in Flames*. Its footage by an unidentified cameraman consisted almost wholly of scenes of war and destruction. Field said upon viewing the film that it was a Soviet propaganda piece, "decidedly left-wing and probably Russian-made as well." There were scenes depicting the Loyalists troops—bolstered by Communist aid—driving Franco's forces from the Sierra de Guadarrama, fascist planes (Italian and German) bombing villages and towns without regard for the helpless civilians unable to escape, hundreds of children being evacuated from Madrid during heavy artillery shelling by Nationalist troops (some sixty children were killed on a single day during the siege of Madrid), and gripping scenes of the defenders of the Alcázar at Toledo under siege.

For the sake of fund-raising, publicity, and impact upon the public, the Dos Passos/Field/Ivens collaboration (entitled *Spain and the Fight for Freedom*) and the Hemingway/Pereda film bore the single title *Spain in Flames*. Dos Passos was credited as the scenarist of the first film, and Pereda and Hemingway, of the second one. Dos Passos spoke briefly of it in a letter to Mary Heaton Vorse: "Have you seen Ivens' and my little picture about the Spanish business? We finally threw it in with an Amkino picture into something called Spain in Flames. It's the first part." Edmund Wilson saw the film and praised it. Not only did he think Dos Passos' film better than the "too-much staged Soviet one"—the *Spain in Flames* Pereda/Hemingway portion—but also called it the "best put-together picture" he had seen. Despite Wilson's reassuring words, Dos Passos was not satisfied by the total effect of the film and was impatient to get on with the new documentary. He knew that by the time he got to Madrid, Hemingway and Ivens would already be shooting, and he worried that Hemingway would influence Ivens to focus upon the battle scenes he had relished in *Spain in Flames* rather than using the war as a backdrop for the common man's struggle to till the soil and survive in the process.

Several nights before Dos Passos and Katy sailed for Europe, they had dinner with Carlo Tresca and Margaret De Silver. "John, they goin' make a monkey outa you . . . a beeg monkey," warned Tresca in reference to Ivens and his cameraman, whereas Dos Passos' concern formerly had rested largely with Hemingway. It was the scenarists who would be selecting the scenes, not Ivens, Dos Passos assured Tresca. He liked Ivens and trusted him to shoot the documentary in the manner upon which they had all agreed. Since Lillian Hellman was to be a scenarist, too, Dos Passos hoped that the two of them could keep in check Hemingway's desire to emphasize the fighting. A Trotskyite, Tresca was wary of anyone affiliated with Communism, which he saw as a blind loyalty superseding any other tie—including a filmmaker's aesthetic integrity. "How can you have control when your director is a Communist party member, when everywhere you go you will be supervised by party members, when everything you do will be for the interest of the Communists?" he asked. Tresca's parting remark added an ominous note to an already somber evening: "If the Communists don't like a man in Spain, right away they shoot him."

Dos Passos and Katy left New York on March 3, 1937, aboard the RMS *Berengaria,* a British liner bound for Southampton. A week later they were in Paris, where he learned that Hemingway was already en route to Madrid, having left Sidney Franklin (a matador and Hemingway's friend) behind to await Martha Gellhorn and escort her into the war zone. He had been impatient to begin his dollar-a-word dispatches through the North American Newspaper Alliance as an "anti-war war correspondent," a label he conceived for himself before leaving Key West. For Hemingway, shooting the documentary with Ivens, Dos Passos, and Hellman was a secondary commitment, although he expected to be able to combine the projects. As it turned out, Hellman took to her bed in Paris with double pneumonia and was unable to join Dos Passos and Hemingway in Madrid for the making of the documentary.

Dos Passos, too, looked forward to getting into Spain, but wanted to check out the prevailing political attitudes in Paris first. He already had talked with Joseph P. Kennedy, the United States ambassador to Great Britain and a fellow passenger aboard the RMS *Berengaria.* Their several conversations could hardly be taken for in-depth discussions of the Spanish crisis, but Dos Passos was convinced based on what little dialogue they did exchange that regardless of how sympathetic the British people were toward the Loyalist government, the country's official position would remain one of strict neutrality. From Bernard Baruch, also en route to England, Dos Passos gained additional insight. As one of America's elder statesmen and a millionaire entrepreneur on an international scale, Baruch was skilled at taking economic and political pulses. After talking with Baruch and Kennedy, Dos Passos was not optimistic that the new documentary film he envisioned making would have any effect on President Roosevelt's stand on nonintervention.

Before leaving Paris, Dos Passos interviewed Léon Blum, the French Premier, and met with a number of leftist and conservative leaders who represented each of the diverse political factions in France. Many feared that a civil war was dangerously close to erupting in France also. Their apprehensions and loyalties mirrored the stances he knew existed in Spain and revealed a fairly even division in the political consciousness of the French people, whose Popular Front government perched upon a shaky foundation. After three weeks in Paris, Dos Passos told Katy good-bye and boarded a train for Perpignan, a remote town in southeastern France. He was to meet two French truck drivers for the two-day trip from the French border to Valencia, Spain's provisional capital. The rendezvous point and time for him to meet his French drivers was high noon April 4, 1937, at the Café Continental, the local bus stop in Perpignan. The café was "a regular operatic smugglers' cave" with all the trappings of international intrigue, he said later. The so-called convoy he was to join turned out to be two trucks, one laden with gas masks destined for Loyalist forces in Madrid and the other, with field telephones and die-making machinery. The truck in which Dos Passos rode was allowed to cross the border at Cerbère with relatively few questions asked, but the other vehicle was detained. Before long, Dos Passos and his driver had crossed the easternmost ridges of the Pyrenees, wended their way as unobtrusively as possible along the narrow road hugging the Mediterranean coast, and on the third day, were in Valencia.

Dos Passos intended to tarry in Valencia only long enough to talk with the Minister of Foreign Affairs, Julio Álvarez del Vayo (who invited him to lunch the next day and arranged his transportation to Madrid); check in with the foreign press office to receive his instructions from the censor regarding his deportment as a correspondent; and look up his friend José Robles, who was in Spain on vacation with his family when the war broke out. Robles had elected to take leave from his teaching post at Johns Hopkins University and stay on in Spain to help the Republican government in whatever way seemed most feasible. In view of the disparate political factions throughout Spain, Dos Passos sensed that he should make discreet inquiries regarding his friend's whereabouts and became vaguely disquieted when he had difficulty determining even where Robles lived and ferreted out only that Robles had moved from Madrid in November when Francisco Largo Caballero, Premier and head of the Spanish Socialist party, elected to take all the government files to Valencia after Madrid fell under siege. Robles had worked first as a cultural attaché with the Ministry of War, where he was asked to serve as interpreter for General Ian Antonovich Berzin, known in Spain only as Goriev—the ranking Soviet general. Robles' work was highly classified, and even his wife had no clear idea what he did. Dos Passos finally located Robles' dreary apartment in a poor section of Valencia. Especially disturbing was the fact that no one had informed him of Robles' arrest. Márgare Robles, his wife, looking disheveled and distraught, greeted Dos Passos with a tearful embrace and told him that Robles had been arrested several weeks earlier. After spending countless hours at the police station and in the offices of every influential person she knew who might possibly be able to shed some light upon her husband's abduction, she learned only that he was being held under conditions of great secrecy. Where he was incarcerated and why remained a mystery. Once more Carlo Tresca's words came to mind: "If the Communists don't like a man in Spain, right away they shoot him." Señora Robles was convinced that her husband was loyal to the Spanish republic, but feared that he was in jeopardy because his brother was an officer in Franco's army. The fact that they had been estranged for almost a decade was perhaps unknown to the authorities, she reasoned.

Dos Passos assured Márgare Robles that he would be judicious in seeking the details of his friend's fate, then hastened to the office of Del Vayo, who "professed ignorance and chagrin" but agreed to look into the circumstances surrounding Robles' arrest. Dos Passos also sought out Pepe Quintanilla, head of the Department of Justice and brother of his friend Luis. Quintanilla acknowledged that he knew something of the case, but assured Dos Passos that he must not worry, since the charges against Robles were of little consequence. While Dos Passos was petitioning official channels for news of Robles, Robles' son, Francisco Robles Villegar (known as "Coco"), was informed secretly that his father was dead. Young Robles' informant was Liston Oak, an American working in Valencia in the Propaganda Department of the Spanish republic. Robles' son was a translator in the same department with Oak, who told him that everyone would be better off if no more questions were asked. When Dos Passos was informed of the rumor, he was determined to get to the bottom of the matter and have verification of Robles' fate. His wife and children were entitled to the truth. As he explained the dilemma later:

> It was not until I reached Madrid that I got definite information from the then chief of the Republican counter-espionage service that Robles had been executed by a "special section" (which I gathered was under control of the Communist party). . . . Spaniards I talked to closer to the Communist party took the attitude that Robles had been shot as an example to other officials because he had been overheard indiscreetly discussing military plans in a café. The "fascist spy" theory seems to be the fabrication of romantic American Communist sympathizers. I certainly did not hear it from any Spaniard.

Dos Passos had Hemingway in mind when he spoke of "romantic American Communist sympathizers." Dos Passos reasoned that "Robles, like many others who were conscious of their own sincerity of purpose, laid himself open to a frame up . . . pushed to the point of execution because Russian secret agents felt that Robles knew too much about the relations between the Spanish war ministry and the Kremlin and was not, from their very special point of view, politically reliable." One of the reasons Dos Passos went on to Madrid when he did—after a week in Valencia seeking answers to Robles' disappearance —was to enlist the aid of Juan Posada, with whom he used to mountain-climb during their student days in Madrid, and now chief of police in the beleaguered city. By this time Dos Passos' interest in filming *The Spanish Earth* (the title hit upon by Archibald MacLeish for their new documentary) was secondary to his search for details of his friend's plight.

Dos Passos made the trip from Valencia to Madrid in a chauffeur-driven Hispano-Suiza assigned to the French journalist André Malraux, who had made a name for himself in Spain for having organized the International Brigades' French air squadron at Alcantarilla. Dos Passos wrote later of piling into the vehicle with luggage, parcels of food, boxes of chocolate, and extra cigarettes. According to Hemingway, they arrived with only four chocolate bars and four oranges. "We damn near killed him," complained Hemingway, who said he had left word in Paris for Dos Passos to bring food with him, since rations were in short supply to outsiders not as adept at foraging as the natives were.

Whatever truth lay in the tale was probably not reflected in Hemingway's version, which was embellished with variations at each retelling during the weeks and months to come. When Lillian Hellman arrived in Madrid in October 1937 during Hemingway's second tour as a journalist, Hemingway complained that Dos Passos had come empty-handed and eaten everyone else's food. Such irresponsibility had caused them to have "an ugly fight," reported Hemingway. Hellman said later that she came bearing two cans each of sardines and liver pâté. The incident served as kindling to ignite Hemingway's various grievances against Dos Passos in the future. He was also put off by what he saw as Dos Passos' "conspicuous inquiries," which were sure to "get everybody into trouble if he persisted." He insisted that such questions about Robles would throw suspicion upon all of them and interfere with the completion of their documentary. According to Josephine Herbst, who arrived in Madrid a few days before Dos Passos, Hemingway urged her to ask Dos Passos to "lay off making inquiries." Herbst told Hemingway that "a reliable source" in Valencia had assured her that Robles' execution was a fact, but that the authorities hoped to keep the truth from Dos Passos for as long as possible because they feared he would denounce their cause, since it was the Loyalists—or those associated with them—who had ordered Robles' execution. Herbst declared that she could not violate the confidence of her informer by conveying the news herself to Dos Passos, but thought that he should be told the truth immediately. Hemingway could tell him, she urged. He could say that someone he had met along the road conveyed the news but furnished no details. Upon reflection, it seemed to Herbst that Hemingway "agreed with too cheerful a readiness."

Hemingway chose a fiesta celebration and luncheon honoring the newly reconstituted Soviet-Spanish 15th International Brigade as the occasion at which to inform Dos Passos that Robles' death had been confirmed. All of the journalists in the vicinity were invited to the propagandistic affair to observe the troops on parade, listen to Soviet ideological speeches by military leaders and officials from the nearby village, and to meet two of Spain's most notable performers—Nina de las Peñas and Pastora Imperio—who were to sing and dance that evening. According to Herbst, it was during the meal that Hemingway told Dos Passos rather offhandedly that there was no need for any more questions because Robles was most assuredly dead. As Hemingway saw it, Robles was guilty of treason and had been caught, tried, and executed. The sooner Dos Passos accepted it, the better it would be for all of them. Whereas time and time again Hemingway had attacked Dos Passos for his naiveté, Herbst was convinced that in Spain, at least, Hemingway was more naive than Dos Passos regarding the current ideologies. She also believed that Hemingway was venturing into areas "better known to people like Dos Passos" (and herself as well) in his annexation of "new realms of experience" with which he was ill-equipped to deal. "Dos Passos was absolutely right in refusing to believe his friend to be guilty of treason," concluded Herbst. Hemingway's callous manner in reporting the execution and his treatment of Dos Passos as a simpleton in regard to the hazards of war offended him more than anything else Hemingway had ever done or said. As he saw it, the only *treason* involved was Hemingway's, in not playing fairly with him. Hemingway had been gulled by the Communists in Spain. He was their "fair-haired boy" to further their future goals in America as well as in Spain.

Even before the Robles incident, Herbst had observed the growing irritation and tension between Dos Passos and Hemingway and concluded that its origin lay deeper than surface differences suggested. She also thought that much of Hemingway's "macho-exuberance" stemmed from the obvious success of his love affair with Martha Gellhorn. The couple had been seen by Herbst and several other journalists emerging from Gellhorn's room in their nightclothes in the midst of a heavy artillery barrage, and no one doubted the nature of their "Papa-Daughter" relationship.

Another Hemingway tale pertaining to Dos Passos' stay in Madrid concerned a telegram reportedly sent to Katy by Dos Passos upon his arrival there. According to A. E. Hotchner, Hemingway's friend and biographer, to whom Hemingway related the story later, the censor sought out Hemingway to ask if the message, "Baby, see you soon," was in code. "No," replied Hemingway. "It just means that Mr. Dos Passos won't be with us very long." Anyone who knew Dos Passos and Katy, however, was aware that of the several pet names he had for his wife, "Baby" was not one of them. Hemingway's version of the two weeks in question continued:

> Dos spent his whole time in Madrid looking for his translator. We all knew he had been shot but no one had the heart to tell Dos, who thought the translator was in prison and went all around checking lists. Finally, I told him. I had never met the translator, nor had I seen him shot, but that was the word on him; well, Dos turned on me like I had shot him myself. I couldn't believe the change in the man from the last time I had seen him in Paris! The very first time his hotel was bombed, Dos packed up and hurried back to France. Of course, we were all damned scared during the war, but not over a chicken-shit thing like a few bombs on the hotel. Only a couple of rooms ever got hit anyway. I finally figured it out that Dos's problem was that he had come into some money, and for the first time his body had become valuable. Fear of death increases in exact proportion to increase in wealth: Hemingway's Law on the Dynamics of Dying.

Hemingway delighted in telling people that Dos Passos had lost no time in deciding that it was dangerous in Spain and that a man could be killed even at his typewriter. He reported that Dos Passos made up much of what he wrote regarding Spain at war, since he had seldom ventured from his hotel room, thus could not have seen it firsthand. Almost everything Hemingway uttered about Dos Passos from then on was largely fabrication. Nor did Dos Passos ever "come into money" in the manner Hemingway implied. More to the point was Hemingway's criticism of Dos Passos for having gone to Hollywood for several months, an interim that led to Dos Passos' prostitution, thought Hemingway. Even more relevant to Hemingway's rancor was that Dos Passos reportedly still owed him some fourteen hundred dollars. He may also have lashed out at Dos Passos because Dos Passos probably made it explicit that he was disappointed in Hemingway's flagrant infidelity to Pauline, who was his and Katy's friend, and he hated to see her hurt.

Dos Passos remained in Madrid for a little over two weeks, but because of the recent turn of events his heart was no longer in the production of the documentary film that had brought him there in the first place. Although he accompanied Ivens, Hemingway, and the cameraman into the battle area along the Madrid-Valencia road several times, Dos Passos was convinced that Hemingway would continue to mastermind the filming as he saw fit. He was particularly put off by Hemingway's leading the entire crew along an exposed, embattled area in full view and range of the rebel forces. Hemingway had luckily calculated that the enemy was taking its siesta and would not bother to attack them.

Before leaving Madrid, Dos Passos urged Ivens and Hemingway to shift their emphasis in the footage they were shooting from scenes of the beleaguered city and its environs to the tiny village of Fuentedueña, which lay nearby between Madrid and Valencia. The land surrounding the village had formerly been owned by ten families, many of whom were killed in the uprising following the military revolt. After the rebellion, local Socialist officials formed a collective out of the land that had lain unworked for generations, and now everyone shared in the tilling, planting, and irrigation of the soil. Before long an extensive irrigation system was installed so that onions, lettuce, tomatoes, peppers, and artichokes could be planted before the dry summer weather set in. "The irrigation project seemed to loom larger than the war in the minds of the mayor and his councilors," observed Dos Passos, who saw that the villagers were more interested in reclaiming the neglected soil and raising their own vegetables than in the broad principles of ideology that divided their leaders and spilled the blood of their hapless countrymen. They farmed within earshot of the hollow popping of guns from the Jarama riverfront and were reminded daily of the war as they shielded the sun from their eyes to watch a plane in the sky or stood motionless while soldiers and munitions rumbled through their village on the road to Madrid.

Dos Passos had little to say to Hemingway when he packed his bag to depart alone for Fuentedueña for a meeting with the farmers of the Socialist co-op and an inspection tour of their irrigation project before proceeding to Valencia. A few hours before leaving, Dos Passos talked with Evan Shipman, a sometime poet and adventurer who was in Madrid after having driven volunteers for the International Brigades into Spain (and being jailed in the process). Shipman jumped at the wrong conclusion concerning Dos Passos' departure. He said later that he had told Dos Passos that he was "courting danger for himself" in talking about the Robles situation and "would do well to leave Spain." His advice reportedly shocked Dos Passos, who "went right out of that restaurant, took the first conveyance he could get, and went back to Paris."

Contrary to Shipman's tale, Dos Passos did not return immediately to Paris, nor did he leave because he feared for his own safety. Dos Passos left because he knew there was little else he could do of a constructive nature so long as a civil war raged in Spain. Before departing Valencia several days later, however, he tried to obtain an official certificate of Robles' death so that his widow could collect the money due her as beneficiary of his life insurance policy (maintained through his professorship at Johns Hopkins University). In effect, Robles was still officially on leave. Although Álvarez del Vayo promised to obtain the necessary documents and forward them to Dos Passos in the United States, a death certificate was never issued—despite repeated efforts by Dos Passos through a variety of official channels—and Márgare Robles was unable to collect on her husband's insurance. Dos Passos regretted the ineffectualness of Ambassador Claude Bowers in not pressuring Del Vayo to produce the death certificate, but he recognized that the ambassador was handicapped in his negotiations with the Spanish republic because he had not remained in the provisional capital of Valencia when the American Embassy moved from Madrid several months after the outbreak of war, but established his office in Biarritz—close to the border, yet in France, nonetheless—from which he and Sir Henry Chilton, the British ambassador to Spain, conducted their Spanish affairs while a skeleton crew kept their embassies open in Valencia (in the fall of 1937 the National Lawyers Guild censured Bowers for his absentee ambassadorship and called for his return to Spain).

In Barcelona, which he had skirted in entering the country, Dos Passos paused briefly to interview Andrés Nin, head of the Partido Obrero de Unificación Marxista (POUM). The news from Spain before Dos Passos left New York was that the POUM was to be liquidated and its leaders tried for conspiracy with Franco, but official charges still had not been made. On April 29, 1937, less than a week after Dos Passos met Nin, Barcelona replaced Madrid as the main battleground of the Spanish Civil War. Communist-Loyalist troops attacked POUM headquarters, arrested its forty-member central committee, declared the POUM illegal, and murdered Nin and other leaders. Before leaving Barcelona, Dos Passos also talked with George Orwell, recently returned from the front with POUM troops with whom he had been fighting. He did not know at the time, however, who the wounded, tubercular Englishman was. Dos Passos recognized Orwell only as a man "about to die" who "allowed himself the ultimate luxury of telling the truth." Having had his fill of "public officials, gulls most of them, or self-deceivers," Dos Passos relished their conversation.

Dos Passos himself engaged in an act of subterfuge to help save a man's life at the border crossing at Cerbère. Liston Oak, who had informed young Robles that his father had been executed, now feared that it was only a matter of time before an execution squad knocked on his door in the dead of night. Oak had asked too many questions and was reported to be politically unreliable, which had prompted him to leave Valencia covertly and present himself at the door of Dos Passos' hotel room with whispered pleas for help in getting out of the country. Oak likened himself to Robles in that he came to Spain to help the Republican government, but had been thwarted because Soviet subversion made it impossible to distinguish a friend from an enemy. Sympathetic with Oak's plight, Dos Passos presented him as his secretary to the border guards, who checked their credentials and allowed them to reenter France.

Dos Passos left Oak in Perpignan and hastened to Antibes to meet Katy and write his final dispatches on Spain before their return together to the United States. In one article, he spoke of his visit to the headquarters of the POUM and of life in the villages through which he had passed along the way. In Pozorubio he had found the villagers boasting of "plenty of bread . . . while in war-torn Madrid, a few miles away, people were starving." A doctor told him that there were no more gentlemen or masters in their village, only comrades. If there were vehicles and gasoline to spare, the people of Madrid could come to Pozorubio and buy all the bread they wanted, lamented the women who operated a bakery. In San Pol de Mar, a small fishing village on the Catalan coast where Dos Passos tarried after leaving Barcelona, the people told him they would be happy if only the fascists and anarchists would let them alone. He wrote of sitting down to a bountiful meal for which everything except the wine and coffee had been grown within the town limits. Here Dos Passos discovered cooperative ventures of agriculture, fishing, chicken farming, retail stores, public baths, showers, a pool parlor, a gymnasium—all municipally operated. Moreover, a Catalonian alliance of cooperatives of long standing had helped unify the people of that province in a unique fashion. The San Pol de Mar villagers were proud that their municipal theater had won a prize at a recent Catalonian drama festival in competition with much larger communities. Dos Passos concluded that the villagers were "the heart of Spain," not the cities with their divisive political factions. Dos Passos collected four essays when he returned home based on his visit to Barcelona and the villages of Pozorubio, Fuentedueña, and San Pol de Mar under the title *The Villages Are the Heart of Spain* and gave them to *Esquire* for publication in a slim, hardback volume subtitled *Speaking Seriously: No. 1 of a Series of Editorial Previews from "Esquire."* The book was distributed as a limited, numbered gift edition in January 1938. The magazine itself carried the essays to its regular readership in the February edition.

Dos Passos was surprised at the sudden appearance of Hemingway at the boat train depot in Paris to see him and Katy off. Hemingway had arrived in the French capital himself only a day or two earlier. Joris Ivens and John Ferno, his cameraman, had shot all of the scenes for *The Spanish Earth* and were leaving soon to take the film to New York for editing. Any thought Dos Passos may have had that Hemingway had come to repair the breach in their friendship was immediately dispelled, however, by his quarrelsome insistence in knowing precisely how Dos Passos intended to write and speak of the Robles affair as well as the overall political situation and exigencies of civil war in Spain. Once more Hemingway donned "the long white whiskers" posture of "sage to child," which had put off Dos Passos and Katy in the past, but never had it been applied so directly as now. Katy found Hemingway's overbearing manner intolerable and reminded him that Dos Passos was no stranger to the necessities of war. Dos Passos answered that he questioned the use of fighting a war for civil liberties when such liberties were being destroyed in the process, and that he would write the truth as he saw it, but was still sorting out what that truth was. Hemingway countered that there was only one stance: Dos Passos was either "with them or against them." Dos Passos merely shrugged his shoulders, a gesture that infuriated Hemingway, who balled his fist at him and glared as though he was on the verge of striking his adversary to the pavement. Instead, he threw a verbal jab and warned that unless Dos Passos changed his tune regarding what he thought he saw happening in Spain, the New York reviewers would crucify him. It was Katy who flung the last word: "Why, Ernest, I never heard anything so despicably opportunistic in my life!"

Hemingway was convinced that Dos Passos was a Trotskyist and lost no time in conveying to friends his disappointment in what he saw as Dos Passos' unreasonable and distorted view of the Spanish situation. He was in Bimini with Pauline and their children when he read Archibald MacLeish's letter, intended to reassure him that Dos Passos was "extremely anxious to cooperate in any way he could, but not to get in anybody else's way" relative to the completion of the documentary. MacLeish was trying to play the peacemaker when he added that Dos Passos was "delighted" that Hemingway was going to narrate the commentary as well as write it (there had been talk that Orson Welles would narrate). "Dos would be very glad I know to give a hand if you want him to," continued MacLeish. "I haven't talked politics with Dos but from the way he talked last night I should say he was no Trotskyist, whatever else he may be, and he certainly is anxious to see as good a picture made as possible."

Although the editing of *The Spanish Earth*—done largely by Ivens—was incomplete, and the music by Virgil Thomson and Marc Blitzstein was yet to be dubbed, Ivens and Hemingway presented a twenty-minute segment of the film at the Second American Writers' Congress on June 4, 1937, in Carnegie Hall. Sponsors of the congress, the League of American Writers, declared its membership open to all antifascist writers of professional standing, but by mid-1937 the organization had become a thoroughly Stalinist-dominated body in spite of a number of Trotskyists among its members and a majority of non-Communists. Over one thousand people were turned away at the door while some thirty-five hundred ticket-holders crowded inside for the opening session, chaired by MacLeish, with Hemingway as the keynote speaker. A rapt audience listened as Hemingway assailed fascism and all who clung to "marvelous exotic doctrines" yet refused "to work at what they profess to believe in" and ran no risks in holding their "skillfully chosen positions." Such ideologies espoused only by typewriter or fountain pen were of little use in the fight against fascism waged by "bullies," insisted Hemingway. Several of his innuendoes were aimed at Dos Passos, who had stayed away. Nor was Liston Oak—who resigned as executive secretary of the League of American Writers upon his harrowing exit from Spain and was another unnamed target—at Carnegie Hall to receive Hemingway's barrage in person. Hemingway talked for seven minutes—his first public speaking engagement—then dashed off stage amidst thundering applause, the Communist party's new literary darling. At the Stork Club afterward, accompanied by Martha Gellhorn, wearing a silver fox cape, Hemingway held forth with "small jab lectures about safe people in New York."

It was largely through the efforts of Gellhorn, who used her friendship with Eleanor Roosevelt as an entree to the President, that *The Spanish Earth* was shown at the White House. On July 8, 1937, Hemingway, Ivens, and Gellhorn took the train to Washington, D.C., for dinner at the White House and a private viewing by the President and several intimates. Although the credits accompanying the fifty-four minute film acknowledged MacLeish, Hellman, and Dos Passos as scenarists, and Hemingway for having written and narrated the commentary, only Hemingway was mentioned as a consultant on the shooting script and as being present on location. Some months later, Dos Passos observed in a letter to Dwight Macdonald at the *Partisan Review* that "the whole story of The Spanish Earth is excessively comic, but it's too long and complicated to tell. The way it was gradually made to appear as if all I'd done in connection with the two movies was sabotage them was a masterpiece of the peculiar mass promotion tactics of our friends the comrats." Whereas the documentary had been conceived primarily to bring the *truth* of the Spanish Civil War to concerned Americans, which in turn might help convince the President to repeal the arms embargo on Spain, what it did in fact, however, was to raise funds for the purchase of Loyalist ambulances and medical supplies. Two days after the White House showing, Hemingway and Ivens took the film to Hollywood, where their fervor fanned the film colony into donations in excess of twenty thousand dollars. Later, the film was banned as a benefit event in such communities as Waterbury, Connecticut, Middlesex County, New Jersey, and Providence, Rhode Island, after local officials called it a propaganda piece to plunge the United States into war. By then, Dos Passos had given up any hope once harbored that the President—the master persuader himself—could be convinced to see the war in Spain as "a rehearsal for deadlier assaults to come."

Dos Passos wrote of having been in Washington, D.C., a few weeks after his return from Spain to talk with several government leaders who felt, as he did, that there was still "a chance of checking the Fascist advance in Europe" if the legal government in Spain was allowed to buy arms from the United States. He experienced encouragement for a time when he encountered quite by chance an American diplomat whose statesmanship he admired who allowed that he had made an appointment with the President expressly for the purpose of trying to convince him of the country's need for a change in foreign policy regarding Spain. The diplomat—who remained unnamed in Dos Passos' account of the incident later—insisted that if the President disagreed with him, he had his resignation in his pocket. There it stayed, concluded Dos Passos wryly. The President's powers of persuasion were "virtually hypnotic." Dos Passos related that he met the same man a few days later at the same spot: "No more talk of ending the blockade. No more talk of resignation. He and the President had agreed perfectly about everything. He had been talked around to 'the larger view.' "

When Dos Passos and Katy returned to Provincetown during the early summer of 1937, rumor had already preceded them that he had abandoned the Loyalist cause. Talk was rampant in the literary community when word filtered down from New York that Dos Passos had stayed away (boycotted, some said) from the Second American Writers' Congress, which thousands had flocked to as a demonstration of their antifascism. A number of Provincetowners concluded that Dos Passos had amply "shown his face" and that they did not like what they saw. The townspeoples' support of the Spanish republic reached new heights after Douglas Roach, their one native who served in the Abraham Lincoln Battalion, died as a result of wounds suffered in action and was given a hero's burial. For two years a hardworking tribe of Provincetowners staged weekly fund-raising parties on behalf of the Loyalists, at which each guest contributed one dollar. Douglas Roach had been the son of the only black family in Provincetown, a town that normally was antiblack and anti-Semitic, but the cause of the Spanish Loyalists cut across color lines and centuries-old prejudices and antipathies that pitted Yankee against Portuguese and now united most of the town. Some one hundred Provincetowners—as well as others from the lower Cape—turned out each week and spilled over into the gardens, patios, and sun decks of private homes among which the parties rotated. For a number of townsfolk it was the major social event of the week as they sipped tea or punch and nibbled open-faced sandwiches and cookies while sharing the latest news from the ever-changing Loyalist front and choice bits of gossip of friends and neighbors. "After paying for our refreshments we often made $75 or more at a single party, which we turned over each week to a Loyalist organization for the purchase of medical supplies, milk for the children, or for whatever else was needed," recalled Grace Pfeiffer Bell, whose first husband, Jack Tworkov, was an artist who had worked with Dos Passos as a prop man for the New Playwrights Theatre. "Dos Passos was supposed to have been such a big Loyalist sympathizer, but he never came to any of these parties," she added ruefully.

Dos Passos offered no excuses to the townspeople among whom he made his home and was often criticized as a result. Most of his close friends knew what lay behind his disillusionment in Spain, but he did not speak publicly of the Robles affair or write of it until two years after his return home because he feared that he might inadvertently endanger Robles' two children and widow, who remained in Valencia. By the time his letter to the editor of *The New Republic,* entitled "Death of José Robles," was published in July 1939, his breach with the literary Left had suffered irreparably, but there were other renegades at his side as well.

In a style that resembled Dos Passos' own, Herbert Solow aptly caught the literary decline of the former lion of the Left in juxtaposition with Hemingway's ascent in an essay entitled "Substitution at Left Tackle: Hemingway for Dos Passos," published in April 1938 in the recently resurrected *Partisan Review,* now a bastion of Trotskyist viewpoint:

> In Spain,
> Dos Passos found bombs horrifying, bloodshed gruesome, anarchists hounded by a Stalinist camarilla, the People's Front conceding to Anglo-French imperialism and suppressing socialism. He consequently criticized the Stalinists to his companion.
> Hemingway found bombs intriguing, bloodshed exciting, anarchists "treasonable," the People's Front noble, socialism nonsense. He consequently denounced his companion.
> Back from Spain,
> Dos Passos published articles criticizing the Communist International, defended the honor of the Spanish anarchists, supported the Trotsky Defense Committee, opposed collective security.
> Hemingway performed at the Communist Party's Writers Congress, joined sixteen C.P.–controlled committees, wrote a play "exposing" the "Fifth Column," fished for tarpon at Key West, and socked Max Eastman.

The Max Eastman reference was to a wrestling match of sorts in the office of Maxwell Perkins when Hemingway's temper flared and he attacked Eastman—his nemesis from time to time over the past four years—for his disparaging remarks concerning his masculinity. The scuffle was well publicized, both by Eastman and Hemingway, which prompted Stewart Mitchell, whom Dos Passos still saw from time to time, to inquire what he thought of the entire affair. "Damn silly that fisticuffs for the press—in fact makes you want to vomit," Dos Passos replied. After receiving a detailed account of the rhubarb from Max Perkins, Fitzgerald observed that Hemingway had done "the same asinine thing that I knew he had it in him to do when he was out here [fund-raising in Hollywood with *The Spanish Earth* film]. . . . He is living at the present in a world so entirely his own that it is impossible to help him. . . . You would think that a man who has arrived at the position of being practically his country's most eminent writer, could be spared that yelping."

Dos Passos was close-mouthed about his break with Hemingway, just as he was with everything of a deeply personal nature. Certainly Bernice Baumgarten was unaware of any problem when she ventured Hemingway's name as a fit choice for a dustjacket blurb to help promote the collected volume, *U.S.A.* Dos Passos replied guardedly that Hemingway was "out for various reasons." To Gerald Murphy, Dos Passos merely volunteered: "You think for a long time you have a friend, and then you haven't."

If there was any doubt that the friendship might ever be revived, Hemingway dispelled it in his letter to Dos Passos from Paris on March 26, 1938:

> I'm sorry I sent you that cable from the boat. It seemed funny when I sent it. Afterwards it seemed only snotty. But I want to speak to you about something that seems to me to be serious. A war is still being fought in Spain between the people whose side you used to be on and the fascists. If with your hatred of communists you feel justified in attacking, for money, the people who are still fighting that war I think you should at least try to get your facts right. In an article just read in the Red Book *[Partisan Review,* which had a red cover] you give the impression that it is a communist run war and you name a Russian General you met. The only trouble about this, Dos, is that Walter is a Pole. . . . You didn't meet any Russian generals. The only reason I can see your attacking, for money, the side that you were always supposed to be on is an unsuppressible desire to tell the truth. Then why not tell the truth? The thing is that you don't find out the truth in ten days or three weeks and this hasn't been a communist run war for a long time. When people read a series of articles running over six months and more from you they do not realize how short a time you were in Spain and how little you saw. That was what made me send the cable but I should have put it in a decent, not a snotty form. . . . For you to try constantly to make out that the war the government is fighting against the fascist Italian, German Moorish invasion is a communist business imposed on the will of the people is sort of viciously pitiful. . . .
>
> Now I am very easy to attack and if you want, instead of trying to get straight on Spain you can simply attack me too. But that won't help you on the road you're going. When people start in being crooked about money they usually end up being crooked about everything. . . .
>
> So this is the end of the letter. If you ever make any money and want to pay me any on what you owe (not the Uncle Gus money when you were ill. I mean others, just small ones, afterwards), why not send thirty dollars if you make three hundred or twenty or ten or any damn thing. . . .
>
> So long, Dos. Hope you're always happy. Imagine you always will be. Must be a dandy life. Used to be happy myself. Will be again. Good old friends. Always happy with the good old friends. Got them that will knife you in the back for a dime. Regular price two for a quarter. Two for a quarter, hell. Honest Jack Passos'll knife you three times in the back for fifteen cents and sing Giovanezza free. Thanks pal. Gee that feel's good. Any more old friends? Take him away, Doc he's all cut. Tell the editor to make Dr. Passos out a check for $250. Thank you Mr. Passos that was very very neat. Come around any time. There's always work here for anyone who thinks as you do.
>
> Yrs. always,
> HEM [signed]

Hemingway blamed Dos Passos for many things that had nothing to do with the Spanish Civil War, although he also beat that particular dead horse to a pulp before the decade was out. In a series of articles for *Ken* (a new leftist magazine published by David Smart, who also published *Esquire),* Hemingway attacked Dos Passos for his supposed naiveté regarding the Robles affair. In the June 16, 1938, issue of *Ken* ("Treachery in Aragón") and in a later *Ken* article, "Fresh Air on an Inside Story," Hemingway derided Dos Passos and libeled him, in an inaccurate account of a tall journalist "with watery eyes, and strips of blond hair pasted carefully across a flat-topped bald head" who came to Valencia in April 1937 and immediately tried to make "liars out of every honest corre-

spondent in Madrid" in a dispatch that charged the Republican government with terror-
izing and shooting thousands of Loyalists. "And this guy (who was 'as white as the under
half of an unsold flounder at 11:00 o'clock in the morning just before the fish market
shuts') had written it without stirring from his hotel the first day he arrived," continued
Hemingway, who insisted that he had exposed the journalist and intercepted the erroneous material as it was being unwittingly smuggled out by a fellow American writer whose
life was endangered by being asked to carry out the sealed dispatch. There was little doubt
in the minds of most leftist readers that the balding journalist was a caricature of Dos
Passos.

21

Departure from the Left, 1937–40

I have come to believe that the CP is fundamentally opposed to our democracy as I see it and that Marxism, though an important basis for the unborn sociological sciences, if held as a dogma, is a reactionary force and an impediment to progress.

Dos Passos to John Howard Lawson
Fall 1937

The Big Money had been in the marketplace for ten months when the Second American Writers' Congress named it the "best novel of the year." Dos Passos, who was not in attendance to accept the accolade in person, was surprised that the predominantly leftist body selected his novel in view of the recent turn of events. Of the five hundred delegates, three hundred fifty cast their ballots for *The Big Money*. Readers of the New York *Times* may have been even more astonished to learn the next day that the year's runaway bestseller, *Gone with the Wind* (which sold more than one million copies compared to *The Big Money*'s twenty thousand copies), had received only one first-place vote.

Dos Passos hoped that the new recognition would prod Harcourt, Brace into bringing out *The 42nd Parallel, 1919,* and *The Big Money* under one cover. Yet by late summer no such agreement had been reached. He was perturbed that his publisher was dragging his heels in the matter. C. A. Pearce, his editor, arranged with Bennett Cerf to reprint all three novels individually in a Modern Library edition reprint, which Dos Passos interpreted as a sign that Harcourt, Brace was "getting discouraged about the whole business and starting to cover its losses." He had been under contract with Harcourt, Brace for five years—since the publication of *1919* in 1932—and thought that his publisher had had "long enough to come up with a workable plan to handle [his] . . . stuff as a whole." As Dos Passos saw it, Pearce's prediction that *The Big Money* would live up to its name was merely wishful thinking, since no one had followed through in promoting the book to its best advantage. In a letter to Bernice Baumgarten, he noted that Steinbeck's *Of Mice and Men* had sold 187,000 copies, compared to *The Big Money*'s 20,000 during the same period. Despite his novel's having been treated well by most critics, it was destined to remain a sow's ear unless Pearce kept his promise and handled the entire canon instead of piecemeal, book by book. Money spent on advertising *The Big Money* was considerable, Dos Passos conceded, but saw such advertising as "the tip of the iceberg" compared to what might be done to promote his work in its entirety. "Damn it, I just don't feel it's my business" to help Harcourt, Brace think up an imaginative and fresh approach to enhance sales, he told Baumgarten. "I write the stuff and I think we've got to get a publisher who's willing to use his brains to try to sell it." Perhaps Bennett Cerf should be approached for the next book, he ventured.

It bothered Dos Passos that no one in sales promotion had picked up on his being *Time*'s cover story when the book first came out. Moreover, they might have noted his election to the National Institute of Arts and Letters in January 1937 or his one-man show of watercolors at the Matisse Gallery in February as a means of increasing his visibility with the book-buying public. The fact that Harcourt, Brace did not come up with a fresh plan to build upon Dos Passos' having written a novel acclaimed the "best book of the year" seemed further testimony to their ineffective tactics. Surely the publication of his last three novels as a trilogy—which he now referred to as *U.S.A.*—could be the "payoff of the whole enterprise." If *U.S.A.* was not published by the spring or fall (at the latest) of 1938, and if a long-term expert plan to promote his work as a whole was not put into effect, he vowed not to publish another book with Harcourt, Brace.

When his publisher brought out *U.S.A.* under one cover (reprinted from the original plates) on January 27, 1938, two months ahead of schedule, Dos Passos was pacified. Although he had fought hard to receive a straight 10 percent of royalties of all books sold, he was forced now to accept a royalty of five cents a copy instead of thirty cents (the book sold for three dollars) because of what Harcourt, Brace termed "unusually high manufacturing costs of *U.S.A.*" According to the adjusted contract, he was to receive a straight 10 percent of the retail price after the sale of 5,000 copies. What Dos Passos did not realize at the time was that Harcourt, Brace published only 5,200 copies as a first edition, compared to the first run by Harper & Brothers at 7,500 of *The 42nd Parallel;* 10,250 of *1919* by Harcourt, Brace (with no second printing); and 10,000 copies of *The Big Money.* The firm's lack of confidence in anticipated sales of *U.S.A.* convinced Dos Passos that he would have to launch his offensive again if his publisher was going to promote the book properly in its new format.

He had earlier proposed that a volume of biographies culled from *U.S.A.* be published; or if that did not interest Harcourt, Brace, he intended to seek permission for the book to be released to "some special edition house." Dos Passos appealed both to his agent and editor, who, he hoped, would approach Donald Brace directly with his ideas. He told Pearce that he thought he had enough objectivity to look at the merchandising problems of his books from an advertising agency's viewpoint. First the salesmen had to get familiar with his books and pay attention to his innovative techniques of style. "They could read and digest Gingrich's piece introducing the Camera Eye things in <u>Esquire</u>. . . . Every one of the half million readers of Esquire is a potential buyer of the book." Dos Passos suggested that Gingrich himself might write something that could be used the way Sinclair Lewis' piece about *Manhattan Transfer* had been. If not Gingrich, they could try to get "some old strong popular novelist of the Booth Tarkington type" to write about it. Baumgarten proposed Hemingway's name, a suggestion Dos Passos vetoed without comment (Baumgarten had no idea an estrangement had taken place of late). Dos Passos also thought that Harcourt, Brace might furnish Gingrich with fifty copies of *U.S.A.* with the request that he send them out to "fifty representative people in different walks of life" whom he would ask to write their impressions of the book for "A Symposium on *U.S.A.*" to be published in *Esquire.* Gingrich replied that it was a good stunt and that he would cooperate, but promised to publish only "the high spots." Harcourt, Brace suggested that Dos Passos stage an autographing at Lord & Taylor's and sign at least fifty copies, but he was not interested. "Sheer nonsense," he replied, then countered with a suggestion that a recording could be made of one of the *U.S.A.* pieces for a "radio book hour." He said he would be willing even to "submit to photographers and interviewers," but would draw the line on a lecture circuit. If he ever "stopped writing and could find nothing better to do," he might consider lecturing as a business, but the two trades were not compatible, he insisted. Dos Passos also complained that Harcourt, Brace seemed to be able to sell other people's books readily enough, and that they probably listened to the New York critics too much. So far as he was concerned, they were "a bunch of dreary fatheads."

Dos Passos and Edmund Wilson commiserated with each other, since Wilson, too, was being published by Harcourt, Brace at the time. When Wilson complained of their publisher's handling of *To the Finland Station* in 1940, Dos Passos replied that perhaps they ought to picket. "Better sue than stew," he added, then on a more serious note told Wilson that it was "a damn dirty trick" that the book had apparently not been well advertised. "If they didn't want to do their best by a hell of an important book, they ought to have had the decency to let you turn it over to some other publisher. . . . To hell with deceitful publishers and magazines that pay two cents a word. What we need is a good five-cent weekly. Tell Mr. New Republic [Malcolm Cowley] that two-cents a word is a damn gyp."

Not only was Dos Passos down on *The New Republic,* in which he had not been published since his "Vag" excerpt from *The Big Money* in 1936 except for his "Letter to the Editor" concerning the Robles affair, but he was also put out by Arnold Gingrich at *Esquire.* In 1937 he had become riled because *Esquire* paid him only half what it had reportedly paid Hemingway for an article. To Arthur Davison Ficke he complained: "The annoying thing about Esquire is that the bastards will publish almost anything, but that they absolutely won't pay. I've managed to raise the ante to $250 but can't get any higher. Hemingway I believe gets $500 (keep this please under the capacious brim of the fellow wordfellow's hat) but they will use stuff that other editors can't stomach. . . . Their regular price is $100." Although Dos Passos' reference to Hemingway reflected their personal quarrel, his objection to *Esquire*'s meager payments to most writers represented what he considered one of the most serious hazards to professional writers. The entire system seemed against them. Dos Passos was especially sensitive to such mistreatment (as he saw it) at this particular time because he was once again casting about for resources on which to live without prostituting himself in the process. He was convinced that he had sufficiently alienated himself from the leftist critics who made up the bulk of those reviewing books of the contemporary period—just as Hemingway had predicted when he flung his malediction at him upon their parting in Paris—thus he asked Baumgarten to insist that Harcourt, Brace get some reviewers for his trilogy who were "outside the general run of critics." He could take their slamming his book, he said, but the "type of review my stuff gets now from the regular critics would kill the sales of the Holy Bible."

Meanwhile, the five hundred dollars Dos Passos had received in July 1937 as an advance against royalties for his next two books was already gone, and he turned once more to his old friends for money. To Stewart Mitchell, who had given him fifty dollars earlier in the year, he petitioned for another small loan. "I ought to be old enough by this time to organize my finances a little more sensibly," he offered, but added that the more he and Katy earned, the higher they lived. "If we didn't our living would be meager indeed. . . . We think of ourselves as continuously on the edge of a big killing of some kind—and in the meantime we are a burden on our friends." In a postscript to John Howard Lawson in one of their several letters in which they exchanged ideologies with mounting fervor in 1937, Dos Passos added: "Gosh thanks for the $200. It was like a heavy shower in a drought—instantly soaked up by the thirsty soil—but it relieved the tension a little. The sheriff and the banker are temporarily out of the living room."

Katy, too, spoke of their financial straits in a letter to Mary Heaton Vorse the day after Dos Passos thanked Lawson for his new loan: "We are broke again, and I can't bear to get up this morning—still in bed at 10:00 a.m., not from sloth, but from what to put on when I'm up. My only black suit is just a gunny sack now and would make a good bird's nest soup if boiled up for the Chinese." To Edmund Wilson in a letter at about the same time, Katy quipped that she wished she had "five beautiful children—all Morgan partners!"

Dos Passos might not have dogged his agent and editor with his various sales promotion schemes had his money situation seemed less bleak, but he was disheartened on several other counts also. Disappointed because he had been unable to arrange for Márgare Robles to collect on her husband's life insurance policy, he then tried to help get her and her children safely to Paris, where his friend and translator Maurice Coindreau promised to look out for them and provide shelter. Robles' son chose to stay in Spain, however, where he was captured while fighting with the Republican militia (young Robles was not freed by Franco's government until 1945). Dos Passos resented his government's unwillingness to aid the Spanish republic while there was still time; yet he was bothered, too, by what he termed its "war spirit," brought on by a "blind enthusiasm of antifascism." In an article published in *Common Sense* in December 1937, which amplified his "Farewell to Europe" statement published in *Common Sense* soon after his return from Spain, Dos Passos insisted that he still felt intense sympathy with the Loyalist cause in Spain, but warned his countrymen not to allow their sympathies to blind them to the complex political situation on the verge of erupting throughout all Europe. "I'm all for sending them ambulances. I'd be for sending them machine guns if there were a way to do it," he said. As it was, ambulances had to be sent illegally. It seemed to him, however, that the American people should temper their help so that the "sufferings of the Spanish people shall not be exploited by any group of politicians (whether or not one agreed with them)," nor should their assistance become a "football of international diplomacy." If the fascists won in Spain, it would mean "the final blotting out of hope for Europe." He also cautioned that the Communists, in helping to unify the disparate anti-Franco factions in Spain through the "tools of enthusiasm and munitions," had also used all the "intricate and bloody machinery of Kremlin policy." Dos Passos saw fascism as a "disease of sick capitalism" that fed on the "war spirit" and could be combated only through intelligent popular government. The best way to fight fascism in Spain was "to expose the Fascist sympathizers in our own State Department and to uncover the forces in the Catholic hierarchy and the banking world which originally put the United States on the side of the enemies of the Spanish people." The place to fight it is "in your home town," he concluded.

To many readers of "The Communist Party and the War Spirit: A Letter to a Friend Who Is Probably a Party Member," Dos Passos' generalizations were a quagmire of rhetoric. John Howard Lawson, to whom the letter might well have been addressed, accused his friend of being on "desperately shaky ground" with his cynical accusations of "people not meaning what they say, of not knowing what they're doing, and being the victims of autocratic plots woven by a single individual or group of individuals in Moscow." Friends and enemies alike of Dos Passos recognized during the winter of 1937–38 that he was on the edge of an important shift that might well affect him and his professional career for the rest of his life. Whereas he had perched for a long time on the fence and swiveled his head from West to East and back again from a relatively safe distance—his trips to the Soviet Union and recent misadventures in Spain notwithstanding—he now locked his eyes into place so that his vision fell upon the United States with far more single-mindedness than ever before. Dos Passos' means of firming up the "desperately shaky ground" on which Lawson alleged that he stood was to tap his own American soil firmly under him. Thus it was with renewed vigor that he returned to his reading of American history and his country's forebears, about whom he intended to write a series of short novels and "a set of historical pieces."

Before the end of 1937 he was already referring to his writings on American history as "The American Base," later entitled *The Ground We Stand On,* as though to dispel once and for all Lawson's criticism of his underpinnings. He was unable to concentrate on his nonfiction chronicles, however, until he cleared up his "old stuff" and got it into a palatable form "in case the public had a taste to buy it." By this time, C. A. Pearce had agreed to publish "a travel omnibus" of excerpts from *Rosinante to the Road Again, Orient Express, In All Countries,* and some eighty manuscript pages that would comprise a new section on Spain. Dos Passos had only to write an introduction to unify the material. He was also impatient to get on with his fictionalized version of his own disillusionment with Communism and what he saw as its dangerous and rapidly growing malignancy in present-day Spain. By the time the collected essays, *Journeys Between Wars,* appeared in April 1938, all of the new Spanish material except "The Fiesta at the Fifteenth Brigade" had already been published in *Esquire.* This essay was the most personal of all in that it was at the fiesta of the 15th Brigade that Hemingway sprang the news that José Robles was dead.

Out of money again in November 1937, Dos Passos managed to get another two thousand dollars—doled out in installments—from his publisher. This time royalties accruing under all existing contracts were thrown into a general account to be applied to his debt balance. He was still in debt for *The Big Money*. Harcourt, Brace owned the rights to *Manhattan Transfer, Orient Express, Panama, or The Adventures of My Seven Uncles, The 42nd Parallel* (published by Harper & Brothers); *1919* and *In All Countries* (published by Harcourt, Brace); *Journeys Between Wars* (not yet published); his "Spanish novel," identified only as a "Novel to follow *The Big Money*" (later entitled *Adventures of a Young Man*); and still another book referred to as a "Nonfiction work to be delivered" *(The Ground We Stand On)*. Dos Passos accepted Harcourt, Brace's money, but thought the indenture unfair. Publishers took risks just as authors did, and he saw no reason for his firm to attempt to recoup its losses against books it had failed to promote adequately by attaching his earnings from books not yet written. It seemed to him another version of the Harlan miner hopelessly in debt to the company store. Only *U.S.A.* was exempt from the list. At five cents a copy as his royalty share, he saw no reason to fall on his knees about it. Dos Passos concluded that once he had worked himself "out of that mess," he would either find another publisher or take up a new trade.

Despite his apprehensions regarding the receptions of *Journeys Between Wars* and *U.S.A.*, and his claim that he did not read reviews, Dos Passos was relatively pleased by the reviews he saw. Many who wrote about his books, especially *Journeys Between Wars*, had never before criticized his work publicly. Most praised the travel book for its descriptive style, his eye for color and pattern, and his "power of characterization"—all superior to his political analysis, noted some reviewers. Hassoldt Davis told readers of the New York *Times Book Review* that *Journeys Between Wars* was the best travel book and "sociological odyssey" of recent years. He commended Dos Passos for combining the "dramatic impetus of a novelist, the perception of a remarkable correspondent and the vigorous, independent curiosity of the great travelers of the past." Lewis Gannett in his "Books and Things" column for the New York *Herald Tribune* warned those who might strain for "clean-cut prophecies, for sharp pros or cons" to look elsewhere. If they were patient and had a mind "already large enough to welcome enlargement," they could survive the platitudes and conclude that travel may enlarge the mind. One could see Dos Passos' evolution as poet, painter, novelist, and interpreter, continued Gannett, who thought his sketches "aflame with color and full of smells and sounds." All were extraordinary for their "personal interpretation of the universe."

The reviews of Michael Gold and Granville Hicks did not surprise him. Their criticism of his political vagaries had mounted since publication of *The Big Money*. Gold used the publication of *U.S.A.* as the occasion to trace Dos Passos' abandonment of the Left and *merde* that lay behind it. Dos Passos hated Communism because "organically he seems to hate the human race," declared Gold in the *Daily Worker*. Hicks launched his attack in low gear, speaking first of such things as the tale in *Journeys Between Wars* of the camel ride from Baghdad to Damascus, which he thought "as pleasant a personal record as can be found in modern literature." Gide, Lawrence, and Huxley wrote travel books that deserved a place among their major writings, said Hicks, but he thought differently about Dos Passos because he "was afraid to draw conclusions" from his observations. Even the Spanish crisis had not shaken him into thought, nor had he written about the issues or distinguished between the Loyalists and the POUM. Hicks was especially irked by Dos Passos' "unabashed detachment"; he saw no excuse for Dos Passos' having come out of Spain "with nothing but a question mark" and for committing himself "to a hysterical isolationism that might almost be called chauvinistic." Hicks also cited Dos Passos' conversation with Dreiser in December (published in *Direction)* as ample evidence of his muddled, shallow thinking, his prejudices, confusion, and blindness —all marked his turn from fellow traveler with a star in his future as "the American Gorki" to a pessimistic, will-o'-the-wisp camp follower whose grasp of economics seemed epitomized in the comment to Dreiser: "Every time there is a rise in wages, prices go up at the A. & P." No one could be more politically unreliable, concluded Hicks.

Other critics, too, picked up Dos Passos' evolving pessimism. Matthew Josephson referred to Dos Passos as the inveterate traveler who never strayed from being himself, "in love with people, with a taste for history and a sharp eye for detail," but found his pessimism disturbing and wondered where it was leading him. Despite impressions conveyed in his writings of this period regarding his so-called abject pessimism, Dos Passos did see daylight at the end of America's tunnel, although he conceded that it would take considerable time to get there. Soon after his return from Madrid, he wrote Claude Bowers, the American ambassador to Spain, that he had "never been much of a flagwaver, but . . . [thought now that] we have more and more cause to congratulate ourselves that we got our parents to born us where they did." It seemed to Dos Passos at this point that politics throughout the world were "about to settle down to the business of plain and fancy massacre," but that the United States was the "only country left where the tension . . . [was] low enough to allow any progress toward solving the problem of how to get anything for the human race out of industrial civilization." Dos Passos had told Dreiser in December that America was "probably the only country where the average guy got the better break," and to Sherwood Anderson he wrote: "If we all have to go into an army I'd rather go into the U.S. Army—I know what that's like. I don't know Mr. Stalin's army from the inside—but it seems kind of creepy to a spectator."

Upon the publication of *U.S.A.* on January 27, 1938, Dos Passos granted several newspaper and radio interviews, but was eager to get on the road again, this time in his own country. Instead of heading south to Key West, as he might have done had he and Hemingway not been estranged, he and Katy set out in their Ford roadster for New Orleans. "Having an absurdly good time riding around in the spring weather and have not heard of a Trotskyist . . . or seen a comrade" since leaving the Hudson Tunnel, he wrote Edmund Wilson. After a week in New Orleans, they moseyed north from town to town, never straying far from the Mississippi. Dos Passos had not been in Louisiana since the assassination of their political "Kingfish," Huey P. Long, in 1935, and he wanted to know how the people were faring under their present governor, Richard Leche. Already Dos Passos was formulating his plan to make Long and his *mise-en-scène* the major ingredient of the novel he wanted to write after finishing his still untitled *Adventures of a Young Man.* In Vicksburg, he mailed a postal card to Chauncey Hackett, a jackleg historian with a background in law and a longtime friend of his and Katy's in Provincetown, whom Hackett's wife described as a "blocked writer who enjoyed helping

Dos with his research." Dos Passos told Hackett that the "principality of the late governor" was "absurdly pleasant." The card depicted Long standing beside the state capitol in
Baton Rouge, where Dos Passos and Katy had tarried several days earlier. After six weeks
on the road, Dos Passos wrote Stewart Mitchell from the Warm Springs Inn in Virginia,
one of their favorite retreats, that there was considerable "life in the old continent yet,"
but cautioned Stewart against spending "too much time in the pestilential fever of the
Eastern seaboard." By this time, Dos Passos was impatient to get back to the Cape to
resume work on *Adventures of a Young Man.*

Back in New York, he learned that the sales of *U.S.A.* totaled 3,524 as of March 12,
1938, and by July 1, they had topped 5,000. If a second printing of *U.S.A.* was not ordered
immediately, however, he saw himself making only a scant sixty dollars on the remaining
200 copies, since his 10 percent royalty did not begin until 5,000 had been sold and only
5,200 had been run. Meanwhile, Harcourt, Brace decided to throw its weight behind the
novel not yet published, *Adventures of a Young Man,* and cast about for a suitable author
to write a positive reappraisal of Dos Passos in a biographical/critical monograph. Harcourt, Brace's publicity director, Helen Taylor, wrote Bernice Baumgarten that they were
stymied on the pamphlet because they were "trying to reach for the stars." If Thomas
Mann did not agree to write it, they would "go after Van Wyck Brooks." Robert Cantwell
insisted that Dos Passos "needed no more boosting from critics of his ilk, but an older,
very distinguished person to tear his shirt over him." Dos Passos had not been impressed
by Brooks's *The Flowering of New England,* which was named "best history of the year"
by the same writers who had selected *The Big Money* as "best novel of 1936–37." He
wrote Edmund Wilson shortly after Brooks's book was published: "I've been trying to
read The Flowering of New England. I've rarely read a book I disliked so much. There's a
kind of female enthusiasm in it I find disgusting. What the devil is it about?" If Dos
Passos were asked about Brooks as a suitable candidate for writing a reappraisal of him, he
probably vetoed him. Later, John Chamberlain was invited to write it, and did.

Despite Harcourt, Brace's efforts to think imaginatively about its promotion of Dos
Passos' books as a whole, the author himself was still far from happy with the poor sales
of *Journeys Between Wars,* published on April 7, 1938. "For Christ sake can that stuff
about twenty years of travel. Not even the sturdiest bookbuyer will stand up under it and
bookbuyers are as feeble as lettuce plants with the wilt this season," he admonished Helen
Taylor when he saw some of the publicity releases. "What interests people this spring is
European politics." The book had been reviewed "all over the place," he continued, yet
could not her people "be induced to sell a few copies? It seems to me a much easier
proposition than U.S.A., but naturally people have to be given an inkling of what's in it."

Dos Passos complained similarly to Bernice Baumgarten. He said that Harcourt,
Brace apparently thought of his "stuff" as a "display article," which they did not attempt
to sell with the enthusiasm that they did their other titles. "Something has just got to be
done about making a fatter living out of my work," he implored. "The wolves . . .
friends of long standing" were no longer content with his basement, but were now
showing "a nasty spirit above ground." The bankers had become "mighty savage." Baumgarten asked Harcourt, Brace for five hundred dollars "because he needs it badly," and
forfeited her own commission so that he might have the full amount. Four months later,

he petitioned for another five-hundred-dollar advance. This time he signed a note for a three-month, interest-free loan, for which he agreed to pay 5 percent interest if the money were not repaid by the first of the year. Distasteful as the idea was to him, Dos Passos even looked into the possibility of a lecture tour. What he learned confirmed his apprehensions. The Leigh Lecture Agency promised to get him three bookings in November and December 1938, but in turn, he had to agree to not give more than one talk on Spain and "preferably none at all." He would also have to commit himself to bookings from November until May and agree to lecture the following season. Half of his one-hundred-dollar or two-hundred-dollar fee was supposed to go to the agency. Dos Passos replied that he got better offers on his own and "turned them down regularly."

An escape from their financial doldrums during the summer of 1938 was made possible by an invitation from Gerald and Sara Murphy to cruise with them in the Mediterranean aboard their schooner, *The Weatherbird*. The entire trip was to be a gift of the Murphys, who were grieving over the death of their son, Patrick, in early 1937 and insisted that they "needed some time with the Dosses," who invariably cheered them up. WE WILL MEET YOU AMONG ANTIQUE CITIES CROWNED WITH ROSES AND LET THERE BE THE SOUND OF FLUTINGS, Dos Passos and Katy cabled the Murphys in late June after boarding their steamship in New York for Naples, Italy, where they agreed to meet. For almost a month they sailed the blue-green waters of the Tyrrhenian Sea from Naples to Sicily. Katy's diary of the trip revealed that she, too, had an eye for color and a flair for description:

> From Naples to Capri the sea is a museum of shipping—henna colored fish nets spread to dry on the gray rocks on the water front. . . . Capri—a tiny blue harbor with a gray volcanic stone mole and gray antique column at the entrance . . . a pretty town. One great pergola of grapes—old stone steps, Roman brick work—umbrella pines, white pink yellow tomato colored houses. . . . The nicest part of the architecture—plain arches, iron work & balconies & steps. In the square up the hill a horrid packed layer cake of races. The Germans are Tyroleans—the Italians horribly small, ugly and devoted to petty larceny, cheating lying and begging—the Blue Grotto jammed with Germans—universally homely and bad-mannered. The Island seems stuffy and crowded. Still smells of Tiberius. . . . Pompeii is just yesterday —has a terrible feeling of violence & disaster. . . . Amalfi is the finest town I've ever seen— a pure medieval city in a great ravine—all built of thick stone—with a curved harbor and wall of stone arches running around the bay. There's an odd fountain in the street, Patron Saint of Fisherman—a statue of the Saint with wooden fish tied to his wrist, a stone bust of a woman with water spouting from her breasts. The people look very medieval. Children very skinny & ragged. Boat loads of indigenes came out and tormented us while we were swimming— particularly disagreeable—insolent older men who stared at the girls and wouldn't give them room to dive or swim. They did not seem like natives of Amalfi but Italian resorts. This riff-raff all deserted us when the Windsor yacht came in. . . . Great sculptured marble clouds pass over Aetna.

Dos Passos had reasoned before leaving for Europe that he could return after some six weeks abroad with a virtually complete manuscript of *Adventures of a Young Man*, but on August 10, 1938, he wrote Baumgarten from the Café de la Laux in Paris that he would be home soon, but thought she ought to start "breaking it to Cap [C. A. Pearce] that '<u>Adventures of etc</u>.' better be put off until early spring. I have a great deal more rewriting to do than I could possibly have imagined and I'm very anxious to have the damn thing right before it goes to press. I'll have it for them during the fall and they'll be able to take their time getting it out." Of his cruise, he said only that it had been a fine one, with "a great deal of sun, seawater and old carved stones." On August 22, the Brooklyn *Daily Eagle* carried a story under the headline: DUCE'S THREAT AMUSES DOS PASSOS:

> Surprised indeed was John Dos Passos when he learned that he had a "kick in the pants" coming to him if he returned to Italy. When told that the editor of *Popolo d'Italia*, Mussolini's mouthpiece, had promised him and Hemingway such treatment the author laughed and said: "That's splendid. I'm all through with Italy. The food is terrible and even the bread is bad. Conditions were worse than I expected. Everybody in Italy seems scared and looks it." Dos Passos thought it odd that he had not been bothered any time during a month's sailing trip along the coast of Italy. Furthermore, he couldn't remember any particular stinging articles or books that he had written about Mussolini or Italy. "Some time ago I wrote that Mussolini was responsible for General Franco in Spain, but I can't see what's wrong about that," added Dos Passos.

The New York *Times* published the story, too, under the caption: DOS PASSOS VISITS ITALY DESPITE THREAT OF EJECTION. When the *Times* reporter asked if Dos Passos had been apprehensive about the warning that he would be "painfully thrown across the border if he set foot in Italy," he said that he had not received such a warning. Whereas Dos Passos was in ill favor because of his criticism of Italy's role in Spain's internal affairs, said the reporter, Hemingway was "persona non grata because of his disparaging remarks about the ability of Italian soldiers." Dos Passos replied that Italy was in bad shape and the people were apprehensive about their future.

In view of his current status in Italy, Dos Passos was surprised to hear in the fall that an Italian house had offered twelve hundred lire for the serial rights to *Journeys Between Wars*. Before he sailed into Italian waters in June, the offer had been broached, whereupon C. H. Brooks, his British agent, wrote Baumgarten: "I don't suppose Mr. Dos Passos counts on selling the Italian rights in view of his anti-Fascist attitude on the Spanish War which is so clearly expressed." Dos Passos considered the offer when it did come a niggardly one (at that time the dollar was worth nineteen lire; therefore he received $63.12 for the sale), but he accepted on the condition that he be sent two sets of serial installments. Additional foreign sales were in the making by year's end. A Swiss firm paid one thousand francs for a German edition of *The Big Money*, an offer of two hundred dollars for the Spanish rights of *The 42nd Parallel* for publication in Argentina was awaiting Dos Passos' signature, and a serial sale for the French rights to *Three Soldiers* was pending. Dos Passos' tale of three American doughboys in Europe during World War I was evoking considerable foreign interest now that the Continent seemed once more on the verge of war. A German publisher, Christian Wegner (whose firm had never before published a Dos Passos book), heard that *Adventures of a Young Man* was in progress and offered to buy it sight unseen, but C. H. Brooks was certain that the book would not be publishable in Germany in view of Dos Passos' political outlook and reportedly discouraged the sale.

Meanwhile, Bennett Cerf had brought out only *The 42nd Parallel* in the Modern Library edition by the end of 1938 and wanted to convert his contract to publish the three books of the trilogy separately to a combined *U.S.A.* volume, since the sale of the trilogy by Harcourt, Brace had "seriously cut into the demand for the separate volumes." Dos Passos was skeptical of the move, however, because he saw it as a threat to sales of the Harcourt, Brace edition. Baumgarten assured him that there would be no loss on the deal, since Cerf would pay enough for the *U.S.A.* rights to compensate for the loss of the advance—yet to be paid—for the two individual titles still unpublished. The question was whether it was better to sell twenty thousand to thirty thousand copies of *U.S.A.* in the Modern Library edition during the upcoming year than to sell some five hundred copies at three dollars and fifty cents each in the regular edition, with the cheap edition to come out still later. Dos Passos decided to accept Cerf's offer.

Another sale in the fall of 1938 was to *Omnibook* for the biographical portraits of *U.S.A.*, to be published under the title "Passing Portraits" in the January issue of *Omnibook Magazine,* for which he was paid $500 (less his agent's commission). Brandt & Brandt reported that his income for 1938 was $2,557, a figure considerably lower than the $4,291 reported the year before. Baumgarten did everything she could to keep her client solvent. Although Dos Passos was grateful for the $500 he had borrowed from Harcourt, Brace, he was rankled that it was a loan rather than a draw against his royalties. He told Baumgarten that winter that he was closing out his checking account with his New York bank (which he had maintained for fifteen years as a convenience both to him and his agent) because he had trouble keeping track of his balance and frequently overdrew his account.

Baumgarten worked hard to sell sections of *Adventures of a Young Man* before it was published, but to little avail. One problem was that Dos Passos was still revising the early segments that had been sent out during the summer and fall for unofficial readings. According to Katy in a letter to Pauline Hemingway on October 31, 1938, Dos Passos was "tearing up everything so I'm thinking of getting him a blackboard so he can just rub it all out every day on the Penelope system." In mid-December she reported to Sara Murphy: "Dos is working like mad but claims to tear up most of the web he spins, like Penelope."

In a note designed to amuse Sara Murphy, Katy described a typical day on the Cape as 1938 drew to a close:

> We sit here modestly on the harbor like wooden ducks in a pond and not even a quack to distinguish us from the scenery. Dos and I have given up conversation and communicate by signs—shivering when the furnace is low, pointing to the door to go walking. Dos rubs his stomach to show he's hungry, and raises an imaginary bottle at five o'clock. I occasionally pretend to be a train to indicate that I want to go to New York and Dos then passes the hat in dumb show. We were momentarily enlivened last week by a visit from Léger and Simone [Fernand Léger and his wife] . . . it was fun, and Léger very comical—but now we've gone back into torpor again. . . . Did I tell you that we had no cold turkey for Thanksgiving because Eliza Poodle ate it? It was an act of sheer hooliganism, as she got it down from a high shelf and had obviously been planning the whole thing while under the table at dinner. . . .

Dos went simply wild and shrieked "That dog's for sale!" He says men feel more intensely about food than women because women have a layer of sub-cutaneous fat and never get really hungry, while men have only a little skin and bone and are hungry practically all the time in a way no woman can ever understand.

Katy used the "wooden ducks in a pond image" in her letter to Pauline Hemingway that fall to describe their uneventful life at present. "Have to be visited by ducks able to fly," she continued in urging Pauline to bring her sons to the Cape and pay them a visit. Hemingway was still married to Pauline, but he was getting ready to return to Spain and to his lover, Martha Gellhorn. He and Pauline had been in Wyoming at the L-Bar-T ranch for several weeks while he finished his drama of Spain, "The Fifth Column," and a collection of stories to be published in the same volume. Each was making an effort to maintain a front that there was some semblance of a marriage between them.

Katy was reminded anew of Hemingway and their estrangement when she and Dos Passos had lunch that fall with Edwin Balmer, an editor at *Redbook* to whom Dos Passos had sent a section of *Adventures of a Young Man*. Balmer had been a friend of hers and also of Hemingway's dating back to their days together in Chicago when Hemingway had first come home from the war. Their several hours at lunch together prompted Katy to jot a nostalgic note to Hemingway: "Oh Wemedge how did we all get where we are, starting from Walloon? And now you're in Indian summer in Wyoming. . . . Had lunch with Balmer without 'McCarty' [a reference to an early, unpublished story of Hemingway's entitled "The Passing of Pickles McCarty," which Hemingway had read to Katy and Balmer when the three of them had been together some twenty years earlier] the other day. Oh Wemedge—Love, Katy." Hemingway never wrote back, and Katy's missive was her last direct communication with her old friend.

Some six weeks later, Katy wrote Pauline that she hoped Pauline had not "forgotten an old school chum whose affections have never varied from their early object. I often wish our husbands were pals as nature intended—and feel bitter about all forms of politics and international warfare, also peace, fascism, democracy and the Kraft-cheese evil. I do not give my views publicly as Dos says he doesn't want a Dorothy Thompson in his home. This hurts me terribly, so I don't say much any more—just sit and chew gum." Katy also quipped about her current impoverished state, which she expected to remedy soon: "Edith Shay and I are engaged on another great money-making scheme which may succeed enough to get us a couple of nice warm dresses by Xmas. We are still wearing light cotton frocks topped by an old frayed sweater, and our hair is straight and long. My nails are nothing but horn and if caught on the corner of 57th and Fifth Avenue I would be put in the zoo. I suppose you are chic as ever and have many fashionable friends." Katy did not elaborate on her fund-raising scheme. She and Edith Shay eventually wrote a novel together, but nothing was published under their coauthorship until an article entitled "New Harmony, Indiana" appeared in *The Atlantic Monthly* in 1940.

Dos Passos interrupted his work on *Adventures of a Young Man* for a trip South the first week of December 1938. The significance of this particular journey might have gone unnoticed had he not mailed a postal card to Edmund Wilson from Warsaw, Virginia, a small town in the Northern Neck of the state that he would not have been in had he not stopped to look over his father's old homestead and to exchange a few pleasantries with his half brother James Madison. More likely, however, he had gone there with the express purpose of checking on his land after hearing that a large portion of it had been sold without his permission or knowledge, then foreclosed on and recovered during the summer of 1938 after a lumber company had denuded it of most of its trees. Seeing his stripped land, Dos Passos decided that he "was being robbed" and was determined to get at the root of it. Bit by bit, the entire story came to light.

Having conveyed his portion of his father's estate to his aunt under an "oral absolute trust that it be managed for his benefit," Dos Passos went to her for money only as a last resort. Mary Lamar Gordon had made a few token payments to her errant nephew over the years "through various means of the moment," but he preferred to borrow from friends than to admit to his aunt that he could not make ends meet on his own. She left the details of management of the Virginia property to her husband, James Riely Gordon, until his death; then her son-in-law, Byron Brown Ralston, took care of it. Ralston was an attorney, and Mary Lamar Gordon happily turned Dos Passos' affairs over to him. In 1926 when a Virginia real estate firm approached Mrs. Gordon with an offer to buy a sizable portion of the land—still held jointly with Dos Passos' half brother Louis—Ralston neither sought Dos Passos' permission nor apprised him of its sale. According to the Westmoreland County Court House records in Montross, Virginia—dated September 15, 1926—some five thousand acres of waterfront property known as Sandy Point Farms, a tract of twenty-three parcels of land fronting fourteen miles along the Potomac River and its estuary, the Yeocomico, were conveyed to The Sandy Point Corporation by Louis Dos Passos and his wife, Grace; and by Mary Lamar Gordon and John R. Dos Passos, Jr., by "two certain deeds of bargain and sale" for a figure reportedly in excess of five hundred thousand dollars. Yet Dos Passos—the true beneficiary of one half of the property—knew nothing of the sale and discovered it only by accident, most likely, some twelve years later.

In the spring of 1937, The Sandy Point Corporation defaulted on its notes for the unpaid balance of the purchase price (after paying over four hundred thousand dollars to the respective mortgagees), whereupon Mrs. Gordon, acting through Ralston as trustee of the mortgage still held by her for her nephew's portion of the sale, collaborated with Louis Dos Passos and brought foreclosure proceedings against the purchaser (now identified as "The Sandy Point Corporation *et al.*"). Louis Dos Passos reportedly had no idea that his half brother was unaware of the various transactions, including the original sale and the foreclosure sale, which followed on August 27, 1938. The two half brothers neither saw one another nor corresponded during these years. Other than their father's blood and joint ownership of land through his bequest, they had little in common and a considerable age difference. Louis knew only that his half brother had relinquished all responsibility for the property and had turned it over to his aunt for management.

In July 1938, Ralston had initiated the foreclosure proceedings, and in late August two large display advertisements announced to readers of the *Richmond Times Dispatch* and the Northern Neck *News* that the five-thousand-acre Sandy Point Farms were to be auctioned at a foreclosure sale from the steps of the Westmoreland County Court House between the hours of 11 A.M. and 12 noon on August 27. Ralston, as a trustee of the mortgage, was named in the advertisement as a special commissioner of the sale ordered in the "Chancery cause of Grace M. Dos Passos and Mary Lamar Gordon." Grace Dos Passos was Louis' wife, to whom he had deeded his share of the property. The name "John Dos Passos, Jr.," did not appear on the foreclosure papers, despite its having been on the original "deed of bargain and sale" in 1926 when The Sandy Point Corporation purchased the land.

The sale at foreclosure did not go through because it failed to produce a bid equal to the amount of the debt. As a result, the mortgagees (now listed as Grace Dos Passos and Mary Lamar Gordon) regained title to the property. A major factor that had figured in the original sale—hundreds of thousands of board feet of virgin oak and pine—was no longer an issue, since almost all of the trees of commercial value had been cut and nothing planted to take their place. The entire Virginia property Dos Passos and his half brother Louis had inherited could have been a veritable gold mine because of the timber alone if the owners—or a proper overseer—had harvested the timber as a crop, treated it against disease and infestation, and cut and replanted the trees on a regular basis. Had their father lived a year or two longer, he probably would have planted seedlings to replace the seventy-five thousand dollars' worth of virgin oak and pine sold in November 1916, just two months before his death. The health of John R. failed significantly immediately after the lumber sale, and the only new trees on that tract took root through nature's happenstance; thus the growth on that portion of the land remained straggly.

The precise date that Dos Passos made his move to regain control over his Virginia property remains unclear, but according to C. Dickerman Williams, a New York attorney and longtime friend who helped him recover the land, Dos Passos insisted that his aunt sign a deed conveying his half interest back to him. "I believe it was Katy who nudged him to try to get his land back," said Williams. "Once Mrs. Gordon gave him the document he sought, he and Katy drove to Montross, Virginia, to file it in the county courthouse. I believe it was then that he inspected the land records and discovered the foreclosure sale, and also the original sale." Dos Passos had been interested in seeing the descriptions and dates that the various parcels of land had been acquired by his father and learned that much of the property had been purchased through his father's private secretary, Joseph J. Schmidt; some of the property had not been transferred to John R.'s name until after his death. But Schmidt was scrupulously honest and bent on looking out for the well-being of his late employer's heirs as well. It was apparently at this time that Dos Passos learned to his great dismay that the five thousand acres constituting Sandy Point Farms, which he thought was his and his brother's all the time, had actually been sold in 1926 and had been back in the family for only a little over three months. Compared to the value of the timber stripped from it, however, the land was worth relatively little. The lumber company had come out the winner despite its having to return the land to its former owners.

Rather than blame his aunt—for whom he still had considerable affection and whom he was reluctant to hurt—Dos Passos concluded that the malevolent character in the whole affair had been her deceased husband, who had undoubtedly counseled her in the original sale. He also saw Byron Ralston as the new villain, since Ralston was an attorney and understood well all the ramifications of the various transactions. In early 1939, Dos Passos consulted Williams regarding what to do next, and Williams advised him to sue for an accounting of the property held in trust for him by his aunt, and for the money now due him. Dos Passos had already concluded from examining the courthouse records involving the original sale and the foreclosure proceedings that over two hundred thousand dollars had already been collected by his aunt as "his share in trust," yet he had seen none of it, and until now, was unaware even of its existence. Williams helped Dos Passos draft a suitable letter to Mary Lamar Gordon declaring his desire for an accounting "so that all money due him could be paid forthwith," but she insisted that there was no money left to turn over to him. Katy told Williams privately that Dos Passos had been vaguely suspicious that "he was being robbed but was too embarrassed to do anything about it" until he came face to face with the evidence in the Montross courthouse.

Meanwhile, Dos Passos begrudged doing anything that took time away from his writing, since he was trying desperately to finish *Adventures of a Young Man* in time for its scheduled June 1, 1939, publication date. As soon as some money came in from that book, he hoped to rid himself of some of his debts, but for now he was forced to borrow enough to meet a mortgage payment due on one of their houses. It was especially frustrating for Dos Passos to have to hound his friends for money when he seemed on the verge of recovering what might have been his own considerable wealth. This time he borrowed from Rumsey Marvin.

Dos Passos worked feverishly on the manuscript of *Adventures of a Young Man* through December—except for his week off when they drove South to the farm in Virginia, then on to Beaufort, South Carolina, to "toast themselves in the sun"—and most of January in order to make his deadline. On January 27, 1939, at 3:30 P.M., he scribbled across the first page of the complete draft the time and date, then bolted from his desk to celebrate with Katy and put it in the mail. By this time, both he and Bernice Baumgarten had tried repeatedly to get excerpts accepted by a number of magazines before the book itself appeared. Most of their efforts were fruitless. Almost every editor to whom material was sent pleaded keen interest in publishing something by Dos Passos in 1939, but not the excerpts submitted. Some magazines, such as *Cosmopolitan*, asked for a bona fide short story. Edward Weeks, editor of *The Atlantic Monthly*, turned down two segments with the comment:

> Luck certainly seems to be against me when it comes to John Dos Passos. I repeat that there is no American writer whose work I should more like to see in the <u>Atlantic</u>, and yet, in this case as formerly, his manuscript does not seem to be available for our purpose. The best episodes in his <u>Adventures of a Young Man</u> have a raw, crude fidelity. This is fundamentally important in a novel with its varied and ever-changing detail, but scenes which would pass without objection in a book, when presented within the short compass of a magazine article, do assume an offensive emphasis which is fair neither to the work in question nor to the reader involved.

Dos Passos needed the money derived from such sales, but he also wanted the exposure as a means of prepublication publicity. While they had been relatively successful in placing segments of earlier novels in periodicals prior to publication of the books themselves, only two fragments of *Adventures of a Young Man* appeared in print before publication date: "The End of the Day," in *Harper's Bazaar*, December 1938, and "Red, White, and Blue Thanksgiving," in the January 1939 (Winter) issue of the *Partisan Review*. Magazines turning down excerpts included *Scribner's Magazine, The Atlantic Monthly, Redbook Magazine, The American Mercury, Harper's Magazine, The Yale Review, Pictorial Review, Esquire, The Saturday Review of Literature, Cosmopolitan, The Virginia Quarterly Review,* and *Story.*

Dos Passos had no quarrel with Harcourt, Brace's promotion campaign of *Adventures of a Young Man* before publication date. *Publishers Weekly* devoted its front page to an announcement of the book, large advertisements were placed in the New York *Times Book Review* and dozens of other papers and magazines, and several thousand copies of John Chamberlain's *John Dos Passos: A Biographical and Critical Essay,* a pamphlet giveaway, were distributed to retail dealers and book buyers across the country. Dos Passos was pleased by Chamberlain's essay, published in a somewhat shorter form in the June 3 issue of *The Saturday Review of Literature,* but Bernice Baumgarten observed to Helen Taylor at Harcourt, Brace on the eve of the novel's publication: "Privately, it disappointed me. I don't think he does right by our Dos." Dos Passos' only worry was that his work as a whole would not be promoted as energetically by Harcourt, Brace as it had been in the past when it was supervised by his editor, C. A. Pearce, who had left the firm shortly before publication of *Adventures of a Young Man.* Dos Passos had no idea who his new editor would be.

Random House brought out its Modern Library paperback edition of *U.S.A.* on March 5, 1939, and promoted it in a double-page spread in the New York *Times Book Review,* which boosted sales of the trilogy and helped promote the new novel soon to be released. Dos Passos also gained visibility as a writer of note upon being named recipient of a $2,500 Guggenheim grant "for the writing of a series of essays on the basis of the present American conceptions of freedom of thought." *The Ground We Stand On,* published August 29, 1941, was the eventual fruit of this award.

Even the publicity brought by the removal of his books from the open shelves of the municipal library in Provincetown because of "organizations" probably stood him in good stead among many readers and potential book buyers. According to his hometown *Advocate* on May 11, 1939:

> The works of John Dos Passos, 1939 Guggenheim fellowship winner, Provincetown resident of fifteen years, and a writer acclaimed by literary critics for his novels and essays on social conditions in America, were removed from the open shelves of the Public Library last week by The Trustees and local civic organizations, including the Catholic Daughters of America and Walter Welsh Council, Knights of Columbus. They are considering the investigation of Dos Passos' books to determine whether they are radical and obscene. . . . Mrs. Catherine Cadose, president of the Catholic Daughters and operator of a local gift shop, told the *Advocate* that her organization and The Knights of Columbus had planned to demand the removal of Dos Passos' *The Big Money,* but on investigation found that the book had already been taken from its place on the shelf with other works of Dos Passos.

The chairman of the Library Book Committee informed the newspaper that he had placed all of Dos Passos' books on reserve after an unnamed Provincetown citizen complained to a library trustee of "dirt" in the offending books. Dos Passos himself was in the Midwest at the time, thus unavailable for comment, but the tempest made front-page headlines on the Cape and prompted two "Letters to the Editor" questioning the whole issue of censorship and defending the right of Provincetowners to read Dos Passos and anyone else they chose from the offerings of the public library. Catherine Cadose later admitted to the *Advocate* that she had not read any of the controversial books and that the entire affair had been blown out of proportion. Without further ado Dos Passos' books were restored to their former shelves in the Provincetown library.

Sales were brisk in the Provincetown Bookshop two weeks later when *Adventures of a Young Man* appeared. The name "Glenn Spotswood," the book's youthful protagonist, wagged on many tongues almost overnight and soon was as familiar to most Provincetowners as the names of their next-door neighbors. Some 8,500 copies of the 10,000 first-edition printing of the novel was sold before publication date, and sales continued at a good pace all summer. Once Hitler swept across Poland and Great Britain and France declared war upon Germany, however, the book-buying public had little heart for *Adventures of a Young Man* or any other book being offered for sale for the first time in the fall of 1939. A victim of the war, the novel was short-lived. There was no second printing.

Although critics of *Adventures of a Young Man* did not bury Dos Passos in the manner of Hemingway's malediction, they hissed and mauled him. Many declared it his weakest novel to date (not counting *Streets of Night,* his Harvard novel), called it a "minor pamphlet" and him a "second-rate novelist," and contrasted it unfavorably with *The Big Money* or the trilogy as a whole. They also faulted it for its shift in narrative technique (there were no "Camera Eyes," "Newsreels," or sketches of actual people, all characteristics they had come to expect of Dos Passos) and declared his fictional people one-dimensional, stereotypic, and unreal. Reviewers lectured the author for his political mistakes, jeered his disillusionment, and attacked him for "fighting battles of left-wing sectarianism." At the head of the pack was Malcolm Cowley, who ignored the book's literary merits and went for its political jugular vein. Cowley insisted that Dos Passos had overreacted to what he saw happening in Spain and that he should have "allowed Hemingway to explain" the Spanish war to him. In effect, Dos Passos had returned home from Spain half-cocked, and *Adventures of a Young Man* was the bent fruit of his misguided thinking. The anonymous reviewer for *Time* was even more explicit: Dos Passos had committed "heresy" in the Marxist camp in writing "Farewell to Europe," which damned the "intricate and bloody machinery of Kremlin policy in Spain," and in the new novel, he had "cooked his goose for good" among the Communists. As "a pariah of American letters," Dos Passos was without peer, thought some critics.

The book itself could hardly have been more timely. All of Republican Spain had unconditionally surrendered by March 31, 1939, to General Francisco Franco and the Spanish Nationalist regime. Franco's government was immediately recognized by the United States and other major powers of the world. Dos Passos' account of an American "innocent slaughtered for his ideals" challenged the pieties of the Popular Front, and the author himself had no illusions regarding the fate of his book and of himself as well at the hands of the critics. A few weeks before *Adventures of a Young Man* was published, Dos Passos told Baumgarten that he was afraid Harcourt, Brace would "muff the novel because it won't please the orthodox leftists who will try to quietly stifle it" and that it would not please any other group of reviewers either. "We must not overrate or underrate the power of ideological intrigue at the moment," he added. In reply to his suggestion that perhaps Henry Wallace or Harold Ickes might be induced to read the book and say a few words about it, Baumgarten replied wryly: "I doubt that their comments would sell any books."

James T. Farrell, a pariah of sorts by his own admission, defended *Adventures of a Young Man* more stalwartly than anyone else in an essay entitled "Dos Passos and the Critics" (published in *The American Mercury*), Farrell interpreted the critics' clamor as "a warning to writers not to stray off the reservations of the Stalinist-controlled League of American Writers." As Farrell saw it, Dos Passos had aptly handled the problem of "maintaining one's integrity in modern America" through his presentation of Glenn Spotswood, who had revolted against the social injustices rampant in America during the 1920s and 1930s and embraced Communism for a time, but fell from grace upon observing the "cynical power politics" and shifting party line of his comrades and refusing to make a blanket promise of loyalty. Rejected by the Party for being politically unreliable, Spotswood remained a radical and fought for the Loyalists in Spain until arrested, then was sent on a senseless mission designed to insure his death. His murder was Dos Passos' fictionalized treatment of the betrayal and execution of his friend José Robles at the hands of those he had sought to serve. An anonymous reviewer for *The North American Review* accused Dos Passos of being too angry at the end of his tale for the conclusion to be "artistically convincing." Farrell's only negative criticism of *Adventures of a Young Man* was Dos Passos' apparent unwillingness to create fully rounded characters. It was a deficiency in his writing in general, said Farrell.

Dos Passos was grateful for Farrell's essay defending the book. "He's a courageous fellow and a damn good polemicist—I love to hear him dust off the jackets of the fellow travelers," he observed to Gene Lyons, editor of *The American Mercury*. Dos Passos was still smarting from Malcolm Cowley's attack upon him when he added: "Everybody knows that Cowley's a Stalinoid and everybody knows that he's a fathead but it's hard to build up a linked deep-rooted plot out of that—though such a plot does exist_de facto to discredit everybody who shows any independence on the left. It's like 'constructive' treason—the sort of thing any crooked lawyer could use in a moment, but damn hard for an honest man to handle. That's the great advantage the Stalinoids have over the rest of us."

It was Cowley's review of *Adventures of a Young Man* and his mention of the José Robles affair that prompted Dos Passos to speak publicly of the death of his friend. He was upset, too, because Robles' son had been captured while fighting for the Loyalists after the execution of his father. Dos Passos feared that young Robles had suffered a similar fate. To Dwight Macdonald, editor of *Partisan Review*, who offered Dos Passos space to address Cowley directly in the event that his "Letter to the Editor" was not published in *The New Republic*, Dos Passos replied: "All I wanted to straighten out was Robles' case. I don't think anything could be gained by arguing with Malcolm Cowley about my mental processes or what influenced them. He has a right to make what deductions he cares to—on the other hand, it should be obvious to any intelligent observer that his deductions are all wet." Edmund Wilson had already attacked Cowley's Stalinist leanings a few months earlier when he wrote him:

> What in God's name has happened to you? I was told some time ago that you were circulating a letter asking endorsements of the last batch of Moscow trials. . . . I don't suppose you're a member of the C. P.; and I can't imagine any other inducement short of bribery or blackmail —which sometimes appears in rather inobvious forms and to which I hope you haven't fallen a victim—to justify and imitate their practices at this time. You're a great guy to talk about the value of a non-partisan literary review after the way you've been plugging the damned old Stalinist line, which gets more and more cockeyed by the minute.

With the signing of the German-Soviet Treaty of Nonaggression on August 23, 1939, a number of leftist writers abandoned their fellow travelers' capes or bolted the Communist party, whose ranks had swelled enormously upon its efforts in support of the Spanish Loyalists and its call for a united front against fascism. Granville Hicks declared his resignation from the Party because of the German-Soviet pact in a "Letter to the Editor" of *The New Republic* on October 4. Hicks was the first of the important leftist literary intelligentsia to unpin his red star, resign from *The New Masses,* and cast about for other means by which to continue to work for what he saw as the good of the American people. Wilson took Cowley to task for remaining in the Stalinist camp in the light of recent developments after reading Cowley's review of Walter Krivitsky's book *In Stalin's Secret Service: An Exposé of Russia's Secret Policies by the Former Chief of the Soviet Intelligence in Western Europe.* As Wilson saw it, the literary editor of *The New Republic* ought to be independent of entanglements of movements and parties, yet he thought Cowley had been "carrying on in a way that matches <u>The New Masses</u> at its worst." Then he spoke of the Robles affair:

> Last summer you were vilifying Robles, about whom you obviously didn't know a thing except what the Stalinists had been pouring into your ear. I knew Robles, who spent a summer up here in Provincetown, and I can't imagine anybody less likely to have worked for the Fascists. His family, as you probably know, played rather an important part in Spanish politics under the Republic; and he had been offered the governorship of a province. He told me that he wouldn't take a job under the Republic, because he knew that it would eventually get to the point of the bourgeois government's suppressing working-class revolts. When I knew him, his left position was quite clear, and he was certainly a man of excellent character. When the war started, he thought he ought to go back, and by the time Dos had arrived, he had been shot. This fact, however, hadn't been made public, and Dos, when he found it out, had the job of breaking it to his wife. There were various things that might have got him into trouble. He had a brother fighting on the Fascist side, and he was one of the few Spaniards who knew Russian, so that he may have known too much. He was personally aristocratic and not at all the sort of person who would be likely to suppress his disapproval. What finished him was probably his enthusiasm for the social revolution, which the Russians were putting down. Now, what do you know about Robles? You promised further revelations when Dos wrote his letter to the <u>N.R.</u>, but they've never been forthcoming. Last week, in the case of Krivitsky, you presented more of what you described as information from reliable sources whom you don't name; but why on earth, after your handling of Robles, should anybody take stock in it? You

write better than the people on the regular Stalinist press, but what you are writing is simply Stalinist character assassination of the most reckless and libelous sort.

Dos Passos had hoped that the sales of *Adventures of a Young Man* might pick up upon what he described as "the wave of disillusionment with the C.P. that seems to be going through liberal and radical circles as a result of the tie-up between Stalin and Hitler." He suggested to Bernice Baumgarten that the trick would be to get "some topline columnist who hadn't read the book to read it and to write about its relation to what's come out. . . . If you have any ideas about how somebody like Pegler or Broun could be interested, call up Brace about it. Chester Kerr said that Assignment in Utopia [Eugene Lyon's new book] didn't sell at all until Dorothy Thompson wrote a column on it. Have had letters from [Carlton] Beals, Ben Stolberg, Evelyn Scott, and various people praising it, but nobody sufficiently headlinish."

Katy decided that she, too, would try to drum up interest in her husband's controversial novel by venturing the same suggestion to Archibald MacLeish that Dos Passos had put to his agent:

> Oh dear I wish I didn't know how busy you are—it's about Dos's book. As you know the critics have pretty generally tried to draw a red herring across the trail but now the red herrings have suddenly turned out to be plain Bismarck herrings. . . . It seems a key moment to point out that the Adventures describes, as Farrell says, the dead end of a historical movement—the Communist Party. This makes valuable reading for people who want to understand what's happened Inside America, as well as Inside Europe. I mean the disillusionment of our generation, which has taken on visible bony form in the Berlin-Moscow pact. Do you think that one of the newspaper columnists might want to tell the true story and bring the whole issue out in the open at this moment in history? Harcourt, Brace wrote Dos about this, but he doesn't know any of the newspaper column boys and anyway, could hardly do anything about it himself. But I remembered you and Ada know Mister Woollcott, and maybe you could write him or [Walter] Winchell and suggest it as a lively topic for discussion right now.

Three weeks later, MacLeish reported that he had given considerable thought to Katy's request, but "had been unable to complete the task." It was a good suggestion, he admitted, but the "difficulty of the moment seems to be that the red herring has turned into a red whale and flattened out all previous roadways, trails and routes." Dos Passos reconciled himself to the probability that *Adventures of a Young Man* would have no second printing, which proved to be the case.

Even before finishing his tale of Glenn Spotswood, Dos Passos already had firmly in mind the title, theme, and substance of the book's sequel, *Number One.* He had decided to make his fictionalized version of Huey P. Long, his title character, the employer of Spotswood's brother, Tyler, but Tyler would be the true protagonist of the novel. He also had a third novel vaguely conceived—*The Grand Design*—which would complete a second trilogy, *District of Columbia,* but the new fiction would have to wait for a while longer, he vowed. His Guggenheim money had been awarded so that he might get on with his nonfiction essays that he intended to weave into a continuous historical narrative to be entitled *The Ground We Stand On.* Once more Dos Passos set his sights on early American history. This time his focus was upon Thomas Paine, who, he decided, did not belong within the major groupings of historical figures on which he wished to concentrate; rather, Paine shored up the ground on which his figures stood. Dos Passos worked quickly to write a fifty-page, biographical/critical essay on Paine for publication in *Common Sense* in two installments in the fall of 1939. The essay appeared in book form as the introduction to *The Living Thoughts of Tom Paine: Presented by John Dos Passos,* published by Cassell & Company in England on February 1, 1940, and brought out simultaneously in the United States by Longmans, Green & Company.

The research and writing of *The Ground We Stand On* was still far from finished in the spring of 1940 when Dos Passos sought a year's renewal of his Guggenheim grant. Instead, he was given five hundred dollars and a three-month reappointment. By this time, his and Katy's life had been complicated financially because they had taken on the responsibility of helping rear two Provincetown youths whose mother had died four years earlier. Christopher ("Beanie"), ten, and Jean, eight, returned from school one day to their home in Truro to discover their mother dead on the bathroom floor. According to friends, Marguerite Kaeselau had a premonition she would die young and habitually "sent her boys to bed without ceremony because she did not want them to become too dependent on her." Although in apparent good health, she died of a heart attack. Charles Kaeselau, an artist, seemed helpless in dealing with the practicalities of life after his wife's death, and various townspeople in Truro and Provincetown who knew and loved Marguerite Kaeselau volunteered to help rear the boys. Reports that Kaeselau was feeding his sons raw hamburger meat "because he knew so little about caring for anybody," said one neighbor, prompted Coulton Waugh to try to adopt Jean, and Phyllis Duganne Given to attempt to adopt Christopher or both boys, but Kaeselau would not hear of it and spoke disparagingly of all who offered to help. When Kaeselau moved to Boston, however, he allowed the boys to live with various families on the lower Cape, yet complained of their "meddling" in his personal affairs. To Eben Given he insisted that he was going to sue Dos Passos and Katy "for alienation of affection of his boys."

Christopher and Jean Kaeselau were not easy to handle. They usually stayed with a family until their father interfered or the patience of a self-proclaimed foster parent grew thin. Guests in homes where the Kaeselaus were housed were told to watch their pocketbooks because wallets and change purses sometimes disappeared. Both boys stayed with Dos Passos and Katy from time to time. "We all marveled that the Dosses managed to do for the boys whatever was needed, even though they never had much money themselves," said Given, who thought that Dos Passos and Katy treated the Kaeselau boys like the "sons they never had, but probably wish for." Christopher was sent to the Reverend Truman Hemingway's school in New Hampshire for "boys with problems" because he got into difficulty with firearms, said Mary Hackett, who remembered riding in the car with Dos Passos and Katy to visit Christopher and her brother, who was also a student at Hemingway's school for a time. "The Dosses were very good to those boys," said Hackett.

During the winter of 1939–40, Jean Kaeselau was staying with Eben and Phyllis Given and Christopher was with Dos Passos and Katy when Dos Passos decided that he could put off no longer his research at the Library of Congress and proposed moving to northern Virginia for several months and putting Christopher in school down there. He had already worked extensively that winter in the library of the Massachusetts Historical

Society in Boston working with a cache of Roger Williams materials for incorporation in *The Ground We Stand On* manuscript, and by mid-January was ready to head South. At year's end, money had been a problem, too. The six months that had passed since *Adventures of a Young Man* was published had required considerably more outgo than his writings had produced, and he was forced to wire Rumsey Marvin for one hundred dollars, which he promised to repay in a week. On January 10, 1940, he wrote for an additional three hundred dollars, but had not been able to pay Marvin back the earlier loan. This time Dos Passos explained:

> By borrow, I mean borrow—because I'm on the edge of considerable (temporary alas) affluence, having managed to recover my War Risk Insurance from my aunt who was "keeping" it for me. It'll be payable to the tune of ten thousand dollars next January and meanwhile I can borrow on it at a low rate of interest. . . . While we await loan from Washington, we are flat here and haunted by the pale faces of bill collectors. Can't borrow from the bank here because it's full of our notes and mortgages. Have to send two hundred to New York Friday to save a batch of holograph . . . from the clutches of a bookshop where I hope to sell it for considerably more.

"The batch of holograph" to which Dos Passos referred consisted of two drafts of *Manhattan Transfer* Edmund Wilson had managed to hock for him several years earlier to help make an insurance payment. Frances Steloff, founder and owner of the Gotham Book Mart, where the manuscripts were awaiting redemption, informed Dos Passos in early January that unless he paid off at least the principal of the debt, she would have to sell the holograph for whatever it would bring. It was at about this time that the manuscript of "Seven Times Round the Walls of Jericho"—the unfinished novel on which Dos Passos and Robert Hillyer had collaborated while in the ambulance service—turned up, and at Hillyer's urging, Dos Passos offered drafts of *Manhattan Transfer* and the unpublished novel to the Widener Library at Harvard University. To Clarence Walton, the rare book and manuscript acquisitions librarian, he wrote that if the manuscripts were to be sold, he would like Widener to "have a chance at them." He also asked for an appraisal. "I realize the position of a contemporary writer has never been less stable than at present, and I have no intention of stepping in front of a truck to enhance the value of my scratchings. If the question is awkward just forget it." Walton replied that Harvard was in no position to purchase the materials and suggested that Dos Passos request Steloff to determine their worth and market them for him. By this time, Dos Passos was tired of dealing with agents and skeptical of commissioning anyone else to act in his behalf. He had begun to think of Bernice Baumgarten as a "luxury" he could not afford during such lean times and considered handling his literary affairs himself. For the time being, however, he decided to leave the holograph with Steloff for safekeeping, after redeeming it for two hundred dollars, and to peddle it himself unless she generated an extraordinary offer.

In his letter to Mitchell asking for another loan, Dos Passos told him that despite the year's having been "full of financial alarums and excursion," the general tone of his finances was "surprisingly firm." He had made up the difference between his earnings and advances by Harcourt, Brace against earlier books—all of which had gone into his "general account"—and had paid back the five hundred dollars he had borrowed from his publisher as an outright loan, but only a pittance remained in his royalties account for *Adventures of a Young Man.* Donald Brace made Dos Passos another interest-free loan of five hundred dollars after the first of the year, yet ventured that he was "a little nervous" upon discovering that *The Ground We Stand On* had been offered as collateral against several advances in the past although the book itself was not under contract. Dos Passos immediately signed a contract for his new book of essays and welcomed the interest-free debt. He wrote Baumgarten: "I don't wish to encourage my publisher in usury," but fretted that with C. A. Pearce no longer with Harcourt, Brace, *The Ground We Stand On* was destined to a fate similar to *Journeys Between Wars* and *Adventures of a Young Man:* poor promotion, small first editions, and no second printings. Perhaps it was time to look around for a new publisher, he suggested to his agent.

Dos Passos had told Mitchell that his "great plans for financial reconstruction and rehabilitation" were in the making, but offered no details. He intended, however, to do far more than retrieve the $10,000 war risk insurance policy from Mary Lamar Gordon, as his letter in mid-January implied: "The policy came. . . . It's much more economical to borrow on it than to cash it now. If I borrow $4,000, interest will be $200 and I'll get a total of $9,800 instead of the $9,270 I'd get now. I haven't seen Aunt Mamie yet but shall tomorrow. Shall try to get hold of Byron [Ralston, his aunt's son-in-law] downtown today and then I'll get out tomorrow to start defrauding the widows and orphans of Pelham." It had now been a year since Dos Passos' chilling discovery that his Virginia property had been sold out from under him, then recovered, but it was still not in his name. His aunt again insisted that there was no money left in the trust account she had maintained for her nephew, and that whatever had been made through the sale to the lumber company in 1926 had been applied to tax debts and other expenses pertaining to the maintenance of the trust and to the foreclosure proceedings in 1938. Mrs. Gordon informed her nephew that Byron Ralston had spent considerable money of his own in securing the title for its true owners, for which he had never been repaid. Ralston's posture as "the injured party" in the entire affair was ridiculous, countered Dos Passos. By this time, rather than admit any culpability in the matter, Ralston answered Dos Passos' demand for an accounting by saying that he was owed $3,919 for his out-of-pocket disbursements and intended to go to court to get a lien against the property if he were not paid. Again Dos Passos placed the matter in the hands of his attorney, C. Dickerman Williams, but urged him to move cautiously because he did not want his aunt hurt in the process.

Meanwhile, Dos Passos had other demands upon his time in addition to his profession as a writer. Margaret De Silver urged him to serve as secretary of the New World Resettlement Fund, a relief organization set up to help resettle several thousand Spanish refugees in South America. As Republican supporters of the old regime, they were Franco's enemies and their lives were in danger if they remained in Spain. Garrison Villard, president of the relief group, asked Dos Passos upon his agreement to work with them to travel to Ecuador to meet with officials there and to inspect potential sites for the refugee colonies, which they envisioned would be self-supporting in a year's time. After the groundwork had been laid and the cost factor considered, letters were to go out under Dos Passos' signature appealing for funds. The opportunity to go to Ecuador appealed to

Dos Passos, but he said that he could not leave the country until he finished a "large chunk of manuscript" for which his Guggenheim money had been awarded.

Dos Passos' new editor was Frank Morley, who asked to read as much of the manuscript of *The Ground We Stand On* as Dos Passos had ready. In turn, Dos Passos hoped that on the basis of some two hundred pages of manuscript, Morley could arrange another advance on the book rather than a loan. He wanted the money so that he could afford to take Katy to Ecuador with him. At present, their plan was for her to stay in Provincetown to await the government loan against his war risk insurance, then to pay off their creditors, while he went on alone to Washington, D. C., to look for a suitable house to rent and a private boarding school for Christopher Kaeselau. It was at this juncture that Dos Passos made another effort to get an accounting from Mary Lamar Gordon and Byron Ralston regarding his Virginia property, then backed off to await developments.

The insurance loan had not arrived and Dos Passos was in New York City before proceeding to Washington when Katy reported:

> Bill collectors are thicker than sea gulls around the door. I'll be firing . . . at them if no money by Monday. Have repulsed Nelson and Oil Man, also Laundry and First National and Rodney, but being encircled by Electric Light and Power and fear mass attack on Monday. Would have wired, but had no money for wire. Mr. Patrick lent me $3.00 Wednesday but that is nearly gone. . . . Well Ape, I suppose you are going around with your rich and fashionable friends (ring-tails) and have little time or thought to spend on a poor proletarian opossum.

Five days after his arrival in Washington, Katy wired that she would stay on the Cape another week instead of coming immediately after getting the bills paid and the house closed upon receiving Dos Passos' loan on his insurance. She explained that she was trying to finish an article she was writing with Edith Shay. Dos Passos chastised her in reply:

> Katy darling—why didn't you tell me you'd be that much longer? . . . Now you've let me make all sorts of plans and it makes me seem such a monkey not having you appear. . . . Why not if you want to make money write another thing for Miss Roberts? [her editor at *Woman's Home Companion*] It's just that you want to stay on the Cape. If that's so, say so and let's arrange for it. Here I've arranged for a school for Beanie [Christopher Kaeselau] and I am just about to get an apartment in Alexandria that would be convenient with car, and very inconvenient without. If you don't intend to come you must wire me at once. I'll just get myself a furnished room. All this delay will make a little trip south so late for me and I'm already beginning to feel a mite rheumatic. . . . Honestly, Katy—it seems sometimes as if so many things were piling up between us it scares me. I hate to be like this. Don't you ever want to do anything I want to do? Forgive the blubber but am rather blue these days and I want a trip, and if you don't get here so we can try out Kaeselau in a school to see if we can leave him there, I'll never get my trip. Don't you see—your annual delay in the winter—which seems to me to be largely automatic—holds up our whole program. And by a little sunlight I can escape the last touches of rheumatiz entirely, so it seems a shame not to do it. Couldn't you think of those things sometimes?

Dos Passos signed his letter "Love, Desperape." By return mail, Katy replied:

> Oh Irascible—what an awful pair of letters you have sent to that poor front-line marsupial. How could I possibly know you had the rheumatick? You were in lovely shape when you left.

I didn't know staying here a week longer would make things difficult for you. . . . You know you told me to plow and have been plowing and planning hard. Oh Ape, please, how are you feeling? It will take a few days to clean and close house but I hope to get off Wednesday or Thursday. . . . I feel awful, but crazy to see you and crazy to go South. Want a little sun myself and some fun. I had an ambition to bring some money in my paw, but better come naked and quick as a flash.

Katy's missive was signed "Katy Anxious Humble-Possum." She added in a postscript: "Oh Ape don't be an Incensape" and signed herself "Katy Hang-Possum," and after still another P.S. ("Will roll South like basking whale. Don't worry Ape—will come like flies"), she identified herself as "Katy Fleetfoot."

During times of stress, Katy's wit never failed her, although she sometimes wilted when too many physical demands were made on her. She did not sulk in her letters in response to Dos Passos' scoldings, but bounced back in good spirits. He probably anguished more than she did after his intemperate words. Katy's sense of humor held her in good stead, too, in dealing with young Kaeselau. The boy was bad about playing truant from school, and when he got put out by Katy over her disciplining him for some infraction of the rules of the house, he sometimes showed up on his father's doorstep in Boston to complain of mistreatment. Charlie Kaeselau usually took his son in for a few days, then packed him off to a boarding school somewhere or sent him back to Provincetown to resume his life with Dos Passos and Katy. Upon one such homecoming, Katy wrote Dos Passos:

> Beanie came home swelled up with boastful pride, yelling, showing off and ordering me around. First remark was "Dad says you are to send these pants to be pressed by a tailor, not give them to that careless Mrs. Breiding." I felt like a cobra and lucky I didn't have the fangs as might of lashed out and struck. But it was pathetic to see his wild joy at getting home. He rushed into his room, turned the light on, examined everything, sang, danced, cheered, took a bath, and sank to sleep holding his Chinese elephant in his hand. A note from Wilsons asks me to dinner Saturday—shall I go? Fear Beanie will fire the house in my absence.

Edmund Wilson, who had married Mary McCarthy in 1938 and was living in Truro with their young son, Rueul, invited Katy to spend a few days with them before she left for Washington, but she declined, saying: "I can't, of course, as I have to control Kaeselau."

Once Katy arrived in Washington with their young charge, Dos Passos fretted that he might not stay in school long enough for them to go to Ecuador. "Beanie is in school once more and pray God he stays there. It's a very nice school with a farm attached, and he may do all right. If so his problems are solved and so are mine," Katy wrote Mary Heaton Vorse a few days after they moved into a large, rambling home at 708 Wolfe Street in Alexandria, which Dos Passos had leased for three months. The house was "inconvenient and rickety, but full of wonderful furniture and glass and china." Dos Passos was especially pleased because it had a garden planted and already laden with fresh vegetables. He settled handily into a routine of driving into the city each morning to work until 1:30 P.M. or 2 at the Library of Congress, then returning home for a late lunch and an afternoon of working in the garden, taking long walks along the Potomac, letter writing, painting, and other change-of-pace activities. By early April he had written some two hundred pages of *The Ground We Stand On,* which he sent to his new editor, then announced that he was off to South America for three weeks.

Katy had hoped to accompany Dos Passos to Ecuador, having extracted a promise from Christopher Kaeselau that he would not run away from school in their absence, but Dos Passos was afraid that Katy would find the long, overland journey from Guyaquil, the port of entry, to Quito, his ultimate destination, much too arduous a trip. Their decision finally was to close the house in Alexandria, drive to Miami, and board a ship for Cristóbal, a seaport in the Canal Zone. Their plan was for Dos Passos to continue alone to Equador from Cristóbal and for Katy to return to New York City on the next northbound steamer. Dos Passos was in Quito when Katy reported that the only good thing about her return journey aboard the "Disgrace Line" (the Grace Line) was that the days were sunny and that in her boredom she had managed "to scratch out an article to good purpose." What she wrote was a travel piece, "They Fly Through the Air," which compared the various airlines servicing the United States and Europe and lightly traced the evolution of flying. Willa Roberts accepted Katy's article for the October 1940 issue of *Woman's Home Companion.* A piece she had worked on earlier, "Fish, Men, and Mystery," was published several weeks after her return to New York in the June issue. By this time, she had also finished the article she had begun in collaboration with Edith Shay before going to Virginia. "New Harmony, Indiana" appeared in the November 1940 issue of *The Atlantic Monthly.* Katy wrote well, but her subjects were light and frothy. Except for her two pictorial serials, she had published no fiction since her marriage. Most of her articles were one thousand to two thousand words in length and relied heavily upon illustrations or photographs. Her observations were couched in a breezy style and laced with statistical trivia. On April 21, 1940, she wrote Dos Passos that she was finishing up her "plane piece at Aunt Mamie's in great luxury and quiet." They had talked previously about the advisability of Katy's calling his aunt upon her return to New York, but Dos Passos was surprised when he read that Katy was ensconced in Pelham among the family he envisioned taking to court if necessary to get his land back in Virginia. As Katy explained it:

> Your Aunt Mary Lamar is certainly a darling. She's not well and I'm glad I'm here. Yesterday she had a heart attack while talking to Lucy Virginia [her daughter] over the phone. I heard her call—ran in—gave her medicine—and put hot applications around her. . . . She came back wonderfully in about twenty minutes. . . . I don't think she ought to be left alone very much. Her heart is certainly very uncertain and she ought to be careful. . . . Lucy V. never came over at all. I suppose it's a good thing as she and Aunt Mamie argue so intensely. I don't know why. Lucy Virginia is studying for the stage and is giving <u>Carmen</u> (in costume) for the Pelham French Club Wednesday. It's not a thing I understand, but she's wrapped up in it and takes singing, dancing, and castanet lessons in New York twice a week at great expense—also reducing at Elizabeth Arden's.

Katy's letter was signed: "Your affectionate north-temperate, no-keepered, ungartered, winter-coated, vitamin-starved down-in-the cornfield howling K. O'Possum of Pelham." On April 23, 1940, she gave Dos Passos an update:

> Everything here is so much the way it was except me and I wish I was on the trip with that Ape and now I'm here in Pelham and it's strange. And Ape that's not all—I haf to go to the

French Club with Aunt Mamie to see Lucy Virginia dance. . . . I'm as uneasy as a dog smelling perfume. . . . Byron came in looking pale and false the other night. I have very little confidence in his ability but more than he has in ours. Aunt Mamie seems to distrust and dislike him, but at the same time he does pretty much run her affairs. . . . Aunt Mamie says Lucy Virginia doesn't like Byron either and never had. I was stunned. Aunt Mamie is a darling and I feel very fond of her and rather worried—will be relieved when you come back and things are settled upwards.

When Katy wrote again, she mentioned the Virginia property:

It is not going to be easy to recover your ole Westmoreland paternal acres, dear Señor, as the big argument is that you're a writer and don't know <u>anything</u> about money and can't be trusted with any kind of business. This goes along with the most alarming stories of a financial nature about Byron. . . . Your aunt says we are "Babes in the Woods." Why do people say that so much? I ain't a Babe. . . . Is it because we aren't so predatory as we ought to be? Well, I don't know that you have to be a sap just because you aren't a crook. . . . I have been almost nowhere except here, working and with Aunt Mamie, who seems much better today—the first time she has seemed so.

Meanwhile, Dos Passos had become disgruntled in Ecuador upon discovering a pirated edition of his articles originally published in *Esquire*. Someone had translated them into Spanish and put them into a book. It was "everywhere in circulation," he told Katy. The country fairly pulsed with "literary gents" who were obviously "behind the times because they still seem to admire the writings of your humble servant." To be admired was one thing, he allowed, but getting no royalties from one's endeavors was quite another. Rather than risk offending the people whose cooperation he was seeking on behalf of the New World Resettlement Fund, he decided not to ask questions about the source of the unauthorized edition, but to let his agent seek redress. He was tired of playing the nice guy while others walked over him, he complained, and said that he would sue the offending publisher if necessary. Dos Passos was also put out by the relief organization's failure to send him money to cover his out-of-pocket expenses in Ecuador, as promised. "The next time Don Desgraciado Gratis comes around, run him out of the house," he wrote Katy on April 29, 1940. You must not stay too long in Pelham. And you must not go see Lucy Virginia make a Carmen of herself. Please go back to New York at once. . . . Give Aunt Mamie my best love but flee the City of Destruction."

Dos Passos and Katy were back on the Cape together in mid-June and worrying about finances once more when he borrowed several hundred dollars again from Donald Brace. He decided, too, to terminate his relationship with Bernice Baumgarten. He explained to her in a letter that "with the state of the literary market and the disappearance of foreign fields," the lean years ahead would not justify the outlay either of her time or his money. "There is absolutely no question in my mind that Brandt and Brandt is the best firm in the business and that you are personally tops in the book field. . . . It's going to give me real pain to bring this long and pleasant relationship to a close." Baumgarten was surprised and hurt when she received her client's letter, but replied with grace: "Of course I am unhappy that I am not to have the handling of your future work. My admiration for your writing made it a particular satisfaction to me, but you are the best judge of the wisest course to follow. All luck to you!" Dos Passos had already told Donald Brace that he intended to negotiate all further business with him, whereupon Alfred Harcourt wrote Baumgarten a commiserating note: "Don [Brace] just told me Dos Passos is slipping from under your wing. I'm sorry, for I know how intelligently, hopefully and wholeheartedly you have fostered his interest. Dos is a fine person, but too inclined to try to force the facts to conform to his wishes. When they don't either his agent or publisher or both gets the blame, and learns to be philosophical." It seemed to Harcourt that it was only a matter of time before Dos Passos severed his relationship with his publisher as well.

Despite Dos Passos' intentions, he found it impossible to function without the advice and cooperation of his agent, on whom he continued to be dependent for several years. Their correspondence during the upcoming year was almost as frequent as it had been before her dismissal, since the Brandt & Brandt files contained the kinds of details that Dos Passos' own fragmentary personal records lacked. "His leaving us . . . was a great blow at the time but I'm getting over it," Baumgarten admitted some eleven months after receiving Dos Passos' severance letter.

Dos Passos took another trip the end of 1940 on behalf of the New World Resettlement Fund, this time to the Dominican Republic to help select Spanish refugee families to be resettled in Haiti. In addition to being secretary to the group, he also was named treasurer of the Joint Campaign for Political Refugees—a combined fund-raising effort of the New World Resettlement Fund and the International Relief Association to appeal for money to "help turn the tide against the bloody-minded tyrants of fascism" so that the "human race" could be differentiated from a "pack of wolves." Thousands of relief dollars poured in when he apprised potential donors of the successful Simón Bolívar Colony in Ecuador (now ten months old) that he had helped establish. Some one hundred fifty additional refugees could be relocated there without increasing the colony's basic overhead expenses, he explained. For five hundred dollars, each refugee could be provided transportation, clothing, housing, medical care, tools, and maintenance for one year, at which time he would be self-supporting and a fully integrated member of the community. Dos Passos also petitioned Claude Bowers to see if Chile, too, would consider admitting political refugees under a similar program. Bowers had been ambassador to Chile since the fall of the Republican government in Spain and was especially sympathetic to the program. A number of letters to the editor appeared in such newspapers and magazines as the New York *Times, The New Republic,* and *The Nation* bearing Dos Passos' signature. Letters soliciting funds also went out to thousands of individuals across the country. Dos Passos assured potential donors that the sponsoring organizations were under no political duress.

During the winter of 1940–41 when he was appealing for funds to help relocate the impoverished and downtrodden Spanish refugees in a colony in which they might work their own land and become self-sufficient again, Dos Passos was also fuming about the present state of affairs concerning his own property in Virginia. Having become increasingly fed up over the years with his need to constantly penny-pinch and borrow, he reasoned that upon gaining his land in Virginia free and clear, he could cease forever relying upon the whims of editors, publishers, reviewers, and book buyers for his sole livelihood. In the spring of 1941 when he learned that Byron Ralston had been successful in attaching a lien against the property, he was furious. Since Ralston claimed that he was owed $3,919 for legal work involving the foreclosure proceedings, Dos Passos countered with his own "Grounds of Defense" claim that Mary Lamar Gordon still held some $60,000 unaccounted for as his trustee, and that if such fees demanded by Ralston were valid, payment should be made by Mrs. Gordon herself, since the debt was incurred when she was trustee. Moreover, Ralston's fees were excessive, insisted Dos Passos. The attachment itself was illegal. The "proper and only Court to grant the relief asked for is a Court of Equity rather than a Court of Law," his petition concluded (filed through his attorney, C. Dickerman Williams), and there the matter stood until the following year.

Dos Passos and Katy were in Wiscasset, Maine, on August 29, 1941, when *The Ground We Stand On* was published. He had outlined the intent of his book to Edmund Wilson, who read the manuscript in its early stages and offered suggestions: "I want to present a fairly rounded picture of . . . Roger Williams and his time (the rise and fall of English republicanism), the rise of the eighteenth-century businessman, Jefferson's reaction to Europe and England, the career of a typical American citizen of the world, Joel Barlow, ending with the check of squirearchical ideas in America on the collapse of Hamilton's bid for power." Given the book's intent, few critics quarreled with its thesis, although several reviewers registered surprise at what they saw as Dos Passos' new attitude toward his country. Many made reference to *Adventures of a Young Man* and marveled that the bitter taste in the author's mouth at the conclusion of his tale of Glenn Spotswood had been transformed into heady optimism when America itself seemed on the brink of world war. Even Malcolm Cowley, who had been ready to write off the checkered career of Dos Passos after *Adventures of a Young Man,* now granted him his intent and concluded that he had undergone a moral crisis and "was perhaps beginning a new career." Cowley pointed out that Dos Passos' training and experience had been as a novelist, reporter, and poet rather than as a historian, but that he had not been trying to "paint an historian's complete picture," but to catch the "interesting character, the fresh and significant detail." The book succeeded despite its flaws, conceded Cowley, because it had accomplished its aim of casting a new light on the present. He did not think *The Ground We Stand On* ranked with *U.S.A.* or *Manhattan Transfer* and termed it inferior to *In All Countries;* yet it had a new quality, "the will to survive," which he liked.

Francis Brown's review, "A Testament of Faith in America," in the New York *Times Book Review* took a similar tack. The means by which Americans could make self-government work was embedded in faith and an invocation of history. The series of essays recapturing the lives and times of such distinguished early Americans as Roger Williams, Benjamin Franklin, Samuel Adams, Thomas Jefferson, Joel Barlow, and Hugh Henry Brackenridge were "truly brilliant," said Brown. The least satisfactory essay was on Brackenridge, agreed most critics, because it was "disproportionately long." Stephen Vincent Benét's review in the New York *Herald Tribune Books* commended *The Ground We Stand On* for providing what "only an eloquent writer can give to history—a sense that the past is alive and the men of the past are alive." According to Benét, Dos Passos had written a "fascinating and extremely readable book . . . with accuracy and candor." Robert Hillyer defined the book for readers of *The Atlantic Monthly* as a "fabric of swift prose, of sudden appearances and departures, of dramatic lights and shadows . . . intelligent in each interpretation of events and important as a record of our hopes for the future." Hillyer saw the core of Dos Passos' political philosophy as the "struggle between constantly forming and re-forming special groups and the self-governing masses" which comprised the "very essence of our political vitality."

Several reviewers faulted the book because it was not more definitive in its thesis. Jacques Barzun, writing for *The Nation,* declared the volume a failure of "point of view, of technique, of proportion, of style," yet he admired its intent. It was a dull book, Barzun concluded. Other critics fairly glowed in their praise. Leon Whipple described it in *Survey Graphic* as "patriotic and inspirational." C. W. Thompson declared in *Catholic World* that it was the most interesting historical book he had read in a long time. "No praise is too high . . . [it is] a brilliant, fascinating panorama of many of the most interesting historical persons in the seventeenth and eighteenth centuries, English and American." Allan Nevins told readers of *The Saturday Review of Literature* that the book was "a valuable contribution to true Americanism," but that the "execution of its admirable intent" was flawed. He was also troubled by the final statement, which he thought Dos Passos could not support. Dos Passos had written that "if we can keep the fabric of a self-governing republic unbroken at home, we are in no danger from the attacks of the slave states of Europe and Asia; if we can't, everything we as Americans have stood for from the beginning will have been in vain."

Dos Passos did not mean to imply that the United States was immune from such attack, but that the country would prevail if self-government was preserved intact. His thesis was no different from his argument put forth to John Howard Lawson many times. In their passionate exchange of letters upon Dos Passos' return from Spain, he had written:

> The real difference between your attitude and mine about politics is that you think the end justifies the means and I think that all you have in politics is the means; ends are always illusory. I think that Anglo-Saxon democracy is the best political method of which we have any, and I'm for or against movements insofar as they seem to me to be consistent with its survival. To survive it's got to keep on evolving. I have come to believe that the CP is fundamentally opposed to our democracy as I see it and that Marxism, though an important basis for the unborn sociological sciences, if held as a dogma, is a reactionary force and an impediment to progress. Fascism is nothing but Marxism inside out and is of course a worse impediment.

In an essay published in *Life* after World War II, "The Failure of Marxism," Dos Passos addressed his readers more fully on the subject. To Edmund Wilson he commented later: "I certainly stirred up a hornet's nest. . . . I don't see why people are so freshly horrified each time because it's the same line I've been pursuing since <u>The Ground We Stand On</u>. . . . It's political methods and not political aims that count."

Dos Passos' new book of historical essays evoked a number of letters from friends. Horsley Gantt wrote from Baltimore that he had learned more history from it than from any book he had read on American history per se. Even with his own University of Virginia background, "Jefferson never meant more than a weak symbol," Gantt continued. "This is one of the most stimulating books I've ever read on history and one I feel is especially timely to raise American morale, unity and self-confidence in a critical moment." Dos Passos' friend Gilbert Seldes read the book and took him to task for his "bigotry." Americans were not Anglo-Saxons, he insisted. "The bedrock habits of Americans were not formed by Anglo-Saxons but by Jews and Portuguese, Bulgars and Italians and Germans and twenty-one races." Dos Passos was unwitting in his bigotry, yet his avowed hatred of prejudice seemed incompatible with his observations in support of his thesis, concluded Seldes. In reply to a letter from Harrison Griswold Dwight, who had caught several historical errors in *The Ground We Stand On,* Dos Passos wrote: "I only wish I'd known you were so well informed about the period before. I'd have been almost nervy enough to inflict upon you proofs: long, dangling, eyestraining, slipping from the hand proofs. That was a hideous blunder about [Chevalier de] Chastellux. I don't know where I got it—anyway it's obvious the minute you speak of it. . . . It reveals the worst kind of historical illiteracy all too plainly. It's much easier to write novels."

Dos Passos was impatient now to move into the writing stage of his next novel, *Number One,* which he saw as a fitting follow-up of his celebration of self-government, *The Ground We Stand On.* The new book would reveal the dangers inherent in allowing an individual too much concentration of power. Huey P. Long's career demonstrated the evils resultant when ends were placed above means and demagoguery was permitted to rage unchecked. Despite his desire to immerse himself in his tale of Machiavellian Louisiana politics of the 1930s, he was also tempted to "report current history within the shadow of the barbed wire" of Europe. Still another book he wanted to write was an in-depth study of Thomas Jefferson and his times.

Although Dos Passos could not afford to go on his own to Europe in the fall of 1941 and he was reluctant to solicit a foreign correspondent's assignment with much of his own work pending, he was delighted when an opportunity to travel about England for a month at someone else's expense literally fell into his lap. A representative of PEN inquired if he would be willing to serve as an American delegate to the International PEN Congress convening in London September 11–13, 1941, and make a speech to the entire assemblage. The principal address was to be given by Thornton Wilder, whose reputation had been boosted in England when *Our Town* was awarded the 1938 Pulitzer Prize for fiction. Wary of public gatherings in which he was expected to perform, Dos Passos might not have accepted the delegate slot had he not also been invited to rove across England as a guest of the British Ministry of Information, which asked him to examine the country in the midst of a war crisis and to write about what he saw. Wilder, too, came at the behest of the British Ministry of Information. Although the two writers had scarcely more than a nodding acquaintance with one another in the United States, when they boarded an American Clipper bound for Lisbon, Portugal—the first leg of their journey—they found themselves elbow to elbow as traveling companions and roommates for almost six weeks.

Cornered at La Guardia Airport on September 5 as they prepared to leave, a New York *Times* reporter queried Dos Passos: "Whom do you favor among the combatants abroad?" Dos Passos snapped back: "Anyone who speaks English." As he saw it, the country with the bombers with the longest range and "capable of achieving the highest altitude" would win the war. Although Roosevelt was not actually "pushing the country into war," he could not "help himself because the whole set-up and drift" was toward war. In fact, the country was already at war, he continued. Yet it would be "a mistake to create an American Expeditionary Force because there is no place to send one." Although Dos Passos had vowed that he would not vote for Roosevelt if he ran for a third term—"I'll never vote for Mr. R. or any of his friends again, not if the devil himself runs against him"—he ended up voting for him anyway in 1940 when Wendell Wilkie was his opponent. "I felt that I did not have a proper choice," explained Dos Passos. He never forgave the President for his neutrality stand and handling of the Spanish Civil War, yet found himself defending him now in America's drift toward war in view of the total situation.

At the PEN congress itself, the responsibilities of a writer during times of war was the major issue. When Storm Jameson, president of the British PEN, proclaimed to delegates from thirty nations at the opening of the session that "if any writer is wanted as a soldier, he has no right to run away to preserve his special skills," a controversy erupted that threatened to break up the proceedings. Jameson insisted that members commit themselves exclusively to propaganda for the Allied cause, a stand opposed by the group known as the humanists, led by E. M. Forster, Rebecca West, and Thornton Wilder. Dos Passos' remarks the second day of the congress, that "authors should be citizens first and writers second," tended to align him with Jameson's group, yet being exclusively a propagandist had no more appeal for him in 1941 than it had a decade earlier when fellow writers on the Left were pleading with him to follow "the Party line." The proceedings were "futile and acrimonious," reported Wilder upon his return. Meanwhile, the New York PEN group complained that they had not been consulted regarding their choice of American delegates, and Henry Seidel Canby, a member of the PEN Executive Board, was reportedly "very huffed" about not being asked to go himself. According to Robert Nathan, president and a charter member of the American Center of PEN, the American club was "a rather feeble affair in those days. . . . We were invited to attend the Congress in Europe that year, but quite before we knew what was happening we were told that Dos and Thornton were to be our delegates. There was never a meeting to vote on it."

Two long articles evolved from Dos Passos' travels across Great Britain at the conclusion of the International PEN Congress. "England in the Great Lull" and "Some Glasgow People" were published in the February and April (1942) issues of *Harper's Magazine.* Dos Passos contended that despite the bombings, the blackout, the rubble he stumbled over in the dark block after block, the people of London were in better shape than they had appeared to be when he was in England four years earlier and war had been quite remote. Their well-being now he attributed to their "great power of resistance in that slow, stolid, self-reliant addiction to routine—the resistance of tough seasoned oak" in the face of adversity. The old complacent order, embodied in the House of Commons, still impeded progress, but the interpenetration of classes had inspired new hope. France had no Winston Churchill, who had helped Britons shore up their "rocky base of English patriotism," said Dos Passos. England had been saved from the fate of France by more than the English Channel. Before leaving London for Glasgow, Scotland, Dos Passos was invited to H. G. Wells's home in Regent's Park to share a partridge and bottle of white wine with him. He said he admired Wells with his "sharp-clipped mustache" and "glaze-blue eyes" that gazed at him with "lizard alertness." Wells had voiced the only protest at the PEN congress when a venerable British speaker ended his interminable address with a toast to "the spirit of liberty that still burned in Buenos Aires, New York, and Barcelona." Dos Passos said that he could hardly believe his ears and that a shiver had run through countless delegates to the congress who had "escaped shooting by the breadth of a hair" and were not antifascist exiles. "All we can do is go on telling the truth when we can," said Wells, whom Dos Passos likened to a "Jeremiah in the wilderness." Dos Passos observed later that "if the English-speaking peoples of the world were to survive," they would need "industrial brains" as well as supremacy in aviation. They would also require "a fresh formula for the application of . . . traditional self-government and all the social habits it implies to the modern industrial setup."

A British reader wrote Frederick Lewis Allen, editor in chief of *Harper's Magazine*, to commend Dos Passos for his series of "glimpses of people and places." Dos Passos had "caught the real truth about the temper of England—there wasn't anything more to be said." The letter was one of a number of positive responses to Dos Passos' articles in *Harper's Magazine*. At this point, Allen wanted him to roam the face of America in the manner in which he had traveled through England and to send in "state of the nation" dispatches for publication each month in the magazine. The idea appealed to Dos Passos, but he was tempted to turn it down because he was impatient to get on with his new fiction, *Number One*, and with his Jefferson biography, in which he had already been steeping himself. Japan's attack upon Pearl Harbor on December 7, 1941, changed that, too.

22

A Nation at War, 1941–44

Pearl Harbor. No way of forgetting that December afternoon. Driving into New York from Long Island I went into a Second Avenue ginmill to make a phone call and heard disaster pouring out over the radio.

The Theme Is Freedom
7 December 1941

Dos Passo was as shocked as millions of other Americans at Japan's heinous two-hour attack upon Pearl Harbor. Although he had despaired of the war spirit kindled for months by the Roosevelt administration and recognized that war was imminent, he saw no excuse for the way America let itself enter the war or for what he later termed the "insane lack of statesmanlike foresight with which the war was conducted from Washington." Casting a ballot for Roosevelt's third term in office was his greatest political blunder, he decided. Had voters not elected to keep him in the White House, he probably would have been recorded as one of history's most remarkable presidents. He was ill-advised and too willful. "Consciously or unconsciously, Roosevelt could find no other way of consolidating the vast power . . . that the success of the New Deal measures brought him, than by leading the country into war." The world would not have been in such a sorry state on the eve of 1942 had the administration applied more pressure to "the French and British politicians who were giving ground before every threat from the dictators" back in 1937 and 1938. "Damn the Japs and the wops and the squareheads—gosh it's a big order," Dos Passos observed in a postscript to Robert Hillyer three days after bombs rained upon Pearl Harbor.

Dos Passos' personal aspirations were always a big order regardless of extraneous events, but he felt more stymied than usual in accomplishing his immediate goals because of a sudden flare-up of rheumatoid arthritis on the heels of a prolonged bout with influenza in mid-January. He had hoped to finish *Number One* by early summer, then travel to Washington, D.C., and points South in preparation for the first of his series of "U.S.A. Now" sketches for *Harper's Magazine,* but poor health necessitated an adjustment to his schedule. For several weeks in February, then again in May, Dos Passos underwent moist-heat treatments in New York City at the hands of Dr. John Currence, the orthopedic specialist who had treated him in the past. He was hospitalized briefly in the spring of 1942 when his condition became so painful that he could barely walk. The "dreadful boilings" sapped his energies, but he took in stride his prescribed meat-free diet and abstention from any form of alcohol. What Dos Passos said he regretted most was Katy's having to stay on the Cape to manage affairs there while he lay ailing in the city.

Almost immediately after the United States' declaration of war, Provincetowners turned out in droves to sign up for civil defense courses. On February 2, 1942, Katy announced to Pauline Hemingway that they were in good spirits and spent most of the time at target practice and driving trucks on the dunes. "This last is my defense course. It's wonderful. Edie [Shay] is taking first aid and so is the boy Kaeselau, who is very adept in bandaging up the dogs. . . . By spring I hope we shall be partly established in our ruined brick hovel in Virginia." In May she wrote Dos Passos, still in New York for his health treatments: "I have the blackout curtains for the whole house and they are going up this afternoon. . . . We have a complete blackout on the waterfront now." Residents on the Cape were jittery. They considered life perilous there during the early months of the war. In January rumor had it that a German submarine was sunk off Highland Light. Katy wrote Dos Passos that "it must be true because dozens of planes appeared and dropped depth charges. We heard shooting somewhere on the back shore this morning, and there is considerable excitement among the population." She also heard a coast guard report that a tanker had been attacked off Wellfleet and "nearly driven ashore at Truro. . . . Chris said he had seen a tanker in the canal on the way home from Boston with a great hole in her side. . . . Convoys passing the back shore are in danger of shelling. . . . That is why Highland Light goes out at night every now and then. The threat of a shell or two through the town is what people seem to be considering. A big British ship was in yesterday, accompanied by a corvette. Even Long Point Light was gone last night." On May 14 Katy spoke of Chauncey Hackett's having gone "rather goon on defense. . . . He prowls the streets all night on blackout patrol and the people at the Defense Center complain of his regulations which are constantly increasing so that they have to fill whole notebooks with reports." Many citizens dropped out of the program after the novelty wore off. Katy mentioned in one letter just getting home "from timing valves over at Jack's."

In May gas rationing went into effect. Dos Passos had expected no special consideration, but was pleased when Katy informed him that instead of the three gallons a week granted most drivers, he had been awarded a "B-3" classification, the category just below "unlimited." The official who disbursed coupons volunteered to Katy: "A feller like him has got to have his car."

Again young Chris Kaeselau was living full-time with Dos Passos and Katy and enrolled in the local public school. They had genuine affection for the boy and reared him in as loving and nurturing an environment as they would have reared a child of their own, but Katy—on whom the brunt of the boy's unruly behavior fell—resented at times the energies expended on his behalf and the responsibility of maintaining a home for him when she would rather have been in the city with her ailing husband or off on a trip with him when he was well. Had Katy not been committed to a literary project in collaboration with Edith Shay during the winter and spring of 1942, she probably would have put Chris back into a boarding school and set out to join Dos Passos. Katy and Edith had decided to collaborate on a historical romance based on the life of Elijah Cobb, a Cape Cod sea captain whose adventures on the high seas involved being captured by a French frigate in 1794, imprisonment in terror-ridden France, and an encounter with the revolutionist Robespierre. The women had happened upon the published memoirs of Cobb, then met one of his descendants who gave them access to a cache of holographs. Katy hoped that she and Edith could put together a prospectus and an initial chapter or two as the basis of a contract with Houghton Mifflin. Robert Hillyer's wife, Dorothy, who had recently become an editor at Houghton Mifflin, encouraged Katy to let her have a first look at it. After Frank Shay went to Washington, D. C., to look for work in early January (with a recommendation from Dos Passos to Archibald MacLeish, recently identified by one reporter as "FDR's poet and war publicist"), Katy invited Edith to stay with her and Chris Kaeselau in Provincetown while they worked together. When Dos Passos wrote to ask Katy if Edith was going to join Shay in Washington, and if not, to see if she would like to stay on in the house with Chris so that Katy could join him in New York City, Katy replied *no* to both questions. Unless Shay found work and she and Edith could get an advance against royalties for their projected novel, Edith could afford neither to leave the Cape or to maintain the house for her and young Kaeselau. "Edie hasn't got a cent—all she has for herself is the pawn ticket Shay sent her for her ring yesterday—that is all she had had from Shay in a year," Katy informed her husband.

She also had two articles she was trying to finish for Willa Roberts, "Science and the Beanstalk" (published in the September 1942 issue of *Woman's Home Companion)* and "Ice Harvest" (February 1942), but her priority was getting enough of their novel on paper so that she and Edith could be free to join their husbands. "I tried hard to place the Boy [Kaeselau] but there was no one who would take him," she lamented in a letter to Dos Passos that spring. "People do not rush forward to volunteer." In another letter she complained: "He interferes with my work because by the time I have bawled him out for not doing things and then have done them myself, hours have passed. . . . I get so exasperated with the lies and excuses and the laziness and selfishness. . . . What a mucker he is, a regular mucker." Dos Passos replied, "That boy's sumpen—wring his neck for me." Katy was especially put out with Chris after having him underfoot during a week-long holiday from school. She wrote Dos Passos:

> The Boy . . . is proving absolutely worthless. I am sick of him—he complains about the least little thing all the time. . . . I sent him out for some wood this morning and he came back with a few handfuls of shingles and a long story about how there wasn't a piece of wood on the beach for miles. I bawled him out and there was an oldtime rage fit and the rush upstairs to pack his suitcase to go to Boston and stay with Dad. Maybe I will just send him. . . . The trouble is that Charlie probably would not take him—he'd say he was going away or something.

Katy warned the youth that if he left, he would regret it later. At lunchtime the boy returned and vowed to reform. Two days later, she gave Dos Passos an update: "He has done better though not well of course. There is not the usual sunshine after storm and I guess it was better that he did return because that same afternoon Paw showed up—down for the weekend. Paw was very nice and he said he wanted to tell us please to take off for the Boy on our income tax—it seems you are allowed to do this so let's do it. Might mean a considerable aid on the tax. After all we have paid out huge sums for the Boy and no end in sight."

When things went well at home, Katy usually used the name "Chris" in referring to their young charge, but when he misbehaved, he was "the Boy" again. "I don't want to please anybody, not even myself," the youth told Katy when she asked why he expected his grade report to be a bad one. Katy regretted that Dos Passos was not on hand to help her discipline him. "When you come home you must be tough too and I believe things will be more agreeable for us all. Just make it easy for him to be good because it's too awful for him when he is bad," she urged. "It is easier to crack down than cope with the new crop of crimes that follow every success of mild reproof. . . . Think the Boy does not like to be responsible even for his own behavior. . . . Ape do try to find out about the Land Corps because we want to get him off as soon as school is out."

Katy was determined to accompany Dos Passos on his next trip to the Northern Neck of Virginia, but she could not if temporary housing was not found for "the Boy." Dos Passos went South three times during the first half of 1942 to deal with the knotty legal problems that had evolved from Byron Ralston's lien against the land as a means of recovering his legal fees as Mary Lamar Gordon's attorney. Another complication was that Dos Passos and his half brother Louis were still trying to settle the division of the property.

The "ruined brick hovel in Virginia" to which Katy referred in her letter to Pauline Hemingway was a two-story house of pre–Revolutionary War vintage situated on a 1,665-acre parcel of land known as Spence's Point. The house had been vacant for years and needed renovation. One problem was solved when Louis agreed to deed over Spence's Point, along with other acreage fronting the Potomac, in exchange for clear title to the inland property, a larger tract. Louis, who needed money more than land, told Dos Passos that he was considering selling some of his portion to the government for use as an airfield (a sale that did not materialize, to Dos Passos' relief). In the fall of 1942 Dos Passos wrote Katy that he wished they could "scrape up a couple of thousand to alleviate Louis' agonies and buy some more land from him." Meanwhile, Ralston had offered to "call it quits" and to withdraw his lien against the property if Dos Passos backed off, too. "My point is that since he started this and has caused us all this expense, he should pay for the mess," countered Dos Passos, who told Katy that Mary Lamar Gordon was insolvent and would go bankrupt if he sued her for an accounting, but that such an action would not hurt her in the long run. "In fact, it may give us an edge on other creditors that might be useful. . . . C. D. [C. Dickerman Williams] is crazy to examine Ralston," he added. According to Dos Passos, Arthur Seeligson, the husband of his mother's sister Lilly, was "going to pension Aunt Mary Lamar after her collapse. I'll chip in—dance of the millions again."

As C. D. Williams explained it later: "The key to the matter regarding Ralston and his legal fees was that 'a lawyer for a trustee must first look to the trustee.' My motion to dismiss Ralston's action in the Circuit Court of Westmoreland County was granted and Dos's suit eventually was tried before Judge Alfred C. Coxe in Federal Court in New York on the basis of the diversity of citizenship of the parties involved. Neither was a bona fide resident of Virginia." Dos Passos did not actually go to court with his suit until 1944. On April 3, 1944, he wrote Robert Hillyer: "The great Virginia lawsuit came to a head last week in the Federal Court with a victory for our side, but like military victories it leaves the mopping up to be done." According to Williams:

> Judge Coxe ruled that the land in question could not be sold because it was held by Mrs. Gordon in trust. In effect, the land was sold illegally and the proceeds from it considered an embezzlement of funds. It came out at the trial that Mrs. Gordon gave money derived from the sale to her daughter, Lucy Virginia Ralston, in the amount of $100 a week as an allowance. The conclusive evidence at the trial was a series of very emotional letters written to Dos by Mrs. Gordon confessing that the money was really his. Judge Coxe said that he would rule for Dos if he had to, but would rather they settle out of court because it was a family matter. In trying to arrive at a settlement, the family offered Dos Passos one of their houses—the older one [at 159 Corlies Avenue in Pelham, New York, where Katy had helped look after Mrs. Gordon when Dos Passos was in Ecuador in 1940]—but he wanted cash. Dos wound up getting only about $9,000 because that was all that was left, but he got a tax deduction for the embezzlement which erased his income tax liability for the year of the trial since a loss from "casualty" (over $100) is deductible from ordinary income.

Dos Passos was in New York City when Katy reported on October 30, 1945, that the lawsuit check was at last in the bank. "They could hardly believe it," she said. "It will take you quite a while to overdraw on that," the bank officer observed dryly.

Along with his determination to get his land back in Virginia and to recoup what losses he could from the trust fund depleted through his aunt's mismanagement, Dos Passos applied fresh resolve to finding a new publisher who would promote him to greater advantage than Harcourt, Brace had done during his six-year tenure with them. Houghton Mifflin was eager to add Dos Passos to its notable stable of writers and to treat him as generously and prominently as possible, but he consented to the move only if the new firm would take over his old books as well as the contracts for *Number One* and *The Grand Design*. Negotiations were already under way when Donald Brace wrote Dos Passos: "I appreciate quite completely how pressing the financial problem has become. We have done our best, I think, and certainly there is no question of our enthusiasm for your work and of our wish to make its publishing successful. We have been particularly proud to be your publisher, and we should face a change with deep regret. . . . However, we don't want to be dog-in-the-manger and stand in the way of your chances to make better arrangements." Harcourt, Brace agreed to release Dos Passos in exchange for $7,185 due the firm for unearned advances against royalties, and to turn over the plates and existing stock remaining of *Manhattan Transfer, Adventures of a Young Man, The Ground We Stand On, Journeys Between Wars, Orient Express, In All Countries, Three Plays,* and *U.S.A.* (including the individual volumes of the trilogy) for an additional $3,750. Plates for *Streets of Night* and *A Pushcart at the Curb* were still at Doubleday, Doran & Company, but plates for his other books had already been destroyed. Dos Passos asked Houghton Mifflin for a number of additional considerations, including a request that all new book advertising include a "box list" of his old books, an agreement to publish the new travel essays he was writing for *Harper's Magazine* as a companion volume to *Journeys Between Wars,* and a $1,500 cash advance to stake him until the publication of *Number One.* In response to Dos Passos' wire that he had just signed his contract with Houghton Mifflin, Katy wrote: "I am indeed delighted that the transfer of a priceless left-winger was effected from the New York Giants to the Boston Braces with fifteen hundred crossing the literary fellow's palm. I hope this will calm and reassure poor Forty-Two." Katy added that she wanted to telephone her congratulations but dared not spend the money for such frivolity, since his savings account was down to $16.93 and she herself was penniless.

Dos Passos' biography of Thomas Jefferson, under contract with the Dial Press rather than Harcourt, Brace, was not affected by his move to Houghton Mifflin. By October 1, 1942, he had received five thousand dollars against royalties, with a final payment of twenty-five hundred dollars upon receipt of the manuscript, which was due August 1, 1942. Dos Passos realized, however, that the scope of the work called for a much longer creative and investigative process than originally anticipated. Scarcely six weeks after the Jefferson manuscript was due at the Dial Press, Dos Passos admitted to Lovell Thompson, his editor at Houghton Mifflin, that he had received veiled threats of a lawsuit from Dial and asked if Houghton Mifflin would consider buying up the contract. When his new firm procrastinated, Dos Passos approached his old publisher, George Doran, who welcomed an opportunity to publish another Dos Passos book and paid off the five thousand dollars charged to the author at Dial without insisting upon a fixed date of delivery.

Dos Passos was eager to resume work on Jefferson as soon as he could establish himself on the farm in Virginia. Spence's Point was to serve as a base of operations so that he would be close both to the University of Virginia in Charlottesville and the Library of Congress. Dos Passos also made it clear to Doubleday Doran that his priority for the next few months would not be Jefferson, but his series of articles for *Harper's Magazine* on America's domestic front. Editor Frederick Lewis Allen was specific regarding the people and issues he wanted Dos Passos to examine. Rumor had it that there was considerable loafing in the shipyards, where it was difficult to check up on workers' activities. They were reportedly playing cards on the job until the sudden appearance of an inspector galvanized them into action. Word had leaked out that officials did not want to bother pushing for the necessary security clearances for aliens or to hire women, whom they would have to jockey about in jobs that did not tax them physically. Blacks, too, were given the runaround despite known labor shortages, and foremen worried that racial tensions might threaten further the morale of the workers. Allen wanted Dos Passos to apply his investigative talents to finding out the truth in such matters at the Fore River Yard of Bethlehem Steel Company in Pennsylvania and the Todd Shipyard Corporation in Bath, Maine, where complaints were rampant, as well as in other war industries across the country. Allen also suggested that Dos Passos' quest include learning if news of the battlefields—such as the recently launched Guadalcanal and North African offensives—

had any direct bearing on the production of workers in their war-industry-related jobs, and what their reactions were to new taxes, gasoline and food rationing, and other privations of the war.

Dos Passos was granted Navy Department clearance when his *Harper's Magazine* editor convinced military officials that his mission was in the best interests of national security. To head off any reluctance to cooperate, Allen wrote letters of introduction to management acknowledging that Dos Passos "used to be regarded as something of a Red," but that he did not detect anything of the sort in him now. "As to his loyalty there is no question." Another letter of endorsement spoke of the fairness with which Dos Passos had approached his material in articles on war-torn England for *Harper's Magazine.* "Most of his friends are in labor or radical circles," but the "terrible radical" tag of the past was no longer applicable, said Allen, who wanted to head off adverse reception by those who remembered Dos Passos' activities in 1941–42 as vice-chairman of the Civil Rights Defense Committee in connection with what was known as the "Minneapolis Case," which involved twenty-nine members of the Socialist Workers Party and leaders of the Motor Transport and Allied Workers Industrial Union Local 544-CIO, all of whom were on trial in Minneapolis for sedition under the Smith Act. As vice-chairman of the committee spearheading the defense and as chief fund-raiser, Dos Passos had signed a protest statement with Carlo Tresca, Margaret De Silver (treasurer of the Civil Rights Defense Committee), Charles R. Walker, and James T. Farrell (chairman), declaring: "Never before in peace-time has the government invoked statutes punishing the mere expression of opinion as it is doing with the Socialist Workers Party. Nor have the Federal authorities ever so flagrantly intervened in a trade union dispute by instituting criminal proceedings against the members of one labor organization, the CIO, on behalf of another, the AFL." Dos Passos thought that the prosecution, led by Attorney General Francis Biddle, and the resultant repression smacked of Attorney General A. Mitchell Palmer's "Red raids" of 1919.

Although Frederick Lewis Allen's observation that most of Dos Passos' friends were in labor or radical circles was an exaggeration, many of them were, and none was more conspicuous in his radicalism than Carlo Tresca, whom Dos Passos made a point to see whenever their paths crossed in New York or on the Cape. On January 11, 1943, Dos Passos wrote Katy that he had met Tresca and Margaret De Silver that day for one of their "long spaghetti lunches" at a Greenwich Village restaurant near the office where Tresca put out his fiery and uncompromising Italian weekly, *Il Martello* (The Hammer). Tresca and his wife were "amazingly well and in fine spirits," said Dos Passos. Possibly while he was writing those very words—a few minutes after 9:30 P.M.—Tresca was leaving his office at Fifteenth Street and Fifth Avenue in the company of an Italian anarchist refugee and headed on foot for a neighborhood tavern. Their scheduled meeting with another antifascist labor leader had failed to materialize, and they were waiting for a traffic light when a gunman approached from behind and fired four .32 caliber bullets into Tresca at close range. Tresca swung around to face his assassin—who fled in a waiting sedan—then died at once from wounds in the head and back. News of Tresca's death blared from newspaper vendors and radios the next morning. Not since the bombing of Pearl Harbor had Dos Passos been so personally shocked, and he rushed to Margaret De Silver's apartment to comfort her and to learn the details of his friend's murder. "Margaret is holding herself together remarkably well. In fact I've never admired anybody so much. I've been trying to hang around a little to see if I can be useful in any way," he wrote Katy on January 12. "I am helping Margaret untangle the various complications of conflicting Italian societies who wanted to have a hand in Carlo's funeral" while the "strangest people" flood the apartment.

Dos Passos had intended to finish reading the galley proofs of *Number One,* then to set out on a swing through the South and Midwest on the first of his two major excursions for *Harper's Magazine;* he delayed his trip, however, to take time to write an appreciation of Tresca for publication in *The Nation* (January 23, 1943). Two years later—Tresca's murder still unsolved—Dos Passos wrote "He Died as a Fighter for Freedom," a tribute that also summarized all that was known and surmised about the case. Dos Passos' personal theory was that Tresca was assassinated by a hired gunman to "stop his voice . . . to keep him from disclosing information that would have been useful to the United States" at the instigation of the "same gang that killed Trotsky in Mexico." Dos Passos conceded that though there was "no certain proof," he was convinced that the Communists planned a takeover of Italy after Mussolini's collapse—expected shortly—and that the American government had made tentative plans to send Tresca in to opppose them. He was also convinced that Tresca was cooperating with the Federal Bureau of Investigation to help "root out the agents of those foreign organizations that were at work among the foreign born in this country," and that it was ultimately as "a fighter for American freedom that he was shot down."

One of the purposes of Dos Passos' second article on Tresca was to implore officials not to drop the investigation:

> The police that started out with such energy have slowed down. The arrested man has been released. The clues have melted away. The newspapers distracted by immense events in Europe and the Pacific have become apathetic. The District Attorney's office has done nothing. Efforts to interest the Attorney General in Washington or the Federal Bureau of Investigation have proved unavailing. The State Government in Albany seems ignorant of the fact that such a murder was ever committed. It is impossible not to get the impression that some organization or some powerful individual is blocking the investigation of Carlo Tresca's murder. We live in a dangerous time. There is a very real danger that in the upheavals of these days the minimum decencies and liberties that all Americans, newspaper editors and labor leaders and politicians and public officials alike, take for granted as the basis of their happiness, may be swept away. We are awake to the danger overseas. Our young men are giving their lives to overcome it. Victories abroad will be of no avail if through cowardice and stupidity and apathy we lose our liberties at home.

Tresca's assassination challenged Dos Passos to examine with renewed fervor the liberties expressed by the American people at home and the forces that threatened to jeopardize them. As a shrewd observer of men and politics, Tresca had warned Dos Passos when he went to Spain to meet Hemingway and the Communist filmmaker Joris Ivens: "John, they gonna make a beeg monkey of you." As Dos Passos saw it, Tresca's prophecy proved true, a painful lesson played out through the murder of José Robles at the hands of the Communists. Now Tresca, too, lay dead, perhaps a Communist-inspired murder. Dos

Passos contended that Tresca had abandoned his stance as a political agitator—preaching violent revolution by an international working class as a means of bringing peace and freedom to the world—for a more realistic and acceptable goal for America's working class: individual freedom. Violence was not an acceptable way to achieve it, insisted Tresca.

Dos Passos was well aware of many of the shortcomings of the New Deal administration and intended to call the shots as he saw them in his "People at War" essays based on his observations throughout the country. An old friend, Gardner Jackson—whose brother, Roland, had been Dos Passos' classmate at Harvard and a traveling companion in Spain before his death in World War I—was now part of the New Deal government and offered to put Dos Passos in touch with various political and military leaders in Washington as soon as he came down from New York. Dos Passos decided to delay his "Washington Sketches" until the summer, however. He was more interested in getting on the road and steering clear of Washington bureaucracy for the time being. His departure was held up briefly while he negotiated with Frederick Lewis Allen for the four specific articles he was to write for *Harper's Magazine.* Allen agreed to give Dos Passos $637.50 for each article, and if they proved a success, to commission him to write four more at the same rate. In view of his projected expenses, Dos Passos considered the payment a paltry sum, but expected to make a book of essays out of them to help recoup his losses. On February 24, 1943, he complained to Robert Hillyer in a letter from New Orleans that he had been "running around over the landscape like crazy," yet still did not feel very much the wiser. "Working my head off writing articles for a miserable rag of a miserly magazine just to get myself a trip," he added. Dos Passos tended to oversimplify his situation in letters to friends. His comments were more revelatory of attitudes than of actual facts.

Number One was due out March 2, 1943, and in characteristic fashion, he preferred not to be on hand for the reviews and interview requests, or lack of them, as the case might be. He hoped that Katy would join him in New Orleans. With money from his first *Harper's Magazine* payment, he wanted to buy an ancient car and drive to Mexico City to catch the pulse of what was going on there, which could be converted into still another article, he theorized. On Valentine's Day Katy wrote from Boston that she had just seen a copy of *Number One:* "The cover just crackles! The book is awfully handsome, too. Title page is wonderful. . . . I never liked the get-up of any of your works so well. They are crazy about it at Mifflin's." Katy was excited, too, because she and Edith Shay had just taken their completed manuscript of *The Private Adventure of Captain Shaw* to Dorothy Hillyer at Houghton Mifflin, who accepted it for publication and exclaimed the firm's pride in having two Dos Passos authors in house at last.

Number One had been out three weeks when a pamphlet released by Houghton Mifflin promoting the book caught up with Dos Passos in Texas. To Robert Hillyer he wrote: "Those little Mifflins have been working like Trojans trying to oil the public esophagus for it [the book], but hardly know yet whether it'll be sweetly swallowed or sourly regurgitated. Nobody ever tried to get anybody to read a book of mine before so it'll be interesting to see what happens." C. A. Pearce and Donald Brace had enthusiastically supported and promoted his books at Harcourt, Brace, but their efforts fell short of what Dos Passos believed could be done. Although his criticism was well founded, from where he sat he was incapable of knowing all of the problems of his publishing house. Diagnosis was one thing, but a workable prescription that would serve the best interests of author as well as publisher was quite another. It was not long before Dos Passos was uttering similar grumblings in reference to Houghton Mifflin's handling of his work.

Advance sales of *Number One* were excellent. Dos Passos' royalty statement for the period ending March 31, 1943 (barely four weeks after publication date) reported a total of 17,197 copies sold in the United States and 350 in Canada. Already the book was in a second printing. Most critics agreed that *Number One* was a good book, but not the author's best. Howard Mumford Jones, writing for *The Saturday Review of Literature,* thought it failed as a novel because of its naive structure and lack of "express conflict." Jones viewed the book as a document, not an art form. *Time*'s anonymous reviewer identified *Number One* as "a sad, harsh, funny companion piece" to *Adventures of a Young Man* and called the title character "the most noisome, best drawn demagogue in U.S. fiction." Mark Schorer also picked up on the comic element in the book, but told readers in *The Yale Review* that Dos Passos probably was not consciously funny. To Robert Hillyer, Dos Passos replied: "I'm delighted you like Number One—I've been hoping it would seem funny to people. Nothing ever seems funny to the critics." Several reviewers faulted the book's narrative method. Schorer thought it "inadequate to express the serious implication of the material." Margaret Marshall, reviewing for *The Nation,* criticized Dos Passos for allowing "another of his dismal drinking young men" (Tyler Spotswood) to serve as the central intelligence of the novel. *The New Yorker*'s reviewer, Clifton Fadiman, called *Number One* a "smoothly geared, expertly written, sharply observed book" and admired the author's creation of Chuck Crawford (the title character) as a successful departure from his usual techniques of characterization. Horace Gregory informed readers of the New York *Times Book Review* that *Number One* was one of the best books he had read in two years and likened its structure and use of irony to Joseph Conrad's *Under Western Eyes.* "Few characters in contemporary fiction are so brilliantly inspired and so faithfully exhibited to public view" as Crawford, observed Gregory. Stephen Vincent Benét, writing for the New York *Herald Tribune Book Review,* applauded *Number One* for its "brilliant portrait" of a corrupt politician as a note of warning of the "particular kind of fascism we could breed in these United States." Several critics were bothered by what they still considered the author's "affectation in coupling words together" and his "vulgarity and sexual realism," as were the anonymous reviewers for *The Atlantic Monthly* and *Commonweal,* but most made no reference to his stylistic techniques already familiar to them.

Even Ernest Hemingway had something good to say about *Number One.* "It's fine to see Dos out working and learning again. His last book was much better," he observed to Archibald MacLeish on June 30, 1943. Hemingway could not resist adding, however, so that MacLeish would not mistake the animus he still felt for Dos Passos: "If his balls are not cut off he will maybe do whatever it was he did best again. And the Portuguese are a hardy race and no man ever hit one a solid blow."

Some $11,000 had gone into advertising *Number One,* reported Lovell Thompson on June 15. "The normal advertising allowance is probably ten per cent of list price. That would mean about $5,000. We are already $6,000 out of line in the advertising," he explained, adding that the firm was still "a few hundred dollars in the hole on the book before overhead." By midyear Dos Passos' debit balance with Houghton Mifflin was down to $3,250, with over $6,000 having been credited since January 1, 1943. He drew $1,000 against his account the first of the year, which prompted Lovell Thompson to tell him that he owed Houghton Mifflin more than $10,000. It would take the sale of 27,500 copies of *Number One* to cover the debt. Dos Passos preferred to think that Houghton Mifflin would promote all of his books rather than rely upon a single new book to put him in the black. There had been plans for a reissue of *Manhattan Transfer*, but the new edition was put off until the fall. On May 27, 1943, Dos Passos drafted a gently chastising letter to Thompson on the matter:

> There are a lot of things I want to talk to you about besides possible future plans for <u>Number One</u>. The more I think about the postponement of <u>Manhattan Transfer</u>, the more discouraging I find it. I would much rather have seen a slash in the advertising budget of <u>Number One</u>. It gives me the feeling that we are falling back into the old speculative "best seller" methods. If you could fish out of your files the memorandum I got up on how I wanted my work handled, before coming over to the friendly fold of the Houghton Mifflin Company, it would give you an idea of the sort of thing I was trying to avoid and the sort of thing I was hoping to accomplish by the transfer. I can quite understand that the paper shortage has raised new complications, but I don't see why they should necessarily be fatal. . . . It's certainly too early to write off your splendid advertising campaign as a loss. What I'm hoping is that it perhaps isn't too late to somewhat change its character.

Thompson explained to Dos Passos that the company had gone considerably out of line in the advertising of *Number One* "as a deliberate action based on our very great interest in your work now and to come. It is an indication of our confidence from every point of view—business and otherwise—in you." Thompson's goal was to hear Dos Passos say what another in-house author recently volunteered: "My problem is not to make any more money in 1943." Thompson assured Dos Passos that it ought to be easy for a writer as gifted as he "to get way over into the black. . . . The black is a pleasant place to be and one in which a writer of your stature belongs." Each new book ought to sell from 30,000 to 50,000 copies, said Thompson. Dos Passos was disturbed by his editor's ambiguous comment that "something should be flowing into the Dos Passos exchequer from Katy's book," a reference to the novel written with Edith Shay. Thompson implied that Katy's royalties ought to be a significant contribution to their joint income, so that Dos Passos would not have to keep "mortgaging his general royalty account."

Dos Passos replied that he was "flabbergasted" at Thompson's suggestion that Katy's contract had anything to do with his own affairs or need for advances in the future. "If my wife's business with Houghton Mifflin and mine aren't kept entirely separate I'm afraid we are likely to run into very grave difficulties."

Thompson, in turn, apologized for his faulty logic but explained that since his own wife's earnings and his went "right into the same old rain barrel and . . . out the same hole at the bottom," he thought of Dos Passos' problem with money the same as if it were his own. "I have no business to do that, but you can see how I might," added Thompson. Dos Passos thought the analogy a weak one, but let it ride. Although he was reluctant to disrupt the harmony of his relationship with his editor, Dos Passos made it clear that he needed additional advances against royalties from time to time on the strength of his future work, even if such books were not actually under contract. Thompson replied that a separate account would have to be set up for each new book under contract, and that advances would be limited to such books.

"I don't know just what to say about your attitude on an advance," retorted Dos Passos:

> This is the first time in twenty odd years of fairly easy dealings with publishers that I find myself in the situation your letter confronts me with. If Houghton Mifflin does not feel enough confidence from a business point of view in my future work to be willing to make advances on it I don't see how we are going to be able to go ahead with the very excellent program we have laid out. I'd hate to have to scatter my publishing around among various houses, because I like the way you are going about it and I think your handling of my complete list is going to prove highly advantageous all around, but I don't see how I'm going to have any alternative. It's only through fairly liberal advances in the past that I have been able to buy the free time necessary for careful and consistent work.

Such exchanges reminded Dos Passos anew of how much he had relied upon Bernice Baumgarten to trouble-shoot and negotiate contracts and advances for him as his agent without his being drawn directly into the controversy. He was convinced that *Number One* would have aroused movie interest if it had been written by any other writer and agreed to give Donald Friede, an agent in Beverly Hills, a six-month option to try to sell the film rights of *State of the Nation,* the book that grew out of his "People at War" series for *Harper's Magazine.* Through Friede he hoped to sell *Number One* as well. During the fall of 1943, he and Katy met with Diarmuid Russell (of Russell & Volkening), who proposed handling both of them, but they decided against it. Dos Passos liked dealing directly with his editor and publisher as a means of short-circuiting the potential for red tape.

Meanwhile, he completed eight essays for *Harper's Magazine* documenting his year-long travels from coast to coast, during which he caught and recorded the heartbeat of a country at war. The pieces bore such titles as "Downeasters Building Ships," "Gold Rush down South," "Grass Roots in the South Are Changing," "New Industries Make New Men," "Washington Evening," and "San Francisco Looks West." He also published articles in *Liberty* ("The Men Who Make the Motors") and in *Fortune* ("Washington Sketches") during the winter of 1943–44 based on his peregrinations that year and included later in *State of the Nation.*

At year's end Dos Passos was once more hard-pressed for money and asked Robert Hillyer to lend him one hundred dollars for about three weeks, pleading that "unaccountable delays in getting paid for some articles" had left him "gasping" and overdrawn at the bank. Almost immediately he rescinded his request, explaining:

> At the last moment a check arrived and the day was saved. This sort of thing always happens to us at Christmas time. We have come to visualize Overdraft as a dreary sort of a character in a long old fashioned nightgown with a quill behind his ear and a ledger under his arm who suddenly starts getting into bed with you in the middle of the night. His feet are clammy. His

B.O. is thoroughly disagreeable. He has a long pendulous nose with a drop perpetually suspended from the end of it. In a world where people get more like hyenas every day it is particularly heart-warming to have you call up with your century neatly packed for relief. I may have to call on you yet but I think I can navigate now until I can drag in a little more money. All in all it's a miracle that I've been able to walk this tightrope so far.

By this time his *State of the Nation* manuscript was three months overdue and Houghton Mifflin was impatient to have it because of the timeliness of the material. Dos Passos had received one thousand dollars upon signing the contract in June 1943 and was due another one thousand dollars when he turned in the manuscript. He calculated that he had three more weeks of work on it when he wrote Hillyer back on January 21, 1944: "Have you still got that little century loose in the bank? This damn book still holds me chained to my desk. What a hideous profession. I've been dragging along all winter in a 'can't get any money till I finish the book, can't finish the book until I get some money' dilemma. Money is the root of considerable discomfort in my life, though hardly of all evil." As Dos Passos saw it, the book was like a jockey "driving his aging race horse on the last lap."

State of the Nation was hailed as Dos Passos' best book ever by a number of critics upon its appearance July 18, 1944. The reviewer for *Time* called it "a report of a miracle" and its section on wartime Washington "a brief masterpiece of social reporting. No U.S. writer can match Dos Passos' use of the hackneyed, senseless, stupefying jargon of political insincerity. Nor is any other writer so quick to detect the process by which ideas harden into clichés, stock answers, pat remarks as offensive as the slamming of a door." Gerald Johnson, writing for the New York *Herald Tribune,* called it "a good book, indeed a very good book. . . . It is doubtful that Dos Passos has ever been more important." The reviewer for the Los Angeles *Times* termed it "a job of super reporting that is captivating readers. Dos Passos always writes in terms of people, and here, in his best and most sincere book, the picture of the people is the picture of America." *Commonweal*'s critic wrote: "After reading his impressionistic but informative book, it is difficult to imagine a reporter who approaches our national scene with greater seriousness. His is no volume in which to seek really rounded portraits of any number of present-day Americans of every walk and section. It is rather an extremely readable series of first-hand impressions that add up to a lot of responsibility for us all." Although the Boston *Sunday Post* commended the book's author as a "clear-eyed, sensitive reporter who submerges his own opinions and allows John Citizen to speak for himself," *The Nation*'s reviewer, Margaret Marshall, pointed out that Dos Passos' conclusions were there in his "Letter to a Friend in the Theaters," which prefaced the book. Edmund Wilson, who took Clifton Fadiman's slot at *The New Yorker,* reviewed the entire canon of Dos Passos (he thought *Adventures of a Young Man* and *Number One* his least satisfactory books), then commended him for having (in the new book) "shrewdly perceived and even dramatized the social phenomena produced by the war—the effect on the American population of going to work for the State—in a way that had not yet been done." The *Virginia Kirkus Service*'s observation that *State of the Nation* was a "provocative and stimulating . . . revealing and disturbing" book that did not attempt to give all the answers, but engaged the reader in a personally significant way, perhaps best depicted the author's intent and achievement.

Negative comments were relatively few. R. H. Gabriel told readers of *The Yale Review* that Dos Passos' "swift succession of small, sharply etched scenes is interesting and stimulating but only moderately illuminating. Social criticism, and even social description, to be useful requires much dull grubbing for facts and more facts to make possible a balanced judgment. The occasional brilliant flash that is reflected from Mr. Dos Passos' surface picture is no substitute for the studied conclusion that emerges from systematic thinking." The reviewer for the New York *Times Book Review*, R. L. Duffus, complained that after "viewing the Dos Passos motion picture," he was at a loss of words to define "just what the plot was all about." *Mademoiselle*'s critic faulted the book for its lack of narrative unity, its "absence of progression and climax," its overall flatness of style, and the author's "determination to remain an outsider. . . . It is excellent but flaccid research." Margaret Marshall thought the book provided "good reading in spite of those funny words of his and the slight monotony of his sensory style after its freshness wears off."

The many positive reviews of *State of the Nation* prompted brisk sales. Houghton Mifflin executive Paul Brooks reported forty-one hundred prepublication copies sold, which he termed "a respectable send-off." Since no more than three thousand copies of Dos Passos' earlier nonfiction books comprised the stock of each first edition, the author was cheered by his publisher's vote of confidence in printing seventy-five hundred copies for a first run, which sold in less than a month. By the end of August, sales totaled more than nine thousand, and *State of the Nation* had earned a berth on the New York *Herald Tribune*'s bestseller list. It was Dos Passos' first nonfiction book to merit a bestseller's tally. Dos Passos was heartened, too, when *Omnibook Magazine* paid one thousand dollars for condensation rights to *State of the Nation* for its September 1944 issue. On September 25, *Life* paid five hundred dollars for an excerpt and ran an eleven-page spread of Dos Passos' text with *Life*'s photographs of the people and regions mirrored in the author's inquisitive tramp across the United States. Released the same day as *State of the Nation* was a reissue of *The Ground We Stand On*, now rejacketed with a new introduction by Dos Passos. The sales of one book boosted the other. Paul Brooks reported that *Manhattan Transfer*, reissued in 1943, was selling well, and that *Number One* would be reissued under a Sundial Press imprint. Although royalties from the Sundial edition would customarily be paid six months after publication, Brooks advanced one thousand dollars when Dos Passos said that he "could use the money."

Again and again during the summer and fall of 1944, Dos Passos prodded his publisher and editor with suggestions for increasing the sales of his back titles. On July 8 he wrote Lovell Thompson that he was "delighted" to hear of Houghton Mifflin's plan to keep *Adventures of a Young Man* and *Number One* "above water even if they needed Mae Wests." Then he suggested a "plush-bottomed" edition of *U.S.A.*, which he thought F. Strobel (who had illustrated *State of the Nation*) could do a good job on if he could be "induced to individualize his style a little more." Dos Passos complained that Strobel's drawings were "marred by a kind of rubber stamp platitude." He also criticized the jacket because it "knocked out the drawing. Not that I mind ugliness per se; but it had the air— to me—of the extreme cheapness of an edition pirated in Chile." He was still smarting from his pirated essays in Ecuador, a problem he had been unable to resolve to his advantage.

Dos Passos' contract for *Number One,* the first book published by his new firm, called for a 15 percent royalty for the first fifty thousand copies and 17.5 percent for everything over. The agreement looked good on paper, but Dos Passos did not think the book would sell enough under its original imprint for him to benefit by the increase. Whereas nearly six thousand copies of the Modern Library edition of *U.S.A.* were sold during the six months ending March 31, 1944, his profit was only $355.32. It seemed to Dos Passos that his next contract should establish a 17.5 percent royalty at a figure significantly less than fifty thousand copies. His next book would be based on travels through the theaters of war, he told Thompson in September 1944, having been asked by *Life* to serve as a navy war correspondent attached to the United States Pacific Fleet. Thompson balked at adjusting the royalty schedule for Dos Passos' war book, however, because he thought it had little likelihood of a movie sale. "If we should alter our standing Dos Passos contract, I'd like to do it on a book where we had a chance to do a campaign which would aim at the movie rights. That must necessarily be fiction." Thompson reported that the firm had already spent 30 percent of its receipts for *State of the Nation* on advertising, a gamble that had paid off. He then proposed a concession for the new nonfiction book contract: "We would like to start you at 17½ percent after 40,000. In the case of the current book this *may* be an academic alteration, but it will mean that you are getting the best contract that Houghton Mifflin ever gives, and that is where we want you to stand."

A few days before Dos Passos left for the West Coast to begin his South Pacific tour as a war correspondent, he and Katy had dinner in Ipswich, Massachusetts, with Lovell Thompson and his wife, Kay. During the course of the evening, they touched upon the problem of Dos Passos' having struggled throughout his professional life to stay out of the red, yet having been unsuccessful much of the time because of matters beyond his control. Dos Passos said that in his profession he had been forced to concern himself with far more than traveling, researching, writing, reading proofs, and giving occasional interviews—all legitimate aspects of his trade about which he had no complaint—but he disliked having to harp to his publishers on getting his book promoted properly. As Dos Passos viewed the problem, the real breakdown involving the sale of his books came in the bookstores themselves, a situation with which he felt powerless to cope. Back in Provincetown after his dinner with Thompson and having thought the matter through once more, he brought up the subject again in a letter to Thompson:

> The more I think about it the more certain I become that the only people who get to buy my books are those who really fight for them. They are very rarely in the windows or on display. The bookstores tend to wait until there's a demand to reorder. There's still more sales resistance at the bookstore level than there is at the customer level. Is there any way that you could check on these hunches? I hate to nag but I have the feeling that nature is being allowed to take its course in the normal routine way in the case of <u>State of the Nation</u> as it was in the case of <u>Number One</u>. . . . I feel that Houghton Mifflin has done an excellent routine job (better than routine on the advertising matter) in these two books, but looking at the record the results are very little better than were the results of Harcourt Brace's very inert routine.

Now we can try to dope out the flaw in the process. Experiment is so much more fun than routine that I can't believe you won't find yourself, in spite of publishing tradition, thinking up new dodges. For the purposes of this argument we have to take for granted that the books are of permanent value and interest to the inhabitants of these states. Particularly about State of the Nation I feel that you are taking it for granted that the book has only temporary interest. I can't argue about that. All I can do is refer you to the people who write as if they liked that part of my work better than any other part, and to the fact that Orient Express is still selling in England after nearly twenty years. If Jonathan Cape can sell Orient Express to a lot of bloody limejuicers I don't see why you can't go on selling State of the Nation to decent Americans for forty years. . . . It means working out a new technique. But hell Lovell that's what you are sitting in that office looking out at those starlings all day for.

Thompson took offense at Dos Passos' offhand final remark and shot back a letter laden with figures detailing the technical aspects of publishing and telling him that they could do no more than they were already doing for him. On November 17, 1944, Dos Passos replied:

Hay Lovell, hold your horses, you don't have to sell me Houghton Mifflin as a publisher. The fact that I'm hanging around nagging you with books and complaining epistles is proof enough that I have a suspicion that you and your starlings are up to something at 2 Park Street. Everything you say about the technical side of publishing is of the greatest interest; in fact it is only the entertainment to be derived from the technical details that makes the grisly headache of trying to make a living by your books at all supportable. Adventures of a Young Man, the biggest flop I ever had from a sales point of view in a novel, sold around nine thousand copies against virtually organized opposition both inside and outside the publishing house. With all the breaks, well-conducted advertising and, in the case of Number One, the best grade A sendoff you had in the house, all we've been able to do is double that figure. The disadvantages of these times are cancelled out by the fact that these are the best bookbuying years on record. I wouldn't have any grounds for argument if we didn't have U.S.A. piling up nine and ten thousand a year sales for the Modern Library. I'm not grumbling about this situation but suggesting that more direct work is needed to change the negative attitude of the majority of bookstores towards my work. I believe in looking carefully into outsiders' hunches. There may be something in them.

From Lovell Thompson's point of view, Dos Passos was incredibly naive regarding the inner workings of a publishing house and what he had a right to expect. "We did as well by Dos as we could," said Thompson in retrospect. "And I don't agree with those who thought his work fell off after *U.S.A.* The nonfiction and two later novels—*Chosen Country* and *Midcentury*—I especially liked. Dos was convinced there was a plot afoot, both within the house and out, to keep his books from selling—that he was blacklisted. You can't keep people from talking, but I'm convinced there was nothing organized."

Sales of *U.S.A.* increased significantly during the summer and fall of 1944 when a member of the Board of Regents of the University of Texas called *U.S.A.* the "dirtiest, most obscene, most perverted book ever written in the English language" and demanded the firing of the professor who recommended it to his sophomore English class. The attack stemmed from an academic freedom and tenure controversy raging in Austin with political ramifications reverberating across the state when the nine-member Board of

Regents led a Red witch-hunt against its liberal president, Homer Price Rainey (members reportedly branded anyone who had voted for Roosevelt an "undesirable" or a "radical"). Rainey was fired November 1, 1944, but could not be removed as a professor of the university because he was tenured. A Texas State Senate investigating committee heard testimony of the offended regent who asserted that "about 1400 or 1500 pages of *U.S.A.* are filled with filth and obscenity. No teacher who would put that book on a list for a sophomore to read is fit to teach in a penitentiary—let alone at the University. As long as I'm regent, I'm going to repress that book and put out any teacher who teaches it." A spokesman for the Southern Association of Colleges and Secondary Schools of Texas sided with the regent. Strident protests were registered by prominent teachers, administrators, and the university itself, whereupon a Committee of Correspondence of the Student Union of the University of Texas released the following statement:

> In reality, *U.S.A.* is a deeply moral book, protesting against materialism and public and private immorality of the Harding-Coolidge-Hoover era. In the novel, sin is depicted in repulsive forms, and the characters who engage in it are neither happy nor prosperous. There are passages in which wrongdoing is depicted in strong language, but to elucidate the ancient text: "The Wages of Sin Is Death." These passages, when taken out of context, can be made to give a completely erroneous impression of the book. Shakespeare, Chaucer, Swift and other great masters of the past can be similarly abused. There is in the book a strong undercurrent of faith in the American way of life.

The controversy was still unresolved during the winter of 1944–45 when an English professor at the University of Texas—who asked Dos Passos not to divulge his name—wrote to apprise him that some six thousand words had been excerpted from his book by a lawyer for the Galveston Chamber of Commerce and by the lieutenant governor of the state and were being circulated. "This seems to me to be a clear violation of copyright," he added. Dos Passos chose not to act upon the infringement, however. He was more interested in knowing that his book was being read than in seeking redress as the injured party. A few months later, the Student Council for Academic Freedom at the University of Texas polled eighty-four leading universities and colleges across the country and learned that sixty-eight of them used *U.S.A.* in their English classes.

Along with news stories of the Texas brouhaha to reach Dos Passos on the Cape before his departure to the Pacific was a letter from James T. Farrell complaining that the Legion of Decency had stirred up a problem involving censorship of the *Studs Lonigan* trilogy. Farrell reported that the novel had originally been one of two hundred books on an approved list by the American Library Association for export to England, but that it had been removed. Dos Passos replied that a letter from a "broadminded cardinal" would be more useful than any statement he might make on Farrell's behalf, but agreed to do what he could.

At the time Dos Passos was waging his own defense of *1919.* Not since his exchange with John Howard Lawson in 1934 regarding their respective stands on Communism and ends versus means had he been assailed so irascibly by a friend as he was now by Robert Hillyer. Some twelve years after *1919* was published, Hillyer read the book for the first time and complained of what he took to be a direct likeness between him and a central character, Richard Savage. Dos Passos defended his method and characterization and denied that there was "much Hillyer in Savage (except for the story of the late General Hillyer that you probably noticed I cribbed from your career and some peace conference courier stories)." Writing novels was "a hell of a business because some people had a mania for finding themselves or their acquaintances in them." It was impossible not to take incidents and traits from the lives of one's friends as well as from oneself, Dos Passos explained, but "that's very different from trying to do a portrait of somebody you know." He told Hillyer that the naming of another major character, Ward Moorehouse (who appeared in the first book of the trilogy), had prompted a New York newspaperman who turned up with the same name to threaten to slay him.

Hillyer was not appeased by Dos Passos' reply and pressed his complaint once more. This time Dos Passos wrote him:

> Dear Robert—it serves you right for departing from your resolution not to read your friends' books. But really you've got it wrong. Savage was a synthetic character as all the characters in my novels are. In developing him a few little touches of Hillyer may have crept in . . . but there was never any intention of producing a portrait or a caricature of my friend Robert Hillyer. You've written novels yourself and you know how you start out with a few notions and anecdotes about somebody you know and then other scraps of the lives of other people get in and a large slice of your own life and then if you are lucky the mash begins to ferment and becomes something quite different. . . . And how could your father have gotten in when I never knew him and I don't think ever heard you speak of him? Gosh Robert you must not let yourself be affected by the literary gossipmongers who are always lifting the skirts of literature and peeping under and giggling and tittering about something that isn't there at all. If you want an affidavit from me that Savage was an imaginary figure and that any resemblances to anybody in the heavens above or the earth beneath or the waters under the earth was purely accidental, I'll gladly give it. But I think the way to treat prying and nosy budding novelists is to slap them down or better, to laugh them off. . . . Don't forget that our novels and schoolrooms aren't all our lives and that we've managed to like each other on a different plane of our lives for thirty years or so. I for one intend to go on liking you.

Despite Dos Passos' placating words, Hillyer remained aloof for several years.

On December 1, 1944, when Dos Passos told Katy good-bye and boarded a plane for San Francisco, he felt somewhat as he had in 1917 in wanting to observe the fighting in Europe and to do whatever he could to help, short of combat, "before things went belly-up." Having covered the war on the domestic front of his country in his series of articles for *Harper's Magazine, Liberty,* and *Fortune* and developed his observations into an organic whole in his book, *State of the Nation,* he was now impatient to commence his tour overseas, this time—unlike his aborted reportage of the civil war in Spain in 1937—as a full-fledged war correspondent. Dos Passos had no desire to cover the war in Europe, which he thought would be played out soon with a victory for the Allies, but he did not want to miss the last of the decisive battles in the South Pacific.

23

Globe-Trotting and a Sad Farewell, 1944–47

Well, here I am all dressed up in my uniform. When I first stepped out of doors I was appalled by the brightness of the buttons: they flashed in the sunlight like lighthouses. . . . And the immensity of the hat—how could I have gotten such a big hat? I suppose I'll get accustomed to this splendor but I feel very odd indeed and tend to duck around corners for fear of being seen and saluted.

Dos Passos to Katy
7 December 1944

Dos Passos was in San Francisco getting ready to board a navy transport plane when he wrote Katy a hurried note and tucked into the envelope a drawing of an ape dangling on one arm from the barrel of a cannon, his buttons gleaming, and waving a handkerchief to his "possum" with the other. Never before had he left Katy with the expectation of their being separated three or four months. He told Katy that he had been reading Tolstoi's *War and Peace* and was beginning to feel like one of its characters, "not a good feeling at all," he added. The war in the South Pacific had been raging for three years, and the anniversary of the bombing of Pearl Harbor was the very day his plane cleared the runway at Benton Field in Alameda, California, and headed for the open sea, its destination Honolulu.

Not having been in uniform for over a quarter of a century, Dos Passos felt as strange in his khaki GI-issue as he had when he first strapped a Sam Browne belt around his custom-made uniform as a gentleman volunteer in the Norton-Harjes Ambulance Corps. Enlisted men barely old enough to shave now eyed him warily and sometimes saluted rather than risk a breach of discipline by ignoring an officer whose rank could not be determined readily. As a war correspondent Dos Passos had no rank, as was the case when he first drove an ambulance in France. Then, as now, he had certain privileges afforded only to officers. As a volunteer driver in an elite outfit during World War I, he had been encouraged not to fraternize with the front-line soldiers, especially the French *poilus,* yet he did whenever he got the chance. Now, as a war correspondent, he knew that the vitality of his dispatches would depend in large measure upon what he was able to pick up in conversations with soldiers, sailors, Seabees, marines—men of all ranks, but especially the privates and noncommissioned officers. Dos Passos discovered quickly that many enlisted men shied away from talking with correspondents, although easygoing, unobtrusive interview techniques and his genial manner sometimes gave him an edge in news gathering that many of the more seasoned journalists lacked. He wrote Katy that he envied the correspondents who were "neatly typing off their manifestos and hurrying to the censor, then to the cable radio and coming back with satisfied faces." Compared to them, he felt like an "amateur softball player who has strayed out on the field in a World Series game."

He also told of having toured a jungle training school with other correspondents escorted by a young lieutenant who sounded like a circus barker announcing upcoming attractions: "jungle living, village fighting, hand-to-hand combat, hip shooting, assault on Jap-fortified area"—all in a two-hour period. The assault looked like the real thing, he added, with "bazookas, bangalores and all." Dos Passos was impatient to be on his way so that he might witness the actual fighting.

From a coral atoll in the Marshall Islands, he wrote on New Year's eve:

> The minute we land on an atoll it begins to look like La Guardia Field. We bring in distillators to distill seawater. We attack the flies and rats. We oil for mosquitoes. We level everything off and establish a city dump. The result isn't picturesque but it's eminently practical so that in the central Pacific at least the islands become extraordinarily healthy. Meanwhile in the place where we are not life goes on as it did a long time ago. The brown Micronesians fish and sail their magnificent outrigger canoes and fatten somewhat on the overflow of our canned goods.

Dos Passos had learned by this time that much of what he imparted to Katy was being censored, and he decided that the safest thing to write home about was the flora and fauna. Katy sometimes complained that what was missing because of the censor's shears was sufficient cause for her to petition him for at least an inkling of what had been cut out. Many observations in Dos Passos' letters showed up in similar fashion in his first two dispatches for *Life:* "Atolls" (March 12, 1945) and "American Marianas" (May 21, 1945).

In his Christmas 1944 letter, Dos Passos enclosed a sketch depicting a solitary ape in a duck-billed cap seated forlornly under a coconut palm on the edge of a beach, his head bent over a notebook. Beneath the wiry figure was the phrase "No Christmas Atoll." Waves, tagged "6,000 miles," stretched out beyond him, and in the lower corner of the drawing was a small "Katy Possum" seated at her desk working industriously with quill pen in hand over a sheaf of papers. At her feet was "Liza-Poodle" and the caption "In Charge of All This and In Charge of All That." The humor expressed in these drawings, pet names, and signatures always provoked a smile even when there was little else over which to rejoice. Typical of Dos Passos' pen names during this period were such signatures as "reluctant literape," "solitary investigape," "lesserless desolape," "aerial navigape," "investigatory affectionape," and "<u>au revoir</u> elevape."

Katy varied her own favorite persona, "Possum," with such closings as "Poor Passionate Poss," "Katy Dos Possum," "Bluestocking" (when she played the novelist and literary sophisticate), and "Frenchy" (the siren). Sometimes she asked Dos Passos which of his women did he want to meet his train or plane. Impatient for his return from the South Pacific, but uncertain as to his precise arrival date, she apologized: "I am afraid you won't be met by Frenchy, as I had hoped, because how can I grow out my fingernails like a lady in time. Bluestocking is here, of course, but you don't want <u>her</u> to meet you. Then there's that Elemental who used to help poor Caliban—she's been around all winter. You used to like her."

Katy had played Bluestocking increasingly that winter after the publication of her and Edith Shay's book, *The Private Adventure of Captain Shaw*. Their publisher, Houghton Mifflin, announced on January 24, 1945, that the book had just been chosen Book of the Month for June for the Book League of America, an affiliate of the Literary Guild, for which Katy and her coauthor were to share the six-thousand-dollar guaranteed royalty. "Oh M. Fish! My dear, you can imagine what airs Bluestocking is giving herself: breakfast in bed and cedar-lined closets in her dressing room (don't you think it would be nice?)." A month later, Katy reported that the book had already sold 10,400 advance copies. She and Edith Shay had earned almost ten thousand dollars between them, including the book club sale. The two women quickly conjured up an idea for another book-length manuscript and presented their proposal to Houghton Mifflin. Katy acknowledged "a certain tenderness in their manner" in that the Houghton Mifflin people had begun to treat her and Edith "like a Persian rug which they had discovered to be of more value than they at first believed." They were no longer "walking on the rug, but had hung it up on the wall for people to see the design." Nonetheless, the rug remembered that it had been walked on "all over . . . for a long time." Everyone at Houghton Mifflin except Ben Ticknor had treated the book like an "ugly duckling" until it began to sell. Katy told her husband that the success of her book had surprised the writing community of Provincetown. "Norman Matson ground his teeth and sat up all night working, he told me next day, and Miss Glower [Susan Glaspell] looked simply stunned" when she heard the news. "It is funny to observe the astonishment of our friends, and Edie says angrily that this is because they never imagined that we could do such a thing and that it seems like <u>dogs walking</u>. Well, maybe it does. . . . I *do* feel rather like a dog walking. But I won't go on the radio or anything." Katy sent Dos Passos a publicity photograph of her and Edith Shay so that he could see for himself what "Bluestocking" looked like in his absence. She was sure that it would provoke the keeper of a lunatic asylum to come after her with his net. "But I won't flee to Hollywood," she promised.

Katy confessed that she missed her husband inordinately, yet hardly knew what to write about: "It all seems so tiny and trivial here with you in the forward areas (wonderful expression!) and everything on such a great scale of men and events. What shall I say to Superape? . . . I wish everything were not so important these days—sometimes I feel as if I were living on the ceiling in the Vatican. . . . It is all so serious and awesome and oversize yet I feel upside down—only a small mammal after all." The only thing she could do was "work every minute" and buy war bonds, she added. Dos Passos suggested that they number their letters so they would know if any had gone astray. "Mail comes remarkably quickly if anybody writes it," he chastised when there were only "two Possum letters" awaiting his arrival on Guam.

Dos Passos' "atoll-hopping" took him to some twenty islands in the South Pacific. From Honolulu he went to Kwajalein and Eniwetok in the Marshall Islands (southwest of Hawaii). After a week in the Marshall Islands he flew still farther south to Tarawa and Makin in the Gilbert Islands, which stretched across the equator. Each time Dos Passos and his fellow newsmen touched down on a new island, they asked: "How was it when the Japs were here?" Three Australian nuns with whom he had tea on New Year's day reported that they would have starved had the natives not brought them food, their own supply at the Catholic mission having been stolen by Japanese troops. One sister reported that she had routed a group of soldiers from their church when she discovered them throwing stones at the statues. "Taboo, taboo," she shouted while poking fingers at their faces with both hands.

Although Dos Passos interrogated many willing natives through English-speaking interpreters as he went from place to place, most of his time was spent observing various military operations. From Majuro he flew in a large amphibian aircraft (a "Dumbo") that routinely accompanied bombers on air strikes to help insure that each plane made it home safely, and if not, to pick up survivors. From the Marianas he flew north over dark lava cliffs and grassy beaches, his eyes straining for signs of yellow from a life raft or a jacket of a downed airman. On one mission he flew over Pagan in the Philippine Sea, where the islands were steeper, wilder, and studded with volcanos, some still smouldering. Beyond them lay the Volcano Islands and Iwo Jima, which they observed at close range several days later from the deck of a battleship.

Dos Passos was one of a number of navy correspondents aboard a battleship in convoy with cruisers and destroyers headed for Iwo Jima, the last major Japanese stronghold between the Micronesian islands and Japan. He wrote Katy on January 23, 1945, from aboard ship that he had been issued ear plugs, a helmet, a Mae West life jacket, asbestos gloves, mask, hood, and "God knows what all into which you are supposed to climb during an attack. It's very confusing. I fumble and stumble around like a centipede in skiboots. . . . Oh Katy we mustn't do too much of this kind of thing separately, but I wouldn't have missed this particular trip for anything in the world." He admitted that during practice alerts he had difficulty getting to his lookout station ("a place called Sky Control") because he was always climbing the wrong ladder and ending up in some strange place off-limits. He said he stayed so busy that it was difficult to find time to write more than random notes, let alone fully developed dispatches. In one letter he wrote of bracing himself for three and a half hours and watching the ship's antiaircraft batteries swivel and fire upon Japanese planes that had managed to get off the ground after bombers had pounded the Iwo Jima airfield. The battleship steered a zigzag course six thousand yards off the beach, its bellowing sixteen-inch guns making coffee cups crumble under the concussion or skitter across a table as salvo after salvo was fired at island targets; then they watched destroyers close in to knock out three Japanese transports lying at anchor. Engulfed in smoke and flames, Iwo Jima looked as though its volcanic center had

Drawing of Dos Passos by Adolph Dehn. (Virginia Dehn)

Katy on the patio after breakfast outside the Arequipa, Provincetown. (Katharine Merrill Smith Durand)

John Dos Passos, war correspondent for Life, 1944–45. (By permission of the University of Virginia Library, Manuscript Division)

Elizabeth and John Dos Passos, March 1952. (Elizabeth Dos Passos)

Lucy Dos Passos and her father. (Elizabeth Dos Passos)

The Dos Passos family with E. E. Cummings at Silver Lake, New Hampshire. (Marion Morehouse Cummings)

Dos Passos at play on G. T. Boyer Ranch in Savery, Wyoming, summer 1964.

Being presented the Peter Francisco Medal in New York City by the Portuguese Continental Union. (Francisco J. Mendonça)

(Richmond News Leader*)*

Dos Passos at work Spence's Point, Virginia. (United Press International)

Dos Passos and Kennydog, May 1970. (Richmond News Leader; *photo by P. A. Gormus, Jr.)*

erupted. The American armada retreated when rain and poor visibility made it advisable to discontinue bombardment. Dos Passos watched the smouldering island disappear into the mist and pulled the plugs from his jangled ears.

In Saipan in the Mariana Islands he inspected a field hospital set up beside an airstrip, then counted eighty-one bombers return from a mission over Japan. It took an hour and twenty minutes for them to land (in pairs every two minutes). With one other correspondent he went out to the runway in a jeep to watch a B-29 that had taken a direct hit land safely and was relieved to see the crew pile out laughing. They saw the waist gunner, unhurt, pick a souvenir of jagged metal from his flak vest. The mission's only casualty was an airman hit in the hand, who was able to walk to the dispensary.

From the Philippines Dos Passos wrote Katy that he was in splendid health and spirits despite "a setback by a silly little accident." He had been clipped on the head by a Piper Cub coming in for a landing on a beach he was roaming. His injuries were slight, he assured Katy: a black eye and a sore, swollen head. "A splendid doctor named January from Massachusetts General" had applied sulfa to his wound and taken a few stitches almost on the spot. He confessed that he had experienced "a near miss" on a mission from Leyte aboard a Mitchell bomber (decorated with an Indian head denoting that the aircraft was in a squadron of "Air Apaches") on a photographic mission over Manila on February 15. A cylinder had blown off the right motor when a 22mm Japanese shell struck the engine, and the crew prepared for a crash landing, but the plane managed to hobble into Lingayen airstrip twenty-five minutes later, having jettisoned its heavy ammunition boxes and snaky belts of cartridges pulled from the machine guns. By the time the story reached the Provincetown *Advocate,* the report was that the plane had been shot down, but managed to land "in a friendly rice field" with no injuries to any of its occupants. A more accurate account was the one published in *Life* April 30, 1945, as a follow-up to Dos Passos' dispatch of March 2. The pilot himself, Major H. H. Brigham, reported the incident in a letter to his brother, who sent it to *Life,* where it was published as a "Letter to the Editor":

> John Dos Passos and I had quite an experience together. About the time our troops were entering Manila, we were asked if we could fly over Manila to see if the Japs were burning the town. . . . As we passed over Santo Tomas we saw quite a gathering and I decided to go back and get some pictures with our belly camera. As we went out over the water to turn, there was a terrific rattling noise. Black smoke poured out of the right engine and I noticed a bullet hole in the left engine. I was all set to ditch her and I could not help but think that if Life's Board of Directors could only see their John now, they would like to hamstring me. Finally, after about ten minutes out, the oil pressure quit pressing, the manifold pressure quit pressing, and the prop ran away. . . . I feathered the prop and we went the rest of the way on one engine. After causing a red alert and a general furor on the radio, we landed safely and with loud sighs of relief. We both kissed the ground.

Katy was beside herself when she heard of Dos Passos' "near misses" and noted that in his letter of February 15 (the afternoon of the incident over Manila), he had made no reference to it. Finally, back in Honolulu on April 3, he said he had written about it in full, then realized that the censors would not have let it go through, thus did not mail it.

"So many other things turned up that I never got around to retelling you about it," he added apologetically.

Dos Passos spent a month in the Philippines, his longest stay in one place during his tour of duty in the Pacific. He rode into Manila on Feburary 5 with the Sixth Army on the heels of the first American troops to reach the city. For three weeks the battle raged before the Japanese surrendered, leaving much of the city in flames. Dos Passos interviewed many prisoners of war newly liberated from Cabanatuan, where some men had survived for three years. In his dispatch of February 7, 1945, he wrote:

> They all looked strangely alike. Their heads looked very large for their bodies. Gray skin hung in folds from skinny necks. Their eyes were large and sunken, the whites clear, the pupils sharp and small, the iris bright. It was as if all the life left in their bodies were concentrated there. . . . We talked to a major sitting on his cot looking down at legs like a pair of golf clubs that stuck out pitifully from his ragged shorts. The prisoners wouldn't be alive today, he said, if it hadn't been that the Japs had gotten panicky and pulled out of the camp three weeks ago. The men in the enlisted men's section looked less exhausted than the men in the officers' section. . . . The three years hadn't borne down quite so hard on them. We roamed around among the tents looking shyly in the men's faces when we passed them, but we couldn't bear to ask any more questions. There seemed no way of phrasing a sentence that would bridge the gap between the life we knew and the life these men had known. Here and there the sergeant stopped a man whom he had seen before, but at the word *correspondent* their faces froze. They immediately remembered something they had to do.

Dos Passos wrote to Gerald and Sara Murphy several days before the Japanese surrender of Manila that the atrocity stories being sent off by "popeyed correspondents" were understated rather than exaggerated. "Burning and pillaging and murdering by the retreating Nips have left the civilians in a heartbreaking plight. . . . This is the grimmest I've seen since South Russia way back in '21." His own dispatch to *Life* failed to make the deadline "due to mysterious delays in San Francisco," he allowed later. "I find myself hot on the wires, struggling with censors, dashing about with copy almost like a war correspondent. . . . The situation is somewhat hectic with stiff fighting still going on in the ashes and a great mob of weeklies, press services, radio people . . . and everybody under heaven trying to rent the surviving buildings and beat each other to the only press left intact." In a note to Katy February 25, 1945, Dos Passos complained about not being able to get his cabled stories published. "I'll be glad to get away from all these correspondents and their endless clacking typewriters, though they are nice fellows most of the time," he added. In early March Manila was secured, and Dos Passos returned to Leyte aboard a C-47 transport. By then two divisions of United States Marines had landed on the beachhead of Iwo Jima and were fighting desperately to take possession of the tiny island, a battle that raged for thirty-six days. Before leaving general headquarters at San Miguel, Dos Passos was granted an interview with the five star general who had vowed to return to Luzon and free the Philippine people, who now cherished the sewing kits, mirrors, and packages of chewing gum, candy, and matches with MacArthur's picture and the message I WILL RETURN on each of thousands of packets distributed over the islands. Dos Passos recorded his impressions of the hero of the Philippines, who claimed to have modeled his life on Robert E. Lee and Stonewall Jackson:

There's an air of breeding about him. He stretches out a small dry hand and greets you with somewhat oldfashioned courtesy. He waves you into a chair and when you are seated he unhurriedly sits down in his rocker again and starts to talk. He talks looking straight ahead of him. His sentences are long with carefully balanced clauses. He rarely pauses for an answer. It's as if our arrival had merely caused him to speak aloud the thoughts that had been working rhythmically in his head as he sat there after the work of the day smoking and looking out at the failing afternoon. Only gradually you discover from the turn of his language that he is acutely aware of his listeners and of their interests and affiliations. There is something disarming in the direct way his rather elaborate thoughts take shape in elaborate phrases.

Impatient to leave the Philippines and head home at last, Dos Passos departed Leyte with an authorization signed by MacArthur, who awarded him an Asiatic-Pacific Service Ribbon for having "added luster to the difficult, dangerous and arduous profession of War Correspondent." Dos Passos' orders were marked "for temporary return to the United States . . . for the purpose of consultation." Although his credentials as a war correspondent were valid until December 31, 1945, he had no intention of returning to the Pacific theater of war. He needed time to finish a long piece on "the great floating base at Ulithi," an atoll of the Caroline Islands, from which his battleship sojourn to Iwo Jima had commenced. Censorship had kept him from sending the story off earlier, but he informed his editor at *Life,* Daniel Longwell, that the censor "was somewhat lifting his curtains on Ulithi." Dos Passos was also developing an extensive narrative about his month in the Philippines, which, he anticipated, would comprise a large chunk of his manuscript of *Tour of Duty,* to be published by Houghton Mifflin as soon as he could pull it together.

Reports of the Yalta Conference in February reached Dos Passos in the Philippines, and Germany's surrender seemed imminent. Newsmen learned that the Soviet Union had agreed to shift its fight from Europe to the Pacific front and to declare war on Japan within three months of the fall of Nazi Germany. Stalin's demands in exchange for his commitment to extend Russia's involvement in the war was disquieting to most observers. Even Katy spoke of Poland's getting short shrift when she mentioned to Dos Passos of having attended a "conference" involving the impending sale of some of the Pelham, New York, property of Mary Lamar Gordon and Byron Ralston as a result of a recent settlement concerning Dos Passos' land in Virginia: "I hope the conference doesn't turn out like Yalta for the Poles." Ringside politicians and lay people alike suspected that the Soviets would never permit Poland the free elections they promised.

President Roosevelt was a sick man by the time he returned from Yalta and reported to Congress his position there. A month later, the President was dead. Dos Passos was being debriefed in San Francisco on April 12, 1945, when the story broke that Roosevelt had touched his forehead and complained softly of a "terrific headache" while poring over a sheaf of papers in preparation for an organizational meeting of the United Nations, then slumped unconscious in his chair and died three hours later, the victim of a cerebral hemorrhage. Soon after the President's death the atrocities of Treblinka, Auschwitz, and Dachau came to light, but no one knew then that the Soviets, too, had been guilty of mass murders of Poles and Jews. Dos Passos was in Provincetown working on his articles for *Life* when he heard the news that Hitler and his bride of one day, Eva Braun, had committed suicide together in an air-raid shelter of the Reich Chancellery in Berlin on April 30.

Back on the Cape with Katy, Dos Passos wrote Edmund Wilson (then in Italy) that he had returned from the Pacific "dizzy from the airplane rides" and bent out of shape from sitting in bucket seats as he winged his way home, but feeling cheered and stimulated, nonetheless. "Saw more attractive and interesting people in the space of a few months than I'd seen in years and came back with considerable confidence in the ability of younger and less important Americans to cope with the terrific problems that face us everywhere." There was much that the American people did not know how to do during such troubled times, he continued, "but the things we do know how to do we do so damn well. . . . Even MacArthur seems to know his business." Yet he was appalled at the overall political picture. "World War II seems to be hurriedly merging into World War III, and as usual we are betraying our friends and feeding up our enemies."

Wilson was disturbed by what he termed Dos Passos' loss of faith in the socialist ideals he had formerly embraced, to which Dos Passos replied that socialism had nothing to do with faith: "Socialism is something we've got . . . like railroads and air conditioning and cancer. . . . As I see it, the problem is how to apply it to the various forms of socialism the world suffers from. What worries me about European socialists is that they don't seem to have advanced beyond the bureaucratic state of mind. . . . We seem to be heading towards monolithic bureaucratic social systems whether they are based on force as in Russia or on persuasion and apathy as in England and the United States." Dos Passos told Wilson that he still retained "unreasoned belief in individual liberty," and that he did not think people had "explored enough in recent years the possibilities of our banal American arbiter-government notion, government as the referee among warring monopolies, cartels, trade unions, etc.," and that he had decided he preferred to live under such a government "than under monolithic socialism even of the most benign cast."

With Germany's surrender at Rheims on May 7, 1945, the country was carved into four zones, and each conqueror eyed the other with suspicion that it may have received the least desirable apportionment of the spoils of war. An international military tribunal set November 20, 1945, for the opening of the Nazi war criminals trials in Nuremberg, and Robert Jackson, chief prosecutor, hailed the event as the first trials in history for "crimes against the peace of the world." *Life* magazine asked Dos Passos to cover it. By this time, he had already finished his Pacific pieces for *Life*, which he expected to comprise the major portion of his new book of essays, *Tour of Duty*, and decided to combine those essays with his observations and notions gleaned from the Allies' waging of peace amid the bleak ruins of Europe to make a substantial book reflecting the situation on both fronts in 1944–45. Meanwhile, Japan had surrendered formally aboard the USS *Missouri* in Tokyo Bay on September 2, and Dos Passos wanted now to observe his fellow Americans in their peace-keeping roles and in their attempt to mete out justice in Nuremberg.

Before leaving the United States on October 10, 1945, he traveled twice with Katy to Westmoreland, Virginia, to look over his newly regained paternal lands and to confer with Walter Griffith, whose uncle had served as overseer when John R. Dos Passos, Sr., was alive. Young Griffith was now in charge of the property. Dos Passos was eager to convert his father's old farm to an income-producing enterprise, since it had lain fallow for many years, whereupon Griffith suggested that he raise Black Angus cattle, which took less attention than farming per se. By fall a large herd of Black Angus and one registered bull were grazing contentedly among the pines on fifteen acres of rye. Katy assured her husband that she would keep up with each new development on the farm and go down herself to look in on things. When he came home, they intended to get the old house there ready to move into themselves. Katy liked the idea of "being in the cattle business." She wrote Dos Passos that some of their friends looked upon their venture as "playing with blue chips."

Katy had never abandoned her predilection for acquiring another house if one came on the market at a good price, and when she learned that the house next door to them at 569 Commercial Street was being put on the market by its owner, William Richey, she could not resist buying it. By now, the book she had written with Edith Shay, *The Private Adventure of Captain Shaw,* had been sold to a book club and was also to be published in England by John Murray. Katy had enough money to purchase the Richey house and also a twelve-foot strip of property owned by Lucy L'Engle on the other side of the Richeys. The strip was hardly large enough to build anything on, nor did she intend to, but Katy liked the idea of owning it and expected to use it for a garden. Susan Glaspell, who had sold it originally to L'Engle, made her agree never to erect any structure or grow anything tall enough to obstruct the view of the harbor from across the street, which was where Susan Glaspell lived. Glaspell told Katy that when she died, she did not care what Katy did with the land. Katy had already sold her house in Truro to Joan Colebrook, a writer, when she extended her holdings on Commercial Street. Dos Passos was in Bad Wiessee, Bavaria, awaiting the start of the Nuremberg trials when Katy donned her newest "Possum" persona, that of land baron: "Oh dear, poor Possum is fat and sassy, purse proud, Shakespearean. The other day I saw him strutting back and forth between his own mansion and the Richey villa saying to himself, 'A plague on both my houses!' He has workmen on the place almost every day but even he cannot find much more to do to improve his establishments. I fear he is obnoxious to many. A little more modesty and self-effacement would become him mightily." The Cape Cod wood-frame house at 569 Commercial Street (three stories, with a detached garage) was in need of repairs, but Katy expected to recoup her investment in short order by renting the house out each summer. Now that gas rationing had been lifted, Provincetowners were bracing for an onslaught of summer tourists. Katy rented the house for one thousand dollars during the summer of 1946, more than she had ever envisioned getting when she bought and refurbished it.

In contrast to his experiences in the South Pacific, Dos Passos was bored by much of his European tour of duty. His first letter to Katy from the Hotel Scribe in Paris on October 12 set the tone for the rest of the trip: "Here I am in a dreary little room. . . . How I miss you now I'm creeping into my damp and lonely straw." Never before had walking the boulevards and streets of Paris seemed "so deadly" and uninspiring. The women were out as usual, dressed now in "vast cardboard hats." Some wore their hair "puffed up on top, the ranks of little curls climbing in steps from the forehead to a peak at the back of the head." He wondered how the civilians survived on wages of three or four thousand francs a month when a meal he had just eaten cost only thirteen francs, since he was a correspondent entitled to U.S. Army rations. The same meal would have cost one hundred francs, plus ration coupons, in what he referred to as a legal restaurant. "It would have been a thousand or more in a black market joint," he told Katy. Upon the eve of his arrival in Paris, Dos Passos attended a press conference for Charles de Gaulle, at which De Gaulle announced his plan to put "seventy-five per cent of everything" into the French Army until it reached a million men. Then he would pay attention to food, industry, and reconstruction. "God knows he may be right. There may be nothing else to do to help his people," lamented Dos Passos, who concluded that there was more to the man than he had suspected: "something sly and old-fashioned."

Before leaving France for Germany the end of October, Dos Passos and a host of other correspondents journeyed to several provinces to observe conditions there. From Biarritz, he wrote Katy that he had a "wonderful room in the palais Napoléon III built for his Empress Eugénie." The palace had been converted into an American university for American soldiers. "America in France is much weirder than America in the Pacific. In spite of what everybody says, I have a notion that the French are pulling themselves together in their own peculiar way." The country seemed on the verge of collapse, yet it did not, he noted. "I haven't much appetite for Europe at present. I want to be home." Germany was more unchanged than he expected. "I suppose what carries Europe through its wars is that the original village economy has never quite broken down. There's a trace of it always to keep people going when the large scale economy collapses." By and large, however, Germany was gloomy, the faces of many of its people "like andirons," he told Katy.

Nuremberg was "particularly horrible . . . a waste of charred and broken buildings. Misery sweats out of the stained and grimy walls. . . . There is a mood you could cut with a knife." He had stopped in Nuremberg only briefly to check into the press camp and look over the preparations for the trials, scheduled to begin November 21, 1945, then left by jeep for Bad Wiessee, a resort village in the foothills of Bavaria near Munich, where he wrote the first of his European pieces for *Life:* "Report on the Occupation." The dispatch was held up, however, until his "Report from Nuremberg" was published, considered by *Life*'s editors to be the priority piece. From Bad Wiessee Dos Passos accompanied two American Military Government (AMG) officers through the Russian Zone to Vienna, which involved a long, bitterly cold ride by jeep over snowy mountain roads. "How do you get along with the Russians?" he asked a grinning American soldier who stopped his jeep as it prepared to cross the Danube. "We get along with 'em all right. They are kinder crude, though. . . . They don't seem eddicated," the youth replied. The "shivering misery of the people in the streets, the burnt-out filigree of Saint Stephen's Cathedral, the shattered baroque facades, the boarded-up shops, the grass-grown ruins" were more touching in Vienna than in the cities in "Germany proper," Dos Passos told Katy.

His next dispatch to *Life*, entitled "Vienna: Broken City," began:

Vienna is heartbreaking. The city has been dying by inches since the collapse of the Hapsburg system in World War One left it a capital without an empire, but even after all these decades of slow strangulation and the Nazi butcheries and the Allied bombings and the brutalities of the Russian armies, it still wears a few of the airs and graces of a metropolis. Vienna is an old musical comedy queen dying in the poorhouse, who can still shape her cracked lips into the confident smile of a woman whom many men have loved, when the doctor makes his rounds of the ward. There is still a touch of Viennese grace about the beautiful old buildings and the manners of the people. . . . In all the poverty and humiliations of the war years the city has not quite forgotten that it once saw great days.

He wrote, too, of the Russians in Vienna. Although he saw them everywhere, he had difficulty getting them to talk with him. "Every Soviet citizen feels that a bitter two-way hostility exists between him and the capitalist world; added to that is the wellfounded and pressing fear in the back of his head that any contact with foreigners will be misinterpreted by the dangerous snoopers of the NKVD." When Dos Passos asked a middle-aged man in a café which of the country's liberators the Viennese liked best, the Austrian replied: "The French—because there are so few of them." He explained that the Viennese people had expected the Americans to bring food and "businesslike vigor to the management of affairs" and the Russians to bring "new ideas, new things, perhaps terrible things, but new." They had expected too much of their liberators, he conceded. "There is nothing new in starvation and looting and murder and rape . . . and bureaucratic stagnation." Many of the people Dos Passos approached shied away from such questions as "How do you get the money to buy rations, and what do you eat?" When he asked a high school principal how he managed to weather the various political changes, the man replied: "Politics is alien to pedagogy." Several journalists who had gone to Budapest while awaiting the opening of the trials showed up in Vienna before Dos Passos left and suggested that he go there for a few days. "Life in Budapest is fantastic and gay in spite of everything," they told him, but he chose to remain in Vienna until time to return to Nuremberg.

From the crumbling, festering city of Nuremberg on November 22, 1945, Dos Passos telescoped his impressions of the opening session in a letter to Katy:

> Robert Jackson's opening for the prosecution yesterday I thought magnificent. A few more speeches like that and the poor old ship of state that's been wallowing rudderless in the trough of the sea will be back on its course. He is really making an effort to make some sense out of what without him would be an act of vengeance. His delivery was amazingly without pomp or self-importance. . . . There was a moment when the Nazis in the prisoners' dock seemed to see themselves for the first time as the world sees them. I'll never forget the look of horror and terror that came over their faces when Jackson read the orders for the massacre of the Jews. Either they had not known what documents were in our possession or something like remorse swept over them for a few minutes. Jackson represented the USA as I like to see it represented. He was reasonable, practical and full of a homey kind of dignity. The Nazis are a strange çrew. Hess looks like a man with some disease of the brain. Streicher and Funk are monstrosities but the rest of them look like men of considerable intellectual brilliance. I had a very good seat and was able to see them very well. Goering's a weird character. He still seems to think he can laugh it all off.

He told Katy that he was going to prepare his "Nuremberg Report" for *Life,* then head home as quickly as possible. "I wonder if they'll print it," he added.

On December 10, 1945, Katy opened her new copy of *Life* and read his published version. She felt as though she, too, were in the courtroom of the old Bavarian Palace of Justice and scrutinizing the faces that had "glared for years from the frontpages of the world":

> There's Goering in a pearlgray doublebreasted uniform with brass buttons and the weazening, leak-balloon look of a fat man who has lost a great deal of weight. Hess's putty face has fallen away till it's nothing but a pinched nose and hollow eyes. Ribbentrop, in dark glasses, has the uneasy trapped expression of a defaulting bank cashier. Streicher's a horrible cartoon of a foxy grandpa. Funk is a little round man with pendulous greyhound jowls and frightened dog's eyes. Schacht glares like an angry walrus. The military men sit up straight and quiet. Except for Hess, who slumps as if in a coma, the accused have an easy expectant look as if they had come to see the play rather than to act in it. Goering is very much the master of ceremonies. He looks around with appreciative interest at every detail of the courtroom. Sometimes his face wears the naughty-boy expression of a repentant drunkard. He is determined to be himself. He bows to an American lady he knows in the press seats. It's a spoiled, genial, outgoing, shrewdly selfsatisfied kind of a face, an actor's face. Not without charm. Nero must have had a face like that.

Dos Passos might have stayed longer in Nuremberg, but he had had enough. He still had another article to write based on his observations in Berlin after leaving Nuremberg, and he was impatient to get on his way. Two jeeps broke down with him en route, and he was forced to hitchhike through icy fog for several hours before the driver of a British lorry delivered him finally to British headquarters in Berlin. Getting out to the American press camp—a "group of dilapidated millionaire nests around a lake" in the suburbs—in the dead of night presented still another challenge. Dos Passos tumbled into his press camp cot "more dead than alive," he whimpered to Katy on November 26. Berlin was a "nightmare city . . . a cold dank hell" in which its "miserable inhabitants with blue lips and hollow eyes" dragged their "little boats of wood" and slogged over the city "under shapeless bundles of things they've taken out of the house to sell to get a little more of something to eat." Outside Berlin's Stettiner Station he was reminded of the liberated Americans he had observed being processed from the concentration camp outside Manila. Hordes of displaced Germans and prisoners of war moved from the train station with their bundles and knapsacks looking out from "staring frightened eyes," their skin draping their bones "like candledrippings."

Before leaving Berlin for Frankfurt on the Main, Dos Passos interviewed Lucius D. Clay, who became the United States commander in chief of the European Command and military governor in Germany. Clay explained something of America's rationale and intent during its occupation of postwar Germany. They had to start "from scratch" in their zone to establish democracy for the German people, he told Dos Passos. Democracy would mean nothing unless it evolved from the lowest level in the villages. The fact that Germany had never allowed local elections was the main reason the Weimar Republic had failed, said Clay. A major problem lay in not knowing whether Germany would become a unified country again or become four separate ones. In a sense, the American occupation forces were only marking time. Grave problems stemmed from the Quadripartite Council —composed of Americans, British, French, and Soviets—trying to administer both Austria and Berlin. An entry in Dos Passos' unpublished "Berlin 1945" notebook revealed not only his thoughts about postwar Germany's problems, but also his concern for America's problems. As he saw it, the United States had made four serious mistakes during its brief history: its failure to abolish slavery in 1776, its method of Reconstruction after the Civil War, its policy toward Mussolini and Hitler, and its policy toward Russian dictatorship. Dos Passos concluded that "he who sups with the devil must need a long spoon—it is time Americans got it through their heads that Democracy and Dictatorship can't cooperate" and that neither form of government was perfect.

Katy was in McClellanville, South Carolina, when Dos Passos arrived in New York City on December 15, 1945, aboard the *Croatan,* a small converted aircraft carrier on which American soldiers were being transported home. He had asked Katy to be waiting for him with civilian clothes and a hotel room reserved, but she had already left with Edith Shay on her trip South before his letter arrived. She had not expected him until just before Christmas and had driven to Spence's Point to carry a few furnishings and to inspect their herd of Black Angus cattle, which, Walter Griffith reported, was thriving. Sara and Gerald Murphy had sent a few pieces of furniture down, too, and Katy was eager to arrange things before moving in for the summer. After leaving the farm, she and Edith drove along the coast "plantation-hopping," as she called it. The new book they were writing together, now entitled "No More the Bugle," was set in part on a South Carolina plantation after the Civil War. Katy had already sent the opening chapter and an outline to Houghton Mifflin, but was skeptical that the new fiction was as good as their previous novel. She hoped that by reinforcing their impressions of the region and absorbing more local color they would be able to finish the book quickly. When Dos Passos finally tracked Katy down by telephone to let her know he was back, she sent a penitent reply that a "homeward hurrying poor Possum" was scampering to greet him.

Dos Passos was weary from his two months of scrambling over the raw countryside of Western Europe and heartsick by all that he had observed there. His four-month tour of the South Pacific had been demanding and even life-threatening at times, yet it was exhilarating as well. In contrast, despite the Allied victory, the mood in Europe was somber. At year's end from Provincetown, where Dos Passos had retreated with Katy—his gloom still upon him—to put together the book of essays to comprise *Tour of Duty,* he wrote Upton Sinclair: "Never felt so much sadder and wiser in my life as after this trip to Europe. Maybe the Russians are right and man is vile and can only be ruled by terror, but I still refuse to believe that everything the West has stood for since the first of the forefathers tumbled out of their leaky boat to do their washing on this beach I'm looking out at as I write must go on the ash heap. My god the tide runs strong against us."

When *Tour of Duty* appeared on August 20, 1946, Dos Passos was poring over the Thomas Jefferson lore at Monticello and at the University of Virginia in Charlottesville. For *Tour of Duty,* Houghton Mifflin published a first edition of eight thousand copies—a larger first printing than any of his other nonfiction books had received—and for the first time in many years he had no quarrel with the promotion of one of his books. *Tour of Duty* sold even better than *State of the Nation* had, boosted as it was by an improved, postwar economy and some ninety reviews, most of them laudatory. Although *Tour of*

Duty was sometimes examined along with the writings of other war correspondents, most critics singled it out for its important differences. The main concern of the book was not the war itself, but the state of mind of the American soldier. Dos Passos allowed the GI to do most of the talking, and from him the reader gleaned the sense of strength and unity in the Pacific operations during the closing months of the war in contrast to the general demoralization in Germany immediately after the war and the United States' "bungling" of events there. "More brilliant than anything else yet attempted in this line . . . probably the best thing Dos Passos has written since he finished *U.S.A.,*" contended Edmund Wilson in *The New Yorker,* a judgment with which a number of other reviewers concurred.

Some critics pointed out that the Stalinists would hate him even more after reading what he had to say about the Russians in the occupied areas, but as John Cort observed to *Commonweal* readers: "It is encouraging to see somebody speak out boldly against the American record in Europe, not simply on the ground of our appeasing the Russians, but also, and perhaps more important, on the ground of cruelty and barbarism and stupidity for which we alone have been responsible." Although the Hartford *Times* called *Tour of Duty* "objective as a paid death notice" and contrasted Dos Passos' technique with that of Ernie Pyle ("who injects himself and his personality into everything he writes"), several reviewers noted that Dos Passos played the impartial observer, yet was highly selective in the conversations he chose to report, thus assuming an editorial stance even when he did not appear to have one.

The author's most explicit posturing was in the European section, "In the Year of Our Defeat," which comprised the last third of the book. In it he reported a conversation between a man of fifty and a young reporter for *The Stars and Stripes* who sought an interview with him. The older man (a Dos Passos persona) was in Paris and on his way home after knocking about postwar Europe in the khaki uniform of a war correspondent. The *Stars and Stripes* reporter, half his age, strolled with him over cold Parisian streets under a darkening sky and ventured his own attitude toward the Soviet Union while asking Dos Passos of his: "The Soviet Union's certainly been a success. You wouldn't deny that, would you, sir? . . . The workers don't need to strike in the Soviet Union. They own the means of production. . . . The Soviet Union is assuring the democratic liberties of the countries in the east of Europe." The older man debated the reporter point by point, but saw his mind "closing up like a clam." The young man pressed on: "But aren't the Russians right in insisting that we stamp out Fascism in Europe?" The war correspondent replied, his frustration mounting, "The only cure for Fascism is liberty. . . . It's only in a free society that life is secure. I don't understand why you boys won't see that. . . . It seems so axiomatic."

Dos Passos ended his book with snippets of conversation picked up in the officers' quarters aboard the cruiser bucking homeward through heavy seas. Again, an older man debated a young one, but this time the older man was a cynical officer who had won his battlefield commission after serving nineteen years as a sergeant. He spoke of the book he could write of the "melting morale of the Army, the sale of Army property, gasoline leaking away into the black market while the fighting was going on," of the looting, and of the mistreatment of civilians. An earnest young lieutenant from Chicago pitched forward in his chair and replied that it was time Americans "wised up" to themselves:

> We're making a mess out of this business. It's all right to arrest the Nazis we've got something criminal on, but can't we try to help out the decent people more? We ought to be helping all Europe—I don't mean just Germany—get on its feet. . . . Instead of giving in to the Russians at every step, we ought to compete with the Russians. I don't mean fight 'em, I mean do our kind of social engineering. We've got to give the world more than they have. . . . If people are prosperous and happy, they won't want to fight a war. . . . One thing I do know. . . . What we are doing since the fighting stopped in Europe is wrong. Two wrongs don't make a right.

The young man's speech served as an *envoi* to the book.

Although the critics spoke admiringly of Dos Passos' style, they were more concerned with his message:

> A style that stings like the flick of a whip . . . lays open the body of war with clean incisions [the Cleveland *News*]. . . . Detail and characterization are so deftly chosen and presented that the reader feels himself present at the scene [the Minneapolis *Sunday Tribune*]. . . . An eloquent commentary on both the clean strength of a well-disciplined army force and the dangerously ineffectual American manner toward the European people [the San Francisco *Argonaut*]. . . . A vivid and powerful warning that we are repeating our mistakes of post-World War I *[The Literary Review]*. . . . Some of the unpleasant truths about the war are most effectively rammed home *[The Wisconsin Library Bulletin]*. . . . His report of Americans at war and after—the "year of our defeat"—could have been published alone. It has the value of timeliness that the first two parts have lost *[The Christian Science Monitor]*. . . . His accurate dialogue frequently carries the kick of a Missouri mule *[The Hartford Courant Magazine]*. . . . I don't know another correspondent who approaches John Dos Passos' skill in putting down the combination of sights, sounds and meanings [The Omaha *World-Herald*]. . . . An admirable technician, he almost always selected an incident so that it would demonstrate the significance of what he saw [the San Francisco *Chronicle*]. . . . One doesn't have to be very old to remember that Dos Passos was once an enthusiastic and uncritical supporter of the Soviet regime. *Tour of Duty* tends to fortify Congreve's contention, "Heaven has no rage like love to hatred turned" [the Chicago *Sun*]. . . . All the Communists who have long had Dos in the *index expurgatorius* will put him further into the Thirteenth Street doghouse. . . . Now I hope Dos Passos can get back to Jefferson . . . to bring the Virginian, with his "passion for peace," alive in our times *[The Nation]*. . . .

Dos Passos was already well into research of Thomas Jefferson for a biography, but was torn between continuing it and beginning the new novel *(The Grand Design)* that would complete his *District of Columbia* trilogy. Having interrupted his study of Jefferson the first time to report on contemporary affairs at home for *Harper's Magazine,* then to observe the American scene in the South Pacific and Western Europe as a war correspondent for *Life,* Dos Passos now felt a responsibility to stay with Jefferson and to remind his readers of the basic principles on which the country had been founded as an object lesson for a more acceptable way of life for contemporary Americans. "The first fifty years of the Republic are of such importance to us now," he wrote Ambassador Claude Bowers, who was a historian and Jefferson scholar as well as a foreign diplomat. Dos Passos had just read Bowers' fourth book on Jefferson, *The Young Jefferson, 1713–1789,* and told him: "I've been working on another aspect of Jefferson's life for some years and now I wish I'd never started because your books do the subject up brown." Dos Passos said that he found Bowers' new book "hellishly accurate" and complimented him on its simplicity and vitality. Only Francis Hirst's *Jefferson: Life and Letters* had been as useful as Bowers' books to him, said Dos Passos, whose concern was Jefferson the man, rather than Jefferson the public servant.

Dos Passos intended to carry his subject only until his fiftieth year, to end his book with Jefferson's resignation as Secretary of State and his retreat to Monticello in 1793, eight years before he became President. Later he might write another volume on Jefferson, he mused. Dos Passos realized that writing about Jefferson could easily evolve into a lifetime project, but he was too much a man of his own century to allow his passion for Jefferson and the early years of the Republic to keep him in dusty archives or in an armchair at home when postwar America needed scrutinizing. Just as the Republic had been on tenuous ground after winning its battle for independence and found that keeping the peace was harder than waging war, so too did Dos Passos consider 1946 a time of crisis for the United States.

Life's request that he follow up his essays on domestic life in America during the war years with a "people at peace" series provided him the occasion to go again to the industrial heart of America to examine the state of the nation so far as labor was concerned. Since industrial profits were reportedly higher in 1946 than at any other time in history, Dos Passos wanted to see what effect such profits had upon the attitudes and lives of the workers themselves. For almost a month he traveled from city to city in the fall of 1946 talking with the man and woman on the street, visiting plants, sitting in on labor meetings, and meeting behind closed doors with businessmen, union officials, and lawyers. Although profits had pumped more money into the economy than ever before, wages barely covered essential spending, and workers were disgruntled that there was nothing left for the luxuries of life. They had seen worse times, but thought that life in the 1920s had been better than what they were experiencing now.

An Irishman at a labor grievance committee meeting told Dos Passos: "We don't want it unless it's forced on us, but if they try to cut real wages or to break up the union we're headed into a fight." Dos Passos talked with many who agreed with a business agent of a truck drivers' union, who insisted that "wages ought to be hitched to the cost of living," but that they could not go on "striking over every damn little thing." Compulsory arbitration or special labor courts might be an answer, he continued. A brick manufacturer proposed that a backlog of six or eight million unemployed would be an apt remedy. Not massive employment, but a "slight recession" would be a better way to get things into line for a gradual buildup of prosperity, countered a lawyer. A company executive who did not want to be identified because union men might protest his means of coping with the rising cost of living declared: "We think we've got the answer: produce more and share the profits." A freight agent asked if workers had ever considered the fact that strikes and slowdowns were blessings in disguise. As he saw it, the difficulties curtailing production helped spread the backlog of consumer demand into the future and eased problems of the economy. Dos Passos listened intently and wove his findings into a composite narrative that revealed much of the frustration, confusion, anger, pigheadedness, and sense of hope voiced by representative Americans of the industrial Midwest as they attempted to answer the question "Where do we go from here?" The question itself became the title of an extensive essay in the January 1947 issue of *Life*.

Meanwhile, the country was entering a phase of peacetime living conceived in the ashes of war, spoken of now as the Cold War and waged by the United States primarily through economic aid to countries threatened by Communist attack or expansion through propaganda, infiltration, and sabotage. The country was especially interested in helping to rebuild war-torn Europe, revive the German economy, and bring its former enemy into a solid anti-Communist alliance. Through the Truman Doctrine—presented to Congress by the President on March 12, 1947—America was able to provide some $400 million in economic relief to Greece and Turkey alone when both countries were endangered by Soviet aggression. Great Britain gave economic and military aid to Greece after World War II, but its own economic crisis forced the country to withdraw all help, a void successfully filled by the Truman Doctrine, followed in 1948 by George C. Marshall's European Recovery Program (Marshall was Secretary of State).

During the summer of 1947, Dos Passos was described by a reporter for the New York *Sunday Mirror* as "one of the moving spirits of The International Rescue and Relief Committee," which had been active since 1933 in "rescuing democratic leaders who opposed Hitler and Mussolini and now had undertaken a similar task in Iron Curtain countries." Through the years Dos Passos had worked with the group (formerly known as the International Relief Association) and its kindred organization, the New World Resettlement Fund, in raising money and inspecting potential sites to help relocate refugees of the Spanish Civil War in South America and in France, but of late he had been more concerned with the need to apprise his fellow Americans of the dangers inherent in Communism and its spread to the United States. His countrymen would be more resistant to the insidious workings of Soviet entrapment at home if they understand more of how Communism operated abroad, he insisted to Sidney Fields, who interviewed him for a feature entitled "Only Human Light on the Red Blackout." As Dos Passos saw it:

> Europe's collapse is complete. Help is needed everywhere. But it's needed most by those who fled the Russians from the Baltic to the Mediterranean. . . . There's a terrible ignorance about world politics. The first need is to understand what the Russians are doing. The next is to save some of the victims. We're hampered by lack of money. What's worse, is the lack of understanding. Too little is done to help those who talk the language of democracy, our language. . . . The Nazis weren't subtle. That was an advantage. The Communists have stolen the whole vocabulary of democracy and use it as a subtle poison. They even have a tremendous operation in South America aimed at encircling us. We are the objective of everything they do. Meanwhile what we do is like trying to shore up a whole sand dune with a few thin planks. The war aimed to destroy aggression and create a peaceful world. It's given birth to a more dangerous enemy of everything America stands for. . . . We don't realize how completely we've lost the war.

In a letter to the editor of the New York *Times Book Review* on March 15, 1947, Dos Passos accused the American press of "playing into the hands of the enemy"— though sometimes inadvertently—by publishing such reviews ("far too often of late") as

Lawrence Lee's of Godfrey Blunden's *A Room on the Route.* The review was couched in such misleading terms that "even a fairly close student of the Soviet Union" would have been discouraged from reading the book and missed "one of the most important novels to appear in English in years." The reviewer had apparently had "certain illusions implanted," so that he "did not dare let himself read a true account of the underside of the Communist dictatorship." Dos Passos warned that an "invisible censorship" existed of certain books that did not adhere to the "pattern of thinking" that Kremlin enthusiasts "have learned from the subtle and diligent propaganda fostered by the Communist Party in this country." It seemed to Dos Passos that a number of newspapers were a part of an organized campaign to smother free discussion of the realities of Soviet life depicted in Blunden's book. If such fanatics for Communist dictatorship with their "Russiaphile censorship" were allowed to go unchecked, warned Dos Passos, World War III was on the way to becoming a reality.

When he mailed his letter to the editor of the New York *Times Book Review,* he was skeptical that it would be published, but when it appeared in the "Editor's Mailbag" column three weeks later, he hardly recognized it. The opening sentence had been amputated in the middle, and the next three hundred words bearing the thrust of his objections were similarly excised. Another one hundred fifty words had also been deleted, which left only an innocuous observation or two having little bearing on his purpose in writing the letter in the first place. Missing were Dos Passos' warnings against such "invisible censorship" imposed by the reviewer, his call for "a fresh review by someone who can be trusted to deliver an unbiased judgment," and every other serious objection he had to the review. To a reader of the "Editor's Mailbag," Dos Passos came off as a querulous letter writer who had "picked up a certain amount of knowledge about the Russian people during a stay in Moscow a number of years ago" and took issue with the reviewer for not agreeing with him that the book contained "moving and brilliant descriptions almost worthy of being set beside Tolstoi's great battlepieces in War and Peace." The "hatchet-job editing of Dos Passos' letter illustrated the very thing he was protesting," observed Isaac Don Levine, who had known Dos Passos since 1926 when Levine issued the call that brought Dorothy Parker, Katherine Anne Porter, Dos Passos, and dozens of other prominent Americans to Boston in support of Sacco and Vanzetti. Levine was now editor of *Plain Talk,* a periodical whose avowed purpose was to fight Marxism and Communism in whatever form it was discovered in the free world.

In a letter to Glenway Wescott on December 27, 1946, Dos Passos warned that the American Writers Association—to which they both belonged—must be "ever vigilant against the threat of Communist infiltration. . . . I've seen the trick turned again and again, in unions during the strikes in this country, in liberal or radical magazines, in the theatre, and in Spain during the Civil War." In the spring of 1947 he followed up his concern with an attack upon the American Authors Authority for being "Communist-inspired." A recent stand taken by the American Authors Authority was "basically a political maneuver" that played into the hands of the Soviets, Dos Passos insisted. "It is very much too bad so many American writers remain ignorant of or indifferent to the political movements that are shaping the world we live in. The ignorance is the main stock in trade of the fanatical Communists who do the work behind the Screen Writers

Guild and the Hollywood center of pro-Soviet propaganda." The only safety lies in "active and aggressive associations that will be ready to meet and thwart the Communist *putsch* at every level." The many non-Communist Hollywood writers must cease being "willing dupes." By this time the House Un-American Activities Committee had begun looking into Communist infiltration of the motion picture industry and the Screen Writers Guild.

Dos Passos spoke out over the air waves as well as in print during the winter of 1946–47. Although he continued to turn down invitations to lecture about his writings (or, as Reginald Cook put it in inviting him to the Breadloaf School of English, to "talk from the novelist's point of view on any phases of American cultural life or literature"), he was quick to accept Lewis Galantiere's invitation to deliver a Christmas or year's end message over Radio Free Europe to the people of Poland, Czechoslovakia, Hungary, Bulgaria, and Romania. Their Eastern European "Voices" (Voice of America) had asked explicitly for him, said Galantiere.

Another of Dos Passos' involvements that winter was spearheading a move in defense of Edmund Wilson's *Memoirs of Hecate County,* which the New York Court of Special Sessions had declared scandalous and obscene. In the process, Wilson's publisher, Doubleday, had a bestseller on its hands. Almost sixty thousand copies had been sold when John S. Sumner and the New York Society for the Suppression of Vice called for the book's removal from all bookshops in the state. Dos Passos had seen his own books banished from the Provincetown library for a time, his *U.S.A.* struck from a reading list at the University of Texas and the center of a censorship controversy during which the president himself was removed for his stand in the matter, James T. Farrell's *Studs Lonigan* trilogy expunged from a list of two hundred books approved for export to England, and now Wilson's book outlawed. Indignant over what he saw as still another injustice, Dos Passos petitioned eight prominent writers and critics to join him on an ad hoc committee in support of Wilson. "If we don't put up a fight now we are in danger of losing all the gains made for freedom of expression in writing during the last twenty years," he wrote Newton Arvin, James T. Farrell, Howard Mumford Jones, Thomas Mann, H. L. Mencken, Ben Stolberg, William York Tindall, and Lionel Trilling in urging them to work with him in an effort to help overturn the two-to-one ruling by the New York Court of Special Sessions through an appeal to the New York Appellate Court filed by Doubleday.

Dos Passos hoped that the committee would influence the Authors' League of America and "other such proud organizations" to go to Wilson's defense. The only financial responsibility of the group was the expense of printing an *amicus curiae* brief being prepared by Carl Rachlin, the attorney who had helped C. D. Williams with the legal work in getting Dos Passos' property settlement in Virginia. Rachlin, a friend of Dos Passos, offered to prepare the brief without fee. Everyone requested to serve on the committee accepted, although Mencken replied skeptically that "such schemes usually only inflame the opposition" and predicted that their "little group would be packed with Communists within two weeks. It is simply impossible to keep such vermin out of the front seats." Farrell agreed to help "because of the principles involved," but told Dos Passos that he did not fancy Wilson's book. If Dos Passos could be instrumental in getting the Authors' League of America to be of assistance where censorship was concerned, Farrell said he would hail him as "the Second Coming of Christ." Wilson did not take the stand in his own defense when the case first came up, for which Farrell faulted him, but Dos Passos replied that Wilson "had been burdened with domestic difficulties" of late and was in Reno at the time getting divorced from Mary McCarthy. When Wilson returned to the Cape soon afterward with still another wife (Elena Mumm Thornton of the Mumm champagne family) and seemed to be enjoying financial freedom for the first time in years, Katy gave him a new nickname. The Christmas season on the Cape had been "unusually brilliant," climaxed by a "great banquet given to welcome back the Bard of Money Hill from Reno with his fair bride," she reported to Henka Farnsworth in a letter of January 5, 1947.

When Houghton Mifflin asked Dos Passos to write a few words for a publicity brochure to accompany a new edition of *U.S.A.* to be released in December 1946, he acknowledged in retrospect that it looked as though what he had really been doing was "trying to defend the Old Seventy-Six." The American Republic had been endangered by "extended Capital" when he wrote the trilogy, but now the foe was "extended Communism," he explained. Dos Passos' editor wanted to capitalize on all this free publicity by bringing out a new edition of *U.S.A.* while the issue of censorship and the recent controversy at the University of Texas were still fresh in readers' minds. At Dos Passos' suggestion, the publishing house contracted Reginald Marsh, whom he admired for his drawings and paintings of contemporary life in New York City and on Coney Island, and for his renderings of burlesque and vaudeville. Dos Passos wanted Marsh given free rein to illustrate *U.S.A.* as he saw fit. Marsh read the book straight through, then read it again, the second time noting the scenes and situations he chose to depict. In a month's time Marsh had produced over five hundred India ink drawings without preliminary sketches, and the new, three-volume boxed edition was in the bookstores in time for Christmas sales.

U.S.A. received considerably less critical attention in its current edition than when the trilogy first appeared, but those who did review it agreed that it was still "one of the greatest of modern American fictional classics" and wrote appreciatively of Marsh's drawings. James Gray's review in the Chicago *Daily News* noted that the "acid of Marsh's irony" matched Dos Passos' own. "It eats into every line, showing that the pageant of the 'boom' years which was supposed to be notable for its brilliance and exuberance was actually one of terrible disintegration and decay. . . . A re-reading of *U.S.A.* does more than increase one's admiration for the author as prophet of doom; it increases one's admiration for him as an artist." Other critics commented on the trilogy's being "in a peculiarly vivid and exciting sense" a portrait of the country. Malcolm Cowley's front-page essay in the New York *Times Book Review* termed Dos Passos' book "the most important and best of the many American novels written in the naturalistic tradition," but made no mention of the author's once being hailed for his "revolutionary vision" or for his role as the leading proletariat writer of the previous decade. Cowley was not happy with what he saw as Dos Passos' attempt to turn up a Communist under every bush or with the direction in which Dos Passos' new conservatism was leading him.

A number of people sought out Dos Passos personally and wrote to him or to

Reginald Marsh of their pleasure in reading the new edition of *U.S.A.*, but Ernest Hemingway was not one of them. His own opinion upon leafing through the book several months after its publication was expressed in a note to Maxwell Perkins: "The Marsh things in Dos's books are absolutely atrocious. . . . I am not surprised Dos's book didn't sell. None of the separate parts did." Hemingway had no concrete information regarding how the new edition was selling, but he remembered Dos Passos' several requests to borrow money when the individual volumes were published, and his animosity for Dos Passos now knew no bounds. Most of Hemingway's attacks were delivered as snide remarks out of Dos Passos' earshot, such as his comment to Perkins that Dos Passos' decline as a writer ran a parallel course to his "increasing dishonesty about money and other things." Hemingway's targets now included Katy and Edmund Wilson. Both men were dishonest, maintained Hemingway, because they allowed themselves to be dominated by women. Wilson's criticism suffered from a "moral decay" comparable to Dos Passos' decline, Hemingway told Perkins, since he was angry at Wilson for having written about him in *The Wound and the Bow: Seven Studies in Literature,* under contract originally with Scribner's, which refused to publish the book unless Wilson withdrew the Hemingway essay. According to a letter from Wilson to Perkins after the book was taken over by Houghton Mifflin: "Hemingway has been raising holy hell about my book. . . . I made only a couple of slight changes in what the lawyer was able to show were misstatements of fact." According to Wilson, Perkins was "afraid of publishing anything about Hemingway, no matter how appreciative, because he carries on like a madman about everything that is written about him."

Dos Passos inadvertently antagonized Hemingway during the summer of 1947, which caused his former friend to lash out at him again. Hemingway became livid when he read in an Associated Press story that William Faulkner had named him *last* in a ranking of "best contemporary writers." Dos Passos, Wolfe, Caldwell, and Faulkner himself had been rated ahead of Hemingway. In an attempt to placate Hemingway, who wrote him an irate letter, Faulkner replied that he had ranked his fellow writers on the basis of "their splendid failure to do the impossible." He had rated Hemingway last because "he stayed with what he knew. He did it fine, but he didn't try for the impossible." Faulkner ranked Wolfe first for having made the most admirable attempt. To refute what he interpreted as a put-down of his courage by Faulkner, Hemingway solicited a statement from General Charles T. Lanham—under whom he had served as a war correspondent on the European front—attesting to his "courage under fire." Still angry, Hemingway submitted to Faulkner his own curious and bizarre assessment of Dos Passos:

> I know what you mean about T. Wolfe and Dos and still can't agree. . . . Dos I always liked and respected and thought was a 2nd rate writer on account of no ear. 2nd rate boxer has no left hand, same as ear to writer, and so gets his brains knocked out and this happened to Dos with every book. Also terrible snob (on acct. of being a bastard) (which I would welcome) and very worried about his negro blood when could have been our best negro writer if would have just been negro as hope <u>we</u> would have.

Dos Passos was in England with Katy when Hemingway and Faulkner parried regarding his rightful place among contemporary American writers. If he was even aware of Faulkner's ranking or of Hemingway's response and accusations, he made no reference to it, nor did Faulkner ever back down on his assessment of either Dos Passos or Hemingway. The rumor that Dos Passos had Negro blood—spread by Hemingway and repeated from time to time by his minions and others who jumped catlike on a morsel of gossip and shook it to death—surfaced even after Dos Passos himself was dead. "Is it true that John Dos Passos' mother was a mulattress?" asked a distant relative of Dos Passos living in Ponta do Sol, in Madeira, Portugal, where his paternal grandfather had been born. An aged aunt of Cyril dos Passos—Dos Passos' cousin—had heard the rumor in the late 1970s that Lucy Sprigg Madison Dos Passos, reportedly of genteel, British/Irish ancestry, was in reality of mixed Caucasian and Negro blood.

Dos Passos was on another assignment for *Life* when he and Katy flew to London on July 15, 1947, to see how Great Britain was faring under the leadership of Clement Attlee, who had unseated Churchill and his Conservative government immediately after the war and was now Prime Minister and head of the British Labour party. When Dos Passos had been in England in 1941 to do a piece for *Harper's Magazine*—"England in the Great Lull"—he commented that the country had been forced to meet "the greatest danger in its history under a government that is short of brains." He was bent now on determining if the British people were aided in their postwar recovery by more intelligent leadership.

For four weeks Dos Passos motored over the countryside in a tiny British car furnished by *Life* (driven usually by Katy) and talked with hundreds of Britons of all economic levels about the state of their nation since the British Labour party came to power. From the industrial centers of the Midlands to the banks of the broad Severn below the Avon and across to southern Wales, he sought out workers and management in coal mines, sheep and dairy farms, factories, small manufacturing companies, shops, pubs, and restaurants in much the same way he had investigated conditions in the industrial Midwest of his own country for his *Life* article "Where Do We Go from Here?"

The basic problem in England was a lack of production, discovered Dos Passos, or as a newspaperman in a mining area put it: "The politicians told them that socialism means paradise and now they are quietly waiting for paradise. . . . We're not getting production because they the working class haven't got a brain in their heads." It seemed to Dos Passos that it was the government who was short of brains, since the government was the working class. The election of the British Labour party was "a revolution that had gone nowhere" and the people were strangling themselves in a "morass of poverty and ineptitude." A manufacturer of snaps and catches for ammunition boxes illustrated the problem of the country's "planned economy" as it affected him: "For seven months we've been corresponding with the Board of Trade for fifty-seven yards of silk and we don't know yet whether we can have it or not. Maybe you've been thinking that the troubles of one little firm turning out a fairly unimportant item aren't important, but multiply these cases by thousands and you'll understand how British economy is being strangled." Civil service employees without any training in industrial production were making the decisions at the Board of Trade and imposing restrictions that penalized production at every turn.

Dos Passos observed repeatedly the validity of Bernard Baruch's remark that "socialism might not succeed in distributing wealth but would certainly distribute poverty." The workers had the "whip hand," explained one employer. "If a man walks out at a quarter to 12:00 it's no use givin' him the sack because the next one'll be just as bad. They'll be no good till we get ten per cent unemployment." There was no incentive to work harder to increase one's income because that brought only higher taxes. "A man doesn't have to work for his children, the state'll take care of them. . . . If he works an extra day he loses almost half of it but if he wins on the races or a football pool he can keep it all." A young industrial worker in the Midlands admitted that it was "frustrating to feel there's no future in your job," that he would "stick it out. . . . There is something in the feeling of being an Englishman, and there's always a chance in the football pool." He had not been able to marry because he could not get a house: "They are to be had but they cost four or five thousand pounds, which is more than I can afford."

Cauliflowers cost a shilling in London, yet were being given away in the rich plain of the Vale of Evesham, Dos Passos discovered. Cabbages were being plowed under because the Minister of Agriculture had not come up with a plan to get food to the people who needed it. German prisoners of war were housed in government camps and "paid a little pocket money" in exchange for their labors on farms and in dairies. They worked better if given a hot meal at noontime, observed one farmer, who said he hated to see them sent home. He hoped that the government would bring in "some displaced persons" to take their place. A young man in London complained in "fluty Oxonian tunes" that England was "the lost island of the Atlantic, sunk in the everlasting ennui." Another criticized the British Broadcasting Corporation for feeding people propaganda that they were working for the leisure they would claim someday. "Teach them how to enjoy their work I say," he countered. At every turn Dos Passos saw evidence that the country was backsliding with dizzying speed into a "regime of misery and servitude such as had not existed in the West since the days of serfdom." Too much concentration of power was the "curse of capitalism," but socialism was not the answer either. "We've got to do better than that," he insisted in an article for *Life* a few weeks after his return home.

From Edinburgh Katy wrote Edith Shay of their strenuous schedule and of being hungry most of the time. "Nobody in the United States has any idea of what is happening here," she continued. "It's the end of free enterprise in Great Britain. . . . The more you see of the Socialist government the more frightening it is." Back in London on August 9, 1947, Katy reported that they were having tea that afternoon with Mary Heaton Vorse, her son, Joel O'Brien, and Griffin Barry. O'Brien had been in England for some time as a radio announcer for the British Broadcasting Corporation and was an enthusiastic supporter of the new government. Katy described him as "coming along. Joe is a big shot and a producer here now, has an English accent, talks on the B.B.C." It seemed to O'Brien then, as well as in retrospect some thirty years after their meeting at the Dorchester, that Dos Passos tended to exaggerate the conditions he found in England after the war: "Dos apparently came over with his mind already made up regarding the Socialist experiment, which had been underway only about a year. Whatever he saw simply reinforced what he already thought. Actually, I was appalled that anyone of Dos's intellect did not question things and weigh more fully what he was told and observed. It was as though his eyes had stopped looking and he was marching to a different drum."

Katy wrote Edith Shay on August 19: "Oh, we are coming home! We sail tomorrow from this distracted island on the Queen Mary." Her only regret in leaving London was that she would miss the publisher's party John Murray wanted to give her to mark the publication of the British edition of *The Private Adventure of Captain Shaw* to be released August 22. Dos Passos' relief to be heading home was registered in a card to Marion Cummings mailed from Southampton: "Westbound thank God." By the time the *Queen Mary* docked in New York, Katy had an article under way based on her own observations and conversations while in England which she hoped to sell to *Woman's Home Companion,* and Dos Passos' first piece for *Life,* "Britain's Dim Democracy," was almost finished. He wanted to spend more time on his second article contracted, which he intended to be a comprehensive polemic on socialism and Communism as betrayals of the "hopes for the better life they once inspired."

Once home, Dos Passos was impatient to take Katy to the farm in Virginia to get acquainted with their growing herd of Black Angus cattle and to begin learning firsthand something of what it took to be a farmer. In England they had liked visiting the old cattle and market town of Aylesbury (near Oxford) and talking with the farmers and drovers, who had fine-looking cattle despite the obvious grain shortages. It was only in talking with the cattle and sheep farmers in England and southern Wales that they perceived any sense of solidity about the country. Katy said that visiting the English farms had given her a "feeling of romantic confidence in the country," which collapsed rapidly once they moved into the industrial section of the Midlands. She, too, looked forward to settling in on the farm, but wanted to finish the new novel on which she had been working with Edith Shay. Half of "No More the Bugle" had already been sent to Houghton Mifflin before Katy left for England. Dos Passos was eager to get *The Grand Design* to Lovell Thompson before the end of the year, since rumor had it that he would be leaving Houghton Mifflin in a few weeks. Dos Passos wanted Thompson there to supervise its promotion to good advantage.

He and Katy had planned to close the house in Provincetown and go to Virginia for the winter, but decided instead to make only a temporary visit to the farm in September, then return to the Cape to finish some projects there before moving to the farm in the early spring on a more permanent basis. Several of their friends on the lower Cape gave small dinner parties for them upon their return from England. "We never knew how long Katy and Dos would stay put so there was always a flurry to welcome them home," said Henka Farnsworth, who invited them to dinner on September 12, 1947. Katy telephoned that morning, however, saying: "Oh Henka, dear, Dos's publisher says he has to be in the city tomorrow, so we will have to postpone our dinner with you and Jerry. Dos said we must leave this afternoon. Then we'll go to Virginia for a few days."

It was midafternoon before they got away, having stopped first at Adelaide and Charles Walker's home in Wellfleet for a few minutes, then on to say good-bye to Edith and Frank Shay. Shay entertained them with a few of the songs he had been collecting for his new book, *American Sea Songs & Chanteys from the Days of Iron Men and Wooden Ships,* an expanded version of *Iron Men and Wooden Ships: Deep Sea Chanties,* then Dos Passos picked up his hat and said that they had to hurry along in order to make by nightfall their favorite inn, The Bee and Thistle, in Old Lyme, Connecticut. "Drive carefully," sang out Edith as Dos Passos steered their gray Chevrolet roadster down the driveway and headed for the Cape Cod highway.

A few minutes after 6 P.M., Shay answered the telephone, listened briefly, then turned to his wife, his face ashen. "It's Dos," said Shay, handing Edith the phone. "Look, Edie . . . Katy's dead," Dos Passos stammered. He was calling from a roadside booth beside Suddard's Garage on Highway 28, just off Elm Street near the town limits of Wareham, Massachusetts, only a few miles beyond Buzzards Bay. Dazed and bleeding about the face, Dos Passos cupped his right eye with his hand as it dangled from its socket. The car horn's blare had roused him from unconsciousness only moments earlier when he peered through his broken glasses and groped for Katy, who had been asleep on his shoulder. He found her sprawled across the shattered windshield, the top of her head practically sliced off, as though with a scalpel. Dos Passos knew at a glance that death had been swift and merciful. The car was telescoped into the rear end of a parked cranberry truck. Police were removing Katy's body from the car when Dos Passos brushed aside questions and solicitous onlookers and made his way to the telephone, thinking only of letting Edith Shay know the horrible truth from him before hearing of it on the news. After talking with Edith, he accompanied his wife's body to Tobey Hospital in Wareham, where a doctor declared her dead on arrival (her skull had been fractured and her brain lacerated). Dos Passos asked to be taken to the Massachusetts Eye and Ear Infirmary in Boston so that he could be treated by Dr. Abraham Pollen, a staff surgeon Katy knew and had once recommended to him.

While receiving first aid at the hospital in Wareham, Dos Passos was able to talk with the police about the accident. No, he had not fallen asleep at the wheel, he insisted. Katy had asked if he was sleepy and had volunteered to drive, but he assured her that he felt fine and was enjoying driving. His speed was moderate when he approached Wareham, rounded two curves, then still another before heading due west down a slight hill. Suddenly a blinding setting sun dropped as though it sat upon the road in front of him. It hovered at eye level, a brilliant fiery ball obscuring everything in his field of vision, even the highway itself, and he had had no time even to brake or swerve when the truck loomed up before them. His face and head took the impact, but the wheel had kept him from sailing through the windshield as Katy had done. Then he blacked out until awakened by the incessant blowing of the horn and discovered Katy's body.

Before leaving for Boston by ambulance, Dos Passos learned that the truck driver and his helper, both of whom were in the cab when struck, suffered head and leg lacerations, but were not severely injured, although the helper was thrown from their vehicle and almost run over when it rolled from the impact. They, too, were rushed to Tobey Hospital for emergency treatment and questioned by the police. According to the police report, neither driver was charged with the accident. The truck had been pulled sufficiently off the highway so that under normal driving conditions it should have posed no hazard to approaching motorists. Dos Passos was not held accountable either. Rather, the accident was attributed to "conditions beyond the driver's control."

News of Katy's death spread rapidly over the lower Cape and throughout New York and New England. Frank Shay called Adelaide and Charles Walker, who had just sat down to dinner, then turned to comfort his wife. Edith was devastated, but remembered

Dos Passos' parting words to her over the phone: "Edie, we must be brave." He had said it quite sternly, aware that Katy had been the love of Edith's life since their early childhood in upper Michigan. He was sure that Edith's sense of loss would know little bounds. He also asked her to call Katy's brother, Bill, and to request Bill to inform Y. K. Smith, Katy's other brother. Edith managed to hold herself together while talking with Bill, then collapsed in tears. "Oh, I had such a dreadful premonition that something terrible was going to happen, but I didn't know what," she told Mary Hackett a few days later.

Radio stations in the area interrupted their regular programs that evening to announce that writer John Dos Passos had been seriously injured in an automobile wreck in which his wife was killed. At 1 A.M. C. D. Williams was awakened by a neighbor who said that he had just heard the news. Williams and his wife, Virginia, were expecting Dos Passos and Katy to arrive at their weekend retreat in Norfolk, Connecticut, in only a few hours. They were to have spent a night with the Williamses before leaving for Virginia. Dos Passos sent them a telegram from the infirmary in Boston early the next morning, saying, CAN'T MAKE IT YOU KNOW WHY. Horsley Gantt, who was anticipating Dos Passos and Katy's arrival in Baltimore a day or two later, also received a wire from Boston. "My son Andy and I rushed right up to his bedside and found him to be just as I expected—a person in shock. Dos was withdrawn and depressed for a long time, and I worried greatly about him," recalled Gantt. "Dos had gone into surgery a few minutes after midnight, Dr. Pollen having determined almost at once that he would be unable to repair his severely damaged right eye. To remove the eye required a four-hour operation."

Friends began to appear in ones and twos at Dos Passos' bedside. Eben Given arrived just before Gantt and was surprised to find him awake, his head swathed in bandages and only his left eye visible through a tiny slot. "Dos, I hate to bring this up," said Given after sitting quietly by his bed for several moments, "but we must make arrangements for Katy's burial."

Dos Passos peered at his friend, then replied softly: "Oh, I had forgotten all about that."

Given urged him to let Katy be buried in the Given family plot at the Snow Cemetery in Truro not far from Given's home. "We have a large lot and it's such a lovely spot high on the hill overlooking both the bay and the ocean. There's no place quite like it on the Cape. I am sure that would please Katy." Dos Passos nodded in agreement, relieved that the problem had been raised and resolved in only a few seconds. "Phyllis said to tell you that she and Henka and Edie and some of the others will handle every detail— you must not worry about a thing."

When Charles Walker and Edmund Wilson came to visit a few hours later, Dos Passos asked them to stop in Wareham to pick up Katy's personal effects. Walker returned to his home that afternoon with Katy's blood-stained purse and coat and put them in his living room closet. "Mercifully, Dos never saw them or even asked about them," said Adelaide Walker. "It was as though they never existed. Then one day, Charles quietly disposed of them and words were never spoken."

Katy's brother Bill and his wife, Marion, arrived late in the evening on September 14 at the hospital in Boston to see Dos Passos before taking the morning steamer across to Provincetown to the funeral. "We were impressed that Dos was wide awake and sitting up in bed with a book held close to his bandaged face learning how to read with his one good eye," said Marion Smith.

On September 15, hundreds of mourners gathered quietly in the living room of Katy's home in Provincetown—or stood in the yard and on the sun porch because they could not get inside the door—while the Reverend William L. Bailey of the Church of St. Mary of the Harbor fittingly eulogized her. At the conclusion of the service, many of her friends filed past the shallow gray closed casket that stood before the fireplace amid wreaths, sprays, and baskets of roses, mums, carnations, snapdragons, lilies of the valley— each arrangement white because Katy was partial to white flowers—and bid her good-bye. Eben Given, Charles Walker, Edmund Wilson, John Foster, and John Worthington bore her casket up the steep hillside beyond the old, white-framed Methodist church of Truro. Frank Shay had wanted to be a pallbearer, too, but decided that he was needed more by Edith, who, he feared, might collapse if he did not walk at her side. Dos Passos—still in the hospital—was in no condition himself to attempt to go to the funeral.

In early October, Jo Hawthorne—Charles Hawthorne's son and an old friend— wrote Dos Passos that he had "put off writing," but to no avail. "It is still no easier to find words. If the service had been held where a piano was available, I would have asked if I might play, which would have said what I wanted far better than this."

Edmund Wilson reported that he had never seen the people of the region so stunned by anything as by Katy's death. Then he spoke of his thoughts at her interment:

> It was a relief to get to the cemetery, which looked so light, clean and dry and yet human up there among the old four-square churches and from which the view was incredibly lovely. The horrible weather we had been having, which seemed to have some connection with what had happened, cleared up and showed the bay all silver in the four o'clock light and the bright waterway winding in between the sands and the marshes. I thought about what the water had meant to us all, and afterwards it took me back as nothing had ever done in all my life on the Cape, and though I have always, by a reflex action, tried to disassociate myself in my own mind, from the rest of the community up here, I had to see that I was part of a local group a good deal more than I had realized or had wanted to be—since it was already a whole life that I had lived here, now going back through many phases for all of twenty-five years—and that Katy had been from a phase now far past yet somehow at the center of it as a principal of imagination and intelligence and beauty and charm—so that her death and the little hilltop cemetery seemed to give the whole thing a kind of dignity such as I did not ordinarily grant it. Everybody seemed much older, both from strain and from losing Katy, who had always remained so young. . . . The worst thing is that really clever and sensitive women are very hard to replace, and that, once you are over forty, you find that you can't bear the idea of living in the country or traveling with even attractive and amiable ones of the kind that you can't really talk to. Katy must have been a wonderful companion—I had the impression that you were never bored with her, and that—rather shy with most other people—she must have been inexhaustibly entertaining with you and inexhaustible in her gift of investing life with something that the statistics don't add up to but that is one of the only reasons why one would like to see life continue on this planet.

Wilson said, too, that he knew something of what Dos Passos was going through because of his own experience after his second wife (Margaret Canby) was killed. "I can't say anything conventionally consoling, because I know how demoralizing it is. But I can tell you that you will get over it and get over the morbid feelings of guilt connected with it— though I never did quite till I remarried, when, in spite of my difficulties with Mary, I began to function normally again."

Friends came often to visit Dos Passos during his ten days at the Massachusetts Eye and Ear Infirmary. Gerald and Sara Murphy, Lloyd and Marion Lowndes, Archibald and Ada MacLeish, C. D. and Virginia Williams, E. E. and Marion Cummings, John P. Marquand, Robert Lowell, Stewart Mitchell, Rumsey Marvin, Dawn Powell, Adelaide Lawson Gaylor, Charles Mayo, and countless others offered condolences, cheered him as best they could, and extended invitations to stay with them when he got out of the hospital and until he decided where he wanted to make his headquarters. Although his and Katy's friends on the Cape hoped that he would return to Provincetown to live, those who knew him best believed that the vivid memories there were far too fresh and painful for him to want to stay there for more than a few days at a time.

Two days after the funeral, Dos Passos began to answer the notes, letters, and telegrams that had poured in. One of his first letters was to Edith Shay. He told her he did not know whether to close the house in Provincetown for the time being and "camp out with various friends" or to go directly to Virginia. "Maybe you'll help me go over Katy's things. . . . Strange what a labor it seems to write a letter even." Everyone who knew Dos Passos believed that only work could save him from his abject grief. To Robert Hillyer he wrote: "This is so much the worst thing that's ever happened to me that it's hard not to just sit in a chair and snivel. Fortunately I have a great deal of work on hand and the good old sheriff right around the corner, so I have to stir my stumps."

Dawn Powell, who wrote that he was constantly in her thoughts, offered two factors she had found "to be glad about": one, that "you are a writer so that agony is of service to you, cruel as our work is; and the other, that you have physical pain to dull the unbearable other kind. I am glad you aren't rich so you can concentrate on some hard-iron thing like making money." It was physical pain and the need of money that had saved her "from going crazy," she allowed.

Dos Passos assured friends that his eye injury was "nothing compared to the other loss." Some thought that his physical impairment was essential to his psychic recovery. Before leaving the hospital Dos Passos was even able to joke with Robert Hillyer about his "wonderful little hunchback physician" who was preparing him a new eye "wired for sound and equipped with radar and a monocle."

Phyllis Given picked up Dos Passos at the home of Robert Lowell in Cambridge on September 26 to drive him to the Cape. "Dos came out, shaken and tear-stained, took one look at the car, and backed away startled," said Eben Given.

> Our pale grey Chevy convertible was just like the one Katy had been killed in. It was a terrible moment for Dos. Then he got in and Phyllis drove him down to our house in Truro, where he stayed. Phyllis wanted to drive him to the cemetery because it was quite a walk from our place, but he insisted on walking and finding it by himself. It was a rigorous climb and Dos was far from having his strength back, but it was something he had to do. He stayed up there for quite a while, and when he got back to the house he said, "I want to get a blue slate stone for her grave."

Charles Mayo, a Provincetown friend who had called Dos Passos in the hospital just before he checked out, said: "Dos, I want you to know my boat is yours if you'll just let me take you out in it for a day." The day after Dos Passos visited Katy's grave, he went to sea with Mayo and his father.

> Everywhere Dos looked, he was reminded of Katy—the harbor, the lighthouse, the beach they had walked, the dunes, the weir traps, the smell of the sea. We dragged rigs, but Dos's arm was still in a splint so he couldn't really fish. He had a patch on his eye still. We left the boat and came ashore in a dory after being out for several hours. We didn't talk much, but as my father and I walked behind him away from the water, I was deeply impressed. There was something about the way Dos carried himself and the way he looked at me that made me know he would leave the Cape and never return to live among us. It was a sad realization.

Mayo drove to the scene of the accident the day after Katy was killed to reenact it in a sense and to confirm the sun's blinding rays. "If that truck had been there when I was coming along, I would have hit it, too," he reported later.

Dos Passos made two trips back to Provincetown a month later. His mission there on October 19 was to meet the owner of a monuments and gravestone company from West Yarmouth, who took him first to see the tablets on the graves of John and Priscilla Alden in the old Myles Standish Cemetery in Duxbury, which his firm had placed there. Dos Passos saw the blue slate stone he wanted and handed his guide a slip of paper bearing the inscription:

KATHARINE SMITH
BELOVED WIFE OF JOHN DOS PASSOS
1894–1947

After leaving the Cape, Dos Passos was driven to the farm in Virginia by Lloyd and Marion Lowndes and stayed for a week in the home of Walter Griffith, who tended his Black Angus cattle and lived with his wife, Nora, in Warsaw. Edith Shay wrote him there to ask if he thought he might eventually return to the Cape to live. "If I tried to avoid all the places I'd been happy with Katy, I'd have to get off the earth because there's nothing lovely in life that doesn't make me think of her. But I'm not going to try to live there for the present," he replied. To Adelaide and Charles Walker he said that fall that "the saddest time of sorrow was remembering happy times, and with Katy there were so many happy times."

He talked with Edith Shay before leaving Provincetown about the article Katy had been working on based on her observations in England and asked if Edith would like to try to finish it for Katy. From Gerald and Sara Murphy's apartment in New York that fall, he wrote: "Edie dear, . . . have you managed to get to those notes of Katy's? Don't do it if it seems too hard, but if you could manage it I'll be delighted to go over the result before you send it off." He also asked her to "think a little about who would have letters of Katy's. I'd love to collect copies of as many as people can find."

Edith had little heart to work on Katy's article and finally gave up on it in despair, but she did begin writing to some of Katy's friends to see if they would send any letters they had saved of hers to Dos Passos. He, too, in writing to thank their friends for expressions of sympathy or for flowers, asked for Katy's letters. Dr. Walter Smith, an aged friend of Katy's father (in whose household Smith lived when Katy was born), replied to a note from Dos Passos that he had no letters, but offered reminiscences instead. He said he had known and loved Katy all her life. "She was a wonderful personality, inheriting much of her father's brainpower and her mother's sweetness and charm. What a companion she must have been for you!" Dos Passos was not surprised when Miller told him that Katy's father had called her at birth his "deep-sea pearl." Canby Chambers replied to Dos Passos' letter with a recollection of their first meeting when she visited him in the American Hospital in Neuilly outside Paris. "Katy brought me pussy willows. . . . The partition between me and earth still seemed so thin then that I was made uncomfortable by more flamboyant flowers, such as lilies or gladioli. These were just right, like so many things about Katy. . . . I still think of her as being more like pussy willows in the Paris springtime than a burst of gladioli."

Dos Passos cherished each letter and reminiscence he collected as though it were a means of defying death and bringing bits and pieces of Katy back to him. He knew that he would want to write about Katy someday—fictionally at least—when he was better able to handle it. Edith Shay seemed less able to cope without Katy than he. She wrote him on October 28:

> Dos, I can't write that I hope you are finding things easier to bear. I know you're not because I am not—really they get harder all the time. I can't help feeling impatience with or kind of cut off from the people who keep telling me that time heals. . . . I don't think people ever get over such a loss, but I do try to believe that, with time, accretions of urgent activities and interests can distract their minds from their grief for periods of time so that they don't continually think about and feel it. . . . I never forget, dear Dos, how on that terrible afternoon, in great agony of body and mind, you said to me, really quite sternly, "Edie, we must be brave." I'm not very, but I try.

In November Edith wrote Dos Passos that she was "floundering terribly" in her efforts to get back to work, which she knew she needed most if she was to recover from her depression, and lamented that she did not have "a really tough index to do, something like The Ground We Stand On. . . . It might kind of toll me back into something more like creative effort." She offered to type for Dos Passos or to do anything for him she could as a means of staying busy. In early December he sent her the manuscript of "The Failure of Marxism," a long article he had recently completed for *Life,* and began referring to her in his letters as "Miss Foley," his private secretary. He addressed her as Edith for their personal exchanges, but shifted to "Miss Foley" when he spoke of the check he was enclosing for her typing services, although she protested that he did not need to pay her.

Christmas was a difficult time for Edith as well as for Dos Passos, who had written her a consoling letter acknowledging his continued abject bereavement, and in reply, Edith wrote on January 15, 1948:

> Dos, when you wrote, "If only I could get over that dreadful feeling of emptiness," it almost made me cry, for I'm afraid you never will, entirely. Nor shall I. I'm afraid I'm too old really ever to learn to live without Kate although I know I must try. I think of her every instant and

to think of her is to miss her unbearably, but she's been so constantly in my heart and mind so long, since before I can remember, I can't break the habit now. All I know to do is to hold hard to everything precious and dear that is left to me—and there is much—and try to believe that life may yet have great satisfaction in store, if never again the old kind of happiness. . . . And Dos dear, it must be consoling to you to remember all the happiness you had with her and particularly how happy she was for so many years. She was always so restless and ambitious and demanding in what she expected of life and particularly of people that when we were girls together I used to wonder if she'd ever find any true contentment. . . . But she certainly had it with you. Over and above your personal happiness together, she found with you everything she wanted and needed most in life. It's terrible to lose that kind of happiness when you've had it, but how much worse never to have it at all. . . . And remember Dos, we've all got to die and, for Katy, it was much better for you to be the one who was left. I'm so lost without her friendship I feel scarcely alive myself most of the time, yet over and over again I thank God, really thank him, that no shadow of our shock and misery ever touched her. . . . Frank's own grief is very deep and his kindness to me and his sympathy these last months have been beyond my power to praise, but he naturally hopes, for my own sake, that I'll soon begin to look forward and not back, so I don't like even to let him know how constantly mournful I am.

According to Edith's stepdaughter, Jean Shay: "Some people on the Cape used to wonder if Edie might someday leave my father and marry Dos if he but crooked his little finger, but she would never have done that. She loved my father very much. Besides, Edie was not Dos's type."

24

At Loose Ends, 1948–49

The fact that I have so much unfinished business in the writing line is the only thing that gives life any plausibility at the moment.

Dos Passos to Robert Hillyer
13 January 1948

In addition to a heavy heart in the weeks and months after his wife's death, Dos Passos was bothered by sudden stabs of pain that seemed unrelated either to the accident or to his chronic rheumatic condition. In early October after returning to New York City from the Cape, he wrote Henry C. Marble, a Boston physician, for advice. Marble replied: "I am not surprised that you are having trouble. It is the usual thing, and often for some weeks after such an injury as you have had, to find sore spots come as if from nowhere." He prescribed rest, sunlight, massage ("without manipulation, for your shoulder"), and as much aspirin as needed for relief. On December 4, 1947, Dos Passos reported to Edith Shay: "My neuralgia or whatever that's been keeping me busy with hot water bottles and aspirin and hot pads for some weeks now is somewhat better." It was at about this time that Dr. Robert Solley, an internist and old friend who lived in Sneden's Landing, New York, suggested to Dos Passos that his physical symptoms of distress were psychological. "Dos had the most extraordinary capacity to recover from the slings and arrows," said Solley. "He accepted without question what I told him and readily gave up the symptoms." According to Solley, Dos Passos had less trouble adjusting to his artificial eye than anyone else he had known. "Dos's first eye was replaced two years later, and muscles behind the eye that had been tied at the initial removal enabled him to move the new eye, which he couldn't do before."

Dos Passo was staying in Sneden's Landing with Lloyd and Marion Lowndes when he was notified that he was one of three new members elected to the American Academy of Arts and Letters and was invited to the luncheon, annual meeting, and ceremony of induction on November 25, 1947. Lifetime membership in the august body was restricted to fifty persons outstanding in the arts, music, and literature. Elected with him were Mahonri M. Young, a sculptor, painter, and graphic artist, and John Taylor Arms, an etcher. Dos Passos replied that he was still "suffering from the backlash" of his accident and declined to attend, but learned later that he was assigned Chair #14, formerly held by the recently deceased Willa Cather. Van Wyck Brooks informed Dos Passos that he had been nominated by Sinclair Lewis, Edna St. Vincent Millay, Eugene O'Neill, Carl Sandburg, and Deems Taylor (Taylor was a composer, writer, and former newspaper-man).

"It's a great pleasure to have a goddaughter," observed Dos Passos in his letter to Edith Shay on December 4 from Sneden's Landing. "Life seems bearable only when I'm working or talking to small children." He and Katy were the godparents of seven-year-old Susan Lowndes, whom he saw off to school each morning and awaited in the afternoon so that they might go sledding together on the hill that led down to the Lowndeses' home. "I'm full of bruises and abrasions from borrowing the children's sleds and coasting with my goddaughter and two small dogs," he wrote Henka Farnsworth, who urged him to come to Sarasota to retreat from what Dos Passos described as "a most amazing arctic winter."

Susan Lowndes recalled:

> It was great fun having Dos with us back then. I remember answering the phone once when Dos's publisher called and saying proudly "Yes, he's here. He's my godfather!" I appreciated his not treating me like a child. For Christmas and birthdays he always brought me books—and it was never children's books. That first winter after the accident he read aloud to me all of the *Iliad* and the *Odyssey*. One time my mother came in and found him reading *Ondine* to me. I was crying and he was mopping his good eye with his handkerchief. Another book he gave me was *War and Peace* for my thirteenth birthday. "If you've already read it, read it again —I always get something new out of it," he suggested. Of course I hadn't read it yet, but I did.

Dos Passos' first long trip after the accident other than brief visits to the farm was to Coon Rapids, Iowa, in late October at the invitation of Roswell ("Bob") Garst, whom he met in 1943 during his "state of the nation" travels to the Midwest for *Life*. He had described Garst then as a "modern super farmer who considered himself a flop if he did not make fifteen dollars an acre a year." Talking with Garst and visiting his farm in the fall of 1943 had whet his own desire to be a successful farmer. He had told Katy that if Garst could do that well with his rich prairie loam, surely they could earn at least two dollars an acre on their tidewater Virginia land.

Walter Griffith, who was still managing Dos Passos' Spence's Point property and tending his Black Angus cattle, went with him to Coon Rapids. "It's wonderful here," Dos Passos wrote Edith Shay on November 5 during their second week on Garst's farm. "Nobody talks about anything but corn and hogs and steers and fertilizer and I'm finding it very educational."

By the time Dos Passos returned East, his essay for *Life*, "Revolution on the Farm"

(August 23, 1948), was well under way. The question he had raised while visiting farm after farm in Iowa and Nebraska with Garst was "What kind of things are you people who grow our food doing to keep up with the increasing needs of this country and the world?" In seeking that answer he was also formulating his reasons for the failure of Marxism in the world and drawing together what he had observed in Socialist England and what he knew of life in other countries where socialism and Communism were failing to meet the basic needs of the people. Dos Passos finished his "Failure of Marxism" article for *Life* before leaving the Garst farm. One of the things that had impressed him about Garst was that he had revolutionized the corn industry, first by the production of hybrid seed corn (which in turn opened his and other people's minds to discover how to produce hybrid pullets and hogs), and by the revolutionary improvements to all kinds of farming and the raising of livestock. Garst had developed a new means of fattening cattle by feeding them ground-up corn cobs (normally discarded) and increasing their weight by 25 percent at less cost than old methods. Everywhere Dos Passos looked he was exposed to revolutionary advances that produced higher yields in farming than ever before. He realized, too, that big-business farming did not have to be at the expense of the "little man," who could be a successful farmer with less labor, more speed, and higher efficiency than ever before, yet not lose his individuality and freedom in the process. After three weeks on the Garst farm and in the surrounding countryside, Dos Passos was eager to put his new liberal education into practice.

Although he made three trips to Spence's Point during the fall and winter of 1947–48 to check on his small herd of cattle and thought seriously about moving to Virginia, he was not ready to cut himself off from friends in the Northeast with whom he had sought refuge. He and Katy had spent a few nights at Spence's Point in the fall of 1946, but the ancient house was strewn with boxes and building materials and other belongings they had moved piecemeal with each trip. He knew that it would be some time yet before he could bring himself to deal with opening the house that he had dreamed for years of sharing with Katy. Meanwhile, looking over the cattle and inspecting the new calves, talking with Griffith about future plans to farm the property, and attending to a few details with his half brother, Louis, regarding their land division were as much as he could handle for the time being.

When John and Adelaide Marquand urged him to drop what he was doing and join them in Nassau in February, Dos Passos accepted. His new novel *(The Grand Design)* was taking much longer to complete than he had anticipated, and he lamented that it was still only about two-thirds finished. He rationalized, too, that by going to Nassau he could look for a house for Sara Murphy, who wanted a tropical retreat comparable to what she had rented in Key West. Sara was not well that winter, and Dos Passos envisioned their taking care of each other and improving their own health in the process. If he went to Nassau, however, he intended to go on to Haiti afterward to work on his novel there in the balmy weather that lured tourists from the United States and Great Britain year-round. But he did not want to go alone. "I wish Eben and Phyllis would go to Haiti—as I hate to go where I've no friends," he wrote Edith in late January. "I'm pathetically dependent on seeing friends just at present." Edith had been typing the manuscript of his novel chapter by chapter and was also doing free-lance editorial work for Houghton Mifflin. She had abandoned any thought of trying to finish alone the novel that she and Katy had worked on together. Dos Passos was relieved that Edith had pulled herself together through the narcotic of work, just as he had, but he knew that living was still difficult for her.

Dos Passos lolled for a month in the tropics and seemed relatively contented so long as he was writing or had someone with him. His letters were filled with observations of island life. After a week in Nassau, he met the Givens and their seven-year-old son, Eben Jr., in Port-au-Prince, where they were joined by three other close friends, Esther Andrews, Canby Chambers, and Dawn Powell. All stayed at the Hôtel Olaffson, which Dos Passos described as "quite funny, full of local characters and rather nice." He admitted to having a set-to one night with a large pale rat over the proprietary rights to his bedpan, but said that his visitor soon "tipped his hat and departed." Each morning Dos Passos worked on his novel, then met the others for lunch and roamed the town looking at the "funniest little houses tiny as rabbit hutches." He wrote Sara Murphy that they resembled old-fashioned valentines with "layer on layer of wooden lace and all sorts of little pinnacles and turrets." The Haitian men were always *"très* correct" and wore coats and ties if they could afford them, he said. To Henka Farnsworth he sent a postcard depicting Haitian women carrying baskets, chairs, cages, and other paraphernalia on their heads: "Wish you were here. It really is a different world. . . . Everybody walks around with chairs and everything else on their heads. Primitive is hardly the word for it. It's paleolithic."

"We had a marvelous time in Haiti, especially after Dawn Powell got there," reported Eben Given. "Dawn was darling—and much funnier always than Dorothy Parker ever imagined being. We were there over Easter, but it wasn't exactly a Christian celebration we observed. We were all fascinated by their cults and talk of voodoo and zombies. The place was seething with black people who surged in from the outlying hills like molten lava. Natives were stacked up all over like cords of firewood."

Dos Passos cut short his Haitian venture to return to Virginia in mid-March to wind up negotiations involving the property division with Louis. Dos Passos ended up with twenty-one hundred acres, which included all of the waterfront property; in the process, he mortgaged the entire spread for $21,500 to compensate Louis for taking the less valuable holdings. He was more determined now than ever before to combine writing and farming for his livelihood and way of life. Keeping his ties with the Cape, as much as he loved his friends there and the Cape itself, would only salt his still painful wounds, he reasoned. As soon as practicable, he intended to give the Provincetown house to Bill Smith. He wanted Edith Shay to have the old "Richey house"—at 569 Commercial Street —which Katy had bought in 1946 with her share of the royalties from *The Private Adventure of Captain Shaw,* and invited her and her husband to move in that winter so they would not be homebound in Wellfleet. The severe storms of snow and ice made getting down from the dunes into Provincetown virtually impossible. Katy had been the driving force in his fight to retain his paternal lands, and now that he had them he intended to carry on what they had started together. He resolved to return to the Cape as soon as possible and begin to sort through the things there that he wanted to ship to Virginia, and to give away the rest.

In the Hotel Ambos Mundos in Havana, where Dos Passos spent the night before returning to the farm, he ran into Tom Heggen, whose *Mr. Roberts* had recently opened on Broadway to rave notices and sell-out crowds. Their only other encounter had been at a Houghton Mifflin luncheon and sales meeting at the Bellevue Hotel in Boston in 1946. Heggen's novel on which his play was based and Dos Passos' *Tour of Duty* were published within a few days of each other, and each author was asked to make a few impromptu remarks about his book to help inspire the sales staff. After Heggen bumbled through his talk with embarrassment, Dos Passos took the floor with similar success. The two men commiserated with one another at the end of the session and did not meet again until Heggen spied Dos Passos by the elevator in the lobby of the Ambos Mundos.

With Heggen was Helen Parker, a tall, stunningly attractive redhead he expected to marry in a few weeks. Parker was still leery of such a commitment, but Heggen looked upon their holidays in Havana as a prehoneymoon and resented what he took to be her outrageous flirtation with Dos Passos when they had barely met. Fiercely jealous of Parker's behavior with other men, Heggen goaded her for being a "literary nymphomaniac." Parker broke with Heggen while they were still in Cuba and returned alone to New York, where she chanced upon Dos Passos again, this time at a publisher's party for Arthur Koestler, who had recently arrived from England. Intrigued by Parker, who spoke knowledgeably and admiringly of his writings—she was a former editor at *Liberty* and now a free-lance writer and book reviewer—Dos Passos invited her to join him and Edmund Wilson for lunch the next day.

In a letter to Edith Shay on April 1, 1948, he reported having seen Wilson in the city upon his return from Havana, but "did not get much conversation with him as most of his time was taken up talking to Arthur Koestler." Dos Passos did not mention that while Wilson was talking with Koestler, he was getting better acquainted with Helen Parker. Eben Given, who knew Parker from her visits to the lower Cape, where she sometimes rented a house, recalled that she was "terribly pretty and very seductive with her lovely green eyes, chestnut-red hair, and a beautiful body. Dos had never known such a woman before, and she made over him inordinately. Helen was half Dos's age and divorced. Her two young sons may have been in need of a father figure. At any rate, Dos was clearly infatuated with Helen for a time, a natural enough rebound after Katy's death—and good for him, I might add."

Dos Passos took Helen Parker out a number of times during the next few months when their paths crossed in New York City, where she kept an apartment on East Thirteenth Street near the river. "I saw their affair as Dos's rather lame attempt to recapture his lost youth," said Given. "Some of us suspected she might even tempt him into marriage. I think he did want a child—something Katy was unable to give him. He wanted to leave something behind that was a part of him besides his writings. In a sense, Helen was an exquisite straw in the wind for Dos."

Dos Passos finished correcting galley proofs for *The Grand Design* in time for its scheduled January 3, 1949, publication date, then dashed to the lower Cape to turn his and Katy's Provincetown house over to Bill and Marion Smith, to whom he had deeded it in the spring. The Smiths were coming to the Cape the first of August, and Dos Passos wanted to get his things out as soon as possible. Having to select which pieces of furniture to ship to Virginia from the house he and Katy had shared for eighteen years and going through the boxes of memorabilia and other things they had accumulated over the years, deciding what to keep and what to give away or discard, was almost more than he could bear. "I didn't know whether I was dead or alive—or care—those last few days on the Cape," Dos Passos wrote Henka Farnsworth the end of August. "I do want to get so I can go back there and see the friendly faces of my friends from time to time," he added. For now, however, he needed to turn his back on Provincetown and its painful reminders. He visited Katy's grave and saw to it that the blue slate stone he had ordered was in place and engraved as he had requested, said good-bye to his friends on the Cape, and headed for New York to set out on a three-month roving tour of South America.

Since his flight to Bogotá, Colombia, was by way of Havana, Dos Passos decided to call Ernest Hemingway to propose a meeting if he and his wife, Mary, were going to be in residence at the La Finca Vigía when he got there. "I was in the final throes of packing when John Dos Passos called from Miami to suggest he come over for a few days," Mary Hemingway wrote in her memoirs, *How It Was.* As she recalled it, her husband told Dos Passos that they were getting ready to sail to Italy, but "he came anyway, a large, subdued-seeming man in our boisterous household, and chatted to Ernest while he wrote scores of predated checks for the Finca's weekly and monthly expenses." Mary Hemingway said that she had looked forward to meeting Dos Passos, since she had been impressed by the "sharp prose" of his books, but found the man himself "disappointing as a companion. . . . If little wit crackled, at least he and Ernest managed to repair some rifts in their friendship." Dos Passos felt relatively good about their encounter, but recognized that their few hours together made for a tenuous bonding at best. He mentioned only casually to Sara Murphy in a letter before leaving Havana on September 7 that he had seen "the good old Monster" at his farewell party aboard the Polish steamship the *Jagiello* that day, and that he seemed "in splendid fettle . . . kept ordering up more giggle-water. . . . The trouble with the party was not the champagne, which was excellent, but the fact that the steamer . . . kept forgetting to leave. First it was 10:30, then 12:00 noon, and then when I had to tear myself away to go about my business, 4 p.m."

Dos Passos was going to South America to "study the competition between government by dictation and government by consent." The Communist tide was receding in Western Europe, but he was not sure what was happening in South America and proposed to *Life* that he examine the current state of affairs in such countries as Colombia, Brazil, Argentina, and Chile in much the same way that he had roved the United States for *Life* during the war, and Great Britain, West Germany, and other European countries after the war. Riots had erupted in Bogotá, Colombia, in April 1948 as a result of the murder of a popular hero, Gaitan. Mob hysteria, accompanied by widespread looting, burning, shooting, and killing, required intervention by government troops when Colombian police were powerless to quell the uprising, which many thought was Communist-inspired. It seemed to Dos Passos that "outside of Montevideo and Buenos Aires, the same malnutrition, the same misery and disease, the same frustrations and strains that produced the crazy April days in Bogotá exist in every large city in Latin America," and unless those who governed by consent could save and improve their existing institutions, Communism might gain considerably more than a toehold there. Dos Passos went first to Bogotá, where he stayed a week and likened the recent revolt to the Lord George Gordon riots in London during the eighteenth century: "There, too, you had a mass of people recently uprooted from a primitive country society, with its rigid frame of conventions and traditions, packed into city slums and set to unaccustomed tasks, crowded and confused by strange stimuli until the tension reached the breaking point." The people of Bogotá seemed ill-prepared to cope with the changes accompanying their evolvement from a provincial city formerly accessible only by muleback to a rapidly expanding metropolis without adequate direction and preparation.

In late September Dos Passos wrote Edith Shay from the Hotel Vogue in Rio de Janeiro: "I'm living here in guilty splendor in the style to which Time, Inc., seems to think I am accustomed. Find lots of pleasant people around and am terribly busy with carrying on investigations and trying to learn the dreadful little language of my paternal ancestors." William W. White, bureau chief of the Time-Life news service, and his wife, Constance, offered to take him into the rugged countryside north of the capital before he set out on his own alone. A week later he flew to Vitória in northeastern Brazil to inspect public health facilities established in the vicinity through the Rockefeller Foundation, which had dedicated itself to the elimination of malaria by eradicating the Gambian mosquito. By train, plane, and jeep, Dos Passos crisscrossed Brazil's vast hinterlands examining gem mines, iron ore deposits, roads, railway lines, water stations, and solid-waste-disposal units, and communicating as best he could in his ancestral tongue with the natives in the villages and towns that sprang up almost overnight as developers pressed into the heart of Brazil. "Brazil is enormous and poor and interesting," he wrote Claude Bowers on October 13. "I'm just finishing up an article here and shall be through the Argentine in about a month." Dos Passos was working then on his next *"Life* Reports" piece, "Pioneers in Brazil" (December 1948), which told of his trek into the new, wild state of Goiás in central Brazil, where he observed a booming new colony carved from the Amazonian jungle by an energetic and innovative road builder, Sayão Araújo, on whom he focused his article.

After a month in Brazil, Dos Passos flew to Buenos Aires, Argentina, which seemed like a different continent entirely. On October 28 he observed to Edith Shay that "after Brazil it's a surprise to find everybody here wearing shoes and looking as if they ate three meals a day." He described Buenos Aires to Sara Murphy as "a large synthetic city" where everyone looked "well fed and well shod and rather stuffy." The people wore disagreeable expressions on their faces, and "no matter how hot it is nobody is allowed to take off his jacket on the street. Even little children have to wear neckties to get into the moving picture theatres and all this is dominated by the extraordinary figures of Mr. and Mrs. Perón." He interviewed both Perón and his wife, who had roused the ire of reformists who insisted she step down as chief aide to her strong-arm husband, but Eva Perón had no intention of abandoning her influential post. "Even in a crisis she's terrific to watch," conceded Dos Passos, whose next article for *Life* was entitled "Visit to Evita" (April 11, 1949). The Peronistas made a point of asking Dos Passos not to identify the Argentine government as a dictatorship, as did Perón himself, who explained that his intent was "to build up a third force between capitalism and communism" which was neither a dictatorship nor fascism. He saw no reason to suppress the Communist party, an action Brazil had taken, because the Communists had no working-class backing and no one listened to them. The landowners and financiers who comprised the oligarchy and had survived Argentina's bloodless coup in 1943 were richer than ever before, pointed out the Peronistas, who said that Perón had spread the prosperity so that the country as a whole had benefited. "The huge German-style restaurants were full of people getting red in the face over gigantic slabs of prime beef," Dos Passos wrote Sara Murphy.

It was late November when he boarded "a funny little old narrow gauge railway" to cross the Andes into Chile. "It was like going through the Rockies and the Alps all piled up together . . . a stupendous trip," he wrote Henka Farnsworth. In Santiago he interviewed President González Videla, who had declared the Communist party illegal even though its members had been responsible for electing him. "What I am trying to do is run a constitutional government between crossfires," he explained. "Here we are trying to cope with all the economic difficulties that come from the stagnation of world trade and inflation and unemployment while the Communists shoot at us from one side and the Fascists, instigated by our friends across the Andes, shoot from the other." González Videla's chief problem was finding "constitutional means to keep the enemies of liberty from destroying the very liberty which has allowed them to become so powerful." When Dos Passos asked what could be done to remedy the acute destitution brought on by rising prices and currency inflation, he replied in an exasperated tone: "If the United States would only lead the way in democracy as she did in technology, we would all sleep much safer in our beds."

Almost everywhere Dos Passos traveled in South America he observed that the bureaucracy threatened to strangle its people just as it did in Socialist England and just as it was in danger of doing in the United States. He also saw that those who were trying to make "government by consent" work effectively voiced an exasperation with the United States similar to that expressed by the President of Chile. Dos Passos blamed his country's State Department for its "fumbling and awkward" policy when it should have been an aggressive one. He saw America's handling of its foreign policy in South America as the same sort of "botch of the peace" he had observed in Europe after the war. American prestige in South America was uncomfortably low, he concluded. One of his new Chilean acquaintances told Dos Passos: "Each time your statesmen make a mistake in Paris or London or Washington, a few more children go hungry in Valparaiso." Dos Passos also noted that whether he was talking to Peronistas, Communists, or nationalists, and whether their form of government was a dictatorship or a democracy, each group appreciated having "the Colossus of the North always at hand as a bloody shirt to draw a crowd with whenever they wanted popular support for self-service measure."

When Claude Bowers (still ambassador to Chile) urged Dos Passos to talk to influential Chileans upon his arrival in Santiago, he declined, saying: "I'm afraid I'm no good as a performing bear for the benefit of the good neighbor policy. . . . When people ask me questions I tend to blurt out what I think." By this time he had finished his essays for *Life* on Brazil and Argentina and decided to save the rest of his impressions for the book he intended to put together upon his return to the States, *The Prospect Before Us,* which he conceived as a series of "lectures" delivered by a fictional persona much like himself and similar to his narrative technique in *Tour of Duty.*

In Lima, Peru, where he stopped for a week on the return leg of his trip, Dos Passos had a chance to observe still another Latin American democracy at work. José Bustamante y Rivero had gained the presidency in 1945 in the first free election in many decades, but shortly before Dos Passos' arrival a new military coup had seated General Manuel Odría as President. By this time—after some thirteen weeks on the road and in the air—Dos Passos was less interested in Peru's politics and economics than in its museums, where "little men kept slamming doors as soon as I stuck my nose in," he complained to Henka Farnsworth in a note from Lima on December 9 after a week in the Peruvian capital. The ceramic art objects, pottery, sculpture, textiles, and incredibly crafted gold and silver workings retrieved from pre-Columbian tombs appealed to him far more than scheduling an interview with Peru's President, although he enjoyed, as usual, his conversations with the local inhabitants. He thought that a good listener was rare in Latin countries. "Fearfully worn out with investigations . . . and with the fact that I'm an early riser and people keep asking you out to dinner at 9:30, which means 11:00—and it's daylight before you get to bed," he grumbled before leaving Lima in mid-December, impatient to be home.

Dos Passos insisted that he seldom read reviews of his books and, once having finished a book, had no desire to sit around discussing it, but he did not mean that he paid no attention to the critical reception of his writings. Good reviews sold books. Bad reviews did not. Moreover, bad ones kept potential readers from buying his other books as well. Yet he was ill-prepared for the uniformly bad reviews that condemned *The Grand Design* for a variety of reasons. None of the reviewers for the major New York newspapers— Orville Prescott, John Hutchens, Maxwell Geismar, Lloyd Morris, William Lavelle—saw fit to commend the book to their readers, nor did Diana Trilling, Lionel Trilling, Granville Hicks, Irving Howe, George Miles, Vance Bourjaily, or the anonymous reviews for *Time, Newsweek, Booklist,* and the *Wisconsin Library Bulletin.* Any pleasure Dos Passos may have felt at being featured on the cover of *The Saturday Review of Literature* on January 8, 1949, faded quickly when he read Henry Morton Robinson's accompanying appraisal:

Time was, when the publication of a novel by John Dos Passos called for the lighting of bonfires on promontories. But no triumphant flare will greet the appearance of his latest work. . . . Mr. Dos Passos deserves something more constructive than mercy. . . . The weakness of *The Grand Design* proceeds not so much from the waning of . . . creative powers— though there is a marked decline here—as from the exhaustion of the genre in which he is working. . . . Mr. Dos Passos cannot, or will not, pass his probe through the skin of naturalism to discover the complex nerves of passion and motive underneath. I am disturbed by the author's evasion of dramatic conflict. . . . I get the feeling (it is purely a guess) that he began this novel long ago, laid it aside in bored desperation, then in an hour of even deeper despair, decided to go through with it. But whatever the reason, *The Grand Design* has the dated quality of a newspaper found at the bottom of a crockery barrel. . . . Man is a socioeconomic creature . . . a psychological mystery, an emotional labyrinth, and a metaphysical challenge. Unless Mr. Dos Passos accepts the challenge, enters the labyrinth, and attempts to unravel the mystery, he cannot hope to be regarded as a continuing force in American letters.

Malcolm Cowley wrote William Faulkner that he had just finished reviewing *The Grand Design* for *The New Republic*. "It is terrible. . . . There have been great novels of disillusionment, like The Possessed, but it doesn't give Dos Passos an edge as it did Dostoevsky; it leaves him flat and trite and unable to feel anything about people except sometimes a dead pity and oftener a cold disgust." *The Grand Design* was no novel, but rather "a political or religious tract in which the characters, instead of being persons, are the bare bones of arguments."

Edmund Wilson told Dos Passos in a personal letter that he considered *The Grand Design* the best of the three in the new trilogy because of the "enormously skillful" writing ("much less burdened by the naturalistic detail of which I used to complain") and for its "swift and subtle presentation of social-political processes." Its weaknesses, however, were several:

> Your characters (in your words) are becoming less and less convincing as human beings. I feel that as you get older it costs you more and more of an effort to imagine the mediocrities that you insist on writing about. Everybody connected with the New Deal was not as mediocre as that, and even in the case of ones who were, I don't think you are the person to write about them, as you haven't enough mediocrity in you to get into the spirit of the thing. I wish there were some Jeffersons, Joel Barlows, and Tom Paines in your fiction nowadays. Above all, as a brilliant conversationalist, why do you persist so in making everybody talk in clichés? Sometimes you give the impression of those writers who like to show off their mastery of the idiom of some African tribe by retailing conversations with the natives. I think, though, that part of the hostility that The Grand Design has aroused has been due to the fact that it has shocked people as blasphemy against the Great White Father [Roosevelt]. He was never any great hero of mine, and I am glad that you have shown up his inadequacies, but there was certainly more to those administrations than anybody could learn from your book.

J. M. Lalley expressed similar sentiments in his review in *The New Yorker*, which prompted Nicholas C. Spanos, a Hollywood attorney who had taken an option on the film rights to *U.S.A.*, to say that the only "fair and honest review" he had seen was *The New Yorker*'s. Spanos said that reading *The Grand Design* confirmed his opinion "of the joker who reviews for *Time*. I particularly couldn't stand his comment that you made the party members too ridiculous to be believable; what he should do is meet a few." When Edith Shay complimented him on the book and spoke of its "unfair reviews," Dos Passos replied: "If you wanted to write a letter to the Saturday Review and one to the New York Times or Tribune complaining about obvious bias, it would be useful. I'm trying to get Houghton Mifflin started on a campaign but I doubt if it will do much good." On February 14 he wrote to thank her for her letter to *The Saturday Review of Literature* and to tell her that "a good deal of rebuttal has come out to even up the critical balance." He said he had "stopped fussing about it and gone on to other things."

Significant rebuttal appeared in the February 13, 1949, issue of the New York *Times Book Review*'s columns "In and Out of Books" by Ralph Thompson and "Speaking of Books" by J. Donald Adams. Thompson pointed out that a cross section of coast-to-coast reviews—some fifty in all—revealed that 55 percent of the critics sent up "a loud chorus of boos," but that 45 percent responded with "loud, brisk applause." Thompson cited such excerpts as "thoroughly objective and memorable" (Cleveland *News*), "thoroughly meaningless and tedious" (Cleveland *Press*), "extraordinarily fine" (Atlanta *Journal*), "shows only the worst side of the picture" (Charlotte *News*), "the writing is a delight" (Washington *Star*), and "cynical and confused" (St. Louis *Star-Times*).

J. Donald Adams vindicated Dos Passos' position by pointing out that no book of late had provoked more sharply divergent reactions than *The Grand Design:*

> There can be little doubt in the mind of anyone who reads carefully and with an open mind both the conflicting reviews of *The Grand Design,* and the book itself, that the unforgivable sin which Mr. Dos Passos has committed in the eyes of those who pour vitriol upon his book is that he has parted company with the gospel according to St. Marx. He is, therefore, a "tired writer who has shot his bolt, he has become a caricaturist rather than a creator of character, he is an old fuddy-duddy who has written 440 extremely tedious and thoroughly meaningless pages." The passionate crusader has been displaced by the "cynical defender of vested interest." It is difficult to read these reviews and to believe that the reviewers are talking about the same book. The only point of agreement is that the novel offers a picture of the New Deal Washington that is for the most part critical and disillusioned in temper. . . . For vitality and vividness I will stack *The Grand Design* against any one of the three panels of *U.S.A.,* which the detractors of this book point to as the shining summit from which Dos Passos has fallen. The technique and the execution are practically identical; all that has changed is the point of view. . . . The reproach that he has abandoned characterization for caricature is one of the most disingenuous or one of the most stupid of the accusations. Dos Passos' strength has never been in the creation of character. . . . If you read *The Grand Design* without ideological blinders, you will see that all that has happened is that Dos Passos has transferred his passionate faith in a revolutionary social system to an equally passionate faith in the capacity of the well-intentioned and determined individual, in cooperation with his fellows, to create a better world. He began as an idealist, with a fundamentally romantic bias, and he still writes like one. He is not primarily a novelist, and never has been; he is a highly perceptive social reporter, with an outstanding gift for descriptive writing, as those who know his books of travel are well aware. When, in the name of common sense and fair play, are we going to learn to value writers for what they are and for what their gifts have endowed them?

Despite its bad reviews, *The Grand Design* received enough critical acclaim to allow it to seesaw for several weeks in the lower half of the New York *Times Book Review* lists of top-ten bestsellers. Its first edition of fifteen thousand copies sold out more rapidly than most of its predecessors had. The book was in its third printing within a few weeks, but its sales did not approach those of the three competitors heading the lists: Lloyd Douglas' *The Big Fishermen,* Irwin Shaw's *The Young Lions,* and Norman Mailer's *The Naked and the Dead.* By this time, Dos Passos had been out of the country for almost a month.

In a letter to Edith Shay in mid-February, Dos Passos said that after another visit to Virginia to look over the cattle, he intended "to toast the carcass for a few days in Nassau . . . with a small side trip to Havana." What he chose not to mention to Edith was that he planned to meet Helen Parker at the Hotel Ambos Mundos in Havana.

"I wouldn't have been surprised if Dos had married Helen down there," reflected Eben Given later. "They were there together for several weeks but came back separately, their brief affair apparently over. Dos never said much about what went sour, but those of us who knew he had gone off with her and read *The Great Days,* the novel he wrote next, guessed something of what the problems were."

Daphne Hellman, Helen Parker's friend in New York City, who also knew Dos Passos, recalled: "The only thing I remember her telling me about Dos was that he fussed mightily about the exact ingredients that went into his salad dressings, and this made Helen impatient. Dos was a charming man—and he never talked to me about salad dressings, so I cannot compare."

Upon his return to New York, Dos Passos invited to lunch a woman he had met through Lloyd and Marion Lowndes in the fall of 1948 before his trip to South America. He had scribbled Elizabeth Hamlin Holdridge's name, address, and telephone number on the back of an envelope mailed to him at the Hotel Ambos Mundos and sketched beside it a configuration of clouds and landscape viewed from the air. Betty Holdridge, a widow with a seven-year-old son, Christopher, had been married to Desmond Holdridge, a writer and photographer until his death in the spring of 1946 in the same automobile accident that killed Marion Lowndes' brother, Emerson ("Tim") Smith. Betty and Desmond—whom she called "Bud"—had been friends of the Lowndeses through Smith, who had gone on a sailing expedition with the Holdridges in the early 1940s.

In introducing Dos Passos to Betty, Marion Lowndes thought that they would be good for each other, since both had lost their spouses in similar fashion and were still in a state of bereavement. She also reasoned that since Betty and her seafaring husband had spent considerable time in the Caribbean and in Brazil, they would have something in common. "I knew that Betty could give Dos some 'steers' about Brazil before he went down there. I thought she might even help Dos learn a little of the native tongue of his ancestors since he said he was going to work on his Portuguese while he was in Brazil." Dos Passos and Betty realized when they saw one another at Sneden's Landing the first time that they had met in an apartment of Lloyd and Marion Lowndes in New York City over tea some years earlier. Betty teased him about his not remembering her, but he insisted he did. He could not imagine forgetting her large, expressive green eyes that twinkled fetchingly when she laughed. Betty was a tall, stately brunette who wore her long, richly textured hair in a French twist and moved with self-assurance. There was a shyness in her manner and a quiet humor that appealed to Dos Passos.

According to Marion Lowndes:

> Dos was on the road considerably during the spring of 1949 after his few weeks in Havana and on the farm in Virginia, but he kept popping in and out on us as he always did. We never thought much about his comings and goings—we were simply happy to have him with us whenever it suited him. I knew that he saw Betty Holdridge several times for lunch or dinner, but I suspected it was getting serious when just the two of us were having breakfast together one morning and Dos said rather absentmindedly, "Betty, these are delicious popovers."

Dos Passos was staying with the Lowndeses while trying to put together an extensive research project for General Mills, a commissioned assignment that took him both before and after his junket to the tropics to Chicago, Minneapolis, Duluth, Atlanta, and San Francisco. The corporation sent him to each of its regional offices and main plants and into the corn and wheat fields of the Midwest so that he might get up a series of articles for publication in their company organ, *Modern Millwheel,* for the story behind their products and how they evolved from fields to mills to grocery shelves. He was also asked to explain something of how the economy was affecting General Mills employees and the country as a whole. After his return from the West Coast in early June, Dos Passos felt a strong need to finish his work for General Mills so that he might get on with his book of reportage, *The Prospect Before Us.* Once more he put out of his mind the Thomas Jefferson book with which he had occupied himself "for too long already," he told Claude Bowers, who pressed upon him each new book about Jefferson and his confreres that caught his eye.

He had collected stacks of materials relative to his General Mills project, but "was having a difficult time making it all gel," Dos Passos admitted to Betty Holdridge over lunch after flying home from California. Betty said she had been typing since her father bought her a machine of her own when she was twelve and offered to help Dos Passos in any way she could. Many people had assisted him over the years in a variety of ways, most of all Katy, but no one had ever suggested secluding herself with him for several days and working elbow-to-elbow nonstop for twelve or more hours at a time until his project was finished, nor had he ever sought such an arrangement.

"We were a team from the beginning," observed Betty Holdridge in recounting the incident later:

I told Dos I had a four-day holiday coming up from my job in the art department at *Reader's Digest,* and he replied "Splendid!" He took a sitting room at the Fifth Avenue Hotel for us to work in and a bedroom for him to sleep in at night and rented a typewriter. We worked every day and it went well. He wrote and organized and I typed and we talked about it as we went along. I was able to recognize "practical repeats." Each night he put me on the train so that I could return home to Kiffy [Christopher], my son, and each morning I came back early and we started again. Finally we finished late the fourth day—we were both starved because we had not stopped for lunch—so we ate at a nice little restaurant; then he walked me to Grand Central to put me back on the train for Mount Kisco. In the station he asked if I'd like a beer and suggested we stop in at Jensen's Haufbrau, which had an entrance inside the station. I thought it very strange of him since we had just eaten a nice supper, but I agreed. We both sipped our beer, then he suddenly reached across the table and took my hand. "Well, is it one for all and all for one?" he asked.

Flabbergasted, I took a deep breath and squeaked, "Yes." Dos's face lit up and mine did, too, and we were quite animated for a moment. Then I looked at my watch and jumped up: "Good heavens, I've got to run!" As soon as I got on the train I got the shakes. I *knew* we could work together, but I thought of our vast differences and all the things we didn't know about each other. He was a famous writer—a man of international reputation who knew many important people—and I was a nobody. There were thirteen years between us, too. I was forty but looked much younger, and he was fifty-three and looked older. There was my son, Kiffy, whom he barely knew. I had a good job and owned my own home in Mount Kisco, having sold the little farm my husband and I had in Maryland. I knew about his farm in Virginia and that that's where he wanted to live, but I really didn't know much about farming. Of course he didn't either, for that matter. Then I thought about the things we did know about each other and what we shared: I knew we both had a fondness for travel and loved the water, and we both knew a lot about South America, and we laughed a lot about the things we did know. By the time I reached Mount Kisco I knew that I wanted very much to marry him. When I told Kiffy what I was going to do, his first reaction was "Will he tell you not to work?" I knew that what Kiffy meant was "Does this mean you'll get to stay home with me?"

Dos Passos said almost nothing of his impending marriage to anyone until a few days before the event itself. The end of July he traveled to the lower Cape to tell Edith and Frank Shay, the Givens, and several other close friends there of his decision. Then he went to Wiscasset, Maine, for a few days of quiet with Lloyd and Marion Lowndes. On July 25, 1949, Dos Passos wrote Sara Murphy: "Betty Holdridge and I are going to get married privately in a corn field and then hurry down to Spence's Point to go to work on the farming and house organization there." Dos Passos and Betty had joked about such a setting for their marriage vows. After all, they were going to be farmers, they reasoned. Actually, Betty had written Desmond Holdridge's younger brother, Lawrence, who lived with his wife, Alice, on a one-hundred-acre horse farm on Chestnut Ridge outside Towson, Maryland, that she and John Dos Passos were being married "in a very simple style ceremony with a justice of the peace, most likely." Alice Holdridge had countered with the suggestion that they come up to Ridgecrest Farm, their home in Baltimore County where Kiffy had spent considerable time with them after the death of his father. She promised to produce a minister for the ceremony, asked if she might give a small reception afterward, and volunteered to keep Kiffy while Dos Passos and Betty got things organized on the farm and took a honeymoon trip to Europe. Betty had assured Dos Passos she had no objections to combining a wedding trip to Italy with an International PEN Congress in Venice.

On Saturday, August 6, 1949, Dos Passos and Betty were married by an Episcopal minister in the dining room of the Holdridge home, a simple ceremony witnessed only by her son Kiffy, her brother, George Hamlin, George's wife, Harriet, and Lawrence and Alice Holdridge. Betty wore a deep blue suit over a white blouse with French cuffs and a rolled collar and had an orchid and rosebud corsage pinned to her lapel. Dos Passos was dressed in a dark two-button suit. Except for a handful of close friends, most people who knew Dos Passos were unaware that he had remarried until they read it in the New York City papers or in *Life* a few days later. He was identified as "a well-known novelist and playwright who made his home in Westmoreland, Virginia," and his bride was "Miss Elizabeth H. Holdridge of Mount Kisco, New York." Immediately after the wedding reception, they told Kiffy good-bye and promised to come get him soon, then set out for Spence's Point.

I have the money-grubbing struggle every year more profoundly. Tough sledding it is trying to scratch up a living out of a piece of land, but like many unpleasant things it's highly instructive. The only way you ever learn anything is getting your nose rubbed in the dirt of it. That's my fate and it's no use grousing about it.

Dos Passos to Edith Shay
1 September 1955

Book III

"MR. JACK"

SQUIRE OF SPENCE'S POINT

1949–70

ELIZABETH HAMLIN HOLDRIDGE DOS PASSOS

She was born Elizabeth Hamlin
in Brooklyn in 1909
on George Washington's birthday.
Her most famous forebear
had piped the rats out of Hamelin
and emptied the town of its children as well
or so the legend went.
William Bradford was still governor of Plymouth Plantation
when Richard and John Hamlin emigrated from England
and sought their fortunes in America,
their ancestors having crossed the channel
from French Normandy or the Rhine
unless they were among the lost of the Children's Crusade.
Elizabeth's father
George Dennison Hamlin
was born in Naples (New York)
was a doctor of medicine
worked hard invited trust made money
yet was never too tired
if a new patient jingled his bell
or summoned him into dark sleety streets
to deliver an infant
to produce a healing potion
or to advise a bereaving husband
to call for a rabbi or priest.

Elizabeth's mother
Fanny Mabel Childs

was born in Utica of English extraction
thought Protestantism a fitting supplement
to her own exemplary manner
traditional to the marrow
thought living a no-nonsense affair
wore her hair severely
treated her children accordingly
moved with a stiff back
a matriarch to her toes.
George Childs Hamlin
was six when he peered suspiciously
at his long-limbed infant sister
(Elizabeth was 5'10" when she stopped growing)
and wondered how her presence
would affect the household.
Her bold green eyes
assured him a confederate
but neither child
breached the icy silence
between their parents
knew little about being kissed and hugged
never doubted that emotions
were to be controlled
learned not to intrude
faced life stoically
knowing that some things pass.

Elizabeth graduated without distinction from Erasmus Hall
a large public high school in Brooklyn
did not want to attend a city college
chose Smith College in Northampton
wanted to know what it was like to live in the country
had enough money to hold her own
did not squander it on clothes or frills
but bought art books majored in art history
remembered some of the things the humanists at Erasmus Hall
had drummed into her
rowed with the crew on Paradise Pond
dated Amherst boys
wore her share of wrist corsages.
Elizabeth was a sophomore when her father died
when her mother's private income dried to a trickle
when she learned she would have to go to work
or have a scholarship to stay in school.

Black Friday compounded her problem
and one-fourth of her class was forced to withdraw
the end of the semester.
But Elizabeth learned to be good with a camera
worked for the Smith Press Board
sold pictures to the New York *Times*
inveigled a scholarship
stood watch duty in the dormitory
took typing at the local business college
was exhausted when she graduated.

Jobs were tough to come by in the thirties
regardless of one's skills.
A rumor that the Brooklyn Museum was losing an employee
brought her running
produced results
impressed Mama Hamlin
who liked having her daughter at home again
who resented the brash intruder
who whirled into the museum
with bags of Indian artifacts
and departed one day with "Bet" Hamlin on his arm
matching him stride for stride.
Desmond ("Bud") Holdridge
knew the tropics
as well as the wicked scar on his cheek
marking an accident at sea
as a teenaged seaman knocked overboard
in a lifeboat drill
handsome quick bright strong ingenious self-made
ordinary seaman at sixteen
licensed sea captain two decades hence
archaeologist astronomer navigator linguist photographer
author editor investigator courier adventurer par excellence.
A new life he promised her
called his first book *Escape to the Tropics.*
They slapped at mosquitoes
between "I do's" and "I will's"
to the man who commissioned roads witnessed documents enforced laws
but never before had asked a man and woman
if they took each other for "husbands and wives"
and "agreed to cooperate"
(nothing more)
his wife a witness in dressing robe and pajamas

in the dead of night on the tiny bush-covered island of St. John
pitch black save for the light from the Commissioner's window.
Pearl Harbor was still tallying its dead
when Christopher was born
("Kiffy," they called him).
Desmond was with Army Intelligence during the war
took his family to Venezuela to live
then to Mexico.
Kiffy was four when his father died
in a car crash
hardly knew him
was used to his comings and goings
had a dim recollection
of a tall man strapping him
into a seat of a plane
spoke Spanish like a native
and was taken for a foreigner
when he returned to Baltimore
where he was born.
Kiffy did not like being teased being thought different
did not like having to share his mother
with a stranger when "Mr. Jack" appeared.

25

Home at Last:
"Mr. Jack" in Virginia, 1949–59

Gentleman farmer? That's a lot of hooey! This place looked like a refugee camp when we got here.

Elizabeth Dos Passos
a recollection, 1977

Dos Passos and his bride of scarcely six hours were tired after the long afternoon drive from the horse farm outside Baltimore, where they had married, to Spence's Point in Westmoreland, Virginia, some one hundred forty miles along heavily traveled U.S. Route 301, then a two-lane road. They wanted to unpack and clean and settle into the ancient, red brick farmhouse (described by a reporter who sought them out shortly after their arrival as a "thin red pencil of a house standing almost ridiculously prim against a background of scrub pine trees, its face to the fields and its back to the Potomac and the distant Maryland shore") before returning to the home of her in-laws by her first marriage for her son, Kiffy. They also needed a little time to themselves before sailing the end of August for Italy to attend the International PEN Congress, a honeymoon of sorts. Dos Passos had warned Elizabeth (he usually called her "Betsy" or "Betty") that the house had not been lived in for many years and lacked certain modern conveniences—it did have electricity, an indoor bathroom, and good running water—but she was ill-prepared for the dusty muddle of boxes, fifteen barrels of books through which they threaded their way in the front hall as though they were crossing a mine field, and the disarray in the bedroom on the right, into which five sofas had been jammed. Stacks of books leaned precariously upon each other on the floor and chairs, opened cartons ranged like haystacks, and assorted furniture yawned from throws.

Before turning off Sandy Point Road upon the dirt lane at Southworth's Store, the little grocery/post office two miles from the house, they stopped to buy a chicken to prepare for dinner. It was too hot to cook on the old-fashioned wood-burning stove in the kitchen, and the kerosene stove upstairs smoked and reeked of fumes. Each time one of them tried to adjust it, the flame went out. They had picked up a block of ice for the icebox—there was no refrigerator—and a bottle of Old Grand-Dad saw them through the preparation of dinner. "By the time we managed to get the stove operating and that chicken cooked, we were pretty drunk," allowed Betty.

They had been married three weeks when Dos Passos found himself the guest of honor at the PEN meeting in Venice. "I knew Dos had a world reputation, but had no idea to what extent until we were mobbed in Venice," said Betty. "There were five hundred people at the conference, and each time we left a session we were followed by what seemed the entire body who wanted a few private words with Dos or simply wanted to observe him. We resorted to making a game out of eluding them. We'd slip off to an out-of-the-way corner for coffee and sit where we could watch his pursuers stream by instead of being watched ourselves." Dos Passos penned a few lines to Gerald and Sara Murphy while in Venice, saying that the city was "as usual, hard to believe, crowded with people, good food, gondolas and large silky ladies floating off every ceiling."

It was Betty's first trip to Italy. In Vicenza, forty miles from Venice, they attended a performance of Monteverdi's *L'Incoronazione di Poppea* in the great opera hall designed by Andrea Palladio, a native of the city. "Vicenza's architecture alone was worth a visit to northern Italy, and Dos had always been intrigued by Venice," said Betty, who appreciated her husband's bent for architecture.

By Thanksgiving they were back in Virginia and beginning to get settled. Dos Passos had already begun a new novel, to be known as *Chosen Country,* and as soon as it was finished he intended to resume work on Thomas Jefferson and get that book out of the way, too. Meanwhile, Betty had been on the road considerably to Mt. Kisco, New York, to get her home sold there, to dispose of some of the furnishings, and to ship the rest to Spence's Point to be crowded in among the things Dos Passos had brought from Provincetown. They also went up together to retrieve Kiffy from his aunt and uncle's home in Baltimore. In mid-November, they rejoiced when they realized Betty was pregnant. "God help us, we are going to build a wing on the house. With a little stranger we'll need more room," Dos Passos wrote Edith Shay. "To finance this folly I'm in a desperate intrigue to sell a small piece of land. . . . After June if all goes well we'll have an extra bath so that visitors won't break their necks on Kiffy's mantraps and a porch from which the problematical stranger can howl at the mockingbirds and crows without driving the grownups of the household to drink before their time (6:00 p.m. sharp)."

When Sara Murphy heard that Dos Passos was to be a father at last, she wrote: "Can't think of <u>anything</u> that would give us more rejoicing. It is just the best news in years! I cannot help hoping (although I've no idea what <u>your</u> feelings are in the matter)—that it's to be a daughter. . . . I can hardly wait!"

Dawn Powell said: "Delighted to hear of your expectations, especially since you'll be needing an extra hand with the cattle. The Sneden ladies [Sneden's Landing] have already gotten to work selecting the proper sex for it, though I thought I would look around a little bit more before voting. I hope Betty keeps well and thinks radiantly, reading poetry and gazing at beautiful objects."

Dos Passos wrote James T. Farrell to thank him for a book and added: "I've married again and settled down in a section of my father's old place—doing some part-time farming via a number of proxies. I like living in the country, and this is about as far away as you can get although it's not more than a hundred miles from Washington."

Parke Rouse, Jr., a reporter who tracked Dos Passos down that winter and requested an interview, referred to him as "Squire of Spence's Point" and said that the Northern Neck natives knew him as "Mister Pasker," the landowner, rather than as a writer. "The idea of a so-called leftist novelist coming to live in ultra-Virginia Westmoreland County might seem surprising," continued Rouse, "but in the house at Spence's Point and in the gray fields which stretch away from it, the author of *Number One* and *Adventures of a Young Man* seems as authentic a part of the landscape as the cedars that line the fields."

Parke Rouse did not discover during his brief visit to Spence's Point that to Dos Passos' friends, neighbors, and business associates on the Northern Neck, he was "Mr. Jack," a name used first by his stepson, Kiffy. Others picked it up, and before long some of the local people began calling Betty "Mrs. Jack." When Edmund and Elena Wilson came down for a weekend, they were taken aback by the "Mr. Jack" tag. According to Adelaide Walker, who experienced a similar reaction when she and her husband visited Spence's Point in 1950: "Bunny came home to the Cape and wrote a poem about 'Mr. Jack.' He said, 'You don't become *Mr. Jack* in Virginia and remain a rebel.' Bunny always thought that had Dos stayed in New York and never moved to Virginia, things might have been different for him. Bunny never stopped quarreling politically with Dos and was disappointed by his turn to the right, a swing begun much earlier, of course. Charles and I avoided political topics with Dos after his move to Virginia, but Bunny always charged right in."

Wilson and his wife arrived in a chauffeur-driven Packard he had hired for the trip from Wellfleet to Spence's Point, a visit that posed something of a dilemma to Betty. Wilson refused to be seated at the table with Mr. Peck, his driver, and Martha Weldon, a black servant, refused "to serve a proper white man in the kitchen." Betty's solution was to feed the Wilsons in the library and Peck in the dining room. "We all felt curdled before the evening was up. Bunny pitched in about something, and since he was our guest, Dos couldn't react to it as strongly as he might have if he were in a club, for instance," recalled Betty. "It was a most peculiar visit and a long weekend. Bunny had no interest in our life at Spence's Point and we could offer him no public entertainment. Dos and Bunny remained friends, but the Wilsons did not return. We confined our meetings to more neutral territory after that."

During their first winter in Virginia, Dos Passos met Bruce Massey, a young local farmer who proposed renting some of his land. Massey, who had little property of his own on which to farm, but made a fair living by contracting rich farmland from others in the area, suggested planting about five hundred acres of open land, bearing the entire cost, and giving Dos Passos 20 percent of the profits. "I didn't need that much land when we started out," said Massey. "Later I cut it to a little over three hundred, then to only a hundred. Finally we found we were most productive in harvesting from fifty to sixty acres a year. Jack had lost money on his farming operation before I took over, so whatever I proposed he generally went along with." They also went into partnership in expanding Dos Passos' herd of Black Angus cattle.

A few weeks before his marriage, Dos Passos wrote Hemingway: "I've taken up farming and find it much more fun than other ways of running into debt. You ought to see me with the Angus cattle I own jointly with a gigantic Negro cattle dealer named Lloyd Thompson. This was a farm of my father's . . . which I got back with the help of the law when other members of the family had cut off the timber and sold off the beach and otherwise despoiled and denuded it. So I go and write articles about how well they farm in Iowa, and use the proceeds for a tractor and barns." The note was one of their few communications after Katy's death. Hemingway responded in a brief letter after hearing of Dos Passos' marriage to Betty, but such exchanges led nowhere so far as their defunct friendship was concerned.

Dos Passos wrote Lloyd and Marion Lowndes, who had been their first houseguests that winter, that six bull calves had joined their herd and one cow had been lost in calving. "It gives this year no heifers—sign of war, people used to say." In the spring he reported that a new bull had started "several calves along the way." He spoke of his satisfaction, too, in having an orchard planted and a garden plowed and disked. "Spence's Point stands up well for us as a winter habitation," he added. At this point Dos Passos' health was excellent, and he had no trace of his former "rheumatics."

The first of April, Dos Passos took Betty and Kiffy to Baltimore for her lying-in. The baby was due in mid-May, but they wanted to be close to Johns Hopkins Hospital in the event that their "little stranger" put in her appearance early. It was difficult to find a suitable furnished house in the early spring because the natives preferred to stay in the city until after the steeplechases. Dos Passos and Betty wanted to be on hand for them, too. In Baltimore, the last three Saturdays of April were highlighted by the Point-to-Point Races sponsored by local landowners. The first was known as My Lady's Manor; next was the Grand National; and last, the Maryland Hunt Cup, the most renowned steeplechase in America. All were amateur races put on by two hunt clubs. In 1950 there was no admission, no grandstand, no tote board, no pari-mutuel betting, and no official purse. Dos Passos described the Baltimore races as "informal gentleman jockey affairs and lots of fun."

They had barely gotten settled in Woodbrook, a commodious home on Meadow Lane in Baltimore, where Dos Passos wrote Edith Shay they were to live in "guilty luxury" for a month, when Horsley Gantt invited them to the steeplechases. Like many others, they arrived early to select their parking so that they could view the race while partaking of a tailgate picnic at their station wagon. Maryland Hunt Cup officials claimed that more cocktails were consumed in Baltimore the last Saturday of April than on any other day of the year. Thousands of cars sought parking on a convenient hill overlooking the four-mile course in Worthington Valley where amateur gentlemen jockeys raced their thoroughbreds over rough terrain, streams, and twenty-two jumps. Gambling was rampant despite the amateur status of the races. The steeplechase season culminated in the Maryland Hunt Cup ball. "Dos was relieved when I told him that I did not care to go to the ball," said Betty. "His memories of having to dress in a tuxedo and spend long evenings at dinner with his father at Delmonico's made his knees weak all over again when he was confronted by an invitation to a formal affair."

After the races, they usually joined friends for drinks and dinner in someone's home. Through Horsley Gantt, they met Hamilton Owens, editor of the Baltimore *Sun* papers, and his wife, Olga, a professional violinist; through Owens, they became friends of Louis and Sara Azrael. Azrael, too, was an editor with the *Sun* papers. They also met Curt Richter, a neuropsychiatrist at Johns Hopkins, whose studies of biological cycles had earned him international recognition, and his wife, Leslie, a steeplechase enthusiast. All became good friends. The men were members of the Hamilton Street Club, where they met weekly for lunch and once a month for dinner, when wives were invited. Soon Dos Passos was a member, too, but he resisted invitations to be their dinner speaker until he had been in the group for some ten years. H. L. Mencken, whom Hamilton Owens had hired when Mencken was new to journalism, was also a member of the Hamilton Street Club. Dos Passos had once described Mencken as a "superannuated dodo," but when he got to know him on a more personal basis in Baltimore, he revised his estimate. Dos Passos shared Mencken's satiric eye and appreciated his ability to cut through claptrap to the heart of a matter.

Meanwhile, Betty felt well throughout her pregnancy and kept up with her active husband without difficulty. "It was usually Dos who insisted we slow down or suggested it was time to take our leave from a dinner party. When there was nothing special planned, we retired early," said Betty. They both liked the Baltimore Symphony Orchestra and chamber music performances and made such evenings out a priority.

"This is to announce the arrival of a tiny squalling leaky little character named Lucy Hamlin Dos Passos," Dos Passos informed Stewart Mitchell on May 21, 1950, when his daughter was six days old. To Mary Heaton Vorse he reported that "the little stranger who has been causing some commotion turned out to be a tiny chit of a girl named Lucy D. P. I want you to meet her." He told Sara Murphy that her godchild looked "more like the Duchess in <u>Alice in Wonderland</u> than the Duchess herself." The infant became known immediately as "Miss Lucy."

Before leaving Spence's Point for Baltimore, Dos Passos and Betty worked with a Richmond architect, F. Scott Rice, on the plans for a large two-story wing to go up on the west end of the house, but construction did not start until they returned to the Northern Neck with Kiffy and the baby. Any thoughts that the new wing would be ready in time for Lucy's christening on September 17 were abandoned, however; the workers had left the job after cutting through a brick wall on the west end of the house where the two structures were to conjoin. Dos Passos never knew if the men simply had taken a holiday or were summoned to another project. "Two weeks later they returned, but rain, dust, pollen, and insects had a field day in the meantime," said Betty, who farmed Lucy out as much as possible to Martha Weldon, who doubled as a nanny when she was not needed for house chores. Betty found it impossible to keep anything clean, including themselves. Compounding the confusion was Silly Sal, an unruly Irish water spaniel they had acquired for Kiffy. Dos Passos warned the Murphys and Lowndeses—Marion Lowndes, too, was to be a godmother—before they came for the christening that "Silly Sal jumps up, gets between your legs, chews everything in sight, steals the carpenter's tools and their lunch boxes, digs up the garden, and does everything a dog should not." Her latest exploit was eating the blueprints for the wing, he added. She also made off with peoples' shoes and ate the clothes off the line. "Sal's appetite is large and disastrous laundry-wise," announced Betty.

Another discomforting factor that summer was the heat. It was so outrageous that they might resort to dunking "the young lady barenaked in George Washington's font" instead of the customary sprinkling by the Reverend William Byrd Lee at Yeocomico Church, Dos Passos wrote the prospective godparents (local historians reported that the nation's first President had been anointed over the same font). Cooling off in the Potomac promised no relief either, said Dos Passos. "It's a poisonous chowder of jellyfish nettles." To Edith Shay, who inquired of the cattle in almost every letter, he replied: "They are hot, we are hot, and the river's a simmering poisonous stew of nettles and weeds, but there are redeeming features. Wish we could ship you some soft crabs." Despite the poor swimming in August, Dos Passos was determined to get out in the Potomac one way or another and bought a tiny sailboat. *The Nitwit* was a miserable little boat and terribly cranky," said Betty. "We rigged it like a sloop and had a devil of a time getting out in it. When people saw us hoisting the sails, they used to line up to watch." Although Betty was a veteran sailor (she had skippered with ease the twenty-two foot sloop *The Parima* with her first husband) and Dos Passos had been at home on the water in a variety of sailing craft, they found that they had about as little control over *The Nitwit* as they did over Silly Sal.

Reclaiming an ancient farmhouse from the wilderness, raising cattle and all of their fresh vegetables for the dinner table, and rearing two children—one an infant—on the banks of a choppy river that hacked away relentlessly at their land—all posed countless problems for Dos Passos and Betty during their first two years in Virginia, but they took them in good stride. Dos Passos' note to Marion Lowndes on New Year's Eve caught both the spirit and letter of their lives at Spence's Point as 1951 rounded the corner:

> You ought to see Lucy in the little red dressing gown. She wears it in the morning and looks very cute standing up in her crib in it, even if she is yelling her head off. My what lungs. . . . Christmas was rather tumultuous. Kiffy and the little Carden boys all fell down the dumb-waiter, mashing Kif's hand. Bob Carden [a neighbor and friend] and I rushed him to Dr. Griffith's. There Bob was met by the news that the field back of his house was on fire. By nightfall, however, everybody was eating rather overdone turkey. No bones broken. Fire out due to timely arrival of the new fire engine from Kinsale. God what a year we face. Here's luck and we need it.

Dos Passos and Betty considered themselves fortunate to have found each other as mates and helpmates with such similar interests and temperaments and, in the process, to have rediscovered themselves. They were comfortable together and they were happy. Their boon was that they were also in love.

Christmas houseguests at Spence's Point even before the new wing was finished were Bill and Marion Smith, who invited Dudley Poore to ride down with them. Poore was working in Washington then, as was Smith, who had recently sold the house in

Provincetown that had once been his and Katy's and was living in Arlington with his wife. In a letter to Hemingway a few days later, Smith reported:

> Marion and I X-mased among John Mutton-Fish Dos Passos on his acres, where he has amongst other things a dandy little seven-month Dos-ette. I am still no judge of such matters, but she seemed like a fine number. Some neighbors foregathered including a guy who had known "Old John R." back in the days when Dos's pa could "ride eleven miles along the river front and never get off his land." Folks down there call M-Fish Jack, which seemed odd to me, but it was fascinating to hear about old John R. He evidently was a power and a powerhouse.

To the natives of Westmoreland County on the Northern Neck who had known John R. the word "powerhouse" was as applicable to "Mr. Jack" as it ever had been to his father. "Until Jack came back here to live," said Bruce Massey, "nobody in these parts could out-pace a timber cruiser. He was a powerhouse walker. He took off like a damned race horse." A timber cruiser's job was to tell the owner how many board feet per acre were in a stand of trees by walking rapidly through the wooded area. Unlike most timber farmers, Dos Passos usually accompanied his timber cruisers. "Both Cleveland Delano and Forrest Patton cruised Jack's timber, and they were rugged walkers, but Jack exhausted them with his energy," said Massey. "When I'd come to get Jack to check something on the farm—it didn't matter whether it was a new calf, a fence that needed mending, a crop, whatever—he'd take off walking. I'd have to call Jack back, saying: 'We haven't got time for that—get in this pick-up!' " Massey said that he could not have hoped for a more energetic and caring business partner. Roswell ("Bob") Garst brought his wife and farm manager to Spence's Point in early 1951 and complimented Dos Passos and Massey on the way they were running things. "We keep pretty busy with farming and lumbering operations to haggle over," Dos Passos reported to the Murphys that winter.

His letters abounded with progress reports of his daughter's achievements during this period. "Miss Lucy is very obstreperous and weighs over eleven pounds," he announced when she was not quite eight weeks old. "Perhaps we should start feeding her whiskey to stunt her growth," he ventured three weeks later after she had gained three pounds. He kept his intimates posted, too, as each new tooth erupted.

Despite his good intentions, Dos Passos was at a loss as to how to relate to his stepson, and welcomed the attention paid him by their neighbor, Robert Carden, who played ball with his own sons and included Kiffy in many of the family's activities. Finally Dos Passos hit upon chess as a means of spending more time with the boy. After Edmund Wilson sent him a book of "helpful hints for chess beginners," Dos Passos replied: "Kiffy beats me almost every night at the slightly rudimentary game we've dreamed up. It fits in very well with the reading of a 35-cent translation of The Iliad."

Kiffy Holdridge had not been fond of school when he was living in Baltimore with his aunt and uncle, but he liked Cople School, the local public elementary school, even less. The level of work being done by his classmates fell short of what Kiffy had already achieved, and he was soon bored and a discipline problem. Dos Passos and Betty did what they could to prod him at home and also tried to help by becoming active in parent-teacher association meetings and in fund-raising to help build a gymnasium for Cople School. At one point Kiffy decided that he would rather be back on his uncle's horse farm and going to school in Baltimore than living in Virginia and vying for his mother's attention. Having to compete with his stepfather was bad enough, reasoned Kiffy, but living with a baby sister who was not a remarkable playmate and who seemed to know all the tricks of making life revolve around her was more than he cared to handle. Fluffy was no longer as entertaining as she had been as a kitten, and Silly Sal was not good for much except making off with things and never bringing them back. His interest had already waned, too, in the wooden swords, shields (his mother had covered them with upholstery sateen), and lances that protruded from all the closets, the remnants of his King Arthur phase.

For Kiffy, the time was ripe to run away from home. What better time to leave, he mused, than in the middle of his birthday party when his friends could be on hand to cover his exit. When Kiffy broached the idea to Billy Carden, Carden wanted to go with him. The party continued for almost two hours without Kiffy, who had left his birthday presents unopened and slipped off with his friend and a cache of provisions and blankets, then headed north in his canoe along the edge of the Potomac. One by one Kiffy's guests moseyed off. Betty had not missed him because the children had been playing in the yard and basement. She had been busy with her own chores and had given little thought to the children after setting up the party, knowing that Kiffy and his friends preferred to be left to their own devices. Finally, Herb Carden, Billy's younger brother, got worried, having seen the boys leave, and decided to tell Kiffy's mother. Soon a full-scale search was launched. Hazel Carden, Billy's mother, described the misadventure:

> Jack and Betty took off in our boat, *The Sea Ranger,* while Bob and I walked the beach. The news spread fast. Soon there were so many boats on the river to help us look that you would have thought it was the Spanish Armada forming. A huge moon came up casting great shadows on the shore, but the wind came up, too, a wild northeaster, and we were frightened. I feared finding two little bodies. Around 2:00 A.M., while people were having a wake of sorts at Spence's Point, Bob and I went back out to search. The land crews were probing the brush and beating the bushes and we were above Bonums when we heard someone yell, "They're here—we've found them!" Treadwell Davis, a local minister, found them asleep in the brush. The wind had driven them back. The canoe took water and they lost their provisions so they set for shore.
>
> When Kiffy was produced to his mother and Jack—Betty had gone upstairs as though resigned to her loss—I'll never forget her calm, unruffled response: "Gee, Fella, don't ever do that again—you really had us worried." Once we knew the boys were safe, everybody called around to make sure everyone knew. It's a small community and people really cared. Bob took hold of Billy and said: "Now Son, first thing in the morning you are going with me to the home of every person who helped look for you to thank them—and to apologize." The whole incident was disturbing to Betty, not only because of Kiffy, but also because it was so disturbing to Jack. Not long after that they sent Kif off to boarding school at Gilman in Baltimore. He was only ten then. It seemed a shame to send him off so young. I think he felt hurt.

"Yes," said Kiffy in retrospect:

> I was hurt by being sent away to school. As a child I was rebellious about a lot of things, and I gave my mother and stepfather a hard time. I also had my oedipal difficulties for a while. I

was jealous of Lucy, yet I liked her at the same time. We didn't get close until she was almost grown, and now we are really good friends. I was on the wrestling team at Gilman, and she wanted me to teach her to wrestle. I did. She was strong and game and she was good. Mr. Jack never knew how to play with me, not being athletic at all. He was not a touching kind of person, not even with Lucy. He might kiss us hello and goodbye where there had been—or was to be—a long absence, but he was never a hugger. I never doubted that Mr. Jack loved me, but neither one of us expressed overtly our affection. I also had a temper that I had to learn to control. My career in the Peace Corps after I finished college lasted only two months because I hit my instructor. I was twenty-two and he was twenty-three.

Dos Passos and Edmund Wilson got along well when they exchanged opinions about what they were reading or exchanged small talk about their families or mutual friends on the Cape whom Dos Passos no longer saw unless he could talk them into coming to Spence's Point for a few days. Eben and Phyllis Given had come down shortly after Wilson's visit with Elena in the company of their chauffeur, William Peck. Knowing Wilson's tendency to goad Dos Passos regarding his political attitudes, Given asked, "How did Bunny's visit go?" Dos Passos said little, but Betty replied that she regretted not being able "to slap a dead fish in Bunny's face when he kept pushing Dos." Dos Passos wrote Wilson upon their departure: "It was great fun having you—you must come often into our benighted Neck. What were the obnoxious political opinions you refer to? I must have been far gone in my glass because I don't remember that you ever gave me a chance to emit a political opinion. . . . I hope you'll explain to me the reason for your strange animus against <u>The New Leader</u>."

Wilson usually threw up his hands at Dos Passos' various political observations and despaired of his perennial attachment for the underdog. Upon Eisenhower's nomination to head the Republican ticket in 1952 (instead of Robert Taft, whom he supported originally), Dos Passos wrote Wilson: "I too was attracted by Stevenson at first, but the more I read his speeches the better I liked Eisenhower's. I'm afraid he'll turn out a subtle bleeding heart, weak where Roosevelt was strong. If you want a continuation of the rule of Roosevelt's epigones, he's the man to vote for for Big Brother. Damn it I wish the candidates would wipe that smile off their faces. I don't see much to smile about as I look out on the world."

Earlier in the year when Archibald MacLeish informed Dos Passos that he no longer understood his politics and that he thought Taft was "an unspeakable hypocrite," Dos Passos replied:

> The reason I'm for Taft rather than Eisenhower is that I think he's a shade less likely to hurry us into 1984 any faster than we're going. Also, I think . . . he's a little more likely to prune the bureaucracy. He has an instinctive antimilitarism that I like. In my opinion the greatest immediate danger we face is a military disaster in the style of France 1940 brought on by a combination of uninstructed politics and military giantism. If we have to have a general I'd rather have MacArthur. He'd bring God in on our side and he would clean at least one clique out of the Pentagon.

MacLeish was not convinced.

Charles and Adelaide Walker visited Spence's Point over Easter in 1951 and met

Betty for the first time. "We liked her immensely and loved seeing Dos's home in Virginia," said Adelaide, who had known Dos Passos well during his most extreme leftist activities.

> Bunny had warned us that Dos had changed since he left the Cape, but it shocked us to hear him attack General George Marshall as a traitor. His condemnation stemmed from Marshall's being Truman's emissary to China after the war, when he was Secretary of Defense. Charles and I expressed straight shock because Dos's view seemed so outlandish, but he didn't back off. We wondered if he really believed what he was saying and thought maybe he was trying the idea on for size, much as he tried book titles out on Charles and Bunny from time to time to see how they set with us.

Elena Wilson thought her husband saw Dos Passos as "a politically dormant patrician." Mary McCarthy, who witnessed a considerable change in Dos Passos' political attitudes while she was married to Wilson, said: "I think Edmund's theory was that Dos's politics had to do with his repudiation of his father. Dos's father was a famous lawyer of Portuguese descent who had identified himself with Anglo-Saxon values. Dos, when young, spoke up for Latin, i.e. Spanish-Portuguese values, turning his back on his father's "Americanization." This changed gradually with Katy's influence. Dos's father had become a proponent of Anglo-Saxon unity, and Dos did, too, rejecting, as Edmund saw it, the "Portuguese" in himself. Edmund couldn't stand this sort of talk. He didn't like seeing Dos turn on himself.

Along with the farming and lumber operations, Dos Passos managed to keep his professional career in gear as a writer. Before moving to Baltimore for the birth of his daughter, Dos Passos wrote Edith Shay on March 18, 1950, that he had had "an epic struggle with the Mifflins about the new contract" for his novel, *Chosen Country,* but that all was serene at last. Another book of essays—his seventh, *The Prospect Before Us*—was due out in the fall. Dos Passos often bounced titles off Edith Shay, too, just as he did with Wilson and Walker. He asked Edith that spring: "What do you think of <u>District of Columbia</u> as a title for the Spotswood three-in-one? For awhile I tried to call it <u>Levers of Power,</u> but that began to sound sort of phony. What does the Colonel [Frank Shay] think? This is about the last chance to change it as I've been popping new titles on the muddled Mifflins about daily for the last two weeks. Since the great battle of the Bulge they've exhibited a saintlike patience."

To finance the new construction on the house in 1950, Dos Passos had agreed to provide twelve pages of text for *Life's Picture History of World War II,* some twenty thousand words in all summarizing every major aspect or development of the war. His full-page text was to be interpolated among the nine hundred to one thousand photographs, for which someone else would write extensive captions to provide additional details. If the editors were satisfied with the first two pages of text, for which he was to be paid one thousand dollars, he was to proceed with the remaining ten. Dos Passos readily accepted the offer, since six thousand dollars would cover the major expenses of the new wing.

Still in Virginia when he agreed to the proposition, a "rush job," Dos Passos requested the resource staff of Time, Inc., to mail him in Baltimore a reliable chronology of the war in chart form to affix to the wall beside his typewriter for instant reference, the diaries of Ernie Pyle, the war books of Bill Mauldin, *Into the Valley: A Skirmish of the Marines* by John Hersey, *Tarawa: The Story of a Battle* by Robert Sherrod, and *The Desert Story*, published by the Great Britain Air Ministry. Dos Passos was fortunate to have Robert Sherrod as a back-up writer and editor who was also preparing the picture text. Sherrod had spent nearly four years as a war correspondent during World War II and had access to classified records for the preparation of a history of Marine Corps aviation. Sherrod went over Dos Passos' text closely, since he had not made an intensive study of the war, despite his having seen much of it firsthand as an observer. According to Sherrod, Dos Passos completed "all twelve pages according to the contract on his own without assistance from anyone working on the text here in Washington." Sherrod said he had "tampered" only slightly with Dos Passos' copy, editing that did not offend him. "Dos Passos appreciated knowing that an authority in the field was reading it before publication so that any possible error could be caught."

Life's Picture History of World War II was published October 16, 1950, to considerable fanfare. Its first printing of 650,000 was the largest first printing in the history of book publishing, reported Arthur Tourtellot, the book's senior editor. By publication date, more than 400,000 copies had been sold. At year's end it was identified as a "run-away best seller." The stipend Dos Passos received for writing the text and the accompanying publicity derived from the book's sales and promotion served him well. He regretted that his own publisher, Houghton Mifflin, did not have the kind of promotion and sales force of the Henry Luce empire.

A headline in the New York *Herald Tribune* on October 4, 1950, declared that Dos Passos had joined Henry A. Wallace on the Soviets' black list. According to the Moscow *Literary Gazette,* they were on its list of "enemies of humanity" and condemned for being "Truman lackeys." Dos Passos was labeled a "literary gangster" who preached the "destruction of humanity with atomic weapons." The Kremlin took note, too, of a statement released by the New York *Times* that winter of Dos Passos' being named a director of a newly formed Citizens' Foreign Relations Committee, which was urging the United States government to break its diplomatic recognition of the Soviet Union and other Communist countries that aid "these usurpers in binding their victims more securely to the chains of inhuman police states." The committee urged employing the "Golden Rule" in meeting Communist subversion in the free world: "We should fight fire with fire" and "do unto others what they are doing unto us." According to the *Times* article, a number of the directors were known for having "frequently criticized United States foreign policy." Dos Passos was the sole writer of the twelve-member group, which included J. Bracken Lee, former governor of Utah (Democrat); Charles Edison, former governor of New Jersey (Democrat); Albert C. Wedemeyer, George E. Stratemeyer, and Charles A. Willoughby, all retired army generals (no mention of political affiliation); Alfred Kohlberg (identified only as a New York importer); and five Republicans of the House of Representatives: Alvin M. Bentley of Michigan, Ralph W. Gwinn of New York, Donald L. Jackson of California, Lawrence H. Smith of Wisconsin, and Wint Smith of Kansas.

In an interview for "New York Close-up" by Jinx Falkenburg and Ted McCrary, Dos

Passos was identified as a former radical who now kept to the middle of the road. He insisted again that he had spent his entire life "trying to escape classification." More and more, however, despite his tendency to shrug off labels, most of his friends and old literary acquaintances in the North interpreted his direction as archconservatism. The Falkenburg/McCrary interview in the New York *Times* was a follow-up to the publication of *The Prospect Before Us,* a collection of twenty-five of Dos Passos' war and postwar travel reports unified by his observations and interpretations as America's best-known social historian and "cracker-barrel philosopher." Although his narrative technique was criticized by a number of reviewers, the majority of the some 125 reviewers across the country liked it and thought it a significant contribution to the times. *Newsweek*'s reviewer likened his "word pictures" to the "bleached, unshadowed, unretouched, unromanticized authenticity of Mathew Brady's great Civil War photographs." *The New Republic*'s critic saw Dos Passos' uncertainties as his strengths: "Unhampered by ideological blinders or by dogma, he gropes to understand, and he believes a solution can be found, although its precise form cannot be discerned." Dos Passos' thesis was that bigness, centralization, and "being done for rather than doing" were the real enemies whether they were found in the Soviet Communist state, the British Socialist state, or the giant American corporation. The result was the same: the dwarfing and frustrating of the individual, his loss of freedom, and abject lack of interest. Dos Passos urged every citizen to ask himself hourly if what he was doing was helping to save the Republic or to hurt it.

Most of the reviewers agreed that Dos Passos had few equals as a reporter. One saw him as "an American Rebecca West," another as a "sort of super-charged Walter Lippmann, telling us the whys and wherefores of our politics and institutions" and doing it well. As Bob Sain expressed it in the Charlotte *News:* "The Dos Passos admirers who were shocked to find The Master writing for Henry Luce's *Life* shouldn't have been. The *Life* Dos Passos wrote for before is gone; the young firebrand who didn't always make sense but always made exciting reading is gone, too; now there is a middle-aged man in Virginia with some wisdom and a good journalistic eye." *Time* saw Dos Passos' position as being similar to that of the late Justice Louis D. Brandeis: "champion of the individual, implacable foe of organized Bigness." Despite the lecturer-audience exchanges' appearing to be a naive gimmick, they provided shrewd, persuasive glimpses in the thinking of the average American citizen, maintained *Time*'s reviewer. Even Granville Hicks, who had been one of his severest critics in recent years and wrote of him twice in 1950 with an overall positive assessment, concluded a long essay in *The Antioch Review* with the statement: "He goes on seeking, and who knows what he may yet find? If there are things he has lost, courage, honesty, and a fundamental generosity of spirit, he has been a true explorer in his day." Hicks told readers of *The New Leader* in a review of *The Prospect Before Us* that he found the "Mr. Lecturer" device clumsy and tiresome and disliked his "childish petulance" in his observations of the New Deal and the British Labour government, but had no quarrel with his basic assumptions. "What must be pointed out is Dos Passos' skillfulness as a reporter and his integrity as a student of the contemporary dilemma. If his stature as a novelist has diminished in recent years, his stature as a man has not." Edgar Ansel Mowrer's review in *The Saturday Review of Literature* began: "If John Dos Passos ever founds a political party he can count on me as a charter member. I do not share his enthusiasm for the sociological approach to situations but I do share his respect for facts and for freedom."

Dos Passos did not bolt the country in his customary fashion upon publication of *The Prospect Before Us,* his first book since his marriage to Betty and since his new life had begun as father, farmer, and country squire. He was in New York having lunch at the Algonquin with book critic Harry Hansen on October 15, 1950, the day before the book appeared. Hansen described him to readers of the Chicago *Sunday Tribune* as "rugged, with big strong features and graying hair—what there was of it." Then he told of Dos Passos' new enterprise as a cattle farmer on land in Virginia inherited from his father. "The farm is the real place to write," said Dos Passos, who insisted that farming was the only form of gambling he enjoyed.

At year's end Dos Passos received a clipping from the Madison (Wisconsin) *Journal* with the headline: FAULKNER VERSUS HEMINGWAY: TOP LITERARY NEWS OF 1950 WAS THE SWITCH IN POSITIONS OF THE TWO FOREMOST AMERICAN WRITERS; TWO RUNNERS-UP, DOS PASSOS AND STEINBECK, LAGGED FAR BEHIND. Critic Warren Beck based his assessment on Faulkner's *Collected Stories,* Hemingway's *Across the River and into the Trees,* Dos Passos' *The Prospect Before Us,* and Steinbeck's *Burning Bright: A Play in Story Form* (his first play). Dos Passos, too, had commented that year upon his three so-called chief competitors in a letter to Edmund Wilson. He spoke first of Wilson's own play, *The Little Blue Light.* "It sure did give me the gooseflesh—as gruesome as 1984. These days I rather tend to rate literary work by the square inches of gooseflesh it brings out on the carcass." Then he mentioned Hemingway's *Across the River and into the Trees,* which he said "brought out the goosepimples in a different way. How can a man in his senses leave such bullshit on the page? Everybody—at least speaking for myself I know I do—writes acres of bullshit but people usually cross it out. It made me wonder whether I really did get all my bullshit into the wastebasket in time." Faulkner's *Intruder in the Dust* made him feel better. "It's such a pleasure to find an American writer that passes middle age without going to pot." Steinbeck had talent as a fictionist, he continued, but "Moravia and Sartre were less uninteresting than Steinbeck." Wilson had said that Steinbeck, Moravia, and Sartre were able reporters of their day, but did not produce great literature. Dos Passos replied that he found it hard to read novels while he was trying to write one, but that he would "work at it." Most of his reading at the time was "in the direction of those Jefferson essays that have long hung fire," he added.

Wilson inquired of Dos Passos that fall if there was something "rather interesting that has been kept out of sight about Jefferson's relations with Negroes." He said he had just learned from Roi Ottley's book *Black Odyssey: The Story of the Negro in America* that Jefferson had several mulatto children. Dos Passos told him that he had not read *Black Odyssey* yet, but was open to enlightenment on the subject. "The evidence seems to point, by the way, against Jefferson's having had any mulatto children," despite his treating them almost as though they were his own. . . . The whole subject is confused by a number of forged letters, one purporting to be from T. J. to G. Washington inviting him to come and see a pretty mulatto girl." Dos Passos said that he remembered visiting Monticello as a boy and being shown such a letter as a "smut item." He decried the attitude of people of English culture toward their "half-breed children." Those from

French, Spanish, and Portuguese cultures "tended to esteem their half-breed children in proportion to their whiteness, but still treated them as humble members of the family." Dos Passos told Wilson that he regretted not having a Kinsey report on Virginia "circa 1750."

A prospective biographer, Charles W. Bernardin, began asking questions in 1950 and sought Dos Passos' cooperation. "I hope Bernardin hasn't made himself a nuisance. He's a distressingly thorough young man," Dos Passos observed to Arthur McComb, who provided Bernardin some anecdotes and opinions for his "Spanish chapter" and sent Dos Passos a copy of what he had said so that it might be contradicted or expunged if he wished. "I did my best to explain to Bernardin that his function was to follow and not precede the undertaker—but since he insists on continuing with his rash enterprise I sent him what data I could remember. As you say, he's polite, appreciative and (I add) industrious. It's his industry I find disarming," Dos Passos told McComb.

On October 23, 1951, when he wrote Hemingway a note of condolence upon hearing of the death of Pauline Hemingway, he added that a "thesis writer from Bradley University" had asked him to fill out a questionnaire about Hemingway's early life. "Being historically minded I usually send these characters what dates I can remember—or do you want me to tell him to make up his own dates?" Hemingway replied that there were dozens of graduate students and "ghouls like Mizener" (inspired by his success with Fitzgerald's biography, *The Far Side of Paradise,* which had just appeared) who wanted to "play buzzards" on him while he was still alive. "I've refused to cooperate with any of them and will not permit publication of any letters nor give them any gen at all. I had a private life until Cowley first intruded on it. But if it hadn't been him it probably would have been someone else."

Had Dos Passos not portrayed Hemingway fictionally in his novel *Chosen Country,* published a month after their friendly exchange of letters that fall, they might have maintained a friendship of sorts until Hemingway's death. Hemingway had closed his last note to Dos Passos with the comment that his telephone number was still Cotorro 17-3 "if you come down here." Hemingway's retaliation to *Chosen Country* was an acerbic attack on Dos Passos in his memoirs, *A Moveable Feast.*

When Archibald MacLeish wrote Dos Passos to congratulate him for having written not only his best novel, but one of "THE best," he asked if Dos Passos had any idea what Hemingway's reaction was to "Georgie," the Hemingway persona. Hemingway himself supplied the answer directly to MacLeish almost a year later: "Dos's last book was so awful that I couldn't write him even in protest. There were quite a few things to say too. Do you think he really wrote it or was it something dear truly dear Katy wrote for The Ladies' Home Journal with Edie Foley?" His observation to Edmund Wilson was stronger still:

> Dos fooled us all I think. But he fooled himself the most. The last book, Chosen Country, made me sick to read. My only hope for him as a writer was that it was a re-write of something dear Katy had written for a Woman's Magazine. That is not a very fine hope. Have you ever seen the possession of money corrupt a man as it has Dos? When Eisenhower received his tax free money from the Democrats for his book he became a Republican. His political development, and that of Dos, have very strange parallels.

In his Christmas card to Bill and Marion Smith that year, Hemingway added in a postscript that in his home in Cuba—La Finca Vigía—he kept "a pack of fierce dogs and cats trained to attack one-eyed Portuguese bastards who wrote lies about their friends."

Most of the reviews of *Chosen Country* were positive compared to those of Dos Passos' last two novels. It was his only published fiction in over a decade, but it was not reviewed nearly so extensively as his most recent book of essays, *The Prospect Before Us.* Several critics agreed with Archibald MacLeish that it was the best book Dos Passos had ever written. Arthur Mizener, whom Hemingway had disparaged, wrote an admiring essay at midyear for *The Saturday Review of Literature* ("The Gullivers of Dos Passos") extolling his worth as a satirist. Since Dos Passos supposedly paid no attention to the critics, Edmund Wilson sent him a copy of the Mizener piece (Mizener was a Princeton graduate, as was Wilson, and a professor of English at Carleton College). Dos Passos thanked Wilson for the article, then quipped: "I immediately felt my pulse and wondered about my blood pressure and rate of alcoholic intake. It all seems normal but you never can tell. I'll have my urine cast at the first opportunity. I have had no call from the mortician, not yet."

When the trilogy *District of Columbia*—comprised of *Adventures of a Young Man, Number One,* and *The Grand Design*—appeared in the spring of 1952, Mizener's essay ("The Gullivers of Dos Passos") served as its introduction. It not only discussed the trilogy, but also presented an admiring overview of Dos Passos' career. Mizener reviewed *Chosen Country* for the New York *Times Book Review,* in which he ventured that the book was "probably Dos Passos' best novel."

Some readers may have been put off by reading reviews that declared *Chosen Country* a boring novel. *Virginia Kirkus Service* called it "abysmally boring" and faulted it for its "loose constructions, non-sequiturs, slipshod writing." Archibald MacLeish suggested that Orville Prescott could not have read the novel before reviewing it for the New York *Times.* "I remember very well what he said, and it has nothing to do with your book," MacLeish wrote Dos Passos. "What bastards. . . . I have nothing but ill words from them. It used to make me unhappier than it does," he added. Dos Passos replied that he had the sensation increasingly of late of "shoving things down a rat hole. I never did read reviews much; now I never read them unless somebody shoves one under my nose. What's the use. By the time the book's published it'll be too late to do anything about the reviewer's complaints even if they happen to make sense."

Edmund Wilson wrote Dos Passos that he and Elena were fascinated by the novel, but found it difficult to judge as a book—for him a rare instance—since he knew so many of the original or "components of the characters." He allowed that he kept seeing the real people on whom they were modeled, which threw him off. "What comes through to me is the Peter Pan fantasy of the Smooleys or the horrors of life with Griffin Barry, which seem to me wonderfully caught, but I can't gauge the effect of all this on a reader who hasn't known them." Wilson chided Dos Passos for another of his "colorless titles" and asked why he was addicted to them. Besides, the phrase "chosen country" was misleading, added Wilson, who also criticized him for his dependence on clichés. Surely Dos Passos could have avoided such "catch phrases and platitudes when dealing with people who are supposed to be clever and charming and sometimes profound and brilliant." Nonetheless, he had never written more "beautifully or fluently—having dropped [his] . . . naturalistic impediments—in evoking sensations and places."

Dos Passos appreciated Wilson's "enlivening remarks," but told him that writing for publication had become increasingly depressing. He said that in his more cheerful moments he tended to think of his books as the "little crosses and sticks in somebody's private dog, cat and pet rabbit burial ground."

On June 11, 1951, he traveled to Northwestern University to accept the degree of Doctor of Humane Letters as a part of the school's formal graduation ceremonies. Six months later, Northwestern University again honored him, this time at its centennial convocation "in recognition of the impress which he has made upon his generation during a lifetime of distinguished service as a resident of one of the States which comprised the Northwest Territory." The honor did little to boost his sagging spirits so far as his career as a writer was concerned, however. Dos Passos wrote Wilson that he had been born in a Chicago hotel room only because his parents happened to be passing through at the time. Of the one hundred "distinguished residents" singled out for the award, Dos Passos was the only writer named in the brief story carried by the New York *Times*. In 1952 Dos Passos was honored by the Phi Beta Kappa chapter at Harvard University, his alma mater, "in recognition of high attainments in liberal scholarship" and traveled to Cambridge for the induction ceremony.

Meanwhile, having turned his attention once more to his book on Thomas Jefferson —determined to get it out of the way before taking on anything else—Dos Passos groused to Wilson in the fall of 1951 that he was finding it "a hell of a lot of work, with only the prospect of another goddamn book to shove down the goddam rathole." He was unhappy, too, because he had been unsuccessful in getting *Chosen Country* serialized. "The regular book market is exceedingly depressed, so we must find other ways of keeping the home fires burning," Betty wrote Marion and Lloyd Lowndes while Dos Passos was in the final stages of the book. The best he managed was a sale to the *Omnibook Magazine,* which published a fifty-page condensation "abridged from the book in the author's own words" (according to the blurb promoting the magazine for its March 1952 issue, which sold for thirty-five cents a copy). It was at this point that Dos Passos decided to ask Bernice Baumgarten at Brandt & Brandt to take him on once more as his agent. He also was unhappy with Houghton Mifflin and decided that Baumgarten could help him find another publisher. Dos Passos had been informed at midyear in 1952 that an error had been made in reporting the sales of *Chosen Country.* The actual sale was twenty-three hundred copies less than the figure first reported. He wrote Lovell Thompson that *Chosen Country* had "the enthusiastic support of your entire publishing house. Furthermore you had a very good press. . . . It certainly doesn't make sense, since Houghton Mifflin made such a poor showing with a novel they did like, to expect them to make a good showing with a novel they don't like." The grievance involved not only the error in reporting sales, but also a novel manuscript that Houghton Mifflin had insisted be revised.

The novel in question was *Most Likely to Succeed,* referred to before its eventual publication by its working title, "Shall Be the Human Race." Despite Dos Passos' resolution to finish *The Head and Heart of Thomas Jefferson,* he had undertaken the writing of a short novel that he thought he could dispense with easily for some ready cash, then planned to return to his Jefferson manuscript. At the heart of the problem, however, was the fact that Dos Passos already had a different novel under contract with Houghton Mifflin, referred to as the "Jasper Milliron" book. Dos Passos wanted his publisher to substitute the *Most Likely to Succeed* manuscript for the "Jasper Milliron" one, and the firm did not agree. Dos Passos then proposed that Houghton Mifflin publish *Most Likely to Succeed* under a new and separate contract, and the house balked at that request, too. On November 9, 1952, he wrote Baumgarten:

> I suspect that Lovell's real objection came to the surface in something he blurted out while we were talking. The H.M. people have a notion that the book will be considered antisemitic because the main character, who turns out to be a pretty unpleasant fellow, is of Jewish origin. Such an attitude is so far from my way of thinking and feeling that I can't help resent the imputation rather hotly. But I'm certainly going over the manuscript very carefully with that imputation in mind. Possibly by building up some of the other characters, who are at present only sketched, the story can be put on a broader base.

Dos Passos served notice to Lovell Thompson that the "present state of affairs" made it imperative for him to seek another publisher.

Dawn Powell put Monroe Stearns at Prentice-Hall onto Dos Passos, as she explained in a letter of November 22, 1952:

> I was beginning to feel that mentioning Monroe Stearns and Prentice-Hall to you and you to Monroe Stearns was like resting casually against a secret button that brought on the whole fire department. . . . I saw Stearns at cocktails yesterday and evidently the whole firm has knocked off all week doing nothing but sewing up a red carpet. He said the 100 pages of your new book were so wonderful he couldn't believe it. He described his feelings on holding the mss. in his very hands like a Raphael and when his wife addressed him he shouted, "Don't speak to me—don't ask me anything—I'm reading a Dos Passos mss."

Several days before seeing Dawn Powell and Monroe Stearns in New York City, Dos Passos asked Bernice Baumgarten to "case the market" for him.

> Of course I won't get my ideal publisher or responsible employee in a publishing firm, but I might as well describe him to you. In politics (which is all important these days), he must be a progressive conservative. A touch of Henry Regnery with more money behind him and perhaps less of "now it can be told." He needn't admire U.S.A. but must show some interest in my later work. Even Lovell thinks The Grand Design was my best book. He must think about distribution and marketing twenty-four hours a day. You have a job cut out for you.

Monroe Stearns informed Dos Passos on November 26 that it would be a signal honor for his firm to add all of Dos Passos' books to their list. "On that list—I revert to my Show Business years for a phrase—you would have the star's dressing room and top billing." In a long, detailed letter, Stearns outlined all the ways Prentice-Hall would promote his books if given the opportunity. "What I think is far more important than all these materialistic statistics," he added, "is the fact that we all, individually and collectively, greatly and sincerely admire your work. It would be a thrilling experience for us to be able to show our admiration by putting all our efforts into working for you." Dos Passos reveled in being courted again. Lovell Thompson played suitor, too, and urged Dos

Passos to finish his Jefferson book before deciding if he needed to make a change. He did not want to release the "Jasper Milliron" contract to another publisher. He was sure that Houghton Mifflin could do more for Dos Passos in the long run than Prentice-Hall or any other publishing house could. He asked how much money Dos Passos needed to "tide him over" and also proposed a $2,500 advance for a "juvenile life of Jefferson to be delivered at his convenience." Thompson saw the volume as a "rest book. . . . It's sometimes a relief to change the form of the problem and to write for different eyes."

The crux of the problem was not simply an incorrect report on the sales of *Chosen Country* or the "Jasper Milliron" contract, however, but Houghton Mifflin's attempt to charge Dos Passos' general account—instead of his *Chosen Country* account—for the royalties of the books supposedly sold, but reported in error. Dos Passos' $10,000 advance on *Chosen Country* was a nonreturnable advance, whereas his actual royalties earned totaled only $8,968.54, based on the 13,929 copies sold. Dos Passos insisted to Bernice Baumgarten, that the deduction for returned and miscounted copies should be taken only from the *Chosen Country* account, not his general account, as had been done. He did not want to go to the expense of getting a lawyer, he said, but was "sick and tired of being accommodating to publishers." As he saw it, Houghton Mifflin had done "everything to make things difficult" and he was not going to "make this operation easy for them." The affair was finally settled in his favor.

Lovell Thompson acknowledged that since the erroneous debit was "at least one element, and a proper one, in Dos's decision to try Prentice-Hall, perhaps I can consider that I have at least paid a price for dozing at the switch and have been sufficiently rebuked." Despite the problems that had arisen between them, their friendship remained intact, and the "Jasper Milliron" book was eventually edited by Thompson and published by Houghton Mifflin under the title *Midcentury*.

Dos Passos was tired of moving from house to house in an attempt to find a publisher who would do for him what he thought was most needed if he was going to be able to keep writing. Monroe Stearns had written enticingly of the advantages of being at Prentice-Hall. They kept their trade list small, and out of fifty books published each year, only ten or twelve were novels. They had nine salesmen who called on bookstores everywhere, regardless of the size of the town or the shop, insisted Stearns. "We ask each of them to read the proofs of every book; thus they can talk to the buyers with authority and enthusiasm. The cordial relations they maintain with these buyers give us the privilege of asking and getting favors from the bookstores which many other publishers are unable to achieve. . . . When a vague customer asks for 'a good book,' the clerk automatically suggests 'the new Dos Passos novel.' " Stearns proposed the kind of promotion Dos Passos had been seeking, and he signed with Prentice-Hall for the publication of *Most Likely to Succeed*.

One of the promotion schemes Stearns applied to the novel was the publication of a six-page pamphlet entitled *John Dos Passos, An Appreciation*, which was distributed nine months before publication of the new novel. It featured miniessays by four significant literary figures whose following represented thousands of diverse readers—Max Eastman, Robert Hillyer, Arthur Mizener, and Dawn Powell—and announced a publication date of

September 27, 1954. Underneath Dos Passos' portrait in the pamphlet was a statement about his writing of the novel:

> Books are written to get something off the man's chest. For many years now, I've been watching with a sort of horrified obsession the development of political delusions in the minds of certain men and women who started out as sane and up-and-coming young people and potential good citizens, but whose lives have by these delusions been thoroughly warped, and the good in them, in my opinion, just about destroyed. Being a man whose business it is to tell stories about people, it is hardly surprising that my puzzlement, my questionings and anguished surmises, and my occasional upsetting discoveries, should, as time went on, have taken on the lineaments of imaginary men and women and that the interweaving of their developing lives should have shaped itself, eventually, into a novel.

Dos Passos' lackluster statement was not conducive to lively advance sales of *Most Likely to Succeed,* nor had Baumgarten been able to sell any segments of the novel except to *Esquire.* Arnold Gingrich bought one excerpt for five hundred dollars, but the novel in general was not one from which segments could be extracted easily. William Maxwell's rejecting it for *The New Yorker* typified the problem and the reactions by magazine editors who saw it. "The Dos Passos story didn't seem right for <u>The New Yorker,</u> largely because there were too many threads connecting it with the book it is a part of. And if you meant you wanted to know what I personally think, I think that here and there is something good, or at least recognizable, but that in general it's a dead piece of writing. But that of course is for you personally," he wrote Baumgarten.

Early reviews of *Most Likely to Succeed* in *Virginia Kirkus Service* and *Library Journal*—on which bookshop managers and librarians often based their orders—failed to ignite sales interest either. The anonymous critic who had branded *Chosen Country* "abysmally boring" for the *Virginia Kirkus Service* was probably the same reader of Dos Passos' new book. The same phrase—"abysmally boring"—was used, to which was added "a dreary tale." *Library Journal* called *Most Likely to Succeed* "incredibly bad," assailed it for its "stale stereotypes" and the "worst kind of assassination." Jed Morris, a playwright and the book's protagonist, was a "repulsive moral coward" without a single redeeming feature. Harold Clurman, writing for *The Nation,* described Morris as "a phony, a mental incompetent, and a moral castrate." Clurman identified Dos Passos' protagonist with the worst features he had seen or imagined to be true as a result of his involvement with the New Playwrights Theatre and his aborted stint in Hollywood. The book was a "wretched piece of work" and also libelous in Dos Passos' treatment of "an important episode from his own life during the late 1920s and early 1930s which impinged upon the character of others." Clurman saw Mike Gold, Francis Faragoh and his wife, Em Jo Basshe, Otto Kahn, and Josef von Sternberg without disguise (a parallel attested to later by John Howard Lawson and his wife, Sue Edmund). *Time*'s anonymous reviewer called *Most Likely to Succeed* a "shrill and savage satire" in which the author at fifty-eight sounded more like a "disappointed lover" than an astute social critic. Granville Hicks threw up his hands at the novel and informed readers of *The New Republic* that the decay of the author's talents was too great to be explained away as "political disillusionment." It was not "the sort of bad novel that good novelists occasionally write," he insisted. Had the author not been identified, a reader might think it the work of a "not very promising beginner." Hicks concluded that readers were confronted in the novel with "nothing less than a literary debacle."

Not many critics found redeeming features in *Most Likely to Succeed.* Florence Bullock, writing for the New York *Herald Tribune Book Review,* thought the book illuminating for its presentation of a "circumstantially authentic historical account of Communist methods" and saw the novel as a "blueprint of the Communist program" in the United States. Robert Gorham Davis informed readers of the New York *Times Book Review* that the experiences in the fiction seemed a "little remote and unreal, like old snapshots looked at too often," but allowed that he admired the characterization despite the failure of the political satire. Paul Engle's review in the Chicago *Sunday Tribune Magazine of Books* declared that the writing appeared "hasty and trite," but thought the novel important for its revelation of the deviousness of the "disciplined disciples of the Marxist conspiracy." The few positive reviews did not send readers into the streets in droves to buy the book, and six months later *Most Likely to Succeed* was still struggling to earn out its advance. When Dos Passos inquired of Bernice Baumgarten regarding his royalty statement, she replied that royalties were not reported if earnings were less than ten dollars.

Edmund Wilson wrote Dos Passos that he enjoyed reading the novel and thought it his most amusing book. "I was certainly pleased that you found a few things to laugh at," answered Dos Passos. "Such criticisms as I saw took it with depressing seriousness." Wilson said he regretted there were "so few goys" among his cast of characters, but thought the "necessity of producing Jewish wisecracks" had an entertaining effect. He was amused, too, by Dos Passos' depiction of Hutchins Hapgood, a long-time resident of the Cape. The ending was unsatisfactory, however. "What is supposed to happen to your hero?"

The book had been out a month when Dos Passos set out on a lecture tour of the Midwest at the instigation of Grayce Sims Peat of the Peat Lecture Bureau, who had asked if she could plan a tour to twenty-five major cities across the United States in the fall of 1954. He had no intention of making lecturing a way of life, but when Peat offered him a guarantee of eight thousand dollars (from which he had to pay his expenses except for transportation), he was tempted to accept. He reasoned that it was a means of promoting his new book as well. Bernice Baumgarten sent a schedule of his appearances to Monroe Stearns at Prentice-Hall with a request that copies of *Most Likely to Succeed* be in the bookshops to herald his arrival in each town and suggested that a window display would be good, too. Once on tour, however, Dos Passos found no one who acknowledged having laid eyes on the novel. He found no books in the bookstores either, he complained, and urged Baumgarten to prod the publisher into getting books to the West coast in time for his talk at the University of Oregon. Stearns, in turn, laid the blame on the bookshops. Of the twelve from whom they had solicited orders for the first half of Dos Passos' tour, not one had placed an order. *Most Likely to Succeed* had been met by "total indifference" in the bookshops, Stearns lamented. Stearns said that the results might have been better had he been furnished with the dates and places of the entire tour, but agreed to rectify matters as best he could for the tag end of the tour.

From Chicago's Bismarck Hotel, Dos Passos wrote Chauncey Hackett: "I'm making a series of speeches in various colleges. Painful, because I find I'm a distressingly bad speaker, but otherwise very interesting. In a little college at Alfred, New York, run by Seventh-Day Baptists, I found the young men surprisingly unstereotyped in their comments. In others they still believe in The New Republic and whatever their professors tell them." From Eugene, Oregon, he scribbled a postal card to Estlin Cummings depicting American Indians fishing in an Oregon river. The photograph was captioned "Soon to be extinct." His message was "I'd soon be extinct, too, if this performance weren't just about over. Lecturing, I find, breeds a profound distaste for the sound of one's own voice, a distaste which every P.A. system distressingly amplifies." It annoyed him that people he met on tour harped on the *U.S.A.* trilogy as though it was the only book he had ever written. When he returned from his tour after two months on the road, Dos Passos wrote Chauncey Hackett that he had finally stopped "bellowing in all those college lecture halls. I can't seem to learn to enjoy the sound of my own vociferations so I suppose I'll never be a lecturer. You occasionally get a few interesting questions from the students afterwards, but more often they are complete whoppers such as 'What is a whole man?'—which only Jesus or Socrates could answer."

One of his suggestions to students was to "go back to the Bible. It's still the best writing we have." He recommended the books of Samuel, Kings, and Ruth, which he thought were splendid narratives. He was partial to the Old Testament. His advice to young writers who wished to produce "great fiction" was to stop imitating those who began writing during the 1920s. "Unless we read books that have been approved by past generations of the human race, we have no standard by which to judge either the books or the TV programs of today." Dos Passos pointed out *Samson Agonistes* as a "wonderful expression of human triumph over failure" and called it Milton's greatest work. Another source of good writing, he continued, was to "listen carefully to popular speech," particularly to people such as "truckdrivers, who are not too much affected by TV," and to remember their "most vigorous and expressive ways of putting things."

Dos Passos also recommended the reading of the nation's founders and spoke of Thomas Jefferson. He had finally finished his Jefferson chronicle, which had been out since February 1954. Never before had he published two books in one year, and he envisioned his current lecture tour as a means of plugging them both. *The Head and Heart of Thomas Jefferson* evoked good reviews for the most part, although several critics judged that Dos Passos had captured the heart of Jefferson, but not the head. Irving Howe's review, "Perils of Americana," informed readers of *The New Republic* that the book's color had been bleached by the author's conservative politics and criticized it for being rambling and formless. The author had apparently interpreted accumulation as method and saw the "absence of theory" as proof of its objectivity, Howe insisted. Others thought the book strong on anecdote, but "slim on analysis." One termed Jefferson's portrait "blurred, inconsistent, and overly simplistic." Yet the majority of reviewers spoke of it in admiring terms. One recommended it for a Pulitzer Prize. Another called it "a triumph, a living biography by a gifted creative writer." Most pointed out that Dos Passos did not intend his book to be a full-dress biography, but rather, as a history of the times, a panoramic biography much like his novels. Others commended its balance and beauty, fair treatment, warmth, and the vividness of its portrait, its revelation of the essence of the man, its brilliance as a historical document, its superb portrait of Jefferson's mind, and its novelistic approach.

Despite its good reviews, sales were "flaccid," Dos Passos informed Robert Hillyer, annoyed that the book into which he had poured "a hell of a lot of irreplaceable time and money" should have such few rewards. A professional writer could not afford to produce books for the sheer satisfaction of pleasing only himself, he said. Hillyer told Dos Passos that *The Head and Heart of Thomas Jefferson* was "even finer" than *The Ground We Stand On,* which he "deeply admired." Hillyer liked Dos Passos' knack for making history "excitingly contemporary."

Dawn Powell wrote Gerald and Sara Murphy that Dos Passos had been in to see her a couple of times that summer "with a load of Thomas Jefferson to trade for a load of Old Grand-Dad." Dos Passos gave away countless copies of his Jefferson book to friends who had contributed in some way to the research, and to others simply because he was in the habit of giving them books each time a new one came out. Stewart Mitchell had been especially helpful with the Jefferson book. As director of the Massachusetts Historical Society in Boston, Mitchell had materials at hand. "Now as to John Adams—you are completely safe in describing him as a short, stubby man, for he stood only a little over 5 feet 6, and was plump—about the size and shape of the late Professor Edward Channing, whom you may remember," Mitchell volunteered in one letter. He said that he had not been able to come up with the breakdown of the members of the Continental Congress by professions, but was working on it.

Dos Passos sent Carl Sandburg an advance copy of *The Head and Heart of Thomas Jefferson,* saying: "Ever since you rescued Lincoln from the embalmers I've had a notion of doing something similar with Jefferson. I haven't the faintest notion whether I have succeeded or failed, but maybe you'll have a chance to take a look at it." Sandburg admired Dos Passos' work and had been one of the five to nominate him to a chair in the National Academy of Arts and Letters. If he ventured an opinion after reading Dos Passos' book on Jefferson, however, he left no record of it.

Meanwhile, once Dos Passos had finished *Most Likely to Succeed,* he set to work on his next novel, *The Great Days,* which had been steeping for some time. In its early stages he referred to it as "Day of Grief," and it was under contract with Prentice-Hall. On January 3, 1955, he sent the completed manuscript to Bernice Baumgarten for forwarding to Monroe Stearns and said that he wanted to talk with Stearns to see what promotion gimmick had been concocted. "Prentice-Hall is probably still smarting from the sales resistance they found on Most Likely to Succeed, but maybe we can think up some fresh approach for them." Two weeks later, Dos Passos met with Stearns, who tactfully suggested that the novel be rewritten or, even better, forgotten as a book and offered somewhere as a periodical sale. Stearns was more explicit in his letter to Baumgarten on January 19, 1955:

> I am not pleased at all with John Dos Passos' The Great Days. . . . The best thing I can say for it is that the hand of the master has not lost its cunning; the literal writing is the equal of Dos's best. Otherwise I feel that it sadly misrepresents his great talents. . . . I find this

novelette to be very incompletely and elliptically told, to present no character of any significance or even sympathy, or to say anything really worth saying. I am also rather offended by what seemed to me quite gratuitous passages dealing with sex acts and natural functions. . . . Too, the fact that so much of the story is told in flashbacks tends to rob the narrative of immediacy, and raises questions which are never completely answered. I got the feeling while I was reading it that I was looking at a stage set on which there were several doors, none of which was ever opened. . . . Not only do I feel it would be a disservice to Dos's literary reputation to publish it, but I think it would just about kill him in the bookstores. <u>Most Likely to Succeed</u> is having only an indifferent success, and as you know, many of the reviews were perfectly dreadful. There were, thank heaven, also plenty of reviewers who agreed with us that it is a fine book. But we should be able to go to the trade with a bang up novel, . . . one that would definitely show that he is still full of his old vigor, not with a pale little package like <u>The Great Days</u>. I have an awful feeling that if Dos's next novel is not a success, he will be through.

Stearns's only suggestion for revision was that the story of Roland Lancaster, a quasi–Dos Passos character, could be developed in a more straightforward manner and the whole novel extended considerably.

Put out by his editor's reaction to *The Great Days,* Dos Passos informed Baumgarten that he would reread his manuscript and decide whether he or Stearns was crazy. Whatever the outcome, he said he was convinced that he must "get disentangled from Prentice-Hall." Again, he outlined to his agent the kind of publisher he needed: one who was willing to print "unfashionable works" and who was interested in "building up a long term proposition" by purchasing the body of his work from Houghton Mifflin. "It would be an expensive proposition for any publisher and I'd probably have to forego any further advances for some time. . . . What I'd like, of course, would be a new and enthusiastic firm, a new Simon and Schuster in its early stages. . . . What do you think of Henry Regnery now? There is a certain flavor of crackpottery about the outfit, but we mustn't forget that today's crackpots become the pundits of tomorrow. The question always is: which ones?"

Dos Passos reminded Baumgarten that his editor's rejection of *The Great Days* manuscript constituted a breach of their agreement, since there was nothing in the contract that called for an acceptable manuscript "only if approved by Stearns." Moreover, the manuscript had been delivered on time. Stearns answered Dos Passos' complaint by saying that he did not intend his suggestions for revision to constitute a rejection. He said he merely wanted the best possible manuscript "for the sake of all concerned" and was willing to wait for another two years, if necessary, "for him to tackle and solve this problem." He reminded Baumgarten that a sizeable advance was at stake, too. Dos Passos agreed that since he had already received five thousand dollars for the book, he would "keep it on ice" while he finished up his current project, then decide what to do about it.

He was under contract for still another book with Doubleday, *The Men Who Made the Nation,* this one more of a panoramic history than his Jefferson book, to be a part of Doubleday's Mainstream of America Series, and also a book of essays bearing the working title "Education of a Radical," to be published by Dodd, Mead & Company. Edward H. Dodd, Jr., wrote Baumgarten on March 7, 1955, that "John Dos Passos came in and we decided to take the plunge. So here's a check [$5,000] for the advance." Two days later, Dos Passos informed Baumgarten that the title had been changed to "Freedom Is the Theme." By the time he finished his manuscript, however, he had reversed the title to read *The Theme Is Freedom,* which he said he preferred because of the rhythm, the sound, and the emphasis. When Dos Passos submitted four titles to Edmund Wilson for his recommendation for the book that became *The Head and Heart of Thomas Jefferson,* Wilson selected "The White Porch of the Republic." It had the most appealing rhythm, he said. Wilson often returned his recommended titles with the syllables marked according to their accents.

The Theme Is Freedom, published on March 26, 1956, was not widely reviewed, but it made a respectable showing. Sales were boosted by Orville Prescott's "Books of the Times" column, from which an excerpt was taken by Dodd, Mead & Company for its display advertising. Prescott called the book an extremely well-written "intellectual autobiography" and termed Dos Passos "a brilliant writer with an impressive flair for striking pictorial images. . . . He not only cares passionately about people, causes and problems; he also needs to act. Throughout his life he has plunged into affairs. . . . Few men can write more vivid and arresting English prose." Dos Passos' essays ranged from his coverage of the Sacco-Vanzetti case to the war in the Pacific and the Nuremberg trials. The book concluded with a new piece, "The American Cause," presented as a reply to several German students who had asked him why they should admire the United States:

> I told them they should admire the United States not for what we were but for what we might become. Selfgoverning democracy was not an established creed, but a program for growth. I reminded them that industrial society was a new thing in the world and that although we Americans had gone further than any people in spreading out its material benefits we were just beginning, amid crimes, illusions, mistakes and false starts, to get to work on how to spread out what people needed much more: the sense of belonging, the faith in human dignity, the confidence of each man in the greatness of his own soul without which life is a meaningless servitude. . . . Faith in self-government, when all is said and done, is faith in the eventual goodness of man.

Dodd, Mead had proposed another book they wanted Dos Passos to write, but he said that it would take an advance of at least twenty-five thousand dollars for him to research and write it. The book was to be a broad study of the situation of the American working man, for which Dos Passos made an extensive outline. It was to have covered the events that had shaped his thoughts, behavior, and feelings as a working man in terms of the "two governments which controlled his life most directly: management and the union." Since such a hefty advance was out of the question, Edward H. Dodd proposed approaching several philanthropic foundations for help in financing the project. On April 14, 1954, letters went out under Dodd's signature to the Twentieth Century Fund, the Rockefeller Foundation, the John Hay Whitney Foundation, the Hill Family Foundation, the Ford Foundation, the Carnegie Corporation of New York, and the Guggenheim Memorial Foundation, but no one offered any money. Dos Passos was forced to scrap the project so far as Dodd, Mead & Company was concerned, but much of what he researched in the process went into his later fiction.

Considerably more energy went into the preparation of *The Men Who Made the Nation* than in *The Theme Is Freedom,* since all of it was original writing for Lewis Gannett's Mainstream of America Series, for which he had signed a contract in 1953. Dos Passos had received $5,000 on signing, then $2,500 in January of 1955, and another $2,500 in 1956. He had begun working on it in earnest when he turned his back on the *Great Days* manuscript rejected by Monroe Stearns. The new history was to be a narrative of the Jefferson period from the surrender of the British in Yorktown to the second administration of Jefferson. On January 6, 1955, Dos Passos wrote Edith Shay that he was "at the stage of being aghast at the difficulty of the job." He wanted to show Jefferson, "mostly from the outside," operating among his peers. He told Gannett that he could send a rough draft of the first half of the book by the end of the summer, and, with luck, would have the entire manuscript ready by February. In November 1955 after reading the first five chapters of what Dos Passos described as "highly provisional," Ken McCormick, Doubleday's editor in chief, wrote him: "Three of us at Doubleday have read, with rising excitement, the first chapters of your Mainstream of America book. It seems to us that you have captured the mood and spirit of the trend of history we are after. . . . We feel that this is going to be one of the best books in the Series, and we are more than delighted with the splendid start you have made."

Gannett wrote that he, too, was delighted with the manuscript:

> You have succeeded marvellously in weaving the contemporary documents into a modern narrative, and in keeping the personalities of the actors in the drama in the foreground. . . . You asked for suggestions, and you have them. But I don't want this note to seem primarily critical. It should appear as a psalm of delight. Your Ground We Stand On and your Jefferson seem to me to have reached ripe fruit in this manuscript. I like your sense of Washington and Jefferson immensely; I like also the minor characters, some of whom weren't familiar to me. And that final benison of Franklin's on the finished job, with its common-sense realization that nothing was or could be perfect, has always given me a lift. It makes a superb conclusion to your story of the convention.

It had been a long time since Dos Passos had heard such praise from an editor, and he felt good about it. Back in 1953 he had observed in a letter to Baumgarten that he "disliked giving Lewis Gannett, who certainly won't be any help to me, a cut in my royalties. It seems to me the publisher ought to pay the editor of their series. If I did this piece of historical narrative, I'd have to do it in my own way and according to my own schedule." A year later, he wrote Baumgarten:

> If you should hear of some part-time consultative job—something like the sinecure Lewis Gannett has editing the Mainstream history books for Doubleday—I'd be obliged if you would let somebody know. These jobs don't occur very often but they do occur. That doesn't mean I'm going to give up writing. I have too much planned ahead for that, but in order to get the freedom of mind to do it, I've got to find something that will produce a reliable income.

Gannett won Dos Passos' respect and friendship as they worked together, and, contrary to Dos Passos' fears, he discovered that they worked harmoniously together. "The book will of course be wholly yours," Gannett had assured him. Dos Passos' editor knew his American history, and his comments on the manuscript were constructive and astute. Of the early material, Gannett suggested: "The Yorktown prologue seems disproportionately long. I had expected to read more of the struggle, through all thirteen nascent states, over ratification. And the Lafayette chapter seemed to give Paris the center of the stage, a bit beyond what my sense of perspective suggested." In his letter of November 13, 1955, he observed: "Your technique of constant quotation from contemporary sources is extraordinarily successful. You put the reader in the period. You do it so well, on the whole, that I felt jolted whenever you made a contemporary reference, used the contemporary we or you, cited Mark Twain, used a twentieth-century word coinage, or referred to the 'judgment of historians.' "

Occasionally Gannett suggested more paragraphing. "They help a reader. I have never felt that either Virginia Woolf or William Faulkner were really helped by many-page paragraphing—or many-page sentences!" He said that he knew a writer had to write his own book and that his tendency might be to "reject a friend's or editor's critical suggestions, but given a bit of time, they sift down through, and while they cannot dictate, they somewhat affect the final result, and the longer they have to sift, the better." In a postscript, Gannett added: "When I reread the opening section, I understood for the first time your fondness for The World Turned Upside Down as a title. . . . But I hope you aren't too firmly set on it." He then asked if the phrase "Birth of a Nation," from D. W. Griffith's film, had any appeal to him. Dos Passos took his title from the name of the piece one of the British regimental bands played when they marched out of Yorktown to surrender. Dos Passos replied that he was open-minded about a title, but he was not impressed by Gannett's suggestion. He accepted Gannett's suggestions with appreciation and grace, saying that he was at "just the stage where editorial criticism is most useful. Your suggestions for more early background on Hamilton, Jefferson, and Franklin are excellent. I'm afraid I'm going to run into a problem on length, but cutting never hurt any book."

After reading the bulk of the manuscript, Gannett wrote: "Pruning always helps, books or apple trees, and I'm afraid, with 623 pages written and two chapters to go, that you will in the end have to face a cutting problem." He told Dos Passos that he had had reservations when his name was first proposed "by the people at Doubleday" to write for "the Series" because he did not know where Dos Passos stood at present: "I had a fear that you might use the period as a sermon against strong federal government. . . . You have preserved a friendly reasonableness toward Thomas Jefferson, Alexander Hamilton, and John Adams, all three, that is rare among historians, and I admire—and like—it no end. . . . You've kept the perspective, and it gives the story a kind of majesty." Gannett believed that Dos Passos would "proudly regard this book as the culmination of a long writing career."

On February 11, 1957, Dos Passos was in New York City to have lunch with LeBaron Barker, Doubleday's executive editor, who was also on the editorial board of its Mainstream of America Series. *The Men Who Made the Nation* had just been published, and it was a celebratory occasion. Barker reported that eighty-five hundred advance copies had already been sold. He was excited, too, about a book Doubleday was publishing by Agnes O'Neill, the playwright's second wife. He had just read the chapter on

Provincetown before meeting Dos Passos, and as they talked, Dos Passos was able to complete some of the anecdotes introduced in Mrs. O'Neill's memoirs, which elicited several reminiscences of his own. It occurred to Barker after lunch that Dos Passos would be a natural to write an autobiography, and he asked Bernice Baumgarten to sound him out on the idea. "He has led an unusually interesting life, has known a great many wonderful people, and God knows he can write well," wrote Barker. Dos Passos mulled the idea over, then replied: "I wonder if he would give us a few months to think it over. In any case I'm not quite ready to do it now. I have many other fish to fry first. The time for that sort of thing is just before senility closes in."

He allowed, too, that his situation at the moment was "fairly good," and that for the first time in years he was not "immediately pressed for cash." He was more interested in talking with Baumgarten about "establishing a more reasonable publishing program." He said that a "movie venture" of his *U.S.A.* trilogy was pending and that he had two more novels already on the drawing board. He also was considering the possibility of doing "a picture book on the men who made the nation" for Prentice-Hall as a means of "getting off the hook," since his novel *The Great Days* was still under contract there. Monroe Stearns had proposed the new book—a coffee table book of sorts, entitled "Prospects of a Golden Age"—as a substitute for the fiction. Dos Passos agreed because it would give him an opportunity to cover some of the same ground he had ploughed in researching *The Men Who Made the Nation*.

He was in fine fettle the day he had lunch with LeBaron Barker not only because of the successful launching of *The Men Who Made the Nation,* but also because he had just been notified of his selection as the recipient of the American Academy and Institute of Arts and Letters' Gold Medal for Fiction. One of the most highly prized awards in the literary field, the medal was conferred only once every five years. It was given in recognition of the entire work of the recipient for his "lasting contribution to American letters." Previous winners were Thornton Wilder, Willa Cather, Booth Tarkington, Edith Wharton, and William Dean Howells. Recipients were selected by the total body of the National Institute of Arts and Letters—two hundred fifty members in all—who already had achieved preeminence in the fields of art, literature, and music.

At the outdoor luncheon beneath an enormous canopy beside the American Academy and Institute of Arts and Letters buildings on Audubon Terrace in upper Manhattan, Dos Passos and Betty were seated with William Faulkner, who was to make the formal presentation of the award at the Joint Annual Ceremonial of the American Academy and Institute of Arts and Letters on May 22, 1957. Marchette Chute, one of the twelve new members being inducted into the National Institute of Arts and Letters, sat with them. Betty concluded that Faulkner (seated beside her) did not care for tall women, since he was short (Faulkner had joined the Canadian Air Force in World War I when no branch of the American armed forces would have him because of his height). Moreover, he gave most women short shrift regardless of their height. "Mr. Faulkner paid little attention to me or to anyone else at the table that day, but sat there as puffed up as a hooded cobra and fidgeted constantly until the wine was served," said Betty. "I offered him my wine, however, and he began to warm up to me. Thereafter, each time the waiter filled Mr.

Faulkner's glass, he filled mine, too, which I passed on to him. It seemed that our glasses were always empty, and we had quite a good time in the process. It was quite a different story at the Ceremonial activities afterward, I might add."

Malcolm Cowley, as president of the National Institute of Arts and Letters, wrote Faulkner on March 2, 1957, to ask him to make the presentation to Dos Passos. His letter was a masterpiece of diplomacy, a characteristic Dos Passos thought lacking in the past. "Dear Bill," began Cowley:

> I wonder whether you could do a little chore this year for the Academy and the Institute. I don't think those august bodies have bothered you in the past, but this is a rather special occasion. This year Dos Passos is being awarded the Gold Medal of the Institute for Fiction. It is almost the highest honor that we award (the only higher one being the Howells Medal, which you received in 1950). . . . I was very pleased when the medal went to Dos Passos, because in recent years his work hasn't been sufficiently recognized—but that's a formal and lukewarm way of putting it; the truth is that he's had to stand up under an intermittent hail of brickbats. Of course his recent work hasn't been up to the level of what he did in the twenties and thirties, but he did a lot then; he took chances; he put other novelists in his lasting debt. And now that he's being given a medal—the first, he says, since he was a boy in school—I'd like to see the occasion made just as big as possible, so that he knows the rest of us haven't forgotten him.
>
> That's why I'm asking whether, as the most distinguished novelist in the Academy, you couldn't make the presentation of the medal. It's not a big chore; about two hundred words would be all that would be required, though of course you'd have to start by being present that afternoon—but that wouldn't be too painful, because it's a pleasant occasion, with good food, drink, and conversation before we go to the platform, to sit there for an hour and a half. But I'd better stop urging and leave it up to you.

Faulkner replied: "I hate like bejesus to face this sort of thing, but maybe when his vocation has been as kind to a bloke as this one has been to me, an obligation such as this is a part of the bloke's responsibility toward it. So, if you are sure I am the man, I will take on the job and do the best I know."

The longer Faulkner sat on the stage of the large auditorium and listened to the interminable proceedings of introductions, presentations of lesser medals, grants, fellowships, special awards, a major address by Salvador de Madariaga (a Spanish writer and diplomat), and the induction of Conrad Aiken and Igor Stravinsky into the academy and twelve into the institute, the less inclined he was to deliver his own presentation address, the finale of the day. Betty, seated down front in the audience, did her best to stay awake, entertained in part by Faulkner, for whom her sympathies increased as the afternoon shadows fell across the stage.

> It seemed that Madariaga branched out on all sorts of topics beyond what he originally intended to say, and he talked for well over an hour. We had already sat through a number of speeches and awards. I found myself watching Mr. Faulkner, who spent practically the entire two hours on the platform screwing himself down in his chair, straightening up and pulling his suit down, examining himself and the various scraps of paper he found in one pocket or another, and twice he simply disappeared to smoke a cigarette—or several—I imagine. Dos was on the stage, too, but things didn't seem to bother him as much. He just went to sleep.

A secretary in the Dodd Room next to the auditorium reported that Faulkner asked her: "How long does *this* go on?" She observed him take his speech out of his pocket, unfold it, peer at what he had written, then scratch out most of it. He emerged and took his place on the stage in time to rise once more and say of Dos Passos without looking at his notes: "Oratory can't add anything to John Dos Passos' stature, and if I know anything about writers he may be grateful for a little less of it. So I'll say, mine is the honor to partake of his in handing this medal to him. No man deserves it more." The speech as Faulkner had written it was published later in the official *Proceedings* of the American Academy and Institute of Arts and Letters:

> The artist, the writer, must never have doubts about where he intends to go; the aim, the dream, must be that high to be worth that destination and the anguish of the effort to reach it. But he must have humility regarding his competence to get there, about his craft and his craftsmanship in it. So the fact that the artist has no more actual place in the American culture of today than he has in the American economy of today, no place at all in the warp and woof, the thews and sinews, the mosaic of the American dream as it exists today, is perhaps a good thing for him, since it teaches him humility in advance, gets him into the habit of humility well ahead whether he would or no; in which case, none of us has been better trained in humility than this man whom the Academy is honoring today. Which proves also that the man, that artist, who can accept the humility, will, must, in time, sooner or later, work through the humility and the oblivion into that moment when he and the value of his life's work will be recognized and honored at least by his fellow craftsmen, as John Dos Passos and his life's work are at this moment. It is my honor to share in his by having been chosen to hand this medal to him. No man deserves it more, and few have waited longer for it.

Uncomfortable as an extemporaneous speaker and not having left the stage to trim down his acceptance speech, Dos Passos delivered what he had prepared in advance for the occasion. "I wonder if any of you have ever noticed that it is sometimes those who find most pleasure and amusement in their fellow man, and have most hope in his goodness, who get the reputation of being his most carping critic," he began, then spoke of the unpopularity of the satirist, whose aim was to prod people into thinking: "In some times and places people have broiled the authors of unpopular works on beds of coals; in other times and places they have tried to educate them into conformity by starving them to death beyond the Arctic Circle." A more merciful way of expressing disapproval was by not buying a man's books, he added. Thus it seemed to him "a handsome gesture on the part of the National Institute of Arts and Letters to pin a medal on [his] . . . lapel." Dos Passos thanked the members warmly and acknowledged that he was "very much touched" by their gesture.

On September 1, 1957, Dos Passos boarded a plane with John Steinbeck and John Hersey to fly to Tokyo as America's official representatives at the twenty-ninth International PEN Congress. The trio—billed as "the three Johns: Dos Passos, Steinbeck, and Hersey"—was given a thunderous ovation when introduced, but Dos Passos was the obvious star of the American delegation and a popular favorite of the entire body. Steinbeck wrote his wife, Elaine, that Dos Passos was being "fawned over." The congress opened in Tokyo, then moved to Kyoto for the second half of the proceedings. In each city Dos Passos found himself trailed and besieged for autographs with even more vigor and perseverance than at the PEN congress in Venice. The two-week trip cost him nothing, and he hoped to parlay it into something useful in his writings. Before leaving Japan, he managed to write two articles for a Tokyo newspaper, which took care of out-of-pocket expenditures not covered by the congress. It was hard "to resist a prepaid excursion," Dos Passos told Robert Hillyer in urging him to bring his wife, Jeanne, to Spence's Point as soon as he returned. Travel of any kind was invigorating, he wrote Hillyer, even his "idiotic flight to Japan." One of the things he said he liked about the trip was the opportunity to get to know Steinbeck and Hersey. Steinbeck reported later that both Dos Passos and Hersey were "wonderful traveling companions," and that Dos Passos was "an angel."

Upon his return home, Dos Passos informed Estlin Cummings that his junket across the Pacific—his first visit to Japan—had left him with "a horrible case of itchy feet" and that he was going to take Betty and Lucy to Mexico as a Christmas "boon." Betty saw it as penance for his frolics in Japan. The first of December they flew to Mexico City, rented a small Ford that "climbed like a lizard and used little gas," and spent most of the month scrambling over mountainous terrain in southwestern Mexico. "Having the time of our lives, not so much being in Mexico as being away from home," Dos Passos wrote Cummings on December 4, 1957. Lucy, now seven, picked up Spanish readily and, according to her father, "reacted strongly to personalities and places."

Awaiting Dos Passos at Spence's Point was an invitation to Brazil from the Instituto Brasil-Estados Unidos for a two-week "good-will tour." He had not been to Brazil since 1948, and he looked forward to the trip. It did not make sense to go for such a short time, however, and he proposed, instead, a tour of at least a month or six weeks. "It would do a good deal more for mutual understanding if I could get around that enormous country a little and lecture in São Paulo or other university centers as well as Rio. I can't manage it unless I can earn enough to pay my way. My wife has lived in Brazil and is as full of enthusiasm as I am for the country, so she can't be left behind on this trip." His own expenses were to be covered by the institute and the Brazilian Foreign Office, but he asked that some paid lectures be arranged and an article or two for a Brazilian newspaper. Writers were poorly paid in Brazil, a representative of the institute informed him, but they would do the best they could. Since he wanted to bring his wife and daughter, they agreed to provide a first-class hotel suite or a furnished apartment. Dos Passos was especially interested in visiting the new capital, Brasília, then being carved out of the wilderness, and arranged with *Reader's Digest* to do an article on it. He was sure that he could get a book out of the trip, too.

By this time he was already involved in a lengthy project for *Reader's Digest* based on the findings of the Senate Committee on Improper Activities in the Labor and Management Fields, headed by John McClellan, the Democratic senator from Arkansas by whose name the committee was popularly known. Labor's rank and file members had written some one hundred thousand letters to the McClellan committee protesting the way their unions were being run and the gross intimidation, fears, and dangers inherent in the union system. Dos Passos examined hundreds of letters received by the committee, talked at length with McClellan, and traveled into the field during the winter and early spring of 1958, much as he had done a quarter century earlier when he went into Harlan County,

Kentucky—except that this time he was not a part of an investigating committee—talking with railroad workers, machinists, cab drivers, musicians, union members all, who were not protesting unions per se, but wanted voluntary union membership and right-to-work laws "with teeth in them." With the cooperation of McClellan, Dos Passos was able to prepare an in-depth report on his findings, which *Reader's Digest* published in its September 1958 issue.

The Brazilians had wanted him to come in June, but he insisted on waiting until he had finished his labor article. "I'm interested first in people and how they live, then in new Brazilian architecture, in popular music, and naturally in new developments in literature, poetry, etc.," Dos Passos informed Leslie F. Warren, executive secretary of the institute, before coming. The United States Information Service agreed to provide transportation and per diem for Dos Passos' travel elsewhere in the country after leaving Rio de Janeiro, where he gave a public lecture, talked at a luncheon for Brazilian writers, journalists, playwrights, poets, professors, art curators, diplomats, and officials and other professionals of countless disciplines—some one hundred in all—and presented a formal address to the august members of the Brazilian Academy of Letters. They stayed nine days in Rio de Janeiro, then set out for the provinces. Dos Passos wrote Estlin Cummings from Recife on August 21, 1958: "We must be crazy but we are enjoying it. Like Mr. Dulles we spend most of our time in the air. The country is enormous. We swim in the ocean and savor the birds and beasts in spite of lectures and welcoming committees." Several paid lectures assured Dos Passos of ample funds to cover expenses incurred by Betty and Lucy.

Brazilian officials were amazed at Dos Passos' energy and ambition to see almost everything the country had to offer. Leslie Warren proposed that he could arrange for them a trip to Brasília, visits to Iguaçu Falls in the South, an on-site inspection of a huge new power development under way in the state of Minas Gerais, a visit to a manganese mining settlement in Amapá (the northernmost state, near the mouth of the Amazon), and even an extremely strenuous trip up the Madeira-Mamoré railroad (a narrow-gauge train built to bring out rubber during the early "rubber days" in Brazil inched around falls and rapids in the Madeira River) to Pôrto Velho. Dos Passos and Betty insisted that they do it all. Lucy—now eight—had already proved herself a seasoned traveler, having taken by this time a variety of excursions with her loose-footed parents, beginning with her first trip in a laundry basket when she was conveyed from Baltimore to Spence's Point as an infant. When officials in Brazil learned that Dos Passos was bringing his young daughter with him, they provided for "alternate entertainment," since they assumed that the activities of her parents would prove either too dull or demanding for her, but she chose to remain with the adults on every occasion.

Upon their return to Spence's Point, Dos Passos wrote Adelaide Walker: "We were all wild about Brazil. Tootoo [Lucy] came home speaking Portuguese better than her Pa." He told Arthur McComb that he had found the Brazilians "as delightful as ever," and had even discovered some Dos Passos cousins in Santos, Brazil, a city of some two hundred thousand on the coast near São Paulo. "We were nearly stuffed to death by them at luncheon," he continued. "We all became very Portuguese in spite of my inability to cope with the intricate little language my paternal ancestors made up." He said he was amazed to discover at age sixty-two that he enjoyed traveling then as much as he had forty years earlier. "There must be something wrong with me," he added. In the book that grew out of his travels in Brazil, written after still another trip there and published in 1963 as *Brazil on the Move,* he said that he had an intense "family feeling for the Brazilians. Perhaps the fact that I had a Portuguese grandfather helps account for it. When people ask me why I keep wanting to go to Brazil, part of the answer is that it's because the country is so vast and so raw and sometimes so monstrously beautiful; but it's mostly because I find it easy to get along with the people."

Dos Passos described his trip to Brazil in 1958 as "a working holiday." It had been a "welcome balm to his spring of <u>sturm</u> and <u>drang</u>," he observed in a letter to Arthur McComb on September 1. His *"sturm* and *drang"* had been his "proverbial struggle to keep the wolf from the door," he noted. Dos Passos had been working on another long book, *Midcentury,* into which much of the material gleaned from his research into labor and union management was to be incorporated, but he kept having to interrupt his narrative in order to work on shorter pieces that had a more immediate cash return. He was notified that summer, however, by the president of the William Volker Fund of Burlingame, California, that he was being awarded a one-year grant of $8,500 (payable quarterly) for work on *Midcentury.* His comment to McComb upon his return from Brazil was that "by some miracle a funny little anonymous foundation on the Pacific Coast has come across with a subsidy. I shall be free—God willing—from the rat race of article writing for a year." On July 24, 1959, he was informed that on the basis of his "good progress report," his grant had been renewed for six months for an additional $4,350 so that he might finish his book in time for a 1960 publication date.

Meanwhile, Dos Passos' eleventh novel, *The Great Days,* appeared in the spring of 1958 while he was immersed in his own personal version of "labor racketeering." He had been undecided about whether to revise his manuscript of *The Great Days* and resubmit it to Monroe Stearns at Prentice-Hall or to send it to Lovell Thompson, still at Houghton Mifflin. "If H-M is going to hold on to the early novels it would seem logical to have them publish this one," he proposed to Bernice Baumgarten. "The thing at the back of my mind is that I want to promote two DP [Dos Passos] readers in the fairly immediate future, one of fiction and one of travel stuff. Plans for a <u>U.S.A.</u> movie may come to a head this month, too," he added in a letter to Baumgarten during the summer of 1957. As Dos Passos saw it, a hard-cover publisher should concentrate on trying to sell "to the 28,000 libraries across the country which buy books." He admitted that he might be wrong about the figures, but wondered why *The Men Who Made the Nation* had sold only thirteen thousand copies in view of its excellent press reviews. "That's not enough to do me any good in these inflationary times. Doesn't even pay my living expenses." Instead of giving *The Great Days* manuscript back to Stearns or offering it to Thompson, however, he decided to try a small, new house, Sagamore Press, which also published reprints. He told Baumgarten that he still was not sure he had told the story he had set out to tell, and that he did not think the book would be any more palatable to the casual reader in its revised state than it was originally. Yet he had done what he thought he must in telling his story as he saw it.

Just as he anticipated, reviewers saw little of note to compliment. Malcolm Cowley, writing for the New York *Times Book Review,* thought readers had a right to expect more than what they got from *The Great Days,* which had no business being housed on the same shelf with *Manhattan Transfer* and *U.S.A.* Despite Dos Passos' smooth style, sharp details, and vivid reporting of the war in flashback, the general concept of the book with its two disparate narrative threads of past and present were insufficiently linked and ineffective. Cowley was put off, too, by the moods of aversion and repulsion that characterized the book. Dos Passos' change in politics over the years was not enough to account for the book's failure, or to excuse it. *Time's* anonymous reviewer declared *The Great Days* the author's "saddest, sorriest novel" and called Dos Passos America's "fallen eagle." Daniel Aaron informed readers of *The New Leader* that he saw nothing convincing about either the characters or their convictions. "The glow had faded from Dos Passos' prose" in proportion to the "repudiation of his beliefs and the dislocation of his values," said Aaron, who already had begun his own intensive study of "writers on the left" and what had become of them.

James T. Farrell came to Dos Passos' defense in an essay for *The New Republic* entitled "How Should We Rate Dos Passos?" He thought it unfair to judge Dos Passos on the basis of immediate political considerations in the manner that most critics had insisted on doing and declared a fresh evaluation in order. To Farrell, *The Great Days* was "ingeniously constructed" and written "with great ease." It was wrong to fault the author for having written a panoramic novel of World War II and its aftermath, yet to expect him to people his tale with in-depth characterization and "strong individuality." Readers should accept Dos Passos for what he did best, which in this case was to create an honest record of the "hope and disappointment of four decades with dignity and seriousness." When Dos Passos' editor at Sagamore Press, Robert Smith, apprised him of Farrell's "immense review," Dos Passos wrote Farrell that he had developed "a sort of amnesia over the years on the subject of reviews," but looked forward to reading this one, since he respected Farrell's opinions.

Edmund Wilson agreed with Dawn Powell's assessment that the girl in the novel, Elsa, was probably one of Dos Passos' best "feminine creations." He said he also liked the "state of mind of the hero, the Cuban characters, and the landscapes," but he did not think the protagonist's quarrel with the New Deal had been well presented. "I seem to remember your accepting at the start the whole New Deal case for intervention, and now you are talking about Roosevelt as a butcher, as you did about Wilson after WWI. Nor did I understand why your reaction against the New Deal should have led you to share—as I thought—something of the panic about Russia, to the point of some tenderness toward McCarthy." Dos Passos answered Wilson's objections point by point. He meant *The Great Days* to represent something of the "inevitable disillusionment with the enthusiasm for airfields and labor-management committees and floating bases and amphibious landings. I still think we have something better to teach the world than the Russians have. The essential thing is the politics of balance and moderation." A good comparison was America's "handling of Puerto Rico with the Russian handling of Hungary." Wilson had been thoroughly put out by Dos Passos' enthusiasm for a time for the Joseph McCarthy investigations. In 1952 Dos Passos had supported Senator Robert Taft on the Republican ticket and joined Max Eastman (another McCarthyite) and John Chamberlain in the formation of an arts and letters committee to help elect Taft. Several months later when Horsley

Gantt's loyalty was called into question, Dos Passos had insisted that "the idea of Dr. Gantt's being a party to or a dupe of the Communist conspiracy in this country is absolutely ludicrous" and signed a sworn affidavit to that effect. In 1954 Dos Passos referred to McCarthy as "that dreadful senator from Wisconsin."

To a reporter from the New York *Times*, Dos Passos said in the fall of 1959:

> People keep asking me whether my political ideas have changed. Of course. Haven't yours? If they haven't where have you been all these years? It's a boring question because none of the political slogans of the Twenties applies to the Fifties. All the concepts have been stood on their heads. "Liberalism," for example, used to be equated with enthusiasm for individual right; now it tends to mean identification with central governing power. This much I can say: though youthful prejudice occasionally led me into what I now see as distortions, on the whole the attitude of mind exhibited by the *U.S.A.* books doesn't seem to me too different from my attitudes today. What has occurred is a complete transformation of the social background. What was white in the Twenties is black in the Fifties and vice versa. The Communists who have a keen nose for heresy "smelled a Lollard" as early as *The Big Money*. I can't see any particular virtue in consistency, but the basic tragedy my work tries to express seems to remain monotonously the same: man's struggle for life against the strangling institutions he himself creates.

Don Ross, a reporter for the New York *Herald Tribune*, asked Dos Passos if his having written the foreword to William F. Buckley, Jr.'s *Up from Liberalism*, published in 1959, represented for him "a seismic swing." Dos Passos replied, "No, I've always been sharp-shooting from the edges. So I find myself in the same situation I was in in the 1920s. I think the only people who have any fresh ideas today are the conservatives." He did not entirely agree with them, but he was "glad they're operating. They are interested in individual liberty," which was his main interest, too, he added. Dos Passos saw himself at the end of the 1950s as a "consistently angry man." When he voted the Communist ticket in 1932, he was "angry about the plight of the coal miners of Harlan County, Kentucky, whose cause the Communists espoused." He said he was angry now about the "plight of the small taxpayer . . . and the plight of the rank and file labor man who was being kicked around by the union bosses," which was the substance of his current manuscript, *Midcentury* (formerly the "Jasper Milliron" book), which Houghton Mifflin wanted to bring out in the fall of 1960. Both its narrative technique and theme—an attack on the misuse and corruption of power—were similar to what he had done in *U.S.A.*

Like it or not, when the lay reader thought of John Dos Passos, he thought of *U.S.A.* Unlike his other works, it had stayed in print most of the time since its publication. It also was the subject of several dramatic adaptations, still another reason that the reading and viewing public tended to associate him more with *U.S.A.* than his other works. The first serious adaptation of *U.S.A.* was made by Paul Shyre. It opened on August 15, 1953, with a two-performance run at the White Barn Theatre in Westport, Connecticut, staged by the repertory company of Lucille Lortel. "Thanks for the clippings. They sound as if you made an interesting show of it," Dos Passos wrote Shyre from Wiscasset, Maine. The two-act production was largely recitative with dramatized sections interspersed among the narratives and read and enacted on a bare stage by three men and two women. An off-stage singer and a band provided background accompaniment from the wings and illustrated the spirit and tempo of the times.

Reviewers applauded the effort, called it a "natural for reading companies on the college circuit." Several noted the similarity of the staging to George Bernard Shaw's *Don Juan in Hell.* "The adaptation deserves additional work and imagination to make it a theatre piece worthy of the novel," wrote one critic, but most theatergoers agreed with Fred Russell, who called it "the most progressive and unique of the dramatic reading programs that are slowly driving a wedge into the traditional format of the legitimate theater." Elliot Hyman, a movie producer, was on hand at the opening and expressed interest in presenting a cinematic version. Shyre sought "lecture presentation rights to U.S.A. until a producer was ready to sign a contract," but Dos Passos declined for the present. Since Houghton Mifflin had been unsuccessful in making a sale on its own, despite the trilogy's having been out for some fifteen years, he wanted his publisher to relinquish its 10 percent interest in the motion picture and dramatic rights to *U.S.A.* He was reluctant to sign away his rights to anyone for the time being, yet was eager to see a dramatic version produced. Bernice Baumgarten informed Dos Passos in the fall of 1953 that Don Moore at Columbia Broadcasting System was interested in acquiring the rights to *Number One* for a television adaptation by "Studio One." These rights, too, were with Houghton Mifflin. Dos Passos urged Baumgarten to get all the subsidiary rights to his works in his own name. He intended to watch his future contracts with greater care to see that he retained all he could. In the spring of 1954, he agreed to a contract with Paul Shyre for a concert-reading version of *U.S.A.,* which he saw as an apt means of stimulating motion picture interest.

On November 14, 1955, Shyre brought his adaptation of *U.S.A.* to New York City for a single evening's performance in the Kaufman Auditorium of the Young Men's Hebrew Association. The production was so well received by New Yorkers that Lucille Lortel—now managing director of the American National Theatre and Academy (ANTA)—asked to present it as its second offering in the new Matinée Series to a nonpaying audience at the Theatre de Lys on Christopher Street "to help lay the groundwork for a representative repertory company in New York built on a subscription audience." The two-hour, two-act production on December 18, 1956, starred Sada Thompson in the Isadora Duncan/Eleanor Stoddard roles for which she had been acclaimed in the 1953 opening at the White Barn Theatre. This time it was staged by Norman Hall, with Lucille Lortel as artistic director. There was no band, only a piano and drums, and many of the tunes that punctuated the period were played from records. Again, the dramatic adaptation was acclaimed a notable achievement. Critics noted that there was no need for "star" billing. Sada Thompson shared the lectern with actors Rae Allen, Norman Rose, Lee Phillips, and Charles Aidman. There were no props, only five chairs, the lectern, and a "sprawling, delicately painted backdrop."

Meanwhile, in the spring of 1956, Dos Passos had granted a year's option to Nicholas C. Spanos for screen rights to the *U.S.A.* trilogy. According to a New York *Times* article on January 4, 1957, Spanos and Shyre planned to confer regarding a road show of Shyre's adaptation with Broadway an eventual destination. Two weeks later, Dos Passos granted Spanos sole control of audio and mechanical rights to *U.S.A.* for a limited option, but began almost at once to prepare his own "suggested treatment" of *U.S.A.* for a film version of the book. For a time it was thought that John Huston was going to produce and direct *U.S.A.* as a film. The author had supposedly prepared "his own screen treatment of the book" and investors were said to be "standing in line to take part in the proposed film production." Dos Passos' "suggested treatment" consisted chiefly of pages cut from a copy of *The Big Money* and taped to legal sheets with interpolations relative to its dramatic format.

While Spanos' "creative package" was being put together in Hollywood, Dos Passos was informed that the Shyre adaptation would probably be allowed to represent the United States on a "twin bill" with O'Neill's *Long Day's Journey Into Night* at the 1957 Paris Theatre Festival. Since the O'Neill play had already been approved by the United States State Department, the request by the American National Theatre and Academy to include Shyre's adaptation on a double bill was ultimately turned down on the basis of insufficient funds. The movie sale was still pending for a revised script of the *U.S.A.* adaptation when Dos Passos decided that he wanted to collaborate with Shyre. "I can't tell whether these additions will work or not, but perhaps you can do some experimenting with them," Dos Passos wrote Shyre during the winter of 1957–58 after rewriting several of the scenes. "As I told you, I felt the present version was so good it was worth doing a little more work on." Soon Dos Passos and Shyre had produced a full-scale revision for Nick Spanos and Howard Gottfried, as co-producers, to present off-Broadway in the fall of 1959.

By mid-September the new version was in rehearsal to open October 26, 1959, in the small theater of the Hotel Martinique on Thirty-second Street at Broadway. "Scoops from U.S.A. I call it, but it will—possibly—be an interesting vaudeville evening," Dos Passos wrote Sara Murphy on October 6. Betty and Lucy, now almost ten, would be with him in New York for opening night, he said. The production opened to rave notices. Billed as a "dramatic revue by John Dos Passos and Paul Shyre," the production starred Sada Thompson, who had played the Isadora Duncan/Eleanor Stoddard roles in its two earlier presentations. *Cue* declared *U.S.A.* the most "exciting uproarious, savagely satiric show of the season, on or off Broadway!" Brooks Atkinson thought it "brilliant." Other opening-night critics used such phrases as "a gem," "fascinating," "exciting," "excellent," "first-rate," and "don't miss it!" to recommend the play to future audiences. *U.S.A.* ran seven and one-half months to enthusiastic viewers. As it neared its two hundredth performance, Howard Gottfried acknowledged that his dilemma was whether to "accede to the requests" by countless other theater companies who wished to produce it, or to tour the present production himself. Requests to produce *U.S.A.* came, too, from West Germany, Austria, Sweden, and Great Britain.

The same date that the *U.S.A.* revue opened in New York City, Dos Passos' publisher, Prentice-Hall, was celebrating the publication of *Prospects of a Golden Age* (1959), which had evolved from the "picture book" originally conceived by Monroe Stearns as a substitute for the manuscript of *The Great Days* into a 266-page history of the Revolutionary generation through 1810, with 150 color illustrations, halftone plates, and line drawings. Although the book was reviewed more as a coffee table item than an in-depth history, it was applauded as an apt and scholarly companion piece to *The Men Who Made the Nation.* Dos Passos told Phil Casey, a reporter for the Washington *Post,* that he was not concerned about sales of his books. His work had never sold well, and he did not expect it to be any different in the future. His daily stint at the writing table was a necessary one, he continued. "I've been trying for years to knock off on Sundays, but I can't seem to. It's a race with senility."

It occurred to Dos Passos at year's end that Paul Shyre might be interested in adapting *Manhattan Transfer,* but nothing came of it. *U.S.A.* was still running strong in the spring of 1961 when Shyre took it on a month's tour of universities and colleges. Back at the Martinique Theatre in May, the play was viewed by a committee of University of Chicago students and faculty who acclaimed it "the most excellent and meaningful play of the current season." As a result, the University of Chicago invited the entire cast to fly to Chicago to present six performances at Mandel Hall. The Dos Passos/Shyre *U.S.A.* was published in full in the June 1960 issue of *Theatre Arts,* along with Dos Passos' piece written for the New York *Times* ("Looking Back on *U.S.A.")* and the directing notes by Paul Shyre.

Although the William Morris Agency expressed interest in arranging a cross-country tour as soon as the revue closed in New York, the tour itself did not materialize. On March 25, 1960, Dos Passos asked Shyre if he had heard that the William Morris Agency was "sponsoring" a Hemingway dramatization that sounded similar to theirs. "It does seem odd that they are willing to buy Hemingway's pig in a poke and are unwilling even to give our production, which has already had a real success of a certain kind, any consideration at all," he grumbled. Dos Passos' reference was to a dramatic treatment of several of Hemingway's "Nick Adams stories" that were being adapted by A. E. Hotchner.

Dos Passos and Hemingway had not seen each other since 1949, and their few letters exchanged since their estrangement in 1938 had been perfunctory. In the fall of 1953 when Van Wyck Brooks asked Dos Passos to serve on a committee to award a gold medal to Hemingway by the American Academy and Institute of Arts and Letters, he replied: "I'd be very pleased to be a member of the committee. As you say, Hemingway is the logical choice." Dos Passos and Betty attended the awards ceremonial on April 26, 1954, but Hemingway was not present to receive his Award of Merit for the Novel and cash prize in person, having recently been on safari in Africa and "too ill" to return from Venice, where he was recuperating, to attend the ceremonial. Dos Passos wrote Cummings that the ceremonial had been "pretty hard to take," but that it had been "relieved by the free bourbon of a high order" and by his pleasure in seeing "such characters as Roger Sessions," whom he had not laid eyes on in twenty-five years. "One of the bitterest things about growing older is the sense of solitude that hedges you about," he wrote Max Eastman that winter. "Old friends harden into fanatics and stop liking you because they don't like the things you say. Sometimes I feel as if I were working down at the bottom of a well." Hemingway was writing his memoirs when he inquired of Archibald and Ada MacLeish what news they had had of Dos Passos of late, then added: "He wrote such an awful ill-written crookedly thought book called <u>Chosen Country</u> that I shouldn't ever write to him."

In the spring of 1961 when Dos Passos read that Hemingway had almost walked into the spinning blades of an airplane propeller, he dropped him a note, saying "Hem, hope this isn't getting to be a habit. Take it easy there. Best of luck. Dos." By then he had heard reports that Hemingway was not well. Four months later, he was in Spain with Betty and Lucy when he read of Hemingway's suicide. Being in Madrid in familiar haunts he once had shared with Hemingway brought back a flood of memories, he wrote Sara Murphy. "Until I read of his poor death, I didn't realize how fond I'd been of the old Monster of Mt. Kisco."

26

As the World Turns:
Speaking His Mind as a Conservative, 1960–69

John Dos Passos was a conundrum. He had a sense of mission, but did not proselytize. He was a sweet-natured man who boiled with a passion.

James Bready to Virginia Spencer Carr
21 March 1977

Having denied countless requests to lecture during his early career, Dos Passos accepted many such invitations during the last fifteen years of his life. He had no desire to go on another organized lecture tour such as he had done for the Peat Lecture Bureau in 1954, but he responded readily to the requests of professors and student leaders who arranged for him to come to their colleges and universities. His fees never exceeded $750 (which Colgate paid him in 1966), but he could be had for less because he appreciated the opportunity that lecturing and reading from his works afforded him in being able to interact with students. Many schools that invited Dos Passos to discuss his views, influences, narrative techniques, and work as a chronicler of his times billed him as "The Radical of the Twenties Who Turned Conservative."

William F. Buckley, Jr., was at Yale University as an alumnus to hear Dos Passos address a group of undergraduates at an honors convocation assembly in 1964. Buckley had been Yale's most prominent radical as a student in the early 1950s, but was now a standard-bearer of conservatism. Dos Passos had been writing for Buckley's magazine, the *National Review*, almost since its inception in 1955. "I think it is the most amusing of the weeklies at present, although I don't always agree with it," he told Myra MacPherson, a reporter for the New Haven *Star*, before his lecture at Yale when asked what he thought of the *National Review*. Buckley was apprehensive regarding Dos Passos' scheduled appearance at Yale because of his "tendency to stammer when he got his anxiety up and/or was agitated in trying to express something. But I should not have worried. Dos may have agreed to *talk,* but what he did was mostly listen. For practically the whole hour it was Dos asking the students questions."

John Chamberlain, who was also in the audience that day, reported: "Dos was not a good speaker, but he was a good listener and he knew how to ask questions. No matter where he was, he was always the novelist and historian looking for new material. I think he wrote to find out what he thought himself." Buckley agreed with Chamberlain that Dos Passos threw ideas out "to test his own inclinations. He sought the company of certain 'non-kooks' who were somewhat intellectual to try his ideas out on. We had some good discussions, but I discovered that the most appropriate thing to do in Dos's presence was not to try to press any paradigm on certain subjects about which his poetic passions were shaping his visions." Buckley said that they only talked right-wing politics once. "Dos pushed me into it when we were out on a boat in Long Island Sound with George Plimpton, who was a liberal." Buckley was convinced that Dos Passos was

> victimized for his political ideas. There was a mind-set about him in those power centers that decide what will be reviewed and what prominence will be given to that which is chosen for review. There is blacklisting in the publishing world, tacit agreement among the cognoscenti. You know such tacit agreement exists when certain worthies get passed over for the Nobel Prize and it goes to Quasimodo, for instance. There is no objective evidence, of course, but one feels a sense of betrayal. Certainly the Nobel Committee maintains a high degree of confidentiality.

Buckley's reference was to Salvatore Quasimodo, Italian poet and essayist, who was awarded the Nobel Prize for literature in 1959.

Dos Passos made no mention in letters that he thought he had been "passed over" by the Nobel Prize Committee or by any other committee, but his friends were fairly certain that he was aware of the various writers to whom the Nobel went year after year, and that he was not one of them. In all, six Americans won the Nobel Prize during Dos Passos' lifetime: Sinclair Lewis in 1930, Eugene O'Neill in 1936, Pearl Buck in 1938, William Faulkner in 1949, Ernest Hemingway in 1954, and John Steinbeck in 1962. Throughout the sixties Dos Passos' friends hoped that he would be awarded it at last, and year by year they noted the announcements: Saint-John Perse, a Frenchman, in 1960; Ivo Andrić, a Yugoslavian, in 1961; Giorgos Seferis, a Greek, in 1963; Jean-Paul Sartre (who declined the prize) in 1964; Mikhail Sholokhov, a Russian, in 1965; Shmuel Josef Agnon, an Israeli, and Nelly Sachs, a Swede, awarded jointly in 1966; Miguel Angel Asturias, a Guatemalan, in 1967; Kawabata Yasunari, a Japanese, in 1968; Samuel Beckett, an Irishman, in 1969; and Aleksandr I. Solzhenitsyn (the second Russian to win in less than a decade) in 1970.

Dos Passos was off the coast of Gibraltar with Betty and Lucy on June 16, 1960, when he wrote Estlin and Marion Cummings to thank them for the flowers they found in their stateroom when they boarded the SS *Italia* in New York, their destination, Venice, Italy, to attend "some doings celebrating Tolstoi." It was "sweet of you to send the flowers," he began. "We are five days out and they are still fresh. It is proving a hellishly comfortable trip—the verandah is everything. I sit out there messing with watercolors while Betty reads more than she has in years and Lucy runs around with an international swarm of wriggly girls. It's the 'grand luxe' and we are certainly enjoying it." Dos Passos had invited his stepson, Kiffy, to accompany them, but he had just finished his freshman year at Randolph-Macon College in Ashland, Virginia, and was working outdoors in Grand Teton National Park in Wyoming for the summer. The crossing had been drizzly, rainy, and blowy, but "we don't give a damn," Dos Passos added in a note to Sara and Gerald Murphy. "We've attended Italian classes religiously every day in the lounge. We eat just a little too much and drink just a wee drop and slip surreptitiously into the pool topside that the officials for some reason always keep roped off." Since Dos Passos' expenses were being covered by the committee sponsoring an international celebration honoring Leo Tolstoi on the fiftieth anniversary of his death, he intended to make of the occasion a six-week vacation excursion with his family. He had just turned in his *Midcentury* manuscript to Houghton Mifflin, which gave him some "loose change" to finance the travels he envisioned for them upon leaving Italy. He looked forward to showing Lucy something of Europe and the culture that had meant a great deal to him in the past and planned to conclude their trip with a visit to Madeira so that he might introduce her to her Portuguese heritage.

In Venice, Dos Passos testified to his debt to Tolstoi. His panoramic canvases had their roots in such works as *War and Peace.* He said that his interest in Tolstoi dated from his early years at Harvard University, and that it had never lessened. By the end of June, he was motoring with Betty and Lucy in a rental car through northern Italy, Switzerland, and northwestern France, the journey not only a vacation, but also a research trip. Dos Passos was already well into his work on a second historical volume for Lewis Gannett's Mainstream of America Series. This one focused on Woodrow Wilson and the events leading up to—and surrounding—World War I. He wanted to look over some of the battlefields, such as Cantigny, Verdun, Belleau Wood, and Château-Thierry, where he had been an ambulance driver over shell-pocked roads more than forty years earlier, and he took pleasure in showing his daughter the scenes of important battles of the remote past that had had an important role in shaping her own country's history. By the end of the second week of July they were headed south along the Rhone to Avignon, then across to Grasse and Nice, where they swam in the Mediterranean before boarding a plane to Lisbon.

Portugal Today, a bimonthly magazine produced by an American public relations firm, published a full-page photograph of Dos Passos alighting from his plane in Lisbon, where he told a reporter that he was on his way to Madeira to visit the countryside of his paternal grandfather, who had lived there until he was a young man. The public relations firm hoped that publicity surrounding Dos Passos' visit would boost Portuguese-American trade and tourism and sent a reporter to query Dos Passos about his Portuguese ancestry and his previous visits to Portugal and Madeira. Dos Passos, in turn, anticipated picking up a few Portuguese-American readers for his new book, *Midcentury,* which he described as "a volume of romantic chronicles," but if they read it with an expectation of finding their homeland mentioned, they were mistaken. Several years later, however, he returned to Portugal for the express purpose of researching the country of his ancestors for the last book published during his lifetime, *The Portugal Story: Three Centuries of Exploration and Discovery*.

In Lisbon, Dos Passos and his family boarded the SS *Moçambique*, a Portuguese steamer that plied the waters regularly to Funchal, a voyage of two and one half days. At the last minute they learned that every available space had been booked and that they would have no place to sleep except a deck chair. Funchal did not have a commercial airport, and it would be a week before the ship could make another run. For a time they thought they would have to cancel their trip, but one of the ship's officers insisted that he would find a place for the "famous American writer" and his family to sleep. The ship was already pulling away from the wharf when the captain's mate escorted them to the wardroom of the ship's officers. "Here you will stay," he said, pointing to a large bare room. "We will put mattresses on the floor and you will sleep as soundly as though you were in your own private stateroom."

"For two nights we slept on the floor to the strains of music piped in over a very loud loudspeaker which ran throughout the night. Somehow we managed, but it was quite an experience," recounted Betty upon their return. In Madeira, they stayed at the same hotel where Dos Passos had stayed with his mother and father while he recuperated from his hernia operation at age seven. He still had distant cousins living in Ponta do Sol, the tiny village of his grandfather's birth, and he wanted to meet them. "As soon as Dos's cousins heard that we had arrived, they called upon us at Reid's Hotel and carried us off to a great festival in Dos's honor. There was a grand luncheon with many courses, and we were served different wines with each course. The meal went on for hours. Then we were carried somewhere else for a huge tea with marvelous iced cakes and other sweets. Finally we were returned to the hotel, but once there, the management welcomed us and wanted to feed us, too. Never had we felt so stuffed," said Betty. The next day they were invited to Ponta do Sol, where they visited Dos Passos' ancestral home. Here the mayor honored him with a century-old medal. Then a plaque was placed above the entrance to the house that read: THIS HOUSE WAS THE BIRTHPLACE OF THE ANCESTORS OF THE EMINENT AMERI-CAN WRITER JOHN DOS PASSOS WHO VISITED THIS MUNICIPALITY ON JULY 20, 1960. HOMAGE OF THE MUNICIPAL CHAMBER.

Among the distant cousins Dos Passos met that week was the family of Maria Amália Pitta Pestana dos Reis, who had recently married Cyril F. dos Passos, a widower. Cyril had been a partner in Dos Passos' father's law firm, but Dos Passos and he had seldom seen each other since John R.'s death. Having renewed his Portuguese connection in Madeira, Dos Passos looked forward to freshening his ties with his paternal family in America, too. Cyril retired from his practice of law to his home in Mendham, New Jersey, to pursue his work as a lepidopterist. He had the largest collection of butterflies in the United States outside the American Museum of Natural History. Lucy, who had been chasing butterflies and collecting them almost since she could walk, was elated when her father took her to visit Cyril and Maria Amália upon their return from Portugal. "Young Lucy and I often corresponded about our butterflies after that first visit," said Cyril. "She had a marvelous curiosity about everything she saw. She was a lovely girl, and her parents brought her up very well. Having a child rather late in his life was one of the best things that ever happened to Jack," observed Cyril when Lucy was a grown woman.

Besides leaving Spence's Point for a month to six weeks each summer to escape the heat and humidity, Dos Passos and Betty had hit upon a workable plan that enabled them to divide their time between Spence's Point and Baltimore so that the children could attend more progressive schools than those in their region of the Northern Neck of Virginia. Kiffy was a boarding student at Gilman and Lucy was about two when they began spending their weekdays in the city and their weekends on the farm. For four years they rented a house at 552 Chateau Avenue in Baltimore and commuted, but the expense of maintaining two households was more than Dos Passos could manage in 1957 and 1958 —leaner than usual years—and he moved his family back to Virginia. Lucy started first grade at Cople School, where Kiffy, too, attended until he was sent to Gilman, but by the end of her second year there, her parents decided that regardless of the cost they would have to put her in a first-rate school. At eight, Lucy was enrolled in Bryn Mawr School in Baltimore, and the family rented a house at 3911 Canterbury Road. "We're back on a weekend commuting schedule that gets rather wearing after a while. When school closes in June it'll be Spence's Point again for us," Betty wrote Henka Farnsworth after they had settled in their new quarters. "Lucy is a third grader, much interested in ballet and ice skating in off hours. This house unfortunately has TV; since we don't have it at home she is going through the period where she sits and sits, oblivious to everything."

Kiffy remembered that it was not until the fall of 1960 that his family owned a television set. "It was right after the U-2 spy incident when Gary Powers was sentenced to ten years in prison. My stepfather was much interested in that, and I recall his watching the news later when Powers was exchanged for a Russian spy. Mr. Jack was always selective in what he watched, and my mother's tastes coincided with his," said Kiffy.

Being in a metropolitan area where he had ready access to major library resources was important to Dos Passos in preparing his historical chronicles. He worked daily at the Enoch Pratt Free Library or the library of the Peabody Institute, and if there was something he could not find in Baltimore, it was only a short drive into Washington, D.C., to work at the Library of Congress. P. W. Filby, director of the Peabody Library, said that he was so pleased to have Dos Passos "ask in his self-effacing manner" if he could use the library that he immediately gave him his own table. When asked to write a piece on what the Peabody Library had meant to him over the years in an "I Speak for the Peabody" series, Dos Passos happily complied. The Peabody was "a scholar's library covering the seminal period during which most of the notions which, for good or ill, govern our thinking today, originated. On top of that, it offers a quiet uncrowded place to work. What more can a man ask?" He also spoke appreciatively of the American public library, "where anybody can go in, and without letters of introduction from learned societies or police identification or the production of a birth certificate, not only be allowed to see the book he wants right away, but have friendly librarians willing to help him find it." He said he had been in enough libraries over the world to know that the American system was unique.

"The people of Baltimore treated John as one of their 'first citizens,' " said Julia Sprigg Cameron, who lived in nearby Bel Air, Maryland. "In the living room or during an outing, John tended to stutter—something he never outgrew—but when he got up in front of a group, it was as though he was a different person. The first formal address I heard him make was to the American Library Association in Baltimore. The applause was thunderous. People even stood in their chairs and cheered—and that's unusual for Baltimore," said Cameron. "When we needed a speaker to dedicate our new Bel Air Library, John was our unanimous choice. We loved his talk—he made us appreciate books in a fresh way. He also made us question our educational system, which had been failing for many years to teach our young people to read." In 1968, Dos Passos donated seventy-five original editions of his books to the Langsdale Library at the University of Baltimore.

Midcentury, the book Dos Passos had been at work on for almost ten years, appeared one month after his sixty-fifth birthday. It was the thirtieth book of his career. Well launched by a front-page review by Harry T. Moore in the New York *Times Book Review* on February 26, 1961, the novel rode the New York *Times* bestseller list for almost four months, having attained its fifth printing before publication date. According to Lovell Thompson, who edited *Midcentury* for Houghton Mifflin: "I liked this last big novel enormously, although *Manhattan Transfer* was probably Dos's best writing as I look back on his books now. *Midcentury* sold better than any other single novel of his—some thirty thousand copies with us—compared to a top of about eighteen thousand for the other books of Dos's published by Houghton Mifflin." Only two other books by Dos Passos were accorded the honor of the cover page of the New York *Times Book Review: Three Soldiers* (in 1921) and *Number One* (in 1943). The dates spanned forty years. "No other writer of the twentieth century approached Dos's stature," insisted Thompson. Harry T. Moore, a research professor at Southern Illinois University who reviewed the book for the New York *Times Book Review*, was a specialist of twentieth-century American literature. His review began:

> Seldom does a writer retrieve a long-lost reputation at a single stroke, but John Dos Passos has probably done just that with *Midcentury*, by far his best novel since he completed the *U.S.A.* trilogy with *The Big Money* in 1936. It is written with a mastery of narrative styles, a grasp of character and a sense of the American scene. In its fictional passages this panoramic novel recaptures the Dos Passos verve and intensity of a quarter-century ago, while the background sections, made up of sociological tidbits and pertinent biographical sketches, show the same Dos Passos skill at manipulating the devices which helped give *U.S.A.* originality and force.

Despite the commercial success of *Midcentury*, its reviews were mixed. Dos Passos reported to Thompson that he was "appalled by the young man they sent up from *Newsweek*. He hadn't read the book and was still looking for McCarthyites under the bed." Judging from the interviewers who had been seeking him out, he added, the book's reception would not be "universal repudiation," but "mixed." The anonymous *Newsweek* reviewer spoke of Dos Passos as the "perennial Lazarus of American letters" who had disappeared from the picture so far as literary criticism was concerned a quarter of a century ago. "If reviewers now consent to notice the books he persists in writing, it is only to ring new changes on the old theme of poor-Dos-is-dead."

Granville Hicks, writing for *Saturday Review*, identified Dos Passos as "a man to whom a cause is necessary" and was less critical of *Midcentury* than of most of his other books. Not since 1931 had Hicks written as supportively of Dos Passos. He said he missed the passion that characterized *U.S.A.,* but thought the other virtues remained. "The biographies, for instance, are terse and revealing, even when one quarrels with some of their judgments. The narratives are based on a knowledge of industrial life few novelists have. . . . Tired and hopeless as he may be, Dos Passos is still a man of solid integrity, saying exactly what he thinks." Hicks especially liked the "good writing" evoked by the character of Blackie Bowman, who represented "the kind of realism to which Dos Passos gave his allegiance."

John K. Hutchens singled Blackie Bowman out as the only character who came alive to the degree that Joe Williams (in *1919)* and Charley Anderson (in *The Big Money)* did, but found "the fire and sweep" missing. Bowman, a garrulous former Wobbly from Greenwich Village, reviewed his life from his bed in a veterans' hospital. The novel's conflict did not involve socialism or Communism versus capitalism. The enemy was the centralization of power in government, business, and labor. "The old technical forms are here, still serviceable. The style is once again simple and delicately strong. The mind is that of the cultivated man of good will. But the fires are banked," concluded Hutchens.

Many critics thought *Midcentury* one of the best American novels of recent years and saw it as a mirror held up to a sick society, a substantial achievement both as fiction and as a record of the temper of the times. Some took pleasure in "the old magic" of *U.S.A.* repeated in the biographical sketches and in some of the narrative scenes, but felt that the characters on the whole were poorly drawn and mouthed banal dialogue. Others had been impressed by Dos Passos' experimental modes in *U.S.A.,* but regretted that he had resurrected them because they suffered by comparison. His imitation of himself did not work well enough to justify the repetition, they rued. According to John Gross in *The New Statesman,* Dos Passos' narrative tricks were devices to launch "a crotchety attack on labor rackets as the root of all un-American evil." Dos Passos sounded "too much like any bilious reactionary down at the country club." Several reviewers faulted him for his cynicism, bitterness, and unrelieved pessimism. Some saw hope at the "end of a long tunnel" if the American society would only heed Dos Passos' writings as a warning. The book was a valuable social document in revealing "the rottenness with the house of labor," despite its failure as a creative work, said another. Robert Stilwell, who wrote perhaps the most condemning review of them all, informed Louisville *Courier-Journal* readers that *Midcentury* was "a dismal hodgepodge of specious thought and outrageously bad craftsmanship, one within which all potential for epic had been either choked by narrow vision or extinguished by wretched artistry." True to his word, Dos Passos saw relatively few of these reviews. "Occasionally someone brought one to his attention which he thought might amuse or interest him, but he had to be hard pressed to read one through," said Betty.

"Lord man, don't worry about reviews," Dos Passos advised William F. Buckley, Jr., after the publication of *Up from Liberalism* in 1959. "Take the advice of an old-timer who has been thoroughly abused by reviewers, alternately abused and ignored, for something like forty years: don't read them. Never answer them. <u>Publico ergo damnatus</u> is the proper motto. A book's a throwaway. Once you get it off your chest you should never give it a thought. There just isn't time." According to Buckley, Dos Passos had encouraged him to "whip the stuff together for publication." Buckley was still addressing him as "Mr.

Dos Passos" when he wrote on September 26, 1958: "I don't know how to express my appreciation to you for the time you spent on that mess of pottage I sent you. . . . I shall never forget the great generosity that you have shown me ever since I first began to importune you several years ago." Later, Buckley admitted being disappointed in Dos Passos' introduction: "I appreciated his help enormously, but the foreword to Up from Liberalism was hyperbolic, and what he said did not follow the basic formula of the book. I confess that I rewrote the final paragraph and told Dos that it had been changed by the publisher to make it more quotable. Dos's introduction had very little to do with the content or the essence of my essays." The paragraph in question was revised to read: "This is not Mr. Buckley's theory. It is mine. Maybe new developments will prove it to be worthless. In any case, the sort of high-spirited analysis offered in this book should prove useful to anyone who is working towards an independent appraisal of this midcentury phenomenon of 'militant liberalism.' " Buckley said that Dos Passos accepted the revision and attributed it to someone's having tried to "take the mashed potatoes out of my mouth." The final sentence of the revised paragraph was placed on the back cover of the dustjacket of the book and attributed to Dos Passos.

On June 17, 1961, Dos Passos was awarded the Peter Francisco Medal by the Portuguese Continental Union of the United States for his "contributions to world literature and to the Luso-American tradition." According to Luís Gomes, supreme president of the group, who made the presentation, the medal was reserved for those who had enhanced the "good name and prestige of Portugal and its people and the people of Portuguese descent in the United States." The two previous recipients of the annual award were John F. Kennedy in 1959 and Basil Brewer, publisher of the New Bedford *Standard-Times,* in 1960. "Dos Passos' integrity, culture and renown—a veritable nimbus of glory—along with all the high virtues of his work and character, certainly add to the prestige of our society," declared Gomes at the awards luncheon in New York City.

In accepting his medal, Dos Passos admitted that until he had been notified of his newly bestowed honor, he had never heard of Pedro Francisco, the Portuguese hero who served with General George Washington in the American Revolution. He said he was ignorant of "many things Portuguese," which he hoped to remedy before he died. He told of being shocked as a small boy to discover that he was one-fourth Portuguese. "That was considered somewhat disreputable in those days," he added. He spoke, too, of his visits to Madeira as a child and, later, to Brazil and Portugal, and of the few classes he attended at the Berlitz School in an attempt to learn the rudiments of his grandfather's language. During Dos Passos' fifteen-minute address, he carefully avoided all controversial topics of the day concerning Portugal. As Harvard professor Francis M. Rogers pointed out: "International affairs where Portugal was concerned were perilous in 1961. A Portuguese luxury liner, the *Santa Maria,* had been seized by opponents of Salazar during the Kennedy Inaugural Ball, and there had been a recent 'black revolt' against Portuguese rule in Angola. Relations had also deteriorated between Portugal and the Indian Union because of Goa, which resulted in Nehru's takeover a few months later." In Dos Passos' audience that day were the consul generals of Portugal and Brazil and the consuls of Portugal in Philadelphia and Boston, as well as other notable Luso-American guests. Officials of the Portuguese Continental Union were aware of Dos Passos' consistent stand against totalitarianism in its myriad forms and were admittedly nervous over what he might say. They might have spared themselves such worries, however. He said nothing inflammatory. "The Portuguese tradition has a certain mildness about it, a lack of the racial and ideological fanaticism that has brought our civilization to the verge of destruction," he said in his concluding statement. "In a time when all the traditions of European humanism are being thrown into the discard, every fragment we can pull out of the wreck becomes valuable as material with which to rebuild Western civilizations. . . . It becomes interesting to find out, too, why Portuguese-speaking peoples who inhabit Brazil are steadily to the fore. The more I study it, the prouder I am of my Portuguese inheritance." Dos Passos' daughter, now eleven, beamed at him from her place at the luncheon table, obviously proud, too, of her Portuguese heritage.

On New Year's Day of 1961, Dos Passos reflected on the state of his country in a letter to Arthur McComb: "I must say I'll see Mr. E. [Eisenhower] retire to Gettysburg without regret. I'm consoling myself over Kennedy by remembering I refused to vote for Franklin D. in 1932 because his platform was so conservative. Maybe the Kennedy clan will behave as Roosevelts in reverse." In the fall of 1962, he spoke of the situation in Cuba. The Soviet Union had just agreed to withdraw its missiles as a result of the United States naval blockade. "The present Cuban snarl is enlivening," he observed to McComb, who shared his political bent. "Do you suppose that Kennedy is preparing to make like a President? I don't trust any of those boys—particularly Robert—who seems to me the dominant figure. Still they'll do anything to win an election—even affront Khrushchev."

Dos Passos' stance did not make him popular with the more liberal members of the academic world of the University of Virginia during his three-week stint as Visiting Author in February of 1963. He had been asked to join the faculty as a Writer-in-Residence in 1956, but declined, pleading that his own literary projects kept him too busy to be of much use to anyone else. The invitation was then extended to William Faulkner, who accepted and remained in the post until 1962. Upon Faulkner's death, Dos Passos was invited once more to the University of Virginia, where faculty members were apprehensive for fear that he would try to foist off his right-wing views upon their students. Jere Real, an undergraduate at the time, recalled hearing two English professors discuss Dos Passos soon after his arrival on campus. "I hear all he does is talk about politics. He doesn't say too much about writing," said one. His colleague replied: "Well, I hope no one goes in to talk with him while he's here." Real went in twice to confer with Dos Passos. "He was very helpful. I had him read twice a short story I had written. He made several suggestions for revision, which I followed, and later, the story was published. But it was clear to me—or so it seemed at the time—that he was far more interested in politics than in literature as a point of discussion. I remember his talking at length about the Kennedy brothers, whom he did not like."

Dos Passos spoke to an overflow audience at the University of Virginia soon after his arrival. Most of the program was a reading of excerpts from *Midcentury*. The students especially liked the "James Dean" section. They also appreciated his "Faulkner: In Memoriam," which he had prepared for delivery at a joint meeting of the National Institute of Arts and Letters and the American Academy of Arts and Letters. Although he answered questions after his address, some thought he replied too briefly or superficially.

When he was asked if he planned to attend the "second bill" of the evening, starring Gus Hall, leader of the Communist party in the United States, who was to address the students as soon as Dos Passos' session adjourned, Dos Passos replied: "Yes, just out of curiosity. We must remember that what he is saying is a lot of guff, but it will be interesting to see what the current line is." He also reiterated his statement made at a press conference in Charlottesville a few hours earlier, that he favored allowing representatives of the Communist and Nazi parties to speak on campus. Throughout his life he insisted that freedom of speech was one of man's most "needful freedoms."

Dos Passos was in Richmond in 1965 to attend a meeting of the Virginia Commission on Constitutional Government—of which he was a member—when he was approached by Jere Real, now a reporter for the Richmond *News Leader*. Real reminded him of their earlier meeting at the university when Dos Passos had helped him with a story. "He was receptive to an interview after the meeting, and we talked for two hours. He spoke bluntly of his belief that the intellectual level of college professors was 'pretty low.' It seemed to him that the current crop of professors and students existed in a sort of vacuum. He didn't think many students knew which end was up so far as world affairs were concerned. As he saw it, the academic community had fallen completely for Communist propaganda."

Despite his criticism of college students and their faculties, Dos Passos was invited repeatedly to their campuses and welcomed. After lecturing at Los Angeles State College, he was asked back in 1964 as a visiting professor for the fall term. For a time he toyed with the idea, since he had in progress then a long, commemorative essay on Lincoln ("Lincoln and His Almost Chosen People") at the request of Allan Nevins for a book of commemorative papers to mark the centennial anniversary of Lincoln's death. Nevins recommended his working at the Huntington Library as a fit resource center for the Lincoln essay and thought it was a good idea to accept the guest professorship, but Dos Passos declined. He was reluctant to disrupt Lucy's education at Bryn Mawr School by taking his family to California, and he did not want to be away from them for three months. He also had other pressing projects at hand. He had finished still another book on Jefferson, published that spring under the title *Thomas Jefferson: The Making of a President,* and was impatient to get on with another novel, which he saw as a continuation of *Midcentury.* It was to be a long novel in the same style as its predecessor. His new Jefferson book was well received by the critics, who reviewed it as a balanced and highly readable biography for youth and young adults.

By this time, Dos Passos had already published another major historical book, *Mr. Wilson's War,* which came out a year after *Midcentury* (November 1962) in Lewis Gannett's Mainstream of America Series. With the exception of a handful of critics, reviewers and lay readers alike spoke of it with enthusiasm. It was described variously as "a blockbuster of a book, lucid and fascinating, scholarly but lively"; "a superb book, with excellent writing and research, of award-winning quality"; "one of Dos Passos' best for sheer craftsmanship, less didactic, more evenly balanced, broader in its philosophical aspects, sounder in its psychological judgments" than his other recent books; "an honest portrayal of Wilson; history, not myth"; "a major history, thoughtfully weighted"; "highly dramatic, fascinating, sensitive selectivity which makes the characters live and breathe"; "a masterful portrait of twenty turbulent years which reads like a first-rate historical novel"; and the plaudits went on and on.

A longtime student of Wilson and a historian/biographer, Arthur S. Link, reviewed *Mr. Wilson's War* for the New York *Times Book Review* some five months after the book itself was published. Link explained that he had meticulously examined the book, since he himself was a biographer of Wilson. It was filled with errors "of nomenclature and fact," he said, due to "Dos Passos' carelessness or failure to assimilate the history of the period." Link praised his treatment of World War I for its "exciting and vivid descriptions." S. L. A. Marshall, also a historian, liked *Mr. Wilson's War* for its "light whimsical touch" and compared its pace, scope, and style to Frederick Lewis Allen's *Only Yesterday*. Marshall thought Dos Passos had caught the mood of the American Expeditionary Forces, which he termed "a light-hearted and gallant army." *Mr. Wilson's War* rode the bestseller lists for several weeks. LeBaron Barker, Dos Passos' Doubleday editor, was well pleased by its reception, as was Gannett, who was told repeatedly that *Mr. Wilson's War* was one of the best—if not *the* best—in his Mainstream of America Series. Dos Passos had worked closely with Gannett, who told him he was pleased that Dos Passos did not "follow the convention of making Wilson a glacial personality." Gannett had known Wilson personally and had gone on bird walks with him when Wilson lived in New Hampshire. "You put some hot blood in his veins, and I like that, though you make him a bit more calculating in his approach to the Presidency than I had conceived to be the case." Gannett was more of a working editor than anyone with whom Dos Passos had dealt. While the book was in progress, Gannett wrote Dos Passos: "If I don't dwell more upon my likes and enthusiasms, that is because you don't want or need—as some authors do— to be praised. You want to hear the questions." One of their strongest arguments involved Dos Passos' choice of titles, but Dos Passos usually had his way. During the 1960s, he did not seek outside advice on his titles, although he routinely tried them out on his wife.

Upon reading Edmund Wilson's *The Cold War and the Income Tax: A Protest,* a pamphlet published in 1963 (Wilson had designated its proceeds to go to A. J. Muste's "peace movement"), Dos Passos wrote William F. Buckley, Jr., that he would like to review it for the *National Review.* "I'd like to use it as a pretext for a preachment on the failure of even our best intellectuals to understand the world they live in," explained Dos Passos. Buckley assented, eager to see what Dos Passos came up with. The review/essay was published on January 28, 1964, entitled "Please Mr. Rip Van Winkle, Wake Up Some More," the title a takeoff on the persona Wilson had assumed for his pamphlet. Before the essay appeared, Dos Passos apprised Wilson of it. "Your protest aroused my patriotic gore [Wilson's book of essays on the Civil War was entitled *Patriotic Gore: Studies in the Literature of the American Civil War]* to the point of causing me to sound off in the *National Review.* I hope you won't find it offensive. I hold up your hands on some rather important points," he ventured. Dos Passos spoke, too, of the "strange and gruesome business" of the assassination of President Kennedy. "The response from the mass misinformers has been to me more gruesome than the nasty crime itself."

Wilson replied that he had not seen Dos Passos' "offensive article" and suggested that he send it to him. "It's been so long now since I've last seen you that I don't know what line you're taking. The last I heard you were receiving a citation from Goldwater, who is surely one of the biggest asses in our asinine country. . . . What do you mean, by the way, by the 'mass misinformers' about the Kennedy assassination?" Wilson harped on Dos Passos' tendency to use abstract phrases without developing his point. After reading Dos Passos' review, Wilson reproached him:

> What danger do you imagine the Soviet Union is threatening us with? . . . I don't under-
> stand how, at your age, you can continue to believe in these bugaboos and see everything in
> terms of melodrama. It seems to me that you are just as gullible as you ever were in the
> twenties. . . . You've been railing against "the liberals" all your life, and my impression is
> that your conception of them is a projection of some suppressed alter ego that you perpetually
> feel you have to discredit. You used to assail this myth from the radical side, and now you
> assail it from the conservative. . . . You ought to dissect your own generalized common-
> places, which seem to me from here identical with the shibboleths of the Goldwater camp.

Wilson's reference to Dos Passos' citation from Goldwater was to the Second Annual Award of the Young Americans for Freedom, which the Republican senator from Arizona presented to Dos Passos on March 7, 1962, at a huge Republican rally at Madison Square Garden. The citation read: "For dedication to the preservation of the heritage of our Nation through consistent support of the principles of freedom and individual dignity." Having aligned himself with Goldwater was bad enough, insisted Wilson, but for Dos Passos to have appeared, also, on the same platform with such a motley crew as Moise Tshombe, President of Katanga; Strom Thurmond, a Democratic senator from North Carolina; ex-President Herbert Hoover; and several others of "strange political persua-sion" or ineptitude seemed ridiculous to Wilson.

Dos Passos answered Wilson's charges by saying that "to continue this argument profitably we would have to agree on a certain number of premises." He said that if Wilson was a "straight Marxist," he would have no trouble. "But in this in between world —between for and against—I find myself bogged. You complain of my use of 'right' and 'wrong.' As a result of the somewhat varied experiences of a longish life I've come to believe—with Jefferson and the eighteenth-century people—that these terms represent something definite in the human makeup, part of the equipment for survival built over generations. We really aren't talking the same language. . . . I'm getting more and more leary of shooting my face in public."

Wilson continued to chastise Dos Passos for not exercising more self-restraint in his political forays and verbal barrages. In response to Dos Passos' piece in the *National Review* covering the Republican Convention, "The Battle of San Francisco" (July 28, 1964), Wilson wrote: "Your article . . . sounded like a teenager squealing over the Beatles. What on earth has happened to you? How can you take Goldwater seriously? His utterances make no sense and never have made any. But you seem to have arrived at a state of pure faith where such questions no longer mean anything."

Morris R. Werner, a friend of both Dos Passos and Wilson who saw both of them during this period, agreed with Wilson: "I think Dos was always politically naive and mushy. His defense of Barry Goldwater was indefensible, and it was inconceivable when he came out for Thomas E. Dewey in 1948. I remember going to a political rally once before that race and being shocked to see Dos on the platform. Dos may have been for the underdog each time, but it simply didn't make good sense. When I mentioned Dos's politics to Bunny Wilson one day, he replied, 'Oh, pish tosh.' "

In the fall of 1963, Dos Passos accompanied James Burnham, a former Communist and perhaps the most controversial of the conservatives writing for the *National Review*, to a three-day meeting in Rome of the Centro di Vita Italiana, where they were joined by Buckley. All three were to present papers. The group had organized to see what could be done to resist the inroads of Communism in Italy, but it also hoped to set up an international anti-Communist body. The United States, Great Britain, Germany, Italy, Portugal, and Poland were represented. Each delegate wore headphones so that he could hear each speech translated into his own language. "At times the proceedings dragged on," said Buckley. "Dos, in his politeness, would not have dreamed of removing his headphones and risk offending someone, though we all got very tired. Finally I noticed Dos switching the translating dial over to German, a language he really did not know. It was his means of coasting just a bit." Wilson, who was in Rome a few months later, was able to read a transcript of Dos Passos' address to the group. "Your lucubration in Rome seems to me an appalling production," taunted Wilson. "I never expected to see you develop into such a hot-air artist."

In 1962, Seymour St. John, headmaster of The Choate School, where Dos Passos himself had been a student, wrote Robert Atmore, one of the school's teachers: "Do you know whether John Dos Passos is a good speaker, and would he be someone we would like to have talk to our Sixth Form sometime? It occurs to me that he is a man we could probably get, and one whom I should be happy to re-ally with the School." Atmore replied: "Suspect he's not very good on a platform. As you know, he is now a die-hard reactionary. I favor his coming for discussion groups and questions." Upon his visit on March 5, 1963, Dos Passos was well received by students and faculty alike. No one felt that he had brought discredit upon the school by his reactionary views, which he handled with restraint. Two years later, Dos Passos was invited back to The Choate School, this time as "alumnus of the year," an honor accompanied by the Alumni Seal Prize. A relatively new award, Dos Passos was its eighth recipient. Other winners included John F. Kennedy, Adlai Stevenson, Alan Jay Lerner, and Seymour St. John, whose father had been headmaster when Dos Passos was there. Some three hundred fifty alumni, students, and faculty crowded into the school's chapel to hear Dos Passos extolled as a "man who has ever held to his basic principles, yet has dared to change with the changing times." Again he visited Choate's English classes—as he had in 1963—and spoke of writing as "hard work." He began his address to the formal body upon accepting his Alumni Seal Prize with the comment that writing was "like setting up milk bottles at fairs for people to throw baseballs at. The result may be excruciating remarks, fitful reviews, and dissatisfaction among some readers. It's one of the more hazardous professions." Had he been living in Russia, he would not have survived after even one of his magazine articles, he told them.

Choate students who met Dos Passos in 1965 were acquainted with one or two of his best-known works, but not many had seen his most recent volume, *Occasions and Protests*, a collection of political essays written over a twenty-year period, which—taken as a whole —was an apt record of his evolving political stance, which had culminated in his recent support of Barry Goldwater. Although the book had been out for six months, lukewarm reviews were still turning up as though editors thought that it ought to be reviewed, but saw no great sense of urgency. John Braine declared in a front-page review of the New York *Times Book Review*—Dos Passos' fourth such review given front-page coverage—on January 10, 1965, that a novelist "should stick to his last." Braine saw no reason for Dos Passos to "lower himself to mouthing common sentiments" in such a "sad, drab book." A novelist should never try to convey his views directly, said Braine, who was especially distressed by the disparity between *Occasions and Protests* and *U.S.A.* Braine described *U.S.A.* as the "great American novel," which he likened to a "mansion built at a time when every other author was building Cape Cod cottages." It was inconceivable to him that the same author had put together both *U.S.A.* and his present book of essays. Most of the other reviewers agreed that the pieces were "competently written," but they took issue with Dos Passos' vision.

Dos Passos told the students at The Choate School that he believed truth to be absolute. It was something for which young people should steadfastly search. "There is no secret formula for truth. The greatest and grandest problem facing America's young today is the choice between what is true and what is not." He warned them to be alert to "hucksters" after the "palatable and the easy in splendid displays" and to recognize that there were "dangerous substitutes for truth in mass advertising." According to D. J. Stewart, who reviewed *Occasions and Protests* for the *National Review,* Dos Passos' foe was anyone who attempted to impose blinders on his vision. Dos Passos' "passion" had consistently been his effort to perceive things as clearly as possible, declared Stewart.

Dos Passos tried not to schedule himself too tightly in his various speaking engagements. If he was in the middle of a major work and could find a suitable stopping point, he enjoyed getting out and finding out anew what students were thinking and doing. Invariably he ran into students who tried to corner him into a conversation about *U.S.A.* While working with the Edward M. House Archives at Yale University in the course of research for *Mr. Wilson's War,* Dos Passos often ate with Howard B. Gotlieb, the director of special collections at the library. "I'll never forget being at lunch with Dos Passos when a student came up and said very formally, 'I wish to address a few words to Mr. Dos Passos, please.' Dos Passos received his visitor cordially, but was put off when the student said, 'I want to talk with you about *U.S.A.*' Dos Passos bristled and replied, 'Why are you reading that now? I've written many books since that one. Why aren't you reading those? I am not a writer of the past.'" As Gotlieb saw it, "Dos Passos had simply had enough of students taking him to task for things he had written earlier which were no longer his political stances." At the University of Florida in 1968, a student bent on impressing Dos Passos during a question and answer session after his formal address ventured: "Mr. Dos Passos, I thought you would be happy to know that *U.S.A.* is on our required reading list in English." His wry reply was simply: "How unfortunate."

In 1965—after an absence of ten years from Cape Cod—Dos Passos took Betty back to visit Eben and Phyllis Given, Edmund Wilson, Henka Farnsworth, the Charles Walkers, and other friends. They stayed with the Givens, who told them upon arrival they were planning a big party for all of their old friends. Two days later—the morning of the party

—Dos Passos was awakened by a violent seizure of gasping and heaves. "We summoned a doctor who lived just over the hill. He was there in record time, gave Dos an injection, and his seizure stopped immediately," recounted Given.

> The doctor prescribed bed rest, foxglove juice—digitalis—and quinine and said he would look in on Dos the next day. I started to call people to cancel the party when Dos insisted that we go ahead with it as planned, and we did. Everyone tiptoed around and we set up the party in the side yard. Meanwhile, Dos was lying in bed in the downstairs bedroom just off the living room looking like a figure in a sarcophagus. Suddenly we looked up from our cups and there was Dos coming out the door, freshly shaved, and wearing a bow tie. He did not intend to miss a thing.

Henka Farnsworth said she was amazed when she heard all the things he had done the day before. "I'm not sure if he sailed, but I know he had a long swim in the ocean, walked seven miles, had another swim later in Gull Pond, and never slowed down a moment."

In a letter that winter to Rumsey Marvin, Dos Passos referred to his ailment as a "heart fit." He said he had had a bout with viral pneumonia in the spring. The infection had settled in his pericardium, and his heart problem stemmed from that. His heart was beating with "alarming irregularities," said the doctor. More rest, good nutrition, and "no snow-shoveling" should keep him going indefinitely, added Dos Passos. He said he intended to do all the things he normally did, except that he would cut down on his research time, "paint more, and go to bed early. After all, I'm on my way to the fatal age and can't expect everything to be beer and skittles."

By this time, a second biographer had appeared on the scene and sought Dos Passos' cooperation. He also began calling on Dos Passos' friends. When Edmund Wilson asked about him, Dos Passos replied: "I'd rather have them wait till they read that death notice in the New York *Times.*" He was working on his own impressionistic memoir in 1965 and was not interested in spending his time with potential biographers, although he did answer their letters and questions from time to time.

On November 26, 1966, *The Best Times: An Informal Memoir* appeared, published by the New American Library. "I have read not only with interest but also with respect for the author as a man," wrote Granville Hicks in his review of Dos Passos' memoir in the *Saturday Review*. "That was not the way I felt about Hemingway when I read *A Moveable Feast,*" Hicks added. The anonymous critic in *The Times Literary Supplement* said that next to *A Moveable Feast, The Best Times* would stand as "the best corrective we are to have of Hemingway's own last judgment beyond the grave. For Dos Passos and Hemingway had been the best of friends before 'the Old Master' began laying down the law, before the importance of being Ernest became too much for any but the tamest of camp followers." Perhaps Dan Wakefield, writing for *The Atlantic Monthly* in an essay entitled "Return to Paradise," caught best the worth and spirit of *The Best Times:*

> In this book there is none of the retrospective backbiting that mars, for instance, *A Moveable Feast,* in which Hemingway seems to write about many old friends, especially Fitzgerald and Gertrude Stein, simply to show his superiority to them, beating his own chest at the expense of others in the most disgusting display of the Hemingway bullyboy bravado. Dos Passos' memoir is free of any such vindictiveness or self-justification. In portraying his old friends with

both their flaws and their virtues, regarding them not as heroes or villains or competitors but talented colleagues, he gives us the best "album" I know of the literary figures of the twenties. He does not attempt to do full-scale portraits of them, any more than he does of himself, but sharp, deft sketches that convey a real sense of the person.

Dos Passos had just submitted the manuscript of *The Shackles of Power: Three Jeffersonian Decades,* his last book in the Mainstream of American Series, before leaving with Betty for the lower Cape. It was a week later that he experienced his first heart seizure. Upon their return home from the Cape, Dos Passos found Lewis Gannett's response to the manuscript awaiting him:

> I think it is the best of the books you have done for us, and that is high praise. It is readable throughout, full of color and of interesting minor characters, some of them hitherto mere names, if that, to me. And over it all broods the figure of Thomas Jefferson, treated with a kind of detached respect that I admire. You delight in his idiosyncracies, as I do; you respect his views, and recognize that he had that rare talent—he could change his mind. I think your use of the Jefferson-Adams letters superb; and I like the coda of de Tocqueville. . . . I admire your easy at-hominess in the period. You know the people and their period. When you say a thing is so, it is, within infinitely minor exceptions, so. Again and again, checking where I had paused to question, I found that you were, despite my first reaction, right. You can write as a novelist, but behind it is always sound scholarship, and that I profoundly respect. . . . My over-all impression is that it is a magnificent book, at once readable and just, beyond any other summary, of Jefferson's influences. I admire your zeal, your energy, your wide-ranging mind. My congratulations!

Gannett had wanted Dos Passos to call his book either "The Age of Jefferson" or "The Era of Jefferson." He thought the title *The Shackles of Power* was "blind." Then he suggested "Thirty Jefferson Years: Three Virginians and an Adams in the White House," but conceded that it was "pretty heavy sledding." Dos Passos insisted on his original title, but agreed to a subtitle, *Three Jeffersonian Decades.* The book was well received upon its publication March 18, 1966, but it was not as universally applauded as *Mr. Wilson's War* had been.

Also published in 1966 was a third book by Dos Passos, *World in a Glass: A View of Our Century,* a collection of excerpts spanning forty years of fiction. His only novels not represented were *One Man's Initiation: 1917, Streets of Night,* and *The Great Days.* Robert Sklar, writing for *The Nation* (January 16, 1967), declared that *World In a Glass* and *The Best Times* would help the reader understand the justification of Jean-Paul Sartre's calling Dos Passos "the greatest writer of his time." The anonymous reviewer for *Virginia Kirkus Review* summarized what he saw as the prevailing attitude toward Dos Passos' career in 1966: "Although Dos Passos has been faulted for the obtrusiveness of his opinions, for the slackness of his documentary style, his work has been both representative and significant, and no one has questioned its essential sincerity, indignation, and 'formidable independence.' "

In an article published in the *National Review* on October 18, 1966, entitled "The New Left: A Spook out of the Past," Dos Passos asked how it was possible for the "stale dogmas of discredited Marxism still to appeal to young people in the colleges." It seemed to him one of history's ironies that it was in the Communist countries that one found today the "oppression of working people that so horrified Marx when he studied early nineteenth-century industrialism in England." Particularly hard to understand was the "sudden recrudescence among American college professors and their students of the leftist delusions of the Nineteen Twenties" despite the obvious ferment in Eastern Europe. He spoke, too, of Boris Pasternak, Milovan Djilas, Andrey Sinyavsky, and others who had been jailed or "hounded to death" for daring to speak candidly on the evils of the system. As Dos Passos saw it, Communist writers were "prisoners of an ideology which makes it impossible for them to draw rational comparisons between man's condition under socialism and under what they still call capitalism." So long as presses remained under police control in the Soviet Union and Eastern Europe, man's basic freedoms were being denied.

When Dos Passos addressed the student body at Colgate College in the fall of 1966 shortly after his latest *National Review* piece, he insisted that the New Left lacked a sense of history. "With all we've learned about the failure of socialism it's astonishing that the same political vocabulary should be used again." He said he had voted the Communist ticket in 1932 because he believed in "voting for the underdog," but explained that he was closer philosophically to the La Follette Progressives than to Marxism. In reply to the editor of *The Colgate Maroon,* who asked if he could tape their discussion after his lecture, Dos Passos declined. "I don't like recorders. I'd rather go through people's heads and have them think with me." A few months later, Dos Passos received a letter from one "Mr. Africa" who sought his current thinking of the New Left. "In my opinion the New Left is hideously mistaken and misinformed about the forces at large in the world today," answered Dos Passos. "It is a distressing waste of the time and idealism of a lot of well-intentioned young people, besides being of great assistance to the enemies of human freedom in the ideological war, so well understood by Ho [Ho Chi Minh] and his supporting powers. Don't ask a man to return, like a dog, to his vomit."

In the spring of 1967, Dos Passos thanked Edmund Wilson for being a "messenger of good tidings." Wilson had written him that he was to be awarded the Feltrinelli Prize, an international prize awarded by the Academia Nazionale dei Lincei, for his "narrative art" of high moral value. It was worth twenty million lire, said Wilson, who had been apprised confidentially of the award by Mario Praz, who was on the committee that selected Dos Passos. It would not be announced until the end of May; therefore Dos Passos must not talk about it, cautioned Wilson. "Twenty million lire, when you boil it down, isn't such a hell of a lot, but—as the man said—it's better than a poke in the eye with a burnt stick. I'll drop a line to Professor Praz," replied Dos Passos.

"Neither Dos nor I was very good at arithmetic when it came to converting lire into dollars," recounted Betty. "It was Lucy who finally calculated the correct amount. Instead of the $3,500 which we thought it was worth, Lucy said it was worth $32,000. Dos was flabbergasted—and also very worried about the tax angle until he learned that international prizes are tax free at both the federal and state levels. The prize was presented on November 14, 1967, and I flew to Rome with him. We would have taken Lucy, but she had just gone off to college and knew that she must not miss her classes."

Shortly after the announcement that Dos Passos was to be awarded the Feltrinelli Prize, Italian journalist Oriana Fallaci traveled to Spence's Point to interview him for

Europeo, a magazine published in Milan. "I remember my emotion during the flight from New York because Dos Passos was one of the myths, literary myths, of my first youth, and when the war was over in Italy and I was a little girl I drank the discovery of American literature, which to me was Faulkner and Dos Passos and Hemingway, and The 42nd Parallel was glued to my mind." Her object in meeting Dos Passos in person was to ask him what he saw as the reasons for the enormous antipathy directed against the United States by much of the rest of the world. She began her interview by observing that few American writers had been as severe with his country as Dos Passos had been. "Your entire work is an act of relentless accusation against America, and through your travels, your studies, and alternating political persuasions, America has always been the focus of your interest as novelist and as historian. Perhaps no one else has your authority to discuss and pronounce upon the hatred which the United States receives from throughout the world."

Dos Passos replied that when he went to Russia in 1928, the Russians "were crazy about Americans." Wherever he went he was treated splendidly, he said. "And the same happened in the Arab countries, when having left Georgia and Armenia, I went down to Persia and through Mesopotamia, then came to Beirut with the caravans. The Arabs loved the United States to the same degree that they hated the English. . . . It was after the Second World War that the hatred against the United States was loosened." The country had not been able to "slow the flood of that hatred because the fuel for hatred was unknown in America. . . . The day the United States should adopt a propaganda machinery similar to that of the communists it should not be a democracy any longer." America had no propaganda machine to fight such propaganda.

Fallaci interrupted: "In other words, you do not see any justification for this hatred of the United States?" Dos Passos replied:

> My god, to accuse ourselves would be to play the game of Moscow, of Peking, of Paris. Good Americans are always inclined to accuse themselves, but the honesty of self-criticism is always implied: *a mea culpa* is judged. Even to speak of pacifism in the United States today is the equivalent of *a mea culpa.* . . . The hatred of which we are the object is unjust and ungrateful. After the Second World War the United States behaved quite decently. . . . It has been the United States which has led the way to the reconstruction of such countries as France, Italy, Germany, Japan, placing at their disposal the best brains and much of its capital. We would delude ourselves if we were to hope that someone might remember this. . . . I too have been very critical of America. But I did when being American was very convenient, very nice, and when America was the recipient of everyone's love. Now I have become quite protective in her regard. . . . The cause for the hatred of America is the power of America. The victory we obtained in World War II left us with great power, and one always hates the powerful.

Dos Passos readily admitted that his country had faults. Such truths had been expressed many times through characters in his novels, in which they were more palatable than truths presented in nonfiction. America's problems lay in the power of the federal government and in trade unions. "There is industrialism, first of all, which I condemned in my first books, and which now is linked at its base with the organization of the mass, woven by bureaucracy, this atrocious power which imposes its creed: spend-spend-spend, tax-tax-

tax, vote-vote-vote. . . . It is the unions on the one side and the government on the other that dominate American society with what I call a television mentality, a superficial mentality." He faulted America's "total lack of leadership." The country had stumbled along without any great statesmen since the end of World War II. Eisenhower was "less than mediocre," he judged; John F. Kennedy was "a disaster." Had Kennedy lived longer, he might have achieved something significant. He had good intentions, but "until the day he was assassinated he did nothing but make horrible mistakes." Lyndon Baines Johnson was "a manipulator without ideals." Compared to such leaders of the fifties and sixties, Harry S Truman was "a great president" who in certain moments "demonstrated courage and virtue of an ancient stamp. When he said something, you believed him." Dos Passos then speculated on who might succeed Johnson to the presidency:

> Robert Kennedy? My God! If John Kennedy was a disaster, then Robert Kennedy is a double disaster: without law, without scruples. He does not have even the attractiveness of the brother; instead, he has all the traits of the father. He is as thirsty for power as the father was for money. And then who? There is Ronald Reagan, the governor of California. He is an extraordinary type, who every day becomes more extraordinary, who was the only one to have an intelligent speech in the campaign of Goldwater. But I prefer to see him continue as governor of California rather than see him in the White House.

Despite America's problems, Dos Passos said that he saw hope for it in its small towns. "Dried plants do not remain dried forever; there is always an era in which they bloom again. There is always a forgotten seed which will germinate. Something is germinating in America, the only country in which the provinces still have a meaning." Cities everywhere were dying, both in Europe and at home, but art, theater, and literature were flourishing in small towns. He said he appreciated the fact that Glassboro, New Jersey, had been selected as the site of the Johnson/Kosygin meeting, rather than New York City or Washington, D.C. America had been "sick," he rued, but it was showing "signs of recovery. To whoever hates America now, I can respond: You hate because you are still sick."

Oriana Fallaci pondered Dos Passos' words that afternoon as she headed back to New York and realized that he at age seventy-one had something important to say to her generation as well as to his. She saw him living then in a kind of "no-man's land: too liberal for conservatives, too conservative for the liberals." Although she wished that she might see him again, she felt that such a likelihood was remote. The novel at which he was then at work—in which he was embedding his "truths" as he explained them—was probably his last novel, she imagined. "Yes, I hope to see you again, to hear you again. People like me, of my generation, need to listen to you."

27

A Final Journey, 1970

There is more to life than just chemistry.

Dos Passos to Lucy
23 May 1970

On February 9, 1970, Dos Passos wrote Elizabeth Austin from Good Samaritan Convalescent Hospital in Baltimore: "Something has been wrong indeed since October, but I seem to be getting over it. Mild heart failure. I've got some very good doctors and they are gradually getting the feeble little pump to working." He explained that he had been in his "convalescent joint" for almost a month and was feeling "remarkably well. . . . This is a horrible life but it is something to be alive." As soon as his heart specialist agreed that he could travel, he said he was flying to Arizona. "But I've had to get used to having my hopes postponed," he added. Meanwhile, he had converted his hospital room into a study, having convinced his doctor that his heart would suffer far less agitation if Betty could bring a typewriter in so that they could work together. He was impatient to finish *Easter Island: Island of Enigmas,* the manuscript that had evolved from his and Betty's trip to Easter Island and to Chile the previous winter. Betty had helped him gather up some fifty photographs and was preparing the final manuscript while he "tied up a few loose ends" from his sickbed or from the chair in which he was allowed to work during brief intervals.

Eben Given invited them back to the Cape to recuperate, and William F. Buckley, Jr., urged them to spend a "recuperative week or two" with him and his wife, Pat, in Switzerland, but Dos Passos declined both entreaties. For the time being, he had to avoid altitudes and cruises and other such levities, but he did intend to go to Arizona. Dos Passos appreciated Buckley's invitation and the prayer issued for his "swift recovery." He was fond of Buckley, whom he had seen intermittently over the years since his "Reminiscences of a Middle-Class Radical" had appeared in an early issue of *National Review* and aligned him with the Conservatives. Upon Buckley's return to New York from Switzerland a few weeks later, Dos Passos decided that he would propose him for membership in the Century Club, to which Dos Passos had belonged for many years. The Century Club might be of some use to Buckley, he mused. "If he doesn't want to fight the liberals who seem to have taken charge of the Century Club, it's all right by me," Dos Passos wrote William L. White, whom he asked to endorse his sponsorship of Buckley. "The more I hear about them the more I feel like resigning. There are better ways of spending $150, particularly as I visit the place about once a year." Upon Buckley's assent, Dos Passos recommended him to the admissions committee:

> Since wit and conversational powers are, as I understand it, qualifications for membership in the Century Association I can't imagine anyone better qualified for membership than Bill Buckley. Since the grand old days of Bob Benchley no one has appeared in the publishing world so full of high spirits and sheer animal warmth. No one held Bob Benchley's occasional political acts against him. There are probably a few mighty men still around old enough to remember them. I hope you will remember that when you are inviting someone to join the Century you are not inviting a bundle of current notions but an entire man with his past behind him and his future before him.

Dos Passos was not privy to the arguments that went on behind the scenes during the admissions committee's deliberations, but his letter was on target and Buckley was invited into membership a few weeks later. "Dear John," said Buckley—one of the few who called him "John"—when he learned of Dos Passos' successful endorsement, "How you can do as much as you do for your friends, with all your preoccupations, is extraordinary." Despite his ill health, Dos Passos continually amazed people by the scope of his concerns and activities while keeping in progress two book-length manuscripts, his Easter Island book and still another novel, *Century's Ebb: The Thirteenth Chronicle.*

Dos Passos wrote Harold Weston and his wife, Faith, on June 25, 1970, that congestive heart failure was "an uphill battle" that he was "sure to lose in the end." Yet he knew he would be "sunk" if he could not keep on working. "I've put to bed a book—delayed— that came out of our last delightful adventure: the trip to Easter Island—January 1969— and I'm putting the finishing touches on a last forlorn Chronicle of Despair. The rank criminal idiocy of the younger generation in this country is more than I can swallow." His views on the younger generation were perhaps best known to his daughter, although Kiffy, his stepson, had been the recipient of several lectures from time to time. Dos Passos had never felt successful in putting his ideas across to his stepson, who recalled that he had been instructed in "the birds and the bees in a taxi when Mr. Jack was on the way to catch a train to see his publisher. At least I *think* that's what he was trying to tell me." Kiffy said that he did not engage him in the topic, since his stepfather seemed embarrassed even to have brought it up. "I was already far ahead of him on the subject."

Kiffy was in his third year of law school at George Washington University in 1970. As an undergraduate he had considered majoring in English, but did not like the emphasis on literary criticism and close textual analysis entailed in such a major. At one time he wanted to be a writer. His father, Desmond Holdridge, had written several books. He also expressed interest in becoming a reporter and worked for a time in the morgue of the Washington *Post.* Kiffy resembled his father, too, in his enamorment of boats. He usually had a small sailing craft of some sort tied up at Sandy Point or at anchor off the house. "I know my stepfather lost patience with me from time to time, though he tried not to show it. When we were apart, we seldom wrote each other. But we understood well how the other had evolved, and we loved each other. The only thing that seemed inconsistent about Mr. Jack when I knew him was his belonging to the Century Club, whose members had mostly acquired their wealth—or so it seemed to me—by having exploited the little man," said Kiffy in retrospect.

Dos Passos frequently engaged his daughter in conversation about contemporary affairs, and they had a comfortable relationship when they talked. While Lucy was a student at Occidental College in California, they wrote each other often, and many of their letters consisted largely of comments on the times. In a letter addressed to "Sweet Rabbit" on May 23, 1970, Dos Passos launched into a subject that had been much on his mind of late:

> Ever since seeing the documentary Woodstock I blame everything on TV. What we are suffering from is the generation weaned and raised on TV. I think one reason you find the orientals, Mexicans, etc. so much more amusing than the poor palefaced WASPs is that they didn't spend those countless hours staring at TV. They learned to play as children. The abuse of narcotics stems in part from an effort to get back into the old TV coma. Woodstock is worth seeing. I'd like to know how it hits you. To me it was endlessly depressing. All those half naked people, young and not so young rejoicing in the fact that there were two hundred thousand of them there. I should think they would have been ashamed to show their underdeveloped muscles. Nobody, except the construction workers who put up the stands, looked as if they had done a decent day's work, plain physical labor, in their lives. It seemed to me that instead of sobbing about how bad the system is, the people of your generation should be trying to develop themselves, physically and mentally and morally into decent human beings. . . .
>
> I read every word of your letter with pleasure and agree with more of it than you think; still I feel it is tragic that the young people have allowed themselves to be led by their elders into this hysteria about Cambodia. It's the first rational military step taken in the whole war, and whether you agree with him or not, President Nixon deserves acclaim instead of obloquy for having had the courage to try it in face of overwhelming Communist-inspired propaganda modeled on the campaign that had its first success among the French at the time of Dienbienphu and Algeria. If Nixon fails it is just this generation that is raising such Cain that will have to bear the brunt of the results. I'll be in my grace re-entering the carbon cycle. . . . I still believe, in that connection, there is more to life than just chemistry.

Another element of American life that Dos Passos found disturbing in 1970 was the black power movement sweeping the nation and the agitation provoked by the Students for a Democratic Society (SDS). He was not surprised when William L. White wrote that a black youth wearing a pistol holster and carrying a gun was killed in a Lawrence, Kansas, grade school as a result of demands for more black cheerleaders at the University of Kansas. White, who saw eye to eye with Dos Passos on most things of public note, told him that he had never seen the country "more split up":

I note where the Premier of Siam is quoted as saying that this country is going through a nervous breakdown, and I can only agree. Even that ass, Earl Warren, who was responsible for much of it, points out that we have never been so divided since the Civil War. I note where moderate Negro leaders are jumping all over Nixon for not having done enough for Civil Rights. And I also note where Strom Thurmond is out jumping on him for having done too much. It may all mean that Nixon is doing the best that any human can do.

P.S. Sensible Negroes here are just as upset about the situation as I am.

Dos Passos insisted that he was not prejudiced against blacks. According to Betty:

Dos got along extremely well with them and was fond of them in personal relationships. A. A. Thompson, a black cattle farmer who helped him get into the cattle business, was a friend, and he was fond of George Smith, a black chieftain type. Most of the blacks on the Northern Neck were descendants of house servants in slavery days, and the ones we have known have always felt a special relationship to their white friends. Lucy's best playmate for years was Martha Weldon's niece, Blanche, and we have stuck by Martha and Harvy through thick and thin for many years.

Upon his death Dos Passos designated $2,500 to go to Martha Weldon in gratitude for her kindnesses to the family. It was the only cash bequest in his will.

Friends of Dos Passos pointed out that he was always put off by rude people, bullies, and hoodlums, no matter what their color. Bruce Massey recalled that on an anniversary of the assassination of Martin Luther King, Jr., a truck full of blacks "went through the town and advised all the merchants who were still open to shut their doors in respect to their fallen leader. Bob Carden refused, and he was threatened with having his store burned down. It was this sort of behavior to which Dos Passos reacted adversely." On April 23, 1969, Dos Passos wrote Marion Lowndes that he was "glad to see that the students and faculty at Cornell at least are reacting against being bullied by the black hoodlums they allowed into the college. The S.D.S. are much more dangerous because they are international coworkers very much under Communistic influence and with a great deal of money (Ford Foundation?) to spend. Who benefits by their 'boyish pranks'? Ho Chi Minh of course."

On December 10, 1969, he made his "usual annual contribution of $350" to Cople Parish in Westmoreland, but this time he informed the vestry that it was "with the understanding that none of the money will go out of Cople Parish to be spent directly or indirectly on the black power movement." Upon the integration of whites and blacks in the schools in Westmoreland County, over 85 percent of the schools became black, said Massey. "We had never had any racial problems on the Northern Neck, and still don't except from outsiders. We were surprised when an actual head count determined that the black population constituted some fifty-five to sixty percent of the entire area."

In the spring of 1968 when a reporter for the Washington *Post* asked how he felt about "the Negro unrest in the country now," Dos Passos replied that he thought it had become "a dangerous situation" which should not have been "allowed to creep up. Our cities are too full with people who are capable only of handling country life. There is no room for cotton pickers in the city. Years ago I walked the streets of Harlem and saw the terrible look of frustration in their faces. This situation should have been stopped on the farm. We should have trained them for city and industrial life there." It seemed to Dos Passos in 1968 that America was going through its "toughest period since the Civil War." Yet he was "rather optimistic about the United States. I have occasion to travel a lot through the nation and I find a tremendous energy and a great deal of life in our people. I don't need to go to Australia yet." When asked if he had any thought of retiring yet, Dos Passos replied, "When the undertaker comes through the door."

It was this same optimism that had struck Robert Solley, the internist and friend Dos Passos had known for fifty years, the last time they saw each other.

> I saw Dos the summer before he died. I had packed him off for home once before after a minor coronary, and he had suffered others since. Dos had no doubts the last time we were together that he was a man about to die. He had many symptoms of circulatory failure as well as heart and kidney problems. Yet despite his ill health, I was struck by his relentless optimism about his country. That he loved his country showed in his face when he talked about the idea of freedom in the United States. I think of him now as I did then. He was the least profane man I ever knew. I saw him as a sort of modern-day Saint Francis.

Dos Passos seemed determined to do as much as he could his last few months of life. "I agree with you that it is important for old friends to see each other at this stage," he wrote Harold Weston in midsummer of 1970. "Old age is no circus." One by one his friends had been dying off: Frank Shay in 1954, Stewart Mitchell in 1957, Robert Hillyer in 1961, Estlin Cummings in 1962, Gerald Murphy in 1964, Dawn Powell in 1965, Hamilton Owens in 1967, Lloyd Lowndes in 1968. His half brother, Louis Dos Passos, died in 1957, and his other half brother, James Madison, in 1962. The death of each person to whom he had been close evoked from Dos Passos a private or public tribute. From Rio de Janeiro upon reading Cummings' obituary, he wrote Marion Cummings:

> I can hardly believe it yet. Though I didn't see him very often, it leaves a great hole in my life. I had grown fonder of him through the years. As to your life, what can I say? As I know from experience the greatest pain carries with it its own antidote. Somehow we manage to live. I'm so happy that we had that pleasant little time together at Silver Lake. Cummings and his pet chipmunk. . . . The memory is very vivid—the porch the table the vines Cummings' face and the chipmunk with his cheeks stuffed with peanuts. Nothing can take these things away. Love, Dos.

Among his literary colleagues, Dos Passos outlived every major American writer of his generation except Edmund Wilson (who died in 1972) and James T. Farrell (who died in 1979). "To tell the truth, the only painful thing about the approach of old age is time's massacre of my friends," he observed to Arthur McComb upon Cummings' death.

Dos Passos had surprised Adelaide and Charles Walker in February of 1970 when he telephoned them from the Good Samaritan Convalescent Hospital in Baltimore to say that he wanted to bring Betty to Tucson for a month's vacation and asked their help in finding them an apartment. The Walkers had been retreating to southern Arizona for five years to escape the Cape Cod winters. Julia Sprigg Cameron and her husband, Brodnax, were in Tucson, too, in 1970, since the Arizona climate was ideal for Brodnax's respiratory problems. "Knowing how sick Dos had been, we were astonished when he announced on arrival that he wanted to attend Tucson's big rodeo celebration coming up in a day or two. He had just checked himself out of the hospital and we expected him to see the city from a wheelchair or our automobile," said Adelaide Walker, who helped find a first-floor apartment so that Dos Passos would not have to climb stairs. "Julia stocked it with fresh flowers and food, then went to the airport with Brodnax and a wheelchair to meet Dos and Betty's plane. You can imagine our surprise when we learned that he had no intention of going home to rest—he wanted to see the city first, to scrutinize the architecture, which he loved, and to visit our wonderful ancient mission, San Xavier del Bac. Why the man acted as though he had never been sick. They attended *La Fiesta de los Vaqueros,* Tucson's championship rodeo, and two concerts in succession." The Walkers saw little resemblance of Dos Passos' behavior as a heart patient to that of other sufferers of heart disease, including Charles Walker himself, who had been ailing for some time. "So far as I could tell, John's only concession to ill health was taking a nap in the late afternoon and retiring fairly early if there was no concert. He wore us healthy ones out," recalled Julia Cameron. "After the rodeo, he moved right back into his regular work routine. He was at his typewriter early every morning, but at noon happily stopped for a picnic lunch which we all had together," she added.

Lucy came to Tucson from Occidental College during her spring holidays to join them. She was a botany major with a concentration in landscape design, which she loved because it allowed her to be outdoors much of the time. Lucy told her parents that she would not be returning to Baltimore or to Spence's Point in June, but would go directly to Boston instead. She had lined up a job at the Harvard Arboretum for the summer. Her parents were pleased that she was going to be gainfully employed in something she enjoyed doing that would enhance her career as well. They told her that if her father's health held, they would drive to the Cape that summer for a fling with friends, then visit her in Boston before proceeding to Maine in August.

Dos Passos' doctor did not want him to spend the entire summer in Virginia because of the heat and humidity, but agreed to some light gardening for Dos Passos upon their return to Spence's Point in the spring. He had advised his patient to lose weight during the winter of 1969–70, and Dos Passos had lost almost forty pounds, which left him weak in the process. Since he was not supposed to climb stairs, Betty ordered a motorized chair-glide installed on their steep staircase, a contraption they referred to as his "private railroad." Dos Passos rode it with some embarrassment, never quite comfortable with the compromise his malfunctioning heart had forced upon him. Each morning he worked at a large circular desk in his study, then ate a light lunch, painted, swam, and usually gardened. Each day he walked briskly over his property—his gait much as it had always been—then rested as he saw fit.

Edmund Wilson, who had suffered a heart attack in 1970, welcomed Dos Passos to "the Cape Cod Cardiac Writers Association, recently organized by Paul Chavchavadze, Charley Walker, and myself." Wilson said that rumors attributed Dos Passos' heart problem to his Easter Island expedition, but his own opinion was that Dos Passos had strained himself in his recent "public statement that Spiro Agnew is the 'greatest Greek since Pericles.' " Wilson was putting him on, but Dos Passos had been quoted by a Richmond *Times-Dispatch* staff writer as having said: "It's refreshing to hear Mr. Agnew tell the truth. He is a mighty valuable fellow. Maybe he is proving that we need more Greeks in government." Agnew was apprised of Dos Passos' statement and sent him a note of appreciation for his "kind sentiments."

Whereas Wilson informed Dos Passos that he himself was leading "a most enjoyable life" since his heart attack and had had his bed moved downstairs so that he had only "to crawl from the bed to the writing table," Charles Walker reported—now home from Tucson—"Bunny is behaving characteristically. He had a serious heart attack and consented to go to the Hyannis Hospital, then walked out after three days before they could complete their diagnosis. Twice he has celebrated feeling slightly better by consuming a quart of whiskey." Dos Passos wrote Wilson on April 25, 1970, that he would be "delighted to become a member of the Cape Cod chapter of the Exalted Order of Digitalis Users" since he was already doing daily obeisance to the triumvirate of chlorthalidone, digoxin, and allopurinol, but asked Wilson not to blame Easter Island for his trouble, despite his having come down with a serious throat infection, which he attributed in part to his having choked on a piece of turkey at an American Embassy luncheon in Santiago after leaving Easter Island.

"I've had what I hope is a small setback. This heart business is tricky," Dos Passos wrote Harold Weston, who had urged him and Betty to visit in their vacation retreat in Canada on their way either to or from Maine that summer. "My doctor hopes to have me straightened out in a couple of weeks, but you never know. My theory still is that any kind of action is better than none." He had reserved a cottage at Head Tide, Maine, for the month of August and wanted to get on the road before the midsummer heat set in. "Sometimes I can't help rejoicing in the fact that I'm not likely to live much longer," he wrote Lois Sprigg Hazell, who visited them in the spring upon their return from Tucson.

"It pained me to see Dos failing so, though he never complained to us or gave in to his illness," said Manoel Cardozo, an old friend who accompanied Dos Passos' cousin to Virginia. Cardozo was head of the history department at Catholic University of America and an Azorean Portuguese whom Dos Passos found helpful in his research for *The Portugal Story: Three Centuries of Exploration and Discovery,* published in April of 1969.

Dos Passos and Betty set out for Maine the end of July in 90° F weather, and it was the same temperature in New England when they arrived. The heat had forced them to bypass everyone but Lucy en route, and they proceeded as quickly as possible to Head Tide. Dos Passos wrote Harold Weston, who had been expecting them, that he had had "a few very bad days" when they reached Maine, which he attributed largely to the weather, but the heart specialist with whom his Johns Hopkins Hospital physician had put him in touch was skeptical of endorsing his remaining in such a remote area. It made more sense for him to return to Baltimore, where his health could be monitored more closely. Dos Passos insisted that he "felt quite himself again," but Betty agreed with the doctor that they ought to return home.

By the end of August they were back in their little apartment in the Village of Cross Keys in Baltimore. Dos Passos wrote Weston that they had "crept most of the way, driving from medico to medico" and resting as much as possible en route with Betty doing all of the driving. Upon reexamination by his Baltimore physician, Dos Passos was ordered back into Good Samaritan Convalescent Hospital, where he spent most of September. Horsley

Gantt visited him there almost every day, knowing that his condition was steadily deteriorating. On September 21, Gantt mentioned to Dos Passos that he would be away for a few days in Virginia, his boyhood home. "Dos looked at me with a wistful expression as though he were thinking, 'Ah, to be able to go home to Virginia just one more time," recounted Gantt later. "I returned to my study after leaving his bedside that day and wrote in my journal: 'He is so weak . . . he talks so slowly . . . can hardly totter. I shall miss him terribly—my best friend.' "

Meanwhile, Dos Passos resented his infirm condition and was impatient to do his recuperating in his own bed. He insisted that he had some rearranging to do on his last book of fiction, *Century's Ebb: The Thirteenth Chronicle,* but Betty urged him not to worry about it. She said she would do whatever was necessary to get it into an acceptable form. The book was under contract with Houghton Mifflin, but Lovell Thompson was no longer there. He had started his own publishing house, Gambit, with offices in Ipswich, a small town outside Boston. Thompson told Dos Passos that he would like to publish *Century's Ebb* himself in the event that he might be receptive to making such a move (eventually Gambit did publish *Century's Ebb*).

On September 27, 1970, Dos Passos and Betty left the hospital and returned to their apartment. Although pale and in considerable discomfort, he was in good spirits and insisted on their accepting a dinner invitation by Julia and Brodnax Cameron, who asked if he felt like letting Betty drive them to Bel Air that very evening. "Jack had always taken to Brodnax's sense of humor, and we hoped that the outing might be good for him," related Julia later. Brodnax recalled that Dos Passos was more subdued than usual and seemed to be in some pain, but said nothing of it. "It wasn't like him not to be able to stand before us at the mantel and thrash about as he talked, his head and whole body entering into the conversation. It was early when we told them goodnight. We did not know then, of course, that it was goodbye as well."

The next morning Dos Passos arose a little after seven o'clock, and Betty served him a glass of fresh orange juice in the living room, then fixed a full-scale breakfast of cantaloupe, boiled eggs, croissants, and coffee, which they enjoyed together at the table. He said that he felt good and had slept well. They watched part of "The Today Show" on television and decided to order a copy of Robert Ardrey's *The Social Contract: A Personal Inquiry into the Evolutionary Sources of Order and Disorder.* "I think I'd like to read the paper now," he said, and Betty hastened to the car and drove to the little arcade of shops in the Village of Cross Keys only a few hundred yards away. In less than ten minutes she was back with a Baltimore *Sun* in her hand. The instant she walked in the door, Betty saw him slumped on the floor before his chair.

Moving quickly to the telephone, she called Horsley Gantt, who had just returned from Virginia. "I was at Dos's side in less than five minutes and attempted to revive him, but I realized the moment I saw him that there was little chance that he might regain consciousness, let alone survive. There was no need for an ambulance. I knew that his death had been swift and merciful." Gantt said that they had talked of late about death and his philosophy of the unknown. "I had brought him Hume and Berkeley, books he had asked for. I never got the feeling that Dos feared death, but he certainly liked living and he refused to stay down. He said to me once: 'There's so much yet undone, and as long as I have life, I'm going to keep doing it.' I thought again of what Dos said about retirement: 'That'll be the day the undertaker carries me out the door.' "

29 September 1970

IN THE WORLD:

President Nasser of Egypt died yesterday in Cairo of what was described as a massive heart attack. His death followed the end of a meeting in the Egyptian capital in which an accord was reached for a cease-fire in Jordan.

Official Washington had no quick or ready answers for what effect President Nasser's death would have for his country, the Middle East or the peace of the world.

Anwar Sadat, the Egyptian vice president who succeeds President Nasser, goes back to the days when he and Mr. Nasser were part of a group of officers plotting the overthrow of King Farouk.

Israelis are skeptical of the Cairo agreement between King Hussein and the Guerrillas.

Representative L. Mendel Rivers (D., S.C.) says the U.S. should take military action to bar construction of a Soviet nuclear submarine base in Cuba.

IN THE NATION:

President Nixon writes college heads asking them to heed advice of J. Edgar Hoover on campus troubles.

The Senate Government Operations Committee approved a bill creating the White House Council of Consumer Affairs and an independent consumer protection service.

The House passed a bill to center government programs on environment in new Environmental Protection Agency.

A federal hearing examiner ruled for the first time that a northern school district violated the federal civil rights laws and should have its federal aid cut off.

IN THE CITY AND STATE:

John Roderigo Dos Passos, author of the trilogy, U.S.A., and other works that present a panoramic view of the first half of the Twentieth Century, died in Baltimore. He was 74.

Baltimore Sun

JOHN DOS PASSOS
1896–1970

1 October 1970
The leaves were burnt-orange and red,
some already withered on the bough,
the morning air crisp
the sky robin's-egg blue
when mourners entered by two's and three's
the silent, gray-stoned Trinity Episcopal Church
in Towson, Maryland,
where cries and prayers of wounded Union soldiers
once resounded,
to pay tribute
to husband, father, friend.

The media came with cameras and notepads,
but gravitated to the living,
noted that it was the Bishop of Maryland
who read from the Book of Common Prayer,
who eulogized in simple words
the man whose ashes lay before them,
the last of his lineage
without heir-apparent,
the literary giants of a half century
having fallen, one by one:
Wolfe, Fitzgerald, Lewis, Hemingway, Faulkner, Dos Passos.

"Would you assess the literary work of John Dos Passos?"
queried a reporter
as William F. Buckley, Jr., left the house of worship.
"I knew him primarily as a friend—

ask Chamberlain here," he replied,
nodding to his companion.

"Along with the sadness one feels a surge of anger
at the way the liberal obituary writers treated his career,"
declared Chamberlain, who had treaded a path similar
to his friend now dead;
the old liberals did not forgive Dos Passos
for changing with his times,
treated him as one who had sold out
when he knew his right foot from his left,
ignored his later career,
did not understand what contemporary chronicles were all about,
did not understand how such a man could have fought for labor
then cried out against its leaders fifty years later,
did not understand that bigness as an instrument of power
inevitably led to destruction,
whether corporation presidents, Communists, government officials, or labor leaders
called the plays;
did not understand that Dos Passos' whole way of life was a seeking
(he never claimed to have all the answers,
but ventured what he thought,
and admitted his mistakes);
an idealist to the end,
a disappointed optimist,
an individualist
who loved his country more than life itself.
"If C. D. Batchelor were active," said Buckley,
"he would have done a drawing of the Statue of Liberty
weeping over his loss; this irreparable loss."

7 October 1970
On the Northern Neck of Virginia,
the family and friends and neighbors of "Mr. Jack"
gathered at the ancient Yeocomico Church
near the edge of Dos Passos Farms,
where he had held his daughter over the font for her christening,
where his stepson had been confirmed,
where he had stood as a youth and followed his mother's body
outdoors to the churchyard for interment,
where his ashes now were interred beside his mother's grave.

"We were all lucky
that the end came mercifully fast," said his wife.
"We had twenty-one wonderful years together,
and that's a lot to lean on."

Notes and Sources

Notes and sources are keyed to the text by page number and lead-in phrase. Abbreviations used of frequently cited people, collections, and books by John Dos Passos:

AAIAL	American Academy and Institute of Arts and Letters, JDP Collection
AMcC	Arthur McComb
BA	Boston Athenaeum, R. Stewart Mitchell Collection
BU	Boston University, Mugar Memorial Library, Paul Shyre Collection
BB	Bernice Baumgarten
DP	Dudley Poore
EDP	Elizabeth ("Betty") Dos Passos
EEC	E. Estlin Cummings
EEH	Edward E. Harding
EH	Ernest Hemingway
EH	*Ernest Hemingway: A Life Story* by Carlos Baker (New York: Scribner's, 1969)
EW	Edmund Wilson
GU	Georgetown University, The University Library, Special Collections, JBS/JDP Papers
HBJ	Harcourt Brace Jovanovich
HU	Harvard University, Houghton Library
HUW	Harvard University, Widener Library
IU	Indiana University, The Lilly Library
JBS	James Brown Scott
JBW	*Journeys Between Wars* (New York: Harcourt, Brace, 1938)
JDP	John Dos Passos
JFK	John F. Kennedy Library, EH Collection
JHL	John Howard Lawson
JRDP	John Randolph Dos Passos
KDP	Katharine Dos Passos
LC	Library of Congress
LSMDP	Lucy Sprigg Madison Dos Passos

PBU	*The Prospect Before Us* (Boston: Houghton Mifflin, 1950)
PCU	Portuguese Continental Union of the United States of America
PU	Princeton University Library
RM	W. Rumsey Marvin
RN	Robert Nathan
SI	University of Southern Illinois at Carbondale, Morris Library, Collection of JHL
SU	Syracuse University, The George Arents Research Library, Robert Hillyer Collection
SUNYAB	State University of New York at Buffalo, the Poetry Collection of Lockwood Memorial Library
TBT	*The Best Times: An Informal Memoir* (New York: New American Library, 1966)
TIF	*The Theme Is Freedom* (New York: Dodd, Mead, 1956)
TOD	*Tour of Duty* (Boston: Houghton Mifflin, 1946)
UPA	University of Pennsylvania, Charles Patterson Van Pelt Library
UT-HRC	University of Texas, Humanities Research Center
UVA	University of Virginia, Alderman Library, JDP Collection
VSC	Virginia Spencer Carr
WSU	Wayne State University, Walter P. Reuther Library, Archives of Labor History and Urban Affairs, Mary Heaton Vorse Collection
YUB	Yale University, Beinecke Rare Book and Manuscript Library
YUS	Yale University, Sterling Memorial Library Manuscripts and Archives

BOOK I

PROLOGUE AND CHAPTER 1

Unlesss otherwise noted, genealogy for Prologue and Chapter 1 are derived from the following sources and interviews:

Cyril F. dos Passos to VSC, interviews, Oct. 25, 1977, Aug. 17, 1978, Mendham, N.J.; letters, Mar. 2, Mar. 16, 1978;

Mary Dos Passos Singleton to VSC, interview, Oct. 25, 1977, Summit, N.J.; letters, Feb. 8, Mar. 13, 1978;

Florence Schmidt de Bottari (daughter of Joseph J. Schmidt) to VSC, Mar. 7, May 17, 1978, Yonkers, N.Y.;

John David Dos Passos to VSC, interview, Nov. 14, 1977, Delmar, N.Y.;

George William Bricka to VSC, interview, Mar. 14, 1978, New Rochelle, N.Y.; letters, May 31, July 11, 1978, Mar. 17, 1980;

Lois Sprigg Hazell to VSC, interviews, Mar. 22, 24, May 5, 30, 1977, Aug. 20, 1978, Chevy Chase, Md.; letters, Jan. 20, July 12, 1977, Feb. 20, Sept. 7, 1978; unpublished, undated diary; undated article, "Rebel Gun in White House," publication unknown;

Julia Sprigg Cameron to VSC, interviews, May 29, Sept. 29, Oct. 23, 1977, Bel Air, Md.; letters, Sept. 18, 1977, Mar. 19, 1978;

James C. Sprigg, Jr., telephone interview, Sept. 23, 1978, Smithfield, Va.; letters, Apr. 7, Sept. 26, 1978; "Preliminary Application," The Virginia Society of the Sons of the American Revolution, July 18, 1930;

Lucy Virginia Gordon Ralston to VSC, interviews, Mar. 16, Mar. 23, 1978, Pelham, N.Y.

PAGE

3 *I want you* . . . . : JRDP to Ida Little Pifer, Apr. 24, 1912, UVA.

12 "Louis is a very nice boy . . .": James Madison to Lucy Sprigg Madison, Feb. 13, 1885, UVA.

13 Death of Ryland R. Madison: Hall of Records Commission, Annapolis, Md.

13 Horseback-riding accident, JRDP: New York *Times*, Dec. 27, 1889.

14 According to official records, the birth went . . . : Cook County Courthouse, Chicago, Ill.

14 "Absolutely not! I would swear . . .": Lucy Virginia Gordon Ralston to VSC, interview, Mar. 23, 1978, Pelham, N.Y.

14 Mary Hays Dos Passos' alleged emotional illness refuted by Mary Dos Passos Singleton, George W. Bricka, and Cyril F. dos Passos, interviews cited for Prologue and Chapter 1.

CHAPTER 2

Unless otherwise noted, the genealogical sources for Prologue and Chapter 1 apply for Chapter 2:

PAGE

15 Jack Madison grew up . . . : Kate Gee and Sophia Louisa Meakin, letters, UVA.

17 "Absolutely not—your husband will . . .": George W. Bricka to VSC, interview, Mar. 1978, New Rochelle, N.Y.

18 For a time he owned . . . : Cyril F. dos Passos to VSC, interview, Aug. 17, 1978, Mendham, N.J.

19 Schmidt took care of . . . : Florence Schmidt de Bottari to VSC, Mar. 7, 1978.

19 "I was very glad . . .": JRDP to Ida Little Pifer, June 14, 1901, UVA.

19 Lois was amused by her cousin . . . : Lois Sprigg Hazell to VSC, interview, Mar. 22, 1977, Chevy Chase, Md.

20 "My mother and I have come . . .": *TBT*, p. 10.

21 "Poor Fannie—the link . . .": JRDP to Ida Little Pifer, Aug. 4, 1902, UVA.

CHAPTER 3

23 "When you write me, I drop everything . . .": Lucy Sprigg Madison to JRDP, July 1903, UVA.

24 "Eyes and heart were . . .": Lucy Sprigg Madison to JRDP, undated letter, UVA.

24 "How hard I tried . . .": Undated essay submitted to Charles T. Copeland, professor of English 12, Harvard, UVA.

25 "How do you like . . .": Lucy Sprigg Madison to Jack Madison, May 17, 1906, UVA.

26 "When I said Judge Parker . . .": *TBT*, pp. 8–9.

26 At the end of his . . . : Peterborough Lodge School records, UVA.

CHAPTER 4

Unless otherwise noted, information pertaining to Jack Madison's years at Choate are derived from the Dos Passos Collection, The Choate School Archives of The Andrew Mellon Library, Wallingford, Conn.; Lee Sylvester, archivist, interview, Mar. 22, 1978; letters, Mar. 28, Apr. 24, 1978.

PAGE

27 Enamored of the sea . . . : *TBT*, p. 14.

28 "Have you received . . .": JRDP to Jack Madison, Jan. 21, 1910, UVA.

29 His one close friend . . . : *TBT*, p. 12.

29 "A chill of half delicious fright . . .": *The Choate Alumni Bulletin*, Fall 1965, p. 30.

30 During one such moment . . . : Lucy Sprigg Madison to Jack Madison, undated letter, UVA.

31 James's chief problem . . . : Lois Sprigg Hazell to VSC, interview, May 5, 1977, Chevy Chase, Md.; James C. Sprigg, Jr., telephone interview, Sept. 23, 1978, Smithfield, Va.; Cyril F. dos Passos to VSC, interview, Aug. 17, 1978.

31 He rarely drank hard liquor . . . : Cyril F. dos Passos to VSC, interview, Oct. 25, 1977.

31 John R. had outfitted . . . : *TBT*, p. 13; Cyril F. dos Passos to VSC, interview, Oct. 25, 1977; EDP, interview, Spence's Point, Westmoreland, Va., Feb. 16, 1977.

32 "Beavers were something . . .": *TBT*, p. 13.

32 In one letter he spoke . . . : JRDP to Jack Madison, undated letter, UVA.

32 "I have missed your letters . . .": Lucy Sprigg Madison to Jack Madison, undated letter, UVA.

33 "Each letter from you . . .": JRDP to Lucy Sprigg Madison, undated letter, UVA.

33 When the animal escaped . . . : JRDP to Jack Madison, undated letter, UVA.

34 "Commit Virgil to memory . . .": JRDP to Jack Madison, undated letter, UVA.

34 "Be careful, my darling . . .": Lucy Sprigg Madison to Jack Madison, undated letter, UVA.

35 "Oh Jack, it is necessary . . .": Lucy Sprigg Madison to Jack Madison, Jan. 18, 1910, UVA.

35 "My darling Jack . . .": Lucy Sprigg Madison to Jack Madison, undated letter, UVA.

35 Lil Cragin was with . . . : JRDP to Lucy Sprigg Madison, undated letter, UVA.

35 "I am sorry not . . .": JRDP to Jack Madison, undated letter, UVA.

36 Later, Jack's Greek teacher . . . : Mrs. George C. St. John to Charles W. Bernardin, July 24, 1943, The Choate School Archives of The Andrew Mellon Library.

CHAPTER 5

38 The events immediately preceding . . . : miscellaneous letters and cards to and from JRDP, Lucy Sprigg Madison, and Jack Madison, Mar. 5–May 15, 1910, UVA.

39 With him was George L. Wolfe . . . : marriage certificate of JRDP and Lucy Sprigg Madison, June 19, 1910, UVA.

40 Perhaps his most telling entry . . . : diary, Apr. 9, 1911, UVA.

41 "Mr. St. John said goodbye . . .": diary, June 17, 1911, UVA.

42 "I should like the Baby . . .": Jack Madison to LSMDP, undated postcard mailed from Rome, UVA.

43 Jack's reply was a . . . : Mar. 28, 1912, UVA.

44 The postal cards and letters . . . : diary signed by Jack Madison during his "Grand Tour," UVA.

44 In none of his letters . . . : *TBT*, pp. 15–16.

44 Home at last . . . : *TBT*, p. 17.

45 "We have made history . . .": JRDP to LSMDP, July 13, 1912, UVA; see also *TBT*, p. 22.

BOOK II

Opposite title page: The first flood . . . : JDP to Jon Bracker, May 23, 1970, UVA.

CHAPTER 6

Unless otherwise noted, general resources for JDP's years at Harvard: the University Archives of Pusey Library of Harvard University and the Houghton Library, collections of JDP, E. Estlin Cummings, the *Harvard Monthly,* and the Norton-Harjes Ambulance Corps; also Richard Bissell, *You Can Always Tell a Harvard Man* (New York: McGraw-Hill, 1962); Rollo Walter Brown, *Harvard Yard in the Golden Age* (New York: Current Books, 1948); Samuel Eliot Morison, *Three Centuries of Harvard: 1636–1936* (Cambridge: Harvard University Press, 1936).

PAGE

52 Robert Nathan, a classmate . . . : RN to VSC, Sept. 7, 1948.

53 "Don't get too husky . . .": JDP to RM, Dec. 6, 1915, UVA.

54 The then prevailing attitude . . . : RN to VSC, July 18, 1980.

56 A yellowed copy . . . : *TBT*, p. 23.

56 Rather, he delighted in . . . : JDP made reference in his diary, as well as in miscellaneous letters to friends during this period, to many of the books he was reading.

57 "The Almeh," *Harvard Monthly,* July 1913, pp. 172–79.

58 "Allow me to offer . . .": John Walcott to JDP, June 21, 1913, UVA.

58 Such new friends . . . : DP to VSC, Apr. 12, 1979; see also Charles W. Bernardin, "John Dos Passos' Harvard Years," *The New England Quarterly,* Mar. 1954, pp. 3–26.

59 In a letter to a . . . : JDP to RM, May 29, 1916, UVA.

59 In another letter he spoke of . . . : JDP to RM, Fall 1915, UVA.

60 To a prep school acquaintance . . . : JDP to RM, Feb. 21, 1916, UVA.

60 "The Honor of the Klepht," *Harvard Monthly,* Feb. 1914, pp. 158–63.

61 As an editor of . . . : Bliss Perry, *And Gladly Teach* (Boston: Houghton Mifflin, 1935).

62 After a second stroke . . . : JRDP to JDP, undated letter, UVA.

62 James apprised his . . . : James Madison to JDP, Feb. 28, 1914, UVA.

63 James wrote of his . . . : James Madison to JDP, Mar. 20, 1914, UVA.

63 In a letter to a prep school . . . : JDP to RM, Oct. 5, 1915, UVA.

64 Also living on "The Gold Coast" . . . : Clyde Kenneth Hyder, *George Kittredge: Teacher and Scholar* (Lawrence: University of Kansas Press, 1962), pp. 44–47.

65 Dos Passos and his friends . . . : DP, diary, UVA; RN to VSC, June 13, July 7, 1978.

65 Nathan was next in line . . . : RN to VSC, Sept. 7, 1978.

65 Cummings had lived with . . . : see Richard S. Kennedy, *Dreams in the Mirror: A Biography of E. E. Cummings* (New York: Liveright, 1980); Charles Norman, *E. E. Cummings: The Magic Maker* (New York: Little, Brown, 1958); see also Richard S. Kennedy, "E. E. Cummings at Harvard: Studies," *Harvard Library Bulletin,* July 1976, pp. 267–97.

66 His next submission . . . : a review of *Insurgent Mexico, Harvard Monthly,* Nov. 1914, pp. 67–68.

67 "Copey"—as most of . . . : J. Donald Adams, *Copey at Harvard* (Cambridge: The Riverside Press, 1960).

68 Of a later piece . . . : Charles Townsend Copeland to JDP, Jan. 18, 1915, UVA.

70 Alumnus Theodore Roosevelt . . . : *First Flowering: The Best of the Harvard Advocate,* Richard M. Smoley, ed. (Reading, Mass.: Addison-Wesley, 1977).

70 The most important pronouncement . . . : Wright McCormick to JDP, Mar. 13, 1915, UVA.

70 Variously interpreted, "An Aesthete's . . .": "Letter to the Editor," the *Harvard Crimson,* undated, UVA.

71 "It would make young men . . .": JDP to RM, Aug. 24, 1916, UVA.

72 While the nation was . . . : Mary Harris to JDP, May 12, 1915, UVA.

73 Years later he was able to write . . . : *1919* (New York: Harcourt, Brace, 1932), "Camera Eye 28," pp. 8–9.

74 Lucy's will left . . . : filed in the Holding Probate Court of the Supreme Court of the District of Columbia, No. 22659, Adm. Doc. 53.

76 On the train home . . . : JDP to RM, Aug. 28, 1915, UVA.

77 Dos Passos could have . . . : RM to VSC, interview, Nov. 18, 1978, Columbus, Ohio.

77 As Boylston Professor . . . : "P.S. to Dean Briggs," in *College in a Yard,* Brooks Atkinson, ed. (Cambridge: Harvard University Press, 1957).

78 "At this moment I'd . . .": JDP to RM, Jan. 26, 1916, UVA.

78 His letters were soon . . . : JDP to RM, undated letter, 1916, UVA.

78 The two friends continued . . . : several hundred letters from JDP to RM and from RM to JDP are in UVA.

79 Submissions were passed . . . : RN to VSC, interview, Aug. 2, 1979, Beverly Hills, Calif.

79 When the Poetry Society . . . : Rollo Walter Brown, *Dean Briggs* (New York: Harper & Brothers, 1926); see also Atkinson, *College in a Yard.*

80 The majority of its meetings . . . : diary, DP, UVA.

81 Malcolm Cowley, a freshman . . . : Malcolm Cowley, *And I Worked at the Writer's Trade: Chapters of Literary History* (New York: Viking, 1978), pp. 37–38.

85 "The poems must stand as . . .": EEC to JDP, undated letter, UVA.

92 In response to one "Mr. Oliver" . . . : JDP to "Dear Mr. Oliver," undated letter, Special Collections, Mugar Memorial Library, Boston University.

93 He was more explicit . . . : JDP to RM, Feb. 20, 1917, UVA.

CHAPTER 7

95 When Dos Passos invited . . . : JDP to RM, July 30, 1916, UVA.

96 He also shared with . . . : JDP to RM, July 9, 1916, UVA.

96 To Arthur McComb, his . . . : JDP to AMcC, Aug. 2, 1916, UVA.

96 Years later when . . . : *TBT*, p. 24.

96 "I kept mounting my fiery . . .": *TBT*, p. 25.

97 A reader could not survive . . . : "Against American Literature," *The New Republic,* Oct. 14, 1916, pp. 269–71.

98 John R. wrote frequently . . . : JRDP to Mary Harris, Sept. 19, 1916, UVA.

99 To Arthur McComb he . . . : JDP to AMcC, undated letter, 1916, UVA.

99 "I might suggest, Mr. Pacifist . . .": JDP to AMcC, undated letter, 1916, UVA.

100 Before leaving for Spain . . . : JDP to RM, Sept. 28, 1916, UVA.

100 "I did not care to wait . . .": JRDP to Mary Harris, Oct. 14, 1916, UVA.

CHAPTER 8

102 As he saw it . . . : Cyril F. dos Passos to VSC, interview, Oct. 25, 1977, Mendham, N.J.

102 Passengers slept in their . . . : JDP to RM, Oct. 25, 1916, UVA.

102 "A friend married . . .": JDP to RM, Sept. 28, 1916, UVA.

103 In the spring of 1916 . . . : Richard S. Kennedy, *Dreams in the Mirror: A Biography of E. E. Cummings* (New York: Liveright, 1980), p. 111.

103 Cummings' biographer, Richard Kennedy . . . : Kennedy, *Dreams in the Mirror,* p. 193.

103 "If one is feeling well . . .": JDP to RM, Aug. 24, 1916, UVA.

103 He acknowledged his frustration . . . : JDP to RM, Nov. 3, 1916, UVA.

104 Dos Passos was taking . . . : diary, Nov. 1916, UVA.

104 By mid-November he was . . . : JDP to RM, Nov. 13, 1916, UVA.

105 "I've never been anywhere . . .": JDP to RM, Dec. 4, 1916, UVA.

105 Dos Passos was bored . . . : JDP to RM, Dec. 4, 1916, UVA.

105 "I've never seen such . . .": *TBT*, pp. 30–31.

106 Winter had already set . . . : *TBT*, pp. 33–34.

106 The trio debated that . . . : *TBT*, pp. 33–34; see also *Rosinante to the Road Again* (New York: George H. Doran, 1922), pp. 9–23.

108 Charles Evans Hughes . . . : The Adamson Bill provided that an eight-hour workday was to be standard only for most railroad workers.

109 According to George Bricka . . . : George W. Bricka to VSC, interview, Mar. 14, 1978, New Rochelle, N.Y.

109 "John R. never let . . .": Florence Schmidt de Bottari to VSC, Mar. 7, 1978.

CHAPTER 9

111 After the shock . . . . : JDP to RM, Jan. 31, 1917, UVA.

112 The same page in the . . . . : New York *Times*, Jan. 28, 1917, sec. 7, p. 3.

113 John R. lay not far . . . . : Woodlawn Cemetery Archives, Jerome Avenue at 233d Street, Woodlawn (Yonkers), N.Y.; JRDP "Beach Plot": Sec. 34-35-47-48, four from Central Avenue, four from Lake Avenue.

114 The same inaccuracies were . . . : Henry Wollman, "John Dos Passos" (spoken before the New York County Lawyers Assoc., May 3, 1917), reprinted as "Judge and Lawyer: A Record of Bench and Bar" in *Case and Comment*, July 1917, pp. 162–65.

114 On March 9 the will . . . : JRDP will probated at Westmoreland County (Virginia) Court House, Book No. 79, pp. 105–11; see Book No. 50, *Deeds and Wills*, p. 481.

115 She avoided the word "lover" . . . : Lois Sprigg Hazell to VSC, interview, Mar. 24, 1977, Chevy Chase, Md.

115 When young Jack Madison . . . : Lois Sprigg Hazell to VSC, interview, May 5, 1977, Chevy Chase, Md.

115 Although Cyril dos Passos . . . : Cyril F. dos Passos to VSC, interview, Oct. 25, 1977, Mendham, N.J.

115 But as Joseph Schmidt's daughter . . . : Florence Schmidt de Bottari to VSC, Mar. 7, 1978.

115 "I spent several weeks at Cintra . . .": The fact that John R. gave his yacht and his Virginia farm Portuguese names makes it clear that he retained a "memory" of his Portuguese heritage.

115 "I was unaware then . . .": Florence Schmidt de Bottari to VSC, Mar. 7, 1978.

115 Similarly, Louis Dos Passos . . . : Mary Dos Passos Singleton to VSC, interview, Oct. 25, 1977, Summit, N.J.

116 The document read: . . . : JRDP to American Security and Trust Co., Washington, D.C., Nov. 20, 1915, UVA.

116 Relations continued to be . . . : Mary Dos Passos Singleton to VSC, interview, Oct. 25, 1977, Summit, N.J.; Cyril F. dos Passos to VSC, interview, Aug. 17, 1978, Mendham, N.J.

117 Years later, Dos Passos . . . : JDP to Charles Norman, *E. E. Cummings: The Magic Maker* (New York: Little, Brown, 1958), p. 68.

117 Upon the President's declaration . . . : JDP to RM, April 10, 1917, UVA.

118 As he expressed it . . . : *TBT*, pp. 46–47.

118 Despite evidence to the . . . : "Writing Schools," (unsigned article), *The Times Literary Supplement*, April 8, 1965.

118 He and Wright McCormick . . . : JDP to RM, April 28, 1917, UVA.

118 "Don't believe the New York *Times* . . .": JDP to RM, undated letter, 1917, UVA.

119 Dos Passos wrote in his memoirs . . . : *TBT*, pp. 45–46.

119 These were heady times . . . : JDP to AMcC, undated letter, AAIAL.

119 In a new introduction . . . : "Introduction, 1968" to *One Man's Initiation: 1917* (Ithaca: Cornell University Press, 1969), pp. 2–3.

120 To Arthur McComb . . . : JDP to AMcC, undated letter, AAIAL.

120 McComb replied that . . . : AMcC to JDP, May 12, 1917, UVA.

120 Dos Passos urged Poore . . . : JDP to DP, May 8, 1917, UVA.

120 Another was an essay . . . : Waldo Frank to JDP, June 6, 1917, UVA.

121 Information regarding the sale of Dos Passos' maternal home in Washington, D.C., to JBS: GU.

121 Dos Passos never knew . . . : Robert Land, letters to diplomatic and consular officers of the United States, Great Britain, and France, June 15, 1917, UVA.

121 To Arthur McComb he urged . . . : JDP to AMcC, June 20, 1917, AAIAL.

122 To Rumsey Marvin he confessed . . . : JDP to RM, June 20, 1917, UVA.

CHAPTER 10

123 "Where're we going, boys? . . .": *YMCA Songbook*, distributed to the men aboard the SS *Chicago*, June 20, 1917, from Private Collection of William H. Harding, Princeton, Mass.; William H. Harding to VSC, Apr. 10, 1978.

123 He had been aboard . . . : JDP to AMcC, June 20, 1917, AAIAL.

124 "The trip was one long . . .": *TBT*, p. 48.

124 After a week at sea . . . : JDP to AMcC, June 28, 1917, AAIAL.

125 In a long letter to McComb . . . : JDP to AMcC, June 28, 1917, AAIAL.

125 "I have no more memories . . .": diary, June 27, 1917, UVA.

126 As the vessel entered . . . : *TBT*, pp. 47–48.

126 He found it amusing . . . : *TBT*, pp. 48–49.

127 Wartime Paris was new . . . : *TBT*, pp. 49–50.

127 The Norton-Harjes organization . . . : Special Collection, the Norton-Harjes Ambulance Corps, HU.

128 Together they set off . . . : diary, 1917, UVA; JDP to RM, July 12, 1917, UVA.

128 He could not shake easily . . . : diary, 1917; see also *One Man's Initiation*, p. 54.

128 Cummings and a new friend . . . : William Slater Brown to VSC, interview, Aug. 2, 1978, Machias, Maine.

129 Sandricourt was an . . . : diary, July 1917, UVA.

129 When mail caught up . . . : Wright McCormick to JDP, Aug. 15, 1917, UVA.

130 As he saw it . . . : JDP to RM, July 12, 1917, UVA.

130 He wrote one day . . . : diary, July 31, 1917, UVA.

130 In early August . . . : diary, Aug. 2, 1917, UVA.

131 Drivers and vehicles . . . : diary, Aug. 3, 1917, UVA.

131 Later, in a novel of . . . : *One Man's Initiation*, pp. 107–8.

132 Drivers pored over maps . . . : EEH, diary, from the Private Collection of William H. Harding, Princeton, Mass.

132 Dos Passos' section . . . : diary, Aug. 1917, UVA; EEH, diary, miscellaneous entries, 1917.

133 Just before going into action . . . : EEH, diary, Aug. 11, 1917.

134 On August 15, 1917 . . . : diary, Aug. 1917, UVA; EEH, diary, miscellaneous entries, 1917.

134 Dos Passos lamented . . . : diary, Aug. 26, 1917, UVA.

135 "Dead men all around . . .": EEH, diary, Aug. 17, 1917.

135 After a week in the field . . . : JDP to RM, Aug. 23, 1917, UVA.

136 "According to ambulanciers . . .": J. Sibley Watson to VSC, May 24, 1979.

136 It took them fifteen . . . : EEH, diary, Aug. 17, 1917.

138 Dos Passos wrote Rumsey Marvin . . . : JDP to RM, Aug. 17, 1917, UVA.

138 Two days after Norton's letter . . . : EEH, diary, Aug. 29, 1917; see also "Facing Death Unarmed: William Allen White Pays Tribute to Work of American Ambulance in France," Toledo (Ohio) *Blade*, Oct. 13, 1917.

139 On September 12 . . . : JDP to AMcC, Sept. 12, 1917, AAIAL.

139 It also provided him . . . : discharge certificate, Oct. 20, 1917, UVA.

139 Dos Passos had hoped to see . . . : William Slater Brown to VSC, interview, Aug. 2, 1978, Machias, Maine; see also JDP to Mrs. Edward Cummings, Dec. 16, 1917, EEC Collection, HU.

140 Dos Passos acquired a new friend . . . : diary, Oct. 1917; Mrs. Thomas Pym Cope to VSC, interview, July 31, 1978, Lincoln Center, Mass.

140 "The wistfulness of russet . . .": JDP to RM, Nov. 12, 1917, UVA.

140 When Marvin asked him . . . : JDP to RM, July 17, 1918, UVA.

141 While attempting to back . . . : *TBT*, p. 59.

141 A second accident occurred . . . : diary, Feb. 20, 1918, UVA.

141 Before leaving Marseilles . . . : *TBT*, p. 59; diary, Nov. 14, 1917, UVA.

141 In Milan at last . . . : diary, Dec. 7, 1917, UVA.

142 "Fiat 4, Fiat 4 . . .": JDP to RM, Dec. 20, 1917, UVA.

142 If they discovered silverware . . . : diary, May 14, 1918, UVA.

142 In a letter to Arthur McComb . . . : JDP to AMcC, Dec. 31, 1917, AAIAL.

142 One day he hiked high . . . : diary, Feb. 5, 1918, UVA.

143 Dos Passos found that . . . : diary, Feb. 8, 1918, UVA; Sidney Fairbanks to VSC, Aug. 6, 1980.

143 "Something in preachifying . . .": JDP to RM, undated letter, UVA.

143 "It was the fifth time . . .": *One Man's Initiation*, pp. 110–11.

144 When Rumsey Marvin expressed . . . : JDP to RM, Mar. 6, 1918, UVA.

144 Dos Passos glowered . . . : Mary Keyt Isham, "Passivism Diagnosed as Disease of the Mind," New York *Times Magazine*, Dec. 30, 1917, pp. 11–12, UVA.

144 Another newspaper clipping . . . : Several hundred newspaper clippings are among the JDP manuscripts and letters, UVA.

144 Wright McCormick wrote . . . : Wright McCormick to JDP, Sept. 29, 1918, UVA.

144 When dinner conversation . . . : diary, Jan. 28, 1918, UVA.

144 "I sympathize with him . . .": JDP to Mrs. Edward Cummings, EEC Collection, HU.

145 Apprehension on his own . . . : diary, Jan. 29, 1918, UVA.

145 The letter that led to his . . . : Dos Passos to José ("Pepe") Giner, undated, spring 1918, UVA; translated from French by Caryl Lloyd.

146 Appended to the letter . . . : Major Bates to Major Guy Lowell, undated, UVA.

146 The two gasoline stoves . . . : JDP to RM, Dec. 30, 1917, UVA; JDP to AMcC, Dec. 31, 1917, AAIAL; diary, Jan. 3, 1918, UVA.

147 "I've gone quite dippy . . .": JDP to RM, undated letter, UVA.

147 Fifty years later . . . : *TBT*, p. 62.

148 At the end of a catalogue . . . : diary, Jan. 25, 1918, UVA.

148 To the authorities he . . . : *TBT*, p. 68; see also diary, Mar. 1, Mar. 15, 1918; JDP to AMcC, July 12, 1918, AAIAL.

148 Dos Passos' job was the . . . : *TBT*, p. 70.

148 For a month he argued . . . : JDP to AMcC, Aug. 10, 1918, AAIAL.

148 The fact that Wright McCormick . . . : Wright McCormick to JDP, Aug. 15, 1917, UVA.

149 Mary Lamar Gordon sought the help . . . : Correspondence pertaining to JDP's delinquent status with draft board and frequent exchange of letters between JBS and Mary Lamar Gordon are at GU.

149 "Bobby's a lieutenant . . .": JDP to JHL, Aug. 11, 1918, SI.

149 Scott appealed to the . . . : undated "memorandum" to Postmaster Burleson and to Senator Claude Swanson, GU.

149 He made one final . . . : JDP to JBS, July 31, 1918, GU.

149 Before leaving Paris . . . : JDP to AMcC, undated letter, AAIAL.

150 Perhaps his most . . . : *TBT*, p. 71.

151 He would have to face . . . : JDP to JBS, Aug. 24, 1918, GU.

CHAPTER 11

153 "If only Aunt Mamie . . .": JDP to JBS, Aug. 24, 1918, GU.
153 So fervent were his pleas . . . : JDP to JBS, Aug. 29, 1918, GU.
154 To jostle his memory . . . : diary, Aug. 24–26, 1918, UVA.
155 Marvin had taken . . . : RM to VSC, interview, Nov. 18, 1978, Columbus, Ohio.
156 As a newly inducted member . . . : diary, Sept. 27, 1918; see also JDP to AMcC, Sept.
   28, 1918, AAIAL.
156 Unless a waiver . . . : JBS to Mary Lamar Gordon, Sept. 3, 1918, GU.
156 Meanwhile, he complained . . . : JDP to JBS, Sept. 28, 1918, GU.
156 "Organization is death . . .": JDP to AMcC, Oct. 5, 1918, AAIAL.
157 After Mrs. Gordon wired . . . : JDP to JBS, Sept. 28, 1918, GU.
157 Her job was to convince . . . : JBS to Mary Lamar Gordon, Oct. 4, Nov. 12, Dec. 3,
   1918, GU.
157 To help insure . . . : diary, Sept., Oct. 1918, UVA.
158 McComb's reply from the . . . : AMcC to JDP, Nov. 15, 1918, UVA.
158 McComb was even more . . . : AMcC to JDP, Dec. 14, 1918, UVA.
158 When he told Cope . . . : Thomas Pym Cope to JDP, Aug. 29, 1918, UVA.
159 "I've no doubt you've . . .": Edward Massey to JDP, Nov. 1, 1918, UVA.
159 Leaving Camp Crane . . . : diary, Nov. 11, 1918, UVA.
160 He was convinced . . . : *TBT*, p. 74.
160 Dos Passos' acting quartermaster . . . : *TBT*, p. 75.
161 Dos Passos vowed . . . : JDP to DP, Dec. 22, 1918, UVA.
161 Marcus S. Goldman, a private first class . . . : Marcus S. Goldman, Oral History Tape
   (RS15/7/33—353-412), University Archives, University of Illinois at Urbana-Champaign.
161 Dos Passos liked Barry . . . : *TBT*, p. 77.
162 A new addition to their . . . : *TBT*, p. 77.
162 He intended to enlarge . . . : JDP to DP, May 21, 1919, UVA.
162 Meanwhile, he applied . . . : JDP to RM, July 13, 1919, UVA.
162 Paris in the spring . . . : JDP to DP, May 14, 1919, UVA.
163 For a time, Dos Passos . . . : *TBT*, p. 76.
163 After an interview with . . . : JBS to Robert Woods Bliss, June 21, 1919, GU.
163 "I am sorry that he . . .": Mary Lamar Gordon to JBS, July 15, 1919, GU.
164 "You are the first person . . .": JDP to JBS, July 4, 1919, GU.
164 To evade the military . . . : *TBT*, p. 78.
166 Wright McCormick complained to . . . : Wright McCormick to JDP, undated letter,
   1919, UVA.
166 "If you want to . . .": JDP to RM, Oct. 15, 1919, UVA.
167 One night he sat alone . . . : *TBT*, p. 80.
168 "It would be fun . . .": *A Pushcart at the Curb* (New York: George H. Doran, 1922),
   pp. 123–24.
168 When he wanted most to play . . . : *TBT*, p. 81.
169 He needed seventy-five pounds . . . : JDP to George Allen & Unwin, Dec. 15, 1919, *The
   Fourteenth Chronicle: Letters and Diaries of John Dos Passos,* ed. Townsend Ludington
   (Boston: Gambit, 1973), p. 272.
170 "They published a perfect . . .": Robert Hillyer to JDP, Jan. 9, 1920, UVA.
170 "To get away with a . . .": JDP to Stewart Mitchell, Feb. 17, 1920, BA.
170 Dos Passos had begun to think . . . : JDP to JHL, undated letter, 1920, SI.
170 Here he met up . . . : JDP to JHL, Mar. 26, 1920, SI.
171 In May he was back . . . : JDP to Stewart Mitchell, May 13, 1920, BA.
171 "The printers refuse . . .": JDP to Thomas P. Cope, undated letter, 1920, UVA.

171 He said later . . . : An authorized edition, complete and unexpurgated, with a new introduction by JDP and drawings from his Paris sketchbook of 1918, was published by Cornell University Press in 1969; see correspondence from JDP to Robert Elias, who suggested the edition and assisted in its editing, at the Cornell University Library, Ithaca, New York, 1958–67.

CHAPTER 12

173 The balmy journey northward . . . : JDP to JHL, Sept. 12, 1920, SI.

175 Cummings' paternity was kept secret . . . : See Richard S. Kennedy, *Dreams in the Mirror: A Biography of E. E. Cummings* (New York: Liveright, 1980), pp. 410–30.

175 "I feel so proud . . .": Kate Gee to JDP, Nov. 16, 1920, UVA.

176 *Three Soldiers* made the rounds . . . : *TBT,* p. 85.

176 "If you people give . . .": JDP to Eugene F. Saxton, Mar., 1921, JDP Collection, HU.

176 By this time, Dos Passos . . . : Extensive correspondence from Brandt & Kirkpatrick, Carl Brandt, and Brandt & Brandt dating from 1919 in UVA.

177 Almost on the spur . . . : *TBT,* p. 86.

178 Even in good weather . . . : JDP to RM, undated letter, 1920, UVA.

178 "Dos went first . . .": EEC to Mrs. Edward Cummings, May 17, 1921, EEC Collection, HU.

179 "Wish to God my father . . .": JDP to Robert Hillyer, July 3, 1921, SU.

179 Hibben told Dos Passos . . . : *TBT,* pp. 90–91.

180 "I'm no more a journalist . . .": JDP to RM, undated letter, 1921, UVA.

180 The black market . . . : *TBT,* p. 93.

180 From Tiflis, Dos Passos . . . : *TBT,* p. 94.

181 "War had ground the country . . .": *TBT,* p. 95.

183 He wrote almost everyone . . . : JDP to Robert Hillyer, Nov. 4, 1921, SU.

183 "I've decided that this wandering . . .": JDP to Thomas P. Cope, Nov. 13, 1921, UVA.

184 "Arabic is the most difficult . . .": JDP to RM, Dec. 8, 1921, UVA.

186 Van den Arend envied . . . : Frederick van den Arend to JDP, Dec. 13, 1921, UVA.

186 According to Cummings . . . : EEC to Mrs. Edward Cummings, Feb. 26, 1922, EEC Collection, HU; see also *Selected Letters of E. E. Cummings,* ed. F. W. Dupee and George Stade (New York: Harcourt, Brace & World, 1969), pp. 63–64.

187 "Since it seems to be . . .": JDP to Sherwood Anderson, Jan. 7, 1922, Sherwood Anderson Collection, Newberry Library, Chicago.

187 "This is the truest damn book . . .": Inscription of personal copy of *Three Soldiers,* Collection of Kenneth Holditch, New Orleans, La.

CHAPTER 13

189 He told Edmund Wilson . . . : Edmund Wilson to F. Scott Fitzgerald, May 26, 1922, *Letters on Literature and Politics, 1912–1972,* ed. Elena Wilson (New York: Farrar, Straus & Giroux, 1977), p. 85.

189 Dos Passos wrote Arthur McComb . . . : April 25, 1922, AAIAL.

189 Dos Passos hid . . . : JDP to RM, undated letter, Mar. 1922, UVA.

190 "Never had so much . . .": JDP to AMcC, undated letter, May 1922, AAIAL.

190 Stewart Mitchell did not allow . . . : "Spain from the Air" (a review of *Rosinante to the Road Again), The Dial,* June 1922, pp. 640–41.

190 Louis Untermeyer appreciated . . . : "Four Poets," *Bookman,* Dec. 1922, p. 495.

190 Mark Van Doren thought . . . : "In Line," *The Nation,* Nov. 15, 1922, p. 530.

191 "The gesture did not . . .": DP to VSC, Apr. 9, 1979.

191 "Dudley and I are in Greenwich . . .": JDP to AMcC, undated letter, May 1922, AAIAL.

191 "I've never liked . . .": JDP to AMcC, Apr. 25, 1922, AAIAL.

191 "You are now a capitalist . . .": AMcC to JDP, Apr. 25, 1922, UVA.

192 Adelaide Lawson thought he . . . : Adelaide Lawson Gaylor to VSC, interview, Aug. 16, 1979, Glenwood Landing, Long Island, N.Y.

192 "It was at Ogunquit . . .": Elizabeth Burroughs Woodhouse to VSC, interview, Aug. 15, 1978, Little Compton, R.I.

192 "Come and bring . . .": JDP to F. Scott Fitzgerald, in F. Scott Fitzgerald Papers, PU.

192 On Wilson's invitation . . . : JDP to EW, Edmund Wilson Collection, YUB.

192 "There were a great many . . .": RN to VSC, Mar. 20, 1979.

193 Nathan, too, was living . . . : RN to VSC, interview, Aug. 1, 1979, Beverly Hills, Calif.

193 James Sibley Watson's wife, Hildegarde . . . : James Sibley Watson to VSC, July 27, 1979.

194 The only thing that had impressed . . . : JDP to JHL, undated letter, SI.

194 "Like the young monk . . .": JDP to Mildred Sweeney, Mar. 8, 1923, UVA.

194 "There was an instant affinity . . .": Crystal Ross Dabney to VSC, telephone interview, Aug. 13, 1980.

195 By early June he was . . . : Donald Ogden Stewart, *By a Stroke of Luck* (New York: Paddington Press, 1975), pp. 116–18; see also *TBT,* p. 140.

195 Dos Passos was not impressed . . . : *TBT,* p. 145.

195 Murphy had invited . . . : *TBT,* p. 146.

196 "I was shy and I hated . . .": *TBT,* pp. 146–47.

196 Cummings' propensity for . . . : *TBT,* p. 133; JDP to Charles Norman, Sept. 29, 1957, UVA; EEC to William Slater Brown, *Selected Letters of E. E. Cummings,* ed. F. W. Dupee and George Stade (New York: Harcourt, Brace & World, 1969), p. 74; Charles Norman, *E. E. Cummings: The Magic Maker* (New York: Little, Brown, 1958), pp. 180–81.

197 The Murphys had left . . . : Calvin Tomkins, *Living Well Is the Best Revenge* (New York: Viking, 1971), pp. 33–36; *TBT,* pp. 148–50.

198 Dos Passos returned to . . . : *TBT,* pp. 127–30.

200 "One arrives on foot . . .": JDP to Germaine Lucas-Championnière, Apr. 3, 1924, in Townsend Ludington, *John Dos Passos: A Twentieth Century Odyssey* (New York: Dutton, 1980), p. 231.

200 "I'll never forget . . .": *TBT,* pp. 198–99.

201 Before leaving New Orleans . . . : JDP to RM, undated letter, UVA.

201 Upon arrival in Pamplona . . . : *TBT,* pp. 154–56; Stewart, *By a Stroke of Luck,* pp. 131–33.

202 He was happiest . . . : *TBT,* p. 156.

203 He was in Cap d'Antibes . . . : JDP to JHL, undated letter, SI.

203 De Beaumont was easily . . . : Tomkins, *Living Well,* p. 41.

204 Her affair with Édouard Jozen . . . : Tomkins, *Living Well,* p. 42.

204 "By this time Scott . . .": *TBT,* pp. 151–52.

204 Fernand Léger, who came . . . : Tomkins, *Living Well,* p. 96.

205 When he heard that . . . : JDP to RM, undated letter, UVA.

206 "We were sweethearts . . .": Crystal Ross Dabney to VSC, telephone interview, Aug. 13, 1980.

206 Still in the house during . . . : *TBT,* pp. 164–65.

206 She addressed him usually . . . : Crystal Ross to JDP, Apr. 5, 1925, UVA. Some fifteen notes and letters from Ross to JDP, most of them undated, from 1925 to 1929, are at UVA.

208 "I'm crazy to take . . .": JDP to RM, undated letter, UVA.

209 He said later that he had . . . : Carlos Baker, *Ernest Hemingway: A Life Story* (New York: Scribner's, 1969), p. 153.

210 "I have just bid . . .": Pauline Pfeiffer to Katharine F. Smith, UVA.

210 "I never understood exactly . . .": JDP to RM, undated letter, Apr. 1926, UVA.

211 Back in Cap d'Antibes . . . : *TBT*, pp. 150–51.

212 From the Villa America . . . : JDP to JHL, undated letter, SI.

212 "Have been working like . . .": EH to William B. Smith, Jr., Dec. 3, 1925, Collection of Marion Hammett Smith, Arlington, Virginia.

212 "I certainly laughed . . .": *TBT*, p. 158.

212 "I love it, but . . .": F. Scott Fitzgerald to Max Perkins, undated letter, in *Dear Scott/ Dear Max: The Fitzgerald-Perkins Correspondence*, ed. John Kuehl and Jackson Bryer (New York: Scribner's, 1971), p. 127.

212 As Dos Passos put it . . . : *TBT*, p. 157.

213 "Trash doesn't come . . .": Fitzgerald to Perkins, Feb. 20, 1926, Kuehl and Bryer, *Dear Scott/Dear Max*, p. 134.

213 *"Liberty, Post, Cosmopolitan . . .":* EH to William B. Smith, Jr., Dec. 3, 1925, Collection of Marion Hammett Smith.

213 The preceding winter Hemingway . . . : "Through Hemingway's Vorarlberg," *Skiing*, Nov. 1967, pp. 141–45; *TBT*, pp. 158–59.

213 Cummings sketched elephants . . . : Many of Cummings' sketches can be found in the EEC Collection, HU.

213 Despite his joking . . . : *TBT*, pp. 161–63.

215 Fitzgerald described *Manhattan Transfer* . . . : Fitzgerald to Perkins, Dec. 30, 1925, in Kuehl and Bryer, *Dear Scott/Dear Max*, p. 128.

215 "In Europe, *Manhattan Transfer* . . .": Fragment of manuscript, undated, JFK.

215 After its British edition . . . : D. H. Lawrence, a review of *Manhattan Transfer, Calendar of Modern Letters*, Apr. 1927, UVA.

215 Dos Passos was in Fez . . . : JDP to EH, Feb. 26, 1926, JFK.

216 "I don't expect much more . . .": JDP to EH, Mar. 8, 1926, JFK.

216 He was in Tangier when . . . : *TBT*, pp. 163–64; see also *Dos Passos and "The Revolting Playwrights"* by George A. Knox and Herbert M. Stahl, in *Essays and Studies on American Language and Literature* (American Institute, Upsala University, Sweden, 1964).

217 Their few days together . . . : *TBT*, pp. 158–59.

217 When he learned later . . . : JDP to EH, Nov. 10, 1926, JFK.

217 Some thirty years after . . . : EH, *A Moveable Feast: Sketches of the Author's Life in Paris in the Twenties* (New York: Scribner's, 1964), pp. 207–9; see also pp. 198–211.

CHAPTER 14

219 The criticism leveled . . . : Reviews and additional background involving the New Playwrights Theatre and individual plays found in JDP Collection, UVA; Collection of Steven Zebrock (Alan Brock) Hastings-on-Hudson, N.Y.; Collection of Em Jo Basshe/Dos Passos Papers, McKeldin Library, University of Maryland; Collection of JHL, SI; playbills and other materials relative to New Playwrights Theatre in the Theatre Collection of the Library and Museum of the Performing Arts, the New York Public Library at Lincoln Center; see also Michael Hamilton Palmer, *The Dramatic, Literary, and Historical Significance of John Dos Passos' Three Plays and Their Relationship to the Major Works* (Ann Arbor, Mich.: University Microfilms, 1975).

220 Early in the year . . . : Daniel Aaron, *Writers on the Left* (New York: Oxford University Press, 1961), pp. 99–102; see also JDP to Maurice Becker, Feb. 1925, in Papers of the

American Fund for Public Service (The Garland Fund), Manuscript and Archives Division, The New York Public Library.

221 His first essay . . . : "The *New Masses* I'd Like," *The New Masses,* June 1926, p. 20.

222 Dos Passos was convinced . . . : "The Pit and the Pendulum," *The New Masses,* Aug. 1926, p. 30.

222 Marvin also invited . . . : RM to VSC, interview, Nov. 18, 1978, Columbus, Ohio; C. Dickerman Williams to VSC, interview, Nov. 16, 1977; the Richmond *News,* "Hiking Author Says Radio Robs Hatteras of Graves," June 29, 1926, p. 4; "Recollections of a Walk Around Cape Hatteras by Rumsey Marvin," undated, UVA; C. Dickerman Williams to RM, Mar. 2, Apr. 3, 1967; JDP to RM, Mar. 13, Apr. 3, 1967, UVA.

223 "You are probably going to hate . . .": JDP to Robert Hillyer, undated letter, SU.

223 "I've written a damn priggish . . .": JDP to EH, Nov. 10, 1926, JFK.

224 "The funny thing about . . .": JDP to EH, Jan. 16, 1927, JFK.

224 "What the hell . . .": EH to JDP, Feb. 16, 1927, UVA.

225 "I'm as dumb . . .": JDP to JHL, undated letter, SI.

225 "I'm in deeper and deeper . . .": JDP to EH, Mar. 27, 1927, JFK.

225 From St. Thomas . . . : JDP to EH, June 9, 1927, JFK.

226 Incensed by the committee's . . . : "An Open Letter to President Lowell," *The Nation,* Aug. 4, 1927, p. 176; published in part in the New York *Times,* Aug. 8, 1927; see also *Facing the Chair: Story of the Americanization of Two Foreignborn Workmen* (Boston: Sacco-Vanzetti Defense Committee, 1927); "They Are Dead Now," *The New Masses,* Oct. 1927, p. 7.

226 The Citizens National Committee . . . : Isaac Don Levine to VSC, interview, Aug. 22, 1978, Waldorf, Md.; miscellaneous clippings from Isaac Don Levine Collection, Waldorf, Md.

227 Most of the picketers . . . : Michael Gold, "Lynchers in Frockcoats," *The New Masses,* Sept. 3, 1927, p. 6.

227 Many of the picketers . . . : Katherine Anne Porter, "The Never Ending Wrong," *The Atlantic,* June 1977, pp. 37–64; see also Anne Cheney, *Millay in Greenwich Village* (University: University of Alabama Press, 1975), pp. 128–29.

227 Dos Passos was arrested . . . : Allen Churchill, *The Literary Decade* (Englewood Cliffs, N.J.: Prentice-Hall, 1972), pp. 273–75; see also Francis Russell, "The 'Second Trial' of Sacco and Vanzetti, *Harvard Magazine,* May–June 1978, pp. 50–54; JDP, "Sacco and Vanzetti," a review of *The Life and Death of Sacco and Vanzetti* by Eugene Lyons, *The New Masses,* Nov. 1927; *TBT,* pp. 166–69, 172–73.

228 "You can't imagine . . .": JDP to EW, Sept. 19, 1927, YUB; EW, *The Twenties* (New York: Farrar, Straus & Giroux, 1975), pp. 388–89.

229 "America is a land of . . .": "America," a poem by David Gordon, which JDP attached to letters to a number of friends in the fall and winter of 1927–28, UVA; he also sent copies of "Excerpt from Court Record in Connection with the Sentencing of David Gordon," dated June 10, 1927, UVA.

230 "America our nation has been beaten . . .": *The Big Money* (New York: Harcourt, Brace, 1936), "Camera Eye #50," pp. 413–14.

230 "The theatre and trying to write . . .": JDP to Robert Hillyer, undated letter, SU.

231 When Hemingway left Europe . . . : *EH,* pp. 191–94; *TBT,* pp. 198–202.

231 The swarthy complexion . . . : Manoel Cardozo to VSC, interview, Mar. 20, 1977, Washington, D.C.

232 "Pleased to have met you . . .": Katharine F. ("Katy") Smith to JDP, June 22, 1928, UVA.

CHAPTER 15

235 Adolph Dehn's caricature . . . : Collection of Virginia Dehn; Virginia Dehn to VSC, interview, Dec. 30, 1978, New York, N.Y.

235 He had gone to Key West only . . . : *TBT*, p. 173.

235 "I'm a dead letter . . .": JDP to RM, undated letter, UVA.

236 By the end of May 1928 . . . : *TBT*, pp. 173–74.

237 Before leaving Leningrad . . . : W. Horsley Gantt to VSC, interviews, Mar. 31, 1977, Mar. 12, Aug. 19, 1978, Baltimore, Md., *TBT*, pp. 177–78.

238 Dos Passos posed a number . . . : diary, miscellaneous entries, summer and fall, 1928; see also *In All Countries* (New York: Harcourt, Brace, 1934), Sections I and II, pp. 3–72.

239 "On a trip of this kind . . .": *TBT*, p. 184.

240 Dos Passos left the group . . . : *TBT*, pp. 187–93.

241 "Soon after I met Dr. Gantt . . .": formal statement prepared for the House Un-American Activities Committee, Jan. 22, 1953, UVA.

241 Gantt conveyed to Dos Passos . . . : *TBT*, pp. 191–93; JDP to EEC, undated letter, EEC Collection, HU. See also Evelyn S. Ringold, "American Pavlov," *Today in Psychiatry,* Sept. 1977, pp. 1–3; Phyllis K. Wilson, "Horsley Gantt, Student of Pavlov, Active Researcher at 84," *Hopkins Medical News,* Mar. 1977, pp. 3–5; W. Horsley Gantt, "A Scientist's Last Words," in *Legacies in the Study of Behavior,* ed. Joseph Warren Cullen (Springfield, Ill.: Charles C. Thomas, 1974), pp. 46–61.

242 Whereas Gantt allowed himself . . . : W. Horsley Gantt to VSC, interview, Mar. 12, 1978, Baltimore, Md.

243 They saw him as the American . . . : Malcolm Cowley, *A Second Flowering: Works and Days of the Lost Generation* (New York: Viking, 1973), p. 84.

244 Eugene Lyons was in Moscow . . . : Eugene Lyons to VSC, telephone interview, July 10, 1978; see also Eugene Lyons, *The Red Decade: The Stalinist Penetration of America* (Indianapolis: Bobbs-Merrill, 1941), p. 129; Daniel Aaron, *Writers on the Left* (New York: Oxford University Press, 1961), pp. 231–32.

244 Dos Passos was more interested . . . : JDP to EEC, undated letter, HU.

244 When he returned home . . . : "The New Theater in Russia," *The New Republic,* Apr. 16, 1930, pp. 236–40.

245 By contrast, New Yorkers . . . : "They Want Ritzy Art," *The New Masses,* June 1928, p. 13; see also "Towards a Revolutionary Theatre," *The New Masses,* Dec. 1927, p. 20.

247 "They want to say goodbye . . .": "Passport Photo," *In All Countries,* pp. 3–6.

247 He was pressed again . . . : Valia Gerasimova to JDP, Feb. 25, 1929, UVA.

247 "How could I answer that . . .": *TBT*, p. 196.

248 As for himself, he . . . : JDP to EH, Dec. 24, 1928, JFK.

248 Hemingway replied that . . . : EH to JDP, undated letter, UVA.

248 "My old man shot himself . . .": Hemingway's father died Dec. 6, 1928; see also *EH*, pp. 198–200.

CHAPTER 16

249 Em Jo Basshe had declared . . . : JHL to JDP, Dec. 28, 1928, UVA; see also undated memorandum by Em Jo Basshe (nine pages), Em Jo Basshe Papers, McKeldin Library, University of Maryland.

250 "Don't ever write . . .": Dos Passos to Robert Hillyer, undated letter, SU.

252 Once the dust had settled . . . : "Did the New Playwrights Theatre Fail?" *The New Masses,* Aug. 1929, p. 13.

252 "For God's sake . . .": EH to JDP, Feb. 9, 1929, UVA.

252 He was pleased with himself . . . : A. Scott Berg, *Max Perkins: Editor of Genius* (New York: E. P. Dutton, 1978), pp. 140–41, 158–59.

252 Strater also painted . . . : Henry Strater to VSC, June 12, 1979, Apr. 1, 1980; Lorene Thompson to VSC, interview, Sept. 10, 1979, Key West, Fla.; Otto ("Toby") and Betty Bruce to VSC, interview, Sept. 10, 1979, Key West, Fla.

253 Hemingway's sister, Madelaine . . . : Madelaine Hemingway Miller to VSC, telephone interview, May 15, 1979; see also Madelaine Hemingway Miller, *Ernie: Hemingway's Sister Sunny Remembers* (New York: Crown, 1975), pp. 112–17; *TBT,* pp. 199–202.

254 Upon leaving Key West . . . : JDP to RM, Apr. 29, 1929, UVA.

254 As he explained later . . . : JDP to David Sanders, in *Writers at Work: The Paris Review Interviews,* ed. George Plimpton, 4th ser. (New York: Viking, 1976), p. 81; see also pp. 67–69.

255 "Dos with his withered . . .": EW, *The Twenties* (New York: Farrar, Straus & Giroux, 1975), pp. 429–30; Richard S. Kennedy, *Dreams in the Mirror: A Biography of E. E. Cummings* (New York: Liveright, 1980), p. 303.

256 On June 11, Vorse . . . : diary, WSU.

256 The name "Smooley" . . . : Background on Edith Foley, Stella Roof, and their move to the Cape with Katy Smith derived chiefly from interviews with Frances Foley Dickinson, Aug. 13, 1978, and letters of Jan. 21, July 4, 1978, Feb. 4, 1980, Wellfleet, Mass.; Isabel Foley Whelan, Nov. 6, 1977 and Aug. 10, 1978, Provincetown, Mass.; Eben Given, Nov. 6, 1977, Aug. 9, Aug. 12, 1978, Truro, Mass.; and miscellaneous correspondence between Katy Smith and Edith Foley, 1923–25, UVA; background on the William Benjamin Smith family: Marion Hammett Smith, interviews, Mar. 24, Aug. 21, 1978, Arlington, Va.; Katharine Smith Durand, interview, Mar. 21, 1977, Norfolk, Va.; Warren Browne, *Titan vs. Taboo: The Life of William Benjamin Smith* (Tucson: Diogenes, 1961); and miscellaneous papers in Collection of Marion Hammett Smith, Arlington, Va.

257 "The group at Smooley Hall . . .": Hutchins Hapgood, *A Victorian in the Modern World* (New York: Harcourt, Brace, 1939), pp. 513–17.

257 The Smooleys submitted . . . : miscellaneous published short stories in JDP Collection, UVA.

257 "I want a pint of whiskey . . .": Eben Given to VSC, interview, Aug. 9, 1978, Truro, Mass.

258 The Smooleys had an ancient . . . : Jerry and Henka Farnsworth to VSC, interview, Feb. 9, 11, 1979, Sarasota, Fla.

258 Katy gave a party . . . : diary, June 11, 1929, WSU.

258 Perhaps the only friend . . . : Frederick van den Arend to JDP, July 23, 1929, UVA.

259 Their plan when he . . . : DP to VSC, Nov. 10, 1981.

259 She allowed that she . . . : Katy Smith to JDP, June 28, 1929, UVA.

260 "Lift up your heads . . .": Katy Smith to JDP, July 9, 1929, UVA.

260 The family farmhouse . . . : Bill Smith to Henka Farnsworth, July 17, 1929, Collection of Henka Farnsworth.

261 "I am afraid hourly . . .": Katy Smith to JDP, July 25, 1929, UVA.

261 The trio was ready . . . : Bill Smith to Henka Farnsworth, "daily graph of emotions" indicating highs and lows of journey, July 2–Aug. 7, 1929, Collection of Henka Farnsworth.

261 Edith and Stella served . . . : Bill Smith to EH, Oct. 4, 1929, JFK.

261 Smith's chief function as . . . : Marion Hammett Smith to VSC, interview, Aug. 21, 1978, Arlington, Va.

261 "I feel so swell . . .": JDP to EH, Aug. 22, 1929, JFK.

262 The truth of the . . . : Official birth records in St. Louis, Mo., verify the birth of Katharine Foster Smith on October 24, 1891; see also Browne, *Titan vs. Taboo.*

262 "That two hundred . . .": JHL to JDP, Aug. 30, 1929, UVA.

262 Hemingway was in Paris . . . : JDP to EH, Oct. 24, 1929, JFK.
263 The book's matchless narrative . . . : "Books" (a review of *A Farewell to Arms*), *The New Masses*, Dec. 1929, p. 16.

CHAPTER 17

265 "The Great Depression . . .": *TBT*, p. 205.
266 "Keep money away from . . .": EH to JDP, Sept. 4, 1929, UVA.
267 "For anyone who was fond . . .": *TBT*, p. 203.
267 McAlmon reportedly accused . . . : *EH*, pp. 206–7; Nancy Milford, *Zelda* (New York: Harper & Row, 1970), pp. 190–91.
267 To compound the situation . . . : Morley Callaghan, *That Summer in Paris* (New York: Coward-McCann, 1963), pp. 211–54; Isabel Paterson, "Turns with a Bookworm," *New York Herald Tribune Books*, Nov. 24, 1929.
268 By this time . . . : Calvin Tomkins, *Living Well Is the Best Revenge* (New York: Viking, 1971), pp. 112–33, 127–28.
268 The Murphys had troubles . . . : *TBT*, pp. 202–3; Tomkins, *Living Well*, pp. 120–23; Honoria Murphy Donnelly to VSC, interview, May 31, 1977.
268 Determined to carry on . . . : *EH*, p. 207; *TBT*, p. 203.
268 Donald Ogden Stewart, *By a Stroke of Luck* (New York: Paddington Press, 1975), pp. 186–87.
269 When Dos Passos returned . . . : *TBT*, pp. 203–4; "Homer of the Transsiberian," *The Saturday Review of Literature*, Oct. 16, 1926, pp. 202, 222; see also Jay Bochner, *Blaise Cendrars: Discovery and Re-Creation* (Toronto: University of Toronto Press, 1978).
270 In Paris, a telegram . . . : Brandt & Brandt to JDP, Jan. 20, 1930, UVA; Patience Ross to Brandt & Brandt, undated letter, UVA.
271 The few passengers . . . : *TBT*, p. 204.
271 "It is not a book . . .": Mary Ross, "Books," *New York Herald Tribune Books*, Feb. 23, 1930, p. 30.
272 The author's "smashing disregard . . .": George Curry, Brooklyn *Daily Eagle*, Feb. 26, 1930, p. 22.
272 He believed that the novel . . . : John Chamberlain, *New York Times Book Review*, Mar. 2, 1930, p. 5.
272 The book's haphazard style . . . : Henry Hazlitt, *The Nation*, Mar. 12, 1930, p. 298.
272 Upton Sinclair (whom Dos Passos . . . : *The New Masses*, Apr. 5, 1930, pp. 18–19.
272 Most remarkable about . . . : *The New Republic*, Mar. 26, 1930, pp. 156–58.
272 V. S. Pritchett saw Dos Passos . . . : *Spectator*, Sept. 27, 1930, pp. 421–22.
273 It is unlikely . . . : Fitzgerald to Max Perkins, May 1, 1930, *Dear Scott/Dear Max: The Fitzgerald-Perkins Correspondence*, ed. John Kuehl and Jackson Bryer (New York: Scribner's, 1971), p. 166.
273 Blaise Cendrars was exuberant: Cendrars to JDP, July 18, 1930, UVA; translated by Caryl Lloyd.
273 "The poetry of Blaise Cendrars . . .": *Panama, or The Adventures of My Seven Uncles* (New York: Harper, 1931), "Translator's Foreword," pp. vii–viii.
275 A number of letters to . . . : JDP to Eugene Saxton, three undated letters, 1930, JDP Collection, HU.
275 "You said it . . .": JDP to John Herrmann and Josephine Herbst, undated letter, UT-HRC.
275 The countryside was "gray and . . .": EW, *The Thirties* (New York: Farrar, Straus & Giroux, 1980), p. 20.
275 "Their big bare fresh . . .": EW, *The Thirties*, pp. 31–32.
275 Margaret once told Wilson . . . : EW, *The Thirties*, pp. 20, 23–24.

276 "Dos has finally come . . .": EW, *Letters on Literature and Politics, 1912–1972,* ed. Elena Wilson (New York: Farrar, Straus & Giroux, 1977), pp. 199, 202.

277 "You have undoubtedly read . . .": JDP to Donald Davidson as "Dear Friend," September 1930, Donald Davidson Papers, Joint Universities Libraries, Nashville, Tenn.

279 The proposal now . . . : *EH,* pp. 214–17; *TBT,* pp. 204–5.

280 His first letter to . . . : JDP to KDP, Oct. 24, 1930, UVA.

280 Only the day before . . . : KDP to JDP, Oct. 31, 1930, UVA.

281 Even Stella Roof . . . : Jerry Farnsworth to VSC, interview, Feb. 11, 1979, Sarasota, Fla.

281 "More matches were made . . .": Henka Farnsworth to VSC, interview, Feb. 11, 1979, Sarasota, Fla.

281 Henka Farnsworth had her own . . . : RN to VSC, interview, Aug. 2, 1979, Beverly Hills, Calif.

281 "If you didn't sleep with . . .": Jean Shay to VSC, interview, July 26, 1978, New York City.

281 Before Phyllis Duganne came . . . : Eben Given to VSC, interview, Nov. 6, 1977.

282 He considered them . . . : Mary McCarthy to VSC, interview, Aug. 3, 1978, Castine, Maine.

282 "Katy was too pleased . . .": Jean Shay to VSC, interview, Mar. 18, 1978, New York City.

282 After Margaret's death . . . : EW, *The Thirties,* p. 257.

282 Hutchins Hapgood observed that Shay . . . : Hapgood, *A Victorian in the Modern World* (New York: Harcourt, Brace, 1939), p. 513.

282 They were married . . . : Frances Foley Dickinson to VSC, Feb. 4, 1980.

283 She and Smith had once . . . : Hapgood, *A Victorian in the Modern World,* p. 513.

283 "*They* is a lot of rainbows . . .": KDP to Henka Farnsworth, Feb. 9, 1931, UVA.

283 "Clurman and Crawford and Strasberg . . .": Dawn Powell to JDP, undated letter, UVA.

283 The Group Theatre, conceived . . . : Harold Clurman to VSC, interview, Nov. 5, 1977, New York City.

283 When the Theatre Guild released . . . : Paul Green to VSC, interview, July 22, 1978, Chapel Hill, N.C.

284 "It does seem a pity . . .": Patience Ross to Carol Brandt, Dec. 10, 1931, UVA.

284 Dos Passos also pushed . . . : Patience Ross to BB, Nov. 6, 1931, UVA; JDP to BB, Dec. 10, 1931, UVA.

284 They had considered buying . . . : KDP to Henka Farnsworth, Feb. 9, 1931, UVA.

285 "Eben is going to pay . . .": KDP to Henka Farnsworth, Feb. 9, 1931, UVA.

285 When they checked into their . . . : Eben Given to VSC, interview, Aug. 12, 1978, Truro, Mass.; see also Carleton Beals, *Glass Houses: Ten Years of Free Lancing* (Philadelphia: J. B. Lippincott, 1938), pp. 248–49.

285 He learned that summer . . . : *EH,* p. 219.

285 Pauline's "Uncle Gus" . . . : *EH,* p. 221.

285 Although she did not push . . . : C. Dickerman Williams to VSC, interview, July 30, 1978, Norfolk, Conn.

286 Moreover, having read a . . . : Lucy Virginia Ralston to VSC, interview, Mar. 23, 1978, Pelham, N.Y.

286 The book was already . . . : Thomas B. Wells to Eugene Saxton, Dec. 11, 1931, JDP Collection, HU.

286 "I'll be down in New York . . .": JDP to Eugene Saxton, undated letter, JDP Collection, HU.

286 The problem was not censorship . . . : BB to Patience Ross, Apr. 11, 1932, UVA.

286 Upon Harcourt, Brace's assumption . . . : BB to Patience Ross, Dec. 11, 1931, UVA.

287 In his new post . . . : "An Appeal for Aid," *The New Republic,* Aug. 5, 1931, p. 318;

see also Irving Bernstein, "Catastrophe in Coal," in *The Thirties,* ed. Don Congdon (New York: Simon & Schuster, 1962), pp. 49–54; W. A. Swanberg, *Dreiser* (New York: Scribner's, 1965), pp. 384–87.

287 After his initial plea . . . : JDP to KDP, Sept. 2, Sept. 7, 1931, UVA.

288 The entire situation . . . : Charles R. Walker, " 'Red' Blood in Kentucky: Why 100% Americans Turn Communist," *Forum,* Jan. 1932, pp. 18–23; "We Went to Harlan," *The New Masses,* Dec. 1931, p. 3.

288 As Dos Passos reported later . . . : "Harlan County Sunset," in *In All Countries* (New York: Harcourt, Brace, 1934), pp. 190–98; see also "Harlan: Working Under the Gun," *The New Republic,* Dec. 2, 1931, pp. 62–67; "In Defense of Kentucky," *The New Republic,* Dec. 16, 1931, p. 137; also Adelaide Walker to VSC, interview, Nov. 8, 1978, Wellfleet, Mass.

291 Both in January and . . . : Form letters (addressee unidentified) dated Jan. and Feb. 1932 in UT-HRC, and in the Noel Sullivan Papers, Bancroft Library, University of California at Berkeley.

291 Edmund Wilson had been . . . : EW, *The Thirties,* p. 147; KDP to JDP, Nov. 3, Nov. 12, 1931, UVA.

291 Upon observing them . . . : Beals, *Glass Houses,* pp. 248–49.

292 When he was in . . . : KDP to JDP, Nov. 9, 1931, UVA.

292 "I am on the hermit side . . .": KDP to JDP, Nov. 12, 1931, UVA.

293 Provincetowners were accustomed . . . : Phil Alexander to VSC, interview, Nov. 7, 1977, Provincetown, Mass.; Oliver Austin to VSC, interview, Jan. 29, 1978, Gainesville, Fla.; Grace Bell to VSC, interview, Nov. 6, 1977, Provincetown, Mass.; Eben Given to VSC, interview, Aug. 9, 1978, Truro, Mass.

293 He told in his diary . . . : EW, *The Thirties,* p. 49–50.

293 Only Edmund Wilson . . . : "Dahlberg, Dos Passos and Wilder," *The New Republic,* Mar. 26, 1930, pp. 156–58.

294 According to Eben Given . . . : Eben Given to VSC, interview, Nov. 6, 1977, Truro, Mass.

294 "My first meeting with Dos Passos . . .": Edward Dahlberg, *Confessions of Edward Dahlberg* (New York: George Braziller, 1971).

294 For a week he cruised . . . : JDP to KDP, Feb. 13, 1932, UVA; see also "Atlantic Fisheries," *Fortune,* Apr. 1935, pp. 69–73+.

295 "There are plenty of buzzards . . .": EH to JDP, Jan. 17, 1932, UVA.

295 "I kept having the feeling . . .": JDP to EH, undated letter, JFK.

295 Katy turned the trip . . . : "Just over the Border," *Woman's Home Companion,* Sept. 1932, pp. 12–13, 36.

295 Traveling across country . . . : Their journey was marked by a series of postal cards from JDP and KDP to EW; many of them contained only topical limericks, UVA.

296 "A lot of the characters . . .": JDP to EH, undated letter, JFK.

296 "The book is bloody splendid . . .": EH to JDP, Mar. 26, 1932, UVA.

296 "Having a 200-seed stake . . .": EH to JDP, Mar. 26, 1932, UVA.

296 Several years later, Hemingway . . . : EH to JDP, undated letter, UVA.

296 A letter awaiting . . . : Tad Edwards to JDP, Mar. 14, 1932, UVA.

297 "What a reading! . . .": Blaise Cendrars to JDP, Mar. 12, 1932, UVA, translated by Caryl Lloyd.

297 "More than any of us . . .": Matthew Josephson to JDP, Mar. 21, 1932, UVA; see also Matthew Josephson, "A Sad 'Big Parade,' " *The Saturday Review of Literature,* Mar. 19, 1932, p. 8.

297 Upton Sinclair's assessment . . . : Upton Sinclair to JDP, Apr. 3, 1932, UVA.

298 Malcolm Cowley called *1919* . . . : "The Poet and the World," *The New Republic,* Apr. 27, 1932, pp. 303–5.

298 "Don't let a twirp . . .": EH to JDP, May 30, 1932, UVA.

298 Henry Hazlitt apprised readers . . . : "Panorama," *The Nation,* Mar. 23, 1932, p. 344.

298 "The language of *1919* . . .": John Chamberlain, "John Dos Passos' Experiment with the 'News' Novel," *New York Times Book Review,* Mar. 13, 1932, p. 2.

298 Leighton saw no . . . : "An Autopsy and a Prescription," *The Hound and Horn,* July–Sept. 1932, pp. 519–39.

298 Most of Dos Passos' fellow-traveling . . . : Granville Hicks, "John Dos Passos," *Bookman,* Apr. 1932, pp. 32–34; Michael Gold, "The Education of John Dos Passos," *The English Journal,* Feb. 22, 1932, pp. 87–97.

299 Dos Passos' final comment . . . : JDP to Fredericka Pisek Field, Nov. 29, 1932, HU.

300 "It persuades me once . . .": Aleksandr Fadeev to JDP, Dec. 12, 1932, UVA.

300 "Everyone here that reads . . .": Walt Carmon to JDP, Dec. 1, 1932, UVA.

300 "I have the first and only copy . . .": James McCann to JDP, Mar. 24, 1932, UVA.

301 In a second letter . . . : James McCann to JDP, Sept. 18, 1932, UVA.

301 "The sight of the veterans . . .": Gladwin Bland to JDP, Aug. 3, 1932, UVA.

301 Dos Passos' treatment . . . : "Washington and Chicago. Part I: The Veterans Come Home to Roost. Part II: Spotlights and Microphones," *The New Republic,* June 29, 1932, pp. 177–79.

303 "At Ford's production . . .": *The Big Money* (New York: Harcourt, Brace, 1936), pp. 55–56.

304 Dos Passos was on hand . . . : "Four Nights in a Garden: A Campaign Yarn," *Common Sense,* Dec. 5, 1932, pp. 20–22.

306 According to Malcolm Cowley . . . : *The Dream of the Golden Mountains: Remembering the 1930's* (New York: Viking, 1980), p. 110.

306 A month later an expanded . . . : *Culture and Crisis: An Open Letter to the Writers, Artists, Teachers, Physicians, Engineers, Scientists and Other Professional Workers of America* (League of Professional Groups for Foster and Ford, 1932); see Daniel Aaron, *Writers on the Left* (New York: Oxford University Press, 1961), pp. 196–98; full list of signers on p. 423.

306 "As the literal-minded young men . . .": *TIF,* p. 101.

307 As treasurer of . . . : "Help the Scottsboro Boys," *The New Republic,* Aug. 24, 1932, p. 49; "The Two Youngest," *The Nation,* Aug. 24, 1932, p. 172.

307 "Day and night it comes . . .": Paul Green to JDP, Oct. 26, 1932, UVA; Paul Green to VSC, interview, July 22, 1978, Chapel Hill, N.C.

308 "After supper people sit . . .": "The Radio Voice," *Common Sense,* Feb. 1934, p. 17.

308 "He's no cripple . . .": JDP to EW, May 16, 1933, YUB.

309 "Brought Katy up here . . .": JDP to EH, Apr. 24, 1933, JFK.

309 "Oh AntiChrist it's so awful . . .": KDP to EW, Apr. 19, 1933, YUB.

309 It was Wilson who . . . : JDP to EW, May 10, May 16, 1933, YUB; EW to JDP, May 11, 1933, UVA; KDP to JDP, May 14, 1933, UVA.

309 Among Dos Passos' visitors . . . : JDP to KDP, May 15, 1933, UVA; JDP to EH, May 10, 1933, JFK.

309 "I do not think . . .": F. Scott Fitzgerald to Max Perkins, Jan. 30, 1933, Kuehl and Bryer, *Dear Scott/Dear Max,* p. 179.

310 "You haven't been in the . . .": F. Scott Fitzgerald to Max Perkins, May 14, 1932, Kuehl and Bryer, *Dear Scott/Dear Max,* p. 176.

310 "Don't tell Ernest because . . .": F. Scott Fitzgerald to Max Perkins, Jan. 19, 1933, Kuehl and Bryer, *Dear Scott/Dear Max,* p. 177.

310 Word spread rapidly among . . . : Susan Glaspell to JDP, undated letter, UVA; Gerald Murphy to JDP, Mar. 9, 1933, UVA.

310 "You certainly fooled the banks . . .": EH to JDP, undated letter, UVA.

311 "It will all be perfectly . . .": EH to JDP, undated letter, UVA; see also *EH,* p. 239.

311 Scribner's owed him . . . : EH to JDP, undated letter, UVA.

311 Once he heard about . . . : EH to JDP, undated letter, UVA.

311 "Jesus Hem it's mighty . . .": JDP to EH, May 3, 1933, JFK.

311 After consulting *Black's Medical* . . . : EH to JDP, undated letter, UVA.

312 "Say Hem I didn't want . . .": JDP to EH, May 10, 1933, JFK.

312 Gingrich had been editing . . . : *EH,* pp. 236, 240, 244.

312 When the doctors ordered . . . : JDP to EH, May 10, 1933, JFK.

312 "John Dos Passos is in Spain . . .": "Backstage with *Esquire," Esquire,* Fall 1933, p. 115.

313 On May 25, 1933, Dos Passos . . . : JDP to KDP, May 17, 1933, UVA; JDP to EH, May 10, May 18, 1933, JFK.

313 "Gerald and Sara went . . .": JDP to EH, May 18, 1933, JFK.

313 When he and Katy sailed . . . : bank statement, Chemical Bank & Trust, Provincetown, Mass., May 22, 1933, UVA.

CHAPTER 18

315 Gerald and Sara Murphy . . . : *TBT,* pp. 149–50, 209. Calvin Tomkins, *Living Well Is the Best Revenge* (New York: Viking, 1971), pp. 93–112; also assorted photographs of Gerald and Sara Murphy with their children and friends at Villa America; see also Honoria Murphy Donnelly, *Sara and Gerald: Villa America and After* (New York: Times Books, 1983).

316 In view of the poor sales . . . : JDP to EH, May 25, 1933, JFK.

316 He looked forward now . . . : *TBT,* p. 226.

316 The new Republican regime had . . . : *In All Countries* (New York: Harcourt, Brace, 1934), pp. 119–68; *JBW,* pp. 304–29.

316 "We don't want any more . . .": To Spaniards, America was not the United States of America, but Hispanic America. Cuba was the destination of many Spanish immigrants, as was Argentina; some went to Brazil.

317 Writing about Spain also . . . : *TBT,* pp. 221–24.

318 They had just come upon . . . : *TBT,* pp. 227–28.

318 After an exchange of several cables . . . : JDP to EH, Aug. 3, 1933, and undated cable, JFK; *EH,* pp. 244–45.

318 Dos Passos spoke later . . . : *TBT,* pp. 219–20.

318 For the time being . . . : critical commentary for leaflet of Quintanilla exhibition at the Pierre Matisse Gallery, New York, Nov. 20–Dec. 4, 1934.

319 *"Cochecito de venta cender"* . . . : *TBT,* pp. 228–29.

319 "Tell Jinny I'll send . . .": JDP to EH, undated postal card, JFK.

319 "I wish to God my father . . .": JDP to Robert Hillyer, July 3, 1921, SU.

CHAPTER 19

321 "Getting better every day . . .": JDP to EH, undated letter, JFK.

321 After conferring with his . . .": JDP to Charles A. Pearce, undated letter, HBJ.

322 He wrote Hemingway . . . : JDP to EH, undated letter, JFK.

322 "I don't want them to pull . . .": JDP to BB, Apr. 21, 1934, UVA.

322 "I hope you don't feel . . .": BB to Patience Ross, June 22, 1934, UVA.

322 "I followed all his suggestions . . .": Charles A. Pearce to BB, May 3, 1934, UVA.

323 "I never lecture . . .": JDP to Charles A. Pearce, undated letter, HBJ.

323 To reassure her client . . . : BB to JDP, May 9, 1934, UVA.

323 "It is supposed to be . . .": BB to JDP, May 4, 1934, UVA; see also JDP to BB, Apr. 27, 1934, UVA.

323 A secretary at Brandt & Brandt . . . : BB to Charles A. Pearce, May 4, May 8, 1934, UVA; Charles A. Pearce to BB, May 9, 1934, UVA.

324 "We managed to get Constable . . .": Patience Ross to BB, Feb. 13, 1934, UVA.

324 "Say do you think . . .": JDP to EH, Aug. 20, 1934, JFK.

324 Hemingway cautioned him . . . : EH to JDP, undated letter, UVA.

324 "Mr. Dos Passos counts . . .": BB to C. H. Brooks, Aug. 3, 1934, UVA; see Brandt & Brandt statement regarding foreign translations as of Sept. 13, 1934, UVA.

324 "There's a vague rumor . . .": JDP to C. H. Brooks, undated letter, UVA; BB to C. H. Brooks, Dec. 18, 1934, UVA.

325 "I send my stuff . . .": quoted by BB to C. H. Brooks, Dec. 18, 1934, UVA.

325 "Mr. Dos Passos does . . .": A. M. Heath to BB, Aug. 24, 1934, UVA.

325 Heath said that he . . . : C. H. Brooks to BB, May 4, May 24, 1934, UVA.

325 The book had already . . . : S. Fischer Verlag to Brandt & Brandt, Apr. 25, 1934, UVA.

325 Theodore Dreiser had pursued . . . : assorted letters from JDP to Dreiser, UPA, dating from Apr. 1933–Nov. 1934; and from Dreiser to JDP during the same period, UVA.

325 Bernice Baumgarten suggested . . . : BB to JDP, Mar. 3, 1934, UVA.

326 "Just before Mr. Dos Passos . . .": BB to B. A. Bergman, Mar. 5, 1934, UVA; B. A. Bergman to Brandt & Brandt, Feb. 15, 1934, UVA.

326 She asked for . . . : BB to Harry Hartwick, Mar. 12, 1934, UVA.

326 Dos Passos asked Baumgarten . . . : JDP to BB, Mar. 19, 1934; Carl Van Doren to JDP, Mar. 12, 1934, UVA; BB to Van Doren, Mar. 20, 1934, UVA.

326 Dos Passos also began . . . : BB to Harold S. Zimmerman, Orrville, Ohio, Nov. 9, 1934.

326 "Say—if you people . . .": JDP to Malcolm Cowley, Mar. 16, 1934, SUNYAB; see also "Good Books That Almost Nobody Has Read," *The New Republic,* Apr. 18, 1934, p. 281.

327 He had written Dorothy Dudley . . . : JDP to Dorothy Dudley, Mar. 10, 1933, University of Rochester Library, Rochester, N.Y.

327 When Dos Passos reviewed William Rollins' . . . : "The Business of a Novelist," *The New Republic,* Apr. 4, 1934, p. 220.

327 "The only excuse for . . .": "Statements of Belief," *Bookman,* Sept. 1928, p. 26.

328 "Christ Almighty, it seems . . .": JHL to JDP, Jan. 24, 1934, UVA.

328 Lawson insisted that . . . : JHL to JDP, Apr. 9, 1934, UVA; see also JHL to JDP, thirteen-page undated letter, UVA.

329 "Oh possum I'm not . . .": JDP to KDP, undated letter, 1934, UVA; JDP to EH, July 27, 1934, JFK; *TBT,* pp. 214–15.

329 Dos Passos was quick to . . . : JDP to EH, July 27, 1934, JFK.

329 He wrote Estlin Cummings . . . : JDP to EEC, Sept. 20, 1935, EEC Collection, HU.

329 From his room at the . . . : JDP to KDP, undated letter, UVA.

330 Since almost everyone . . . : JDP to KDP, Aug. 6, 1934, UVA.

330 "Communism for the high-salaried . . .": *TBT,* p. 215.

330 Twelve hours after . . . : "Dr. W. B. Smith, Former M.U. Teacher, Dies: Professor Emeritus of Tulane Succumbs at 83," St. Louis *Post-Dispatch,* Aug. 6, 1934; for details of death and will, see Warren Browne, *Titan vs. Taboo: The Life of William Benjamin Smith* (Tucson: Diogenes, 1961); also Katharine Smith Durand to VSC, interview, July 22, 1978, Norfolk, Va.; JDP to EH, Aug. 20, 1934, JFK.

331 He was especially struck by . . . : JDP to EEC, undated letter, EEC Collection, HU.

331 "Gosh I wish you'd . . .": JDP to EW, Aug. 24, 1934, YUB.

331 Before leaving Hollywood . . . : JDP to C. A. Pearce, Sept. 18, 1934, HBJ.

332 Dos Passos wrote Fitzgerald . . . : JDP to F. Scott Fitzgerald, Oct. 19, 1934, PU.

332 "Hem's in wonderful shape . . .": JDP to Gerald and Sara Murphy, Oct. 30, 1934, Honoria Murphy Donnelly Collection, McLean, Va.

332 Fulgencio Batista y Zaldívar was "grabbing . . .": JDP to EW, Nov. 2, Nov. 15, 1934, YUB.

332 To Robert Cantwell, then an . . . : JDP to Cantwell, Nov. 14, 1934, University of Oregon Library, Eugene, OR.

332 She could not find . . . : radiogram, JDP to KDP, Nov. 9, 1934, Frances Foley Dickinson Collection, Wellfleet, Mass.

332 "Please Katy, let's have . . .": JDP to KDP, Nov. 9, 1934, UVA.

332 "Oh my dearest M. Fish . . .": KDP to JDP, undated letter, UVA.

333 Edith, her husband, Frank . . . : KDP to JDP, undated letter, UVA; unless otherwise noted, Katy's stay at 314 East Fifty-third Street, New York City, is derived from six undated letters to JDP, UVA.

333 Wilson had been living there . . . : EW to Phelps Putnam, Nov. 23, 1933, EW, *Letters on Literature and Politics, 1912–1972,* ed. Elena Wilson (New York: Farrar, Straus & Giroux, 1977), p. 232; EW to JDP, Jan. 11, 1935, UVA.

334 "You don't say what you're . . .": JDP to KDP, undated letter, UVA.

334 "I am reasonably sure that . . .": W. Horsley Gantt to VSC, interview, Mar. 19, 1978, Baltimore, Md.

335 "I can't understand your not . . .": JDP to KDP, undated letter, UVA.

335 "Oh my dear M. Fish I might as well . . .": KDP to JDP, Nov. 28, 1934, UVA.

335 To Estlin Cummings he explained . . . : JDP to EEC, undated letter, EEC Collection, HU.

336 "If you like the stuff . . .": JDP to Malcolm Cowley, Nov. 13, 1934, SUNYAB.

336 Pressed for time, Cowley took . . . : letters dated Nov. 13–Dec. 12, 1934, and undated letters pertaining to Quintanilla exhibition and Dos Passos' letter published in *The New Republic* found in SUNYAB, and at UVA.

336 It was Hemingway who had . . . : *EH,* p. 267.

336 "Hemingway and I both feel . . .": JDP to Malcolm Cowley, Dec. 12, 1934, SUNYAB.

337 Dos Passos was introduced to . . . : Antonio Gattorno to VSC, Oct. 24, 1978; see also *EH,* pp. 264–65, 267.

337 Dos Passos was in New York . . . : EH, *Gattorno: With 38 Reproductions and a Few Critical Opinions* (Havana: Ucar, Garcia y Cia, 1935), pp. 91–92.

337 "As he's entirely unknown here . . .": JDP to Waldo Frank, undated letter.

338 "I never forgot Dos Passos' help when . . .": Antonio Gattorno to VSC, June 2, 1979.

338 The Kremlin was not . . . : JDP to EW, undated letter, YUB.

338 The two men exchanged . . . : See EW to JDP, EW, *Letters,* Jan. 11, Jan. 31, Feb. 26, May 9, 1935, pp. 255–60, 263–68.

340 Their first attempt to . . . : *TBT,* pp. 210–14; also *EH,* pp. 271–73; JDP to Patrick Murphy, undated letter, Honoria Murphy Donnelly Collection, McLean, Va.

340 Dos Passos decided that they . . . : JDP to EH, undated letter, JFK.

340 Horsley Gantt arranged . . . : W. Horsley Gantt to VSC, interview, Mar. 12, 1978, Baltimore, Md.

340 Pauline Hemingway dashed off a cryptic . . . : Pauline Hemingway to EH, undated letter, JFK.

340 In mid-May after Katy . . . : JDP to EH, undated letter, JFK.

340 Katy did not return immediately . . . : KDP to JDP, undated letter, UVA.

341 "Poor kid—tortured with knives . . .": Archibald MacLeish to JDP, undated letter, UVA.

341 "You've been so brave . . .": JDP to Gerald and Sara Murphy, undated letter, Honoria Murphy Donnelly Collection, McLean, Va.

341 "Gerald was nearly crushed . . .": KDP to JDP, undated letter, UVA.

341 He was moved to the Trudeau . . . : KDP to JDP, undated letter, UVA.

341 "How mortifying, but . . .": KDP to Y. K. Smith, note on undated letter, UVA.

342 Dos Passos had sent Katy . . . : JDP to KDP, undated letter, UVA.

342 According to records kept . . . : Brandt & Brandt to JDP, Feb. 14, 1935, Feb. 17, 1936.

342 "I sure hope you can sell . . .": JDP to BB, May 6, 1935, UVA.

342 His tone changed after . . . : BB to JDP, assorted letters from each editor June 12, 1935–Dec. 16, 1935, UVA.

342 "I hope the Margo Dowling section . . .": JDP to BB, Aug. 18, 1935, UVA.

342 *Cosmopolitan* replied to his . . . : BB to JDP, July 30, 1935, UVA.

343 A typical note began . . . : JDP to BB, Sept. 7, 1935, UVA.

343 Dos Passos wrote Hemingway that . . . : JDP to EH, July 23, 1935, JFK.

343 "I've been working pretty steadily . . .": JDP to KDP, Aug. 2, 1935, UVA.

343 "I don't seem to have . . .": JDP to KDP, undated letter, UVA.

344 Katy was exuberant when . . . : KDP to JDP, Aug. 5, 1935, UVA.

344 "Birds that fly too high . . .": Marion Smith Lowndes to VSC, interview, Nov. 9, 1977, Wiscasset, Maine.

344 "I have quite a lot of cash . . .": Sara Murphy to JDP, undated letter, UVA.

344 "Friends are the dearest things . . .": Sara Murphy to EH, Sept. 18, 1935, JFK.

344 Dos Passos joined Katy in . . . : JDP to KDP, Oct. 17, 1935, UVA.

344 Dos Passos was "so superior . . .": C. A. Pearce to BB, Sept. 30, 1935, UVA.

344 Baumgarten told Dos Passos . . . : BB to JDP, Apr. 2, Nov. 25, 1935, UVA.

345 "Oh Ape, a terrific trip . . .": KDP to JDP, Jan. 23, 1936, UVA.

345 "Oh please, don't be a literary . . .": JDP to KDP, Feb. 15, 1936, UVA.

345 "People we haven't seen for years . . .": KDP to JDP, Jan. 29, 1936, UVA.

346 "Ape, it's not absolutely sewed . . .": KDP to JDP, undated letter, UVA.

346 "I am thinking of getting false whiskers . . .": JDP to KDP, undated letter, UVA.

347 "Dr. Antix fixed me . . .": JDP to KDP, Jan. 29, 1936, UVA.

347 "I don't know quite where . . .": JDP to KDP, Feb. 2, 1936, UVA.

347 "What a blow from Indian Giver . . .": KDP to JDP, undated letter, UVA.

347 She was in the city . . . : JDP to KDP, Feb. 2, 1936, UVA.

347 Their financial distress . . . : London attorney (signature illegible) to JDP, Feb. 28, 1936, UVA.

348 Hemingway complained later . . . : EH to JDP, June 10, 1936, UVA.

348 "Gosh Hem, it was a tough . . .": JDP to EH, May 21, 1936, JFK.

348 "Will make a good trip . . .": EH to JDP, July 16, 1936, UVA.

349 Cantwell drove a staff . . . : Robert Cantwell to JDP, July 5, 1936, UVA; C. A. Pearce to BB, July 15, 1936, UVA.

349 The other literary figures . . . : Time, Inc., Archives were made available to VSC, July 24, 1978, New York City.

349 "What's all this nonsense . . .": JDP to C. A. Pearce, Sept. 22, 1936, HBJ.

349 John Howard Lawson wrote . . . : JHL to JDP, undated letter, UVA.

349 Scott Fitzgerald said . . . : F. Scott Fitzgerald to JDP, Sept. 21, 1936, UVA.

349 Edmund Wilson called . . . : EW to JDP, July 22, 1936, UVA.

350 "I guess I ought to . . .": JDP to EW, July 24, 1936, YUB.

350 Malcolm Cowley reviewed . . . : "Afterthoughts on Dos Passos," *The New Republic,* Sept. 9, 1936, p. 134.

350 T. S. Matthews (in an anonymous . . . : *Time,* Aug. 10, 1936, pp. 51–53.

351 Herschel Brickell informed . . . : *Review of Reviews,* Sept. 1936, p. 12.

351 The Brooklyn *Daily Eagle*'s . . . : Alvah C. Bessie, Brooklyn *Daily Eagle,* "Dos Passos and Democracy," Aug. 23, 1936.

351 "Dos and I have gone . . .": KDP to EW, Aug. 24, 1936, YUB.

351 She likened their holidays . . . : KDP to Pauline Hemingway, Sept. 15, 1936, JFK.

351 "One came to tell . . .": KDP to Sara Murphy, Nov. 2, 1936, UVA.

351 Upon reading Wilson's recent . . . : JDP to EW, June 27, 1936, YUB.

352 When he wrote Theodore Dreiser . . . : JDP to Theodore Dreiser, July 8, 20, 1936, UPA.

352 In September he wrote Fitzgerald . . . : JDP to F. Scott Fitzgerald, undated letter, PU.

352 "Can't get out there . . .": JDP to EH, undated letter, JFK.

352 Dos Passos was still nursing . . . : JDP to C. A. Pearce, undated letter, HBJ.

352 Moreover, a week before . . . : Margaret G. Cuff to BB, July 23, 1936, UVA; BB to JDP, July 24, 1936, UVA.

353 "Suppose you have an author . . .": JDP to C. A. Pearce, undated letter, HBJ.

353 One of the most enthusiastic personal . . . : Alfred Harcourt to BB, quoted by BB to JDP, July 20, 1936, UVA; see also Charles A. Pearce to BB, July 15, 1936, UVA.

353 Insull was "of English . . .": BB to JDP, July 20, 1936, UVA.

354 "I rather wish I'd put . . .": JDP to BB, Aug. 3, 1936, UVA.

354 AUTHOR HYSTERICAL, PRESUME . . . : Michael Sadleir to Constable, Nov. 10, 1936; BB to Michael Sadleir, Nov. 9; Michael Sadleir to BB, Nov. 23, Dec. 22, 1936, UVA.

354 In late December C. A. Pearce . . . : On December 17, 1936, Pearce qualified his earlier sales figure of 20,000: "I overestimated sales of The Big Money, I guess. Total is 18,900 to Dec. 12, and we have sold several hundred this week," Charles A. Pearce to JDP, UVA.

354 Although his current novel . . . : JDP to EH, Jan. 9, 1937, JFK.

355 "She made nothing on the . . .": John Hughes Hall to VSC, July 26, 1979.

355 "Oh Katy please let's not run . . .": JDP to KDP, undated letter, UVA.

355 Dos Passos had recently borrowed . . . : JDP to Stewart Mitchell, undated letter, BA.

355 Katy had gone for health . . . : KDP to JDP, Nov. 29, 1936, UVA; KDP to Mary Heaton Vorse, Dec. 9, 1936, WSU.

CHAPTER 20

357 Dos Passos was asked by . . . : JDP to Norman Thomas (telegram) Nov. 24, 1936; copy at UVA.

357 Dos Passos insisted that he . . . : Dos Passos to Roger Baldwin (telegram), Nov. 24, 1936, Special Manuscript Collection (Spanish Refugee), Butler Library, Columbia University of the City of New York.

357 Katy told Mary Heaton Vorse . . . : Dec. 9, 1936, WSU.

358 "I hope you get to go. . . .": JDP to EH, undated letter, JFK; the New York *Times*, Feb. 28, 1937, p. 30.

358 Spain's civil war . . . : For a comprehensive account of Spain's civil war, see Hugh Thomas, *The Spanish Civil War* (New York: Harper & Row, 1961).

360 When Dos Passos finally effected . . . : JDP to EW, Mar. 9, 1937, YUB.

360 Bernice Baumgarten wrote . . . : BB to JDP, Jan. 28, 1937, UVA; JDP to BB, Feb. 6, 1937, UVA.

360 "Their ends are not my . . .": JDP to EW, Mar. 9, 1937, YUB.

360 Dos Passos may have been upset . . . : "Dos Passos States His Political Creed, Laying Emphasis Upon Preservation of Civil Liberties," New York *World-Telegram*, Feb. 20, 1937; Brooklyn Public Library Archives.

360 As Mary McCarthy told it . . . : Mary McCarthy, *On the Contrary* (New York: Farrar, Straus & Giroux, 1976), pp. 94–99; see also Alan M. Wald, *James T. Farrell: The Revolutionary Years* (New York: New York University Press, 1978), p. 62.

361 Among the fifty signatures . . . : *The New Masses,* Feb. 16, 1937, p. 1.

361 "Members are telephoned day . . .": James T. Farrell to EH, Feb. 9, 1937, JFK.

362 Actually, Dos Passos would have liked . . . : JDP to EW, Mar. 9, 1937, YUB.

362 MacLeish was also chairman . . . : Archibald MacLeish to VSC, Feb. 15, 26, Mar. 6, June 13, 1978; MacLeish to EH, Feb. 15, 1937, JFK.

362 Since the Spanish news service to apprise . . . : William O. ("Bill") Field to VSC, interview, July 30, 1978, Carmel, N.Y.

362 Meanwhile, Dos Passos had . . . : W. O. ("Bill") Field to VSC, interview, July 30, 1978, Carmel, N.Y.

362 "Ivens has just come . . .": JDP to Theodore Dreiser, Apr. 25, 1937, UPA.

362 Hemingway, too, had been invited . . . : *EH*, p. 300; JDP to EH, telegram, Feb. 11, 1937, JFK.

362 NANA had promised him . . . : *EH*, p. 299.

363 "It was by now visible . . .": Matthew Josephson, *Infidel in the Temple: A Memoir* (New York: Knopf, 1967), p. 431–33; according to Baker, *EH*, Hemingway and Gellhorn left Key West separately (p. 299).

363 Hemingway was now being . . . : the New York *Times*, Jan. 12, 1937, p. 4.

363 In December Arnold Gingrich . . . : *EH*, pp. 298–99.

363 At the suggestion . . . : Lillian Hellman, *An Unfinished Woman: A Memoir* (Boston: Little, Brown, 1969), p. 66.

364 Hemingway had worked on . . . : W. O. Field to VSC, interview, July 30, 1978, Carmel, N.Y.

364 According to Field . . . : W. O. Field to VSC, interview, Apr. 26, 1978.

364 Meanwhile, Hemingway had . . . : *EH*, pp. 299–300.

364 "Have you seen Ivens' . . .": JDP to Mary Heaton Vorse, Mar. 8, 1937, WSU.

365 "John, they goin' make a . . .": *TIF*, p. 116.

365 He knew that by the time . . . : *EH*, p. 300; see also Arturo Barea, *The Forging of a Rebel* (New York: Reynal & Hitchcock, 1946), p. 653.

365 Before leaving Paris . . . : *Journeys Between Wars* (New York: Harcourt, Brace, 1938), pp. 361–63.

366 The café was "a regular . . .": *TIF*, pp. 118–20.

366 Dos Passos intended to tarry . . . : *TIF*, pp. 123–30.

367 "It was not until I reached . . .": "Letter to the Editor," *The New Republic*, July 1939, pp. 308–9.

367 Dos Passos made the trip . . . : *JBW*, pp. 361–63.

367 "We damn near killed him. . . .": EH to A. E. Hotchner, *Papa Hemingway* (New York: Random House, 1966), p. 132.

368 When Lillian Hellman arrived . . . : Hellman, *An Unfinished Woman*, p. 101.

368 He was also put off . . . : Josephine Herbst, "The Starched Blue Sky of Spain," *Noble Savage*, Feb. 1960, p. 93.

368 Herbst told Hemingway . . . : Herbst, "Starched Blue Sky of Spain," pp. 96, 97, 108.

368 All of the journalists . . . : *TIF*, pp. 131–36.

368 Whereas time and time . . . : Herbst, "Starched Blue Sky of Spain," p. 93.

368 "Dos Passos was absolutely . . .": Herbst, "Starched Blue Sky of Spain," p. 93.

369 According to A. E. Hotchner . . . : *Papa Hemingway*, p. 132.

369 Dos Passos remained in Madrid . . . : Herman Shumlin to VSC, telephone interview, Aug. 10, 1978; letter, Oct. 13, 1978.

370 "The irrigation project seemed . . .": *TIF*, p. 139.

370 A few hours before leaving . . . : Josephson, *Infidel in the Temple*, p. 483.

370 Before departing Valencia . . . : Dos Passos to Claude Bowers, July 21, 1937, IU; Bowers to JDP, Aug. 27, 1937, UVA.

371 In Barcelona, which he . . . : *TIF*, pp. 140–46.

371 Sympathetic with Oak's plight . . . : *TIF*, p. 146.

371 In one article, he spoke . . . : "The Villages Are the Heart of Spain," *Esquire*, Feb. 1938, pp. 32–33, 151–53; also *JBW*, pp. 382–94.

372 Dos Passos was surprised . . . : see notes for *Century's Ebb: The Thirteenth Chronicle* (Boston: Gambit, 1975), UVA; also Dos Passos' fictionalized version of this incident and his involvement in Spain during the Spanish Civil War in *Century's Ebb*, pp. 46–99; *JBW*, pp. 330–94; *TIF*, pp. 113–49; KDP to EW, Nov. 8, 1937, YUB.

372 MacLeish was trying to . . . : MacLeish to EH, undated letter, JFK.

373 A rapt audience listened . . . : Daniel Aaron, *Writers on the Left* (New York: Oxford University, 1961), p. 360; Margaret De Silver to JDP, undated letter, UVA; Dawn Powell to JDP, undated letter, UVA.

373 It was largely . . . : the New York *Times,* July 25, 1937, Sec. 10, p. 4.

373 Some months later . . . : JDP to Dwight MacDonald, undated letter, Partisan Review Collection, Alexander Library, Rutgers, The State University of New Jersey, Camden.

373 Although the credits . . . : *The Spanish Earth* can be viewed by appointment through the Film Archives, Museum of Modern Art, New York City.

373 Later, the film was banned . . . : the New York *Times,* Jan. 30, 1937; see also Mar. 25, p. 27; May 19, p. 10; July 21, p. 12.

374 Dos Passos wrote of having . . . : *TIF,* p. 149.

374 For two years a hardworking . . . : Grace Pfeiffer Bell to VSC, interview, Nov. 6, 1977, Provincetown, Mass.

374 Dos Passos offered no . . . : Grace Pfeiffer Bell to VSC, Sept. 4, 1977 interview, Provincetown, Mass.; Toni Willison to VSC, Aug. 14, 1976; Jerry Farnsworth to VSC, interview, Feb. 11, 1979, Sarasota, Fla.

375 The Max Eastman reference . . . : Max Eastman, *Great Companions* (New York: Farrar, Straus and Cudahy, 1942), pp. 41–76; *EH,* pp. 241–43.

375 "Damn silly that fisticuffs . . .": JDP to Stewart Mitchell, undated letter, BA.

375 After receiving a detailed . . . : Max Perkins to F. Scott Fitzgerald, Aug. 24, 1937; F. Scott Fitzgerald to Max Perkins, Sept. 3, 1937; in *Dear Scott/Dear Max: The Fitzgerald-Perkins Correspondence,* ed. John Kuehl and Jackson Bryer (New York: Scribner's, 1971), pp. 237–41.

375 Dos Passos was close-mouthed . . . : JDP to BB, undated letter, UVA.

376 "I'm sorry I sent you . . .": EH to JDP, Mar. 26, 1938, UVA; see also EH, *Selected Letters* (New York: Scribner's, 1981), pp. 463–65.

376 . . . in a later *Ken* article . . . : "Fresh Air on an Inside Story," *Ken,* Sept. 22, 1938.

CHAPTER 21

379 *The Big Money* had been . . . : the New York *Times,* June 7, 1937, p. 2; June 9, p. 24.

379 C. A. Pearce, his editor . . . : BB to Audrey Heath, Oct. 8, 1937, UVA; BB to JDP, July 29, 1937, UVA.

380 Despite his novel's . . . : JDP to BB, Oct. 12, 1937, UVA.

380 "Damn it, I just don't . . .": JDP to BB, July 3, 1937, UVA.

380 Moreover, they might have . . . : "Academician, Author in One-Man Show," Brooklyn *Daily Eagle,* Feb. 7, 1937, Sec. C, p. 8.

380 According to the adjusted . . . : BB to Harcourt, Brace, Dec. 3, 1937, UVA.

380 Dos Passos appealed both . . . : JDP to BB, July 3, 1937, UVA.

381 Dos Passos also thought . . . : BB to Charles A. Pearce, Dec. 10, 1937, UVA; JDP to BB, Oct. 12, 1937, UVA.

381 He said he would be willing . . . : JDP to BB, Oct. 12, Nov. 5, 1937, UVA.

381 "Better sue than stew . . .": JDP to EW, undated letter, YUB.

381 "The annoying thing about *Esquire* . . .": JDP to Arthur Davison Ficke, Sept. 29, 1937, YUB.

382 He could take their slamming . . . : JDP to BB, Aug. 1, 1937, UVA.

382 "I ought to be old enough . . .": JDP to Stewart Mitchell, Sept. 27, 1937, BA.

382 "Gosh thanks for the $200 . . .": JDP to JHL, Nov. 4, 1937, SI.

382 "We are broke . . .": KDP to Mary Heaton Vorse, Nov. 5, 1937, WSU.

382 To Edmund Wilson . . . : KDP to EW, Nov. 8, 1937, YUB.

383 John Howard Lawson, to whom . . . : JHL to JDP, Sept. 14, 1937, UVA.

384 Hassoldt Davis told readers . . . : the New York *Times Book Review,* Apr. 24, 1938, p. 9.

384 Lewis Gannett in his . . . : New York *Herald Tribune,* Apr. 13, 1938, p. 13.

384 The reviews of Michael Gold . . . : Michael Gold, "The Keynote to Dos Passos' Works," *Daily Worker,* Feb. 26, 1938, p. 7; Granville Hicks, "The Moods and Tenses of John Dos Passos," *The New Masses,* Apr. 26, 1938, pp. 22–23.

385 Matthew Josephson referred . . . : "Grim Interlude," *The New Republic,* Apr. 27, 1938, p. 365.

385 Soon after his return . . . : JDP to Claude Bowers, Sept. 5, 1937, IU.

385 Dos Passos had told Dreiser . . . : JDP to Theodore Dreiser, undated letter, UPA.

385 "If we all have to go . . .": JDP to Sherwood Anderson, undated letter, Anderson Papers, Newberry Library, Chicago, Ill.

385 "Having an absurdly good . . .": JDP to EW, Mar. 3, 1938, YUB.

385 In Vicksburg, he mailed . . . : JDP to Chauncey Hackett, Mar. 12, 1938, UVA; interview, Mary Hackett to VSC, Aug. 10, 1978, Provincetown, Mass.

386 After six weeks on . . . : JDP to Stewart Mitchell, Mar. 1938, BA.

386 Harcourt, Brace's publicity . . . : Helen Taylor to BB, Mar. 15, 1938, UVA.

386 He wrote Edmund Wilson . . . : JDP to EW, Feb. 6, 1937, YUB.

386 "For Christ sake can . . .": JDP to Helen Taylor, undated letter, UVA.

386 "Something has just got . . .": JDP to BB, undated letter, UVA.

386 Baumgarten asked Harcourt, Brace . . . : memo to "FL" from BB, Apr. 13, 1938, UVA.

386 Four months later . . . : BB to JDP, Sept. 29, 1938, UVA.

387 The Leigh Lecture Agency . . . : BB to JDP, Sept. 26, 1938, UVA.

387 Dos Passos replied . . . : JDP to BB, Sept. 30, 1938, UVA.

387 WE WILL MEET YOU . . . : KDP to Sara Murphy, May 20, 1938, UVA.

387 "From Naples to Capri . . .": diary, KDP, July–Aug. 1938, UVA.

388 "Dos Passos Visits Italy . . .": the New York *Times,* Aug. 23, 1938, p. 15.

388 In view of his current . . . : BB to JDP, Oct. 10, 1938, UVA.

388 Before he sailed into . . . : C. H. Brooks to BB, June 10, 1938, UVA.

388 A Swiss firm paid . . . : BB to JDP, May 5, Sept. 12, 1938, UVA.

388 A German publisher . . . : C. H. Brooks to BB, Nov. 28, 1938, UVA.

389 Meanwhile, Bennett Cerf . . . : BB to JDP, Dec. 7, 1938, UVA.

389 Dos Passos was skeptical . . . : JDP to BB, Dec. 7, 1938, UVA.

389 Another sale in the fall . . . : M. M. Geffen to BB, Nov. 4, 1938, UVA.

389 Brandt & Brandt reported . . . : BB to JDP, Sept. 27, 1938, UVA.

389 He told Baumgarten that . . . : JDP to BB, Oct. 4, 1938, UVA.

389 "Dos is working like mad . . .": KDP to Pauline Hemingway, Oct. 31, 1938, JFK.

389 "We sit here modestly . . .": KDP to Sara Murphy, Dec. 15, 1938, UVA.

390 "Oh Wemedge how did we . . .": KDP to EH, Sept. 17, 1938, JFK.

390 Katy also quipped . . . : KDP to Pauline Hemingway, Oct. 31, 1938, JFK.

390 She and Edith Shay . . . : *The Private Adventure of Captain Shaw* (Philadelphia: The Blakiston Company, 1945); "New Harmony, Indiana," *The Atlantic Monthly,* Nov. 1940, pp. 604–11.

391 Having conveyed his portion . . . : C. Dickerman Williams to VSC, interviews, Nov. 16, 1977, New York City; July 31–Aug. 1, 1978, Norfolk, Conn.; also letters, C. Dickerman Williams to VSC, Apr. 25, 29, 1982.

391 Louis Dos Passos reportedly . . . : Mary Dos Passos Singleton to VSC, interview, Oct. 25, 1977.

392 The sale at foreclosure . . . : C. Dickerman Williams to VSC, Apr. 25, 1982.

392 "I believe it was Katy . . .": C. Dickerman Williams to VSC, interview, July 31, 1978, Norfolk, Conn.

392 Dos Passos had been interested . . . : see miscellaneous deeds in Westmoreland County

Court House, Montross, Va.: Deed Book 79, pp. 142, 145, 398, 404, 405; also "Amended Grounds of Defense: Byron B. Ralston vs. John R. Dos Passos, et al.," Feb. 17, 1942, and other assorted deeds: Deed Book 85, pp. 218, 222, 241, 243; Deed Book 89, p. 123; miscellaneous clippings provided by Mary Dos Passos Singleton.

393 "Luck certainly seems . . .": Edward Weeks to BB, Nov. 25, 1938, UVA.

393 Magazines turning down . . . : miscellaneous correspondence, BB to JDP, UVA.

393 Dos Passos' only worry . . . : BB to JDP, May 11, 1939, UVA.

395 At the head of the . . . : Malcolm Cowley, "Disillusionment," *The New Republic,* June 14, 1939, p. 163.

395 The anonymous reviewer for *Time* . . . : "Heresy," *Time,* June 5, 1939, pp. 86, 88.

395 A few weeks before . . . : JDP to BB, Mar. 23, 1939, UVA.

396 In reply to his suggestion . . . : BB to JDP, Mar. 24, 1939, UVA.

396 As Farrell saw it . . . : James T. Farrell, "Dos Passos and the Critics," *The American Mercury,* August 1939, pp. 489–94.

396 Dos Passos was grateful . . . : JDP to James T. Farrell, undated letter, UPA.

396 "He's a courageous fellow . . .": JDP to Eugene Lyons, undated letter, IU.

396 "All I wanted to straighten . . .": JDP to Dwight MacDonald, undated letter, Collection of Dwight MacDonald, YUB.

397 "What in God's name . . .": EW to Malcolm Cowley, Oct. 20, 1938, *Letters on Literature and Politics, 1912–1972,* ed. Elena Wilson (New York: Farrar, Straus & Giroux, 1977), p. 310.

397 As Wilson saw it . . . : EW to Malcolm Cowley, Jan. 26, 1940, Wilson, *Letters,* pp. 357–58.

398 He suggested to Bernice . . . : JDP to BB, Aug. 27, 1939, UVA.

398 "Oh dear I wish . . .": KDP to Archibald MacLeish, Sept. 8, 1939, Archibald MacLeish Collection, LC.

398 It was a good suggestion . . . : Archibald MacLeish to KDP, Sept. 30, 1939, Archibald MacLeish Collection, LC.

399 Charles Kaeselau, an artist . . . : Eben Given to VSC, interview, Nov. 6, 1977, Truro, Mass.; Mary Hackett to VSC, interview, Aug. 10, 1978, Provincetown, Mass.; Hazel Hawthorne Werner to VSC, interview, Aug. 8, 1978, Provincetown, Mass.

400 "I realize the position . . .": JDP to Clarence Walton, Feb. 22, 1940, Manuscript Collection, HUW.

400 For the time being . . . : JDP to Clarence Walton, Feb. 22, 1940, HUW.

400 In his letter to Mitchell . . . : JDP to Stewart Mitchell, Jan. 10, 1940, BA.

401 Donald Brace made Dos Passos . . . : BB to JDP, Apr. 11, 1940, UVA.

401 "The policy came . . .": JDP to KDP, Jan. 20, 1940, UVA.

401 Again Dos Passos placed . . . : C. Dickerman Williams to VSC, interview, July 31, 1978, Norfolk, Conn.

401 Margaret De Silver urged . . . : JDP to KDP, undated letter, UVA; see also "Dear Mr. Milgram" from JDP as treasurer of the Joint Campaign for Political Refugees, Workers Defense League Collection, WSU; JDP to BB, Apr. 4, 1940, UVA.

402 In turn, Dos Passos hoped . . . : JDP to BB, Apr. 4, 1940, UVA.

402 "Bill collectors are thicker . . .": KDP to JDP, Jan. 19, 1940, UVA.

402 "Katy darling—why didn't . . .": JDP to KDP, Jan. 28, 1940, UVA.

402 "Oh Irascible—what an awful . . .": KDP to JDP, Feb. 1, 1940, UVA.

403 "Beanie came home swelled . . .": KDP to JDP, undated letter, UVA.

403 "Beanie is in school . . .": KDP to Mary Heaton Vorse, Feb. 14, 1940, UVA.

403 By early April he had written . . . : JDP to BB, Apr. 5, 1940, UVA.

404 Dos Passos was in Quito . . . : KDP to JDP, Apr. 16, 1940, UVA.

405 "It is not going to be easy . . .": KDP to JDP, Apr. 26, 1940, UVA.

405 Someone had translated . . . : JDP to KDP, Apr. 17, 1940, UVA.

405 Dos Passos was also put out . . . : JDP to KDP, May 1, 1940, UVA.

405 He decided, too, to terminate . . . : JDP to BB, June 15, 1940, UVA.

405 "Of course I am unhappy . . .": BB to JDP, June 18, 1940, UVA.

406 "Don [Brace] just told . . .": Alfred Harcourt to BB, June 18, 1940, UVA.

406 "His leaving us . . .": BB to Patience Ross, May 8, 1941, UVA.

406 Dos Passos also petitioned . . . : JDP to Claude Bowers, undated letter, IU.

407 Since Ralston claimed . . . : Westmoreland County Court House Records, Montross, Va.: "Order of Publication," June 17, 1941; "Bill of Particulars," Oct. 17, 1941; "Amended Grounds of Defense," Feb. 17, 1942.

407 Dos Passos outlined the . . . : JDP to EW, undated letter, YUB.

407 Even Malcolm Cowley . . . : "Ancestors," *The New Republic*, Sept. 1, 1941, p. 282.

407 Francis Brown's review . . . : the New York *Times Book Review*, Aug. 31, 1941, p. 5.

407 According to Benét . . . : Stephen Vincent Benét, "Dos Passos: Evolution of an American," New York *Herald Tribune Books*, Sept. 21, 1941, p. 6.

407 Robert Hillyer defined the book . . . : "Bookshelf," *The Atlantic Monthly*, Nov. 1941.

408 Jacques Barzun, writing for . . . : "Using the Past," *The Nation*, Sept. 13, 1941, pp. 227–28.

408 Leon Whipple described . . . : "History for Our Times," *Survey Graphic*, Oct. 1941, pp. 531–32.

408 C. W. Thompson declared . . . : *Catholic World*, Nov. 1941, p. 244.

408 Allan Nevins told . . . : "Roots of Democracy," *The Saturday Review of Literature*, Sept. 15, 1941, p. 6.

408 "The real difference . . .": JDP to JHL, undated letter, SI.

408 In an essay published . . . : "The Failure of Marxism," *Life*, Jan. 19, 1948, pp. 96–98+.

408 To Edmund Wilson he . . . : JDP to EW, Mar. 2, 1948, YUB.

408 Horsley Gantt wrote . . . : W. Horsley Gantt to JDP, Nov. 10, 1941, UVA.

409 Gilbert Seldes read . . . : Gilbert Seldes to JDP, Oct. 7, 1941, UVA.

409 In reply to a . . . : JDP to Harrison Griswold Dwight, Dec. 10, 1941. Harrison Griswold Dwight Collection, Amherst College Library, Amherst, Mass.

409 Cornered at La Guardia . . . : the New York *Times*, Sept. 8, 1941, p. 6.

410 "I'll never vote for Mr. R. . . .": JDP to Claude Bowers, undated letter, IU.

410 "I felt that I did not . . .": JDP to David Sanders, *The Paris Review Interviews: Writers at Work*, ed. George Plimpton, 4th ser. (New York: Viking Press, 1976), pp. 67–89.

410 At the PEN Congress . . . : the New York *Times*, Sept. 12, 1941, p. 12; Sept. 14, p. 28; Oct. 19, p. 3; see also JDP to KDP, Oct. 14, 1941, UVA.

410 According to Robert Nathan . . . : RN to VSC, Dec. 4, 1979; also Thornton Wilder to JDP, Oct. 29, 1941, UVA.

411 A British reader wrote . . . : Frederick Lewis Allen to JDP, Feb. 4, 1942, Harpers Collection, LC.

411 At this point, Allen . . . : Frederick Lewis Allen to JDP, Jan. 17, 1942, Harpers Collection, LC.

CHAPTER 22

413 Casting a ballot . . . : *TIF*, pp. 161–62.

413 "Damn the Japs and . . .": JDP to Robert Hillyer, Dec. 10, 1941, SU.

414 In January rumor had . . . : KDP to JDP, Jan. 24, 1942, UVA.

415 "Edie hasn't got a cent . . .": KDP to JDP, Feb. 20, 1942, UVA.

415 "I tried hard to place the Boy . . .": KDP to JDP, May 14, 1942, UVA.

415 "He interferes with . . .": KDP to JDP, Feb. 20, 1942, UVA.

416 Katy regretted that Dos Passos . . . : KDP to JDP, May 14, 1942, UVA.

416 Louis needed money . . . : JDP to KDP, May 8, Nov. 18, 1942, UVA.

416 Meanwhile, Ralston reportedly . . . : JDP to KDP, June 6, 1942, UVA.

417 As C. D. Williams explained . . . : C. Dickerman Williams to VSC, Apr. 29, 1982.

417 "The great Virginia lawsuit . . .": JDP to Robert Hillyer, Apr. 3, 1944, SU.

417 "Judge Cox ruled . . .": C. Dickerman Williams, to VSC, Apr. 25, 1982.

417 Houghton Mifflin was eager . . . : Robert Linscott to Ferris Greenslet, Jan. 3, 1942, Houghton Mifflin Collection, HU.

417 "I appreciate quite completely . . .": Donald Brace to JDP, Jan. 15, 1942, UVA.

418 Dos Passos asked Houghton . . . : JDP to Robert Linscott, Jan. 18, 1942, Houghton Mifflin Collection, HU.

418 "I am indeed delighted . . .": KDP to JDP, Feb. 19, 1942, UVA.

418 Scarcely six weeks after . . . : Lovell Thompson to Paul Brooks, Sept. 23, 1943, Houghton Mifflin Collection, HU.

418 Rumor had it . . . : Frederick Lewis Allen to JDP, Nov. 12, 1942, Harpers Collection, LC.

418 Allen wanted Dos Passos . . . : Frederick Lewis Allen to JDP, miscellaneous letters dated Mar. 23, May 26, 1942; Jan. 5, 15, 26, May 20, 26, Aug. 23, 1943, Harpers Collection, LC.

419 To head off any reluctance . . . : Frederick Lewis Allen to "To Whom It May Concern," Jan. 13, 1943; Frederick Lewis Allen to Tell Berna, Jan. 15, 1943; Frederick Lewis Allen to Lt. Commander Walter Karig, Nov. 9, 1942, Harpers Collection, LC.

419 As vice-chairman of the committee . . . : "To a Liberal in Office," *The Nation*, Sept. 6, 1941, pp. 195–97.

420 Two years later . . . : *TIF*, pp. 174–78; see also JDP's "Foreword" to *Who Killed Carlo Tresca* (New York: Tresca Memorial Committee, 1945), pp. 4–6.

421 Allen agreed to give . . . : Frederick Lewis Allen to JDP, Feb. 9, 1943, Harpers Collection, LC.

421 Katy was excited . . . : KDP to JDP, Jan. 27, 29, Feb. 4, 6, 1943, UVA; also undated letter, Dorothy Hillyer to KDP, UVA.

421 "Those little Mifflins . . .": JDP to Robert Hillyer, Mar. 24, 1943, SU.

422 Howard Mumford Jones, writing . . . : "Sound-Truck Caesar," *The Saturday Review of Literature*, Mar. 6, 1943, pp. 7–8.

422 *Time*'s anonymous reviewer . . . : "The People Are You!" *Time*, Mar. 15, 1943, p. 78.

422 Mark Schorer also picked . . . : *The Yale Review*, Summer 1943, pp. x–xii.

422 "I'm delighted you like . . .": JDP to Robert Hillyer, Mar. 24, 1943, SU.

422 Margaret Marshall, reviewing . . . : "Notes by the Way," *The Nation*, Mar. 13, 1943, p. 384.

422 *The New Yorker*'s reviewer . . . : Clifton Fadiman, "Dos Passos—Burma & Dieppe," *The New Yorker*, Mar. 6, 1943, pp. 65–66.

422 Horace Gregory informed readers . . . : "Dos Passos and the Demagogue," the New York *Times Book Review*, Mar. 7, 1943, pp. 1, 18.

422 Stephen Vincent Benét, writing . . . : "He Gets to the Senate with a Hillbilly Band," New York *Herald Tribune Book Review*, Mar. 7, 1943, p. 3.

422 Several critics were bothered . . . : "Demagogue at Work," *The Atlantic Monthly*, Apr. 1943, p. 146; "Wanted: A Dynamism," *Commonweal*, Mar. 5, 1943, pp. 497–98.

422 "It's fine to see Dos . . .": EH to Archibald MacLeish, June 30, 1943, Archibald MacLeish Collection, LC.

423 Thompson explained to . . . : Lovell Thompson to JDP, June 4, 1943, Houghton Mifflin Collection, HU.

423 Dos Passos was disturbed . . . : JDP to Lovell Thompson, June 13, 1943, Houghton Mifflin Collection, HU.

423 Thompson, in turn, apologized . . . : Lovell Thompson to JDP, June 15, 1943, Houghton Mifflin Collection, HU.

424 "This is the first time . . .": JDP to Lovell Thompson, June 18, 1943, Houghton Mifflin Collection, HU.

424 He was convinced . . . : JDP to Ira Rich Kent, Feb. 2, 20, 1944, Houghton Mifflin Collection, HU.

424 During the fall . . . : Diarmuid Russell to JDP, Oct. 1943, UVA.

424 At year's end . . . : JDP to Robert Hillyer, Dec. 23, Dec. 26, 1943, SU.

425 The reviewer for *Time* . . . : "Reports of a Miracle," *Time,* July 31, 1944, pp. 91–92, 94–96.

425 Gerald Johnson, writing . . . : "Round the Perimeter of the Republic," *Weekly Book Review* (New York *Herald Tribune),* July 23, 1944, p. 3.

425 The reviewer for the Los Angeles *Times* . . . : Irene Elwood, "Men Who Had Look-See Reveals State of Nation," July 30, 1944, p. 14.

425 *Commonweal*'s critic wrote . . . : "America's Urgent Problems," *Commonweal,* Aug. 25, 1944, pp. 449–50.

425 Although the Boston *Sunday Post,* . . . : P. J. Searles, "What Americans Are Thinking," Boston *Sunday Post,* July 23, 1944.

425 *The Nation*'s reviewer . . . : Margaret Marshall, "Notes By the Way," *The Nation,* July 29, 1944, p. 131.

425 Edmund Wilson, who took . . . : "Dos Passos' Reporting," *The New Yorker,* July 29, 1944, pp. 57–58, 61.

425 The *Virginia Kirkus Service*'s observation . . . : *Virginia Kirkus Service,* May 15, 1944, p. 227.

426 Negative comments were . . . : R. H. Gabriel, "Surveying the Nation," *The Yale Review,* Winter 1944–45, pp. 348–51.

426 The reviewer for . . . : R. L. Duffus, the New York *Times Book Review,* July 23, 1944, p. 3.

426 *Mademoiselle*'s critic faulted . . . : Anonymous review, *Mademoiselle,* Sept. 1944.

426 Margaret Marshall thought . . . : *The Nation,* July 29, 1944, p. 58

426 Houghton Mifflin executive . . . : Paul Brooks to JDP, July 19, 1944, Houghton Mifflin Collection, HU.

426 By the end of August . . . : Lovell Thompson to JDP, Aug. 31, 1944, Houghton Mifflin Collection, HU.

426 Dos Passos was heartened . . . : Ira Rich Kent to JDP, Sept. 12, 1944, Houghton Mifflin Collection, HU.

427 His next book would . . . : JDP to Lovell Thompson, Sept. 29, 1944, Houghton Mifflin Collection, HU.

427 "The more I think about . . .": JDP to Lovell Thompson, Nov. 11, 1944, Houghton Mifflin Collection, HU.

428 "We did as well by . . .": Lovell Thompson to VSC, interview, Nov. 1, 1979, Ipswich, Mass.

428 The attack stemmed from . . . : John Gunther, *Inside U.S.A.* (New York: Harper & Brothers, 1947), pp. 857–58.

429 Strident protests were . . . : *"U.S.A."* Brochure published by Houghton Mifflin upon publication of three-volume edition, Nov. 26, 1946, p. 27.

429 The controversy was still . . . : David Lee Clark to JDP, Dec. 29, 1944, UVA.

429 Farrell reported that . . . : James T. Farrell to JDP, undated letter, UVA; JDP to James T. Farrell, Nov. 2, 1944, UPA.

430 Dos Passos defended . . . : JDP to Robert Hillyer, Nov. 3, 1944, SU.

CHAPTER 23

432 He wrote Katy that he envied . . . : JDP to KDP, Jan. 13, 1945, UVA.

432 He also told . . . : JDP to KDP, Dec. 23, 1944, UVA.

432 "The minute we land . . .": JDP to KDP, Dec. 31, 1944, UVA.

433 "I am afraid you won't . . .": KDP to JDP, Mar. 23, 1945, UVA.

433 Their publisher, Houghton . . . : Paul Brooks to KDP, Feb. 13, 1945, UVA.

433 They were no longer . . . : KDP to JDP, Mar. 23, 1945, UVA.

433 Each time Dos Passos . . . : *TOD*, pp. 28–29.

435 The mission's only casualty . . . : *TOD*, pp. 74–75.

435 From the Philippines . . . : JDP to KDP, Mar. 2, 1945, UVA.

435 By the time the story . . . : "Plane Bearing John Dos Passos Downed While on Photo Mission over Manila," Provincetown *Advocate,* Mar. 1, 1945.

435 "John Dos Passos and I . . .": Major H. H. Brigham to *Life* ("Letter to the Editor"), Apr. 30, 1945.

436 "They all looked strangely . . .": *TOD*, pp. 134–35.

436 Dos Passos wrote to Gerald . . . : JDP to Gerald and Sara Murphy, Feb. 21, 1945; Collection of Honoria Murphy Donnelly, McLean, Va.

436 "I find myself hot on . . .": JDP to KDP, Feb. 15, 1945, UVA.

437 "There's an air of breeding . . .": *TOD*, pp. 169–71.

437 Impatient to leave . . . : General Douglas MacArthur to JDP, Sept. 23, 1945, UVA.

437 "I hope the conference . . .": KDP to JDP, Mar. 7, 1945, UVA.

438 "Saw more attractive . . .": JDP to EW, May 18, 1945, YUB.

438 "Socialism is something we've . . .": JDP to EW, July 19, 1945, YUB.

439 Katy liked the idea . . . : KDP to JDP, Nov. 8, 1945, YUB.

439 By now, the book she . . . : KDP to JDP, Jan. 12, 1945, UVA. Paul Brooks at Houghton Mifflin wired KDP that "authors' share of guaranteed royalty will be $6,000," Jan. 12, 1945, UVA.

439 Susan Glaspell, who had sold . . . : Barnstable County Courthouse, Barnstable, Mass. Deed Book 618, p. 403; Deed Book 454, p. 380.

439 "Oh dear, poor Possum . . .": KDP to JDP, Nov. 9, 1945, UVA.

440 Nuremberg was "particularly . . .": JDP to KDP, Nov. 3, 1945, UVA.

440 He had stopped in Nuremberg . . . : JDP to KDP, Nov. 4, 1945, UVA.

440 "How do you get . . .": *TOD*, p. 207.

440 "Vienna is heartbreaking. . . .": *TOD*, pp. 279–95.

441 "Every Soviet citizen . . .": *TOD*, p. 282.

441 "The French—because there . . .": *TOD*, p. 292.

441 "I wonder if they'll . . .": JDP to KDP, Nov. 22, 1945, UVA.

442 Hordes of displaced . . . : *TOD*, p. 325.

442 Clay explained something . . . : *TOD*, pp. 321–22.

443 An entry in Dos Passos' . . . : unpublished notebook, "Berlin 1945," undated entry, UVA.

443 When Dos Passos finally . . . : KDP to JDP, Dec. 16, 1945, UVA.

443 "Never felt so much sadder . . .": JDP to Upton Sinclair, Dec. 30, 1945, IU.

444 "More brilliant than . . .": EW, *The New Yorker,* Aug. 24, 1946, p. 55.

444 "It is encouraging . . .": John Cort, *Commonweal,* Sept. 20, 1946, p. 556.

444 Although the *Hartford Times* . . . : Marian Murray, "Grand Reporting on War Fronts by Dos Passos," the *Hartford Times,* Aug. 17, 1946.

444 "The Soviet Union's certainly . . .": *TOD*, pp. 327–30.

445 "The first fifty . . .": JDP to Claude Bowers, June 27, 1945, IU.

446 *Life*'s request that he . . . : "Where Do We Go from Here?" *Life,* Jan. 27, 1947, pp. 95–97+.

447 "Europe's collapse is . . .": Sidney Fields, "Light on the Red Blackout," the New York *Times*, July 15, 1947.

448 The opening sentence had . . . : "From the Editor's Mailbag," the New York *Times Book Review*, Apr. 6, 1947, p. 26; original letter from JDP to Editor, the New York *Times Book Review*, Mar. 15, 1947, in Private Collection of Isaac Don Levine, Waldorf, Md.

448 The "hatchet-job editing . . .": Isaac Don Levine to VSC, interview, Aug. 22, 1978, Waldorf, Md.

448 In a letter to Glenway Wescott . . . : JDP to Glenway Wescott, Dec. 27, 1946, in Max Eastman Collection, IU; see also statement by JDP to the American Writers Association, Apr. 8, 1947, warning that a recent stand taken by the American Authors Authority was "basically a political maneuver" that played into the hands of the Soviet Union, Max Eastman Collection, IU.

449 Although he continued to turn . . . : R. L. Cook to JDP, Nov. 6, 1945, Abernethy Library, Middlebury College, Middlebury, Vt.; a second invitation extended Nov. 10, 1946, to which Dos Passos replied: "The trouble is I'm not good at standing up and giving tongue and I just never do it."

449 Their Eastern European "Voices" . . . : Lewis Galantiere to JDP, Dec. 15, 1946, UVA.

449 Indignant over what . . . : JDP to William York Tindall, Jan. 10, 28, 1947, Special Manuscript Collection, Tindall, Columbia University of the City of New York; acceptances received from Lionel Trilling to JDP, Jan. 16, 1947, UVA; Benjamin Stolberg to JDP, Jan. 13, 1947, UVA; James T. Farrell to JDP, Jan. 15, 1947, UVA; William York Tindall to JDP, Jan. 27, 1947, UVA; H. L. Mencken to JDP, Jan. 13, 27, 1947, UVA; see also the New York *Times*, May 17, 1947, p. 13; Nov. 14, 1947, p. 20.

450 Marsh read the book . . . : publicity brochure, *U.S.A.* (Boston: Houghton Mifflin, 1946), p. 29.

450 James Gray's review . . . : Chicago *Daily News*, Dec. 4, 1946.

450 Cowley was not happy . . . : Malcolm Cowley, the New York *Times Book Review*, Jan. 19, 1947, p. 1.

451 "The Marsh things in Dos's . . .": EH to Max Perkins, Apr. 28, 1947, EH, *Selected Letters* (New York: Scribner's, 1981), p. 431.

451 "Hemingway has been raising . . .": EW to Max Perkins, July 3, 1941, *Letters on Literature and Politics, 1912–1972*, ed. Elena Wilson (New York: Farrar, Straus & Giroux, 1977), p. 388.

451 According to Wilson, Perkins . . . : EW to Florine Katz, Mar. 1, 1941, Wilson, *Letters*, p. 387.

451 Hemingway became livid . . . : *EH*, p. 461; see also Harvey Breit, "A Walk with Faulkner," the New York *Times Book Review*, Jan. 30, 1955, p. 4.

451 "I know what you mean . . .": EH to William Faulkner, July 23, 1947, EH, *Selected Letters*, p. 619.

452 An aged aunt of . . . : Francis Rogers to VSC, interview, Aug. 1, 1978, Belmont, Mass.

452 When Dos Passos had been in . . . : "England in the Great Lull," *Harper's Magazine*, Feb. 1942, pp. 235–44.

452 He discovered that . . . : "Where Do We Go from Here?" *Life*, Jan. 1947, pp. 95–96+; "Britain's Dim Dictatorship," *Life*, Sept. 29, 1947, pp. 120–122+.

453 Too much concentration . . . : "The Failure of Marxism," *Life*, Jan. 19, 1948, pp. 95–98+.

453 "Nobody in the United States . . .": KDP to Edith Shay, Aug. 6, 1947; Collection of Isabel Foley Whelan, Provincetown, Mass.

453 "Dos apparently came over . . .": Joel O'Brien to VSC, interview, Aug. 12, 1978, Provincetown, Mass.

454 In England they . . . : KDP to Edith Shay, Aug. 1, 1947; Collection of Isabel Foley Whelan, Provincetown, Mass.

454 "We never knew how . . .": Henka Farnsworth to VSC, Feb. 11, 1979, interview, Sarasota, Fla.

454 It was midafternoon before . . . : Adelaide Walker to VSC, interview, Nov. 5, 1977, Wellfleet, Mass.

455 A few minutes after . . . : Eben Given to VSC, interview, Nov. 6, 1977, Truro, Mass.; Adelaide Walker to VSC, interview, Nov. 5, 1977, Wellfleet, Mass.; Isabel Foley Whelan, interview, Nov. 6, 1977, Provincetown, Mass.; Jerry and Henka Farnsworth, interview, Feb. 9, 1979, Sarasota, Fla.

455 Before leaving for Boston . . . : the Provincetown *Advocate* carried a detailed report of the accident on September 18, 1947, p. 1; see also the Boston *Sunday Herald,* Sept. 13, 1947.

455 Edith was devastated . . . : Eben Given to VSC, interview, Nov. 6, 1977.

456 "Oh, I had such . . .": Mary Hackett to VSC, interview, Aug. 10, 1978, Provincetown, Mass.

456 At 1 A.M. C. D. Williams . . . : C. Dickerman Williams to VSC, interview, Nov. 16, 1977, Norfolk, Conn.

456 "My son Andy and I . . .": W. Horsley Gantt to VSC, interview, Mar. 31, 1977, Baltimore, Md.

456 Eben Given arrived just . . . : Eben Given to VSC, interview Nov. 6, 1977, Truro, Mass.

456 When Charles Walker came . . . : Adelaide Walker to VSC, interview, Nov. 5, 1977, Wellfleet, Mass.

456 "We were impressed . . .": Marion Hammett Smith to VSC, interview, Mar. 24, 1978, Arlington, Va; see also Marion Hammett Smith, "Recollections of Dos," *Connecticut Review,* Apr. 1975, pp. 21–24.

457 "It is still no easier . . .": Jo Hawthorne to JDP, Oct. 8, 1947, UVA.

457 "It was a relief . . .": EW to JDP, Nov. 24, 1947, UVA.

458 "Maybe you'll help . . .": JDP to Edith Shay, Sept. 17, 1947, Collection of Isabel Foley Whelan.

458 "This is so much the worst . . .": JDP to Robert Hillyer, Sept. 19, 1947, SU.

458 It was physical pain . . . : Dawn Powell to JDP, Sept. 17, 1947, UVA.

458 Dos Passos assured friends . . . : JDP to Katharine Smith Durand, Sept. 18, 1947, Collection of Katharine Smith Durand, Norfolk, Va.

458 Some thought his physical . . . : Robert Solley to VSC, interview, Mar. 21, 1978, Old Saybrook, Conn.

458 Before leaving the hospital . . . : JDP to Robert Hillyer, Sept. 19, 1947, SU.

458 "Dos came out, shaken . . .": Eben Given to VSC, interview, Nov. 6, 1977, Truro, Mass.

459 "Dos, I want you to know . . .": Charles Mayo to VSC, interview, Nov. 6, 1977, Provincetown, Mass.

459 "If I tried to avoid . . .": JDP to Edith Shay, Oct. 8, 1947, Collection of Isabel Foley Whelan.

459 To Adelaide and Charles . . . : JDP to Adelaide and Charles Walker, undated letter, UVA.

459 "Edie dear, . . . have you . . .": JDP to Edith Shay, Oct. 3, 1947, Collection of Isabel Foley Whelan.

460 "She was a wonderful personality . . .": Walter Miller to JDP, Oct. 6, 1947, UVA.

460 "Katy brought me pussy willows . . . : Canby Chambers to JDP, Oct. 18, 1947, UVA.

460 "Dos, I can't write . . .": Edith Shay to JDP, Oct. 28, 1947, UVA.

460 In early December . . . : JDP to Edith Shay, Dec. 3, 1947, Collection of Isabel Foley Whelan.

461 According to Edith's stepdaughter . . . : Jean Shay to VSC, interview, July 26, 1978, New York City.

CHAPTER 24

463 "I am not surprised . . .": Henry C. Marble to JDP, Oct. 10, 1947, UVA.
463 "Dos had the most extraordinary . . .": Robert Solley to VSC, interview, Mar. 21, 1978, Old Saybrook, Conn.
464 Dos Passos replied . . . : JDP to Van Wyck Brooks, Nov. 24, 1947, UPA.
464 Susan Lowndes recalled . . . : Susan Lowndes to VSC, interview, Nov. 9, 1977, Wiscasset, Maine.
465 When John and Adelaide Marquand . . . : JDP to Chauncey Hackett, Feb. 11, 1948, UVA.
465 He rationalized, too, . . . : JDP to Edith Shay, Mar. 2, 1948, Collection of Isabel Foley Whelan.
465 "I wish Eben and Phyllis . . .": JDP to Edith Shay, Jan. 22, 1948, Collection of Isabel Foley Whelan.
466 All stayed at the . . . : JDP to Edith Shay, Mar. 17, 1948, Collection of Isabel Foley Whelan.
466 "Wish you were here. . . .": JDP to Henka Farnsworth, Mar. 1, 1948, Collection of Henka Farnsworth, Sarasota, Fla.
466 "We had a marvelous time . . .": Eben Given to VSC, interview, Aug. 12, 1978, Truro, Mass.
466 Dos Passos cut short . . . : JDP to Edith Shay, Mar. 17, 1948, Collection of Isabel Foley Whelan; JDP to John and Ruth Herrmann, Mar. 18, 1948, UT-HRC.
466 As soon as practicable . . . : JDP to Bill and Marion Smith, Apr. 16, 1949, PU; also Marion Smith to VSC, interview, Aug. 21, 1978, Arlington, Va.
467 In the Hotel Ambos Mundos . . . : John Leggett, *Ross & Tom: Two American Tragedies* (New York: Simon & Schuster, 1974), pp. 322–23, 386, 392–94; also John Leggett to VSC, interview, Aug. 5, 1978, Manchester, Mass.; JDP to John Leggett, July 11, 1970, University of Iowa Libraries, Iowa City, Iowa.
467 "I saw their affair . . .": Eben Given to VSC, interview, Aug. 9, 1978, Truro, Mass.
468 "I didn't know whether . . .": JDP to Henka Farnsworth, Aug. 28, 1948, Collection of Henka Farnsworth.
468 The Smiths were coming . . . : JDP to Edith Shay, July 22, 1948, Collection of Isabel Foley Whelan.
468 "I was in the final throes . . .": Mary Hemingway, *How It Was* (New York: Alfred A. Knopf, 1976), pp. 220–21.
468 Dos Passos was going . . . : *PBU*, p. 133; see also pp. 135–38.
469 "I'm living here in guilty . . .": JDP to Edith Shay, Sept. 24, 1948, Collection of Isabel Foley Whelan.
469 A week later he flew . . . : *PBU*, pp. 138–76; see also "Pioneers in Brazil," *Life*, Dec. 20, 1948, pp. 5–6.
469 "Brazil is enormous . . .": JDP to Claude Bowers, Oct. 13, 1948, IU.
469 The people wore disagreeable expressions . . . : JDP to Sara Murphy, Nov. 7, 1948, Collection of Honoria Murphy Donnelly.
469 "Even in a crisis . . .": "Visit to Evita," *Life*, Apr. 11, 1949, pp. 27–28+.
470 "The huge German-style . . .": JDP to Sara Murphy, Nov. 7, 1948, Collection of Honoria Murphy Donnelly.
470 "It was like going through . . .": JDP to Henka Farnsworth, Nov. 28, 1948, Collection of Henka Farnsworth.
470 In Santiago he interviewed . . . : *PBU*, pp. 215–23.
470 "I'm afraid I'm no good . . .": JDP to Claude Bowers, Oct. 28, 1948, IU.
471 "Fearfully worn out . . .": JDP to Henka Farnsworth, Dec. 9, 1948, Collection of Henka Farnsworth.

471 "Time was, when the . . .": Henry Morton Robinson, *The Saturday Review of Literature,* Jan. 8, 1949, p. 9.

472 "Your characters (in your words) . . .": EW to JDP, Jan. 27, 1949, UVA.

472 J. M. Lalley expressed similar . . . : J. M. Lalley, *The New Yorker,* Jan. 8, 1949, p. 69.

472 Spanos said that reading . . . : Nicholas C. Spanos to JDP, Jan. 29, 1949, UVA.

472 "If you wanted to write . . .": JDP to Edith Shay, Jan 21, 1949, Collection of Isabel Foley Whelan.

473 J. Donald Adams vindicated . . . : "Speaking of Books," the New York *Times Book Review,* Feb. 13, 1949, p. 2.

473 In his letter to Edith Shay . . . : JDP to Edith Shay, Feb. 14, 1949, Collection of Isabel Foley Whelan.

473 "I wouldn't have been surprised . . .": Eben Given to VSC, interview, Aug. 12, 1978, Truro, Mass.

474 "The only thing I remember . . .": Daphne Hellman (Mrs. Hsio-Wen Shih) to VSC, July 1, 1978.

474 In introducing Dos Passos to Betty . . . : Marion Lowndes to VSC, interview, Nov. 9, 1977, Wiscasset, Maine.

474 Dos Passos and Betty realized . . . : EDP to VSC, interview, Dec. 10, 1976, Westmoreland, Va.

475 "I told Dos I had . . .": EDP to VSC, interview, Dec. 10, 1976, Westmoreland, Va.

476 Alice Holdridge had countered . . . : Alice Vorperian to VSC, interview, Aug. 25, 1978, Staunton, Va.

476 Except for a handful . . . : EDP to VSC, interview, Dec. 10, 1976, Westmoreland, Va.

476 He was identified as . . . : "John Dos Passos to Wed," the New York *Times,* Aug. 6, 1949; see also Baltimore *News American* for photograph and caption story, Aug. 7, 1949.

BOOK III

PROLOGUE

PAGE

480 Unless otherwise indicated, all material in Book III pertaining to Elizabeth ("Betty") Dos Passos and John Dos Passos from their marriage in 1949 until his death in 1970 has been derived from interviews with Elizabeth Dos Passos on July 10, 1976; Feb. 16–17, 1977; July 24, 1978, (Spence's Point) Westmoreland, Va.; Apr. 7–8, 1980, Farmville, Va.; and from some two dozen letters from Elizabeth Dos Passos to VSC from Nov. 17, 1976, through Feb. 1, 1983.

483 "Kiffy did not like . . .": Christopher Holdridge to VSC, interview, Mar. 18–19, 1977, Richmond, Va.

CHAPTER 25

486 "Can't think of *anything* . . .": Sara Murphy to JDP and EDP, Nov. 24, 1949, UVA.

486 "Delighted to hear of . . .": Dawn Powell to JDP and EDP, undated letter, UVA.

487 "I've married again and . . .": JDP to James T. Farrell, Jan. 24, 1950, UPA.

487 "The idea of a . . .": Parke Rouse, Jr., "Dos Passos Digs In," clipping provided by Katharine Smith Durand, Norfolk, Va.; publication (newspaper and date) unknown.

487 "Bunny came home . . .": Adelaide Walker to VSC, interview, Aug. 8, 1978, Wellfleet, Mass.

487 "We all felt curdled . . .": EDP to VSC, interview, Feb. 17, 1977, Westmoreland, Va.

487 "I didn't need that much . . .": R. Bruce Massey to VSC, interview, July 24, 1978, Hague, Va.

488 "I've taken up farming . . .": JDP to EH, June 23, 1949, JFK.

488 Hemingway responded in a brief . . . : EH to JDP, Sept. 17, 1949, UVA.

488 "It gives this year . . .": JDP to Lloyd and Marion Lowndes, Feb. 23, 1950, UVA.

489 After the races . . . : W. Horsley Gantt to VSC, interview, Aug. 19, 1978, Baltimore, Md.; Olga Owens to VSC, interview, Mar. 21, 1977, Baltimore, Md.; Louis and Sara Azrael to VSC, Mar. 20, 1977, Baltimore, Md.; Curt Richter to VSC, interview, Mar. 21, 1977, Baltimore, Md.

489 Dos Passos had once described Mencken . . . : JDP to EW, Dec. 23, 1934, YUB.

489 "This is to announce . . .": JDP to Stewart Mitchell, May 21, 1950, BA.

489 To Mary Heaton Vorse . . . : JDP to Mary Heaton Vorse, undated letter, WSU.

489 He told Sara Murphy . . . : JDP to Sara and Gerald Murphy, May 20, 1950, Collection of Honoria Murphy Donnelly.

489 Betty farmed Lucy out . . . : EDP to VSC, interview, Feb. 16, 1977, Westmoreland, Va.; Martha and Harvy Weldon to VSC, Feb. 16, 1977, Tucker Hill, Va.

489 Compounding the confusion . . . : JDP to Lloyd and Marion Lowndes, Aug. 31, 1950, UVA.

490 It was so outrageous . . . : JDP to Sara and Gerald Murphy, Aug. 12, 1950, Collection of Honoria Murphy Donnelly; see also JDP to Lloyd and Marion Lowndes, Aug. 13, 1950, UVA.

490 "It's a poisonous chowder . . .": JDP to Marion Lowndes, Aug. 5, 1950, UVA.

490 "They are hot, we are hot . . .": JDP to Edith Shay, undated postcard, Collection of Isabel Foley Whelan.

490 "You ought to see . . .": JDP to Marion Lowndes, Dec. 31, 1950, UVA.

491 "Marion and I X-mased . . .": Bill Smith to EH, Jan. 12, 1951, JFK.

491 "Until Jack came back . . .": R. Bruce Massey to VSC, interview, July 24, 1978, Hague, Va.

491 "Miss Lucy is very obstreperous . . .": JDP to Edith Shay, July 9, 1950, Collection of Isabel Foley Whelan.

491 He was at a loss . . . : Hazel Carden to VSC, interview, July 24, 1978, Warsaw, Va.

491 Kiffy Holdridge had not been . . . : Christopher Holdridge to VSC, interview, Mar. 18, 1977, Richmond, Va.; also EDP to VSC, Feb. 17, 1977, Westmoreland, Va.

492 Finally, Herb Carden . . . : recollections of their adventure by Herb Carden and William T. Carden to VSC, interview, July 24, 1978, Warsaw, Va.

492 "Jack and Betty took off . . .": Hazel Carden to VSC, interview, July 24, 1978, Warsaw, Va.

492 "I was hurt by being . . .": Christopher Holdridge to VSC, interview, Mar. 17, 1977, Richmond, Va.

493 Eben and Phyllis Given had come down . . . : Eben Given to VSC, interview, Oct. 12, 1978, Truro, Mass.; see also Dawn Powell to Sara Murphy, May 7, 1951, Collection of Honoria Murphy Donnelly.

493 "It was great fun having you . . .": JDP to EW, May 22, 1951, YUB.

493 Upon Eisenhower's nomination . . . : JDP to EW, Sept. 14, 1952, YUB.

493 "The reason I'm for Taft . . .": JDP to Archibald MacLeish, Feb. 5, 1952, LC.

494 "We liked her immensely . . .": Adelaide Walker to VSC, interview, Aug. 8, 1978, Wellfleet, Mass.

494 Elena Wilson thought her husband . . . : Elena Wilson to VSC, interview, Aug. 10, 1978, Wellfleet, Mass.

494 "I think Edmund's theory . . .": Mary McCarthy to VSC, interview, Aug. 3, 1978, Castine, Maine.

494 "What do you think of . . .": JDP to Edith Shay, Mar. 18, 1950, Collection of Isabel Foley Whelan.

494 If the editors were satisfied . . . : assorted materials, Time-Life Archives, New York City.

495 According to Sherrod . . . : Robert Sherrod to VSC, Oct. 23, 1978.

495 At year's end . . . : Orville Prescott, "Books of the Times," New York *Times,* Dec. 8, 1950; Prescott identified *Life's Picture History of World War II* as the most popular book published in 1950.

495 The Kremlin took note . . . : "Citizens Group Asks U.S. to End Red Ties," the New York *Times,* Feb. 11, 1951.

495 In an interview for . . . : Tex McCrary and Jinx Falkenburg, "New York Close-Up," the New York *Times,* Nov. 8, 1950, p. 27.

496 *Newsweek's* reviewer likened . . . : "Political Traveler," *Newsweek,* Oct. 23, 1950, pp. 102–3.

496 "Unhampered by ideological . . .": V. O. Key, Jr., "The Problem of Our Times," *The New Republic,* Dec. 4, 1950, pp. 19–20.

496 "The Dos Passos admirers . . .": Bob Sain, "The Curious Case of John Dos Passos," Charlotte (North Carolina) *News,* Dec. 30, 1950.

496 *Time* saw Dos Passos' position . . . : "The Traveller," *Time,* Oct. 30, 1950, pp. 108–9.

496 "He goes on seeking . . .": Granville Hicks, "The Politics of John Dos Passos," *The Antioch Review,* Spring 1950, pp. 85–98.

496 "What must be pointed out . . .": Granville Hicks, "Dos Passos as a Lecturer," *The New Leader,* Dec. 11, 1950.

496 "If John Dos Passos ever . . .": Edgar Ansel Mowrer, "Liberty and Democratic Participation," *The Saturday Review of Literature,* Nov. 4, 1950, pp. 14–15.

497 At year's end Dos Passos . . . : Warren Beck, "Faulkner Versus Hemingway," Madison (Wisconsin) *Journal,* Dec. 24, 1950.

497 "It sure did give me . . .": JDP to EW, July 19, Aug. 1, 1950, YUB.

497 Wilson had said that . . . : EW to JDP, July 21, 1950, UVA.

497 Wilson inquired of Dos Passos . . . : EW to JDP, Sept. 5, 1950, UVA.

497 "The evidence seems to point . . .": JDP to EW, Sept. 19, 1950, YUB.

498 "I hope Bernardin . . .": JDP to Arthur McComb, undated letter, UVA.

498 Hemingway replied that there were dozens . . . : EH to JDP, Oct. 30, 1951, UVA.

498 Hemingway's retaliation to *Chosen Country* . . . : EH, *A Moveable Feast: Sketches of the Author's Life in Paris in the Twenties* (New York: Scribner's, 1964), pp. 207–11.

498 When Archibald MacLeish wrote . . . : Archibald MacLeish to JDP, undated letter, UVA.

498 "Dos's last book was . . .": EH to Archibald MacLeish, Oct. 5, 1952, LC.

498 "Dos fooled us all . . .": EH to EW, Nov. 8, 1952, YUB.

499 In his Christmas card . . . : EH to Bill and Marion Smith, Dec. 1952, PU.

499 Arthur Mizener, whom Hemingway . . . : "The Gullivers of Dos Passos," *The Saturday Review of Literature,* June 30, 1951, pp. 6–7, 34–36.

499 "I immediately felt my pulse . . .": JDP to EW, July 6, 1951, YUB.

499 Mizener reviewed *Chosen Country* . . . : "Dos Passos' Story of the Yearning That Makes Americans," New York *Times Book Review,* Dec. 2, 1951, p. 7.

499 *Virginia Kirkus Service* called . . . : review of *Chosen Country,* Oct. 15, 1951, p. 622.

499 "I remember very well . . .": Archibald MacLeish to JDP, undated letter, UVA.

499 Dos Passos replied that . . . : JDP to Archibald MacLeish, Feb. 5, 1952, LC.

499 "What comes through to me . . .": EW to JDP, Nov. 27, 1951, UVA.

500 Dos Passos appreciated Wilson's . . . : JDP to EW, Dec. 13, 1951, YUB.

500 On June 11, 1951, he traveled . . . : miscellaneous news clippings pertaining to Dos

Passos' honorary degree at Northwestern University and his award at Northwestern's centennial convocation (Dec. 2, 1951), UVA.

500 He was honored in 1952 . . . : certificate of Phi Beta Kappa initiation, Harvard University, June 14, 1952, UVA.

500 Meanwhile, having turned . . . : JDP to EW, Sept. 15, 1951, YUB.

500 "The regular book market . . .": EDP to Lloyd and Marion Lowndes, Feb. 21, 1951, UVA.

500 He also was unhappy . . . : JDP to BB, Nov. 9, 1952, UVA.

500 He wrote Lovell Thompson . . . : JDP to Lovell Thompson, Nov. 29, 1952, UVA.

501 "Of course I won't get . . .": JDP to BB, Nov. 9, 1952, UVA.

501 Lovell Thompson played suitor . . . : Lovell Thompson to JDP, Nov. 6, 1952, UVA; also BB to JDP, Nov. 25, 1952, UVA.

502 His actual royalties earned . . . : BB to R. H. Roberts, Jan. 21, 1953, UVA; Lovell Thompson to BB, Feb. 3, 1952, UVA.

502 He did not want . . . : JDP to BB, Jan. 7, 1953, UVA.

502 Despite the problems . . . : Lovell Thompson to VSC, interview, Nov. 1, 1967, Ipswich, Mass.

502 "We ask each of them . . .": Monroe Stearns to JDP, Nov. 26, 1952, UVA.

503 Arnold Gingrich bought . . . : BB to JDP, Jan. 7, 1953, UVA.

503 "The Dos Passos story . . .": William Maxwell to BB, Dec. 16, 1952, UVA.

503 The same phrase—"abysmally boring" . . . : *Virginia Kirkus Service,* June 1, 1954, p. 345.

503 *Library Journal* called . . . : Louis Barron, *Library Journal,* Aug. 1954, pp. 1399–1400.

503 Harold Clurman, writing . . . : "Communists by Dos Passos," *The Nation,* Oct. 9, 1954, p. 310.

503 *Time*'s anonymous reviewer . . . : "Portrait," *Time,* Sept. 27, 1954, p. 102.

503 Granville Hicks threw . . . : "Dos Passos: Fruits of Disillusionment," *The New Republic,* Sept. 27, 1954, pp. 17–18.

504 Florence Bullock, writing . . . : New York *Herald Tribune Book Review,* Sept. 26, 1954, p. 3.

504 Paul Engle's review in . . . : Chicago *Sunday Tribune Magazine of Books,* Oct. 3, 1954, p. 4.

504 When Dos Passos inquired . . . : BB to JDP, June 5, 1955, UVA.

504 "I was certainly pleased . . .": JDP to EW, Nov. 6, 1954, YUB.

504 Wilson said he regretted . . . : EW to JDP, Nov. 1, 1954, UVA.

504 He had no intention . . . : BB to JDP, Nov. 16, 1953; see also *Program,* The Management of the American Platform, Jan. 1954, p. 7, Library and Musuem of the Performing Arts, The New York Public Library at Lincoln Center.

504 He found no books . . . : BB to Monroe Stearns, Nov. 1, 1954, UVA; Monroe Stearns to BB, Nov. 3, 1954, UVA.

505 "I'm making a series . . .": JDP to Chauncey Hackett, Oct. 31, 1954, UVA.

505 From Eugene, Oregon . . . : JDP to EEC, Nov. 10, 1954, EEC Collection, HU.

505 When he returned . . . : JDP to Chauncey Hackett, undated letter, UVA.

505 One of his suggestions . . . : Frank L. Hayes, "Books: Go Back to the Bible, It's Still the Best Writing Says Author Dos Passos," Chicago *Daily News,* undated clipping, Collection of Mary Dos Passos Singleton, Summit, N.J.; also JDP to EW, Nov. 23, 1954, YUB.

505 The author had apparently . . . : Irving Howe, "Perils of Americana," *The New Republic,* Jan. 25, 1954, pp. 16–17.

506 Despite its good . . . : JDP to Robert Hillyer, undated letter, SU; also Robert Hillyer to JDP, Aug. 30, 1954, UVA.

506 Dawn Powell wrote . . . : Dawn Powell to Gerald and Sara Murphy, undated letter, Collection of Honoria Murphy Donnelly.

506 "Now as to John Adams . . .": Stewart Mitchell to JDP, Dec. 19, 1952, UVA.

506 Dos Passos sent Carl Sandburg . . . : JDP to Carl Sandburg, Dec. 20, 1953, Sandburg Collection, University of Illinois at Urbana-Champaign.

507 Put out by his . . . : JDP to BB, Jan. 23, 1955, UVA.

508 When Dos Passos submitted . . . : EW to JDP, Apr. 30, 1953, UVA.

508 Sales were boosted by . . . : Orville Prescott, "Books of the Times," Mar. 30, 1956.

508 "I told them they . . .": *TIF*, pp. 261–62.

508 Dodd, Mead had . . . : Florence Bonime to JDP, Jan. 12, 1953, UVA; copies of Edward H. Dodd's letters seeking help from philanthropic foundations on Dos Passos' behalf at UVA.

509 "Three of us at Doubleday . . .": Ken McCormick to JDP, Nov. 12, 1955, UVA.

509 "You have succeeded marvellously . . .": Lewis Gannett to JDP, Oct. 11, 1955, Collection of Lewis Gannett, HU.

509 Back in 1953 he . . . : JDP to BB, June 4, 1953, UVA.

509 "If you should hear . . .": JDP to BB, Mar. 15, 1954, UVA.

509 "The book will of course . . .": Lewis Gannett to JDP, May 3, 1955, Collection of Lewis Gannett, HU.

510 "The Yorktown prologue . . .": Lewis Gannett to JDP, Oct. 11, 1955, Collection of Lewis Gannett, HU.

510 He accepted Gannett's . . . : JDP to Lewis Gannett, Nov. 15, 1955, Collection of Lewis Gannett, HU.

510 "Pruning always helps . . .": Lewis Gannett to JDP, Apr. 15, 1956, Collection of Lewis Gannett, HU.

510 Barker reported that eighty-five hundred . . . : BB to JDP, Feb. 14, 1957, UVA.

511 "I wonder if he would . . .": JDP to BB, undated letter, UVA.

511 He also was considering the possibility . . . : JDP to BB, Mar. 12, 1957, UVA.

511 He was in fine fettle . . . : "Dos Passos Wins Institute Gold Medal," publicity release, Feb. 11, 1957, AAIAL; New York *Times,* Feb. 12, 1957.

511 Betty concluded that Faulkner . . . : EDP to VSC, interview, Apr. 7, 1980, Farmville, Va.

512 "I wonder whether you could . . .": Malcolm Cowley to William Faulkner, *The Faulkner-Cowley File: Letters and Memories, 1944–1962* (New York: Viking, 1968), pp. 142–43; Faulkner's undated reply, pp. 143–44.

512 "It seemed that Madariaga . . .": EDP to VSC, interview, Apr. 7, 1980, Farmville, Va.

513 A secretary in the Dodd . . . : Cowley, *Faulkner-Cowley File,* p. 145.

513 "The artist, the writer . . .": *Proceedings,* 2d ser., no. 2, American Academy of Arts and Letters, National Institute of Arts and Letters, 1958, p. 192.

513 "I wonder if any of you . . .": "Acceptance by John Dos Passos," *Proceedings,* p. 193.

513 Steinbeck wrote his wife . . . : Elaine Steinbeck to VSC, Aug. 11, 1977.

513 In each city Dos Passos found . . . : EDP to VSC, July 24, 1978, Westmoreland, Va.

514 It was hard "to resist a . . .": JDP to Robert Hillyer, Aug. 25, 1957, SU.

514 Steinbeck reported later . . . : John Steinbeck to Elaine Steinbeck, Sept. 1, 1957, *Steinbeck, A Life in Letters,* ed. by Elaine Steinbeck and Robert Wallsten (New York: Viking, 1975), p. 566.

514 "It would do a good deal . . .": JDP to Leslie Frank Warren, Feb. 3, 1958, UVA.

514 Writers were poorly paid . . . : Leslie Frank Warren to JDP, May 8, 1958, UVA.

514 By this time he was already . . . : "What Union Members Have Been Writing Senator McClellan," *Reader's Digest,* Sept. 1958, pp. 25–32.

515 "I'm interested first . . .": JDP to Leslie Frank Warren, June 23, 1958, UVA.

515 Leslie Warren proposed . . . : Leslie Frank Warren to JDP, May 2, 1958, UVA.

515 "We were all wild . . .": JDP to Adelaide Walker, undated letter, UVA.

515 "We were nearly stuffed . . .": JDP to Arthur McComb, Sept. 1, 1958, UVA.

516 In the book that grew . . . : *Brazil on the Move* (Garden City, N.Y.: Doubleday, 1963), p. 14.

516 He was notified that summer . . . : H. W. Luhnow to JDP, June 25, 1958, UVA.

516 "If H-M is going to hold . . .": JDP to BB, July 7, 1957, UVA.

516 Malcolm Cowley, writing . . . : "Success That Somehow Led to Failure," New York *Times Book Review,* Apr. 13, 1958, pp. 4–5, 45.

517 *Time*'s anonymous reviewer . . . : "Fallen Eagle," *Time,* Mar. 13, 1958, pp. 89–90.

517 Daniel Aaron informed . . . : "Dos Passos Obsessed," *The New Leader,* June 2, 1958, p. 24.

517 James T. Farrell came to . . . : "How Should We Rate Dos Passos," *The New Republic,* Apr. 28, 1958, pp. 17–18.

517 When Dos Passos' editor at . . . : JDP to James T. Farrell, May 3, 1958, UPA.

517 Edmund Wilson agreed . . . : EW to JDP, Apr. 13, 1958, UVA.

517 Dos Passos answered Wilson's . . . : JDP to EW, Apr. 19, 1958, YUB.

517 Several months later . . . : JDP to House Un-American Activities Committee, Jan. 22, 1953, Collection of W. Horsley Gantt, Baltimore, Md.

518 "People keep asking . . .": "Looking Back on *U.S.A.,*" New York *Times,* Oct. 25, 1959, Sec. 2, p. 5.

518 Don Ross, a reporter . . . : "John Dos Passos: A Consistently Angry Man Who's 'Always Sharpshooting from the Edges,' " New York *Herald Tribune,* Oct. 25, 1959.

518 "Thanks for the clippings . . .": JDP to Paul Shyre, Sept. 21, 1953, BU; many clippings and letters tracing the evolvement of several dramatic productions of *U.S.A.* are in this collection.

519 "The adaptation deserves additional . . .": Rita Hassan, "Review, *U.S.A.,*" *Show Business,* Aug. 17, 1953, p. 6.

519 Elliot Hyman . . . was . . . : Harold Hornstein, "Dos Passos' *U.S.A.* Leaves Past's Spectre at White Barn," Westport *Town Crier,* Aug. 18, 1953.

519 Shyre sought "lecture . . .": JDP to Paul Shyre, Apr. 13, 1954, BU.

519 Bernice Baumgarten informed . . . : BB to JDP, Oct. 7, 1953, UVA.

519 By the spring of 1954 . . . : JDP to Paul Shyre, Apr. 13, 1954, BU.

520 Dos Passos' "suggested tratment" . . . : Dos Passos' dramatic version of *U.S.A.* in UVA; another major repository of documents, playbills, and clippings pertaining to *U.S.A.* as a dramatic review is the Library and Museum of the Performing Arts, Lincoln Center.

520 "As I told you . . .": JDP to Paul Shyre, Feb. 17, 1958, BU.

521 Dos Passos told Phil Casey . . . : "Dos Passos Speeds Up His Pen After 4 Decades of Writing," Washington *Post,* July 16, 1959, p. 1B.

521 "I'd be very pleased . . .": JDP to Van Wyck Brooks, Nov. 14, 1953, UPA.

521 Hemingway was not present . . . : New York *Times,* Mar. 24, 1954.

521 Dos Passos wrote Cummings that the ceremonial . . . : JDP to EEC, May 31, 1954, EEC Collection, HU.

521 "One of the bitterest things . . .": JDP to Max Eastman, Dec. 25, 1953, IU.

521 "He wrote such an awful . . .": EH to Archibald and Ada MacLeish, Oct. 29, 1954, LC.

522 "Hem, hope this isn't . . .": JDP to EH, Apr. 28, 1961, JFK.

522 "Until I read of his poor . . .": JDP to Sara Murphy, Aug. 1961, Collection of Honoria Murphy Donnelly.

CHAPTER 26

523 "John Dos Passos was a conundrum . . .": James Bready to VSC, interview, Mar. 21, 1977, Baltimore, Md.

523 His fees never exceeded . . . : Dos Passos lectured at Colgate University on Nov. 10,

1966; see *The Colgate Maroon,* Nov. 10, Nov. 17, 1966; also JDP to Joseph Slater, June 18, July 4, Nov. 1, 1966, Everett Needham Case Library, Colgate University, Hamilton, N.Y.

523 William F. Buckley, Jr. . . . : two unidentified clippings at UVA: "Dos Passos Here May 14 to Speak at Honors Convocation Assembly" and an article by John Chamberlain, Apr. 27, 1967.

523 "I think it is the most amusing . . .": JDP to Myra MacPherson, New Haven *Star,* clipping undated, YUS.

523 Buckley was apprehensive . . . : William F. Buckley, Jr., to VSC, interview, Aug. 15, 1978, New York City.

524 John Chamberlain, who was . . . : John Chamberlain to VSC, interview, Aug. 16, 1978, New York City.

524 "Dos pushed me into it . . .": William F. Buckley, Jr., to VSC, interview, Aug. 15, 1978, New York City.

525 He looked forward . . . : EDP to VSC, interview, July 24, 1978, Westmoreland, Va.

525 *Portugal Today,* a bimonthly . . . : *Portugal Today,* July–August, 1960, PCU.

526 In Lisbon, Dos Passos . . . : EDP to VSC, interview, July 24, 1978, Westmoreland, Va.

526 Among the distant cousins . . . : Cyril F. and Maria Amália dos Passos to VSC, interview, Aug. 17, 1978, Mendham, N.J.; background information on JDP's Portuguese background provided by Francis M. Rogers to VSC, interview, Aug. 1, 1978, Belmont, Mass.; see also Francis M. Rogers, *The Portuguese Heritage of John Dos Passos* (Boston: PCU, 1976); Francis M. Rogers, *Atlantic Islanders of the Azores and Madeiras* (North Quincy, Mass.: Christopher Publishing House, 1979), pp. 258, 294, 325–26.

526 "Young Lucy and I . . .": Cyril F. dos Passos to VSC, interview, Aug. 17, 1978, Mendham, N.J.

527 "We're back on a weekend . . .": EDP to Henka Farnsworth, Jan. 3, 1958, Collection of Henka Farnsworth.

527 "It was right after . . .": Christopher Holdridge to VSC, interview, Mar. 19, 1977, Richmond, Va.

527 P. W. Filby, director . . . : P. W. Filby to VSC, Mar. 2, 1978.

527 When asked to write . . . : "I Speak for the Peabody," Peabody Institute Library, Mar. 7, 1961; see also Frank N. Jones to JDP, Mar. 17, 1961, UVA.

527 "The people of Baltimore treated . . .": Julia Sprigg Cameron to VSC, interview, Sept. 29, 1977, Bel Air, Md.

528 According to Lovell Thompson . . . : Lovell Thompson to VSC, interview, Nov. 1, 1977, Ipswich, Mass.

528 "Seldom does a writer . . .": Harry T. Moore, "The Return of John Dos Passos," New York *Times Book Review,* Feb. 26, 1961, pp. 1, 51.

528 "He hadn't read the book . . .": JDP to Lovell Thompson, Jan. 20, 1961, Houghton Mifflin Collection, HU; "The Sands of Power," *Time,* Mar. 3, 1961, p. 91.

528 The anonymous *Newsweek* . . . : "Out of the Past," *Newsweek,* Feb. 27, 1961, p. 93.

528 Not since 1931 had Hicks . . . : Granville Hicks, "Of Radicals and Racketeers," *The Saturday Review,* Feb. 25, 1961, pp. 25–26.

529 "The old technical forms are . . .": John K. Hutchens, New York *Herald Tribune,* Feb. 27, 1961, p. 21.

529 Dos Passos sounded "too much . . .": John Gross, "Past Masters," *The New Statesman,* Oct. 27, 1961, pp. 614–15.

529 Robert Stilwell, who wrote . . . : "A Massive Failure Difficult to Assay," Louisville *Courier-Journal,* Mar. 5, 1961.

529 "Occasionally someone brought . . .": EDP to VSC, interview, Feb. 16, 1977, Westmoreland, Va.

529 "Lord man, don't . . .": JDP to William F. Buckley, Jr., Dec. 7, 1959, YUS.

530 "I appreciated his help . . .": William F. Buckley, Jr., to VSC, interview, Aug. 15, 1978, New York City.

530 "This is not Mr. Buckley's theory . . .": *Up from Liberalism* (New York: McDowell, Obolensky, 1959), Foreword.

530 According to Luís Gomes . . . : "Modest Dos Passos Gets Pedro Francisco Award," *Sunday Standard-Times* (New Bedford, Mass.), June 18, 1961, pp. 1+; extensive clippings and photograph collection, PCU.

530 "International affairs where Portugal . . .": Francis M. Rogers is the Nancy Clark Smith Professor of the Language and Literature of Portugal at Harvard University; especially helpful is his chapter "Peter Francisco Award and the Heritage," in *The Portuguese Heritage of John Dos Passos* (Boston: PCU, 1976), pp. 31–36; see also Francis M. Rogers, *Americans of Portuguese Descent: A Lesson in Differentiation* (New York: Sage, 1974).

531 "The present Cuban snarl . . .": JDP to Arthur McComb, Nov. 2, 1962, UVA.

531 He had been asked . . . : JDP to Robert Hillyer, Apr. 29, 1956, SU.

531 Upon Faulkner's death . . . : JDP to Arthur McComb, Feb. 12, 1963, UVA; see also "Dos Passos Lectures at Virginia U. In His Debut as Writer in Residence," Washington *Post,* Feb. 10, 1963; "Mr. Dos Passos and the U.S.A.," Feb. 10, *Ledger-Dispatch* (Norfolk, Va.).

531 "He was very helpful . . .": Jere Real to VSC, interview, Aug. 12, 1978, Provincetown, Mass.; also letter, Mar. 10, 1978.

531 Dos Passos spoke . . . : Nancy St. Clair, "Dos Passos Lauds Faulkner in Talk," Charlottesville (Virginia) *Progress,* Feb. 9, 1963.

532 "He was receptive . . .": Jere Real to VSC, Oct. 6, 1978; see also Jere Real, "Intellectuals Misled?—A Red 'Success' " (undated clipping, spring, 1965), Richmond *News Leader,* Collection of Jere Real.

532 Nevins recommended his . . . : JDP to Allan Nevins, Jan. 31, 1964, Special Manuscript Collection, Nevins Professional Collection, Butler Library, Columbia University of the City of New York.

532 He was reluctant to disrupt . . . : EDP to VSC, interview, Feb. 16, 1977, Westmoreland, Va.

533 A longtime student of . . . : Arthur S. Link, New York *Times Book Review,* Apr. 7, 1963, p. 41.

533 Marshall thought Dos Passos . . . : S. L. A. Marshall, *The Saturday Review,* Dec. 29, 1962, p. 42.

533 Dos Passos had worked closely . . . : Lewis Gannett to JDP, Jan. 18, 1961, Lewis Gannett Collection, HU.

533 "I'd like to use it . . .": JDP to William F. Buckley, Jr., Nov. 20, 1963, YUS.

533 "Your protest aroused . . .": JDP to EW, Dec. 24, 1963, YUB.

533 "It's been so long . . .": EW to JDP, Jan. 18, 1964, UVA.

534 "What danger do you . . .": EW to JDP, Feb. 1, 1964, UVA.

534 Having aligned himself . . . : See "Conservative Rally Will Honor Hoover," New York *Times,* Jan. 2, 1962; "An Objection by Goldwater Led to Cancellation of Walker Talk," New York *Times,* Feb. 14, 1962.

534 "But in this in between . . .": JDP to EW, Apr. 18, 1964, YUB.

534 "Your article . . . sounded like a teenager . . .": EW to JDP, Sept. 15, 1964, UVA.

534 "I think Dos was always . . .": Morris R. Werner to VSC, interview, Mar. 5, 1978, New York City.

535 "At times the proceedings . . .": William F. Buckley, Jr., to VSC, interview, Aug. 15, 1978, New York City; considerable correspondence relative to the Rome meeting of the Centro di Vita Italiana in the Buckley Collection, YUS.

535 "Your lucubration in Rome . . .": EW to JDP, Mar. 18, 1964, UVA.

535 "Do you know whether . . .": Seymour St. John to Robert Atmore, Apr. 13, 1962, The Choate School Archives of The Andrew Mellon Library, Wallingford, Conn.

535 He began his address . . . : manuscript of JDP's address in The Choate School Archives of The Andrew Mellon Library; see also New York *Times,* May 9, 1965; New Haven *Register,* May 9, 1965; *The Morning Record* (Meriden, Conn.), May 10, 1965.

536 According to D. J. Stewart . . . : "Elbow Room for the Eye," *National Review,* Dec. 1, 1964, pp. 1072–73.

536 "I'll never forget being . . .": Howard B. Gotlieb to VSC, interview, Nov. 3, 1977, Boston, Mass.

536 "Mr. Dos Passos, I thought . . .": "Novelist Dos Passos Visits UF," Florida *Alligator,* undated clipping; see also tape recording of JDP's informal talk to gathering of faculty and students, Mar. 1, 1968, in the University Libraries, Rare Book and Manuscript Collection, University of Florida, Gainesville.

537 "We summoned a doctor . . .": Eben Given to VSC, interview, Aug. 12, 1978, Truro, Mass.

537 His heart was beating . . . : JDP to RM, Nov. 21, 1965, UVA.

537 "I'd rather have them wait . . .": JDP to EW, Apr. 26, 1965, YUB.

537 "I have read not only . . .": Granville Hicks, "John Dos Passos Reminisces," *The Saturday Review,* Nov. 26, 1966, pp. 33–34.

537 The anonymous critic in . . . : "Kilroy Was Here," *The Times Literary Supplement,* Mar. 31, 1968.

537 "In this book there is none . . .": Dan Wakefield, "Return to Paradise," *The Atlantic Monthly,* Feb. 1967, pp. 102–4, 106, 108–10.

538 "I think it is the best . . .": Lewis Gannett to JDP, July 1, 1965, Lewis Gannett Collection, HU.

538 "Although Dos Passos has been faulted . . .": *Virginia Kirkus Review,* July 1, 1966, p. 644.

539 "With all we've learned . . .": *The Colgate Maroon,* Case Library Archives, Colgate University, Hamilton, N.Y.

539 "In my opinion the New Left . . .": JDP to "Dear Mr. Africa," Oct. 22, 1967, Manuscripts, Special Collections, University of California, Santa Barbara.

539 In the spring of 1967 . . . : JDP to EW, Apr. 12, 1967, YUB; EW to JDP, Apr. 6, 1967, UVA.

539 "Neither Dos nor I . . .": EDP to VSC, interview, Dec. 10, 1976, Westmoreland, Va.

540 "I remember my emotion . . .": Oriana Fallaci to VSC, Feb. 1, 1979.

540 She began her interview by observing . . . : "Why Is America So Hated?" *Europeo* (Milan, Italy), July, Aug., 1967 (published in Italian and translated for VSC by Mario R. Mion, Dec. 9, 1982); see also "3 Writers Assess U.S. For Italians: Dos Passos, Bradbury and Mailer Discuss Antipathy," by Robert C. Doty, New York *Times,* Sept. 3, 1967.

541 Oriana Fallaci pondered . . . : Oriana Fallaci to VSC, Feb. 1, 1979.

CHAPTER 27

543 Dos Passos appreciated Buckley's . . . : William F. Buckley, Jr., to JDP, Jan. 29, 1970, YUS; JDP to Buckley, Feb. 4, 1970, YUS.

543 He was fond of . . . : "Reminiscences of a Middle-Class Radical," *National Review,* Jan. 18, 1956, pp. 9–11.

544 "If he doesn't want to fight . . .": JDP to William L. White, May 12, 1970, *The Fourteenth Chronicle: Letters and Diaries of John Dos Passos,* ed. Townsend Ludington (Boston: Gambit, 1973), pp. 637–38.

544 "Since wit and conversational . . .": JDP to the Committee on Admissions, The Century Association, July 17, 1970, UVA.

544 "How you can do as much . . .": William F. Buckley, Jr., to JDP, July 22, 1970, YUS.

544 Despite his ill health . . . : *Easter Island: Island of Enigmas* (Garden City, N.Y.: Doubleday, 1971); *Century's Ebb: The Thirteenth Chronicle* (Boston: Gambit, 1975).

544 "I've put to bed . . .": JDP to Harold Weston, June 25, 1970, UVA.

544 Dos Passos had never . . . : Christopher Holdridge to VSC, interview, Mar. 19, 1977, Richmond, Va.

545 His father, Desmond Holdridge . . . : *Feudal Island* (New York: Harcourt, Brace, 1936); *Escape to the Tropics* (New York: Harcourt, Brace, 1937); *Witch in the Wilderness* (New York: Harcourt, 1937); *Northern Lights* (New York: Viking, 1939); *End of the River* (New York: Harcourt, Brace, 1940); and several others.

546 "I note where the Premier . . .": William L. White to JDP, July 20, 1970, UVA.

546 Friends of Dos Passos . . . : R. Bruce Massey to VSC, interview, July 24, 1978, Hague, Va.; Hazel Carden to VSC, interview, July 24, 1978, Warsaw, Va.; Margaret Devereaux to VSC, Aug. 25, 1978; Manoel Cardozo, interview, Mar. 12, 1978, Washington, D.C.

547 It seemed to Dos Passos in 1968 . . . : John Davenport, "Four Decades After Three Soldiers," Washington *Post,* May 5, 1968, pp. 24–26, 28.

547 "I saw Dos the summer . . .": Robert Solley to VSC, interview, Mar. 21, 1978, Old Saybrook, Conn.

547 "I agree with you . . .": JDP to Harold Weston, July 10, 1970, UVA.

547 "I can hardly believe it yet . . .": JDP to Marion Cummings, Sept. 6, 1962, EEC Collection, HU.

547 "Knowing how sick . . .": Julia Sprigg Cameron to VSC, interview, Sept. 29, 1977, Bel Air, Md.

548 He rode it with some embarrassment . . . : EDP to VSC, interview, Feb. 16, 1977, Westmoreland, Va.

549 "Bunny is behaving characteristically . . .": Charles R. Walker to JDP, May 2, 1970, UVA.

549 "I've had what I hope . . .": JDP to Harold Weston, July 10, 1970, UVA.

549 "It pained me to see . . .": Manoel Cardozo to VSC, interview, Mar. 20, 1977, Washington, D.C.

549 By the end of August . . . : JDP to Harold Weston, Aug. 23, 1970, UVA.

550 "Dos looked at me . . .": W. Horsley Gantt to VSC, interview, Aug. 19, 1978, Baltimore, Md.

550 Thompson told Dos Passos . . . : Lovell Thompson to VSC, interview, Nov. 1, 1977, Ipswich, Mass.

550 "Jack had always taken . . .": Julia Sprigg Cameron and Brodnax Cameron to VSC, interview, Sept. 29, 1977, Bel Air, Md.

550 "I was at Dos's side . . .": EDP to VSC, interview, July 24, 1978, Westmoreland, Va.

550 "I had brought him Hume . . .": W. Horsley Gantt to VSC, interview, Aug. 19, 1978, Baltimore, Md.

SOME WORDS AFTER

555 "If C. D. Batchelor were . . .": William F. Buckley, Jr., "The Passing of Dos Passos: A Time for Liberty's Tears," *National Review,* Oct. 1, 1970.

Dos Passos' death was front-page news in almost every major newspaper in the country; see especially New York *Times,* Sept. 29, 1970; Washington *Post,* Sept. 29, 30, 1970; Baltimore *Sun,* Sept. 29, Oct. 1, 1970; *International Herald Tribune* (Paris), Sept. 29, 1970; *Newsweek* and *Time,* Oct. 12, 1970; Chicago *Tribune,* Sept. 29, 1970; *National Review,* Oct. 20, 1970; *The New American,* Oct. 11, 1970.

Index